WORKS ON JAPANESE

By

MR. AND MRS. ORESTE VACCARI

COMPLETE COURSE OF
JAPANESE CONVERSATION-GRAMMAR

CORSO COMPLETO
GRAMMATICA DELLA LINGUA GIAPPONESE
(Edizione Italiana)

GIAPPONESE IN FRETTA E FURIA
(Edizione Italiana)

JAPANESE READERS

STANDARD KANJI
AN EASY METHOD TO LEARN CHINESE-JAPANESE CHARACTERS

BRUSH UP YOUR JAPANESE
A UNIQUE, PIONEERING PUBLICATION

PLASTIC KANJI CARDS
A PRACTICAL METHOD TO QUICKLY LEARN
CHINESE-JAPANESE CHARACTERS

THE NEW UP-TO-DATE
ENGLISH-JAPANESE CONVERSATION DICTIONARY

CONCISE
ENGLISH-JAPANESE—JAPANESE-ENGLISH
500 pages—   DICTIONARY   —3½×2 inch
(in roman and Japanese symbolic characters)

JAPANESE IN A HURRY
A QUICK APPROACH TO SPEAKING JAPANESE

DICTIONNAIRE PRATIQUE ET MIS A JOUR
de la
CONVERSATION FRANCO-JAPONAISE

漢　和　英　大　辞　典
A. B. C. JAPANESE-ENGLISH DICTIONARY

PICTORIAL
CHINESE-JAPANESE CHARACTERS
A NEW AND MOST FASCINATING METHOD
TO LEARN IDEOGRAPHS

JAPANESE ON RECORD
(A set of three 10-inch records for practical lessons)

See at the end of this book the description of each of
the above mentioned works.

AN ENTIRELY RESET
AND GREATLY ENLARGED EDITION

COMPLETE COURSE

OF

JAPANESE
CONVERSATION-GRAMMAR

A NEW AND PRACTICAL METHOD OF LEARNING
THE JAPANESE LANGUAGE

BY

ORESTE VACCARI

GRADUATED AT THE ORIENTAL UNIVERSITY OF NAPLES (ITALY)

AND

MRS. ENKO ELISA VACCARI

GRADUATED AT THE FRIENDS' GIRLS' SCHOOL AND
ATHÉNÉE FRANÇAIS (DEPARTMENT OF ENGLISH) OF TOKYO

Published by
VACCARI'S LANGUAGE INSTITUTE
170, 2-chome, Harajuku, Shibuya-ku, TOKYO

SOLD BY THE PUBLISHERS

and

MARUZEN CO., LTD.
2-chome, Nihonbashi, Chuo-ku, TOKYO

CHARLES E. TUTTLE CO.
3, 1-chome, Kanda Jimbocho, Chiyoda-ku TOKYO

KYOBUNKAN
4-chome, Ginza, Chuo-ku, TOKYO

JENA SEIKO CO., LTD.
4, 5-chome, Ginza, Chuo-ku, TOKYO

KEGAN PAUL, TRENCH, TRUBNER & COMPANY
43, Great Russell Street, LONDON, W. C. 1.

Published by
Vaccari's Language Institute

Copyright by
Oreste Vaccari

First Edition, January 1937
Tenth Edition September 1952
(Revised and Enlarged)
Twelfth Edition, October 1955
Thirteenth Edition. October 1956
Fourteenth Edition, January 1958
Fifteenth Edition, May 1959
Sixteenth Edition, January 1961
Seventeenth Edition, July 1961
Eighteenth Edition, January 1963

Nineteenth Edition, April 1964
(Entirely reset and greatly enlarged)

Printed in Japan by
Dai Nippon Printing Company
Tokyo

PREFACE

"Look it up in Vaccari's" has come to mean the last word in Japanese language study.

The foreign student who tries to learn Japanese without a Vaccari text to guide and instruct him is simply asking for punishment. The student may have access to all the Japanese grammar and syntax there is, but only in this COMPLETE COURSE OF JAPANESE CONVERSATION GRAMMAR will he also find the indispensable traffic signal to direct him smoothly and accurately on his way. With Mr. and Mrs. Vaccari to chart his language course, the foreign student of Japanese cannot possibly get lost or confused, and, moreover, he reaches his destination by the shortest possible route.

Previous editions of this grammar already looked as if they had covered all the Japanese ground that needed covering for a sound knowledge of the language. But the sweeping changes that have occurred in Japan in recent years have had their impact also on the language, and this new edition, with two hundred additional pages of new details on Japanese language, besides giving further help to those who are willing to pursue its study to the very end, represents the authors' successful endeavour to keep abreast of Japan's linguistic response to the changes. The student of this new edition can, therefore, be perfectly confident that he is studying the Japanese language of the day, as currently spoken and written by educated native-born.

To enable the student to acquire a correct pronunciation from the outset, the perfectionist authors have, in this reset edition, used graphic accents to indicate syllabic stresses and appropriate emphases. The importance of this original and extremely effective approach to correct Japanese accentuation can scarcely be overestimated. There are many Sino-Japanese characters which, though differently accented in speech, are transliterated into roman letters of exactly the same spelling. Knowing where to put the proper stress on these deceptive homonyms can make all the difference between correct Japanese and an embarrassing word puzzle.

After many years of research in Japanese phonetics, the authors have finally succeeded in establishing definite and accurate rules (pp. 651-734) for dispelling the uncertainties of Japanese pronunciation. Before the application of the Vaccari system used in this grammar, many foreign students of the Japanese language had to rely on "near enough" methods to learn how to pronounce Japanese. Even if they did have a native-born teacher for personal tuition, they lacked, nevertheless, a grammar of reference and study in which the precise accent of Japanese words was clearly indicated. This new Vaccari system of Japanese accentuation is undoubtedly a valuable contribution to a better study of Japanese language.

Whether the student aspires to a thorough knowledge of the Japanese language, or whether he just wants to learn enough to meet more casual requirements, this grammar equips him to attain either objective.

PETER RUSSO, Ph. D.

Former Professor of Occidental Languages at the Tokyo University of Commerce; former Examiner in Japanese at the University of Melbourne.

. . . .

Ma di quest' acqua convien che tu bei,
Prima che tanta sete in te si sazii.
DANTE, Par. xxx

. . . .

But first behoves thee of this water drink,
Or e'er that longing be allay'd.
DANTE, Par. xxx

INTRODUCTION
to the Reset and Enlarged Edition

Thirty years ago the first edition of this book was published. Since then, new editions, some revised and enlarged, have followed almost yearly. No other book for the study of Japanese has been reprinted so many times, a sufficient testimony to the favour it has found among students and teachers of the language.

Encouraged by the proven success of its method and the ever growing demand, the authors decided, a few years ago, to extend the grammar's scope of study without in any way complicating its processes. The result is the present volume, the nineteenth edition, entirely reset and enlarged with about two hundred more pages of new grammatical information and additional reading matter of general and topical interest.

Some of the exclusive and important features of this new volume may be summarised as follows:

All Japanese words in roman letters of two or more syllables have their proper stress indicated by a graphic accent. From the beginning of his study, the student is thus able to absorb the correct pronunciation of Japanese in the same effortless manner that he learns to pronounce his mother tongue.

For the first time in any text for the study of Japanese language, definite rules are provided on the essential aspect of Japanese accentuation. See Pages 675-757.

Of particular significance in this volume is the care the authors have taken to bring the study of the Japanese language up to date. Obsolete terms have been discarded, and all words and terms in the translation exercises and reading matter conform with modern usage. New coinages and expressions, introduced since the Pacific War, are also blended with the exercises in such a way as to make their Japanese context familiar to the foreign student.

It is the hope of the authors that this book, as well as facilitating the study of the Japanese language, will also contribute to friendly understanding between the people of Japan and the people of all other countries.

Mr. and Mrs. ORESTE VACCARI

PREFACE
to the first edition of Vaccari's Japanese Grammar.

To those of us who are engaged in fostering among foreign peoples a more thorough and enlightened understanding of Japan and the Japanese, this new grammar book is a source of much encouragement. Mr. and Mrs. Vaccari have brought out, after much intelligent labour, what I would like to regard as the most complete book to date for the study of Japanese and have, thereby, provided an effective and practical guide toward a basic study of the Japanese nation and people.

Final judgement on the real merits of a book of this nature should not be passed by one to whom Japanese is the mother tongue. It should be reserved for the student of the language who, after thoughtful perusal of the book, discovers by his own experiences, how helpful it has proved to him. Objectively considered, however, this grammar possesses many points of merit. The method introduced by the authors is not only scientific, but human, for while the particulars of the language have been fully treated and illustrated with practical examples and exercises in natural and logical order, they have, at the same time, been regulated in each lesson according to the measure of partial efforts of the mind.

The Japanese taught in this book has struck me as being of the best commonly accepted diction to-day. I have, furthemore, found that the lessons consist of expressions of facts which are deeply imprinted upon the mental background of every individual. These expressions, when learned by the student, are therefore certain to prove of practical value in his daily mingling with the Japanese people.

The authors have introduced a new idea of giving all the sentences in the book in Japanese characters and Roman transliteration with their respective English translation, an innovation most likely to prove very helpful.

Mr. and Mrs. Vaccari have published a book of high merit and may be regarded as the initiators of a new system for teaching Japanese.

COUNT AYSKE KABAYAMA

Chairman of the Board of Directors,
The Kokusai Bunka Shinkokai
(The Society for International Cultural Relations)

FOREWORD
to the former editions of Vaccari's Japanese Grammar

Japan's international status and the exceptional industry and talent of its people give the Japanese language a special significance. It is a specific key to the understanding of a country and people destined to have an ever increasing impact on word affairs.

In spite of these demonstrable facts, the study of the Japanese language by foreigners has not been receiving the attention it warrants. The reason is not far to seek. In brief, it is because, until recent years, there have been no suitable, comprehensive texts for the study of Japanese, or for reducing the complexities of this difficult language to comparatively simple terms.

Until this complete grammar of Japanese appeared, foreign students had to depend for their Japanese language study on books of the scholars of long ago, texts which by now are largely archaic and inadequate to yield satisfactory results. Furthermore, the foreign student has been the more handicapped in that the Japanese themselves have not yet produced a complete treatise on their own language.

To overcome these serious gaps in Japanese language study, the authors of this grammar spent several years in research and inquiry into current Japanese idiom, spoken and written. The result is the present complete grammar of Japanese, which remains the first in its field, and is acknowledged by world scholars, as the one comprehensive text for the study of modern Japanese.

The grammar is made up of sixty-two lessons, covering the full range of grammatical rules, vocabulary and translation exercises. The authors have, however, replaced the orthodox-approach to the Japanese language study with new scientific methods which enable the student to absorb the spoken and written language with far greater ease and precision. Among the unique features of the grammar, for instance, is the transliteration with *kanji* (Chinese characters) of every Japanese example and exercise given in roman letters, so that the student may, if he desires, learn the language also as it is written by Japanese.

This volume does not follow a stricktly grammatical order, but grammar has been given in each lesson as the necessity arises, passing immediately into practice with the given examples and exercises, embodying itself in actual facts and in habitual locutions to which one has recourse many times a day.

Nothing has been overlooked in the authors' efforts to make this grammar a practical and efficient guide to anyone wishing to make a thorough study of the language as currently spoken and written by educated Japanese.

Mr. and Mrs. ORESTE VACCARI

It is considered in Japan a great privilege and coveted honor to obtain, and be placed at the beginning of a literary work, a motto written by a minister in charge, other high official of the government or other personage of noted fame in the country.

In consideration of the cultural character of this volume, the Minister of Education has granted such a privilege and honor to their authors.

To fully understand the meaning of the motto reproduced in the photogravure, one must refer to the "Manyoshu," the most ancient (VII century A. D.) collection of Japanese poems, one of which says that "Words have a soul, and may create any kind of emotion, among which happiness is supreme."

NOTE. Brush writing is, in Japan, considered a real art, not less noble and prized than the art of painting in Western countries.

Brush writing is taught to Japanese since their first school days, and many are those who fervently and assiduously practice it, just for art's sake, until their oldest age. Prominent men do not neglect this art and not few are those who devote themselves to the profession of teachers of such a branch of learning.

Every year are held in Japan exhibitions of specimens of brush writing of famous mottos or short poems, and the best among them are awarded prizes as in Western countries prizes are awarded to the best paintings.

It is considered in Japan a great privilege and coveted honor to obtain and be placed at the beginning of a literary work, a motto written by a minister in charge, other high official of the government or other personage of noted fame in the country.

In consideration of the cultural character of this volume, the Minister of Education has granted such a privilege and honor to their authors.

To fully understand the meaning of the motto reproduced in the photogravure, one must refer to the "Manyoshu", the most ancient (VII century A.D.) collection of Japanese poems, one of which says that "Words have a soul and may create any kind of emotion among which happiness is supreme".

NOTE. Brush writing is in Japan considered a real art, not less noble and prized than the art of painting in Western countries.

Brush writing is taught to Japanese since their first school days, and many are those who fervently and assiduously practice it, just for art's sake, until their oldest age. "Prominent men do not neglect this art" and not few are those who devote themselves to the profession of teachers of such a brush of learning

Every year are held in Japan exhibitions of specimens of brush writing of famous mottos or short poems, and the best among them are awarded prizes as in Western countries prices are awarded to the best paintings.

Photogravure of a motto written especially for this book by His Excellency Toh Matsunaga, the Minister of Education of Japan.

The motto reproduced above, which, in typographic characters correspond to 言靈の幸 and in roman characters to KOTO DAMA NO SACHI, signifies HAPPINESS IN THE SPIRIT OF LANGUAGE.

CONTENTS

ORTHOGRAPHY
AND
PRONUNCIATION

Orthography and Pronunciation

The Japanese adopted the Chinese ideographic script, called *kanji* 漢字, in the third century of our era, when the code of Confucian philosophy and the literature embodying it were introduced into Japan.

Through the Chinese ideograms there came into existence, about the close of the eighth century, two syllabaries called *katakaná* 片仮名 and *hiraganá* 平仮名, both of which have a common appellation : *kaná* 仮名.

Although every Japanese word could be written with *kaná,* these have not supplanted the ideograms, but play only a minor role beside them, their use being generally restricted to indicate verbal inflections and to write some of the adverbs and prepositions, most of the conjunctions, and the interjections.

The *katakana* characters are now generally used in writing foreign names, words of foreign derivation and telegrams, while the *hiragana* characters are used in other cases.

The characters of the Japanese language, like those of the Chinese, are arranged in columns, beginning on the right-hand side of the page and running from top to bottom and from right to left. Some books, however, especially those that treat of mathematics, medical science, chemistry, and mechanics, are written from left to right and in horizontal lines, as European languages are.

In 1885, a society was organized by foreigners and Japanese for the purpose of effecting a substitution of the Roman system of writing for the Chinese and Japanese scripts. However, the romanization of the Japanese writing is still very far from being a reality, its use being at present restricted to a few books, a very few magazines and to Japanese bilingual dictionaries.

There are three systems of romanization of the Japanese writing, but the one adopted for this book is that followed by almost all the *rōmaji* ローマ字 (roman characters) dictionaries.

In the first of the following tables are given the *katakana* characters arranged in the Japanese order of the *go-jū-on* 五十音 "the fifty sounds." Under each *katakana* is given the corresponding *hiragana,* and under that the equivalent in roman letters.

Katakana and *Hiragana*

Table I

ワ わ wa	ラ ら ra	ヤ や ya	マ ま ma	ハ は ha	ナ な na	タ た ta	サ さ sa	カ か ka	ア あ a
ヰ ゐ i	リ り ri	イ い i	ミ み mi	ヒ ひ hi	ニ に ni	チ ち chi	シ し shi	キ き ki	イ い i
ウ う u	ル る ru	ユ ゆ yu	ム む mu	フ ふ fu	ヌ ぬ nu	ツ つ tsu	ス す su	ク く ku	ウ う u
ヱ ゑ e	レ れ re	エ え e	メ め me	ヘ へ he	ネ ね ne	テ て te	セ せ se	ケ け ke	エ え e
ン ん n / ヲ を wo	ロ ろ ro	ヨ よ yo	モ も mo	ホ ほ ho	ノ の no	ト と to	ソ そ so	コ こ ko	オ お o

The first *hiragana* characters in the cases of the following table, although considered obsolete, are still used by some Japanese in their cursive writing. For comparison, the corresponding modern *hiragana* characters have been placed below the obsolete ones.

Table II

し shi	さ sa	え e	ま ma	の no	た ta	わ wa	と to	に ni	い i
す su	き ki	て te	こ ko	く ku	な na	か ka	ち chi	ほ ho	は ha

By putting two small marks or a small circle on the right side of the upper part of certain syllables, their sound is modified.

The two small marks are called *nigori* 濁, and the small circle is called *maru* 丸 or *handaku* 半濁.

Table III

ヴァ ア va	パ ぱ pa	バ ば ba	ダ だ da	ザ ざ za	ガ が ga
ヴィ イ vi	ピ ぴ pi	ビ び bi	ヂ ぢ ji	ジ じ ji	ギ ぎ gi
ヴ ヴ vu	プ ぷ pu	ブ ぶ bu	ヅ づ zu	ズ ず zu	グ ぐ gu
ヴェ エ ve	ペ ぺ pe	ベ べ be	デ で de	ゼ ぜ ze	ゲ げ ge
ヴォ オ vo	ポ ぽ po	ボ ぼ bo	ド ど do	ゾ ぞ zo	ゴ ご go

N. B. The separate column on the left includes four combinations of characters representing the sounds of the consonant *v* with the four vowels *a, i, e,* and *o,* and one single character to represent the sound of *v* and *u,* all of which are used only to write foreign words.

In writing words of foreign derivation, the sound of **di,** as in the word *dictation,* may be represented by the symbol ヂ or ディ·

    birudingu ビルヂング or ビルディング   building

By the combination of certain syllables with *ya* ヤ, *yu* ユ, and *yo* ヨ, other sounds are obtained. In this case the characters corresponding to *ya*, *yu*, and *yo* are written in a smaller size than the characters with which they are combined.

Table IV

リャ りゃ rya	ミャ みゃ mya	ヒャ ひゃ hya	ニャ にゃ nya	チャ ちゃ cha	シャ しゃ sha	キャ きゃ kya
リュ りゅ ryu	ミュ みゅ myu	ヒュ ひゅ hyu	ニュ にゅ nyu	チュ ちゅ chu	シュ しゅ shu	キュ きゅ kyu
リョ りょ ryo	ミョ みょ myo	ヒョ ひょ hyo	ニョ にょ nyo	チョ ちょ cho	ショ しょ sho	キョ きょ kyo
	ピャ ぴゃ pya	ビャ びゃ bya	ヂャ ぢゃ ja	ジャ じゃ ja	ギャ ぎゃ gya	
	ピュ ぴゅ pyu	ビュ びゅ byu	ヂュ ぢゅ ju	ジュ じゅ ju	ギュ ぎゅ gyu	
	ピョ ぴょ pyo	ビョ びょ byo	ヂョ ぢょ jo	ジョ じょ jo	ギョ ぎょ gyo	

Note that all the Japanese characters transliterated with roman letters and containing *y* in the body of the syllable, have diphthongal sounds.

PRONUNCIATION
Short Vowels

A, a   is pronounced as **a** in *father.*
E, e   as in the first syllable of the words *enamel, enemy, edge, melody.*
I, i   as **e** in *me, be.*
O, o   as in *oasis, opinion, original.*
U, u   as in *put, push, pull, full.*

The *u* of the syllable *su* is almost silent when followed by a syllable beginning with *k,* and the *u* of the syllable *ku* is, in certain words, almost silent when followed by a syllable beginning with *s.*

U is almost silent also in the verbal suffix *masu* マス, as in *tabemasu (tabemas′)* 食べマス I eat, *ikimasu (ikimas′)* 行キマス I go.

sukoshi (s′koshi) 少シ little   *suki*   *(s′ki)*   好キ   I like
takusan (tak′san) 沢山 much   *okusan (ok′san)* 奥サン Madam

In such cases the almost silent *u* will be, in this book, distinguished by a curve placed above, as shown below:

sŭkóshi 少シ little   **sŭkí**   好キ   I like
takŭsán 沢山 much   **ókŭsan** 奥サン Mrs., Madam
ikimásŭ   行キマス I go
kakimásŭ 書キマス I write

In certain words, and invariably in the suffix *máshĭta* マシタ, also the vowel *i* is almost silent, as in **shĭtá** *(sh'ta)* 下 *under,* in which case the *i* will similarly be distinguished by a curve, as in the following examples:

ikimáshĭta 行キマシタ I went   *mimáshĭta* 見マシタ I saw

The graphic accent placed on one of the vowels of each of the above words given as phonetic examples, indicates the force of utterance to be laid on their stressed syllables.

Long Vowels

The long vowels are characterized by a line placed above them.
Ā, ā   as in *park, lark, spark.*
Ē, ē   as the sound of **a** in *ape, fame, same* or *ay* in *day, may, say.*
Ō, ō   as in *so, old,* and as **oa** in *oats, oath.*
Ū, ū   as **oo** in *boom, soon, broom, spoon.*

The long vowel *e* is often written *ei.*

The long sound of *i* (pron. **ee,** as in **beer**) is generally written *ii.*

okāsan	オ母サン	mother	*ōkii*	大キイ	big, large
obāsan	オバアサン	grandmother	*kōsan*	降参	surrender
nēsan	姉サン	elder sister	*ureshii*	ウレシイ	glad, happy
kēsan	ケーサン	paper weight	*kanashii*	カナシイ	sad
eikō	栄光	glory	*joyū*	女優	actress
heitai	兵隊	soldier	*kūshū*	空襲	air raid
kōhei	公平	impartiality	*mōbaku*	盲爆	blind bombing
kōkei	光景	a scene	*sabishii*	淋シイ	lonesome
sōkei	総計	total amount	*niisan*	兄サン	elder brother

Note that it is essential to distinguish long from short vowel sounds, if one wishes to speak the Japanese language intelligibly. Many words written with short vowels have a different meaning when written with long vowels.

koshi	腰	the waist	*kōshi*	孝子	dutiful child
kósei	個性	personality	*kōsei*	校正	proof reading
súji	筋	muscle	*sūji*	数字	a numeral, a figure
bóshi	拇指	thumb	*bōshi*	帽子	hat
kuki	茎	a stalk	*kūki*	空気	air
kosúi	湖水	a lake	*kōsui*	香水	perfume
kúro	黒	black	*kurō*	苦労	suffering
tóru	取ル	to take	*tōru*	通ル	to go through
toshi	年	year	*tōshi*	投資	investment

When writing Japanese with *kaná,* the sound of the long vowel *a* may be represented by the symbol **ア,** placed after the character containing the long vowel, as in the following examples:

obāsan	オバアサン	grandmother
okāsan	オカアサン	mother

The sound of the long vowel *o* may be represented in five ways, as shown in Table V and Table VI, and the long vowel *u* in two ways, as given in Table IX.

The different ways of representing the sound of the long vowels *o* and *u* are indiscriminately used by the Japanese, both in writing and in printing. However, to avoid confusion, the sound of the long vowel *o* and *u* will be represented in this book in one way only, as given in the upper division of each of the following tables.

Katakaná

Table V

rō	yō	mō	pō	bō	hō	nō	dō	tō	zō	sō	gō	kō	ō
ロオ	ヨオ	モオ	ポオ	ボオ	ホオ	ノオ	ドオ	トオ	ゾオ	ソオ	ゴオ	コオ	オオ
ロウ	ヨウ	モウ	ポウ	ボウ	ホウ	ノウ	ドウ	トウ	ゾウ	ソウ	ゴウ	コウ	オウ
ラウ	ヤウ	マウ	パウ	バウ	ハウ	ナウ	ダウ	タウ	ザウ	サウ	ガウ	カウ	アウ
ラフ	ヤフ	マフ	パフ	バフ	ハフ	ナフ	ダフ	タフ	ザフ	サフ	ガフ	カフ	アフ
ロフ	ヨフ	モフ	ポフ	ボフ	ホフ	ノフ	ドフ	トフ	ゾフ	ソフ	ゴフ	コフ	オフ

OBSOLETE SPELLING

ō
ヲウ
ワウ
ヲウ
ワフ
ヲフ

Hiraganá

Table VI

rō	yō	mō	pō	bō	hō	nō	dō	tō	zō	sō	gō	kō	ō
ろお	よお	もお	ぽお	ぼお	ほお	のお	どお	とお	ぞお	そお	ごお	こお	おお
ろう	よう	もう	ぽう	ぼう	ほう	のう	どう	とう	ぞう	そう	ごう	こう	おう
らう	やう	まう	ぱう	ばう	はう	なう	だう	たう	ざう	さう	がう	かう	あう
らふ	やふ	まふ	ぱふ	ばふ	はふ	なふ	だふ	たふ	ざふ	さふ	がふ	かふ	あふ
ろふ	よふ	もふ	ぽふ	ぼふ	ほふ	のふ	どふ	とふ	ぞふ	そふ	ごふ	こふ	おふ

OBSOLETE SPELLING

ō
をう
わう
わう
わふ
をふ

Katakaná

Table VII

ryō	myō	pyō	byō	hyō	nyō	chō	shō	gyō	kyō	jō		jō
リョウ	ミョウ	ピョウ	ビョウ	ヒョウ	ニョウ	チョウ	ショウ	ギョウ	キョウ	ジョウ		ヂョウ
リャウ	ミャウ	ピャウ	ビャウ	ヒャウ	ニャウ	チャウ	シャウ	ギャウ	キャウ	ジャウ	OBSOLETE SPELLING	ヂャウ
レウ	メウ	ペウ	ベウ	ヘウ	ネウ	テウ	セウ	ゲウ	ケウ	ゼウ		デウ
レフ	ミフ	ペフ	ベフ	ヘフ	ネフ	テフ	セフ	ゲフ	ケフ	ゼフ		デフ

Hiraganá

Table VIII

ryō	myō	pyō	byō	hyō	nyō	chō	shō	gyō	kyō	jō		jō
りょう	みょう	ぴょう	びょう	ひょう	にょう	ちょう	しょう	ぎょう	きょう	じょう		ぢょう
りゃう	みゃう	ぴゃう	びゃう	ひゃう	にゃう	ちゃう	しゃう	ぎゃう	きゃう	じゃう	OBSOLETE SPELLING	ぢゃう
れう	めう	ぺう	べう	へう	ねう	てう	せう	げう	けう	ぜう		でう
れふ	みふ	ぺふ	べふ	へふ	ねふ	てふ	せふ	げふ	けふ	ぜふ		でふ

Table IX

ryū	myū	pyū	byū	hyū	nyū	jū	chū	jū	shū	gyū	kyū	yū
リ ュ ウ	ミ ュ ウ	ピ ュ ウ	ビ ュ ウ	ヒ ュ ウ	ニ ュ ウ	ヂ ュ ウ	チ ュ ウ	ジ ュ ウ	シ ュ ウ	ギ ュ ウ	キ ュ ウ	ユ ウ
リ フ	ミ フ	ピ フ	ビ フ	ヒ フ	ニ フ	ヂ フ	チ フ	ジ フ	シ フ	ギ フ	キ フ	ユ フ

The sound of all long vowels may also be represented, when writing in *kana*, by a bar placed immediately after the syllable containing the long vowel, especially when writing certain words of foreign derivation, as shown in the following examples:

bīru	ビール	beer
erebētā	エレベーター	elevator
kōhī	コーヒー	coffee
sŭtēshon	ステーション	station
taipŭraitā	タイプライター	typewriter
tēburu	テーブル	table

Note that words of foreign derivation generally maintain the accent upon the syllable corresponding to the one stressed in the original foreign word.

When a *kaná* character is repeated in succession in the same word, the duplicated character is represented by the symbol ヽ.

háha ハヽ mother   **chichí** チヽ father

When writing Japanese in horizontal lines, a word written in *kaná* may be regularly repeated with syllabic characters, as for instance **iró-iró** イロイロ *various*, **kutá-kutá** クタ クタ *worn out* but when writing Japanese in vertical lines, the repetition is indicated by a long mark resembling the character 〈 (ku) of the *hiraganá* syllabary, as shown on the right side of this explanation.

The symbol ヽ takes the *nigori* when it is used to indicate that the sound of the duplicated character is altered according to Table III.

Ex: *kagamí* カゞミ mirror   *kogotó* コゞト a scolding

Also the symbol used to indicate the repetition of a word takes the *nigori* when the sound of the first character of the duplicated word is altered according to Table III. The words vertically written on the right of this explanation correspond to the ones given below.

ト ク
キ ニ
〱 〱

kuníguni クニグニ countries   *tokidokí* トキドキ now and then

The repetition of a *kanji* is indicated by the symbol 々 .

iró-iró 色々 various   *tabí-tabí* 度々 often

Consonants

The consonants *b, d, j, k, m, n, p,* and *t,* are pronounced as they are in English.

G is always pronounced hard as in *garland.* Ex. *gakú* 額 framed picture, *géki* 劇 a drama, *gímu* 義務 duty, *gógo* 午後 afternoon. When *g* is in the body of a word, it is generally pronounced as if it were preceded by a faint sound of **n**. Ex. *kagó* (*ka_ngo*) 籠 cage, *kagamí* (*ka_ngami*) 鏡 mirror.

F is pronounced with the two lips a little apart, and one's lower and upper teeth almost in contact, not with the lower lip and the upper teeth as Western people pronounce it.

H is always pronounced aspirated as in *hope.*

The symbol ン, corresponding to the sound of *n,* is pronounced *m* before *b, p* and *m.*

シンブン *shimbún* newspaper ワンパクナ *uámpaku-na* naughty
センモンカ *semmonká* specialist   ホンモノ *hommonó* genuine article

R is not pronounced as distinctly as it is in English; it approaches the sound of **l**, but until one hears it from a Japanese, it is better not to try to pronounce it differently from the natural way one is accustomed to.

The sound of **l** does not exist in the Japanese language, and when foreign words containing this consonant are to be written with *kana* characters, the **r** symbols are used.

Labrador *Raburadorú* ラブラドル lamp   *rámpu* ランプ
London *Róndon* ロンドン   lemonade *remonēdo* レモネード

S before a vowel, is always pronounced as in *salmon, self, solar.*

Sh is pronounced as in *shaft, sheep.*

Ch is pronounced as in *cherry, chief, choice.*

The syllable **wa** is pronounced as in *waft*, and the syllable **wo,** which is used to indicate the accusative case, is pronounced as **wo** in *worship*, when it follows a word ending in **n,** but when it follows a word ending in a vowel, the **w** is almost silent.

wakái	ワカイ	young	*waraú*	ワラウ	to laugh
hon wo	ホンヲ	the book	*umá wo*	ウマヲ	the horse

Y is pronounced as in English in the words *yacht, yell, yonder, you*. When **y** is preceded by **i,** both letters should be pronounced distinctly to avoid mistaking their combined sound for that of some of the diphtongs given in Table IV.

biyóin	美ビ容ヨ容院ン	beauty parlour	*byóin*	病ビョ院ウ院ン	hospital
kíyō	器キ用ヨ用ウ	skilful	*kyō*	今日(キョウ)	to-day

Z is pronounced as in *zeal, zodiac, zone.*

Double Consonants

Care must be taken to distinguish single from double consonants, as many words that have single consonants change meaning when these are pronounced double. The double consonants are pronounced in Japanese as they are in Italian, that is, they are stressed by holding for a moment the vocal organs in the position required to pronounce them.

kóka	古コ歌カ	an old song	*kokká*	国コ歌カ	national anthem
isó	磯ソ	beach	*issō*	一ソ層ソ	more
sóto	外ト	outside	*sottó*	ソット	softly
tokú	徳ク	virtue	*tokkú*	トック	already
hikakú	比ヒ較カ	comparison	*hikkáku*	引ヒ搔カク	to scratch

The small *katakaná* on the right side of the above *kanji* indicate the pronunciation of the latter.

The phonetic syllables attached to ideograms, whether written with *katakaná* or *hiraganá*, are called **furiganá** 振リ仮カ名ナ, and until shortly after the end of the Pacific War, were used in most newspapers and printed books to indicate the pronunciation of the *kanji*.

Since 1947, following the written language reforms approved by the Japanese Diet (See page 15), practically all newspapers, most of the magazines and books intended for the learned and average class of readers, have been printed, in conformity with the new law, without *furigand*, except in the case of unfamiliar *kanji*.

However, the *furiganá* is still being used in books and magazines intended for a less learned class of readers.

Katakaná and *hiraganá* cannot be mixed in the same composition, so that the *furiganá* must be written with the characters of the same syllabary used with the ideograms.

The double consonants are indicated by having the affected character preceded by a small ッ (*tsu*), as shown in the above five words on the right.

The double pronunciation of **ch** is represented in roman characters by **tch** and in *kaná* characters by ッ placed before the affected syllable.

kotchí	コッチ	here	*dótchi*	ドッチ	which
atchí	アッチ	there	*mátchi*	マッチ	matches

Accentuation

Some of the early studies of the Japanese language expressed the view that the syllables of Japanese words bear scarcely any accentuation. This error concerning Japanese accentuation has been carried over into later studies, mainly because of inadequate research into this important aspect of the language.

The fact is that syllabic stresses vary in any words containing two or more syllables, no matter what the language may be.

To the untrained Western ear, the comparatively unemotional manner of speaking of the Japanese may appear to lack syllabic stress. When their emotions are aroused, however, the Japanese stress their syllables clearly and specifically.

If Japanese words are not correctly accented, they sound as oddly foreign to Japanese ears as, say, the English language sounds to English ears when spoken by French students who may tend to stress the last syllables of English words according to French usage.

The correct stress on Japanese syllables is the more important in that the Japanese language contains numerous words which, although spelled with the same letters, have different meaning according to the position of the stressed syllable.

The examples given below, which represent only a very small number of words spelled with the same letters but having different meaning according to the position of their stressed syllable, will demonstrate how necessary it is to know the right accentuation of Japanese words.

ása	朝	morning	*asá*	麻	flax, hemp
haná	花	flower	*hána*	端	the outset. beginning

háshi	橋	a bridge	*háshi*	箸	chopsticks
ippái	いっぱい	full, up to the brim	*ippai*	一杯	one cupful
kagú	嗅ぐ	to smell	*kágu*	家具	furniture
karasu	枯らす	to let wither	*kárasu*	烏	a crow
kashí	貸し	loan	*káshi*	樫	oak tree
kaú	買う	to buy	*káu*	飼う	to keep (animals)
kijí	雉子	a pheasant	*kíji*	記事	article (of newspaper)
kirú	着る	to wear. put on	*kíru*	切る	to cut
nashí	梨	a pear	*náshi*	無し	without
magó	孫	grandchild	*mágo*	馬子	pack-horseman
omoí	重い	heavy	*omói*	思い	emotion, feeling
séki	席	seat, pew	*sekí*	咳	cough
shimai	姉妹	sisters	*shimái*	仕舞	end, close
tátsu	立つ	to stand up	*tatsú*	竜	dragon
új i	氏	family stock	*uji*	蛆	larva
yói	良い	good	*yoi*	宵	early evening

To provide the student with the essential approach to correct pronunciation, the authors have had a graphic accent printed on the stressed syllable of the Japanese words given throughout the book.

This new and unique feature will prove to be of great benefit to the student, as he will be able, from the very beginning of his study, and without mental effort, to pronounce the words he gradually learns, correctly and intelligibly to Japanese ears.

Before the publication of this new and enlarged edition of Vaccari's Japanese Grammar, no book, either compiled by Japanese or foreign scholars, treated, to any appreciable extent, the subject of phonetics of the Japanese language.

This apparent neglect was probably due to the long and wearisome work required to elaborate and establish for the first time phonetic rules of a difficult language as the Japanese language is.

The task of filling this gap was taken up some years ago by the authors of this book, and the result of their researches is indicated not only by the accent placed on the Japanese words used throughout this volume, but also by the ascertained and important phonetic rules given at its end, from page 651 to page 733.

The phonetic study of Western languages has been well established for centuries. Better Western dictionaries use special marks to stress the syllables of polysyllabic words. The study of Japanese phonetics, scientifically based, has however been overlooked by Oriental scholars, whether Japanese or foreigner.

The authors offer this first comprehensive and systematic exposition of Japanese phonetics in the hope that it will facilitate the processes of accurate study and usage.

JAPANESE LANGUAGE REFORMS
Limitation of Chinese Characters

With a view to simplifying the Japanese script, an Investigating Commettee, under the auspices of the Education Ministry, drew up, in November 1946, a list of 1850 essential characters.

The list[1] was approved by the Diet in 1947 as the only characters to be used by newspapers, magazines and in official documents.

Of the 1850 characters, the most common ones, 881 in all, are to be taught to, and learned by, all boys and girls during the nine years of their compulsory education.

Since the use of several thousands of different ideographs is indeed a serious obstacle to popular education, their reduction in number is welcome.

If in future the limited number of characters is still reduced untill they are abolished outright, the Japanese could then use one of their two easy native syllabaries or adopt the alphabetic system for their written language. Their culture would be immensely benefitted and their national progress would be by far more rapid.

Present *Kaná* Spelling
Géndai Kanazukaí

(*géndai* present, *kaná* Japanese letters, *zukái* spelling)

The Japanese Ministry of Education also ruled that some *kana* letters should be considered obsolete and substituted by others, of the same Japanese sillabary but of the same sound, as indicated below:

Obsolete spelling			Present spelling		
Katakaná	*Hiraganá*		*Katakaná*	*Hiraganá*	
ヰ	i	ゐ	イ	i	い
ヱ	e	ゑ	エ	e	え
ヲ	o	を	オ	o	お

Examples:

Obsolete spelling			Present spelling	
Katakana	*Hiragana*	**Meaning**	*Katakaná*	*Hiraganá*
ヰマス	ゐます		イマス	います
imásŭ	*imásŭ*	there is	*imásŭ*	*imásŭ*
エホン	ゑほん		エホン	えほん
ehón	*ehón*	picture book	*ehón*	*ehón*

---

1. The list of the 1850 characters, in brush and printed styles, is given in Vaccari's publication "STANDARD KANJI," with their transliteration in roman characters, English translation and in their compound kanji-words. See the description of this publication at the end of this book.

The *Katakaná* ヲ and its *Hiraganá* equivalent を, although considered obsolete, are used, according to the directives of the Ministry
of Education, only when they indicate the accusative case.

肉ヲ食ベマス ｝*Nikú wo tabemás*.
肉を食べます ｝I eat meat.

Before the language reform was decided, the letter ヘ (へ) *he,*
which is pronounced with aspirate *h,* was also used in several cases
in place of エ or エ (ゑ or え), pronounced *e* without aspiration,
as for instance in the word *káeru* カヘル (かへる) to return.

According to the reform, however, the letter ヘ should be used
only when it represents the sound of *he* with aspirate *h,* so that
the word *káeru* is now supposed to be written カエル (かえる).

It is only to indicate the terminal point towards which movement
is made, in which case it corresponds to the English preposition **to,**
that the letter ヘ is pronounced *e* without aspiration.

東京ヘ来マシタ. ｝*Tōkyō e kimáshĭta.*
東京ヘ来ました. ｝I came to Tokyo.

大阪ヘ行キマシタ.｝*Ōsaka e ikimáshĭta.*
大阪ヘ行きました.｝I went to Osaka.

Romanization of the Language

As already stated in the foreword, there are three systems of
romanization of the Japanese language. Of the three, however, the
Hepburn system is by far the most widely used, both in Japan as
well as abroad, for which reason it has been adopted for this volume
and for all Vaccari's books on Japanese.

Below, the syllables of the three systems that are differently spelled
are given for comparison:

Hepburn Spelling	Nippon Spelling	Kunrei Spelling
cha	tya	tya
chi	ti	ti
chu	tyu	tyu
cho	tyo	tyo
fu	hu	hu
ja	dya	zya
ji	di	zi
ju	dyu	zyu

Hepburn Spelling	Nippon Spelling	Kunrei Spelling
jo	dyo	zyo
sha	sya	sya
shi	si	si
shu	syu	syu
sho	syo	syo
tsu	tu	tu

According to the Kunrei system, long vowels are distinguished by a circumflex accent instead of a dash as used according to the Hepburn and Nippon systems.

In considering these language reforms, the student should not come to the conclusion that the use of the Chinese characters and *kaná* will soon see their end in Japan.

Most books will continue to be printed with as many characters as they were printed in the past. People who received their school education before the recent reforms will continue using the same number of ideographs and *kaná* in their private dealings as they have been accustomed to.

Moreover, if one wishes to read any book, magazine or newspaper issued up to the time of the reforms, one must know the characters they contain.

Therefore, the reforms mentioned above should be understood only as the first attempts made towards the simplification of the written language. Many years, however, will have to go by before the final goal is reached.

HOW TO WRITE JAPANESE CHARACTERS

The Japanese characters are written from left to right and from top to bottom, with the exception of the katakana symbols ン (n) and シ (shi), whose final strokes are written upward.

KATAKANA

STROKES				Completed Characters
1°	2°	3°	4°	
ア	ア			ア a
イ	イ			イ i
ウ	ウ	ウ		ウ u
エ	エ	エ		エ e
オ	オ	オ		オ o
カ	カ			カ ka
キ	キ	キ		キ ki
ク	ク			ク ku

HIRAGANA

STROKES				Completed Characters
1°	2°	3°	4°	
あ	あ	あ		あ a
い	い			い i
う	う			う u
え	え			え e
お	お	お		お o
か	か	か		か ka
き	き	き		き ki
く				く ku

KATAKANA

STROKES				Completed Characters
1°	2°	3°	4°	
ケ	ケ	ケ		ケ ke
コ	コ			コ ko
サ	サ	サ		サ sa
シ	シ	シ		シ shi
ス	ス			ス su
セ	セ			セ se
ソ	ソ			ソ so
タ	タ	タ		タ ta
チ	チ	チ		チ chi
ツ	ツ	ツ		ツ tsu

HIRAGANA

STROKES				Completed Characters
1°	2°	3°	4°	
け	け	け		け ke
こ	こ			こ ko
さ	さ			さ sa
し				し shi
す	す			す su
せ	せ	せ		せ se
そ				そ so
た	た	た	た	た ta
ち	ち			ち chi
つ				つ tsu

KATAKANA

	STROKES			Completed Characters
1°	2°	3°	4°	
テ	テ	テ		テ te
ト	ト			ト to
ナ	ナ			ナ na
ニ	ニ			ニ ni
ヌ	ヌ			ヌ nu
ネ	ネ	ネ	ネ	ネ ne
ノ				ノ no
ハ	ハ			ハ ha
ヒ	ヒ			ヒ hi
フ				フ fu

HIRAGANA

	STROKES			Completed Characters
1°	2°	3°	4°	
て				て te
と	と			と to
な	な	な	な	な na
に	に	に		に ni
ぬ	ぬ			ぬ nu
ね	ね			ね ne
の				の no
は	は	は		は ha
ひ	ひ			ひ hi
ふ	ふ	ふ	ふ	ふ fu

KATAKANA

STROKES				Completed Characters
1°	2°	3°	4°	
ヘ				ヘ he
ホ	ホ	ホ	ホ	ホ ho
マ	マ			マ ma
ミ	ミ	ミ		ミ mi
ム	ム			ム mu
メ	メ			メ me
モ	モ	モ		モ mo
ヤ	ヤ			ヤ ya
ユ	ユ			ユ yu
ヨ	ヨ	ヨ		ヨ yo

HIRAGANA

STROKES				Completed Characters
1°	2°	3°	4°	
ヘ				ヘ he
ほ	ほ	ほ	ほ	ほ ho
ま	ま	ま		ま ma
み	み			み mi
む	む	む		む mu
め	め			め me
も	も	も		も mo
や	や	や		や ya
ゆ	ゆ	ゆ		ゆ yu
よ	よ			よ yo

KATAKANA   HIRAGANA

STROKES				Completed Characters	STROKES				Completed Characters
1°	2°	3°	4°		1°	2°	3°	4°	
ラ	ラ			ラ ra	ら	ら			ら ra
リ	リ			リ ri	り	り			り ri
ル	ル			ル ru	る				る ru
レ				レ re	れ	れ			れ re
ロ	ロ	ロ		ロ ro	ろ				ろ ro
ワ	ワ			ワ wa	わ	わ			わ wa
丰	卅	荓	卉	ヰ i	ゐ				ゐ i
ユ	卫	ヱ		ヱ e	ゑ				ゑ e
ラ	ヲ	ヲ		ヲ wo	を	を	を		を wo
ン	ン			ン n	ん				ん n

STROKES					Completed Characters
1°	2°	3°	4°	5°	
一					一 1
二	二				二 2
三	三	三			三 3
四	四	四	四	四	四 4
五	五	五	五		五 5
六	六	六	六		六 6
七	七				七 7
八	八				八 8
九	九				九 9
十	十				十 10

JAPANESE
CONVERSATION–GRAMMAR

First Lesson　第^ダ_イ一^イ_ッ課^カ

The Japanese language has no article and, except in a very few cases, no distinction is made between singular and plural nouns. Thus, **hon** 本^ホ_ン *book*, may mean *a book, the book, books,* or *the books.* (See Lesson 10.)

The conjunction **and** is expressed by **to** ト.

Vocabulary

book	*hon*	本^ホ_ン	inkstand	*inkitsubó*	インキ壷^ツ_ボ
box	*hakó*	箱^ハ_コ	man	*otokó*	男^オ_ト^コ
bread	*pan*	パン	meat	*nikú*	肉^ニ_ク
butter	*báta*	バタ	pen	*pen*	ペン
chair	{ *isú*	椅^イ子^ス	pencil	*empitsú*	鉛^エ_ン筆^ピ_ツ
	koshikaké	腰^コ_シ掛^カ_ケ	spoon	*sají*	匙^サ_ジ
fish	*sakaná*	魚^サ_カ^ナ	table	*téburu*	テーブル
fork	*fóku*	フォーク	woman	*onná*	女^オ_ン^ナ

Exercise　*Renshū* 練^レ_ン習^シ_ュ^ウ

1. Hon to pen.　**2.** Isú to téburu.　**3.** Otokó to onná.　**4.** Sají to fóku.
5. Pan to báta.　**6.** Nikú to sakaná.　**7.** Empitsú to pen.　**8.** Hakó to inkitsubó.

1. 本トペン.　**2.** 椅子トテーブル.　**3.** 男ト女.　**4.** 匙トフォーク.
5. パントバタ.　**6.** 肉ト魚.　**7.** 鉛筆トペン.　**8.** 箱トインキ壷.

1. A book and a pen.　**2.** The chair and the table.　**3.** Men and women.
4. The spoon and the fork.　**5.** Bread and butter.　**6.** Meat and fish.
7. Pencils and pens.　**8.** The boxes and the inkstand.

Second Lesson 第ダイ二ニ課カ

The **nominative** case is generally indicated by the particle *wa* ハ (postposition) placed after the subjective word.

As a rule, the syllable ハ is pronounced **ha,** but when indicating the nominative, it is pronounced **wa** as in the English word *waft.*

To Have *mótsu* 持ツ
Present Tense

I have	*Watakŭshí wa mótte imásŭ*	私ハ持ッテイマス
You have	*Anáta wa mótte imásŭ*	貴方ハ持ッテイマス
He has	*Káre wa mótte imásŭ*	彼ハ持ッテイマス
She has	*Káno-jo wa mótte imásŭ*	彼女ハ持ッテイマス
It has	*Soré wa mótte imásŭ*	ソレハ持ッテイマス
We have	*Watakŭshitachí wa mótte imásŭ*	私達ハ持ッテイマス
You have	*Anátatachi wa mótte imásŭ*	貴方達ハ持ッテイマス
They have	*Kárera wa mótte imásŭ*	彼等ハ持ッテイマス

Mótte 持ッテ means *having* or *holding,* and *imásŭ* イマス corresponds, in this particular case, to *am, is, are,* so that *Watakŭshí wa mótte imásŭ* 私ハ持ッテイマス translated literally, corresponds to *I am having* or *I am holding=***I have.**

Note that it is only as an auxiliary, as in the above case, that *imásŭ* イマス corresponds to *to be.* When expressing relation of subject and attribute *to be* is translated by *désŭ* デス. See Lesson 5.

Watakŭshí is often shortened into **watashí,** especially in familiar speech.

Káno-jo translated literally means **that woman.**

Watakŭshitachí is often shortened to **watashitachí.**

Watakŭshidómo or **watashidómo** 私共 may be used instead of *watakŭshitachí* or *watashitachí* 私達, in which case the expressions ending in *domo* 共 suggest humbleness.

Káre (he), *káno-jo* (she) and *kárera* (they) are literary expressions. In colloquial speech **he** and **she** are generally expressed by **anó-katá** アノ方 (that person) and **they** by **anó-katatachí** アノ方達 (those persons). In less polite speech *anó-hĭtó* アノ人 may be used instead of *anó-katá,* and *anó-hĭtotachí* アノ人達 instead of *anó-katatachí.*

See Lesson 10, Page 55 for more details on the Japanese personal pronouns.

The negative of the present tense of the verb **to have** is formed by *mótte imasén* 持ッテイマセン.

I have not	*Watashí wa mótte imasén*	私ハ持ッテイマセン
You have not	*Anáta wa mótte imasén*	貴方ハ持ッテイマセン
He has not	*Káre wa mótte imasén*	彼ハ持ッテイマセン
She has not	*Káno-jo wa mótte imasén*	彼女ハ持ッテイマセン
It has not	*Soré wa mótte imasén*	ソレハ持ッテイマセン
We have not	*Watashitachí wa mótte imasén*	私達ハ持ッテイマセン
You have not	*Anátatachi wa mótte imasén*	貴方達ハ持ッテイマセン
They have not	*Kárera wa mótte imasén*	彼等ハ持ッテイマセン

Imasén イマセン is the negative form of *imásŭ* イマス, so that **mótte imasén** 持ッテイマセン, translated literally, corresponds, in this particular case, to *having* or *holding am, is, are* **not.**

As it may be seen from the verb forms, there are no verbal inflections to distinguish number or person. Both must be determined from the context. Personal pronouns before verbs are often omitted, but they are generally used when it is necessary to avoid ambiguity.

The **accusative,** or *objective case,* is indicated by the postposition *wo* ヲ. (See Page 12 for pronunciation of *wo* ヲ。)

> *Nominative :* the book *hon* **wa** 本ハ
> *Accusative :* the book *hon* **wo** 本ヲ
> I have the book. *Watashí* **wa** *hon* **wo** *mótte imásŭ.*
> 私　　ハ　本　ヲ　持ッテ　イマス。

When two or more words are joined by the conjunction **to,** only the last word takes the case particle.

> I have a book and a pencil. *Watashí wa hon* **to** *empitsŭ* **wo** *mótte imásŭ.*
> 私　ハ　本　ト　鉛筆　ヲ　持ッテ　イマス。

Note the construction of the Japanese sentence : **subject + object + verb.**

Vocabulary

apple	*ringó*	リンゴ	pear	*nashí*	梨ナシ
boy	*otokonokó*	男ノ子	picture	*e*	絵エ
clock	*hashiradokéi*	柱時計	saucer	*chatakú*	茶托
cup	*koppú*	コップ		*kōhīzará*	コーヒー皿
	kōhījawán	コーヒ茶椀	water	*mizú*	水ミズ
glass	*garaśu no koppú*	ガラスノコップ	hot water	*o-yu*	オ湯
milk	*gyūnyū*	牛乳	watch[1]	*tokéi*	時計
	míruku	ミルク		*kaichūdokéi*	懐中時計

1 *tokéi* general name for watch, *kaichūdokéi* pocket watch, *udedokéi* 腕時計 wristwatch

Exercise *Renshū* 練_{レン}習_{シウ}

1. Watashí wa báta to pan wo mótte imásŭ. **2.** Anáta wa empitsú to pen wo mótte imásŭ. **3.** Onná wa gyūnyū to mizú wo mótte imásŭ. **4.** Otokonokó wa empitsú to e wo mótte imásŭ. **5.** Watashitachí wa hon to e wo mótte imásŭ. **6.** Anáta wa hashiradokéi to kaichūdokéi wo mótte imásŭ. **7.** Anókatatachí wa tēburu to koshikaké to pen to ínki to inkitsubó wo mótte imásŭ. **8.** Anáta wa ringó to nashí wo mótte imásŭ. **9.** Otokonokó wa kōhījawán to kōhīzara wo mótte imásŭ.

1. 私ハバタトパンヲ持ッテイマス. **2.** 貴方ハ鉛筆トペンヲ持ッテイマス. **3.** 女ハ牛乳ト水ヲ持ッテイマス. **4.** 男ノ子ハ鉛筆ト絵ヲ持ッテイマス. **5.** 私達ハ本ト絵ヲ持ッテイマス. **6.** 貴方ハ柱時計ト懐中時計ヲ持ッテイマス. **7.** アノ方達ハテーブルト腰掛トペントインキトインキ壺ヲ持ッテイマス. **8.** 貴方ハリンゴト梨ヲ持ッテイマス. **9.** 男ノ子ハコーヒー茶椀トコーヒー皿ヲ持ッテイマス.

1. I have the butter and bread. **2.** You have the pencil and pen. **3.** The woman has the milk and water. **4.** The boy has the pencil and picture. **5.** We have the book and picture. **6.** You have a clock and a watch. **7.** They have the table, chair, pen, ink, and inkstand. **8.** You have an apple and a pear. **9.** The boy has a cup and a saucer.

Third Lesson 第_{ダイ}三_{サン}課_カ

The Adjective of Quantity *some*.

Some is expressed by *íkuraka* 幾ラカ joined to a noun by the particle **no** ノ.

íkuraka no mizú	幾ラカノ水	some water
íkuraka no kamí	幾ラカノ紙	some paper

Watashí wa **íkuraka no** gyūnyū wo mótte imásŭ.   I have some milk.
私   ハ   幾ラカ   ノ   牛乳   ヲ 持ッテイマス.

This construction is not often used in ordinary speech. The object before *íkuraka* 幾ラカ without *no* ノ is preferred.

Watashí wa gyūnyū **wo** íkuraka mótte imásŭ.
私   ハ   牛乳   ヲ   幾ラカ   持ッテ イマス.

As *some* is often omitted in English before a noun used in a partitive sense, so is *íkuraka* 幾ラカ in Japanese, without altering much the meaning of the sentence.

Watashí	*wa*	*gyūnyū*	*wo*	*íkuraka*	*mótte*	*imásŭ.*	I have **some** milk.

私　　ハ　　牛乳　　ヲ　　幾ラカ　持ッテ　イマス.

| *Watashí* | *wa* | *gyūnyū* | *wo* | *mótte* | *imásŭ.* | I have milk. |

私　　ハ　　牛乳　　ヲ　　持ッテ　イマス.

To Have

Past Tense *Kakó-jisō* 過ヵ去ヨ時ジ相ゾ

I had	*Watashí wa mótte imáshĭta*	私ハ持ッテイマシタ
You had	*Anáta wa mótte imáshĭta*	貴方ハ持ッテイマシタ
He had	*Káre wa mótte imáshĭta*	彼ハ持ッテイマシタ
She had	*Káno-jo wa mótte imáshĭta*	彼女ハ持ッテイマシタ
It had	*Soré wa mótte imáshĭta*	ソレハ持ッテイマシタ
We had	*Watashitachí wa mótte imáshĭta*	私達ハ持ッテイマシタ
You had	*Anátatachi wa mótte imáshĭta*	貴方達ハ持ッテイマシタ
They had	*Kárera wa mótte imáshĭta*	彼等ハ持ッテイマシタ

Literary translated, ***mótte imáshĭta*** 持ッテイマシタ corresponds to *having* or *holding was* or *were*, and the whole expression indicates the past tense of **to have**.

Negative Past Tense

I had not	*Watashí wa mótte imasén déshĭta*	私ハ持ッテイマセンデシタ
You had not	*Anáta wa mótte imasén déshĭta*	貴方ハ持ッテイマセンデシタ
He had not, etc	*Káre wa mótte imasén déshĭta*	彼ハ持ッテイマセンデシタ

Mótte imasén déshĭta 持ッテイマセンデシタ corresponds to *having*, or *holding was* or *were* **not**, and the whole expression stands for the negative form of the past tense of **to have**.

Otokonokó	*wa*	*kamí*	*wo*	*mótte*	*imáshĭta.*	The boy had paper.

男ノ子　　ハ　　紙　　ヲ　　持ッテ　イマシタ.

| *Onnanokó* | *wa* | *ínki* | *wo* | *mótte* | *imasén* | *déshĭta.* | The girl had no ink. |

女ノ子　　ハ　インキ　ヲ　持ッテイマセン　デシタ.

The Conjunction *and*

When the conjunction ***and*,** instead of joining two nouns, joins two clauses, it is translated by ***soshĭté*** ソシテ and not by *to* ト.

| *Otokonokó* | *wa* | *ringó* | *wo* | *mótte* | *imáshĭta* | ***soshĭté*** | *onnanokó* | *wa* | *nashí* |

男ノ子　　ハ　リンゴ　ヲ　持ッテイマシタ　ソシテ　女ノ子　ハ　　梨

wo *mótte imáshĭta.*　　　　　　The boy had an apple **and** the girl had a pear.

ヲ　持ッテ　イマシタ.

Soshĭté ソシテ may also be used after the final *to* ト placed between the last two of a series of nouns:

| *Watashí* | *wa* | *garasú* | *no* | *koppú* | **to** | *kōhijawán* | **to** | *gyūnyū* | **to** | *pan* | **to** |

私　　ハ　　ガラス　ノ　コップ　ト　コーヒー茶椀ト　牛乳　ト　パン ト

soshĭté *sají* *wo* *mótte imáshĭta.*　　　I had a glass, cup, milk,

ソシテ　匙　ヲ　持ッテ　イマシタ.　　　　　bread **and** a spoon.

Vocabulary

boy	*otokonokó*[1]	男オコノ子コ	mother	*okāsan*	オ母カサン
cake	*o-káshi*[2]	オ菓カ子シ	paper	*kamí*	紙カミ
chalk	*hakubokú*	ハクボク	salt	*shió*	塩シオ
coffee	*kōhī*	コーヒー	sugar	*satō, o-satō*	砂サ糖ト, オ砂糖
father	*otōsan*	オ父トサン	tea	*o-cha*[2]	オ茶チャ
fruit	*kudámono*	果ク物モノ	vinegar	*su*	酢ス
girl	*onnanokó*[1]	女オナノ子コ	wine	*budōshu*	葡ブ萄ド酒シュ

give me   *kudasái*   下サイ
Give me the pencil.   *Empitsú wo kudasái.*   鉛筆ヲ下サイ

Exercise *Renshū* 練レ習シウ

1. Watashí wa íkuraka no pan wo mótte imáshĭta soshĭté otokonokó wa báta wo mótte imáshĭta. **2.** Otōsan wa o-cha wo mótte imáshĭta soshĭté okāsan wa kōhī wo mótte imáshĭta. **3.** Watashí wa kudámono wo mótte imásŭ. **4.** Onnanokó wa nashí wo mótte imáshĭta. **5.** Otōsan wa kudámono to o-káshi wo mótte imáshĭta. **6.** Otōsan to okāsan wa gyūnyū to budōshu wo mótte imáshĭta. **7.** Anáta wa mizú to gyūnyū wo mótte imáshĭta. **8.** Otokonokó to onna-no-kó wa hakó wo mótte imáshĭta. **9.** O-satō wo íkuraka kudasái. **10.** Onnanokó wa hakubokú wo mótte imáshĭta. **11.** Shió to su wo kudasái.

1. 私ハ幾ラカノパンヲ持ッテイマシタソシテ男ノ子ハバタヲ持ッテイマシタ. **2.** オ父サンハオ茶ヲ持ッテイマシタソシテオ母サンハコーヒーヲ持ッテイマシタ. **3.** 私ハ果物ヲ持ッテイマス. **4.** 女ノ子ハ梨ヲ持ッテイマシタ. **5.** オ父サンハ果物トオ菓子ヲ持ッテイマシタ. **6.** オ父サントオ母サンハ牛乳トブドウ酒ヲ持ッテイマシタ. **7.** 貴方ハ水ト牛乳ヲ持ッテイマシタ. **8.** 男ノ子ト女ノ子ハ箱ヲ持ッテイマシタ. **9.** オ砂糖ヲ幾ラカ下サイ. **10.** 女ノ子ハハクボクヲ持ッテイマシタ. **11.** 塩ト酢ヲ下サイ.

1. I had some bread and the boy had some butter. **2.** The father had tea and the mother had coffee. **3.** I have fruit. **4.** The girl had some pears. **5.** The father had the fruit and cake. **6.** The father and mother had the milk and wine. **7.** You had the water and milk. **8.** The boy and girl had some boxes. **9.** Give me some sugar. **10.** The girl had some chalk. **11.** Give me the salt and vinegar.

---

1 The syllable *no* of the words *otokonokó* and *onnanokó* may be written between dashes: *otokó-no-ko, onná-no-ko.*

2 As a rule, *o,* before a word, indicates polite speech. Before certain words, however, as in the case of *o-cha* and *o-káshi,* the letter *o* is used without any idea of politeness. See Honorifics, Lesson 34.

Fourth Lesson 第ダイ四ヨン課カ

Interrogative Form

The **interrogative form** is indicated by the particle *ka* カ placed at the end of a declarative sentence.

Have you?	*Anáta wa mótte imásŭ ka.*	貴方ハ持ッテイマスカ
Have you not?	*Anáta wa mótte imasén ka.*	貴方ハ持ッテイマセンカ
Had you?	*Anáta wa mótte imáshĭta ka.*	貴方ハ持ッテイマシタカ
Had you not?	*Anáta wa mótte imasén déshĭta ka.*	貴方ハ持ッテイマセンデシタカ

NOTE. About the same stressed tone of voice as used on the first words of an English interrogative sentence, generally a verbal expression, has to be laid on the final part of an interrogative Japanese sentence, since it terminates with the principal verb of the interrogation. And the highest pitch of the interrogation has to be laid on the interrogative particle *ka.*

Anáta wa pan wo mótte imásŭ ka.   Have you bread?
貴方 ハ パン ヲ 持ッテ イマス カ.
Senséi wa hakubokú wo mótte imáshĭta ka.   Had the teacher the chalk?
先生 ハ ハクボク ヲ 持ッテ イマシタ カ.

The **personal pronoun** is generally omitted whenever there is no ambiguity, as explained in Lesson 2, so that the first sentence in the above examples may be expressed as follows:

Pan wo mótte imásŭ ka.

When answering a question the personal pronoun is rarely used.

    (Anáta wa) *pan wo mótte imásŭ ka.*

Hái, pan wo mótte imásŭ.	Yes, I have bread.
ハイ, パン ヲ 持ッテ イマス.	
Iié, pan wo mótte imasén.	No, I have no bread.
イヽエ, パン ヲ 持ッテ イマセン.	

As in English, so in Japanese, the object may be omitted when answering a question:

Gyūnyū wo mótte imásŭ ka.	Have you milk?
牛乳 ヲ 持ッテ イマス カ.	
Hái, mótte imásŭ. ハイ, 持ッテイマス.	Yes, I have.
Iié, mótte imasén. イヽエ, 持ッテイマセン.	No, I have not.
Kudámono wo mótte imáshĭta ka.	Had you fruit?
果物 ヲ 持ッテ イマシタ カ.	
Hái, mótte imáshĭta. ハイ, 持ッテイマシタ.	Yes, I had.
Iié, mótte imasén déshĭta.	No, I had not.
イヽエ, 持ッテイマセン デシタ.	

The adjective of quantity **any** in interrogative sentences is translated, as *some* is, by *ikuraka.* In negative answers **any** is not translated.

Anáta *wa* *pan* *wo* ***íkuraka*** *mótte* *imásŭ* *ka.*   Have you **any** bread?
貴方　ハ　パン　ヲ　幾ラカ　持ッテ　イマス　カ.

Otōsan *to* *okāsan* *wa* *satō* *wo* ***íkuraka*** *mótte* *imáshĭta* *ka.*
オ父サント　オ母サン　ハ　砂糖　ヲ　幾ラカ　持ッテ　イマシタ　カ.
   Had the father and mother any sugar?

Hái, ***íkuraka*** *mótte* *imáshĭta.*   Yes, they had **some.**
ハイ,　幾ラカ　持ッテ　イマシタ.

Iié, *mótte* *imasén* *déshĭta.*   No, they hadn't any.
イ丶エ, 持ッテ　イマセン　デシタ.

Vocabulary

blackboard	*kokubán*	黒板	knife *náifu*	ナイフ
cap *bōshi*	帽子		oil *aburá*	油

Exercise   *Renshū* 練習

1. Anáta wa hon to pen wo mótte imásŭ ka. **2.** Onná-no-hĭtó[1] wa pan wo mótte imásŭ ka.—Hái, íkuraka mótte imásŭ.—Iié, mótte imasén. **3.** Inki wo mótte imásŭ ka.—Hái, mótte imásŭ.—Iié, mótte imasén. **4.** Otokó-no-hĭtó[2] wa isú to tēburu wo mótte imásŭ ka.—Hái, mótte imásŭ.—Iié mótte imasén. **5.** Otokó-no-ko wa nikú wo mótte imásŭ ka.—Hái, íkuraka mótte imásŭ.—Iié, mótte imasén. **6.** Aburá to su wo kudasái. **7.** Anáta wa satō wo íkuraka mótte imáshĭta ka.—Hái, íkuraka mótte imáshĭta.—Iié, mótte imasén déshĭta. **8.** Anó katá wa kamí to empitsú wo mótte imáshĭta ka.—Hái, mótte imáshĭta. —Iié, mótte imasén déshĭta. **9.** Anó katá wa náifu to fōku wo mótte imáshĭta ka.—Hái, mótte imáshĭta.—Iié, mótte imasén déshĭta. **10.** Watashitachí wa kokubán to hakubokú wo mótte imásŭ ka.—Hái, mótte imásŭ.—Iié, mótte imasén.

1. 貴方ハ本トペンヲ持ッテイマスカ. **2.** 女ノ人ハパンヲ持ッテ
イマスカ.—ハイ,　幾ラカ持ッテイマス.—イ丶エ,　持ッテイマセン.
3. インキヲ持ッテイマスカ.—ハイ,　持ッテイマス.—イ丶エ持ッテイ
マセン. **4.** 男ノ人ハ椅子トテーブルヲ持ッテイマスカ.—ハイ,　持ッ
テイマス.—イ丶エ,　持ッテイマセン. **5.** 男ノ子ハ肉ヲ持ッテイマス
カ.—ハイ,　幾ラカ持ッテイマス.—イ丶エ,　持ッテイマセン. **6.** 油ト
酢ヲ下サイ. **7.** 貴方ハ砂糖ヲ幾ラカ持ッテイマシタカ.—ハイ,　幾ラ
カ持ッテイマシタ.—イ丶エ,　持ッテイマセンデシタ. **8.** アノ方ハ紙
ト鉛筆ヲ持ッテイマシタカ.—ハイ,　持ッテイマシタ.—イ丶エ,　持ッテ
イマセンデシタ. **9.** アノ方ハナイフトフォークヲ持ッテイマシタカ.

---

1 When speaking of a woman *Onná-no-hĭtó* is generally used instead of *onná,* which in Japanese sounds vulgar. *Onná,* however, may be used when *woman* is in opposition to *man.*

2 *Otokó-no-hĭtó* is preferable to *otokó,* which sounds impolite. *Otokó,* however, is generally used when *man* is in opposition to *woman.*

一ハイ，持ッテイマシタ．—イヘエ，持ッテイマセンデシタ．**10.** 私達
ハ黒板トハクボクヲ持ッテイマスカ．—ハイ，持ッテイマス．—イヘエ，
持ッテイマセン．

1. Have you the book and pen? **2.** Has the woman any bread?—Yes,
she has some.—No, she hasn't any. **3.** Have you any ink?—Yes, I have
some.—No, I haven't. **4.** Has the man the chair and the table?—Yes, he
has.—No, he hasn't. **5.** Has the boy any meat?—Yes, he has some.—No, he
hasn't. **6.** Give me the oil and vinegar. **7.** Had you any sugar?—Yes, I
had.—No, I hadn't. **8.** Had he the paper and pencil?—Yes, he had.—No,
he hadn't. **9.** Had she the knife and fork?—Yes, she had.—No, she hadn't.
10. Have we the blackboard and chalk?—Yes, we have.—No, we have not.

Fifth Lesson 第五課

	TO BE	
Present		**Past**
désŭ デス �	*déshĭta* デシタ ⎫
da ダ ⎬ am, are, is	*dátta* ダッタ ⎬ was, were

Kudámono wa oishíi désŭ.
果物　　ハ オイシイ デス.

The fruit **is** tasty.

Haná wa utsŭkushíi désŭ.
花　　ハ　美シイ　　デス.

Flowers **are** beautiful.

Ténki wa yói déshĭta.
天気　ハ　ヨイ　デシタ.

The weather **was** fine.

Kodomó wa rikō déshĭta.
子供　ハ　利口　デシタ.

The children **were** clever.

Uchí wa ōkii déshĭta ka.
家　　ハ 大キイ デシタ　カ.

Was the house large?

Hái ōkii déshĭta.
ハイ，大キイ デシタ.

Yes, it **was** large.

Ojisán wa kanemochí désŭ ka.
伯父サン ハ　金持　デス　カ.

Is the uncle rich?

Hái, kanemochí désŭ.
ハイ，　金持　　デス.

Yes, he **is** rich.

Désŭ and **déshĭta** are used by anybody and on every occasion;
however, **da** instead of *désŭ*, and **dátta** instead of *déshĭta* are used
in familiar speech among men and young boys, rarely by women.

We advise the beginner to refrain from using these abbreviated forms of
désŭ and *déshĭta* until he has learned by careful observation when it is proper
to use them.

Japanese women use words with softer sounds than those used by men,
whenever the language permits to do so. Japanese men, especially in familiar
conversation, have more liberty of speech than women, and when the occasion
permits they use words that sound more robust when uttered.

   To a beginner, the difference between the speech of a Japanese woman and
that of a man is not noticeable, but to one accustomed to the sounds of the
Japanese language this difference gives charm to the speech of Japanese women.

   If one tries to study the difference in sound between *désŭ* and *da*, and *déshĭta*
and *dátta*, one cannot but notice that *désŭ* and *déshĭta* sound much softer than
da and *dátta*.

There is and There are

   orimásŭ オリマス   *imásŭ* イマス   *arimásŭ* アリマス

   When referring to human beings **there is** and **there are** are
translated by ***orimásŭ*** オリマス or ***imásŭ*** イマス, in which case
the use of *orimásŭ* オリマス indicates a higher degree of polite
speech than is indicated by *imásŭ* イマス.

   When referring to animals ***imásŭ*** イマス is generally used. It
is only when one wishes to show special consideration or respect
towards the person whose animals one speaks of, that, in referring
to them, ***orimásŭ*** オリマス may be used instead of *imásŭ* イマ
ス. This may be the case when speaking of one's superior's or
one's master's horse, dog, etc.

   Arimásŭ アリマス is used when referring to inanimate objects.

   Nouns preceded by *there is, there are* are followed by the particle
ga, which also indicates the *nominative case*. (See Lesson 28)

*Kodomó **ga** orimásŭ ka.* (or *imásŭ ka.*)		Is there a boy?
子供　ガ　オリマス　カ.　　（イマス　カ）		
*Hái, kodomó **ga** orimásŭ.* (or *imásŭ.*)		Yes, there is a boy.
ハイ，子供　ガ　オリマス.　　（イマス）		
*Nezumi **ga** imásŭ ka.*	ネズミガイマスカ.	Are there rats?
Hái, imásŭ.	ハイ，イマス.	Yes, there are.
*Isŭ **ga** arimásŭ ka.*	椅子ガアリマスカ.	Are there chairs?
Hái, arimásŭ.	ハイ，アリマス.	Yes, there are.

   Arimásŭ アリマス corresponds also to the present of **to have**
and is used instead of *mótte imásŭ* 持ッテイマス when referring to
animate beings.

*Otōsan wa musŭkó **ga** **arimásŭ**.*	The father has a son.
オ父サン　ハ　息子　ガ　アリマス.	
*Watashí wa inú **ga** **arimásŭ**.*	I have a dog.
私　ハ　犬　ガ　アリマス.	
*Watashitachí wa ōmu **ga** **arimásŭ**.*	We have a parrot.
私達　　ハ　オームガ　アリマス.	

   As shown in the three above examples, when ***arimásŭ*** アリマ
ス is used to translate **to have**, its object is followed by ***ga*** ガ and
not by ***wo*** ヲ. The postposition ***wo*** ヲ is used after the object
when **to have**, translated by ***mótte imásŭ*** 持ッテイマス, refers to
the possession of inanimate things.

In colloquial speech, however, ...*ga arimásŭ* ガアリマス is often used even when **to have** refers to inanimate things.

Watashí	*wa*	*uchí*	*ga*	*arimásŭ.*	I have a house.
私	ハ	家	ガ	アリマス.
Watashitachí	*wa*	*niwá*	*ga*	*arimásŭ.*	We have a garden.
私達	ハ	庭	ガ	アリマス.

As an independent word, **arimásŭ** アリマス means **there is** or **there are**, so that, literally translated, the two above sentences would correspond to *There is a house for me*, and *There is a garden for us.*

There was and There were

orimáshĭta オリマシタ   *imáshĭta* イマシタ   *arimáshĭta* アリマシタ

What has been said as to the use of *orimásŭ, imásŭ, arimásŭ,* may be applied to the use of *orimáshĭta, imáshĭta, arimáshĭta: ***orimáshĭta** or **imáshĭta** is used for persons; **imáshĭta** for animals; **arimáshĭta** for inanimate objects.[1]

Kodomó ga orimáshĭta ka. (or *imáshĭta ka.*)	{ Was there a child?
子供　ガ　オリマシタ　カ.　(イマシタ　カ)	{ Were there children?
Hái, kodomó ga orimáshĭta. (or *imáshĭta.*)	{ Yes, there was a child.
ハイ、子供　ガ　オリマシタ.　(イマシタ)	{ Yes, there were children.
Nezumí ga imáshĭta ka.	{ Was there a rat?
ネズミ　ガ　イマシタ　カ.	{ Were there rats?
Hái, nezumí ga imáshĭta.	{ Yes, there was a rat.
ハイ、ネズミ　ガ　イマシタ.	{ Yes, there were rats.
Isú ga arimáshĭta ka.	{ Was there a chair?
椅子　ガ　アリマシタ　カ.	{ Were there chairs?
Hái, arimáshĭta.	{ Yes, there was.
ハイ、アリマシタ.	{ Yes, there were.

N. B. The use of *orimásŭ* and *orimáshĭta* indicates a higher degree of politeness than is indicated by *imásŭ* and *imáshĭta.*

Arimáshĭta アリマシタ corresponds also to the past of **to have** and is used instead of *mótte imáshĭta* 持ッテイマシタ when referring to animate beings.

Watashí	*wa*	*umá*	*ga*	*arimáshita.*	I had a horse.
私	ハ	馬	ガ	アリマシタ.
Watashitachí	*wa*	*jochū*	*ga*	*arimáshita.*	We had a maidservant.
私達	ハ	女中	ガ	アリマシタ.

---

1 When fictitious persons are introduced at the beginning of an imaginary story, *arimáshĭta,* and not *imáshĭta,* is used in referring to them, even though they are supposed to have existed as living beings in the past, as in the well known expression: *Once upon a time there was an old man, etc.* In this case the fictitious persons are considered as inanimate objects.

It is understood that all notes given regarding the use of *arimásŭ* アリマス apply also to the use of *arimáshĭta* アリマシタ.

Vocabulary

candle	*rōsoku*	ローソク	cheap	*yasúi*	安イ
cat	*néko*	猫	diligent	*kimbén*	勤勉
daughter	*musŭmé*	娘	intelligent	*kashikói*	賢イ
garden	*niwá*	庭	large	*ōkii*	大キイ
house	*uchí, ié*	家	poor	*bímbō*	貧乏
newspaper	*shimbún*	新聞	rich	*kanemochí*	金持
son	*musŭkó*	息子	small	*chiisái*	小サイ
university	*daigakú*	大学	tasty	*oishíi*	オイシイ

Bring me...... (*Watakŭshí ni*) *mótte kité kudasái.* (私ニ)持ッテ来テ下サイ

Translated literally, **mótte kité kudasái** corresponds to *having coming please=bring......please.*

Bring me a chair. *Isú wo mótte kité kudasái.* 椅子ヲ持ッテ来テ下サイ
Bring me some water. *Mizú wo mótte kité kudasái.* 水ヲ持ッテ来テ下サイ
I am satisfied. *Watakŭshí wa manzokú désŭ.* 私ハ満足デス

Exercise *Renshū* 練習

1. Watashí wa bímbō désŭ soshĭté anáta wa kanemochí désŭ. **2.** Otokó-no-ko wa kashikói désŭ. **3.** Nikú wa yasúi déshĭta ka.—Hái, yasúi déshĭta. **4.** Otokó-no-ko to onná-no-ko wa kimbén désŭ. **5.** Uchí wa chiisái déshĭta ka.—Hái, chiisái déshĭta. **6.** Kudámono wa oishíi déshĭta ka. **7.** Daigakú ga arimásŭ ka.—Hái, arimásŭ. **8.** Niwá ga arimáshĭta ka.—Hái, arimáshĭta. **9.** Onná-no-ko ga orimásŭ ka.—Hái, orimásŭ. **10.** Shimbún wo mótte kité kudasái. **11.** Anáta wa manzokú désŭ ka.—Hái, manzokú désŭ. **12.** Kodomó wa néko ga arimásŭ ka.—Hái, néko ga arimásŭ. **13.** Watashitachí wa ié to niwá ga arimáshĭta.

1. 私ハ貧乏デスソシテ貴方ハ金持デス. **2.** 男ノ子ハ賢イデス. **3.** 肉ハ安イデシタカ.—ハイ, 安イデシタ. **4.** 男ノ子ト女ノ子ハ勤勉デス. **5.** 家ハ小サイデシタカ.—ハイ, 小サイデシタ. **6.** 果物ハオイシイデシタカ. **7.** 大学ガアリマスカ.—ハイ, アリマス. **8.** 庭ガアリマシタカ.—ハイ, アリマシタ. **9.** 女ノ子ガオリマスカ.—ハイ, オリマス. **10.** 新聞ヲ持ッテ来テ下サイ. **11.** 貴方ハ満足デスカ.—ハイ, 満足デス. **12.** 子供ハ猫ガアリマスカ.—ハイ, 猫ガアリマス. **13.** 私達ハ家ト庭ガアリマシタ.

1. I am poor and you are rich. **2.** The boy is intelligent. **3.** Was the meat cheap?—Yes, it was cheap. **4.** The boy and girl are diligent. **5.** Was the house small?—Yes, it was small. **6.** Was the fruit tasty? **7.** Is there a university?—Yes, there is. **8.** Was there a garden?—Yes, there was. **9.** Is there a girl?—Yes, there is. **10.** Bring me a newspaper. **11.** Are you satisfied?—Yes, I am satisfied. **12.** Has the child a cat?—Yes, he has a cat. **13.** We had a house and a garden.

Sixth Lesson 第ダイ六ロク課カ

Negative Form of To Be *Désŭ*

The negative form of *désŭ* (am, is, are) is *de wa arimasén* デハアリマセン and *de wa arimasén déshĭta* デハアリマセンデシタ is the negative form of *déshĭta* デシタ (was, were).

Grammatically analyzed, the first element *de* デ of the two negative expressions is the root of *désŭ* デス to be; *wa* ハ substantivizes the preceding word, so that *de wa* デハ corresponds to *the being* or *to be* (noun); *arimasén* アリマセン in this case corresponds to *am*, *is* or *are not*, and *arimasén déshĭta* アリマセンデシタ to *was or were not*.

De wa arimasén デハアリマセン then would correspond to *the being is not* (=am, is, are not), and *de wa arimasén déshĭta* デハアリマセンデシタ to *the being was not* (=was, were not).

In language regarded below the standard of cultivated speech, *jā arimasén* ジァアリマセン is used instead of *de wa arimasén* デハアリマセン and *jā arimasén déshĭta* ジァアリマセンデシタ instead of *de wa arimasén déshĭta* デハアリマセンデシタ.

Watashí wa Yamadá de wa arimasén.   I am not Mr. Yamada.
私　ハ　山田　デ　ハ　アリマセン.   (I Yamada the being is not.)
Hakubokú de wa arimasén.   It is not chalk.
ハクボク　デ　ハ　アリマセン.   (Chalk the being is not.)
Watashí wa kanemochí de wa arimasén.   I am not rich.
私　ハ　金持　デ　ハ　アリマセン.   (I rich the being is not.)
Káre wa kimbén de wa arimasén.   He is not diligent.
彼　ハ　勤勉　デ　ハ　アリマセン.   (He diligent the being is not.)
Káno-jo wa rikō de wa arimasén déshĭta.   She was not clever.
彼女　ハ　利口デ　ハ　アリマセン　デシタ.   (She clever the being was not.)
Watashitachí wa bímbō de wa arimasén déshĭta.   We were not poor.
私達　　ハ　貧乏デ　ハ　アリマセン　デシタ. (We poor the being was not.)

Note that *de wa arimasén* or *de wa arimasén déshĭta* is used only when the word that precedes the negative is a noun, as in the first two examples or an *adjective of quality* that does not belong to the group of words classified as **true adjectives.** See

Lesson 21 on the *Adjective of Quality and its Adverbial Form*, pages 128 and 129.

There is (was) not, There are (were) not

there is not there are not	⎧ *orimasén* ⎨ *imasén* ⎩ *arimasén*	オリマセン イマセン アリマセン
there was not there were not	⎧ *orimasén déshĭta* ⎨ *imasén déshĭta* ⎩ *arimasén déshĭta*	オリマセンデシタ イマセンデシタ アリマセンデシタ

Referring to human beings, *orimasén* オリマセン and *imasén* イマセン are used, *orimasén* indicating a higher degree of polite speech than is indicated by *imasén*; referring to animals only *imasén* イマセン is used, while *arimasén* アリマセン is used when referring of inanimate objects.

kokó ni コヽニ here　　　　　　**sokó ni** ソコニ there
　　　asokó ni アソコニ over there

Sokó ni kodomó ga orimásŭ ka. ソコ ニ　子供　ガ　オリマス　カ.	Is any child there?
Kokó ni kodomó ga orimasén. コヽ ニ　子供　ガ　オリマセン.	There is no child here.
Sokó ni kodomotachí ga imásŭ ka. ソコ ニ　　子供達　　ガ イマス カ.	Are any children there?
Kokó ni kodomotachí ga imasén. コヽ ニ　子供達　　ガ イマセン.	There are no children here.
Néko ga sokó ni imásŭ ka. 猫　ガ ソコニ イマス カ.	Is a cat there?
Asokó ni keikán ga orimáshĭta ka. アソコ ニ 警官　ガ オリマシタ カ.	Was a policeman over there?
Asokó ni keikán ga orimasén déshĭta. アソコニ 警官　ガ オリマセン デシタ.	There was no policeman over there
Sokó ni inú ga imasén déshĭta ka. ソコニ 犬 ガ イマセン デシタ カ.	Was not a dog there?
Inú ga sokó ni imasén déshĭta. 犬　ガ ソコニ イマセン デシタ.	There was no dog there.
Mĭzú ga arimasén. 水　ガ アリマセン.	There is no water.
Ki ga arimasén. 木　ガ アリマセン.	There are no trees.
Gyŭnyū ga arimasén déshĭta. 牛乳　ガ アリマセン デシタ.	There was no milk.
Ringó ga arimasén déshĭta. リンゴ ガ アリマセン デシタ.	There were no apples.

The above negative forms *arimasén* and *arimasén déshĭta* are also used in expressing the negative meaning of the verb **to have.**

Otōsan wa musŭkó ga arimásŭ ka.　Has the father a son?
オ父サン ハ 息子 ガ アリマス カ.
　Otōsan wa musŭkó ga arimasén.　The father has not a son.
オ父サン ハ 息子 ガ アリマセン.
Anáta wa inú ga arimáshĭta ka.　Had you a dog?
貴方 ハ 犬 ガ アリマシタ カ.
　Watashí wa inú ga arimasén déshĭta.　I had no dog.
私 ハ 犬 ガアリマセン デシタ.

Vocabulary

aunt	obá	伯母	policeman	omáwarisan[1]	オ巡リサン	
child	kodomó	子供		keikán[2]	警官	
doctor	ishá	医者	people	hĭtóbito	人々	
green-grocer	yaoyá	八百屋	person	hĭtó	人	
horse	umá	馬	soldier	heitaí	兵隊	
match	mátchi	マッチ	student	séito[3]	生徒	
monkey	sáru	猿		gakŭséi[4]	学生	
			wolf	ōkami	狼	

Exercise *Renshū* 練習

1. Ishá ga orimásŭ ka.—Hái, orimásŭ.—Iié, orimasén. 2. Heitaí ga imásŭ ka.—Hái, imásŭ.—Iié, imasén. 3. Keikán ga orimáshĭta ka.—Hái, orimáshĭta.—Iié, orimasén déshĭta. 4. Séito ga imáshĭta ka.—Hái, imáshĭta.—Iié, imasén déshĭta. 5. Umá ga imásŭ ka.—Hái, imásŭ.—Iié, imasén. 6. Ōkami ga imáshĭta ka.—Iié, ōkami ga imasén déshĭta. 7. Inkitsubó ga arimásŭ ka.—Hái, arimásŭ.—Iié, arimasén. 8. Mátchi ga arimásŭ ka.—Mátchi ga arimasén. 9. Ishá wa musŭmé ga arimásŭ ka.—Iié, musŭmé ga arimasén. Musŭkó ga arimásŭ. 10. Ojisán ga arimásŭ ka.—Iié, arimasén. Obá ga arimásŭ. 11. Yaoyá wa sáru wo mótte imásŭ. 12. Watashitachí wa kodomó ga arimasén.

1. 医者ガオリマスカ.—ハイ, オリマス.—イヽエ, オリマセン. 2. 兵隊ガイマスカ.—ハイ, イマス.—イヽエ, イマセン. 3. 警官ガオリマシタカ.—ハイ, オリマシタ.—イヽエ, オリマセンデシタ. 4. 生徒ガイマシタカ.—ハイ, イマシタ.—イヽエ, イマセンデシタ. 5. 馬ガイマスカ.—ハイ, イマス.—イヽエ, イマセン. 6. 狼ガイマシタカ.—イヽエ, 狼ガイマセンデシタ. 7. インキ壷ガアリマスカ.—ハイ, アリマス.—イヽエ, アリマセン. 8. マッチガアリマスカ.—マッチガアリマセン. 9. 医者ハ娘ガアリマスカ.—イヽエ, 娘ガアリマセン.

---

1 colloq. speech　2 formal speech　3 pupil　4 scholar (one who attends a school)

息子ガアリマス． **10.** 伯父サンガアリマスカ．―イヽエ，アリマセン．
伯母ガアリマス． **11.** 八百屋ハ猿ヲ持ッテイマス． **12.** 私達ハ子供ガ
アリマセン．

1. Is there a doctor?—Yes, there is.—No, there is not. **2.** Are there soldiers?
—Yes, there are.—No, there are not. **3.** Was there a policeman?—Yes, there
was.—No, there was not. **4.** Were there students?—Yes, there were.—No,
there were not. **5.** Is there a horse?—Yes, there is.—No, there is not.
6. Were there wolves?—No, there were no wolves. **7.** Is there an inkstand?—
Yes, there is.—No, there is not. **8.** Are there matches?—No, there are no
matches. **9.** Has the doctor a daughter?—No, he has not a daughter; he has
a son. **10.** Have you an uncle?—No, I have not; I have an aunt. **11.** The
green-grocer has a monkey. **12.** We have no children.

Seventh Lesson　第イ七チ課カ

Demonstrative Adjectives and Pronouns

	Adjectives				Pronouns	
this	**konó**	コノ		this	**koré**	是レ, コレ
these	**korérano**	是レ等ノ		these	**koréra**	是レ等ヲ
that	{ **anó**	アノ		that	{ **aré**	アレ
	{ **sonó**	ソノ			{ **soré**	ソレ
those	{ **arérano**	アレ等ラノ		those	{ **aréra**	アレ等ヲ
	{ **sorérano**	ソレ等ラノ			{ **soréra**	ソレ等ヲ

Sonó, sorérano, soré, soréra, are used when indicating objects
that are near to the persons spoken to, or when referring to things
previously spoken of. **Sonó, sorérano**, have often the meaning
of a weak *that* or *those*, and correspond in many cases to the English
the when this article refers to something already mentioned.

Anó アノ, *arérano* アレ等ノ, *aré* アレ, *aréra* アレ等 are used when
referring to objects that are far from the speaker and the person
spoken to.

The other demonstrative adjectives and pronouns are used as in
English.

Konó sakaná wa umái désŭ.　　　This fish is tasty.
コノ　魚　ハ　旨イ　デス．

Korérano hon wa omoshirói désŭ.　These books are interesting.
是等ノ　本　ハ　面白イ　デス．

Anó nikú wa mazúi désŭ.　　　That meat is tasteless.
アノ　肉　ハ　マヅイ　デス．

Arérano kimonó wa takái désŭ.　Those kimonos are dear.
アレ等ノ　着物　ハ　高イ　デス．

Sonó bōshi wa chiisái désŭ.
ソノ 帽子 ハ 小サイ デス.

Sorérano empitsú wa nagái désŭ.
ソレ等ノ 鉛筆 ハ 長イ デス.

Koré wa oishíi désŭ.
コレ ハ オイシイ デス.

Koréra wa mazúi désŭ.
コレ等 ハ マヅイ デス.

Aré wa takái désŭ.
アレ ハ 高イ デス.

Aréra wa takái désŭ.
アレ等 ハ 高イ デス.

Soré wa yasúi désŭ.
ソレ ハ 安イ デス.

Soréra wa yasúi désŭ.
ソレ等 ハ 安イ デス.

That hat is small.

Those pencils are long.

This is tasty.

These are tasteless.

That is dear.

Those are dear.

That is cheap.

Those are cheap.

Most adjectives ending in *i* may be used predicatively in the present tense, without being followed by *désŭ*. This omission, however, renders the speech less polite. See Lesson 10, Page 58.

Konó sakaná wa **umái.**
コノ 魚 ハ 旨イ.

Korérano hon wa **omoshirói.**
コレ等ノ 本 ハ 面白イ.

Anó nikú wa **mazúi.**
アノ 肉 ハ マヅイ.

Sonó bōshi wa **chiisái.**
ソノ 帽子 ハ 小サイ.

Aré wa **utsŭkushíi.**
アレ ハ 美シイ.

This fish is tasty.

These books are interesting.

That meat is tasteless.

That hat is small.

That is beautiful.

The plural form of the demonstrative adjectives and pronouns is not used in Japanese as often as in English. In most cases the singular instead of the plural form is used.

Konó hon wa omoshirói.
コノ 本 ハ 面白イ.

{ **This** book is interesting.
{ **These** books are interesting.

Anó kimonó wa takái.
アノ 着物 ハ 高イ.

{ **That** kimono is dear.
{ **Those** kimonos are dear.

Sonó bōshi wa chiisái.
ソノ 帽子 ハ 小サイ.

{ **That** hat is small.
{ **Those** hats are small.

Koré wa umái.
コレ ハ 旨イ.

{ **This** is tasty.
{ **These** are tasty.

Soré wa yasúi.
ソレ ハ 安イ.

{ **That** is cheap.
{ **Those** are cheap.

It is only when the singular form of the demonstrative adjective or pronoun might appear ambiguous that the plural form is used.

Korérano	*ié*	*wa*	*furúi.*	These houses are old.
コレ等ノ	家	ハ	古イ.	
Sorérano	*kodomó*	*wa*	*otonashíi.*	Those children are quiet.
ソレ等ノ	子供	ハ	オトナシイ.	

In using the singular form in the two above sentences, it may be thought that one is speaking of only one house or child.

Note that even with the plural demonstrative adjective the following noun is used in the singular.

It is only by practice that one can learn when it is preferable to use the plural form instead of the singular.

Vocabulary

lantern(paper)	*chōchin*	チョウチン	interesting	*omoshirói*	面ナ白シロイ
mountain	*yamá*	山ヤマ	new	*atarashíi*	新アラシイ
ship	*fúne*	船フネ, 舟フネ	old¹	{ *furúi*	古フルイ
big	*ōkii*	大オオキイ		{ *toshiyorí*	年ト寄ヨリ
brave	*isamashíi*	勇イサマシイ	quiet²	{ *otonashíi*	オトナシイ
dear(expensive)	*takái*	高タカイ		{ *shízuka-na*	静シヅカナ
far	*tōi*	遠トオイ	tasteless	*mazúi*	マヅイ

Is that a university? *Soré wa daigakú désŭ ka.* ソレハ大学デスカ.
    It is. *Sō désŭ.* ソーデス (*lit.* So is.)

Exercise *Renshū* 練レン習シュウ

1. Konó yamá wa utsŭkushíi. **2.** Korérano heitaí wa isamashíi. **3.** Anó hĭtó wa ōkii. **4.** Sonó onná wa bímbō désŭ. **5.** Sonó daigakú wa tōi déshĭta ka.—Hái, tōi déshĭta. **6.** Sonó fúne wa chiisái déshĭta ka.—Hái, chiisái déshĭta. **7.** Arérano gakŭséi wa rikō désŭ. **8.** Koré wa Fújisan désŭ. **9.** Koré wa yasúi désŭ ka.—Takái désŭ. **10.** Aré wa chōchin désŭ ka.—Sō désŭ. **11.** Soré wa atarashíi désŭ ka.—Furúi désŭ. **12.** Aré wa takái déshĭta ka.—Yasúi déshĭta. **13.** Sonó uchí wa ōkii déshĭta ka.—Iié, chiisái déshĭta. **14.** Otōsan wa toshiyorí désŭ ka.—Iié, wakái désŭ.—Okāsan wa toshiyorí désŭ. **15.** Sorérano kodomó wa otonashíi déshĭta.

1. コノ山ハ美シイ. **2.** コレ等ノ兵隊ハ勇マシイ. **3.** アノ人ハ大キイ. **4.** ソノ女ハ貧乏デス. **5.** ソノ大学ハ遠イデシタカ.—ハイ, 遠イデシタ. **6.** ソノ舟ハ小サイデシタカ.—ハイ, 小サイデシタ. **7.** アレ等ノ学生ハ利口デス. **8.** コレハ富士山デス. **9.** コレハ安イデスカ.—高イデス. **10.** アレハチョウチンデスカ.—ソーデス. **11.** ソレハ新シイデスカ.—古イデス. **12.** アレハ高イデシタカ.—安イデシタ.

---

1 *Toshiyorí* said of age; *furúi* in other cases.
2 *Otonashíi* said of people and animals; *shízuka-na* of people and places.

13. ソノ家ハ大キイデシタカ.—イ丶エ, 小サイデシタ. **14.** オ父サン
ハ年寄デスカ.—イイエ, 若イデス.—オ母サンハ年寄デス. **15.** ソレ
等ノ子供ハオトナシイデシタ.

1. This mountain is beautiful. **2.** These soldiers are brave. **3.** That man
is big. **4.** That woman is poor. **5.** Was the university far?—Yes, it was
far. **6.** Was the ship small?—Yes, it was small. **7.** Those students are
clever. **8.** This is Mount Fuji. **9.** Are these cheap?—They are dear. **10.** Is
that a paper-lantern?—It is. **11.** Is that new?—It is old. **12.** Was that dear?
—It was cheap. **13.** Was the house large?—No, it was small. **14.** Is the
father old?—No, he is young.—The mother is old. **15.** Those children were
quiet.

Eighth Lesson   第ダイ 八ハチ 課カ

Cardinal Numbers

1	*ichí*[1]	一 *or* 壱	*hǐtótsu*	一ツ
2	*ni*	二 *or* 弐	*fǔtatsú*	二ツ
3	*san*	三 *or* 参	*mitsú, mittsú*	三ツ
4	*shi, yo, yon*	四	*yotsú, yottsú*	四ツ
5	*go*	五	*itsútsu*	五ツ
6	*rokú*	六	*mutsú, muttsú*	六ツ
7	*shichí, nána*	七	*nanátsu*	七ツ
8	*hachí*	八	*yatsú, yattsú*	八ツ
9	*ku* or *kyū*	九	*kokónotsu*	九ツ
10	*jū*	十 *or* 拾	*tō*	十

The first set of numerals is of Chinese, and the second set of Japanese,
derivation.

shi 四 *four* and *shichí* 七 *seven* are in some cases avoided because their
similarity in sound may lead to confusion. When avoided, their equivalent
yo or *yon* for *four*, and *nána* for *seven*, are used.

Shi is also discarded sometimes to avoid that in combination with the following noun it may be mistaken for some homonymous word, or from a
superstitious fear of the homonym *shi* 死 *death*.

The first set of numerals is generally used for counting.

Korérano pen wo kazóete kudasái.   Count these pens, please.
コレ等ノ ペン ヲ カゾエテ 下サイ.

Ichí, ni, san, shi, go. 一, 二, 三, 四, 五,   One, two, three, four, five, etc.

---

1 To indicate money values on notes, certificates, contracts, cheques, receipts, or
to indicate prices of goods, the figures 壱, 弐, 参 and 拾 are almost invariably used
instead of the simpler ones 一, 二, 三 and 十, which may be easily altered.

The second set is used only for things, not for persons, and they usually follow the noun. In case they precede the noun they may take the particle **no** but more often than not *no* is omitted.

There are three ways of counting from one to ten. However, the two given above are generally used in modern Japanese, while the third one, which will be given later, is obsolete, and rarely used.

Isú ga arimásŭ ka.	椅子ガアリマスカ.	Are there chairs?
Hái, **mittsŭ** *arimásŭ.*	ハイ，三ツアリマス.	Yes, there are three.
Ringó wo **mittsŭ** *mótte imásŭ.*	リンゴ ヲ 三ツ 持ッテ イマス.	
Mittsu no *ringó wo mótte imásŭ.*	三ツ ノ リンゴ ヲ 持ッテ イマス.	I have three apples.
Mittsŭ *ringó wo mótte imásŭ.*	三ツ リンゴ ヲ 持ッテ イマス.	

Above eleven there is only one set of numerals, which is formed by the first ten numerals of Chinese derivation.

11	*jū-ichí*	十一		26	*ni-jū-rokú*	二十六
12	*jū-ni*	十二		27	*ni-jū-shichí*	二十七
13	*jū-san*	十三		28	*ni-jū-hachí*	二十八
14	*jū-shi* or *jū yon*	十四		29	*ni-jū-ku*	二十九
15	*jū-go*	十五		30	*san-jū*	三十 *or* 卅
16	*jū-rokú*	十六		31	*san-jū-ich*	三十一
17	*jū-shichí*	十七		32	*san-jū-ni*	三十二
18	*jū-hachí*	十八		34	*san-jū-shi*	三十四
19	*jū-ku*	十九		37	*san-jū-shichí*	三十七
20	*ni-jū*	二十 *or* 廿		40	*shi-jū* or *yonjū*	四十
21	*ni-jū-ichí*	二十一		41	*shi-jū-ichí*	四十一
22	*ni-jū-ni*	二十二		43	*shi-jū-san*	四十三
23	*ni-jū-san*	二十三		45	*shi-jū-go*	四十五
24	*ni-jū-shi*	二十四		50	*go-jū*	五十
25	*ni-jū-go*	二十五		51	*go-jū-ichí*	五十一

Numeratives

When counting objects, the Japanese often use a class of words called *numeratives*, whose function may be compared to that of the English *head* in the expression *six head of cattle*.

The following are among the most common numeratives:

Nin 人 *person*, used to indicate human beings, as in

ichí-nin 一人, *ni-nin* 二人. *san-nin* 三人, *yo-nin* 四人, etc.

Hĭtóri 一人 and **fŭtári** 二人 are more commonly used than *ichí-nin* and *ni-nin*, although the Chinese character used is the same.

Between the numerative and the noun following *no* ノ is used.

Hĭtóri no kodomó ga imásŭ. 一人ノ子供ガイマス. There is one child.
San-nín no kodomó ga imásŭ.三人ノ子供ガイマス. There are three children.

Hĭkí 匹 *fellow*, used in counting animals (quadrupeds, fishes, insects).

Note that when a numeral is followed by a noun or numerative, the end sound of the numeral and the first sound of the noun or numerative, may either or both suffer modification, as in the following examples. See Lesson 41.

ippikí 一匹 one, *ni-hikí* 二匹 two, *san-bikí* or *sámbiki* 三匹 three, *shi-hikí* 四匹 four, *go-hikí* 五匹 five, *rokú-hiki* or *roppikí* 六匹 six, *shichí-hiki* 七匹 seven, *hachí-hiki* 八匹 eight, *ku-hikí* 九匹 nine, *jippikí* 十匹 ten.

Inŭ ga imásŭ ka.   犬ガイマスカ.   Are there any dogs?
Shi-hikí imásŭ.   四匹イマス.   There are four.

A noun in the objective case is generally put before the numerative without *no*, although the numerative before the object is grammatically correct.

Watashí wa inú wo *ippikí* mótte imásŭ.   I have one dog.
私　　ハ　犬　ヲ　　一匹　　持ッテイマス.

Anó onná-no-hĭtó wa néko wo *sámbiki* mótte imásŭ.   That woman
アノ　女ノ人　　ハ　猫　ヲ　　三匹　　持ッテイマス.   has three cats.

or

Watashí wa *ippikí no* inú wo mótte imásŭ.
私　　ハ　一匹　　ノ　犬　ヲ　持ッテ　イマス.

Anó onná wa *sámbiki no* néko wo mótte imásŭ.
アノ　女　ハ　三匹　　ノ　猫　ヲ　持ッテイマス.

Wa 羽 *feather*, used in counting birds.

ichí-wa 一羽 one, *ni-wa* 二羽 two, *sámba* 三羽 three, *shi-wa* or *yómba* 四羽 four, *go-wa* 五羽 five, *rokú-wa* or *róppa* 六羽 six, *shichí-wa* 七羽 seven, *hachí-wa* 八羽 eight, *ku-wa* 九羽 nine, *jíppa* 十羽 ten.

Watashí wa háto wo *ichí-wa* mótte imásŭ.   I have one pigeon.
私　　ハ　鳩　ヲ　　一羽　持ッテイマス.

Senséi wa ahirú wo *sámba* mótte imáshĭta.   (Our) teacher
先生　ハアヒルヲ　　三羽　持ッテイマシタ.   had three ducks.

Satsú 冊 *volume*, used in counting books.

issatsú 一冊 one, *ni-satsú* 二冊 two, *san-satsú* 三冊 three, *yon-satsú* or *shi-satsú* 四冊 four, *go-satsú* 五冊 five, *rokú-satsú* 六冊 six, *naná-satsú* or *shichí-satsú* 七冊 seven, *hassatsú* 八冊 eight, *kyū-satsú* 九冊 nine, *jissatsú* 十冊 ten.

Watashí wa hon ga *issatsú* arimásŭ.
私　　ハ　本　ガ　　一冊　　アリマス.   } I have
                                                        one book.
or

Watashí wa hon wo *issatsú* mótte imásŭ.
私　　ハ　本　ヲ　　一冊　持ッテイマス.

Hassatsú no hon ga arimásŭ. 八冊ノ本ガアリマス. There are eight books.

A numeral may, when the meaning is clear, be followed by a numerative without the object:

> *Anáta wa hon wo mótte imásŭ ka.*   Have you books?
> 貴方 ハ 本 ヲ 持ッテイマス カ.
>
> ***Jissatsŭ*** *mótte imásŭ.* 十冊持ッテイマス.   I have ten.

Hon 本 *trunk,* used in counting round, long objects, as trees, sticks, legs, fingers, needles, cigars, fans, ropes, etc.

> *íppon* 一本, *ni-hon* 二本, *sámbon* 三本, *shi-hon* or *yon-hon* 四本,
> *go-hon* 五本, *róppon* 六本, *shichí-hon* or *nanáhon* 七本, *hachí-hon*
> 八本, *ku-hon* or *kyū-hon* 九本, *jíppon* 十本.
>
> *Uchíwa wo* ***íppon*** *mótte kité kudasái.* Bring me one fan.
> ウチワ ヲ 一本 持ッテ 来テ 下サイ.
>
> *Hári wo* ***go-hon*** *kudasái.* 針ヲ五本下サイ. Give me five needles.

Mái 枚 *pieces,* used in counting flat things, as paper, cloth, clothes, blankets, coins, boards, dishes, etc. This numerative does not suffer any alteration.

> *ichí-mái* 一枚, *ni-mái* 二枚, *san-mái* or *sámmai* 三枚.
>
> *Kamí wo* ***yo-mái*** *kudasái.* 紙ヲ四枚下サイ. Give me four sheets of paper.
> *Mōfu wo* ***rokŭ-mái*** *mótte kité kudasái.* Bring me six blankets.
> 毛布 ヲ   六枚   持ッテ 来テ 下サイ.

There are about thirty numeratives used to indicate the groups into which objects are classified. For a full list of numeratives see Lesson 41.

The Conjunction *and.*

When three or more nouns follow one another and the last two are joined by **and**, this word may be translated by both Japanese conjunctions, *to* ト and *soshĭté* ソシテ, following each other in succession. When using the double conjunction *to soshĭté* トソシテ the speaker's voice dwells a little on the first conjunction *to* ト. The use of *to soshĭté* トソシテ corresponds more or less to the use of the English **and then.**

> *Watashí wa ringó to nashí* **to soshĭté** *orénji ga sŭkí désŭ.*
> 私   ハ リンゴ ト 梨 ト ソシテオレンヂガ 好キ デス.
> I like apples, pears, and oranges.

> *Watashí wa inú ni-hikí to néko sámbiki* **to soshĭté** *háto róppa mótte imásŭ.*
> 私 ハ 犬 二匹 ト 猫 三匹 ト ソシテ 鳩 六羽持ッテイマス.
> or
> *Watashí wa ni-hikí no inú to sámbiki no néko* **to soshĭté** *róppa no háto wo*
> 私   ハ 二匹 ノ 犬 ト 三匹 ノ 猫 ト ソシテ 六羽 ノ 鳩 ヲ
> *mótte imásŭ.* I have two dogs, three cats, and six pigeons.
> 持ッテ イマス.

Without the use of *soshĭté* ソシテ no pause should be made after uttering the last conjunction *to.*

> *Watashí wa inú ni-hikí to néko sámbiki* **to** *háto róppa mótte imásŭ.*

When the numerative is used, the last two words of a succession of nouns may be joined by *soshité* ソシテ only, without *to* ト.

Watashí wa inú ni-hiki to néko sámbiki soshité háto róppa mótte imásŭ.

Note that the case-particle *wo* may be used or omitted after a noun that precedes a numerative. Ex.:

Watashí wa inú wo ippiki mótte imásŭ.
Watashí wa inú ippiki mótte imásŭ. } I have a dog.

Vocabulary

blanket	*mōfu*	毛布	fan	{ *sensú*[3]	扇子	
				uchíwa[4]	ウチワ	
canary	*kanariyá*	カナリヤ	goldfish	*kíngyo*	金魚	
cane	{ *tsúe*[1]	杖	goose	*gachō*	鵞鳥	
	sŭtékki[2]	ステッキ	needle	*hári*	針	
cow	*meushi*	牝牛	pigeon	*háto*	鳩	
dish	{ *sará*	皿	sheep	*hitsují*	羊	
	o-sará	オ皿	umbrella	{ *kōmorigasa*[5]	コウモリ傘	
duck	*ahirú*	アヒル		*amagása*[6]	雨傘	

Exercise   *Renshū* 練習

1. Anó onná-no-hĭtó wa san-nin kodomó ga arimásŭ. **2.** Watashí wa musŭkó ga fŭtarí to musŭmé ga yo-nin arimásŭ. **3.** Séito ga imáshĭta ka.—Go-nin séito ga imáshĭta. **4.** Watashitachí wa go-hiki no umá to sámbiki no ushí to soshĭté ni-jippikí no hitsují wo mótte imásŭ. **5.** Anó otokó-no-ko wa roppikí no inú to ni-hikí no néko ga arimásŭ. **6.** Watashí wa kíngyo ga jū-sámbiki arimásŭ. **7.** Anáta wa gachō wo mótte imáshĭta ka.—Jū-rokú-wa mótte imáshĭta. **8.** Anó onná-no-ko wa háto wo ni-jū-go-wa mótte imásŭ. **9.** Watashí wa kanariyá wo rokú wa mótte imáshĭta. **10.** Ahirú ga imáshĭta ka.—Hái, jíppa imáshĭta. **11.** Hon wo mótte imásŭ ka.—Go-satsú hon wo mótte imásŭ. **12.** Empitsú ga arimásŭ ka.—Hái, empitsú ga shi-hon to pen ga sámbon arimásŭ. **13.** Sŭtékki wo mótte imásŭ ka.—Sŭtékki wo shi-hon mótte imásŭ. **14.** Amagása wo ni-hon mótte kité kudasái. **15.** Mōfu wo ni-mái kudasái. **16.** O-sará ga arimásŭ ka.—Jū-mái arimásŭ. **17.** Kamí wo jū-go-mái mótte kité kudasái.

1. アノ女ノ人ハ三人子供ガアリマス. **2.** 私ハ息子ガ二人ト娘ガ四人アリマス. **3.** 生徒ガイマシタカ.—五人生徒ガイマシタ. **4.** 私達ハ五匹ノ馬ト三匹ノ牛トソシテ廿匹ノ羊ヲ持ッテイマス. **5.** アノ男ノ子ハ六匹ノ犬ト二匹ノ猫ガアリマス. **6.** 私ハ金魚ガ十三匹アリマス. **7.** 貴方ハ鵞鳥ヲ持ッテイマシタカ.—十六羽持ッテイマシタ. **8.** アノ女ノ子ハ鳩ヲ廿五羽持ッテイマス. **9.** 私ハカナリヤヲ六羽持

---

1 cane for support **2** walking stick **3** folding fan **4** round, non-folding fan
5 Western style umbrella **6** Japanese style, made of paper

ッテイマシタ. **10.** アヒルガイマシタカ.―ハイ, 十羽イマシタ. **11.** 本
ヲ持ッテイマスカ.―五冊本ヲ持ッテイマス. **12.** 鉛筆ガアリマスカ.
―ハイ, 鉛筆ガ四本トペンガ三本アリマス. **13.** ステッキヲ持ッテイ
マスカ―ステッキヲ四本持ッテイマス. **14.** 雨傘ヲ二本持ッテ来テ下
サイ. **15.** 毛布ヲ二枚下サイ. **16.** オ皿ガアリマスカ.―十枚アリマ
ス. **17.** 紙ヲ十五枚持ッテ来テ下サイ.

1. That woman has three children. **2.** I have two sons and four daughters.
3. Were there any students?—There were five students. **4.** We have five
horses, three cows, and twenty sheep. **5.** That boy has six dogs and two
cats. **6.** I have thirteen goldfish. **7.** Had you any geese?—I had sixteen
geese. **8.** That girl has twenty-five pigeons. **9.** I had six canaries. **10.** Were
there any ducks?—Yes, there were ten ducks. **11.** Have you any books?—
I have five books. **12.** Are there any pencils?—Yes, there are four pencils
and three pens. **13.** Have you any canes?—I have four canes. **14.** Bring
me two umbrellas. **15.** Give me two blankets. **16.** Are there any dishes?—
There are ten. **17.** Bring me fifteen sheets of paper.

Ninth Lesson　第ダ九ク課カ

Much, Many

Both **much** and **many** are translated by **takŭsán** followed by **no**
when used as adjectives of quantity before a noun:

much milk	**takŭsán no** gyūnyū	沢山ノ牛乳
many flowers	**takŭsán no** haná.	沢山ノ花

Anáta wa **takŭsán no** *o-kané wo mótte imásŭ ka.*
貴方　ハ　　沢山　　ノ　オ金　ヲ　持ッテイマス　カ.
　　Have you much money?

Iié, **takŭsán** *mótte imasén.*　　　　No, I have not much.
イ丶エ, 沢山　　持ッテイマセン.

Takŭsán no *mōfu ga arimásŭ ka.*　　Are there many blankets?
沢山　　ノ　毛布　ガ アリマス カ.

Hái, **takŭsán no** *mōfu ga arimásŭ.*　　Yes, there are many blankets.
ハイ, 沢山　　ノ　毛布　ガ アリマス.

Hái, **takŭsán** *arimásŭ.*　　　　　　Yes, there are many.
ハイ, 沢山　　アリマス.

Anó hĭtó wa **takŭsán no** *jímen wo mótte imáshĭta ka.*
アノ　人　ハ　　沢山　　ノ　地面　ヲ　持ッテ　イマシタ　カ.
　　Had that man much land?

Iié, **takŭsán** *mótte imasén déshĭta.*　　No, he had not much.
イ丶エ, 沢山　持ッテイマセン デシタ.

Hái, **takŭsán** *mótte imáshĭta.*　　　Yes, he had much.
ハイ,　　沢山　　持ッテ イマシタ.

How much, How many

When asking the quantity of something, **how much** is translated by *ikura* イクラ or by the more polite word *ikahodó* イカホド. Both *ikura* and *ikahodó* may precede or follow the noun they refer to. When they precede the noun these two words may be followed by *no*.

Satō ga ikahodó arimásŭ ka. 砂糖 ガ イカホド アリマス カ.	**How much** sugar is there?
Nikú wo ikura mótte imásŭ ka. 肉 ヲ イクラ 持ッテイマス カ. *Ikura nikú wo mótte imásŭ ka.* イクラ 肉 ヲ 持ッテイマス カ.	**How much** meat have you?

The construction used in the first two sentences is the one generally used in ordinary conversation.

When asking the price of something, *ikura* or *ikahodó* is put after the numeral or object inquired about.

Konó sakaná wa ikura désŭ ka. コノ 魚 ハ イクラ デス カ. *Konó sakaná wa ikahodó désŭ ka.* コノ 魚 ハ イカホド デス カ.	How much is this fish? How much for this fish? How much does this fish cost?
Hyakú yen désŭ. 百 円 デス.	One hundred yen.
Hĭtótsu ikura. or *Hĭtótsu ikahodó.* 一ツ イクラ, 一ツ イカホド. *Hĭtótsu ikura (ikahodó) désŭ ka.* 一ツ イクラ (イカホド) デス カ.	How much for one?

How much and **how many** may be expressed also by *dóno-kuraí* ドノクライ, which is sometimes pronounced *dóno-guraí* ドノグライ.

Mizú ga dóno-kuraí arimásŭ ka. 水 ガ ドノクライ アリマス カ.	**How much** water is there?
Yon kokú arimásŭ. 四 石 アリマス.	There are four koku.[1]
Kōhī wo dóno-kuraí mótte imásŭ ka. コーヒーヲ ドノクライ 持ッテイマス カ. *Dóno-kuraí(no) kōhī wo mótte imásŭ ka.* ドノクライ(ノ) コーヒー ヲ 持ッテイマス カ.	**How much** coffee have you?
Go póndo mótte imásŭ. 五 ポンド 持ッテ イマス.	I have five pounds.
San gin mótte imásŭ. 三 斤 持ッテ イマス.	I have three kin.[2]

---

1 One *kokú* is about 36 lbs. **2** One *kin* is about 1½ lb.

*Hĭtó   ga   **dóno-kurai**   imáshĭta   ka.*
人　ガ　ドノクライ　イマシタ　カ.

__Dóno-kurai__ (no) hĭtó ga imáshĭta ka.
ドノクライ　（ノ）　人　ガ　イマシタ　カ.

}How many people were there?

Yon-jū-nin ĭmáshĭta. or *Shi-jū-nin orimáshĭta.*   There were forty people.
四十人　イマシタ.　　四十人　オリマシタ.

The word **kurai** implies an approximate quantity, so that **dóno-kurai**
really means *about how much, about how many;* however, the Japanese sometimes use this expression when in English the word *about* would not be used.

Japanese people are fond of using expressions conveying a vague idea of
approximation, uncertainty or ambiguity, as if they were afraid of using
expressions which, while giving the exact conception of what one wants or is
asking, might, in their belief, give the person spoken to an impression of
abruptness or impoliteness.

Dóno-kurai.   ドノクライ   { (About) how much ?
                                  { (About) how many ?

Konó-kurai.   コノクライ   { (About) so much.
                                  { (About) so many.

How many?

How many is also translated by *íkutsu* イクツ, or by *íku* 幾 or
nan 何 followed by the numerative and the noun. *Ikutsu, íku,* or
nan ask for the exact number, not an approximation.

*Tamágo ga **íkutsu** arimásŭ ka.*
卵子　ガ　イクツ　アリマス　カ.

__Íkutsu__ (no) tamágo ga arimásŭ ka.
イクツ　（ノ）　卵子　ガ　アリマス　カ.

}How many eggs are there?

The first construction is preferred and is more colloquial.

Ni-jū arimásŭ.   There are twenty.
廿　アリマス.

*Séito ga **íku-nin** imásŭ ka.*
生徒　ガ　幾人　イマス　カ.

__Íku-nin__ (no) séito ga imásŭ ka.
幾人　（ノ）　生徒　ガ　イマス　カ.

}How many students are there?

Séito ga san-jū-nin imásŭ.   There are thirty students.
生徒　ガ　三十人　イマス.

San-jū-nin imásŭ.   There are thirty.
三十人　イマス.

Takŭsán (no) tamágo ga arimáshĭta.   There were many eggs.
沢山　（ノ）　卵子　ガ　アリマシタ.

__Íkutsu__ arimáshĭta ka.   **How many** were there?
イクツ　アリマシタ　カ.

Go-jū arimáshĭta.   There were fifty.
五十　アリマシタ.

Takŭsán (no) séito ga orimáshĭta.
沢山　（ノ）生徒　ガ　オリマシタ.

There were many students.

Iku-nin orimáshĭta ka.
幾人　オリマシタ　カ.

How many were there?

San-jū-nin orimáshĭta.
三十人　オリマシタ.

There were thirty.

Anó hĭtó wa umá ga íku-hikí arimásŭ ka.
アノ　人　ハ　馬　ガ　幾匹　アリマス　カ.

Anó hĭtó wa umá ga nan-biki arimásŭ ka.
アノ　人　ハ　馬　ガ　何匹　アリマス　カ.

Anó hĭtó wa nan-biki (no) umá ga arimásŭ ka.
アノ　人　ハ　何匹　（ノ）馬　ガアリマスカ.

Anó hĭtó wa íku-hikí (no) umá ga arimásŭ ka.
アノ　人　ハ　幾匹　（ノ）馬　ガアリマスカ.

How many horses has that man?

Jippikí (no) umá ga arimásŭ.
十匹　（ノ）馬　ガ　アリマス.

He has ten horses.

Jippikí arimásŭ. 十匹アリマス.

He has ten.

Anáta wa hon wo íku-satsú mótte imásŭ ka.
貴方　ハ　本　ヲ　幾　冊　持ッテイマス　カ.

Anáta wa hon wo nan-satsú mótte imásŭ ka.
貴方　ハ　本　ヲ　何　冊　持ッテイマス　カ.

Anáta wa íku-satsú (no) hon wo mótte imásŭ ka.
貴方　ハ　幾冊　（ノ）本　ヲ持ッテイマスカ.

Anáta wa nan-satsú (no) hon wo mótte imásŭ ka.
貴方　ハ　何冊　（ノ）本　ヲ持ッテイマスカ.

How many books have you?

Kyū-satsú (no) hon wo mótte imásŭ.
九冊　（ノ）本　ヲ　持ッテイマス.

I have nine books.

Kyū-satsú mótte imásŭ. 九冊持ッテイマス.

I have nine.

Note that the numerative used in a question is generally used in the answer.
Ikutsu is generally used when asking the quantity of things that we can handled, as round-shaped fruit, eggs, glasses, electric bulbs, boxes, etc. Whenever possible however, *nan* or *íku* with the numerative is used.

Vocabulary

chicken	*niwatorí*	鶏	money	*kané*	金	
egg	*tamágo*	卵		*o-kané*	オ金	
farmer	*nōfu*	農夫	pig	*butá*	豚	
knife	*náifu*	ナイフ	pound	*póndo*	ポンド	
land	*tochí*	土地	strawberry	*ichigó*	苺	

How old are you?	*Anáta wa o-íkutsu désŭ ka.*	貴方ハオイクツデスカ.
	Anáta wa nan-sái désŭ ka.	貴方ハ何才デスカ.

I am eighteen.　*Jū-hachí désŭ.*　十八デス.

I am twenty-two years old. *Ni-jū-ni-sái désŭ.*　二十二才デス.

I am twenty.　*Hátachi désŭ.* or *Ni-jū désŭ.*　廿デス. 二十デス.

When the word *sái* 才 is used for asking somebody's age, it is generally repeated in the answer. Note that the word *sái* is more of the literary style.

In telling one's years *hátachi* is often used for twenty.

Exercise   *Renshū*   練レ 習シウ

1. Heitaí ga takŭsán orimásŭ ka.—Hái, orimásŭ.—Iié, takŭsán orimasén. **2.** Takŭsán ki ga arimáshĭta ka.—Hái, takŭsán arimáshĭta.—Iié, takŭsán arimasén déshĭta. **3.** Iku-hon arimáshĭta ka.—Yon-jū-go-hon arimáshĭta. **4.** Dóno-kuraí pan ga arimásŭ ka.—Rokú póndo guraí arimásŭ. **5.** Konó bōshi wa íkura désŭ ka.—Ni-sen yen désŭ. **6.** Shió wo dóno-kuraí mótte imásŭ ka. —Jū-go póndo guraí mótte imásŭ. **7.** Kodomó ga iku-nin imáshĭta ka.—San-jū-go-nin imáshĭta. **8.** Isú wo mótte kité kudasái.—Ikutsu désŭ ka.[1]—Tō guraí. **9.** Rōsoku wo nan-bon mótte imásŭ ka.—Jū-sámbon mótte imásŭ. **10.** Anó nōfu wa ushí wo nan-biki mótte imáshĭta ka.—Ushí wo ni-jippikí to hitsují wo yon-jū-go-hikí to butá wo jū-go-hikí soshĭté niwatorí wo san-jū-go-wa mótte imáshĭta. **11.** Konó yōfuku wa íkura désŭ ka.—Yon man yen désŭ. **12.** Sará to naífu to sají wa íkutsu arimásŭ ka.—Sará ga ni-jū-go-mái, naífu ga jū-ni-hon, fōku ga jū-hachí-hon soshĭté sají ga jíppon arimásŭ. **13.** Empitsú wo sámbon mótte kíte kudasái. **14.** Anáta wa íkutsu désŭ ka.—Jū-go désŭ. **15.** Arérano kodomotachí wa takŭsán ichigó wo mótte imásŭ. (Colloquially *Anó* instead of *Arérano*)

1. 兵隊ガ沢山オリマスカ.—ハイ，オリマス.—イヽエ，沢山オリマセン. **2.** 沢山木ガアリマシタカ.—ハイ，沢山アリマシタ.—イヽエ，沢山アリマセンデシタ. **3.** 幾本アリマシタカ.—四十五本アリマシタ. **4.** ドノクライパンガアリマスカ.—六ポンドグライアリマス. **5.** コノ帽子ハイクラデスカ.—二千円デス. **6.** 塩ヲドノクライ持ッテイマスカ.—拾五ポンドグライ持ッテイマス. **7.** 子供ガ幾人イマシタカ.—卅五人イマシタ. **8.** 椅子ヲ持ッテ来テ下サイ.—イクツデスカ.—十グライ. **9.** ローソクヲ何本持ッテイマスカ.—十三本持ッテイマス. **10.** アノ農夫ハ牛ヲ何匹持ッテイマシタカ.—牛ヲ廿匹ト羊ヲ四十五匹ト豚ヲ十五匹ソシテ鶏ヲ卅五羽持ッテイマシタ. **11.** コノ洋服ハイクラデスカ.—四万円デス. **12.** 皿トナイフト匙ハイクツアリマスカ.—皿二十五枚，ナイフガ十二本，フォークガ十八本，ソシテ匙ガ十本アリマス. **13.** 鉛筆ヲ三本持ッテ来テ下サイ. **14.** 貴方ハイクツデスカ.—十五デス. **15.** アレ等ノ子供達ハ沢山苺ヲ持ッテイマス.

1. Are there many soldiers?—Yes, there are.—No, there are not many. **2.** Were there many trees?—Yes, there were many.—No, there were not many. **3.** How many were there?—There were forty-five. **4.** How much bread is there?—There are about six pounds. **5.** How much does this hat cost?—It

---

1 When in English *how much* or *how many* is used alone as in this case, in Japanese *désŭ* generally follows the adverb of quantity.

costs two thousand yen.   **6.** How much salt have you?—I have about fifteen pounds.   **7.** How many children were there?—There were thirty-five. **8.** Bring me some chairs.—How many?—(About) ten.   **9.** How many candles have you?—I have thirteen.   **10.** How many cows had that farmer?—He had twenty cows, forty-five sheep, fifteen pigs, and thirty-five chickens. **11.** How much does this suit cost?—It costs forty thousand yen.   **12.** How many dishes, knives, and spoons are there?—There are twenty-five dishes, twelve knives, eighteen forks, and ten spoons.   **13.** Bring me three pencils. **14.** How old are you?—I am fifteen years old.   **15.** Those children have many strawberries.

Tenth Lesson   第十課

Plural   *Fukusū*   複フク数スウ

In the first lesson it has been said that except in very few cases, no distinction is made between singular and plural number. When the plural number is to be expressed, it is done by adding certain suffixes to the noun.

These suffixes, arranged in decreasing order of politeness, are: *gatá* 方, *tachí* 達, *shū* 衆, *dómo* 共, *ra* 等. All of these are used of persons. In rare cases *ra* is used to indicate the plural of things.

lady	*fujín*	婦フ人ジン	ladies	*fujingatá*	婦人方ガタ
parent	*oyá*	親オヤ	parents	*oyatachí*	親達タチ
retainer	*kérai*	家ケ来ライ	retainers	*keraitachí*	家来達
merchant	*akíndo*	商アキ人ンド	merchants	*akindoshū*	商人衆シウ
student	*séito*	生セイ徒ト	students	*séitora*	生徒等ラ

Note that *shū* is an obsolete suffix, very rarely used in modern speech.

Although these suffixes are very little used in forming the plural of nouns, their singular form being used instead, as already explained in the first lesson, they are, however, used often in forming the plural of personal pronouns:

| I | *watakŭshí* 私 *watashí* 私 | we | *watakŭshitachi* 私 達 *watashitachi* 私 達 *watakŭshidómo* 私 共 *watashidómo* 私 共 |
| **you** | *anáta* 貴方 | you | *anatagatá* 貴方々 *anátatachi* 貴方達 |

Bóku 僕ボク instead of *watashí* and *kimi* 君キミ instead of *anáta*, are often used by young men in familiar speech among themselves. *Omaé* 才前マエ instead of *anáta* is used in vulgar speech when talking to inferiors.

Anatagatá is generally used when speaking to people of higher or of the same rank. *Anátatachi* is generally used when speaking to inferiors, as a teacher to his students, or when speaking to friends, children, etc.

he *káre*　彼ｶﾚ　　they ｛ *káretachi*　彼ｶﾚ達ﾀﾁ
　　　　　　　　　　　　　　 kárera　彼ｶﾚ等ﾗ

Káretachi is rarely used. When **they** has to be expressed by a plural personal pronoun, *kárera* is preferred. However, the Japanese personal pronouns corresponding to *he, she, it*, and *they* are generally avoided and their equivalents are used instead :

he	｛that person	*anó katá* / *anó hǐtó*	アノ方ｶﾀ / アノ人ﾋﾄ
	that gentleman	*anó shínshi*	アノ紳ｼﾝ士ｼ
	that man	*anó otokó*	アノ男ｵﾄｺ
	that old person	*anó rōjin*	アノ老ﾛｳ人ｼﾞﾝ
	that fellow	*anó yátsu*	アノ奴ﾔﾂ

Anó yátsu may be contracted into **aitsŭ** 彼奴, アイツ

she	that lady	*anó fujín*	アノ婦ﾌ人ｼﾞﾝ
	that person	*anó katá*	アノ方ｶﾀ
	that woman	*anó onná*	アノ女ｵﾝﾅ
	that girl	*anó musŭmé*	アノ娘ﾑｽﾒ
	that young lady	*anó ojōsan*	アノオ嬢ｼﾞｮｳサン
	that old lady	*anó rōfujin*	アノ老ﾛｳ婦ﾌ人ｼﾞﾝ

they	*anó o-katagatá*	アノオ方々	(very polite speech)
	anó katagatá	アノ方々	(polite speech)
	anó katatachí	アノ方達	(less polite speech)
	anó hǐtotachí	アノ人達	(ordinary speech)

Instead of the personal pronouns of the third persons singular or their equivalents, the name of the person referred to is very often used, and is indeed, the best way to translate *he* or *she*.

Anó o-katagatá is used in very polite speech, *anó katagatá* and *anó katatachi* are used in ordinary polite conversation, and *anó hǐtotachí* is used often speaking of friends or inferiors.

it	｛that child	*anó ko*	アノ子
	that	*soré*	ソレ

A Few, A Little

A few and **a little** are rendered by *sŭkóshi* 少ｽｺｼ or *sŭkóshi bákari* 少ｽｺｼバカリ. *Bákari* バカリ means *only*, so that the expression *sŭkóshi bákari* could be translated also by **a few only**.

Anó ojōsan wa sŭkóshi haná wo mótte imásŭ.
アノ オ嬢サン ハ　少シ　花　ヲ 持ッテ イマス.
Anó ojōsan wa haná wo sŭkóshi mótte imásŭ.
アノ オ嬢サン ハ 花　ヲ　少シ 持ッテ イマス.
｝ She has **a few** flowers. (That young lady has......)

Anó onná wa haná wo **sŭkóshi bákari** *mótte imásŭ.*
アノ 女 ハ 花 ヲ 少シ バカリ 持ッテ イマス.
 She (that woman) has **a few** flowers.

Anó otokó wa nikú wo **sŭkóshi** *mótte imásŭ.*   He (that man)
アノ 男 ハ 肉 ヲ 少シ 持ッテ イマス. has **a little** meat.

Anó rōjin wa íkuraka hon ga arimásŭ ka.   Has he (that old person)
アノ 老人 ハ イクラカ 本 ガ アリマス カ. any books?

Hái, **sŭkóshi bákari** *arimásŭ.*   Yes, he has **a few**.
ハイ, 少シ バカリ アリマス.

Few, Little

Few and **little** are both translated by **sŭkóshi shĭká** 少シシカ
or **sŭkóshi kirí** 少シキリ (*lit.* but few, but little) followed by the
verb in the negative.

Note that **few** and **little** mean respectively **not many, not much**, which
explains the use of the negative verb.

Takŭsán no kodomó ga imásŭ ka.   Are there many children?
沢山 ノ 子供 ガ イマス カ.

Iié, **sŭkóshi shĭká** *imasén.* or   ⎫
イ丶エ, 少シ シカ イマセン. ⎬ No, there are **few**.
Iié, **sŭkóshi kirí** *imasén.* ⎨ There are **but few**.
イ丶エ, 少シ キリ イマセン. ⎭

Anó obāsan wa takŭsán no pan wo mótte imásŭ ka.
アノ オバアサン ハ 沢山 ノ パン ヲ 持ッテ イマス カ.
 Has that old woman much bread?

Iié, **sŭkóshi shĭká** *mótte imasén.*   No, she has **little**.
イ丶エ, 少シ シカ 持ッテ イマセン.

Anó hĭtotachí wa íkuraka pan wo mótte imásŭ ka. Have they
アノ 人達 ハ イクラカ パン ヲ 持ッテ イマス カ. any bread?

Hái, **sŭkóshi bákari** *mótte imásŭ.*   Yes, they have **a little**.
ハイ, 少シ バカリ 持ッテ イマス.

Several

Several is translated by **go-rokú** 五六 (five or six) followed by
the numerative, or by **sū** 数 (literary style).

several children	⎰ *sū-nin no kodomó*	数人ノ子供
	⎱ *go-rokú nin no kodomó*	五六人ノ子供
several books	⎰ *sū-satsŭ no hon*	数冊ノ本
	⎱ *go-rokú satsú no hon*	五六冊ノ本
several pencils	⎰ *sū-hon no empitsú*	数本ノ鉛筆
	⎱ *go-roppón no empitsú*	五六本ノ鉛筆
several blankets	⎰ *sū-mái no mōfu*	数枚ノ毛布
	⎱ *go-rokú mái no mōfu*	五六枚ノ毛布

several dogs $\begin{cases} \textit{sū-hiki no inú} \\ \textit{go-roppiki no inú} \end{cases}$ 数匹ノ犬

五六匹ノ犬

Anó onná-no-hǐtó wa **go-rokú hikí** *no néko ga arimáshǐta.*
アノ　女ノ人　ハ　五六　匹ノ　猫　ガ　アリマシタ.
That woman had **several** cats.

Adjectives of Quality

Most adjective in Japanese end in *i*, as *chiisái* 小サイ small, *ōkii* 大キイ large. See Lesson 20.

Anó uchí wa **chiisái** *désǔ.* アノ家ハ小サイデス. That house is small.
Ōkii *hakó wo mótte kité kudasái.*   Bring me a large box.
大キイ箱　ヲ持ッテ来テ下サイ.

This class of adjectives may be used predicatively without **désǔ** or **déshǐta**, as already stated in Lesson 7, page 43.

Anó uchí wa **chiisái**   アノ家ハ小サイ.   That house is small.
Konó hakó wa **ōkii**   コノ箱ハ大キイ.   This box is large.

The Conjunction *and*

The conjunction **and** may also be translated by **ya** ヤ instead of *to* ト, after each noun except the last, when it is used to join two or more nouns that are not given as a complete list. In that case it is implied that other similar things are implied but not named.

Sonó fujín wa inú **ya** *néko ga sǔkí désǔ.*   ソノ婦人ハ犬ヤ猫ガ好キデス.
    That lady is fond of dogs **and** cats (besides other animals that she may be fond of).

Pen to *empitsú wo mótte kité kudasái.*   ペント鉛筆ヲ持ッテ来テ下サイ.
    Bring me a pen **and** a pencil. (and nothing else is implied).

In this last example *ya* ヤ could not be used because *pen* and *pencil* form a complete list of what I want.

Ya ヤ is not used when the nouns are preceded or followed by a numerative.

When mentioning two or more nouns that do not form a complete list, **danó** ダノ may be used instead of *ya* ヤ.

Inú **danó** *néko* **danó** *ga sǔkí désǔ.*   I am fond of dogs **and** cats.
犬　ダノ　猫　ダノ　ガ　好キ　デス.

As **danó** is not a refined expression, it is better to avoid it in polite conversation.

A Few Verbs

Yomimásǔ.   読ヨミマス   I, you, we, they read.   He, she, it reads.
Sǔkí désǔ.   好スキデス   I, you, we, etc. like.   He, she likes.
Kiraimásǔ.   嫌キライマス   I, you, etc. dislike.   He, she dislikes.
Kirái désǔ.   嫌キライデス   I, you, etc. dislike.   He, she dislikes.

When using *sŭkí désŭ*, *kirái désŭ*, the object is followed by *ga* ガ; when using *kiraimásŭ* the object is followed by *wo* ヲ. Since *kiraimásŭ* indicates a stronger dislike than *kirái désŭ*, it is not often used.

Anó ojíisan wa takŭsán no hon wo yomimásŭ.
アノオヂイサンハ　沢山　ノ　本　ヲ　読ミマス.
That old man reads many books.

Anó kodomotachí wa kudámono ga sŭkí désŭ.   Those children like fruit.
アノ　子供達　ハ　果物　ガ　好キ　デス.

Anó otokó wa tabakó ga kirái désŭ.   That man dislikes tobacco.
アノ　男　ハ　タバコ　ガ　嫌イ　デス.

Anó obāsan wa tabakó wo kiraimásŭ.   That old woman dislikes tobacco.
アノオバアサンハ　タバコ　ヲ　嫌イマス.

Vocabulary

bottle	bin[1]	ビン	maid-servant	o-tétsudaı	オ手伝イ	
	tokkurí[1]	徳ッ利ヶリ	merchant	shōnin	商シゥ人ニン	
cook	ryōrinin	料リゥ理リ人ニン	nephew	oí	甥オイ	
	kókku[2]	コック	parents	oyá	親オヤ	
doll	ningyō	人ニン形ギゥ		ryōshin	両リゥ親シン	
friend	tomodachí	友トモ達ダチ	servant	meshitsŭkái	召メシ使ツイカ	
	yūjin[3]	友ユゥ人ジン	street	machí[4]	町マチ	
gentleman	shínshi	紳シン士シ		tōri[5]	通トゥリ	
lady	fujín	婦フ人ジン	tobacco	tabakó	タバコ	
lord (feudal)	tonosamá	殿トノ様サマ	to read	yómu	読ョム	
man-servant	génan	下ゲ男ナン				

Exercise   *Renshū*   練レン習シゥ

1. Iku-nin kodomó ga imásŭ ka.—Jū-ni-nin kodomó ga imásŭ. 2. Anó tonosamá wa takŭsán no kérai ga arimáshĭta. 3. Anó rōfujin wa nan-nin meshitsŭkái ga arimásŭ ka.—Anó katá wa jochū go-nin to génan shichí-nin to ryōrinin ga fŭtarí arimásŭ. 4. Anó hĭtó wa takŭsán no bōshi ga arimásŭ ka.—Iié, sŭkóshi kirí.[6] 5. Anó rōjin wa oí ga arimásŭ ka.—Hái, arimásŭ.— Hái, sū-nin arimásŭ. 6. Anátatachi wa takŭsán no uchí wo mótte imásŭ. Watashitachí wa sŭkóshi shĭká mótte imasén. 7. Senséi wa hakubokú wo mótte imáshĭta ka.—Sukóshi mótte imáshĭta. 8. Anó tōri wa nagái déshĭta. 9. Konó empitsú wa mijikái. 10. Soréra no ningyō wa takái désŭ. 11. Shimbún wo

---

1 *Bin* indicates any kind of bottles; *tokkurí* used only to indicate the bottle for Japanese wine, *saké* **2** from the English *cook* **3** The word *yūjin* is used only by men when speaking of their friends **4** *machí* street with houses or shops **5** *tōri* thoroughfare **6** The negative verb after *kirí* or *shĭká*, in this case *mótte imasén*, may be omitted when its omission is clearly understood, as in this example.

sŭkóshi mótte kité kudasái. **12.** Anó shínshi wa hon wo sŭkóshi kirí yomimasén. **13.** Anó hĭtó wa konó niwá ga sŭkí désŭ. **14.** Konó budōshu wa
takái. **15.** Sonó fujingatá wa kodomó ga sŭkí désŭ. Anó katatachí wa néko
ga kirái désŭ. **16.** Gyūnyū ga arimásŭ ka.—Go roppón arimásŭ. **17.** Sokó
ni pen ya empitsú ya kamí ga arimáshĭta. **18.** Watashitachí wa yói hĭtó ga
sŭkí désŭ. **19.** Watashidómo wa warŭi hĭtó wo kiraimásŭ. **20.** Satō sŭkóshi
to mizú wo sŭkóshi mótte kité kudasái. **21.** Anó fujín wa nan sái désŭ ka.
—San-jissái désŭ.

1. 幾人子供ガイマスカ.—十二人子供ガイマス. **2.** アノ殿様ハ沢山
ノ家来ガアリマシタ. **3.** アノ老婦人ハ何人召使ガアリマスカ.—アノ
方ハ女中五人ト下男七人ト料理人ガ二人アリマス. **4.** アノ人ハ沢山
ノ帽子ガアリマスカ.—イ丶エ, 少シキリ. **5.** アノ老人ハ甥ガアリマ
スカ.—ハイ, アリマス.—ハイ, 数人アリマス. **6.** 貴方達ハ沢山ノ家
ヲ持ッテイマス. 私達ハ少シシカ持ッテイマセン. **7.** 先生ハハクボ
クヲ持ッテイマシタカ.—少シ持ッテイマシタ. **8.** アノ通リハ長イデ
シタ. **9.** コノ鉛筆ハ短カイ. **10.** ソレラノ人形ハ高イデス. **11.** 新
聞ヲ少シ持ッテ来テ下サイ. **12.** アノ紳士ハ本ヲ少シキリ読ミマ
セン. **13.** アノ人ハコノ庭ガ好キデス. **14.** コノブドウ酒ハ高イ.
15. ソノ婦人方ハ子供ガ好キデス. アノ方達ハ猫ガ嫌イデス. **16.** 牛
乳ガアリマスカ.—五六本アリマス. **17.** ソコニペンヤ鉛筆ヤ紙ガア
リマシタ. **18.** 私達ハ善イ人ガ好キデス. **19.** 私共ハ悪イ人ヲ嫌イマ
ス. **20.** 砂糖少シト水ヲ少シ持ッテ来テ下サイ. **21.** アノ婦人ハ何
才デスカ.—三十才デス.

1. How many children are there?—There are twelve children. **2.** That
lord had many retainers. **3.** How many servants has that old lady?—She
has five maid-servants, seven men-servants, and two cooks. **4.** Has she many
hats?—No, she has few. **5.** Has that old man any nephews?—Yes, he has.
—Yes, he has several. **6.** You (pl.) have many houses. We have few.
7. Had the teacher any chalk?—He had a little. **8.** That street was long.
9. This pencil is short. **10.** Those dolls are dear. **11.** Bring me a few newspapers. **12.** That gentleman reads few books. **13.** He likes this garden.
14. This wine is dear. **15.** They (those ladies) like children. They dislike
cats. **16.** Have you any milk?—Yes, I have several bottles. **17.** There
were there pens, pencils and some paper. **18.** We like good people.
19. We dislike bad people. **20.** Bring me a little sugar and some water.
21. How old is that lady?—She is thirty years old.

Eleventh Lesson　第十一課

Possessive Adjectives
Shoyū-keiyōshi 所^シ有^ユ形^ケ容^ヨ詞^シ

Possessive adjectives are formed by adding *no* ノ to the personal pronouns.

my	*watakŭshí no*	私ノ		**our**	*watakŭshitachí no*	私達ノ
	watashí no	私ノ			*watashitachí no*	私達ノ
your	*anáta no*	貴方ノ			*watakŭshidómo no*	私共ノ
his	*káre no*	彼ノ		**your**	*anatagatá no*	貴方々ノ
	anó katá no	アノ方ノ			*anátatachi no*	貴方達ノ
	anó otokó-no-hĭtó no	アノ男ノ人ノ		**their**	*kárera no*	彼等ノ
	anó-hĭtó no	アノ人ノ			*anó katatachí no*	アノ方達ノ
her	*kánojo no*	彼女ノ			*anó hĭtotachí no*	アノ人達ノ
	anó katá no	アノ方ノ			*kánojora no*	彼女等ノ
	anó onná-no-hĭtó no	アノ女ノ人ノ			*kánojotachi no*	彼女達ノ
	anó fujín no	アノ婦人ノ				

In the tenth lesson it was stated that **káre** and **kárera** are generally avoided when indicating the third person singular and plural of the personal pronoun. The same may be said of the possessive adjectives *his*, *her*, and *their*. Therefore, instead of **káre no** and **kárera no**, such equivalents as *anó katá no*, *anó otokó no*, *anó katatachí no*, etc., or still better, the names of the persons referred to, followed by *no* ノ, are used. See in the tenth lesson the equivalents given for **he** and **she**, and the remarks made on these two pronouns.

Watashí no *bōshi wo mótte kité kudasái.*　　Bring me my hat, please.
私　ノ 帽子 ヲ 持ッテ 来テ 下サイ.

Watashí wa **anáta no** *hon wo mótte imásŭ.*　　I have your book.
私　ハ 貴方 ノ 本 ヲ 持ッテイマス.

Anó fujín no *kimonó wa kírei désŭ.*　　That lady's kimono is pretty.
アノ 婦人 ノ 着物 ハ キレイ デス.

Watashidómo no *senséi wa ōkii uchí wo mótte imásŭ.*
私共　　 ノ 先生 ハ 大キイ 家 ヲ 持ッテイマス.
Our teacher has a large house.

Anó hĭtotachí no *inú wa otonashíi désŭ.*　　Their dogs are quiet.
アノ　 人達　 ノ 犬 ハ オトナシイ デス.

When speaking of family relations the Japanese use certain expressions to designate their own relatives, and other expressions when speaking of the relatives of the persons spoken to, or of a third person, without using possessive adjectives :

chichí	父	}my father (ordinary speech)
chichioyá	父チ親オ	
otōsan	オ父サン	}my father (polite speech)
otōsama	オ父ゥ様マ	
otōsan	オ父サン	your, his, *or* her father
go-sompú samá	御ゴ尊ソン父ゥ様マ	your father (very polite)
Otōsan!	オ父サン！	Father! Papa!
háha	母	}my mother (ordinary speech)
hahaoyá	母ハ親オ	
Okāsan!	オ母サン	Mother! Mama!
okāsan	オ母サン	my, your, his, *or* her mother
okāsama	オ母様	your, his, *or* her mother (very polite)
kánai	家内	}my wife
sái ; tsúma	妻	
ókŭsama	奥様	your, *or* his wife
uchí, takú	内, 宅	my husband
dannasamá	ダンナ様サ	your husband
go-shújin	御主人	your husband, your master
ottó	夫オト	husband (correlative of wife)
tsúma	妻ツ	wife (correlative of husband)
segaré	伜セガレ	}my son
musŭkó	息子	
go-shisóku	御ゴ子シ息ソ	your son (literary style)
musŭkosán	息ムス子コサン	your son (ordinary speech)
musŭmé	娘	my daughter
ojōsan	オ嬢サン	your daughter

Its

The possessive adjective **its** is translated by *sonó* ソノ.

Watashí wa issatsú no hon wo mótte imásŭ.   **Sonó** *pēji wa kiiró désŭ.*
私 ハ 一冊 ノ 本 ヲ 持ッテイマス. ソノ 頁 ハ 黄色 デス.
I have a book. **Its** pages are yellow.

Musŭkó wa ié wo mótte imásŭ.   **Sonó** *mádo wa chiisái.*
息子 ハ 家 ヲ 持ッテイマス. ソノ 窓 ハ 小サイ.
My son has a house. **Its** windows are small.

A better translation of **its**, and one that is generally used both in spoken and written style, is indicated by *sonó* followed by the noun which the pronoun **its** refers to. In this case the noun is put in the genitive with *no*.

Watashí wa issatsú no hon wo mótte imásŭ.   **Sonó** *hon* **no** *pēji wa*
私 ハ 一冊 ノ 本 ヲ 持ッテイマス. ソノ 本 ノ 頁 ハ
kiiró désŭ. I have a book. **Its** pages are yellow.
黄色 デス.

Musŭkó wa ié wo mótte imásŭ.   **Sonó** *ié* **no** *mádo wa chiisái.*
息子 ハ 家 ヲ 持ッテイマス. ソノ 家 ノ 窓 ハ 小サイ.

In......*ni* ニ, *no náka ni* ノ中ニ

When speaking of closed objects, like boxes, drawers, etc., *no náka ni* ノ中ニ is used. In this case *náka* 中 corresponds to *inside*. When speaking of open places, like fields, prairies, etc., only *ni* is used. When speaking of places that have an enclosure, like gardens, and of places like rooms, theatres, etc., both *ni* and *no náka ni* ノ中ニ may be used. In this case *no náka ni* is emphatic.

*Sonó hakó **no náka ni** empitsú ga arimásŭ.* ソノ 箱 ノ 中 ニ 鉛筆 ガ アリマス.	**In** that box there are pencils.
*Konó hataké **ni** takŭsán no haná ga arimásŭ.* コノ 畑 ニ 沢山 ノ 花 ガ アリマス.	**In** this field there are many flowers.

*Niwá **ni** ki ga arimásŭ.* or *Niwá **no náka ni** ki ga arimásŭ.*
庭 ニ 木 ガ アリマス.　　庭 ノ 中 ニ 木 ガ アリマス.
There are trees **in** the garden.

*Fŭtarí no kodomó ga konó heyá (**no náka**) **ni** imáshĭta.*
二人 ノ 子供 ガ コノ 部屋 (ノ 中) ニ イマシタ.
There were two children **in** this room.

When referring to a place where action is performed, **in** is translated by *de* デ。

*Watashí no musŭme wa sonó heyá **de** nemásŭ.* 私 ノ 娘 ハ ソノ 部屋 デ 寝マス.	My daughter sleeps **in** that room.

at......*ni* ......ニ, ...*de* ......デ

When **at** refers to a place where something or somebody is or stays, *ni* ニ is used, while *de* デ is used when referring to a place where action is performed.

*Watashí no kodomó wa gakkō **ni** imásŭ.* 私 ノ 子供 ハ 学校 ニ イマス.	My children are **at** school.
*Ima chichí wa uchí **ni** imásŭ.* 今 父 ハ ウチ ニ イマス.	My father is now **at** home. (*lit.* Now, father home **at** is.)
*Gekijō **de** mátte imáshĭta.* 劇場 デ 待ッテ イマシタ.	I was waiting **at** the theatre. (*lit.* Theatre **at**, waiting was.)
*Ichiba **de** konó sakaná wo kaimáshĭta.* 市場 デ コノ 魚 ヲ 買イマシタ.	I bought this fish **at** the market. (*lit.* Market **at**, this fish bought.)

On, Upon

......*no ué ni* ......ノ上ニ, ...*no ué de*...... ノ上デ

No ué ni ノ上ニ is used when referring to a place where something or someone is or stays, while *no ué de* ノ上デ is used when referring to a place where action is performed.

Anáta no bōshi wa sonó isú no ué ni arimásŭ.
アナタ ノ 帽子 ハ ソノ 椅子 ノ 上 ニ アリマス.
Your hat is **on** that chair.

Néko ga isú no ué de neté imásŭ.   The cat is sleeping **on** the chair.
猫 ガ 椅子 ノ 上 デ ネテ イマス.   (*lit.* Cat, chair **on**, sleeping is.)

Kodomó ga kaigán de asondé imáshǐta.   The children were playing **on**
子供 が 海岸 デアソンデイマシタ.   the beach.
(*lit.* Children, beach **on**, playing were.)

With verbs of motion, such as *to run, to fly, to pass*, etc., **no ué wo** ノ上ヲ is used.

Néko ga yáne no ué wo hashítte imásŭ.
猫 ガ 屋根 ノ 上 ヲ 走ッテ イマス.
A cat is running **on** the roof. (*lit.* Cat, roof's **on**, running is.)

From the above example it may be seen that with verbs of motion, **on** or **upon** is used, in the Japanese translation, as a noun in the accusative case.

Over and Above

To indicate that something is **over** or **above** something else, **no ué ni** ノ上ニ is used.

Dentō wa tsŭkué no ué ni sagátte imásŭ.   An electric lamp is
電燈 ハ 机 ノ 上 ニサガッテイマス.   (hanging) **over** the desk.
(*lit.* Electric-lamp, desk over, hanging is.)

Chōjō wa kúmo no ué ni déte imásŭ.   The top of the mountain rises
頂上 ハ 雲 ノ 上 ニ 出テイマス.   **above** the clouds.
(*lit.* Summit, clouds above emerging is.)

When, however, the thing that is *over* or *above* something else has contact with another body, as a bridge whose both ends rest on supports of some kind, only **ni**=is used:

Sonó nagaré ni hashí ga kakátte imásŭ.
ソノ 流レ ニ 橋 ガ カカッテ イマス.
There is a bridge **over** that stream. (*lit.* That stream over, bridge lying is.)

With verbs of motion, such as *to run, to fly, to pass*, etc., *over* and *above* are translated by **no ué wo** ノ上ヲ.

Hikōki ga hataké no ué wo tondé imásŭ.   An airplane is flying **over**
飛行機 ガ 畑 ノ 上 ヲ 飛ンデイマス.   (*or* above) the field.
(*lit.* Airplane, field's above, flying is.)

As in the case of *on* and *upon*, **over** and **above** are used, in the preceding and similar sentences, as nouns in the accusative case.

Below and Under

......*no shǐtá ni* ......ノ下ニ, ...*no shǐtá de* ......ノ下デ

No shǐtá ni ノ下ニ is used when referring to something that is or stays **below** or **under** something else, while **no shǐtá de** ノ下デ

is used when referring to a place where action is performed.

Hashí **no shǐtá** *ni kawá ga arimásǔ.* **Under** the bridge there is
橋　　ノ　下　ニ　川　ガ　アリマス.　　　a river.

Watashitachí **no shǐtá** *ni utsǔkushíi taní ga arimáshǐta.*
私達　　　ノ　下　ニ　美シイ　谷　ガ　アリマシタ.
A beautiful valley was **below** us. (Us **below**, beautiful valley was.)

Hashí **no shǐtá** *de mátte imáshǐta.*　　I was waiting **under** the bridge.
橋　　ノ　下　デ　待ッテイマシタ.　　(*lit.* Bridge under, waiting was.)

With verbs of motion such as *to run, to fly, to pass,* etc., *below*
or *under* is translated by **no shǐtá wo** ノ下ヲ.

Jidōsha ga rikukyō **no shǐtá** *wo tōrimáshǐta.*　　The motorcar passed
自動車　ガ　陸橋　ノ　下　ヲ　通リマシタ.　**under** the elevated bridge.
(*lit.* Motorcar, elevated-bridge's under passed.)

Also in this last case *under* is used, in the Japanese translation, as a noun
in the accusative case.

Vocabulary

Nouns		
bedroom	*shinshitsú*	寝室
bridge	*hashí*	橋
field	*hataké*	畑
kimono	*kimonó*	着物
kitchen	*daidokoró*	台所
motor-car	*jidōsha*	自動車
page	*pēji*	頁
river	*kawá*	河,[1] 川[2]
room	*heyá*	部屋
school	*gakkō*	学校

teacher	*senséi*	先生
window	*mádo*	窓
Adjectives		
beautiful	*utsǔkushíi*	美シイ
near	*chikái*	近イ
pretty	{ *kírei*	キレイ
	{ *kírei-na*	キレイナ
yellow	*ki-iró*	黄色
Verbs		
to dislike	*kiraú*	嫌ウ
I dislike	*kirái désǔ*	嫌イデス

Exercise *Renshū* 練習

1. Anáta no shinshitsú wa ōkii désǔ. **2.** Watashí no daidokoró wa chiisái
désǔ. **3.** Koréra no séito wa kimbén désǔ. Kárera no gakkō wa tōi désǔ.
4. Anáta no musǔmé-san wa utsǔkushíi ningyō wo mótte imásǔ. **5.** Anáta
no danná-samá wa niwá ni imásǔ. **6.** Anó otokó-no-ko wa kírei na tokéi wo
mótte imásǔ. Káre no otōsan wa kanemochí désǔ. **7.** Okásan! Pan wo
kudasái. **8.** Anáta no okāsan wa wakái désǔ ka.—Hái, wakái désǔ. **9.** Chichí wa umá ga hachí-hiki arimásǔ. Chichí wa umá ga sǔkí désǔ. **10.** Musǔkó
wa jidōsha wo mótte imáshǐta. **11.** Watashí wa konó uchí ga kirái désǔ.
Konó uchí no heyá wa chiisái désǔ. **12.** Konó hakó no náka ni empitsú ga
go-hon arimáshǐta. **13.** Anó niwá ni ki ga nan-bon arimáshǐta ka.—Jū-ni

---

1 河 a large liver **2** 川 a small river

hon arimáshĭta. **14.** Watashí no musŭkó no gakkō wa chikái désŭ. **15.** Anáta no ókŭsan no zasshí wa anó tsŭkué no ué ni arimásŭ. **16.** Otōsan! Dōzo sen-yen kudasái. **17.** Warewaré wa sóra no shĭtá ni orimásŭ. **18.** Sóra wa warewaré no ué ni arimásŭ. **19.** Anáta no jibikí wa anó tēburu no shĭtá ni arimásŭ. **20.** Watashí no niwá ni takŭsán no haná ga arimásŭ. Watashi-tachí wa haná ga sŭkí désŭ. **21.** Anáta no musŭmé-san to mŭsukó-san wa niwá ni orimásŭ. O-futarí tomó[1] ki no shĭtá ni orimásŭ. **22.** Takŭsán no torí ga anó oká no ué wo tondé imásŭ.[2]

1. 貴方ノ寝室ハ大キイデス. **2.** 私ノ台所ハ小サイデス. **3.** コレ等ノ生徒ハ勤勉デス. 彼等ノ学校ハ遠イデス. **4.** 貴方ノ娘サンハ美シイ人形ヲ持ッテイマス. **5.** 貴方ノダンナ様ハ庭ニイマス. **6.** アノ男ノ子ハキレイナ時計ヲ持ッテイマス. 彼ノオ父サンハ金持デス. **7.** オ母サン! パンヲ下サイ. **8.** 貴方ノオ母サンハ若イデスカ.— ハイ, 若イデス. **9.** 父ハ馬ガ八匹アリマス. 父ハ馬ガ好キデス. **10.** 息子ハ自動車ヲ持ッテイマシタ. **11.** 私ハコノ家ガ嫌イデス. コノ家ノ部屋ハ小サイデス. **12.** コノ箱ノ中ニ鉛筆ガ五本アリマシタ. **13.** アノ庭ニ木ガ何本アリマシタカ.—十二本アリマシタ. **14.** 私ノ息子ノ学校ハ近イデス. **15.** 貴方ノ奥サンノ雑誌ハアノ机ノ上ニアリマス. **16.** オ父サン! ドーゾ千円下サイ. **17.** 我々ハ空ノ下ニオリマス. **18.** 空ハ我々ノ上ニアリマス. **19.** 貴方ノ字引ハアノテーブルノ下ニアリマス. **20.** 私ノ庭ニ沢山ノ花ガアリマス. 私達ハ花ガ好キデス. **21.** 貴方ノ娘サント息子サンハ庭ニオリマス. オ二人トモ木ノ下ニオリマス. **22.** 沢山ノ鳥ガアノ丘ノ上ヲ飛ンデイマス.

1. Your bedroom is large. **2.** My kitchen is small. **3.** These students are diligent. Their school is far. **4.** Your daughter has a beautiful doll. **5.** Your husband is in the garden. **6.** That boy has a pretty watch. His father is rich. **7.** Mother! Give me some bread. **8.** Is your mother young?—Yes, she is young. **9.** My father has eight horses. He likes horses. **10.** My son had a motor-car. **11.** I dislike this house; its rooms are small. **12.** In this box there were five pencils. **13.** How many trees were there in that garden? —There were twelve. **14.** My son's school is near. **15.** Your wife's magazines are on that desk. **16.** Father! Please give me one thousand yen. **17.** We are below the sky. **18.** The sky is above us. **19.** Your dictionary is under that table. **20.** In my garden there are many flowers. We like flowers. **21.** Your daughter and son are in the garden. They are both under a tree. **22.** Many birds are flying over that hill.

---

1 *fŭtarí tomó* both; the *o* before this expression is an honorific 2 *tondé imásŭ* are flying (*lit.* flying are)

Twelfth Lesson 第十二課

Where ?

Dóko ドコ, *dóko ni* ドコニ, *dóko de* ドコデ, *dóko wo* ドコヲ

What has been said in the preceding lesson as to the use of the postpositions *ni* ニ, *de* デ, *wo* ヲ after *no ué* ノ上 (on, over, above) and *no shǐtá* ノ下 (below, under), applies also to *dóko* ドコ (where).

Dóko ni ドコニ is therefore used referring to a place where something or someone is or stays, *dóko de* ドコデ when referring to a place where action is performed, and *dóko wo* ドコヲ with verbs of motion, such as *to run, to fly, to pass,* etc.

Note that no postpositions are used when *dóko* ドコ is followed by *désǔ* デス (is, are) or *déshǐta* デシタ (was, were).

Nagásaki-shi wa **dóko** *ni arimásǔ ka.* 長崎市　ハ　ドコ　ニ　アリマス　カ. *Nagásaki-shi wa* **dóko** *désǔ ka.* 長崎市　ハ　ドコ　デス　カ.	Where is the city of Nagasaki ?
Kyūshū **ni** *arimásǔ.* or *Kyūshū désǔ.* 九州　ニ　アリマス.　　九州　デス.	It is **in** Kyushu.
Dóko **ni** *chichí wa imásǔ ka.* ドコ　ニ　父　ハ　イマス　カ.	Where is my father ?
Niwá **ni** *imásǔ.* 庭　ニ　イマス.	He is **in** the garden.
Dóko **de** *koré wo kaimáshǐta ka.* ドコ　デ　コレ　ヲ　買イマシタ　カ.	Where did you buy this ? (Where this bought ?)
Dóko **wo** *sagashimáshǐta ka.* ドコ　ヲ　サガシマシタ　カ.	Where did you search ? (*sagashimáshǐta* past of *to search*)

Dóko ドコ takes the postposition *e* ヘ, instead of *wo* ヲ, when followed by verbs of motion that indicate direction towards a place, as *to go, to come* for instance.

Note that the postposition *e* ヘ is used after all adverbs of place whenever direction towards a locality is to be expressed.

Dóko *e ikimásǔ ka.* ドコ　ヘ　行キマス　カ.	Where do you go? (*ikimásǔ* 行 キマス I, you, we, they go ; he, she goes)
Gakkō *e ikimásǔ.* 学校　ヘ　行キマス.	I go **to** school.

When a question is connected with another question, the conjunction *and* is generally translated by *soshǐté* ソシテ or *sorekará* ソレカラ, as in the following example :

*Watashí no bōshi wa **dóko ni** arimásŭ ka.*　　**Where** is my hat?
私　ノ　帽子　ハ　ドコ　ニ　アリマス　カ.

Anó bōshikake ni arimásŭ.　　It is on that hatrack.
アノ　帽子掛　ニ　アリマス.

Soshĭté (or *sorekará*) *watashí no sŭtékki wa.*　　**And** my stick?
ソシテ　(ソレカラ)　私　ノ　ステッキ　ハ.

Here *Kokó* ココ

There *Asokó* アソコ, *Sokó* ソコ

These three adverbs take different postpositions as ***dóko*** ドコ, according to the various cases described above.

Asokó アソコ is used when the thing or the person referred to is far from both the speaker and the person spoken to, while ***sokó*** ソコ is used when the thing or person referred to is far from the speaker and near the person spoken to.

*Watashí no bōshi wa **dóko ni** arimásŭ ka.*
私　ノ　帽子　ハ　ドコ　ニ　アリマス　カ.
*Watashí no bōshi wa **dóko désŭ** ka.*　} **Where** is my hat?
私　ノ　帽子　ハ　ドコ　デス　カ.

Kokó *ni arimásŭ.*　コヽニアリマス.
Kokó désŭ.　コヽデス.　} It is **here.**

Asokó ni *arimásŭ.*　アソコニアリマス.
Asokó désŭ.　アソコデス.　} It is **there.**

Sokó *ni arimásŭ.*　ソコニアリマス.
Sokó désŭ.　ソコデス.　} **There** it is.

*Kodomotachí wa **dóko ni** imásŭ ka.*　　**Where** are the children?
子供達　ハ　ドコ　ニ　イマス　カ.

*Asokó **ni** imásŭ.*　アソコニイマス.　　They are **there.**

Dóko *de sonó saifú wo mitsŭkemáshĭta ka.*
ドコ　デ　ソノサイフ　ヲ　見ツケマシタ　カ.
　　Where did you find that purse? (*mitsŭkemáshĭta* past of *mitsuke·rú* to find)

Kokó *de mitsŭkemáshĭta.*　　I found it **here.**
コヽ　デ　見ツケマシタ.

Asokó (*Sokó*) *de mitsŭkemáshĭta.*　　I found it **there.**
アソコ　(ソコ)　デ　見ツケマシタ.

Kokó *e irasshái.*　コヽヘイラッシャイ. Come **here.**=Come to this place.
(*irasshái* イラッシャイ is the imperative of both verbs *to go* and *to come*)
(See page 162)

Asokó (*Sokó*) *e irasshái.* Go **there.**
アソコ　(ソコ)　ヘイラッシャイ.

*Senshū watashí wa **kokó wo** tōrimáshĭta.*　　Last week I passed by **here.**
先週　私　ハ　コヽ　ヲ　通リマシタ.
　(*tōrimáshĭta* past of *tōru* to pass by—*kokó* used here as accusative noun)

Kokó wo *gorán nasái.*   コヽヲゴランナサイ.   Look **here**. (*gorán nasái* is a polite imperative expression for *look!*)

All three adverbial expressions may be used also in the nominative case, as in the following examples:

Kokó wa *samúi.*   コヽハ寒イ.   It is cold **here**.=This place is cold.
(*samúi* corresponds to the adjective *cold* as well as to the expression *it is cold*)
Asokó (*Sokó*) ***wa*** *atsúi.*   アソコ(ソコ)ハ暑イ.   It is hot **there**.=That place is hot. (*atsúi*=hot, it is hot)

Ordinal Numbers

The *ordinal numbers* are formed by the *Chinese cardinal numbers*, preceded or not by the word ***dái*** 第 and followed by ***bammé*** 番目 or ***ban-me***. *Bammé* is a contraction of *ban-me*.

Ban 番 stands for *number* and ***me*** 目 for *gradation*. ***Dái*** 第 means *order* or *ordinal*, and its use is emphatic.

Ichí-bammé 一番目 given below for *the first*, would then correspond, translated literally, to: *one, number of gradation*, and ***dái-ichí-bammé*** 第一番目 would emphasize the "*order of the first gradation number.*"

1st	ichí-bammé	一 番 目	or	dái-ichí-bammé	第 一 番 目
2nd	ni-ba-mmé	二 番 目	"	dái-ni-bammé	第 二 番 目
3rd	san-bammé	三 番 目	"	dái-san-bammé	第 三 番 目
4th	yo-bammé	四 番 目	"	dái-yon-bammé	第 四 番 目
5th	go-bammé	五 番 目	"	dái-go-bammé	第 五 番 目
6th	rokú-bammé	六 番 目	"	dái-rokú-bammé	第 六 番 目
7th	shichí-bammé	七 番 目	"	dái-shichí-bammé	第 七 番 目
8th	hachí-bammé	八 番 目	"	dái-hachí-bammé	第 八 番 目
9th	ku-bammé	九 番 目	"	dái-ku-bammé	第 九 番 目
10th	jū-bammé	十 番 目	"	dái-jū-bammé	第 十 番 目
11th	jū-ichí-bammé	十一番目	"	dái-jū-ichí-bammé	第十一番目
12th	jū-ni-bammé	十二番目	"	dái-jū-ni-bammé	第十二番目

Between the ordinal number and the following noun, the particle *no* is used.

Ni-bammé *no hakó wa ōkíi.* or *Dái-ni-bammé **no** hakó wa ōkíi.*
二番目　ノ　箱　ハ　大キイ.　　第二番目　ノ　箱　ハ　大キイ.
The second box is large.

Go-bammé *no hakó wa chiisái.* or *Dái-go-bammé **no** hakó wa chiisái.*
五番目　ノ　箱　ハ　小サイ.　　第五番目　ノ　箱　ハ　小サイ.
The fifth box is small.

Ni-bammé *no musŭmé wa Pékin ni imásŭ.* ⎫
二番目　ノ　娘　ハ　北京　ニイマス.　　⎬ My second daughter is
Dái-ni-bammé *no musŭmé wa Pékin ni imásŭ.* ⎪ in Peking.
第二番目　ノ　娘　ハ　北京　ニイマス.　　⎭

When a numerative is used with an ordinal number, *ban* is omitted.

Ni-hon-me no *empitsú* wo *kudasái.*
二本目　　ノ　　鉛筆　　ヲ　　下サイ.

Dái-ni-hon-me no *empitsú* wo *kudasái.*
第二本目　　　ノ　　鉛筆　　ヲ　　下サイ.

} Please give me
the second pencil.

Sámbiki-me no *inú* wa *asokó* ni *imásŭ.*
三匹目　　　ノ　　犬　　ハ　アソコ　ニ　イマス.

Dái-sámbiki-me no *inú* wa *asokó* ni *imásŭ.*
第三匹目　　　ノ　　犬　　ハ　アソコ　ニ　イマス.

} The third dog is there.

Vocabulary

	Nouns					
bank	*ginkō*	銀行	stick	*sŭtékki*	ステッキ	
city	*shi*	市		**Adjectives**		
dictionary	*jibikí*	字引	black	*kurói*	黒イ	
handkerchief	*hankechí*	ハンケチ	brown	*chairó*	茶色	
hatrack	*bōshikake*	帽子掛	cold	*samúi*	寒イ	
hill	*oká*	丘	cool	{ *suzushíi*	涼シイ	
letter	*tegamí*	手紙		{ *tsumetái*	冷タイ	
place	{ *bashó*	場所	grey	*nezumiiró*	鼠色	
	{ *tokoró*	所	hot	*atsúi*	暑イ	
purse	*saifú*	財布	warm	*atatakái*	暖カイ	
			white	*shirói*	白イ	

Exercise *Renshū* 練習

1. Hakodaté shi wa dóko désŭ ka.—Hokkaidō désŭ. **2.** Anáta no musŭko-sán wa dóko ni imásŭ ka.—Gakkō ni imásŭ. **3.** Konó tegamí wa dóko ni arimáshĭta ka.—Soré wa anáta no tsŭkué no ué ni arimáshĭta. **4.** Konó tebúkuro wa dokó ni arimáshĭta ka.—Anó hakó no náka ni arimáshĭta. **5.** Watashí no shimbún wa dóko désŭ ka.—Sonó isú no ué ni arimásŭ. **6.** Tōkyō Ginkō wa dóko désŭ ka.—Sokó désŭ. **7.** Kokó ni anáta no saifú ga arimásŭ. Sokó ni anáta no hankechí to bōshi ga arimásŭ. **8.** Kokó wa suzushíi désŭ ka.—Hái, suzushíi désŭ. **9.** Sokó wa atatakái désŭ ka.—Hái, atatakái désŭ. **10.** Dái-san-gan[2] wo kudasái. **11.** Dái-ni-bammé no musŭkosán wa dóko désŭ ka.—Ōsaka ni orimásŭ. **12.** Shi-hikí no umá ga imásŭ. Dái-ichí-ban-me wa shíro[3], dái-ni-ban-me wa kúro[3], dái-san-ban-me wa chairó, dái-yo-ban-me wa nezumí iró désŭ. **13.** Watashí no kamiíré wa dóko ni arimáshĭta ka.—Dái-san-ban-mé no tsŭkué no ué ni arimáshĭta. **14.** Dái-ichí-ban-me no fujín wa watashí no senséi désŭ. **15.** Anáta no uchí wa dóko désŭ ka.—Asokó désŭ. **16.** Watashí no kodomotachí wa dóko ni orimáshĭta ka.—Kokó ni orimáshĭta.

---

1 *Suzushíi* said of weather; in other cases *tsumetái* is used. 2 Modified pronunciation of *kan* (*volume*). 3 When two or more true adjectives are in succession and all depend on one verb, as in this sentence, their final *i* is dropped.

1. 函館市ハドコデスカ.—北海道デス. **2.** 貴方ノ息子サンハドコ
ニイマスカ.—学校ニイマス. **3.** コノ手紙ハドコニアリマシタカ.—ソ
レハ貴方ノ机ノ上ニアリマシタ. **4.** コノ手袋ハドコニアリマシタカ.
—アノ箱ノ中ニアリマシタ. **5.** 私ノ新聞ハドコデスカ.—ソノ椅子ノ
上ニアリマス. **6.** 東京銀行ハドコデスカ.—ソコデス. **7.** コヽニ貴方
ノ財布ガアリマス. ソコニ貴方ノハンケチト帽子ガアリマス. **8.** コ
コハ涼シイデスカ.—ハイ, 涼シイデス. **9.** ソコハ暖カイデスカ.—ハ
イ, 暖カイデス. **10.** 第三巻ヲ下サイ. **11.** 第二番目ノ息子サンハドコ
コデスカ.—大阪ニオリマス. **12.** 四匹ノ馬ガイマス. 第一番目ハ白,
第二番目ハ黒, 第三番目ハ茶色, 第四番目ハ鼠色デス. **13.** 私ノ紙入
ハドコニアリマシタカ.— 第三番目ノ机ノ上ニアリマシタ. **14.** 第一
番目ノ婦人ハ私ノ先生デス. **15.** 貴方ノ家ハドコデスカ.—アソコデ
ス. **16.** 私ノ子供達ハドコニオリマシタカ.—コヽニオリマシタ.

1. Where is the city of Hakodate?—It is in Hokkaido. **2.** Where are your
sons?—They are at school. **3.** Where was this letter?—It was on your desk.
4. Where were these gloves?—They were in that box. **5.** Where is my
newspaper?—There it is on that chair. **6.** Where is the Tokyo Bank?—
There it is. **7.** Here is your purse; there are your handkerchiefs and hat.
8. Is it cool here?—Yes, it is cool. **9.** Is it warm there?—Yes, it is warm.
10. Give me the third volume. **11.** Where is your second son?—He is in
Osaka. **12.** There are four horses: the first one is white, the second one is
black, the third one is brown, and the fourth is grey. **13.** Where was my
pocketbook?—It was on the third desk. **14.** The first lady is my teacher.
15. Where is your house?—It is there. **16.** Where were my children?—They
were here.

Thirteenth Lesson   第十三課

Interrogative pronouns and Adjectives

Gimón daiméishi to gimón keiyōshi

疑問代名詞ト疑問形容詞

dónata	ドナタ	Who? (in polite speech)
dáre	ダレ	Who? (in ordinary speech)
dóre	ドレ	}Which? (among several)
dóno	ドノ	

Dóre ドレ is used as a *pronoun*, *dóno* ドノ as an *adjective*.

    Dóre děsǔ ka.   ドレデスカ.   Which is it?

      Dóno haná děsǔ ka.   ドノ花デスカ.   Which flower?

dóchira	ドチラ	Which? (of the two)
dótchi	ドッチ	(used as pronoun)

Dóchira ドチラ is more polite than *dótchi* ドッチ.

dóchira no	ドチラノ	Which? (of the two)
dótchi no	ドッチノ	(used as adjective)
dónata no	ドナタノ	Whose?
dáre no	ダレノ	
náni or *nan*	何, 何ン	What? (pronoun)
nan no[1]	何ンノ	What? (adjective)

When used subjectively, *dónata, dáre, dótchi, dóchira, náni* do not require any particle when followed by *désŭ*; they take *ga* in other cases. *Ga* is also used after the subject of a sentence in answer to a question that has one of the above interrogatives except when *désŭ* is used.

Konŏ hĭtŏ wa dónata (dáre) désŭ ka.	Who is this person?
コノ 人 ハ ドナタ (ダレ) デス カ.	
Watashĭ no tomodachĭ désŭ. 私ノ友達デス.	He is my friend.
Dónata (dáre) ga anŏ heyá ni imásŭ ka.	Who is in that room?
ドナタ (ダレ) ガ アノ 部屋 ニ イマス カ.	
Háha ga imásŭ. 母ガイマス.	My mother is there.
Dóre ga sŭkí désŭ ka. ドレガ好キデスカ.	Which do you like?
Koré ga sŭkí désŭ. コレガ好キデス.	I like this.
Dóno hon ga omoshirói désŭ ka.	Which book is interesting?
ドノ 本 ガ 面白イ デス カ.	
Anŏ hon ga omoshirói. アノ本ガ面白イ.	That book is interesting.
Anŏ hikidashĭ ni náni ga arimásŭ ka.	What is there in that drawer?
アノ 引出シ ニ 何 ガ アリマス カ.	
Shashín ga arimásŭ. 写真ガアリマス.	There are photographs.
Koré wa nan désŭ ka. コレハ何ンデスカ.	What is this?
Koré wa nan no shokúbutsu désŭ ka.	What plant is this?
コレ ハ 何ン ノ 植物 デス カ.	
Koré wa nettái shokúbutsu désŭ.	It is a tropical plant.
コレ ハ 熱帯 植物 デス.	

Kochirá コチラ or *kotchí* コッチ instead of *koré* コレ, *achirá* アチラ or *atchí* アッチ instead of *aré* アレ, and *sochirá* ソチラ or *sotchí* ソッチ instead of *soré* ソレ are often used in answer to *dóchira* ドチラ.

The use of *kochirá* コチラ, *achirá* アチラ and *sochirá* ソチラ is more polite than the use of *kotchí* コッチ, *atchí* アッチ and *sotchí* ソッチ.

---

1 See Lesson 31, page 218.

Dóchira (*dótchi*) *ga anáta no bōshi désŭ ka.*   **Which** is your hat?
ドチラ（ドッチ）ガ 貴方 ノ 帽子 デス カ.

Kochirá ga watashí no bōshi désŭ.   This is my hat.
コチラ ガ　私　ノ 帽子 デス.

Dóchira no kimonó ga sŭkí désŭ ka.   **Which** kimono do you like?
ドチラ ノ　着物　ガ 好キ デス カ.

Kochirá ga sŭkí désŭ.　コチラガ好キデス.　I like **this**.

Achirá ga sŭkí désŭ.　アチラガ好キデス.　I like **that**.

All the above interrogative pronouns, followed by the particle **no** ノ, may be used as interrogative or demonstrative adjectives:

Sochirá (*sotchí*) **no** *hakó ni náni ga arimásŭ ka.*   What is there in
ソチラ（ソッチ）ノ 箱 ニ 何 ガ アリマス カ.   **that** box?

Kochirá (*kotchí*) **no** *hakó ni tokéi ga arimásŭ.*   In **this** box there
コチラ（コッチ）ノ 箱 ニ 時計 ガ アリマス.   is a watch.

It and **they** are generally omitted in answers. When *it* or *they* is expressed, the *demonstrative pronoun* or the noun used in the question *is repeated* in the answer.

Aré wa dónata no (*dáre no*) *kutsú désŭ ka.*   Whose shoes are **those**?
アレ ハ ドナタ ノ（ダレノ）靴 デス カ.

Aré wa watashí no kutsú désŭ.
アレ ハ　私　ノ　靴　デス.

Watashí no kutsú désŭ. 私ノ靴デス.   }**They** are my shoes.

Watashí **no** *désŭ.*　私ノデス.　**They** are mine.

Aré wa dáre no uchí désŭ ka.   Whose house is **that**?
アレ ハ ダレノ 家 デス カ.

Watashí **no** *désŭ.*　私ノデス.　**It** is mine.

When a noun is omitted, as in the last two answers, **no** ノ has the function of a *pronoun*.

Possessive Case   *Shoyūkaku* 所有格

The *possessive case* is formed by adding the particle **no** ノ to the possessor.

Watashí **no** *níisan* **no** *uchí.*　私ノ兄サンノ家.　My elder brother's house.

Anáta **no** *tomodachí* **no** *jidōsha.* 貴方ノ友達ノ自動車. Your friend's motorcar.

In a few cases, the use of **no** ノ alters the meaning of a word without it, as in the following expressions:

otōsan **no** *ko* a father's child   *obasán* **no** *ko* an aunt's child
オ父サン ノ 子   オバサン ノ 子

otōsan-ko   a father's pet child   *obasán-ko*   an aunt's pet child
オ父サン子   オバサン子

Tarō   wa   otōsan-ko   désŭ.   Taro is my father's pet child.
太郎　　ハ　オ父サン子 デス.

Hanakó   wa   okāsan-ko   désŭ.   Hanako is my mother's pet child.
花子　　　ハ　オ母サン子 デス.

Káre   wa   watashí   no   obasán   no   ko   désŭ.   He is my aunt's child (son).
彼　　ハ　　私　　ノオバサンノ 子 デス.

Indefinite Pronouns
Futéi daiméishi 不定代名詞

dónata ka   ドナタカ ｝somebody (in positive and interr. sentences)
dáre ka   ダレカ   ｝anybody (in interrogative sentences)
dónata mo   ドナタモ ｝everybody, anybody
dáre mo   ダレモ   ｝ (with positive verb)
dónata mo   ドナタモ ｝nobody, not anybody
dáre mo   ダレモ   ｝ (with negative verb)

See the beginning of this lesson for the use of *dónata* and *dáre.*

*Anó heyá ni **dónata ka** (dáre ka) imásŭ ka.*
アノ 部屋 ニ ドナタ カ (ダレカ) イマス カ.
　　Is there somebody (*or* anybody) in that room?

*Hái, **dónata ka** imásŭ.* ハイ, ドナタカイマス.   Yes, there is somebody.

*Iié, **dónata mo** (dáre mo) imasén.*   ｝No, there is nobody.
イイエ, ドナタ モ (ダレ モ) イマセン.   ｝No, there is not anybody.

***Dónata mo** imásŭ.*   ドナタモイマス.   Everybody is in.

***Dónata mo** (dáre mo) imasén.*   Nobody is in.
ドナタ　モ (ダレ モ) イマセン.   (*lit.* Everybody is not in.)

When **everybody** is used in the interrogative, it is translated by
minásan 皆サン (polite) or by **miná** 皆 (less polite). *Miná,*
which also corresponds to *all,* is often pronounced *minná* ミンナ,
in which case it is emphatic.

***Minásan** wa dóko ni imásŭ ka.*   Where is everybody?
皆サン　　ハ ドコ ニイマス カ.

***Minásan** wa asokó ni imásŭ.*   Everybody is there.
皆サン　　ハ アソコニイマス.

Vocabulary

bag	*fukuró*	袋フク		secretary	*hishó*	秘ヒ書ショ
flag	*hatá*	旗ハタ		shirt	*shátsu*	シャツ
mirror	*kagamí*	鏡カガミ		shoe	*kutsú*	靴クツ
office	*jimúsho*	事ジ務ム所ショ		trousers	*zubón*	ズボン
overcoat	*gaitō*	外ガイ套トウ		vase (for flowers)	*kabín*	花カ瓶ビン

Who are you? *Anáta wa dónata désŭ ka.* 貴方ハドナタデスカ.

I am Mr. Sumikura. *Watashi wa Sumikurá[1] désŭ.* 私ハ角倉デス.

Are you Mr. Fukushima? *Anáta wa Fukushimá San désŭ ka.*
貴方　ハ　福島　サンデス カ.

No, I am not Mr. Fukushima; I am Mr. Ishikawa.
Iié, watashí wa Fukushimá de wa arimasén.   Ishikawá désŭ.
イ丶エ、 私　ハ　福島　デ ハ アリマセン.　石川　デス.

What colour is this book? *Konó hon wa naní iró désŭ ka.*
コノ 本 ハ 何 色 デス カ.

It is yellow. *Kiiró désŭ.* 黄色デス.

What colour are those flowers? *Sonó haná wa nani iró désŭ ka?*
ソノ 花 ハ 何 色 デス カ.

They are red. *Aka désŭ.* 赤デス.

Exercise *Renshū* 練習

1. Dáre ga watashí no jibikí wo mótte imásŭ ka.—Anáta no otōsan ga mótte imásŭ. **2.** Anó fujín wa dónata désŭ ka.—Háha dèsŭ. **3.** Koréra no kodomó wa dáre désŭ ka.—Watashí no musŭkó to musŭmé désŭ. **4.** Watashí no inkitsubó wo mótte imásŭ ka.—Iié, mótte imasén.—Dáre ga mótte imásŭ ka. —Anáta no nēsan ga mótte imásŭ. **5.** Dóchira ga anáta no gaitō désŭ ka. —Kótchi désŭ. **6.** Dóchira ga otōsan no shátsu désŭ ka.—Kochirá désŭ. **7.** Dótchi no inú ga sŭkí désŭ ka.—Kochirá ga sŭkí désŭ. Achirá wa kirái désŭ. **8.** Anó fukuró no náka ni náni ga arimásŭ ka.—Chiisái kagamí to hankechí ga arimásŭ. **9.** Koré wa nan désŭ ka.—Soré wa kabín désŭ. **10.** Koré wa dáre no zubón désŭ ka.—Anáta no désŭ. **11.** Anáta wa dáre no tokéi wo mótte imáshĭta ka.—Watashí no áni no tokéi wo mótte imáshĭta. **12.** Anáta no obasán no uchí wa dóko désŭ ka.—Anó ōkina niwá no náka désŭ. **13.** Uchí no o-ishá no musŭkosán wa Indonéshiya ni imásŭ. **14.** Watashí no senséi no gakkō wa anó tōri ni arimásŭ. **15.** Anáta no heyá ni dáre ka imásŭ.—Dáre désŭ ka.—Anáta no ojisán désŭ. **16.** Jimúsho ni dáre ka imásŭ ka.—Hái, anáta no hishó ga imásŭ. **17.** Machí ni takŭsán no hĭtó ga imáshĭta. Minná chiisái hatá wo mótte imáshĭta. **18.** Anó ié ni dáre ka imásŭ ka.—Iié, imasén.

1. ダレガ私ノ字引ヲ持ッテイマスカ.—貴方ノオ父サンガ持ッテイマス. **2.** アノ婦人ハドナタデスカ.—母デス. **3.** コレ等ノ子供ハダレデスカ.—私ノ息子ト娘デス. **4.** 私ノインキ壺ヲ持ッテイマスカ.—イ丶エ, 持ッテイマセン.—ダレガ持ッテイマスカ.—貴方ノ姉サンガ持ッテイマス. **5.** ドチラガ貴方ノ外套デスカ.—コッチデス. **6.** ドチラガオトウサンノシャツデスカ.—コチラデス. **7.** ドッチノ犬ガ好キデスカ.—コチラガ好キデス. アチラハ嫌イデス. **8.** アノ袋ノ中ニ何ガアリマスカ.—小サイ鏡トハンケチガアリマス. **9.** コレハナン

---

1 In telling one's own name the title of courtesy *San* is not used.

デスカ．—ソレハ花瓶デス．　**10.** コレハダレノズボンデスカ．—貴方ノ
デス．　**11.** 貴方ハ誰ノ時計ヲ持ッテイマシタカ．—私ノ兄ノ時計ヲ持
ッテイマシタ．　**12.** 貴方ノ伯母サンノ家ハドコデスカ．—アノ大キナ
庭ノ中デス．　**13.** ウチノオ医者ノ息子サンハインドネシヤニイマス．
14. 私ノ先生ノ学校ハアノ通リニアリマス．　**15.** 貴方ノ部屋ニダレカ
イマス．—ダレデスカ．—貴方ノ伯父サンデス．　**16.** 事務所ニダレカイ
マスカ．—ハイ，貴方ノ秘書ガイマス．　**17.** 町ニ沢山ノ人ガイマシタ．
皆ンナ小サイ旗ヲ持ッテイマシタ．　**18.** アノ家ニダレカイマスカ．—
イヽエ，イマセン．

1. Who has my dictionary?—Your father has it. **2.** Who is that lady?—
She is my mother. **3.** Who are these children?—They are my sons and
daughters. **4.** Have you my inkstand?—No, I have not.—Who has it?—
Your elder sister has it. **5.** Which is your overcoat?—This is. **6.** Which
are your father's shirts?—These are. **7.** Which dog do you like?—I like
this. I do not like that. **8.** What is there in that bag?—There is a small
mirror and some handkerchiefs. **9.** What is this?—It is a flower vase.
10. Whose trousers are these?—They are yours. **11.** Whose watch had you?
—I had my elder brother's watch. **12.** Where is your aunt's house?—It is in
that large garden. **13.** Our doctor's son is in Indonesia. **14.** My teacher's
school is in that street. **15.** There is somebody in your room.—Who is it?
—It is your uncle. **16.** Is there anybody in my office?—Yes, your secretary
is there **17.** There were many people in the street. Everybody had a small
flag. **18.** Is there anybody in that house?—No, there isn't.

Fourteenth Lesson　第十四課

Yes and No

We have already given the Japanese translation of **yes** and **no**
(*hái* ハイ and *iié* イヽエ).

Whenever a question is put in the affirmative, the Japanese translation of these two adverbs corresponds to the English. However,
when the question is put in the negative, *hái* ハイ is used for **no**,
and *iié* イヽエ for **yes**:

Anáta wa inú ga arimasén ka.	貴方ハ犬ガアリマセンカ．	Haven't you a dog?
Hái, arimasén.	ハイ，アリマセン．	**No,** I have not.
Iié, arimásŭ.	イイエ，アリマス．	**Yes,** I have.

This opposite use of **yes** and **no** in answer to a negative question may seem
strange at first; however, if we consider the use of these adverbs from a Japanese point of view, we shall soon understand.

To a negative question in English, the positive or negative answer refers to what is said in the answer, that is: if the thought answer is positive, we use the positive adverb *yes*, while if the thought answer is negative we use the negative adverb *no*.

In Japanese, however, to the same question *Haven't you a dog?*, the positive or negative adverb in the answer refers to the negative idea expressed in the question. Therefore, when the Japanese answer ***Hái, arimasén*** (Yes, I have not.), the affirmative adverb *hái* (yes) means *It is true (that I haven't)*; when they answer ***Iié, arimásŭ*** (No, I have.), the negative adverb *iié* (no) means: *It is not true (that I haven't)*, therefore I have.

Anáta wa ojōsan ga arimasén ka.		Have you not a daughter?
貴方　ハ オ嬢サン ガ アリマセン カ.		
Hái, arimasén.	ハイ、アリマセン.	**No,** I have not.
Iié, arimásŭ.	イイエ、アリマス.	**Yes,** I have.
Konó niwá ni sakurá ga arimasén déshĭta ka.		Wasn't there a cherry tree in this garden?
コノ　庭 ニ　桜　ガアリマセンデシタ カ.		
Hái, arimasén déshĭta. ハイ、アリマセンデシタ.		**No,** there was not.
Iié, arimáshĭta.	イイエ、アリマシタ.	**Yes,** there was.
Sonó kodomotachí wa hahaoyá ga arimasén ka.		Haven't those children a mother?
ソノ　子供達　ハ　母親　ガアリマセン カ.		
Hái, arimasén.	ハイ、アリマセン.	**No,** they haven't.
Iié, arimásŭ.	イイエ、アリマス.	**Yes,** they have.

But

As an adversative conjunction ***but*** is generally translated by ***ga*** ガ.

Watashí wa taitéi ása kōhī wo nomimásŭ ga chichí to háha wa
私　ハ　大抵　朝コーヒーヲ　飲ミマス　ガ　父　ト　母　ハ
o-cha wo nomimásŭ.　　　I generally drink coffee in the morning, **but** my father
オ茶　ヲ　飲ミマス.　　　and mother drink tea.

Instead of ***ga*** one may use ***kéredomo*** ケレドモ, which seems to be more emphatic than ***ga***. ***Kéredomo*** corresponds also to **however**.

Anáta wa pen wo mótte imásŭ ka. Have you a pen?
貴方　ハ　ペン　ヲ　持ッテイマス カ.

*Iié, pen wa[1] mótte imasén, **kéredomo** empitsú wo mótte imásŭ.*
イイエ、ペン　ハ　モッテイマセン ケレドモ　鉛筆　ヲ　持ッテイマス.
No, I have not a pen **but** I have a pencil.

*Watashí no uchí wa chiisái désŭ, **kéredomo** (or **ga**) sumiyói[2] désŭ.*
私　ノ　家　ハ　小サイ　デス　ケレドモ　（ガ）住ミヨイ デス.
My house is small; **however,** it is comfortable.

But, as well as **however,** may be translated also by ***shikáshi*** 併シ or by the more formal expression ***shikáshi nágara*** 併シナガラ.

---

1 See Lesson 20, page 123 for the use of *wa* instead of *wo*.
2 *sumiyói* comfortable to live in

In colloquial language both *shikáshi* and *shikáshi nágara* may be used by men, but not by women, while *ga* and *kéredomo* may be used by anybody:

Watashí wa tsúma ga arimásŭ **shikáshi** *kodomó ga arimasén.*
私 ハ 妻 ガ アリマス 併シ 子供 ガ アリマセン.
I have a wife **but** have no children.

Possessive Adjective

When speaking in English of the shopkeepers from whom we generally buy our home supplies, the possessive adjective is used:

> **Our** baker has brought the bread.
> **Your** grocer sells too dear.

In Japanese, however, instead of *our*, **uchí no** ウチノ (of the home) is used, and, instead of *your*, **o-takú no** オ宅ノ (of your home) is used.

Uchí no *sakanayá wa yasúi désŭ.*   Our fishmonger is (sells) cheap.
ウチ ノ 魚屋 ハ 安イ デス.

O-takú no *nikúya wa takái.*   Your butcher is (sells) dear.
オ宅 ノ 肉屋 ハ 高イ.

The *possessive adjective*, however, is used in Japanese as in English, when we indicate a shopkeeper that generally supplies the needs of a single person, and not of the whole family.

Watashí no *yōfukuya wa jōzu désŭ.*   My tailor is skilful.
私 ノ 洋服屋 ハ 上手 デス.

Anáta no *tokoyá wa dóko désŭ ka.*   Where is your barber?
貴方 ノ 床屋 ハ ドコ デス カ.

Sonó tōri ni kutsúya ga arimásŭ.   In that street there is a shoemaker.
ソノ 通リ ニ 靴屋 ガ アリマス.

Note that *ya,* at the end of the words *sakanayá, nikúya, yōfukuya,* and *tokoyá,* means **shop.** However, these words also indicate the persons that keep the shops, so that *sakanayá* means both *fishmonger* and the *shop selling fish;* the same may be said of the other three words.

In sentences like the ones given above, the Japanese *refer to the shop* and not to the shopkeeper, which explains the use of *arimásŭ* instead of *imásŭ,* in the last example. (It has been said already that *arimásŭ* is used for things, and *imásŭ* or *orimásŭ* for persons and animals. See Lesson 5)

When addressing a shopkeeper, the word **san** サン is placed after the word indicating the trade or occupation he or she is engaged in.

Pan-ya **San,** *pan wo ni-kin todókete*[1] *kudasái.*
パン屋 サン パン ヲ 二斤 届ケテ 下サイ.
(Mr. Baker) please deliver two kin[2] of bread.

---

1 *todókete kudasái* = please deliver   **2** one *kin* = about one pound

Wish to have and Want to have

hoshíi, hoshíi désŭ, hoshíi no désŭ.[1]
欲シイ，欲シイ　デス，欲シイ　ノ　デス.

The three expressions are here given in their increasing degree of politeness. The object of any of the three expressions is followed by *ga.*

Anáta wa náni ga hoshíi (no) désŭ ka.   What do you wish to have?
貴方　ハ　何　ガ　欲シイ（ノ）デス　カ.

Udedokéi ga hoshíi. 腕時計ガ欲シイ.   I wish to have a wrist-watch.

Bíru ga hoshíi désŭ. ビールガ欲シイデス.   I wish to have some beer.

Dóchira ga hoshíi désŭ ka.   Which do you wish to have?
ドチラ　ガ　欲シイ　デス　カ.

Kochirá ga hoshíi désŭ. コチラガ欲シイデス.   I wish to have this one.

With, In company with

...... *to* ト, ... *to isshó* ト一緒, ... *to isshó ni* ト一緒ニ

The three expressions are here given in their increasing degree of emphatic force.

Ojōsan wa dóko ni imásŭ ka.   Where is your daughter?
オ嬢サン　ハ　ドコ　ニ　イマス　カ.

Okāsan to niwá ni imásŭ.
オ母サント　庭　ニ　イマス.
                                        She is in the garden **with** her
Okāsan to isshó ni niwá ni imásŭ.   mother.
オ母サント　一緒　ニ　庭　ニ　イマス.

Chichí wa obá to isshó ni imásŭ.   My father is **with** my aunt.
父　ハ　伯母ト　一緒　ニ　イマス.

Ni is dropped after *isshó* when *désŭ* is used.

Otōsan to isshó déshĭta. オ父サント一緒デシタ. I was **with** my father.

With (instrumental) *de* デ

Me de mimásŭ.   眼デ見マス.   We see **with** our eyes.
Mimí de kikimásŭ. 耳デ聞キマス.   We hear **with** our ears.
Koppú de mizú wo nomimásŭ.   We drink water **with** a cup.
コップ　デ　水　ヲ　飲ミマス.   (Cup with water drink.)

Vocabulary

Nouns					
barber	tokoyá	床屋	boiled egg	*yudé-tamágo*	ユデ玉子
butcher	nikúya	肉屋	ear	*mimí*	耳
cherry tree	*sakurá no ki*	桜ノ木	eye	*me*	眼

1 This third expression is emphatic and used by women.

exercise[1]	undō	運ウ動ド	tailor	yōfukuya	洋ヨ服フ屋ヤ	
	renshū	練レ習シウ	time	himá	暇ヒマ	
	renshū-mondai	練習問モ題ダイ		jikán	時ジ間カン	
fishmonger	sakanayá	魚サナ屋ヤ	tongue	shĭtá	舌シタ	
fountain	funsuí	噴フン水スイ	**Adjectives**			
gas	gásu	ガス	comfortable[3]			
library[2]	toshókan	図ト書シヨ館カン	happy	shiawasé	仕シ合アワセ	
	toshóshitsu	図ト書シヨ室シツ		kōfuku	幸コウ福フク	
nose	haná	鼻ハナ	unhappy	fukō	不フ幸コウ	
parrot	ōmu	オウム		fushiawasé	不フ仕シ合アワセ	
rose	bará	バラ	**Verbs**			
shoemaker	kutsúya	靴クツ屋ヤ	to correct	naósu	直ナオス	

The rose smells good (sweet). *Bará wa yói niói* (or *kaorí*) *ga shimásŭ.*
バラ ハ ヨイ ニオイ (香リ) ガ シマス.
(*lit.* Rose good smell makes.)

Gas smells bad. *Gásu wa iyá-na niói ga shimásŭ.*
ガス ハ イヤナ 臭イ ガ シマス.

Have you time to write a letter? *Tegamí wo káku jikán ga arimásŭ ka.*
手紙 ヲ 書ク 時間 ガ アリマス カ.
(*lit.* Letter to write time have?)

No, I have no time now. *Iié, íma arimasén.* イイエ, 今アリマセン.
(*lit.* No. now Iaven't.)

Yes, I have time. *Hái arimásŭ.* ハイ, アリマス. (Yes, have)

Exercise *Renshū* 練習

1. Konó tōri ni kutsúya ga arimasén ka.—Iié, arimásŭ.—Hái, arimasén.
2. Kokó ni funsuí ga arimasén déshĭta ka.—Iié, arimáshĭta.—Hái, arimasén
déshĭta. **3.** Anáta no otōsan wa ōkii toshóshitsu wo mótte imasén ka.—Iié,
mótte imásŭ.—Hái, mótte imasén. **4.** Anó fujín wa jochū ga san-nin arimasén
déshĭta ka.—Iié, arimáshĭta.—Hái, arimasén déshĭta. **5.** Anáta wa ōmu wo
ni-wa mótte imasén déshĭta ka.—Hái, mótte imasén déshĭta, kéredomo háto
wo ni-wǝ mótte imáshĭta. **6.** Watashí wa chichí wa[4] arimásŭ ga háha ga
arimasén. **7.** Anó rōjin wa kanemochí désŭ shikáshi anó hĭtó wa fushiawasé
désŭ. **8.** Uchí no kutsúya wa bímbō désŭ ga kōfuku désŭ. **9.** Uchí no

---

1 *undō*=physical exercise; *renshū* or *renshū-mondai*=study, lesson
2 *toshókan* public library; *toshóshitsu* private library
3 The word *comfortable* is rendered in Japanese by a verb indicating *what the
thing spoken of is comfortable for,* followed by the adjective *yói* ヨイ (*good* or *it is
good*), so that *comfortable for living in* as a house, a place, etc., is translated by *sumí*
住ミ (from *súmu* to live)+*yói* ヨイ=*sumiyói* 住ミヨイ=*good to live in.* *Comfortable
for wearing,* as suits, dresses, and kimonos, is translated by *ki* 着 (from *kirú* to wear)
+*yói* ヨイ=*kiyói*=good to wear. *Comfortable* (shoes) *hakiyói* 穿キヨイ; (hats)
kaburiyói 被リヨイ (*kabúru* to put on, wear); for sleeping *neyói* (*nerú,* to sleep) etc.
4 See Lesson 20, page 123.

sakanayá wa sakaná wo mótte imasén déshĭta ka.—Iié, mótte imáshĭta.—Hái.
mótte imasén déshĭta. **10.** Náni ga hoshíi no désŭ ka.—Sūpu to yudé-tamágo
ga hoshíi désŭ. **11.** Anáta no chiisái musŭmesán wa náni ga hoshíi no désŭ
ka.—Amé ga hoshíi no désŭ. **12.** Anáta no musŭkosán wa senséi to isshó
désŭ. **13.** Haná de kagimásŭ. **14.** Warewaré wa nikú wo fóku to náifu de
tabemásŭ. **15.** Haná wa yói niói ga shimásŭ. **16.** Inki wa yói niói ga shimasén. **17.** Konó renshūmondai wo naósu jikán ga arimásu ka.—Hái. jikán ga
arimásŭ.—Iié, arimasén. **18.** Shĭtá de ajiwaimásŭ.

1. コノ通リニ靴屋ガアリマセンカ.—イヽエ，アリマス.—ハイ，ア
リマセン. **2.** コヽニ噴水ガアリマセンデシタカ.—イヽエ，アリマシ
タ.—ハイ，アリマセンデシタ. **3.** アナタノオ父サンハ大キイ図書室
ヲ持ッテイマセンカ.—イヽエ，持ッテイマス.—ハイ，持ッテイマセ
ン. **4.** アノ婦人ハ女中ガ三人アリマセンデシタカ.—イヽエ，アリマ
シタ.—ハイ，アリマセンデシタ. **5.** 貴方ハオウムヲ二羽持ッテイ
マセンデシタカ.—ハイ，持ッテイマセンデシタ. ケレドモ鳩ヲ二羽
持ッテイマシタ. **6.** 私ハ父ハアリマスガ母ガアリマセン. **7.** アノ老
人ハ金持デス. 然シアノ人ハ不仕合セデス. **8.** ウチノ靴屋ハ貧乏デ
スガ幸福デス. **9.** ウチノ魚屋ハ魚ヲ持ッテイマセンデシタカ.—イヽ
エ，持ッテイマシタ.—ハイ，持ッテイマセンデシタ. **10.** 何ガ欲シ
イノデスカ.—スープトユデ玉子ガ欲シイデス. **11.** 貴方ノ小サイ娘
サンハ何ガ欲シイノデスカ.—飴ガ欲シイノデス. **12.** 貴方ノ息子サ
ンハ先生ト一緒デス. **13.** 鼻デ嗅ギマス. **14.** 我々ハ肉ヲフォークト
ナイフデ食ベマス. **15.** 花ハヨイニオイガシマス. **16.** インキハヨイ
ニオイガシマセン. **17.** コノ練習問題ヲ直ス時間ガアリマスカ.—ハ
イ，時間ガアリマス.—イヽエ，アリマセン. **18.** 舌デ味ワイマス.

1. Is there not a shoemaker in this street?—Yes, there is.—No, there is
not. **2.** Was there not a fountain here?—Yes, there was.—No, there was not.
3. Hasn't your father a large library?—Yes, he has.—No, he has not.
4. Hadn't that lady three servants?—Yes, she had.—No, she hadn't. **5.** Hadn't
you two parrots?—No, I hadn't, but I had two pigeons. **6.** I have a father,
but I have no mother. **7.** That old man is rich, but he is unhappy. **8.** Our
shoemaker is poor, but he is happy. **9.** Hadn't our fishmonger any fish?—
Yes, he had.—No, he hadn't. **10.** What do you want to have?—I want to
have some soup and boiled eggs. **11.** What does your little daughter wish to
have?—She wishes to have some candy. **12.** Your son is with his teacher.
13. We smell with the nose. **14.** We eat meat with fork and knife.
15. Flowers smell good. **16.** Ink does not smell good. **17.** Have you time to
correct this exercise?—Yes, I have time.—No, I haven't. **18.** We taste with
our tongue.

Fifteenth Lesson 第十五課

The verb *Dōshi* 動ドゥ 詞シ

The Japanese verb has **no infinitive**. In dictionaries verb forms are given in the **present tense** of the indicative mood, invariably ending in the sound *u*.

tabéru	食タベル	to eat	I, you, we, they eat; he, she, it eats
míru	見ミル	to see	I, you, we, they see; he, she, it sees
tobú	飛トブ	to fly	I, you, we, they fly; he, she, it flies
nómu	飲ノム	to drink	I, you, we, they drink; he, she, it drinks

As is may be seen, there is no distinction as to person.

For the convenience of grammatical explanation, we shall call this form of the present tense of the indicative mood *simple present,* to distinguish it from another present, formed with a suffix which is given in the next page.

*Nippónjin wa háshi de **tabéru.*** The Japanese eat with chopsticks.
日本人　ハ　箸　デ　食ベル.　(*lit.* Japanese chopsticks with eat.)

*Denshobáto wa háyaku **tobú.*** The carrier-pigeon flies fast.
伝書鳩　ハ　速ク　飛ブ.　(*lit.* Carrier-pigeon fast flies.)

*Watashitachí wa koppú de mizú wo **nómu.*** We drink water with a cup.
私達　ハ　コップ　デ　水　ヲ　飲ム.　(We cup with water drink.)

*Me de **míru.*** 眼デ見ル. We see with our eyes. (*lit.* Eyes with see.)

Classification of Japanese Verbs

Japanese verbs are divided into **two classes**. To **Class I** belong the verbs whose simple present ends in *ru* preceded by a syllable ending in *e* or *i*.

de-ru	=*déru*	出デル	to go out
i-ru	=*irú*	居イル	to be, there is (are)
mi-ru	=*míru*	見ミル	to see
mi-e-ru	=*miéru*	見ミエル	to be visible
ta-be-ru	=*tabéru*	食タベル	to eat

To **Class II** belong verbs whose simple present has the next to the last syllable ending in either *a, o,* or *u.*

sa-ku	=*sakú*	咲サク	to bloom
ka-u	=*kaú*	買カウ	to buy
to-bu	=*tobú*	飛トブ	to fly
nu-ru	=*nurú*	塗ヌル	to paint, to plaster, to daub, etc.

Among this second class of verbs there are some that end in *ru* like those of *Class I,* but in this case *ru* is preceded by another syllable ending in one of the vowels *a, o,* or *u,* as *nurú* 塗ヌル to paint, to plaster, or by two vowels, as *káeru* 帰ルル, to return.

There are several verbs like *miéru* belonging to *Class I,* and as *káeru* belonging to *Class II.* The correct classification of such verbs can be learned only by study and practice.

Class I

By dropping the final syllable *ru* of the verbs of this class, we obtain their **simple verbal stems**:

tabéru	食ベル	to eat	*tabe*	食ベ
míru	見ル	to see	*mi*	見

And by adding the suffix *másŭ* マス to the verbal stem, we obtain a second form of the **present tense** of verbs of Class I. The *u* of *másŭ* is almost silent.

tabemásŭ	食ベマス	I, you, we, they eat; he, she, it eats
demásŭ	出マス	I, you, we, they go out; he, she, it goes out
mimásŭ	見マス	I, you, we, they see; he, she, it sees

The *negative form* of the second present tense is obtained by adding the suffixed *masén* マセン to the verbal stem.

tabemasén	食ベマセン	I, you, etc. do not eat; he, etc. does not eat
demasén	出マセン	I, you, etc. do not go out; he, etc. does not go out
mimasén	見マセン	I, you, etc. do not see; he, etc. does not see

Phonetic Rule. The stress on the *a* of the suffix *másŭ* and on the *e* of the negative suffix *masén* is regularly maintained throughout the conjugation of Japanese verbs.

This second form of the present is used in colloquial speech more than the simple present and is considered more polite.

Nippónjin wa háshi de **tabemásŭ.** The Japanese eat with chopsticks.
日本人 ハ 箸 デ 食ベマス.

Ōbeijin wa háshi de **tabemasén.** Western people do not eat with
欧米人 ハ 箸 デ 食ベマセン.   chopsticks.

Denshobáto wa háyaku **tobimásŭ.** The carrier pigeon flies fast.
伝書鳩 ハ 速ク 飛ビマス.

Gachō wa háyaku **kakemasén.** The goose does not run fast.
ガチョウ ハ 速ク 駈ケマセン.

Me de **mimásŭ.** 眼デ見マス.   We see with our eyes.

Kuraí tokoró de monó ga **miemasén.** ⎰ In dark places things are not seen.
暗イ 所 デ 物 ガ 見エマセン. ⎱ In dark places we do not see (things).

Me de monó wo **mimásŭ.** 眼デ物ヲ見マス. We see things with our eyes.

From the last two examples it may be seen that *míru* 見ル takes the accusative particle *wo* ヲ, while *miéru* 見エル takes the nominative particle *ga* ガ. *Míru* is an active verb, *miéru* (=to be seen) corresponds to the passive form of " to see," which explains the different use of *wo* and *ga.*

Class II

The verbs belonging to this class are divided into **six groups,** and have an **enlarged verbal stem** in *i,* as shown below:

Group 1	*kógu*	漕ヨグ	to row	*kogi*	漕ギ
	káku	書カク	to write	*kaki*	書キ
Group 2	*dásu*	出ダス	to take out	*dashi*	出シ
	kasú	貸カス	to rent	*kashi*	貸シ
Group 3	*tátsu*	立タツ	to stand	*tachi*	立チ
	mátsu	待マツ	to wait	*machi*	待チ
Group 4	*tobú*	飛トブ	to fly	*tobi*	飛ビ
	yómu	読ヨム	to read	*yomi*	読ミ
	shinú	死シヌ	to die	*shini*	死ニ
Group 5	*áru*	アル	to be, there to be	*ari*	アリ
	yabúru	破ヤブル	to tear	*yaburi*	破リ
Group 6	*iú*	云イウ	to say	*ii*	云イ
	kaú	買カウ	to buy	*kai*	買イ
	núu	縫ヌウ	to sew	*nui*	縫イ

The final *u* of the verbs of **group 6** is always preceded by another vowel.

Note that with the exception of the verbs belonging to **group 2** and **group 3,** the extended verbal stem of the verbs of Class II is formed by changing the termination *u* of the verb into *i.* Verbs of **group 2** change *su* ス into *shi* シ, and verbs of **group 3** change *tsu* ツ into *chi* チ.

By adding the suffix *másŭ* マス for the positive, and *masén* マセン for the negative, to the enlarged stem in *i* of the verbs of Class II, we obtain their second present tense.

kakimásŭ	書カキマス	I write	*kakimasén*	書キマセン	I do not write
dashimásŭ	出ダシマス	I take out	*dashimasén*	出シマセン	I do not take out
tachimásŭ	立タチマス	I stand	*tachimasén*	立チマセン	I do not stand
yomimásŭ	読ヨミマス	I read	*yomimasén*	読ミマセン	I do not read
arimásŭ	アリマス	there is	*arimasén*	アリマセン	there is not
yaburimásŭ	破ヤブリマス	I tear	*yaburimasén*	破リマセン	I do not tear
kaimásŭ	買カイマス	I buy	*kaimasén*	買イマセン	I do not buy

Examples

*Watashí wa takŭsán no tegamí wo **kakimásŭ.***   I write many letters.
私 ハ 沢山 ノ 手紙 ヲ 書キマス.

*Musŭmé wa takŭsán no tegamí wo **kakimasén.***   My daughter does not
娘 ハ 沢山 ノ 手紙 ヲ 書キマセン. write many letters.

*Watashí wa Mainichi to Asahí shimbún wo **yomimásŭ.***
私 ハ 毎日 ト 朝日 新聞 ヲ 読ミマス.

I read the Mainichi and the Asahi newspapers. (*Mainichi* and *Asahi* **are the** titles of two of the most important newspapers in Japan.)

Chichí wa zasshi wo **yomimasén.**   My father does not read magazines.
父　ハ　雑誌　ヲ　読ミマセン.

Watashitachí wa hitsuyō-na monó wo **kaimásŭ.** We buy useful things.
私達　ハ　必要　ナ　物　ヲ　買イマス.

Watashidómo wa fuhitsuyō-na monó wo **kaimasén.**   We do not buy
私共　ハ　不必要　ナ　モノ　ヲ　買イマセン.   useless things.

Often, Generally, Sometimes

often   **tabitabi** 度々, **shibashiba** (formal speech) 屡々,
        yóku (colloq. speech) ヨク
generally **taitéi**   大抵, **taigái** 大概
        sometimes **tokidoki** 時々

Watashí wa **tabitabi** *shibaí e ikimásŭ.*   I often go to the theatre.
私　ハ　度々　芝居　ヘ　行キマス.

Chichi wa **taitéi** *yūgata tegamí wo dashimásŭ.* My father generally posts
父　ハ　大抵　夕方　手紙　ヲ　出シマス.   his letters in the evening.

Háha wa **taigái** *(taitéi) ása kōhī wo nomimásŭ.*
母　ハ　大概　(大抵)　朝コーヒーヲ　飲ミマス.
My mother generally drinks coffee in the morning.

Watashidómo wa anó kojikí wo **tabitabi** *tōri de mimásŭ.*
私共　ハ　アノ　乞食　ヲ　度々　通リ　デ　見マス.
We often see that beggar in the street.

Nippón de wa **tokidoki** *saigaí[1] wo tomonáu[2] jishín ga arimásŭ.*
日本　デ　ハ　時々　災害　ヲ　トモナウ　地震　ガ　アリマス.
In Japan sometimes there are disastrous earthquakes.

Nichiyō wa **dóko** *e ikimásŭ ka.*   Where do you go on Sunday?
日曜　ハ　ドコ　ヘ　行キマス　カ.

Taitéi Atami e ikimásŭ.   I generally go to Atami.
大抵　熱海　ヘ　行キマス.

Vocabulary

	Nouns				
beer	bīru	ビール	earthquake	jishín	地震
beggar	kojikí	乞食	evening	yūgata / yóru	夕方 / 夜
carrier-pigeon	denshobáto	伝書鳩	foot	ashí	足
chimney	entotsú	煙突	ham	hámu	ハム
chopsticks	háshi	箸	language[3]	kotobá	言葉
club	kúrabu	クラブ	novel	shōsetsu	小説

---

1 calamity, disaster **2** to accompany, to go with; *saigaí wo tomonáu jishín* earthquake accompanied by disaster **3** In compounds *go* 語 is used instead of *kotobá*, as in **Nihón-go** 日本語 the Japanese language.

piano	*pianó*	ピアノ
poetry	*shi*	詩シ
violin	*vaiorín*	ヴァイオリン

Adjectives

disastrous	*saigaí wo tomonáu*	
		災害ヲトモナウ
useful	*hitsuyō-na*	必ヒッ要ヨウナ
useless	*fuhitsuyō-na*	不フ必ヒッ要ヨウナ

Adverbs

| fast | *háyaku* | 速ハヤク |

Verbs

to clean	*migakú*	ミガク
to go	*ikú*[1]	行イク
	yukú[2]	行ユク
to play[3]	*asobú*	遊アソブ
	hikú	弾ヒク
to speak	*hanásu*	話ハナス
to walk	*arúku*	歩アルク

Do you speak French?   *Anáta wa Fŭransú-go wo hanashimásŭ ka.*
       貴方   ハ   フランス語   ヲ   話シマス   カ.

Yes, I do.   Yes, I speak it.   *Hái, hanashimásŭ.*   ハイ, ハナシマス.

No, I don't.   No, I do not.   *Iié, hanashimasén.*   イイエ, ハナシマセン.

How do you do?   *Go-kigén wa ikága désŭ ka.*   御機嫌ハイカガデスカ.

     (*lit.* Your health how is?—*kigén* state of one's health, *ikága* how?)

How are you?   *Ikága désŭ ka.*   イカガデスカ.

I am very well, thank you.   *Arigatō, tasshá désŭ.*   *Arigatō jōbu désŭ.*
       アリガトウ 達者 デス. アリガトウ 丈夫 デス.

     (*tasshá, jōbu* healthy, well and strong, hale and hearty, etc.—*jōbu* is more colloquial than *tasshá*.)

Good-bye.   *Sayonára.*   サヨナラ.

Exercise   *Renshū*   練習

1. Anáta wa Nihón-go wo hanashimásŭ ka.—Iié, Nihón-go wa[4] hanashima-sén ga Shiná-go wo hanashimásŭ. **2.** Bīru wo nomimásŭ ka.—Iié, nomimasén, kéredomo budōshu wo nomimásŭ. **3.** Ashí de arukimásŭ. **4.** Warewaré wa náifu to fōku de nikú wo tabemásŭ. **5.** Asa náni wo tabemásŭ ka.—Taitéi hámu to tamágo to yakí-pan wo tabemásŭ. **6.** Dáre ga anáta no kutsú wo migakimásŭ ka.—Jochū ga migakimásŭ. **7.** Nan de tabemásŭ ka.—Kuchí de tabemásŭ. **8.** Anáta no musŭmesán wa yūgata náni wo shimásŭ ka.—Taitéi hon wo yomimásŭ. **9.** Anáta wa tabitabí Nikkō e ikimásŭ ka.—Iié, tabitabí ikimasén ga Háyama e tabitabí ikimásŭ. **10.** Anáta wa yūgata taitéi dóchira e ikimásŭ ka.—Taitéi kúrabu e ikimásŭ. **11.** Anáta no ojōsan wa pianó wo hikimásŭ ka.—Pianó wa hikimasén ga vaiorín wo hikimásŭ. **12.** Anáta wa íkutsu kotobá wo hanashimásŭ ka.—Shi-ka-kokú[5]-gó hanashimásŭ : Itarī-gó, Furansú-go, Supéin-go, soshĭté Eigó désŭ. **13.** Anáta wa tokidokí shōsetsu wo yomimásŭ ka.—Hái, tokidokí yomimásŭ, kéredomo shi wo móttó[6] yomimásŭ.

---

1 *ikú* colloq. speech   **2** *yukú* formal speech   **3** *asobú* for amusements; *hikú* for musical instruments   **4** See Lesson 20 page 123 for the use of *wa* instead of *wo*.   **5** *Shi-ka-kokú* 四カ国 four countries, *Shi-ka-kokú-go* 四カ国語 the languages of four countries   **6** *mótto* モット in this case means *more often*

Watashí wa shi ga sŭkí désŭ. **14.** Ani to watashí wa tabitabí Kamakurá e ikimásŭ. Kamakurá wa chiisái shi désŭ. **15.** Anó entotsú no ué no torí ga miemásŭ ka.—Miemasén. **16.** Konó kimonó wa íkura désŭ ka.—Ni-man yen désŭ.—Takái désŭ.—Sayonára.

1. 貴方ハ日本語ヲ話シマスカ.—イヽエ, 日本語ハ話シマセンガ支那語ヲ話シマス. **2.** ビールヲ飲ミマスカ.—イヽエ, 飲ミマセン, ケレドモブドウ酒ヲ飲ミマス. **3.** 足デ歩キマス. **4.** 我々ハナイフトフォークデ肉ヲ食ベマス. **5.** 朝, 何ヲ食ベマスカ.—大抵ハムト玉子トヤキパンヲ食ベマス. **6.** 誰ガ貴方ノ靴ヲミガキマスカ.—女中ガミガキマス. **7.** 何ンデ食ベマスカ.—口デ食ベマス. **8.** 貴方ノ娘サンハ夕方何ヲシマスカ.—大抵本ヲ読ミマス. **9.** 貴方ハ度々日光ヘ行キマスカ.—イヽエ, 度々行キマセンガ葉山ヘ度々行キマス. **10.** 貴方ハ夕方大抵ドチラヘ行キマスカ.—大抵クラブヘ行キマス. **11.** 貴方ノオ嬢サンハピアノヲ弾キマスカ.—ピアノハ弾キマセンガヴァイオリンヲ弾キマス. **12.** 貴方ハイクツ言葉ヲ話シマスカ.—四ヵ国語話シマス. イタリー語, フランス語, スペイン語ソシテ英語デス. **13.** 貴方ハ時々小説ヲ読ミマスカ.—ハイ, 時々読ミマス, ケレドモ詩ヲモット読ミマス. 私ハ詩ガ好キデス. **14.** 兄ト私ハ度々鎌倉ヘ行キマス. 鎌倉ハ小サイ市デス. **15.** アノ煙突ノ上ノ鳥ガ見エマスカ.—見エマセン. **16.** コノ着物ハイクラデスカ.—弐万円デス.—高イデス.—サヨナラ.

1. Do you speak Japanese?—No, I do not speak Japanese, but I speak Chinese. **2.** Do you drink beer?—No, I do not, but I drink wine. **3.** We walk with our feet. **4.** We eat meat with knives and forks. **5.** What do you eat in the morning?—I generally eat ham and eggs and toast. **6.** Who cleans your shoes.—My servant cleans them. **7.** With what do you eat?—I eat with my mouth. **8.** What does your daughter do in the evening?—She generally reads books. **9.** Do you often go to Nikkō?—No, I do not, but I often go to Hayama. **10.** Where do you generally go in the evening?—I generally go to the club. **11.** Does your daughter play the piano?—She does not play the piano, but she plays the violin. **12.** How many languages do you speak?—I speak four languages: Italian, French, Spanish, and English. **13.** Do you sometimes read novels?—Yes, I do sometimes, but I more often read poetry. I like poetry. **14.** My elder brother and I often go to Kamakura. Kamakura is a small city. **15.** Do you see a bird on top of that chimney? —No, I do not. **16.** How much does this kimono cost?—It costs 20,000 yen. —It is dear.—Good-bye.

Sixteenth Lesson 第十六課

Past tense *káko* 過ヵ去ㄱ

The positive form of the **past definite** of all verbs is obtained by adding the suffix *máshĭta* マシタ to the simple stem of verbs of Class I and the *i*-stem of verbs of Class II, and the negative form by adding *masén déshĭta* マセンデシタ.

What in Japanese corresponds to the English **past tense** corresponds also to the **perfect tense.**

Phonetic Rule. The stress on the first *a* of the suffix *máshĭta* is regularly maintained throughout the conjugation of Japanese verbs in the past tense.

Class I
Positive Conjugation

dĕru	出ル	*de*	出	*demáshĭta*	出マシタ	I went out
mĭru	見ル	*mi*	見	*mimáshĭta*	見マシタ	I saw
irú	居ル	*i*	居	*imáshĭta*	居マシタ	(there) was, were

Negative

demasén déshĭta	出マセンデシタ	I did not go out
mimasén déshĭta	見マセンデシタ	I did not see
imasén déshĭta	居マセンデシタ	(there) was not, were not

Class II
Positive Conjugation

káku	書ク	*kaki*	書キ	*kakimáshĭta*	書キマシタ	I wrote
dásu	出ス	*dashi*	出シ	*dashimáshĭta*	出シマシタ	I took (*or* put) out
tátsu	立ツ	*tachi*	立チ	*tachimáshĭta*	立チマシタ	I stood
yómu	読ム	*yomi*	読ミ	*yomimáshĭta*	読ミマシタ	I read
tóru	取ル	*tori*	取リ	*torimáshĭta*	取リマシタ	I took
áru	アル	*ari*	アリ	*arimáshĭta*	アリマシタ	(there) was
óru	居ル	*ori*	居リ	*orimáshĭta*	居リマシタ	(there) were
kaú	買ウ	*kai*	買イ	*kaimáshĭta*	買イマシタ	I bought

Negative

kakimasén déshĭta	書キマセンデシタ	I did not write
dashimasén déshĭta	出シマセンデシタ	I did not take (*or* put) out
tachimasén déshĭta	立チマセンデシタ	I did not stand
yomimasén déshĭta	読ミマセンデシタ	I did not read
torimasén déshĭta	取リマセンデシタ	I did not take

arimasén déshĭta	アリマセンデシタ	{ (there) was not
orimasén déshĭta	オリマセンデシタ	{ (there) were not
kaimasén déshĭta	買イマセンデシタ	I did not buy

Examples

Dáre ga konó tegamí wo kokó ni okĭmáshĭta ka. Who (has) put this
誰 ガ コノ 手紙 ヲ ココニ 置キマシタ カ. letter here?

O-tétsudai ga okĭmáshĭta. オ手伝イガ置キマシタ. The maid (has) put it

Késa náni wo tabemáshĭta ka. { What did you eat this morning?
ケサ 何 ヲ 食ベマシタ カ. { What have you eaten this morning?

Sakaná to góhan wo tabemáshĭta. { I ate fish and rice.
魚 ト 御飯 ヲ 食ベマシタ. { I have eaten fish and rice.

Gichō wa enzetsú wo hajimemáshĭta. The chairman began (to deliver)
議長 ハ 演説 ヲ 始メマシタ. a speech.

Kinō anáta wa yófuku wo kaimáshĭta ka. Did you buy a suit
キノウ貴方 ハ 洋服 ヲ 買イマシタ カ. yesterday?

Iié, kaimasén déshĭta. イイエ, 買イマセンデシタ. No, I did not.

Watashí no tegamí wo dashĭmáshĭta ka. Did you post my letter?
私 ノ 手紙 ヲ 出シマシタ カ.

Iié, máda dashĭmasén déshĭta. No, I have not posted it yet.
イイエ, マダ 出シマセン デシタ. (*máda* not yet, with negative verb)

Kyō gakkō e ikĭmáshĭta ka. { Have you been to school to-day?
キョウ 学校 ヘ 行キマシタ カ. { Did you go to school to-day?

Iié, gakkō e ikĭmasén déshĭta. No, I did not go to school.
イイエ, 学校 ヘ 行キマセン デシタ.

Senshū eppeishikí ga arimasén déshĭta ka.—Arimáshĭta.
先週 閲兵式 ガ アリマセン デシタ カ.—アリマシタ.
Wasn't there a military review last week?—There was.

Sensei wa dóko ni imáshĭta ka. Where was the teacher?
先生 ハ ドコニ イマシタ カ.

Gakkō ni imáshĭta. 学校ニイマシタ. He was in the school.

Desiderative

By affixing *tái* 度タイ to the simple stem of verbs of Class I and
to the extended stem in *i* of the verbs of Class II, we obtain the
desiderative form.

The suffix *tái* means *like to, wish to, should like to.*

Phonetic Rule. Verbs in the desiderative conjugation with *tái* are stressed
on the *a* of the said suffix.

Class I

míru	見ミル	*mi*	見	*mitái*	見度イ	I, you, etc. wish to see
tabéru	食タベル	*tabe*	食ベ	*tabetái*	食ベ度イ	I, you, etc. wish to eat

Class II

káku	書ク	**kaki** 書キ	*kakitái* 書キ度イ	I, you, etc. wish to write
dásu	出ス	**dashi** 出シ	*dashitái* 出シ度イ	I, you, etc. wish to take out
tátsu	立ツ	**tachi** 立チ	*tachitái* 立チ度イ	I, you, etc. wish to stand
yómu	読ム	**yomi** 読ミ	*yomitái* 読ミ度イ	I, you, etc. wish to read
tóru	取ル	**tori** 取リ	*toritái* 取リ度イ	I, you, etc. wish to take

For the negative form of the desiderative see Lesson 22.

Désŭ デス generally follows the verb in the desiderative form, and the object of a desiderative verb may be followed by *wo*, or by *ga* when the object is to be emphasized.

Shōsetsu wo yomitái désŭ. 小説ヲ読ミ度イデス. } I wish to read a novel.
Shōsetsu ga yomitái désŭ. 小説ガ読ミ度イデス. }

Uenó no dōbutsuen wo (or *ga*) *mitái désŭ.*   I wish to see the Ueno
上野 ノ 動物園 ヲ （ ガ）見度イ デス.   Zoological Garden.

Without **désŭ** the desiderative form is less polite.

Nihón shokú ga tabetái. 日本食ガ食べ度イ.   I wish to eat Japanese food.

No ノ sometimes follows the verb in the desiderative form.

*Dóchira no hon ga **yomitái** no désŭ ka.*   Which book do you wish
ドチラ ノ 本 ガ 読ミタイ ノ デス カ.   to read?

*Kochirá ga **yomitái** (**no**) désŭ.*   I wish to read this one.
コチラ ガ 読ミ度イ （ノ）デス.

The use of **no** ノ, as in the two above examples, gives the sentence a tone of gentleness, for which reason it is more of the feminine speech than men's.

It and Them

When **it** and **them,** in answer to a question, are used in the objective case, their translation is omitted in Japanese.

Sashimí[1] ga sŭkí désŭ ka. 刺身ガ好キデスカ.   Do you like raw fish?

Hái, sŭkí désŭ. ハイ, 好キデス.   Yes, I like **it.**

Iié, sŭkimasén. イイエ, 好キマセン.   No, I do not like **it.**

Iié, kirái désŭ. イイエ, 嫌イデス.   No, I dislike **it.**

Dáre ga konó shátsu wo koshiraemáshĭta ka.   Who made this shirt?
誰 ガ コノ シャツ ヲ コシラエマシタ カ.

Háha ga koshiraemáshĭta. 母ガコシラエマシタ.   My mother made **it.**

Dóko de koréra no hon wo kaimáshĭta ka.   Where did you buy
ドコ デ コレ等 ノ 本 ヲ 買イマシタ カ.   these books?

Marúzen de kaimáshĭta.   I bought **them** at the Maruzen Book Store.
丸善 デ 買イマシタ.

---

1 *sashimí* sliced raw fish

The conjunction *and*

When two or more clauses are joined by **and,** the **verbal suffix** is sometimes used only for the verb of the last clause; in the other clause or clauses only the **verbal stem** is used. This construction generally indicates a habit, and it is possible only when the verbs are used in the same tense.

*Asa chichí wa cha wo **nómi**, watashí wa kōhī wo nomi**másŭ.***
朝　父　ハ　茶　ヲ　飲ミ，　私　　ハコーヒーヲ　飲ミマス.
In the morning my father drinks tea **and** I drink coffee.

*Mái ása chichí wa cha wo **nómi**, háha wa gyūnyū wo **nómi**, watashí*
毎　朝　父　ハ　茶　ヲ　飲ミ，　母　ハ　牛乳　ヲ　飲ミ，　私
*wa kōhī wo nomi**másŭ.*** Every morning my father drinks tea, my mother
ハコーヒーヲ　飲ミマス.　　　　drinks milk, **and** I drink coffee.

As it may be seen, the conjunction **and** is not used in such Japanese sentences as the above. **And,** however, may be translated by ***soshīté*** ソシテ, in which case the **verbal suffix** may be used for the stems of the verbs of all the clauses or only for the stem of the verb of the last clause. In such a case, the voice should dwell a little on the word ***soshīté*** ソシテ, as it is done in the case of the English expression....**and then**....

*Musŭkó wa hirumá ginkō de hataraki (másŭ), **soshīté**, yóru daigakú*
息子　ハ　ヒルマ　銀行　デ　仂キ　(マス)　ソシテ　夜　　大学
e ikimásŭ. (hirumá daytime, during the day; ginkō bank. yóru nighttime, at
ヘ　行キマス.　　night; daigakú university)
During the day my son works in a bank **and** in the evening he goes to the university.

When two adjectives not belonging to the class of true adjectives are used predicatively and joined by the conjunction **and,** it is the second adjective that is followed by *désŭ* デス or *déshīta* デシタ, as the case may be, while the first adjective is followed by *de* デ, which is the stem of the two verbal expressions. This is done for euphonic reason, that is, for not repeating the sound of the same word.

Anó onná wa namakemonó de o-sháberi désŭ. That woman is lazy
アノ　女　ハ　ナマケ者　　デオシャベリデス.　**and** talkative.

Vocabulary

	Nouns					
building	{ *tatémono*	建物	furniture	*kágu*	家具	
	birudingú	ビルディング	home	*katéi*	家庭	
cinema	{ *éiga*	映画	jewel	*hōseki*	宝石	
	shínema	シネマ	rice	*komé*[3]	米	
cousin	*itóko*	{ 従兄弟[1]	school building	*kōsha*	校舎	
		{ 従姉妹[2]	shirt	*shátsu*[4]	シャツ	
			work	*shigotó*	仕事	

1 male cousin　**2** female cousin　**3** *komé* 米 raw rice; *góhan* 御飯 or *meshĭ* 飯 cooked rice. The word *meshí* is considered vulgar.　**4** *Kínu no shátsu* 絹ノシャツ silk shirt; *momén no shátsu* 木綿ノシャツ cotton shirt

Verbs

to find	sagasú	探_ガ^サス	every day	mái nichí	毎_イ^マ日_チ^ニ

to find	sagasú	探ガサス
to finish	{ oe·rú	終オエル
	{ shimaú	仕シ舞マウ
to put into	...no náka ni ire·rú	...ノ中ニ入レル
to sell	urú	売ウル
every night	mái ban	毎イマ晩バン
every evening	{ mái ban	毎イマ晩バン
	{ mái yū	毎イ夕ユウ

every day	mái nichí	毎マ日ニチ
every morning	mái ása	毎マ朝ア
this morning	késa	ケサ
to-day	{ kyō	キョウ
	{ kónnichi	今ヲ日ニチ
yesterday	{ kinō	昨日(キノウ)
	{ sakújitsu	昨ザ日ジツ
last evening	{ sakúban	昨ザ晩バン
	{ yūbe	ユウベ

Exercise *Renshū* 練習

1. Yūbe dekakemasén déshĭta ka.—Iié, dekakemáshĭta. Shibaí e ikimáshĭta.
—Hái, dekakemasén déshĭta. Uchí ni imáshĭta. 2. Shibaí ni takŭsán hĭtó
ga imáshĭta ka.—Hái, takŭsán imáshĭta. 3. Anáta wa náni wo urimáshĭta
ka.—Furúi kágu wo urimáshĭta. 4. Ikutsu tamágo wo kaimáshĭta ka.—Tō
kaimáshĭta. 5. Watashí wa kinō omoshirói shōsetsu wo yomimáshĭta.
6. Anáta no kodomó ga anáta no kínu no shátsu wo yaburimáshĭta. 7. Anáta
no shigotó wo oemáshĭta ka.—Iié, máda oemasén déshĭta. 8. Dáre no saifú
wo mitsŭkemáshĭta ka.—Anáta no musŭmesán no saifú wo mitsŭkemáshĭta.
9. Dáre ga watashí no hōseki wo konó hakó e iremáshĭta ka.—Anáta no
o-tétsudai ga iremáshĭta. 10. Inú ga watashí no heyá ni imáshĭta ka.—Iié, inú
wa imasén déshĭta ga néko ga imáshĭta. 11. Watashí no jibikí wa dóko ni
arimáshĭta ka.—Anáta no tsŭkué no ué ni arimáshĭta. 12. Watashí no itóko
wa anáta to isshó ni imáshĭta ka.—Iié, anó katá no senséi to isshó ni imáshĭta.
13. Kokó ni sū-ko[1] no kaichūdokei ga arimásŭ. Dóre ga kaitái désŭ ka.—
Koré ga kaitái désŭ. 14. O-cha wo nomitái désŭ ka.—Iié, o-cha wa nomítaku
arimasén ga kōhī ga íppai nomitái désŭ. 15. Anáta no musŭmesán wa dóko
e ikitái no désŭ ka.—Eiga e ikitái no désŭ. 16. Námbon empitsú ga kaitái
no désŭ ka.—Go-hon kaitái no désŭ. 17. Watashí no musŭkó wa Itarī-go ga
naraitái no désŭ. 18. Watashí no tebúkuro wo mitsŭkemáshĭta ka.—Iié, mi-
tsŭkemasén déshĭta.—Hái, mitsŭkemáshĭta.—Dóko ni arimáshĭta ka.—Anáta
no shindái no ué ni arimáshĭta. 19. Atarashíi kōsha wo mimáshĭta ka.—Iié,
mimasén déshĭta.—Hái, mimáshĭta. 20. Watashí wa ása shimbún wo yómi
yūgata hon wo yomimásŭ.

1. ユウベ出カケマセンデシタカ.—イヽエ, 出カケマシタ. 芝居ヘ
行キマシタ.—ハイ, 出カケマセンデシタ. 家ニイマシタ. 2. 芝居ニ
沢山人ガイマシタカ.—ハイ, 沢山イマシタ. 3. 貴方ハ何ヲ売リマシ
タカ.—古イ家具ヲ売リマシタ. 4. イクツ玉子ヲ買イマシタカ.—十買
イマシタ. 5. 私ハキノウ面白イ小説ヲ読ミマシタ. 6. 貴方ノ子供ガ
貴方ノ絹ノシャツヲ破リマシタ. 7. 貴方ノ仕事ヲ終エマシタカ.—イ

---

1 *ko* 個 is the numerative used in counting watches, clocks, and other things that
have no special auxiliary numeral, as bundles, parcels, etc.

イエ，マダ終エマセンデシタ．　8．誰ノ財布ヲ見ツケマシタカ．一貴方
ノ娘サンノ財布ヲ見ツケマシタ．　　9．誰ガ私ノ宝石ヲコノ箱ヘ入レマ
シタカ．一貴方ノオ手伝イガ入レマシタ．　10．犬ガ私ノ部屋ニイマシタ
カ．一イイエ，犬ハイマセンデシタガ猫ガイマシタ．　11．私ノ字引ハド
コニアリマシタカ．一貴方ノ机ノ上ニアリマシタ．　12．私ノイトコハ貴
方ト一緒ニイマシタカ．一イイエ，アノ方ノ先生ト一緒ニイマシタ．
13．ココニ数個ノ懐中時計ガアリマス．ドレガ買イタイデスカ．一コ
レガ買イ度イデス．　14．オ茶ヲ飲ミ度イデスカ．一イイエ，オ茶ハ飲
ミ度クアリマセンガコーヒーガ一杯飲ミ度イデス．　15．貴方ノ娘サン
ハドコヘ行キ度イノデスカ．一映画ヘ行キタイノデス．　16．何本鉛筆
ガ買イタイノデスカ．一五本買イタイノデス．　17．私ノ息子ハイタリ
ー語ガ習イタイノデス．　18．私ノ手袋ヲ見ツケマシタカ．一イイエ，
見ツケマセンデシタ．一ハイ，見ツケマシタ．一ドコニアリマシタカ．一
貴方ノ寝台ノ上ニアリマシタ．　19．新シイ校舎ヲ見マシタカ．一イイ
エ，見マセンデシタ．一ハイ，見マシタ．　20．私ハ朝，新聞ヲ読ミ．夕
方本ヲ読ミマス．

1. Did you not go out last night?—Yes, I went out. I went to the theatre.
—No, I did not go out. I remained at home. 2. Were there many people
at the theatre?—Yes, there were many. 3. What did you sell?—I sold my
old furniture. 4. How many eggs did you buy?—I bought ten. 5. Yesterday
I read an interesting novel. 6. Your child tore your silk shirt. 7. Did you
finish your work?—No, I have not finished it yet. 8. Whose purse did you
find?—I found your daughter's purse. 9. Who put my jewels into this box?
—Your maid did. 10. Was my dog in my room?—No, your dog was not
in your room, but your cat was there. 11. Where was my dictionary?—It
was on your desk. 12. Was my cousin with you?—No, he was with his
teacher. 13. Here are several watches; which do you wish to buy?—I wish
to buy this one. 14. Do you wish to drink tea?—No, I do not wish to drink
tea, but I wish to drink a cup of coffee. 15. Where does your daughter
wish to go?—She wishes to go to the cinema. 16. How many pencils do
you wish to buy?—I wish to buy five. 17. My son wishes to learn Italian.
18. Did you find my gloves?—No, I did not find them.—Yes, I found them.
—Where were they?—They were on your bed. 19. Did you see the new
school building?—No, I did not see it.—Yes, I saw it. 20. In the morning
I read the newspapers and in the evening I read books.

A Japanese Proverb.

Kangén wa gujín wo yorokobásu. 甘言ハ愚人ヲ喜バス． *lit.*
Honeyed words delight fools. =*Fair words please fools.* (*kangén*
甘言 sweet words, *gujín* 愚人 a fool, *yorokobásu* 喜バス to delight)

Seventeenth Lesson 第十七課

English Prepositions and Adverbs

In

In Lesson 11 it has been said that **in** is translated by *no náka ni* ノ中ニ when speaking of closed objects, by only *ni* ニ when speaking of open places like fields, etc., and by both *ni* ニ and *no náka ni* ノ中ニ when speaking of places that have an enclosure, like gardens, etc., or places like rooms, theatres, etc.

Anó niwá ni sū-hon no ki ga arimásŭ.   **In** that garden there are
アノ 庭 ニ 数本 ノ 木 ガ アリマス.   several trees.

*Anáta no kimonó wa watashí no tansú **no náka ni** arimásŭ.*
貴方 ノ 着物 ハ 私 ノタンスノ 中 ニ アリマス.
Your kimono is **in** my wardrobe.

In the above examples and in those in Lesson 11 the preposition **in** refers to the place where a thing stays or exists. However, when **in** refers to a place where an action is performed, *de* デ, instead of *ni* ニ, is used. Also *dóko* ドコ (Where?) is followed by *de* when this adverb asks for the place where an action is or was performed, as already explained in Lesson 11.

*Sonó utsŭkushíi kása wo **dóko** de kaimáshĭta ka.*
ソノ 美シイ 傘 ヲ ドコ デ 買イマシタ カ.
Where did you buy that beautiful umbrella? (action performed)

Ōsaka de kaimáshĭta. 大阪デ買イマシタ. I bought it **in** Osaka.

Konó saifú wo tōri de mitsŭkemáshĭta.   I found this purse
コノ 財布 ヲ 通リデ 見ツケマシタ.   **in** the street.

Takŭsán no jokŏin¹ ga anó kōjō de hatarakimásŭ.   Many girls work
沢山 ノ 女工員 ガ アノ 工場 デ 仂キマス.   **in** that factory.

When emphasis is to be expressed *ni* ニ or *de* デ is followed by *wa* ハ.

*Nihón **ni** wa takŭsán no onsén ga arimásŭ.*   **In** Japan there are many
日本 ニ ハ 沢山 ノ 温泉 ガ アリマス.   hot springs. (existence)

*Nihón **de** wa hĭtó ga o-komé wo takŭsán tabemásŭ.*   **In** Japan people eat
日本 デ ハ 人 ガ オ米 ヲ 沢山 食ベマス.   much rice. (action)

In is also translated by *no* ノ, the postposition corresponding to **of** when used to indicate possession, as in the following examples:

---

1 *jokōin* a factory girl

*Suzumé ga takŭsán uchí no niwá **no** ki no ué ni imáshĭta.*
雀　ガ　沢山　ウチノ　庭　ノ　木ノ　上　ニ　イマシタ.
Many sparrows were on a tree **in** (=of) my garden.
(*lit.* Sparrows many, my garden's tree on, were.)

*Anáta no mégane wa watashí no heyá **no** tsŭkué no ué ni arimáshĭta.*
貴方　ノ　眼鏡　ハ　　私　ノ　部屋　ノ　机　ノ　上　ニ　アリマシタ.
Your eyeglasses were on the desk **in** (=of) my room.

*Bóku no shirói zubón wa shinshitsú **no** yōfuku-dánsu no náka ni arimáshĭta.*
僕　ノ　白イヅボンハ　　寝室　　ノ　洋服ダンスノ　中　ニアリマシタ.
My white trousers were in the wardrobe **in** (=of) my bedroom.

From *karà* カラ

*Dokó **karà** kimáshĭta ka.* ドコカラ来マシタカ. Where did you come **from**?

*Kyōto **karà** kimáshĭta.*　京都カラ来マシタ.　I came **from** Kyōto.

*Ameriká **karà** Nihón e takŭsán no kankō-kyakú ga kimásŭ.*
アメリカ　カラ　日本　ヘ　沢山　ノ　　観光客　　ガ　来マス.
Many tourists come to Japan **from** America.

*Kyō watashí wa nagái tegamí wo ojiisan **karà** moraimáshĭta.*
キョウ　私　　ハ　長イ　手紙　ヲオジイサンカラ　　貰イマシタ.
To-day I have had (received) a long letter **from** my grandfather.

Till, Until, To (as far as), *máde* マデ

*Watashí wa máinichi uchí kára éki **máde** arukimásŭ.*
私　　ハ　毎日　ウチ　カラ　駅　マデ　　歩キマス.
Every day I walk from my home **to** the station.

*Kinō uchí de anáta wo yūgata **máde** machimáshĭta.*
キノウ家　デ　貴方　ヲ　夕方　マデ　　待チマシタ.
Yesterday I waited for you at my home **until** evening.

*Kyō **máde**.* キョウマデ.　　　　**Till** to-day.

Before (place and time), In front of

......*no máe ni* ......ノ前ニ ......*no máe de* ......ノ前デ

Reminder: *Ni* ニ after *máe* 前 is used when referring to a place where a thing stays or exists, while *de* デ is used when referring to a place where action is performed.

*Watashí no ié **no** máe **ni** yūbinkyoku ga arimásŭ.*
私　　ノ家ノ　前　ニ　　郵便局　　ガ　アリマス.
In front of my house there is a postoffice. (existence)

*Watashí wa anáta wo éki **no** máe **de** machimáshĭta.*
私　　ハ　アナタ　ヲ　駅　ノ　前　デ　　待チマシタ.
I waited for you **in front of** the station. (action performed)

With verbs of motion, as *to walk, run, fly,* etc. *máe* 前 is followed by the postposition *wo* ヲ.

Watashí wa Kyūjō no máe wo arúite imáshĭta.
私 ハ 宮城 ノ 前 ヲ 歩イテ イマシタ.
I was walking **before** the Imperial Palace.

When *máe* 前 refers to time the postposition *ni* may be omitted, while it is always omitted when *désŭ* デス or *déshĭta* デシタ is used,.

Ichí nen máe. 一年前. One year **before**.

Teikokú Hóteru wa dóko désŭ ka. Where is the Imperial Hotel?
帝国 ホテル ハ ドコ デス カ.

Hibiyá Kōen no máe désŭ. It is **in front of** Hibiya Park.
日比谷 公園 ノ 前 デス.

Behind

......*no ushiró ni* ......ノ 後ニ ......*no ushiró de* ......ノ 後デ

Reminder: *Ni* ニ after *ushiró* 後 is used when referring to a place where a thing stays or exists, while *de* デ is used when referring to a place where action is performed.

Uchí no ushiró ni o-miyá ga arimásŭ. **Behind** my house there is
ウチ ノ 後 ニ オ宮 ガ アリマス. a shrine.

Anáta no otōsan ni rájio hōsōkyoku no ushiró de o-me ni
アナタ ノ オ父サン ニ ラジオ 放送局 ノ 後 デ オ目 ニ
kakarimáshĭta. I met your father **behind** the radio station. (*o-me ni kakáru* オ
カカリマシタ. 目ニカカル polite speech for .....*ni áu* ......ニ会ウ to meet)

With verbs of motion, as *to walk, run, fly,* etc. *ushiró* 後 is followed by the postposition *wo* ヲ.

Takŭsán no heitaí ga heiéi no ushiró wo hashítte imáshĭta.
沢山 ノ 兵隊 ガ 兵営 ノ 後 ヲ 走ッテ イマシタ.
Many soldiers were running **behind** the barracks.

When *désŭ* デス or *déshĭta* デシタ is used no postposition is required.

Tōkyō Ginkō hontén wa dóko désŭ ka. Where is the head office of
東京 銀行 本店 ハ ドコ デス カ. Tokyo Bank?

Mitsŭkóshi no ushiró désŭ. 三越ノ後デス. It is **behind** Mitsukoshi.
(Mitsukoshi is the name of a large Department store in Tokyo.)

When? *ítsu* 何ィ時ッ

Itsu Asamá Marú wa tsŭkimáshĭta ka. Wnen did the (ship)
イツ 浅間 丸 ハ 着キマシタ カ. Asama Maru arrive?

Sakŭjitsu tsŭkimáshĭta. 昨日着キマシタ.　　She arrived yesterday.

Itsu kyōkai e ikimásŭ ka.　　**When** do you go to church?
イツ　教会　ヘ行キマス　カ.

Nichiyō ni ikimásŭ. 日曜ニ行キマス.　I go **on** Sunday.

On before one of the days of the week is translated by *ni* ニ.

Why? *náze* 何ヲ故ニ

Because *kará* カラ, *nóde* ノデ, *názenaraba* ナゼナラバ

All the three conjunctions are used by both men and women; however, *nóde* ノデ is more of the feminine speech.

Náze anáta wa kinō jimúsho wo yasumimáshĭta[1] ka.
ナゼ　アナタ　ハ キノウ 事務所　ヲ　　休ミマシタ　カ.
Why were you absent from the office yesterday?

Byōki déshĭta **kará.** or *Byōki déshĭta* **nóde.**　　**Because** I was ill.
病気　デシタ　カラ,　　病気　デシタ　ノデ.

Náze nihónjin wa sakurá-no-haná wo shōsan[2] shimásŭ ka.
ナゼ　日本人　ハ　　桜ノ花　　ヲ　賞讃　シマス　カ.
Why do the Japanese admire the cherry blossoms?

Názenaraba nihónjin ni tótte[3] sakurá-no-haná wa samuraí séishin[4] no
ナゼナラバ　日本人　ニトッテ　桜ノ花　　ハ　士　精神　ノ
shōchō[5] désú.　　**Because,** to Japanese, the cherry blossom symbolizes the spirit
象徴　デス.　　of the samurai. (*séishin* spirit, *shōchō* symbol)

Názenaraba ナゼナラバ is always placed at the beginning of the sentence, while *kará* カラ and *nóde* ノデ are placed at the end, so that the last sentence may be translated as follows:

Nihónjin ni tótte sakurá-no-haná wa samuraí séishin no shōchō désŭ
日本人　ニトッテ　桜ノ花　　ハ　士　精神　ノ　象徴　デス
kará (nóde). (*lit.* To Japanese, cherry blossom, samurai spirit's symbol
カラ　(ノデ).　is because.)

Both *názenaraba* ナゼナラバ and *kará* カラ or *nóde* ノデ may be concurrently used in the same clause, which is thus rendered more emphatic.

Názenaraba nihónjin ni tótte sakurá-no-haná wa samuraí séishin no
ナゼナラバ　日本人　ニ トッテ　桜ノ花　　ハ　士　精神　ノ
shōchō désŭ kará (nóde).　　(See Note on next page.)
象徴　デス カラ　(ノデ).

---

1 *yasúmu* 休ム to rest from labour, to take a day off, to lie idle　**2** *shōsan* 賞讃 praise, admiration; *shōsan surú* to admire, to extol, to praise　**3** *ni tótte* ニトッテ to
4 *séishin* 精神 spirit, mind　**5** *shōchō* 象徴 symbol

Note. To understand the reason of the symbolization given above, one must consider this fact: The petals of the cherry blossom leave their calix when still fresh and at the best of their vigour and beauty, and twirling in the air, as if dancing and unmindful of their approaching end, give, to those looking at them, a show of gaity and merriment before touching the ground that will be their grave. They thus give their young life for a good cause: to show beauty to people, unlike all other flowers whose petals cling to their calix until they wither and rot, as if afraid to die.

Similarly it may be said of the old samurai, who, when still in full vigour, was always ready to give his life for a good cause, just like the cherry blossoms.

Vocabulary

Nouns

carpenter	dáiku	大工	shrine	*jínja* (Lit.)	神社	
church	kyōkai	教会		*o-miyá* (Colloq.)	御宮	
country[1]	*inaká*	田舎	sister[5]	*nēsan*	姉	
	kuní	国		*imōto*	妹	
entrance[2]	*iriguchí*	入口	spirit	séishin	精神	
	génkan	玄関	star	hoshí	星	
factory	kōjō	工場	station	*éki*	駅	
factory girl	jokōin	女工員		*sŭtēshon*	ステーション	
holiday[3]	*yasumí*	休	steamer[6]	*fúne*	船	
	saijitsú	祭日		*kisén*	汽船	
hospital	byōin	病院	sun	taiyō	太陽	
hotel[4]	*hóteru*	ホテル	symbol	shōchō	象徴	
	yadoyá	宿屋	wardrobe	tansú	タンス	
market	íchiba	市場				

Adjectives

moon	tsŭkí	月	
park	kōen	公園	busy	isogashíi	忙シイ
pond	iké	池	courageous	isamashíi	勇シイ
ring	yubiwá	指輪	ill, sick	byōki	病気
road	*dōro*	道路	wide	hirói	広イ
	michí	道			

Verbs

motor ship	hatsudōki-sen	発動機船
to arrive	tsŭkú	着ク
to live	súmu	住ム

In the morning. *Asa (ni).* 朝(ニ)   During the day. *Hirumá; chŭkan* 昼間
In the afternoon. *Gógo (ni).* 午後(ニ)   At home.   *Uchí ni.*   家ニ

---

1 *inaká* rural district; *kuní* one's native land **2** *iriguchí* way in, as opposed to way out, entrance to public places; *génkan* entrance of a house **3** *yasumí* recess, holiday, vacation, day off; *saijitsú* national holiday, red letter day **4** *hóteru* foreign style hotel; *yadoyá* Japanese style hotel or lodging house, inn **5** *nēsan* elder sister; *imōto* younger sister **6** *fúne* any vessel; *kisén* steamer

In the evening. *Yūgata (ni).* 夕方(ニ) In the country. *Inaká ni.* 田舎ニ
At night *or* During the night. *Yóru* 夜, *Yóru no aidá ni.* 夜ノ間ニ or *yakán* 夜間
I was at home. *Uchí ni imáshĭta.* 家ニイマシタ.
I was resting at home. *Uchí de yasúnde imáshĭta.* 家デ休ンデイマシタ.
I thank you very much. *Taihén arigatō gozaimásŭ.* 大変アリガトウゴザイマス.
Not at all. *Dō itashimáshĭte.* ドウイタシマシテ.

Exercise *Renshū* 練習

1. Nagásaki kará no fúne wa ítsu tsŭkimásŭ ka.—Gógo tsŭkimásŭ. **2.** Itsu anáta wa íchiba e ikimásŭ ka.—Asa íchiba e ikimásŭ. **3.** Konó yubiwá wo dóko de mitsŭkemáshĭta ka.—Tōri de mitsŭkemáshĭta. **4.** Anó kōjō de nan-nin no dáiku ga hataraité[1] imásŭ ka.—Yon-jū-go nin. **5.** Tōkyō kará Yoko-hamá máde no dōro wa hirói désŭ. **6.** Senshū watashí wa Kyōto kará Ōsaka máde arukimáshĭta. **7.** Tōkyō-ekí no máe ni ōkikute rippá-na tatémono ga arimásŭ. **8.** Anáta no uchí wa dóko désŭ ka.—Anó yūbinkyoku no máe désŭ. **9.** Teikokú Hóteru no máe ni chiisái iké ga arimásŭ. **10.** Nikúya wa sakanayá no máe ni kimáshĭta. **11.** Anáta no kodomosán wa ítsu gakkō e ikimásŭ ka.—Asa ikimásŭ.—Soshĭté ítsu gakkō kará kaerimásŭ ka.—Gógo gakkō kará kaerimásŭ. **12.** Anáta no ushiró ni ōkina inú ga imásŭ. **13.** Eki wa soréra no tatémono no ushiró désŭ. **14.** Itsu taiyō wa terimásŭ[2] ka.—Taiyō wa hirumá terimásŭ. **15.** Tsŭkí to hoshí wa yóru kagayakimásŭ.[3] **16.** Náze kinō uchí e kimasén déshĭta ka.—Isogashíi déshĭta nóde. **17.** Náze koréra no séito wa gakkō e ikimasén ka.—Kyō wa saijitsú désŭ kará. **18.** Senséi[4] wa uchí ni imásŭ ka.—Iié, uchí ni imasén. Byōin e ikimáshĭta. **19.** Anáta no níisan wa dóko ni súnde imásŭ[5] ka.—Inaká ni súnde imásŭ. Ani wa nōfu désŭ. **20.** Náze imōtosan to isshó ni kimasén déshĭta ka.—Imōtotachi wa uchí de isogashíi déshĭta nóde. **21.** Dōzo mátchi wo kudasái.—Arigatō gozaimásŭ.—Dō itashimáshĭte.

1. 長崎カラノ船ハイツ着キマスカ.—午後着キマス. **2.** イツ貴方ハ市場へ行キマスカ.—朝市場へ行キマス. **3.** コノ指輪ヲドコデ見ツケマシタカ.—通リデ見ツケマシタ. **4.** アノ工場デ何人ノ大工ガ仂イテイマスカ.—四十五人. **5.** 東京カラ横浜マデノ道路ハ広イデス. **6.** 先週私ハ京都カラ大阪マデ歩キマシタ. **7.** 東京駅ノ前ニ大キクテ立派ナ建物ガアリマス. **8.** 貴方ノ家ハドコデスカ.—アノ郵便局ノ前デス. **9.** 帝国ホテルノ前ニ小サイ池ガアリマス. **10.** 肉屋ハ魚屋ノ前ニ来マシタ. **11.** 貴方ノ子供サンハイツ学校へ行キマスカ.—朝行キマス.—ソシテイツ学校カラ帰リマスカ.—午後学校カラ帰リマス.

---

1 *hataraité imásŭ* 仂イテイマス are working.—*hatarakú* 仂ク to work
2 *Téru* 照ル to shine, generally said of the sun.
3 *Kagayáku* 輝ク to shine, to glitter, etc., said of anything bright, whether it be the sun, the moon, precious stones and metals, or other shining objects.
4 *Senséi* 先生 means teacher, but is also a respectful title used in addressing doctors, professors or other learned persons.
5 *súnde imásŭ* 住ンデイマス are living, from *súmu* 住ム to live (in a place), to dwell

12. 貴方ノ後ニ大キナ犬ガイマス． **13.** 駅ハソレ等ノ建物ノ後デス．
14. イツ太陽ハ照リマスカ．—太陽ハ昼間照リマス． **15.** 月ト星ハ夜
輝キマス． **16.** ナゼ，キノウ家ヘ来マセンデシタカ．—忙シイデシタ
ノデ． **17.** ナゼコレ等ノ生徒ハ学校ヘ行キマセンカ．—キヨウハ祭日
デスカラ． **18.** 先生ハ家ニイマスカ．—イヽエ，家ニイマセン． 病院
ヘ行キマシタ． **19.** 貴方ノ兄サンハドコニ住ンデイマスカ．—田舎ニ
住ンデイマス． 兄ハ農夫デス． **20.** ナゼ妹サント一緒ニ来マセンデシ
タカ．—妹達ハ家デ忙シイデシタノデ． **21.** ドウゾマッチヲ下サイ．
アリガトウゴザイマス．—ドウイタシマシテ．

1. When does the steamer from Nagasaki arrive?—She arrives in the
afternoon. **2.** When do you go to the market?—I go to the market in the
morning. **3.** Where did you find this ring?—I found it in the street.
4. How many carpenters work in that factory?—Forty-five. **5.** The road from
Tokyo to Yokohama is wide. **6.** Last week I walked from Kyoto to Osaka.
7. In front of Tokyo station there are large and fine buildings. **8.** Where is
your house?—It is in front of that post-office. **9.** Before the entrance of the
Imperial Hotel there is a small pond. **10.** The butcher came before the fishmonger. **11.** When do your children go to school?—They go to school in
the morning.—And when do they come back from school?—They come back
from school in the afternoon. **12.** There is a big dog behind you. **13.** The
station is behind those buildings. **14.** When does the sun shine?—The sun
shines during the day. **15.** The moon and the stars shine during the night.
16. Why did you not come to my home yesterday?—Because I was busy.
17. Why do not these students go to school?—Because to-day is a holiday.
18. Is the doctor at home?—No, he is not at home. He went to the hospital.
19. Where does your elder brother live?—He lives in the country. He is a
farmer. **20.** Why did you not come with your sisters?—Because they were
busy at home. **21.** Give me a match, please.—Thank you very much.—Not
at all.

A Japanese Proverb

Gō ni itté wa gō ni shĭtagáe. 郷ニ入ッテハ郷ニ従ヘ． *lit.* In
a village entering, to the village obey. = Obey the customs of a
place where you go. *Do in Rome as the Romans do.* (*gō* 郷 village,
ni ニ in, to, *irú* 入ル to enter, *shĭtagáu* 従ウ to obey)

Eighteenth Lesson　第十八課

One and That

The pronoun **one** after *this* and *that* is often omitted in translating into Japanese.

It may be here pointed out that the omission of *one* after *this* and *that* often occurs in English.

Dóchira (dótchi) ga anáta no hon désŭ ka.　Which is your book?
ドチラ （ドッチ） ガ　貴方　ノ　本　デス　カ.

Kochirá (kotchí) désŭ. コチラ （コッチ） デス.　This (is). This **one** (is).

Achirá (atchí) désŭ.　アチラ （アッチ） デス.　That (is). That **one** (is).

Kokó ni ningyō ga fŭtatsú arimásŭ ; dóchira ga sŭkí désŭ ka.
ココ ニ　人形 ガ　二ツ　アリマス　ドチラ　ガ　好キ デス　カ.
Here are two dolls ; which **one** do you like?

Kochirá (kotchí) ga sŭkí désŭ.　I like this **one**.
コチラ （コッチ） ガ　好キ デス.

One may, however, be translated by *hō* 方 or *no hō* ノ方.

Dóchira ga anáta no bōshi désŭ ka. Konó hō désŭ ka, anó hō désŭ ka.
ドチラ　ガ　貴方　ノ　帽子 デス　カ.　コノ　方 デス カ, アノ 方 デス カ.
or *Dótchi ga anáta no bōshi désŭ ka. Kotchí no hō désŭ ka, atchí no*
ドッチ ガ　貴方　ノ　帽子 デス　カ.　コッチ　ノ　方 デス カ, アッチ ノ
hō désŭ ka.　Which is your hat, this **or** that?
方 デス　カ.　*or* Which is your hat, this **one** or that **one**?

Kotchí no hō désŭ. or *Kochirá no hō désŭ.*　This is. This **one**.
コッチ　ノ　方 デス.　コチラ　ノ　方 デス.

As there is no distinction between singular and plural **these** and **those** are translated as **this** and **that**.

Dóchira ga (or *dóchira no hō ga*) *anáta no tebúkuro désŭ ka. Kochirá*
ドチラ　ガ　（ドチラ　ノ　方 ガ）　貴方　ノ　　手袋　デス カ.　コチラ
no hō désŭ ka, achirá no hō désŭ ka. (or *konó hō désŭ ka, anó hō*
ノ　方 デス カ, アチラ ノ　方 デス カ.　　（コノ　　方 デス カ, アノ　方
désŭ ka.)　Which are your gloves, these **or** those.
デス　カ.）

Kochirá no hō désŭ. コチラノ方デス.　These (are).

Note that the conjunction **or,** as in the two above questions, has been omitted in the Japanese translation. This omission often occurs in similar sentences as in the two questions given above and the one in the next page.

Fŭransú-go   wo   hanashimásŭ   ka   Ei-gó   wo   hanashimásŭ   ka.
フランス語 ヲ　話シマス　カ　英語 ヲ　話シマス　カ.
Do you speak French **or** English?
(*lit.* French do you speak, English do you speak?)

Fŭransú-go   wo   hanashimásŭ. フランス語ヲ話シマス.   I speak French.

The expressoins ......**is not that of** and ......**are not those of,**
followed by the name of the possessor, are rendered by ......*no de*
wa arimasén ノデハアリマセン.

*Korĕ   wa   watashí   no   jibikí   dĕsŭ,   anáta   no   tomodachí   **no   de   wa***
コレ ハ　私　ノ 字引 デス, 貴方 ノ　友達　ノ デ ハ
arimasĕn.   This is my dictionary and not your friend's.
アリマセン.   (*or* not that of your friend)

After a qualifying adjective **one** or **ones** is generally translated
by *no hŏ* ノ方 or *hŏ no* 方ノ. *No* ノ in this case is a contraction
of *monó* モノ *thing.*

Watashí   no   bōshi   wo   móttĕ   kitĕ   kudasái.   Bring me my hat,
私　ノ　帽子　ヲ　持ッテ 来テ 下サイ.   (*or* hats) please.

*Kurói   **no**   dĕsŭ   ka,   shirói   **no**   dĕsŭ   ka.*
黒イ　ノ　デス　カ、白イ　ノ　デス　カ.

*Kurói   **hō**   dĕsŭ   ka,   shirói   **hō**   dĕsŭ   ka.*
黒イ 方 デス カ、白イ 方 デス カ.

*Kurói   **hō**   **no**   dĕsŭ   ka,   shirói   **hō**   **no**   dĕsŭ   ka.*
黒イ 方 ノ デス カ、白イ 方 ノ デス カ.

The black **one** (ones)
or the white **one**
(ones)?

*Kurói   **no**   dĕsŭ.* or *Kurói   **hō**   dĕsŭ.*   The black **one** (ones).
黒イ　ノ　デス.　　黒イ　方 デス.

*Watashí   wa   takái   bōshi   wo   kaimáshĭta   ga   otóto   wa   yasúi   **no**   wo*
私　ハ　高イ　帽子　ヲ　買イマシタ ガ　弟　ハ　安イ ノ ヲ
kaimáshĭta.   I bought an expensive hat but my younger brother bought
買イマシタ.   a cheap **one.**

Chichí   no   tábi[1]   *to   háha   **no   to**   wo   móttĕ   kitĕ   kudasái.*
父　ノ 足袋 ト　母　ノ ト　ヲ　持ッテキテ 下サイ.
Bring me my father's and my mother's socks.

Note that *háha no to wo* 母ノトヲ in the last sentence means *and those of
my mother* in the accusative case.

*Anó   tsŭkuĕ   no   uĕ   ni   watashí   no   empitsú   to   **sensĕi   no   to**   ga   arimásŭ.*
アノ 机　ノ 上 ニ　私　ノ　鉛筆 ト　先生 ノ ト ガ アリマス.
On that desk there are my pencils and those of my teacher.
On that desk there are my pencil and my teacher's pencil.

The conjunction *or*

At the beginning of this lesson, in illustrating how to translate
the pronoun **one,** three examples have been given in which the

---
1 *tábi* Japanese kind of socks

translation of the conjunction **or** has been omitted.

This omission occurs also in other cases, as in expressions of indefinite meaning similar to the following ones :

<table>
<tr><td>two **or** three</td><td>*ni-san*</td><td>二三</td><td></td><td>four **or** five</td><td>*shi-go*</td><td>四五</td></tr>
<tr><td></td><td>two **or** three times</td><td>*ni-san* do</td><td></td><td>二三度</td></tr>
<tr><td></td><td>four **or** five people</td><td>*shi-go* nin</td><td></td><td>四五人</td></tr>
<tr><td></td><td>five **or** six years</td><td>*go-rokú* nen</td><td></td><td>五六年</td></tr>
</table>

*Anáta no heyá ni **ni-san nin** no fujín ga imáshĭta.*
貴方　ノ　部屋　ニ　二三　人　ノ　婦人　ガ　イマシタ.
There were two **or** three ladies in your room.

*Watashí no tomodachí wa **shi-go** nen Chūgoku ni imáshĭta.*
私　ノ　友達　ハ　四五　年　中国　ニ　イマシタ.
My friend was in China four **or** five years.

The indefinite idea as expressed in the above examples may be emphasized by using the interrogative particle *ka* カ placed after the first numerative or after the word following the first numeral, as in the sentences below.

The particle *ka* カ would then correspond to **or ;** however, in such cases, it should be uttered in a tone of interrogation, as if one were asking oneself which of the two expressed numbers might be the correct one. Ex :

*Anáta no heyá ni **fŭtarí ka,** san-nin no fujín ga imáshĭta.*
貴方　ノ　部屋　ニ　二人　カ，　三人　ノ　婦人　ガ　イマシタ.
(I am not sure whether) there were two **or** three ladies in your room.
(*lit.* Your room in, two persons?, three ladies there were.)
(*fŭtarí* is here used instead of *ni-nin* for euphonic reason)

*Watashí no tomodachí wa **yo-nen ka,** go-nen Burajirú ni imáshĭta.*
私　ノ　友達　ハ　四年　カ　五年　ブラジル　ニ　イマシタ.
(I am not sure whether) my friend was in Brazil four **or** five years.

Or is sometimes translated by *to* ト.

*Pan **to** góhan **to** dóchira ga sŭkí désŭ ka.*　　Which do you like
パン　ト　ゴハン　ト　ドチラ　ガ　好キ　デス　カ.　　bread **or** rice?
Pan ga sŭkí désŭ. パンガ好キデス.　　I like bread.

Or may also be translated by ***soretómo*** ソレトモ, which is an emphatic expression.

*Asa náni wo nomimásŭ ka. O-chá désŭ ka **soretómo** kōhī désŭ ka.*
朝　何　ヲ　飲ミマス　カ.　オ茶　デス　カ　ソレトモ　コーヒーデス　カ.
Which do you drink in the morning tea **or** coffee?

Kōhī wo nomimásŭ. コーヒーヲ飲ミマス.　　I drink coffee.

For (in favour of) *no tamé ni* ノタメニ

*Konó kimonó wo dáre **no tamé** ni kaimáshĭta ka.*　**For** whom did you
コノ　着物　ヲ　ダレ　ノ　タメ　ニ　買イマシタ　カ.　　buy this kimono?

Anáta no tamé ni. 貴方ノタメニ   **For** you.

Anáta no musŭmesán wa konó haná wo watashí no tamé ni mótte
貴方 ノ 娘サン ハ コノ 花 ヲ 私 ノ タメ ニ持ッテ
kimáshĭta.   Your daughter brought these flowers **for** me.
来マシタ.

Whom and Whose

Whom is translated by *dónata* ドナタ or *dáre* 誰 followed by the particles corresponding to the postpositions required to indicate the appropriate case.

Dónata is used in polite speech, *dáre* in ordinary speech. (See Lesson 13)

Whom?	*Dónata (dáre) wo*	ドナタ（誰）ヲ
For whom?	*Dónata (dáre) no táme ni*	ドナタ（誰）ノタメニ
From whom?	*Dónata (dáre) kará*	ドナタ（誰）カラ
To whom?	*Dónata (dáre) ni*	ドナタ（誰）ニ
With whom? {	*Dónata (dáre) to*	ドナタ（誰）ト
	Dónata (dáre) to isshó ni[1]	ドナタ（誰）ト一緒ニ
Whose?	*Dónata (dáre) no*	ドナタ（誰）ノ

Dáre wo mimáshĭta ka. 誰ヲ見マシタカ.   **Whom** did you see?

Konó tegamí wo dáre kará uketorimáshĭta ka.
コノ 手紙 ヲ 誰 カラ 受取リマシタ カ.   **From whom** did you receive this letter?

Anó kozútsumi wo dáre ni okurimáshĭta ka.
アノ 小包 ヲ 誰 ニ 送リマシタ カ.   **To whom** did you send that parcel?

Dónata to (or *Dónata to isshó ni*) *shibaí e ikimáshĭta ka.*
ドナタ ト （ドナタ ト 一緒 ニ） 芝居 ヘ 行キマシタ カ.
With whom did you go to the theatre?

Obāsan to (isshó ni) ikimáshĭta.
オバアサント （一緒 ニ） 行キマシタ.   I went with my grandmother.

Koré wa dáre no bōshi désŭ ka.
コレ ハ 誰 ノ 帽子 デス カ.   **Whose** hat is this?

Watashí no bōshi désŭ. 私ノ帽子デス.   It is my hat.

Something, Anything, Nothing

As indefinite pronouns **something** in the positive, and **anything** in the positive-interrogative form, are translated by *náni ka* 何カ.

Náni ka kudasái. 何カ下サイ.   Give me **something**.

Náni ka yói monó wo mótte imásŭ ka.
何 カ ヨイ 物 ヲ 持ッテイマス カ.   Have you **anything** good?

Hái, mótte imásŭ. ハイ, 持ッテイマス.   Yes, I have.

---

1 *to isshó ni* is an emphatic expression

Anything in a positive sentence is translated by *nan de mo* 何ンデモ.

Nan de mo sŭkí désŭ. 何ンデモ好キデス.   I like **anything**.

Nan de mo dekimásŭ. 何ンデモ出来マス.   He can do **anything**.

Idiom : *Nan de mo yoroshíi.* 何ンデモヨロシイ. **Anything** will do.

Nothing, or **not anything,** is translated by *náni mo* 何モ when the verb is in the negative.

Náni ka arimásŭ ka. 何カアリマスカ.   Is there something?

Náni mo arimasén.   There is **nothing**. There is **not anything**.
何　モ　アリマセン.

Náni ka mótte imásŭ ka. 何カ持ッテイマスカ.   Have you something?

Náni mo mótte imasén.   I have **nothing**. I have **not anything**.
何　モ　持ッテイマセン.

Náni mo 何モ is pronounced *nanni mo* to render it emphatic.

To Have

In English the verb **to have** is often used with the meaning of *to eat, to drink* or *to receive*. In Japanese the corresponding verbs *tabéru* 食ベル (to eat), *nómu* 飲ム (to drink), and *uketorú* 受取ル or *moraú* 貰ウ (to receive), are used as the case may require.

Késa sakaná wo tabemáshĭta. This morning I **had** fish.
ケサ　魚　ヲ　食ベマシタ.

Watashí wa taitéi hirú[1] ni o-cha wo nomimásŭ. I generally **have**
私　ハ　大抵　昼　ニ　オ茶　ヲ　飲ミマス.　　tea at lunch.

Kinō ōkina nímotsu wo ryōshin kará uketorimáshĭta.
キノウ大キナ　荷物　ヲ　両親　カラ　受取リマシタ.
Yesterday, I **had** a large parcel from my parents.

Instead of *tabéru* or *nómu*, the verb *itadakú* 頂ク is often used by the first person in humble speech or referring to an inferior person, as a servant, for instance.

Anáta wa o-hirú[2] wo tabemáshĭta ka. **Have** you **had** your lunch?
貴方　ハ　オ昼　ヲ　食ベマシタ　カ.

Hái, itadakimáshĭta. ハイ, 頂キマシタ.   Yes, I **had** it.

Mēdo wa o-cha wo mō itadakimáshĭta ka. Has the maid **had**
メード　ハ　オ茶　ヲ　モウ　頂キマシタ　カ.　　tea already?

Hái, itadakimáshĭta. ハイ, 頂キマシタ.   Yes, she has **had** it.

---

1 *hirú* noon ; *hirú ni* at noon *or* at lunch time
2 *o-hirú* in this example is an abbreviation of *o-hirú góhan* noon's meal

Vocabulary

Nouns

charcoal	*sumí*	炭 ス ミ
coal	*sekitán*	石 キ 炭 タ ン
coal dealer	*sekitán-ya*	石 キ 炭 タ ン 屋 ヤ
grandmother	*obāsan*	オ バ ア サ ン
neighbour	*o-tonarí*	オ 隣 ト ナ リ
parcel	*kozútsumi*	小 コ 包 ヅ ミ

sock[1]	{ *kutsushĭtá*	靴 ク ツ 下 シ タ
	tábi	足 タ 袋 ビ
tool	*shigotó-dōgu*	仕 シ 事 ゴ ト 道 ド ウ 具 グ
year	*nen*	年 ネ ン

Verbs

to receive	*uketorú*	受 ウ ケ 取 ト ル

English lessons   *Eigó no kéiko*   英語ノ稽古
to take lessons   *kéiko wo surú*   稽古ヲスル
What is your name?   *O-namaé wa nan to osshaimásŭ ka.*
         オ名前 ハ 何 ン トオッシャイマス カ.
My name is Joseph.   *Jósefu to iimásŭ.*   ジョセフトイイマス.
Just now.   *Chōdo íma.* 丁度今. or *Tattá íma.* (colloq.) タッタ今.
A little while ago.   A short time ago.   *Chottó máe ni.* (colloq.) 一寸前ニ.
Shibáraku máe ni. 暫ク前ニ. or *Sŭkóshi máe ni.* 少シ前ニ.

Exercise   *Renshū* 練習

1. Dóchira ga anáta no okāsan no atarashíi kimonó désŭ ka, kochirá désŭ ka achirá désŭ ka.—Achirá désŭ. **2.** Dótchi ga anáta no shigotó-dōgu désŭ ka, kotchí no hō désŭ ka, atchí no hō désŭ ka.—Kotchí désŭ. **3.** Watashí no tebúkuro wo kudasái.—Dóchira désŭ ka.—Kurói hō désŭ. **4.** Anáta no imōtosan wa dótchi no bōshi wo kaimáshĭta ka, chiisái no désŭ ka ōkíi no désŭ ka.—Ōkii no désŭ. **5.** Konó jibikí wa anáta no désŭ ka soretómo anáta no senséi no désŭ ka.—Senséi no désŭ. **6.** Koré wa watashí no hankechí désŭ. Imóto no de wa arimasén. **7.** Watashí wa tokidokí chairó no kutsú wo hakimásŭ ga taitéi kurói no wo hakimásŭ. **8.** Anáta wa taitéi yūgata náni wo shimásŭ ka, uchí ni imásŭ ka soretómo dekakemásŭ ka.—Taitéi uchí ni imásŭ. **9.** Murá no ié wa chiisái ga tokái no wa ōkii. **10.** Empitsú wo ni-sámbon mótte kité kudasái. **11.** Anó hakó ni pen ga arimásŭ ka.—Hái, shi-go hon arimásŭ. **12.** Niwá ni íku-nin guraí onnanokó ga imásŭ ka.—Fŭtarí ka san-nin imásŭ. **13.** Koré wa dáre no umá désŭ ka.—Watashí no shújin no désŭ. **14.** Konó o-kané wa dáre no tamé ni désŭ ka.—Nikúya no tamé ni désŭ. **15.** Anáta wa dáre ni anáta no furúi yōfuku to kutsú wo yarimáshĭta ka.—Kojikí ni. **16.** Dáre to gakkō e ikimásŭ ka.—O-tonarí no musŭkosán to. **17.** Sekitán wo dóko kará kaimásŭ ka.—Anó sekitán-ya kará. **18.** Kinō anáta wa shibaí de dónata to isshó déshĭta ka.—Oji to. **19.** Náni ka yói monó wo kudasái.—Náni ga hoshíi désŭ ka.—Nan de mo yoroshíi désŭ. **20.** Anáta wa dóchira ga hoshíi désŭ ka kōhī désu ka soretómo o-cha désŭ ka.—Kōhī ga hoshíi désŭ. **21.** Dóchira de Nihón-go no kéiko wo shimásŭ ka.—Anó gakkō de. **22.** O-namaé wa nan to osshaimásŭ ka.—Uiriyamusú to iimásŭ.

---

1 *kutsushĭtá* foreign sock; *tábi* Japanese sock   2 *soretómo* ソレトモ or

1. ドチラガアナタノオ母サンノ新シイ着物デスカ, コチラデスカア
チラデスカ.—アチラデス. **2.** ドッチガ貴方ノ仕事道具デスカコッチ
ノ方デスカアッチノ方デスカ.—コッチデス. **3.** 私ノ手袋ヲ下サイ.—
ドチラデスカ.—黒イ方デス. **4.** 貴方ノ妹サンハドッチノ帽子ヲ買イ
マシタカ, 小サイノデスカ大キイノデスカ.—大キイノデス. **5.** コノ
字引ハ貴方ノデスカソレトモ貴方ノ先生ノデスカ.—先生ノデス.
6. コレハ私ノハンケチデス. 妹ノデハアリマセン. **7.** 私ハ時々茶色
ノ靴ヲハキマスガ大抵, 黒イノヲハキマス. **8.** 貴方ハ大抵夕方何ヲ
シマスカ. 家ニイマスカソレトモ出カケマスカ.—大抵家ニイマス.
9. 村ノ家ハ小サイガ都会ノハ大キイ. **10.** 鉛筆ヲ二三本持ッテ来テ
下サイ. **11.** アノ箱ニペンガアリマスカ.—ハイ, 四五本アリマス.
12. 庭ニ幾人位, 女ノ子ガイマスカ.—二人カ三人イマス. **13.** コレハ
誰ノ馬デスカ.—私ノ主人ノデス. **14.** コノオ金ハ誰ノタメニデスカ.
—肉屋ノタメニデス. **15.** 貴方ハ誰ニ貴方ノ古イ洋服ト靴ヲヤリマシ
タカ.—乞食ニ. **16.** 誰ト学校へ行キマスカ.—オ隣リノ息子サント.
17. 石炭ヲドコカラ買イマスカ.—アノ石炭屋カラ. **18.** キノウ貴方
ハ芝居デドナタト一緒デシタカ.—伯父ト. **19.** 何カヨイモノヲ下サ
イ.—何ガ欲シイデスカ.—何ンデモヨロシイデス. **20.** 貴方ハドチラ
ガ欲シイデスカコーヒーデスカソレトモオ茶デスカ.—コーヒーガ欲
シイデス. **21.** ドチラデ日本語ノ稽古ヲシマスカ.—アノ学校デ.
22. オ名前ハ何トオッシャイマスカ.—ウイリヤムスト云イマス.

1. Which is your mother's new kimono, this one or that one?—That one.
2. Which are your working tools, these or those?—These. **3.** Give me my
gloves.—Which ones?—The black ones. **4.** Which hat did your younger
sister buy, the small one or the large one?—The large one. **5.** Is this your
dictionary or your teacher's?—It is my teacher's. **6.** These are my handkerchiefs and not those of my younger sister. **7.** I sometimes wear brown shoes,
but I generally wear black ones. **8.** What do you generally do in the evening
do you stay at home or do you go out?—I generally stay at home. **9.** The
houses of a village are small, but those of a city are large. **10.** Bring me
two or three pencils. **11.** Are there any pens in that box?—Yes, there are
four or five. **12.** How many girls are there in the garden?—(I am not sure
whether) there are two or three. **13.** Whose horses are these?—They are
my master's. **14.** For whom is this money?—It is for our butcher. **15.** To
whom did you give your old suit and shoes?—To a beggar. **16.** With whom
do you go to school?—With our neighbour's son. **17.** From whom do you
buy your coal?—From that coal-dealer. **18.** With whom were you at the
theatre yesterday?—With my uncle. **19.** Give me something good.—What
do you wish to have?—Anything will do. **20.** Which do you wish to have
coffee or tea?—I wish to have coffee. **21.** Where do you take Japanese
lesson?—At that school. **22.** What is your name?—My name is Williams.

Nineteenth Lesson　第十九課

Possessive Case　*Shoyū-kakú* 所有格

In Lesson 13 it has been said that the possessive case is formed by placing the particle *no* ノ after the noun indicating the possessor.

Ishá no ié wa ōkii. 医者ノ家ハ大キイ.　The doctor's house is large.

When two or more nouns in the possessive case are used one after the other, the particle *no* ノ is repeated after each noun.

Watashí no tomodachí no ishá no ié wa rippá désŭ.

私　ノ　友達　ノ 医者 ノ　家ハ　立派デス.

My friend's doctor's house is fine.

The particle *no* ノ also translates the verb **to belong to**:

Konó tsŭkué wa ojí no tomodachí no désŭ. コノ机ハ伯父ノ友達ノデス.

This desk belongs to my uncle's friend. (*lit.* This desk is my uncle's friend's.)

In this case, however, *no* ノ before *désŭ* デス is a contraction of *monó* モノ (thing), so that the literal translation of the above sentence is *This desk is my uncle's friend's property, or thing.*

Monó モノ, in the meaning of *thing*, as well as its abbreviation *no* ノ, is used to form possessive pronouns. In this case, *no monó* ノモノ or simply *no* ノ, follows the personal pronoun as shown below. Note that the use of *no monó* ノモノ is emphatic.

Koré wa dónata no bóshi désŭ ka.　**Whose** hat is this?
コレ ハ ドナタ ノ 帽子 デス カ.

Watashí no (monó) désŭ. 私ノ（モノ）デス.　　It is **mine**.
Anáta no (monó) désŭ. 貴方ノ（モノ）デス.　　It is **yours**.
Anó katá no désŭ. アノ方ノデス.　　It is **his**.
Káno-jo no désŭ. 彼女ノデス.　　It is **hers**.
Watashitachí no désŭ. 私達ノデス.　　It is **ours**.
Anatatachí no désŭ. 貴方達ノデス.　　It is **yours**.
Anó katatachí no désŭ. アノ方達ノデス.　　It is **theirs**.

Désŭ デス may be omitted in familiar speech.

Koré wa dáre no hon (désŭ ka). コレハダレノ本（デスカ.)
　　　　　　　　　　　　　　　　　　Whose book (is this)?
Watashí no (monó désŭ). 私ノ（モノデス).　　(It's) **mine.**
Anáta no (monó désŭ). 貴方ノ（モノデス).　　(It's) **yours.**

Such expressions as *a friend of mine, one of my friends,* etc., are simplified in Japanese and expressed by *watashi no tomodachi* (my friend), etc. Whenever possible the name of the intended friend or other person, as the case may be, should be mentioned.

Watashí no tomodachí no Takáhashi San wa sakunén Itarī e ikimáshĭta.

私　ノ　友達　ノ　高橋　サン ハ　昨年 イタリー ヘ 行キマシタ.

My friend Mr. Takahashi went to Italy last year.

Between

......*no aidá ni* ......ノ間ニ ......*no aidá de* ......ノ間デ

Ni ニ after *aidá* 間 is used when referring to something that exists between two places or things, while *de* デ is used when referring to an action performed between two places or things.

Nagoyá wa Tōkyō to Ōsaka (to) **no aidá ni** *arimásŭ.*
名古屋 ハ 東京 ト 大阪 （ト） ノ 間 ニ アリマス.
Nagoya is **between** Tokyo and Osaka.
    (*lit.* Nagoya, Tokyo and Osaka –and– between is.)

Uchí no niwá to tonarí no niwá (to) **no aidá ni** *kakíne ga arimásŭ.*
家 ノ 庭 ト 隣リ ノ 庭 （ト） ノ 間 ニ 垣根 ガ アリマス.
Between my garden and my neighbour's garden there is a fence.

Anáta no kodomosán wa watashí to watashí no otōto (to) **no aida**
貴方 ノ 子供サン ハ 私 ト 私 ノ 弟 （ト） ノ 間
ni *imáshĭta.*   Your child was **between** me and my younger brother.
ニ イマシタ.

Tōkyō to Yokohamá **no aidá de** *resshá jíko ga okorimáshĭta.*
東京 ト 横浜 ノ 間 デ 列車 事故 ガ 起リマシタ.
A railway accident has occurred **between** Tokyo and Yokohama.
    (*resshá* railway, *jíko* accident, *okorimáshĭta* past of *okóru* 起ル to happen)

With verbs of motion, such as *to walk, to run, to fly,* etc., **no aidá wo** ノ間ヲ is used:

Watashí wa sonó nagái heí **no aidá wo** *arukimáshĭta.*   I walked bet-
私 ハ ソノ 長イ 塀 ノ 間 ヲ 歩キマシタ.   ween the two long walls.

Among

......no aidá ni *(de)* ......ノ間ニ（デ） **......no náka ni** *(de)*
......ノ中ニ（デ） **......no uchí ni** *(de)* ......ノウチニ（デ）

Ni ニ in each of the three expressions is used when referring to something that is or exists among other things, while *de* デ is used when referring to an action performed among various things.

Note that the expression with **uchí** ウチ is more of the literary style.

Anáta no jibikí ga watashí no hon **no aidá** *(náka, uchí)* **ni** *arimáshĭta.*
アナタノ 字引 ガ 私 ノ 本 ノ 間 （中、 ウチ） ニ アリマシタ.
Your dictionary was **among** my books.

Go-rokú nin no kodomotachí ga yabú **no aidá** *(náka, uchí)* **ni** *imáshĭta.*
五六 人 ノ 子供達 ガ ヤブ ノ 間 （中、 ウチ） ニ イマシタ.
Some children were **among** the bushes.

Go-rokú nin no kodomotachí ga yabú **no náka** *(aidá, uchí)* **de** *asondè*
五六 人 ノ 子供達 ガ ヤブ ノ 中 （間、 ウチ） デアソンデ
imáshĭta.   Some children were playing **among** the bushes. (action performed.)
イマシタ.   (*yabú* bush, *asondè imáshĭta* were playing)

Sonó kané wa kyōdai **no aidá** *(náka, uchí)* **de** *bumpái saremáshĭta.*
ソノ 金 ハ 兄弟 ノ 間 （中、 ウチ） デ 分配 サレマシタ.
The money was divided **among** the brothers. (*bumpái sarerú* to be divided)

Note that **náka** 中 and **uchí** ウチ have the idea of closeness in space, for which reason, when **among** refers to things that are well separated from one another, only the expression with **aidá** 間 is generally used, as in the following example:

*Sorérano shimájima **no aidá de** go-sō no gyosén ga shizumimáshĭta.*
ソレ等ノ　島々　　ノ　　間　デ　五隻ノ　漁船　　ガ　　沈ミマシタ.

Five fishing boats sank **among** those islands. (*sō* 雙 numerative for boats,
gyosén fishing boat, *shizumimáshĭta* past of *shizumú* 沈ム to sink)

Only

bákari バカリ, *daké* ダケ, *nómi*[1] ノミ

Anáta wa otōsan to okāsan ga arimásŭ ka.　　Have you a father
貴方　　ハ　オ父サント　オ母サンガ　アリマス　カ.　　　　and mother?

*Iié, chichí **bákari** désŭ.* イイエ, 父バカリデス.
No, I have **only** a father. No, only my father. (*lit.* No, father only is.)

Takŭsán no tegamí wo kakimáshĭta ka.　　Did you write many letters?
沢山　　ノ　手紙　　ヲ　書キマシタ　カ.

*Iié, ittsū **daké**.* イイエ, 一通ダケ.　　No, **only** one.

N. B. For letters the numerative *tsū* 通 is used. *Ittsū* 一通 one letter, *ni-
tsū* 二通 two letters, *san-tsū* 三通 three letters, etc.

All

Miná 皆, *zémbu* 全部, *súbete*[1] 総テ, スベテ
(*miná* pronounced *minná* when emphasis is to be expressed)

Miná**, **súbete and ***zémbu*** do not take any particle when, used
as the subjects or the object of a clause or sentence, indicate the
whole of something or all the individuals of a group.

> *Miná kimáshĭta.*　皆来マシタ.　　⎫
> *Zémbu kimáshĭta.*　全部来マシタ.　⎬ **All** came.
> *Súbete kimáshĭta.*　総テ来マシタ.　⎭

*Kodomotachí wa **miná** (**zémbu**, **súbete**) tabemáshĭta.*　The children
子供達　　　ハ　　皆　　（全部,　　　総テ）食ベマシタ.　　ate **all.**

When in polite speech one refers to persons, **all** is translated by
minásan 皆サン or ***zémbu no katá*** 全部ノ方 or ***súbete no katá***
総テノ方. *Kata,* in this case, stands for *person, individual.*

> ***Minásan** kimáshĭta.*　　　　　　皆サン来マシタ.　　**All** came.
> ***Zémbu no katá** ga kimáshĭta.* 全部ノ方ガ来マシタ. ⎫**All** (the persons)
> ***Súbete no katá** ga kimáshĭta.* 総テノ方が来マシタ. ⎰came

When used as adjectives ***zémbu*** and ***súbete*** take *no* before a
noun :

> ***Zémbu no*** (or ***súbete no***) *kudámono wo tabemáshĭta.*　I ate **all**
> 全部　　ノ　　（総テ　　　ノ）　果物　　ヲ　食ベマシタ.　　the fruit.

---

1 literal expression

Miná no 皆ノ before a noun has not the function of an adjective of quantity as *zémbu no* 全部ノ or *súbete no* 総テノ has. *Miná no* indicates only the possessive case of *miná* used as a noun :

Miná no kudámono wo tabemáshĭtu.   I, you, he, etc. ate the fruit
皆   ノ   果物   ヲ   食ベマシタ.   of all (the people).

However, *miná,* as well as *zémbu,* and *súbete,* when placed after the noun, corresponds to the English adjective **all.** In this case *no* is omitted.

Kudámono wo miná (zémbu, súbete) tabemáshĭta.   I ate **all** the fruit.
果物   ヲ   皆   (全部,   総テ)   食ベマシタ.

Séito wa miná (zémbu, súbete) Tennō-Héika wo haikán ni[1] *ikimáshĭta.*
生徒 ハ   皆   (全部,   総テ) 天皇 陛下 ヲ   拝観 ニ 行キマシタ.
All the students went to see the Emperor.

Sometimes the particle *wa* ハ may be put after *miná, zémbu,* or *súbete,* followed by a negative verb, in which case the inference is that each of the three expressions refers only to a part of the whole one speaks about.

Miná wa (Zémbu wa, Súbete wa) wakarɩmasén.   I do not
皆   ハ (全部   ハ, 総テ ハ) 解リマセン.   understand it **all.**

Without the particle *wa, Miná wakarimasén* means *I do not understand any part of it. I don't understand it at all.*

Not All

When this expression depends on the verb **to be,** without being followed by an adjective, the subject of the sentence is followed by one of the words *miná, zémbu,* or *súbete,* preceded or not by *no,* to which the periphrastic expression *de wa arimasén* デハアリマセン is added :

Konó hóndana no hon ga watashí no hon (no) zémbu de wa arimasén
コノ 本棚 ノ 本 ガ 私   ノ 本 (ノ) 全部   デ ハアリマセン
Not all my books are in this bookshelf.
(*lit.* Of this bookshelf the books, my books all are not.)

When an adjective follows **to be,** or when **not all** depends on another verb. the adjective, or the verb, is followed by *no de wa arimasén* ノデハアリ マセン. In this particular case *no* stands for *the fact.*

Konó yonónaka de súbete no hĭtó ga kashikói no de wa arimasén.
コノ 世ノ中 デ 総テ ノ 人 ガ 賢イ ノ デ ハ アリマセン.
In this world **not all** people are wise. (In this world all people wise, the fact is not.)

Watashí no musŭmé zémbu ga gakkō e ikú no de wa arimasén.
私   ノ 娘   全部 ガ 学校 ヘ行クノ デ ハ アリマセン.
Not all my daughters go to school. (My daughters all to school go, the fact is not.)

---

1 *haikán ni ikú* 拝観ニ行ク to go and see (in very polite speech)   2 When a noun precedes *miná, zémbu* or *súbete,* the particle. *no* may be omitted.

No ノ may be replaced by the word *wáke* ワケ, which is more emphatic.

Konó yonónaka de miná (súbete, zémbu) no hǐtó ga kashikói wáke de
コノ 世ノ中 デ 皆 （総テ， 全部）ノ 人 ガ 賢イ ワケ デ
wa arimasén. In this world **not all** people are wise.
ハ アリマセン． (*lit.* In this world **all** people wise are not.)

Watashí no musǔmé zémbu (miná, súbete) ga gakkō e ikú wáke de
私 ノ 娘 全部 （皆， 総テ）ガ 学校 ヘ行ク ワケ デ
wa arimasén. **Not all** my daughters go to school.
ハ アリマセン． (*lit.* My daughters **all** to school to go is **not.**)

Some

Some may be translated by *áru* 或ル when it corresponds to *a certain unknown* or *unspecified*.

áru hǐtó 或ル人 some man   *áru tokoró* 或ル所 some place
áru kuní 或ル国 some country   *áru hon* 或ル本 some book

When **some** is used in the meaning of *some do and some do not*, besides being translated by *áru* 或ル, it may be translated, in increasing degree of emphasis, by *ni yotté* ニヨッテ placed after the noun it modifies, and by both *áru......ni yotté* 或ル......ニヨッテ, as in the following examples.

Aru haná wa nói ga arimasén.
或ル 花 ハ 匂イ ガ アリマセン．
Haná ni yotté wa nói ga arimasén.
花 ニ ヨッテ ハ 匂イ ガアリマセン．   } {Some flowers have no smell.
Aru haná ni yotté wa nói ga arimasén.
或ル 花 ニ ヨッテ ハ 匂イ ガアリマセン．

Some is idiomatically translated in the following expressions:

ítsǔka イツカ some day   *chikái uchí ni* 近イウチニ **some** of these days
shibáraku シバラク for **some** time   *sū nen máe* 数年前 **some** years ago
yáku ni-jū máiru 約二十哩 **some** twenty miles
oyosó hyakú satsú no hon 凡ソ百冊ノ本 **some** hundred books

Every

As a distributive adjective before a noun indicating persons or things, **every** is generally translated by *dóno* ドノ ......*mo* モ.

Dóno heitaí mo teppō to guntō to wo mótte imáshǐta. **Every** soldier had a
ドノ 兵隊 モ 鉄砲 ト 軍刀 ト ヲ持ッテ イマシタ．   gun and a sword.
Dóno hakó mo kará dèshǐta. **Every** box was empty.
ドノ 箱 モ 空 デシタ．

In literary style, **every** is translated by *káku* 各.

kakkokú 各国 every country (*káku*+*kokú*=*kakkokú*)
kakushō 各省 every ministry (*shō* 省 a government ministry)
kákuchi 各地 every place (*chi* 地 a spot, a place)
kákujin 各人 everyone, every person (*káku*+*jin*=*kákujin*)
Sekái kákuchi kará. 世界各地カラ From every corner of the earth.
Soré wa kákujin ga shirubéki désŭ. Everybody should know it.
ソレハ各人ガ知ルベキデス。

With words indicating periods of time, **every** is translated by *mái* 毎.

every day	*mái nichí* 毎日	every morning	*mái ása* 毎朝
every week	*mái shū* 毎週	every evening	*mái yū* 毎夕
every month {	*mái tsŭkí* 毎月	every night	*mái ban* 毎晩
	mái getsú 毎月	every year	*mái nen* 毎年

See Lesson 42 for the use of *góto* instead of *mái.*

Every Time

Every time is translated by *tabí ni* 度ニ, pronounced *tambí ni* 度ンビニ when emphasis is to be expressed.

Watashí wa omoté ni déru tabí ni anó ōkina inú wo mikakemásŭ.
私 ハ 表 ニ 出ル 度 ニ アノ大キナ 犬 ヲ 見カケマス.
Every time I go out I notice that big dog.

Omoté 表 corresponds to *outside*, and followed by *ni* ニ or *e* ヘ, and *déru* 出ル the whole expression means *to go* or *come* out of a house, hall, theatre, etc.

Everyone, Everybody

In Lesson 13 we have said that the indefinite pronouns **everyone** and **everybody** are translated by *dónata mo* ドナタモ and *dáre mo* ダレモ. By inserting the particle *de* デ between *dónata* ドナタ or *dáre* ダレ and *mo* モ, both pronouns become emphatic and would correspond to the English emphatic expression **everyone of them.**

Dáre de mo kōfuku ga sŭkí désŭ.   **Everybody** (*or* everyone)
ダレ デ モ 幸福 ガ 好キ デス.   likes happiness.
Dáre de mo (*dónata de mo*) *dekimásŭ.*   **Everybody** can do it.
ダレ デ モ (ドナタ デ モ) 出来マス.

Dáre de mo ダレデモ or *dónata de mo* ドナタデモ is generally avoided with a negative verb, *dáre mo* ダレモ or *dónata mo* ドナタモ being used instead.

Dónata mo imasén. ドナタモイマセン. Nobody is in.
(*lit.* Everybody is not.)

The difference between the expressions *dónata de mo* ドナタデモ, *dáre de mo* ダレデモ and *miná* 皆 *súbete* 総テ or *zémbu* 全部 is more or less the difference that exists between the English expressions **everyone** and **all**. The first two expressions are thus more emphatic than the last three.

Watakushí no kyōdai wa dáre de mo Fŭransú-go wo hanashimásŭ.
私 ノ 兄弟 ハ ダレ デ モ フランス語 ヲ 話シマス.
Everyone of my brothers speaks French.

Watakushí no kyōdai wa zémbu (miná, súbete) Fŭransú-go wo hanashimásu.
私 ノ 兄弟 ハ 全部 （皆, 総テ）フランス語 ヲ 話シマス.
All my brothers speak French.

Korérano gakŭséi wa miná (zémbu, súbete) kimbén désŭ.
コレ等ノ 学生 ハ 皆 （全部, 総テ） 勤勉 デス.
Everyone of these students is diligent. *or* **All** these students are diligent.

Everything

Everything is translated by *nan de mo* 何ンデモ:

Anó misé wa nan de mo yasúi désŭ. アノ店ハ何ンデモ安イデス.
In that shop **everything** is cheap. (That shop everything is cheap.)

Everything may also be translated by *miná, zémbu, súbete.*

Sonó dorobō wa kínko no náka no monó wo miná (zémbu, súbete)
ソノ 泥棒 ハ 金庫 ノ 中 ノ 物 ヲ 皆 （全部, 総テ）
nusumimáshĭta.   That thief stole **everything** from the safe.
盗ミマシタ.   (*lit.* That thief the things inside the safe all stole.)

Vocabulary

Nouns					
brother[1]	*kyōdai*	兄弟	safe	*kínko*	金庫
country[2]	*kuní*	国	shop	*misé*	店
crowd	*hĭtogomí*	人込	smell	*niói*	匂イ
employee	*jimúin*	事務員	store	*misé*	店
fence	*heí*	塀		**Adjectives**	
gun	*teppō*	鉄砲	charitable	*jizénshin no áru*	慈善心ノアル
manager	*shiháinin*	支配人	dishonest	*fushōjiki-na*	不正直ナ
photograph	*shashín*	写真	honest	*shōjiki-na*	正直ナ
pocket	*kakŭshí*	カクシ	lazy (person)	*namakemonó*	ナマケモノ
	pokétto	ポケット	wise	*kashikói*	賢イ

---

1 *kyōdai* brothers; *nίisan* generally used for one's own as well as. for other people's *elder brother*; *áni* used only for *my elder brother*; *otōtosan* used for other people's *younger brother*; *otōto* used only for *my younger brother*.

2 *kuní* for geographical region, kingdom, empire; *o-kuní* 御国 your native country; *kuní* 国 or *watashi no kuní* 私ノ国 my country

Verbs

to lose $\begin{cases} nakusúru & 無ナクスル \\ ushinaú & 失ウシナウ \end{cases}$

to notice[1] $\begin{cases} chúi surú & 注ュ意ィスル \\ mikake·rú & 見ミカケル \end{cases}$

to steal *nusúmu* 盗ヌスム

Adverbs

formerly *móto* 元モト

a good deal of, a great deal of $\begin{cases} takŭsán no & 沢山ノ \\ taryō no \text{ (Lit. expression)} & 多量ノ \end{cases}$

a good many of, a great many of

What have you? *Náni wo anáta wa mótte imásŭ ka.*
何 ヲ 貴方 ハ 持ッテイマス カ.

This is all that I have. *Koré wa watashí ga mótte irú zémbu désŭ.*
コレ ハ 私 ガ 持ッテイル 全部 デス.

I have nothing at all. *Watashí wa náni mo mótte imasén.*
私 ハ 何 モ 持ッテイマセン.

How much all together? *Miná (zémbu) de íkura désŭ ka.*
皆 (全部) デイクラ デス カ.

Five thousand yen. *Go Sen yen désŭ.* 五千円デス.

Did you see the new bridge? *Atarashíi hashí wo górán ni narimáshĭta ka.*
新シイ 橋 ヲ 御覧 ニ ナリマシタ カ.

Górán ni náru 御覧ニナル is the polite form of *miru* 見ル *to see.*

Exercise *Renshū* 練習

1. Anáta no mēdo no ottó wa shōjiki de wa arimasén déshĭta ka.—Hái, fushōjiki de namakemonó[2] déshĭta. **2.** Tanaká San no yūjin no okāsan wa musŭmesán to go-isshó ni anó fúne ni imásŭ. **3.** Uchí no musŭkó no senséi no uchí wa anó tatémono no ushiró ni arimásŭ. **4.** Konó saifú wa dónata no désŭ ka.—Soré wa anáta no otōsan no o-tomodachí no désŭ. **5.** Taiheiyō wa Ameriká to Ajiyá no aidá ni arimásŭ. **6.** Panamá únga wa kitá-Ameriká to minamí-Ameriká to no aidá ni arimásŭ. **7.** Konó shashín wo dóko de mitsŭkemáshĭta ka.—Anáta no hon no aidá de mitsŭkemáshĭta. **8.** Ani wo górán ni narimáshĭta ka.—Anó hĭtogomí no náka de mimáshĭta. **9.** Námbiki inú wo kátte[3] imáshĭta ka.—Móto ippikí daké kátte[3] imáshĭta ga íma wa shi-hikí kátte imásŭ. **10.** Itóko ga takŭsán arimásŭ ka.—Iié, fŭtarí daké désŭ. Fŭtarí tomó[4] kanemochí de takŭsán no o-kané wo mótte imásŭ. **11.** Watashí no gakkō no senséi wa minná Kyōto e ikimáshĭta. **12.** Watashí wa kakŭshí ni sen yen mótte imáshĭta ga minná nakushimáshĭta. **13.** Ima ikahodó o-kané wo mótte imásŭ ka.—Koré wa watashí ga mótte irú zémbu désŭ. **14.** Bóku no yūjin wa minná zenryō désŭ ga miná bímbō désŭ. **15.** Satō ni-póndo to kōhī ippóndo kudasái. Minná de íkura désŭ ka.—Issén go-jū yen désŭ. **16.** Musŭ-kosán wa minná gakkō e ikimásŭ ka.—Minná ga gakkō e ikú no de wa arimasén. Chōnan wa anó kōjō de hataraité imásŭ. **17.** Zémbu no hĭtó ga

---

1 *chūi surú* to observe, to pay attention; *mikakerú* to happen to see **2** idler, lazy fellow **3** sub. of *káu* 飼う to keep (animals) **4** *fŭtarí tomó* both, they

jizénshin ga áru no¹ de wa arimasén. **18.** Mái-yū watashí wa kúrabu e ikimásŭ.
19. Mái ása anó oterá e takŭsán no hĭtó ga ikimásŭ. **20.** Dóno ié ni mo to
to mádo ga arimásŭ. **21.** Watashí no séito wa minná Nihón-go wo hanashimásŭ.
Minná kimbén désŭ. **22.** Minásan wa dóko ni imáshĭta ka.—Miná niwá ni
imáshĭta. **23.** Shiháinin wa jimúshitsu ni imáshĭta ka.—Iié, irasshaimasén²
déshĭta.—Jimúintachi wa jimúsho ni imáshĭta ka.—Iié, miná dekaketé imáshĭta.
Jimúsho ni wa dáre mo imasén déshĭta. **24.** Anó misé³ wa nan de mo takái
désŭ. **25.** Watashí no kuní wa Itarī désŭ.

1. 貴方ノメードノ夫ハ正直デハアリマセンデシタカ.—ハイ, 不正
直デナマケ者デシタ. **2.** 田中サンノ友人ノオ母サンハ娘サント御一緒
ニアノ船ニイマス. **3.** ウチノ息子ノ先生ノ家ハアノ建物ノ後ニアリ
マス. **4.** コノ財布ハドナタノデスカ.—ソレハ貴方ノオ父サンノオ友
達ノデス. **5.** 太平洋ハアメリカトアジヤノ間ニアリマス. **6.** パナマ
運河ハ北アメリカト南アメリカトノ間ニアリマス. **7.** コノ写真ヲド
コデ見ツケマシタカ.—貴方ノ本ノ間デ見ツケマシタ. **8.** 兄ヲ御覧ニ
ナリマシタカ.—アノ人込ノ中デ見マシタ. **9.** 何匹犬ヲ飼ッテイマシ
タカ.—元一匹ダケ飼ッテイマシタガ今ハ四匹飼ッテイマス. **10.** イト
コガ沢山アリマスカ.—イヽエ, 二人ダケデス. 二人共金持デ沢山ノオ
金ヲ持ッテイマス. **11.** 私ノ学校ノ先生ハ皆ンナ京都ヘ行キマシタ.
12. 私ハカクシニ千円持ッテイマシタガ皆ンナナクシマシタ.
13. 今, イカホドオ金ヲ持ッテイマスカ.—コレハ私ガ持ッテイル全
部デス. **14.** 僕ノ友人ハ皆ンナ善良デスガ皆貧乏デス. **15.** 砂糖二
ポンドトコーヒー一ポンド下サイ. 皆ンナデイクラデスカ.—一千五
十円デス. **16.** 息子サンハ皆ンナ学校ヘ行キマスカ.—皆ンナガ学校
ヘ行クノデハアリマセン. 長男ハアノ工場デ仂イテイマス. **17.** 全部
ノ人ガ慈善心ガアルノデハアリマセン. **18.** 毎夕私ハクラブヘ行キマ
ス. **19.** 毎朝アノオ寺ヘ沢山ノ人ガ行キマス. **20.** ドノ家ニモ戸ト窓
ガアリマス. **21.** 私ノ生徒ハ皆ンナ日本語ヲ話シマス. 皆ンナ勤勉デ
ス. **22.** 皆サンハドコニイマシタカ.—皆, 庭ニイマシタ. **23.** 支配人
ハ事務室ニイマシタカ.—イヽエ, イラッシャイマセンデシタ.—事務
員達ハ事務所ニイマシタカ.—イヽエ, 皆, 出カケテイマシタ. 事務
所ニハダレモイマセンデシタ. **24.** アノ店ハ何ンデモ高イデス.
25. 私ノ国ハイタリーデス.

1. Was not your maid-servant's husband honest?—No, he was dishonest
and lazy. **2.** Mr. Tanaka's friend's mother is on that ship with her daughter.
3. My son's teacher's house is behind that building. **4.** Whom does this
purse belong to?—It belongs to your father's friend. **5.** The Pacific Ocean

---

1 *jizénshin ga áru* charitable   **2** *irasshaimasén déshĭta* polite form for *orimasén*
déshĭta   **3** *ni* is suppressed—*lit.* That store everything is dear.

is between America and Asia. **6.** The Panama Canal is between North and
South America. **7.** Where did you find this photo?—I found it among your
books. **8.** Did you see my elder brother?—Yes, I saw him in the crowd.
9. How many dogs had you?—I had only one but now I have four. **10.** Have
you many cousins?—No, I have only two. They are rich; they have a great
deal of money. **11.** All the teachers of my school went to Kyoto. **12.** I had
one thousand yen in my pocket but I lost all. **13.** How much money have
you now?—This is all that I have. **14.** All my friends are good, but everyone
of them is poor. **15.** Give me two pounds of sugar and one pound of coffee.
How much all together?—One thousand fifty yen. **16.** Do all your sons go to
school?—Not all of them go to school. My eldest son works in that factory.
17. Not all people are charitable. **18.** I go to the club every evening. **19.** Every
morning a great many people go to that temple. **20.** Every house has doors
and windows. **21.** Everyone of my students speaks Japanese. They are all
diligent. **22.** Where was everybody?—Everybody was in the garden. **23.** Was
the manager in his office?—No, he was not.—And were his employees in the
office?—No, everybody was out. Nobody was in the office. **24.** In that store
everything is dear. **25.** My native country is Italy.

Twentieth Lesson　第廿課

Adjectives of Quality

Seishitsú-keiyōshi　性ッ質ッ形ケ容ョ詞シ

In Lesson 10 we have said that most adjectives of quality end in
i. This class of adjectives, called **true adjectives,** have the *i* preceded by one of the vowels *a, i, o, u,*

sam*úi* 寒イ cold		*tōi*	遠イ far
tak*ái* 高イ tall, expensive		*utsŭkushíi* 美シイ beautiful	

These adjectives, besides being used attributively, are also used
predicatively, as shown in Lesson 10.

tōi kuní 遠イ国 a far country	*samŭi hi* 寒イ日 a cold day
Anó tatémono wa **takái.** アノ建物ハ高イ.	That building **is tall.**
Konó torí wa **utsŭkushíi.** コノ鳥ハ美シイ.	This bird **is beautiful.**

Adjectives ending in *ei,* as *kírei* キレイ (pretty), are not classed
as true adjectives. They belong to the class described below, and
when used attributively they take *na,* as *kírei-na ojōsan* a pretty girl.

Quasi-Adjectives

Besides the *true adjective* there is another class of adjectives called
quasi-adjectives. The *quasi-adjective* is a noun followed by *na* or *no.*

báka-na	馬鹿ナ	foolish	*rikō-na*	利口ナ	clever
búrei-na	無礼ナ	impolite	*shínsetsu-na*	親切ナ	kind
iyá-na	嫌ナ	disagreeable	*shōjiki-na*	正直ナ	honest
hontō-no	ホントウノ	true	*úso-no*	嘘ノ	untrue

There is no exact rule by which one may understand which nouns are made adjectives with **na** ナ and which with **no** ノ. Only by consulting a dictionary, by study and by practice may one learn the right usage of the two postpositions to form quasi-adjectives.

Konó haná wa iyá-na niói ga shimásŭ.	This flower smells bad.
コノ 花 ハ 嫌ナ 臭イ ガ シマス.	(*niói ga surú* to smell)
Aré wa shōjiki-na rōdōsha désŭ.	That is an honest workman.
アレ ハ 正直 ナ 労伇者 デス.	
Koré wa hontō-no hanashí désŭ.	This is a ture story.
コレ ハホントウノ 話 デス.	

This second class of adjectives do not require **na** or **no** when followed by *désŭ, déshĭta* or their negative form. (See Lesson 6.)

Konó kodomó wa rikō désŭ. コノ子供ハ利口デス.   This boy is clever.

Koré wa hontō désŭ. コレハホントウデス.   This is true.

Anáta wa shínsetsu désŭ. 貴方ハ親切デス.   You are kind.

Konó kodomó wa rikō de wa arimasén.   This boy is not clever.
コノ 子供 ハ 利口 デ ハ アリマセン.

Koré wa hontō de wa arimasén.   This is not true.
コレ ハ ホントウデ ハ アリマセン.

Anáta wa shínsetsu de wa arimasén.   You are not kind.
貴方 ハ 親切 デ ハ アリマセン.

Anáta wa shínsetsu de wa arimasén déshĭta.   You were not kind.
貴方 ハ 親切 デ ハ アリマセン デシタ.

When two or more quasi-adjectives are used predicatively in succession, only the last one is followed by **désŭ,** or **déshĭta,** as the case may be, while the others are followed only by **de,** which is the root of both *désŭ* and *déshĭta*. This rule is observed to avoid repeating the same verbal expression. In such cases, the last adjective is generally preceded by the expression **sonó ué** ソノ上 *besides* or *also*.

Uchí no o-tétsudai wa shōjiki de, shínsetsu de, sonó ué rikō désŭ.
ウチ ノ オ手伝イ ハ 正直 デ, 親切 デ, ソノ 上 利口 デス.
Our servant is honest, kind, and **also** clever.

This construction may be employed also when one of the adjectives is used attributively before a noun, as in the following example:

*Sonó otokó wa báka **de**, iyá-na yátsu[1] **de**, **sonó ué busahō da**.*

ソノ 男 ハ 馬鹿 デ, 嫌 ナ 奴 デ, ソノ 上 無作法 ダ.

That man is foolish, disagreeable, and **also** impolite. (*busahō impolite*)

Da ダ instead of *désŭ* is here used to make the less polite verbal form of *to be* agree with the rather uncomplimentary qualities of the person spoken of.

Compare with the construction given for the translation of two consecutive adjectives used predicatively. Lesson 16, Page 91.

A great many quasi-adjectives in **no** ノ are obtained from names of countries, material nouns, and nouns of places.

Kínu no *kutsushĭtá wo mótte kité kudasái.*   Bring me (some)

絹 ノ 靴下 ヲ 持ッテ 来テ 下サイ.   silk stockings.

Kyūshū no *hitótachi wa wakarinikúi hōgen wo hanashimásŭ.*

九州 ノ 人達 ハ 解リ難イ 方言 ヲ 話シマス.

The people of Kyūshū speak a difficult dialect.

(*wakarinikúi* difficult to understand, *hōgen* dialect)

By affixing the word **nikúi** 難イ (hard, difficult, troublesome) to the stem of verbs of Class I and to the *i*-stem of verbs of Class II, the Japanese form a great number of adjectives indicating difficulty or troublesomeness in doing the thing specified by the verb.

míru	見ル	*minikúi*	見難イ	difficult to see
yómu	読ム	*yominikúi*	読ミ難イ	difficult to read
wakáru	解ル	*wakarinikúi*	解リ難イ	difficult to understand

Adjectives indicating facility in doing the thing specified by the verbs are formed by affixing the word **yasúi** (easy) to verbal stems.

míru	見ル	*miyasúi*	見易イ	easy to see
wakáru	解ル	*wakariyasúi*	解リ易イ	easy to understand

Another class of adjectives is formed by adding the termination **rashíi** ラシイ to adjectives, nouns, verbs, and adverbs. The termination *rashíi* added to nouns or verbs has the meaning of the English terminations *ish*, *ly*, or of such words as *appearing, seeming, looking like*, etc.

otokó	男	man	*otokorashíi*	男ラシイ	manly
onná	女	woman	*onnarashíi*	女ラシイ	womanly, womanish
kodomó	子供	child	*kodomorashíi*	子供ラシイ	childish, child-like
báka	馬鹿	fool	*bakarashíi*	馬鹿ラシイ	foolish
sō	ソウ	so	*sōrashíi*	ソウラシイ	appearing to be so
takái	高イ	expensive	*takairashíi*	高イラシイ	it seems it is expensive

1 *iyá-na yátsu* disagreeable person.

From the above examples it may be seen that adjectives, nouns and adverbs do not suffer any alteration when adding *rashíi.*

As to verbs, when expressed in positive form, the termination *rashíi* ラシイ is added to their simple present, and when expressed in the negative, *rashíi* is added to their negative form ending in *nai* ナイ. The negative form of verbs with the suffix *nai* ナイ is illustrated in the following lesson.

dekíru 出来ル			it seems it can be done
to be able	*dekirurashíi*	出来ルラシイ	it seems he (she, etc.) can do
can			(it)
dekínai			it seems it cannot be done
出来ナイ	*dekinairashíi*	出来ナイラシイ	it seems he (she, etc.) cannot
cannot			do (it)
déru 出ル			it seems he (she, it) is coming
to come out	*derurashíi*	出ルラシイ	out
to go out			it seems they are coming (going) out
dénai 出ナイ			it seems he (she, it) is not coming out
not to	*denairashíi*	出ナイラシイ	
come out			it seems they are not coming (going) out
kíru 来ル	*kururashíi*	来ルラシイ	it seems he (she, it) is coming
to come (irr. verb)			it seems they are coming
kónai 来ナイ			it seems he (she, it) is not coming
not to come	*konairashíi*	来ナイラシイ	
			it seems they are not coming

Material Adjectives

Busshitsú-keiyōshi 物ッ質ッ形ケ容ョ詞シ

When a material adjective is used before a noun, **no** ノ between the two words is generally used in colloquial speech, but it is omitted in literary style.

kin **no** tokéi	金ノ時計		*kindokéi*	金時計	a gold watch
gómu **no** kutsú	ゴムノ靴		*gomugutsú*	ゴム靴	rubber shoes
burikí **no** kan	ブリキノ罐		*burikí-kan*	ブリキ罐	tin can
kínu **no** íto	絹ノ糸		*kínu-íto*	絹糸	silk thread

For the rules on phonetic changes as given above in the case of the compound words *gomugutsú* and *kindokéi*, see Lesson 41.

In several cases, when **no** ノ is omitted, different words are used as adjectives to qualify a noun.

ki no shindái	木ノ寝台	wooden	*ishí no ié*	石ノ家	stone
mokuséi shindái	木製寝台	bed	*sekizō káoku*	石造家屋	house

When the material adjective is used predicatively it may be followed by *désŭ* or *de arimásŭ:*

Konó tokéi wa kin désŭ. コノ時計ハ金デス. 〕
Konó tokéi wa kin de arimásŭ. 〉This watch is gold.
コノ 時計 ハ 金 デ アリマス. 〕

Material adjectives used predicatively may be followed by the word *séi* 製 which means *made of.*

Sonó tokéi wa ginséi déshĭta. 〕
ソノ 時計 ハ 銀製 デシタ. 〉That watch was silver.
Sonó tokéi wa ginséi de arimáshĭta. 〉That watch was made of
ソノ 時計 ハ 銀製 デ アリマシタ. 〕silver.

Very

taihén	大変	*hijō ni*	非常ニ
nakanaká	ナカナカ	*totemó*	トテモ

Taihén 大変 is used in any style of speech; *hijō ni* 非常ニ is more of the literary style and when used in ordinary conversation it is more of men's than women's speech; *nakanaká* ナカナカ is colloquial and *totemó* トテモ is colloquial and emphatic.

Konó nikú wa taihén (hijō ni) yawarakái.   This meat is **very** tender.
コノ 肉 ハ 大変 (非常 ニ) 柔カイ.

Kyō wa totemó (hijō ni) samúi.   To-day is **very** cold.
キョウハ トテモ (非常 ニ) 寒イ.

Konó mondaí wa nakanaká muzukashíi.   This problem is
コノ 問題 ハ ナカナカ ムヅカシイ.   **very** difficult.

Too (*adv.* exceedingly) *amari* アマリ

Konó michí wa amari semái.   This road is **too** narrow.
コノ 道 ハ アマリ 狭イ.

Sonó kimonó wa amari takái.   That kimono is **too** dear.
ソノ 着物 ハ アマリ 高イ.

Too, Also (conjunctions)

Too and **also** in the meaning of *likewise* are translated by *mo* モ after a noun or pronoun.

Yūbe shibaí e ikimáshĭta.   Last night I went to the theatre.
ユウベ 芝居 ヘ 行キマシタ.

Watashí mo ikimáshĭta. 私モ行キマシタ.   I **also** went.

Koré **mo** *kaimásŭ.* コレモ買イマス.   I will buy this **too.**
                                              (*lit.* This **also** I buy.)

The **future** may sometimes be translated by the Japanese **present,** as in the last example.

The Cases *Kakú* 格カ

In previous lessons we have shown how to form all the cases except the **dative.** Here we will give the full declention of the personal pronoun and the noun.

Personal Pronoun

Nom.	*watashí **wa, ga***	私ハ, **ガ**	I
Acc.	*watashí **wo***	私ヲ	me
Gen.	*watashí **no***	私ノ	my
Dat.	*watashí **ni*** *watashí **no tamé ni***	私ニ 私ノ**タメ**ニ	to me for me
Abl.	*watashí **kará*** *watashí **to** (isshó ni)*	私**カラ** 私ト（一緒ニ）	from me with me

Noun

Nom.	*senséi **wa** or **ga***	先生ハ, **ガ**	the teacher
Acc.	*senséi **wo***	先生ヲ	the teacher
Gen.	*senséi **no***	先生ノ	the teacher's
Dat.	*senséi **ni*** *senséi **no tamé ni***	先生ニ 先生ノ**タメ**ニ	to the teacher for the teacher
Abl.	*senséi **kará*** *senséi **to** (isshó ni)*	先生**カラ** 先生ト（一緒ニ）	from the teacher with the teacher

*Isshó **ni*** is an emphatic expression and may be omitted when emphasis is not required.

*Anáta **wa** watashí **wo** yobimáshĭta ka.*   Did you call me?
貴方　ハ　私　ヲ　呼ビマシタ　カ.

Iié, yobimasén déshĭta.   No, I did not call you.
イイエ, 呼ビマセンデシタ.

*Konó kimonó **wo** anáta **no tamé ni** kaimáshĭta.*   I bought this
コノ　着物　ヲ　貴方　ノ　タメ　ニ　買イマシタ.   kimono **for** you.

*Sonó dorobō **wa** watashí **kará** kané **wo** torimáshĭta.*
ソノ　泥棒　ハ　私　カラ　金　ヲ　取リマシタ.
That thief stole (took) some money from me.

*Dáre **ga** anáta **to** isshó **ni** imáshĭta ka.*   Who was **with** you?
誰　ガ　貴方　ト　一緒　ニ　イマシタ　カ.

*Watashí **no** musŭmé déshĭta.* 私ノ娘デシタ.   It was my daughter.

In some cases *wa* ハ, instead of *wo* ヲ, is used to indicate the **accusative** as, for instance, when one wishes to lay stress on the object, especially when two clauses of a sentence are connected by the adversative conjunction **but** or **however**. Ex:

O-chá wo nomimásŭ ka. オ茶ヲ飲ミマスカ.   Do you drink tea?

O-cha wa nomimasén ga kōhī wo nomimásŭ.   I do not drink tea,
オ茶 ハ 飲ミマセン ガコーヒーヲ 飲ミマス.   **but** I drink coffee.

Anáta wa Uenó kōen no Dōbutsu-en wo mimáshĭta ka.
貴方 ハ 上野 公園 ノ 動物園 ヲ 見マシタ カ.
Have you seen the Zoological Garden at Ueno Park?

Iié, Dōbutsu-en wa mimasén déshĭta ga Kokuritsú Hakubutsukán wo
イイエ, 動物園 ハ 見マセン デシタ ガ 国立 博物館 ヲ
mimáshĭta.   No, I haven't seen the Zoological Garden, **but** I have seen the
見マシタ.   National Museum.

Chichí wa jidōsha wo kaimáshĭta.   My father has bought a motor-car.
父 ハ 自動車 ヲ 買イマシタ.

Fōdo wo kaimáshĭta ka. フォードヲ買イマシタカ.   Did he buy a Ford?

Iié, Fōdo wa kaimasén déshĭta ga Byúkku wo kaimáshĭta.
イイエ, フォードハ 買イマセンデシタ ガ ビュック ヲ 買イマシタ.
No, he did not buy a Ford; (**but**) he bought a Buick.

Wa is also used after the object of the verb when an unexpressed adversative clause is implied:

Anáta wa sofŭtó karā wo tsŭkaimásŭ ka.   Do you wear soft collars?
貴方 ハ ソフトカラー ヲ 使イマス カ.

Iié, watashí wa sofŭtó karā wa tsŭkaimasén.   No, I do not wear
イイエ, 私 ハ ソフトカラー ハ 使イマセン.   soft collars.

In the above answer "*I do not wear soft collars*," there is the implication that I wear some other kind of collars. Even in this case the stress is on the object.

The *dative* with *ni* ニ is sometimes made emphatic by adding to it the expression *tótte wa* トッテハ:

Soré wa watashí ni tótte wa ichí dáiji[1] désŭ.   It is a very important
ソレ ハ 私 ニトッテ ハ 一 大事 デス.   matter **to** me.

Sen yen guraí anó kanemochí ni tótte wa nan de mo arimasén.
千 円 位 アノ 金持 ニトッテ ハ 何ン デ モアリマセン.
A thousand yen is nothing **to** a man of his wealth.

Anó hĭtó ni tótte wa o-saké wa kusurí désŭ.   *Saké*[2] is a medicine
アノ 人 ニトッテ ハ オ酒 ハ 薬 デス.   **with** him.
(Said of a person whose drinking wine is beneficial to his health.)

Wa may also replace the postposition *ga* when, followed by *árŭ,* it indicates the accusative. This also occurs when the object is

1 *ichí dáiji* a matter of vital importance   **2** *Saké* name of Japanese wine made from rice.

emphasized.

Anáta wa inú ga arimásŭ ka. 貴方ハ犬ガアリマスカ.   Have you a dog?

Iié, inú wa arimasén ga néko ga ni-hikí arimásŭ.
イイエ, 犬 ハ アリマセンガ 猫 ガ 二匹 アリマス.
No, I have not a dog, but I have two cats.

O-níisan wa kurumá ga arimasén ka.   Hasn't your elder
オ兄サン ハ 車 ガ アリマセン カ.   brother a coach?

Kurumá wa arimásŭ ga umá ga arimasén.   He has a coach
車 ハ アリマス ガ 馬 ガ アリマセン.   but has no horses.

Wa followed by **áru** is also used instead of **ga áru** after the
object, when an unexpressed adversative clause is implied:

Kegawá no gaitō ga arimásŭ ka.   Have you a fur coat?
毛皮 ノ 外套 ガ アリマス カ.

Iié, kegawá no gaitō wa arimasén.   No, I have not a fur coat.
イイエ, 毛皮 ノ 外套 ハ アリマセン.

In the above answer there is the implication that although I have
not a fur coat, I may have a coat made of some other material.

To Give and the **Dative Case**

The verb *to give* is translated by *agerú* 上ゲル, *yarú* ヤル,
and *kudasáru* 下サル.

When the person giving is in a lower social position than the one receiving,
agerú is used, while *yarú* is used when the person giving is in a superior
social position. *Agerú,* however, is generally used by the first person when
speaking to the second person or of a third person, even if the receiver is
an inferior, as for instance, a servant. In this case the use of *agerú* is
observed for some consideration towards the person spoken to notwithstanding
his or her inferior social standing.

Agerú and *yarú* are also used when the second person gives to a third
person, or when the third person gives to the second person. In this case
also, when the giver is in a higher position than the receiver, *yarú* is used,
while *agerú* is used if the giver is in a lower station than the receiver.

Kudasáru 下サル or *kurerú* 呉レル is used when the first person is given
or receives from the second or third person. *Kurerú* 呉レル is less polite
than *kudasáru* 下サル. See Lesson 34 for polite verbs.

Watashí wa kírei-na haná wo okāsan ni agemáshĭta.
私 ハ キレイナ 花 ヲ オ母サンニ 上ゲマシタ.
I gave some beautiful flowers to my mother.

Watashí wa anó kawaisō-na hĭtó ni o-kané wo yarimáshĭta.
私 ハ アノカワイソウナ 人 ニ オ金 ヲ ヤリマシタ.
I gave some money to that poor man. (*kawaisō-na* poor, miserable)

Sensĕi wa konó hon wo watashí ni **kudasaimáshĭta.**
先生 ハ コノ 本 ヲ 私 ニ 下サイマシタ.
My teacher gave me this book.

Dáre ga sonó yubiwá wo anáta ni **agemáshĭta ka.** Who gave you
誰 ガ ソノ 指輪 ヲ 貴方 ニ 上ゲマシタ カ. that ring?

Obá ga watashí ni **kuremáshĭta.** My aunt gave it to me.
伯母 ガ 私 ニ 呉レマシタ.

Adjectives and Adverbs of Quantity

very much	*hijō ni takŭsán*	or	*taihén takŭsan*	
	非ヒ常ジョウニ 沢タ山サン		大タイ変ヘン 沢タ山サン	
too much, too many	*amarí takŭsán*	or	*ōsugíru*	
	アマリ 沢タ山サン		多オ過スギル	
very little	*hijō ni sŭkunái*	or	*taihén sŭkunái*	
	非ヒ常ジョウニ 少スクナイ		大タイ変ヘン 少スクナイ	

too little, too few
{ *amarí sŭkunái* or *sŭkuná sugíru*
　アマリ 少スクナイ 　　少スクナ 過スギル
{ *amarí sŭkóshi*
　アマリ 少スコシ

Anáta wa **amarí takŭsán** *(no) empitsú wo mótte imásŭ; sŭkóshi watashí*
貴方 ハ アマリ 沢山 (ノ) 鉛筆 ヲ 持ッテイマス, 少シ 私
ni kudasái. You have **too many** pencils; give me some.
ニ 下サイ.

Anáta wa **amarí sŭkóshi** *kuremáshĭta; mō sŭkóshi kudasái.*
貴方 ハ アマリ 少シ 呉レマシタ モウ 少シ 下サイ.
You gave me **too few**; give me some more.

Vocabulary

Nouns			disagreeable *iyá-na*	嫌イヤナ
			foolish *báka-na*	馬バ鹿カナ
action	*okonaí*	行オコナイ	impolite { *shitsúrei-na*	失シツ礼レイナ
cotton	*momén*	木モ綿メン	{ *búrei-na*	無ブ礼レイナ
cotton shirt	*momén no shátsu*		kind *shínsetsu-na*	親シン切セツナ
		木綿ノシャツ	manly *otokorashíi*	男オトコラシイ
deed	*okonaí*	行オコナイ	narrow *semái*	狭セマイ
news	*hōchi*	報ホウ知チ	splendid *subarashíi*	素ス晴バラシイ
silk	*kínu*	絹キヌ	tender *yawarakái*	柔ヤワラカイ
smell	*niói, kaorí*	臭ニオイ; 香カオリ	true *hontō-no*	ホントウノ
story	*hanashí*	話ハナシ	untrue *úso-no*	嘘ウソノ
	Adjectives		Verbs	
difficult	*muzukashíi*	ムズカシイ	to admire *homé・ru*	ホメル

| to seem | mié•ru | 見ミエル | to smell | niói ga surú | ニオイガスル |
| to show | misé•ru | 見ミセル | to wear | ki•rú | 着キル |

Mótto kamí ga hoshíi désŭ ka.—Mō takŭsán désŭ.   Mō irimasén.

モット　紙　ガ　欲シイ　デス　カ.—モウ　沢山　デス.　モウイリマセン.

Do you wish to have any more paper?—I have enough.   I wish no more.

Mō hóshiku arimasén.   I do not wish to have any more.

モウ　欲シク　アリマセン.　 (lit. Any more desirous am not.)

Mō íppai mizú wo kudasái.   Give me one more glass of water.

モウ　一杯　水　ヲ　下サイ.　 (lit. More one-glassful water give me.)

Konó haná wa íi niói ga shimásŭ.   These flowers smell good.

コノ　花　ハイイニオイ　ガ　シマス.　(These flowers good smell make.)

Anó haná wa iyá-na niói ga shimásŭ.   Those flowers smell bad.

アノ　花　ハ　イヤナニオイガ　シマス.　(Those flowers bad smell make.)

Exercise *Renshū* 練習

1. Anó otokó wa ítsumo taihén bakarashíi hanashí wo shimásŭ. **2.** Eki no máe ni subarashíi tatémono ga arimásŭ. **3.** Kokó wa taihén shízuka désŭ. Watashí wa shízuka-na tokoró ga sŭkí désŭ. **4.** Sonó fŭtarí no Ōsaka no shínshi wa hijō ni yūfuku-na[1] shōnin désŭ. **5.** Anáta wa kínu no shátsu wo kimásŭ ka, soretómo momén désŭ ka.—Watashí wa momén no wo kimásŭ. **6.** O-kyakú wa konairashíi désŭ. **7.** Kimí no okonaí wa kodomorashíi. **8.** Konó hōdō[2] wa hontōrashíi désŭ. **9.** Nihón-go wa taihén muzukashíi désŭ. **10.** Konó hakó wa amarí semái désŭ. Ōkii hō wo mótte kité kudasái. **11.** Konó sūpu wa amarí atsúi désŭ. **12.** Konó ié wa amarí chiisái désŭ. Watashí wa sŭkimasén. **13.** Sakúban watashí wa éiga e ikimáshĭta.— Watashí mo. **14.** Konó heyá no mádo wa amarí semái soshĭté to wa amarí ōkii. **15.** Anáta no oí ni náni wo agemáshĭta ka.—Kin no tokéi wo yarimáshĭta. **16.** O-takú wa chikái désŭ ka.—Iié, taihén tōi désŭ. **17.** Konó kírei-na kimonó wo dáre no tamé ni tsŭkurimáshĭta ka.—Suzukí San no ókŭsan no musumesán no tamé ni tsŭkurimáshĭta. **18.** Anáta wa watashí no musŭkó to isshó ni gakkō e ikimáshĭta ka.—Iié, watashí wa áni to isshó ni ikimáshĭta. **19.** Anó Itarī no fujín wa tabitabí o-kané wo mazushíi hĭtó ni yarimásŭ. **20.** Anáta no ojisán wa náni ka anáta ni kuremáshĭta ka.—Iié, náni mo kuremasén déshĭta.—Hái, konó omócha wo kuremáshĭta. **21.** Anáta wa amarí takŭsán pan wo mótte imásŭ. Ikuraka kudasái. Anáta wa amarí sŭkóshi kuremáshĭta. Mō sŭkóshi kudasái. **22.** Mótto kōhī ga hoshíi désŭ ka.—Hái, mō íppai kudasái. **23.** Haná wa yói kaorí ga shimásŭ ga ínki wa warúi niói ga shimásŭ. **24.** Anáta no obāsan wa náni wo anáta ni misemáshĭta ka.—Takŭ- sán no utsŭkushíi e wo misemáshĭta. **25.** Mótto o-káshi ga hoshíi désŭ ka. —Iié, mō hóshiku arimasén. **26.** Anó kōen ni wa taihén kírei-na ki ga arimásŭ. Watashí wa tabitabí asokó e ikimásŭ. **27.** Dáre démo otokorashíi okonai wo homemásŭ.

---

1 *yūfuku-na* rich, wealthy   **2** news

1. アノ男ハイツモ大ヘン馬鹿ラシイ話ヲシマス. **2.** 駅ノ前ニ素晴ラシイ建物ガアリマス. **3.** コヽハ大変静カデス. 私ハ静カナ所ガ好キデス. **4.** ソノ二人ノ大阪ノ紳士ハ非常ニ裕福ナ商人デス. **5.** 貴方ハ絹ノシャツヲ着マスカ, ソレトモ木綿デスカ.―私ハ木綿ノヲ着マス. **6.** オ客ハ来ナイラシイデス. **7.** 君ノ行イハ子供ラシイ. **8.** コノ報道ハホントウラシイデス. **9.** 日本語ハ大変ムヅカシイデス. **10.** コノ箱ハ余リ狭イデス. 大キイ方ヲ持ッテ来テ下サイ. **11.** コノスープハアマリ熱イデス. **12.** コノ家ハアマリ小サイデス. 私ハ好キマセン. **13.** 昨晩私ハ映画ヘ行キマシタ.―私モ. **14.** コノ部屋ノ窓ハアマリ狭イソシテ戸ハアマリ大キイ. **15.** 貴方ノ甥ニ何ヲ上ゲマシタカ.―金ノ時計ヲヤリマシタ. **16.** オ宅ハ近イデスカ.―イヽエ, 大変遠イデス. **17.** コノキレイナ着物ヲ誰ノタメニツクリマシタカ.―鈴木サンノ奥サンノ娘サンノタメニツクリマシタ. **18.** 貴方ハ私ノ息子ト一緒ニ学校ヘ行キマシタカ.―イヽエ, 私ハ兄ト一緒ニ行キマシタ. **19.** アノイタリーノ婦人ハ度々オ金ヲ貧シイ人ニヤリマス. **20.** 貴方ノ伯父サンハ何カ貴方ニ呉レマシタカ.―イヽエ, 何モ呉レマセンデシタ.―ハイ, コノオモチャヲクレマシタ. **21.** 貴方ハアマリ沢山パンヲ持ッテイマス. 幾ラカ下サイ. 貴方ハアマリ少シ呉レマシタ. モウ少シ下サイ. **22.** モットコーヒーガ欲シイデスカ.―ハイ, モウ一杯下サイ. **23.** 花ハヨイ香リガシマスガインキハ悪イ臭イガシマス. **24.** 貴方ノオバアサンハ何ヲ貴方ニ見セマシタカ.―沢山ノ美シイ絵ヲ見セマシタ. **25.** モットオ菓子ガ欲シイデスカ.―イヽエ, モウ欲シクアリマセン. **26.** アノ公園ニハ大変キレイナ木ガアリマス. 私ハ度々アソコヘ行キマス. **27.** 誰デモ男ラシイ行イヲホメマス.

1. That man always tells very foolish stories. **2.** In front of the station there are splendid buildings. **3.** This place is very quiet. I like quiet places. **4.** Those two Osaka gentlemen are very rich merchants. **5.** Do you wear silk shirts or cotton ones?—I wear cotton ones. **6.** The guest does not seem to come. **7.** Your action is childish. **8.** This news seems to be true. **9.** The Japanese language is very difficult. **10.** This box is too narrow. Bring me a large one. **11.** This soup is too hot. **12.** This house is too small. I do not like it. **13.** Last night I went to the cinema.—I also. **14.** The windows of this room are too narrow and the door is too large. **15.** What did you give to your nephew?—I gave him a gold watch. **16.** Is your house near? —No, it is very far. **17.** For whom did you make these beautiful dresses?— I made them for Mrs. Suzuki's daughter. **18.** Did you go to school with my son?—No, I went with my elder brother. **19.** That Italian lady often gives money to the poor. **20.** Did your uncle give you anything?—No, he did not give me anything.—Yes, he gave me these toys. **21.** You have too much bread; give me some. You gave me too little. Give me some more. **22.** Do you wish to have any more coffee?—Yes, give me one more cup. **23.** Flowers

smell good but ink smells bad. 24. What did your grandmother show you?
—She showed me many beautiful pictures. 25. Do you wish to have any
more cake?—No, I do not wish to have any more. 26. In that park there
are very beautiful trees. I often go there. 27. Everybody admires manly deeds.

Twenty-first Lesson   第廿一課

The Adjective of Quality and its Adverbial Form

By dropping the final *i* of a **true adjective** we obtain its **stem,**
and by adding the termination *ku* to the stem we obtain its
adverbial form.

In order to explain this Japanese adverbial transformation, the
corresponding English forms are given, even though all are not
in actual use.

	Adjective		Stem		Adverbial form	
hot	*atsúi*	暑い[1] 熱い[1]	*atsu*	*átsuku*	暑く 熱く	hotly
cold	*samúi*	寒い	*samu*	*sámuku*	寒く	coldly
white	*shirói*	白い	*shiro*	*shíroku*	白く	whitely
late	*osoí*	遅い	*oso*	*osokú*	遅く	lately
short	*mijikái*	短い	*mijika*	*mijíkaku*	短く	shortly
tall	*takái*	高い	*taka*	*tákaku*	高く	highly
long	*nagái*	長い	*naga*	*nágaku*	長く	longly
beautiful	*utsŭkushíi*	美しい	*utsukushi*	*utsŭkúshiku*	美しく	beautifully

See **phonetic rule** on adverbial form of adjectives, Page 676.

The adverbial form of the true adjective precedes the verb.

> *Sakurá no haná wa háru utsŭkúshiku sakimásŭ.*
> 桜　の　花　は　春　美しく　咲きます.
> In spring cherry blossoms bloom beautifully.

> *Anó kutsúya wa yóku hatarakimásŭ.*　That shoemaker works hard.
> あの　靴屋　は　よく　仂きます.　(*yóku* from *yói* = well)

The adverbial form of true adjective is used to translate adjectives
of quality used adverbially:

> *Sámuku narimáshĭta.*　　　　It has become cold.
> 寒く　成りました.　　　　　　(coldly became.)

> *Resshá wa osokú tsŭkimáshĭta.*　The train arrived late.
> 列車　は　遅く　着きました.　　(Train late arrived.)

---

1 Both Chinese characters are pronounced *atsúi*; however, the first one is used
in reference to weather, while the second one is used is other cases.

Késa chichí wa taihén háyaku dekakemáshǐta.

けさ 父 は 大変 早く 出かけました.

My father went out very early this morning. (*hayái* early)

Anó hǐtó wa amarí tákaku shinamonó wo urimásǔ.

あの 人 は あまり 高く 品物 を 売ります.

He sells his goods too dear. (*shinamonó* goods, *urimásǔ* sells)

Momén to keorimonó no nedán ga hijō-ni yásuku narimáshǐta.

木綿 と 毛織物 の 値段 が 非常に 安く なりました.

The price of cotton and woolen cloth has become very cheap.

(*momén* cotton cloth, *keorimonó* woolen cloth, *nedán* price, *yasúi* 安い cheap)

Anó otokó no hǐtó wa ítsumo amarí nágaku shaberimásǔ.

あの 男 の 人 は いつも あまり 長く しゃべります.

That man always talks too long. (*shabéru* しゃべる to talk, to chat)

The adverbial form of the *true adjective* is also used to translate the **comparative adverbs** repeated in pairs and joined by the conjunction *and*:

Natsú wa hi ga dandán mijíkaku narimásǔ.

夏 は 日 が 段々 短く 成ります.

In summer the days become **shorter and shorter**.

(*lit.* Summer, days gradually shortly become.)

Asa táiyō wa dandán tákaku agarimásǔ.   In the morning the sun

朝 太陽 は 段々 高く 上がります.   rises **higher and higher**.

(*lit.* Morning, the sun gradually highly rises.)

Undō surú kotó ni yotté hǐtó wa karadá ga dandán tsúyoku narimásǔ.

運動 する 事 によって 人 は 体 が だんだん 強く なります.

By doing physical exercise one becomes **stronger and stronger**.

(*lit.* Exercise to do by, persons the body strong becomes)

Hǐtó wa namákete irú to sonó séishin ga dandán yówaku narimásǔ.

人 は なまけている と その 精神 が だんだん 弱く なります.

Continual laziness makes one's mind **weaker and weaker**.

(*lit.* A man being lazy is when, his mind gradually weak becomes.)

Saikín kikō ga dandan átsuku nátte kimáshǐta.

最近 気候 が だんだん 暑く なって 来ました.

Lately the weather has become **hotter and hotter**.

(*saikín* lately, *nátte kúru*=becoming to come=to become)

When in English the comparative adverb is repeated, as in the above examples, the Japanese adverbial form of the adjective may be repeated to render the sentence more emphatic:

Natsú wa hi ga dandán mijíkaku mijíkaku narimásǔ.

(*lit.* In summer the days gradually shortly shortly become.)

Asa táiyō wa dandán tákaku tákaku agarimásǔ.

(*lit.* Morning, the sun gradually highly highly rises.)

Conjugation of True Adjectives

Japanese true adjectives are conjugated like verbs, and have their tenses and moods.

Past of True Adjectives

The past of the true adjective is obtained in three ways:

1. By adding *déshĭta* でした or *no déshĭta* のでした to the adjective;
2. by adding *arimáshĭta* ありました to the adverbial form;
3. by adding *katta* かった or *katta no déshĭta* かったのでした to the stem.

Present	Stem	Past		
samúi 寒い it is cold	*samu* 寒	*samúi déshĭta* *samúi no déshĭta* *sámuku arimáshĭta* *sámukatta* *sámukatta no déshĭta*	寒いでした 寒いのでした 寒くありました 寒かった 寒かったのでした	} It was cold.
takái 高い it is dear.	*taka* 高	*takái déshĭta* *takái no déshĭta* *tákaku arimáshĭta* *tákakatta* *tákakatta no déshĭta*	高いでした 高いのでした 高くありました 高かった 高かったのでした	} It was dear.

Of the five past forms given above, the ones with *no déshĭta, arimáshĭta* are the most polite.

Negative Conjugation of True Adjectives

By adding *arimasén* ありません or *nái* ない to the adverbial form of the true adjective we obtain the **negative** form of the **present**. Both *arimasén* and *nái* mean **there is not,** but when they follow the adverbial form of the true adjective they mean **is not:**

takái 高い it is dear	*tákaku arimasén* *tákaku nái*	高くありません 高くない	} it is not dear
samúi 寒い it is cold	*sámuku arimasén* *sámuku nái*	寒くありません 寒くない	} it is not cold

The negative form with *arimasén* is more polite than the one with *nái*.

Nái ない which means **there is not,** is conjugated like a true adjective, and its past is *nákatta* なかった **there was not.**

By adding *arimasén déshĭta* ありませんでした or *nákatta* なかった to the adverbial form of true adjectives, we obtain their **negative past.**

tákaku arimasén déshĭta 高くありませんでした `|`
tákaku nákatta 高くなかった `}` it was not dear

sámuku arimasén déshĭta 寒くありませんでした `|`
sámuku nákatta 寒くなかった `}` it was not cold

Nái ない may be followed by *désŭ* です or *no désŭ* のです for the present, and *déshĭta* でした or *no déshĭta* のでした for the past. *Nákatta* なかった may be followed by *no déshĭta* のでした. The use of *désŭ, no désŭ, no déshĭta* after *nái* or *nákatta* render the negative more polite.

sámuku nái (no) désŭ. 寒くない(の)です.   it is not cold
sámuku nái (no) déshĭta. 寒くない(の)でした. `|`
sámuku nákatta no déshĭta. `}` it was not cold
寒く なかった の でした. `|`

Note that when we use *désŭ* です after *nái* ない, *no* の may be omitted:

Sámuku nái désŭ. 寒くないです.   *Sámuku nái déshĭta.* 寒くないでした.

However, when we use *nákatta* なかった, *no* の cannot be omitted before *déshĭta* でした.

Omoshíroku nákatta no déshĭta.   It was not interesting.
面白く なかった の でした.   (*omoshirói* interesting)

Utsŭkúshiku nákatta no déshĭta.   It was not beautiful.
美しく なかった の でした.   (*utsukushíi* beautiful)

Examples

Sonó hanashí wa omoshíroku nái (no) désŭ. (or......*omoshíroku arimasén.*)
その 話 は   面白く ない (の) です.   (面白く ありません.)
That story is not interesting.

Anáta no te wa tsumetakŭ[1] nái (no) désŭ ka.   Are your hands
貴方 の 手 は   冷たく   ない (の) です か.   not cold?

Hái, tsumetakŭ arimasén.
はい, 冷たく ありません. `|`
`}` No, they are not cold.
Hái, tsumetakŭ nái (no) désŭ. `|`
はい, 冷たく ない (の) です.

---

1 Adv. form of *tsumetaí* 冷い cold to the touch; *samúi* 寒い cold, in other cases.

Anáta no kimonó wa mijíkaku **arimasén ka.** (or......*nái (no) désŭ ka.*)
貴方　の　着物　は　短かく　ありません　か.　　（ない（の）です　か.）
Isn't your kimono short?

Hái, mijíkaku **arimasén.** はい, 短かくありません.　）
Hái, mijíkaku **nái** (*no*) *désŭ.* 　　　　　　　＞ No, it is
はい,　短かく　ない　（の）　です.　　　　　）　not short.

Sonó ryokō wa nágaku **nái** (*no*) *déshĭta.* 　）
その　旅行　は　長く　ない　（の）　でした.　　）
Sonó ryokō wa nágaku **arimasén** *déshĭta.* 　＞ That trip was
その　旅行　は　長く　ありません　でした.　　｝ not long.
Sonó ryokō wa nágaku **nákatta** *no déshĭta.* 　）
その　旅行　は　長く　なかった　の　でした.　　）

Anó hĭtó no ié wa yásuku **arimasén** *déshĭta.* 　）
あの　人　の　家　は　安く　ありません　でした.　｝
Anó hĭtó no ié wa yásuku **nái** (*no*) *déshĭta.* 　＞ His house was
あの　人　の　家　は　安く　ない　（の）　でした.　｝ not cheap.
Anó hĭtó no ié wa yásuku **nákatta** *no déshĭta.* 　）
あの　人　の　家　は　安く　なかった　の　でした.　）

Sonó mondaí wa muzukáshiku **nái** (*no*) *déshĭta.* 　）
その　問題　は　むづかしく　ない　の　でした.　　）
Sonó mondaí wa muzukáshiku **arimasén** *déshĭta.* 　＞ That problem
その　問題　は　むづかしく　ありません　でした.　｝ was not
Sonó mondaí wa muzukáshiku **nákatta** *no déshĭta.*｝ difficult.
その　問題　は　むづかしく　なかった　の　でした.　）

The Japanese being fond of **periphrastic forms,** even such accumulated periphrases are found as:

Samúi no de wa nái no désŭ. 　寒いのではないのです.　I am not cold.
Samúi no de wa nái no déshĭta. 寒いのではないのでした.　I was not cold.

Negative Conjugation of Verbs with
nai ない and *nakatta* なかった

Nai and **nakatta,** instead of **masén** and **masén déshĭta,** are
used also in the negative conjugation of verbs. *Nai* and *nakatta*
are, in this case, placed after the simple stem of verbs belonging
to Class I, and after an enlarged stem in *a* of verbs belonging to
Class II. **Nai** and **nakatta** may be followed by **no désŭ** or **no
déshĭta,** as in the case of the adverbial form of adjectives.

Phonetic Rule

Verbs that in their simple present form are stressed on the second last syllable, as *míru*, *kógu*, for instance, maintain the stress on the final vowel of their stem when adding *nai* or *nakatta,* while the negative form of verbs whose simple present is stressed on their final *u*, as *irú*, *kasú*, for instance, has the stress on the first syllable of the suffixes *nai* and *nakatta*. Observe this rule graphically applied in the list of verbs given below.

Class I

		Stem	Negative Present		Negative Past	
míru	見る	*mi*	*mínai*	見ない	*mínakatta*	見なかった
to see		見	I do not see		I did not see	
tabéru	食べる	*tabe*	*tabénai*	食べない	*tabénakatta*	食べなかった
to eat		食べ	I do not eat		I did not eat	
irú	いる	*i*	*inái*	いない	*inákatta*	いなかった
there is		い	there is not		there was not	

Class II

			Stem	Negative Present		Negative Past	
1	*kógu*	漕ぐ	*koga*	*kogánai*	漕がない	*kogánakatta*	漕がなかった
	to row		漕が	I do not row		I did not row	
	káku	書く	*kaka*	*kakánai*	書かない	*kakánakatta*	書かなかった
	to write		書か	I do not write		I did not write	
2	*dásu*	出す	*dasa*	*dasánai*	出さない	*dasánakatta*	出さなかった
	to take out		出さ	I do not take out		I did not take out	
	kasú	貸す	*kasa*	*kasanái*	貸さない	*kasanákatta*	貸さなかった
	to rent		貸さ	I do not rent		I did not rent	
3	*tátsu*	立つ	*tata*	*tatánai*	立たない	*tatánakatta*	立たなかった
	to stand		立た	I do not stand		I did not stand	
	mátsu	待つ	*mata*	*matánai*	待たない	*matánakatta*	待たなかった
	to wait		待た	I do not wait		I did not wait	
4	*tobú*	飛ぶ	*toba*	*tobanái*	飛ばない	*tobanákatta*	飛ばなかった
	to fly		飛ば	I do not fly		I did not fly	
	yómu	読む	*yoma*	*yománai*	読まない	*yománakatta*	読まなかった
	to read		読ま	I do not read		I did not read	
	shinú	死ぬ	*shina*	*shinanái*	死なない	*shinanákatta*	死ななかった
	to die		死な	He does not die		He did not die	
5	*áru*	ある	......	*nái*	ない	*nákatta*	なかった
	there is			there is not		there was not	
	tóru	取る	*tora*	*toránai*	取らない	*toránakatta*	取らなかった
	to take		取ら	I do not take		I did not take	
6	*iú*	云う	*iwa*	*iwanái*	云わない	*iwanákatta*	云わなかった
	to say		云わ	I do not say		I did not say	
	kaú	買う	*kawa*	*kawanái*	買わない	*kawanákatta*	買わなかった
	to buy		買わ	I do not buy		I did not buy	
	núu	縫う	*nuwa*	*nuwánai*	縫わない	*nuwánakatta*	縫わなかった
	to sew		縫わ	I do not sew		I did not sew	

Note that the negative form with *masén* and *masén déshita* is more polite than the one with *nai* and *nakatta*. The negative present with *nai,* corresponds, in degree of politeness, to the simple present in *u.*

See Lesson 30 for the affirmative form corresponding in degree of politeness to the negative past with *nakatta.*

Being the formation of the negative past with *nakatta,* more simple and easier to remember than the corresponding affirmative form, we have preferred to follow what might be called an antithetical grammatical order.

Examples

Anó kojikí wa monó wo iwanái.   That beggar does not speak.
あの 乞食 は 物 を 云わない.   (*lit.* That beggar thing doesn't say.)

Konó akambō wa máda arukánai.   This baby does not walk yet.
この 赤ん坊 は まだ 歩かない.   (*arúku* to walk)

Konó búnshō wo wakaránai.   I do not understand
この 文章 を わからない.   this sentence.

Yūbe anó kaigō e dáre mo kónakatta.
ゆうべあの 会合 へ だれ も 来なかった.
　Nobody came to the meeting last night.
　　(*kaigō* meeting, *kónakatta* irregular past of *kúru* 来る to come)

Fúji no rempeijō de heitaí wo mínakatta ka.
富士 の 練兵場 で 兵隊 を 見なかった か.
Did you not see the soldiers at Fuji military ground?

Hái, mínakatta no déshita.   No, I did not see them.
はい、見なかった の でした.

Izen Nippónjin wa yōshoku wo tabénakatta. (or *tabénai no déshita.*)
以前 日本人 は 洋食 を 食べなかった. （食べない の でした.）
Formerly the Japanese did not eat foreign food.

Chichí wa anó otokó ni kané wo kasanákatta (*no déshita.*)
父 はあの 男 に 金 を 貸さなかった （の でした.）

or *Chichí wa anó otokó ni kané wo kasanái* (*no*) *déshita.*
父 はあの 男 に 金 を 貸さない （の） でした.
My father did not lend any money to that man.

Tō-séiki no hajimé máde hĭtó wa sóra wo tobanákatta (*no déshita.*)
当世紀 の はじめ まで 人 は 空 を 飛ばなかった （の でした.）

or *Tō-séiki no hajimé máde hĭtó wa sóra wo tobanái* (*no*) *déshita.*
当世紀 の はじめ まで 人 は 空 を 飛ばない （の） でした.
　Until the beginning of this century man did not fly through the sky.
　　(*tō* 当 this, the present; *séiki* 世紀 century)

Tō 当 for *this, the present* or *the current,* in reference to a period of time, is of the written or literary style. It is used especially in such expressions as:

tō-ji 当時 at the present time, nowadays
tō-getsŭ 当月 this *or* the current month
tō-nen 当年 this *or* the current year

Another negative conjugation of the present tense of verbs is formed by adding *nu* ぬ instead of *nai*, to the verbal stem:

tabéru 食べる *tabénai* 食べない *tabénu* 食べぬ I do not eat
káku 書く *kakánai* 書かない *kakánu* 書かぬ I do not write

See **phonetic rule** on negative form with *nu,* Page 678.

Negative verbs formed with *nai* or *nu* are used especially when followed by *uchi ni* うちに *while, during, before,* or by *toki ni* 時に, *when.* In other cases, the negative conjugation with *masén* is preferred in polite conversation.

Examples

Kurumá ga tomaranŭ (or *tomaranái*) *uchi ni tobioríru no wa abunái*
車 が 止まらぬ （止まらない）うち に 飛び降りるの は 危い
désŭ. It is dangerous to jump off the car **while** it is in motion.
です。 (The car does not stop while, to jump off dangerous is.)

Kurakú naránu (or *naránai*) *uchi ni kaerimashō.*
暗く ならぬ （ならない）うち に 帰りましょう。
Let's go home **before** dark. (Dark does not become while, let us return.)

Jimúsho ni watashí ga oránu (or *oránai*) *toki ni jimúintachi wa*
事務所 に 私 が おらぬ （おらない）時 に 事務員達 は
namakerurashíi[1] *désŭ.* It seems that **when** I am not in the office my employees
なまけるらしい です。 are idle.

Vocabulary

Nouns			Adjectives		
aeroplane	*hikōki*	飛行機	long	*nagái*	長イ
baby	*akambō*	赤ン坊	short	*mijikái*	短カイ
dress	*kimonó*	着物	slow	*norói*	ノロイ
hand	*te*	手	useless	*múeki-na*	無益ナ
magazine	*zasshí*	雑誌	**Verbs**		
plant	*shokúbutsu*	植物	to become	*náru*	成ル
spring (season)	*háru*	春	to borrow	*kari·rú*	借リル
trip	*tabí*	旅	to get up	*okí·ru*	起キル
	ryokō	旅行	to grow	*haéru*	生エル
turtle	*káme*	亀	to lend	*kasú*	貸ス
wall	*kabé*	壁	to rain	*áme ga fúru*	雨ガ降ル
foreign dress	*fujín fukú*	婦人服	dressmaker	*yōsaishi*	洋裁師
				fujín fukúya	婦人服屋

---

1 *namakéru* なまける, to be idle; *rashíi* or *rashíi dèsŭ*=it seems, it appears

What did he say?   *Nan to iimáshĭta ka.* 何んと云いましたか.

He said nothing at all. *Nan to mo iimasén déshĭta.* 何んとも云いませんでした.

There is nothing.   *Náni mo nái.* 何もない.

It is nothing at all.   *Nan de mo nái.* 何んでもない.

It makes no difference to me. *Nan to mo nái.* 何んともない.

Exercise *Renshū* 練習

1. Ḥikōki wa taihén háyaku tobimásŭ. **2.** Káme wa hijō-ni nóroku aruki-másŭ. **3.** Anáta no heyá no kabé wo náni iró ni nurimáshĭta ka.—Shíroku nurimáshĭta. **4.** Watashí wa mái ása taihén háyaku okimásŭ. **5.** Háru hi wa dandán nágaku narimásŭ ga yóru wa dandán mijíkaku narimásŭ. **6.** Kinō wa sámukatta ga kyō wa atatakái désŭ. **7.** Anáta no te wa tsumetái désŭ. O-yu ga hoshíi désŭ ka.—Dōzo o-yu wo mótte kité kudasái. **8.** Anáta wa amarí osokú gakkō e tsŭkimasén déshĭta ka.—Hái, tsŭkimasén déshĭta. **9.** Anó shōnin wa shinamonó wo amarí tákaku urimasén ka.—Hái, amarí tákaku urimasén. **10.** Senshū kimí wa atarashíi yōfuku wo kawanákatta ka. —Iié, kaimáshĭta. **11.** Anáta no heyá wa sámuku arimasén ka.—Hái, sámuku arimasén. **12.** Sakújitsu Yokohamá wa taihén átsuku arimasén déshĭta ka.— Hái, átsuku arimasén déshĭta. Suzúshikatta no déshĭta. **13.** Náze sonná ni yukkúri arukimásŭ ka.—Tsŭkárete imásŭ nóde. **14.** Konó hĭtótachi wa Nihón-go wo hanashimasén; Chōsen-go daké hanashimásŭ. **15.** Súbete no torí wa háyaku tobimásŭ ka.—Iié, súbete no torí ga háyaku tobú no de wa arimasén. Torí ni yotté wa[1] (Aru torí wa) yukkúri tobimásŭ. **16.** Hĭtó wa taitéi múeki-na monó wo kaimasén. **17.** Takŭsán no zasshí wo o-yomí[2] ni narimásŭ ka. —Zasshí wa takŭsán yomimasén ga mái nichí iroiró no shimbún wo yomimásŭ. **18.** Anáta no yōsaishi ga konó yōfuku wo tsŭkurimáshĭta ka.—Iié, tsŭkuri-masén déshĭta. Watashí ga tsŭkurimáshĭta. **19.** Nágaku machimáshĭta ka.— Iié, nágaku machimasén déshĭta. **20.** Konó otokonokó wa kyō náni mo tabemasén déshĭta. Sŭkóshi byōki désŭ. **21.** Konó hon wo mō yomimáshĭta ka.—Iié, máda yomimasén déshĭta. **22.** Anáta no okāsan wa budōshu wo nomimasén ka.—Hái, nomimasén. **23.** Anáta no otōsan wa ása o-cha wo nomimasén ka.—Iié, nomimásŭ kéredomo kōhī wa nomimasén. **24.** Kyónen wa áme ga takŭsán furimasén déshĭta, shikáshi kotoshí wa taihén furimáshĭta. **25.** Kimí wa bóku no ojí kará kané wo karinákatta ka.—Karimasén déshĭta, kéredomo bóku no obá kará karimáshĭta. **26.** Kansō[3] shĭtá tochí ni wa shokúbutsu wa haénai.

1. 飛行機は大変速く飛びます. **2.** 亀は非常にのろく歩きます.
3. 貴方の部屋の壁を何色に塗りましたか.—白く塗りました. **4.** 私は
毎朝大変早く起きます. **5.** 春, 日は段々長く成りますが夜はだん
だん短かくなります. **6.** きのうは寒かったがきょうは暖かいです.
7. 貴方の手は冷たいです. お湯が欲しいですか.—どうぞお湯を持っ

---

1 *ni yotté wa* after a noun means *some* **2** *o-yomi ni náru* polite for *yómu* to read **3** *kansō* 乾燥 dryness; *kansō shĭtá* 乾燥した dried; *kansō surú* to dry

て来て下さい. **8.** 貴方はあまり遅く学校へ着きませんでしたか.—はい, 着きませんでした. **9.** あの商人は品物をあまり高く売りませんか.—はい, あまり高く売りません. **10.** 先週君は新しい洋服を買わなかったか.—いゝえ, 買いました. **11.** 貴方の部屋は寒くありませんか.—はい, 寒くありません. **12.** 昨日横浜は大変暑くありませんでしたか.—はい, 暑くありませんでした. 涼しかったのでした. **13.** なぜそんなにゆっくり歩きますか.—疲れていますので. **14.** この人達は日本語を話しません. 朝鮮語だけ話します. **15.** すべての鳥は速く飛びますか.—いゝえ, すべての鳥が速く飛ぶのではありません. 鳥によっては (或る鳥は) ゆっくり飛びます. **16.** 人は大抵無益な物を買いません. **17.** 沢山の雑誌をお読みになりますか.—雑誌は沢山読みませんが毎日色々の新聞を読みます. **18.** 貴方の洋裁師がこの洋服をつくりましたか.—いゝえ, つくりませんでした. 私がつくりました. **19.** 長く待ちましたか.—いゝえ, 長く待ちませんでした. **20.** この男の子はきょう何も食べませんでした. 少し病気です. **21.** この本をもう読みましたか.—いゝえ, まだ読みませんでした. **22.** 貴方のお母さんはぶどう酒を飲みませんか.—はい, 飲みません. **23.** 貴方のお父さんは朝お茶を飲みませんか.—いゝえ, 飲みます, けれどもコーヒーは飲みません. **24.** 去年は雨が沢山降りませんでした然し, 今年は大変降りました. **25.** 君は僕の伯父から金を借りなかったか.—借りませんでした, けれども僕の伯母から借りました. **26.** 乾燥した土地には植物は生えない.

1. Aeroplanes fly very fast. **2.** Turtles walk very slowly. **3.** What colour did you paint the walls of your room?—I painted them white. **4.** Every morning I get up very early. **5.** In spring the days become longer and longer, but the nights become shorter and shorter. **6.** Yesterday it was cold, but to-day it is warm. **7.** Your hands are cold; do you want some hot water? —Yes, bring me some hot water, please. **8.** Did you not arrive at school too late?—No, I did not arrive too late. **9.** Doesn't that merchant sell his goods too dear?—No, he does not sell them too dear. **10.** Didn't you buy a new suit last week?—Yes, I did. **11.** Isn't it cold in your room?—No, it is not cold. **12.** Wasn't it very hot yesterday in Yokohama?—No, it was not. It was cool. **13.** Why do you walk so slowly?—Because I am tired. **14.** These people do not speak Japanese. They speak only the Korean language. **15.** Do all birds fly fast?—No, not all birds fly fast. Some birds fly slowly. **16.** Generally people do not buy useless things. **17.** Do you read many magazines?—I do not read many magazines, but I read several newspapers everyday. **18.** Did your dress-maker make this dress?—No, she did not make it; I made it. **19.** Did you wait long for me?—No, I did not wait long. **20.** This boy has not eaten anything to-day. He is a little sick. **21.** Have you read this book already?—No, I have not read it yet. **22.** Does not your mother drink wine?—No, she does not. **23.** Does your father not drink tea in the morning?

—Yes, he does, but he does not drink coffee. **24.** Last year it did not rain much, but this year it has rained very much. **25.** Did you not borrow any money from my uncle?—I did not borrow any money from him, but I borrowed some from my aunt. **26.** Plants do not grow on dry land.

Twenty-second Lesson　第廿二課

Desiderative Conjugation

In Lesson 16 it has been shown that the **desiderative form** of verbs in the present tense is obtained by adding *tai* たい to the simple verbal stem of verbs of Class I, and to the *i*-stem of verbs of Class II.

Class I

míru 見る　to see　*mi* 見　*mitái* 見たい　I wish to see

Class II

yómu 読む　to read　*yomi* 読み　*yomitái* 読みたい　I wish to read

surú[1] する　to do　*shi* し　*shitái* したい　I wish to do

The termination *tai* たい is conjugated as a true adjective. Its past form is *takatta* たかった, and its adverbial form is *taku* たく, which, followed by *nái* ない or *nákatta* なかった, is used to form the negative tenses. Both *takatta* and *taku* are joined to the simple stem of vervs of Class I and to the *i*-stem of verbs of Class II, as shown below.

See **phonetic rules** on words in the desiderative form, Page 679.

Positive		Negative	
Present			
mitái　I wish to see 見たい		*mítaku-nái*　I do not wish to see 見たくない	
yomitái　I wish to read 読みたい		*yomítaku-nái*　I do not wish to read 読みたくない	
shitái　I wish to do したい		*shitakú-nái*　I do not wish to do したくない	
Past			
mítakatta　I wished to see 見たかった		*mítaku-nákatta*　I didn't wish to see 見たくなかった	
yomítakatta　I wished to read 読みたかった		*yomítaku-nákatta*　I didn't wish to read 読みたくなかった	
shitákatta　I wished to do したかった		*shitakú-nákatta*　I didn't wish to do したくなかった	

---

1 *Surú* is an irregular verb.

What has been said in the previous lesson of the conjugation of the true adjective, applies also to the conjugation of verbs in the desiderative form.

Here below are given the different forms of the present and past tenses of the desiderative conjugation, both in the positive and negative.

Míru 見る   To See

míru 見る   *mi* 見   *mitái* 見たい   I wish to see

Present

Positive		Negative	
I wish to see, etc.		I do not wish to see, etc.	
mitái	見たい	*mítaku-nái*	見たくない
mitái désŭ	見たいです	*mítaku-nái désŭ*	見たくないです
mitái no désŭ	見たいのです	*mítaku-nái no désŭ*	見たくないのです
mítaku arimásŭ	見たくあります	*mítaku arimasén*	見たくありません

Past

I wished to see, etc.	I did not wish to see, etc.
mitái déshĭta	*mítaku-nái déshĭta*
見たいでした	見たくないでした
mitái no déshĭta	*mítaku-nái no déshĭta*
見たいのでした	見たくないのでした
mítaku arimáshĭta	*mítaku arimasén déshĭta*
見たくありました	見たくありませんでした
mítakatta	*mítaku nákatta*
見たかった	見たくなかった
mítakatta no déshĭta	*mítaku nákatta no déshĭta*
見たかったのでした	見たくなかったのでした

Yómu 読む   To Read

yómu 読む   *yomi* 読み   *yomitái* I wish to read

Present

I wish to read, etc.		I do not wish to read, etc.	
yomitái	読みたい	*yomítaku-nái*	読みたくない
yomitái désŭ	読みたいです	*yomítaku-nái désŭ*	読みたくないです
yomitái no désŭ	読みたいのです	*yomítaku-nái no désŭ*	読みたくないのです
yomítaku arimásŭ	読みたくあります	*yomítaku arimasén*	読みたくありません

Past

I wished to read, etc.	I did not wish to read, etc.
yomitái déshĭta	*yomítaku-nái déshĭta*
読みたいでした	読みたくないでした
yomitái no déshĭta	*yomítaku-nái no déshĭta*
読みたいのでした	読みたくないのでした

I wished to read, etc.	I did not wish to read, etc.
yomítaku arimáshǐta	*yomítaku arimasén déshǐta*
読みたくありました	読みたくありませんでした
yomítakatta	*yomítaku-nákatta*
読みたかった	読みたくなかった
yomítakatta no déshǐta	*yomítaku-nákatta no déshǐta*
読みたかったのでした	読みたくなかったのでした

Surú する To Do (irr. verb)

surú する *shi* し *shǐtái* したい I wish to do

Present

I wish to do, etc.		I do not wish to do, etc.	
shǐtái	したい	*shǐtakú-nái*	したくない
shǐtái désǔ	したいです	*shǐtakú-nái désǔ*	したくないです
shǐtái no désǔ	したいのです	*shǐtakú-nái no désǔ*	したくないのです
shǐtakú arimásǔ	したくあります	*shǐtakú arimasén*	したくありません

Past

I wished to do, etc.	I did not wish to do, etc.
shǐtái déshǐta	*shǐtakú-nái déshǐta*
したいでした	したくないでした
shǐtái no déshǐta	*shǐtakú-nái no déshǐta*
したいのでした	したくないのでした
shǐtakú arimáshǐta	*shǐtakú arimasén déshǐta*
したくありました	したくありませんでした
shǐtákatta	*shǐtakú-nákatta*
したかった	したくなかった
shǐtákatta no déshǐta	*shǐtakú-nákatta no déshǐta*
したかったのでした	したくなかったのでした

Of all the forms of the conjugation of the desiderative verb given above, the ones with *désǔ* です and *déshǐta* でした are preferred in ordinary speech.

The object of the desiderative verb may take *ga* が or *wo* を. In using *ga* が the object is emphasized.

Examples

Anáta wa Nippón no rekishí ga yomitái désǔ ka.
貴方 は 日本 の 歴史 が 読みたい です か.
Do you wish to read the history of Japan?

Hái, yomitái désǔ. はい, 読みたいです.   Yes, I wish to read it.

Náze sonó kimonó wo kaitakú-nái no désǔ ka.   Why do you not wish
なぜ その 着物 を 買いたくない の です か.   to buy that kimono?

Amarí takái kará. あまり高いから.   Because it is too dear.

Sŭkiyakí[1] *ga tabétakatta kará yūbe Tōkyō Káikan e ikimáshĭta.*
すき焼 が 食べたかった から ゆうべ 東京 会館 へ 行きました.
As I wished to eat *sukiyaki* last night I went to the Tokyo Kaikan.[2]

Ténki ga warúi déshĭta kará dekaketaku-nákatta no déshĭta.
天気 が 悪い でした から 出かけたくなかった の でした.
As the weather was bad we did not wish to go out.

Konó-aidá Kamakurá e ikimáshĭta ga oyogítaku-nái déshĭta.
この間 鎌倉 へ 行きました が 泳ぎたくない でした.
The other day I went to Kamakura,[3] but I did not wish to swim.

Anáta wa anó ié wo uritakú arimáshĭta ka.   Did you wish to sell
貴方 は あの 家 を 売りたくありましたか.   that house?

Iié, uritakú arimasén déshĭta.   No, I did not wish to sell it.
いいえ, 売りたくありませんでした.

With the negative conjugation of desiderative verbs, as well as true adjectives, the paraphrase *no de wa arimasén* のではありません is sometimes used by women, but rarely by men.

Samúi no de wa arimasén. 寒いのではありません.   It is not cold.

Sámukatta no de wa arimasén.
寒かった の で は ありません.
Sámukatta no de wa arimasén déshĭta.
寒かった の で は ありません でした.
}It was not cold.

Hanashĭtái no de wa arimasén.   I do not wish to speak.
話したい の で は ありません.

Hanashĭtákatta no de wa arimasén.
話したかった の で は ありません.
Hanashĭtákatta no de wa arimasén déshĭta.
話したかった の で は ありません でした.
}I did not wish to speak.

The expression *no de wa arimasén*, translated word for word, corresponds to : **the fact** (*no*), **to be** (*de-wa*), **is not** (*arimasen*).

The first example *Samúi no de wa arimasén* would then correspond, awkwardly as it may sound, to *The fact that it is cold —to be is not.* Or, in plain English: *It is not the case to say that it is cold.*

The inclination, intention or desire to do something is expressed in a milder and more gentle form by affixing *to omóu* と思う to the verb in the desiderative form. In such cases, the inclination, intention, or desire is generally indicated in English by such expressions as *I should like to, I am* or *feel inclined to, I feel like, I have a desire to, I intend to,* etc.

Méron wo tabetái to omoimásŭ.   }I feel like eating melon.
メロン を 食べたい と 思います.   }I have a desire to eat melon. Etc.

1 slices of meat eaten while cooking in an iron pan **2** *Tokyo kaikan* name of a fashionable restaurant in Tokyo. **3** A fashionable summer resort on the sea near Tokyo.

To omóu と思う after a verb in the desiderative form means, literary translated, *I, you, we, etc. think so.*

Méron wo tabetái to omoimásŭ.   (*lit.* Melon, I wish to eat, so I think.)
メロン を 食べたいと　思います.

Sonó jidōsha wo kaitái to omoimáshĭta ga kané ga arimasén déshĭta.
その 自動車 を買いたいと　思いました　が　金　がありませんでした.
I wished to buy that motor-car but I had no money (to buy it).

Séngetsu anáta wa Hokkaidō e ikitái to omoimasén déshĭta ka.
先月　貴方　は　北海道　へ行きたいと　思いません　でした　か.
Did you not intend (wish) to go to Hokkaido last month?

Omoimasén déshĭta. 思いませんでした.   I did not.

Instead of *to omóu* と思う, we may use *omóu* 思う only, without *to* と, after the simple stem of verbs of Class I, and after the *i*-stem of verbs of Class II, followed by *taku* たく, the adverbial form of *tai* たい.

Sashimí[1] *wo tabétaku omoimasén ka.*   Don't you wish to eat
刺身　を　食べたく　思いません　か.   some *sashimi*[1]?

Iié, tabétaku omoimásŭ. いゝえ, 食べたく思います.   Yes, I do.

Yūbe watashí wa Kabukizá e ikitakú omoimáshĭta.
ゆうべ 私　は　歌舞伎座 へ 行きたく　思いました.
Last night I wished to go to the Kabuki theatre.

The intention is more clearly expressed by the word *tsumori* つもり, which means **intention**, followed by *désŭ* or *déshĭta.* In a negative sentence *tsumorí* つもり is followed by *wa arimasén* はありません or , if emphasis is to be expressed, by *de wa arimasén* ではありません.

Píano wo kaú tsumorí (de) wa arimasén ka.   Don't you intend
ピアノ を買う　つもり　(で)　は　ありません　か.   to buy a piano?

Píano wo kaú tsumorí (de) wa arimasén déshĭta ka.
ピアノ を買う　つもり　(で)　は　ありません　でした　か.
Did you not intend to buy a piano?

The word *tsumorí* may be used also after the desiderative.

Sonó fujingatá wa dekaketái tsumorí désŭ ka.   Do those ladies wish
その　婦人方　は　出かけたい　積り　です　か.   to go out?
or Do those ladies intend to go out?

Iié, dekaketái no de wa arimasén.   No, they do not wish to
いゝえ, 出かけたいの　で　は　ありません.   go out.

The verb in the desiderative followed by the expression *tsumorí désŭ* or *no de wa arimasén* indicates a higher degree of politeness than is indicated by the simple present of the verb followed by the same expressions.

The desire, wish, or eagerness to do something is also expressed by the suffix *garu* がる, placed after the simple stem of verbs of Class I and after the *i*-stem of verbs of Class II, followed by *ta* た (*tai* たい after dropping *i* い).

---

1 *sashimí* sliced raw fish

The termination *tagáru* たがる indicates a stronger desire than is indicated by the desiderative termination *tai* たい, and corresponds to such expressions as *to be eager to, to be fond of, to be anxious to, to be dying* (=*curious*) *to,* etc.

míru 見る	*mi-tagáru* 見たがる	*mitagáru* 見たがる	I am, he is, eager to see, etc. you are eager to see, etc.
yómu 読む	*yomi-tagáru* 読みたがる	*yomitagáru* 読みたがる	I am, he is, eager to read, etc. you are eager to read, etc.
surú する	*shi-tagáru* したがる	*shĭtagáru* したがる	I am, he is, eager to do, etc. you are eager to do, etc.

The termination *gáru* がる is regularly conjugated like a verb:

Present

mitagarimásŭ	見たがります	I am, he is, eager
mitagáru no désŭ	見たがるのです	to see, etc.
mitagarimasén	見たがりません	
mitagaránai	見たがらない	I am not,
mitagaránai désŭ	見たがらないです	he is not
mitagaránai no désŭ	見たがらないのです	eager to see, etc.

Past

mitagarimáshĭta	見たがりました	I, he was eager
mitagáru no déshĭta	見たがるのでした	to see, etc.
mitagátta	見たがつた	
mitagarimasén déshĭta	見たがりませんでした	
mitagaránakatta	見たがらなかった	
mitagaránakatta no déshĭta	見たがらなかったのでした	I, he was not eager to see, etc.
mitagaránai déshĭta	見たがらないでした	
mitagaránai no déshĭta	見たがらないのでした	

Uchí no kodomó wa Uenó no Hakurankái e ikitagarimásŭ.
うち の 子供 は 上野 の 博覧会 へ 行きたがります.
Our children have a strong desire to go to the Ueno Exhibition.

Anáta wa chiisái tokí ni otogibánashi wo yomitagarimáshĭta.
貴方 は 小さい 時 に おとぎ話 を 読みたがりました.
When you were young (small) you were eager to read fairy stories.

Watashí wa káigai ni itá tokí ni kuní e kaeritagátta monó désŭ.
私 は 海外 にいた 時 に 国 へ 帰りたがった もの です.
When I was abroad I felt a great desire to return to my native country.

The termination *garu* がる may be added also to true adjectives after dropping their final *i*. In this case the suffix *garu* がる intensifies the meaning expressed by the adjectives.

samúi cold 寒い	*samugáru* 寒がる	to feel very cold to suffer much from the cold

atsúi warm 暑い	*atsugáru* 暑がる	{ to feel very hot to suffer much from the heat
kurushíi painful 苦しい	*kurushigáru* 苦しがる	} to feel much pain to suffer much from pain

Anó kodomó wa samugarimásŭ.
あの 子供 は 寒がります。
   } That child feels very cold.
    That child suffers much from the cold.

Sonó byōnin wa takái netsú de kurushigarimáshĭta.
その 病人 は 高い 熱 で 苦しがりました。
  The patient suffered much from high fever.

Sonó shirogumá wa atsugátte imáshĭta.
その 白熊 は 暑がって いました。
  That white bear was suffering much from the heat.

The intensified desiderative of verbs with *tagaru* たがる is regularly used for the negative form.

ikú to go 行く	*ikitagarimasén* 行きたがりません	} I, you, etc. do not intend to go I, you, etc. do not wish at all to go.
tabéru to eat 食べる	*tabetagarimasén* 食べたがりません	} I, you, etc. do not intend to eat I, you, etc. do not wish at all to eat.
míru to see 見る	*mitagarimasén* 見たがりません	} I, you, etc. do not intend to see I, you, etc. do not wish at all to see.

Watashí wa asokó e ikitagarimasén.
私 は あそこ へ 行きたがりません。
I do not wish at all to go there.—I positively do not wish to go there.

Substantivizing Verbs and Adjectives

A verb, as well as a true adjective, in its desiderative form, may be substantivized by substituting its final *i* for *sa* さ, as in the following examples:

áu 会う	to meet	*aitái* 会いたい	*aitása* 会いたさ	the desire to meet
arúku 歩く	to walk	*arukitái* 歩きたい	*arukitása* 歩きたさ	the desire to walk
míru 見る	to see	*mitái* 見たい	*mítasa* 見たさ	the desire, eagerness to see
kaú 買う	to buy	*kaitái* 買いたい	*kaitása* 買いたさ	the desire, eagerness to buy
akaruí 明るい	bright		*akarúsa* 明るさ	brightness, condition of being bright
furúi 古い	old		*fúrusa* 古さ	antiquity, oldness

hosói 細い	thin	*hósosa* 細さ	thinness	
omoshirói 面白い	interesting	*omoshírosa* 面白さ	the condition of being interesting	
wakái 若い	young	*wákasa* 若さ	youth, youthfulness	

Quasi-adjectives do not suffer any alteration when substantivized by the suffix *sa*.

jōbu	丈夫	strong	*jōbusa*	丈夫さ	strength
jōzu	上手	skilful	*jōzusa*	上手さ	skilfulness
rikō	利口	clever	*rikōsa*	利口さ	cleverness
kimbén	勤勉	diligent	*kimbensá*	勤勉さ	diligence
shōjiki	正直	honest	*shōjikisa*	正直さ	honesty

The substantivized verbal and adjectival expressions render possible the formation of sentences whose meaning has to be translated into English with words that, rather often, do not correspond to those of the original Japanese text, but only portray its idea, as shown in the follwoing few examples:

Kowái-monó mítasa de káre wa chottó nozoité mimáshĭta.
怖いもの　見たさ　で　彼　は　ちょっと　覗いて　見ました.
Curiosity overcame fear, and he had a peep at it.
(*lit.* Fearful thing, by eagerness to see, he a little peeping looked.)

Sonó heyá no akarúsa wa chōdo hirumá no yō déshĭta.   That room was as bright as daytime.
その部屋の　明るさ　は　丁度　昼間　のようでした.
(*lit.* That room's brightness just day-like was.)

When

As a conjunction, **when** is translated by *tokí* 時 or *tokí ni* 時に. The particle *ni* after *tokí* is used when emphasis is to be expressed.

1. *Watashí wa Kánada ni itá tokí ni Nihón-go wo naraimáshĭta.*
　私　は　カナダ　にいた　時　に　日本語　を　習いました.
When I was in Canada I studied Japanese.

2. *Musŭkó ga anáta no uchí e ittá tokí mínasan wa o-dekaké déshĭta.*
　息子　が　貴方　のうちへ行った　時　皆さん　は　お出かけ　でした.
When my son went to your home everybody was out.

Note that the subject of the clause introduced by **when** takes *wa* は if it is also the subject of the second clause, as in example **1**; however, the subject of the clause introduced by **when** takes *ga* が if it is different from the subject of the second clause, as in example **2**.

If **when** introduces a habit or a customary occurrence it is translated by *to* と placed after the simple present of the verb it precedes.

Ishiyamá San wa watashí ga náni ka chūkoku wo surú to ítsudemo
石山　さん　は　私　が　何　か　忠告　を　する　と　いつでも
okorimásŭ. **When** I give Mr. Ishiyama any advice he always gets angry.
怒ります.

Anó otokó wa nómu[1] to súgu yoimásŭ.[2] **When** that man drinks *saké*
あの　男　は　飲む　と　すぐ　酔います.　he soon gets drunk.

How To

The expression **how to + a verb,** is rendered into Japanese by adding the termination **katá** 方 to the simple stem of verbs of Class I and to the *i*-stem of verbs of Class II.

Anáta wa kanjí no kakikatá wo shĭtté imásŭ ka.
貴方　は　漢字　の　書き方　を　知っています　か.
Do you know **how to** write Chinese characters?
(*lit.* You, *kanjí* the way of writing do you know?)

Konó hakó no akekatá wo shĭtté imásŭ ka. Do you know **how**
この　箱　の　開け方　を　知っています　か.　to open this box?
(*lit.* This box the way of opening do you know?)

Iié, soré no akekatá wo shirimasén. No, I do not know
いゝえ,それの　開け方　を　知りません.　**how to** open it.

Vocabulary

	Nouns				
			weather	*ténki*	天気
advice	*chūkoku*	忠告	winter	*fuyú*	冬
exhibition	*hakurankái*	博覧会		**Verbs**	
history	*rekishí*	歴史	to approach	*chikazúku*	近ヅク
melon	*méron*	メロン	to earn	*mōke·ru*	儲ケル
music	*ongakú*	音楽	to hear	*kikú*	聞ク
noise	*otó*	音	to like	*konómu*	好ム
priest	*shimpú[3]*	神父	to sing	*utaú*	歌ウ
	bōsan[3]	坊サン	to swim	*oyógu*	泳グ
relative	*shinsekí*	親戚	to tease	*ijime·rú*	虐メル
swallow	*tsubamé*	ツバメ			

entirely black *makkúro* 真黒; entirely red *makká* 真赤; entirely white *masshíro* 真白; therefore *soré désŭ kará* それですから, *désŭ kará* ですから, *soré de* それで; to make a noise *otó wo tatéru* 音を立てる; to make too much noise *otó wo tatesugirú* 音を立て過ぎる. You are making too much noise. *Anáta wa amarí otó wo tatesugité imásŭ.* 貴方は余り音を立てすぎています. *Amarí,* which means *too much,* is here used for emphasis.

---

1 *Nómu* 飲む "*to drink*" may be used, as it is in the above sentence, with the meaning of *to drink saké* (the chief alcoholic beverage of the Japanese), or any other liquor. **2** *yóu* 酔う to get drunk **3** *shimpú* Catholic priest; *bōsan* Buddhist priest

an English-Japanese dictionary *Ei-wa jitén* 英和辞典; a Japanese-English dictionary
Wa-éi jitén 和英辞典; to be thirsty *nodó ga kawáku* 喉がかわく; I am thirsty
Nódo ga kawakimáshĭta. 喉がかわきました (*lit.* The throat got dry.)

Exercise *Renshū* 練習

1. Dónata ni hanashí¹ ga shĭtái no désŭ ka.—Shiháinin ni hanashí ga
shĭtái no désŭ. **2.** Náze anáta wa itóko to dekaketakú-nái no désŭ ka.—Naze-
náraba itóko wa ítsudemo watashí wo ijimemásŭ kará. **3.** Dáre ga takŭsán
no o-kané wo mōketái no désŭ ka.—Dáre de mo o-kané wo takŭsán mōketái
no désŭ. **4.** Dáre ka kimáshĭta ka.—Hái, o-takú no dáiku ga kimáshĭta soshĭté
anáta ni hanashí ga shĭtákatta no déshĭta. **5.** Náze yūbe gakká wo benkyō-
shĭtakú-nákatta no déshĭta ka.—Tsŭkárete imáshĭta nóde. **6.** Nódo ga kawakimáshĭta mizú ga nomitái désŭ.—Budōshu wo nomítaku arimasén ka.—Ima
wa takŭsán désŭ. Nódo ga kawáita tokí ni wa mizú ga nomitái no désŭ.
7. Anó kodomotachí ni kudámono wo yarimáshĭta ga tabetagarimasén déshĭta.
8. Kómban watashí wa omoté e détaku arimasén. Uchí ni itái désŭ.
9. Watashí wa Nihón-go no senséi wo hōmon² shĭtái no désŭ. **10.** Kinō watashí
wa kázoku to isshó ni Atamí e ikitákatta no déshĭta ga Ōsaka kará shinsekí
no monó³ ga kimáshĭta nóde uchí ni imáshĭta. **11.** Watashí wa Kánada
ni itá tokí Nihón-go wo benkyō surú tsumorí wa arimasén déshĭta ga
íma Nihón ni kimáshĭta nóde Nihón-go wo benkyō shĭtái to omoimásŭ.
12. Samúi tokí ni wa ōku⁴ no hĭtó wa ása háyaku okíru no wo konomimasén.
13. Anáta wa Wa-éi jitén wo kaú tsumorí de wa arimasén déshĭta ka.—Hái,
watashí wa Wa-éi jitén wa mótte imásŭ. Watashí wa Ei-wa jitén wo kaitákatta
no déshĭta. **14.** Náze sonná-ni otó wo tatéru no désŭ ka. Anáta wa ongakú
wo kikitakú arimasén ka.—Anná ongakú wo kikitakú arimasén. Anó onga-
kukatachí wa jōzu ni ensō⁵ surú kotó wo shirimasén. **15.** Tsubamé wa samúi
tokoró ni súmu no wo sŭkimasén, désŭ-kará fuyú ga chikazúku to atatakái
kunĭ-guní⁶ e ikimásŭ. **16.** Chōsenjin wa masshiròi kimonó wo kirú no ga
sŭkí désŭ. **17.** Katoríkku no shimputachí wa ítsumo makkúro-na yōfuku wo
kimásŭ. **18.** Itsu anáta wa o-kuní e káeru tsumorí désŭ ka.—Kotoshí wa
kuní e káeru tsumorí wa arimasén ga rainén wa káeru to omoimásŭ.

1. どなたに話がしたいのですか.—支配人に話がしたいのです.
2. なぜ貴方はいとこと出かけたくないのですか.—なぜならばいとこ
はいつでも私を虐めますから. **3.** 誰が沢山のお金を儲けたいのです
か.—誰でもお金を沢山儲けたいのです. **4.** 誰か来ましたか.—はい,
お宅の大工が来ましたそして貴方に話がしたかったのでした. **5.** な
ぜ, ゆうべ学課を勉強したくなかったのでしたか.—疲れていました
ので. **6.** 喉がかわきました水が飲みたいです.—ぶどう酒を飲みたく
ありませんか.—今はたくさんです. 喉がかわいた時には水が飲みたい

---

1 *hanashí wo surú*=*hanásu*=to speak   2 *hōmon surú* 訪問する to pay a visit
3 *shinsekí no monó* relatives; in this case *monó* means *people, folks*   4. *ōku no* many
5 *ensō surú* to play, to give a performance, a recital   6 *kuni-guni* plural of *kuni*
country

のです. **7.** あの子供達に果物をやりましたが食べたがりませんでし
た. **8.** 今晩私はおもてへ出たくありません. うちにいたいです. **9.** 私
は日本語の先生を訪問したいのです. **10.** きのう，私は家族と一緒に
熱海へ行きたかったのでしたが大阪から親戚の者が来ましたのでうち
にいました. **11.** 私はカナダにいた時，日本語を勉強するつもりはあ
りませんでしたが今，日本に来ましたので日本語を勉強したいと思
います. **12.** 寒い時には多くの人は朝早く起きるのを好みません.
13. 貴方は和英辞典を買うつもりではありませんでしたか.—はい，
私は和英辞典は持っています，私は英和辞典を買いたかったのでした.
14. なぜそんなに音を立てるのですか. 貴方は音楽を聞きたくありま
せんか. —あんな音楽を聞きたくありません. あの音楽家達は上手に
演奏する事を知りません. **15.** つばめは寒い所に住むのを好きませ
ん，ですから冬が近づくと暖かい国々へ行きます. **16.** 朝鮮人は真白
い着物を着るのが好きです. **17.** カトリックの神父達はいつも真黒な
洋服を着ます. **18.** いつ，貴方はお国へ帰るつもりですか.—今年は国
へ帰るつもりはありませんが来年は帰ると思います.

1. To whom do you wish to speak?—I wish to speak to the manager.
2. Why do you not wish to go out with your cousin?—Because he always
teases me. **3.** Who wishes to earn much money?—Everybody wishes to earn
much money. **4.** Did anybody come?—Yes, your carpenter came; he wished
to speak to you. **5.** Why did you not wish to study your lesson last night?—
Because I was tired. **6.** I am thirsty; I wish to drink some water.—Don't
you wish to drink wine?—Not now; when I am thirsty I wish to drink
water. **7.** We gave some fruit to those children, but they did not wish to
eat it. **8.** To-night I do not feel like going out; I wish to remain at home.
9. I should like to pay a visit to my Japanese teacher. **10.** Yesterday I
intended to go to Atami with my family, but as some of my relatives came
from Osaka, we remained at home. **11.** When I was in Canada I had no
intention of studying Japanese, but as I am now in Japan I wish to study it.
12. When it is cold many people do not like to get up early in the morning.
13. Did you not intend to buy a Japanese-English dictionary?—No, I have
a Japanese-English dictionary, but I did intend to buy an English-Japanese
dictionary. **14.** Why are you making so much noise? Don't you like to
hear music?—I do not wish to hear such music. Those players do not know
how to play well. **15.** Swallows do not like to live in cold places; therefore,
when winter approaches they go to warm countries. **16.** The Koreans like
to wear pure white dresses. **17.** Catholic priests always wear jet black dresses.
18. When do you intend to go back to your native country?—I have no
intention of going back to my native country this year, but next year I shall
go back.

Twenty-third Lesson 第廿三課

The Subordinate

We will now explain the formation of the **subordinate,** a peculiarity of the Japanese verb, without which it is difficult to form long sentences.

The **subordinate** of verbs of **Class I** is formed by adding the termination *te* て to verbal stems.

See **phonetic rules** on verbs in their subordinate form, Page 680.

míru 見る	to see, to watch	*mi* 見	*míte* 見て	⎫
tabéru 食べる	to eat	*tabe* 食べ	*tábete* 食べて	⎭

Progressive Conjugation

By adding *imásŭ* います or *orimásŭ* おります (is, are), *imáshĭta* いました or *orimáshĭta* おりました (was, were), to the *subordinate* of verbs, we obtain the present and past tenses of the **progressive conjugation.** In such cases the subordinate corresponds to the present participle of English verbs.

míte imásŭ	見ています	⎫ I am watching
míte orimásŭ	見ております	⎭
tábete imásŭ	食べています	⎫ I am eating
tábete orimásŭ	食べております	⎭
míte imáshĭta	見ていました	⎫ I was watching
míte orimáshĭta	見ておりました	⎭
tábete imáshĭta	食べていました	⎫ I was eating
tábete orimáshĭta	食べておりました	⎭

The *subordinate* with *imásŭ* います is generally used in ordinary conversation, while with *orimásŭ* it is used in polite speech.

*Ōzei no hĭtó ga yakyū wo **míte imásŭ.*** (*yakyū* 野球 baseball game)
大勢 の 人 が 野球 を 見て います.
Many people are watching the baseball game.

*Keibá wo **míte imáshĭta.*** I was watching the horse race.
競馬 を 見て いました.　(*keibá* 競馬 horse race)

*Soréra no kodomotachí wa kudámono wo **tábete imásŭ.*** Those children
それ等 の 子供達 は 果物 を 食べて います. are eating fruit.

Jimúsho kará kaerimáshĭta tokí ni uchí no monó[1] *wa o-káshi wo **tábete***
事務所 から 帰りました 時 に うちの 者 はお菓子 を 食べて
imáshĭta. When I returned from the office my family were eating cakes.
いました.

---

1 *uchí no monó* the people, the folk, at my home = my family

The **subordinate** of verbs of **Class II** is formed by changing the last syllable of the simple present into different terminations according to the group they belong to.

Progressive Conjugation

	Subordinate	Present	Past
kógu 漕ぐ to row (boat)	*kóide* 漕いで rowing	*kóide imásŭ* 漕いでいます I am rowing	*kóide imáshĭta* 漕いでいました I was rowing
káku 書く to write	*káite* 書いて writing	*káite imásŭ* 書いています I am writing	*káite imáshĭta* 書いていました I was writing
dásu 出す to take out	*dáshĭte* 出して taking out	*dáshĭte imásŭ* 出しています I am taking out	*dáshĭte imáshĭta* 出していました I was taking out
kasú 貸す to loan, rent	*kashĭté* 貸して renting	*kashĭté imásŭ* 貸しています I am renting	*kashĭté imáshĭta* 貸していました I was renting
tátsu 立つ to stand	*tátte* 立って standing	*tátte imásŭ* 立っています I am standing	*tátte imáshĭta* 立っていました I was standing
mátsu 待つ to wait	*mátte* 待って waiting	*mátte imásŭ* 待っています I am waiting	*mátte imáshĭta* 待っていました I was waiting
tobú 飛ぶ to fly	*tondé* 飛んで flying	*tondé imásŭ* 飛んでいます I am flying	*tondé imáshĭta* 飛んでいました I was flying
yómu 読む to read	*yónde* 読んで reading	*yónde imásŭ* 読んでいます I am reading	*yónde imáshĭta* 読んでいました I was reading
shinu[1] 死ぬ to die	*shindé* 死んで dying	*shindé imásŭ* 死んでいます He is dead	*shindé imáshĭta* 死んでいました He was dead
áru ある to be	*átte* あって being	Not used with *imásŭ* or *orimásŭ* います おります	
urú 売る to sell	*utté* 売って selling	*utté imásŭ* 売っています I am selling	*utté imáshĭta* 売っていました I was selling
yabúru 破る to tear	*yabútte* 破って tearing	*yabútte imásŭ* 破っています I am tearing	*yabútte imáshĭta* 破っていました I was tearing

(Groups numbered in the margin: 1, 2, 3, 4, 5)

---

1 The verb *shinú* followed by *imásŭ* or *imáshĭta* indicates a condition. The progressive conjugation of *shinú* is formed with the subordinate of the verb *kakáru* かかる *to be about to, to be impending. Shiní kakátte imásŭ* I am dying; *Shiní kakátte imáshĭta* I was dying. Note that *shinú* is the only Japanese verb ending in *nu.*

iŭ 云う to say	*itté* 云って saying	*itté imásŭ* 云っています I am saying	*itté imáshĭta* 云っていました I was saying
kaŭ 買う to buy	*katté* 買って buying	*katté imásŭ* 買っています I am buying	*katté imáshĭta* 買っていました I was buying

6

Note that the verbs of *groups* **1, 2, 3, 4,** and **5** drop the last syllable when forming the subordinate, and that the verbs of *group* **1** in *gu* and *group* **4** in *bu, mu* and *nu,* have the subordinate ending in *de* で instead of *te* て. Verbs of *groups* **3, 5,** and **6** have their subordinate termination written with **double** *t.*

See **phonetic rules** on subordinate forms, Page 656.

Examples

Náni wo káite imásŭ ka. 何を書いていますか. What are you writing?

Tomodachí ni tegamí wo káite imásŭ. 友達 に 手紙 を 書いて います. I am writing a letter to a friend.

Sensêi ga irasshaimáshĭta[1] tokí ni watashí wa Nihón-go no renshū 先生 がいらっしゃいました時 に 私 は 日本語 の 練習 *mondaí wo káite imáshĭta.* When my teacher arrived I was writing 問題 を 書いて いました. my Japanese language exercise.

Keikán ga ítsumo anó tatémono no máe ni tátte imásŭ. 警官 が いつも あの 建物 の 前 に 立って います. A policeman is always standing before that building.

Asa háyaku kará imá-máde anáta wo mátte imáshĭta. 朝 早く から 今迄 貴方 を 待って いました. I have been waiting for you from early morning until now.

Gorán nasái! Hikōki ga go-dái[2] watashitachí no ué wo tondé imásŭ. 御覧 なさい! 飛行機 が 五台 私達 の 上 を 飛んで います. Look! Five aeroplanes are flying above us.

Anáta no o-jōsan wa sŭkóshi máe ni o-heyá de hon wo yónde imáshĭta. 貴方 のお嬢さんは 少し 前 に お部屋で 本 を 読んで いました. Your daughter was reading a book in her room a little while ago.

Anó otokó wa kutsushĭtá wo taihén yásuku utté imásŭ. あの 男 は 靴下 を 大変 安く 売って います. That man is selling socks very cheap.

Anó fujín wa náni wo itté imáshĭta ka. What was that lady saying? あの 婦人 は 何 を云って いました か.

Kiité imasén déshĭta. 聞いていませんでした. I was not listening.

The **subordinate** of *surú* する (to do, *irr. verb*) is *shĭté* して.

---

1 *Irrasháru* いらっしゃる "to go" *or* "to come" is a polite verb used for the 2nd and 3rd persons. See lesson 35, page 262. **2** *dái* is the numerative used for counting aeroplanes or cars

Anáta wa náni wo shǐté imásǔ ka.   What are you doing?
貴方 は 何 を して います か.

Benkyō shǐté imásǔ.   勉強しています.   I am studying.

Another form of *progressive present*, used in ordinary conversation, is obtained by using *irǔ no désǔ* いるのです or *óru no désǔ* おるのです instead of *imásǔ* います or *orimásǔ* おります after the subordinate. *No désǔ* のです after *irǔ* いる or *óru* おる is sometimes omitted in vulgar speech.

Progressive Present Tense

tabéru	*tábete*	*tábete irǔ (óru) no désǔ*
食べる	食べて	食べて いる (おる) の です
to eat	eating	I am eating
káku	*káite*	*káite irǔ (óru) no désǔ*
書く	書いて	書いている(おる) の です
to write	writing	I am writing
mátsu	*mátte*	*mátte irǔ (óru) no désǔ*
待つ	待って	待っている (おる) の です
to wait	waiting	I am waiting

Progressive Past Tense

yómu	*yónde*	*yónde irǔ (óru) no déshǐta*
読む	読んで	読んで いる (おる) の でした
to read	reading	I was reading
urú	*utté*	*utté irǔ (óru) no déshǐta*
売る	売って	売っている (おる)の でした
to sell	selling	I was selling

Anáta wa dónata wo mátte óru no désǔ ka.   Whom are you
貴方 は どなた を 待って おる の です か.   waiting for?

Háha wo mátte irǔ no désǔ.   I am waiting for my mother.
母 を 待って いる の です.

Séito wa miná Eigó no hon wo yónde óru no désǔ.
生徒 は 皆 英語の 本 を 読んで おる の です.
All students are reading English books.

Still another form of progressive conjugation, used in ordinary conversation, is formed by adding to the subordinate *irǔ tokoró désǔ* いるところです or *óru tokoró désǔ* おるところです for the present, and *irǔ tokoró déshǐta* いるところでした or *óru tokoró déshǐta* おるところでした for the past.

Present

tábete irǔ (óru) tokoró désǔ	食べている(おる)ところです	I am eating
káite irǔ (óru) tokoró désǔ	書いている(おる)ところです	I am writing
mátte irǔ (óru) tokoró désǔ	待っている(おる)ところです	I am waiting
yónde irǔ (óru) tokoró désǔ	読んでいる(おる)ところです	I am reading
utté irǔ (óru) tokoró désǔ	売っている(おる)ところです	I am selling

Past

tábete irú (óru) tokoró déshǐta 食べている(おる)ところでした I was eating

káite irú (óru) tokoró déshǐta 書いている(おる)ところでした I was writing

mátte irú (óru) tokoró déshǐta 待っている(おる)ところでした I was waiting

yónde irú (óru) tokoró déshǐta 読んでいる(おる)ところでした I was reading

utté irú (óru) tokoró déshǐta 売っている(おる)ところでした I was selling

*Ima o-kyakǔsamá wa o-cha wo **nónde irú tokoró désǔ.***
今　　お客様　　は　お茶　を　飲んで　いる　ところ　です。
The guests **are** now **drinking** tea.

Yūbe Tanaká San no tokoró e ikimáshǐta tokí (ni) Tanaká San wa
ゆうべ　田中　さん　の　ところ　へ行きました　時　(に)　田中　さん　は
*watashí ni tegamí wo **káite irú tokoró déshǐta.***
私　に　手紙　を　書いて　いる　ところ　でした。
When I went to Mr. Tanaka's last night, he **was writing** a letter to me.

The **subordinate** corresponds also to the **perfect participle** of English verbs:

míru	見る	to see	*míte*	見て	seeing, having seen
tabéru	食べる	to eat	*tábete*	食べて	eating, having eaten
nómu	飲む	to drink	*nónde*	飲んで	drinking, having drunk
oerú	終える	to finish	*oeté*	終えて	finishing, having finished
táipu de útsu タイプで打つ		to typewrite	*táipu de útte* タイプで打って		typing, having typed

(*táipu* タイプ short for *typewriter, de* で with, *útsu* 打つ to strike)

*Shigotó wo **oeté** dekakemáshǐta.* 仕事を終えて出かけました.
I finished the work and went out. (*lit.* The work having finished, I went out.)

*Kusurí wo **nónde** nemáshǐta.* 薬を飲んで寝ました.
I drank the medicine and went to bed.
(*lit.* The medicine having drunk, went to bed.)

*Tegamí wo táipu de **útte** shiháinin ni watashimáshǐta.*
手紙　を　タイプ　で　打って　支配人　に　渡しました.
I typewrote the letter and gave it to the manager.
(*lit.* The letter with typewriter having struck, to the manager handed.)

The subordinate of verbs is also formed by adding *máshǐte* **まして,** instead of *te* **て,** to the simple stem of verbs of Class I, and to the *i*-stem of verbs of Class II.

míru	見る	to see	*mi*	見	*mimáshǐte*	見まして	=*míte* 見て
káku	書く	to write	*kaki*	書	*kakimáshǐte*	書きまして	=*káite* 書いて

The subordinate with *máshǐte* **まして** may be used in place of the shorter form with the termination *te* **て** in all cases except

to form the progressive conjugation. The subordinate with *máshĭte*
is more polite than the shorter form with *te.*

Dōmo o-jamá wo itashimáshĭte sumimasén.[1]   I am sorry to disturb you.
どうも お邪广 を 致しまして すみません。
(*lit.* Much obstruction having made, it is unpardonable.)

This sentence is very much used by Japanese, and corresponds to the
English *excuse me, I beg your pardon for interrupting you, for giving you
trouble,* and similar expressions.

Subordinate followed by *arimásŭ.*

The subordinate may be followed by *arimásŭ* あります instead
of *imásŭ* います. In this case, however, instead of expressing
a progressive action, the construction with *arimásŭ* あります
expresses a condition that is the result of an action, which in
English may be expressed by *to be* and an adjectival participle or
by a passive perfect tense.

The following comparative examples will show the different function of *imásŭ* and *arimásŭ* placed *after a subordinate.*

1) *O-tétsudai wa anáta no heyá wo sōji shĭté imásŭ.*   The maid **is cleaning**
お手伝い は 貴方 の 部屋を 掃除 して います   your room.
Anáta no heyá wa sōji shĭté arimásŭ.   Your room **is cleaned.**
貴方 の 部屋 は 掃除 して あります.   Your room **has been cleaned.**

2) *Hon wo katazŭkete*[2] *imásŭ.*   I **am putting** the books in good order.
本 を 片づけて います.
Hon wa katazŭkete[2] *arimásŭ.*   The books **are** (put) in good order.
本 は 片づけて あります.   The books **have been put** in good order.

3) *Gakŭséi ga haná wo katté imásŭ.*   The students **are buying** flowers.
学生 が 花 を 買つて います.
Haná wa katté arimásŭ.   The flowers **are bought.**
花 は 買つて あります.   The flowers **have been bought.**

4) *Mómban wa mon ni kagí*[3] *wo kákete imásŭ.*   The gatekeeper **is lock-**
門番 は 門 に 鍵 を かけて います.   **ing** the gate.
Mon ni kagí ga kákete arimásŭ.   The gate **is locked up.**
門 に 鍵 が かけて あります.   The gate **has been locked up.**

5) *Kókku wa nikú wo kizandé*[4] *imásŭ.*   The cook **is chopping** the meat.
コック は 肉 を きざんで います.
Nikú wa kizandé arimásŭ.   The meat **is chopped.**
肉 は きざんで あります.   The meat **has been chopped.**

If the condition is to be expressed in the *past* or in the *negative,*
the **past** or **negative** form of *arimásŭ* is used accordingly.

---

1 *o-jamá wo itasú* お邪广を致す to cause disturbance; *sumánai* 済まない to be
unpardonable; *sumimasén* 済みません I am sorry 2 *katazukéru* 片づける to put
(things, room) in order 3 ......*ni kagí wo kakéru*...... に鍵をかける to lock (*ni* to,
kagí key or lock, *kakéru* to apply, to put) 4 *kizamú* to chop

1) *O-tétsudai wa anáta no heyá wo sōji shĭté imáshĭta.*   The maid **was clean-**
お手伝い は 貴方 の 部屋 を 掃除 して いました.   **ing** your room.

Anáta no heyá wa sōji shĭté arimáshĭta.   Your room **was cleaned.**
貴方 の 部屋 は 掃除 して ありました.   Your room **had been cleaned.**

2) *Hon wo katazúkete imáshĭta.*   I **was putting** the books in good order.
本 を 片づけて いました.

Hon wa katazúkete arimáshĭta.   The books **were** in good order.
本 は 片づけて ありました   The books **had been put** in good order.

3) *Mómban wa mon ni kagí wo kákete imáshĭta.*   The gatekeeper **was**
門番 は 門 に 鍵 を かけて いました.   **locking** the gate.

Mon ni kagí ga kákete arimáshĭta.   The gate **was locked.**
門 に 鍵 が かけて ありました.   The gate **had been locked.**

The *subordinate* followed by **arimásŭ** may also indicate a simple
fact or condition that is not the result of an action, as in the following example.

Anó tatéfuda ni nan to káite arimásŭ ka.   What **is written** on that
あの 立札 に 何んと 書いて あります か.   board?

"Konó tochí urimonó" to káite arimásŭ.   It **is written**: "This plot
この 土地 売物 と 書いて あります.   of land is for sale."

Vocabulary

Nouns			Verbs		
accountant	*kaikeí-gakarí*	会計係	to be in a hurry	*isóide irú*	急イデイル
construction	*kenchikú*	建築	to cry	*nakú*	泣ク
contractor	*ukeóinin*	請負人	to frighten	*odorokásu*	オドロカス
custom	*fūshū*	風習	to give up	*yame·rú*	止メル
idea	*mokutekí*	目的	to make	*koshirae·rú*	コシラエル
motor-boat	*mōtā-bōto*	モーターボート	to prepare	*yōi surú*	用意イスル
photograph	*shashín*	写真	to return	*káeru*	帰ル
postman	*yūbin-ya*[1]	郵便屋		Adverbs	
	yūbin-haitatsufú	郵便配達夫	about	}*bákari* (suffix)	バカリ
race	*kyōsō*	競走	excitedly	*kōfun shĭte*	興奮シテ
to run a race	*kyōsō surú*	競走スル			

Exercise *Renshū* 練習

1. Sonó heyá de náni wo shĭté imásŭ ka.—Shashín wo genzō shĭté[2] imásŭ.
2. Anáta no otōsan wa dóko ni imásŭ ka.—Niwá de shimbún wo yónde
imásŭ. **3.** Soshĭté anáta no ojōsan wa.—Musŭmé wa heyá de jibún no kimonó
wo koshiraeté imásŭ. **4.** Góran nasái! San-zō[3] no mōtā-bōto ga kyōsō shĭté

---

1 *yūbin-ya* (colloq.)   2 *genzō surú* to develop (negatives films)   3 *zō* 艘 is the
numerative for ships; *sō* is pronounced *zō* after *san*

imásŭ. **5.** Náze sonná ni háyaku arúite imásŭ ka.—Isói de orimásŭ nóde.
6. Náze anáta no gakká wo benkyō shimasén ka.—Mō benkyō shǐté shimaimáshǐta. **7.** Anó kōjō de nan-nin no otokó ga hataraité imásŭ ka.—Go-jū
nin bákari[1] hataraité imásŭ. **8.** Anó hǐtó-bitó wa náni-go de hanáshǐte imásŭ
ka.—Chōsen-go de hanáshǐte imásŭ. **9.** Dáre ga anáta wo yondé imásu ka.
—Háha ga watashí wo yondé imásŭ. Háha wa shokudō de shokutakú no
yōi wo shǐté imásŭ. **10.** Dáre ga anáta ni hanáshǐte imáshǐta ka.—Yūbin-ya
ga hanáshǐte imáshǐta. **11.** Sakúban (yūbe) o-takú de dónata ga anná ni otó
wo tátete imáshǐta ka.—Yūbe, takú de wa dáre mo otó wo tátete imasén
déshǐta. Go-rokú nin no tomodachí ga dánsu[2] wo shǐté imáshǐta. **12.** Aréra
no rōdōshatachi wa anó furúi tatémono no sóto de náni wo shǐté imáshǐta ka.—
Arérano hǐtotachí wa atarashíi ginkō wo kenchikú surú tokoró no ukeóinin wo
mátte imáshǐta. **13.** Kōchō-senséi[3] ga warewaré no kumí e háitte kitá tokí ni
séito wa minná tátte imáshǐta. **14.** Anáta no ákachan wa náze naité imáshǐta
ka.—Uchí no inú ga odorokáshǐta no désŭ. **15.** Watashí ga shiháinin no jimu-
shitsú e háitta tokí ni, shiháinin wa kōfun shǐté[4] kaikéi-gákari ni hanáshǐte
imáshǐta. **16.** Dáre ka watashí wo yondé imáshǐta ka.—Dáre mo yondé imasén
déshǐta. **17.** Kyónen anáta wa Shiná-go wo benkyō shǐte imasén déshǐta ka.
—Hái, Shiná-go wo benkyō shǐté imasén déshǐta. Chōsen-go wo benkyō shǐté
imáshǐta. Watashí wa Chōsen no fūshū wo kenkyū[5] surú tamé ni ni-nen
kan achirá e ikú tsumorí déshǐta. Kéredomo Tōkyō de amarí isogáshiku
narimáshǐta nóde achirá e ikú kangáe wo yamemáshǐta.

1. その部屋で何をしていますか.―写真を現像しています. **2.** 貴方
のお父さんはどこにいますか.―庭で新聞を読んでいます. **3.** そして
貴方のお嬢さんは.―娘は部屋で自分の着物をこしらえています.
4. 御覧なさい！三艘のモーターボートが競争しています. **5.** なぜそ
んなに速く歩いていますか.―急いでおりますので. **6.** なぜ貴方の学
課を勉強しませんか.―もう勉強してしまいました. **7.** あの工場で何
人の男が仂いていますか.―五十人ばかり仂いています. **8.** あの人々
は何語で話していますか.―朝鮮語で話しています. **9.** 誰が貴方を呼
んでいますか.―母が私を呼んでいます. 母は食堂で食卓の用意をして
います. **10.** 誰が貴方に話していましたか.―郵便屋が話していまし
た. **11.** 昨晩（ゆうべ）お宅でどなたがあんなに音を立てゝいました
か.―ゆうべ宅では誰も音を立てゝいませんでした. 五六人の友達がダ
ンスをしていました. **12.** あれ等の労仂者達はあの古い建物の外で何
をしていましたか.――あれ等の人達は新らしい銀行を建築するところ
の請負人を待っていました. **13.** 校長先生が我々の組へ入って来た時
に生徒はみんな立っていました. **14.** 貴方の赤ちゃんはなぜ泣いてい
ましたか.―うちの犬がおどろかしたのです. **15.** 私が支配人の事務室

---

1 *bákari* about   2 *dánsu* foreign social dance ; *odorí* 踊り Japanese native dance
3 *kōchō-senséi* director of a school   4 *kōfun surú* to be excited   5 *kenkyū surú*
to study, to make scientific researches

へ入った時に支配人は興奮して会計係に話していました. **16.** 誰か私
を呼んでいましたか. ―誰も呼んでいませんでした. **17.** 去年貴方は
支那語を勉強していませんでしたか.―はい, 支那語を勉強していませ
んでした. 朝鮮語を勉強していました. 私は朝鮮の風習を研究するた
めに二年間あちらへ行くつもりでした. けれども東京であまり忙しく
なりましたのであちらへ行く考えをやめました.

1. What are you doing in that room?—I am developing films (photo-
graph.) 2. Where is your father?—He is in the garden reading the newspaper.
3. And where is your daughter?—She is in her room making a kimono for
herself. 4. Look! Three motor-boats are running a race. 5. Why are you
walking so fast?—Because I am in a hurry. 6. Why are you not studying
your lesson?—I have studied it already. 7. How many men are working in
that factory?—About fifty men are working there. 8. What language are
those people speaking?—They are speaking Korean. 9. Who is calling you?
—My mother is calling me. She is in the dining-room preparing the table
for dinner. 10. Who was speaking to you?—The postman was speaking to
me. 11. Who was making so much noise in your house last night?—Nobody
was making noise in my house last night. A few friends of mine were dancing. 12. What were all those workmen doing outside that old building?—
They were waiting for the contractor who is to construct the new bank.
13. When the director of the school entered our class all the students were
standing. 14. Why was your baby crying?—Our dog frightened it.
15. When I entered my manager's office, he was speaking excitedly to our
accountant. 16. Was anybody calling me?—Nobody was calling you.
17. Were you not studying Chinese last year?—No, I was not studying
Chinese; I was studying Korean. I intended to go to Korea to study the
customs of the country for two years. However, as I have become too
busy here in Tokyo, I have given up my idea of going there.

A Japanese Proverb

Torá wa shindé kawá wo nokóshi, hïtó wa shindé na wo nokósu.
虎 は 死んで 皮 を のこし, 人 は 死んで 名 を のこす
The tiger, on his death, leaves his pelt; man, on his death,
  leaves his name.

(*torá* 虎 tiger; *shindé* 死んで sub. of *shinú* 死ぬ to die; *kawá* 皮 skin,
pelt; *nokóshi* のこし stem of *nokósu* のこす to leave; *na* 名 name, repu-
tation, etc.)

(Translation of the English counterpart: *Man dies but his name remains.*)

Hïtó wa shindé mo na wa nokóru. 人は死んでも名はのこる。

(*lit.* Man, even dying *or* also after death, his name remains.)

Twenty-fourth Lesson　第廿四課

The Subordinate (continued)

In the previous lesson we have shown **four ways to form** the progressive conjugation:

1. *Ima minná wa kyakumá de* **odotté imásŭ.**
   今　皆　は　客間　で　踊って　います.

2. *Ima minná wa kyakumá de* **odotté irŭ.**
   今　皆　は　客間　で　踊って　いる.

3. *Ima minná wa kyakumá de* **odotté irŭ no désŭ.**
   今　皆　は　客間　で　踊って　いる　の　です.

4. *Ima minná wa kyakumá de* **odotté irŭ tokoró désŭ.**
   今　皆　は　客間　で　踊って　いる　ところ　です.

Everybody **is** now **dancing** in the parlour.

Now, by adding to the **simple present** of a verb the expression *tokoró désŭ* for the present and *tokoró déshĭta* for the past, the Japanese convey the idea of the **immediate future** as expressed in English by *to be going to, to be just going to, to be about to, to be on the point of*, and kindred forms. Examples:

1. In the parlour the musicians are about to play and the people are waiting for the music to start. I am outside the parlour with a friend of mine, but as I wish to see the people begin their dancing, I say to him:

Kyakumá e mairimashō; íma minná ga odorŭ tokoró désŭ.
客間　へ　参りましょう.　今　皆　が　踊る　ところ　です.

Let's go to the parlour; everybody is now **going to dance.**

N.B. *Máiru* 参る is a humble verb used by the first person when speaking to one's superiors or when referring to persons of lower social standing, as one's servants, for instance, and it corresponds to the ordinary verb *ikŭ* 行く *to go* or *kŭru* 来る *to come.* See page 162. *Ga* is used after *minná* instead of *wa,* as in the four previous sentences, because the subject (in this case *everybody—minná*) stands more prominent in the thought of the speaker than the predicate *is now going to dance.* See Lesson 28, page 189 on *Wa* and *Ga.*

2. Suppose you are going to pay a visit to Mr. X., and that upon arriving at the door of his house he opens it and appears in front of you, as if intending to leave his home. A little surprised you say to him:

Oya, o-dekaké ni nárū tokoró désŭ ka.　　Oh, are you going out?
おや, お出かけ　に　なる　ところ　です　か.

Hái. dekakerŭ tokoró désŭ.　　Yes, I am going out.
はい. 出かける　ところ　です.

O-dekaké ni náru is the polite form for *dekakerŭ* 出かける *to go out.*

O-shokují¹ wa sumimáshĭta ka.   Have you finished your meal?
お食事 は 済みました か.   Have you had your dinner, etc.

Iié, korekará hajimerú tokoró désŭ.   No, I am now
いゝえ、これから 始める ところ です.   **going to start.**

Watashí wa shigotó wo oemáshĭta; sampó ni dekakerú tokoró désŭ.
私 は 仕事 を終えました. 散歩 に 出かける ところ です.
I have finished my work; I am (now) **going out** for a walk.

Yūbe Suzukí San ga takú e kimáshĭta tokí ni watashí wa chōdo
ゆうべ 鈴木 さん が 宅 へ 来ました 時 に 私 は 丁度
nerú tokoró déshĭta.   When Mr. Suzuki came home last night
寝る ところ でした.   **I was** just **going to bed.**

The expression **to have just finished** (followed by a gerund) is also translated by *tokoró désŭ* or *déshĭta.*

3. Suppose you have been taking a bath and are now coming out of the tub, or that, having come out of it, you are about to dry or are drying your body. Someone of your family asks you whether you have finished your bath:

O-fúro wa sumimáshĭta ka.   Have you finished your bath?
お風呂 は 済みました か.

and you answer:

Ima agarú tokoró désŭ. 今あがるところです.   **I have just come out.**

or *Ima fúro kará déru tokoró désŭ.*   I have just come out of the bath.
今 風呂 から 出る ところ です.

(*agarú* あがる to come up, to rise, to ascend.—In the above example, the use of this verb gives the idea of *rising from the water.*)

Even if a part of your body is still in the water, as you are coming out, you may use either of the two answers given above.

In some cases, to indicate an action that is taking place at the moment we speak, one may use either the immediate future, formed with *tokoró désŭ,* or the present tense, while in English only the progressive tense is used. This occurs especially when the statement indicating the progressive action is connected with some previous occurrence or arrangement:

O-kyakŭsamá ga kimásŭ. or *O-kyakŭsamá ga kúru tokoró désŭ.*
お客様 が 来ます.   お客様 が 来る ところ です.
The guests are coming.

What is said in the above sentence is evidently connected with some previous arrangement. In fact, to say "The guests are coming," indicates that we must have been expecting them, following some previous understanding that they would come.

When in English the expression **to be going to,** followed by a verb, refers to a pending action, the present tense is used in Japanese:

Ashĭtá Ōsaka e ikimásŭ.   To-morrow I am going to Osaka.
あした 大阪 へ 行きます.   To-morrow I shall go to Osaka.

---

1 *Shokují* 食事 means *meal* and may be used to translate any of the words *breakfast, lunch,* or *dinner.*

Kómban watashí wa Nihón-go no senséi wo tazunemásŭ.

今晩　　私　　は　日本語　の　先生　を　　訪ねます.

To-night I am going to visit my Japanese teacher.

(*tazunéru* 訪ねる to call on a person, at a house; to visit)

Often the Japanese subordinate, followed by a verb, forms an expression corresponding in meaning to a single English verb:

déte ikú	出て行く	= *déru*	to go out
déte kúru	出て来る	= *déru*	to come out
káette kúru	帰って来る	= *káeru*	to return
kurabeté míru	比べてみる	= *kuraberú*	to compare
mótte kúru	持って来る		to bring
tótte kúru	取って来る		to fetch
tsureté ikú	連れて行く		to take, to lead to ⎫ person or
tsureté kúru	連れて来る		to bring with ⎭ animal

Examples

Senséi wa kyōshitsu kará déte ikimáshĭta.   Our teacher went

先生　は　　教室　　から　出て　行きました.   out of[1] the class room.

Anáta wa ítsu Ōsaka kará káette kimáshĭta ka.

貴方　は　いつ　大阪　から　帰って　来ました　か.

When did you return from Osaka?

Sakúban tsúma to isshó ni káette kimáshĭta.   I came back last

昨晩　　妻　と　一緒　に　帰って　来ました.   night with my wife.

Júnsa wa dorobō wo keisatsú e tsureté ikimáshĭta.

巡査　は　泥棒　を　　警察　へ　連れて　行きました.

The policeman took the thief to the police station.

The subordinate followed by a verb corresponds at times to English expressions formed by a verb and a present participle or an adverb:

Arúite kimáshĭta.	歩いて来ました.	I came walking.
Hashítte ikimáshĭta.	走って行きました.	He went running.
Naité hanashimáshĭta.	泣いて話しました.	He spoke crying.
Yorokónde tabemáshĭta.	喜んで食べました.	He ate gladly.

There are some verbs which, when used in the subordinate with *imásŭ,* *orimásŭ* or the less polite verbal forms *irú* or *óru,* do not indicate progressive tenses, but denote a condition resulting from an action. The most common of these verbs are:

dekakerú 出かける	*dekaketé imásŭ*	出かけています ⎫ he is out
to go out	*dekaketé irú*	出かけている ⎭
dekíru 出来る	*dékite imásŭ*	出来ています ⎫ it is ready,
to be done, ready	*dékite irú*	出来ている ⎭ done, completed

---

1 To go out of = to go out from (in Japanese)

déru	出る	*déte imásŭ*	出ています	it is out (buds, leaves, etc.)
to go out, come out		*déte irú*	出ている	he is out
káeru	帰る	*káette imásŭ*	帰っています	he is back
to return		*káette irú*	帰っている	he has returned
kúru	来る	*kité imásŭ*	来ています	he is here
to come		*kité irú*	来ている	he has come
shinú	死ぬ	*shindé imásŭ*	死んでいます	he is dead
to die		*shindé irú*	死んでいる	
ikú	行く	*itté imásŭ*	行っています	he is out
to go		*itté irú*	行っている	he has gone

N. B. For brevity, the forms with *orimásŭ* and *óru* have been omitted.

Examples

1. *Watashí ga o-ishá no uchí e ikimáshĭta tokí ni o-ishá wa dekaketé*
私 が お医者 の 家 へ 行きました 時 に お医者 は 出かけて
imáshĭta.   When I went to the doctor's house he was out.
いました.

Otōsan wa orimásŭ ka.—Iié, dekaketé orimásŭ.   Is your father in?—
お父さん は おります か.—いゝえ, 出かけております.   No, he is out.

Dáiku wa máda kimasén ka.—Iié, kité imásŭ.
大工 は まだ 来ません か.—いゝえ, 来ています.
Haven't the carpenters come yet?—Yes, they are here. (*or* They have come.)

2. *Yōfukuya ni ikimáshĭta tokí ni watashí no atarashíi yōfuku wa máda*
洋服屋 に行きました 時 に 私 の 新しい 洋服 は まだ
dékite imasén déshĭta.   When I went to the tailor's my new suit was
出来て いません でした.   not yet finished.

3. *Otōsan wa dóchira ni ikimáshĭta ka.—Éiga ni itté imásŭ.*
お父さん は どちら に 行きました か.—映画 に行っています.
Where did your father go?—He has gone to (*or* He is at) the cinema.

In Lesson 15, it has been said that the preposition **to,** indicating *motion to* or *towards a place*, is translated by *e* へ, as in the first example above (**1**). **To,** however, may also be translated by *ni* に, as in the last two examples (**2** and **3**), and the difference in the use of the two postposition is the following: When a place we go to is considered in its material sense, the postposition *e* へ is used, while *ni* に is used when a place is considered in its abstract sense, that is, when it is considered as the seat of the activity or purpose it is used for.

In example **1** then, *the doctor's house* is considered as a dwelling and not the place where the doctor performs his profession, in which case *e* へ is used to translate **to**; in example **2** one refers to the tailor's working establishment and not his dwelling, which may be somewhere else, and in example **3**, in answering *He has gone to the cinema.*, it is understood that *the father* went there to see the show and not the building where it is held.

What has been said above is the rule as it should be. However, as this rule is not strictly observed, the postposition *e* へ is sometimes used instead of *ni* に.

Both the progressive conjugation of the above verbs and their immediate future meaning *to be going to, to be on the point of, to be about to......*, etc. are formed only with *tokoró désŭ.*

déru tokoró désŭ	出るところです	{ he is going out { he is about to go out
déru tokoró déshĭta	出るところでした	he was going out, etc.
dekíru tokoró désŭ	出来るところです	it is being completed, etc.
dekíru tokoró déshĭta	出来るところでした	it was almost ready, etc.
kúru tokoró désŭ	来るところです	he is coming, etc.
shinú tokoró désŭ	死ぬところです	he is dying, etc.
ikú tokoró désŭ	行くところです	he is going to (a place)
ikú tokoró déshĭta	行くところでした	he was about to go to......

For brevity's sake only the third person singular is given as translations of the above Japanese expressions.

To Go and To Come

Ikú or *yukú* 行く and *kúru* 来る, as we have shown with various examples, ordinarily mean *to go* and *to come*, both of which verbs may also be translated by *máiru* 参る or *irassháru* いらっしゃる.

As both *máiru* and *irassháru* express the double idea of *to go* and *to come*, it is only from the context that one can understand the intended meaning.

Irassháru is an honorific verb used when politely speaking to the second or of a third person, even though the person spoken to and the one spoken of may not be of higher social rank.

Note that polite speech is also used in Japanese when speaking of, or to one's own parents, elder brothers and sisters, and elder relatives.

Máiru 参る is a humble verb used when speaking of oneself, or when speaking of a third person towards whom there is no necessity to use polite speech.

People towards whom polite speech is not necessary are one's own sons, younger brothers and sisters, servants, small shopkeepers and their clerks, and still lower class people. Examples:

Isshūkan ni nan-do Nihón-go gakkō e irasshaimásŭ ka. (pol. speech)
一週間 に 何度 日本語 学校 へ いらっしゃいますか。
How many times a week do you **go** to the Japanese language school?

Isshūkan ni san-do mairimásŭ.   I **go** there three times a week.
一週間 に 三度 参ります.

Itsu matá irasshaimásŭ ka.   When will you **come** again?
いつ また いらっしゃいますか。

*Raishū matá **mairimásu**.* 来週　また　参ります.	I shall **come** again next week.
*Senséi wa dóko e **irasshaimáshĭta** ka.* 先生　は　どこ　へいらっしゃいましたか.	Where **did** the teacher **go**?
*Kōchō-shitsú e **irasshaimáshĭta**.* 校長　室　へいらっしゃいました.	He **went** to the director's room.

*Kinō dóchira e **irasshaimáshĭta** ka.* きのうどちら　へいらっしゃいましたか. *Kinō dóchira e **ikimáshĭta** ka.* きのうどちら　へ　行きました　か.	Where **did** you **go** yesterday?
*Yokohamá e **mairimáshĭta**.* 横浜　へ　　参りました. *Yokohamá e **ikimáshĭta**.* 横浜　へ　行きました.	I **went** to Yokohama.

*Kodomotachí wa dóko e **mairimáshĭta** ka.* 子供達　は　どこへ　　参りました　か.	Where **did** my children **go**?
*Hibiyá Kōen e **irasshaimáshĭta**.* 日比谷　公園　へいらっしゃいました.	They **went** to Hibiya Park.

The last sentence ending in the polite verb *irasshaimáshĭta* いらっしゃいました, is supposed to have been expressed by a servant speaking to his or her master or by a person of equal or lower social standing answering an enquiry.

*O-tétsudai wa dóko e **mairimáshĭta** ka.* お手伝い　は　どこへ　　参りました　　か. *O-tétsudai wa dóko e **ikimáshĭta** ka.* お手伝い　は　どこへ　行きました　か.	Where **did** the servant **go**?
*Ichiba e kaimonó ni **mairimáshĭta**.* 市場　へ　買物　に　参りました. *Ichiba e kaimonó ni **ikimáshĭta**.* 市場　へ　買物　に　行きました.	She **went** to the market for shopping.

Idiomatic Use of *irasshái*

Irasshái. いらっしゃい.	Come here. Welcome.
Matá irasshái. またいらっしゃい.	Please come again.
Yóku irasshaimáshĭta. よくいらっしゃいました.	I am pleased to see you. You are welcome.
Mátte irasshái. 待っていらっしゃい.	Please wait.
Anáta wa dónata de irasshaimásu ka. 貴方　は　どなた　でいらっしゃいますか.	Who are you? Whom have I the honour of addressing?
Go-shújin wa irasshaimásu ka. 御主人　はいらっしゃいますか.	Is your master in?

Hái, irasshaimásŭ. はい、いらっしゃいます．　Yes, he is in.

Ima shimbún wo yónde irasshaimásŭ. He is now reading the newspaper.
今，新聞を読んでいらっしゃいます．　(Speaking of a superior.)

Vocabulary

Nouns					
			prayer	*inorí*	祈リ
branch (of tree)	*edá*	枝エダ	seat	*séki*	席セキ
brim	*fuchí*	縁フチ	**Verbs**		
clerk[1]	⎰*jimúin*	事務員ジムイン	to begin	*hajime·rú*	始ハジメル
	⎱*ten-in*	店員テンイン	to burn ⎰tr.	*moyasú*	燃モヤス
crater	*kakō*	火口カコウ		⎱intr.	*moe·rú*	燃モエル
guide	*annaishá*	案内者アンナイシャ	to go back	*modóru*	戻モドル
manager	*shiháinin*	支配人シハイニン	to hurry	*isógu*	急イソグ
parlour	⎰*kyakumá*	客間キャクマ	to leave[2]	*dé·ru*	出デル
	⎱*ōsetsuma*	応接間オウセツマ	to treat	*taigū surú*	待遇タイグウスル

in such a hurry *sonná ni isói-de* そんなに急いで; to say one's prayers *o-inorí wo surú* お祈りをする; to go to pray at a temple, to visit a temple *o-mairí ni ikú* お詣りに行く; to go shopping *kaimonó ni ikú* 買物に行く．

Exercise　*Renshū* 練習

1. Isogí nasái! Resshá ga hasshá surú tokoró désŭ yo.[3]　**2.** Kinō tōri de o-me ni kakátta[4] tokí anáta wa dóchira e irassháru tokoró déshĭta ka.—Tomo-dachí no Inoué San no tokoró e ikú tokoró déshĭta.　**3.** Shízuka ni[5] nasái! Senséi ga kimásŭ yo!　**4.** Sonná ni isói-de dóko e ikú no désŭ ka.—Jimúsho e ikú tokoró désŭ.　**5.** O-ishá ga kúru tokoró désŭ.　**6.** Sā![6] Séki e modori-mashō! Ongakú ga íma hajimarú tokoró désŭ.　**7.** Sakúban anáta no go-ryōshin ga takú e irasshaimáshĭta tokí ni watashí wa chōdo éki e ikú tokoró déshĭta.　**8.** Anó jishín ga okótta[7] tokí watashitachí wa yū no o-inorí wo shĭté itá[8] tokoró déshĭta.　**9.** Sonó néko wo dóko e tsureté[9] ikú no désŭ ka.—Byōki désŭ kará byōin e tsureté ikú tokoró désŭ.　**10.** Ráigetsu watashí wa Chūgoku e ikimásŭ.　**11.** Itsu atarashíi jidōsha wo kaú no désŭ ka.[10]—Raishū kaimásŭ.

---

1 *Jimúin* is a clerk of an office; *ten-in* is a clerk of a store.　**2** to leave, said of trains, *hasshá surú* 発車する; of ships *shuppán surú* 出帆する; *déru* 出る may be used for both trains and ships　**3** In familiar speech *yo* is sometimes put at the end of a sentence to render it emphatic.　**4** *o-me ni kakátta=o-me ni kakarimáshĭta；o-me ni kakáru* お目にかゝる to meet (somebody)　**5** *shízuka ni* quietly: *nasái* imperative of *nasáru* なさる, to do　**6** *Sā!* Come! Come now!　**7** *okótta=okori-máshĭta*　**8** *shĭté itá=*were doing, were saying　**9** *tsureté* subord. of *tsurerú* 連れる, to take (with)　**10** *Itsu......kaú no désŭ ka.* lit. "When......to buy, the thing or the fact is?" *No*, after *kaú*, stands for *koto* 事 (the fact, thing.)

12. Dáre ga kúru no désŭ ka.—Kimí no tokoyá ga kúru[1] tokoró désŭ. **13.** Háru wa ki no edá kará mídori no wakába ga demásŭ. **14.** Warewaré ga Kyōto kará káetta[2] tokí ni ié ga yakemáshĭta. **15.** Annaishá wa fŭtarí no Amerikajín no yūrankyakú wo kakō no fuchí e tsureté ikimáshĭta. **16.** Konó depāto no ten-intachí wa miná yorokónde[3] hatarakimásŭ názenaraba shiháinin ga ítsumo minná wo yóku taigū shimásŭ[4] nóde. **17.** Anáta no ojōsan wa dóchira désŭ ka.—Musŭmé wa ikébana no gakkō ni itté imásŭ. **18.** Dónata ga dekakerú no désŭ ka.—Dáre mo dekakemasén.—Déwa dáre ga to wo akemáshĭta ka.—Kazé de akimáshĭta. **19.** Watashí no atarashíi kutsú wa dekiagarimáshĭta[5] ka.—Máda dekiagarimasén. **20.** Náni ka tabetái désŭ. Itsu shokují ni narimásŭ ka.—Súgŭ[6] shĭtakú ga dekíru tokoró désŭ. **21.** Anáta to anáta no okāsan wa ashĭtá dóchira e irasshaimásŭ ka.—Nikkō e o-mairí ni ikimásŭ. **22.** Nára e ittá kotó ga arimásŭ ka.—Máda désŭ. Raishū ikimásŭ. **23.** Anáta wa ítsu Nagasakí kará o-kaerí ni narimáshĭta ka.—Sakúban. **24.** Anáta no otōsan wa máinichi jimúsho e ikimásŭ ka.—Iié, nichiyōbi wa jimúsho e ikimasén. **25.** Okāsan wa o-takú désŭ ka.—Iié, háha wa dekaketé orimásŭ. **26.** Shitsúrei[7] désŭ ga anátasama wa dónata désŭ ka.—Watakŭshí wa Robinson désŭ. **27.** Sangū senséi ni o-hanashí ga shĭtái no désŭ.—Dōzo kokó de chottó o-machí[8] kudasái. **28.** Gurantó San, ikága désŭ ka.—Arigatō, okagesamá de jōbu désŭ.—Dōzo, matá irasshái.

1. 急ぎなさい！列車が発車する所ですよ！ **2.** きのう通りでお目にかかった時貴方はどちらへいらっしゃる所でしたか.—友達の井上さんの所へ行く所でした. **3.** 静かになさい！先生が来ますよ！ **4.** そんなに急いでどこへ行くのですか.—事務所へ行く所です. **5.** お医者が来る所です. **6.** さあ！席へもどりましょう！音楽がいま始まる所です. **7.** 昨晩貴方の御両親が宅へいらっしゃいました時に私は丁度駅へ行く所でした. **8.** あの地震が起った時私達は夕のお祈りをしていた所でした. **9.** その猫をどこへ連れて行くのですか.—病気ですから病院へ連れて行く所です. **10.** 来月私は中国へ行きます. **11.** いつ新しい自動車を買うのですか.—来週買います. **12.** 誰が来るのですか.—君の床屋が来る所です. **13.** 春は木の枝から緑の若葉が出ます. **14.** 我々が京都から帰った時に家が焼けました. **15.** 案内者は二人のアメリカ人の遊覧客を火口の縁へ連れて行きました. **16.** このデパートの店員達は皆喜んで働きますなぜならば支配人がいつも皆をよく待遇しますので. **17.** 貴方のお嬢さんはどちらですか.—娘は活花の

---

1 *Kúru* 来る is the only verb which, followed by the expression *tokoró désŭ* or *tokoró déshita*, indicates progressive action and not immediate future. 2 *káetta*= *kaerimáshĭta* from *káeru* 帰る, to return   3 *yorokónde*=willingly, from *yorokóbu* 喜ぶ, to be glad   4 *taigū surú* 待遇する to treat   5 *dekiagarú* 出来上がる to be ready, to be completed, to be finished   6 *súgu* soon   7 *shitsúrei désŭ ga*......I beg your pardon, but......   8 *O-machí kudasái*. Wait. (polite form)

学校に行っています. **18.** どなたが出かけるのですか.—だれも出か
けません.—ではだれが戸を開けましたか.—風で開きました. **19.** 私
の新しい靴は出来上りましたか.—まだ出来上りません. **20.** 何か食
べたいです. いつ食事になりますか.—すぐ支度が出来る所です.
21. 貴方と貴方のお母さんは明日どちらへいらっしゃいますか.—日光
へお詣りに行きます. **22.** 奈良へ行った事がありますか.—まだです.
来週行きます. **23.** 貴方はいつ長崎からお帰りになりましたか.—昨
晩. **24.** 貴方のお父さんは毎日事務所へ行きますか.—いゝえ, 日曜日
は事務所へ行きません. **25.** お母さんはお宅ですか.—いゝえ, 母は出
かけております. **26.** 失礼ですが貴方様はどなたですか.—私はロビ
ンソンです. **27.** 山宮先生にお話しがしたいのです.—どうぞこゝで
一寸お待ち下さい. **28.** グラントさんいかゞですか.—ありがとうお
かげ様で丈夫です.—どうぞまたいらっしゃい.

1. Hurry up; the train is going to leave. 2. Where were you going when
I met you in the street yesterday?—I was going to see my friend Mr. Inouye.
3. Keep quiet; the teacher is coming. 4. Where are you going in such a
hurry?—I am going to the office. 5. The doctor is coming. 6. Let's go
back to our seats; the music is now going to begin. 7. When your parents
came to visit me last night, I was just going to the station. 8. When the
earthquake occurred we were saying our evening prayers. 9. Where are you
going to take that cat?—I am going to take it to the hospital as it is sick.
10. Next month I am going to China. 11. When are you going to buy the
new motor-car?—I am going to buy it next week. 12. Who is coming?—
Your barber is coming. 13. In spring green leaves come out of the branches
of trees. 14. Our house burned down upon our return from Kyoto. 15. A
guide took the two American tourists to the brim of the crater. 16. All the
clerks of this department store work willingly because the manager always
treats them well. 17. Where is your daughter?—She is at (has gone to) the
flower arrangement school. 18. Who is going out?—Nobody is going out.—
And who opened the door?—The wind opened it. 19. Are my new shoes
ready?—They are not ready yet. 20. I wish to eat something. When will
dinner be ready?—It will be ready soon. 21. Where are you and your
mother going to-morrow?—We are going to visit Nikko temple. 22. Have
you been to Nara?—Not yet. I am going next week. 23. When did you
return from Nagasaki?—Last night. 24. Does your father go to the office
every day?—No, he does not go on Sunday. 25. Is your mother in?—No,
she is out. 26. Whom have I the pleasure of speaking to?—I am Mr.
Robinson. 27. I wish to speak to Professor Sangu.—Please, wait here a
moment. 28. How do you do. Mr. Grant.—Very well, thank you.—Please
come again.

Twenty-fifth Lesson　第廿五課

Negative Subordinate

The negative subordinate is formed by adding **nakute** 無くて or **なくて,** **nai de** 無いで or **ないで,** or **zu ni** ずに to the simple stem of the verbs of Class I, and to the **a**-stem of the verbs of Class II.　The negative subordinate corresponds to the negative present and perfect participle of English verbs, or to the present participle preceded by the adverb *without.*

See **phonetic rules** on the negative subordinate form, Page 681.

Class I

míru 見る	*mi* 見	*mínakute* 見なくて	*mínai de* 見ないで	*mízu ni* 見ずに

not seeing, not having seen / without seeing / without having seen

tabéru 食べる	*tabe* 食べ	*tabénakute* 食べなくて	*tabénai de* 食べないで	*tábezu ni* 食べずに

not eating, not having eaten / without eating / without having eaten

Class II

káku 書く / *kaka* 書か	*kakánakute* 書かなくて / *kakánai de* 書かないで / *kákazu ni* 書かずに	not writing, not having written / without writing / without having written
dásu 出す / *dasa* 出さ	*dasánakute* 出さなくて / *dasánai de* 出さないで / *dásazu ni* 出さずに	not taking *or* putting out / not having taken *or* put out / without taking out, etc.
mótsu 持つ / *mota* 持た	*motánakute* 持たなくて / *motánai de* 持たないで / *mótazu ni* 持たずに	not having, not having had / without having / without having had
yómu 読む / *yoma* 読ま	*yománakute* 読まなくて / *yománai de* 読まないで / *yómazu ni* 読まずに	not reading, not having read / without reading / without having read
yabúru 破る / *yabura* 破ら	*yaburánakute* 破らなくて / *yaburánai de* 破らないで / *yabúrazu ni* 破らずに	not tearing, not having torn / without tearing / without having torn
kaú 買う / *kawa* 買わ	*kawanákute* 買わなくて / *kawanái de* 買わないで / *kawazú ni* 買わずに	not buying, not having bought / without buying / without having bought

Irregular Verbs

surú する	⎰ *shinákute* ⎨ *shinái de* ⎱ *sézu ni*	しなくて しないで せずに	⎰ not doing, not having done ⎨ without doing ⎱ without having done
áru ある	*nákute* *nái de*	無くて 無いで	⎰ there being no...... ⎱ there having been **no**......

Examples

Késa chichí wa shimbún wo yómazu ni jimúsho e dekakemáshĭta.
けさ 父 は 新聞 を 読まず に 事務所 へ 出かけました.
This morning my father went to the office **without reading** the newspaper.

Yūbe zutsū ga shimáshĭta nóde yūhan wo tabénai de nemáshĭta.[1]
ゆうべ 頭痛 が しました ので 夕飯 を 食べない で 寝ました.
As I had a headache last night, I went to bed **without eating** supper.

Taihén isóide orimáshĭta nóde saifú wo mótazu ni dekakemáshĭta.
大変 急い で おりました ので 財布 を 持たず に 出かけました.
As I was in a great hurry I went out **without taking** my purse.

Kodomó wa sŭkóshi byŏki dèsŭ kará kyō wa tsurenái de mairimásŭ.
子供 は 少し 病気 です からきょうは 連れない で 参ります.
As my child is a little ill to-day I shall go out **without taking** it with me.

Benkyō sézu ni manabú kotó wa dekimasén. 勉強せずに学ぶ事は出来ません.
Without studying it is impossible to learn.
    (*lit.* Without studying, to learn, the thing cannot be done.)

Note that the verbal form ending in *zu* ず, as given at the beginning of this lesson, but without the postposition *ni* に, is used in literary style in place of *masén* ません, the ending used to form the negative of the present tense of verbs.

tabéru 食べる	to eat	*tábezu* (=*tabemasén*) 食べず（食べません）	does not *or* do not eat
káku 書く	to write	*kákazu* (=*kakimasén*) 書かず（書きません）	does not *or* do not write
yómu 読む	to read	*yómazu* (=*yomimasén*) 読まず（読みません）	does not *or* do not read

More illustrations of the use of the positive and negative subordinate.

By adding *wa* to the subordinate, an emphasized subordinate is formed. The **emphatic subordinate** corresponds to the emphasized verbs in English.

---

1 *nemáshĭta* past of *nerú* 寝る to sleep, to fall asleep, to go to bed, to go to sleep

Sonná ni rambō ni nímotsu wo **torí-atsŭkatté wa** *náka no monó ga*
そんな に 乱暴 に 荷物 を 取扱って は 中 の 物 が
kowaremásŭ.   If you handle the parcel so roughly its contents will break.
こわれます.   (*lit.* So roughly the parcel handling, the inside things break.)

Isóide **ikanákute wa** *kishá ni maniaimasén.*[1] Unless we hurry we shall
急いで 行かなくて は 汽車 に間にあいません. not catch the train.
    (*lit.* Hurridly without going the train we miss.)

Kō **shĭté wa,** *ikága désŭ ka.*   How would it be if I did it in this way?
こうして は, いかゞ ですか.   (*lit.* This way the doing, how is it?)

    Soré wa kekkō désŭ. それは結構です. That would be all right.

Konná árashi no ban ni **déte itté wa** *abunái désŭ.*
こんな 嵐 の 晩 に 出て行っては 危い です.
    It is dangerous to go out in such a stormy night.
        (*Konná árashi no ban ni* = On such a stormy night)

N. B. The termination *te* て together with *wa* は is pronounced, in familiar
speech, *cha* ちゃ, and *de wa* では, *jā* じゃ.

The subordinate followed by such expressions as *tamarimasén*
堪りません or *tamaranái* 堪らない (not to be endured), *shikatá
ga arimasén* 仕方がありません, *shikatá ga nái* 仕方がない,
shiyō ga arimasén 仕様がありません or *shiyō ga nái* 仕様が
ない (there is nothing to be done, there is no help for it) conveys
the idea of *too, awfully, extremely, unbearably, terribly*, etc.

Note that *tamarimasén* 堪りません or *tamaranái* 堪らない is the negative
form of *tamarŭ* 堪る to bear, to endure, which verb, however, is never used
in the positive form. *Shikatá* (or *shiyō*) *ga arimasén* 仕方 (仕様) があり
ません or *shikatá* (*shiyō*) *ga nái* 仕方 (仕様) がない, translated literally,
corresponds to *a way* or *a method there is not* (*shikatá* 仕方 or *shiyō* 仕様 a
way, a method; *arimasén* ありません there is not).

The termination *imasén* in such expressions is preferable to *nái*.
By adding *désŭ* to *tamaranái, shikatá ga nái* or *shiyō ga nái*, these
expressions become more polite, and are preferable.

Futsŭká kan danjikí wo shĭté imásŭ kará o-naká ga **suité tamarimasén.**
二日 間 断食 をしています から お腹 が 空いて 堪りません.
As I have been fasting for two days I am terribly hungry.
    (*lit.* Two days fast doing am because, the abdomen having become empty,
    cannot endure.—*sŭkú* 空く to become empty, *o-naká ga sŭkú* to be hungry)

Sakúban kará ha ga **ítakute shikatá ga arimasén.**
昨晩 から 歯 が 痛くて 仕方 が ありません.
I have been suffering from a terrible toothache since last night.
    (*lit.* Since last night the teeth having ached, it cannot be endured.)

Kutabírete shiyō ga nái. くたびれて仕様がない.   I am too tired.

─────────────
1 *kishá ni maniáu* to be in time for the train

Nódo ga kawáite[1] tamarimasén.   I am awfully thirsty.
喉　が　かわいて　　堪りません.
      (*lit.* The throat having become dry it cannot be endured.)

The above expressions may also mean **there is no use**...... In this case the subordinate is followed by **mo** も.

Kómban itté mo shikatá ga nái désŭ.   It's no use going to-night.
今晩　行っても　　仕方　が　ない　です.
      (*lit.* To-night, even going, there's no use.)

Naité mo shikatá ga arimasén.   It's no use crying.
泣いて　も　仕方　が　ありません.   (Crying even, there's no use.)

Shimpái shŭté mo shikatá ga nái désŭ.   It's no use worrying.
心配　　して　も　　仕方　が　ない　です.
      (*lit.* Worry doing even, there's no use.)

The expression *shikatá ga arimasén* or *shikatá ga nái*, with or without *désŭ*, is very often used alone in answer to some remark or statement, meaning **There is no help for it.** or **It can't be helped.**

Kómban Kabukizá no kippú wa miná urikiré[2] désŭ.
今晩　歌舞伎座　の　切符　は　皆　売り切れ　です.
To-night all tickets for the Kabuki theatre are sold out.

Shikatá ga arimasén. 仕方がありません.   **It can't be helped.**

The affirmative emphatic subordinate followed by one of the words *ikemasén* いけません, *ikenái* いけない (it will not do), *narimasén* なりません, *naránai* ならない (it is not, it won't do) means **not to be allowed** or **must not.**

Hĭtó no kaó wo mitsumeté wa narimasén.   We must not stare
人　の　顔　を　見つめて　は　なりません.   people in the face.
      (*lit.* People's face the staring is not allowed.—*mitsumerú* 見つめる to stare at)

Sonná ni isóide tábete wa ikemasén.   You **must not eat** so quickly.
そんな　に　急い　で　食べて　は　いけません.
      (*lit.* So hurridly the eating will not do.)

Tōkyō de wa dénsha no náka de tabakó wo sutté wa ikemasén.
東京　で　は　電車　の　中　で　煙草　を　吸って　は　いけません.
In Tōkyō one is not allowed to smoke in the street-car.
      (*lit.* In Tokyo street-car inside, tobacco the inhaling won't do.)

Instead of the subordinate followed by one of the words *ikemasén*, *ikenái*, etc., one may use the simple present, followed by *kotó wa narimasén* 事はなりません or *naránai* ならない, or *kotó wa ikemasén* 事はいけません or *ikenái* いけない. However, the forms with the subordinate are preferred.

Hĭtó no tegami wo akerú kotó wa narimasen. (or. ....*aketé wa*
人　の　手紙　を　開ける　事　は　なりません.   (開けて　は

---

1 *nódo* throat, *kawáku* かわく to dry up; *nódo ga kawáku* 喉がかわく to be or to feel thirsty   2 *urikiréru* to be sold out

narimasén.) One **must not open** other people's letters.
なりません.) (*lit.* People's letters the opening won't do.)

*Konó heyá ni **háiru kotó wa ikemasén.*** (or ......*háitte wa ikemasén.*)
この 部屋 に 入る 事 は いけません. （入って は いけません.）
You **must not enter** this room.

The negative emphatic subordinate followed by *ikemasén, ike-nái,* or *narimasén, naránai* means **to be obliged** or **must.**

*Mō jikí ni[1] okyakŭsamá ga kimásŭ kará shokují no shǐtakú wo **shinákute[2]***
もうじきに お客様 が 来ます から 食事 の 仕度 を しなくて
wa naránai. As the guests will soon come, we **must make** preparations
は ならない. for dinner.
(*lit.* Soon guests come because, dinner's preparations not-making, won't do.)

Vocabulary

Nouns			Verbs		
animal	*dōbutsu*	動物	to be tired	*kutabiré·ru*	クタビレル
anxiety	*shimpaí*	心配			
face	*kaó*	顔	to cry	*nakú*	泣ク
			to earn	*mōke·ru*	儲ケル
headache	*zutsū*	頭痛	to get tired	*tsŭkaré·ru*	疲レル
health	*kenkō*	健康	to handle	*toriatsŭkaú*	取扱ウ
permission	*kyóka*	許可	to move	*ugokásu*	動カス
storm	*árashi*	嵐	to open	*ake·rú*	開ケル
ticket	*kippú*	切符	to permit	*yurúsu*	許ス
Adjectives			to be permitted	*yurusaré·ru*	許サレル
dangerous	*abunaí*	危ブナイ	to run[3]	*hashíru*	走ル
deep	*fukái*	深カイ	to stare at	*mitsume·rú*	
healthful	*kenkō ni yoroshíi*				見ツメル
	健康ニヨロシイ		to treat	*atsŭkaú*	扱ウ

to fast *danjikí wo surú* 断食をする；to have a headache *zutsū ga surú* 頭痛がする；to be hungry *onaká ga sŭkú* お腹が空く；Imperial Palace *Kyūjō* 宮城

Exercise *Renshū* 練習

1. Késa watashí wa asahán wo tábezu ni jimúsho e ikimáshǐta. **2.** Yūbe nágaku benkyō shimáshǐta ka.—Iié, shimasén déshǐta. Okyakú ga átta nóde gakká wo benkyō sézu ni neté shimaimáshǐta. **3.** Me wo akenákute **wa** miemasén. **4.** Ashí wo ugokásazu ni wa arukemasén. **5.** Hatarakanákute wa o-kané wo mōkeru kotó ga dekimasén. **6.** Isói-de gekijō e ikanái to kippú ga urikiremásŭ yo![4] **7.** Dōbutsu wo sonná ni rambō-ni atsŭkatté (*or* atsŭkaú no) wa migurushíi[5] désŭ. **8.** Yábun osokú neté (*or* nerú no) wa

---

1 *mō jikí ni* soon **2** *shǐtakú wo surú* to make preparations **3** said of people, animals, vehicles, ships etc. **4** *Yo* is an emphatic interjection sometimes used in familiar speech at the end of a sentence. **5** *migurushíi* disgraceful, shameful

kenkō ni yoroshikú arimasén.   **9.** O-imōtosan to go-isshó ni irasshátte wa ikága désŭ ka.—Soré wa kékkō désŭ.   **10.** Amarí aói (*or* jukusánai) kudámono wo tabéru no (*or* tábete) wa kenkō ni gái¹ ga arimásŭ.   **11.** Ichí nichí-jū arukí-dōshi² déshĭta nóde totemó tsŭkaremáshĭta.   Watashí wa mō nemashō. **12.** Anáta no kodomosantachí wa gakkō kará káetta (kaerimáshĭta) tokí ni totemó o-naká ga suité imáshĭta.   **13.** Dóchira e o-dekaké désŭ ka.—Uenó no Toshókan e mairimásŭ.—Kyō wa saijitsú de Toshókan wa shimátte imásŭ kará itté mo mudá³ désŭ yo.   **14.** Meshitsŭkái⁴ wa náni wo kowashimáshĭta ka.—Garasú no koppú wo kowashimáshĭta.—Shikatá ga arimasén.   **15.** Kurumá ga hashítte irú uchí-ni tobiórite⁵ wa ikemasén.   **16.** Konó jimúsho de wa tabakó wo sutté wa ikemasén. (*or*......tabakó wo suú kotó wa yurusárete imasén.) **17.** Hĭtó ga hanáshĭte irú tokí-ni jamá⁶ wo shĭté wa ikemasén.   **18.** Tokubetsú no kyóka náku shĭté wa Kyūjō e háiru kotó wa yurusaremasén.   **19.** Yanai San ga irasshaimásŭ kará éki e o-mukaé ni iká-nákereba narimasén.   **20.** Konó ringó wa máda aói désŭ kará tábete wa ikemasén yo.   **21.** Kawá wa totemó fukái kará sóba e itté wa ikemasén.   **22.** Watashí wa Itarí ni itá (=imáshĭta) tokí totemó Nihón e kitákatta⁷ no déshĭta.

1. けさ私は朝飯を食べずに事務所へ行きました. **2.** ゆうべ長く勉強しましたか.—いゝえ，しませんでした. お客があったので学課を勉強せずに寝てしまいました. **3.** 眼を開けなくては見えません. **4.** 足を動かさずには歩けません. **5.** 仂かなくてはお金を儲ける事が出来ません. **6.** 急いで劇場へ行かないと切符が売切れますよ！ **7.** 動物をそんなに乱暴に扱って（扱うの）は見苦しいです. **8.** 夜分遅く寝て（寝るの）は健康によろしくありません. **9.** お妹さんと御一緒にいらっしゃってはいかゞですか.—それは結構です. **10.** あまり青い（熟さない）果物を食べるの（食べて）は健康に害があります. **11.** 一日中歩き通しでしたのでとても疲れました. 私はもう寝ましょう. **12.** 貴方の子供さん達は学校から帰った（帰りました）時にとてもお腹が空いていました. **13.** どちらへお出かけですか.—上野の図書館へ参ります.—今日は祭日で図書館は閉まっていますから行っても無駄ですよ. **14.** 召使は何をこわしましたか.—ガラスのコップをこわしました.—仕方がありません. **15.** 車が走っているうちに飛び降りてはいけません. **16.** この事務所では煙草を吸ってはいけません. （......煙草を吸う事は許されていません.） **17.** 人が話している時に邪广をしてはいけません. **18.** 特別の許可なくしては宮城へ入る事は許されません. **19.** 柳井さんがいらっしゃいますから駅へお迎えに行かなければなりません. **20.** このりんごはまだ青いですから食べてはいけませ

---

1 *gái* injury, harm   **2** *dōshi* throughout, all through   **3** *mudá* futility, uselessness **4** *meshitsŭkái* man *or* woman servant, domestic   **5** *tobioríru* to jump down, leap down   **6** *jamá wo surú* to inconvenience, obstruct, interrupt somebody   **7** past of *kitái* wish to come

んよ. **21.** 河はとても深いから側へ行ってはいけません. **22.** 私はイタリーにいた（いました）時とても日本へ来たかったのでした.

1. This morning I went to the office without eating breakfast. **2.** Did you study long last night?—No, I did not. As there were guests at home I went to bed without studying my lesson. **3.** Without opening our eyes we cannot see. **4.** Without moving our legs we cannot walk. **5.** If we do not work we cannot earn money. **6.** If you do not go hurridly to the theatre the tickets will be sold out. **7.** Treating animals so roughly is shameful. **8.** Going to bed late at night is not healthful. **9.** How would it be if you would come with your younger sister?—That would be all right. **10.** Eating too green fruit is harmful to health. **11.** As I have been walking all day I am awfully tired. I am now going to bed. **12.** Your children were awfully hungry when they came back from school. **13.** Where are you going?—I am going to the Ueno Library.—It's no use going there; to-day being a holiday the Library is closed. **14.** What has the servant broken?—She has broken some glasses.—It can't be helped. **15.** You must not jump off the car while it is running. **16.** In this office one is not allowed to smoke. **17.** You must not interrupt people while they are speaking. **18.** One is not allowed to enter the Imperial Palace without a special permission. **19.** As Mr. Yanai is coming we must go to the station to meet him. **20.** As these apples are still green you must not eat any. **21.** As the river is too deep you must not go near to it. **22.** When I was in Italy I had a great desire to come to Japan.

Twenty-sixth Lesson　第廿六課

The Subordinate (continued)

Placed after the *subordinate*, **mo** も corresponds to **even if, though, although**.

Ashǐtá áme ga fútte mo Kamakurá kembutsú ni ikimásǔ.
あした 雨 が 降って も 鎌倉 見物 に 行きます.
To-morrow I will go sightseeing to Kamakura **even if it rains**.
  (*lit.* To-morrow rain falling even, Kamakura sightseeing for, I go.)

Chǐchí wa tóshi[1] wo tótte mo hijō-ni génki désǔ.
父 は 年 を 取って も 非常に 元気 です.
Although my father is old he is very energetic.
  (*lit.* Father, years taking although, very energetic is.)

Chǐchí wa tóshi wo tótte ité[1] mo hijō-ni génki désǔ.
父 は 年 を 取っていて も 非常に 元気 です.
Although my father is old he is very energetic.

Ani wa takǔsán tábete mo yaseté imásǔ.　**Although** my elder brother
兄 は 沢山 食べて も やせて います.　　eats much he is thin.

---

1 *tóshǐ wo tóru* 年を取る to become old (*toshí* years, *tóru* to take)

An emphatic translation of the above conjunctions is obtained by using a finite verb followed by the expression *nimo kakawarazú* にも拘らず, instead of the *subordinate* followed by *mo*. *Nimo kakawarazú* corresponds also to such expressions as **in spite of, notwithstanding, no matter how, nevertheless.**

Chichí wa tóshi wo tótte irú[1] *nimo kakawarazú hijō ni génki désŭ.*
父 は 年 を取っている にも 　拘らず 　非常 に 元気 です.
Although (In spite of the fact that) my father **is** old he is very energetic.

Ani wa takŭsán tabéru nimo kakawarazú yaseté imásŭ.
兄 は 沢山 食べる にも 　拘らず 　やせて います.
Although (In spite of the fact that) my elder brother **eats** much he is thin.

Watashí no tomodachí no Kanedá San wa ōi[2] *ni benkyō shĭtá nimo*
私 の 友達 の 金田 さん は 大い に 勉強 した にも
kakawarazú rakudái[3] *shimáshĭta.*　　My friend Kaneda failed in his examina-
拘らず 落第 しました.　　tion notwithstanding his great diligence.
　　　(*lit.* My friend Mr. Kaneda, much study did **although**, failed in the examination.)

The *affirmative subordinate* followed by *mo* (sometimes in very colloquial speech without *mo*) and one of the adjectives *ii* いゝ, *yói* よい, *yoroshíi* よろしい has the concessive meaning of **may.**

Ima asondé mo ii désŭ ka. 今遊んでもいゝですか.　　**May** I play now?
　　(*lit.* Now playing **even if**, alright is it?)

Hái, asondé mo yoroshíi.　　Yes, you **may** play.
はい, 遊んで も よろしい.　　(*lit.* Yes, playing even is alright.)

Kómban éiga e itté mo yoroshíi désŭ.　　You **may** go to the cinema
今晩 映画へ行って も よろしい です.　　to-night.

In the last example **may** has been used to give permission. When, however, **may** does not indicate permission but rather the convenience or the advisability of doing something, the principal verb is translated by the *simple present*, followed by *hō ga yói* 方がよい or *yoroshíi* よろしい.

O-nokorí ni nátte watashidómo to isshó ni hirú no shokují wo shĭté irasshái,
お残り になって 私共 と 一緒 に 昼 の 食事 をしていらっしゃい,
soshĭté kará káeru hō ga yói deshō. (or *káeru hō ga yoroshíi deshō.*)
そして から 帰る 方 がよいでしょう. (帰る 方がよろしいでしょう.)
　　Please stay with us for lunch; and then you **may** go back home.

Nokóru 残る to stay; *nokorí* the remainder, remaining; *nátte* is the subord. of *náru* なる to become・ *O-nokorí ni nátte kudasái.* Please remain. This expression is often used in colloquial speech. *Shokují wo surú* 食事をする to have a meal; *irasshái* いらっしゃい please.

The *negative subordinate* followed by *mo* and one of the adjectives *ii, yói, yoroshíi* means **need not, without even.**

Kyō wa o-ténki ga warúi kará sentakú wo shinákute mo yoroshíi.
きょう は お天気 が 悪い から 洗濯 を しなくて も よろしい.
　　As the weather is bad you **need not** wash to-day.

---

1 *toshí wo tótte irú* 年を取っている to be old　**2** *ōi ni* synonym of *takŭsán* much; *ōi ni benkyō surú* to study much　**3** *rakudái surú* to fail in an examination

Atatakái kará haorí[1] wo kinákute mo yoroshíi désŭ.
暖かい　から　羽織　を　着なくて　も　よろしい　です。
As it is warm you need not wear the haori.[1] (*kirú* 着る to wear)

Concessive subordinates standing in pairs correspond to **whether** ......**or.**

Anáta wa itté mo ikanákute mo kamaimasén.   I do not care **whether**
あなた　は　行って　も　行かなくて　も　かまいません.   you go **or** not.
    (*lit.* Going even if, not going even if, do not mind *or* do not care.)

Katté mo kawanákute mo kamaimasén.   I don't care **whether** you
買って　も　　買わなくて　　も　かまいません.   buy it **or** not.
    (*lit.* Buying even if, not buying even if, do not mind *or* do not care.)

When the conjunction **however** qualifies some adjective or adverb, it is translated by *ikura* いくら, and the verb following is used in the subordinate with *mo.*

Ikura watashí wa benkyō shité mo, áni wo shinógu[2] kotó ga
いくら　私　は　勉強　して　も，　兄　を　しのぐ　事　が

dekimasén.   **However** hard I may study I cannot surpass my elder brother.
出来ません.   (*lit.* How much I, study doing though, elder brother, etc.)

Kará から placed immediately after a subordinate corresponds to **after.**

Koréra no tegamí wo taipuraitā de útte kará watashí no tokoró e
これ等　の　　手紙をタイプライターで打ってから　　私　　の　　所　へ

mótte kité kudasái.   **After** you have typed (after typing) these letters, please
持って来て下さい.   bring them to me (to my place).

From the above sentence it may be seen that one action follows another in normal succession of time, that is, when the letters are written the writer is to go to the manager's room. In this and similar cases only *kará* follows the subordinate. However, when between the recurrence of the two events a period of time, whether short or long, intervenes, *kará* is generally followed by *áto-de* 後で, an expression corresponding to *subsequently, later* or *afterwards.* In such cases, in English, the two clauses are joined by the conjunction **and** and the adverb **then.**

Anáta no kozútsumi wo uketotté kará áto-de anáta no tegamí wo
貴方　の　　小包　　を　受取って　から　　後　で　貴方の　手紙　を

itadakimáshĭta.   I received your parcel **and then** your letter arrived. *or*
頂きました.   Your letter arrived after I received your parcel.

Note that when *kará* does not immediately follow the subordinate, but follows a finite verb or an adjective or an adjective followed by *désŭ* or *déshĭta,* it means **because** or **as.**

---

1 *Haori* a Japanese half coat worn over the other clothing. 2 *shinógu* to surpass, to be superior to

Kyō　Asamá　Marú　ga　Yokohamá　ni　tsŭkimásŭ　kará　watashí　wa
きょう　浅間　丸　が　横浜　に　着きます　から　私　は

tomodachí　wo　mukaé　ni　ikimásŭ.
友達　を　迎え　に　行きます.

As the Asama Maru **arrives** at Yokohama to-day, I am going there and meet
my friends.

Sakúban　ojí　ga　Ōsaka　e　tachimáshĭta　kará　Tōkyō　ekí　e　miokurí[1]
昨晩　伯父　が　大阪　へ　立ちました　から　東京　駅　へ　見送り

ni　ikimáshĭta.　　　　**As** my uncle **was leaving** last night for Osaka, I went to
に　行きました.　　　　Tokyo station to see him off.

Konó　kimonó　wa　amarí　takái　désŭ　kará　kaimasén.
この　着物　は　あまり　高い　です　から　買いません.

As this kimono **is too dear** I am not going to buy it. (*lit.* I don't buy it.)

Konó　kutsú　wa　sŭkóshi　chiisái　kará　torikaeté　kudasái.
この　靴　は　少し　小さい　から　取替えて　下さい.

As these shoes **are a little small** (for me), please change them.

Kará から, placed after a subordinate, corresponds also to **since,
from the time......** In this case, instead of **kará** one may use *irai*
以来, which expression is restricted to the meaning of *since then,
from the time downward, ever since.* ***Irai,*** however, is more of the
literary speech.

Watashí　wa　Nihón　e　mairimáshĭte　kará　(or　irai)　taihén　kenkō
私　は　日本　へ　参りまして　から　（以来）　大変　健康

ni　narimáshĭta.　　**Since I came** to Japan I have become very healthy.
に　なりました.　　(*máiru* to come; *kenkō ni náru* to become healthy)

Sometimes the relation of the subordinate to a finite verb is that
of cause and effect. It then corresponds to the finite verb followed
by **kará** (because).

Kodomó　ga　sawáide　(sawágu　kará)　anáta　ga　itté　irú　kotó　ga　wakarimasén.
子供　が　騒いで　（騒ぐ　から）　貴方　が　云っている　事　が　解りません.

As the children are making a noise I don't understand what you are saying.
(*lit.* The children making noise, what you are saying I don't understand.)

Anó　hĭtó　wa　rambō-na　kotó　wo　shĭté　(surú　kará)　komarimásŭ.
あの　人　は　乱暴　な　事　を　して　（する　から）　困ります.

The rough manner of that man troubles me. (*komáru* 困る to be troubled)
(*lit.* That man, rough manners doing—*or* to do because—, troubled I am.)

The subordinate followed by the word **kudasái** 下さい, corresponding to the English **please,** expresses a mild imperative, which
is generally used in Japanese when making a request, an entreaty,
and even when giving an order. See Imperative, Lesson 40, page 316.

*Sŭkóshi **mátte kudasái.*** 少し待って下さい.　　**Please wait** a moment.

---

1 *miokurí ni ikú* 見送りに行く to go to see (a person) off

Anáta no empitsú wo kashǐté kudasái.　　**Please lend** me your pencil.
貴方 の 鉛筆 を かして 下さい.

Konó heyá wo háyaku háite kudasái.　　**Please sweep** this room
この 部屋 を 早く 掃いて 下さい.　　quickly.

The imperative formed with *kudasái* is rendered more polite, or more emphatic, by the word *dōzo* どうぞ placed at the beginning of the sentence. *Dōzo......kudasái* corresponds more or less to the English expression *Please be so kind as to......*

Dōzo, jibikí wo kashǐté kudasái.　　Please be so kind as to lend me
どうぞ, 字引 を かして 下さい.　　your dictionary.

Dōzo, o-sakí e itté kudasái.　　Please go first.
どうぞ, お先 へ行って 下さい.

Sometimes *dōka* どうか, instead of *dōzo* どうぞ, is heard in ordinary conversation, but it does not convey any greater idea of politeness than does the one word *kudasái*.

In public announcements, written or verbal, in offices, theatres, and other public places, the word *kudasái* may be followed by *máse* ませ, to render the request more polite. *Kudasái-máse* 下さいませ may also be used by women in very polite speech and in letters. Men never use this word.

Go-yō ga arimáshǐtara go-enryó náku **mōshitsǔketé** kudasái-máse.
御用 が ありましたら 御遠慮 なく 申しつけて 下さいませ.
If you have any business please **call upon** us without hesitation.

> (*lit.* Affair if you have, without hesitation, tell us please. *enryó* hesitation, reserve; *náku* without; *mōshi-tsǔkéru* to tell, to order, to instruct)

Hondá Samá, o-dénwa de gozaimásǔ kará, dōzo génkan máde oidé
本田 様, お電話 で 御座います から, どうぞ 玄関 迄 御出で
kudasái-máse. Mr. Honda, a telephone call for you; **please go** to the entrance.
下さいませ.　　(Announcement in public gathering.)

Dōzo o-himá no setsú o-asobí ni oidé kudasái-máse.
どうぞ 御暇 の 節 御遊び に 御出で 下さいませ.
> When you have time, **please call on** me. (*lit.* Please, spare time when, recreation for, coming favour me.—*himá* spare time, *setsú* on the occasion of=when)

The **negative imperative** with *kudasái,* or with both *dōzo* and *kudasái,* is formed by using the *negative present* with *nái* followed by *de.*

Dōzo watashí wo matánai de kudásai.　　**Please do not wait** for me.
どうぞ 私 を 待たない で 下さい.

Dōzo konó tegamí wo dasánai de kudásai.　　**Please do not post** this
どうぞこの 手紙 を 出さない で 下さい.　　letter.

Sonná ōki-na otó wo taténai de kudasái.　　**Please do not make** such
そんな 大きな 音 を 立てない で 下さい.　　a big noise.

> (*otó wo tatéru* 音を立てる to make a noise, *lit.* to raise a noise)

When two or more subordinates follow one another, and are used as the first part of imperative verbal expressions, it is only the last one that takes **kudasái** 下さい。

> *Tamagó wo ichı dāsu* **katté kité kudasái.** **Please buy** a dozen eggs.
> 玉子 を 一 ダース買って 来て 下さい。
>
> (*lit.* Eggs one dozen buying, coming please.)

> *Suzuki San no ókŭsan no tokoró e* **itté,** *konó kozútsumi wo* **ageté,**
> 鈴木 さん の 奥さん の 所 へ行って, この 小包 を 上げて,
>
> *háyaku* **káette**[1] **kité kudasái.**   Go to Mrs. Suzuki, give her this parcel, and
> 早く 帰って 来て 下さい。   come back home quickly.
>
> (*lit.* Mr. Suzuki's wife's place to, going, this parcel giving, quickly returning, coming please.)

When the verbs of two or more clauses are intended to express the same tense, it is the last verb only that takes the termination of tense, while the other verbs are expressed in the subordinate.

> *Hanáya e* **itté** *haná wo* **katté** *uchí e* **kaerimáshıta.**
> 花屋 へ行って 花 を 買って うちへ 帰りました。
> I went to the florist, bought some flowers and returned home.

> *Kudámono wo* **katté** *yóku* **aratté tabemáshıta.**
> 果物 を 買って よく 洗って 食べました。
> I bought some fruit, washed it well and ate it.

In similar sentences, when it is the verb **to be** that is intended to express the same tense, **de** is used instead of *désŭ* or *déshĭta*, in all clauses except the last one of the sentence, which is done for euphonic reason.

> *Anáta no kimonó wa* **kínu de,** *watashí no wa keorí* **désŭ.**
> 貴方 の 着物 は 絹 で, 私 の は 毛織 です。
> Your kimono is silk, mine is woolen.

> *Chichí wa bímbō* **de,** *oǐ wa kanemochí* **déshĭta.** My father was poor, my
> 父 は 貧乏 で, 伯父 は 金持 でした。   uncle was rich.

From these two examples we see that **de** is used both for the *present* and for the *past tense*, so that before hearing the last verb we cannot know whether the verb in the previous clause is intended to be in the present or past.

Vocabulary

Nouns

cinerama	*shineramá*	シネラマ	florist	*hanáya*	花ハ屋ヤ
energy	*génki*	元ゲン気キ	spear	*yari*	槍ヤリ
envelope	*fūtō*	封フウ筒トウ	telephone	*denwá*	電デン話ワ
fire	*hi*	火ヒ	trunk	*kabán*	鞄カバン

---

1 *káette kúru* 帰って来る (*lit.* returning to come) to return

				Verbs		
valise	*tesagé-kabán*	手テ提サゲ鞄カバン		to exchange	*torikae·rú*	取トリ替カエル
vegetables	*yasái*	野ヤ菜サイ		to mend (repair)	*naósu*	直ナオス
	Adjectives			to mend (patch)	*tsugú*	継ツグ
energetic	*génki-na*	元ゲ気キナ		to snow	*yukí ga fúru*	雪ユキガ降フル
learned	*monoshirí*[1]	物モ識シリ		to surpass	*shinógu*	凌シノグ
rough	*rambō-na*	乱ラン暴ボウナ		to wash	*araú*	洗アラウ

to go sightseeing *kembutsú ni ikú* 見物に行く; to typewrite *taipŭraitā de útsu* タイプライターで打つ; to rain fire=to rain spears *yarí ga fúru* 槍が降る; to become thin *yaserú* やせる; to pack *nizúkuri surú* 荷造りする; the movies *éiga* 映画; letter-paper *retā pēpa* レターペーパ; to take a hot bath *o-furó ni háiru* お風呂に入る (*furó* bath, bathtub; *o-furó ni háiru*=to enter the bath *lit.*)

Exercise *Renshū* 練習

1. Anó hĭtó wa takŭsán hon wo yómu nímo kakawarazú monoshirí de wa nái. **2.** Tatoé[2] yarí ga fútte mo watashí wa ikimásŭ. **3.** Chichí wa taihén hatarakú nímo kakawarazú mōkeru no wa sŭkunái désŭ. **4.** Anáta ga takŭsán benkyō shĭté mo Nihón-go wo ichí-nen de wa oboeraremasén.[3] Nihón-go wa taihén muzukashíi désŭ. **5.** Háitte mo yoroshíi désŭ ka.—Hái, yoroshíi désŭ. **6.** Kimí no jibikí wo karité mo yoroshíi désŭ ka.—Hái, yoroshíi désŭ. Kéredomo ashĭtá máde-ni kaesá-nákute[4] wa ikemasén. **7.** Anáta no shigotó wo oemáshĭta ka.—Hái, oemáshĭta.—Déwa, mō uchí e káette mo yoroshíi désŭ. **8.** Kyō wa yukí ga furimásŭ kará o-uchí e káerazu ni kómban kokó e tomatté irasshái soshĭté ashĭtá kaerí nasái. **9.** Anó otokó wa hataraité mo hataraká-nákute mo nenjū[5] kané ga arimasén. **10.** Anáta no hōseki wo minná utté mo kamaimasén[6] ga anáta no hon wo utté wa ikemasén. **11.** Watashí wa Nihón e kité írai[7] máda Kabuki-zá wo míte imasén. Kon-ya kóso[8] wa mi ni ikimásŭ. **12.** Koréra no kabán wo nizúkuri shĭté kará éki e okutté kudasái. —Anáta no tesagé-kabán mo éki e okurimashō ka.—Iié, tesagé-kabán wa jibún de[9] mótte ikimásŭ. **13.** Kimí wa o-kané ga nái kará bóku ga sŭkóshi kashĭté agemashō. **14.** Konó ié wa watashí ni wa amarí ōki-sugimásŭ[10] kará chiisái no wo karimashō. **15.** Anó onná-no-ko wa amarí shaberisugimásŭ kará hĭtóbito wa sŭkimasén. **16.** Tomodachí to isshó ni shineramá e itté mo íi désŭ ka.—Yoroshíi ga amarí osokú káette wa ikemasén. **17.** Dōzo retā-pēpa to

---

1 *monoshirí* means learned man, but followed by *désŭ* it may be used as an adjective **2** *tatoé* even if **3** potential of **obóeru** to commit to memory, to learn **4** *káesu* to return, to give back **5** *nenjū* the whole year, always **6** *kamaimasén* I don't care **7** *írai* since **8** *kóso* indeed, the very; *kon-ya kóso* this very evening **9** *jibún de* by myself **10** *ōki-sugíru* 大き過ぎる to be too large; *sugíru* to go beyond, to be in excess. *Sugíru* 過ぎる, added to the stem of verbs, the stem of true adjectives, or to a noun followed by *ga*, signifies excess of an action, quality or quantity. *Satō ga ō-sugimásŭ.* There is too much sugar (in it). *ii-sugíru* 言い過ぎる to say too much, to overstate; *taká-sugíru* 高過ぎる to be too high

fūtō wo kaí ni itté kudasái.   18. Go-shújin wa irasshaimásŭ ka.—Hái, irasshaimásŭ.—O-hanashí ga shĭtái no désŭ ga.¹ (or Chottó o-me ni kakaritái no
désŭ ga.¹)—Dōzo o-kaké ni nátte chottó kokó de o-machí kudasái.   Ima
shújin wa o-furó ni háiru tokoró désŭ kará.   19. Dōzo, koréra no hon ni
sawaranái de kudasái.   20. Anáta wa késa náni wo shimáshĭta ka.—Watashí
wa íchiba e itté yasái to o-sakaná wo katté kimáshĭta.—Déwa sakúban wa náni
wo shimáshĭta ka.—Yūbe wa anáta no yōfuku wo tsuidé kará nemáshĭta.
21. Anó hĭtó wa go-nen mo Fŭransú ni orimáshĭta nímo kakawarazú Fŭransú-
go ga dekimasén.—Manabú tamé ni wa benkyō shinákute wa narimasén.

1. あの人は沢山本を読むにも拘らず物識りではない. **2.** たとえ槍
が降っても私は行きます. **3.** 父は大変伨くにも拘らず儲けるのは少
いです. **4.** 貴方が沢山勉強しても日本語を一年では覚えられません.
日本語は大変むづかしいです. **5.** 入ってもよろしいですか.—はい,
よろしいです. **6.** 君の字引を借りてもよろしいですか.—はい,よろ
しいです.けれどもあした迄に返さなくてはいけません. **7.** 貴方の
仕事を終えましたか.—はい,終えました.—ではもう家へ帰ってもよろ
しいです. **8.** きょうは雪が降りますからおうちへ帰らずに今晩ここ
へ泊っていらっしゃいそしてあした帰りなさい. **9.** あの男は伨いて
も伨かなくても年中金がありません. **10.** 貴方の宝石を皆売っても構
いませんが貴方の本を売ってはいけません. **11.** 私は日本へ来て以来
まだ歌舞伎座を見ていません.今夜こそは見に行きます. **12.** これ等
の鞄を荷造りしてから駅へ送って下さい.—貴方の手提鞄も駅へ送りま
しょうか.—いゝえ,手提鞄は自分で持って行きます. **13.** 君はお金が
無いから僕が少し貸してあげましょう. **14.** この家は私にはあまり大
き過ぎますから小さいのを借りましょう. **15.** あの女の子は余りしゃ
べり過ぎますから人々は好きません. **16.** 友達と一緒にシネラマへ
行ってもいいですか.—よろしいがあまり遅く帰ってはいけません.
17. どうぞレターペーパと封筒を買いに行って下さい. **18.** 御主人は
いらっしゃいますか.—はい,いらっしゃいます.—お話しがしたいの
ですが(一寸お目にかゝりたいのですが.)—どうぞお掛けになって
一寸こゝでお待ち下さい.今,主人はお風呂に入るところですから.
19. どうぞこれらの本に触らないで下さい. **20.** 貴方はけさ,何をし
ましたか.—私は市場へ行って野菜とお魚を買って来ました.—では,
昨晩は何をしましたか.—ゆうべは貴方の洋服を継いでから寝ました.
21. あの人は五年もフランスにおりましたにも拘らずフランス語が出
来ません.—学ぶためには勉強しなくてはなりません.

---

1 A sentence expressing the desire of obtaining a favour, or of having one's
request granted, may sometimes end elliptically by *ga* (but). In such a case the
unexpressed idea suggests some fear, on the part of the speaker, that the request
may cause trouble or embarrassment. *Ga* used in this way indicates polite speech.

1. Although that man reads many books he is not learned. **2.** I will go even if it should rain fire. **3.** Although my father works much, he earns little. **4.** Even if you study much, you cannot learn Japanese in one year. The Japanese language is very difficult. **5.** May I enter?—Yes, you may. **6.** May I borrow your dictionary?—Yes, you may, but you must return it to me by to-morrow. **7.** Have you finished your work?—Yes, I have.—Then you may go home. **8.** As it is snowing to-day you need not go home; you may remain here for to-night and go home to-morrow. **9.** Whether that man works or not, he is always without money. **10.** I don't care whether you sell all your jewels, but you must not sell your books. **11.** Since I came to Japan I have not seen the Kabuki theatre. To-night I must go there. **12.** After you have packed these trunks send them to the station.—May I send also your valises to the station?—No, I will take the valises with me. **13.** As you have no money I am going to lend you some. **14.** As this house is too large for me, I am going to rent a small one. **15.** As that girl talks too much, people do not like her. **16.** May I go with my friend to the cinerama?—Yes, you may, but you must not come home too late. **17.** Please go and buy some letter paper and envelopes. **18.** Is your master at home? —Yes, he is.—I wish to speak to him.—Sit down please and wait here for a moment. My master is just going to take a bath. **19.** Please do not touch these books. **20.** What have you done this morning?—I went to the market, bought some vegetables and fish and returned home.—And what did you do last night?—Last night I mended your suits and went to bed. **21.** Although that man was in France five years, he does not speak French.—In order to learn one must study.

Twenty-seventh Lesson 第廿七課

The Subordinate (continued)

Subordinate of Adjectives

Adjectives of quality in *i*, as already shown, are conjugated like verbs, and their subordinate is obtained by adding *te* to their *adverbial form*.

See phonetic rules on adjectives in their subordinate form, Page 682.

Adjective		Adverb		Subordinate		
atsúi 熱い hot		*átsuku* 熱く		*átsukute* 熱くて being hot		
samúi 寒い cold		*sámuku* 寒く		*sámukute* 寒くて being cold		
nái[1] 無い there is not		*náku* 無く		*nákute* 無くて not there being		

The negative of the subordinate of such adjectives is formed by adding *nákute* to the adverbial form.

---

1 *Nái* is conjugated as a true adjective. (Lesson 21)

átsuku 熱く *átsuku-nákute* 熱くなくて not being hot
sámuku 寒く *sámuku-nákute* 寒くなくて not being cold

When there are two predicative adjectives in a sentence, only the last one is used in its predicative form, the first being in the subordinate. In such English expressions the two adjectives are joined by the conjunction *and*.

Konó	*kudámono*	*wa*	*yásukute*	*umái désŭ.*
この	果物	は	安くて	旨い です.

This fruit is cheap **and** tasty.

Konó	*shōsetsu*	*wa*	*mijikakute omoshirói.*
この	小説	は	短かくて 面白い.

This novel is short **and** interesting.

In similar sentences, if the adjectives do not belong to the class of true adjectives, which, as already stated, may be used in the subordinate form, they are followed by *de,* with the exception of the last one. which is followed by *désŭ, déshĭta,* or *deshō,* as the case may be.

Konó	*kikái*	*wa*	*jōbu*	*de kanzén désŭ.*	
この	機械	は	丈夫	で 完全 です.	

This machine is strong **and** perfect. (*kanzén* perfect)

Anó	*hĭtó*	*wa*	*gōyoku*	*de namakemonó désŭ.*	
あの	人	は	強欲	で なまけ者 です.	

That man is greedy **and** lazy. (*gōyoku* greedy)

When the predicates of two or more clauses are adjectives, or partly adjectives and partly verbs, intended to express the same tense, only the last adjective or verb takes the predicative form, the other adjectives or verbs being in the subordinate form.

1. *Yukí wa shírokute súsu wa kŭrokute sóra wa aói désŭ.*
   雪 は 白くて 煤 は 黒くて 空 は 青い です.
   Snow is white, soot is black, the sky is blue.

2. *Chichí wa i ga wárukute byōin ni háitte imásŭ.*
   父 は 胃が 悪くて 病院 に 入って います.
   As my father is suffering from stomach trouble, he is staying at the hospital.
   (*lit.* My father his stomach being bad, in the hospital, having entered, is.)

In example 1, and in similar sentences with all *predicative adjectives,* even if the last adjective is followed by *désŭ* or *déshĭta.* instead of the subordinate. it is preferable to use the adverbial form for all adjectives except the last one in the sentence.

Yukí wa shíroku súsu wa kŭroku sóra wa aói désŭ.
雪 は 白く 煤 は 黒く 空 は 青い です.

When in the sentence there is an adjective and a verb. as in example 2, the adverbial form of the adjective is not used. In such cases. however, instead of the subordinate of the adjective we may use the true adjective, followed by *kará* から or *nóde* ので.

Chichí wa i ga warúi kará (or *nóde*) *byōin ni háitte imásŭ.*
父 は 胃が 悪い から (ので) 病院 に 入って います.
As my father is suffering from stomach trouble, he is staying at the hospital.
(*lit.* My father the stomach bad because, in the hospital, having entered, is.)

Chichí wa i ga warúi kará byōin e ikimáshĭta.
父　は胃が　悪い　から　病院 へ行きました.
As my father is suffering from stomach trouble, he went to the hospital.

If the first verb of a sentence is in the desiderative, the same
may be used in the subordinate.

Watashí wa Nihón-go ga naraitákute tamarimasén kará dōzo yói
私　は 日本語　が　習いたくて　たまりません からどうぞよい
senséi ni shōkai¹ shĭté kudasái.   As I am eager to learn Japanese,
先生 に 紹介　して 下さい.   please introduce me to a good teacher.

   (*lit.* I, Japanese language, wishing to learn cannot endure because, please,
   good teacher to, introduction doing please.—*naráu* 習う to learn, *naraitá-*
   kute 習いたくて wishing to learn, *tamarimasén* たまりません cannot
   endure)

In such cases, however, it is preferable to use the desiderative
form with *tai* たい followed by *kará* から.

Watashí wa Nihón-go ga naraitái kará dōzo yói senséi ni shōkai
私　は　日本語　が　習いたい　から どうぞよい 先生 に　紹介
shĭté kudasái.   (*lit.* I Japanese language wish to learn because, please good
して 下さい.   teacher to, introduce.)

In sentences with more than one verb and one or more predicative
adjectives, the *subordinate* may be used for both verbs and adjectives, but it is not possible to use the adverbial form of the adjectives
if the verbs are used in the subordinate.

Netsú ga átte, me ga ítakute, sonó ué memái² ga shimásŭ kará,
熱　があって,眼 が　痛くて,　その 上 めまい が　します から,
gakkō e ikú kotó ga dekimasén. As I have fever and sore eyes, and as I
学校 へ行く 事　が 出来ません.　feel dizzy besides, I cannot go to school.

   (*lit.* Having fever, the eyes aching, on the top of that—besides—being dizzy,
   to school to go the thing cannot.)

Netsú ga átte, me ga ítakute, sonó ué memái ga shimáshĭta kará,
熱　があって,眼 が　痛くて,　その 上 めまい が　しました から,
gakkō e ikú kotó ga dekimasén déshĭta.
学校 へ行く 事　が 出来ません でした.
As I had fever and sore eyes, and I felt dizzy besides, I couldn't go to school.

In sentences like the preceding ones, we may, however, use the
adverbial form of the adjective if the first verb is used without the
suffix *másŭ.*

Netsú ga ári³ me ga ítaku, sonó ué memái ga shimásŭ kará gakkō
熱　があり眼 が　痛く,　その上 めまい が　します から 学校
e ikú kotó ga dekimasén.
へ行く 事　が 出来ません.

---

1 *shōkai surú* to introduce　**2** *memái ga surú* to have dizziness　**3** *ári＝arimásŭ*
without the suffix *másŭ*

Netsú ga ári me ga ítaku, sonó ué memái ga shimáshĭta kará
熱　が　あり　眼　が　痛く,　その　上　めまい　が　しました　から
gakkō e ikú kotó ga dekimasén déshĭta.
学校　へ行く　事　が　出来ません　でした.

The subordinate and the following verb or predicative adjective often stand to each other in the relation of cause and effect.

Konó mondaí wa muzukáshikute wakarimasén.
この　問題　は　むづかしくて　解りません.
This problem is so difficult that I cannot understand it.
(*lit.* This problem being difficult I don't understand it.)

or: *Konó mondaí wa muzukashíi kará* (or *nóde*) *wakarimasén.*
この　問題　は　むづかしい　から　（ので）　解りません.

Konó shi wa mijikakute ankí-shiyasúi désŭ. As this poem is short,
この　詩　は　短かくて　暗記しやすい　です. it is easy to memorize.
(*lit.* This poem being short, easy-to-memorize is.—*ankí* learning by heart)

or: *Konó shi wa mijikái kará (nóde) ankí-shiyasúi désŭ.*
この　詩　は　短かい　から　（ので）　暗記しやすい　です.

The *subordinate of adjectives* followed by the postposition *mo* も has the force of the **concessive,** and corresponds to **although, though, even if, even though.** Compare with *subordinate of verbs* followed by *mo* も. (See Lesson 26.)

Anó hĭtó wa karadá wa chíisakute mo tsuyói désŭ.
あの　人　は　体　は　小さくて　も　強い　です.
Although his body is **small** he is strong.
(*lit.* That man the body being small though, strong is.)

Watashí no itóko wa wákakute mo taihén gakúmon[2] ga arimásŭ.
私　のいとこ　は　若くて　も　大変　学問　が　あります.
Even though my cousin is **young,** he is very learned.

The *affirmative subordinate of adjectives* followed by *mo* も and one of the adjectives *ii* いゝ, *yói* よい, *yoroshíi* よろしい means **it will likewise do.** Compare with subordinate of verbs followed by the same adjectives. (See Lesson 26, page 174)

Nagái empitsú ga iriyō de wa arimasén kará, mijikakute mo
長い　鉛筆　が　入用　で　はありません　から,　短かくて　も
yoroshíi désŭ. As I need not have a long pencil, a short one will likewise do.
よろしい　です. (*lit.* A long pencil, need as there is not, even being short is good.)

The *subordinate of adjectives* followed by *wa* は and by an *intransitive* (mostly negative) *verb,* or a *predicate noun* or an *adjective,* indicates a condition. Compare with subordinate of verbs followed by *wa* は. (See Lesson 25, page 168)

---

1 *ankí surú* to memorize, *ankí-shiyasúi* easy to memorize **2** *gakúmon* learning, *gakúmon ga áru* learned

Karadá ga wárukute wa kōfuku de wa arimasén.　If one is sick one
体　　が　　悪くて　　は　幸福　で　はありません.　is not happy.
(*lit.* The body being bad happy being is not.)

Kaichūdokei ga amarí ōkikute wa mochinikúi[1] *désŭ.*
懐中時計　が　余り　大きくて　は　持ちにくい　です.
If a watch is too large it is inconvenient to carry.
(*lit.* A watch being too large troublesome to carry is.)

Akarí ga kurákute wa yóku yómu kotó ga dekimasén.
あかりが　暗くて　は　よく　読む　事　が　出来ません.
If the light is dim one cannot read well.
(*lit.* The light being dim well to read the thing cannot.)

Shimbún ga nákute wa sekái no jísei[2] *wo wakarimasén.*
新聞　が　無くて　は　世界　の　時勢　を　解りません.
Without newspapers we cannot know what is going on in the world.
(*lit.* Newspapers there not being, the trend of the world we don't understand.)

The *subordinate affirmative of adjectives* followed by *wa* は and *ikemasén* いけません, *ikenái* いけない, *narimasén* なりません or *naránai* ならない, means *not to be allowed, must not* or *won't do.* Compare with subordinate of verbs followed by the same words. (See Lesson 25, page 170)

Kimonó ga sonná ni kitánakute wa ikemasén.　A dress must not
着物　が　そんなに　汚くて　は　いけません.　be so dirty.
(*lit.* A dress so much being dirty won't do.)

Nerú no wa amarí osókute wa narimasén.　One must not go to
寝る の　は　余り　おそくて　は　なりません.　sleep too late.
(*lit.* To sleep too much being late must not.)

The *subordinate of verbs* in the *desiderative* is obtained by adding *takute* たくて to the simple stem of verbs of Class I, and to the *i*-stem of verbs of Class II.

See **phonetic rules** on verbs in their subordinate-desiderative form, Page 682.

Class I

míru	見る	*mi*	見	*mítakute*	見たくて	wishing to see
tabéru	食べる	*tabe*	食べ	*tabétakute*	食べたくて	wishing to eat

Class II

káku	書く	*kaki*	書き	*kakitákute*	書きたくて	wishing to write
dásu	出す	*dashi*	出し	*dashitákute*	出したくて	wishing to take out
tátsu	立つ	*tachi*	立ち	*tachitákute*	立ちたくて	wishing to stand
tobú	飛ぶ	*tobi*	飛び	*tobitákute*	飛びたくて	wishing to fly
tóru	取る	*tori*	取り	*toritákute*	取りたくて	wishing to take
kaú	買う	*kai*	買い	*kaitákute*	買いたくて	wishing to buy
surú	する	*shi*	し	*shitákute*	したくて	wishing to do

1 *mochinikúi* inconvenient to carry; *mochí* from *mótsu* to hold, to have; *nikúi* difficult, troublesome　**2** *jísei* the tendency of the times

The *subordinate of the desiderative* is generally followed by one of the expressions *tamarimasén* たまりません, *tamaranái* たまらない, *shikatá ga arimasén* 仕方がありません, *shikatá ga nái* 仕方がない, each of them meaning *it is unbearable, it is irresistible, it cannot be borne, it cannot be endured* and other expressions of similar meaning.

Instead of *shikatá ga nái* 仕方がない the more colloquial *shiyō ga nái* 仕様がない may be used.

Watashí wa Nihón-go ga **naraitákute** *tamarimasén.*
私　は　日本語　が　習いたくて　　たまりません.
I have a great desire to learn Japanese. (*naráu* 習う to learn, *naraitákute* wishing to learn) (*lit.* I, the Japanese language wishing to learn I cannot endure.)

Watashí wa kuní e **kaeritákute** *shikatá ga arimasén.*
私　は　国　へ　帰りたくて　　仕方　が　ありません.
My desire to return to my native country is so great that I cannot endure it.
(*lit.* To my country wishing to return cannot be endured.)

Itté mítakute tamaranái (or *shikatá ga nái*).   I wish very much to
行って　見たくて　　たまらない　　　（仕方　がない）.　　go and see it.
or I wish so much to go and see it that I cannot endure the desire any longer.
(*lit.* Going, wishing to see, cannot endure.)

Bīru ga **nomitákute shikatá ga arimasén.**   I am dying for a glass
ビールが　飲みたくて　　仕方　がありません.　　*or* a drink of beer.
(*lit.* Beer wishing to drink it is unbearable.—*nómu* 飲む to drink)

Kaitákute tamarimasén (or *shikatá ga arimasén.*)   I want to buy
買いたくて　　たまりません　　　（仕方　がありません）.　　it badly.
or I have a great desire to buy it. (*lit.* Wishing to buy, it cannot be endured.)

The *subordinate of the desiderative* form of verbs may be followed by *mo* も, when one wishes to give the clause or sentence a concessive meaning. See Lesson 26, page 173 and Lesson 27, page 184, for subordinate of verbs and adjectives followed by *mo*.

Sakúban tegamí wo **kakitákute mo** *kamí mo fūtō mo arimasén déshĭta*
昨晩　手紙　を　書きたくて　も　　紙　も　封筒　もありませんでした
kará yamemáshĭta.   Last night, although I had a desire to write a letter,
から　やめました.　　　I had to give it up as I had neither paper nor envelopes.
(*lit.* Last night, a letter although greatly wishing to write, as there was no paper nor envelopes, I gave it up.)

Zutsū no tamé ni gakkō e **ikitákute mo** *ikú kotó ga dekimasén déshĭta.*
頭痛　の　ため　に　学校　へ　行きたくて　も　行く　事　が　出来ませんでした.
Although I wished to go to school, I could not go on account of my headache.
(*lit.* Headache on account of, to school wishing to go although, to go the thing I could not.)

Adjectives in the subordinate form are also used with *tamari-masén* たまりません, *shikatá ga arimasén* 仕方がありません and their more colloquial forms, as in the following examples.

Anó niói wa kusákute tamarimasén.   I cannot bear that bad smell.
あの 臭い は くさくて たまりません.   (*kusái* くさい smelling bad)
    (*lit.* That smell, smelling bad, I cannot bear—*or* it cannot be endured.)

Nemúkute tamaranái (or *shikatá ga nái*).   I am irresistibly sleepy.
眠くて 堪らない (仕方 が ない).
    (*lit.* Being sleepy, it is unbearable.—*nemuí* 眠い sleepy, *nemúkute* 眠くて being sleepy)

Atsukute shikatá ga arimasén.   It is unbearably hot.
暑くて 仕方 がありません. I cannot stand this heat.
    (*lit.* Being hot, it cannot be endured.—*atsúi* 暑い hot)

Vocabulary

Nouns						
camel	*rakudá*	ラクダ		lonesome	*sabishíi*	淋シイ
desert	*sabakú*	沙漠		shallow	*asaí*	浅イ
dizziness	*memái*	メマイ		tough	*kataí*	硬イ
examination	*shikén*	試験		uninteresting	*omoshíroku nái*	
sight, view	*késhiki*	景色				面白クナイ
stomach	*i*	胃		**Verbs**		
tuition	*gesshá*	月謝		to blow (wind)	*fúku*	吹ク
Adjectives				to ford	*arúite watarú*	
						歩イテ渡ル
careful	*chūibukái*	注意深イ		to cross	*koe·rú*	越エル
expensive	*kōka*	高価		to memorize	*obóe·ru*	覚エル

beautiful sight *yói késhiki* よい景色; common sense *jōshiki* 常識; to have sore eyes *me ga itái* 眼が痛い; to feel mortified *zannén ni omóu* 残念に思う; to make fun of *báka ni surú* 馬鹿にする; to be fordable *arúite watarerú* 歩いて渡れる

Exercise   *Renshū* 練習

1. Konó hanashí wa nágakute omoshíroku arimasén.   **2.** Ráion wa tsúyokute yūki[1] ga arimásŭ.   **3.** Bará wa utsŭkúshikute kaorí ga yói désŭ.   **4.** Daiyamóndo wa utsŭkúshikute kōka désŭ.   **5.** Sonó kawá wa asákute arúite wataremásŭ. **6.** Níisan wa me ga itái nóde uchí de neté imásŭ.   **7.** Ame ga hídoku fúri (*or* fútte), michí ga wáruku (*or* wárukute) sonó ué kazé ga fúite itá nóde tomodachí no ié ni ikú kotó ga dekimasén deshĭta. **8.** Hakoné wa késhiki ga yóku, takŭsán no onsén ga ári, sonó ué yói yadoyá ga arimásŭ kará takŭsán no hĭtó ga ikimásŭ.   **9.** Takú no meshitsŭkái wa taihén chūibúkakute kesshĭté

---

1 *yūki ga áru* to be courageous; *yūki* courage

o-sará ya koppú wo kowáshĭta kotó ga arimasén. **10.** Nihón-jin wa kireizukí de kimbén[1] de soshĭté yūkan[2] désŭ. **11.** Watashí no kurói yōfuku wa yásu-katta ga nágaku mochimáshĭta.[3] **12.** Chūrippu wa kírei démo kaorí ga arima-sén. **13.** Watashí wa ōkii heyá wa irimasén kará chiisái no démo yoroshíi désŭ. **14.** Konó nikú wa katákute taberarénai.[4] **15.** Kutsú ga amarí chiisái to fuyúkai[5] désŭ. **16.** Rakudá náshi de sabakú wo koerú no wa muzukashíi désŭ. **17.** Katéi wo motánu[6] monó wa sabishíi. **18.** Hĭtó wa tábezu ni wa ikirarénai. **19.** Jōshiki náshi de wa nanigotó[7] mo dekínai. **20.** Anáta wa anó namakemonó[8] ni sonná ni takŭsán kané wo yaranái hō ga yói. **21.** Nihón wo ryōkai surú[9] ni wa Nihón-go wo yóku shiranákute wa ikemasén. **22.** Anó hĭtó ga watashí wo báka ni shĭtá nóde watashí wa totemó okorimáshĭta. **23.** Bóku wa shikén ni rakudái shĭtá nóde totemó zannén désŭ. **24.** Senséi ni gesshá wo haraitákute mo ginkō ni ikú no wo wasuremáshĭta nóde haráu kotó ga dekimasén. **25.** Watashí wa Kánada ni imáshĭta tokí totemó Nihón-go ga naraitákatta nóde Nihón-jin no senséi no tokoró e benkyō ni[10] ikimáshĭta.

1. この話は長くて面白くありません．**2.** ライオンは強くて勇気があります．**3.** ばらは美しくて香りがよいです．**4.** ダイヤモンドは美しくて高価です．**5.** その川は浅くて歩いて渡れます．**6.** 兄さんは眼が痛いので家で寝ています．**7.** 雨がひどく降り（降って）道が悪く（悪くて）その上風が吹いていたので友達の家に行く事が出来ませんでした．**8.** 箱根は景色がよく，沢山の温泉があり，その上よい宿屋がありますから沢山の人が行きます．**9.** 宅の召使は大変注意深くて決してお皿やコップをこわした事がありません．**10.** 日本人はきれい好きで勤勉でそして勇敢です．**11.** 私の黒い洋服は安かったが長くもちました．**12.** チューリップはきれいでも香りがありません．**13.** 私は大きい部屋は要りませんから小さいのでもよろしいです．**14.** この肉は硬くて食べられない．**15.** 靴が余り小さいと不愉快です．**16.** らくだなしで沙漠を越えるのはむづかしいです．**17.** 家庭をもたぬ者は淋しい．**18.** 人は食べずには生きられない．**19.** 常識なしでは何事も出来ない．**20.** 貴方はあのなまけ者にそんなに沢山金をやらない方がよい．**21.** 日本を了解するには日本語をよく知らなくてはいけません．**22.** あの人が私を馬鹿にしたので私はとても怒りました．**23.** 僕は試験に落第したのでとても残念です．**24.** 先生に月謝を払いたくても銀行に行くのを忘れましたので払うことが出来ません．**25.** 私はカナダにいました時，とても日本語が習いたかったので日本人の先生のところへ勉強に行きました．

---

1 diligent   **2** *yūkan* bravery; *yūkan-na* brave; *na* is omitted when followed by *désŭ*   **3** *mótsu* to last   **4** *taberarénai* cannot be eaten   **5** *fuyúkai* uncomfortable   **6** *motánu* without having, not having, without   **7** anything   **8** lazy fellow   **9** *ryōkai surú* to understand   **10** *benkyō ni* to study

1. This story is long and uninteresting. **2.** Lions are strong and courageous. **3.** Roses are beautiful and fragrant. **4.** Diamonds are beautiful and expensive. **5.** That river is shallow and can be forded. **6.** As my elder brother has sore eyes he is staying at home in bed. **7.** As it was raining heavily, the roads were bad, and the wind was blowing, we could not go to our friend's home. **8.** As there are beautiful sights at Hakone, many hot springs and good hotels, many people go there. **9.** Our servant is very careful, and has never broken any dish or glass. **10.** The Japanese are cleanly, diligent and courageous. **11.** Although my black suit was cheap it lasted long. **12.** Even though tulips are beautiful they have no fragrance. **13.** As I do not need a large room, a small one will do. **14.** This meat is so tough that it cannot be eaten. **15.** If one's shoes are too small they are uncomfortable. **16.** Without camels it is difficult to cross a desert. **17.** If one has no home one feels lonesome. **18.** One cannot live without eating. **19.** Without common sense a man cannot do anything. **20.** You must not give so much money to that lazy man. **21.** In order to understand Japan you must know the Japanese language well. **22.** I was very angry with him for making fun of me. **23.** Having failed in my examination I feel greatly mortified. **24.** Although I intend to pay the tuition to my teacher I am unable to do so because I forgot to go to the bank. **25.** When I was in Canada, as I ardently wished to learn the Japanese language, I went to a Japanese teacher's to study it.

Twenty-eighth Lesson   第廿八課

Wa は and *Ga* が

We have already said that *wa* は and *ga* が are used to indicate the *nominative case*. We will now give definite rules illustrating the use of these two postpositions.

It may be said that in most sentences replying to an interrogation, introduced by one of the interrogative pronouns *dáre* 誰, *dónata* どなた (who), *dótchi* どっち, *dóchira* どちら, *dóre* どれ, *dóno* どの (which), *náni* 何 (what), in the nominative case, the **subject** is followed by *ga* が.

Dáre ga kimáshǐta ka. 誰が来ましたか。 **Who** has come?

Senséi ga kimáshǐta. 先生が来ました。 The **teacher** has come.

Tsǔkué no ué ni náni ga arimásǔ ka. 机 の 上 に 何 が ありますか。 **What** is there on the desk?

Tegamí ga arimásǔ. 手紙があります。 There are **letters**.

Dóchira no hon ga sǔkí désǔ ka. どちら の 本 が 好き です か。 **Which** book do you like?

Kochírá ga sǔkí désǔ. こちらが好きです。 I like **this** one.

Questions represented by one of the interrogative pronouns **who, what, which** may be implied before expressing the idea words. For example: When somebody comes to our home, and the maid servant announces a guest, she will say: *Tanaka San ga irasshaimáshǐta.* 田中さんがいらっしゃいました. *Mr. Tanaka has come.*

In this sentence the question *Who has come?* may be supposed to have been asked before the servant announces Mr. Tanaka. In such a case *ga* が follows the subject.

O-ishá   ga   irasshaimáshǐta.   **The doctor** has come.
お医者 がいらっしゃいました. (Supposing we were expecting him.)

As a general rule, in question about the predicate, the subject is followed by *wa* は. In such a case the question may actually be asked or presumed to have been asked by *what?* in the accusative, or by one of the adverbs *how? dō* どう, *ikága* いかゞ, *where* dóko.

Anáta wa náni wo shǐté imásǔ ka.	**What** are you doing?
貴方　は　何　を　して　います　か.	
Watashí wa benkyō shǐté imásǔ.	I am **studying.**
私　　は　勉強　して　います.	
Otōsan wa ikága désǔ ka.	**How** is your father?
お父さん　は　如何　です　か.	
Chichí wa jōbu désǔ. 父は丈夫です.	My father is **well.**
Eki wa dóko désǔ ka. 駅はどこですか.	**Where** is the station?
Eki wa anó hashí no mukō désǔ.	The station is **beyond**
駅　は　あの　橋　の　向う　です.	**that bridge.**

In all the above sentences it is the **predicate**, that is, **that which is said about the subject,** that stands prominent. From the above examples with *ga* が and *wa* は we may see that the question of the use of these two postpositions is essentially one of subject and predicate.

When the subject stands prominent in the thought of the speaker, being the centre of gravity in the sentence, *ga* が is used after it, while *wa* は is used when the predicate is the centre of gravity.

In the sentence **Who** *has come? Dáre ga irasshaimáshǐta ka.*, the interrogative pronoun **who,** stands prominent in the sentence. In fact we wish to know **Who is he** *that has come.* Here the predicate *has come* takes a secondary place in the sentence.

In the other sentence **What** *are you doing? (Anata wa náni wo shǐte imásǔ ka.)* the interrogative pronoun **what,** or the predicate, stands more prominent in the sentence than the personal pronoun *you,* the subject. In fact, in asking such a question we wish to know *what is the thing* that *you are doing.* The subject **you** takes a secondary place in the sentence and hence takes *wa* は.

Therefore, in order to form accurate ideas of the use of *ga* が and *wa* は, it is of the greatest importance to think clearly whether it is the subject or the predicate that stands more prominent in the sentence. This rule applies in almost all cases, as may be seen from the following examples, and those given in the succeeding lesson.

In clauses whose subjects stand in opposition to each other, *ga* が is used after both subjects, while *wa* は is used if the predicates of both clauses stand in opposition to each other.

This rule agrees with what has been said at the beginning of this lesson.

Konó shátsu no uchí de **dóchira** *ga asá de* **dóchira** *ga momén*
この シャツ の うち で どちら が 麻 で どちら が 木綿

désŭ ka.   **Which** of these shirts are linen and **which** cotton?
です か.   (*lit.* These shirts among, which linen are, which cotton are?)

Koréra *ga asá de* **aréra** *ga momén désŭ.*   **These** are linen, **those**
これ等 が 麻 で あれ等 が 木綿 です.   are cotton.

In both sentences it is the subject **which,** in the question, and **these** and **those,** in the answer, that stand prominent. In fact, we wish to know **which are the shirts** *that are made of linen and* **which** *of cotton.* In the answer *these* and *those* are emphasized.

In the following sentence:

Konó shátsu **wa** *asá de aré* **wa** *momén désŭ.*   These shirts are **linen**
この シャツ は 麻 で あれ は 木綿 です.   those are **cotton.**

the centre of gravity is in the predicates, **linen** and **cotton.** In fact we wish to state that **it is linen** and **it is cotton** that has been used to make these shirts.

Note that the last example is not connected wish the previous two, but is an independent statement, with the emphasis upon the predicative words, **linen** and **cotton.**

In European languages this emphasis is obtained by stress. We may then say that what in European languages is accomplished by **emphasis** and **tone** is in great part accomplished in Japanese by the use of the particles *ga* が and *wa* は.

Wa は is used in elliptical interrogative sentences with nouns only.

Suppose you send your servant to buy bread and meat. She brings you the bread but not the meat. You say: *Nikŭ wa* 肉は. (And the meat? or What about the meat?). Here the centre of gravity in the elliptical sentence lies in the unexpressed predicate **What is the thing** that happened to the meat? or **What about** the meat?

Wa は is used after the subject noun when mention is made of its nature, its characteristics, as in sentences such as the following:

Ráion *wa atsúi kuní ni sumimásŭ.*   Lions live in hot countries.
ライオン は 暑い 国 に 住みます.

Nippón wa utsŭkushíi kuní désŭ.   Japan is a beautiful country.
日本　は　美しい　国　です.

In the two above sentences it is the predicate, or what is said of the lion and Japan, that stands prominent, which again confirms the given rule of the use of *wa* and *ga*.

Vocabulary

Nouns

anchor	*ikarí*	錨イリカ
banana	*bánana*	バナヽ
eaves	*nokí*	軒キ
penholder	*penjikú*	ペン軸ジク
platinum	*pŭrachiná*	プラチナ

Verbs

to attack	*tobikakáru*	飛トビカカル

to awake	*samé·ru*	サメル
to grow	*seichō surú*	成セイ長チョウスル
to tame	*narásu*	馴ナラス
to be tamed	*narasaré·ru*	馴ナラサレル

Adverbs

fiercely	*monosúgoku*	物モノスゴク
willingly	*yorokónde*	喜ヨロコンデ

bear *kumá* 熊クマ; black bear *kurogumá* 黒クロ熊グマ; white bear *shirogumá* 白シロ熊グマ; railway fare *kisháchin* 汽車賃; foreign clothes *yōfuku* 洋服; stringed instrument *íto no hatté áru gakkí* 糸の張ってある楽器; to be at anchor *teihakú shĭté irú* 碇泊している; municipal office, city hall *shiyákusho* 市役所; to obey *fukujū surú* 服従する

Exercise *Renshū* 練習

1. Dónata ga anáta no heyá de anáta ni hanáshĭte imáshĭta ka.—Dónata mo watashí ni hanáshĭte imasén déshĭta. Watashí wa hĭtóri de gakká wo benkyō shĭté imáshĭta. 2. Shiyákusho wa dóko désŭ ka.—Anó hashí no sóba désŭ. 3. Retāpēpā to fūtō to penjikú to wo kái ni itté kudasái.—Kokó ni kamí to fūtō ga arimásŭ.—Penjikú wa.—Penjikú wo kaú no wo wasuremáshĭta. 4. Fukúi San wa máda kimasén ka.—Iié, sŭkóshi máe ni irasshaimáshĭta ga mátte irarenákatta[1] nóde o-kaerí ni narimáshĭta. O-híru kará matá irasshaimásŭ. 5. Konó kusarí wa gin désŭ. Aré wa pŭrachiná désŭ. 6. Bánana wa Nihón no Honshū ni wa seichō shimasén. Ogasawará-shotō ni seichō shimásŭ. 7. Konó sakaná wa iyá-na niói ga shimásŭ kará tábete wa ikemasén. 8. Nihón de wa sakurá wa haná no ō-samá de arimásŭ. 9. Bíwa to wa nan désŭ ka. —Soré wa íto no hatté áru Nihón no gakkí désŭ. Géndai de wa[2] góku wázuka[3] no hĭtó ga bíwa wo hikú daké désŭ. 10. Otōsama wa ikága désŭ ka.—Arigatō, okagesamá[4] de tasshá désŭ. Ishá ga chichí wa shigokú[5] kenkō da to mōshimáshĭta. 11. Kokó ni tokéi ga san-ko arimásŭ ga dóre ga ichibán sŭkí désŭ ka.—Koré ga ichibán sŭkí désŭ. 12. Hachijū nen máe máde Nihón-jin wa yōfuku wo kimasén déshĭta. Ima wa taitéi no hĭtó ga kité imásŭ. 13. Tsubamé ga uchí no nokí shĭtá ni su wo tsŭkútte[6] imásŭ. 14. Dóko no kuní ni mo zen-nin[7] mo ári akú-nin[8] mo arimásŭ. 15. Watashí ga yadoyá ni tsŭkimáshĭta tokí ni anáta no tegamí wa máda kité imasén déshĭta.

---

1 *mátte irarerú* to be able to wait **2** *géndai de wa* nowadays **3** *góku wázuka* very few **4** *okagesamá de* by your kind influence, thanks to you **5** *shigokú* very, exceedingly **6** *su wo tsŭkúru* to build a nest **7** good people **8** bad people

16. Kyō minató ni Itarī no fúne ga teihakú shĭté imásŭ ka.—Hái, ni-sō teihakú shĭté imásŭ. **17.** Nikkō máde kisháchin wa íkura déshĭta ka.—Go-hyakú yen déshĭta. **18.** Dáiku wa shigotó wo oemáshĭta ka.—Iié, héi daké wa deki-máshĭta ga mon wa máda désŭ. **19.** Kōshi[1] wa Shinájin de ári Sháka[2] wa Indójin de arimáshĭta. **20.** Ōsaka wa ōkikuté taihén hanká-na[3] tokái désŭ. **21.** Káji ga okorimáshĭta[4] tokí o-kyakú wa kyakumá de odotté imáshĭta. **22.** O-tétsudai wa ichí-nichí-jū hatarakí-dōshi[5] déshĭta nóde íma wa taihén tsŭká-rete imásŭ. Ima ni ni ikú tokoró désŭ. **23.** Móto Nihónjin wa pan wo tabemasén déshĭta ga Porutogarú-jin ga Nihón ni kité kará pan wo tsŭkútte tabé-hajimemáshĭta. Géndai[6] de wa takŭsán no Nihónjin ga máinichi pan wo tábete imásŭ. **24.** Shirogumá wa fuyú no aidá kōri no náka no aná[7] ni nemásŭ. Háru ga kúru to tōmin[8] kará sáme taihén kūfuku wo kanjí[9] hĭtó ni áeba monosúgoku tobikakarimásŭ. **25.** Nihón ni wa kurogumá ga imásŭ. Kurogumá wa Hokkaidō no yamayamá ni[10] súnde imásŭ. Kurogumá wa narasaréru to kikén de wa arimasén yorokónde sonó shújin ni fukujū shimásŭ.

1. どなたが貴方の部屋で貴方に話していましたか.—どなたも私に話していませんでした.　私は一人で学課を勉強していました.　**2.** 市役所はどこですか.—あの橋のそばです.　**3.** レターペーパーと封筒とペン軸とを買いに行って下さい.—こゝに紙と封筒があります.—ペン軸は.　—ペン軸を買うのを忘れました.　**4.** 福井さんはまだ来ませんか.—いいえ，少し前にいらっしゃいましたが待っていられなかったのでお帰りになりました.　おひるからまたいらっしゃいます.　**5.** このくさりは銀です.　あれはプラチナです.　**6.** バナヽは日本の本州には成長しません.　小笠原諸島に成長します.　**7.** この魚は嫌な臭いがしますから食べてはいけません.　**8.** 日本では桜は花の王様であります.　**9.** 琵琶とは何んですか.—それは糸の張ってある日本の楽器です.　現代では極僅かの人が琵琶をひくだけです.　**10.** お父様は如何ですか.—ありがとう，おかげ様で達者です.　医者が父は至極健康だと申しました.　**11.** こゝに時計が三個ありますがどれが一番好きですか.—これが一番好きです.　**12.** 八十年前まで日本人は洋服を着ませんでした.　今は大抵の人が着ています.　**13.** つばめがうちの軒下に巣をつくっています.　**14.** どこの国にも善人もあり悪人もあります.　**15.** 私が宿屋に着きました時に貴方の手紙はまだ来ていませんでした.　**16.** きよう港にイタリーの船が碇泊していますか.—はい，二雙碇泊しています.　**17.** 日光まで汽車賃はいくらでしたか.—五百円でした.　**18.** 大工は仕事を終えましたか.—いゝえ，塀だけは出来ましたが門はまだです.　**19.** 孔子は支那人であり釈迦は印度人でありました.　**20.** 大阪は大きくて大変繁華な都会です.　**21.** 火事が起りました時お客は客間で

---

1 Confucius　2 Buddha　3 busy　4 *okóru* to happen, to break out, to start　5 all through, throughout　6 *géndai* now　7 *aná* hole, cave　8 winter sleep　9 *kūfuku wo kanjirú* to feel hungry　10 *yamayamá ni irú* to frequent the mountains

踊っていました．　22．お手伝いは一日中働き通しでしたので今は大変
疲れています．今寝に行くところです．　23．元，日本人はパンを食べ
ませんでしたがポルトガル人が日本に来てからパンを造って食べ始めま
した．現代では沢山の日本人が毎日パンを食べています．24．白熊は
冬の間氷の中の穴に寝ます．春が来ると冬眠からさめ，大変空腹を感
じ人に会えば物すごく飛びかゝります．　25．日本には黒熊がいます．
黒熊は北海道の山々に住んでいます．黒熊は馴らされると危険ではあ
りませんよろこんでその主人に服従します．

1. Who was in your room speaking to you?—Nobody was speaking to me.
I was alone studying my lesson. 2. Where is the city hall?—It is near that
bridge. 3. Go and buy some letter-paper, envelopes and a penholder.—Here
are the paper and envelopes.—And the penholder?—I forgot to buy it.
4. Hasn't Mr. Fukui come yet?—Yes, he came a short time ago, but he could
not wait and so he left. He will come again this afternoon. 5. This chain
is silver, that is platinum. 6. Bananas do not grow in Japan proper. They
grow in the Bonin Islands. 7. This fish smells bad; you mustn't eat it.
8. In Japan the cherry blossom is the king of flowers. 9. What is the *biwa*?
—It is a Japanese stringed instrument. Nowadays only a few people play
the *biwa*. 10. How is your father?—He is well, thank you. The doctor found
him in very good health. 11. Here are three watches; which do you prefer?
—I prefer this one. 12. Until eighty years ago the Japanese did not wear
foreign clothes. Now nearly all Japanese wear them. 13. A swallow is building its nest under the eaves of our house. 14. In every country there are
good people and bad people. 15. When I reached the hotel your letter had
not arrived yet. 16. Is there any Italian ship at anchor in the harbour to-day?
—Yes, there are two. 17. What was the railway fare to Nikko?—Five
hundred yen. 18. Has the carpenter finished his work?—No, the fence is
done, but the gate is not done yet. 19. Confucius was a Chinese and
Buddha was an Indian. 20. Osaka is a large and very busy city. 21. When
the fire started the guests were dancing in the hall. 22. As the maid has
been working the whole day she now feels very tired. She is just going to
bed. 23. Formerly the Japanese did not eat bread. When the Portuguese
came to Japan, they began to make and eat it. Now many Japanese are
accustomed to eating bread every day. 24. In winter the white bear sleeps
in a cave in the ice. When spring comes he awakes from his winter sleep
and feeling very hungry, he fiercely attacks men when he meets them.
25. In Japan there are black bears. They frequent the mountains in Hokkaido.
When the black bear is tamed he is not dangerous, and willingly obeys his
master.

Twenty-ninth Lesson　第廿九課

Wa and *Ga* (continued)
More Illustrations

A. Suppose that you expect the visit of somebody, Mr. Omura for instance. At the appointed time you return home and ask the servant:

Ōmura San *wa* kimáshĭta ka.　　*Did* Mr. Omura *come ?*
大村　さん　は　　来ました　　か.

The servant answers:

Iié, Ōmura San *wa irasshaimasén déshĭta ké*redomo Satō San ga
いゝえ, 大村さん　はいらっしゃいませんでした　けれども　佐藤　さん　が
*ir*asshaimáshĭta.　　No, Mr. Omura *did not come*, but **Mr. Sato** has come.
いらっしゃいました.

The emphasis in your question *Did Mr. Omura come?* falls on the predicate **come,** and similarly it falls on the predicate of the first clause of the answer **did not come,** in the answer given by the servant, while in the second clause of the answer *Mr. Sato has come.*, the emphasis falls on the subject **Sato San,** whom you did not expect, and so **Sato San** stands more prominent than the predicate *has come*, and therefore it takes *ga.*

We repeat, that whenever the emphasis falls on the **subject,** this is followed by *ga,* while when the emphasis falls on the **predicate** the subject takes *wa.*

B. Sometimes the use of *ga* and *wa* depends on the mind of the speaker.

Suppose that I have in front of me two or more objects of which one immediately attracts my attention because of its beauty. Wishing to manifest my admiration to somebody who is with me, I say, pointing to the admired object:

Koré *wa* kírei désŭ.　これはきれいです.　　This is *beautiful.*

In this sentence the emphasis falls on the predicate *kírei désŭ, is beautiful.* In fact, it is the beauty of the object that has attracted my attention, though I may not have paid enough attention to the other objects to compare them accurately. In saying "This is beautiful.", I have expressed my admiration from impulse rather than from a careful examination of the objects in front of me.

However, were I to compare the artistic beauty of the objects, before expressing an opinion, whether asked or supposed to be asked, then, even though I do not actually ask somebody "Which is beautiful, ?" it may be imagined that I have put such a question to myself. In this case, if I say "**This** is beautiful.", the emphasis falls on the subject **This** (to the exclusion of the other objects), which will therefore be followed by *ga,* according to the rule given in the previous lesson:

Koré *ga* kírei désŭ.　これがきれいです.

The above illustration explains the reason why the interrogative pronouns *dónata, dáre, dóno,* etc. and the subjects in answer to such interrogatives, are followed by *ga,* as said in Lesson 13, page 72.

C. In a question about the subject represented by something already spoken of, and in answer to the same question, the subject is followed by *ga.*

For instance, suppose we are going to see a school of which we have already spoken, and that on approaching a certain building I wish to ask whether the building is the school in question. I may ask :

1. *Koré ga sonó gakkō désŭ ka.* これがその学校ですか. Is **this** the school?

2. *Hái, koré ga sonó gakkō désŭ.*   Yes, **this** is the school.
はい, これ が その 学校 です.

3. *Iié, koré wa sonó gakkō de wa arimasén.*   No, this is not
いゝえ, これ は その 学校 で は ありません.   the school.

Iié, sō de wa arimasén.   No, it isn't.
いゝえ, そうで は ありません.

However, if in a similar question the subject has not been spoken of before, but is introduced in the question for the first time, *wa* is used after the subject :

4. *Koré wa nan désŭ ka.* これは何ですか.   What is this?

5. *Koré wa gakkō désŭ.* これは学校です.   This is a school.

From the above illustration we may clearly see that in example **1.** *Is this the school ?*, the emphasis in the sentence falls on this, as it does in answer **2** while in examples **4** and **5,** the emphasis falls on the predicates and not on the common subject *koré* (this), which therefore takes *wa.*

In answer **3** the emphasis falls on the predicate *is not a school,* and not on the subject *this.* (This *is not the school* spoken of.)

In all the above examples it is again demonstrated that the question of when to use *ga* and when *wa* is, as a general rule, a question of emphasis, whether on the subject or on the predicate.

After words indicating division of time *wa* is used when there is contrast with other periods of time :

Kónnichi wa yói o-ténki désŭ.   It is fine weather to-day.
今日 は よい お天気 です.   (compared with yesterday or other days)

Séngetsu wa samúi déshĭta.   Last month it was cold.
先月 は 寒い でした.   (compared with this or another month)

When there is no idea of contrast, words indicating division of time are used without being followed by any particle.

Séngetsu Nikkō e ıkimáshĭta.   Last month I went to Nikkō.
先月 日光 へ 行きました.

In this last sentence it is simply stated that at a certain time I went to Nikkō, without any reference to any other time. If however, we say : *Last month I did not go to Nikkō.* then *wa* is used,

Séngetsu wa Nikkō e ikimasén déshĭta.

because in this case there is the idea of comparison, as the sentence may imply that I am accustomed to go to Nikko periodically but did not go there last month.

In sentences in which the subject followed by *wa* is illustrated, the predicate may contain a word followed by *ga.*

Zō wa me ga chiisái. 象 は 眼 が 小さい.	⎧ The elephant has small eyes. ⎨ (The elephant the eyes are small.) ⎩ As to the elephant its eyes are small.
Nippón wa yamá ga ōi. 日本 は 山 が 多い.	⎧ Japan is mountainous. ⎨ (Japan, mountains are many.) ⎩ As to Japan its mountains are many.

Many expressions with *ga,* corresponding to English adjectives, have become idiomatic:

génki ga yói	元気がよい	(vitality is good)	vigorous, vivacious
ijí ga warúi	意地が悪い	(temper is bad)	ill-natured
ki ga mijikái	気が短かい	(spirit is short)	quick-tempered
kokoromochí ga yói	心持がよい	(feeling is good)	comfortable
kuchí ga warúi	口が悪い	(mouth is bad)	sarcastic
séi ga hikúi	背が低い	(stature is low)	short
séi ga takái	背が高い	(stature is high)	tall
tsugō ga yói	都合がよい	(circumstances are good)	convenient
tsugō ga warúi	都合が悪い	(circumstances are bad)	inconvenient
yōjin ga yói	用心がよい	(caution is good)	careful
yokú ga fukái	欲が深い	(greed is deep)	avaricious

When a word in the nominative is to be emphasized, it may be followed by the emphatic particle ***kóso*** こそ, in place of *ga* or *wa.* ***Kóso*** corresponds to *the very, just, indeed,* and other similar expressions. Examples:

Watashí kóso o-wabí[1] wo shi-nákereba narimasén.   It is I (and not you)
私 こそ お詫び を しなければ なりません.   that must apologize.
  (*lit.* I indeed, apology if I don't make, it won't do.)

Kóndo kóso seikō[2] shi-nákereba narimasén.   This very time I must
今度 こそ 成功 しなければ なりません.   succeed.
  (*lit.* This very time success if I don't make won't do.)

Toshí kóso wakái ga káre wa nakanaká no binwankú[3] désŭ.
年 こそ 若い が 彼 は なかなか の 敏腕家 です.
  Young as he is, he is a very capable man.
    (*lit.* The years indeed young, but very capable man he is.)

---

1 *o-wabí* apology; *o-wabí wo surú* to make an apology   **2** *seikō* success; *seikō surú* to make a success   **3** *binwanká* capable man

Sonó hanashí **kóso** *watashí ga kanégane kikitákatta monó désŭ.*
その 話 こそ 私 が かねがね聞きたかったもの です.
That is the very story I wanted to hear. (*kanégane* beforehand)
(*lit.* That very story I beforehand wished to hear, the thing is.)

Soré **kóso** *chōdo o-atsuraé-muki*[1] *désŭ.*   That is the very thing for us.
それ こそ 丁度 お誂え向き です.
That is the very thing for our purpose. (That the very, just ideal is.)

For other rules and details given in this book on the use of *wa* and *ga*, we refer the student to the index.

To See *míru* 見る, To be seen *miéru* 見える.

Míru (to see, to perceive by the eye) is a transitive verb, and its object is placed in the accusative.

Watashí wa ōkami **wo mimáshĭta.**   I saw a wolf.
私 はおおかみを 見ました.

Miéru 見える, the passive of *to see* (to be seen, to be visible), has its subject always followed by *ga* が.

Kokó kará Fújisan **ga miemásŭ.**   Mount Fuji is visible from here.
こゝ から 富士山 が 見えます.

The passive form of *to see* is used in Japanese more than in English. Even when we would say *I see, I can see Mount Fuji from here.*, in Japanese the passive is used as in the preceding example.

Miéru 見える means also *to seem, to appear, to look* (intr.). In this case the subject takes *wa* は.

Anáta **wa** *tsŭkárete*[2] **miemásŭ.**   You look tired.
貴方 は 疲れて 見えます.   (You being tired look.)

Anó uchí **wa** *chíisaku* **miemásŭ.**   That house appears to be small.
あの うち は 小さく 見えます.   That house looks small.

Watashí ni **wa** *amarí ōkiku* **miemásŭ.**   It looks too big to me.
私 に は 余り 大きく 見えます.   (To me too greatly looks.)

Anó musŭmé **wa** *gaijín no yō-ni* **miemásŭ.**[3]   That girl looks like
あの 娘 は 外人 のように 見えます.   a foreigner.

When **to see** is used with the meaning of *to meet, to have an interview with* (*somebody*), it is translated by *o-me ni kakáru* お目にかゝる, or the less polite ......*ni áu* ......に会う.

Anáta wa Arimá Taishō ni Meijí Jingū de **o-me ni kakarimáshĭta ka.**
貴方 は 有馬 大将 に 明治 神宮 で お目に かゝりました か.
Did you see (meet) Admiral Arima at the Meiji Shrine?

Hái, o-me ni kakarimáshĭta.   Yes, I met him.
はい, お目に かゝりました.   Yes, I saw him.

---

1 *atsŭraé-mukí* suitable, ideal   2 *tsŭkaréru* 疲れる to be tired   3 ......*no yō-ni miéru* ......のように見える to look like

Kinō watashí wa tōri de, omoigakénaku[1] mukashí no tomodachí ni
きのう　私　は　通り　で，思いがけなく　昔　の　友達　に
aimáshĭta.　Yesterday I unexpectedly met in the street an old friend of mine.
会いました.

Vocabulary

	Nouns					
			famous	*yūmei-na*	有ユゥ名メィナ
body (physical)	*karadá*	体カダラ	fashionable	*tōseimuki no*	
bud	*me*	芽メ			当トゥ世セ向ムキノ
dramatist	*gikyokŭká*	戯ギ曲キョク家カ	important	*taisetsú-na*	大タィ切セッナ
feeling(s)	*kanjō*	感カン情ジゥョ	noble	*kōshō-na*	高コゥ尚ショゥナ
gentleman	*shínshi*	紳シン士シ		**Verbs**	
grammar	{ *buntén*[2]	文ブン典テン	to acquire	*é·ru*	得エル
	{ *bumpō*[3]	文ブン法ポゥ	to consider	*kangáe·ru*	考カガエル
landlord	*yánushi*	家ヤ主ヌシ	to destroy	*sokonáu*	損ゾナゥウ
mind	*shinréi*	神シン霊レィ	to divide	*bunkái surú*	分ブン界カィスル
peninsula	*hantō*	半ハン島トゥ	to love	*aisúru*	愛アィスル
play (theat.)	*gikyokú*	戯ギ曲キョゥ	to protect	*fuségu*	防フゼグ
skin (fur)	*kegawá*	毛ケ皮ガゥ	to put forth	*fukú*	吹フク
universe	*úchū*	宇ゥ宙チゥゥ	to touch	*sawarú*	サワル
wisdom	*chié*	知チ慧エ	to use	*mochii·rú*	用モチィル

daily life *nichí-jō seikatsú*; ancient customs *kódai no fūshū*; distinguished-looking *hĭtogará no yói*; conservatory of music *ongakú gakkō*; to be considered *kangaeraré·ru*; summer resort *hishóchi*; quick tempered *kimijiká*; western countries *seiyōshokoku*

Exercise *Renshū* 練習

1. Samúi kuníguni[4] de wa ō-mukashí kará hĭtó wa sámusa wo fuségu[5] tamé ni kegawá wo mochiité imáshĭta. 2. Dōgu náshi de shigotó wa sŭkóshi kirí dekimasén.[6] 3. Seiyōshokoku[7] de wa pan wo takŭsán tabemásŭ ga Nihón Shína Ĭndo de wa pan wo sŭkóshi kirí tabemasén. 4. Kínsen[8] wo aisúru kotó wa hĭtó no súbete no kōshō-na kanjō wo sokonaimásŭ. 5. Kangáezu ni dokŭshó[9] surú kotó wa chié wo éru ni wa yakudatánu.[10] 6. Marúzen wa konó Nihóngo-buntén no itté-hambaitén[11] désŭ. 7. Dáiku wa kimáshĭta ka.—Iié, dáiku wa kimasén déshĭta, kéredomo ishĭyá ga kimáshĭta. 8. Pen to ínki wa chiisái monó désŭ ga warewaré no nichijō seikatsú ni wa taihén taisetsú désŭ. 9. Chikámatsu Monzaemón wa hijō ni yūmei-na Nihón no gikyokŭká déshĭta. Chikámatsu Monzaemón wa takŭsán no gikyokú wo kakimáshĭta soshĭté

---

1 *omoigakénai* 思いがけない unexpected **2** as a book **3** as a science **4** *kuníguni* is the plural of *kuní* country **5** *sámusa wo fuségu tamé ni* to protect oneself from the cold **6** lit. Tools without, work only little cannot. **7** Western countries **8** money **9** *dokŭshó surú* to read books **10** *yakudátsu* to be of use; *yakudatánai* of no use **11** sole agent

Nihón no Shēkusupiya to kangaerárete imásŭ. **10.** Kójiki wa kódai Nihón no rekishí désŭ. Móshi Nihón no kódai no fūshū wo shiritái náraba Kójiki wo yomá-nákereba[1] narimasén. **11.** Kurói yōfuku wo kitá anó hĭtogará no yói shínshi wa dónata désŭ ka.—Anó katá wa yūmei-na Itarī no ongakŭká desŭ. Anó katá wa jū-nen máe ni Nihón ni kité íma wa Uenó no Ongakú Gakkō de seigakú[2] wo oshieté imásŭ.—Anó katá no o-namaé wa nan to iimásŭ ka. —Komerī Sénsei to iimásŭ. **12.** Takú no yánushi wa taihén yokú ga fukái. **13.** Kamakurá wa dónna tokoró désŭ ka.—Kamakurá wa Tōkyō ni chikái tōseimuki no hishóchi désŭ. Watashí wa mái-nen natsú Kamakurá e ikimásŭ. **14.** Háru ga kúru to súbete no ki wa me wo fukimásŭ. **15.** Chōsen hantō wa Nihónkai[3] to Kōkai[4] to wo bunkái shĭté imásŭ. **16.** Shinréi wa zen[5] úchū ni michí-watatté[6] irú. **17.** Koré ga Shímbashi éki désŭ ka.—Iié, tsugí[7] no éki ga Shímbashi désŭ. **18.** Hĭtó wa kimijiká no hĭtó wo konomimasén. **19.** Nihón no onná wa gáishĭte[8] séi ga hikúi. **20.** Anó inú wa seishitsú[9] ga warúi désŭ. Sawaranái hō ga yói désŭ. **21.** Anó ki wa fúruku miemásŭ. **22.** Kóndo no Itarī táishi ni o-aí ni narimáshita ka.—Iié, o-me ni kakarimasén. Myōnichi o-me ni kakáru tsumorí désŭ. Kyō táishi wa Fŭransú táishi to Nikkō e ikaremáshĭta.[10] **23.** Sakuyá Ōsaka ni ōkii jishín ga arimáshĭta.

1. 寒い国々では大昔から人は寒さを防ぐために毛皮を用いていました. **2.** 道具なしで仕事は少しきり出来ません. **3.** 西洋諸国ではパンを沢山食べますが日本，支那，印度ではパンを少しきり食べません. **4.** 金銭を愛する事は人の総ての高尚な感情を損います. **5.** 考えずに読書する事は知慧を得るには役立たぬ. **6.** 丸善はこの日本語文典の一手販売店です. **7.** 大工は来ましたか.—いゝえ，大工は来ませんでしたけれども石屋が来ました. **8.** ペンとインキは小さいものですが我我の日常生活には大変大切です. **9.** 近松門左衛門は非常に有名な日本の戯曲家でした. 近松門左衛門は沢山の戯曲を書きましたそして日本のシェークスピヤと考えられています. **10.** 古事記は古代日本の歴史です. 若し日本の古代の風習を知りたいならば古事記を読まなければなりません. **11.** 黒い洋服を着たあの人柄のよい紳士はどなたですか.—あの方は有名なイタリーの音楽家です. あの方は十年前に日本に来て今は上野の音楽学校で声学を教えています.—あの方のお名前は何んと云いますか.—コメリー先生と云います. **12.** 宅の家主は大変欲が深い. **13.** 鎌倉はどんな所ですか.—鎌倉は東京に近い当世向きの避暑地です. 私は毎年夏鎌倉へ行きます. **14.** 春が来ると総ての木は芽を吹きます. **15.** 朝鮮半島は日本海と黄海とを分界しています. **16.** 神霊は全宇宙に満ちわたっている. **17.** これが新橋駅ですか.—いゝえ，次の駅が新橋です. **18.** 人は気短かの人を好みません.

---

1 *yomá-nákereba narimasén* you must read (if you do not read it won't do) 2 vocal music 3 Sea of Japan 4 Yellow Sea 5 whole 6 *michí-watarú* to pervade 7 next 8 generally 9 *seishitsú ga warúi* bad tempered, ill natured 10 *ikarerú* polite for *ikú*

19. 日本の女は概して背が低い．　**20.** あの犬は性質が悪いです．　さわらない方がよいです．　**21.** あの木は古く見えます．　**22.** こんどのイタリー大使にお会いになりましたか．—いゝえ，お目にかゝりません．明日お目にかかるつもりです．　きょう大使はフランス大使と日光へ行かれました．　**23.** 昨夜大阪に大きい地震がありました．

1. In cold countries, man has, from very ancient time, used skins of animals to protect his body. **2.** Without tools man can do very little work. **3.** In Western countries people eat much bread, but in Japan, China and India, people eat little. **4.** Love of money destroys all noble feelings in any man. **5.** Without thinking, reading is of little use in acquiring wisdom. **6.** Maruzen is the sole agent for this Japanese Grammar. **7.** Have the carpenters come? —No, they haven't, but the masons have come. **8.** Pen and ink are small things but they are very important in daily life. **9.** Monzaemon Chikamatsu was a Japanese dramatist of great fame. He wrote many plays, and is considered the Shakespeare of Japan. **10.** The Kojiki[1] is the history of ancient Japan. If you wish to know the old customs of Japan you must read that book. **11.** Who is that distinguished-looking man wearing a black coat?— He is a famous Italian musician. He came to Japan ten years ago, and now he teaches singing at the Ueno Conservatory of music.—What is his name? —Maestro Comelli. **12.** My landlord is very avaricious. **13.** What kind of a place is Kamakura?—It is a very fashionable summer resort near Tokyo. I go there every summer. **14.** When spring comes all trees put forth buds. **15.** The Peninsula of Korea separates the Sea of Japan from the Yellow Sea. **16.** Mind pervades the whole universe. **17.** Is this Shimbashi station?—No, the next station is Shimbashi. **18.** We do not like quick-tempered people. **19.** Japanese women are generally short. **20.** That dog is ill-natured. It is better not to touch it. **21.** That tree looks old. **22.** Have you met the new Italian Ambassador?—No, I have not. To-morrow I am going to meet him. To-day he has gone to Nikkō with the French Ambassador. **23.** Last night there was a big earthquake in Osaka.

A Japanese Proverb

Tákaki ni noború wa hikúki yóri.　高きに登るは低きより。
lit. To a height to ascend, low spot from. = Begin from a low spot to ascend a height. = *He who would climb the ladder must begin from the bottom.* (*tákaki* 高き height, *ni* に to, *noború* 登る to ascend, *hikúki* 低き low spot, *yóri* より from)

---

1 The *Kójiki* is the name given to a book containing the cronicles of ancient Japan. It was produced under the Emperor *Gemmyō* in 712 A. D. The word *Kojiki* means "Record of Ancient Matters."

Thirtieth Lesson　第卅課

Past Tense　*Káko*　過去

Besides the positive form of the past tense obtained with *máshĭta* ました (Lesson 16), there is another one used in familiar speech, which is formed by substituting the final *e* of the subordinate of the verb for an *a*.

The negative form, corresponding, in degree of politeness, to this past, is obtained with *nakatta* なかった, as already shown in Lesson 21. P. 131.

See phonetic rules on this second past form, Page 678 and 683.

Class I

		Subordinate	Positive Past		Negative Past	
míru 見る	to see	*míte* 見て	*míta* 見た	saw	*mínakatta* 見なかった	did not see
tabéru 食べる	to eat	*tábete* 食べて	*tábeta* 食べた	ate	*tabénakatta* 食べなかった	did not eat
irú[1] いる	to be	*ité* いて	*itá* いた	was	*inákatta* いなかった	(there) was not

Class II

			Subordinate	Positive Past		Negative Past	
1	*kógu* 漕ぐ	to row	*kóide* 漕いで	*kóida* 漕いだ	I rowed	*kogánakatta* 漕がなかった	did not row
	káku 書く	to write	*káite* 書いて	*káita* 書いた	I wrote	*kakánakatta* 書かなかった	did not write
2	*kesú* 消す	to put out[2]	*keshĭté* 消して	*keshĭtá* 消した	I put out	*kesanákatta* 消さなかった	did not put out
	kasú 貸す	to rent	*kashĭté* 貸して	*kashĭtá* 貸した	I rented	*kasanákatta* 貸さなかった	did not rent
3	*tátsu* 立つ	to stand	*tátte* 立って	*tátta* 立った	I stood	*tatánakatta* 立たなかった	did not stand
	mátsu 待つ	to wait	*mátte* 待って	*mátta* 待った	I waited	*matánakatta* 待たなかった	did not wait
4	*tobú* 飛ぶ	to fly	*tondé* 飛んで	*tondá* 飛んだ	I flew	*tobanákatta* 飛ばなかった	did not fly
	yómu 読む	to read	*yónde* 読んで	*yónda* 読んだ	I read	*yománakatta* 読まなかった	did not read
	shinú 死ぬ	to die	*shindé* 死んで	*shindá* 死んだ	He died	*shinanákatta* 死なゝかった	did not die

---

1 We remind the student that *irú* and *óru* are used for animate, and *áru* for inanimate, things. **2** to put out light, fire, *or* to extinguish

óru おる	to be	*ótte* おって	*ótta* おった	I was	*oránakatta* おらなかった	(there) was not
5	*áru* ある	to be	*átte* あって	*átta* あった	I was	*nákatta* 無かった	(there) was not
	tóru 取る	to take	*tótte* 取って	*tótta* 取った	I took	*toránakatta* 取らなかった	did not take
	iú 云う	to say	*itté* 云って	*ittá* 云った	I said	*iwanákatta* 云わなかった	did not say
6	*kaú* 買う	to buy	*katté* 買って	*kattá* 買った	I bought	*kawanákatta* 買わなかった	did not buy
	núu 縫う	to sew	*nútte* 縫って	*nútta* 縫った	I sewed	*nuwánakatta* 縫わなかった	did not sew
	surú する	to do	*shĭté* して	*shĭtá* した	I did	*shinákatta* しなかった	did not do

This past form is especially used, by both men and women, when it is followed by *toki* 時 or *toki ni* 時に (when), *kará* から or *nóde* ので (because). In other cases, however, it is used only by men in familiar speech. To Japanese ears this short form of past as given above sounds harsh and abrupt, for which reason it is avoided in polite speech.

Examples

*Watashí wa anó jidōsha wo **míta toki** ni kaitái to omoimáshĭta*
私　は　あの　自動車　を　見た　時　に　買いたいと　思いました
*ga o-kané ga **nákatta** nóde yamemáshĭta.* (*yamerú* to give up, to desist,
が　お金　が　無かった　ので　やめました.　　as from an attempt)
　　When I saw that motor-car I wanted to buy it, but as I had no money I gave it up.

*Sonó gaikokú shisetsú ga éki ni **tsŭíta toki** (ni) gunshū wa "banzái" wo*
その　外国　使節　が　駅　に　着いた　時　(に)　群集　は　万歳　を
sakebĭmáshĭta.　　When the Foreign Delegation arrived at the station the crowd
叫びました.　　shouted "banzai."[1] (*sakébu* to shout, *shisetsú* delegation)

*Bóku wa yūbe Ginzá[2] de atarashíi bōshi wo **kattá.***
僕　はゆうべ銀座　で　新しい　帽子　を　買った.
　　Last night I bought a new hat on Ginza.[2]

When using this past form in the interrogative, the particle *ka* is often precede by *no,* which renders the sentence more familiar and more pleasing to the ear.

*Kimí wa kinō éiga e **ittá no ka.***　　Did you go to the cinema
君　はきのう映画へ行った　の　か.　　　yesterday?

Iié, bóku wa ikanákatta. いゝえ, 僕は行かなかった.　　No, I did not go.

---

1 *Banzái,* which, translated literally, means "ten thousand years," corresponds to the expressions: *Long live! Long life to......! Hurrah! Hip, hip, hurrah!* etc.
2 The busiest and most popular thoroughfare in the city of Tokyo.

*Omaé wa dóko de konó saifú wo **nusánda** **no** **ka.***
お前 は どこ で この 財布 を 盗んだ の か.
Where did you steal this purse? (*nusúmu* to steal)

Nusánda *no de wa arimasén.* **Hirottá** *no désŭ.* I did not steal it;
盗んだ の で は ありません. 拾った の です. I found it.

Note that *bóku* 僕 and *kimí* 君 are used in familiar speech by young men,
and that *omaé* お前 is used in speaking to inferiors, which justifies the use of
the less polite form of the past, in the above three examples. See Lesson 10
for the use of the personal pronouns *bóku* 僕, *kimí* 君, and *omaé* お前.

At the end of an interrogative sentence the particle *ka* is rather often
omitted by women in very familiar speech. In this case, however, the particle
no is used. In very familiar speech even the principal verb may be omitted
when answering a question.

*Dóko e **ikú no.*** どこへ行くの.   Where are you going?

Kaimonó ni. 買物に.   I am going shopping.

*Sakúban anáta wa dóko e **ittá no.***   Where did you go last night?
昨晩 貴方 は どこ へ 行った の.

Ongakŭkái e. 音楽会へ.   To the concert.

Progressive Past Tense

By substituting the suffix *imáshĭta* いました for *itá* いた after
the subordinate of verbs, we obtain a second progressive form of
the past. The negative is formed by adding *inákatta* いなかった,
instead of *imasén déshĭta* いませんでした, to the subordinate.

Standard Form		**Familiar Form**
tábete imáshĭta 食べていました	was, were eating	*tábete itá* 食べていた
tábete imasén déshĭta 食べていませんでした	was. were not eating	*tábete inákatta* 食べていなかった
káite imáshĭta 書いていました	was, were writing	*káite itá* 書いていた
káite imasén déshĭta 書いていませんでした	was, were not writing	*káite inákatta* 書いていなかった
keshĭté imáshĭta 消していました	was, were extinguishing	*keshĭté itá* 消していた
keshĭté imasén déshĭta 消していませんでした	was, were not extinguishing	*keshĭté inákatta* 消していなかった
tátte imáshĭta 立っていました	was, were standing	*tátte itá* 立っていた
tátte imasén déshĭta 立っていませんでした	was, were not standing	*tátte inákatta* 立っていなかった
tondé imáshĭta 飛んでいました	was, were flying	*tondé itá* 飛んでいた

tondé imasén déshĭta 飛んでいませんでした	was, were not flying	*tondé inákatta* 飛んでいなかった
tótte imáshĭta 取っていました	was, were taking	*tótte itá* 取っていた
tótte imasén déshĭta 取っていませんでした	was, were not taking	*tótte inákatta* 取っていなかった
katté imáshĭta 買っていました	was, were buying	*katté itá* 買っていた
katté imasén déshĭta 買っていませんでした	was. were not buying	*katté inákatta* 買っていなかった

In degree of politeness, the progressive past with *itá* いた and *inákatta* いなかった corresponds to the past formed by the subordinate with its final *e* changed into *a*. The corresponding negative is formed with *nákatta* なかった.

Watashí ga ása no shokují wo tábete itá tokí ni jishín ga okorimashĭta.
私　が朝の　食事　を　食べていた　時に　地震が　起りました.
While I was eating breakfast an earthquake occurred.

Hibarí ga sóra tákaku tondé itá.　　Larks were flying high up in
ひばり　が　空　高く　飛んで　いた.　　the sky.

Kodomó wa kudámono wo tábete itá.　The children were eating fruit.
子供　は　果物　を　食べて　いた.

Compound Tenses

The Japanese language has no compound tenses as most European languages have. What in Japanese corresponds to our **past tense** corresponds also to our **perfect tense.** (See Lesson 16.)

I ate	*tabemáshĭta*	食べました
I have eaten	*tábeta*	食べた
I did not eat	*tabemasén déshĭta*	食べませんでした
I have not eaten	*tabĕnakatta*	食べなかった

Kinō no ása náni wo tabemáshĭta ka.　What did you eat
きのうの　朝　何　を　食べました　か.　yesterday morning?

Sakaná to góhan wo tabemáshĭta.　I ate fish and rice.
魚　と　御飯　を　食べました.

Anáta wa mō asahán wo tabemáshĭta ka.　Have you eaten
貴方　は　もう　朝飯　を　食べました　か.　breakfast already?

Iié, máda asahán wo tabemasén déshĭta.　No, I haven't eaten
いゝえ，まだ　朝飯　を　食べません　でした.　my breakfast yet.

Iié, máda désŭ. いゝえ，まだです.　　No, not yet.

What in Japanese corresponds to our **progressive past** (the subordinate followed by *imáshĭta* いました or *itá* いた) is also used for the **pluperfect.**

1. *Nippón ni kúru máe ni watashí wa Kánada ni jū-nen* **súnde imáshǐta**
日本 に 来る 前 に 私 は カナダ に 十年 住んで いました
(or itá).   Before I came to Japan I **had lived** (*or* been) ten years in Canada.
(いた).

2. *Watashí ga uchí ni tsúita tokí kázoku no monó wa súdeni[1]* **dekaketé**
私 が うち に 着いた 時 家族 の 者 は すでに 出かけて
imáshǐta.   When I arrived at home my family **had** already **gone out.**
いました.

3. *Anáta ga kimáshǐta máe ni watashi wa súdeni shigotó wo* **oeté**
貴方 が 来ました 前 に 私 は すでに 仕事 を 終えて
imáshǐta *(itá).*   Before you came I **had** already **finished** my work.
いました (いた).

4. *Ishá ga kitá máe ni byōnin wa* **shindé imáshǐta** *(itá).*
医者 が 来た 前 に 病人 は 死んで いました (いた).
Before the doctor came the patient **had died.**

5. *Watashí ga anó bengoshí ni tōri de átta máe ni watashí wa súdeni*
私 が あの 弁護士 に 通り で会った 前 に 私 は すでに
anó hǐtó no jimúsho e ni-do mo **itté imáshǐta** *(itá).*
あの 人 の 事務所 へ 二度 も 行って いました (いた).
I **had** already **been** to that lawyer's office twice before I met him in the street.

In Japanese, when the verb in the pluperfect indicates an action that is completely finished before the subsequent action takes place, the verb *shimaú* 仕舞う *to finish,* is often used after the subordinate of the principal verb. In this case the verb *shimaú* may be used in all its past forms: *shimatté imáshǐta* 仕舞っていました, *shimatté itá* 仕舞っていた, *shimaimáshǐta* 仕舞いました, *shimattá* 仕舞った, according to the degree of politeness. This rule may then be applied to examples 2, 3, 4 and 5, where the actions expressed by the verbs in the pluperfect were completely finished before the subsequent action took place.

Accordingly, the last verbs in the Japanese sentences 2, 3, 4 and 5, may be changed as follows:

2. ...... *dekaketé shimatté imáshǐta*	出かけて仕舞っていました
dekaketé shimaimáshǐta	出かけて仕舞いました
dekaketé shimatté itá	出かけて仕舞っていた
dekaketé shimattá	出かけて仕舞った
3. ...... *oeté shimatté imáshǐta*	終えて仕舞っていました
oeté shimaimáshǐta	終えて仕舞いました
oeté shimatté itá	終えて仕舞っていた
oeté shimattá	終えて仕舞った
4. ...... *shindé shimatté imáshǐta*	死んで仕舞っていました
shindé shimaimáshǐta	死んで仕舞いました
shindé shimatté itá	死んで仕舞っていた
shindé shimattá	死んで仕舞った

---

1 *súdeni* すでに already—See Lesson 31 p. 218 for the use of *súdeni*.

	itté shimatté imáshīta	行って仕舞っていました
5.	*itté shimaimáshīta*	行って仕舞いました
	itté shimatté itá	行って仕舞っていた
	itté shimattá	行って仕舞った

However, when the verb in the pluperfect indicates an action that was still in progress when the subsequent action took place, as in example 1 (*I had lived ten years in Canada before I came to Japan.*), the verb *shimaū* 仕舞う cannot be used, because the idea of a completed action is not implied.

When translating like sentences into Japanese, the clause expressing an action following that expressed by the pluperfect verb, comes first.

In English such a sentence as:

Before the doctor came | the patient had died.

may be expressed by inverting the order of the clauses:

The patient had died | before the doctor came.

without change of meaning. In Japanese, however, the clause *Before the doctor came* must come first.

There is another form of past tense in Japanese, which is used in familiar and friendly speech.

This form is obtained by changing the termination *ta* た of the past form of verbs of Class I and Class II into *chatta* ちゃった.

Class I		**Regular Past**	**Familiar Past**	
míru 見る	to see	*míta* 見た	*míchatta* 見ちゃった	saw
tabéru 食べる	to eat	*tábeta* 食べた	*tábechatta* 食べちゃった	ate
irú いる	to be	*itá* いた	*ichattá* いちゃった	was, were

Class II			**Regular Past**	**Familiar Past**	
Group 1	*káku* 書く	to write	*káita* 書いた	*káichatta* 書いちゃった	wrote
Group 2	*kesú* 消す	to put out	*keshītá* 消した	*keshīchattá* 消しちゃった	put out
	kasú 貸す	to rent	*kashītá* 貸した	*kashīchattá* 貸しちゃった	rented
	surú する	to do	*shītá* した	*shīchattá* しちゃった	did

Verbs in the past that end in *tta* った, change this termination into *tchatta* っちゃった.

Group 3	*tátsu* 立つ	to stand	*tátta* 立った	*tátchatta* 立っちゃった	stood
	mátsu 待つ	to wait	*mátta* 待った	*mátchatta* 待っちゃった	waited
Group 5	*áru* ある	to be	*átta* あった	*átchatta* あっちゃった	was, were
	tóru 取る	to take	*tótta* 取った	*tótchatta* 取っちゃった	took
Group 6	*iú* 云う	to say	*ittá* 云った	*itchattá* 云っちゃった	said
	kaú 買う	to buy	*kattá* 買った	*kacthattá* 買っちゃった	bought
	núu 縫う	to sew	*nútta* 縫った	*nátchatta* 縫っちゃった	sewed

Verbs in the past that end in *da* change this termination into *jatta.*

Group 1	*kógu* 漕ぐ	to row	*kóida* 漕いだ	*kóijatta* 漕いじゃった	rowed
Group 4	*tobú* 飛ぶ	to fly	*tondá* 飛んだ	*tonjattá* 飛んじゃった	flew
	yobú 呼ぶ	to call	*yondá* 呼んだ	*yonjattá* 呼んじゃった	called
	shinú 死ぬ	to die	*shindá* 死んだ	*shinjattá* 死んじゃった	died

The above past form has been given for grammatical information only. It will not be used in the examples nor in the exercises.

Vocabulary

Nouns

bandit	*bázoku*	馬バ賊ゾク
booty	*emonó*	エモノ
collar	*karā*	カラー
corner	*kádo*	角カド
enemy	*tekí*	敵テキ
fireman	*shōbōfu*	消シヨ防ボウ夫フ
laundryman	*sentakuyá*	洗セ濯タク屋ヤ
lawyer	*bengóshi*	弁ベン護ゴ士シ
missionary	*dendōshi*	伝デン道ドウ師シ
museum	*hakubutsŭkán*	博ハク物ブツ館カン
pamphlet	*shōzasshi*	小シヨ冊サッ子シ
	panfŭrétto	パンフレット
restaurant	*ryōri-ya*	料リヨ理リ屋ヤ

sailor	*súihei*	水スイ兵ヘイ
storm	*árashi*	嵐アラシ
traveller	*ryokōsha*	旅リヨ行コウ者シヤ
underwear	*shĭtagi*	下シタ着ギ
village	*mura*	村ムラ

Adjectives

severe	*sugói*	凄スゴイ
imperial	*teishitsú*	帝テイ室シツ

Verbs

to borrow	*haishakú surú*	拝ハイ借シヤク スル
to climb	*noború*	登ノボル
to evacuate	*hiki-agé·ru*	引ヒキ揚アゲル
to distribute	*kubáru*	配クバル

to flee	nigé·ru	逃゠ゲル	to remember	obóe·ru	覚オボエル
to occur	okóru	起オコル	to rescue	kyūjo surú	
to pursue	tsuiseki surú	追ツイ跡キセスル			救キュウ助ジョスル
to overtake	oitsúku	追オイ着ツク	to ring	narasú	鳴ナラス
to remain	todomáru	留トドマル	to shout	sakébu	叫サケブ

to lose (miss) one's way *michí ni mayóu*; to suffer much, to go through hardships *nangí wo surú*; mounted police *kibajúnsa*; farmer's house *nōka*; to accompany *tsureté ikú*

Exercise *Renshū* 練習

1. Watashí no toránku to kabán wo éki e mótte ikimáshĭta ka.—Hái, mótte ikimáshĭta, soshĭté chíkki[1] (áifuda) wa kokó ni arimásŭ. **2.** Sentakuyá wa bóku no shátsu wo mótte kimáshĭta ka.—Iié, mótte kimasén déshĭta. Karā to shĭtagí wo mótte kimáshĭta ga shátsu wa mótte kimasén déshĭta. **3.** Watashí wa ítsu déshĭta ka[2] konó machí wo tōrimáshĭta ga soré ga ítsu de átta ka oboemasén. **4.** Tekí ga sonó shi ni shinnyū[3] shĭtá tokí shímin wa súdeni hikiágete imáshĭta. **5.** Shōbōfu ga tōchaku[4] shĭtá tokí ni ié wa súdeni yaké-óchite[5] imáshĭta. **6.** Michí ni mayótta[6] ryokōshatachi wa warewaré ga kárera wo kyūjo shĭtá máe ni súdeni zúibun hídoku nangí wo shĭté itá no déshĭta. **7.** Wága kibajúnsa ga tōchaku shĭtá máe ni súdeni bázoku wa emonó wo mótte nígete shimatté itá. Kibajúnsa wa kárera wo ichi-nichí-jū[7] tsuiseki shĭtá ga oitsúku kotó ga dekínakatta. **8.** Warewaré ga yamá wo nobotté itá tokí ni sugói árashi ga hajimarimáshĭta.[8] Warewaré wa nōka ni hínan[9] wo shimáshĭta soshĭté akurú ása[10] máde sokó ni todomarimáshĭta. **9.** Ginzá wo arúite itá tokí ni san-nin no Igirisú no súihei wo mimáshĭta. Bóku wa eigó de sonó hĭtótachi ni hanashimáshĭta. Sorekará sonó hĭtótachi wo Ueno Kōen e tsureté ikimáshĭta. Kárera wa Hakubutsŭkán[11] wo mitagátte[12] imáshĭta. **10.** Anó hĭtó wa anáta ni náni wo kuremáshĭta ka.—Shōzasshi (Panfŭrétto) wo kuremáshĭta. Anó hĭtó wa Igirisujín no dendōshí désŭ. Anó hĭtó wa tabitabí anó tatémono no kádo ni tátte panfŭrétto wo kubátte imásŭ. **11.** Késa no shimbún wo mō o-yomí ni narimáshĭta ka.—Iié, máda. Náze désŭ ka.—Nan-demó arimasén. Haishakú shĭtákatta no déshĭta.—Mótte irasshái; sokó no tēburu no ué ni arimásŭ. **12.** Konó ié ni nágaku o-sumái désŭ ka.—Go-nen kokó ni súnde orimásŭ. **13.** Chūzenji e tabitabí ikimáshĭta ka.—Iié, tabitabí de wa arimasén. Honnó[13] ni-san-do désŭ.—Natsú asokó e wa takŭsán gaikokujín ga ikimásŭ. **14.** Tōkyō ni kúru máe ni watashí wa Ōsaka ni jū-nen súnde imáshĭta. **15.** Kimí ga yobirín[14] wo narashĭtá tokí ni bóku wa Nihón-go no hon-yakú[15] wo oeté shimatté dekakerú tokoró déshĭta. Bóku wa ryōriya e itté yūhan wo tabeyō[16] to omótte itá no déshĭta. **16.** Anáta no dempō wo uketorú máe ni

---

1 *chíkki* or *áifuda* check **2** *ítsu déshĭta ka* sometime past **3** *shinnyū surú* to enter, penetrate into **4** *tōchaku surú* to arrive **5** *yaké-ochíru* to be burned down **6** *michí ni mayótta* that had lost the way=the lost...... **7** *ichi-nichí-jū* the whole day **8** *hajimarú* to begin **9** *hínan wo surú* to take shelter **10** *akurú ása* next morning **11** *Hakubutsŭkán* Museum **12** *mitagátte irú* to wish, want to see **13** only **14** bell **15** translation **16** *tabeyō* I will eat; *to omótte itá no déshĭta* I had thought

watashí wa ni-do mo éki e itté imáshǐta. **17.** Nikái de náni wo shǐté imáshǐta ka. Anáta ga amarı otó wo tátete[1] itá nóde watashí wa benkyō surú kotó ga dekimasén déshǐta.—Bóku wa hataraité imáshǐta. Ki no hakó wo tsǔkútte itá no désǔ. **18.** Nihón ni kúru máe ni watashí wa Nihón-go wo ni-nen kan benkyō shimáshǐta ga, Nihón-go ga amarí muzukashíi nóde watashí ga Nihón-go wo hanáshǐte mo Nihón-jin ni wa yóku tsūjimasen[2] déshǐta shi watashí mo Nihón-jin no hanásu no ga yóku wakarimasén déshǐta. Shikáshi ima wa Nihón-go wo hanásu kotó mo káku kotó mo soshǐté ryōkai[3] surú kotó mo yóku dekimásǔ.

1. 私のトランクと鞄を駅へ持って行きましたか.—はい，持って行きました. そしてチッキ（合[がふ]札[さつ]）はこゝにあります. **2.** 洗濯屋は僕のシャツを持って来ましたか.—いゝえ，持って来ませんでした. カラーと下着を持って来ましたがシャツは持って来ませんでした. **3.** 私はいつでしたかこの町を通りましたがそれがいつであったか覚えません. **4.** 敵がその市に侵入した時市民はすでに引揚げていました. **5.** 消防夫が到着した時に家はすでに焼け落ちていました. **6.** 道に迷った旅行者達は我々が彼等を救助した前にすでに随分ひどくなんぎをしていたのでした. **7.** 我が騎馬巡査が到着した前にすでに馬賊はえものを持って逃げてしまっていた，騎馬巡査は彼等を一日中追跡したが追いつく事が出来なかった. **8.** 我々が山を登っていた時にすごい嵐がはじまりました. 我々は農家に避難をしましたそして翌る朝までそこに留まりました. **9.** 銀座を歩いていた時に三人のイギリスの水兵を見ました. 僕は英語でその人達に話しましたそれからその人達を上野公園へ連れて行きました彼等は博物館を見たがっていました. **10.** あの人は貴方に何を呉れましたか.—小冊子（パンフレット）を呉れました. あの人はイギリス人の伝道師です. あの人は度々あの建物の角に立ってパンフレットを配っています. **11.** けさの新聞をもうお読みになりましたか.—いゝえ，まだ. 何故ですか.—何んでもありません. 拝借したかったのでした.—持っていらっしゃい. そこのテーブルの上にあります. **12.** この家に長くお住いですか.—五年こゝに住んでおります. **13.** 中禅寺へ度々行きましたか.—いゝえ，度々ではありませんほんの二三度です.—夏あそこへは沢山外国人が行きます. **14.** 東京に来る前に私は大阪に十年住んでいました. **15.** 君が呼鈴を鳴らした時に僕は日本語の翻訳を終えてしまって出かけるところでした. 僕は料理屋へ行って夕飯を食べようと思っていたのでした. **16.** 貴方の電報を受取る前に私は二度も駅へ行っていました. **17.** 二階で何をしていましたか. 貴方があまり音を立てゝいたので私は勉強

---

1 *otó wo tatéru* to make a noise **2** *tsūjiru* to make oneself understood; *Nihónjin ni wa yóku tsūjimásén déshǐta* I could not make myself well understood by the Japanese. **3** *ryōkai surú* to understand

する事が出来ませんでした．—僕は仂いていました．　木の箱を造って
いたのです．　**18.** 日本に来る前に私は日本語を二年間勉強しましたが
日本語が余りむづかしいので私が日本語を話しても日本人にはよく通
じませんでしたし私も日本人の話すのがよく解りませんでした．然し
今は日本語を話す事も書く事もそして了解する事もよく出来ます．

1. Did you take my trunk and valises to the station?—Yes, I took them,
and here are the checks. **2.** Has the laundryman brought my shirts?—No,
he hasn't. He brought your collars and underwear, but not the shirts. **3.** I
have sometimes passed by this street, but I do not remember when. **4.** When
the enemy entered the city, the citizens had already evacuated it. **5.** When
the firemen arrived the house was already burned down. **6.** The lost travellers
had already suffered a great deal when we rescued them. **7.** The bandits
had already fled with their booty when our mounted police arrived. The
police pursued them the whole day but they could not overtake them. **8.** While
we were climbing the mountain, a severe storm began. We took shelter in
a farmer's house, and remained there until the next morning. **9.** While I was
walking on Ginza I saw three British sailors. I spoke to them in English
and then accompanied them to Ueno Park. They wanted to see the Museum.
10. What has that man given you?—He has given me some pamphlets. He
is an English missionary. He often stands at the corner of that building
distributing pamphlets. **11.** Have you already read the newspaper this morning?
—No, I haven't. Why?—Oh, nothing, I only wished to borrow it.—You may
have it; there it is on the table. **12.** Have you lived in this house long?—
I have lived here five years. **13.** Have you often been to Chūzenji?—No, not
often, only two or three times.—Many foreigners go there in summer.
14. Before I came to Tōkyō I had lived ten years in Osaka. **15.** When you
rang the bell I had already finished my Japanese translation and was ready
to go out. I wanted to go to the restaurant for dinner. **16.** Before I received
your telegram I had gone to the station twice. **17.** What were you doing
upstairs? You were making so much noise that I could not study.—I was
working; I was making some wooden boxes. **18.** Before I came to Japan
I had studied the Japanese language for two years. But as the language is
very difficult, the Japanese did not understand me well when I spoke to
them, and I understood very little when they spoke to me. Now, however,
I speak, write and understand Japanese quite well.

A Japanese Proverb

Akuji mi ni káeru. 悪事身に帰る *lit.* Evil to the body returns.
=Evil returns to one who has done it.=*They hurt themselves that
hurt others.* (*ákuji* 悪事 evil, *mi* 身 body, *ni* に to, *káeru* 帰る to
return)

Thirty-first Lesson   第卅一課

Progressive Conjugation

Perfect Tense   *Génzai Kanryō*   現在完了

What in Japanese corresponds to the English perfect tense of the progressive conjugation is obtained by using the word **zuttó** ずっと (all the time, continuously) before the present or past tense formed by the *subordinate* and the suffix *imásŭ* or *imáshĭta*.

Note that the word **zuttó** is rather emphatic and may be omitted whenever emphasis is not needed.

> *Zuttó hataraité imásŭ* (or *imáshĭta*.) I have been working.
> ずっと　働いて　います　（いました.） (continuously)
>
> *Zuttó benkyō shĭté imásŭ* (or *imáshĭta*.) I have been studying.
> ずっと　勉強　して　います　（いました.） (continuously)
>
> *Watashí wa ichí nichí-jū zuttó hataraité imásŭ* (or *imáshĭta*.)
> 私　は　一　日中　ずっと　働いて　います　（いました）.
> I have been working the whole day.

The idea of the Japanese in using the past of the progressive conjugation even when the action expressed by the verb is not completely finished, is that when one speaks one interrupts the action one is performing, an interruption which renders the action spoken of, a momentary past event. On the other hand, the use of the present conveys the idea that the action continues even while the performer is speaking.

The use of both the past and the present for the translation of the progressive perfect tense is possible only when the progressive action is performed by the speaker. However, when one refers to an action that is being performed by a third person, then only the present is used, because the action will not have any interruption when one speak of it, as shown in the two following examples.

> *Anó onná wa ichí jikán bákari* (or *guraí*) *zuttó shabétte imásŭ.*
> あの　女　は　一　時間　ばかり　（位）　ずっとしゃべっています.
> That woman has been chatting for about an hour. (and is still chatting)
>
> *Anó o-ishá wa konó byōin ni jū-nen bákari zuttó tsutómete[1] imásŭ.*
> あの　お医者　は　この　病院　に　十年　ばかり　ずっと　勤めて　います.
> That doctor has been working at this hospital for about ten years. (and he is still working here.)

Pluperfect Tense   *Káko Kanryō*   過去完了

The **pluperfect** of the progressive conjugation is the same as the

---

1 *tsutoméru* to serve an office, in an office, to be in the service of, to do professional work; *hatarakú* to work, used for professional as well as ordinary manual work

pluperfect of the ordinary conjugation of verbs as given in the previous lesson, that is, it is formed by adding *imáshĭta* or *itá* to the *subordinate*.

Note that the forms with **shimaú** 仕舞う are not used in the progressive conjugation.

súnde imáshĭta or **itá** 住んで　いました　　　いた	I had been living
benkyō shĭté imáshĭta or **itá** 勉強　　して　　いました　（いた）	I had been studying

Tōkyō ni kúru máe ni watashí wa Kyōto ni súnde imáshĭta.
東京　に　来る　前　に　私　　は　京都　に　住んで　いました.
Before coming to Tōkyō I **had been living** in Kyōto.

*Ani wa Kemburijí Daigakú e ikú máe ni Tōkyō Daigakú de **benkyō***
兄　は　ケンブリヂ　大学　へ行く　前　に　東京　大学　で　　勉強
shĭté imáshĭta.   Before going to Cambridge University my elder brother **had**
して　いました.   **been studying** at the Tōkyō University.

The progressive conjugation is formed also by adding **nágara**
ながら or **tsutsu** つゝ to the simple stem of verbs of Class I and
the *i*-stem of verbs of Class II. In this case, both suffixes **nágara**
ながら and **tsutsu** つゝ correspond to **while**.

Note that *tsutsu* つゝ is used in literary style.

tabéru to eat —*tabenágara* or *tábetsutsu* while eating 食べる　　　　　食べながら　　　食べつゝ	
waraú to laugh—*warainágara* or *waráitsutsu* while laughing 笑う　　　　　笑いながら　　　笑いつゝ	

*Anó hĭtó wa **tabenágara** (tábetsutsu) mo hon wo yomimáshĭta.*
あの　人　は　食べながら　（食べつゝ）　も　本　を　読みました.
He kept on reading even while (he was) eating.

*Watashidómo wa ōji wo **katarinágara** (katáritsutsu) yo wo fukashimáshĭta.*
私共　　は往時を　語りながら　　（語りつゝ）夜　を　ふかしました.
We sat up till late, (while) talking of bygone days. (*katarú* 語る to talk, to
narrate, *yo wo fukásu* 夜をふかす to sit up till late at night, *yo* 夜 night)

For, During

When **for** has the meaning of *during*, and is followed by a word
or words expressing a period of time, it is translated by **kan** 間 or
no aidá[1] 間. In this case, both **kan** and **aidá** correspond to
interval, period.

Tō ka kan. or **Tō ka no aidá.** 十　日　間　　　十　日　の　　間	**For** (during) ten days. For a period of ten days.

---

1 Although the two words *kan* and *aidá* are pronounced differently, they are
written with the same Chinese character. The use of *aidá* is more colloquial than *kan*.

Yo nen **kan.** or *Yo nen* **no aidá.**   **For** (during) four years.
四　年　間　　　四　年　の　間

Ni shū **kan.** 二週間   **For** (during) two weeks.

For euphonic reason **no aidá** is not used after **shū** 週 week.

Watashí no ojí wa anó iĕ ni **san-nen kan** (*san-nen no* **aidá**) *súnde*
私　の伯父　は　あの家　に　三年　　間　（三年　　の　　間）住んで
imásŭ.   My uncle has been living in that house **for** three years.
います.

Konó hon wo **mikká kan** (*mikká* **no aidá**) *yónde imásŭ.*
この　本　を　三日　　間　（三日　の　　間）　読んでいます.
I have been reading this book **for** three days.

Warewaré no tomodachí wa **ni-shū kan** *bákari ái ni kimasén.*
我々　の　　友達　　は　　二週　　間　ばかり会いに　来ません.
Our friends have not come to see us **for** two weeks.

Chichí wa byōki de **tō ka kan** *neté imásŭ.*   My father has been ill in
父　は　病気　で　十　日　間　寝ています.   bed **for** ten days.

In the last example, *de* で after the word *byōki* 病気, has to be considered
as the abbreviation of *désŭ-kará* ですから, meaning *is because.* The literal
translation of the example would then be: *Father sick is because, for ten days'
period in bed is.* (*nerú* 寝る to be confined to one's bed, to be laid up
with illness, etc.—*Nerú* 寝る means also *to sleep, to go to sleep.*)

When an action is finished at the end of a stated period of time, the postposition *de* で is added to **kan** 間. The postposition *ni* に, however, may
be used after **kan** 間 as well as after **aidá** 間.

Konó hon wŏ **tō ka kan ni** (*tō ka kan de, tō ka kan* **no aidá**
この　本　を　十　日　間　に（十　日　間　で,　十　日　間　の　間
ni) *yomimáshĭta.*   I read (have read) this book **in** (within) ten days.
に）読みました.

Within (not longer in time than......)

Inai de 以内で, *ínai ni* 以内に, *kan de* 間で, *kan ni* 間に

De で after *ínai* 以内 or **kan** 間 is used when *within* refers to action
performed, while *ni* に is used in other cases.

Káre wa go-fun **ínai ni** *kokó e kimásŭ.*   He will be here **within**
彼　は　五分　以内　に　こゝへ　来ます.   five minutes.
     (*lit.* He five minutes within here comes.)

Watashí wa konó shigotó wo **yokká kan de** (*ínai de,* etc.) *oemáshĭta.*
私　は　この　仕事　を　四日　　間　で（以内　で,）　終えました.
I have finished this work **within** four days. (action performed)

Konó yōfuku wo **muiká kan de** (*ínai de,* etc.) *koshiraeté kudasái.*
この　洋服　を　六日　　間　で（以内　で,）　こしらえて下さい.
Please make this suit **within** six days. (action to be performed)

While

Aidá (*ni*) 間 (に), *Uchí* (*ni*) 内 (に), *Toki* (*ni*) 時 (に)

When two or more clauses in a sentence, one of which introduced by **while,** indicate actions continuous for a certain period of time, only *aidá ni* 間に or *toki ni* 時に is used.

1. *Watashí ga hataraité itá aidá ni* (or *toki ni*) *ryōshin wa nemutté*
私　　が　仂いて　いた　間　　に　　　（時　に）　両親　は　ねむって
imáshĭta. While I was working **my parents** were sleeping.
いました.

However, when the clause following the one introduced by *while* expresses an action that occurred at a certain moment, while another action was in progress, then, any of the three expressions *aidá ni, uchí ni,* or *toki ni* may be used.

2. *Watashí ga hataraité itá uchí ni (aidá ni,* or *toki ni) ryōshin*
私　　が　仂いて　いたうち　に　（間　に,　　　時　に）　両親
wa nemáshĭta. While I was working **my parents** went to bed.
は　寝ました.

3. *Warewaré ga anó yamá ni nobotté itá toki ni (aidá ni, uchí ni)*
我々　　が　あの　山　に　登っていた　時　に　（間　に, うち に）
yuki ga furidashimáshĭta.[1] While **we** were climbing the mountain **it** began
雪　が　降り出しました.   to snow.

4. *Anáta ga dekaketé itá toki ni (aidá ni, uchí ni) konó dempō ga*
貴方　が　出かけていた　時　に　（間　に, うち に）この　電報　が
kimáshĭta. Wh..e **you** were out **this telegram** came.
来ました.

Note that in the above cases **2, 3** and **4** the actions expressed by the clauses following the ones introduced by **while** (*went to bed, it began to snow, the telegram came*) require some time for completion. In these and similar cases the three expressions *aidá ni, uchí ni, toki ni* may be used. However, if the action expressed by the clause following the one introduced by *while* happens suddenly, only *toki ni* is generally used, as in the two examples below. Sometimes *aidá ni* is also used, but *uchí ni* is not, as in example **1,** in which, two actions are in progress at the same time.

5. *Watashí wa michí wo yokogítte itá toki ni korondé ashí wo kegá*
私　　は　道　を　横ぎつて　いた　時　にころんで　足　を　怪我
shimáshĭta. While I was crossing the street I fell and hurt my leg. (*yokogíru*
しました.   横ぎる to cross, to go across a street, etc., *korobú* ころぶ to
fall, *kegá wo surú* 怪我をする to get wounded or hurt, *kegá* 怪我 wound)

6. *Watashí wa jimúsho e ikú toki ni anáta no otōsan ni aimáshĭta.*
私　　は　事務所　へ行く　時　に　貴方　のお父さんに会いました.
While I was going to the office I met your father.

In very familiar speech, and in sentences similiar to the examples **2, 3,** and **4, while** may be translated by **ma ni** 間に, as in the following two examples :

---

1 *furidasú* to begin to fall, as rain, snow

7. *Káre* ***ga*** *rúsu no* ***ma ni*** *dorobō ga hairimáshĭta.*　　While **he** was absent
彼　が　留守　の　間　に　泥棒　が　入りました.　　a thief entered.

8. *Watashí* ***ga*** *neté irú* ***ma ni*** *anó katá wa déte ikimáshĭta.*
私　がねている　間　に　あの　方　は　出て　行きました.
He left while **I** was sleeping.

In Lesson 22, page 145, it has been said that the subject of a clause introduced by **when** takes *wa* は if it is also the subject of the second clause, but takes *ga* が if the subjects of the two clauses are different. The same rule applies to the subject introduced by **while.**

Accordingly, the subjects of the clauses introduced by **while** in the examples 1, 2, 3, 4, 7 and 8 are followed by the postposition *ga* が because the subjects of their second clauses are different, and the subjects of the clauses introduced by **while** in the examples 5 and 6 are followed by *wa* は because they are also the subjects of the second clauses. As to the second clause in the Japanese translation, its subject may take *ga* が if it is to be emphasized.

How Long?

Dóno kurai[1] どの位, *Dóno kurai nágaku* どの位長く

Dóno kuraí どの位 is an abbreviation of *dóno kuraí nágaku* どの位長く.

Dóno kuraí nágaku watashí wo mátte imáshĭta ka.
どの　位　長く　私　を　待って　いました　か.
How long have you been waiting for me?

Anáta wa Nihón-go wo dóno kuraí benkyō shĭté imásŭ ka.
貴方　は　日本語　を　どの　位　勉強　して　います　か.
How long have you been studying Japanese?

Watashi wa Nihón-go wo ichí nen bákari benkyō shĭté imásŭ.
私　は　日本語　を　一　年　ばかり　勉強　して　います.
I have been studying Japanese for about one year.

Note that in the first example the Japanese for *have been waiting* is in the past tense, because when the question is asked the act of waiting is finished, while in the other two examples the present is used because the act of studying continues and will continue even after the question is asked.

Since

kará から, *írai* 以来

Kará is generally used in ordinary conversation, while *írai* is used in formal speech and in literary style.

---

1 *kuraí* is sometimes pronounced *guraí*

Watashi wa sengetsu kará anáta no otōsan ni aimasén.
私　は　先月　から　貴方　のお父さんに会いません.
I haven't seen (*lit.* I don't meet) your father since last month.

Dóno kuraí nágaku Tōkyō ni súnde imásŭ ka.   How long have you been
どの　位　長く　東京　に　住んでいます　か.   living in Tōkyō?

Watashí wa sakunén kará Tōkyō ni súnde imásŭ.
私　は　昨年　から　東京　に　住んでいます.
I have been living in Tōkyō since last year.

Since then is translated by *Sonó toki kará*......その時から or
by *Sonó toki írai* その時以来 in formal speech.

Watashí no Nihón-go no senséi wa ni-nen máe ni Indo e ikimáshĭta.
私　の　日本語　の　先生　は　二年　前　に　印度へ行きました.

Sonó toki kará tegamí ga ichí-do mo kimasén.
その　時　から　手紙　が　一度　も　来ません.

My Japanese teacher went to India two years ago; **since then** I haven't received
any letter from him. (*lit.* since then letter even one time does not come.)

Relative Interrogative Adjectives

What......? What kind of......? What sort of......?

Dónna......どんな. *Dō yū*......どうゆう, *Dō yū yō-na*......どうゆう様な

These three Japanese expressions are given in their increasing
degree of politeness. *Dónna* is the most common in ordinary
speech.

Dónna (dō yū or dō yū yō-na) hon ga hoshíi désŭ ka.
どんな　（どうゆう，どうゆう様な）　本　が　欲しい　です　か.
What kind of a book do you wish to have?

Nihón rekishí ga hoshíi désŭ.   I wish to have a history of Japan.
日本　歴史　が　欲しい　です.

Dónna (dō yū, dō yū yō-na) tebúkuro wo okāsan ni agemáshĭta ka.
どんな　（どうゆう，どうゆう様な）　手袋　をお母さんにあげました　か.
What kind of gloves did you give your mother?

Kawá no tebúkuro wo agemáshĭta.   I gave her leather gloves.
革　の　手袋　を　上げました.

Other expressions corresponding in meaning to **What kind, sort of......**, are
Dónna shúrui no どんな種類の and *Dō yū shúrui no*......どうゆう種類
の, which are especially used when one wishes to know some details of the
object one inquires about. *Shúrui* 種類 means *a kind, a sort, a class, a species,*
a type, etc.

Dō yū shúrui no inú wo kaimashĭta ka.   What sort of a dog did
どうゆう　種類　の　犬　を　買いました　か.   you buy?

Shirói tériya wo kaimáshĭta.   I bought a white terrier.
白い　テリヤ　を　買いました.

Dónna shírui no hon ga kodomó ni wa yói désŭ ka.
どんな　種類　の　本　が　子供　に　は　よい　です　か.
What kind of books are good for children?

Omoshírokute tamé ni náru[1] hon ga yói désŭ.
面白くて　ため　に　なる　本　が　よい　です.
Interesting and instructive books are good (for children).

What......? What kind of......? What sort of......? may be translated also
by *Nan no......* 何んの (See Lesson 13, page 72), which, however, is not so
emphatic as the other synonymous expressions given above.

Yūbe shibai de nan no géki wo mimáshĭta ka.
ゆうべ　芝居　で　何ん　の　劇　を　見ました　か.
What play did you see last night at the theatre?

Puchiní no O-chō-Fújin wo mimáshĭta.   I saw Puccini's "Madame
プチニ　の　お蝶　夫人　を　見ました.   Butterfly."

Anáta no senséi wa anáta ni nan no hon wo agemáshĭta ka.
貴方　の　先生　は　貴方　に　何ん　の　本　を　上げました　か.
What book did your teacher give you?

Nihón no fūshū ni tsúite no hon wo kudasaimáshĭta.
日本　の　風習　に　ついて　の　本　を　下さいました.
He gave me a book on Japanese customs.   (*fūshū* customs, manners)

When the English preposition on is used with the meaning of *in reference
to, in relation to, with respect to* or *about,* it is translated by *ni tsúite......* に
ついて, as in the last sentence.

Still

In ordinary conversation and in ordinary written style the adverb
still may be translated by any of the expressions *íma-mo* 今も,
íma-de-mo 今でも, or *máda* まだ, while in formal speech or in
literary style it is translated by *íma-mo náo* 今も尚.

Anáta wa íma-mo Shiná-go wo benkyō shĭté imásŭ ka.
貴方　は　今　も　支那語　を　勉強　して　います　か.
Are you **still** studying Chinese?

Iié, yamemáshĭta. いゝえ, 止めました.   No, I gave it up.

Already *mō* もう, *súdeni* すでに
......yet *máda* まだ

Mō is used in ordinary conversation; *súdeni* in formal speech
or in literary style.

Kutsúya wa watashí no kutsú wo mō koshiraemáshĭta ka.
靴屋　は　私　の　靴　を　もうこしらえました　か.
Has the shoemaker **already** made my shoes?

---

1 *tamé ni náru* instructive

Iié, máda désŭ. いゝえ、まだです.   No, not yet.

Iié, máda koshiraemasén déshĭta.   No, he has not made them yet.
いゝえ、まだ こしらえません でした.

In Japanese the expression not yet without the principal verb is translated
by *máda* and the affirmative verb, instead of the negative form, as shown
in the above example.

Watashí ga anáta no dempō wo uketottá tóki ni wa mō kaban wo
私 が 貴方 の 電報 を 受取った 時 に は もう 鞄 を
éki e okutté shimatté imáshĭta.   When I received your telegram I had already
駅 へ 送ってしまっていました.   sent my trunks to the station.

In sentences like the preceding one, in which one clause is expressed with
the adverb already, the same adverb is often omitted in the Japanese translation, so that the above sentence may be expressed as follows:

Watashí ga anáta no dempō wo uketottá tókí ni wa kabán wo éki
私 が 貴方 の 電報 を 受取った 時 に は 鞄 を 駅
e okutté shimatté imáshĭta.
へ 送って しまって いました.

Used to......

Used to is not translated into Japanese, and the English verb
that follows used to is put in the progressive past, which gives the
meaning conveyed by this expression.

Watashí wa shokují no tokí pan daké tábete imáshĭta ga íma de
私 は 食事 の 時 パン だけ 食べて いました が 今 で
wa góhan mo tabemásŭ.   I used to eat for dinner only bread, but now I also
は 御飯 も 食べます.   eat rice.

(*lit.* I, dinner time, bread only eating was, but now rice also eat.)

Used to may be translated also by the principal verb in its simple present
form, followed by *shūkan* 習慣 habit and *déshĭta.*

Anáta wa ása náni wo nómu shūkan déshĭta ka.
貴方 は 朝 何 を 飲む 習慣 でした か.
What were you accustomed to drink in the morning? (What used you......?)
(*lit.* You, morning, what to drink habit was?)

O-cha wo nómu shūkan déshĭta ga íma wa kōhī wo nomimásŭ.
お茶 を 飲む 習慣 でした が 今 はコーヒーを 飲みます.
I used to drink tea, but now I drink coffee.

When *désŭ* is used after *shūkan* the sentence has a present meaning, and
corresponds to *I am in the habit of......,* or *I am accustomed to.. ...*

Asa háyaku okíru shūkan désŭ.   I am in the habit of rising early in
朝 早く 起きる 習慣 です.   the morning.

(*lit.* Morning, early to rise habit is.)

In colloquial speech, used to may be expressed by the past tense of the verb
in consideration, followed by *monó déshĭta* ものでした, as in the following
example.

*O-cha wo **nónda monó déshĭta** ga íma wa kōhī wo nomimásŭ.*
お茶 を 飲んだ もの でした が 今 はコーヒーを 飲みます.
I used to drink tea but now I drink coffee.

Vocabulary

Nouns			Verbs		
audience	*chōshū*	聴衆	to build	*kenchikú surú*	建築スル
detective	*tantéi*	探偵	to chat	*shabéru*	シャベル
hope	*kibō*	希望	to complete	*kanséi surú*	完成スル
meeting	*kaigō*	会合	to emigrate	*imín surú*	移民スル
orator	*kōensha*	講演者	to insult	*bujokú surú*	
season	*jíki*	時期			侮辱スル
striker	*higyōsha*	罷業者	to rise	*tachiagarú*	
telegram	*dempō*	電報	to stand (get) up	立チ上ガル	
workman	*shokunín*	転人			

invitation card *shōdaijō* 招待状; to look for, to search *sagasú* 探ス; business man *jitsugyōka* 実業家; tourist *man-yū-sha* 漫遊者 or *kankō kyakú* 観光客; to walk up and down *ittári kitári surú* 行ツタリ来タリスル.

Exercise *Renshū* 練習

1. Konó hashí wo dóno kuraí nagaí aidá[1] kenchikú shĭté imásŭ ka.—Ichínen guraí zuttó kenchikú shĭté imásŭ. Ima wa hotóndo kanséi shimáshĭta. 2. Anó otokó wa ichí-jikán guraí tōri wo ittári kitári shĭté imásŭ. Anáta wa anó hĭtó wo shĭtté imásŭ ka.—Iié, shirimasén ga tantéi darō to omoimásŭ. 3. Kánada ni ikú máe ni watashí wa Itarí ni súnde imáshĭta. 4. Nihón-go wo naraí hajimerú máe ni Shiná-go wo benkyō shĭté imáshĭta. 5. Káko[2] sanjūnen-kan takŭsán no Nihón-jin ga Burajirú[3] e imín shimáshĭta. 6. Kantō chihō wa takŭsán áme ga zuttó futté imásŭ ka.—Hái, yokká bákari zuttó futté imásŭ. Ima wa nyūbai désŭ. Konó jíki ni wa taigái áme ga takŭsán furimásŭ. 7. Isshūkan ínai ni watashí no atarashíi tsŭkué wa dekimásŭ ka.—Iié. dekimasén ga tō ka ínai ni tsŭkurimásŭ. Uchí no shokunín ga fŭtarí séngetsu kará zuttó byōki désŭ. 8. Kōensha ga enzetsú[4] wo shĭté itá tokí ni chōshū no náka no fŭtarí no otokó ga tachiagatté kōensha wo bujokú shihajimetá. 9. Miná ga neté itá aidá ni dorobō ga háiri kané wo zémbu nusúnda. 10. Watashí no atarashíi tebúkuro wo mitsŭkemáshĭta ka.—Iié, hōbō sagashĭté imásŭ ga mitsŭkarimasén.[6] 11. Anó otokó wa dóno kuraí nágaku anó to no sóba ni tátte imásŭ ka.—Oyosó[7] jíppun-kan guraí asokó ni zuttó tátte imásŭ. 12. Sanjū-nen máe máde wa takŭsán no Nihón-jin ga Ameriká Gasshūkoku[8] e

---

1 *dóno kuraí nagaí aidá* how long, *lit.* How long during 2 *káko* past. *Káko jū-go-nen* During the last fifteen years. 3 Brazil 4 *enzetsú wo surú* to make a speech 5 everywhere 6 *mitsŭkarimasén* they cannot be found 7 about 8 *Ameriká Gasshūkoku* The U. S. of America, *gasshūkoku* a federal state

imín shĭtá monó désŭ.   Sonó go[1] wa gakŭséi, jitsugyōka, man-yūsha bákari ga Hokubéi e itté orimásŭ.   **13.** Anáta wa máda kabán wo nizúkuri shĭté irú no désŭ ka.—Iié, mō nizúkuri wo oemáshĭta.   **14.** Keikán ga tōchaku shĭtá tokí ni wa higyōsha wa súdeni kaigō wo oeté imáshĭta.   **15.** Dónna shátsu ga kaitái no désŭ ka.—Kínu no shátsu ga kaitái désŭ.—Kokó ni yói no ga arimásŭ.   **16.** Uchí no obāsan wa íkite[4] itá tokí ni omoshirói hanashí wo takŭsán shĭté kuretá monó déshĭta.   **17.** Anó katá ga budōshu wo susumetá[5] tokí ni watashí wa súdeni bĭru wo ni-hái mo nónde shimatté imáshĭta nóde soré wo nómu kotó ga dekimasén déshĭta.   **18.** Inochi ga áru aidá wa kibō ga arimásŭ.

1. この橋をどの位長い間建築していますか. ――一年位ずっと建築しています. 今は殆ど完成しました.　**2.** あの男は一時間位通りを行ったり来たりしています. 貴方はあの人を知っていますか.—いゝえ, 知りませんが探偵だろうと思います.　**3.** カナダに行く前に私はイタリーに住んでいました.　**4.** 日本語を習い始める前に支那語を勉強していました.　**5.** 過去三十年間沢山の日本人がブラジルへ移民しました.　**6.** 関東地方は沢山雨がずっと降っていますか.—はい, 四日ばかりずっと降っています. 今は入梅ですこの時期には大概雨が沢山降ります.　**7.** 一週間以内に私の新しい机は出来ますか.—いゝえ, 出来ませんが十日以内に造ります. うちの転人が二人先月からずっと病気です.　**8.** 講演者が演説をしていた時に聴衆の中の二人の男が立ち上って講演者を侮辱し始めた.　**9.** 皆が寝ていた間に泥棒が入り金を全部盗んだ.　**10.** 私の新しい手袋を見つけましたか.—いゝえ, 方々探していますが見つかりません.　**11.** あの男はどの位長くあの戸のそばに立っていますか.—凡そ十分間位あそこにずっと立っています.　**12.** 三十年前迄は沢山の日本人がアメリカ合衆国へ移民したものです. その後は学生, 実業家, 漫遊者ばかりが北米へ行っております.　**13.** 貴方はまだ鞄を荷造りしているのですか.—いゝえ, もう荷造りを終えました.　**14.** 警官が到着した時には罷業者はすでに会合を終えていました.　**15.** どんなシャツが買い度いのですか.—絹のシャツが買い度いです.—こゝによいのがあります.　**16.** うちのおばあさんは生きていた時に面白い話を沢山してくれたものでした.　**17.** あの方がぶどう酒を勧めた時に私はすでにビールを二杯も飲んでしまっていましたのでそれを飲む事が出来ませんでした.　**18.** 命がある間は希望があります.

1. How long have they been building this bridge?—They have been building it for about a year. It is almost finished. **2.** That man has been walking up and down the street for an hour. Do you know him?—No, I do not

---

1 *sonó go* since then **2** *nizúkuri surú* to pack **3** *tōchaku surú* to arrive **4** *ikíru* to live **5** *susumerú* to offer

know him, but I think he is a detective. **3.** Before going to Canada I had been living in Italy. **4.** Before beginning the study of the Japanese language, I had been studying Chinese. **5.** During these last thirty years many Japanese have been emigrating to Brazil. **6.** Has it been raining much in the Kanto district?—Yes, it has been raining for about four days. Now we are in the "nyūbai" season, and during this season it generally rains much. **7.** Can you make my new desk within a week?—No, I cannot, but I can make it within ten days. Two of my workmen have been ill since last month. **8.** While the orator was speaking two men in the audience rose and began to insult him. **9.** While everybody was sleeping a thief broke into the house and stole all our money. **10.** Have you found my new gloves?—No, I have been looking for them everywhere, but I cannot find them. **11.** How long has that man been standing near that door?—He has been standing there for about ten minutes. **12.** Until thirty years ago many Japanese used to emigrate to the United States. Since then, only students, business men and tourists have gone to North America. **13.** Are you still packing your trunks?—No, I have already finished packing them. **14.** When the police arrived the strikers had already finished their meeting. **15.** What kind of shirts do you wish to buy?—I wish to buy some silk shirts.—Here are some good ones. **16.** When my grandmother was living she used to tell us many interesting stories. **17.** I had already drunk two glasses of beer when he offered me a glass of wine, but I could not drink it. **18.** While there is life there is hope.

ON MEETING PEOPLE

The English **hello,** when used to greet people, has no corresponding word in Japanese. Instead, one has to use one of the expressions *O-hayō* お早う (Good morning), *Kónnichi-wa* 今日は. (Good day) or *Kómban-wa* 今晩は. (Good evening), according to the time of the day.

Minásan, kónnichi-wa. 皆さん，今日は. Hello everybody. (*lit.* Everybody, to-day.)

Kómban-wa, dóchira e. 今晩は，どちらへ. Good evening; where are you going? (*Dóchira e* is an abbreviation of *Dóchira e irasshaimásŭ ka.* どちらへいらっしゃいますか. or *Dóchira e ikimásŭ ka.* どちらへ行きますか. (*lit.* Where you go?)

When **hello** is used to call somebody's attention, especially in connection with the telephone, it is translated by *móshi-móshi* もしもし.

Móshi-móshi, kōban wa dóko désŭ ka. もしもし，交番はどこですか. Hello, could you tell me where is a police box? (*lit.* Hello, police-box where is?)

Móshi-móshi, anáta wa Tanaká-san désŭ ka. もしもし，あなたは田中さんですか. Hello, are you Mr. Tanaka? (*lit.* Hello, you Mr. Tanaka are?)

Móshi-móshi, dónata désŭ ka. もしもし，どなたですか. Hello, who's speaking?

Móshi-móshi, kikoemásŭ ka. もしもし聞こえますか. Hello, can you hear me?

Thirty-second Lesson 第卅二課

Future *Mírai* 未来

The future is formed by adding the suffix *mashō* ましよう to the simple stem of verbs of Class I, and to the *i*-stem of verbs of Class II, or by adding, with decreasing degree of politeness, *deshō* でしょう or *darō* だろう to the simple present.

The negative form is indicated by adding the suffix *masén deshō* ません でしよう, to the simple stem of verbs of Class I, and to the *i*-stem of verbs of Class II, or by adding one of the expressions *nái deshō* ないでしょう, *nái darō* ないだろう or *nakarō* なかろう to the simple stem of verbs of Class I, and to the *a*-stem of verbs of Class II. The negative form with the suffix *nakarō,* which is the least polite of the negative forms of the future. is sometimes used by men, but it is avoided by women.

Note that the first two forms of the positive future have only one common form for their negative—See *phonetic rule,* Page 684.

Class I

Déru 出る   To Go Out

I shall go out		I shall not go out	
demásŭ deshō	出ますでしょう	*demasén deshō*	出ませんでしょう
demashō	出ましょう	*demasén deshō*	出ませんでしょう
déru deshō	出るでしょう	*dénai deshō*	出ないでしょう
déru darō	出るだろう	*dénai darō*	出ないだろう
		denakarō	出なかろう

Tabéru 食べる   To Eat

I shall eat		I shall not eat	
tabemásŭ deshō	食べますでしょう	*tabemasén deshō*	食べませんでしょう
tabemashō	食べましょう	*tabemasén deshō*	食べませんでしょう
tabéru deshō	食べるでしょう	*tabénai deshō*	食べないでしょう
tabéru darō	食べるだろう	*tabénai darō*	食べないだろう
		tabenakarō	食べなかろう

Irú いる   To Be (in a place), There To Be

I shall be	There will be	I shall not be	There will not be
imásŭ deshō	いますでしょう	*imasén deshō*	いませんでしょう
imashō	いましょう	*imasén deshō*	いませんでしょう
irú deshō	いるでしょう	*inái deshō*	いないでしょう
irú darō	いるだろう	*inái darō*	いないだろう
		inakarō	いなかろう

Class II
Group 1   *Káku* 書く   To Write

I shall write		I shall not write	
kakimásŭ deshō	書きますでしょう	kakimasén deshō	書きませんでしょう
kakimashō	書きましょう	kakimasén deshō	書きませんでしょう
káku deshō	書くでしょう	kakánai deshō	書かないでしょう
káku darō	書くだろう	kakánai darō	書かないだろう
		kakanakarō	書かなかろう

Group 2   *Dásu* 出す   To Take (or Put) Out

I shall take (put) out		I shall not take (put) out	
dashimásŭ deshō	出しますでしょう	dashimasén deshō	出しませんでしょう
dashimashō	出しましょう	dashimasén deshō	出しませんでしょう
dásu deshō	出すでしょう	dasánai deshō	出さないでしょう
dásu darō	出すだろう	dasánai darō	出さないだろう
		dasanakarō	出さなかろう

Group 3   *Tátsu* 立つ   To Stand

I shall stand		I shall not stand	
tachimásŭ deshō	立ちますでしょう	tachimasén deshō	立ちませんでしょう
tachimashō	立ちましょう	tachimasén deshō	立ちませんでしょう
tátsu deshō	立つでしょう	tatánai deshō	立たないでしよう
tátsu darō	立つだろろ	tatánai darō	立たないだろう
		tatanakarō	立たなかろう

Group 4   *Tobú* 飛ぶ   To Fly

I shall fly		I shall not fly	
tobimásŭ deshō	飛びますでしょう	tobimasén deshō	飛びませんでしょう
tobimashō	飛びましょう	tobimasén deshō	飛びませんでしょう
tobú deshō	飛ぶでしょう	tobanái deshō	飛ばないでしょう
tobú darō	飛ぶだろう	tobanái darō	飛ばないだろう
		tobanakarō	飛ばなかろう

Group 5   *Tóru* 取る   To Take

I shall take		I shall not take	
torimásŭ deshō	取りますでしょう	torimasén deshō	取りませんでしょう
torimashō	取りましょう	torimasén deshō	取りませんでしょう
tóru deshō	取るでしょう	toránai deshō	取らないでしょう
tóru darō	取るだろう	toránai darō	取らないだろう
		toranakarō	取らなかろう

Óru おる　To Be (in a place)　There To Be

I shall be	There will be		I shall not be	There will not be
orimásŭ deshō	おりますでしょう		*orimasén deshō*	おりませんでしょう
orimashō	おりましょう		*orimasén deshō*	おりませんでしょう
óru deshō	おるでしょう		*oránai deshō*	おらないでしょう
óru darō	おるだろう		*oránai darō*	おらないだろう
			oranakarō	おらなかろう

Group 6　Kaú 買う　To Buy

I shall buy			I shall not buy	
kaimásŭ deshō	買いますでしょう		*kaimasén deshō*	買いませんでしょう
kaimashō	買いましょう		*kaimasén deshō*	買いませんでしょう
kaú deshō	買うでしょう		*kawanái deshō*	買わないでしょう
kaú darō	買うだろろ		*kawanái darō*	買わないだろう
			kawanakarō	買わなかろう

Irregular Verbs

Aru ある　There To Be

There will be			There will not be	
arimásŭ deshō	ありますでしょう		*arimasén deshō*	ありませんでしょう
arimashō	ありましょう		*arimasén deshō*	ありませんでしょう
áru deshō	あるでしょう		*nái deshō*	無いでしょう
áru darō	あるだろう		*nái darō*	無いだろう
			nakarō	無かろう

Désŭ です　To Be

I shall be			I shall not be	
deshō	でしょう		*nái deshō*	無いでしょう
darō	だろう		*nái darō*	無いだろう
			nakarō	無かろう

Surú する　To Do

I shall do			I shall not do	
shimásŭ deshō	しますでしょう		*shimasén deshō*	しませんでしょう
shimashō	しましょう		*shimasén deshō*	しませんでしょう
surú deshō	するでしょう		*shinái deshō*	しないでしょう
surú darō	するだろう		*shinái darō*	しないだろう
			shinakarō	しなかろう

Another negative future is indicated by adding the suffix *masu-mái* ますまい to the simple stem of verbs of Class I, and to the *i*-stem of verbs of Class II. Still another negative future is formed by adding *mái* まい to the simple stem of verbs of Class I, and to the simple present of verbs of Class II.

Class I

| *míru*
見る | *mimasumái*
見ますまい | *mimái*
見まい | I shall (probably) not see |
| *tabéru*
食べる | *tabemasumái*
食べますまい | *tabemái*
食べまい | I shall (probably) not eat |

Class II

káku 書く	*kakimasumái* 書きますまい	*kakumái* 書くまい	I shall (probably) not write
dásu 出す	*dashimasumái* 出しますまい	*dasumái* 出すまい	I shall (probably) not take out
mátsu 待つ	*machimasumái* 待ちますまい	*matsumái* 待つまい	I shall (probably) not wait
yobú 呼ぶ	*yobimasumái* 呼びますまい	*yobumái* 呼ぶまい	I shall (probably) not call
áru ある	*arimasumái* ありますまい	*arumái* あるまい	It will (probably) not be there
iú 言う	*iimasumái* 言いますまい	*iumái* 言うまい	I shall (probably) not say

These forms of the negative future with *masumái* and *mái* are little used however, and when used, the one with the suffix *masumái* is preferable to the other with *mái*.

This form of negative future with *masumái* ますまい and *mái* まい may be also used when volition is to be expressed, as in the following two examples, and it is only from the context that one may know whether the verbs with such suffixes express probability or will.

> *Watashí wa ni-do to[1] sokó e ikimasumái* (or *yukumái*).
> 私 は 二 度 と そこ へ 行きますまい   (行くまい).
> I will not go there again. (*lit.* I two times there will not go.)

> *Watashí wa anó hĭtó ni mō aimasumái.*   I will not see him again.
> 私 は あの 人 に もう 会いますまい.
> (*lit.* I that person again will not meet.)

The suffixes *masumái* and *mái* are also used in a considerable number of expressions which, properly translated into English, do

---

1 *to* is here used as an emphatic particle

not require a future construction, as in the following examples.

Tábun sō de wa **arimasumái** (or **arumái**).   I do not think so.
多分 そうで は ありますまい   （あるまい）.
　　(*lit.* Perhaps so to be, will not.)

The above sentence may be translated also as: *I dare say not.—I suppose not.—I fear not.—I doubt it.*

Konó mondaí ni tsúite wa **hanashimasumái.**   I'd rather not tell you
この　問題　に ついて　は　　話しますまい.   about this matter.
　　(*lit.* This matter about will not tell.)

Anó katá no ryōshin wa kanemochí de wa **arimasumái** (or **arumái**).
あの　方 の　両親　は　　金持　で は ありますまい　（あるまい）.
I don't think his parents are rich.
　　(*lit.* That person's parents rich to be—probably will not be.)

Fúru deshō ka. 降るでしょうか.   Do you think it will rain?
　　(*lit.* Will it rain?)

Furimasumái (or **furumái**).   No, I hope not.
降りますまい　　（降るまい）.   (*lit.* Probably it will not rain.)

Anó byōnin wa tasúkáru déshō ka.   Will the patient live?
あの　病人　は　　助かる でしょうか.

Tasúkarimasumái.   No, I am afraid he will not live.
助かりますまい.   (*lit.* Probably he will not live.)

(*tasúkáru* 助かる to be saved, to survive a disaster, etc., to escape with one's life, to live)

Káre wa shōjiki de wa **arimasumái** or **arumái.**
彼　は 正直 で　は ありますまい　　あるまい.
I doubt if he is honest. I doubt his honesty.
　　(*lit.* He honest to be probably will not be.)

The above examples have been given just to show some of the cases in which the two suffixes in question may be used. However, since they are sparingly used, they will be avoided in the examples and exercises of this book.

The future tense in Japanese is generally used only when the future action is not decidedly certain, or when we wish to express probability, and it is for this reason that all the future forms given in this lesson are called **probable future.**

Kotoshí wa shōyo[1] ga **demasén deshō.**   This year we shall probably not
今年　は 賞与　が　出ません でしょう.   be given any bonus.

Kómban éiga e ikimashō ka.   Shall we go to the cinema to-night?
今晩　映画 へ行きましょうか.

Hái, ikimashō. Okāsan ga isshó ni ikú deshō.
はい, 行きましょう. お母さんが 一緒 に 行くでしょう.
Yes, we shall go; mother will go with us.

---

1 *shōyo* bonus

*Anó hĭtó wa rainén nyūei[1] **suru darō.***   Next year that man will enter
あの 人 は 来年 入営 する だろう.   the barracks.

*Ashĭtá áme ga **fúru deshō.***   It will probably rain to-morrow.
あした 雨 が 降る でしょう.

*Kotoshí wa komé ga yasŭi **darō.***   Rice will likely be cheap this year.
今年 は 米 が 安い だろう.

An idea of greater uncertainty may be indicated by the word
tábun 多分 (perhaps), before the future tense:

*Ashĭtá áme ga **tábun fúru deshō.***   It may rain to-morrow.
あした 雨 が 多分 降る でしょう.   Perhaps it will rain to-morrow.

When a future occurrence is sure to happen, the **present,** instead
of the future, is used.

*Ashĭtá Nikkō e **ikimásŭ.***   To-morrow I will go to Nikkō.
あした 日光 へ 行きます.

*Itsu Nagásaki kará no fúne wa Yokohamá ni **tsŭkimásŭ** ka.*
いつ 長崎 からの 船 は 横浜 に つきます か.
When will the boat from Nagasaki arrive at Yokohama?

*Myōasa **tsŭkimásŭ.*** 明朝つきます.   She will arrive to-morrow morning.

The future is used when asking for an opinion as to the probability of a future occurrence.

*Anó gakŭséi wa rainén Tōkyō Daigakú e **háiru deshō** ka.*
あの 学生 は 来年 東京 大学 へ 入る でしょうか.
Do you think that student will enter the Tokyo University next year?

Háiru deshō. 入るでしょう.   I think he will.

The future formed with *mashō* is often used in announcing a
decision just made by the speaker, or in inviting the cooperation of
another person. In this case the future may corresponds to the
imperative.

*Osói kará **kaerimashō.***   It is late; I (*or* let's go back) will go back.
遅い から 帰りましょう.   (*lit.* As it is late I (we) will go back.)

*Keibá wo mi ni **ikimashō** ka.*   Shall we go and see the horse races?
競馬 を 見 に 行きましょうか.   (*keibá* horse race)

*Hái, **ikimashō.*** はい, 行きましょう.   Yes, let's go.

The future in *deshō* and *darō* is used as a *probable present.*

*Anó gaijín wa Nihón-go wo **hanásu deshō.***
あの 外人 は 日本語 を 話す でしょう.
Probably (it is possible that) that foreigner speaks Japanese.
or I think that foreigner speaks Japanese.

Another form of future is formed by adding *yō* よう to the simple

---

1 *nyūei surú* to enter the barracks, to enlist in the army

stem of verbs of Class I, and *ō* to the verbs of Class II, after dropping their final *u*. Verbs ending in *tsu* drop *su* when taking *ō*. This form of future generally indicates volition.

Class I

míru	見る	to see	*mi*	*miyō*	見よう	I will see

Class II

káku	書く	to write	*kak*	*kakō*	書こう	I will write
kasú	貸す	to lend	*kas*	*kasō*	貸そう	I will lend
tátsu	立つ	to stand	*tat*	*tatō*	立とう	I will stand
yobú	呼ぶ	to call	*yob*	*yobō*	呼ぼう	I will call
tóru	取る	to take	*tor*	*torō*	取ろう	I will take
kaú	買う	to buy	*ka*	*kaō*	買おう	I will buy

Irregular Verbs

kúru	来る	to come	*koyō*	来よう	I will come
surú	する	to do	*shiyō*	しよう	I will do

This future form, being considered vulgar, is not used in good conversation, but it is used by men in familiar speech. Women do not use it. However, followed by *to omoimásŭ* (I think), it is often used in ordinary conversation by both men and women.

Yakyū[1] no shiai[2] wo mi ni bóku to isshó ni kimásŭ ka.
野球 の 試合 を 見 に 僕 と 一緒 に 来ます か.
Will you come with me to see the baseball match?

Ā, ikō. あー, 行こう. Yes, I will. *or* Yes, let's go.

Kané ga irú nará kasō to Nakamurá Kun ga bóku ni ittá.
金 が 要る なら 貸そうと 中村 君 が 僕 に 言った.
Mr. Nakamura said that he would lend me money if I needed it.
   (*lit.* Money if you need I will lend so Mr. Nakamura to me said.)

Kómban ojisán wo tazuneyō to omoimásŭ. I think I will pay a visit
今晩 伯父さんを 訪ねよう と 思います.   to my uncle to-night.

Ishihara San no ókŭsan ni tegamí wo kakō to omoimásŭ.
石原 さん の 奥さん に 手紙 を 書こうと 思います.
I think I will write a letter to Mrs. Ishihara.

Anó jidōsha wo kaō to omoimásŭ. I think I will buy that motor-car.
あの 自動車 を 買おうと 思います.

This form of future, followed by *to surú,* is used also in ordinary conversation when it is followed by *toki (ni)*. In this case, such a construction indicates the immediate future formed with *to be about to, to be on the point of,* and similar expressions. Compare the use of this future with the use of the shorter past form followed by *toki (ni)*, as given in Lesson 30, page 203.

---

1 *yakyū* baseball **2** *shiai* match

Watashí ga dekakeyō to shítá toki ni Tanaká San wa kimáshǐta.
私　が　出かけよう　と　した　時　に　田中　さん　は　来ました.
When I was about to go out Mr. Tanaka came. (*dekakerú* to go out)

Shokují wo shiyō to shítá toki ni ōkina jishín ga okorimáshǐta.
食事　を　しよう　と　した　時　に　大きな　地震　が　起りました.
When I was about to eat a strong earthquake occurred.

There is in Japanese another future form, which conveys the idea of probability, and refers to an action that probably has been, or was, already completed. This is called the probable past and is formed by adding *mashǐtarō* ました ろう to the simple stem of verbs of Class I, and to the *i*-stem of verbs of Class II, or by adding *deshō* or *darō* to the past form of the verb, or by the subordinate followed by *itá deshō, darō,* or by *imáshitarō* いました ろう.

The probable past may also be formed by adding *tarō* たろう to the simple stem of verbs of Class I, and to the *i*-stem of verbs of Class II. This last form of the probable past is, however, used only by men in very familiar speech.

The negative form of the probable past is obtained by adding, in decreasing degree of politeness, *masén déshita deshō* ませんでしたでしょう, or *masén déshitarō* ませんでしたろう to the simple stem of verbs of Class I, and to the *i*-stem of verbs of Class II; by adding *nákatta deshō* なかったでしょう or *nákatta darō* なかっただろう to the simple stem of verbs of Class I, and to the *a*-stem of verbs of Class II; by adding *imasén déshitarō* いませんでしたろう or *inákattarō* いなかったろう to the subordinate, or by adding *nákattarō* なかったろう or *nakarō* なかろう to the simple stem of verbs of Class I, and to the *a*-stem of verbs of Class II. This last form is used only by men in very familiar speech.

All the above mentioned future forms are given here below:

Probable Past

Tabéru 食べる   To Eat
Positive

Tabemáshǐta deshō	食べましたでしょう	⎫ He, she has
Tabemáshǐtarō	食べましたろう	⎭ probably eaten.
Tábete itá deshō (darō)	食べていたでしょう（だろう）	⎱ You, they have
Tábete imáshǐtarō	食べていましたろう	⎰ probably eaten.
Tábeta deshō	食べたでしょう	⎱ He, you, they
Tábetarō	食べたろう	⎰ probably ate.

Negative

Tabemasén déshǐta deshō	食べませんでしたでしょう	
Tábete imasén déshǐtarō	食べていませんでしたろう	⎱ He has probably
Tabemasén déshǐtarō	食べませんでしたろう	⎰ not eaten. etc,
Tábete inákattarō	食べていなかったろう	⎱ He probably did
Tabénakatta deshō (darō)	食べなかったでしょう（だろう）	⎰ not eat. etc.
Tabénakattarō	食べなかったろう	

Anó hĭtó wa **dekakemáshĭtarō.**   Probably that man has gone out.
あの 人 は 出かけましたろう.

Káku 書く   To Write
Positive

Kakimáshĭta deshō	書きましたでしょう	
Kakimáshĭtarō	書きましたろう	He has probably
Káita deshō (darō)	書いたでしょう(だろう)	written. etc.
Káite itá deshō (darō)	書いていたでしょう(だろう)	He probably
Káite imáshĭtarō	書いていましたろう	wrote. etc.
Káitarō	書いたろう	

Negative

Kakimasén déshĭta deshō	書きませんでしたでしょう	
Kakimasén déshĭtarō	書きませんでしたろう	He has probably
Kakánakatta deshō (darō)	書かなかったでしょう(だろう)	not written. etc.
Káite imasén déshĭtarō	書いていませんでしたろう	He probably did
Káite inákattarō	書いていなかったろう	not write. etc,
Kakánakattarō	書かなかったろう	

O-imōto San wa Kabukizá no kippú wo **kaimáshĭta deshō ka.**
お妹 さん は 歌舞伎座 の 切符 を 買いました でしょうか.
Do you suppose that your younger sister has bought the tickets for the Kabuki
theatre ?

Hái, tábun **kaimáshĭta deshō.**   Yes, perhaps she has bought them.
はい, 多分 買いました でしょう.

Conjugation of True Adjective
Probable Future

The future of true adjectives is formed by adding to them the word
deshō or **darō,** or by adding the termination **karō** to their form
without their final *i*. The negative is formed by adding **nái deshō,**
nái darō, or **nakarō** to the adverbial form of the adjective :

warúi 悪い   bad

It will be bad		It will not be bad	
warúi deshō	悪いでしょう	*wáruku nái deshō*	悪くないでしょう
warúi darō	悪いだろう	*wáruku nái darō*	悪くないだろう
warukarō	悪かろう	*wáruku nakarō*	悪くなかろう

Probable Past

The positive form of the probable past is obtained by adding **katta deshō,**
katta darō, or **kattarō** to the true adjective after dropping its final *i*.

The negative form is obtained by adding *nákatta deshō*, *nákatta darō*, or *nákattarō* to the adverbial form of the adjective:

It was probably bad   Probably it was not bad

wárukatta deshō   *wáruku nákatta deshō*
悪かった でしょう   悪く なかったでしょう

wárukatta darō   *wáruku nákatta darō*
悪かった だろう   悪く なかっただろう

wárukattarō   *wáruku nákattarō*
悪かったろう   悪く なかったろう

Konogoró úmi ga areté imásŭ kará sakaná wa takái deshō.
この頃 海 が 荒れています から 魚 は 高い でしょう.
As the sea has been stormy during the past few days, fish will probably be dear.

Anáta ga Hokkaidō wo ryokō-chū yukí ga takŭsán furimáshĭta kará
貴方 が 北海道 を 旅行 中 雪 が 沢山 降りました から
sámukatta deshō.   As it snowed much in Hokkaido it was probably cold
寒かった でしょう.   while you were travelling there.
     (*lit.* You, Hokkaido traveling-while, snow much fell because, it was cold probably.)

Progressive Future

The *Progressive future* is formed by the subordinate followed by *imashō*, *irú deshō*, or *irú darō*. The negative form is obtained by the subordinate followed by *inái deshō*, *inái darō*, or *imasumái*.

Yoshidá San wa máda nemutté irú deshō kará íma ikanái hō ga
吉田 さん は まだ 眠って いるでしょうから 今 行かない方 が
ii deshō.   As Mr. Yoshida will likely be still sleeping, it is better not to go
いゝでしょう.   to see him now. (*lit.* Mr. Yoshida, still as he will likely be
     sleeping, not to go, good will be.)

Shiháinin wa tattá íma kyūkeishitsu ni ikimáshĭta; tábun shimbún wo
支配人 は たつた 今 休憩室 に 行きました, 多分 新聞 を
yónde irú deshō to omoimásŭ.
読んで いるでしょうと 思います.
     The manager just now went to the rest room; I think he will probably be
     reading the newspaper.

If

When **if,** at the beginning of a sentence, expresses a condition, it is translated by *móshi* 若し, and its dependent verb is followed by *nára* なら or *náraba* ならば. The subject of an if-clause is generally followed by *ga.* (See Lesson 47 for subjunctive.)

Móshi anáta ga kimbén de áru náraba senséi wa yorokóbu deshō.
もし 貴方 が 勤勉 で ある ならば 先生 は 喜ぶでしょう.
If you are diligent your teacher will be pleased.

Móshi anáta no gakká wo benkyō shinái náraba obóenai darō.
もし 貴方 の 学課 を 勉強 しない ならば 覚えないだろう.
If you do not study your lessons you will not learn (remember).

Móshi *anáta* *ga* ***ikú* *náraba*** *watashí* *mo* *ikimásŭ.*
もし　貴方　が　行く　ならば　　私　　も　行きます.
If you go I'll go too. (*lit.* If you go, I also go.)

Note that the *if-clause* is always put at the beginning of the sentence, even when in English it is placed at the end. We cannot say, for instance, *I will go if you go*; we must say, as in the above example: *If you go I will go.*

When **if** is used in English for making an admission, it is omitted in the Japanese translation, as in the following example:

Watashí *wa* *bímbō* *de* *wa* *áru* *kéredomo* *kōketsu* *désŭ.*
私　　は　貧乏　で　は　ある　けれども　高潔　です.
If I am poor, I am honourable. (*lit.* I am poor but I am honourable.)

If is also omitted in the Japanese translation when in English it is used with the meaning of **whether,** in asking a question in indirect narration:

Anó *otokó* *wa* *bōshi* *ga* *dóko* *ni* *áru* *ka* *watashí* *ga* *shĭtté* *irú* *ka* *to*
あの　男　は　帽子　が　どこ　に　ある　か　私　　が　知っているか　と
kikimáshĭta.　　That man asked me **if** (whether) I knew where his hat was.
聞きました.　　(*lit.* That man: "My hat where is it, do you know?" so he asked me.)

Watashí *wa* *anó* *fujín* *ga* *Fŭransú-go* *wo* *shĭtté* *irú* *ka* *dō-ka* *kiité*
私　　は　あの　婦人　が　フランス語　を　知って　いるかどうか聞いて
mimáshĭta.　　I asked that lady **if** (whether) she knew French. (*lit.* I, that lady,
みました.　　"French do you know, how is it?" asking I tried.)

From the preceeding two examples it may be seen that in Japanese the *indirect form of narration* is turned into the *direct form.*

The conjunctions **whether** and **if** when used in alternative clauses may also be translated by ***ka* *dō-ka*** かどうか.

Durante-San *wa* *Nihón-go* *wo* *o-hanashi* *ni* ***náru***[1] ***ka* *dō-ka*** *anáta* *wa*
デユウランテさんは　日本語　を　お話し　に　なる　かどうか　貴方　は
shĭtté *imásŭ* *ka.*　　Do you know **whether** Mr. Durante speaks Japanese?
知っています　か.

Hanako *San* *ga* *o-heyá* *ni* ***irú* *ka* *dō-ka*** *go-zónji* *désŭ* *ka.*
花子　さん　が　お部屋　に　いる　かどうか　御存じ　です　か.
Do you know **whether** Miss Hanako is in her room?

Hái, *irasshaimásŭ.*[2]　はい、いらっしゃいます.　　Yes, she is.

The word ***káshira*** かしら *I wonder if* is frequently used in Japanese in familiar speech after a verb in the present, past, or future to indicate a doubtful but probable event:

Senséi *wa* *máda* *gakkō* *ni* ***irú* *káshira.***　**I wonder if** the teacher is
先生　は　まだ　学校　に　いる　かしら.　　still in the school.

---

1 *o-hanashí* *ni* *náru* お話しになる polite form for *hanásu*, to speak　**2** *irasshai-másŭ* polite form for *orimásŭ*

Senséi wa **kimásh̆ta kashira.**   I **wonder if** our teacher has come.
先生 は 来ました かしら.

Tsugí no Orimppíkku wa Tōkyō de **hirakaréru kashira.**
次 のオリンピック は 東京 で 開かれる かしら.
   I wonder if the next Olympic games will be held in Tokyo.

Yūbe Yamadá San wa Ōsaka e **tátta kashira.**
ゆうべ 山田 さん は 大阪 へ立った かしら.
   I wonder if Mr. Yamada left for Osaka last night.

All the above sentences and similar ones are rendered more polite by using *deshō* before the word **kashira:**

Senséi wa máda gakkō ni **irú deshō kashira.**
先生 は まだ 学校 に いるでしょう かしら.
   (*lit.* The teacher still in school, will he be, I wonder.)

Senséi wa **kimásh̆ta deshō kashira.** 先生は来ましたでしょうかしら.
   (*lit.* The teacher will he have come, I wonder.)

Tsugí no Orimppíkku wa Tōkyō de **hirakaréru deshō kashira.**
次 のオリンピック は 東京 で 開かれる でしょう かしら.
   (*lit.* Next Olimpic games in Tokyo, will be opened, I wonder.)

Yūbe Yamadá San wa Ōsaka e **tátta deshō kashira.**
ゆうべ 山田 さん は 大阪 へ立ったでしょう かしら.
   (*lit.* Last night Mr. Yamada for Osaka will he have left, I wonder.)

Vocabulary

Nouns			Adjectives		
accident	*jíko*	事ジ故コ	clean	*kírei-na*	キレイナ
bonus	*shōyo*	賞ショウ与ヨ	honourable	*kōketsu*	高コウ潔ケツ
incense	*kō*	香コウ	**Verbs**		
laundry	*sentakuyá*	洗セン濯タク屋ヤ	to be dirty	*yogore·rú*	汚ヨゴレル
lunch[1]	{ *hiruhán*	昼ヒル飯ハン	to be stormy	*are·rú*	荒アレル
	ránchi	ランチ	to visit	*ukagaú*	伺ウカガウ
picnic	*ensokú*	遠エン足ソク	**Adverbs**		
restaurant	*ryōriya*	料リョウ理リ屋ヤ	recently	*saikín*	最サイ近キン
sea	*úmi*	海ウミ	some day	*íma-ni*	イマニ
wound	*kegá*	怪ケ我ガ	surely	*kittó*	キット

statue of Buddha *daibutsú* 大ダイ仏ブツ; learned man *gakŭshá* 学ガク者シャ; full bloom *mankaí* 満マン開カイ; to go on foot *arúite-ikú* 歩アルイテ行ク; to go by train *resshá de ikú* 列車レッシャデ行ク; to go by boat *fúne de ikú* 船フネデ行ク; to be (get) injured *kegá wo nasáru* 怪我ヲナサル; to go on a picnic *ensokú ni ikú* 遠足ニ行ク; Japanese food *Nihón-shokú* 日本食; foreign food *yōshoku* 洋食; incense burner *kōro* 香コウ炉ロ; to sail for Australia *Ōsutorariya e shuppán surú* オーストラリヤへ出帆スル.

---

1 *Hiruhán*, and less commonly *chūjiki* 中食, are the ordinary words for lunch, while *ránchi*, a corruption of the English word *lunch*, is generally used to indicate foreign style noon meal.

Exercise   *Renshū* 練習

1. Kyō wa samúi désŭ. Ashĭtá wa tábun yukí ga fúru deshō. **2.** Anó misé
de konná kamí wo urú deshō ka.—Urú to omoimásŭ.—Urú to omoimasén.
3. Anáta no otōsan wa anó jidōsha wo kaú deshō ka.—Ima kawanái deshō to
omoimásŭ. Chichí wa saikín atarashíi kágu wo watashidómo no atarashíi ié
no tamé ni kaimáshĭta kará íma wa amarí genkín[1] ga nái to omoimásŭ.
—Watashí wa anáta no otōsan wa aré wo kaú darō to omoimásŭ yo.
4. Hiruhán wa dóko e ikimashō ka.—Tōkyō Kaikán[2] e ikimashō. Asokó wa
taihén yói ryōriya désŭ soshĭté gaikokujín ga takŭsán asokó e ikimásŭ.
5. Watashí wa Nára ni[3] itté Daibutsú to sorekará yūmei-na kōen to ga mitái
désŭ.—Déwa[4] raishū ikimashō.—Hái, mairimashō. **6.** Shanhái kará kúru
fúne wa mō Yokohamá ni tsúita deshō ka.—Tábun tsúita deshō.—Máda tsŭkánai deshō. **7.** Mō ikkágetsu mo[5] áme ga furimasén kará kotoshí wa o-komé
ga fusakú[6] deshō. **8.** Bóku no itóko wa ása kará ban máde benkyō bákari
shĭté imásŭ kará íma-ni kittó gakŭshá ni náru deshō. **9.** Uenó kōen no
sakurá wa ni-san nichí no uchí ni mankaí ni náru deshō.—Déwa asátte
ikimashō.—Ē[7] ikimashō.—Arúite ikimashō ka.—Iié, jidōsha de ikimashō.
10. Hánako San ga jidōsha jíko de kegá wo nasátta sō désŭ.—Déwa kómban
omimái[8] ni ikimashō. **11.** Móshi ashĭtá áme nárabā[9] ensokú ni ikú kawarí ni
éiga e ikimashō. **12.** Kómban wa yōshoku no kawarí ni Nihón-shokú wo
tabemashō. Watashí wa tokidokí Nihón-shokú wo tabéru no ga sŭkí désŭ.
13. Anáta wa konó kōro wo o-kái ni narimásŭ ka.—Móshi yásukereba[10] kaimashō.—Sen-yen ni shĭté okimashō.[11] **14.** Móshi Shibusawá San ga kómban
o-mié[12] ni narimasén náraba myōnichi ukagatté mimashō. **15.** O-isogí ni
naránu to resshá ni noriokuremásŭ yo. **16.** Dóchira e oidé désŭ ka.—Sampó
ni ikimásŭ.—Go-isshó ni ikimashō ka.—Hái, isshó ni irasshái. **17.** Kírei-na
shátsu wo mótte kité kudasái.—Anáta no shátsu wa minná yogoreté imáshĭta
kará sentakuyá e mótte ikimáshĭta. Ima itté atarashíi no wo katté kimashō
ka.—Itté hĭtótsu katté kité kudasái. **18.** Itsu Ōshū e o-tachí désŭ ka.—Ráigetsu tachimásŭ. **19.** Yōfukuya wa ítsu atarashíi yōfuku wo mótte kimásŭ
ka.—Ashĭtá mótte kúru deshō to omoimásŭ. **20.** Anáta ga tomodachí ni
yóku shimasén náraba tomodachí wa anáta ni yóku shinái deshō.

1. きょうは寒いです．あしたは多分雪が降るでしょう．**2.** あの店
でこんな紙を売るでしょうか.—売ると思います.—売ると思いません.
3. 貴方のお父さんはあの自動車を買うでしょうか.—今買わないでし
ょうと思います．父は最近新しい家具を私共の新しい家のために買い
ましたから今は余り現金が無いと思います.—私は貴方のお父さんは
あれを買うだろうと思いますよ．**4.** 昼飯はどこへ行きましょうか.—
東京会館へ行きましょう．あそこは大変よい料理屋ですそして外国

---

1 ready money   2 *Tōkyō Kaikán* a fashionable restaurant in Tokyo.   3 *Ni* is
sometimes used instead of *e* with verbs of motion.   4 *déwa* then   5 This *mo* is
used here as an emphatic particle.   6 a poor harvest   7 *Ē* is a familiar interjection
corresponding to *Yes, Oh yes, All right, Very well, Yes, I see.*   8 *o-mimái ni ikú*
to go and visit   9 *áme náraba* if it rains   10 if it is cheap   11 *shĭté okimashō* is an
idiom and means "I shall let you have it."   12 *o-mié ni náru* to come

人が沢山あそこへ行きます. **5.** 私は奈良に行って大仏とそれから有名な公園とが見たいです.—では来週行きましょう.—はい，参りましょう. **6.** 上海から来る船はもう横浜に着いたでしょうか.—多分着いたでしょう.—まだ着かないでしょう. **7.** もう一ケ月も雨が降りませんから今年はお米が不作でしょう. **8.** 僕のいとこは朝から晩まで勉強ばかりしていますからいまにきっと学者になるでしょう. **9.** 上野公園の桜は二三日のうちに満開になるでしょう.—ではあさって（明後日）行きましょう.—えゝ，行きましょう.—歩いて行きましょうか.—いゝえ，自動車で行きましょう. **10.** 花子さんが自動車事故で怪我をなさったそうです.—では今晩お見舞に行きましょう. **11.** 若しあした雨ならば遠足に行く代りに映画へ行きましょう. **12.** 今晩は洋食の代りに日本食を食べましょう. 私は時々日本食を食べるのが好きです. **13.** 貴方はこの香炉をお買いになりますか.—若し安ければ買いましょう.—千円にしておきましょう. **14.** 若し渋沢さんが今晩お見えになりませんならば明日伺って見ましょう. **15.** お急ぎにならぬと列車に乗り遅れますよ. **16.** どちらへお出でゝすか.—散歩に行きます.—御一緒に行きましょうか.—はい，一緒にいらっしゃい. **17.** きれいなシャツを持って来て下さい.—貴方のシャツは皆んな汚れていましたから洗濯屋へ持って行きました. 今，行って新しいのを買って来ましょうか. —行って一つ買って来て下さい. **18.** いつ欧州へお立ちですか.—来月立ちます. **19.** 洋服屋はいつ新しい洋服を持って来ますか.—あした持って来るでしょうと思います. **20.** 貴方が友達によくしませんならば友達は貴方によくしないでしょう.

1. It is cold to-day; to-morrow it will probably snow. **2.** Do you think they sell paper like this at that shop?—I think they do.—I don't think they do. **3.** Do you think your father will buy that motor-car?—I don't think he will buy it now. He has recently bought new furniture for our new house, and he has not much ready money now.—I expect he will buy it. **4.** Where shall we go for lunch?—Let's go to the Tōkyō Kaikan; it is a very good restaurant, and many foreigners go there. **5.** I wish to go to Nara and see the large statue of Buddha and the famous park.—Let's go there next week. —Yes, let's go. **6.** Do you suppose that the boat from Shanghai has already arrived at Yokohama?—Perhaps she has.—I don't think she has. **7.** As it has not rained for a month the rice crop will be poor this year. **8.** As my cousin is studying hard from morning till night, I am sure that some day he will become a learned man. **9.** The cherry blossoms at Ueno Park will be in full bloom in two or three days.—Then let's go there the day after to-morrow.—Yes, let us.—Shall we go there on foot?—No, we shall go by motor-car. **10.** I have heard that Miss Hanako has been injured in a motor-car accident.—Let's go and visit her this evening. **11.** If it rains to-morrow we shall go to the cinema instead of going on a picnic. **12.** To-night we shall eat Japanese food instead of foreign food. I like to eat Japanese food sometimes. **13.** Will you buy this incense burner?—I shall buy it if it is cheap.—I will give it to you for one thousand yen. **14.** If Mr. Shibusawa does not come to-night we shall go and visit him to-morrow. **15.** If you do not hurry you will miss the train. **16.** Where will you go now?—I will go to take a walk.—Shall I come with you?—Yes, you may come with me. **17.** Bring me a clean shirt.—All your shirts were dirty and I took them to the laundry. Shall I go and buy a new one?—Yes, go and buy one, please. **18.** When will you sail for Europe?—I will sail for Europe next month. **19.** When will the tailor bring me my new suit?—I think he will bring it to-morrow. **20.** If you are not good to your friends they will not be good to you.

Thirty-third Lesson 第卅三課

Relative Pronouns *Kankéi Daiméishi* 関係代名詞

There are no relative pronouns is Japanese. Where in English a relative clause is used, the Japanese prefix the verb of the relative clause to the noun or pronoun which in English would be the antecedent. The verb will thus become an adjective.

Nominative
Who, Which, That

Kimáshĭta otokó...... 来ました 男	The man that (who) came...... (*lit.* Came man......)
Yónde imásŭ musŭmé...... 読んでいます 娘	The girl that (who) is reading...... (*lit.* Reading girl......)
Ashĭtá tsukú fúne...... あした 着く 船	The ship that (which) arrives to-morrow...... (*lit.* To-morrow arrives ship......)

The object in an English relative clause is put in Japanese before the verb, as in non-relative clauses.

> ***Hon wo yónde imásŭ*** *shōjo wa Chōsenjin désŭ.*
> 本 を 読んで います 少女 は 朝鮮人 です.
> The girl **that (who) is reading a book** is a Korean.
> (*lit.* Book reading girl Korean person is.)

The above relative phrases and example may be rendered in Japanese also by the word ***tokoró no*** ところの placed before the affected noun. In such cases, the expression *tokoró no* might be said to correspond to a relative pronoun. This construction, however, seems to be more of the literary style, and may therefore be neglected in ordinary conversation.

Below are given the above examples in the new form:

   Kimáshĭta **tokoró no** *otokó*......   The man **that** came......
   来ました　ところ　の　男

   Yónde imásŭ **tokoró no** *musŭmé*......   The girl **that** is reading......
   読んでいます　ところ　の　娘

   Ashĭtá tsŭkú **tokoró no** *fúne*......   The ship **that** arrives to-morrow......
   あした　着く　ところ　の　船

   Hon wo yónde imásŭ **tokoró no** *shōjo wa Chōsenjin désŭ.*
   本　を　読んでいます　ところ　の　少女　は　朝鮮人　です.

In the examples given below, illustrating how to translate relative clauses with the other relative pronouns, the expression *tokoró no* ところの will be in parentheses, just to show the place it should be, were one to use it.

Accusative
Whom, Which, That

In Japanese, relative clauses with relative pronouns in the accusative have the same construction as is used when translating relative clauses with relative pronouns in the nominative.

   Watashí ga **mimáshĭta** (***tokoró no***) **fujín wa** *anáta no okāsan*
   私　が　見ました　（ところ　の）　婦人　は　貴方　のお母さん
   déshĭta.   The lady **whom** I saw was your mother.
   でした.   (*lit.* **I-saw-lady** your mother was.)

   Anáta ga máinichi **nómu** (***tokoró no***) **o-cha wa** *Táiwan kará*
   貴方　が　毎日　飲む　（ところ　の）　お茶　は　台湾　から
   kúru no désŭ.   The tea **that** (which) you drink every day comes from
   来る　の　です.   Formosa.
      (*lit.* You–every–day–**drink–tea** from Formosa comes.)

Compare the two following relative clauses in which both the nominative and accusative relative pronouns have the same antecedent.

   Watashí wo **mimáshĭta** (***tokoró no***) **fujín wa** *anó ki no ushiró*
   私　を　見ました　（ところ　の）　婦人　は　あの木　の　うしろ
   ni imáshĭta.   The lady **who** saw me was behind that tree.
   に　いました.   (*lit.* **Me–saw–lady** that tree behind was.)

   Watashí ga **mimáshĭta** (***tokoró no***) **fujín wa** *anó ki no ushiró*
   私　が　見ました　（ところ　の）　婦人　は　あの木　の　うしろ
   ni imáshĭta.   The lady **whom** I saw was behind that tree.
   に　いました.   (**I–saw–lady** that tree behind was.)

The antecedent of a relative clause in English requires, when translated into Japanese, the proper postposition to indicate the required case.

   Watashí wa kĕsa **kitá** (*tokoró no*) **otokó wo** *mimáshĭta.*
   私　は　けさ　来た　（ところの）　男　を　見ました.
   I saw the man **that** came this morning.

Késa **kimáshĭta** *(tokoró no)* **hĭtó wa** *chichí désŭ.*
けさ 来ました （ところの） 人 は 父 です.
The man **that** came this morning was my father.

Késa **kitá** *(tokoró no)* **otokó to** *hanashimáshĭta.*
けさ 来た （ところ の） 男 と 話しました.
I spoke with the man **that** came this morning.

Késa **kitá** *(tokoró no)* **otokó kará** *konó haná wo kaimáshĭta.*
けさ 来た （ところ の） 男 から この 花 を 買いました.
I bought these flowers from the man **that** came this morning.

Uchí no kodomó wa késa **kitá otokó to** *isshó ni Uenó Kōen e*
うち の 子供 は けさ 来た 男 と 一緒 に 上野 公園へ
ikimáshĭta.   My children went to Ueno Park with the man **that** came this
行きました.   morning.

What

Kinō anó gakkō de **okótta** *(tokoró no)* **kotó wa** *minná wo odorokase-*
きのうあの 学校 で 起った （ところの） 事 は みんな を 驚かせ
máshita.[1]   **What happened** in that school yesterday surprised everybody.
ました. (*lit.* Yesterday at that school happened thing surprised all.)

Anó ko ga **ittá** *(tokoró no)* **kotó wo** *anáta wa wakarimáshĭta ka.*
あの 子 が 言った（ところの） 事 を 貴方 は 解りました か.
Did you understand **what** that boy **said?**

Iié, ittá (tokoró no) **kotó wo** *wakarimasén déshĭta.*
いゝえ, 言った（ところの） 事 を 解りません でした.
No, I did not understand **what he said.**

Anáta ga **ittá** *(tokoró no)* **kotó wa** *hontō de wa arimasén déshĭta.*
貴方 が 言った（ところの） 事 は 本当 で はありませんでした.
What you said was not true.

Anáta ga **osshátta** *(tokoró no)* **kotó wo** *dōzo kurikaeshĭté kudasái.*
貴方 がおっしゃった（ところ の） 事 を どうぞくり返して 下さい.
Please repeat **what you said.** (*kurikaesú* to repeat)

Anáta no otōsan ga **ittá** *(tokoró no)* **kotó wo** *anáta ni o-hanashí*
貴方 のお父さんが 言った（ところの） 事 を 貴方 に お話し
shimashō.   I will tell you **what** your father **said.**
しましょう.

N. B. The subject of a clause with the relative pronoun **what** in the accusative is followed by **ga,** as in the preceding examples.

In some cases, the relative pronoun **what** may have to be turned
into an interrogative pronoun, as in the following example:

Anó onná-no-ko ga **náni wo** *hoshíi no ka watashí wa shirimasén.*
あの 女の子 が 何 を 欲しいのか 私 は 知りません.
I do not know **what** that girl wants.
(*lit.* That girl, **what** does she want?, I do not know.)

---

1 *odorokaséru* 驚かせる to cause surprise

Whose

*Koré wa íma hijō-ni ninkí no áru (**tokoró no**) shōsetsu no sakká désŭ.*
これ は 今 非常 に 人気 の ある（ところ の） 小説 の 作家 です。
This is the author **whose** novels are now very popular.
> (*lit.* This, now very popular are novels' author is.)
>> *ninkí* popularity; *ninkí no áru* popular; *shōsetsu* novel; *sakká* writer.

Aré wa anó hĭtó no umá ga sakunén no dābĭ keibá de yūshō shĭtá
あれ は あの 人 の 馬 が 昨年 のダービー競馬 で 優勝 した
(tokoró no) fugō désŭ.   That is the millionaire **whose** horse won last year's
（ところ の） 富豪 です。   Derby. (*lit.* That, that man's horse, in last year's
Derby horse race won millionaire is.)
> (*Dābĭ* Derby; *keibá* horse-race; *yūshō surú* to win; *fugō* millionaire)

*Konó gakkō wa ryōshin ga bimbō de áru (**tokoró no**) kodomó daké*
この 学校 は 両親 が 貧乏 である（ところ の） 子供 だけ
ga nyūgaku wo yurusaremásŭ.   In this school are admitted only children
が 入学 を 許されます。   **whose** parents are poor.
> (*lit.* This school, parents poor are (whose) children only admission-into-the-
> school is allowed.)
>> (*nyūgaku wo yurusaréru* to be allowed to enter a school)

Jínsei wo yūeki-na shigotó wo surú tamé ni tsŭkaerú hĭtó wa kōfuku
人生 を 有益 な 仕事 を する ため に 使える 人 は 幸福
ni chigainái.
にちがいない。
A man **whose** life is spent in doing a useful work must indeed feel happy.
> (*lit.* One's life, useful work in order to do, that is spent man, is happy, there
> is no mistake.—*jínsei* man's life, existence; *yūeki-na* useful; *tsŭkaerú*
> passive of *tsŭkaú* 使う to make use of, to employ, to spend, etc.)

Relative Pronouns Preceded by Prepositions

At the beginning of this lesson it has been said that *tokoró no*
ところの may be considered to correspond to English relative pronouns. The same expression may be used also in translating relative
clauses with the said pronouns preceded by prepositions. However,
as the construction with *tokoró no* would become rather pedantic,
it is generally avoided.

Below are given a few examples of sentences with relative pronouns
preceded by prepositions and translated with *tokoró no* in parentheses.

*Anáta ga sonó katá **ni tsŭite** o-hanashí shĭté irú (**tokoró no**) fujín*
貴方 が その 方 について お話し して いる（ところ の） 婦人
wa watashí no senséi désŭ.   The lady **about whom** you are speaking is my
は 私 の 先生 です。   teacher.
> (*lit.* You, that person–about–talk–doing–are–lady (**of whom**) my teacher is.)

*Moritá-San wa watashí ga dái-on wo úketa (**tokoró no**) katá désŭ.*
森田さん は 私 が 大恩 を 受けた（ところ の） 方 です。
Mr. Morita is a person **from whom** I received a great favour.
> (*lit.* Mr. Morita, I–great–favour–received–(**from whom**) person is.)

*Anáta ga konó tegamí wo o-uketorí ni nátta (**tokoró no**) tsŭkái no*
貴方 が この 手紙 を お受取り に なった（ところ の）使 の

monó wa watashí no otōto désŭ. The messenger **from whom** you received
者 は 私 の 弟 です. this letter is my younger brother.

    (*o-uketorí ni náru* polite for *uketorú* 受取る to receive)
    (*lit.* You, this–letter–received–(**from whom**) messenger's person, my younger
    brother is.)

*Aré wa watashí ga anáta ni o-hanashí shǐtá (**tokoró no**) Fŭransú*
あれ は 私 が 貴方 に お話し した（ところ の）フランス

no fujín désŭ. That is the French lady **of whom** I spoke to you.
の 婦人 です.   (*lit.* That, I to you talk I made (**of whom**) French lady is.)

*Koré wa watashí ga isshó ni ryō wo shǐtá (**tokoró no**) seinén*
これ は 私 が 一緒 に 猟 を した（ところ の）青年

désŭ. This is the young man **with whom** I hunted.
です.   (*lit.* This, I–together–hunting–made–(**with whom**) young man is.)

*Anó shōnen ga nigedashǐtá (**tokoró no**) mádo.* The window **from which**
あの 少年 が 逃げ出した（ところ の）窓. the boy escaped.

    (*lit.* The boy–escaped–(**from which**) window.)

*Aré wa watashí ga máe ni súnde itá (**tokoró no**) uchí désŭ.*
あれ は 私 が 前 に 住んでいた（ところ の）家 です.

That is the house **in which** I previously lived.
[*lit.* That, I–before–living–was–(**in which**) house is.]

*Anáta ga ki wo kitté irú (**tokoró no**) óno wa amarí omói désŭ.*
貴方 が 木 を 切っている（ところ の）斧 は 余り 重い です.

The hatchet **with which** you are chopping wood is too heavy.
    (*lit.* You wood cutting are (**with which**) hatchet too heavy is.)

In many cases, the relative clause formed by a preposition and
a relative pronoun cannot be translated in what in Japanese would
correspond to a relative construction, as in the examples given above.
For illustration's sake, two of such cases are given below:

Anáta no o-hanashí no sonó dorobō wa tsŭkamarimáshǐta.
貴方 の お話 の その 泥棒 は つかまりました.

The thief **of whom** you speak has been arrested.
    (*lit.* Your talk of that thief was arrested=The thief of your talk was arrested.)

Sonó jíko no giséisha san-jū nin no uchí yo-nin wa shinimáshǐta.
その 事故 の 犠牲者 三十 人 の 内 四人 は 死にました.

In that accident there were thirty victims, four **of whom** died.
    (*lit.* Of that accident victims, thirty among, four died.=Among thirty victims
    in that accident, four persons died.)

In order to minimize the difficulty in translating a compound
sentence with a relative clause into Japanese, the most practical
way is to make a separate sentence of each clause.

For instance, a sentence like this:

**That man, who so suddenly attained to greatness, had a very unhappy
childhood.**

could, without change of its meaning, be expressed thus:

1. That man had a very unhappy childhood. 2. He suddenly attained to greatness.

And this is the way that similar English compound sentences with relative clauses are generally expressed in Japanese.

The above sentence would then be translated as follows:

1. *Anó hĭtó no kodomó-jidái wa hijō ni fukō dĕshĭta.* **2.** *Káre wa totsuzén*
あの 人 の 子供時代 は 非常 に 不幸 でした. 彼 は 突然
idái ni narimáshĭta.   (*lit.* 1. That man's childhood very unhappy was. 2. He
偉大 に なりました.   suddenly to greatness became.—*náru* to become)

A few more illustrations are here given:

That man, whom I have offended, was my best friend.

Anó hĭtó wa watashí no ichibán íi tomodachí dĕshĭta. Watashí wa káre
あの 人 は 私 の 一番 いゝ 友達 でした. 私 は 彼
wo okorásete shimaimáshĭta.   That man was my best friend. I have offended
を 怒らせて しまいました.   him. (*lit.* That man my No. 1 good friend was.
            I, him causing-to-be-offended ended by.-*okoraséru* to cause to be offended)

This safe box, of which I have the key, holds important documents.

Konó kínko wa jūyō-na shorúi ga háitte imásŭ. Watashí ga sonó kagí wo
この 金庫 は 重要な 書類 が 入っています. 私 が その 鍵 を
mótte imásŭ.   This safe box holds important documents. I have its key.
持っています.   (*lit.* This safe important documents are put in. I its key have.)

Nippón téikoku wa Jínmu Tennō ni yotté kensetsú saremáshĭta. **Konó**
日本 帝国 は 神武 天皇 によって 建設 されました. この
Tennō *wa konó kuni no saishó no tōchisha de arimáshĭta.*
天皇 は この 国 の 最初 の 統治者 で ありました.
        The Japanese Empire was founded by the Emperor Jimmu, **who** was the first
        ruler of this country. (*lit.* The Japanese Empire by Jimmu Tennō was founded.
        This Emperor, of this country the first ruler was.)
        ni yotté by; *kensetsú sarerú* to be founded; *saishó* first; *tōchisha* ruler

Nikkō e ikú kaidō ni wa takŭsán no sugí no ki ga arimásŭ. **Koréra**
日光 へ行く 街道 に は 沢山 の 杉 の 木 が あります. これ等
wa oyosó sam-byakú nen máe ni ueraretá monó dĕsŭ.
は 凡そ 三百 年 前 に植えられたもの です.
        Along the road to Nikko there are a great many cryptomeria trees, **which** were
        planted about three hundred years ago. (*lit.* To Nikko that goes road many
        cryptomeria trees there are. These about three hundred years before were
        planted.)
        kaidō road; *oyosó* about; *uerererú* to be planted

That (conjunction)

There is no word in Japanese corresponding to the conjunction **that**. The following examples will show how to translate sentences that have this conjunction:

Watashí no senséi wa watashí ga konó hon-yakú wo surú kotó ga
私 の 先生 は 私 が この 翻訳 を する 事 が
dekíru to iú kotó wo utagatté imásŭ. My teacher doubts **that** I can make
出来る という 事 をうたがっています. this translation.

    (*lit.* My teacher, I, this translation to make can, the thing doubts.)

Watashí wa anáta ga pianó wo hikú kotó ga o-dekí ni náru no wo
私 は 貴方 が ピアノ を 弾く 事 が お出来に なる の を
shirimasén déshĭta. I did not know **that** you could play the piano.
知りません でした. (*hikú* to play an instrument)

    (*lit.* I, you, piano to play you can the thing I did not know.)

Anáta no okāsan wa niwá ni oidé ni náru to omoimásŭ.
貴方 のお母さん は 庭 においでに なる と 思います.
I think **that** your mother is in the garden.

    (*lit.* Your mother in the garden is, so I think.)

Anáta no ojisán wa kómban korarénai to watashí ni iimáshĭta.
貴方 の伯父さんは 今晩 来られない と 私 に 言いました.
Your uncle told me **that** he could not come to-night.

    (*lit.* Your uncle to-night cannot come so to me said.)

Nakamurá San wa Eikokú e ikú **sō désŭ.** I hear **that** Mr. Nakamura
中村 さん は 英国 へ行くそう です. is going to England.

Shimbún ni yorú to[1] kómban árashi ga áru **sō désŭ.**
新聞 によると 今晩 嵐 が あるそう です.
The papers say **that** we shall have a storm this evening.

Sō désŭ at the end of a sentence, as in the last two examples, means *I hear, they say,* or *it is said.*

Vocabulary

Nouns					
			victory	*shōri*	勝シヨウ利リ
admiral	*kaigún-taishō*	海軍大将	warship	*gúnkan*	軍グン艦カン
company	*kaishá*	会カイ社シヤ	**Verbs**		
concert	*ongakŭkái*	音オン楽ガク会カイ	to admit	*yurúsu*	許ユルス
foundation	*kisó*	基キ礎ソ	to be admitted	*yurusaré·ru*	許ユルサレル
message	*kotozuké*	言コトヅケ	to break	*kowásu*	コワス
noble class	*kízoku*	貴キ族ゾク	to believe	*shinjí·ru*	信シンジル
president	*shachō*	社シヤ長チヨウ	to doubt	*utagaú*	ウタガウ
sailor	*súihei*	水スイ兵ヘイ	to dress	*kise·rú* (tr.)	着キセル
speaker	*kōensha*	講コウ演エン者シヤ	to honour	*sonkéi surú*	尊ソン敬ケイスル
translation	*hon-yakú*	翻ホン訳ヤク	to recognize	*mioboe·rú*	見ミ覚オボエル
truth	*shínjitsu*	真シン実ジツ	to translate	*yakusúru*	訳ヤクスル

the other day *senjitsú;* at last, at length, finally *yattó;* peer, nobleman *kízoku;* Peers' School *Gakushūin;* entrance (admission) into a school *nyūgaku;* sons, children *shitei* (lit.); naval battle *kaisén;* to return (to a place) *káette ikú*

---

1 *ni yorú to* or *ni yoréba* によれば according to; *yorú* よる to be based upon, to depend on, to be founded on

Exercise   *Renshū* 練習

1. Tattá[1] íma déte ittá otokó wa dáre désŭ ka (*or* dáre déshĭta ka).—Sentakuyá désŭ (*or* déshĭta). Sentakuyá wa anáta no kírei ni nátta sentakú monó wo mótte kimáshĭta. **2.** Anó fujín wo anáta wa go-zónji[2] désŭ ka.—Hái, shĭtté orimásŭ. Anó fujín wa gorokú-satsú no Doitsú-go no hon wo Nihón-go ni hon-yakú[3] nasaimáshĭta tokoró no senséi désŭ. (That lady several German books into Japanese translation made–who–, teacher is.) **3.** Anáta ni o-hanashí ga shĭtái to iú otokó-no-ko ga kité imásŭ.[4] (To you talk wish–to–do, so to say boy has come.=A boy has come saying he wishes to talk to you.)—Anáta wa anó hĭtó wo shĭtté imású ka.—Iié, shirimasén. **4.** Kinō watashí ga katté kitá[5] atarashíi kimonó wo kodomó ni kiseté kudasái. (*kimonó wo kodomó ni kiserú* dress on the child to put) **5.** Senshū watashitachí ga Yokohamá de míta Fŭransú no gúnkan wa mō Honkón ni tsŭkimáshĭta. **6.** Senjitsú Kimurá San no ókŭsan ga anáta ni kudasátta koppú wo fŭtatsú meshitsŭkái[6] ga kowashimáshĭta. —(The other day Kimura's wife to you gave–cups–two, the servant broke.) Shikatá ga arimasén. **7.** Anó wakái fujín wo mioboeté imásŭ ka.—Iié, aré wa dónata désŭ ka.—Anó katá wa kinō ongakŭkái de o-me ni kakátta Burajirú táishi no reijō[7] désŭ. (That person yesterday at the concert met Brazilian ambassador's daughter is.) **8.** Kimí ga Itarī-go no jibikí wo karitá tokoró no gakŭséi ga kité kimí ni hanashitái sō désŭ.—(You Italian dictionary borrowed from whom, having come to you wishes to talk, so is.) Chottó mátte kudasái to itté kudasái. **9.** Kinō anáta ga Ginzá wo go-isshó ni arúite itá wakái gofujín wa dónata désŭ ka (*or* déshĭta ka).—(Yesterday, you Ginza together walking was young lady, who is?) Anó katá wa uchí no kaishá no shachō no ojōsan désŭ (*or* déshĭta). **10.** Watashí wa yattó anó shínsetsu-na hĭtó ni aimáshĭta, sonó hĭtó kará watashí wa nakushĭtá saifú wo uketottá no déshĭta. (I at last that kind person I met; that person from, I lost purse received the fact was.) **11.** Kōensha ga hánshĭte irú kotó wo wakarimásŭ ka.— (The speaker telling things do you understand?) Kōensha ga itté irú kotó no zémbu wa wakarimasén ga sŭkóshi wa wakarimásŭ. Anó hĭtó wa amarí háyaku shaberímásŭ.[8] **12.** Kimí ga ittá kotó wo nanní-mo shinjimasén[9] yo. —Shínjite mo shinjínakute mo bóku ga íttá kotó wa shínjitsu désŭ. **13.** Anó otokó ga ittá kotó wo hanásu kotó ga dekimásŭ ka.—O-hanashí dekimasén. Anó hĭtó wa Shiná-go de hanashĭmáshĭta soshĭté watashí wa Shiná-go wo shirimasén. **14.** Anó fujín wa ojōsan ga jidōsha jíko de nakunararetá[10] katá désŭ. (That lady, the daughter motor-car accident by died, person is.) **15.** Konó gakkō wa kízoku no shitéi daké ga séito to shĭté nyūgaku wo yurusárete imáshĭta. Koré wa Gakushūin to yobareté[11] imásŭ. **16.** Watashí ga íma súnde irú uchí no hĭtó wa Shiná-jin désŭ. (I now–living–am–house–of person, Chinese is.) Konó hĭtó wa Ameriká e ni-jū-nen máe ni itté kyónen Nihón e kimáshĭta. Konó hĭtó wa Eigó wo totemó[12] tasshá ni[13] hanashimásŭ.

---

1 *tattá ima* just now   2 *go-zónji* you know (pol.)   3 *hon-yakú nasáru*=*hon-yakú surú* or *yakusúru* to translate   4 *kité imásŭ* there is (after coming)   5 *katté kitá* having bought I came (home)   6 man or maid servant   7 *reijō* very polite for *musŭmé* daughter   8 *háyaku shabéru* to speak too fast   9 *shinjíru* to believe 10 *nakunarú* to die, to get lost   11 *yobarerú* to be called   12 very   13 *tasshá ni* skillfully, with proficiency

17. Anáta ga anáta no otōsan no kotozuké wo uketottá anó súihei wa myōnichi Burajirú e káette ikimásu. (You, your–father's–message–received–that–sailor, to-morrow to Brazil returning is going.) Sonó hǐtó wa móshi anáta ga otōsan e náni-ka okuritái náraba mótte itté agerú to iimáshǐta.—Arigatō, déwa myōchō[1] watashí wa fúne ni itté anó katá ni o-me ni kakarimashō. **18.** Súiko Jotéi (Seireki[2] 593–628) no miyó[3] ni Nihón wo osámete oráreta[4] (tokoró no) sesshō[5] Shōtoku Táishi[6] wa netsuretsú-na[7] Bukkyō shínja[8] déshǐta. Shōtoku Táishi no sesshō jidái[9] ni Bukkyō wa Nihón-kokujū ni hiromári,[10] sonó tokí írai Nihón kokumín no shuyō-na shūkyō[11] to narimáshǐta. Shōtoku Táishi wa nihónjin no tamé ni saishó no kempō[12] wo o-tsŭkurí ni narimáshǐta.[13] **19.** Nihón Téikoku no kisó wo tsukútta Tokugawá Iyeyasú wa shódai[14] no Tokugawá shōgun de arimáshǐta.

1. たった今，出て行った男は誰ですか（誰でしたか）.—洗濯屋です（でした）.洗濯屋は貴方のきれいになった洗濯物を持って来ました. **2.** あの婦人を貴方は御存じですか.—はい，知っております.あの婦人は五六冊の独逸語の本を日本語に翻訳なさいました所の先生です. **3.** 貴方にお話がしたいという男の子が来ています.—貴方はあの人を知っていますか.—いゝえ，知りません. **4.** きのう私が買って来た新しい着物を子供に着せて下さい. **5.** 先週私達が横浜で見たフランスの軍艦はもう香港に着きました. **6.** 先日木村さんの奥さんが貴方に下さったコップを二つ召使がこわしました.—仕方がありません. **7.** あの若い婦人を見覚えていますか.—いゝえ，あれはどなたですか.—あの方はきのう音楽会でお目にかゝったブラジル大使の令嬢です. **8.** 君がイタリー語の字引を借りたところの学生が来て君に話したいそうです.—ちょっと待って下さいと言って下さい. **9.** きのう貴方が銀座を御一緒に歩いていた若い御婦人はどなたですか（でしたか）.—あの方はうちの会社の社長のお嬢さんです（でした）. **10.** 私はやっとあの親切な人に会いましたその人から私は失くした財布を受取ったのでした. **11.** 講演者が話している事を解りますか.—講演者が言っている事の全部は解りませんが少しは解ります.あの人は余り早くしゃべります. **12.** 君が言った事を何んにも信じませんよ.—信じても信じなくても僕が言った事は真実です. **13.** あの男が言った事を話す事が出来ますか.—お話し出来ません.あの人は支那語で話しました，そして私は支那語を知りません. **14.** あの婦人はお嬢さんが自動車事故で亡くなられた方です. **15.** この学校は貴族の子弟だけが生徒として

1 to-morrow morning　2 Christian Era, A.D.　3 reign, period　4 *osámete oráreta* respectful for *osamemáshǐta*, past of *osaméru* to rule over, to govern　5 regent　6 Prince　7 fervent, ardent 8 believer　9 period, epoch　10 *hiromáru* to spread　11 *sonó tokí írai* since then; *kokumín* the people, the nation; *shuyō-na* the main; *shūkyō* religion 12 *saishó no* the first; *kempō* constitution 13 *o-tsŭkurí ni narimáshǐta* respectful for *tsŭkurimáshǐta* past of *tsukúru* to make　14 *shódai* the first

入学を許されていました．これは学習院と呼ばれています．**16.** 私が今住んでいる家の人は支那人です．この人はアメリカへ廿年前に行って去年日本へ来ました．この人は英語をとても達者に話します．**17.** 貴方が貴方のお父さんの言づけを受取ったあの水兵は明日ブラジルへ帰って行きます．その人は若し貴方がお父さんへ何かおくりたいならば持って行ってあげると言いました．―ありがとう．では明朝私は船に行ってあの方にお目にかゝりましょう．**18.** 推古女帝の御代に日本を治めておられた（ところの）摂政聖徳太子は熱烈な仏教の信者でした．聖徳太子の摂政時代に仏教は日本国中に広まり，その時以来日本国民の主要な宗教となりました．聖徳太子は日本人のために最初の憲法をおつくりになりました．**19.** 日本帝国の基礎を作った徳川家康は初代の徳川将軍でありました．

1. Who was the man that just went out?—He was the laundryman. He brought your clean laundry. **2.** Do you know that lady?—Yes, I do. She is the teacher that translated several German books into Japanese. **3.** There is a boy who wishes to speak to you.—Do you know him?—No, I don't. **4.** Please dress the child with the new dress that I bought yesterday. **5.** The French warship that we saw last week in Yokohama has already reached Hong-kong. **6.** The servant has broken two of the cups that Mrs. Kimura gave you the other day.—It can't be helped. **7.** Do you recognize that young lady?—No, who is she?—She is the Brazilian Ambassador's daughter, whom we met yesterday at the concert. **8.** The student from whom you borrowed the Italian dictionary has come and wishes to speak to you.—Tell him to wait for a moment. **9.** Who was the young lady you were walking with yesterday on Ginza?—She was the daughter of the president of our company. **10.** At last I met the kind person from whom I received my lost purse. **11.** Do you understand what the speaker is saying?—I understand a little but not all that he is saying. He speaks too fast. **12.** I don't believe anything of what you told me.—Believe it or not, what I told you is true. **13.** Can you tell me what that man said?—I cannot; he spoken in Chinese and I do not know Chinese. **14.** That is the lady whose daughter died in a motor-car accident. **15.** In this school were admitted only students whose parents belonged to the nobility. It is called the Peers' School. **16.** The man in whose house I am now living is a Chinese. He went to America twenty years ago and came to Japan last year. He speaks English very well. **17.** The sailor from whom you received your father's message is returning to Brazil to-morrow. He told me that if you wish to send something to your father he will deliver it to him.—Thank you; to-morrow morning I will go and meet him on the boat. **18.** Prince regent Shotoku, who governed Japan during the reign of Empress Súiko (A.D. 593–628), was a fervent believer in Buddhism. During Prince Shotoku's regency Buddhism spread throughout Japan and since then it has been the main religion of the Japanese people. Prince Shotoku framed the first constitution for the Japanese. **19.** Ieyasu Tokugawa, who laid the foundation of the Japanese Empire, was the first Tokugawa Shōgun.

Thirty-fourth Lesson　第卅四課

Titles of Courtesy　*Sonshō* 尊称

The word *San* さん is used after names of persons and corresponds to either *Mister, Mistress,* or *Miss.*

San is a contraction of *Samá* 様, which is to-day rarely used in the colloquial. *Samá* is, however, generally used in the written style. In formal written style the word *donó* 殿 instead of *samá* is used, and corresponds to *Esquire.*

Kun 君 is used instead of *San* among boys, students, or other young men on intimate terms.

In speaking of married ladies, it is necessary to use such circumlocution as : *Yamada San no ŏkŭsan,* or *ŏkŭsama* (Mr. Yamada's wife, *or* Mrs. Yamada.)

Sometimes in formal conversation, and very often in the written language, *fujin* 夫人 (lady) is used after family names. In formal written style *reifujin* 令夫人 instead of *fujín* may be used.

Mrs. Ota { *Ōta San no ŏkŭsan, Ōta San no ŏkŭsama, Ōta San no fujín, Ōta fujín, Ōta reifujín*

What corresponds to our Christian name, is in Japanese put after the family name.

Ōta Tsúruko fujín.　太田鶴子夫人　Mrs. **Tsúruko** Ōta

When one is asked about one's name or identity, the title of courtesy is omitted in the answer.

Anáta wa dónata de gozaimásŭ ka.　Who are you?
貴方　は　どなた　で　ございます　か.

Watashí wa Kurosawá désŭ.　I am Mr. Kurosawa.
私　は　黒沢　です.

O-namaé wa nan to osshaimásŭ ka.　What is your name?
お名前　は　何ん　とおっしゃいますか.

Yamadá to mōshimásŭ.　My name is Mr. (Miss,
山田　と　申します.　Mrs) Yamada.

(*mōshimásŭ*, present of *mōsu* 申す -to say, to tell, a verb indicating humility when speaking to one's superiors, or just used to show respect towards the person spoken to)

In addressing teachers, professors, and doctors the word *senséi* 先生 (teacher) is used.

Doctor Otani　*Ōtani Senséi* 大谷先生

Honorifics
O and *Go*

In polite conversation, when referring to things or persons which belong, or are related, to those whom we address, respect is indicated by prefixing the phonetic sound of *o* or *go* to the noun indicating the possessed object.

The sound *o* is generally prefixed to Japanese words, while *go* is prefixed to words of Chinese origin. Sometimes however, *o* is prefixed to words of Chinese derivation and *go* to pure Japanese words.

Go is always represented by the Chinese symbol 御, while *o* may be represented by the same Chinese symbol 御 or by the Japanese letter お.

Only by practice can one know when it is fitting to use the honorific *o* お and when *go* 御.

The following is a list of the most common words which, by themselves, indicate possessions of the first person, but when preceded by the honorific *o* or *go* indicate possessions of the second or third person.

> *takú* 宅   or *uchí* 家   my home, husband, family, house
>
> *o-takú* お宅   or *o-uchí* お家   your home, husband, family, house

O-takú de wa minásama ikága désŭ ka.   How are the members of your
お宅 で は 皆様 いかが です か.   family?
(*lit.* At your home, everybody how is?)

O-kagesamá de takú de wa miná jōbu désŭ.   Everybody is well,
お蔭様 で 宅 で は 皆 丈夫 です.   thank you.
(*lit.* Thanks to your favour, at my home, everybody healthy is.)

takú no (*uchí no*) *toshiyorí* 宅 の（家 の）年寄	our aged parents, *or* grandparents the old people at our home
o-takú no (*o-uchí no*) *o-toshiyorí* お宅 の（お家 の）お年寄	your aged parents, *or* grandparents
takú no kodomó 宅の子供	my *or* our child
o-kosán (*o-kodomosamá*) お子さん（お子供様）	your child
takú no kodomotachí 宅の子供達	my *or* our children
o-takú no kodomosantachí お宅 の 子供さん達	your children
o-takú no o-kodomosantachí お宅 のお子供さん達	your children
o-takú no o-kosantachí お宅 の お子さん達	your children
áni (*nísan*) 兄（兄さん）	my elder brother

o-aníisan[1] (o-níisan) お兄さん（お兄さん）		your elder brother
ané (nēsan) 姉（姉さん）		my elder sister
o-anēsan[1] (o-nēsan) お姉さん（お姉さん）		your elder sister

imōto 妹	my younger sister	o-imōto (o-imōtosan) お妹 （お妹さん）	your younger sister
tegami 手紙	a letter (written by me)	o-tegami お手紙	your letter
takú no niwá 宅 の 庭	our garden	o-takú no o-niwá お宅 の お庭	your garden
kuni 国	my country	o-kuni お国	your country
kázoku 家族	my family	go-kázoku 御家族	your family
ryōshin 両親	my parents	go-ryōshin 御両親	your parents
shinrui 親類	my relatives	go-shínrui 御親類	your relatives
kyōdai 兄弟	my brothers	go-kyōdai 御兄弟	your brothers
kyōdai 姉妹	my sisters	go-kyōdai 御姉妹	your sisters

When referring to an object belonging to a third person, before the word preceded by *o* or *go*, some other word indicating the possessor must be used.

Usuda San no o-takú wa Ōmori désŭ. or:
臼田 さん の お宅 は 大森 です。

Usudá San no o-takú wa Ōmori ni arimásŭ.
臼田 さん の お宅 は 大森 に あります。

} Mr. Usuda's house is in Omori.

Makŭmorin San no o-kuni wa Kánada désŭ.
マクモリン さん の お国 は カナダ です。

Miss Macmorine's native country is Canada.

The honorific *o* and *go* used in the following expressions have lost the idea of doing honour to the persons addressed, and may be said to have become a part of the words they precede.

With some words these honorifics are invariably used by women and children, while men may dispense with them.

o-bon お盆	the tray	o-ténki	お天気	the weather
o-cha お茶	the tea	o-tentō samá	お天道様	the sun
o-hashí お箸	the chopsticks	o-tsŭkisamá	お月様	the moon
o-káshi お菓子	the cake	o-yu	お湯	hot water
o-komé お米	the rice	go-han	御飯	boiled rice, meal

Some words of certain common expressions, as the following ones for instance, are always preceded by *o* or *go*.

---

1 In very polite conversation, instead of *san*, the more formal title of courtesy *samá* is used: *o-aníisama* お兄様 *o-anēsama* お姉様

O-kagé-samá de	Thanks to you......, Owing to......, Thanks to
お蔭様　で	your kind assistance......
O-tasshá de.	{ I hope you will keep well.
お達者　で	{ I wish you good health.
Go-chisō samá.	{ Thank you for your kind entertainment.
御馳走　様	{ I have enjoyed your dinner very much.
Go-kurō samá. 御苦労様	Many thanks for your trouble.

The honorific *o* before adjectives and verbs is very often used by women in polite as well as in ordinary conversation, while men use it only occasionally when speaking to superiors.

Anáta no o-jōsan wa o-kírei désŭ ne.[1]	Your daughter
貴方　の　お嬢さん　は　おきれい　です　ね.	is beautiful.
(Kyō wa) o-atsúi désŭ. (きようは) お暑い です.	It is hot (to-day).
(Kyō wa) taihén o-samúi désŭ.	It is very cold (to-day).
(きようは)　大変　お寒い　です.	
(Kyō wa) íi o-ténki désŭ.	It is fine (to-day).
(きようは) いゝ お天気　です.	

When verbs are preceded by the honorific *o*, it is the simple stem of verbs of Class I and the *i*-stem of verbs of Class II that are used:

| *Dōzo go-énryo*[2] *náku o-agarí*[3] *kudasái.* | Please help yourself. (*lit.* Please, |
| どうぞ 御遠慮　なく お上がり　下さい. | without reserve, eat.) |

A verb preceded by the honorific *o* is often followed by the particle *ni* and the verb **náru なる (成る)**, which, as an independent verb, means *to become, to come into being, to turn out, to result in*, etc. The honorific *o* followed by the stem of a verb and the expression *ni náru,* forms a polite substitute for the ordinary inflection of a verb.

Itsu Ōsaka kará o-kaerí ni narimáshĭta ka.	When did you return
いつ 大阪 から　お帰り　に　なりました　か.	from Osaka?
Kinō kaerimáshĭta. きのう帰りました.	I returned yesterday.

Sonó o-shigotó wa ítsu o-sumí ni náru deshō ka.
その　お仕事　は　いつ　おすみ　に　なる　でしょうか.
When will that (your) work be finished? (*súmu* to end, to be concluded, to be finished, to come, be brought to an end, etc.)

---

1 *Ne,* after a verb or adjective at the end of a sentence, is emphatic, and corresponds to the English *Is it not? Is it? Does it? Doesn't it? Don't you think so?* etc. This interjection is generally used by women and children, although men use it occasionally; however, whether by women or men, *ne* is used only in familiar speech. The above sentence with *ne* may be translated by *Your daughter is really beautiful.*
2 *enryó* reserve, hesitation; *go-enryó náku* without hesitation **3** The verb *agarí* is often used instead of *tabéru* when offering food; *o-agarí kudasái* is more polite than *o-tabé nasái.*

Raishū máde ni súmu deshō.   It will be finished by next week.
来週 まで に すむでしょう.

Honorific Verbs

In Japanese certain special verbs are used in speaking to superiors or to persons to whom we wish to show politeness and respect.

The verbs of this class are: *Gozáru* 御座る, *nasáru* なさる, *kudasáru* 下さる, *irassháru* いらっしゃる, *itasú* 致す.

Gozáru 御座る

The stem of this verb is *gozai* 御座い, and is inflected only with *másŭ*.

	Present	
Positive	**Negative**	
gozaimásŭ 御座います	*gozaimasén*	御座いません
	Past	
gozaimáshĭta 御座いました	*gozaimasén déshĭta* 御座いませんでした	
	Future	
gozaimashō 御座いましょう	*gozaimasén deshō* 御座いませんでしょう	
	Subordinate	
gozaimashĭté 御座いまして	*gozaimasén déshĭte* 御座いませんでして	
	gozaimasén de[1] 御座いませんで	

In former times, the stem of *gozáru* 御座る was *gozari* 御座り, and this form is found with verbal suffixes (*gozarimásŭ* 御座ります, *gozarimáshĭta* 御座りました, etc.) in old literature and is used in modern times on the stage when classical plays are given.

Gozáru is the polite form of the verb *áru* (*to have* or *there to be*), and *de gozáru* is the polite equivalent of *de áru* or *désŭ* (*to be*). All these expressions are used indiscriminately of the 1st, 2nd and 3rd persons in polite speech.

Anáta wa musŭkosán ga **gozaimásŭ ka.**
貴方 は 息子さん が 御座います か.
Have you any sons?

Hái, watashí wa musŭkó ga **gozaimásŭ.**
はい, 私 は 息子 が 御座います.
Yes, I have sons.

Iié, musŭkó ga **gozaimasén.**
いゝえ, 息子 が 御座いません.
No, I haven't any sons.

Sonó ojōsan wa taihén rikó de **gozaimásŭ.**
そのお嬢さんは 大変 利口 で 御座います.
That girl is very clever.

---

1 *Gozaimasén de* is less polite than *gozaimasén déshĭte.*

Anáta wa Roshiyá-jin de wa gozaimasén ka.   Are you not Russian?
貴方　は　ロシヤ人　で　は　御ざいません　か.

Iié, watashí wa Itari-jin de gozaimásŭ.   No, I am an Italian.
いゝえ，私　はイタリー人で　御ざいます.

Rainén Tōkyō ni hakuránkái ga gozaimashō ka.
来年　東京　に　博覧会　が　御ざいましょうか.
Will there be an exhibition next year in Tokyo?

Iié, gozaimasén deshō.   No, there will not be.
いゝえ,御ざいませんでしょう.

Nakamura San no ókŭsama wa inú ga taihén o-sŭkí de gozaimásŭ
中村　さんの　奥様　は　犬　が　大変　お好き　で　御ざいます
ga néko wa o-kirái de gozaimásŭ.   Mrs. Nakamura likes dogs, but hates
が　猫　は　お嫌い　で　御ざいます.   cats.

The following expressions with *gozaimásŭ* are very common in daily conversation.

Ikága de gozaimásŭ ka.	如何で御ざいますか.	How do you do?
Arigatō gozaimásŭ.	ありがとう御ざいます.	Thank you very much.
Tasshá de gozaimásŭ.	達者で御ざいます.	I am well.
Sayō de gozaimásŭ.	左様で御ざいます.	That it so. It is so.

Sometimes, instead of *Arigatō gozaimásŭ*, one may say *Arigatō zonjimásŭ* (from *zonjíru* 存じる to know).

Go-zónji and *zonjimásŭ* are often used in the following expressions:

Go-zónji désŭ ka. 御存じですか.   Do you know (it, about it)?

Hái, zónjite orimásŭ.   Yes, I know (it, about it).
はい, 存じて おります.

Iié, zonjimasén. いゝえ, 存じません.   No, I don't know.

Go-zónji no tōri. 御存じの通り.   As you know.

Go-zónji no hazú désŭ.   You ought to know.
御存じ　の　筈　です.

Go-zónji de wa arimasén ka.   Don't you know about it?
御存じ　で　はありません　か.

Hái, zonjimasén. はい, 存じません.   No, I don't know.

Gozáru may follow a verb in the subordinate:

Góhan wa mō niemáshĭte gozaimásŭ.   The rice is already
御飯　は　もう　煮えまして　御ざいます.   boiled (cooked).
(*nierú* 煮える to boil, be boiled, to cook, be cooked)

Sonó hon wa daijí ni shimatté gozaimásŭ.   That book is kept
その　本　は　大事　に　仕舞って　御ざいます.   carefully.
(*shimaú* 仕舞う to put away, stow away, keep, save, store, etc.)

Contracted Adverbial Form

In Lesson 21 we have said that the adverbial form of the true adjective is obtained by dropping the termination *i* and adding **ku**.

hayái 早い   early   *haya* 早   *háyaku* 早く

Now, by dropping **k,** and contracting the two vowels at the end of the word into one long vowel as shown below, we obtain the **contracted adverbial form** of the adjective, which is used with the polite verb *gozáru*.

$$a+u=\bar{o} \qquad u+u=\bar{u}$$
$$i+u=\bar{u} \qquad o+u=\bar{o}$$

hayái	early	*háyaku*	*haya+u*	*hayō*
早い		早く	早+う	早う
utsŭkushíi	beautiful	*utsŭkúshiku*	*utsŭkushi+u*	*utsŭkushū*
美しい		美しく	美し+う	美しう
furúi	old	*fúruku*	*furu+u*	*furū*
古い		古く	古+う	古う
kurói	black	*kúroku*	*kuro+u*	*kurō*
黒い		黒く	黒+う	黒う

O-hayō gozaimásŭ.   お早う御ざいます.   Good morning. (*lit.* It is early.)

Anáta no kimonó wa **utsŭkushū gozaimásŭ.**   Your kimono is
貴方 の 着物 は 美しう 御ざいます.   beautiful.

Konó kabín wa furū gozaimásŭ ka.   Is this flower vase old?
この 花瓶 は 古う 御ざいます か.

Iié, atarashū gozaimásŭ.   No, it is new.
いゝえ, 新しう 御ざいます.

Watashí no atarashíi kutsú wa **kurō gozaimásŭ.**   My new shoes
私 の 新しい 靴 は 黒う 御ざいます.   are black.

Verbs in the desiderative form, before *gozáru* 御ざる, may be used in their adverbial form in **ku** or in their contracted form in *o*.

míru	to see	*mitái*	*mítaku*	*mitō*
見る		見たい	見たく	見とう
yómu	to read	*yomitái*	*yomítaku*	*yomitō*
読む		読みたい	読みたく	読みとう
ikú	to go	*ikitái*	*ikitáku*	*ikitō*
行く		行きたい	行きたく	行きとう

Note that while the contracted form of adjectives is the only one used before *gozáru* 御ざる, both contracted and adverbial forms are used in the case of desiderative verbs before the same honorific verb.

Although the contracted form of desiderative verbs is considered to be very polite, its use is becoming rather old fashioned, while their adverbial form is becoming more common. It is for this reason that the contracted form has been put in parentheses in the following examples.

*Konná shízuka-na ban ni wa hĭtóri de hon ga **yomítaku** (or **yomitō**)*
こんな 静か な 晩 に は 一人 で 本 が 読みたく （読みとう）
gozaimásŭ.   On such a quiet night I like to be alone and read books.
御ざいます.

*Kon-ya wa samúi kará omoté e **ikitakú** (or **ikitō**) **gozaimasén.***
今夜 は 寒い から 表 へ 行きたく （行きとう） 御ざいません.
As it is cold to-night I do not wish to go out. (*omoté* outdoors)

*Anáta wa watashí to isshó ni Nihón no shibaí wo **mítaku** (or **mitō**)*
貴方 は 私 と 一緒 に 日本 の 芝居 を 見たく （見とう）
gozaimásŭ ka.   Do you wish to see a Japanese drama with me?
御ざいます か.   (*shibaí* a play, drama, show, theatre, playhouse)

*Hái, taihén **mítaku** (or **mitō**) **gozaimásŭ.***   Yes, I wish very much
はい, 大変 見たく （見とう） 御ざいます.   to see it.

Vocabulary

assistance	*o-kagé*	才蔭カゲ		plum	*umé*	梅ウ
drama	*shibaí*	芝シ居イ		saucer	*chatakú*	茶托

botanical garden *shokubutsú-en* 植物園;   pickled plums *umeboshí* 梅干;   old fashioned people *kyūshiki-na hĭtótachi* 旧式な人達;   Thanks to your assistance *O-kagesamá de* お蔭様で;   temple (of the head) *komekamí* こめかみ

As it is the custom among many English speaking people to use remarks about the weather as expressions of salutation upon meeting, so is the custom with many Japanese. On a hot day they would then say:

     O-atsū gozaimásŭ.   お暑う御ざいます.   It is hot (today).

and on a cold day: ***O-samū gozaimásŭ.***   お寒う御ざいます.   It is cold.

Exercise   *Renshū* 練習

1. Késa éki e ikú tokí ni Watanabé San no ókŭsan ni o-me ni kakarimáshĭta. Anó katá mo Atamí e oidé ni náru tokoró déshĭta nóde[1] go-isshó ni mairimáshĭta. **2.** Anáta wa dónata de gozaimásŭ ka.—Watakŭshí wa Négishi de gozaimásŭ. **3.** Ōmura Senséi wa ráigetsu Itarī e irrasshaimásŭ. Senséi wa ráinen no háru Tōkyō e o-kaerí ni narimásŭ ga o-jōsan wa ongakú kenkyū[2] no tamé ni Itarī ni ni-nen kan o-todomarí ni[3] náru deshō. **4.** O-kuní wa dóchira de gozaimásŭ ka.—Itarī de gozaimásŭ. **5.** Go-ryōshin wa o-tasshá de gozaimásŭ ka.—Hái, arigatō, ryóshin wa tasshá de gozaimásŭ. **6.** Anáta no go-kázoku wa máda Hakoné kará o-kaerí ni narimasén ka.—Hái, kaerimasén. Kázoku wa Hakoné ni ráigetsu máde irú deshō. **7.** Go-shújin wa Nagásaki e o-idé ni náru no de wa gozaimasén ka.—Mairitákatta no de gozaimáshĭta ga taihén isogashíi nóde getsumatsú máde Tōkyō ni orimásŭ. **8.** Kotoshí no fuyú wa taihén samúi deshō to shimbún ga itté orimásŭ. **9.** Dōzo, o-yu[4] wo

---

1 *oidé ni náru tokoró déshĭta nóde* as she was going   2 *ongakú kenkyū* study of music
3 *o-todomarí ni náru deshō* will remain   4 hot water

mótte kité kudasái. Te wo araitái no désŭ. **10.** O-kagesamá de zeikán ni tsutomeguchí[1] ga gozaimáshĭta. **11.** Kyō wa taihén otonashikattá[2] kará o-káshi wo agemashō.—Arigatō. **12.** Onorāto San no ókŭsan wa taisō[3] go-shínsetsu-na go-fujín désŭ. **13.** Dóko ni watashí no bōshi wa gozaimásŭ ka.—Kokó ni anáta no o-bōshi wa gozaimásŭ. **14.** Anáta no musŭkó-san wa o-ikutsú de irasshaimásŭ ka.—Musŭkó wa nanátsu (shichí-sái) de gozaimásŭ. **15.** Konó saifú wa dónata no de gozaimásŭ ka.—Soré wa anó go-fujín no de gozaimásŭ. **16.** Uenó Kōen no sakurá ga mankaí de gozaimásŭ. **17.** Matsu-shimá e irasshaimáshĭta ka.—Iié, máda de gozaimásŭ. Raishū máiru hazú de gozaimásŭ. **18.** O-hayō gozaimásŭ. Otōsama wa o-tasshá de gozaimásŭ ka.—Arigatō, chichí wa aikawarazú[4] tasshá de gozaimásŭ. **19.** Sonó kimonó wa takái désŭ ka.—Iié, o-takakú arimasén. O-yasú[5] gozaimásŭ. Sen-go-hyakú yen de gozaimásŭ.—Déwa kaimashō. **20.** O-takú wa tōi désŭ ka.—Iié, taihén chikō gozaimásŭ. **21.** Konó chawán to chatakú wa kírei désŭ. Koréra wa taihén yasú gozaimáshĭta. **22.** Shiná-go wo go-zónji désŭ ka.—Iié, zonjimasén. **23.** Watashí wa o-cha wo o-kyakú-sama ni sashiagemáshĭta.[6] **24.** Kyō watashí wa Shiná-ryōri ga tabetō gozaimásŭ. **25.** Kyō anáta wo watashí to isshó ni shokubutsú-en wo gorán ni naritáku[7] gozaimasén ka.—Iié, taihén mítaku zonjimásŭ. **26.** Nihón no kyūshiki-na hĭtótachi wa zutsū[8] ga shimásŭ tokí ni umeboshí wo komekamí ni harimásŭ.[9]

1. けさ，駅へ行く時に渡辺さんの奥さんにお目にかゝりました．あの方も熱海へお出でになるところでしたので御一緒に参りました．**2.** 貴方はどなたで御ざいますか．—私は根岸で御ざいます．**3.** 大村先生は来月イタリーへいらっしゃいます．先生は来年の春東京へお帰りになりますがお嬢さんは音楽研究のために，イタリーに二年間おとゞまりになるでしょう．**4.** お国はどちらで御ざいますか．—イタリーで御ざいます．**5.** 御両親はお達者で御ざいますか．—はい，ありがとう，両親は達者で御ざいます．**6.** 貴方の御家族はまだ箱根からお帰りになりませんか．—はい，帰りません，家族は箱根に来月までいるでしょう．**7.** 御主人は長崎へお出でになるのでは御ざいませんか．—参りたかったので御ざいましたが大変忙しいので月末まで東京におります．**8.** 今年の冬は大変寒いでしょうと新聞が言っております．**9.** どうぞお湯を持って来て下さい．手を洗いたいのです．**10.** お蔭様で税関に勤め口が御ざいました．**11.** きようは大変おとなしかったからお菓子を上げましょう．—ありがとう．**12.** オノラートさんの奥さんは大層御親切な御婦人です．**13.** どこに私の帽子は御ざいますか．—こゝに貴方のお帽子は御ざいます．**14.** 貴方の息子さんはお幾つでいらっしゃいますか．—息子ゝ七つ（七才）で御ざいます．**15.** この財布

---

1 a situation, a position 2 *otonashíi* quiet, obedient, good tempered 3 very, very much, exceedingly 4 as usual 5 *yasúi* cheap 6 *sashiagerú* to give, present, offer 7 *gorán ni naritái* wish to see 8 headache 9 *harú* to stick

はどなたので御ざいますか．—それはあの御婦人ので御ざいます．
16. 上野公園の桜が満開で御ざいます．**17.** 松島へいらっしゃいま
したか．—いゝえ，まだで御ざいます．来週参る筈で御ざいます．
18. お早う御ざいます．お父様はお達者で御ざいますか．—ありがと
う，父は相変らず達者で御ざいます．**19.** その着物は高いですか．—
いゝえ，お高くありません．お安う御ざいます．千五百円で御ざいま
す．—では買いましょう．**20.** お宅は遠いですか．—いゝえ，大変近う
御ざいます．**21.** この茶椀と茶托はきれいです．これ等は大変安う
御ざいました．**22.** 支那語を御存じですか．—いゝえ，存じません．
23. 私はお茶をお客様に差上げました．**24.** きよう私は支那料理が食
べとう御ざいます．**25.** きよう貴方は私と一緒に植物園を御覧になり
たく御ざいませんか．—いゝえ，大変見たく存じます．**26.** 日本の旧式
な人達は頭痛がします時に梅干をこめかみに張ります．

1. This morning while I was going to the station I met Mrs. Watanabe.
She also was going to Atami, so we travelled together. **2.** Who are you?—
I am Mr. Negishi. **3.** Professor Omura will leave Japan for Italy next month.
He will come back to Tokyo next spring, but his daughter will remain in
Italy for two years to study music. **4.** What is your native country?—Italy
is my native country. **5.** Are your parents well?—Yes, they are well, thank
you. **6.** Haven't your family come back from Hakone yet?—No, they haven't.
They will remain at Hakone until next month. **7.** Isn't your husband going
to Nagasaki?—He wanted to go, but as he is very busy, he will remain in
Tokyo until the end of the month. **8.** The newspapers say the weather will
be very cold this winter. **9.** Bring me some hot water, please. I want to
wash my hands. **10.** Thanks to your assistance I have obtained a position
at the Custom House. **11.** You have been very good to-day. I am going
to give you a cake.—Thank you. **12.** Mrs. Onorato is a very kind lady.
13. Where is my hat?—Here is your hat. **14.** How old is your son?—My
son is seven years old. **15.** Whose purse is this?—It is that lady's. **16.** The
cherry blossoms at Ueno Park are in full bloom. **17.** Have you been to
Matsushima?—No, I have not been there yet. I intend to go there next
week. **18.** Good morning, is your father in good health?—Thanks, my father
is in his usual good health. **19.** Is that kimono dear?—No, it is not dear, it
is cheap. The price is 1,500 yen.—I will buy it then. **20.** Is your house far
away?—No, it is very near. **21.** These cups and saucers are pretty and they
were very cheap. **22.** Do you know Chinese?—No, I don't. **23.** I have
offered the tea to the guest. **24.** To-day I wish to eat Chinese food.
25. Don't you wish to see the botanical garden with me to-day?—Yes, I wish
very much to see it. **26.** In Japan, old fashioned people stick pickled plums
on their temples when they have a headache.

Thirty-fifth Lesson　第丗五課

Honorifics (continued)

Nasáru なさる　To Do

This honorific verb is used as an auxiliary indicating an action of the second or third person.

Anáta wa kotoshí no natsú dóchira e o-dekaké nasaimásŭ ka.
貴方　は　今年　の　夏　どちら　へ　お出かけ　なさいます　か.
Where will you go this summer? (*dekakerú* to go out, take an outing)

Watashi wa Hokkaidō e ikú tsumorí désŭ.　I intend going to
私　は　北海道　へ　行く　つもり　です.　Hokkaido.

Nasáru is added to the simple stem of verbs of Class I, as in the above example, and to the *i*-stem of verbs of Class II. The suffix *másŭ* is generally used after *nasáru,* whose stem is *nasái* なさい. *O* precedes the stem of the verb that is used before this honorific auxiliary.

Conjugation

Present

Positive		Negative	
nasaimásŭ	なさいます	*nasaimasén*	なさいません
nasáru	なさる	*nasaránai*	なさらない

Past

Positive		Negative	
nasaimáshĭta	なさいました	*nasaimasén déshĭta*	なさいませんでした
nasátta	なさった	*nasaránakatta*	なさらなかった

Future

nasaimashō	なさいましょう	*nasaimasén deshō*	なさいませんでしょう
nasáru deshō	なさるでしょう	*nasaránai deshō*	なさらないでしょう

Subordinate

nasaimáshĭte	なさいまして	*nasaimasén déshĭte*	なさいませんでして
nasátte	なさって	*nasaránakutte*	なさらなくって

Anáta wa Nihón no shimbún wo tokidokí o-yomí nasaimásŭ ka.
貴方　は　日本　の　新聞　を　時々　お読み　なさいます　か.
Do you sometimes read Japanese newspapers?

Iié, yomimasén. いゝえ, 読みません.　No, I do not read them.

Anáta wa konó kabín wo o-kaı nasaimashō ka.   Will you buy this
貴方　は　この　花瓶　を　お買い　なさいましょうか．   flower-vase?

Iié, kaimasén, kéredomo konó katá ga o-kái nasáru deshō.
いゝえ，買いません，けれどもこの　方　が　お買い　なさる　でしょう．
No, I am not going to buy it, but this gentleman will likely buy it.

Nasáru may also be used, instead of **surú**, when this auxiliary
forms a verbal expression with a noun, which, in this case, is
generally preceded by the honorific **go.**

Ano gaijín wa Nihón-go wo go-benkyō nasaimáshĭta ka.
あの　外人　は　日本語　を　御勉強　なさいました　か．
Did that foreigner study Japanese?

go-benkyō nasáru＝benkyō surú＝to study

Iié, nasaimasén déshĭta.   No, he did not.
いゝえ，なさいません　でした．

Anáta wa Shiná-go wo go-benkyō nasaimásŭ ka.   Do you study
あなた　は　支那語　を　御勉強　なさいます　か．   Chinese?

Hái, benkyō shĭté imásŭ. はい，勉強しています． Yes, I do (study it).

Iié, benkyō shĭté imasén. いゝえ，勉強していません． No, I do not (study it).

In the above question the honorific verb *nasáru* なさる has been used for
respect towards the person spoken to, while the ordinary verb *surú* する has
been used in the two answers supposed to be given by the first person, who,
logically, need not use honorific verbs when speaking of himself.

Fukudá San wa kinō otōsan to go-isshó ni Méijĭ Jingū wo go-sampái
福田　さん　はきのうお父さんと　御一緒　に　明治　神宮　を　御参拝
nasaimáshĭta.   Yesterday Mr. Fukuda went with his father to worship at
なさいました．   the Meiji shrine.

go-sampái nasáru＝sampái surú＝to worship, to visit a shrine

Nasáru is often used in the following idiomatic expressions:

Dō nasaimáshĭta ka.   {What has happened to you?
どうなさいました　か．   {What's the matter with you?

Anáta no íi yō-ni nasái.   Do as you please.
貴方　のいゝようになさい．

Kō nasaimasén ka.   {Don't you like to do it this way?
こうなさいませんか．   {How do you like to do it this way?

Dō nasaimásŭ ka.   {What will you do?
どうなさいます　か．   {What are you going to do about this?

Although **nasáru** is a polite verb, the imperative **nasái** is not
polite, neither when used by itself nor when it follows a verbal
stem. The polite imperative of *nasáru* is **nasátte kudasái.**

Mō osói kará o-kaerí nasátte kudasái.   As it is late, please go home.
もう遅い　から　お帰り　なさって　下さい．

The imperative **nasái** なさい sounds rude even when speaking

to inferiors, however, it is commonly used when speaking to one's own children.

> *Shi nasái.* しなさい Do it. *Ikí nasái.* 行きなさい Go.
>
> *Tabé nasái.* 食べなさい Eat. *Yamé nasái.* 止めなさい Stop it.

(*shi* し stem of *surú* する to do; *ikí* 行き stem of *ikú* 行く to go; *tabé* 食べ stem of *tabéru* 食べる to eat; *yamé* 止め stem of *yamerú* 止める to discontinue, to give up, desist, etc.)

By using the honorific *o* お before the stem of a verb followed by *nasái* なさい, the expression becomes rather gentle, and may be used when speaking to inferiors, as a teacher addressing his students, a person talking to his servants, etc.

> *O-tabé nasái.* お食べなさい.   *O-yamé nasái.* お止めなさい.

A more honorific verb than *nasáru* is *asobasú* 遊ばす, which corresponds to the English expression *to be pleased* or *to deign* (to do something).

> *Kyō náni wo nasaimásŭ ka.* What are you going to do to-day?
> きょう 何 を なさいます か.
>
> *Kyō náni wo asobashimásŭ ka.* What will you deign to do to-day?
> きょう 何 を 遊ばします か.
>
> *Anáta no go-shujinsamá wa dóko e o-dekaké asobashimáshǐta ka.*
> 貴方 の 御主人様 は どこ へ お出かけ 遊ばしました か.
> Where has your master been pleased to go?
>
> *Gozensamá*[1] *wa Tokugawá kōshaku no oyashikí*[2] *e o-dekaké asobashi-*
> 御前様 は 徳川 公爵 の お屋敷 へ お出かけ 遊ばし
> *máshǐta.* My lord was pleased to go to Prince Tokugawa's.
> ました. (*lit.* My lord, Tokugawa Prince's mansion to was pleased to go.)

Kudasáru 下さる

Used as an independent verb, *kudasáru* means *to give, to bestow*, and may refer to the first as well as the second and third persons. Its stem is *kudasái* 下さい, which, as already shown, is also a polite imperative.

Conjugation

Present

Positive		Negative	
kudasaimásŭ	下さいます	*kudasaimasén*	下さいません
kudasáru	下さる	*kudasaránai*	下さらない

Past

kudasaimáshǐta	下さいました	*kudasaimasén déshǐta*	下さいませんでした
kudasátta	下さった	*kudasaránakatta*	下さらなかった

---

1 *gozensamá* my lord   2 *o-yashikí* mansion

Future

	Positive		Negative

Positive   Negative

kudasaimashō 下さいましょう   *kudasaimasén deshō* 下さいませんでしょう

kudasáru deshō 下さるでしょう   *kudasaránai deshō* 下さらないでしょう

kudasáru darō 下さるだろう   *kudasaránai darō* 下さらないだろう

Subordinate

kudasaimáshĭte 下さいまして   *kudasaimasén déshĭte* 下さいませんでして

kudasátte 下さって   *kudasaránakutte* 下さらなくって

Examples

Eikokú taishikán no hisho ga tabitabí watashí ni gaikokú no yūbin
英国 大使館 の 秘書 が 度々 私 に 外国 の 郵便
kitté wo kudasaimásŭ.   A secretary of the British Embassy often gives
切手 を 下さいます.   me foreign postage stamps.

Kinō kyōkai de bókushi-san ni o-me ni kakarimáshĭta toki ni bókushi-
きのう 教会 で 牧師さん に お目 に かゝりました 時 に 牧師
san wa konó séisho wo watashí ni kudasaimáshĭta.
さん は この 聖書 を 私 に 下さいました.
   Yesterday when I met the pastor at the church, he gave me this Bible.

Móshi mo konó hon ga go-fuyō náraba watashi ni kudasaimasén
若し も この 本 が 御不用 ならば 私 に 下さいません
deshō ka.   If you do not want this book won't you give it to me?
でしょうか.   (*lit.* If this book unnecessary is, to me will you not give?)

The action of giving is expressed, except when the receiver is the first person, by the verb *agerú* 上げる in ordinary polite speech, and by *sashiagerú* 差上げる in very polite speech. Both verbs are conjugated with the suffix *másŭ*.

Haná wo kudasaimasén ka.   Will you not give me a flower?
花 を 下さいません か.   (*lit.* Flower don't you give me?)
Hái, takŭsán agemashō.   Yes, I will give you many.
はい, 沢山 上げましょう.
Anó kakémono wo Hanazonó kōshaku ni sashiagemáshĭta.
あの 掛物[1] を 花園 公爵 に 差上げました.
   I gave that kakemono[1] to Prince Hanazono.

Kudasáru may be used after the subordinate of both *agerú* and *sashiagerú.*

Konó o-miyagé wo ókŭsama ni ageté kudasái.   Please give this present
この お土産 を 奥様 に 上げて 下さい.   to your wife.
Dōzo konó shiná[2] wo go-shújin ni sashiageté kudasái.
どうぞ この 品 を 御主人 に 差上げて 下さい.
   Please give this thing to your master.

---

1 A picture usually higher than wide, suitable for hanging on a wall. **2** The word *shiná* means *an article, goods, wares, stocks,* but it may be used to translate also the word *thing* when used in a material sense.

As an auxiliary verb **kudasáru** means *to condescend*, or *to be pleased to do*, and denotes that the action of the 2nd or 3rd person is done, or meant to be done in favour of the speaker. In this case **kudasáru** either follows the stem of another verb, which is then preceded by *o* or *go*, or its subordinate without honorifics.

Senjitsú sashiagemáshǐta hon wo **o-yomí kudasaimáshǐta** *ka.*
先日　差上げました　本　を　お読み　下さいました　か.
Did you read the book that I gave you the other day.?
    (*lit.* The other day I gave you book, were you pleased to read?)

Obāsan wa tokidokí otogí-banashí wo **shǐté kudasaimásǔ.**
おばあさんは　時々　おとぎ話　を　して　下さいます.
My grandmother is often pleased to tell us fairy stories.
(*otogí-banashí* fairy tales; *otogí-banashí wo surú* to tell fairy tales)

Samúi kará mádo wo **shǐmete kudasái.**   As it is cold please close
寒い　から　窓　を　しめて　下さい.   the window.

Kóndo no nichiyō ni hakubutsukán e **tsureté itté[1] kudasái.**
今度　の　日曜　に　博物館　へ　連れて　行って　下さい.
    Next Sunday please take me to the museum.

Watashí ga hon wo kakimáshǐta tokí ni Shidehará danshakú wa soré
私　が　本　を　書きました　時　に　幣原　男爵　は　それ
ni jobún wo **káite kudasaimáshǐta.**   (*danshakú* baron; *jobún*
に　序文　を　書いて　下さいました.   preface)
    When I wrote my book Baron Shidehara kindly wrote a preface to it.

The following sentences with **kudasáru** are often used in daily conversation :

Mátchi wo **kudasaimasén** *ka.*   Could you favour me with a match?
マッチ　を　下さいません　か.   Would you please give me a match?

Senséi wa imōto ni konó hon wo **kudasaimáshǐta.**
先生　は　妹　に　この　本　を　下さいました.
    The teacher gave this book to my younger sister.

Kása wo o-kashí **kudasaimasén** *ka.*   Would you please lend me
傘　を　お貸し　下さいません　か.   your umbrella?

Sō shǐté **kudasáreba[2]** *kekkō désǔ.*   If you would kindly do so,
そう　して　下されば　結構　です.   that would suit me very well.

Kinō shújin wa watashí ni konó kimonó wo **katté kudasaimáshǐta.**
きのう主人　は　私　に　この　着物　を　買って　下さいました.
    Yesterday my master did me the favour of buying this kimono for me.

Kurerú, instead of *kudasáru*, is used in less polite speech. Its stem is **kure,** which takes *másǔ* when conjugated. The imperative of **kurerú** is also **kure,** which, often preceded by *o* is attached to the subordinate of other verbs and is generally used when wishing to speak to one's own inferiors in a friendly manner.

---

1 *tsureté ikú* 連れて行く to take, to accompany   **2** *kudasáreba* subjunctive of *kudasáru—lit.* So doing, if you favour me, very well is.

Furukawá san **wa** *bóku* **wo** *tokidokí sŭkiyakí*[1] **wo** *tábe ni Ginzá e*
古川 さん は 僕 を 時々 すき焼 を 食べ に 銀座 へ
tsureté itté kuremásŭ.   Mr. Furukawa often takes me to Ginza for eating
連れて 行って くれます.   *sŭkiyaki.*

Séngetsu shachō[2] *wa watashí no gekkyū wo ageté kuremáshita.*
先月 社長 は 私 の 月給 を 上げて くれました.
Last month the director of our company kindly raised my salary.

Konó tegamí wo dáshĭte o-kuré.   この手紙を出しておくれ. Post this letter.

Bōshi wo mótte kité o-kuré.   帽子を持って来ておくれ. Fetch my hat.

Among well bred people, even when speaking to inferiors, *o-kuré*
is avoided, and *kudasái* is used instead.

Irassháru いらっしゃる
To Be (in a place), To Come, To Go

This verb is used either in polite reference to the person addressed,
or to a third person. The stem is *irasshái,* which is also the
imperative form.

De irassháru でいらっしゃる is the polite form of *désŭ* です
when referring to someone's identity.

Anáta wa dónata de irasshaimásŭ ka. or *dónata désŭ ka.*   Who **are**
貴方 は どなた でいらっしゃいますか. どなた ですか.   you?

Watashí wa Yamadá désŭ. 私は山田です.   ⎫

Watashí wa Yamadá de gozaimásŭ. (polite)   ⎬ I am Mr. Yamada.
私 は 山田 で 御ざいます.   ⎭

Okadá senséi wa dóko e irasshaimáshĭta ka.   Where did Prof.
岡田 先生 は どこ へいらっしゃいましたか.   Okada go?

Byōin e irasshaimáshĭta.   He **went** to the hospital.
病院 へいらっしゃいました.

Russō Hákase wa Téikoku Hóteru ni irasshaimásŭ.
ルッソー博士 は 帝国 ホテル に いらっしゃいます.
Doctor Russo **is staying** at the Imperial Hotel.

Go-shújin wa irasshaimásŭ ka.   Is your master **in**?
御主人 は いらっしゃいますか.

Hái, irasshaimásŭ. はい, いらっしゃいます.   Yes, he **is in**.

Iié, irasshaimasén. いゝえ, いらっしゃいません. No, he **is not in**.

Anó gaikokujín wa dóchira kará irasshaimáshĭta ka.
あの 外国人 は どちら から いらっしゃいましたか.
Where did that foreigner **come** from?

Sóren kará irasshaimáshĭta.   He **came** from the Soviet Union.
ソ連 から いらっしゃいました.

---

1 Sliced beef cooked with a special Japanese sauce. **2** *shachō* president, director
of a company; the possessive adjective *our* has been omitted because in this sentence
it is understood that the speaker speaks of the director of the company he works for

Anáta wa dóko e **irasshaimásŭ** *ka.*[1]   Where are you **going**?
貴方　は　どこ　へいらっしゃいます　か.

Ginzá e kaimonó ni **mairimásŭ**.   I am going shopping to Ginza.
銀座　へ　買物　に　参ります.　(*kaimonó* purchase, shopping; *ni* for)

The verb **máiru** 参る, used in the last example, ordinarily meaning *to come* (*kúru*) or *to go* (*ikú*), is also used by the speaker as a verb of humility.

Irassháru いらっしゃる is used with other verbs when politely speaking to the second or of a third person. In this case, the verb preceding *irassháru* is in the subordinate, and the expression formed by the two verbs indicates progressive action or a condition in reference to the present.

hanáshĭte irassháru	話していらっしゃる	to be speaking
káette irassháru	帰っていらっしゃる	to be returning
kiité irassháru	聞いていらっしゃる	to be listening
míte irassháru	見ていらっしゃる	to be seeing
shĭté irassháru	していらっしゃる	to be doing
tábete irassháru	食べていらっしゃる	to be eating

Go-shújin wa náni wo **shĭté irasshaimásŭ** *ka.*   What **is** your master
御主人　は　何　を　して　いらっしゃいます　か.   **doing?**

Shújin wa hon wo **yónde irasshaimásŭ**.   My master **is**
主人　は　本　を　読んで　いらっしゃいます.   **reading** a book.

When **irassháru** いらっしゃる is used in the past, its combination with the preceding verb in the subordinate besides indicating a progressive past action or a past condition, it indicates also a completed past action.

Nakayamá Senséi ga **hanáshĭte irasshaimáshĭta** *tokí ni dentō ga*
中山　　先生　が　話して　いらっしゃいました　時　に　電燈　が
kiemáshĭta.   While Professor Nakayama **was speaking** the lights went off.
消えました.　(progressive past)

Ikedá Hákase wa mō Karuizawá kará **káette irasshaimáshĭta** *ka.*
池田　博士　は　もう　軽井沢　から　帰って　いらっしゃいました　か.
Has Dr. Ikeda already **returned** from Karuizawa? (condition)

Hái, **káette irasshaimáshĭta**.   Yes, he **has returned.**
はい,　帰って　いらっしゃいました.

Iié, máda **káette irasshaimasén.**   No, he **hasn't returned** yet.
いゝえ,　まだ　帰っていらっしゃいません.

Ashĭtá **káette irasshaimásŭ**.   He will **return** to-morrow.
あした　帰って　いらっしゃいます.

Nikkō de Tōshōgū wo **míte irasshaimáshĭta** *ka.*
日光　で　東照宮　を　見て　いらっしゃいました　か.
Have you **seen** Tōshōgū shrine in Nikkō? (completed action)

---

1 This is a common expression often used as a salutation when meeting in the street, without intending to actually inquire where one is going.

Iié, míte mairimasén déshǐta.   No, I haven't seen it.

いゝえ, 見て参りません でした.

*Itsu anáta wa Fukúoka kará **káette irasshaimáshǐta** ka.*

いつ 貴方 は 福岡 から 帰って いらっしゃいました か.

When did you return from Fukuoka? (completed action)

Kinō káette mairimáshǐta.   I returned yesterday.

きのう帰って 参りました.

Irasshái is invariably used as a salutation by servants and waiters of hotels and restaurants when meeting their guests, but it may also be used by anybody when meeting a guest who calls. In both cases **Irasshái** means "Welcome." **Irasshái** is also used, as in the following example, when a guest is leaving.

Guest—*Sayō-nára, o-jamá[1] shimáshǐta.*

左様なら, お邪广 しました.

    Good-bye, and excuse me for having troubled you.

    (*lit.* Good-bye; hindrance I made.)

Host—*Dō itashimáshǐte. Dōzo matá **irasshái**.*

どう 致しまして. どうぞ また いらっしゃい.

    Not at all. Please **come** again.

The following common expressions of salutation with **máiru** and **irassháru** are also used by members of the same family when one of them leaves home.

*Itté **mairimásǔ**.*   I am leaving. I am going. Good-bye.

行って 参ります.   (Spoken by the one leaving.)

*Itté **irasshái**.*   Good-bye. All right, good-bye *or* you may go.

行っていらっしゃい.   (Spoken by those remaining at home.)

On returning home one would generally say: **Tadáima** 只今 short for *Tadáima kaerimáshǐta,* meaning: *I returned just now.* The other members of the family would answer: *O-kaerí nasái* お帰りなさい (You have come back), which corresponds to "Welcome home."

Other common expressions with **irassháru** are:

*Yóku **irasshaimáshǐta**.*   You are welcome.

よく いらっしゃいました.   We are very glad to see you.

*Minásan go-jōbu de **irasshaimásǔ** ka.*   Are you all well?

皆さん 御丈夫 でいらっしゃいます か.   Is everybody at home well?

*Háyaku káette **irasshái**.*   (Please,) come back soon.

早く 帰っていらっしゃい.

Itasú 致す To Do

Itasú is another polite verb and humbly indicates the action of the first and third persons. Its stem is **itashi** 致し, which takes only *másǔ* in the conjugation. **Itasú** is a humble synonym of *surú*.

---

1 *jamá wo surú* to inconvenience another, to obstruct another; *hǐtó no shigotó no jamá wo surú* 人の仕事の邪广をする to interrupt somebody's work

*Watashí wa máinichi konó heyá wo sōji **itashimásŭ.***
私　は　毎日　この　部屋　を　掃除　致します.
I clean this room every day. (*sōji surú* to clean, sweep)

*Konó hon wo dō **itashimashō** ka.*　　What shall I do with this book?
この　本　を　どう　致しましょう　か.

Sonó hóndana e shimatté kudasái.　　Please, put it in that bookshelf.
その　本柵　へ　仕舞って　下さい.

Itasú 致す is used in literary style in the meaning of *to bring about, to make* or *to cause*, as in the following examples:

*hĭtó wo shi ni **itasú*** 人を死に致す　to cause a person's death
*chikará wo **itasú*** 力を致す **to** make an effort
*ryūsei wo **itasu*** 隆盛を致す to cause prosperity

*Sonó hĭtó ga kónnichi no ryūsei wo **itashĭtá** no wa nan de áru ka.*
その　人　が　今日　の　隆盛　を　致した　の　は　何　で　ある　か.
What has brought that man to his present prosperity?
(*lit.* That man, to-day's prosperity that has made-or caused-what is?)

The following sentences with ***itasú*** are often used in daily conversation, to make apology for a fault, to seek indulgence for, etc.

*Shitsúrei **itashimáshĭta**.*[1]　　Excuse me. I beg your pardon.
失礼　致しました.　　　　　　(*lit.* Impoliteness I did.)

*Tsúi shitsúrei **itashimáshĭta**.*　　Excuse me, I didn't do it on purpose.
つい　失礼　致しました.　　　　Excuse me, I did it unconsciously.
　　　　　　　　　　　　　　　(*tsúi.* unintentionally, carelessly, etc.)

*Dō **itashimáshĭte.***　　Don't mention it. Not at all.
どう　致しまして.

Surú

When there is no necessity of speaking humbly *surú* is used. *Surú* denotes the action of the first and third person, and also of the second person, if this is an inferior, or an intimately connected person.

*Watashí wa máinichi konó heyá wo sōji **shimásŭ**.*
私　は　毎日　この　部屋　を　掃除　します.

*Konó hon wo dō **shimashō** ka.* この本をどうしましょうか.

Compare with examples above under *itasú* 致す.

Vocabulary

Nouns			chain	*kusarí*	鎖クリ
attention	*ki*	気キ	company	*kaishá*	会カイ社シャ
Christmas	*Kurisumasú*	クリスマス	curio	*kottō*	骨コッ董トウ

---
1 *shitsúrei surú* 失礼する to be impolite

earrings	*mimikázari*	耳ミ飾カザリ	generous	*kimaé ga yói*	気前ガヨイ
lecture	*kōen*	講コウ演エン	historical	*rekishitekí*	歴史的
pastor	*bókushi*	牧ボク師シ	naval	*káigun*	海カイ軍グン
pin	*pin*	ピン	prominent	*erái*	偉エライ
preface	*jobún*	序ジョ文ブン		**Verbs**	
premier	*sōridaijin*	総理大臣	to bark	*hoé·ru*	吠ホエル
viscount	*shíshaku*	子シ爵シャク	to fetch	*mótte kúru*	持ッテ来ル
	Adjectives				
annoying	*urusái*	煩ウルサイ			

to be shopping *kaimonó wo surú* ; cloisonne vase *shippōyaki no utsuwá* ; prominent people *erái katágata* ; fairy tales *otogí-banashí* ; autumnal tints *kōyō* ; to put on autumnal tints *kōyō surú* ; to go sightseeing *kembutsú ni yukú* ; vice-admiral *kaigún-chūjō* ; postage stamp *kitté* ; our company *wága sha*.

Exercise　*Renshū*　練習

1. Nichiyō wa dō nasaimásŭ ka.—Kamakurá e mairimásŭ. Soshĭté anáta wa.—Watakŭshí mo Kamakurá e mairimásŭ. **2.** Go-shújin wa mō Kōbe e o-tachí[1] ni narimáshĭta ka.—Iié, máda désŭ. Kómban o-tachí nasaimásŭ. **3.** Anáta wa tabitabí shōsetsu wo o-yomí nasaimásŭ ka.—Iié, yomimasén ga tabitabí rekishitekí no hon wo yomimásŭ. **4.** Kurosawá San ni dónna hon wo sashiagemáshĭta ka.—Séngetsu kattá Nihón rekishí wo sashiagemáshĭta. **5.** Anáta wa Nihón-go wo taihén o-jōzu[2] ni o-hanashí ni narimásŭ ne. Dónata ga anáta no sénséi désŭ ka.—Satō San ga watashí no sénséi désŭ. **6.** Kaimonó wo nasáru tokí ni ki wo o-tsŭké[3] ni narimasén[4] to kakéne[5] wo saremásŭ yo. **7.** Osanái San wa taihén shínsetsu-na katá désŭ. Fuyú no aidá ítsumo yói ringó to báta wo Hokkaidō kará okutté kudasaimásŭ. **8.** Anáta ga Kurisumasú ni okutté kudasaimáshĭta go-hon wa taihén omoshiró gozaimáshĭta. Watashí wa mō sukkári[6] yónde shimaimáshĭta. **9.** Yamadá San no ókŭsama ga sakú-jitsu o-tazuné[7] kudasaimáshĭta. Ókŭsama wa Shanhái de o-kái asobashĭtá konó utsŭkushíi Shiná kottō wo kudasaimáshĭta. **10.** Konó hakó ga go-fuyō[8] náraba watashí ni kudasaimasén deshō ka.—Watashí wa irimasén kará yoro-kónde sashiagemásŭ. **11.** Anó shippōyaki no utsuwá wo dónata ni sashiage-máshĭta ka.—Inoué shíshaku ni sashiagemáshĭta. **12.** Dōzo konó mimikázari wo anáta no ojōsan ni sashiageté kudasái. **13.** Redoman San wa watashí no musŭkó ni Ei-go wo oshieté kudasaimáshĭta. Anó katá wa hijō ni yūmei-na sénséi de Tōkyō de jū-nen bákari mo Ei-go wo oshieté irasshaimásŭ. **14.** Konó inú wo achírá e yatté[9] kudasaimasén ka. Amarí hóete urusái désŭ. **15.** Wága sha no atarashíi (kóndo no) shachō wa hijō ni kimaé ga yói désŭ. Shachō wa warewaré ni shōyo wo takŭsán kudasaimáshĭta. **16.** Anáta no haorí wa taihén kírei désŭ. Dóchira de o-kái ni narimáshĭta ka.—Kattá no de wa

1 stem of *tátsu* 立つ to leave　**2** *jōzu ni* skifully, very well　**3** *ki wo tsŭkeru* to pay attention　**4** *ni narimasén to* if you do not　**5** *kakéne wo surú* to overcharge **6** completely, entirely　**7** *tazunéru* 訪ねる to visit, *o-tazuné* visit　**8** *fuyō* unnecessary, not wanted　**9** *achirá e yarú* to take away—*lit.* This dog yonder taking away, don't you favour me?

arimasén. Okadá San no ókŭsama ga kudasátta no désŭ. **17.** Anáta no kusarí wo kudasáru náraba konó kin no pin wo sashiagemashō. **18.** Watashí ga kōen wo itashimáshĭta tokí ni takŭsán no erái katágata ga kikí ni[1] koraremáshĭta[2]. **19.** Nikkō no mómiji ga íma utsŭkúshiku kōyō[3] shihajimemáshĭta. Kóndo no nichiyōbi ni watashí to isshó ni kembutsú ni irasshaimasén ka.— Hái, yorokónde go-isshó ni kembutsú ni mairimashō. Mómiji wa íma ga taihén utsŭkushíi sō désŭ. **20.** Senjitsú Chichibŭ Marŭ de Nakayamá hakŭshakú ga Béikoku kará káette irasshaimáshĭta. Onají fúne de wága Chūbei[4] Yamadá táishi mo kikokú[5] saremáshĭta. **21.** Makurin káigun chūjō wa saikín[6] goshinkyū[7] nasaimáshĭte íma wa káigun táishō de irasshaimásŭ. **22.** Ima enzetsú[8] wo nasátte irassháru katá wa dónata désŭ ka.—Anó katá wa Hiratá sōridaijin désŭ. **23.** Anáta ga séngetsu Kyūshū e yukaremáshĭta[9] tokí Unzén to Beppú to wo gorán ni narimáshĭta ka.—Hái, mimáshĭta. **24.** Hĭtó-samá ga o-hanashí wo nasátte irassháru tokí ni wa ki wo tsŭkéte uketamawáru[10] monó désŭ.

1. 日曜はどうなさいますか.—鎌倉へ参ります. そして貴方は.—私も鎌倉へ参ります. **2.** 御主人はもう神戸へお立ちになりましたか.—いゝえ, まだです. 今晩お立ちなさいます. **3.** 貴方は度々小説をお読みなさいますか.—いゝえ, 読みませんが度々歴史的の本を読みます. **4.** 黒沢さんにどんな本を差上げましたか.—先月買った日本歴史を差上げました. **5.** 貴方は日本語を大変お上手にお話しになりますね. どなたが貴方の先生ですか.—佐藤さんが私の先生です. **6.** 買い物をなさる時に気をおつけになりませんと掛値をされますよ. **7.** 小山内さんは大変親切な方です. 冬の間いつもよいりんごとバタを北海道から送って下さいます. **8.** 貴方がクリスマスに送って下さいました御本は大変面白う御ざいました. 私はもうすっかり読んで仕舞いました. **9.** 山田さんの奥さまが昨日お訪ね下さいました. 奥さまは上海でお買い遊ばしたこの美しい支那骨董を下さいました. **10.** この箱が御不用ならば私に下さいませんでしょうか.—私は要りませんから喜んで差上げます. **11.** あの七宝焼の器をどなたに差上げましたか.—井上子爵に差上げました. **12.** どうぞこの耳飾りを貴方のお嬢さんに差上げて下さい. **13.** レッドマンさんは私の息子に英語を教えて下さいました. あの方は非常に有名な先生で東京で十年ばかりも英語を教えていらっしゃいます. **14.** この犬をあちらへやって下さいませんか. 余り吠えてるうるさいです. **15.** わが社の新しい (こんどの) 社長は非常に気前

---

1 *kikí ni* to hear, for the purpose of hearing **2** *koraréru* polite for *kúru* to come **3** *shihajiméru* しはじめる to begin to do, *utsŭkúshiku kōyō shihajimemáshĭta* began to put on autumnal tints beautifully **4** *chūbei* residing in the United States, accredited to the U.S.A. This word is used only for government officials. **5** *kikokú sarerú* polite for *kikokú surú* to return to one's country **6** *recently* **7** *shinkyū surú* to promote, to be promoted **8** *enzetsú wo nasátte irasshárú* polite for *enzetsú wo shĭté irú* to be delivering a speech **9** *yukarerú* polite for *yukú* to go **10** *ki wo tsŭkéte* attentively; *uketamawáru* polite for *kikú* to listen

がよいです．社長は我々に賞与を沢山下さいました．　**16.** 貴方の羽織
は大変きれいです．どちらでお買いになりましたか．―買ったのではあ
りません．岡田さんの奥様が下さったのです．　**17.** 貴方の鎖を下さる
ならばこの金のピンを差上げましょう．　**18.** 私が講演を致しました時
に沢山の偉い方々がきゝに来られました．　**19.** 日光のもみじが今美し
く紅葉しはじめました．こんどの日曜日に私と一緒に見物にいらっしゃ
いませんか．―はい，喜んで御一緒に見物に参りましょう．もみじは今
が大変美しいそうです．　**20.** 先日秩父丸で中山伯爵が米国から帰っ
ていらっしゃいました．同じ船でわが駐米山田大使も帰国されました．
21. マクリン海軍中将は最近御進級なさいまして今は海軍大将でいら
っしゃいます．　**22.** 今演説をなさっていらっしゃる方はどなたですか．
―あの方は平田総理大臣です．　**23.** 貴方が先月九州へ行かれました時
雲仙と別府とを御覧になりましたか．―はい，見ました．　**24.** 人様がお
話しをなさっていらっしゃる時には気をつけてうけたまわるものです．

1. What will you do on Sunday?—I will go to Kamakura, and you?—I
will also go. **2.** Has your master already left for Kobe?—No, not yet; he is
leaving to-night. **3.** Do you often read novels?—No, I do not, but I often
read historical books. **4.** What book did you give Mr. Kurosawa?—I gave
him a history of Japan, which I bought last month. **5.** You speak Japanese
very well; who is your teacher?—Mr. Sato is my teacher. **6.** If you do not
pay attention when you are shopping, you will be overcharged. **7.** Mr. Osanai
is a very kind person: In winter he always sends us nice apples and butter
from Hokkaido. **8.** The book that you sent me at Christmas is very interesting. I have already read it through. **9.** Mrs. Yamada came yesterday and
paid me a visit. She gave me this beautiful Chinese curio, which she bought
in Shanghai. **10.** If you do not want this box will you not give it to me?
—I do not need it and I will give it to you with pleasure. **11.** To whom
did you give that cloisonne vase?—I gave it to Viscount Inoue. **12.** Please
give these earrings to your daughter. **13.** Mr. Redman taught my son English.
He is a very well known professor, and has been teaching English in Tokyo
for about ten years. **14.** Will you please take this dog away? He barks too
much and annoys me. **15.** The new president of our company is very
generous: he gave us a large bonus. **16.** Your haori is very beautiful; where
did you buy it?—I did not buy it; Mrs. Okada gave it to me. **17.** If you
give me your chain I shall give you this gold pin. **18.** When I gave my
lecture many prominent people came to hear it. **19.** The maple trees at Nikko
are now putting on their beautiful autumnal tints; will you not go with me
to see them next Sunday?—Yes, I shall willingly go with you and see them.
They told me that the maple trees are very beautiful now. **20.** The other
day Count Nakayama returned from America by the Chichibu Maru. Mr.
Yamada, our Ambassador to the United States, also came by the same boat.
21. Vice-admiral Maclean has recently been promoted and he is now an
admiral. **22.** Who is the man that is now delivering the speech?—He is

premier Hirata. **23.** When you went to Kyushu last month did you see
Unzen[1] and Beppu?—Yes, I did. **24.** When a person is speaking to us we
should listen attentively.

Thirty-sixth Lesson   第卅六課

To Do and To Make

Surú only indicates action, not the making of material objects,
which is indicated by *tsŭkúru* 造る or *koshiraerú* 拵える. Therefore *surú* corresponds to *to do* as well as *to make* when in English
the latter verb has an abstract meaning.

amímono wo surú	編物をする	to do knitting
báka-na kotó wo surú	馬鹿な事をする	to do a silly thing
saihō wo surú	裁縫をする	to do needlework
shigotó wo surú	仕事をする	to do work
shōbai wo surú	商売をする	to do business
shínsetsu wo surú	親切をする	to do a kindness
shínsetsu ni surú	親切にする	to do a kindness (*lit.* to do kindly)

Ichí-nichi-jū áme ga fútte imáshĭta nóde watashí wa uchí de amímono
一日中 雨 が 降っていました ので 私 は うちで 編物
wo shĭté imáshĭta. As it rained the whole day I remained at home
を して いました. knitting.

Móshi sonná báka-na kotó wo surú náraba watashí wa zekkō[2] shimásŭ.
若し そんな 馬鹿な 事 を する ならば 私 は 絶交 します.
If you do such a silly thing I'll break up friendship with you.

Dáredemo shōbai wo surú ni wa shihón ga irimásŭ.
誰でも 商売 を する に は 資本 が 要ります.
To do business one needs capital. (Anyone business to do capital needs.)

Hĭtó no shínsetsu wo mu ni shĭté wa ikemasén.
人 の 親切 を 無 に して は いけません.
Do not avail yourself unnecessarily of people's kindness.
(People's kindness bringing to naught won't do.—*mu ni surú* to bring to naught)

Anó hĭtó wa iroiró shínsetsu ni shĭté kuremáshĭta. He did me many
あの 人 は 色々 親切 に して くれました. kindnesses.

doryokú wo surú	努力をする	to make an effort
enzetsú wo surú	演説をする	to make a speech

---

1 *Unzén* and *Beppú* are the names of two famous Japanese hot-spring resorts.
2 *zekkō surú* to break up friendship

sensō wo surú	戦争をする	to make war
jamá wo surú	邪广をする	to hinder, make obstructions
kaimonó wo surú	買物をする	to make a purchase
keisán wo surú	計算をする	to make a calculation
ryokō wo surú	旅行をする	to make a journey
shazaí wo surú	謝罪をする	to make an apology
shǐtakú wo surú	支度をする	to make preparations
yakǔsokú wo surú	約束をする	to make a promise

Mukashí wa yóku shūkyō no tamé ni **sensō wo shimáshǐta** *ga íma de wa*
昔　は　よく　宗教　の　ために　戦争　を　しました　が　今　では
shūkyō sensō wa arimasén.   Formerly people often made war for their reli-
宗教　戦争　は　ありません.   gions, but now there are no religious wars.

Kinō no ása ítsumo no tōri gakkō ni ikí, gógo wa tomodachí to
きのう　の　朝　いつも　の　通り　学校　に　行き,　午後　は　友達　と
Ginzá e **kaimonó wo surú** *tamé ni ikimáshǐta.*
銀座　へ　買物　を　する　ために　行きました.
　　Yesterday morning I went to school as usual, and in the afternoon I went
　　shopping on Ginza with a friend. (*lit.* Yesterday morning as usual I went
　　to school, the afternoon with friend to Ginza to make purchase I went.)

Yakǔsokú wo shǐtá *tokí ni wa kanarazú[1] mamorá-nákereba narimasén.*
約束　を　した　時　には　必ず　守らなければ　なりません.
　　When you make a promise you must by all means keep it.

Tokugawá Kōshaku wa Bankokú Sekijújisha Taikái[2] de rippá-na **enzetsú**
徳川　公爵　は　万国　赤十字社　大会　で　立派な　演説
wo nasaimáshǐta.   Prince Tokugawa made a splendid address at the Inter-
を　なさいました.   national Red Cross Congress. (*Nasáru* is here used
　　　　　　　　　　　instead of *surú* in respect to the Prince.)

Surú is used in many expressions which may be translated into
English by a single verb, by a verb and its object, by a verb and
a particle, or a verb and an adverbial expression.

In parentheses is given the translation of the word preceding *surú* する,
which verb may correspond to *to make* or *to do*.

anshín surú	安心する	to feel at ease (peace of mind)
dendō surú	伝道する	to preach the Gospel (missionary work)
dōi surú	同意する	to agree (agreement, assent)
hanashí wo surú	話をする	to speak (talk, chat, speech)
hon-yakú surú	翻訳する	to translate (translation)
jisatsú wo surú	自殺をする	to commit suicide (suicide)
kegá wo surú	怪我をする	to get wounded (wound)
kenká wo surú	けんかをする	to quarrel (quarrel)

---

1 *kanarazú* by all means   **2** *Bankokú Sekijújisha Taikái* International Red Cross
Congress; *bankokú* international, *sekijújisha* red cross, *taikái* congress

kushámi wo surú くしゃみをする to sneeze (sneezing, sneeze)

mané wo surú 真似をする to imitate (imitation, mimicry)

sekí wo surú 咳をする to cough (a cough)

Sakúban michí wo arúite orimáshĭta tokĭ ni ishí ni tsumazuité kegá 昨晩 道 を 歩いておりました 時 に 石 に つまづいて 怪我 *wo shimáshĭta.* Last night while I was walking in the street I stumbled を しました. over a stone and got hurt. (*tsumazukú* to stumble)

Nihón de fukuín wo hajímete dendō shĭtá no wa Porutogarú no 日本 で 福音 を 初めて 伝道 した の は ポルトガル の *senkyōshitachi déshĭta.* The Portuguese missionaries were the first to preach 宣教師達 でした. the Gospel in Japan. (*fukuín* gospel)

Nihónjin wa amarí kenká wo shimasén, názenaraba Nihónjin wa 日本人 は 余り けんか を しません, なぜならば 日本人 は *jiséishin wo yōi ni[1] ushinaimasén.* The Japanese rarely quarrel, because they 自制心 を 容易 に 失いません. do not easily lose their self-control. (The Japanese too much quarrel do not make because the Japanese self-control easily do not lose.—*jiséishin* self-control, *ushinaú* to lose)

Shimbún ni yoréba Mihará-yamá de takŭsán no hĭtó ga jisatsŭ wo 新聞 に よれば 三原 山 で 沢山 の 人 が 自殺 を *shimáshĭta.* According to the newspapers many people have commited しました. suicide at Mihara Mountain.[2]

Surú is sometimes used as a neuter verb, in which case the subject is followed by **ga.**

otó ga surú 音がする there is, to produce a noise

fukutsū ga surú 腹痛がする to have a stomach-ache

zutsū ga surú 頭痛がする to have a headache

warúi kokoromochí ga surú 悪い心持がする to have a bad feeling

yói kokoromochí ga surú よい心持がする to have a good feeling

Note that all the above expressions indicate conditions related to our senses and are generally translated into English by the verb *to have*. Even the first expression "There is a noise," might be paraphrased by "I have a noise about me."

Kinō amarí zutsū ga shimáshĭta kará benkyō wo shimasén déshĭta. きのうあまり 頭痛 が しました から 勉強 を しません でした. Yesterday I did not study because I had a severe headache.

Tabesugirú to fukutsū ga shimásŭ. If we overeat we have 食べ過ぎる と 腹痛 が します. stomach-ache.

Sakúban niwá de hen-na otó ga shimáshĭta kará déte míru to 昨晩 庭 で 変 な 音 が しました から 出て 見る と *ayashíi otokó ga nígete ikimáshĭta.* 怪しい 男 が 逃げて 行きました. Last night, upon hearing a strange noise in the garden, I went out and saw

---

1 *yōi ni* easily   **2** Mihara is the name of an active volcano in the island of Oshima, about 60 miles S.W. of Tokyo.

a suspicious-looking man running away. (*lit.* Last night in the garden a strange noise as there was, when I went out to see a suspicious-looking man was running away.)

For euphonic reasons, **surú** becomes **zuru** or **jiru** when preceded by a syllable ending in **n.**

Words ending in **zuru** are generally used in literary style, while those ending in **jiru** are used in colloquial speech.

anjíru	案じる	}to be anxious	*kanjirú*	感じる	}to feel
anzúru	案ずる		*kanzúru*	感ずる	
kinjirú	禁じる	}to prohibit	*hanjíru*	判じる	}to judge
kinzúru	禁ずる		*hanzúru*	判ずる	
konjíru	混じる	}to mix	*shinjíru*	信じる	}to believe
konzúru	混ずる		*shinzúru*	信ずる	

zonjíru	存じる	}to know
zonzúru	存ずる	

*Ishá wa watashí ga tabakó wo suú kotó wo **kinjimáshita.***
医者 は 私 が 煙草 を 吸う 事 を 禁じました.
My doctor prohibited me from smoking tobacco.

*Háyaku kaeránai to ryōshin ga **anjimásŭ** kará koré de o-itomá[1] shimásŭ.*
早く 帰らない と 両親 が 案じます からこれ で お暇 します.
If I do not go home soon my parents will be anxious about me, so I must say good-bye. (*lit.* Quickly don't return if, my parents are anxious because, with this I say good-bye.)

Several common idioms are formed with **surú,** the most important of which are:

Dō shĭté	どうして	How?
Kō shĭté	こうして	In this way
Dō shĭté-mo	どうしても	By all, any means
......*ni shĭté wa*	......にしては	As for......
Sō shĭté......	そうして......	and, and then......
Sō shĭtára......	そうしたら......	}So then......, If so......,
Sō surú-to......	そうすると......	}If that is so......,
Sō suréba	そうすれば......	}In that case......

*Konó e wa anáta **ni shĭté wa** amarí jōzŭ désŭ ne.*
この 絵 は 貴方 に して は 余り 上手 です ね.
This picture is too well drawn for your ability. (*ilt.* This picture, as for you, too well drawn, isn't it?)

*Watashí wa toshí **ni shĭté wa** séi ga takái.*
私 は 年 に して は 背 が 高い.
I am tall for my age. (As for my years the height is tall.)

---

1 *itomá surú* to leave, to say good-bye (to)

Sō surú to anáta wa kotoshí daigakú wo déta to iú no désŭ ne.
そう する と 貴方 は 今年 大学 を 出た というの です ね.
So then, you have finished the university this year, haven't you?
(*lit · So then, you this year university left, so to say is, isn't it?)

Sō surú to watashí wa go-ji máde ni sokó e ikú no désŭ ka.
そう する と 私 は 五時 迄 に そこ へ行く の です か.
Am I to understand that I must be there by five?
(Then, I by five, there to go am I?)

Followed by a positive verb, the expression *dō shǐté-mo* means *by all
means*, and followed by a negative verb it has the meaning of *by no means,
or cannot possibly*.

Dō shǐté-mo Nihón-go wo naraitái désŭ. I wish **by all means** to
どうして も 日本語 を 習いたい です. learn Japanese.

Dō shǐté-mo anó byōnin wa naorimasén. That patient **cannot
possibly** recover.
どうして も あの 病人 は 治りません.

Other common sentences in which *surú* is used are the following:

Soré wa watashí no surú kotó désŭ. That is my business.
それ は 私 の する 事 です. You needn't attend to it.

Náni wo surú no désŭ ka. What do you mean by this behaviour?
何 を する の です か. What are you going to do?

Soré wa Nihón de wa shitsúrei-na kotó désŭ to shǐté arimásŭ.
それ は 日本 で は 失礼 な 事 です と して あります.
That is considered impolite in Japan. (That in Japan impolite thing is, so
doing there is.)

The stem of *surú* (*shi*) followed by certain verbs forms various
verbal expressions, some of which are the following:

shi-agéru	仕上げる	to finish, to complete one's work
shi-naósu	仕直す	to do over again
shi-sokonáu	仕損う	} to do wrong, to fail
shi-sonjíru	仕損じる	
shi-nikúi	仕にくい	difficult to do

When a verb of motion denotes an act done in order that a certain
purpose may be accomplished,—such verbs as *to go, to come, to send*,
etc.,—the purpose may be expressed by the simple stem of verbs of
Class I and the *i*-stem of verbs of Class II, followed by *ni*.

Tenrankái wo mi ni irasshaimáshǐta ka. Did you **go to see** the
展覧会 を 見 にいらっしゃいましたか. Exhibition?

O-tétsudai wa o-sakaná wo kai ni ikimáshǐta. The maid-servant **went to
お手伝い は お魚 を 買い に 行きました. buy** some fish.

Sakúban watashí wa Nihónshoku wo tábe ni ryōriya e ikimáshǐta.
昨晩 私 は 日本食 を 食べ に 料理屋 へ行きました.
Last night I **went** to a restaurant **to eat** Japanese food.

When an infinitive follows a verb that is not of motion, and has
the implied meaning of *for the purpose of* or *in order to*, it is

translated by the simple present followd by the expression *tamé*
ni ために. In this ease, *tamé ni* corresponds to the two English
phrases.

*Watashí no kabán wo éki e **hakobú tamé ni** pōtā wo yondé kudasái.*
私 の 鞄 を 駅へ 運ぶ ため にポーターを 呼んで 下さい.
Call a porter **to take** my trunks to the station.

Konó hakó ni kugí wo útsu tamé ni kanazuchí ga irimásŭ.
この 箱 に 釘 を 打つ ため に 金鎚 が 要ります.
I **need** a hammer (in order) **to nail** this box.

Anáta no shátsu wo tsŭkúru tamé ni konó kínu no kiré wo kaimáshĭta.
貴方 のシャツを 造る ため にこの 絹 の切れを 買いました.
I **bought** this silk cloth (in order) **to make** some shirts for you.

The simple present followed by *tamé ni* is also used to translate
the expression *that one may* followed by a verb.

*Hĭtó wa **tabéru tamé** ni ikíru no de wa nákute ikíru tamé ni*
人 は 食べる ため に生きるの で は 無くて 生きる ため に
tabéru no désŭ.   Man does not live **that he may eat** but eats **that he may live.**
食べる の です.   (*lit.* Man in order to eat, to live not being, in order to live
                 to eat is.)

Vocabulary

Nouns			Adjectives		
business	shōbai	商ショ売バイ	patient	gamanzuyói	我慢強イ
chill	samuké	寒サム気ケ	rare	maré-na	稀マレナ
customer	kyakú	客キャク	religious	shūkyō no	宗教ノ
complexion	kaoiró	顔カオ色イロ	splendid	rippá-na	立リッ派バナ
family	kázoku	家カ族ゾク	silly	báka-na	馬バ鹿カナ
habit	shūkan	習シュ慣カン	**Verbs**		
occupant	jōkyaku	乗ジョ客キャ	to be anxious	shimpái surú	心シン配パスル
promise	yakŭsokú	約ヤ束ソク	to crash	shōtotsu surú	衝突スル
religion	shūkyō	宗シュ教キョウ	to greet	áisatsu surú	挨アイ拶サツスル
suicide	jisatsú	自ジ殺サツ	to prohibit	kinji·rú	禁キンジル
treatment	taigū	待タイ遇グウ	to stumble	tsumazukú	ツマヅク

to break friendship *zekkō surú*; to give good service *yói taigū wo surú*; to make
calculations *keisán wo surú*; self-control *jiséishin*; to be able to keep a promise
yakŭsokú wo : mamoréru;   'bus *básu*; to feel chilly *samuké ga surú*; to catch a
cold *kazé wo hikú*; to say good-bye, to take leave *o-itomá surú*; to be too nice, too
good *yosugíru*; to listen *mimí wo katamukéru;* to become rare *maré-ni náru*

Exercise   *Renshū* 練習

1. Yóku[1] báka-na kotó wo iú hĭtó ni mimí wo katamukéru no wa iyá

---

1 *yóku* often, very often (colloquial speech)

désŭ.[1] **2.** Hĭtó ga shínsetsu ni shĭté kurerú to ureshíi monó désŭ. **3.** O-kyakú ni yói taigū wo shinái náraba shōbai wa hanjō[2] shimasén. **4.** Nihón-jin wa sorobán de keisán wo shimásŭ. **5.** Enzetsú wo surú máe ni chōshū ni áisatsu wo surú no wa shūkan désŭ. **6.** Ryokō wo surú máe ni wa shĭtakú wo shimásŭ. **7.** Nihón-go kará Ei-go ni hon-yakú surú no wa yasashíi désŭ ga Ei-go wo Nihón-go ni seikakú[3] ni hon-yakú surú no wa muzukashíi désŭ. **8.** Mukashí sekái no hĭtóbito wa shíbashiba sensō wo shimáshĭta. Géndai wa sensō ga maré ni narimáshĭta. **9.** Yakŭsokú wo surú máe ni wa sonó yakŭsokú ga mamoréru ka dō-ka wo yóku kangáe-nákereba ikemasén. Takŭsán no hĭtó ga kangáezu-ni yakŭsokú wo shimásŭ. **10.** Kinō yukí ga fútte itá sáichū[4] ni shi no básu ga ki ni shōtotsu shĭté jōkyaku zémbu kegá wo shimáshĭta. **11.** Nihón-jin wa taihén monoshízuka de gamanzuyói désŭ kará métta ni[5] kenká wo shimasén. Watakŭshí wa Nihón ni san-jū-nen mo súnde imásŭ ga hĭtó ga tōri de kenká wo shĭté irú no wo mimasén. **12.** Sakúban watashí wa kazé wo hiité samuké ga shimáshĭta kará shokují wo sézu-ni[6] nemáshĭta. **13.** Shibaí e go-isshó ni yukimásŭ ka.—Yukitái no désŭ ga háha ga yábun osokú déte imásŭ kotó wo kinjité orimásŭ kará. Yóru osokú máde gaishutsú[7] shĭté irú no wa watashí no kenkō ni yóku nái to háha wa mōshite orimásŭ. **14.** O-kaerí ni nátta hō ga yói deshō. Súgu o-kaerí ni naránai to go-ryōshin ga go-shimpai[8] wo nasáru deshō.—Déwa[9] o-itomá shimásŭ. Sayōnara. **15.** Déwa[10] tōtó Ameriká e irassháru no désŭ ne.—Hái, ashĭtá Hawái Marú de tachimásŭ. **16.** Nakamurá San wa Nihón-jin to-shité[11] wa amarí iró ga shirosugimásŭ shi séi mo takasugimásŭ[12] ne. **17.** Konó shigotó wo dō itashimashō.[13]—Kō nasái. **18.** Tōkyō cháku[14] no jikán wo o-shirasé[15] kudasái, sō suréba éki máde o-mukaé ni[16] demásŭ. **19.** Konó yōfuku wo isshūkan ínai ni[17] shi-ágete moraitái. **20.** Watashí wa Nihón e itté Nihón-go wo shi-agetái to omótte imásŭ. **21.** Konó heyá ga kurái nóde shigotó ga shi-nikúi désŭ. **22.** Nihón no katéi de wa ítsumo kodomó wa jūjun ni[18] shi-tsŭkeraremásŭ.[19] **23.** Séite[20] wa kotó wo shi-sonjíru. **24.** Anó otokó wa nan no tamé ni kokó e kimáshĭta ka.—Anó otokó wa dáiku désŭ. Uchí no máe ni atarashíi mon wo tsŭkúru tamé ni kimáshĭta. **25.** Watashitachí wa manabí ni gakkō e yukimásŭ. *or* Watashitachí wa manabú tamé ni gakkō e yukimásŭ.

1. よく馬鹿な事を言う人に耳を傾けるのは厭です. **2.** 人が親切にしてくれると嬉しいものです. **3.** お客によい待遇をしないならば商売ははんじょうしません. **4.** 日本人はそろばんで計算をします. **5.** 演説をする前に聴衆に挨拶をするのは習慣です. **6.** 旅行をする前には支度をします. **7.** 日本語から英語に翻訳するのは易しいですが英語を日本語に正確に翻訳するのはむづかしいです. **8.** 昔，世界の

1 *iyá désŭ* do not like **2** *hanjō surú* to do good business **3** accurately **4** *sáichū ni* while **5** *métta ni* rarely **6** *shokují wo sézu-ni* without eating **7** *gaishutsú surú* to go out of doors **8** *shimpai surú* to be anxious **9** *déwa* then, well **10** *déwa* so **11** *to-shĭté wa* for **12** *séi ga takasugirú* to be too tall **13** *Ka* at the end of a question is sometimes omitted in familiar speech. **14** arrival **15** *shiraserú* to let know **16** *mukaé ni déru* to go and meet **17** *ínai ni* within **18** *jūjun ni* to obedience **19** *shi-tsukeraréru* to be trained **20** *séku* to hurry; *séite wa* being in a hurry; *kotó wo shi-sonjíru* you do things wrong

人々はしばしば戦争をしました．現代は戦争が稀になりました．
9. 約束をする前にはその約束が守れるかどうかをよく考えなければ
いけません．沢山の人が考えずに約束をします．**10.** きのう雪が降っ
ていた最中に市のバスが木に衝突して乗客全部怪我をしました．
11. 日本人は大変物静かで我慢強いですから滅多にけんかをしません．
私は日本に三十年も住んでいますが人が通りでけんかをしているのを
見ません．**12.** 昨晩私はかぜを引いて寒気がしましたから食事をせず
に寝ました．**13.** 芝居へ御一緒に行きますか．―行きたいのですが母
が夜分おそく出ています事を禁じておりますから．夜おそく迄外出し
ているのは私の健康によくないと母は申しております．**14.** お帰りに
なった方がよいでしょう．直ぐお帰りにならないと御両親が御心配を
なさるでしょう．―では，お暇します．さようなら．**15.** では到頭ア
メリカへいらっしゃるのですね．―はい，明日ハワイ丸で立ちます．
16. 中村さんは日本人としては余り色が白すぎますし背も高過ぎます
ね．**17.** この仕事をどういたしましょう．―こうなさい．**18.** 東京着
の時間をお知らせ下さい，そうすれば駅迄お迎えに出ます．**19.** こ
の洋服を一週間以内に仕上げて貰いたい．**20.** 私は日本へ行って日本
語を仕上げたいと思っています．**21.** この部屋が暗いので仕事がし
にくいです．**22.** 日本の家庭ではいつも子供は従順にしつけられま
す．**23.** 急いては事を仕損じる．**24.** あの男は何んのためにこゝへ来
ましたか．―あの男は大工です．うちの前に新しい門を造るために来ま
した．**25.** 私達は学びに学校へ行きます．(私達は学ぶために学校へ行
きます．)

1. We do not like to listen to people who often say silly things. **2.** When
a person does a kindness to us we feel happy. **3.** If we do not give good
service to our customers we cannot do good business. **4.** The Japanese make
calculations with the "soroban."[1] **5.** Before making a speech it is customary
to greet the audience. **6.** Before making a journey we make preparations.
7. It is easy to translate Japanese into English but it is difficult to accurately
translate English into Japanese. **8.** In ancient times the people of the world
often made war. In modern times wars have become rare. **9.** Before making
a promise we must think well whether we can keep it. Many people make
promises without thinking. **10.** Yesterday while it was snowing a city bus
crashed against a tree and all occupants were wounded. **11.** The Japanese
are very quiet and patient, and they rarely quarrel. I have lived thirty years
in Japan without ever seeing people quarreling in the street. **12.** Last night,
as I had a cold and felt chilly I went to bed without eating. **13.** Will you
come with me to the theatre?—I should like to go but my mother has
prohibited me from staying out late at night. She said it is not good for my

---

1 *sorobán* a frame with balls sliding on thin bamboo sticks for performing arith-
metical calculations

health to stay out late at night. **14.** You had better go home. Your parents will be anxious about you if you do not go back soon.—I am going; good-bye. **15.** So, you are going to America at last.—Yes, I am leaving tomorrow by the Hawai Maru. **16.** For a Japanese Mr. Nakamura has too fair a complexion and he is too tall. **17.** How shall I do this work?—Do it in this way. **18.** Let me know the time you will arrive in Tōkyō, so that I may meet you (at the station). **19.** I wish to have this suit made within a week. **20.** I have been thinking of going to Japan to complete my study of Japanese. **21.** As it is dark in this room, it is difficult to work. **22.** In Japanese families children are always trained to obedience. **23.** Haste is waste. **24.** What did that man come here for?—That man is a carpenter. He came to make a new gate in front of our house. **25.** We go to school to learn.

Thirty-seventh Lesson 第卅七課

To Get

A great many English expressions with **get** are turned into Japanese by the verb *náru* なる, *to come into being, to become, to turn out*. Others are translated in different ways.

to get cold	*sámuku náru*	寒くなる
to get warm	*atatákaku náru*	暖かくなる
to get sick	*byōki ni náru*	病気になる
to get well	*yóku náru*	良くなる
to get rich	*kanemochí ni náru*	金持になる
to get angry	*okóru*	怒る
to get information	*jōhō wo éru*	情報を得る
to get knowledge	*chíshiki wo éru*	知識を得る
to get old	*toshí wo tóru* (of people)	年を取る
	toshiyorí ni náru (of people)	年寄になる
	fúruku náru (of things)	古くなる

Náru 成る（なる）

Náru 成る generally follows either the adverbial form of an adjective or of a verb in the desiderative, or an adverbial construction. This may be seen from the translation of most of the above expressions with *get*, and in the following examples:

akakú náru	赤くなる	to turn red; to blush
áoku náru	青くなる	to turn blue; to turn pale
damé ni náru	駄目になる	to get out of order / to become useless
ikitakú náru	行たくなる	to get a desire to go

éraku náru	偉くなる	to become a great man
kusurí ni náru	薬になる	to become wholesome
o-ténki ni náru	お天気になる	to turn out fine (weather)
yóku náru	良くなる	to become better; to improve
yukí ni náru	雪になる	to turn to snow
okáshiku narimáshǐta	おかしくなりました	⎰It became funny; I, he, etc. ⎱felt inclined to laugh

Náru is very often used both in written and spoken style. Though it may be translated into English in a great many ways, the idea evident in nearly all cases is, as stated at the beginning of this lesson, *to come into being, to become* or *to turn out.* The following are a few of the most common sentences with **náru**:

*Watashí no musǔkó wa ongakǔká ni **náru** tsumorı désǔ.*
私 の 息子 は 音楽家 に なる つもり です.
My son intends to be (*or* to **become**) a musician.

*Tōkyō e kité kará nan nen ni **narimásǔ** ka.*   How long have you
東京 へ来て から 何 年 に なります か.   been in Tokyo?
(*lit.* To Tokyo since you came, how many years has it **become**?)

*Mō isshū-kan de man ichí nen ni **narimásǔ**.*   Another week will make
もう 一週間 で 満 一 年 に なります.   a full year.
(*lit.* More one week, full one year **becomes.**)

*Watashí wa kóndo no tanjōbi de hátachi ni **narimásǔ**.*
私 は 今度 の 誕生日 で 廿才 に なります.
I shall be twenty years old my next birthday.
(*lit.* I next birthday by, twenty **become.**)

*Kurakú **naránu** uchí ni o-kaerí nasái.*   You had better go home before
暗く ならぬ 内 に お帰りなさい.   it gets dark.
(*lit.* Dark it doesn't **become** while, return.)

*Rokú ni shichí wo tasú to jū-san ni **narimásǔ**.*   Six plus seven
六 に 七 を 足すと 十三 に なります.   make thirteen
(*lit.* To six, seven if to add, thirteen **becomes.**)   (*tasú* to add)

*Hǐtó no iú tōri ni bákari **náru** hǐtó wa seikō shinái.*
人 の 言う通り に ばかり なる 人 は 成功 しない.
A man who simply follows the opinion of other people will not succeed.
(*lit.* People's saying like only **becomes** man, success does not make.)

*Samúi to byōki ni **narimásǔ**.*   ⎰When it gets cold I become ill.
寒い と 病気 に なります.   ⎱The cold weather makes me ill.

*Anáta wa jikí ni oyogéru yō-ni **narimásǔ**.*   You will soon be
貴方 は 直 に 泳げるように なります.   able to swim.
(*lit.* You soon to swim in order to **become.**)

*Hidói árashi ni wa **naránai deshō**.*   I don't think it will be
ひどい 嵐 に は ならない でしょう.   a severe storm.
(*lit.* Severe storm in probably will not **become.**)

*Mattakú iyá-ni **nátte shimaimáshĭta**.*   I have become thóroughly
全く　厭　に　なって　しまいました.   disgusted.
   (*lit.* Entirely disgusted **becoming** I ended by.)

*Dō shĭté kō **nátta** no désŭ ka.*   How did it happen so?
どうしてこうなった　の　です　か.

*Anó kotó wa dō **narimáshĭta** ka.*   What has **become** of that affair?
あの　事　は　どう　なりました　か.

Náru is often used after the desiderative in its adverbial form:

*Nihón e ikitakú **narimáshĭta**.*   I have formed a desire to go to
日本　へ　行きたく　なりました.   Japan.

Náru in the past tense may be translated, according to circumstances, by the English past or present. In the latter case, the
adverb **now** is often used.

*Damé ni **narimáshĭta**.*   { It is of no use now.
駄目　に　なりました.   { It has **become** useless.

*Dekínaku **narimáshĭta**.*   { It has **become** impossible.
出来なく　なりました.   { It is now impossible.

Náru is sometimes rendered by the English passive:

*o-sewasamá ni **náru***   to be assisted
お世話様　に　なる   (*sewá* help, aid, assistance)

O-sewasamá ni narimáshĭta. お世話様になりました. is a common
expression often used by Japanese in giving thanks for a favour received,
however small it may be, and it corresponds to *I owe you much for your
kindness.—I am much obliged to you for your assistance.—Thank you for your
kind help.*

In some cases ***náru*** corresponds also to the verb **to be**:

*Ōki-na sensō ni wa **naránai deshō**.*   I don't think it will be
大きな　戦争　に　は　ならない　でしよう.   a big war.

*Ato hĭtóri daké ni **narimáshĭta**.*   There is only one person left.
あと　一人　だけ　に　なりました.   (After, one person only has become.)

*Karadá no tamé ni **narimásŭ**.*   It is good for one's health.
体　の　ために　なります.   (The body, for the benefit of, becomes.)

  (*tamé ni* ために for the sake, benefit or good of; for one's good, sake or interest;
to one's own advantage, etc.)

The expression ***yo-ni náru*** ようになる *to become like, to become
so* has several uses. Some of the most common are illustrated in
the following sentences;

*Konná chíisa-na murá ni mo éiga-kan ga dekíru **yō-ni narimáshĭta**.*
こんな　小さ　な　村　に　も　映画館　が　出来る　ように　なりました.
Even such a small village has begun to have the cinema.
  (*lit.* Such a small village in even, cinema to be able, it became like.)

Ima[1] *ni góku wázuka no jikán*[2] *de sekái wo isshū*[3] *surú kotó ga dekíru*
今 に ごく 僅か の 時間 で 世界 を 一週 する 事 が 出来る
yō-ni náru deshō.   Some day we shall be able to travel around the world
ように なる でしよう.   within a few hours.

Yoshidá San no bótchan wa kotoshí kará shōgakkō e ikú yō-ni
吉田 さん の 坊ちゃん は 今年 から 小学校 へ 行く ように
narimáshìta.   Mr. Yoshida's son began to attend the primary school from
なりました.   this year. (......to school to go, so has become.)

Anáta wa konogoró Nihón-go wo nakanaká jōzu-ni hanásu yō-ni
貴方 は この頃 日本語 を なかなか 上手 に 話す ように
narimáshìta.   Recently you have become very skilful in speaking Japanese.
なりました.   (*lit.* You recently Japanese language very skilfully to speak,
so have become)

Alternative

By adding the termination *tari* たり to the simple stem of verbs
of Class I, and by substituting the final *e* of the subordinate of
the verbs of Class II for the termination *ari* あり, we obtain the
alternative verbal form, also called **frequentative.**

The alternative is mostly used in pairs, and serves to express
actions that follow one another in succession.

In most cases the alternative corresponds to the conjunction *and*, or to the
English **sometimes......sometimes, once......then again, now......then, partly......
partly, as well as.**

Verbs in the alternative are generally followed by *surú.*

The negative of the alternative is indicated by the termination *nakattari*
なかったり, added to the simple stem of verbs of Class I and to the *a*-stem
of verbs of Class II.—See *phonetic rule*, Page 684.

Alternative of Verbs of Class I

				Positive		Negative	
tabéru	食べる	*tabe*	食べ	*tábetari*	食べたり	*tabénakattari*	食べなかったり
míru	見る	*mi*	見	*mítari*	見たり	*mínakattari*	見なかったり

Alternative of Verbs of Class II

káku	書く	{	*káite*	書いて	P.[4]	*káitari*	書いたり
			kaká	書か	N.[5]	*kakánakattari*	書かなかったり
yómu	読む	{	*yónde*	読んで	P.	*yóndari*	読んだり
			yomá	読ま	N.	*yománakattari*	読まなかったり
dásu	出す	{	*dáshìte*	出して	P.	*dáshìtari*	出したり
			dasá	出さ	N.	*dasánakattari*	出さなかったり

---

1 *íma ni* some day, in the future **2** *góku wázuka no jikán de* in a few hours
góku very; *wázuka* few; *jikán* hours **3** *isshū surú* to go around **4** *P.*=positive
5 *N.*=negative

mátsu	待つ	*mátte*	待って	P.	*máttari*	待ったり
		matá	待た	N.	*matánakattari*	待たなかったり
tóru	取る	*tótte*	取って	P.	*tóttari*	取ったり
		torá	取ら	N.	*toránakattari*	取らなかったり
kaú	買う	*katté*	買って	P.	*kattári*	買ったり
		kawá	買わ	N.	*kawanákattari*	買わなかったり
áru	ある	*átte*	あって	P.	*áttari*	あったり
				N.	*nákattari*	なかったり

Examples

Anáta wa taigaí yóru náni wo shimásŭ ka. What do you generally do
貴方 は 大がい 夜 何 を します か. in the evening?

Watashí wa hon wo **yóndari**, *tegamí wo* **káitari**, *sampó ni*
私 は 本 を 読んだり, 手紙 を 書いたり, 散歩 に
dekaketári shimásŭ.   Sometimes I read books, sometimes I write letters,
出かけたり します.   and sometimes I go out for a walk.

Kōfuku-na tokí ni wa watashitachí wa hĭtó to **hanáshitari, warattári,**
幸福 な 時 に は 私達 は 人 と 話したり, 笑ったり,
utattári, odottári shĭtakú[1] *kanjimásŭ.*[2]
歌ったり, 踊ったり したく 感じます.
    When we are happy we feel a desire to talk with people, to laugh, to sing
    and to dance.

Nihón de wa hĭtó no máe de haná wo **kandári**, *akubí wo* **shĭtári**
日本 で は 人 の 前 で 鼻 を かんだり, あくび を したり
surú *no wa taihén shitsúrei désŭ.* In Japan blowing one's nose or yawning be-
する の は 大変 失礼 です.   fore people is considered very impolite.
(*haná wo kamú* 鼻をかむ to blow one's nose; *akubí wo surú* あくびをする to
yawn, *akubí* あくび yawn or yawning)

Anó hĭtó wa heyá no náka wo **ittári kitári shĭté** *imáshĭta.*
あの 人 は 部屋 の 中 を 行ったり 来たり して いました.
He was walking up and down the room.
    (That person the inside of the room now going, now coming was doing.)

Watashí wa heyá wo **háitari fuitári shĭté** *orimáshĭta.*
私 は 部屋 を 掃いたり 拭いたり して おりました.
I was sweeping and wiping (the floors of) the rooms.

Sonná ni nágaku **nenákattari tabénakattari shĭté** *ité wa karadá*
そんな に 長く 寝なかったり 食べなかったり して いては 体
ni dokú désŭ.   Going without eating and sleeping for such a long time is very
に 毒 です.   bad for the body. (*dokú* harm, injury)

Hon wo **yóndari** *niwá wo sampó* **shĭtári shĭté** *ichí nichí wo*
本 を 読んだり 庭 を 散歩 したり して 一 日 を
sugoshimáshĭta.[3]   I spent the day reading and strolling in the garden.
過しました.   (*sampó surú* to walk, to stroll)

---

1 *shitakú*, from *shitái* したい (desiderative of *surú* する) wish to do **2** *kanjirú*
感じる to feel **3** *sugósu* 過す to spend (the day, one's time, etc.)

The negative alternative expressing the idea of *not to do this nor to do that*, is obtained as follows:

1. By the simple stem of verbs of Class I and the *i*-stem of verbs of Class II, followed by **mo** も +the stem of the second verb+**mo**+the negative of *surú* する.

2. By the positive alternative form of the verbs as given above, followed by the negative of *surú* する.

*Kyō wa **nómi mo tábe mo shinákatta.***
きょうは 飲み も 食べ も しなかった. ⎫ To-day I have **neither**
*Kyō wa **nóndari tábetari shinákatta.*** ⎬ drunk **nor** eaten.
きょうは 飲んだり 食べたり しなかった. ⎭

*Kinō kimochí ga wárukute, hon wo **yómi mo**, tegamí wo **káki mo***
きのう気持ち が 悪くて、 本 を 読み も、 手紙 を 書き も
shinákatta. (or......*hon wo **yóndari**, tegamí wo **káitari shinákatta.***)
しなかった. (本 を 読んだり, 手紙 を 書いたり しなかった.)
    Yesterday I did not feel well and did **neither** read a book **nor** write a letter.

When one has to express the idea of *not to be able to do this nor to be able to do that*, the positive form of the alternative of the verbs may be used, followed by *surú kotó ga dekimasén* する事が出来ません.

*Anó hǐtó wa hon wo **yóndari**, tegamí wo **káitari** surú kotó ga*
あの 人 は 本 を 読んだり, 手紙 を 書いたり する 事 が
dekimasén.   That man **can neither** read a book **nor** write a letter.
出来ません.

True adjectives may be used in the alternative form, by adding the termination *kattari* to their stem:

	Stem		Alternative
atatakái 暖かい warm	*atataka* 暖か	*atatakakáttari* 暖かかったり
samúi 寒い cold	*samu* 寒	*sámukattari* 寒かったり

*Konogoró wa **sámukattari atatakakáttari** shǐté tenkō ga taihén*
この頃 は 寒かったり 暖かかったり して 天候 が 大変
fujún désǔ.   The weather has been very unsettled lately: now cold and then warm.
不順 です.   (*lit.* Lately, now cold now warm doing, the weather very unsettled is.)

Verbs in the alternative form may be used also when there is no idea of repeated action. In this case the alternative generally indicates a mild reproach, or disapproval.

*Nan no tsumorí de anó furúi tsǔkué wo **kattári** shimáshǐta ka.*
何ん の つもり で あの 古い 机 を 買ったり しました か.
    What on earth did you buy that old desk for?
    (*lit.* What purpose for, that old desk buying you did?)
*Sonná atsúi monó wo **tábetari** surú to (shǐté wa) shǐtá wo yakimásǔ.*
そんな 熱い もの を 食べたり する と (して は) 舌 を 焼きます.
    If you eat such hot food you will burn your tongue.
    (*lit.* Such hot thing eating if you do, the tongue you will burn.)

The intended meaning in the last sentence is: *You shouldn't eat such hot food because you might burn your tongue.*

In ordinary language the above two sentences would be translated as follows:

Nan no tsumorí de anó furúi tsŭkué wo kaimáshǐta ka.
何んの つもり であの 古い 机 を 買いました か.
Why did you buy that old desk?

Sonná atsúi monó wo tábete wa shǐtá wo yakimásŭ.
そんな 熱い もの を 食べて は 舌 を 焼きます.

Vocabulary

Nouns			Adjectives		
affair	mondaí	問題	fresh	shinsén-na	新鮮ナ
baseball	yakyū	野球	important	jūdai-na	重大ナ
assistance	joryokú	助力	instructive	yūeki-na	有益ナ
condition	{ guaí	工合	lazy	namákete	ナマケテ
	{ jōtai	状態		**Verbs**	
driver[1]	unténshu	運転手	to celebrate	iwái wo surú	祝ヲスル
lighthouse	tōdaí	燈台	to decide	kime·rú	定メル
need	hitsuyō	必要	to remain	okare·rú	置カレル
notice	keijí	掲示	to win	yūshō surú	優勝スル
sacrifice	giséi	犠牲		**Adverbs**	
stenographer	sokkishá	速記者	gradually	dandán	ダンダン
workman	rōdōsha	労仂者	thoroughly	mattakú	全ク
to be postponed	enkí ni náru	延期になる	to dismiss	káiko surú	解雇する
to recover	o-naori ni náru	お治りになる	to need	hitsuyō to surú	必要とする
to advise	chŭkoku surú	忠告する	to be angry	okótte irú	怒っている
to be exited	kōfun surú	興奮する	as it is	sonó mamá	そのまま

as hard as one can, with all one's might *isshōkemmei* 一生懸命
to address oneself to, to accost, to speak to *hanashí kakerú* 話し掛ける

Exercise   *Renshū*   練習

1. Hǐtó wa okótte irú tokí ni wa yóku kangáeru kotó ga dekimasén. **2.** Okāsan wa ikága désŭ ka.—Yoroshíi hō désŭ ga ishá wa áto[2] isshūkan guraí neté irú yō-ni[3] chūkoku shimáshǐta. **3.** Ani wa ni-jū-nen máe ni Aruzenchín e itté isshōkemmei hataraité kanemochí ni narimáshǐta. **4.** Anáta wa shinsén-na kūki no náka e dekaketé yukú kotó wo sézu ni shūjitsu[4] konó chíisa-na heyá ni irú to byōki ni narimásŭ yo. **5.** Watashí wa Nambéi e itté hatarakú tsumorí déshǐta ga Nihón ni irú kotó ni kimemáshǐta. Watashí no ryōshin ga dandán toshí wo tóri watashí no joryokú wo hitsuyō to shǐté orimásŭ nóde.

---

1 driver of vehicles **2** *áto isshūkan* another week **3** *neté irú yō-ni* to remain in bed (*lit.* so as to remain in bed) **4** *shūjitsu* all day

6. Chíshiki wo éru saizén no hōhō[1] wa yūeki-na hon wo yómu kotó désŭ.
7. Konó jūdai-na hōdō wo éru tamé ni wa ōinaru[2] giséi ga harawaremáshĭta.[3]
8. Anó mondaí wa dō narimáshĭta ka.—Aré wa ízen[4] to onají jōtai no mamá[5] désŭ. Tōbun no aidá[6] aré wa mikáiketsu[7] no mamá de okarerú[7] to omoimásŭ.
9. Koréra no rōdōshatachi wa taihén namákete yóku hatarakimasén kará watashí wa mattakú iyá-ni nátte[8] shimaimáshĭta.   Ashĭtá kárera wo káiko shimashō.
10. Watashí wa ni-jū-go ni náru musŭmé ga arimásŭ.   **11.** Jū-san ni náru[9] watashí no ói ga ráigetsu hĭtóri de Burajirú e yukimásŭ.   **12.** Senjitsú no jishín de o-takú wa dō mo narimasén[10] déshĭta ka.—Hái, takú wa dō mo narimasén déshĭta.   **13.** Hirái San no o-jōsan no kekkón wa dō narimáshĭta ka.—Kúgatsu máde enkí ni narimáshĭta.   **14.** Késa o-kárada no guaí wa ikága désŭ ka.— Máda yóku arimasén.—Súgu ni o-naorí ni náru deshō.—Arigatō gozaimásŭ.
15. Yūbe Ginzá-dōri de ōzei no gakŭséi ga ōki-na kóe de[11] utattári sawáidari shĭté irú no wo mimáshĭta.   Náze anná ni kōfun shĭté itá no ka wakarimasén déshĭta.—Tábun yakyū-shiái de Wasedá daigakú ni yūshō shĭtá Keiō daigagú no gakŭséi ga o-iwái wo shĭté itá no deshō.   **16.** Anó keijí ni naní ga káite arimásŭ ka.   Dōzo yónde kudasái.—" Untenshú ni hanashí-kaketári shánai[12] de tabakó wo nóndari surú kotó wo kinjimásŭ "[13] to káite arimásŭ.   **17.** Watashí ga háitte kúru máe ni hanáshĭtari warattári shĭté itá no wa dáre désŭ ka.— Sokkishatachí ga o-híru no shokují[14] wo shĭté itá no déshĭta.   **18.** Anó otokó wa ichí-jikán guraí tōri wo ittarí kitári shĭté imásŭ.   Aré wa dáre désŭ ka shĭtté imásŭ ka.—Iié, shirimasén.   **19.** To wo aketári shímetari surú to heyá ga sámuku narimásŭ.   **20.** Tōku no hō de[15] míetari miénaku náttari shĭté irú akarí wa nan désŭ ka.—Aré wa yūmei na Inubō Mísaki no tōdai désŭ.
21. Watashí no móto[16] no Nihón-go no senséi wa Eigó wo yóku yóndari hijō ni ryūchō[17] ni hanáshĭtari shĭtá monó désŭ.

1. 人はおこっている時には，よく考える事が出来ません． **2.** お母さんは如何ですか．—よろしい方ですが医者はあと一週間位寝ているように忠告しました． **3.** 兄は廿年前にアルゼンチンへ行って一生懸命忇いて金持になりました． **4.** 貴方は，新鮮な空気の中へ出かけて行く事をせずに終日この小さな部屋にいると病気になりますよ．**5.** 私は南米へ行って忇くつもりでしたが日本にいる事に決めました．私の両親がだんだん年をとり私の助力を必要としておりますので． **6.** 知識を得る最善の方法は有益な本を読む事です． **7.** この重大な報道を得るためには大いなる犠牲が払われました． **8.** あの問題はどうなりましたか．—あれは以前と同じ状態のまゝです，当分の間あれは未解決のまゝで置かれると思います． **9.** これ等の労忇者達は大変なまけてよく忇きませんから私は全くいやになってしまいました． あした

---

1 *saizén no hōhō* best way; *hōhō* method **2** great **3** *harawaréru* to be paid, *haráu* to pay **4** *ízen* before **5** *jōtai* state, condition, *no mamá* as it was **6** *tōbun no aidá* for the time being **7** *mikáiketsu* unsettled, *okarerú* to be left, to remain **8** *iyá ni nátte* disgusted **9** *jū-san ni náru* thirteen years old **10** *dō mo narimasén déshĭta ka* didn't anything happen to **11** *ōki na kóe de* with loud voice **12** *shánai de* in the coach **13** is prohibited **14** *o-híru no shokují* lunch **15** *tōku no hō de* in the distance **16** *móto no* former, old. **17** *ryūchō ni* fluently

彼等を解雇しましょう. **10.** 私は廿五になる娘があります. **11.** 十三になる私の甥が来月一人でブラジルへ行きます. **12.** 先日の地震でお宅はどうもなりませんでしたか.—はい, 宅はどうもなりませんでした. **13.** 平井さんのお嬢さんの結婚はどうなりましたか.—九月迄延期になりました. **14.** けさお体の工合は如何ですか.—まだよくありません.—直ぐにお治りになるでしょう.—有難うございます. **15.** ゆうべ銀座通りで大勢の学生が大きな声で歌ったり騒いだりしているのを見ました. なぜあんなに興奮していたのか解りませんでした.—たぶん野球試合で早稲田大学に優勝した慶応大学の学生がお祝いをしていたのでしょう. **16.** あの提示に何が書いてありますか. どうぞ読んで下さい.—「運転手に話しかけたり車内で煙草をのんだりする事を禁じます」と書いてあります. **17.** 私が入ってくる前に話したり笑ったりしていたのは誰ですか.—速記者達がお昼の食事をしていたのでした. **18.** あの男は一時間ぐらい通りを行ったり来たりしています. あれは誰ですか知っていますか.—いゝえ, 知りません. **19.** 戸を開けたり閉めたりすると部屋が寒くなります. **20.** 遠くの方で見えたり見えなくなったりしている明りは何ですか.—あれは有名な犬吠岬の燈台です. **21.** 私の元の日本語の先生は英語をよく読んだり非常に流暢に話したりしたものです.

1. When people get angry they can not think well. **2.** How is your mother?—She is getting well, but the doctor has advised her to remain in bed for another week. **3.** My elder brother went to Argentina twenty years ago, worked hard and got rich. **4.** If you remain in this small room the whole day without going out in the fresh air, you will get ill. **5.** I intended to go to South America and work there, but I have decided to remain in Japan. As my parents are getting old they need my assistance. **6.** The best way to get knowledge is to read instructive books. **7.** This important information was obtained at great sacrifice. **8.** What has become of that affair?—It is still in the same state as it was and I believe it will remain unsettled for sometime yet. **9.** These workmen are so lazy and work so badly that I am thoroughly disgusted with them. To-morrow I will dismiss them. **10.** I have a daughter who is now twenty-five years old. **11.** My thirteen years old nephew is going alone to Brazil next month. **12.** Didn't anything happen to your house during the earthquake the other day?—No, my house did not suffer any damage. **13.** What has become of the marriage of Mr. Hirai's daughter?—It was postponed till next September. **14.** How do you feel this morning?—I am not yet well.—I hope you will soon recover.—Thank you. **15.** Last night on Ginza (Street) I saw a great many students singing aloud and making merry. I could not understand why they were so excited.—Perhaps they were students of the Keio University celebrating their victory over Waseda University baseball team. **16.** What is written on that notice? Please read it to me.—" Speaking to the driver or smoking in the coach is strictly prohibited." **17.** Who was talking and laughing just before I entered?—Some of the stenographers who were eating their lunch. **18.** That man has been walking up and down the street for about an hour. Do you know him?— No, I don't. **19.** The room will become cold if you keep opening and closing the door. **20.** What is that light appearing and disappearing in the distance? —It is the well known Inubō-Misaki lighthouse. **21.** My old Japanese teacher used to read well and speak English quite fluently.

Thirty-eighth Lesson   第卅八課

Degrees of Comparison
Hikakú-Kyū 比ヒ較カク級キウ

In making comparisons Japanese adjective are not inflected as they are in English.

The following examples illustrate the way the comparison of adjectives is obtained in Japanese.

Konó haná wa kírei. この　花　は　きれい.	This flower is pretty.
Anó haná wa mótto kírei. あの　花　は　もっと　きれい.	That flower is prettier.
Aré wa mótto kírei. あれ　は　もっと　きれい.	That is prettier.

The word **mótto** corresponds to the English **more**.

When the thing that is compared is mentioned, **no hō ga** の方が may be used instead of *mótto*. **Hō** in this case corresponds to the indefinite pronoun **one**.

Anó haná no hō ga kírei. あの花の方がきれい.　That flower is prettier.
(*lit.* That flower than that **one,** pretty.)

Anó hō ga kírei. あの方がきれい.　That **one** is prettier.
(Compared with another that is less pretty,—is here understood.)

Note that **no** in the last example has been omitted because the thing compared (*haná*) is not mentioned as it is in the previous example, in which case *anó* functions as a pronoun.

The word **mótto** may be used before the adjective when **no hō ga** or **hō ga** is used. **Mótto,** in this case, gives more emphasis to the comparison.

*Anó haná **no hō ga mótto** kírei.*   That flower is prettier.
あの　花　の　方　が　もっときれい。

  (*lit.* That flower, than that one, more pretty.)

*Anó **hō ga mótto** kírei.* あの方がもっときれい。   That is prettier.

Much, before a comparative adjective, is translated by *zuttó* ずっと, which expression corresponds to *by far more.*

*Anó hō ga **zuttó kírei** désŭ.*   That is much prettier.
あの　方　が　ずっと　きれい　です。

  (*lit.* That one by far more pretty is.)

The comparison may be rendered more emphatic by using both words **mótto** and **zuttó.**

*Anó hō ga **mótto zuttó** kírei désŭ.*
あの　方　が　もっと　ずっと　きれい　です。

When an adjective expresses the quality in a higher or lower degree, it may be followed by either **no** の, **hō** 方, or **no hō** の方.

*Kokó ni iroiró no jibikí ga arimásŭ ga, konó **chiisái hō ga** (**no** こゝ　に　色々　の　字引　が　あります　が、　この　小さい　方　が　（の
ga, or **no hō ga**) íi. が、　の　方　が）いゝ。 Here are several dictionaries, but the small one is better than the others (*or* is the best).

  (*lit.* Here several dictionaries are, but the small one is good.)

Hō in a comparison of adjectives may be used as an indefinite pronoun without *ga.*

*Dóchira no empitsú ga o-sŭkí désŭ ka, **nagái hō** désŭ ka, **mijikái** どちら　の　鉛筆　が　お好き　です　か、　長い　方　です　か、　短い
hō désŭ ka. 方　です　か。 Which pencil do you like better, the longer one or the shorter one? (*or*......the long one or the short one?)

*Mijikái **hō** ga sŭkí désŭ.* { I like (better) the shorter one.
短い　方　が　好き　です。 { I like (better) the short one.

No may be used instead of **hō.**

*Dóchira no empitsú ga o-sŭki désŭ ka, **nagái no** désŭ ka, **mijikái** どちら　の　鉛筆　が　お好き　です　か、　長い　の　です　か、　短い
no désŭ ka.—Mijikái **no** ga sŭkí désŭ.
の　です　か。—短い　の　が　好き　です。

If we wish to express an intensified quality as with the words *still better,* **náo** 尚 or *issō* 一層 may be used.

Hánako San no kimonó wa kírei.   Miss Hanako's kimono
花子　さん　の　着物　は　きれい。   is pretty.

Tsúruko San no kimonó wa mótto kírei.   Miss Tsuruko's kimono
鶴子　さん　の　着物　は　もっときれい。   is prettier.

Nátsuko San no kimonó wa náo (issō) kírei. Miss Natsuko's kimono
夏子 さん の 着物 は 尚 (一層)きれい.   is still prettier.

Koré wa íi ga aré wa náo íi. This is good, but that
これ はいゝ があれ は 尚 いゝ.   is (still) better.

When in comparing two things the standard of comparison is named, the higher or lower degree is indicated by the postposition **yóri より** or **yóri mo よりも,** which corresponds to the English ......than used as the second member of a comparison expressing inequality. **Yóri** means, literally, *from,* and **yóri mo** *even from.*

Nihón-go wa Eigó yóri mo muzukashíi. 日本語は英語よりもむづかしい.
The Japanese language is more difficult than English.
    (*lit.* Japanese-language, English-language than, difficult.)

Watashí no uchí wa anáta no yóri mo chiisái désŭ.
私 の 家 は 貴方 の より も 小さい です.
My house is smaller than yours.
    (*lit.* My house, yours than, small is.)

The word expressing the standard followed by **yóri** may be placed at the beginning of the sentence, and the word expressing the compared object may be followed by **hō** (side, a way, a method), which renders the comparison rather emphatic.

Eigó yóri Nihón-go no hō ga muzukashíi.
英語 より 日本語 の 方 が むづかしい.
    (*lit.* English-language than, Japanese-language's side difficult.)

Eigó yóri Nihón-go ga muzukashíi.
英語 より 日本語 が むづかしい.
    (*lit.* English-language than, Japanese-language difficult.)

The Japanese language is more difficult than the English language.

Anáta no uchí yóri watashí no hō ga chiisái.
貴方 の 家 より 私 の 方 が 小さい.
    (*lit.* Your house than, my own small.)

Anáta no uchí yóri watashí no ga chiisái.
貴方 の 家 より 私 の が 小さい.
    (*lit.* Your house than, mine small.)

My house is smaller than yours.

Yóri is also used when one of the things compared is expressed by a verb. In this case **yóri** follows the simple present.

Kikú wa kikanái yóri íi. Kikanái yóri kikú hō ga íi.
聞く は 聞かない よりいゝ. 聞かない より 聞く 方 がいゝ.
    To ask is better than not to ask.
    (*lit.* To ask, not-to-ask than, good. Not to ask than, to ask, the method good.)

Yóri, followed or not by **mo,** is also used in comparing the intensity of two actions expressed by a verb.

Anó otokó wa áni yóri mo mótto hatarakimásŭ. That man works more
あの 男 は 兄 より も もっと 仂きます. than his elder brother.
    (*lit.* That man, his elder brother than, more works.)

Ojí wa watashí yóri anáta wo sŭkí désŭ.   My uncle likes you
伯父 は 私 より 貴方 を 好き です.   better than me.
　　(*lit.* My uncle, me than, you likes.)

Superlative

The superlative is expressed by *ichibán* 一番 (colloq.), meaning
number one, first, or by *móttomo* 最も (Lit.), meaning *most.*

Fújisan wa Nihón de ichibán takái yamá désŭ.
富士山 は 日本 で 一番 高い 山 です.
Mount Fuji is the **highest** mountain in Japan.

Tōkyō wa Nihón-jū[1] de ichibán ōkii tokái désŭ.   Tokyo is the **largest**
東京 は 日本中 で 一番 大きい 都会 です.   city in Japan.
　　(*lit.* Tokyo, Japan throughout in, first big city is.)

Ishikarí-gawá wa Nippón de móttomo nagái kawá désŭ.
石狩川 は 日本 で 最も 長い 川 です.
The Ishikari is the **longest** river in Japan.
　　(*lit.* Ishikari river in Japan most long river is.)

Sonó tokí anó hĭtó wa móttomo tokŭi no tokí déshĭta.
その 時 あの 人 は 最も 得意 の 時 でした.
At that time he was at the zenith of his prosperity.
　　(*lit.* That time that man most prosperity's time was.)

The word *ichí* 一, after a noun of place, also indicates the superlative degree.

Sekái ichi no takái yamá wa Himarayá désŭ.
世界 一 の 高い 山 は ヒマラヤ です.
The highest mountains in the world are the Himalayas.

If the meaning of the sentence is clear, the adjective may be omitted.

Fúji wa Nippón ichí no yamá.   Mount Fuji is the highest mountain in
富士 は 日本 一 の 山.   Japan.

Most, meaning the *majority of,* before a noun, may be translated
by *taigái (no)* 大概 (の), *taitéi (no)* 大抵 (の)

As adverbs, the two expressions *taigái* 大概 and *taitéi* 大抵 correspond
to *generally, generally speaking, mostly, for the most part, in most cases, in the
main, as a rule, principally, chiefly.*

Taigái no gaikoká no gakŭséi wa konó bumpōsho wo mótte imásŭ.
大概 の 外国 の 学生 は この 文法書 を 持って います.
Most foreign students have this grammar. (*gaikokú* foreign)

Watashí wa imá-máde taitéi inaká de kurashimáshĭta.
私 は 今迄 大抵 田舎 で 暮しました.
I have lived in the country most of my days.
　　(*lit.* I until now mostly in the country have lived.)

---

1 *Jū* after a noun of place means *throughout.*

The Most

ichibán ōi 一番多い (colloq.)   *móttomo ōi* 最も多い (Lit.)

As a separate word, *ōi* 多い means **much** or **many,** so that the expression *móttomo ōi* 最も多い, translated literally, corresponds to **most much** or **most many.**

The Least

ichibán sŭkunái 一番少ない(colloq.)   *móttomo sŭkunái* 最も少ない(Lit.)

As a separate word, *sŭkunái* 少ない means **few** or **little,** so that the expression *móttomo sŭkunái* 最も少ない, translated literally, corresponds to **most few** or **most little.**

Anó hĭtó wa **móttomo** *(ichibán) ōi o-kané wo mótte imásŭ.*
あの 人 は 最も （一番） 多い お金 を 持っています.
That man has **the most** money.

Konó hĭtó wa **móttomo** *(ichibán) sŭkunái o-kané wo mótte imásŭ.*
この 人 は 最も （一番） 少ない お金 を 持っています.
This man has **the least** money.

Irregular English Comparatives

The rules given for the formation of the comparative and superlative degrees of Japanese adjectives may be applied to all adjectives, even to those corresponding to English adjectives that form their comparative and superlative irregularly.

good		better		the best	
yói	よい	*mótto yói*	もっとよい	*ichibán yói (íi)*	一番よい(いゝ)
íi	いゝ	*mótto íi*	もっといゝ	*móttomo íi (yói)*	最もいゝ（よい）

bad, ill		worse		the worst	
warúi	悪い	*mótto warúi*	もっと悪い	*ichibán warúi*	一番悪い
				móttomo warúi	最も悪い

little, small (size)		less		the least	
chiisái	小さい	*mótto chiisái*	もっと小さい	*ichibán chiisái*	一番小さい
				móttomo chiisái	最も小さい

little (quantity)		less		the least	
sŭkunái	少ない	*mótto sŭkunái*	もっと少ない	*ichibán sŭkunái*	一番少ない
sŭkóshi	少し	*mótto sŭkóshi*	もっと少し	*móttomo sŭkóshi*	最も少し

far		farther		the farthest	
tōi	遠い	*mótto tōi*	もっと遠い	*ichibán tōi*	一番遠い
				móttomo tōi	最も遠い

up		upper		the uppermost	
ué	上	*mótto ué*	もっと上	*ichibán ué*	一番上
				móttomo ué	最も上

The comparative expressions **better than** and **worse than,** are regularly translated by *yóri* or *yóri mo*......*yói, yóri* or *yóri mo*......*warúi.*

Anáta no kutsú wa watashí no yóri mo yói.
貴方　の　靴　は　私　の　より　も　よい. Your shoes are **better than** mine.

Anáta no kutsú yóri mo watashí no hō ga yói.
貴方　の　靴　より　も　私　の　方　が　よい. My shoes are **better than** yours.
(*lit.* Than your shoes mine are good.)

Watashí no kutsú yóri anáta no kutsú ga yói.
私　の　靴　より　貴方　の　靴　が　よい. Your shoes are **better than** my shoes.
(*lit.* Than my shoes your shoes are good.)

Watashí no atarashíi tokéi wa furúi no yóri mo warúi.
私　の　新しい　時計　は　古い　の　より　も　悪い.
My new watch is **worse than** the old one.
(*lit.* My new watch, the old one than, bad.)

However, in literary style or in formal speech, **better than** is translated by the expression *ni (mo) masáru* に (も) 優る (勝る), and **worse than** by *ni (mo) otóru* に (も) 劣る. The particle *mo* is used when emphasis is to be expressed.

Masáru means *to surpass, to excel, to exceed, to outshine, to be superior to, to outdo,* etc., and *otóru* means *to be inferior to, to be worse than, to be below, to compare unfavourably with,* etc.

Kenkō wa tómi ni (mo) masáru. Health is **better than** wealth.
健康　は　富　に　(も)　優る. (Health to wealth is superior.)

Anó hĭtó wa kemonó ni (mo) otóru. He is **worse than** a beast.
あの　人　は　けもの　に　(も)　劣る. (That person to beast is inferior.)

Both, Either

ryōhō 両方, *dóchira mo* どちらも

Ryōhō 両方 corresponds exactly to **both**, while *dóchira mo* どちらも corresponds more to the expressions **either,** *each of two, the one and the other.*

Anó e ga hoshíi no désŭ ka konó hō désŭ ka. Do you want that picture
あの絵　が　欲しい　の　です　か　この　方　です　か. or this one?
(*lit.* That picture do you want?, this one is?)

Ryōhō hoshíi (no) désŭ. 両方欲しい (の) です. I want **both.**

Dóchira mo hoshíi (no) désŭ. どちらも欲しい (の) です.
(*lit.* The one and the other I want. *or* I want either.)

Anáta wa koré wo kaitái no désŭ ka, aré wo kaitái no désŭ ka.
貴方　は　これ　を買いたいの　です　か，あれ　を買いたいの　です　か.

Do you wish to buy this or that?

(*lit.* You, this want to buy? that want to buy?)

***Dóchira mo** kaitái no désŭ.*   I want to buy **both**.
どちら　も　買いたいの　です.

(*lit.* The one and the other want to buy. *or* Either want to buy.)

When using one or the other of the above two Japanese expressions, it should be considered that the English word **both,** means *the two taken jointly*, while **either** means *the one and the other taken separately*. The same difference of meaning that exists between *both* and *either*, exists between **ryōhō** 両方 and *dóchira mo* どちらも.

Ryōhō 両方 is rendered emphatic by the word **tomó** とも, while the synonymous expression *dóchira mo* どちらも is already emphasized by the particle *mo* も.

Ryōhō tomó *íi désŭ.* *or* **Dóchira mo** *íi désŭ.*
両方　とも　いゝです.   　どちら　も　いゝです.

Both of them **are** good. *or* **Either** of them **is** good.

Note that etymologically analized, the word **ryōhō** 両方 is composed of **ryō** 両, meaning *the two* or *both of them*, and **hō** 方, meaning *part* or *parts*. In translating the expression *both sides* or *either side*, **hō** 方 is replaced by the word *gawá* 側 which means **side**.

*Michí no **ryō-gawá** ni.* 道の両側に. On **both** (*or* either) **sides** of the street.

*Hoshō ga mon no **ryō-gawá** ni tátte imáshĭta.*
歩哨　が　門　の　両　側　に立っていました.

A sentinel was on **both** (*or* either) **sides** of the gate.

Either......or......

.....*ka*.....*ka*......   ......*ka arúiwa*.....*ka*......

·.....か ·.....か ....か　或は　.....か ......

The **ka** か given above to translate the expression **either**......**or,** is the same particle corresponding to the English question mark. The word preceding the particle **ka** should then be given a slight interrogative intonation. **Arúiwa** 或は corresponds exactly to the conjunction **or.**

Arúiwa after **ka** may in any case be omitted.

*Anó hĭtó wa Igirisú-jin **ka** (**arúiwa**) Ameriká-jin **ka** désŭ.*
あの　人　は　イギリス人　か　（或は）　アメリカ人　か　です.

He is **either** English **or** American.

(*lit.* That person English person?—or—American person? is.)

Koré wa hommonó¹ ka (arúiwa) nisemonó² ka wakarimasén.
これ は 本物 か （或は） にせ物 か 解りません.
I don't understand whether this is a genuine thing **or** an imitation.
  (*lit.* This, genuine thing?—or—imitation thing?, I don't understand.)

Dōzo, koré ka aré ka wo eránde kudasái.   Please choose **either**
どうぞこれ か あれ か を 選んで 下さい.   this **or** that.
  (*lit.* Please, this?, that?, choose.)

Neither......nor......

......*mo*......*mo* も......も   *dóchira mo* どちらも

In Lesson 20 it has been said that the word *mo* も corresponds to **also**. As each of the two *mo* of the expression given above has the same meaning, it follows that *mo*......*mo* corresponds to **also ......also**. Followed by a negative verb, *mo*......*mo* translates **neither ......nor.**

Háha wa kōhī mo o-chá mo nomimasén.   My mother drinks **neither**
母 はコーヒーも お茶 も 飲みません.   coffee **nor** tea.
  (*lit.* My mother coffee **also** tea **also** does not drink.)

Watashí wa tómi mo méiyo mo kamaimasén.   I care **neither** for wealth
私 は 富 も 名誉 も かまいません.   **nor** for honours.
  (*lit.* I, wealth **also** honours **also** do not care.)

Anáta wa Nihón-go ka Shiná-go ka wo hanashimásu ka·
貴方 は 日本語 か 支那語 か を 話します か.
Do you speak Japanese or Chinese?
  (*lit.* You, Japanese language? Chinese language do you speak?)

Watashí wa Nihón-go mo Shiná-go mo hanashimasén.
私 は 日本語 も 支那語 も 話しません.
I speak **neither** Japanese **nor** Chinese.
  (*lit.* I, Japanese language **also**, Chinese language **also** do not speak.)

The expression *dóchira mo* どちらも, which, followed by a positive verb, means **either** as already shown above, alters its meaning into **neither......nor** when followed by a negative verb.

Watashí no chichí-háha wa dóchira mo gaikokú e ikimasén déshĭta.
私 の 父母 は どちら も 外国 へ行きませんでした.
Neither my father **nor** my mother has gone abroad.
  (*lit.* My father-mother either one, to foreign country did not go.)

As soon as......   ......*to súgu ni* ......とすぐに

......*shídai* ......次第   ......*ya ína ya* ......や否や

---

1 genuine thing **2** an imitation, a spurious article

In colloquial speech, **as soon as** is translated by a verb in the simple present followed by *to súgu ni* とすぐに. The postposition *ni* に is rather emphatic and may be omitted whenever emphasis is not required.

Konó shigotó wo oerú to súgu (ni) sampó ni dekakemashō.
この　仕事　を終えると　すぐ（に）　散歩　に出かけましょう.
As soon as we **finish** this work we shall go out for a walk.

Anó shigotó wo oeru to súgu (ni) sampó ni dekakemáshĭta.
あの　仕事　を終えると　すぐ（に）　散歩　に出かけました.
As soon as we **finished** that work we went out for a walk.

Watashí wa anó otokó wo míru to sugu ni dáre da ka wakarimáshĭta.
私　はあの　男　を　見る　とすぐ　に誰　だ　か　わかりました.
As soon as I **looked** at that man I recognized him.
(*lit.* I, that man saw as soon as, who is it?, I understood.)

In literary style, **as soon as** may be translated, instead of *to súgu ni*, by a verb in the simple present followed by *ya ína ya* や否や or by the simple stem of verbs of Class I and the *i*-stem of verbs of Class II followed by the word *shídai* 次第.

Táishi wa tōchaku surú ya ína ya taishikán e isóide irasshaimáshĭta.
大使　は　到着　する　や　否　や大使館へ急いでいらっしゃいました.
As soon as the ambassador **arrived** he rushed to the embassy.
(*táishi* ambassador; *tōchaku surú* to arrive; *taishikán* embassy)

Watashí wa anó otokó wo míru ya ína ya dáre da ka wakarimáshĭta.
私　はあの　男　を　見る　や否　や　誰　だ　か　わかりました.
As soon as I **looked** at that man I recognized him.

Konó shigotó wo oerú ya ína ya sampó ni dekakemásŭ. ⎫
この　仕事　を終えるや否　や　散歩　に出かけます.   ⎪ As soon as we
Konó shigotó wo oé shídai sampó ni dekakemásŭ.   ⎬ **finish** this work
この　仕事　を終え　次第　散歩　に出かけます.   ⎪ we shall go out
Konó shigotó wo oerú to súgu (ni) sampó ni dekakemásŭ. ⎪ for a walk.
この　仕事　を終えるとすぐ（に）散歩　に出かけます. ⎭

Ame ga yamí shídai dekakemashō.   **As soon as** the rain **stops** we
雨　が　止み　次第　出かけましょう.   shall go out.
(*áme ga yamú* 雨が止む to stop raining)

A noun, instead of a verb, may precede *shídai* 次第:

Go-tōchaku shídai watashí ni dempō wo kudasái.   **As soon as** you **arrive**
御到着　次第　私　に　電報　を　下さい.   send me a telegram.
(*tōchaku* arrival, *go-tōchaku* your arrival; *dempō* telegram)

During

In Lesson 31, the translation of **during** in reference to a period of time is given as *kan* or *aidá* 間.

There are some Japanese words, however, which, besides indicating time, have also the idea expressed by *during*. Common among such words are the ones below, which may also be expressed according to the rule given in Lesson 31.

during the day   *hirú no aidá* or *hirumá* (colloquial), *chūkan* (Lit.)
　　　　　　　　　　昼の間　　　　　昼間　　　　　　　　　　昼間

during the night   *yóru no aidá* or *yábun* (colloquial), *yakán* (Lit.)
　　　　　　　　　　夜の間　　　　　夜分　　　　　　　　　　夜間

Taiyō wa hirú no aidá (hirumá, chūkan) kagayakimásŭ.
太陽　は　昼　の　間　（昼間，　昼間）　かがやきます.

　　The sun shines **during the day.** (*kagayáku* かがやく to shine, to be radiant)

Yóru no aidá (*yábun* or *yakán*) *tsŭkí to hoshí wo mimásŭ.*
夜　の　間　（夜分　　夜間）　月　と　星　を　見ます.

　　We see the moon and the stars **during the night.** (*tsŭkí* moon, *hoshí* stars)

When not referring to a period of time **no aidá ni** の間に or simply **ni** に may be used.

Anáta no rúsu (no aidá) **ni** *watashí wa uchí wo sōji shimashō.*
あなた　の　留守　（の　　間）　に　私　は　家　を　掃除しましょう.

　　During your absence I will clean the house. (*rúsu* absence; *sōji surú* to clean)

During may also be expressed by the word *chū* 中, often pronounced *jū* 中 for euphonic reason.

ichí nichí-jū 一日中 **during** one day　　*kotoshí-jū* 今年中 **during** this year
ichí nen-jū 一年中 **during** one year　　*fuyú-jū* 冬中 **during** winter
ryokō-chū 旅行中 **during** a trip　　*rúsu-chū* 留守中 **during** the absence

Watashí wa Ōsaka e no ryokō-chū ni kámera wo nakushimáshĭta.
私　は　大阪　への　旅行中　に　カメラ　を　なくしました.

　　I lost my camera during a trip to Osaka. (*nakŭsú* なくす to lose)

Ni に is used after *chū* or *jū* 中 when something is said after **during,** as in the above example.

When something happens suddenly and is of very short duration, as an earthquake, a motorcar accident, etc., while something else is going on, **during** is translated by *saichū ni* 最中に, which word corresponds also to such expressions as *in the midst of, in the height of,* etc.

Keibá no saichū ni fŭtarí no kishú ga kegá wo shimáshĭta.
競馬　の　最中　に　二人　の　騎手　が　怪我　を　しました.

　　During the race two jockeys got wounded. (*keibá* horse races; *kishú* jockey)

Anó jishín no saichū ni go-rokkén no ié ga taoremáshĭta.
あの　地震　の　最中　に　五六軒　の　家　が　倒れました.

　　During the earthquake several houses collapsed.

　　(*jishín* earthquake; *go-rokú* five or six; *ken* 軒 numerative for counting houses; *ié* house; *taoréru* 倒れる to collapse, to tumble)

Vocabulary

Nouns			Adjectives		
continent	*tairikú*	大陸	intelligent	*sōmei*	聰明
earnings	*kasegí*	稼ギ	precious	*tōtoi*	貴イ
Europe	*Ōshū*	欧洲	useful	*yūeki-na*	有益ナ
examination	*shikén*	試驗			
handbag	*tesagé*	手提		Verbs	
preparations	*júmbi*	準備	to come across to see	}*miuke·rú*	見受ケル
prosperity	*tokúi*	得意	to recognize	*mioboe·rú*	見覚エル
skill	*jukurén*	熟練	to run out	*kakedasú*	駈出タス

ryōnin	両人	both persons	*ryōsha*	両者	both persons (*Lit.*)
ryōte	両手	both hands	*ryōashi*	両足	both feet, both legs

Exercise *Renshū* 練習

1. Ōsaka wa Tōkyō kará tōku,[1] Nagasakí wa mótto tōi désŭ. Okinawá wa Nihón Téikoku de Tōkyō kará ichibán tōi tokoró désŭ. 2. Hánako San wa wákaku, Yóshiko San wa mótto wakái désŭ, ga Tsúruko San wa minná no náka de ichibán wakái désŭ. 3. Bōshi wa minná sonná ni takái no désŭ ka.—Iié, Danná San, kochirá no hō wa mótto o-yasúi désŭ. 4. Pári wa ōkii tokái désŭ ga Róndon wa mótto ōkii désŭ. 5. Dóchira no heyá ga yoroshíi désŭ ka, chiisái hō désŭ ka, ōkii hō désŭ ka.—Ōkii hō ga yoroshíi désŭ. 6. Inoué San no o-niwá wa hirói désŭ, Kimurá San no wa mótto hirói désŭ, shikáshi Morinagá San no wa soré yóri mo mótto hirói désŭ. 7. Sakunén kattá kutsú wa séngetsu kattá no yóri mo zuttó yasúi déshĭta. 8. Nihón-jin ni wa Eigó wa Fŭransú-go yóri mo oboeyasúi désŭ. 9. Kin wa tetsú yóri mo tōtoi désŭ ga tetsú wa kin yóri mo mótto yūeki désŭ. 10. Ajiya no jinkō wa Yōroppa no jinkō yóri mo mótto ōi désŭ. 11. Afuriká wa Yōroppa yóri mo mótto ōkii tairikú désŭ ga Ajiya wa soré yóri mo náo ōkii désŭ. 12. Bóku no gakkō ni wa kimí no gakkō yóri mo séito ga mótto takŭsán imásŭ. 13. Watashí ga súnde irú ié wa anáta no uchí yóri mo ōkii désŭ ga anáta no hō ga mótto sumigókochi[2] ga yói désŭ. 14. Watashí wa áni yóri mo mótto hatarakimásŭ nóni[3] áni no hō ga watashí yóri mo mótto kasegimásŭ.—Jukuren-kō[4] wa tatoé[5] sŭkúnaku hataraité mo fujukurenkō[6] yóri mo ítsumo ōku[7] kasegi-másŭ. 15. Sekái no yondaí kásen wa Hokubéi no Mishishippī, Burajirú no Ama-zón, Afuriká no Náiru soshĭté Shína no Yōsukō désŭ. 16. Pári wa Róndon yóri mo furúi tokái désŭ ga Rōma wa Ōshū de ichibán furúi miyakó désŭ. 17. Inaká ni súnde irú takŭsán no Nihón-jin wa kimonó wo kité imásŭ. Ōki-na tokái de daké daibúbun[8] no hĭtó ga yōfuku wo kité imásŭ. 18. Ippán ni[9]

---

1 When two or more true adjectives depend on the same verb, and the clauses of the sentence are not joined by a conjunction, only the last adjective is used in its normal form, while the others are used in their adverbial form. 2 *sumigókochi ga yói* comfortable to live in 3 *nóni* after a verb means *although* 4 skilled workers 5 *tatoé......mo* even if, though 6 unskilled workers 7 *ōku* adverbial form of *ōi* much 8 the bulk, the majority 9 *ippán ni* generally

otokó wa onná yóri mo mótto kasegimásŭ.—Hataké shigotó¹ wo surú hĭtótachi wa ichibán kasegí ga sŭkunái désŭ. **19.** Koré wa Inábata San no ókŭsan no tesagé désŭ ka.—Inábata San no ókŭsan no ka Kúroda San no ókŭsan no ka zonjimasén. **20.** Dóchira ga anáta no tebúkuro désŭ ka, kochirá désŭ ka, achirá désŭ ka.—Dóchira de mo arimasén. Ryōhō to mo Furukawá San no désŭ. **21.** Anáta ga éki e o-tsŭkí ni nátta tokí watashí no musŭkó wa anáta wo mioboeté orimáshĭta ka.—Hái, musŭkosan wa watashí wo gorán ni náru ya ína ya o-wakarí ni narímáshĭta. **22.** Jishín ga hajimattá totán ni² minná tōri e kakedashimáshĭta. **23.** Watashí wa yūgata taiteí uchí ni orimásŭ. Ráigetsu Tōkyō Daigakú de ukéru shikén³ no júmbi wo shĭté orimásŭ.

1. 大阪は東京から遠く，長崎はもっと遠いです．沖縄は日本帝国で東京から一番遠い所です．**2.** 花子さんは若く，好子さんはもっと若いですが鶴子さんは皆んなの中で一番若いです．**3.** 帽子は皆んなそんなに高いのですか．—いゝえ，旦那さん，こちらの方はもっとお安いです．**4.** 巴里は大きい都会ですがロンドンはもっと大きいです．**5.** どちらの部屋がよろしいですか，小さい方ですか大きい方ですか．—大きい方がよろしいです．**6.** 井上さんのお庭は広いです．木村さんのはもっと広いです然し森長さんのはそれよりももっと広いです．**7.** 昨年買った靴は先月買ったのよりもずっと安いでした．**8.** 日本人には英語はフランス語よりも覚え易いです．**9.** 金は鉄よりも貴いですが鉄は金よりももっと有益です．**10.** アジヤの人口はヨーロッパの人口よりももっと多いです．**11.** アフリカはヨーロッパよりももっと大きい大陸ですがアジヤはそれよりも尚大きいです．**12.** 僕の学校には君の学校よりも生徒がもっと沢山います．**13.** 私が住んでいる家は貴方の家よりも大きいですが貴方の方がもっと住み心地がよいです．**14.** 私は兄よりももっと仂きますのに兄の方が私よりももっと稼ぎます．—熟練工はたとえ少なく仂いても不熟練工よりもいつも多く稼ぎます．**15.** 世界の四大河川は北米のミシシッピー，ブラジルのアマゾン，アフリカのナイルそして支那の揚子江です．**16.** 巴里はロンドンよりも古い都会ですがローマは欧州で一番古い都です．**17.** 田舎に住んでいる沢山の日本人は着物を着ています．大きな都会でだけ大部分の人が洋服を着ています．**18.** 一般に男は女よりももっと稼ぎます．—畑仕事をする人達は一番稼ぎが少ないです．**19.** これは稲畑さんの奥さんの手提ですか．—稲畑さんの奥さんのか黒田さんの奥さんのか存じません．**20.** どちらが貴方の手袋ですか，こちらですかあちらですか．—どちらでもありません．両方とも古川さんのです．**21.** 貴方が駅へお着きになった時私の息子は貴方を見覚えておりましたか．—は

---

1 *hataké shigotó* farm work **2** *totán ni* just as **3** *shikén* examination, *ukéru* to receive, *shikén wo ukéru* to undergo an examination

い，息子さんは私を御覧になるや否やお分りになりました．**22.** 地震
が始まったとたんに皆んな通りへ駆け出しました．**23.** 私は夕方大抵
家にいます．来月東京大学で受ける試験の準備をしております．

1. Osaka is far from Tokyo and Nagasaki is farther. (The Island of) Okinawa is the farthest place in the Japanese Empire from the city of Tokyo.
2. Miss Hanako is young, Miss Yoshiko is younger, but Miss Tsuruko is the
youngest of all. **3.** Are all your hats so dear?—No, sir; these are cheaper.
4. Paris is a large city, but London is larger. **5.** Which room will you
have, the smaller one or the larger one?—I will have the larger one.
6. Mr. Inoue's garden is large, Mr. Kimura's is larger, but Mr. Morinaga's
is still larger. **7.** The shoes I bought last year were much cheaper than the
ones I bought last month. **8.** For the Japanese people English is easier to
learn than French. **9.** Gold is more precious than iron, but iron is more
useful than gold. **10.** The population of Asia is greater than the population
of Europe. **11.** Africa is a larger continent than Europe, but Asia is still
larger. **12.** In our school there are more students than in yours. **13.** The
house in which I live is larger than yours, but your house is more
comfortable than mine. **14.** My elder brother earns more than I, although I
work more than he.—Skilled workers always earn more than unskilled ones,
even though they work little. **15.** The four largest rivers in the world are:
The Mississippi in North America, the Amazon in Brazil, the Nile in Africa,
and the Yang-tse-kiang in China. **16.** Paris is a more ancient city than
London, but Rome is the most ancient capital city in Europe. **17.** Many of
the Japanese living in the country wear kimono; only in the large cities
almost all people wear foreign dresses. **18.** Men generally earn more money
than women.—People working on the farm earn the least. **19.** Is this Mrs.
Inabata's handbag?—I do not know whether it is hers or Mrs. Kuroda's. **20.**
Which gloves are yours, these or those?—Neither are mine; both pairs belong
to Mr. Furukawa. **21.** Did my son recognize you when you arrived at the
station?—Yes, he recognized me as soon as he saw me. **22.** As soon as the
earthquake began everybody ran out in the street. **23.** During the evening
I generally remain at home. I am preparing for the examinations that I shall
take next month at the Tokyo University.

A Japanese Proverb

Kané áreba báka mo danná. 金あれば馬鹿も旦那. *lit.* Money
if there is even a fool a master.=*Money makes the man.* (*kané* 金
money, *áreba* あれば if there is, if one has, *báka* 馬鹿 a fool, *mo*
も even, *danná* 旦那 a master.)

Thirty-ninth Lesson　第卅九課

Comparison (continued)

More than, when used to compare two quantities, is translated by either of the expressions *yóri mo takŭsán* よりも沢山, ...*yóri mo ōku* よりも多く, or......*yóri mo yokéi* よりも余計, placed before the word indicating either the quantity being compared, or the second quantity of the comparison. Each of the three expressions corresponds, translated literally, to......**than many** or **than much.**

*Watashí wa anáta **yóri mo takŭsán** (ōku or yokéi) hon wo mótte*
私　は　貴方　より　も　沢山　（多く，　余計）　本　を持って
imásŭ.　　I have **more** books **than** you have.
います.　　(*lit.* I, you than, many books have.)

*Kochirá no kyōkai wa achirá no hō **yóri mo takŭsán** (ōku or*
こちら　の　教会　はあちら　の　方　より　も　沢山　（多く，
yokéi) shínja ga arimásŭ.　　This church has **more** believers **than** that one.
余計）　信者　が　あります.
　　(*lit.* This church, that one more than, many believers has.)

*Watashí wa kōhī **yóri mo takŭsán** (ōku or yokéi) o-cha wo*
私　はコーヒーより　も　沢山　（多く，　余計）　お茶　を
nomimásŭ.　　I drink **more** tea **than** coffee.
飲みます.　　(*lit.* I, coffee than, much tea drink.)

Yóri mo may be separated from *takŭsán, ōku* or *yokéi* by one of the two things compared, as shown here below:

*Watashí wa anáta **yóri mo** hon wo **takŭsán** (**ōku, yokéi**) mótte imásŭ.*
*Kochirá no kyōkai wa achirá no hō **yóri mo** shínja ga **takŭsán** arimásŭ.*
*Watashí wa kōhī **yóri mo** o-cha wo **takŭsán** (**ōku, yokéi**) nomimásŭ.*

Less......Than

In sentences with **less......than,** if the adjective used for the comparison is a true adjective, it is put in its adverbial form, while quasi-adjectives are followed by *de wa* では. Moreover, *yóri mo* よりも (=than) is placed before the adjective, whether in its adverbial form or not, and the following verb is put in its negative form.

*Watashí wa anáta **yóri mo** kashikóku arimasén* (or *nái.*)
私　は　貴方　より　も　賢く　ありません　（ない.）
I am **less** intelligent **than** you. (I, than you, intelligently am not.)

Kóndo no jimúin wa máe no yóri mo shĭnsetsu de wa arimasén.

今度 の 事務員 は 前 の より も 親切 で は ありません.

The new clerck is **less** kind **than** the previous one. (*or*......not so kind as the......)

(*lit.* This time's clerk, the previous one than, kind is not.)

If, instead of adjectives we compare two quantities, **less......than** is translated by *yóri mo......sŭkúnaku* よりも......少なく (...... than, in small *or* smaller quantity=less).

1. *Watashí wa o-cha yóri mo kōhī wo sŭkúnaku nomimásŭ.*

私 は お茶 より も コーヒーを 少なく 飲みます.

I drink **less** coffee **than** tea. (*lit.* I, tea than, coffee less drink.)

2. *Watashí wa anáta yóri mo kané wo sŭkúnaku mótte imásŭ.*

私 は 貴方 より も 金 を 少なく もって います.

I have **less** money **than** you. (*lit.* I, you than, money less have.)

When the comparison of the two quantities depends on the verb *désŭ* です or *déshĭta* でした, instead of *sŭkúnaku,* 少なく, its adjectival form *sŭkunái* 少ない is used.

Kotoshí no komé no shūkaku wa sakunén yóri mo sŭkunái désŭ.

今年 の 米 の 収穫 は 昨年 より も 少ない です.

This year's rice crop is **less than** last year's.

(*lit.* This year's rice crop, last year than, little is.)

Zaikó no kōhī wa o-cha yóri mo sŭkunái déshĭta.

在庫 のコーヒーは お茶 より も 少ない でした.

The stock of coffee was **less than** the stock of tea.

(*lit.* The stock's coffee, tea than, little was.)

zaikó 在庫 stock, stockpile; *zaikó-hin* 在庫品 goods in the stock.

Fewer......Than......

Fewer than is translated in the same way as *less......than.*

3. *Watashí wa nashí wo ringó yóri mo sŭkúnaku kaimáshĭta.*

私 は 梨 を りんご より も 少なく 買いました.

I bought **fewer** pears **than** apples.

Sonó enkái ni fujín yóri mo otokó-no-hĭtó ga sŭkunái déshĭta.

その 宴会 に 婦人 より も 男の人 が 少ない でした.

At the party there were **fewer** men **than** ladies.

(*lit.* That party at, ladies than, male persons few were.)

Note. Negative comparisons like the preceding ones with *yóri mo sŭkúnaku* よりも少なく, are generally avoided by Japanese in preference of a positive construction. Therefore, the above sentences marked **1, 2** and **3** would be generally expressed as follows:

1. *Watashí wa kōhī yóri mo o-cha wo yokéi nomimásŭ.*

(*lit.* I, coffee than, tea much drink.)

2. *Anáta wa watashí yóri mo o-kané wo takŭsán mótte imásŭ.*

(*lit.* You, I than, money much have.)

3. *Watashí wa nashí yóri mo ringó wo yokéi kaimáshĭta.*
　　(*lit.* I, pears than, apples many bought.)

Comparison of Equality

as...............as
as much......as   }   *......to onaji guraí (ni)*
as many......as   }   ......と 同じ 　位　 （に）

Translated literally, the expression......*to onaji guraí* corresponds to......
as the same about (=about the same).

Anáta wa Tanaká San to onaji guraí (ni) fŭtótte imásŭ.
貴方 は 田中 さん と 同じ 　位　 （に） 太って います.
You are (about) **as fat as** Mr. Tanaka.

Suzukí San no obasán wa watashí no obá to onaji guraí zaisán
鈴木 さん の伯母さん は 　私　 の伯母 と 同じ 　位　 財産
wo mótte imásŭ.　　Mr. Suzuki's aunt has (about) **as much** property **as** my aunt.
を 持っています.

Anó gaijín wa anáta to onaji guraí inú wo mótte imásŭ.
あの 外人 は 貴方 と 同じ 　位　 犬 を 持っています.
That foreigner has (about) **as many** dogs **as** you have.

The sameness of the qualities or the quantities compared are expressed with more precision by the word ***chōdo*** 丁度 placed before *onaji guraí.* ***Chōdo*** means *just, exactly, precisely.*

Anáta wa Tanaká San to chōdo onaji guraí (ni) fŭtótte imásŭ.
貴方 は 田中 さん と 丁度 同じ 　位　 （に） 太っています.
You are **just as** fat **as** Mr. Tanaka.

These comparative expressions with *guraí,* however, do not indicate real exactness in the degree of the two qualities, or in the quantities compared, but rather indicate approximation. When we wish to emphasize that the compared qualities are really the same, without the least difference, the expression *to chōdo onaji daké* と丁度同じだけ (as, just the same only) is used.

Konó hakó no náka ni wa anó hakó no náka to chōdo onaji daké
この 箱 の 中 には あの 箱 の 中 と 丁度 同じ だけ
empitsú ga arimásŭ.　　In this box there are **just as many** pencils **as** in that
鉛筆 が あります.　　　　one.
　　(In this box, that box inside as, just the same only, pencils there are.)

The word ***chōdo*** may be separated from the rest of the two comparative expressions.

Anáta wa chōdo watashí to onaji daké torí wo mótte imásŭ.
貴方 は 丁度 私 と 同じ だけ 鳥 を 持って います.
You have **just as many** birds **as** I have.
　　(*lit.* You, just I as, the same only, birds have.)

*Anáta no heyá no ōkisa wa **chōdo** watashí no heyá **to onají**[1] dèsŭ.*
貴方 の 部屋 の大きさは 丁度 私 の 部屋 と 同じ です.
Your room is just as large as mine.
(*lit.* Your room's size, just my room as, the same is.)

The following negative comparative expressions are translated into
Japanese by positive expressions:

no less ......than   no fewer ......than

not less......than   not fewer......than

*......**to chōdo onají gurai**......* (......as, just the same about)
と 丁度 同じ 位

*......**to onají gurai ka soré íjō*** (......as, the same about?—that more)
と 同じ 位 か それ 以上

*......**to onají gurai ka arŭiwa soré íjō*** (......as, the same about? or
と 同じ 位 か 或るいは それ以上 that more)

Soré íjō means *more than that; **ka*** interrogation particle, ***arŭiwa*** *or.*

*Anó hĭtó wa anáta **to chōdo onají gurai** o-kané wo mótte imásŭ.*
あの 人 は 貴方 と 丁度 同じ 位 お金 を 持っています.
That man has **no less** money **than** you.
(*lit.* That person, you as, just the same about, money has.)

*Hánako San wa Tóshiko San **to onají guraí ka soré íjō** rikō de arimásŭ.*
花子 さん は とし子さんと 同じ 位 か それ以上利口であります.
Miss Hanako is **not less** clever **than** Miss Toshiko.
(*lit.* Miss Hanako, Miss Toshiko as, the same about? that more clever is.**)**

If the quantity compared is specified by a number, *to **onají*** or *to **chōdo**,*
is omitted.

*Watashí wa 200 (ni-hyakŭ) satsŭ gurai **ka arŭiwa soré íjō** hon*
私 は 二百 冊 位 か 或るいはそれ 以上 本
wo mótte imásŭ.   I have **no fewer than** 200 books.
を 持っています.   (*lit.* I 200 volumes about? or that more books have.)

Not so......as......   Not as......as......

Both expressions are translated by ***hodó*** 程, which corresponds
to the comparative element **as,** followed by a **negative verb.**

*Anáta no nēsan wa anáta **hodó** benkyō shimasén.*
貴方 の 姉さん は 貴方 程 勉強 しません.
Your elder sister does **not** study **as** much **as** you do.
(*lit.* Your elder sister, you as, study doesn't.)

*Watashí wa anáta **hodó** takŭsán no tomodachi ga arimasén.*
私 は 貴方 程 沢山 の 友達 が ありません。
I have **not as** many friends as you have.
(*lit.* I, you as, many friends have not.)

---

1 Speaking of places that are made to established dimensions, as Japanese rooms
for instance, neither *gurai* nor *daké* may be used after the expression *chōdo onají.*

In comparing a quality represented by a *true adjective*, this is used in its adverbial form and is followed by *arimasén*.

Konó nikú wa anó nikú **hodó yawarákaku arimasén.**
この　肉　は　あの　肉　程　　柔らかく　ありません.
This meat is **not so** tender **as** that.
(*lit.* This meat, that meat as, tenderly is not.)

If the quality compared is represented by a *quasi-adjective*, this is followed by *de wa arimasén*.

Yamáguchi San wa Nakamurá San hodó **kanemochí de wa arimasén.**
山口　さん　は　中村　さん　程　金持　で　は　ありません.
Mr. Yamaguchi is **not so** rich **as** Mr. Nakamura.
(*lit.* Mr. Yamaguchi, Mr. Nakamura as, moneyed-man is not.)

As Well As......

This expression may be translated by......*to onaji gurai* と同じ 位 (......as, the same about), ...*to onájiku* と同じく (......as, similarly), ...*to onaji yō-ni* と同じように (......as, the same as).

Watashí wa Nihón-go wo Shiná-go **to onaji gurai** shĭtté imásŭ.
私　は　日本語　を　支那語　と　同じ　位　知っています.
I know Japanese about **as well** as I know Chinese.
(*lit.* I, Japanese language, Chinese language as, the same about know.)

Nihón wa Eikokú **to onájiku** (or **onaji yō-ni**) úmi ni yotté torikakomareté[1]
日本　は　英国　と　同じく　（同じ　ように）海　によって　取り囲まれて
irú.   Japan like (**as well as**) England, is surrounded by water.
いる.   (*lit.* Japan, England as, similarly (or the same as), by sea is surrounded.)

Other comparative expressions often used in Japanese, are *yō-na* ような (adjective) and *yō-ni* ように (adverb). These expressions, however, do not always correspond to English comparative elements, although they maintain the idea conveyed by the expressions **as, as if, like, so as to, in order to,** as it may be seen from the following examples.

yō-na ような

Yō-na ような corresponds, in most cases, to *kind, sort, such like thing......, such as, like, as.*

Konó **yō-na** shiná. このような品。   An article of this **kind.**
Sonná **yō-na** katté-dōgu.   Kitchen utensils **such as** those.
そんな　ような　勝手道具　　(*katté* kitchen)
Atarashíi hishó wa dónna **yō-na** hĭtó désŭ ka. What sort of man is
新しい　秘書　は　どんな　ような　人　です　か。 the new secretary?
Watashí wa sō iú **yō-na** monó wo kesshĭté kaimasén.
私　はそういう　ような　もの　を　決して　買いません。
I never buy that **sort** of things. (*kesshĭté* never)

---

1 *torikakomú* to surround; *torikakomarerú* to be surrounded; *ni yotté* by

Soré wa imá-máde tábeta kotó no nái yō-na monó déshĭta.
それ は 今 まで 食べた 事 のない ような もの でした.
That was a thing **such as** I never ate before. (That, until now ate the fact
there is not, such thing was.)

Koré wa watashí ga nakŭshĭtá no to onáji yō-na mannenhitsú désŭ.
これ は 私 が 失くした の と 同じ ような 万年筆 です.
This is a similar fountain pen **as** the one I lost. (*nakŭsú* to lose)

Káre wa konó mondaí ni tsúite shĭtté irú yō-na kotó wo iimásŭ.
彼 は この 問題 について 知つている ような 事 を 云います.
He talks as if he knew about this matter. (*mondaí* matter, affair)

Waraitái yō-na ki ga shimáshĭta.   I felt **like** laughing.
笑いたい ような 気 が しました.   (I wish to laugh like, I felt.)

Háha no yō-na aijō.   Affection **of** a mother.
母 の ような 愛情.   (*lit.* Mother's like affection.)

Ténshi no yō-na fujín.   An angel of a woman. (*lit.* Angel-**like** woman.)
天使 の ような 婦人。

Anáta no musŭkosán no yō-na kimbén-na[1] kodomó wa makotó-ni
あなた の 息子さん の ような 勤勉 な 子供 は 誠に
mezurashíi désŭ.   Boys **as** diligent **as** your son are very rare indeed.
珍しい です.   (Your son **as,** diligent boys indeed rare are.)

O-takú no o-jōsan no yō-na otonashíi katá wo míta kotó ga arimasén.
お宅 のお嬢さんの ようなおとなしい 方 を 見た 事 がありません.
I have never seen **so** quiet a person **as** your daughter.
(Your daughter **as,** quiet person, seen thing there is not.)

Nikaí[2] e dáre ka kúru yō-na otó wo kikimáshĭta.
二階 へ 誰 か 来る ような 音 を 聞きました.
I heard a noise **as if** somebody was coming upstairs.
(To the second floor, someone to come **as if,** noise I heard.)

Sonó yō-na (or *Sō iú yō-na*) *kotó wo iú monó de wa arimasén.*
その ような （そういうような） 事 を いうもの で はありません.
You shouldn't say a thing **like** that.
(That **like** thing, to say, the fact to be there is not.＝That is not a thing to
be said. *or* Such a thing is not a thing to be said.)

Konó yō-na (or *Konná*) *keitó[3] wo utté imasén ka.*   Do you not sell woolen
この ような （こんな）毛糸 を売っていませんか.   yarn **like** this?

Neté itá tokí ni kínu wo sáku[4] yō-na kóe de me ga samemáshĭta.
寝ていた 時 に 絹 を さく ような 声 で 目 が さめました.
While I was sleeping I was awakened by a shrill voice.
(Sleeping was when, silk-to-tear-**like** cry by, the eyes awoke.—*me ga saméru* 目
が さめる to awake—*lit.* the eyes become conscious)

yō-ni ように

Yō-ni ように corresponds, in most cases, to *so as to, in order
to, so that one may* and other expressions of similar meaning. In

---

1 *kimbén-na* diligent   **2** second floor, upstairs   **3** woolen yarn   **4** to tear

some cases it indicates the *way* or *manner*.

Watashí wa anáta ga anó jímen wo te ni irareprerú **yō-ni** *shimashō.*
私　は　貴方　が　あの　地面　を　手　に入れられるようにしましよう.
I will see that you get that plot of land.　(*lit.* I, you that land in the hand
to be put so as to, will do.—*te ni irerú* to put into the hand=to obtain, *te
ni irarerú* to be put into the hand=to be obtained)

Watashí wa Mosŭkō ni tenkín surú **yō-ni** *iwaremáshĭta.*
私　は モスコー に　転勤　する　ように　云われました.
It was suggested to me that I might be transferred to Moscow.
(*tenkín surú* to be transferred to another office, *iwarerú* to be told)

Ashĭtá, narubéku kúru **yō-ni** *shimásŭ.*　　I will try and come to-morrow.
あした　なるべく　来る　ように　します.　　　(*narubéku* as far as possible)

Konó dempō wo súgu dásu **yō-ni** *shĭté kudasái.*
この　電報　を　すぐ　出す　ように　して　下さい.
See that this telegram be sent at once. (*dempō wo dásu* to send a telegram)

Káre no chūi wo hikú **yō-ni** *watashí wa káre ni mekúbase shimáshĭta.*
彼　の　注意　を　ひくように　私　は　彼　に　目くばせ　しました.
I winked at him by way of arresting his attention. (*chūi wo hikú* to pull the
attention=to draw, arrest someone's attention; *mekúbase surú* to wink signi-
ficantly at)

Konó **yō-ni.** このように.　　Thus. Like this. In this manner.

Dóno **yō-ni.** どのように.　　How?—In what manner?

Onají **yō-ni** *shĭté kudasái.* Do it in the same way *or* in the same manner.
同じ　ように　して　下さい.

Watashí no yōfuku wo konná **yō-ni** *tsŭkútte moraitái désŭ.*
私　の　洋服　を　こんな　ように　つくってもらいたいです.
I want to have my suit made **like** this.
(My suit such **like,** making wish to get—or to have—is.)

Anó fujín wa néko wo chōdo wágako no **yō-ni** *kawaigarimásŭ.*
あの　婦人　は　猫　を　丁度　わが子　の　ように　可愛がります.
That lady loves her cat as her own baby. (*wágako* one's own child)
(That lady, cat just own-child **like,** loves.—*kawaigáru* to make a pet of)

Go-ryōshin ga ossháru **yō-ni** *nasái.* Do as your parents tell you.
御両親　がおっしゃるように　なさい.　　(Your parents tell **like** do.)

Kyūkō ni ma-ni-áu **yō-ni** *háyaku okimáshĭta.*　I got up early so **as to** be
急行　に　間にあうように　早く　起きました.　　in time for the express.
(Express train for, be in time **as to,** early I got up.)

Isogashíi **yō-ni** *miemásŭ.*　　He seems to be busy. He looks **as if** he were
忙しい　ように　見えます.　　busy. (Busy **as if** he looks.)

Konó shigotó wo ashĭtá máde ni oerú **yō-ni** *shĭté kudasái.*
この　仕事　を　あした　迄　に終えるように　して　下さい.
Please, finish this work by to-morrow.
(This work, to-morrow until by, to finish **in order to,** do please.)

Ima súgu kutsú wo migakú[1] ***yō-ni*** *o-tétsudai ni itté kudasái.*
今 すぐ 靴 を みがく ように お手伝い に云って 下さい.
Tell the maid to polish my shoes at once.
(Now at once, the shoes to polish **in order to,** the servant to, tell please.)

Chichí wa taitéi mái ban no ***yō-ni*** *kúrabu*[2] *e dekaketé ikimásŭ.*
父 は 大抵 毎 晩 の ように クラブ へ出かけて 行きます.
My father generally goes to the club almost every night.
(My father, generally, every evening **as if,** to the club going out goes.)

O-wasuré[3] *monó nái* ***yō-ni*** *negaimásŭ.*   Please do not forget anything.
お忘れ 物 ない ように 願います.
(Forgotten things there-are-not **so as,** I beg.)

Preceded by a negative verb, ***yō-ni*** ように corresponds to *in order not to, so as not to, that one may not......* In such cases, the simple stem of verbs of Class I and the *a*-stem of verbs of Class II are used, followed by the negative suffix ***nai*** ない or ***nu*** ぬ, as shown in the following examples:

Kowasánai[4] ***yō-ni*** *ki wo tsŭkéte koré wo hakondé*[5] *kudasái.*
こわさない ように 気 を つけて これ を 運んで 下さい.
Carry this carefully **so as not to** break it.
(Not-to-break in order to, paying attention carry please.)

Korobanái[6] ***yō-ni*** *nasái.*   Pay attention **not to** fall.
ころばない ように なさい.   (Not to fall in order to, do.)

Kusaránu[7] ***yō-ni*** *koré wo reizōko*[8] *no náka e iré nasái.*
くさらぬ ように これ を 冷蔵庫 の 中 へ入れなさい.
Put this into the icebox to prevent it from getting bad.
(Not to rot **in order to,** this, icebox inside put please.)

Irregular verbs:

surú する to do, *shinái* しない not to do, ***shinái yō-ni*** しないように in order not to do, so as not to do, etc.

kúru 来る to come, *kónai* 来ない not to come, ***kónai yō-ni*** 来ないように in order not to come, so as not to come, etc.

Yō-ni may be used at the end of a sentence, in which case it generally corresponds to *I wish, I hope* and other expressions of similar meaning.

Sonná-ni takŭsán nikú wo tabénai ***yō-ni.***   **I wish** you would not eat
そんなに 沢山 肉 を 食べないように.   so much meat.

Anó katá wo okorasénai ***yō-ni.***   **I hope** you will not offend him.
あの 方 を 怒らせない ように.

(That person not to cause to be offended I hope.)—*okóru* 怒る to be offended, *okoraséru* 怒らせる to offend, to cause to be offended)

---

1 *migakú* みがく to polish 2 *kúrabu* クラブ club 3 *wasurerú* 忘れる to forget, *wasuré monó* 忘れ物 forgotten things 4 *kowásu* こわす to break 5 *hakobú* 運ぶ to carry 6 *korobú* ころぶ to fall 7 *kusáru* くさる to rot 8 *reizōko* 冷蔵庫 icebox

Kazé wo hikanái **yō-ni.**   **I hope** you will not catch a cold.
かぜ を 引かない ように.
(Cold not to catch I hope, I wish.—*kazé wo hikú* かぜを引く to catch a cold)

yō-ni surú ようにする

Hi ga kienái[1] **yō-ni** *shi nasái.*   Don't let that fire go out.
火 が消えない ように し なさい.
(The fire not to go out **in order to,** do please.)

Watashí ga iitsŭkéta[2] **yō-ni** *shimáshĭta ka.* Did you do as I told you?
私　が云いつけたように しました　か.   (I ordered **as,** did you do?)

Myōnichi no sōkai ni wa okurenái[3] **yō-ni** *shĭté kudasái.*
明日　の 総会 に はおくれないように して 下さい.
Please do not be late at to-morrow general meeting.
(To-morrow's general meeting at, not-to-be-late **in order to,** do please.)

Háyaku o-naorí nasáru[4] **yō-ni** *shĭtái monó désŭ.*   I hope you will soon
早く おなおりなさる ように したい もの です.   recover.
(Quickly recovery to become **in order to,** I wish the fact to be.)

Watashí wa ashĭtá kúru **yō-ni** *shimásŭ.*   I will try to come to-morrow.
私　は あした 来る ように します.
(I to-morrow, to come **in order to** I do.)

yō-ni náru ようになる

Konogoró wa hikōki de sekái isshū[5] ga dekíru **yō-ni** *narimáshĭta.*
この頃　は 飛行機 で 世界 一周 が 出来る ように なりました.
Nowadays it is possible to go round the world by airplane.
(Nowadays, airplane by, the world round, to be able **as,** has become.)

Uchí no akambō[6] wa hĭtóri de arúku[7] **yō-ni** *narimáshĭta.*
うち の 赤ん坊 は 一人 で 歩く ように なりました.
Our baby is now able to walk by himself.
(Home baby, alone to walk, **able** has become.)

Dái-tokái de wa taitéi no nihonjín ga yōfuku wo kirú **yō-ni** *narimáshĭta.*
大都会 で は 大抵 の 日本人 が 洋服 を 着るように なりました.
In large cities almost all Japanese have become accustomed to wear foreign clothes. (Large cities in, nearly-every Japanese, foreign suit to wear, **accustomed** have become.)

yō désŭ ようです

Yō désŭ ようです corresponds to *it seems, it looks like, as if.*

Ame ga fúru yō **désŭ.**   It looks **like** rain.
雨 が 降る よう です.   (Rain to fall looks like).

---

1 *kierú* 消える to go out, to die out, said of fire   2 *iitsŭkéru* 云いつける to order, to tell   3 *okurerú* おくれる to be late   4 *o-naorí nasáru* おなおりなさる to recover   5 *sekái isshū* round the world   6 baby   7 to walk.

Pentorá Hákase[1] *wa nihón-go ga taihén o-sŭkí no yō dèsŭ.*
ペントラ 博士 は 日本語 が 大変 お好き の よう です.
  Dr. Pentler seems to like the Japanese language very much.
  (Doctor Pentler Japanese language much likes, **it seems.**)

Koré wa yói kiré no yō dèsŭ.   This seems to be a good cloth.
これ はよい きれ の よう です.   (This good cloth **looks like.**)

Sonó otokó wa tantéi[2] *no yō dèshita.*   That man looked like a detective.
その 男 は 探偵 の よう でした.   (That man detective **as if** was.)

Yō よう after the simple stem of verbs of Class I and after the
i-stem of verbs of Class II gives the meaning of **the way of doing.**

Konó hakó no akè yō ga dō-shĭtè-mo wakarimasén.
この 箱 の 開け よう が どうしても わかりません.
  I don't know how to open this box by any means.
  (This box opening's the way of doing, by any means don't understand.)

Késa wa kutsú no migakí yō ga tarinákatta.[3]
けさ は 靴 の みがき よう が 足りなかった.
  You didn't polish my shoes well enough this morning.
  (This morning, shoes polishing, the way of doing was not enough.)

Anó hĭtó no warai yō ga ki ni irimasén.   I don't like the way
あの 人 の 笑い よう が 気 に入りません.   he smiles.

(That person's laughing the way of doing, feeling into doesn't enter.—*ki ni irú*
気に入る to like, *lit.* to enter *or* touch one's feeling; *ki ni iranái* 気に入らない
not to like, to dislike, *lit.* not to enter *or* not to touch one's feelings.)

The former......the latter
zénsha......*kōsha*...... 前者......後者

The expression *zénsha*......*kōsha* 前者......後者 for **the former
......the latter** is used in written style. In conversation the words
corresponding to *the former......the latter* are generally repeated.

Fújisan to Shiranè-san wa Nippón de ichibán takái yamá dèsŭ. **Fújisan**
富士山 と 白根山 は 日本 で 一番 高い 山 です. 富士山
(*zénsha*) *wa Shizuokakén ni ári, Shiranè-san* (*kōsha*) *wa Yamanashikén ni*
(前者) は 静岡 県 にあり, 白根山 (後者) は 山梨 県 に
arimásŭ. Mount Fuji and Mount Shiranè are the two highest mountains in Japan:
あります. **the former** is in Shizuoka prefecture, **the latter** is in Yamanashi prefecture.

Never, Rarely, Seldom

Never is translated by *késshĭte* 決して or *kátsŭte* かつて; **rarely**
by *tamá ni shĭká* たまにしか or *métta ni* めったに; **seldom**

---
1 *hákase* Doctor (academical degree) **2** detective **3** *tarirú* 足りる to be enough

by *métta ni* めったに. The verb after any of these Japanese expressions is used in the negative.

The use of a negative verb after the above Japanese expressions, whose English corresponding words, in themselves, have a negative meaning, may be compared to the double negative used in expressions of some European languages, as for instance, in the French **Je n'ai jamais vu cela.** *I have never seen that.* (*lit.* I have **not** never seen that.)

Watashí wa **késshĭte** *Shiná-go wo benkyō shĭtá kotó ga* **arimasén.**
私　は　決して　支那語　を　勉強　した　事　が　ありません.
I **never** studied the Chinese language.
  (*lit.* I, never, Chinese language study did, the fact is not.)

Watashí wa **kátsŭte** *anó hĭtó wo máe ni míta kotó ga* **arimasén.**
私　は　かつて　あの　人　を　前　に　見た　事　が　ありません.
I **never** saw that man before.
  (*lit.* I, never that person before saw, the fact there is not.)

Kanekó San wa **métta ni** *watashí no uchí ni kimasén.*
金子　さん　は　めった　に　私　の　家　に　来ません.
Mr. Kaneko **seldom** comes to my house.
  (*lit.* Mr. Kaneko seldom to my house does not come.)

Chichí wa shibaí ni **tamá ni shĭká** *ikimasén.*
父　は　芝居　に　たま　に　しか　行きません.
My father goes to the theatre only on rare occasions.
  (*lit.* My father to theater rarely does not go.)

For a better understanding in the use of the four above expressions, their various corresponding meanings are here given:

késshĭte	決して	never, by no means, in no way, not in the least
métta ni	めったに	rarely, seldom, least likely
kátsŭte	かつて	once, on one occasion, at one time
tamá ni	たまに	once in a while, occasionally, now and then
shĭká	しか	but, no more than, merely, simply
tamá ni shĭká	たまにしか	no more than once in a while=rarely

The expression **késshĭte** 決して (never), **métta ni** めったに (rarely) and **tamá ni shĭká** たまにしか (rarely) may be used only with a negative verb. However, the expressions **kátsŭte** かつて and **tamá ni** たまに without *shĭká* しか, may also be used with a positive verb, as in the following examples:

Kánojo wa **kátsŭte** *joyū* **déshĭta.**   She was **once** (at one time, etc.)
彼女　は　かつて　女優　でした.   an actress.

Kánojo wa **kátsŭte** *joyū de wa* **arimasén déshĭta.**   She **never** was
彼女　は　かつて　女優　で　は　ありません　でした.   an actress.
  (*lit.* She once actress was not.=She never was an actress.)

Watashí wa sonná kotó wo **kátsŭte kikimasén** *déshĭta.*
私　はそんな　事　を　かつて　聞きません　でした.
I have **never** heard such a thing.
  (*lit.* I such a thing once haven't heard.—once haven't=never)

*Pan wo **tamá ni tabemásŭ.***   I eat bread **once in a while.**
パン を たま に 食べます.

*Pan wo **tamá ni shĭka tabemasén,***   I **rarely** eat bread. (=I eat bread
パン を たま に しか 食べません.   no more than once in a while.)

*Watashí wa sonná kotó wo **kátsŭte** kikimáshĭta.*   **At one time** I heard
私   は そんな 事 を かつて 聞きました.   such a thing.
(*lit.* I such thing on one occasion heard.)

Note. The above negative sentences have been given for comparison.

Sometime (or other), Ever
Itsŭka いつか

Itsŭka いつか corresponds also to *some day, sooner or later, in the long run.*

*Anáta wa **ítsŭka** Itarī e o-kaerí ni nárŭ[1] deshō ka.*   Will you **ever** go
貴方 は いつかイタリーへお帰り に なるでしょうか.   back to Italy?

*Watashí wa **ítsŭka** Itarī e káeru deshō.*   I shall go back to Italy
私   は いつかイタリーへ 帰るでしょう.   **sometime.**

Itsŭka いつか is used in the following common expressions:

matá ítsŭka	またいつか	some other time
raishū no ítsŭka	来週のいつか	sometime next week
ítsŭka sonó uchí ni	いつかその中に	one of these days

Without

Before a noun **without** is translated by *náshi de* 無しで.

*Mizŭ **náshi de** (wa) shokúbutsu wa sodátánai.*[2]   **Without** water plants
水   無し で (は)   植物   は 育たない.   do not grow.

Náshi de may be followed by **wa** when the verb of the principal clause is used in the negative, as in the above example, and when emphasis is to be expressed.

*Bōshi **náshi de** dekakemáshĭta.*   He went out **without** his hat.
帽子 無し で 出かけました.

When **without** is used before verbs, it is translated by the expression *zu ni* affixed to the simple stem of verbs of Class I and to the *a*-stem of verbs of Class II. See Lesson 25, page 167

*Chichí wa hĭtó kotó[3] mo iwazŭ **ni** déte yukimáshĭta.*
父 は 一 言 も 言わず に 出て 行きました.
My father went out **without saying** a word.

*Tábezu **ni** nemáshĭta.* 食べずに寝ました.   I went to bed **without eating.**

---

1 *O-kaerí ni nárŭ* お帰りになる polite form for *káeru* to return. **2** *sodátsu* to grow, *sodatánai* not to grow **3** *hĭtó kotó mo* 一言も even a word

Vocabulary

Nouns			Adjectives		
believer	*shínja*	信ｼﾝ者ｼﾞｬ	expensive	*kōka*	高ｺｳ価ｶ
factory	*kōjō*	工ｺｳ場ｼﾞｮｳ	industrialized	*sangyōteki*	産業的
hen	*mendorí*	牝ﾒﾝ鶏ﾄﾞﾘ	patient	*shimbōzuyoi*	辛棒強ｲ
inhabitant	*jūmin*	住ｼﾞｭｳ民ﾐﾝ	skilful	*kíyō-na*	器ｷ用ﾖｳﾅ
knowledge	*chíshiki*	知ﾁ識ｼｷ	strange	*hen-na*	変ﾍﾝﾅ
property	*zaisán*	財ｻﾞｲ産ｻﾝ	unskilful	*hetá-na*	下ﾍ手ﾀﾅ
sheep	*hitsují*	羊ﾋﾂｼﾞ	**Verbs**		
shepherd	*hitsujikaí*	羊ﾋﾂｼﾞ飼ｶｲ	to climb	*noború*	登ﾉﾎﾞﾙ
typhoon	*bōfū*	暴ﾎﾞｳ風ﾌｳ	to deliver	*kubáru*	配ｸﾊﾞﾙ
victim	*higáisha*	被ﾋ害ｶﾞｲ者ｼｬ	to employ	*yatóu*	雇ﾔﾄｳ
wages	*chíngin*	賃ﾁﾝ銀ｷﾞﾝ	to increase	*masú*	増ﾏｽ
fish	{ *uó* (lit.)	魚ｳｵ	**Adverbs**		
	{ *sakaná* (colloq.)	魚ｻｶﾅ	next	*kóndo no*	今ｺﾝ度ﾄﾞﾉ

male factory hand *dankō*; female factory hand (young or of age) *jokōin*; river fish *kawá-uó*; factory boy *shōnenkō*; mother tongue *jikokú-go*; Japan Proper *Honshū*

Exercise *Renshū* 練習

1. Ippán ni Nihón-jin wa nikú yóri mo sakaná wo yokéi ni tabemásŭ. **2.** Asa gyūnyū wo kubáru anó nōfu wa oushí yóri mo meushí wo yokéi mótte imásŭ. **3.** Kyūshū wa Shikóku yóri mo jūmin ga ōi désŭ. **4.** Konó kōjō wa dankō yóri mo jokōin no hō wo yokéi ni yatótte imásŭ. **5.** Mendorí to háto to dóchira ga yokéi (ni) tamagó wo umimásŭ[1] ka shĭtté imásŭ ka.—Shĭtté imásŭ tómo,[2] mendorí no hō ga yokéi (ni) tamagó wo umimásŭ. **6.** Watashí wa anáta yóri mo hetá désŭ ga anáta yóri mo shimbōzuyoi désŭ. Tatoé[3] hijō ni kíyō de nákute mo[3] móshi shimbōzuyoi náraba takŭsán shigotó wo surú kotó ga dekimásŭ. **7.** Ōsaka wa Tōkyō hodó ōkii tokái de wa arimasén ga Tōkyō yóri mo sangyōteki désŭ. **8.** Watashí wa áni yóri mo zaisán ga sŭkunái ga áni yóri mo kōfuku désŭ. **9.** Anó nōfu wa ushí yóri mo umá wo sŭkúnaku mótte imásŭ ga umá no hō ga dóno[4] ushí yóri mo kōka désŭ. **10.** Konó máe no bōfu de higáisha wa sanzén-nin wo kudaranákatta.[5] **11.** Sumidá Kun wa bóku to onají guraí hon wo mótte imásŭ ga kesshĭté hon wo yomimasén kará gakkō wo déte írai chittómo chíshiki wo mashĭté imasén. **12.** Anó hitsujikaí wa dóno kuraí hitsují wo mótte imásŭ ka.—Hyakú-hiki wa kudaranái[5] to omoimásŭ. **13.** Jokōin ya shōnenkō wa dankō yóri mo hatarakemasén kará dankō yóri mo chíngin ga sŭkunái désŭ. **14.** Kabukí-za wa Nihón-gekijō yóri mo ōkiku arimasén ga mótto utsŭkushíi désŭ. **15.** Kawá-uó wa úmi no sakaná yóri mo oishikú arimasén. **16.** Mótto yói heyá ga arimasén ka.— Koré wa konó uchí de ichibán yói heyá désŭ. **17.** Fŭransú-go wo o-hanashí

---

1 *umú* to give birth to, to lay eggs **2** of course **3** *tatoé......nákute mo* even without, *kíyō de nákute mo* even without being skilful **4** *dóno* any of, whichever **5** *kudarú* to be less than, to be inferior to; *kudaranákatta* were no fewer than

ni narimásŭ ka.—Hái, jikokú-go no Itarī-go to onají kuraí ni hanashimásŭ.
18. Ishikarí-gawá to Shinanó-gawá wa Nihón de ichibán nagái kawá désŭ.
Ishikarí-gawá (zénsha) wa Hokkaidō ni ári, Shinanó-gawá (kōsha) wa Honshū
no chūōbu[1] ni arimásŭ. **19.** Fújisan e nobottá kotó ga arimásŭ ka.—Iié, arimasén ga kóndo no natsú nobotté mitái to omoimásŭ. **20.** Watashí wa jū-
ichí-ji máe ni wa métta ni yasumimasén. **21.** Anáta wa tokidokí hikōki de
go-ryokō nasaimasén ka.—Tamá ni shiká shǐmasén ; Ōsaka e hikōki de ni-
do ittá bákari désŭ. **22.** Fukunó San no ókŭsan wa watashí no sóba[2] wo
tōtta tokí ni shiranái furí wo shimáshǐta.—Anó katá wa sŭkóshi hen-na katá
désŭ. Anó katá wa tokidokí ā iú yō-na[3] kotó wo nasaimásŭ. **23.** Shóseki
náshi de wa chíshiki wo takŭsán masú kotó ga dekimasén. **24.** Késa watashí
wa osokú ókita nóde éki e o-kané wo mótazu[4] ni ittá hodó[5] awatemáshǐta.
Sokó de[6] watashí wa ié ni hikikáeshǐte[7] o-kané wo mótte fŭtatabí éki e ikimáshǐta.—Ningén[8] wa awateté irú tokí ni wa kokóro[9] ga yóku hatarakanái
monó désŭ.

1. 一般に日本人は肉よりも魚を余計に食べます. **2.** 朝牛乳を配る
あの農夫は牡牛よりも牝牛を余計もっています. **3.** 九州は四国より
も住民が多いです. **4.** この工場は男工よりも女工員の方を余計に雇
っています. **5.** 牝鶏と鳩とどちらが余計(に)玉子を生みますか知っ
ていますか.—知っていますとも, 牝鶏の方が余計(に)玉子を生みま
す. **6.** 私は貴方よりも下手ですが貴方よりも辛棒強いです. たとえ非
常に器用でなくても若し辛棒強いならば沢山仕事をする事が出来ま
す. **7.** 大阪は東京ほど大きい都会ではありませんが東京よりも産業
的です. **8.** 私は兄よりも財産が少ないが兄よりも幸福です. **9.** あの
農夫は牛よりも馬を少なく持っていますが馬の方がどの牛よりも高価
です. **10.** この前の暴風で被害者は三千人を下らなかった. **11.** 隅田
君は僕と同じぐらい本を持っていますが決して本を読みませんから学
校を出て以来ちっとも知識を増していません. **12.** あの羊飼はどのく
らい羊を持っていますか.—百匹は下らないと思います. **13.** 女工員
や少年工は男工よりも働けませんから男工よりも賃銀が少ないです.
14. 歌舞伎座は日本劇場よりも大きくありませんがもっと美しいです.
15. 川魚は海の魚よりもおいしくありません. **16.** もっとよい部屋が
ありませんか.—これはこの家で一番よい部屋です. **17.** フランス語
をお話しになりますか.—はい, 自国語のイタリー語と同じ位に話しま
す. **18.** 石狩川と信濃川は日本で一番長い川です. 石狩川(前者)は
北海道にあり, 信濃川(後者)は本州の中央部にあります. **19.** 富士山
へ登った事がありますか.—いゝえ, ありませんが今度の夏登って見た

---

1 central part **2** near, by **3** *ā iú yō-na* like that **4** without taking **5** *awaterú* to
be in a hurry, *hodó* such, *ittá hodó awatemáshǐta* I went in such a hurry that
6 *sokó de* therefore **7** *hikikáesu* to return (to the place where one started) and go
back again (where one went first) **8** people, human beings **9** heart, mind

いと思います．　**20.** 私は十一時前にはめったに休みません．　**21.** 貴方は時々飛行機で御旅行なさいませんか．—たまにしかしません．大阪へ飛行機で二度行ったばかりです．　**22.** 福野さんの奥さんは私のそばを通った時に知らない振りをしました．—あの方は少し変な方です．あの方は時時ああいうような事をなさいます．　**23.** 書籍なしでは知識を沢山増す事が出来ません．　**24.** けさ私は遅く起きたので駅へお金を持たずに行った程あわてました．そこで私は家に引返してお金を持って再び駅へ行きました．—人間はあわてゝいる時には心がよく仂かないものです．

1. The Japanese generally eat more fish than meat. **2.** The farmer who delivers us milk in the morning has more cows than oxen. **3.** Kyūshū Island has more inhabitants than Shikoku Island. **4.** This factory employs more girls than men. **5.** Do you know which lay more eggs, hens or pigeons? —Of course I know; hens lay more eggs than pigeons. **6.** I am less skilful than you but I am more patient than you. Even without great skill we can do much work if we are patient. **7.** Osaka is not so large a city as Tokyo, but it is more industrialized. **8.** I have less property than my elder brother, but I feel much happier than he. **9.** That farmer has fewer horses than cows, but each of his horses costs more than any of his cows. **10.** During the last typhoon there were no fewer than three thousand victims. **11.** Mr. Sumida has not less books than I, but as he never reads any of them, he has not increased his knowledge since he left school. **12.** About how many sheep has that shepherd?—I believe he has no less than one hundred. **13.** Factory girls and boys do not work so much as men do; therefore they receive lower wages than men. **14.** The Kabuki theatre is not so large as the Nippon theatre, but it is more beautiful. **15.** River fish is not so tasty as sea fish. **16.** Have you no better room?—This is the best room in the house. **17.** Do you speak French?—Yes, I do, and I speak it as well as I speak Italian, my mother tongue. **18.** The Ishikari and the Shinano are the two longest rivers in Japan; the former is in Hokkaido, the latter is in the central part of Japan proper. **19.** Have you ever climbed Mount Fuji?—No, I have not, but I intend to climb it next summer. **20.** I rarely go to bed before eleven o'clock. **21.** Do you not often travel by airplane?—I seldom do; I have been to Osaka only twice by airplane. **22.** When Mrs. Fukuno passed by me, she pretended she did not know me.—She is rather a strange lady: she often acts like that. **23.** Without books we cannot increase our knowledge very much. **24.** This morning I got up late, and was in such a hurry to go to the station that I left home without taking any money with me. Therefore I returned home, got some money and went to the station again.—When we are in a hurry our mind does not work well.

Fortieth Lesson 第四十課

Shall and Will

In Lesson 32 we have shown that the suffixes *mashō, deshō,* and *darō* are used to form the simple future tense, indicated in English by *shall* for the first and *will* for the second and third persons.

In this lesson we will show how to translate these two auxiliaries when they are used to express volition.

Shall

The future with *mashō, deshō,* and *darō* is used also when *shall* indicates a promise or threat of the speaker.

> *Ashǐtá o-kané wo agerú deshō.* To-morrow you **shall** receive the money
> あした お金 を 上げるでしょう. (from me).
>
> (*lit.* To-morrow I will give you the money.)

> *Watashí no o-tétsudai wa ashǐtá himá wo dasaréru[1] deshō.*
> 私 の お手伝い は あした 暇 を 出される でしょう.
>
> My servant **shall** be dismissed to-morrow. (*lit.* My servant, to-morrow, time will be given.=My servant to-morrow will be dismissed.)

Since passive verbs, as in the second example, are avoided whenever possible and active verbs are preferred, as shown in the first example, the second example will be better translated as follow:

> *Ashǐtá watashí wa o-tétsudai ni himá wo dashimásǔ.* To-morrow I **will**
> あした 私 はお手伝いに 暇 を 出します. **dismiss** my servant.

In this example, the present instead of the future indicates that the mind of the speaker is made up.

When **shall** indicates a command of the speaker, it is translated by adding *nákereba narimasén* なければなりません or *nákereba ikemasén* なければいけません (*lit.* If it is not, it won't do.) to the simple stem of verbs of Class I and to the *a*-stem of verbs of Class II. Also **must** may be translated in the same manner.

In less polite speech, *naránai* ならない is used instead of *narimasén*, and *ikenái* いけない instead of *ikemasén*.

Literally translated, *nákereba* なければ corresponds to *if it isn't*, and *narimasén* なりません and *ikemasén* いけません, as well as their less polite forms, correspond to *won't do, it isn't proper, it isn't right*, and such like expressions. *Nákereba narimasén* then, translated literally, corresponds to *if it isn't so it won't do*.

> *Anáta wa kyō hataraká-nákereba narimasén.* You **shall** (must)
> 貴方 はきよう 仂かなければ なりません. work to-day.

---

1 *himá wo dasaréru* to be dismissed; *himá wo dásu* to dismiss; *himá* time, *dásu* to give, *dasaréru* to be given; *himá wo dasaréru* to be given time=to be dismissed

Watashí no musŭkó wa watashí no iú yō-ni (iú tōri ni) shi-nákereba
私 の 息子 は 私 の言うように(言う通りに) しなければ
narimasén.   My son **shall** (must) do what I tell him to do.
なりません.   (*lit.* My son, my to say like, if he does not do, it won't do.)

The corresponding negative form is obtained by the subordinate of the verb, followed by *ikemasén* or *ikenái.* Compare with negative imperative in this lesson.

Kyō, anáta wa dekaketé wa ikemasén.   You **shall** (must) not go out to-day.
きよう貴方 は 出かけて は いけません.   (*lit.* To-day going out won't do.)

Will

When **will** indicates an action dependent upon the resolution of the speaker, the verb indicating the action is, in Japanese, used in the present, instead of the future.

Ima kará watashí wa mō tabakó wo suimasén.
今 から 私 は もう 煙草 を すいません.
From now on I **will not smoke** any more.
   (*lit.* Now from, I, more *or* again, tobacco do not inhale.)
Watashí no tokéi wa yakú[1] ni tatánai kará kyō atarashíi no wo kaimásŭ.
私 の 時計 は 役 に立たないからきよう新しいの を 買います.
My watch is useless; to-day I **will buy** a new one.
   (*lit.* My watch, utility doesn't hold good because, to-day new one I buy.)

However, if one expresses only a simple intention, without the idea of resolution or determination, then the future with *mashō, deshō,* or *darō* is used. In such a case, **shall** instead of **will** is generally used in English.

Watashí no tokéi wa yakú ni tatánai kará kyō atarashíi no wo kaimashō.
私 の 時計 は 役 に立たないからきよう新しい の を買いましょう.
My watch is useless; to-day I **shall buy** a new one.

Deshō or **darō,** instead of *désŭ,* may be used after the desiderative.

Konó kodomotachí wa íma dekaketái no désŭ ka (or deshō ka).
この 子供達 は 今 出かけたい の です か (でしょうか).
Do these children wish to go out now?
   (*lit.* These children now wish to go out, is it?)
Iié, dekaketái no de wa arimasén.   No, they do not wish to go out.
いゝえ, 出かけたいので はありません.   (No, they wish to go out is not.)
The following is a more polite form for such a question as the one above.

Sonó fujingatá wa íma o-dekaké ni naritái[2] no désŭ (or deshō) ka.
その 婦人方 は 今 お出かけ に なりたい の です (でしょう) か.
Do those ladies wish to go out now?

---

1 *yakú* use, utility; *tátsu* to hold good; *yakú ni tátsu* to be useful; *yakú ni tatánai* to be useless **2** *o-dekaké ni náru* polite for *dekakerú* to go out

When **will** indicates the determination to do something, even against the will of another, the expression *dō-shǐté-mo* (*at any cost, by all means*) or the less polite expression *tómo* (*indeed, of course, certainly*) is used.

Dō-shǐté-mo is used before the verb, *tómo* after it:

Kyō dekaketé wa ikemasén.   You must not (shall not) go out to-day.
きよう出かけて は いけません.

Nan to osshátte[1] mo watashí wa dekakemásǔ tómo.   ⎫
何ん とおっしゃっても　私　　は　出かけます　とも.   ⎪ Whatever you
Nan to osshátte mo dō-shǐté-mo watashí wa dekakemásǔ.   ⎬ may say I will
何んとおっしゃってもどうして も　　私　　は　出かけます.   ⎭ go out.

nan to......mo 何んと......も whatever......

More emphasis is given to **will** if both expressions *dō shǐté-mo* and *tómo* are used in the same clause or sentence.

Nan to osshátte mo dō-shǐté-mo dekakemásǔ tómo.

To translate the expression **will you please**+*a verb*, the Japanese use the principal verb in the subordinate, followed by the negative form of the polite verb *kudasáru* 下さる.

Dōzo anáta no náifu wo kashǐtě kudasaimasén ka.
どうぞ貴方　の　ナイフを　　貸して　　下さいません　か.
Will you please lend me your penknife?
   (*lit.* Please, your knife lending, will you not favour me?)

Ginzá e ittára kō iú fūtō wo nijū mái Itōya de katté kudasaimasén ka.
銀座へ行ったらこういう封筒を廾 枚 伊東屋で買って　下さいません　か.
When you go to Ginza **will you please buy** twenty envelopes like these at Itōya?[2] (*lit.* To Ginza when you go, such envelopes twenty, at Itōya buying do you not do for me?)

Kashikomarimáshǐta. かしこまりました.   With pleasure. Certainly, I will.

The word *kashikomarimáshǐta* comes from *kashikomáru, to obey with respect, to accept with respect,* and is generally used when we wish to show willingness to comply with, or to satisfy, somebody's desire. It corresponds to the two given English translations and similar forms. This expression is used only when speaking to one's superiors.

Imperative

In Lesson 26, page 176, we have said that a mild form of imperative is obtained by the *subordinate of a verb*, followed by *kudasái.* This form of imperative is used when the action expressed by the verb is to be performed in favour of the speaker.

Konó shigotó wo háyaku shǐté kudasái.   **Please do** this work (for me)
この　仕事　を　早く　して　下さい.   quickly.

---

1 *osshátte* subordinate of *ossháru* to say, to speak, to tell **2** *Itōya* is the name of a large stationary store in Tokyo. *Ginza* is the name of the most popular thorough-fare in Tokyo.

Pen wo kashĭté kudasái.   **Please lend** me your pen.
ペン を 貸して 下さい.

When the action expressed by the verb refers to the second or third person, then, instead of *kudasái,* one must use *nasái* なさい, the imperative form of *nasáru* なさる, after the simple stem of verbs of Class I, and the *i*-stem of verbs of Class II.

Note that although *nasái* is derived from the polite verb *nasáru,* its use in the imperative does not indicate politeness, but rather a mild order. By using the honorific *o* before the simple stem of verbs of Class I and the *i*-stem of verbs of Class II followed by *nasái,* the imperative becomes polite. A still more polite form is indicated by the expression *nasátte kudasái,* instead of *nasái.*

Ame ga furánai uchí ni háyaku kaerí nasái.   Before it starts raining
雨 が降らない 内 に 早く 帰り なさい.   **go back** quickly.
   (*lit.* Rain does not fall while, quickly return.)

O-cha ga saménai uchí ni o-nómi nasái.   **Drink** your tea before it
お茶 が 冷めない 内 に お飲み なさい.   gets cold.
   (*lit.* The tea doesn't get cold while, drink.)

Osokú náru to ikemasén kará o-dekaké nasátte kudasái.
遅く なる といけませんから お出かけ なさって 下さい.
   Please go as it may become too late.
   (*lit.* Late if it becomes, won't do because, your going out please do.)

o-dekaké nasáru お出かけなさる polite form for *dekakéru* 出かける to go out.

Among intimate male friends, or when men speak to inferior, the word *tamaé* is sometimes used in place of *nasái. Tamaé* is not used by women.

Kokó wo mi tamaé. こゝを見給え.   **Look** here.

Asobí ni ki tamaé. 遊びに来給え.   **Come** to see me sometimes.

asobú 遊ぶ to amuse oneself; *asobí ni ikú* or *kúru* to pay an informal visit for pleasure

The first person singular of the imperative is expressed by the *subordinate of causative verbs,* followed by *kudasái.* See Causative Verbs, Lesson 43, page 354.

Konó shigotó wo watashí ni saseté kudasái. **Let me do** this work.
この 仕事 を 私 に させて 下さい. (*saserú* to cause to do)

Saseté させて is the subordinate of *saserú* させる, which is the causative form of *surú* する to do.—*shigotó wo surú* 仕事をする to work, *shigotó wo saserú* 仕事をさせる to cause, to allow to work=to let work.

Gaishutsú[1] *saseté kudasái.* 外出させて下さい.   **Let me** go out.

gaishutsú surú 外出する to go out, *gaishutsú saserú* 外出させる to cause or allow to go out=to let go out.

The first person plural of the imperative is expressed by the *future of verbs* formed with the termination *mashō,* as stated in Lesson 32.

---

[1] *gaishutsú* the going out; *gaishutsú surú* to go out of doors; *gaishutsú saserú* to cause to go out

Ikimashō.   行きましょう.   Let us go.

Tabemashō.   食べましょう.   Let us eat.

The negative of this form of the imperative is indicated by the negative future formed with the suffix *masumái.* See Lesson 32.

Ikimasumái.   行きますまい.   Let us not go. (We will not go.)

Tabemasumái.   食べますまい.   Let us not eat. (We will not eat.)

The two most common forms of the negative imperative, used in every day conversation, are obtained by adding to the simple stem of verbs of Class I and the *a*-stem of verbs of Class II the expression *nái hō ga yói* (*désŭ*) ない方がよい（です）, or, as shown in Lessons 15 and 26, *nái de kudasái* ないで下さい.

Nái hō ga yói (*désŭ*) corresponds, in meaning, to......*if you don't it is good=better not to*......Literally translated, ...*nái* corresponds to *not to*......, *hō* the way, the method, *yói* good, *désŭ* is, so that the expresssion *nái hō ga yói* (*désŭ*) corresponds to *not to*......*the way good is.*

Nái de kudasái corresponds to *not to* or *don't please.*

In using *nái hō ga yói,* or *nái hō ga yói désŭ* the imperative takes the form of advice; in using *nái de kudasái* (please don't), the imperative indicates a kind request.

O-saké ga kirái náraba nománai hō ga yói désŭ.
お酒 が 嫌い ならば 飲まない 方 が よい です.
If you do not like saké don't drink it. (*Saké* Japanese wine)
(*lit.* Wine dislike if, not to drink the way good is.)

Hǐtó no máe de sonná ni ōkíi kóe de hanasánai hō ga yói.
人 の 前 でそんな に大きい声 で 話さない 方 が よい.
Do not talk so loud before people. (Before people, with such big voice not to speak is good.)

Konó tegamí wo yománai de kudasái.   Don't read this letter.
この 手紙 を 読まない で 下さい.

Konó heyá kará dénai de kudasái.   Don't go out of this room,
この 部屋 から 出ない で 下さい.   please.

When one wishes to use a stronger form of negative imperative, one may use the subordinate of the verb followed by *wa ikemasén* はいけません or *wa ikenái* はいけない, as shown in Lesson 27.

Konó kudámono wo tábete wa ikemasén; koré wa máda aói désŭ.
この 果物 を 食べて は いけません, これ は まだ 青い です.
Don't eat this fruit; it is still green.

Besides the various forms of the imperative already given, there is another one which is formed as follows: for verbs of Class I, add one of the particles *ro* ろ, *yo* よ, or *na* な, to the simple stem; for verbs of Class II, use the *e*-stem followed or not by *yo,* or add *na* to the *i*-stem.

Note that in this case, the postposition *na* な is the abbreviation of *nasái* なさい, which is the imperative of *nasáru* なさる to do.

Class I

míru 見る   *mi* 見   *Míro.* 見ろ.   *Míyo.* 見よ.   *Miná.* 見な.   Look!
tabéru 食べる   *tabe* 食べ   *Tabéro.* 食べろ.   *Tábeyo.* 食べよ.   *Tabená* 食べな.   Eat!

Class II

káku	書く	*Káke.* 書け.	*Kákeyo.* 書けよ.	*Kakiná.*	書きな.	Write!
dásu	出す	*Dáse.* 出せ.	*Dáseyo.* 出せよ.	*Dashiná.*	出しな.	Take out!
mátsu	待つ	*Máte.* 待て.	*Máteyo.* 待てよ.	*Machiná.*	待ちな.	Wait!
yobú	呼ぶ	*Yobé.* 呼べ.	*Yobéyo.* 呼べよ.	*Yobiná.*	呼びな.	Call!
yómu	読む	*Yóme.* 読め.	*Yómeyo.* 読めよ.	*Yominá.*	読みな.	Read!
tóru	取る	*Tóre.* 取れ.	*Tóreyo.* 取れよ.	*Toriná.*	取りな.	Take!
iú	言う	*Ié.* 言え.	*Iéyo.* 言えよ.	*Iiná.*	言いな.	Speak!

kúru 来る   to come   **Irregular Verbs**   **surú** する   to do

kúru	来る	*Kói* 来い.	*Kóyo.* 来よ.	*Kiná.*	来な.	Come!
surú	する	*Shiró* しろ	*Séyo.* せよ.	*Shiná.*	しな.	Do!

The above are grammatical imperative forms, but as they are considered rude or vulgar, they are rarely used except among young intimate male friends or low class people. The form in *na* preceded by the honorific *o* is used by low class women.

The above forms of the imperative, although vulgar in conversation, are found in the written style, and are invariably used in proverbs.

Isógaba[1] *mawaré.*   { If in a hurry go around.
急がば　廻れ.   { The more haste the less speed.

Zen[2] *wa isóge.*   { Strike while the iron is hot.
善　は　急げ.   { Make hay while the sun shines.
(*lit.* Good things do in haste.—*isógu* 急ぐ to make haste)

The negative of the above imperative forms is indicated by the simple present of the verb, followed by *na.*

Míru-na. 見るな.   Don't look.   *Káku-na.* 書くな.   Don't write.
Tabéru-na. 食べるな.   Don't eat.   *Yobú-na.* 呼ぶな.   Don't call.
Késshĭte úso wo tsŭkú-na. 決して嘘をつくな.   Never tell a lie.
(*lit.* Never lies pour forth—*tsŭkú*, to vomit, to spew, to pour forth)

To give more emphasis to the negative, the word *nákare* 勿れ, which is of the literary style, is used in place of *na.*

Séi wo fundé osoréru[3] *nákare.*   Be just and fear not.
正　を　ふんで　恐れる　勿れ.   Abide by justice and be not afraid.
(*lit.* Justice fulfilling, fear do not.)

---

1 *isógu* to be in a hurry, to hurry; *isógaba* if you are in a hurry; *mawaré* imperative of *mawarú* to go around   **2** *zen* the good, good things   **3** *osoréru* to fear

Impersonal Verbs

English impersonal verbs are, in Japanese, conjugated like any other verbs.

áme ga fúru	to rain	*kaminarí ga narú*	to thunder
雨 が 降る	(rain falls)	雷 が 鳴る	(thunder roars)
araré ga fúru	to hail	*inabíkari ga surú*	to lighten
あられが 降る	(hail falls)	稲光 が する	(lightning makes)

yukí ga fúru 雪が降る   to snow (snow falls)

Kinō kará áme ga túte imásu.   It has been raining since yesterday.
きのうから 雨 が 降っています.

Yūbe araré ga takúsán furimáshĭta.   Last night it hailed heavily.
ゆうべあられ が 沢山 降りました.

Kyūshū de wa yukí ga tamá ni shǐká furimasén.   In Kyushu it rarely
九州 で は 雪 が たま に しか 降りません.   snows.
(*lit.* In Kyushu snow rarely does not fall.)

Vocabulary

Nouns

dentist	*háisha*	歯ハ医イ者シャ
food	*shokuryōhin*	食料品
incense	*sénkō*	線セン香コウ
lightning	*inabíkari*	稲イ子光ビカリ
mosquito-net	*kayá*	蚊カ帳ヤ
rice crop	*beisakú*	米ベイ作サク
good crop	*hōsaku*	豊ホウ作サク
poor crop	*fusakú*	不フ作サク
salary	*gekkyū*	月ゲッ給キュウ
thunder	*kaminarí*	雷カナミリ
toast (bread)	*yakipán, tōsŭto*	焼ヤキパン, トースト

value	*káchi*	価カ値チ

Verbs

to bite	*kuitsŭkú*	クイツク
to hail	*hyō ga fúru*	雹ヒョウ ガ降ル
	araré ga fúru	アラレガ降ル
to hang up (mosquito-net)	*tsurú*	吊ツル
to pardon	*yurúsu*	許ユルス
to raise (price, salary)	*age·rú*	上アゲル

Adverbs

immediately	*súgu (ni)*	直グ (ニ)

old fashioned *kyūshiki-na;* to hang up a mosquito-net *kayá wo tsurú*

Exercise *Renshū* 練習

1. Anó otokó wa watashí no kanjō wo taihén gaishimáshĭta[1] kará watashí wa kesshĭté anó hĭtó wo yurushimasén.—Tatoé anó hĭtó ga anáta no kanjō wo gáishĭte mo yurúshĭte[2] yarubéki désu. Móshi anáta no kanjō wo gáishĭta mónó wo yurúshĭte yaréba anáta wa totemó kimochí ga yóku narimásu yo. **2.** Késa asahán ni náni wo meshiagarimásu[3] ka.—Hámu to

---

1 *kanjō wo gaisúru* to offend 2 *yurúshĭte yarú* is more colloquial than *yurúsu* to pardon; *yurúshĭte yarubéki* you should pardon 3 *meshiagarú* polite for *tabéru* used only for the second and third person

tamagó to tōsuto to kōhī wo itadakimásŭ. **3.** O-kyakŭsamá wa kómban uchí ni o-tomarí deshō ka.—O-tomarí ni narimasén; jikí ni o-kaerí ni narimásŭ. **4.** Kóndo no shachō wa warewaré no gekkyū wo ageté kururú[1] to omoimásŭ ka.—Hakkíri-to[2] wa wakarimasén ga jimúsho no renjū[3] wa shachō ga ageté kururú darō to omótte imásŭ. **5.** Kimí wa otōsan kará itadaitá anó kin no shigarettó kēsu wo utté wa ikemasén ne.—Anáta wo shitsubō[4] saserú no wa zannén[5] désŭ ga bóku wa urō to omoimásŭ. Bóku wa anó shigarettó kēsu wo iranái shi matá sŭkí mo shimasén. Soré-ni[6] bóku wa yūeki-na[7] shóseki ga kaitái no désŭ ga jūbun-na kané ga nái no désŭ. Hitsuyō no nái[8] monó wa warewaré ni wa nan no káchi mo arimasén. **6.** Dannasamá, kabán no shĭtakú ga dekimáshĭta. Kóndo wa náni wo itashimashō.—Kōtsū Kōsha[9] e itté Shimonosekí yukí no nitō no kippú[10] wo ni-mái katté go-ji ni éki de watashí wo mátte i[11] nasái. **7.** Ame ga hídoku fútte[12] imásŭ nóni watashí wa íma súgu uchí e kaeráneba narimasén. Anáta no kása wo kómban kashĭté itadakerú deshō ka.—Hái, kashĭté agemashō. **8.** Kyō anáta ga háisha e irasshátta tokí ni dōzo konó tegamí wo senséi ni sashiageté[13] kudasái.—Hái, sashiagemashō, soshĭté senséi ni nan to mōshimashō[14] ka.—Nánni-mo osshárazu ni táda[15] tegamí daké ageté kudasái. **9.** Watashí ga benkyō shĭté irú tokí ni wa dōzo amarí otó wo sasenái[16] de kudasái. **10.** Watashidómo ga káette kúru máe ni o-heyá wo zémbu sōji shĭté okí[17] nasái. **11.** Anáta wa o-yasumí ni náru máe ni otōsan ni tegamí wo o-kakí nasái.—Hái, kakimásŭ. **12.** Ame no tamé ni[18] íchiba e ikú no ga iyá náraba[19] ikanái de mo yoroshíi. Shokuryōhin wa jūbun futsŭká bun[20] guraí arimásŭ kará. **13.** Anó inú to asondé wa ikemasén. Anó inú wa kitanái shi soré ni kuitsukú ka-mo shiremasén. **14.** Heyá ga samúi kará to wo akebanashí[21] ni shĭté wa ikemasén. **15.** Konó natsú takŭsán hyō ga furimáshĭta kará kotoshí wa o-komé ga fusakú deshō to hĭtóbito wa omótte imásŭ. **16.** Hokkaidō wa Nihón-jū no dóko yóri[22] mo yukí ga ōku furimásŭ. **17.** Nihón de wa kaminarí ga nattá tokí kyūshiki-na hĭtótachi wa kayá wo tsutté sonó náka ni háiri kaminarí ga yamú[23] máde senkō wo taitá[24] monó déshĭta. **18.** Natsú tabitabí inabíkari ga suréba komé ga hōsaku da to Nihón no nōfu wa shínjite imásŭ.

1. あの男は私の感情を大変害しましたから私は決してあの人を許しません.—たとえあの人が貴方の感情を害しても許してやるべきです. 若し貴方の感情を害した者を許してやれば貴方はとても気持がよくなりますよ. **2.** けさ, 朝飯に何を召上りますか.—ハムと玉子とトー

---

1 *ageté kururú* to raise, in favour of the speaker 2 *hakkíri-to wa* for sure 3 *renjū* several members of the staff of a company, of an office 4 *shitsubō saserú* to disappoint 5 *zannén désŭ* I am sorry, I regret 6 *soré ni* besides 7 *yūeki-na* useful 8 *hitsuyō no nái* useless 9 *Kōtsū Kōsha* Travel Bureau 10 *nitō no kippú* 2nd class ticket 11 *mátte irú* to be waiting, *i* is the stem of *irú* 12 *áme ga hídoku fúru* to rain hard 13 *sashiagerú* polite for to give. 14 *mōsu* humble for to say 15 just 16 *saserú* to cause to be done 17 *sōji shĭté okí nasái* lit. clean and finish (cleaning) 18 *tamé ni* on account of 19 *iyá náraba* if you don't like 20 *fŭtsuká bun* ration for two days 21 *akebanashí ni surú* to leave open 22 *dóko yóri mo* in any other part 23 *yamú* to be over, to end 24 *takú to* burn, to kindle

ストとコーヒーをいただきます．　**3.** お客様は今晩うちにお泊りで
しょうか．―お泊りになりません，ぢきにお帰りになります．　**4.** 今度
の社長は我々の月給を上げてくれると思いますか．―はっきりとは解
りませんが事務所の連中は社長が上げてくれるだろうと思っていま
す．　**5.** 君はお父さんから頂いたあの金のシガレットケースを売って
はいけませんね．―貴方を失望させるのは残念ですが僕は売ろうと思
います．僕はあのシガレットケースを要らないし又好きもしません．
それに僕は有益な書籍が買い度いのですが充分な金がないのです．必
要のないものは我々には何んの価値もありません．　**6.** 旦那様鞄の支
度が出来ました．今度は何を致しましょう．―交通公社へ行って下関
行の二等の切符を二枚買って，五時に駅で私を待っていなさい．　**7.**
雨がひどく降っていますのに私は今すぐ家へ帰らねばなりません．
貴方の傘を今晩貸して頂けるでしょうか．―はい，貸して上げましょ
う．　**8.** きょう貴方が歯医者へいらっしゃった時にどうぞこの手紙を
先生に差上げて下さい．―はい，差上げましょう，そして先生に何んと
申しましょうか．―何もおっしゃらずに只手紙だけ上げて下さい．　**9.**
私が勉強している時にはどうぞ余り音をさせないで下さい．　**10.** 私共
が帰って来る前にお部屋を全部掃除しておきなさい．　**11.** 貴方はお休
みになる前にお父さんに手紙をお書きなさい．―はい，書きます．　**12.**
雨のために市場へ行くのが嫌ならば行かないでも宜しい．食料品は充
分二日分位ありますから．　**13.** あの犬と遊んではいけません．あの犬
は汚いしそれにくいつくかも知れません．　**14.** 部屋が寒いから戸を開
けばなしにしてはいけません．　**15.** この夏沢山雹が降りましたから今
年はお米が不作でしょうと人々は思っています．　**16.** 北海道は日本中
のどこよりも雪が多く降ります．　**17.** 日本では雷が鳴ったとき旧式な
人達は蚊帳を吊ってその中に入り雷が止む迄線香をたいたものでした．
18. 夏，度々稲光がすれば米が豊作だと日本の農夫は信じています．

1. That man has offended me greatly and I will never pardon him.—Even
though he has offended you, you should pardom him. If you pardon those
that have offended you, you will feel happier. **2.** What will you have for
breakfast this morning?—I will have ham and eggs, toast and coffee. **3.** Will
the guests remain at our home for the night?—No, they will not. They will
soon leave. **4.** Do you think that our new president will raise our salary?
—I do not know for sure, but several employees in our office think he will.
5. You mustn't sell the gold cigarette case that your father gave you.—I am
sorry to disappoint you, but I will sell it. I don't need that cigarette case
and I do not like it; besides, I intend to buy some useful books and have
not sufficient money. What we do not need has no value for us. **6.** The
trunks are ready, Sir. What shall I do now?—You, are to (shall) go to the
Travel Bureau, buy two 2nd class tickets for Shimonoseki, and wait for me

at the station at five o'clock. **7.** It is raining hard and I must return home immediately. Will you please lend me your umbrella for to-night?—Yes, I will lend it to you. **8.** When you go to the dentist to-day will you please give him this letter?—Yes, I will, and what shall I tell him?—Nothing, just give him the letter. **9.** When I am studying please do not make too much noise. **10.** Clean all the rooms before we come back. **11.** Before you go to bed write a letter to your father.—Yes, I will. **12.** If you do not wish to go to the market on account of the rain, don't go; we have enough food for another two days. **13.** Do not play with that dog; he is dirty and he may bite you. **14.** Don't leave the door open; it is (too) cold in this room. **15.** As it has hailed much this summer, people think that there will be a poor rice crop this year. **16.** In Hokkaido it snows more than in any other part of Japan. **17.** When it thundered, old-fashioned people in Japan used to hang up their mosquito-nets and remain inside of them, burning incense until the roaring of the thunder was over. **18.** Japanese farmers believe that when it lightens very often in summer, their rice fields will yield good crops.

Forty-first Lesson　第四十一課

Numerals　*Sūshi*　数ズゥ詞シ

There are in Japanese three sets of numbers from one to ten, two of which have been already given in Lesson 8. The three sets are here given for comparison. The third set is an abbreviation of the second.

1	一 or 壱	*ichí*	一つ	*hĭtótsu*	一	*hi*	
2	二 or 弐	*ni*	二つ	*fŭtatsú*	二	*fŭ*	
3	三 or 参	*san*	三つ	*mĭtsú, mittsú*	三	*mi*	
4	四	*shi, yo, yon*	四つ	*yotsú, yottsú*	四	*yo*	
5	五	*go*	五つ	*itsútsu*	五	*íi*	
6	六	*rokú*	六つ	*mutsú, muttsú*	六	*mu*	
7	七	*shichí*	七つ	*nanátsu*	七	*naná, na*	
8	八	*hachí*	八つ	*yatsú, yattsú*	八	*ya*	
9	九	*ku, kyū*	九つ	*kokónotsu*	九	*kokóno, kóno*	
10	十 or 拾	*jū*	十	*tō*	十	*tō*	

See Lesson 8, page 45, for remarks on the various Japanese translations of *four* and *seven*. Here we may add that *ku* 九 nine, is often pronounced *kyū*.

From *eleven* upward only one set of numbers is used. In Lesson 8 the numbers of this set are given up to 50. Below is a list of larger numbers.

50	五十	*go-jū*	52	五十二	*go-jū-ni*
51	五十一	*go-jū-ichí*	53	五十三	*go-jū-san*

60	六十	*rokú-jū*	1,002	千二	*issén-ni*
70	七十	*shichí-(naná)jū*	1,003	千三	*issén-san*
80	八十	*hachí-jū*	2,000	二千	*ni-sen*
90	九十	*ku-(kyū)jū*	3,000	三千	*san-zen*
100	百	*hyakú*	4,000	四千	*yon-(shi)sen*
101	百一	*hyakú-ichí*	5,000	五千	*go-sen*
102	百二	*hyakú-ni*	6,000	六千	*rokú-sen*
103	百三	*hyakú-san*	7,000	七千	*shichí-(naná)sen*
200	二百	*ni-hyakú*	8,000	八千	*hassén*
300	三百	*sam-byakú*	9,000	九千	*kyū-sen*
400	四百	*yon-(shi)hyakú*	10,000	一万	*ichí-man*
500	五百	*go-hyakú*	20,000	二万	*ni-man*
600	六百	*roppyakú*	30,000	三万	*san-man*
700	七百	*shichí-(naná)hyakú*	40,000	四万	*yon-man, yo-man*
800	八百	*happyakú*	50,000	五万	*go-man*
900	九百	*kyū-hyakú*	100,000	十万	*jūman*
1,000	千	*sen* or *issén*	200,000	二十万	*ni-jū-man*
1,001	千一	*issén-ichí*	1,000,000	百万	*hyakú-man*

375 三百七十五 *sam-byakú-naná-jū-go;* 531 五百卅一 *go-hyakú-san-jū-ichí;* 649 六百四十九 *roppyakú-yon-jū-kyū;* 891 八百九十一 *happyakú-kyū-jū-ichí;* 3,478 三千四百七十八 *san-zen-yon-hyakú-naná-jū-hachí;* 8,266 八千二百六十六 *hassén-ni-hyakú-rokú-jū-rokú;* 45,748 四万五千七百四十八 *yon-man-go-sen-naná-hyakú-yon-jū-hachí;* 139,648 十三万九千六百四十八 *jū-san-man-kyū-sen-roppyakú-yon-jū-hachí;* 1,863,783 百八十六万三千七百八十三 *hyakú-hachí-jū-rokú-man-san-zen-naná-hyakú-hachí-jū-san.*

Kotoshí   wa   seirekí   sen-kyū-hyakú-rokujū-ichi   nen   de   Nihón-rekí   no   ni-sen-
今年 は 西暦   千九百六十一   年 で 日本暦 の 二千
roppyakúnijū-ichi   nen   désū.   We are now in the year 1961 of the Christian Era,
六百二十一   年 です。 or in the year 2621 of the Japanese Era.
(*lit.* This year, Christian-era 1961 year is, Japanese-era 2621 year **is.**)

From the list of numbers given above, it may be observed that in some cases the end sound of a numeral and the first sound of the following number are modified. These phonetic alterations occur also when the word following the altered number is a noun.
The rules of these phonetic changes are given below:

ichí	becomes	*it*	⎫	before	*jū*	”	”	*jip*	⎫	before
hachí	”	”	*hat*	⎬ *ch, t,*		*hyakú*	”	”	*hyap*	⎬ **f or h**
jū	”	”	*jit*	⎭ *ts*		*sen*	”	”	*sem*	⎭
ichí	”	”	*ip*	⎫		*ichí*	becomes	*ik*	⎫	
san	”	”	*sam*	⎬ before		*rokú*	”	”	*rok*	⎬ before
rokú	”	”	*rop*	⎭ **f or h**		*hachí*	”	”	*hak*	⎭ **k**

jū	becomes	*jik*	
hyakú	" "	*hyak*	}before **k**

ichí	" "	*is*	}before	*san*	becomes	*sam*	}before
hachí	" "	*has*	**s** or **sh**	*sen*	" "	*sem*	**m** or **b**
jū	" "	*jis*					

After *san* or *sen,* words beginning with the letters *f, h, k, s, sh* generally undergo the following changes:

f or *h*	becomes	*p*	*s*	becomes	*z*
k	" "	*g*	*sh*	" "	*j*

Numeratives

In Lesson 8, page 45, we have given a few numeratives of Chinese origin, which are used with the first set of numbers as given at the beginning of this lesson. Below we will give some more numeratives often used in daily conversation.

Hái 杯 *cup,* used in counting cupfuls or glassfuls of liquid.

> *Ippai* 一杯, *níhai* 二杯, *sámbai* 三杯, *shíhai* or *yónhai* 四杯, *góhai* 五杯, *róppai* or *rokúhai* 六杯, *shichíhai* or *nanáhai* 七杯, *hachíhai* 八杯, *kuhái* or *kyūhai* 九杯, *jíppai* 十杯, *hyakuhái* or *hyáppai* 百杯, etc. *Námbai.* 何杯. How many cupfuls?
>
> *Nódo ga kawakimáshǐta kará mizú wo íppai mótte kité kudasái.* 喉 が かわきました から 水 を 一杯 持って 来て 下さい. As I am thirsty, please bring me a glass of water.

Ban 晩 *night.*

> *Hǐtóban* 一晩, *fǔtabán* 二晩, *mibán* 三晩, *yobán* 四晩. One night, two nights, three nights, four nights. Above four both the Chinese and Japanese numbers are used to count nights. *Ikuban.* 幾晩. *Námban.* 何晩. How many nights?
>
> *Teikokú Hóteru ni fǔtabán imáshǐta.* 帝国 ホテル に 二晩 いました. I was two nights at the Imperial Hotel.

Bin びん *bottle.*

> *Hǐtóbin* 一びん, *fǔtabín* 二びん, *míbin* 三びん, etc. One bottle, two bottles, three bottles.—*Nán* (or *íku*) *bin.* 何 (幾) びん. How many bottles?—*San-jū-gobin.* 卅五びん. Thirty-five bottles.

Chō 挺 *a piece,* used in counting scissors, pistols, saws.

> *hasamí itchō* 鋏一挺 a pair of scissors.
> *nokogirí nichō* 鋸二挺 two saws.

Chakú, 着, used in counting suits, dresses.

> *itchakú* 一着 a suit of clothes, *yōfuku ni-chakú* 洋服二着 two suits of clothes, *ōbā san-chakú* オーバー三着 three overcoats

Dái 台 *a stand*, used in counting vehicles of any description.

Ichídai 一台, *nídai* 二台, *sándai* 三台, etc.

Nán (íku) dai. 何 (幾) 台. How many (vehicles)?

Jidōsha wo **nídai** *yondé kudasái.*　Please call two motor-cars.
自動車 を 二台 呼んで 下さい.

Do 度 *time*.

Ichidó 一度, *nidó* 二度, *sándo* 三度, *yodó* 四度, etc. Once *or* one time, twice *or* two times, three times, four times, etc.—*Nán* (or *íku*) *do.* 何 (幾) 度. How many times?

Anáta wa Nikkō e **nándo** *(ikudo) irasshaimáshĭta ka.*
貴方 は 日光 へ 何 度 (幾度)いらっしゃいましたか.
How many times did you go to Nikko?

Godó ikimáshĭta. 五度行きました.　I went there five times.

Instead of *do* one may use *tabi,* which is written with the same Chinese character 度. With *tabi* only the Japanese numbers are used from one to four, while both the Chinese and the Japanese numbers may be used from five to ten.

Hĭtótabi, fŭtatabí, mĭtabi, yótabi, itsútabi or *gótabi, mútabi* or *rokŭtabí, nanátabi* or *shichítabi, yátabi* or *hachítabi, kokónotabi* or *kyūtabi, tótabi* or *jittabí.* Once, twice, three times, etc.—*Nántabi* 何度 or *Íkutabi* 幾度 How many times?

Ikudo-mo many times; *ikudo-mo ikudo-mo* time after time

E 重 *fold, ply*.

Hĭtóe 一重 single or one fold, *fŭtaé* 二重 double or two fold, *mié* 三重 treble or three fold, *yoé* 四重 four fold, etc.

This numeral is also read *jū,* and is used only with numbers of Chinese derivation. *Ichijū* 一重 single or one time, *nijū* 二重 double, twice, *sanjū* 三重 three times, *shijū* 四重 four times, etc.

Furí 振 used in counting swords.

kataná hĭtófuri 刀一振 a (one) sword, *kataná mífuri* 刀三振 three swords.

Counting swords with the numerative *furí* 振 is now considered obsolete and the numerative **hon** 本 is generally used instead. The two above examples will thus be: *kataná íppon* 刀一本 one sword, *kataná sámbon* 刀三本 three swords.

Hakó 箱 *a box*.

Hĭtóhako 一箱, *fŭtáhako* 二箱, *míhako* 三箱, *yónhako* or *yóhako* 四箱, etc. One box, two boxes, three boxes, four boxes, etc.
Ikuhako. 幾箱. or *Námbako.* 何箱. How many boxes?

Jō 畳 *a mat*, used in counting Japanese floor mats (uniformly 3 ft. × 6 ft.).

> *Ichijō* 一畳, *ni-jō* 二畳, *sanjō* 三畳, etc.   One mat, two mats, etc.
> *Nan* (*íku*) *jō*. 何 (幾) 畳.   How many mats?—*Jū-rokujō* 十六畳 Sixteen mats.
>
> *Konó heyá wa* **nánjō** *désŭ ka.*   How large is this room?
> この 部屋 は 何畳 です か.   (*lit.* This room how many mats is it?)
> *Rokŭjō désŭ.* 六畳です.   It is a six-mat room.

Kagó 籠 basket.

> *kudámono hĭtókago* 果物一籠 or *hĭtókago no kudámono* 一籠の果物 a basket of fruit, *fŭtakagó no ringó* 二籠のりんご two baskets of apples.

Kan 巻 *a volume*, used in counting books of a single work or reels of moving-picture film.

> *dái ikkán* 第一巻 the first volume, *éiga sángan monó* 映画三巻物 three reels (of film).

Maki 巻 *a roll*, used in counting rolls of silk or other cloth.

> *kínu hĭtómaki* 絹一巻, *hĭtómaki no kínu* 一巻の絹 a roll of silk.

Méi 名 *a person* used in literary style for counting persons.

> *ichímei* 一名 one person, *ni-jūmei* 二十名 twenty persons,
> *san-jū-gómei giséisha* 三十五名犠牲者 thirty-five victims.

Sokŭ 足 *foot*, used in counting coverings for the feet, as socks, stockings, shoes, etc.

> *Issokú* 一足, *nísoku* 二足, *sánzoku* 三足, *shísoku* or *yónsoku* 四足, *gósoku* 五足, *rokŭsoku* 六足, *shichísoku* or *nanásoku* 七足, *hassokú* 八足, *kyūsoku* 九足, *jissokú* 十足.   One pair, two pairs, three pairs, etc., of shoes, etc.
> *Nánzoku* 何足 or *Íkusoku*. 幾足.   How many pairs?
>
> *Yŭbe Ginzá de atarashíi kutsú wo* **issokú** *to kutsushĭtá wo* **nísoku**
> ゆうべ 銀座 で 新しい 靴 を 一足 と 靴下 を 二足
> *kaimáshĭta.*   Last night on Ginza I bought a new pair of shoes and two pairs
> 買いました.   of stockings.

Tsŭkí 月 *a month.*

Hĭtótsŭki 一月, *fŭtatsŭkí* 二月, *mĭtsŭki* 三月, etc.   One month, two months, three months, etc.   *Íkutsŭki.* 幾月.   How many months? *Hantsŭkí.* 半月. Half a month.

With *tsŭkí* the Chinese numbers are not used, but they are used with *ka-getsú* ヵ月, which also serves to indicate a number of months.

Ikkágetsu 一ヵ月 one month, *nikágetsu* 二ヵ月 two months, *sanká-getsu* 三ヵ月 three months, *yonkágetsu* or *shikágetsu* 四ヵ月 four months, etc. *Nán* (or *íku*) *kagetsu*. 何(幾)ヵ月. How many months?
In the above examples the *kana* ヵ functions as a numerative.

Zen 膳 used in counting bowls of rice, and pairs of chopsticks.

   góhan ichízen 御飯一膳 a bowl of rice
   háshi nízen 箸二膳 two pairs of chopsticks

More

When a comparison is implied, **more** is translated by *koré, aré, soré* followed by *ijō* 以上 or by *yóri mo* よりも (more than this, more than that). *Mótto* もっと may follow *ijō* or *yóri mo*. *No* may be used after *ijō* and before the noun following, but not after *yóri*.

Anáta wa **koré** *yóri mo* (*koré ijō*) *mótto o-kané wo mótte imásŭ ka.*
貴方 は これ より も (これ 以上) もっと お金 を 持っています か.
or *Anáta wa* **mótto** *o-kané wo mótte imásŭ ka.* Have you any **more** money?
貴方 は もっと お金 を 持っています か.

Mō sŭkóshi. もう少し.   **A little more,** some more.

Mótto takŭsán. もっと沢山.   { **Much more..** / A great deal more.

Hái, **mō sŭkóshi** *mótte imásŭ.*   Yes, I have **a little more.**
はい、もう 少し 持っています.

Hái, **mótto takŭsán** *mótte imásŭ.*   Yes, I have **much more.**
はい、もっと 沢山 持っています.

Mótto *o-kané wo kudasái.* もっとお金を下さい.
Koré ijō (**Koré yóri** mo) *o-kané wo kudasái.*   } Please give me **more** money.
これ 以上（これ より も）お金 を 下さい.

Mō takŭsán もう沢山 is an idiom, and means: "No more" or "I do not wish any more, thank you."

Mótto o-káshi wo o-agari[1] kudasái.   Please have some **more** cake.
もっと お菓子 を お上り 下さい.   (*lit.* More cake raise please.)

Arigatō, **mō takŭsán** (*désŭ.*)   Thank you, I have had plenty.
ありがとう、もう 沢山 （です）.   I wish **no more.**

Any more with a negative verb, is translated by *mō, koré ijō, koré yóri,* or *mō koré ijō* もうこれ以上, *mō koré yóri mo* もうこれよりも.

Anáta wa **mótto** (*koré ijō, koré yóri mo*) *o-kané wo mótte imásŭ ka.*
貴方 は もっと（これ 以上、これ より も）お金 を 持っています か.
Have you **any more** money?

---

1 *agarí* from *agarú* to raise; *o-agarí kudasái* lit. transl.=raise please=raise the food to your mouth and eat it—This expression is used in polite speech when offering food or drink.

Mō mótte imasén. もう持っていません.

Koré íjō (koré yóri) mótte imasén.
これ 以上（これ より）持って いません.

Mō koré íjō (koré yóri) mótte imasén.
もう これ 以上（これ より）持って いません.

} I haven't **any more.**
I have **no more.**

Mō sen yen kudasái. もう千円下さい.   Please give me a thousand yen **more.**

Koré wa watashí no mótte irú zémbu désŭ.   This is all that I have.
これ は 私 の持っている 全部 です.   (*lit.* This my having all is.)

When used after a number, the adverb **more** is translated by *mō* もう or *áto* あと. *Mō* may be used in all cases, while *áto* is used only when *more* suggests the idea that one speaks of the remainder, the rest, or what is left of a certain number of things spoken of, or existing before.

Mō hĭtótsu. もう一つ }
Ato hĭtótsu. あと一つ } One more.

Mō mittsú. もう三つ }
Ato mittsú. あと三つ } Three more.

Ato íkutsu ringó wo otōtosan ni agemáshĭta ka.—Mō (átó) hĭtótsu.
あと 幾つ りんご を 弟さん に 上げました か.—もう（あと）一つ.
How many **more** apples did you give your little brother?—One **more.**

With *mō* or *áto,* numeratives are regularly used according to the rules given in this and previous lessons.

Mō námbon empitsú ga hoshíi désŭ ka.—Mō sámbon.
もう 何本 鉛筆 が 欲しい です か.—もう 三本.
How many more pencils do you want?—**Three more.**

Ato námbon empitsú wo mótte imásŭ ka.—Ato sámbon.
あと 何本 鉛筆 を 持って います か.—あと 三本.
How many more pencils have you?—**Three more.** (and no more.)

If one of the adverbs *once, twice, three times, four times,* etc. precedes *more,* the word *do* 度 is put after the Chinese number.

Mō ichí do. もう一度. }
Ato ichí do. あと一度. } Once more.

Mō sándo. もう三度. }
Ato sándo. あと三度. } Three more.

How much more? or *How many more?* is translated by *Mō* (or *Ato*) *dóno kuraí, Mō* (or *Ato*) *dóno kuraí ōku,* or *Mō* (or *Ato*) *dóno kuraí takŭsán.*

Anáta wa mō dóno kuraí (ōku, takŭsán) zasshí wo mótte imásŭ ka.
貴方 は もう どの 位（多く, 沢山）雑誌 を 持っていますか.
How many **more** magazines have you?

Mō sánsatsu mótte imásŭ. もう三冊持っています.   I have three **more.**

How many more?, when used with a numerative, is translated by *Mō* (or *Ato*) *íku* or *Mō* (or *Ato*) *nan.* Without a numerative only *Mō* (or *Ato íkutsu*) is used.

Anáta wa mō (áto) nan (íku) satsú hon wo mótte imásŭ ka.
貴方 は もう（あと）何（幾）冊 本 を 持って います か.
How many **more** books have you?

Mō (or *Ato*) *gósatsu mótte imásŭ.*   I have five **more**.
もう （あと） 五冊 持っています.

When **more** indicates a greater quantity, it is translated by *yokéi*
余計, or *mótto yokéi* もっと余計.

Dóchira no hakó ga **yokéi** *háiru*[1] *deshō ka.*   Which box will hold
どちら の 箱 が 余計 入る でしょうか.   (the) **more**?

Kochirá no hō ga **yokéi** *hairimásŭ.*   This holds (the) **more**.
こちら の 方 が 余計 入ります.

Vocabulary

	Nouns				
bedroom	*shinshitsú*	寝室	resident	*kyojūsha*	居住者
bride	*hanáyome*	花嫁	total	*gōkei*	合計
bridegroom	*hanamúko*	花婿	wave	*namí*	波 (浪)[2]
coast	*kaigán*	海岸	wooden clog	*getá*	下駄
cup	*sakazukí*	杯	**Adjectives**		
Diet	*Gíkai*	議会	liquid	*ekitái*	液体
flour	*koná*	粉	nutritious	*jiyō no áru*	滋養ノアル
niece	*méi*	姪	**Prepositions and Adverbs**		
religion	*shūkyō*	宗教	along	*ni sottá*	ニ沿ッタ
			lately	*chikágoro*	近頃

House of Councillors *Sangí-in*; House of Representatives or Lower House *Shūgi-in*; member of the Upper or Lower House *giín*; electoral district *senkyóku*; to elect or return *senshutsú surú*; political party *seitō*; a seat in the Diet *gisekí*; Shinto shrine *jínja*; Buddhist temple *terá*; Christian church *Kirisŭtó-kyō no kyōkai*; wedding ceremony *kekkón shikí*; entrance of a house *génkan*; drawing room *ōsetsuma*; living room *chanomá*; a study, a library *shosai*; bed-room *shinshitsú*; tidal wave *tsunamí*

Exercise   *Renshū* 練習

1. Nihón no Sangí-in wa ni-hyakú-go-jūmei no giín kará naritachí[3] Shūgi-in wa yon-hyakú-rokú-jū-naná-méi no giín kará naritatté imásŭ. **2.** Nihón zénkoku[4] wa hyakú-jū-ku no senkyóku ni wakárete imásŭ, soshĭté káku[5] senkyóku wa sannín kará gonín máde no giín wo Gíkai e senshutsú shimásŭ. **3.** Nihón no jinkō wa sen-kyū-hyakú-rokujū-san nen ni oyosó kyū-sen yon-hyakú man-nin de átta. Nihón no jinkō wa mainén yáku[6] hyakumánnin zōka surú[7] to yosokú sareté[8] óri, shĭtagátte[9] sen-kyū-hyakú naná-jūnen ni wa ichíoku no jinkō wo mótsu kotó ni náru de arō.[10] **4.** Nihón ni wa hachí-man-naná-sen

---

1 *háiru* to hold   **2** 波＝small wave, 浪＝big wave   **3** ......*kará naritatsú* to be composed of, to consist of (*lit.* to be composed from, to consist from)   **4** *zénkoku* the whole country   **5** *káku* each   **6** *yáku* about   **7** *zōka surú* to increase   **8** *yosokú surú* to estimate, *yosokú sarerú* to be estimated, *yosokú sareté óri* has been estimated and......   **9** *shĭtagátte* consequently   **10** *mótsu kotó ni náru de arō* will have (*lit.* to have, the fact to become will be)

-happyakú no jínja to naná-man-ni-sen-kyū-hyakú-jū-hachí no téra to san-zen-
yon-hyakú-go-jū-yon no kirisūto-kyō kyōkai to ga arimásŭ.   **5.** Fúji-san wa
oyosó ichí-man-ni-sen jakú[1] arimásŭ.   **6.** Nihón no shakú wa Eikokú no fíto
yóri mo sŭkóshi nagái désŭ.   **7.** Sen kyū-hyakú-rokujū-nen jū gatsú ichí-nichí[2]
no Nihón ni okéru[3] gaijín kyojūsha no sōkei-sū[4] wa rokú-jū-yon-man-naná-
hyakú hachijū-san nin de arimáshĭta. Konó uchí go-jū-roku-man-kyū-sen sanjū-
yo nin wa Kankokújin, yon-man-rokusén gojū-ni nin wa Chūgokujin, soshĭté
ni-man-go-sen roppyakú kyūjū-naná nin wa Ō-Béi[5] shókoku-jin[6] déshĭta.   **8.**
Nihón de wa kekkón-shikí no toki hanáyome hanamúko wa saké wo sámbai
zutsú nomikawashimásŭ.[7] Koré wa " San-san-ku-do no sakazukí gotó "[8] to
yobareté orimásŭ.   **9.** Béikoku ni irú méi ni Nihón no getá issokú to tábi
nísoku okurō to omoimásŭ.   **10.** Konó kutsushĭtá wa issokú íkura désŭ ka.—
100 yen désŭ.—Rokŭsokú kaimashō.   **11.** Gorán nasái! Hikōki ga jū-ni-dái
anó oká no ué wo tondé imásŭ.   **12.** Anáta no atarashíi ié no heyá wa dóno
kuraí ōkii désŭ ka.—Génkan ga sanjō, ōsetsuma ga jūjō, chanomá ga hachijō,
shosái ga rokujō, soshĭté shinshitsú ga jū-nijō désŭ.   **13.** Nihón no kitá kaigán
ni sottá takŭsán no murá ga tsunamí de sarawaremáshĭta.[9]   **14.** Uchí no
kázoku wa taitéi ichí nichí ni gyūnyū wo hachíhon nomimásŭ. Gyūnyū wa
móttomo yói taihén jiyō no áru ekitái shokúmotsu désŭ.   **15.** Chikágoro dóno
kuraí torí wo o-kái ni narimáshĭta ka.—Mō amarí kaimasén déshĭta. Sámba
dáke.   **16.** Batā ga mótto hoshíi désŭ ka.—Iié, mō takŭsán désu. Jūbun
itadakimáshĭta, arigató.   **17.** Konó gōkei wa átte[10] imasén kará mō ichidó
yarinaoshí nasái.[11]   **18.** Dótchi no fukuró ni koná ga yokéi hairimásŭ ka,
koré désŭ ka anó hō désŭ ka.—Ryōhō tomó onají désŭ.

1. 日本の参議院は二百五十名の議員から成り立ち，　衆議院は四百六
十七名の議員から成り立っています．　**2.** 日本全国は百十九の選挙区に
分かれています．そして各選挙区は三人から五人迄の議員を議会へ選出
します．**3.** 日本の人口は千九百六十三年に凡そ九千四百万人であった，
日本の人口は毎年約百万人増加すると予測されており，従って千九百七
十年には一億の人口を持つ事になるであろう．　**4.** 日本には八万七千八
百の神社と七万二千九百十八の寺と三千四百五十四のキリスト教教会と
があります．**5.** 富士山は凡そ一万二千尺あります．　**6.** 日本の尺は英国
のフィートよりも少し長いです．　**7.** 千九百六十年十月一日の日本に於
ける外人居住者の総計数は六十四万七百八十三人でありました．この中，
五十六万九千三十四人は韓国人，四万六千五十二人は中国人，そして二
万五千六百九十七人は欧米諸国人でした．　**8.** 日本では結婚式の時花嫁
花婿は酒を三杯ずつ飲み交します．　これは「三々九度の盃事」と呼ばれ

---

1 *jakú=shakú* foot (measure)   **2** *ichi-nichi* first day of the month   **3** *ni okéru* in
formal speech used instead of *ni* (in)   **4** *sōkei-sū* total number   **5** Ō-*Béi* Europe
and America；　Ō=*Ōshū* Europe, *Béi=Béikoku* America   **6** *shókoku* various countries,
shókoku-jin people of various countries   **7** *nomikawasú* to exchange drinks, to drink
by turns   **8** *gotó=kotó* thing, affair (in this case *gotó* means ceremony, celebration)
9 *sarawarerú* to be swept away   **10** *átte imasén* is not correct, *átte irú* to be correct
11 *yarinaósu* to try and correct.

ております．　**9.** 米国にいる姪に日本の下駄一足と足袋二足送ろうと
思います．　**10.** この靴下は一足幾らですか．—百円です．—六足買い
ましょう．　**11.** 御覧なさい！飛行機が十二台あの丘の上を飛んでい
ます．　**12.** 貴方の新しい家の部屋はどの位大きいですか．—玄関が三
畳，応接間が十畳，茶の間が八畳，書斎が六畳，そして寝室が十二畳で
す．　**13.** 日本の北海岸に沿った沢山の村がつなみでさらわれました．
14. うちの家族は大抵一日に牛乳を八本飲みます．　牛乳は最もよい大
変滋養のある液体食物です．　**15.** 近頃どのくらい鳥をお買いになり
ましたか．—もう余り買いませんでした．　三羽だけ．　**16.** バターがも
っと欲しいですか．—いゝえ，もう沢山です．充分頂きました，ありが
とう．　**17.** この合計は合っていませんからもう一度やりなおしなさい．
18. どつちの袋に粉が余計入りますかこれですかあの方ですか．—両
方とも同じです．

1. The Japanese House of Councillors is composed of 250 members, and
the House of Representatives of 467 members. 2. The whole of Japan is
divided into 119 electoral districts, and each district returns from three to five
members to the House of Representatives. 3. In 1963 the population of Japan
was about ninety-four million. It is estimated that the Japanese population
increases about a million every year and that by 1970 Japan will therefore
be inhabited by one hundred million people. 4. In Japan there are 87,800
Shinto shrines, 72,918 Buddhist temples and 3,454 Christian churches. 5. Mount
Fuji is about 12,000 feet high. 6. The Japanese "shaku" is a little longer
than the English "foot." 7. On October the first, 1960, the total number of
foreign residents in Japan was 640,783. Of these, 569,034 were Koreans,
46,052 Chinese, 25,697 of European and American countries. 8. In Japan,
when a wedding ceremony is celebrated, the bride and bridegroom drink, by
turns, three cups, of *sake* (Japanese wine). This is called "The ceremony of
the three-times-three exchange of nuptial cups." 9. I am going to send my
niece in America a pair of Japanese wooden clogs and two pairs of *tabi*
(Japanese socks). 10. How much does a pair of these socks cost?—100 yen.
—I will buy six pairs. 11. Look! A dozen aeroplanes are flying above that
hill. 12. How large are the rooms of your new house?—The entrance hall is
a three-mat room, the drawing room ten mat, the living room eight-mat,
the study six-mat, and the bed room twelve. 13. Many villages along the
northern coast of Japan have been swept away by tidal waves. 14. My family
generally drink eight bottles of milk every day. Milk is the best and the most
nutritious liquid food. 15. How many more birds have you bought lately?—
Not many more; only three. 16. Do you wish to have some more butter?—
No, I do not wish any more. I have had enough; thank you. 17. This
total is not correct; try once more. 18. Which bag holds more flour this one
or that?—They both hold the same.

Forty-second Lesson 第四十二課

The Four Rules *Shisoku* 四則

Addition *Kuwaezán* 加え算, (*Lit.*) *kahō* 加法.

3+5=8 *San ni go wo kuwaerú (to)*[1] *hachí.* (*lit.* To three, five if we add,
三 に 五 を 加える （と） 八. eight.—*kuwaerú* to add)

Substraction *Hikizan* 引き算, (*Lit.*) *gempō* 減法.

12—5=7 *Jū-ni kará go hikú (to)*[1] *shichi.* (*lit.* Twelve from, five if we
十二 から 五 引く（と） 七. deduct, seven.—*hikú* to deduct)

A substraction may also be worded as follows:

12—5=7 *Jū-ni mainasú go ikōru shichí.* (*lit.* Ten minus five equals seven.
十二 マイナス 五 イコール七. —*mainasú* minus, *ikōru* equals)

Multiplication *Kakézan* 掛け算, (*Lit.*) *jōhō* 乗法.

4×5=20 *Shi ni go wo kakéru (to) ni-jū.*
四 に 五 を 掛ける（と）二十.
(*lit.* Four by five if we multiply, twenty.—*ni*......*kakéru* to multiply by)

Division *Warizan* 割算, (*Lit.*) *joho* 除法.

45÷5=9 *Yon-jū-go wo go de warú (to) kyū.*
四十五 を 五 で 割る（と）九.
(*lit.* Forty-five, by five if we divide, nine.—*warú* to divide)

A division may also be worded as follows:

45÷5=9 *Yon-jū-go warú go wa kyū.* 四十五割る五は九.

The four arithmetic operations may be mentioned in one single word, formed by the first syllable of each of the four expressions given above:

kagenjōjo (*ka-gen-jō-jo*) 加減乗除

Fractional Numbers

Bunsū 分数 (*bun* 分 part, *sū* 数 number)

½ *nibún no ichí* 二分の一 (*lit.* of two parts, one)
⅓ *sambún no ichí* 三分の一 (*lit.* of three parts, one)
¾ *yombún no ni* 四分の二 (*lit.* of four parts, two)

San-jū-ni no yombún no san wa íkutsu désŭ ka. How much is ¾ of 32?
三十二 の 四分 の 三 は いくつ です か.
(*lit.* 32 of, of four parts three, how much is?=Of 32, of 4 parts 3, how much is it?)

---

1 *to* may be omitted, but when used it corresponds to *if*

When a number is followed by a fraction without specifying what they represent, the numerative *ka* か is used between the number and the fraction, as in the following example:

4⅓   *yon **ka** sambún no ichí*   四か三分の一

In cases as the above, the numerative *ka* might be considered to take place of the conjunction **and** (four **and** one third).

When the thing that the number and fraction represent is mentioned, the numerative *ka* か is not used, as in the following example:

5¾ miles—*go máiru yombún no san* (*lit*. four miles, of four parts, three.)
五マイル 四分 の 三

Ordinal Numbers

Ordinal numbers are formed by placing the word ***bammé*** 番目 after the cardinal numbers, preceded or not by ***dái*** 第, as given in Lesson 12, page 69. ***No*** is used before the noun that follows the ordinal number.

*Hachí-**bammé** no denchū.*	八番目の電柱.	⎫
***Dái**-hachí-**bammé** no denchū.*	第八番目の電柱.	⎬ The eighth electric pole.
***Dái-hachí** denchū.*	第八電柱.	⎭

*Anó rétsu no **dái-ichí-bammé** no katá wa miyasamá désŭ.*
あの 列 の 第一番目 の 方 は 宮様 です.
The first person in that line is an Imperial prince.
(*lit*. Of that line the first person, prince is.)

*Konó kádo kará **go-bammé** no ié wa watashí no uchí désŭ.*
この 角 から 五番目 の 家 は 私 の 家 です.
The fifth house from this corner is my house.
(*lit*. From this corner the fifth house, my house is.)

Note the following expressions, which may be used both as adjectives and nouns:

saishó no	最初の	the first, the first one
tsugí no	次の	the next, the next one
áto no	後の	the one after
máe no	前の	the one before
sáigo no	最後の	⎫
ichibán shimái no	一番しまいの	⎬ the last, the last one
ichibán owarí no	一番終りの	⎭

Chūshingura[1] no ichibán shimái no makú[2] wa taihén omoshirói désŭ.
忠臣蔵 の 一番 しまい の 幕 は 大変 面白い です.
The last scene of Chūshingura is very interesting.

---

1 *Chūshingura* is the name of the most popular Japanese drama, telling the story of forty-seven devoted retainers, who sacrificed their lives to avenge their wronged master. See page 619 for description of this story. **2** *makú* scene

The order of succession of sovereigns is indicated by the ordinal number, followed by the word *sei* 世. *Dái* before the number indicating the order of succession may be omitted.

Edowādo dái-hássei	エドワード第八世	Edward VIII
Jōji rokú-séi	ジョージ六世	George VI

Idiomatic Usage

Ichí—, *dái-ichí* 第一, *ichíban* 一番, *dái-ichíban* 第一番 without being followed by *me* 目, may be used idiomatically with a superlative meaning, as expressed in the following examples:

Káre wa sekái ichí (dái-ichí, ichíban, dái-ichíban) no káshu[1] désŭ.
彼　は　世界　一　（　第一,　一番,　第一番　）　の　歌手　です.
He is No. 1 (A1, the best, etc.) singer in the world.

Káre wa tōshi[2] dái-ichí (ichíban, etc.) no fugō désŭ.
彼　は　当市　第一　（　一番;　）　の　富豪　です.
He is the richest man in our city.

Káre wa ichíban (dái-ichí, etc.) no séito désŭ.   He is the top
彼　は　一番　（　第一;　）　の　生徒　です.   (No. 1, etc.) student.

Kánojo wa kúrasu[3] dái-ichí (ichíban, etc.) désŭ.
彼女　は　クラス　第一　（　一番;　）　です.
She is the best (the top, etc.) of the class.

ichíban de shikén[4] ni gōkaku[5] surú   to pass an examination first
一番　で　試験　に　合格　する   on the list

ichíban shōbu[6] 一番勝負   contest decided by a single game

Jōji rokú-séi ga sen-kyū-hyakú-go-jū-ni nen ni-gatsú muiká ni hōgyo asoba-
ジョージ六世が　千九百五十二　年　二月　六日　に　崩御　遊ば

saretá[7] sokkokú karé no ōjo[8] wa Erizabesú niséi, sunáwachi, Eikokú joō[9] to
された　即刻　彼　の　王女　は　エリザベス　二世,　即ち,　英国　女王と

nararemáshĭta.   George VI died on February 6th, 1952 and upon his demise
なられました.   his daughter became Elisabeth II, Queen of England.

Years and Eras

The Japanese count the years by *eras*, which correspond to the reigns of the emperors that have ruled Japan since its foundation as an empire in the year 660 B. C.

The present era is called *Shōwa* 昭和, and began on the 26th of December, 1926.

The *Méiji* 明治 Era began in 1868 and ended on the 30th of July, 1912.

The *Taishō* 大正 Era, which preceded the present Era, began on July 31st, 1912, and ended on the 25th of December, 1926.

---

1 singer 2 city 3 class 4 examination 5 *gōkaku surú* to succeed in (an examination) 6 game, contest 7 *hōgyo asobasarerú* to demise 8 *sokkokú* immediately, at once; *ōjo* daughter of a sovereign 9 *joō* queen

Nihón no Kinjō Héika no Go-sokuishikí wa Shōwa sannén jū-ichĭ-gatsŭ
日本　の　今上　陛下　の　御即位式　は　昭和　三年　十一　月

tōka ni Kyōto de ageraremáshĭta. (*sokuishiki* enthronment ceremony;
十日　に　京都　で　挙げられました.   *Go* honorific)

    The ceremony for the enthronement of the present Emperor of Japan was held in Kyoto on the 10th of November, 1928 (the third year of the Shōwa Era).

    The years of the Christian era are named by the word **seireki** 西暦 (Western Calendar), followed by the cardinal number indicating the year.

Kotoshí wa seireki *sen* (or *issén*) *kyū-hyakú-rokujū-ichı* *nen désŭ.*
今年　は　西暦　千　（一千）　九百六十一　年　です。
    We are now in the year 1961. (*lit.* This year Western calendar 1961 year is.)

half a year	*han toshí, han nen* (Lit.)	半年, 半年
this year	*kotoshí, honnén* (Lit.)	今年, 本年
last year	*kyónen, sakunén* (Lit.)	去年, 昨年
next year	*rainén*	来年
the following year	{ *akurú-toshí* { *yokunén* (Lit.)	明くる年 翌年
the year before last	*otótoshi, issakú nen* (Lit.)	一昨年(おととし), 一昨年
the year after next	*sarainén*	再来年

    When words indicating divisions of time are used subjectively they are followed by *wa* or *ga* according to the rules already given governing these two postpositions. However, they are not followed by any postposition when they are used adverbially.

Kotoshí wa *urūdoshi désŭ kará sakunén yóri mo ichí-nichí ōi désŭ.*
今年　は　閏年　です　から　昨年　より　も　一日　多いです。
    This year, being leap year, is one day longer than last year.

Sakunén wa *honnén yóri mo áme ga takŭsán furimáshĭta.*
昨年　は　本年　より　も　雨　が　沢山　降りました.
    Last year it rained more than this year.
    (Last year, this year than, rain much fell.)

Watashí wa **rainén** *Yōroppa e mairimásŭ.*   Next year I shall
私　は　来年　ヨーロッパへ　参ります.   go to Europe.

The Four Seasons of The Year
Shiki 四季

háru	春	spring	*áki*	秋	autumn
natsŭ	夏	summer	*fuyŭ*	冬	winter

    When named in combination, the four seasons are also called: **shun-ka-shū-tō** 春夏秋冬, an expression of Chinese origin.

Ichí nen wa shikí ni wakárete imásŭ.   The year is divided into four
一　年　は　四季　に　分かれて　います。   seasons.

Háru wa ichí nen-jū de ichibán yói kisétsu¹ désŭ.   Spring is the best season
春　は　一　年　中で　一番　よい　季節　です。   of the year.

The Day and its Divisions

day	*hirú* 昼 *hirumá* 昼間		to-day	*kyō* きょう *kónnichi*²	今日
morning	*ása* 朝		to-night	*kon-ya* 今夜 *kómban*²	今晩
noon	{ *shōgo* 正午² { *hirú* 昼		to-morrow	*ashĭtá* あした *myōnichi*²	明日
afternoon	*gógo* 午後		yesterday	*kinō* きのう *sakújitsu*²	昨日
evening	*yū* 夕 *yūgata* 夕方		this morning	*késa* けさ *konchō*²	今朝
night	*yóru* 夜 *yábun* 夜分		this evening	*kómban* 今晩 *kyō no yūgata* きょうの夕方
midnight	*yonaká* 夜中		last night	*sakúban* 昨晩 *sakuyá* 昨夜 *yūbe* ゆうべ

to-morrow morning	*ashĭtá no ása*	あしたの朝 *myōchō*²	明朝
to-morrow before noon	*ashĭta no gozén*	あしたの午前 *myōgozen*²	明午前
to-morrow afternoon	*ashĭtá no gógo*	あしたの午後 *myōgogo*²	明午後
to-morrow evening	*ashĭtá no yūgata*	あしたの夕方 *myōyū*²	明夕
to-morrow night	*ashĭtá no ban*	あしたの晩 *myōban*²	明晩
yesterday morning	*kinō no ása*	きのうの朝 *sakuchō*²	昨朝
the day before yesterday	*ototói* おととい *issakújitsu* (Lit.)	一昨日
the day after to-morrow	*asátte* さあって *myōgonichi* (Lit.)	明後日
three days ago	*issakú-sakújitsu*	一昨々日
three years ago	*issakú-sakunén*	一昨々年
three nights ago	*issakú-sakuyá*	一昨々夜

Dōzo myōgonichi oidé kudasái.   Please call on me the day after to-morrow.
どうぞ　明後日　お出で下さい。

Ototói Sumidá-gawá no atarashíi hashí no kaitsūshiki³ wo mimáshĭta.
おととい　隅田川　の　新しい　橋　の　開通式　を　見ました。
The day before yesterday I saw the ceremony for the opening of the new bridge over the Sumida river.

Kyō wa taihén íi o-ténki désŭ.   We are having a very fine day.
きょうは　大変　いゝお天気　です。   The weather is very fine to-day.

The Days of the Week

Monday	*getsuyō(bi)*	月曜(日)	from	*getsu*	moon	and	*yōbi*
Tuesday	*kayō(bi)*	火曜(日)	from	*ka*	fire	and	*yōbi*
Wednesday	*suiyō(bi)*	水曜(日)	from	*sui*	water	and	*yōbi*
Thursday	*mokuyō(bi)*	木曜(日)	from	*moku*	wood	and	*yōbi*
Friday	*kin-yō(bi)*	金曜(日)	from	*kin*	gold	and	*yōbi*
Saturday	*doyō(bi)*	土曜(日)	from	*do*	earth	and	*yōbi*
Sunday	*nichiyō(bi)*	日曜(日)	from	*nichi*	sun	and	*yōbi*

1 *kisétsu* season   **2** literary style   **3** *kaitsūshiki* opening (inauguration) ceremony

Bi 日 modified pronunciation of *hi* 日 day; *yōbi* 曜日 day of week.

Kyō wa náni yōbi désŭ ka.   What day of the week is to-day?
きょうは 何 曜日 です か。

Kyō wa kayōbi désŭ. きょうは火曜日です。   To-day is Tuesday.

On, used before days of the week, is translated by *ni.*

Watashí wa Nihón-go no kéiko wo getsuyōbi, suiyōbi, kin-yōbi ni shimásŭ.
私 は 日本語 の 稽古 を 月曜日、 水曜日、 金曜日 に します。
I take Japanese lessons **on** Mondays, Wednesdays, and Fridays.

Taigái nichiyōbi ni wa Nikkō e ikimásŭ.   **On** Sundays I generally go
大概   日曜日 に は 日光 へ行きます。   to Nikkō.

When two or more days of the week are mentioned in succession
the termination *yōbi* may be omitted. *Getsuyōbi* may be shortened
also into *getsu.*

Watashí wa Itarī-go no kéiko wo getsu, sŭi, kin ni shimásŭ.
私   はイタリー語の 稽古 を 月、 水、 金 に します。
I take Italian lessons on Mondays, Wednesdays, and Fridays.

this week	*konshū*	今週	the week before last	*sen-sen-shū*	先々週
next week	*raishū*	来週	the week after next	*rái-rái-shū*	来々週
last week	*senshū*	先週	three weeks ago	*san-shū-kan máe*	三週間前

The Months

January	*ichigatsú*	一月	July	*shichigatsú*	七月
February	*nigatsú*	二月	August	*hachigatsú*	八月
March	*sángatsu*	三月	September	*kúgatsu*	九月
April	*shigatsú*	四月	October	*jūgatsu*	十月
May	*gógatsu*	五月	November	*jū-ichigatsú*	十一月
June	*rokugatsú*	六月	December	*jū-nigatsú*	十二月

this month	*kongetsú*	今月	last month	*séngetsu*	先月
next month	*ráigetsu*	来月	three months ago	*san-ka-getsú máe*	三ヶ月前
	the month before last	*sen-séngetsu*	先々月
	the month after next	*rái-ráigetsu*	来々月

Séngetsu kará Nihón-go no benkyō wo shĭté imásŭ.
先月   から 日本語 の 勉強 を して います。
Since last month I have been studying Japanese.

Sen-séngetsu Indo kará tomodachí to isshó ni Nippón e kimáshĭta.
先々月   インド から 友達   と 一緒 に 日本 へ 来ました。
The month before last I came to Japan from India with a friend.

The months may be counted with the numerals of both Chinese and Japanese origin, as given below ·

ikkágetsu	一か月	*hĭtótsŭki*	一月	one month
ni-kágetsu	二か月	*fŭtatsŭkí*	二月	two months
san-kágetsu	三か月	*mĭtsŭki*	三月	three months
shi-(yon)-kágetsu	四か月	*yótsŭki*	四月	four months
go-kágetsu	五か月	*itsútsŭki*	五月	five months
rokkágetsu	六か月	*mútsŭki*	六月	six months
shichí-(naná)-kágetsu	七か月	*nanátsŭki*	七月	seven months
hakkágetsu	八か月	*yátsŭki*	八月	eight months
ku-kágetsu	九か月	*kokónotsŭki*	九月	nine months
jikkágetsu	十か月	*tótsŭki*	十月	ten months
jū-ikkágetsu	十一か月	*jū-ichítsŭki*	十一月	eleven months

Before the language reforms were promulgated (See Page 15), instead of the *hiragana* symbol か, the symbol ケ was used, which symbol is the upper left part of the character 箇, which was, and is still now, used as a numerative for counting bundles, parcels, round shaped fruits, cakes of soap and other such things that can be handled.

The Days of the Month

1 st	{*ichinichi*	一日	16 th	*jū-rokunichí*	十六日	
	{*tsuitachí*	朔日	17 th	*jū-shichinichí*	十七日	
2 nd	*futsŭká*	二日	18 th	*jū-hachinichí*	十八日	
3 rd	*mikká*	三日	19 th	*jū-kunichí*	十九日	
4 th	*yokká*	四日	20 th	*hatsŭká*	廿日	
5 th	*itsŭká*	五日	21 st	*ni-jū-ichinichí*	二十一日 （廿一日）	
6 th	*muiká*	六日	22 nd	*ni-jū-ninichí*	二十二日 （廿二日）	
7 th	*nanoká*	七日	23 rd	*ni-jū-sannichí*	二十三日 （廿三日）	
8 th	*yōka*	八日	24 th	*ni-jū-yokká*	二十四日 （廿四日）	
9 th	*kokonoká*	九日	25 th	*ni-jū-gónichi*	二十五日 （廿五日）	
10 th	*tōka*	十日	26 th	*ni-jū-rokunichi*	二十六日 （廿六日）	
11 th	*jū-ichinichí*	十一日	27 th	*ni-jū-shichinichí*	二十七日 （廿七日）	
12 th	*jū-ninichí*	十二日	28 th	*ni-jū-hachinichí*	二十八日 （廿八日）	
13 th	*jū-sannichi*	十三日	29 th	*ni-jū-kunichí*	二十九日 （廿九日）	
14 th	*jū-yokká*	十四日	30 th	*san-jūnichí*	三十日 （卅日）	
15 th	*jū-gonichí*	十五日	31 st	*san-jū-ichinichí*	三十一日 （卅一日）	

The first day of the month is called *tsuitachí* 朔日, and the last day of the month *misoká* 晦日. The first day of the year is called *ganjitsŭ* 元日 or *gantán* 元旦, (*Lit.*) and the last day of the year *ō-misoká* 大晦日.

Nihón de wa ō-misoká no ban jū-ni-ji kará jóya no kané[1] ga naridashimásŭ.

日本 で は 大晦日 の 晩 十二時 から 除夜 の 鐘 が 鳴り出します.

In Japan, on the last day of the year at 12 o'clock at night all temple bells begin to ring.

naridásu 鳴り出す *to begin to ring*—This verb is formed by the stem of ***narú*** 鳴る to sound, to ring, to peal and ***dásu*** 出す, which verb, used here as a suffix, corresponds to *to begin to*...... Many compound verbs are formed with the suffix ***dásu*** 出す as in the case of ***naridásu*** 鳴り出す.

Ganjitsŭ *ni wa Nihon-jū dokó no uchí de mo zōni[2] wo tabemásu.*

元日 に は 日本中 どこ の 家 で も 雑煮 を 食べます.

On New Year's Day in Japan, people in all houses eat *zoni*.

The two expressions *What day of the month......? How many days......?* are translated by ***Nan nichí......, Iku nichí......,*** or ***Ikka......***

*Kyō wa **nan nichí** (íku nichí, íkka) désŭ ka.*   What day of the month

きようは 何 日 (幾 日, 幾日) です か.   is it to-day?

*Ōsaka ni **íku nichí** gurai go-taizái[3] désŭ ka.*   About how many days will

大阪 に 幾 日 位 御滞在 です か.   you stay in Osaka?

(*lit.* In Osaka, how many days about your sojourn is it?)

Ago

The adverb **ago,** when used to indicate a past period of time specified in days, months, or years, is translated by ***máe*** 前 (before):

*Yokká **máe**.*   Four days ago.   *Rokkágetsu **máe**.*   Six months ago.

四日 前.   六ヶ 月 前.

*Go-nen **máe**.*   Five years ago.   *Mítsŭki **máe**.*   Three months ago.

五 年 前.   三 月 前.

When the period of time is specified in weeks, ***máe*** is preceded by the word ***kan*** 間.

San-shū-kan máe.   三週間前.   Three weeks ago.

Isshū-kan máe.   一週間前.   One week ago.

If the period of time is specified in hours, ***kan*** forms one single word with ***ji,*** which means *hour.*

Ni-jikán máe.   二時間前.   Two hours ago.

Ni-san-jikán máe.   二三時間前.   Two three hours ago.

As a separate word ***jikán*** 時間 means *time.*

Common indefinite expressions ending in **ago** in English and ***máe*** in Japanese are the following:

---

1 *Jóya* 除夜 New Year's Eve, the watch night; *jóya no kané* the watch night bell, the bell speeding the old year   2 *dóko no......de mo* in whichever......, *uchí* house; *zōni* traditional soup eaten on New Year's Day   3 sojourn

zuttó máe	ずっと前	a long time ago
shibáraku máe	暫く前	sometime ago
sūjitsu máe	数日前	a few, several days ago

Sonná ni máe de wa arimasén.   Not so long ago as that.
そんな に 前 で は ありません.   It is not so long ago.

The past time suggested by any of these expressions is, as in English, in relation to the subject spoken of, so that "a long time ago," may mean any period of time from a few hours to centuries. Examples:

Ima okimáshǐta ka. or *Ima o-okí ni narimáshǐta ka.*   Did you just get
今 起きました か.   今 お起きに なりました か.   up?

Iié, zuttó máe ni okimáshǐta.   No, I got up a long time ago.
いゝえ, ずっと前 に 起きました.

Haradá san no go-ryōshin wa zuttó máe ni nakunarimáshǐta.
原田 さん の 御両親 は ずっと 前 に 亡くなりました.
Mr. Harada's parents died a long time ago.

Anáta no o-jōsan wa Igirisú e irasshátta to shibáraku máe ni
貴方 の お嬢さん は イギリスへいらっしゃったと 暫く 前 に
ukagaimáshǐta.   Sometime ago they told me that your daughter had gone to
伺いました.   England.
   (*lit.* Your daughter to England went, so sometime before I heard.)

Musŭmé wa Eikokú e wa mairimasén déshǐta ga Itarī e ongakú no
娘 は 英国 へ は 参りません でした がイタリーへ 音楽 の
kenkyū ni mairimáshǐta.   She did not go to England, but she went to Italy
研究 に 参りました.   to study music.

Sūjitsu máe ni konó tokoró de jū-go-ken ié ga yakemáshǐta.
数日 前 に この 所 で 十五軒 家 が 焼けました.
A few days ago fifteen houses were burnt in this district.

Other common expressions indicating a past period of time are *móto* 元, *ízen* 以前 *formerly, once*, and *mukashi* 昔 *in olden days, in days gone by*. *Móto, ízen,* and *mukashi* may all be used to translate the expression *a long time ago*. Note that *móto* is used in ordinary, *ízen* in formal, speech.

Móto watashí wa anó apāto ni súnde imáshǐta.
元 私 は あのアパートに住んでいました.
Formerly I lived in that apartment house.

Sonó hanashí wa ízen (móto) kikimáshǐta (ukagaimáshǐta).
その 話 は 以前 (元) 聞きました (伺いました).
I heard that story a long time ago.

Konó shiró wa mukashí kizukaremáshǐta.   This castle was built a long
この 城 は 昔 築かれました.   time ago.
   kizúku 築く to build, *kizukaréru* 築かれる to be built

Expressions indicating periods of time, preceded or not by the preposition *for* or *during*, are formed with the word *kan* 間 (interval, period), as shown in the following examples: (See Lesson 31.)

mikká-kan	三日間	(for *or* during a period of) three days
yon-kágetsu-kan	四か月間	(for *or* during a period of) four months
jūnen-kan	十年間	(for *or* during a period of) ten years

Vocabulary

Nouns

apprentice	*kozō*	小ㇱ僧ゾウ
Buddhism	*Bukkyō*	仏ブッ教キョウ
building	*kenchikubutsú*	建ケン築チク物ブツ
chivalry	*bushidō*	武ブ士シ道ドウ
chrysanthemum	*kikú*	菊キク
emblem	*shōchō*	象ショウ徴チョウ
era, period	*miyó*	御ミ代ヨ
Far East (the)	*Kyokutō*	極キク東トウ
municipality	*shiyákŭsho*	市シ役ヤク所ショ
owner	*mochínushi*	持モチ主ヌシ
prize	*shō*	賞ショウ
purity	*junketsú*	純ジュン潔ケツ
ruler	*tōchisha*	統トウ治チ者シャ

season	*jíki*	時ジ季キ
show	*tenrankái*	展テン覧ラン会カイ
symbol	*shirushí*	印シン
throne	*mi-kurái*	御ミ位クラ

Verbs

to celebrate	*iwáu*	祝イウ
to exhibit	*shuppín surú*	出品スル
to last	*tsuzukú*	続ツク
to open / to inaugurate	*hiráku*	開ヒラク
to receive	*uké·ru*	受ウケル
to rule over	*osamé·ru*	治オサメル
to set up	*narabe·rú*	並ナラベル
to venerate	*uyamáu*	敬ウヤマウ

the reigning (Emperor) *Kinjō*; emperor *tennō*; His, Her, Your Majesty *Héika*; His Majesty the reigning Emperor *Kinjō Tennō Héika*; The name of a dead emperor is generally followed by the word *Tennō*; to succeed to the throne *mi-kurái ni o-tsŭkí ni náru*; to rule over *osamé ni náru*; great, illustrious *erái*; knightly honour *búshi no méiyo*; potted chrysanthemums *hachiué no kikú*; Europe *Yōroppa*; Australia *Ōsŭtorariya*; North America *Hokubéi*; South America *Nambéi*; Doll's Festival *Hiná Matsurí*; wooden stand *ki no dái*; knightly *búshi no*; honour *méiyo*

Exercise *Renshū* 練習

1. Kinjō Tennō Héika wa dái hyakú-ni-jū-yo dái-me no Nippón Téikoku no tōchisha de irasshaimásŭ.[1] Héika wa sen-kyū-hyakú-ichí-nen shi-gatsú ni-jū-ku nichí ni o-umaré ni narimáshĭta,[2] soshíte sen-kyūhyaku-ni-jū-go-nen jū-ni gatsú ni-jū-go nichí ni chichigími[3] Taishō Tennō ga o-kakuré[4] ni nátta tokí mikurái ni o-tsŭkí ni narimáshĭta. **2.** Méiji Tennō wa yon-jū-go-nen kan Nihón wo o-osamé ni nári issén-kyū-hyakú-ni-nen shichí-gatsú-san-jū-nichí ni hōgyo asobasaremáshĭta.[5] Méiji Tennō wa Nihón no ichibán erái tennō to

---

1 *irasshaimásŭ* used instead of *áru*   **2** *o-umaré ni náru* polite for *umarerú* to be born   **3** *chichigími* very polite for father and only used in literary style   **4** *o-kakuré ni náru* to die, to pass away, used when referring to members of the Imperial family   **5** *hōgyo asobasarerú* to demise, pass away, used only when referring to an emperor's demise

shĭté Nihón kokumín kará uyamawárete[1] oraremásŭ. **3.** Nihón no dái ni-jū-
kyū-dái no tennō wa Kimméi Tennō déshĭta. Kimméi Tennō wa seirekí
go-hyakú-yon-jū-nen kará go-hyakú-nána-jū-ni-nen máde konó kuní wo o-osamé[2] ni nararemáshĭta. Kimméi Tennō no míyo ni Bukkyō ga Nihón e hairimáshĭta. **4.** Sen-kyū-hyakú-ni-jū-san-nen ku-gatsú tsuitachí ni dái-jishín ga
okorimáshĭta. Konó dái-jishín[3] no tokí ni oyosó kyū-man-nin guraí no hĭtó
ga Tōkyō to Yokohamá de shinimáshĭta. Konó dái-jishín ízen ni wa Tōkyō
to Yokohamá ni wa ōki-na tatémono wa amarí nákú[4] taitéi no[5] dōro wa
sémakatta[6] no déshĭta. Kónnichi Tōkyō wa Kyokutō ni okéru[7] móttomo
utsukushíi tokái de ári takŭsán no ōki-na kenchikubutsú, hirói dōro, utsukushíi
kōen ga arimásŭ. **5.** Nihón ni wa ichí-nen-jū shikí wo tsūjite[8] utsukushíi
haná ga arimásŭ, ga móttomo yói haná no jíki wa háru sakurá no haná no
mankaí surú tokí désŭ. Nihón de wa sakurá no haná wa junketsú no shirushí
de ári bushidō to búshi no méiyo no shōchō de arimásŭ. **6.** Mái nen jū-ichí-
gatsú hajimé ni Tōkyō-to[9] shusái no motó[10] ni kikú no haná no tenrankái
ga Hibiyá Kōen de hirakaremásŭ.[11] Konó tenrankái ni wa takŭsán no
hachiué no kikú ga shuppín saremásŭ,[12] soshĭté ichibán utsŭkushíi haná no
mochínushi ga shō wo ukemásŭ. **7.** Nihón, Chūgoku, Roshiyá, Yōroppa,
Hokubéi de wa jū-nigatsú, ichigatsú, nigatsú wa fuyú no tsŭkí désŭ ga
Ōsŭtorariya to minamí Afuriká to Nambéi de wa natsú no tsŭkí désŭ. **8.** Mái-
nen sángatsu mikká ni, chiisái musŭmé no áru taitéi no Nihón no katéi[13]
de wa " Hiná Matsurí " wo iwaimásŭ. Konó matsurí no tokí ni katéi no
musŭmé no yorokobí no tamé ni[14] chiisái ningyō ga ki no dái no ué ni
naraberaremásŭ.[15] **9.** Nihón no ichibán samúi jíki wa ichigatsú no itsŭká
ka muiká kará hajimarí hatsŭká kan tsuzukimásŭ. Konó samúi jíki wa
kan to yobaremásŭ. **10.** Oyosó san-jū nen guraí máe máde Nihón de wa ichigatsú no jū-go-nichí, jū-rokú-nichí to shichigatsú no jū-go, jū-rokú nichí to
wa *Yabuirí* to itté jochū ya génan ya kozō no han-toshí me no yasumibí[16]
déshĭta.

　　1. 今上天皇陛下は第百廿四代目の日本帝国の統治者でいらっしゃ
います. 陛下は千九百一年四月二十九日にお生れになりました. そし
て千九百二十五年十二月二十五日に父君大正天皇がおかくれになった
時御位におつきになりました. **2.** 明治天皇は四十五年間日本をお治
めになり，一千九百十二年七月卅日に崩御遊ばされました. 明治天皇
は日本の一番偉い天皇として日本国民から敬われておられます.
3. 日本の第二十九代の天皇は欽明天皇でした欽明天皇は西暦五百四
十年から五百七十二年迄この国をお治めになられました. 欽明天皇の

---

1 *uyamawárete oraréru* to be venerated, respected　**2** *o-osamé ni nararéru* polite for
osaméru to rule　**3** *dái-jishín* big earthquake　**4** *amarí nákú* few　**5** *taitéi no*
most　**6** *sémakatta no déshĭta* were narrow　**7** *ni okéru* used in formal speech
instead of *ni* in　**8** *tsūjite* all through ; *shikí wo tsūjite* through all the four seasons
9 *Tōkyō-to* Tokyo metropolis　**10** *shusái no motó ni* under the auspices of　**11** *hirakaréru* to be opened, inaugurated, as an exhibition, etc.　**12** *shuppín sarerú* to be
exhibited　**13** family　**14** *yorokobí no tamé ni* for the enjoyment　**15** *naraberarerú*
to be set up　**16** holiday, day of rest

御代に仏教が日本へ入りました．4. 千九百廿三年九月朔日（一日）に
大地震が起りました．この大地震の時に凡そ九万人位の人が東京と横
浜で死にました．この大地震以前には東京と横浜には大きな建物は余
りなく大抵の道路はせまかったのでした．今日東京は極東に於ける最
も美しい都会であり沢山の大きな建築物，広い道路，美しい公園があ
ります．5. 日本には一年中四季を通じて美しい花がありますが最も
よい花の時季は春桜の花の満開する時です．日本では桜の花は純潔の
印であり武士道と武士の名誉の象徴であります．6. 毎年十一月初め
に東京都主催の下に菊の花の展覧会が日比谷公園で開かれます．この
展覧会には沢山の鉢植の菊が出品されますそして一番美しい花の持主
が賞を受けます．7. 日本，支那，ロシヤ，ヨーロッパ，北米では十二
月，一月，二月は冬の月ですがオーストラリヤと南アフリカと南米で
は夏の月です．8. 毎年三月三日に，小さい娘のある大抵の日本の家
庭では「雛祭」を祝います．この祭の時に家庭の小さい娘の喜びの為
に小さい人形が木の台の上に並べられます．9. 日本の一番寒い時期
は一月の五日か六日から初まり廿日間続きます．この寒い時期は「寒」
と呼ばれます．10. 凡そ三十年ぐらい前まで日本では一月の十五日，
十六日と七月の十五，十六日とは「藪入」と言って女中や下男や小僧
の半年目の休み日でした．

1. His Imperial Majesty Hirohito[1] is the one hundred and twenty-fourth
ruler of the Japanese Empire. He was born on April 29th, 1901, and succeeded
to the throne on the death of his father, the Emperor Taisho, on December
25th, 1925. 2. Emperor Meiji ruled over Japan for forty-five years; he died
on July 30th, 1912. The Emperor Meiji is venerated by all Japanese people
as the greatest emperor of Japan. 3. The 29th Emperor of Japan was Kimmei, who ruled this country from the year 540 to the year 572 A. D. During
the Kimmei Era Buddhism was introduced into Japan. 4. On September 1st,
1923 a great earthquake occurred. During that great earthquake about 90,000
people perished in Tokyo and Yokohama. Before the great earthquake Tokyo
and Yokohama had few large buildings, and most of their streets were
narrow. To-day Tokyo is the most beautiful city in the Far East, and has
many large buildings, wide streets and fine parks. 5. In Japan there are
beautiful flowers in all the four seasons of the year, but the best season for
flowers is spring, when the cherry flowers are in full bloom. In Japan the
cherry blossom is the symbol of purity and the emblem of chivalry and
knightly honour. 6. Every year at the beginning of November, a chrysanthemum show is opened at Hibiya Park under the auspices of the Tokyo metro-

---

1 Translate: His Majesty the present Emperor (*Kinjō Tennō Héika*), omitting
the proper name. In Japanese conversation and even in written style, the name of
the reigning emperor is rarely mentioned. The reigning emperor is referred to as
"His Majesty the Present Emperor."

police. During this show many potted chrysanthemum plants are exhibited and the owners of the most beautiful ones receive prizes. **7.** December, January, and February are winter months in Japan, China, Russia, Europe and North America, but they are summer months in Australia, South Africa, and South America. **8.** Every year, on the 3rd of March, most Japanese families with little daughters celebrate the Doll's Festival. During this festival small dolls are set up on wooden stands for the enjoyment of the little girls in the home. **9.** The real cold season in Japan is supposed to begin on the 5th or the 6th of January, and to last twenty days. This cold season is called *kan*. **10.** In Japan until about thirty years ago, the 15th and 16th of January and the 15th and 16th of July, were the days for the *Yabuiri*, or the semi-annual holidays for maid-servants, boy-servants and apprentices.

Forty-third Lesson   第四十三課

The Hours of the Day

Hour *ji* 時	Minute *fun* 分	Second *byō* 秒
ichí-jíkan 一時間 one hour	*nífun* 二分 two minutes	
san-jíkan 三時間 three hours	*jūbyō* 十秒 ten seconds	

When indicating a period of hours the word **kan** is always used, but it may be omitted when indicating a number of minutes or seconds. **Kan** 間, as used in the above expressions, means *duration*, so that *ichí-ji-kan* 一時間 corresponds to *one hour's duration*.

The word **fun** undergoes the following orthographic changes:

ippun 一分 one minute, *nífun* 二分 two minutes, *sámpun* 三分 three minutes, *yómpun* or *shífun* 四分 four minutes, *gófun* 五分 five minutes, *róppun* 六分 six minutes, *shichífun* or *nanáfun* 七分 seven minutes, *hachífun* 八分 eight minutes, *kyūfun* 九分 nine minutes, *jíppun* 十分 ten minutes.

jū-gófun	十五分	a quarter of an hour
han-jíkan	半時間	half an hour
yon-jū-gófun	四十五分	three quarters of an hour

Examples

Ichí nichí wa ni-jū-yo-jíkan désŭ.
一　日　は　二十四時間　です。
(*lit.* One day twenty-four hours is.)

In one day there are twenty-four hours.

Ichí-jíkan wa rokú-jíppun désŭ.   In one hour there are sixty minutes.
一時間　は　六十分　です.

Ippun wa rokú-jū-byō désŭ.   One minute contains sixty seconds.
一分　は　六十秒　です.

Watashí wa anáta wo ni-jíkan-han mátte imáshĭta.
私　は　貴方　を　二時間半　待っていました.
I waited for you two hours and a half.

When indicating the time of day *kan* is not used.

Ima nánji désŭ ka.   今, 何時ですか.   What time is it now?
Ichíji désŭ.   一時です.   It is one o'clock.
Sánji désŭ.   三時です.   It is three o'clock.
Góji-han désŭ.   五時半です.   It is half past five.

Every

In Lesson 19, page 113, it has been stated that the distributive
adjective **every** is translated by *mái* 毎 placed before nouns indicating periods of time.

mái nen   毎年   every year

Every may be translated also by *góto-ni* placed after the noun
indicating a period of time, which, in this case, is preceded by a
numeral whenever a day of the week or a month of the year is
mentioned. When *mái* is used, the postposition *ni* may follow
the name of the days of the week, but is generally omitted in other
cases.

mái jíkan	毎時間	*ichí jíkan góto-ni*	一時間毎に	every hour
mái nichí	毎日	*ichí nichí góto-ni*	一日毎に	every day
mái shū	毎週	*isshūkan góto-ni*	一週間毎に	every week
mái getsú	毎月	*ikkágetsu góto-ni*	一か月毎に	every month
mái kayōbi	毎火曜日	*kayō(bi) góto-ni*	火曜(日)毎に	every Tuesday

Examples

Watashí wa mái shū (or *isshūkan góto-ni*) *ikkái ikébana[1] no kéiko*
私　は　毎　週　（一週間　毎　に）　一回　活花　の　稽古
wo shimásŭ.   I take flower arrangement lessons once every week.
を　します.   (*kéiko wo surú* to practice, to take lessons)

Tóshiko San wa mái doyōbi (ni) uchí ni kimású.
とし子　さん　は　毎　土曜日　（に）　家　に　来ます.
Tóshiko San wa doyōbi góto-ni uchí ni kimású.
とし子　さん　は　土曜日　毎　に　家　に　来ます.
} Miss Toshiko comes to our home every Saturday.

[1] flower arrangement

Mái suiyōbi (ni) éiga e yukimásŭ.
毎　水曜日　（に）映画へ　行きます.　⎫

Suiyōbi góto-ni éiga e yukimásŭ.　⎬ I go to the cinema every
水曜日　毎　に　映画へ　行きます.　⎭ Wednesday.

*Konó shibaí no puroguramú wa **mái mokuyōbi** (ni) kawarimásŭ.*
この　芝居　の　プログラム　は　毎　木曜日　（に）替ります.

or *Konó shibaí no puroguramú wa **mokuyōbi góto-ni** kawarimásŭ.*
この　芝居　の　プログラム　は　木曜日　毎　に　替ります.

The program of this theatre changes every Thursday.

Mái kin-yōbi (ni) or *Kin-yōbi góto-ni yūransen ga Yokohamá kará*
毎　金曜日　（に）　金曜日　毎　に　遊覧船　が　横浜　から

Okinawá e demásŭ.   Every Friday an excursion steamer leaves Yokohama for
沖縄　へ　出ます.   Okinawa.

If the numeral is above **one,** the distributive adjective **every** is translated by *góto-ni* only.

futsŭká góto-ni	二日毎に	every two days
rokú shū kan góto-ni	六週間毎に	every six weeks
jikkágetsu góto-ni	十か月毎に	every ten months
ni-jū nen góto-ni	廿年毎に	every twenty years

*Haréi suiséi wa **naná-jū-go** nen-me **góto-ni** ichidó arawaremásŭ.*
ハレイ　彗星　は　七十五　年目　毎　に　一度　現われます.

Halley's comet appears once in every seventy-five years.

*Yokohamá yukí no dénsha wa Tōkyō kará **gófun góto-ni** demásŭ.*
横浜　行の　電車　は　東京　から　五分　毎　に　出ます.

An electric train leaves Tokyo for Yokohama every five minutes.

When used before words that do not indicate periods of time, **every** is translated by *góto-ni.* Also in this case the construction with *mai* is not used.

Ichí-go wo masú[1] ***góto-ni*** go yen harawáneba narimasén.*
一語　を　増す　毎　に　五　円　払わねば　なりません.

You must pay five yen for every additional word.

*Kúroda San wa áu hĭtó **góto-ni** musŭkó no jimán*[2] *wo shimásŭ.*
黒田　さん　は　会う　人　毎　に　息子　の　自慢　を　します.

Mr. Kuroda boasts of his son to every man he meets.
(*lit.* Mr. Kuroda, to meet person every, son's boast does.)

*Watashí no otōto wa kotó **góto-ni** seikō shimásŭ.*
私　の　弟　は　事　毎　に　成功　します.

My younger brother succeeds in every thing he undertakes.
(*lit.* My younger brother, thing every, success makes.)

---

1 *masú* to increase, to augment   **2** *jimán wo surú* to boast

Idioms

taitéi mái-nichí	大抵毎日	almost every day
taitéi no kodomó	大抵の子供	almost every child
ichí-nichí óki	一日置き	every other day
ichí-nichí ni ni-do	一日に二度	twice a day
hirú to yóru	昼と夜	day and night

Kyō wa ashĭtá wa to itté imá-máde nobashimáshĭta.
きよう は あした は と云って今 迄 延ばしました.
It has been put off from day to day.
(*lit.* To-day, tomorrow, so saying until now adjourned.)

Taitéi no otokonokó wa konó hanashí wo shĭtté imásŭ.
大抵 の 男の子 は この 話 を 知っています.
Almost every boy knows this story. (Most boys this story know.)

Jūji jíppun máe désŭ. 十時十分前です.   It is ten minutes before ten.

Jū-ichíji jū-gofun máe désŭ.   It is a quarter before eleven.
十一時 十五分 前 です.

Jū-ichíji jū-gófun sugí[1] désŭ.   It is fifteen minutes past eleven.
十一時 十五分 過ぎ です.

Sánji níjippun sugí désŭ.   It is twenty minutes after three.
三時 二十分 過ぎ です.

Yonaká no jū-niji jū-nifun sugí désŭ.   It is twelve minutes past
夜中 の 十二時 十二分 過ぎ です.   midnight.

Nán-ji ni Kōbe kará resshá ga tsŭkimáshĭta ka.
何時 に 神戸 から 列車 が 着きました か.
At what o'clock did the train from Kobe arrive?

Resshá wa hachíji-yon-jū-gófun ni[2] tsŭkimáshĭta.   The train arrived at 8.45.
列車 は 八時四十五分 に 着きました.

Watashí wa jū-níji no resshá de Tōkyō wo tachimásŭ.
私 は 十二時 の 列車 で 東京 を 立ちます.
I shall leave Tokyo by the twelve o'clock train. (*tátsu* to leave, to depart)

Konó tokéi wa jíppun susundé imásŭ.   This clock is ten minutes fast.
この 時計 は 十分 進んで います.   (This clock ten minutes advances.)

Watashí no tokéi wa gófun okureté imásŭ.   My watch is five minutes
私 の 時計 は 五分 後れて います.   slow.

ása no kishá	朝の汽車	} the morning train
gozén no resshá	午前の列車	
gógo no kishá	午後の汽車	} the afternoon train
gógo no resshá	午後の列車	
yakō resshá	夜行列車	} the night train
yógisha	夜汽車	

---

1 *sugí* past, after **2** at

jikán wo awasé·ru 時間を合わせる   ⎫
tokéi wo awasé·ru 時計を合わせる   ⎬ to set a watch

tokéi wo makú   時計を巻く   to wind a watch

Instead of......*kawari ni* 代りに

No is placed before *kawari ni* when this expression is preceded by a noun, but it is omitted when *kawari ni* is preceded by a verb.

Mugiwará bōshi no kawari ni fuerutó bōshi wo kaimáshǐta.
麦わら 帽子 の 代り に フエルト 帽子 を 買いました.
Instead of a straw hat I bought a felt hat.

Jūji no resshá de shuppatsú surú kawari ni yūgata no resshá de
十時 の 列車 で 出発 する 代り に 夕方 の 列車 で
shuppatsú shimásǔ.   **Instead of** leaving by the ten o'clock train I shall leave by
出発 します.   the evening train.

    (*lit.* Ten o'clock's train by, departure to do instead, evening's train by departure I do.)

Bakabánashi wo shǐté jikán wo tsubusú kawari ni kokó e kité konó
ばか話 を して 時間 を つぶす 代り に ここへ来て この
shigotó wo shiagéru[1] no wo tetsudái[2] nasái.
仕事 を し上げる の を 手伝い なさい.
Come here and help me finish this work **instead of** wasting time with your silly talk. (*lit.* Silly-talk doing, time to dissipate instead, here coming, this work to finish help do.)

Before

When **before** indicates position, or when used to indicate the time, it is translated by *máe* or *máe ni,* as already shown in previous lessons.

When the idea of **before** indicates a relation between two events, in addition to *máe* or *máe ni,* one may use *ízen* 以前, which is more literary in style.

Tokugawá jidái ízen (máe) Tōkyō wa chíisana machí de átta.
徳川 時代 以前 (前) 東京 は 小さな 町 であった.
Before the Tokugawa era Tokyo was a small town.

Watashí wa Nihón ni kúru máe (ízen) ni Nihón-go wo naraimáshǐta.
私 は 日本 に 来る 前 (以前) に 日本語 を 習いました.
Before I came to Japan I studied Japanese.

When **before** indicates an action of short duration that immediately precedes or has preceded another action, only *máe* or *máe ni* is used.

---

1 *shiagéru* to finish   **2** *tetsudáu* to help

Nihón-jin *wa* *o-miyá* *ni* *máiru* **máe** **ni** *seisuí* *de* *te* *wo* *araí* *kuchí* *wo*
日本人　は　お宮　に　参る　前　に　清水　で　手　を　洗い　口　を

susugimásŭ.　　**Before** approaching a Shinto shrine, the Japanese wash their hands
すすぎます.　　and rinse their mouth with fresh water. (*lit.* The Japanese, Shinto-
　　　　　　　shrine to, to go before, with clear water hands wash and mouth
　　　　　　　rinse.)

A verb preceded by **before,** whether referring to the present or the
past may be translated by the simple present, followed by *máe ni*
or *ízen ni,* or by its negative form in *nái* followed by *uchí ni*
うちに, which is more colloquial.

Watashí *wa* *Nitobé* *Hákase* *ga* *nakunarú* *mikká* **máe** **ni** (*ízen* **ni**)
私　は　新渡戸　博士　が　亡くなる　三日　前　に　(以前　に)

o-me *ni* *kakarimáshĭta.*　　I met Dr. Nitobe three days **before** he died.
お目　に　かゝりました.　　(I, Dr. Nitobe, to die 3-days before, met.)

Dénsha *ga* **tomaranái** **uchí** **ni** *oríru* *no* *wa* *kikén* *désŭ.*
電車　が　止らない　うち　に　降りるの　は　危険　です.
It is dangerous to get off the streetcar **before** it stops.
(*lit.* Streetcar does not stop while, to alight danger is.)

The expression **the same as before** is translated by *ízen no tōri*
以前の通り or *máe no tōri* 前の通り.

Anáta *wa* *íma* *mo* *ízen* **no** *tōri* *Nippón* *Yūsen* *Kaishá*[1] *de* *hataraité*
貴方　は　今　も　以前　の　通り　日本　郵船　会社　で　仂いて

imásŭ *ka.*　　Are you still working at the Nippon Yūsen Kaisha?
います　か.　　(You, now even, the same as before N.Y.K. at working are you?)

Hái, **máe** **no** *tōri* *íma* *mo* *asokó* *de* *hataraité* *imásŭ.*
はい, 前　の　通り　今　も　あそこ　で　仂いて　います.
Yes, I am still working there the same as before.
(*lit* Yes, the same as before, now even, there working am.)

After

When **after** indicates position without motion it is translated by
ushiró ni 後に (behind), when it refers to a place where action
is performed, it is translated by *ushiró de* 後で, and with verbs
of motion, as *to go, come, walk,* etc., it is translated by *ushiró*
wo 後を.

Watashí *no* *uchí* *no* **ushiró** *ni* *jínja* *ga* *arimásŭ.*　　**After** my house
私　のうちの　後　に　神社　が　あります.　　there is a shrine.

The postposition *ni* に is omitted when *désŭ* です or *déshĭta* でした is used:

Watashí *no* *uchí* *wa* *anó* *jínja* *no* *ma-ushiró* *désŭ.*　My house is just
私　のうち　は　あの　神社　の　まうしろ　です.　**after** that shrine.
(*Ma* ま, as a prefix before *ushiró* うしろ, corresponds to **just.**)

---

1 The *Nippon Yūsen Kaishá* is name of the biggest Japanese steamship company.

*Jidōsha-jíko ga anó kōban no súgu **ushiró de** okorimáshĭta.* (*Jíko* accident,
自動車事故 が あの 交番 の すぐ うしろ で 起りました. *kōban* police box)
A motorcar accident occurred right **after** that police box.

*Hén-na yōsu no otokó ga watashí no **ushiró wo** arúite imáshĭta.*
変な 様子 の 男 が 私 の 後 を 歩いて いました.
A suspicious looking man was walking **after** (behind) me.
(*hén-na*, suspicious looking, *yōsu no* of aspect *or* appearance)

When **after** is used to indicate the time of day it is translated
by *sugí* 過ぎ, as shown at the beginning of this lesson.

*Jūji **sugí** nará ítsudemo o-tazuné kudasái.*   Please call on me at any time
十時 過ぎ なら いつでも お訪ね 下さい.   **after** ten o'clock.

(Ten o'clock after, at any time, your visiting do please.)

In the meaning of *subsequent to*, **after** may be translated by *sugí ni* すぎに.

*Anó katá wa higuré **sugí ni** kimáshĭta.*   He came **after** sunset.
あの 方 は 日ぐれ すぎ に 来ました.   (*higuré* sunset)

A verb preceded by **after** may be translated by the *subordinate*
with *kará* or *nochí* 後, or by the *past form* followed by *áto de*
or by the literary expression *nochí ni.*

*Konó shigotó wo **oeté kará** watashí no jímusho e kité kudasái.*
この 仕事 を 終えて から 私 の 事務所 へ 来て 下さい.
After you have finished this work, (please) come to my office.
(*lit.* This work having finished after, to my office come please.)

or *Konó shigotó wo **oetá áto de** watashí no jímusho e kité kudasái.*
この 仕事 を 終えた 後 で 私 の 事務所 へ 来て 下さい.

*Ni-kai ni watarú tsuyói jishín no **nochí ni** tsunamí ga sū-ka-son no*
二回 に わたる 強い 地震 の 後 に つなみ が 数か村 の
gyosón wo osoimáshĭta.   **After** two strong earthquake shocks a tidal wave
漁村 を おそいました.   struck several fishing villages.
(*ni-kaí ni watarú* two in succession, *jishín* earthquake shocks, *tsunamí* tidal wave,
gyosón fishing village, *sū* several, *ka-son* numerative for counting villages, *osoú* おそ
う to attack, to strike)

*Mikká **nochí ni.*** 三日後に   Three days **after.**

When **after** precedes a noun or pronoun it is translated by *áto kará.*

*Pán-ya wa sakanayá no **áto kará** kimáshĭta.*   The baker came **after**
パン屋 は 魚屋 の 後 から 来ました.   the fishmonger.

Used adverbially, *áto kará* corresponds also to **after** in the meaning of
later or *later in time.*

Ato kará mairimásŭ. 後から参ります.   I shall go **later** (after).

In literary style, **after**, placed before or following expressions indicating or
suggesting periods of time or as a synonym of *afterward* and *later on*, may
be translated by the postposition *go* 後. In ordinary colloquial speech, instead of *go* 後 one may use *nochí* のち and in more colloquial speech *áto*
あと may be used.

sonó **go** (sonó **nochí,** sonó **áto**)   after that, after that time,
その 後 (その　　のち，　その　あと)   since then

sorekará ni-nen **go** (**nochí, áto**)   after two years, two years after
それから　二年　後　(のち，　あと)

yū-shoku **go** (yū-shokú **no** nochí or **no** áto) after the evening meal
夕食　後　(夕　食　の　のち，　　の　あと)

In the meaning of *because of*, **after** may be translated by....**no désŭ kará**
のですから or by the literal expression....**ijō** 以上.

Kō nátta **no désŭ kará** (**ijō**), *watashí wa káre ni wa kuchí wo*
こう なつた の です から (以上) 私　は　彼　に　は　口　を
kikimasén.
ききません.

 After (Because of) this I will not speak to him. (*lit.* So became, is because,
 I to him do not speak.—*kuchí wo kikú* to speak, in rather slangy speech)

In the meaning of *in spite of*, **after** may be translated by **ni mo kaka-**
warazŭ にもかかわらず.

Watashí ga zúibun sewá wo shǐtá **ni mo kakawarazŭ** *sonó néko*
私　が ずいぶん 世話 を した に　も　かかわらず　その 猫
wa shinimáshǐta. **After** (In spite of) all my care the cat died.
は 死にました. (*sewá wo surú* to take care of, to look after)

In the meaning of *next in importance to*, **after** may by translated by....
ni tsuidé に次いで

Tōkyō **ni tsuidé** *no dái-tokái.* The largest city **after** Tokyo.
東京　に　次いで　の　大都会

Idiomatic usage:

after all **kekkyokŭ** 結局
the day after **akuruhí** (colloq.) あくる日, **yokujitsŭ** (*Lit.*) 翌日
one after another **tsuzuité** 続いて
in after years **kōnen** 後年
in after days **gojitsŭ** 後日
soon after **mamónaku** まもなく

Besides
hoká ni 外に ué ni 上に

Hoká ni 外に is generally used to translate **besides** when
followed by a noun or pronoun; **ué ni** 上に is generally used in
other cases.

Konó **hoká ni** *náni mo hóshiku arimasén.* I care for nothing **besides**
この　外　に　何　も　欲しくありません. this.
 (*lit.* This besides, nothing desired there isn't.)

Sonó **hoká ni** *máda takŭsán arimásŭ.* I have much more **besides** that.
その　外　に　まだ　沢山　あります.
 (*lit.* That besides, still much there is.)

Bóku   no   hoká   ni   mō   hĭtóri   o-kyakŭsamá   ga   arimásŭ.
僕　の　外　に　もう　一人　　お客様　　が　あります.
There is another visitor **besides** me. (Me besides, still another visitor there is.)

Gekkyū   no   hoká   ni   nan   no   shūnyū   mo   nái.　　He has no income **besides**
月給　の　外　に　何　の　収入　も　ない.　　his salary.
(*lit.* Salary besides, no other income hasn't.—*nan no......mo* no other)

Sonó   hoká   ni   ossháru   kotó   ga   arimásŭ   ka.—Iié,   arimasén.
その　　外　におつしやる事　が　ありますか.—いゝえ, ありません.
Besides that have you anything to say?—No, I haven't.

Kánojo   wa   wákakute   kanemochí   de   áru   ué   ni   utsŭkushíi   désŭ.
彼女　は　若くて　　金持　　である上　に　美しい　です.
She is young, rich and beautiful **besides**.
(She young, rich is; besides beautiful is.)

Jitsugyōka   de   átta   ué   ni   ongakŭká   de   mo   átta.
実業家　であった上　に　音楽家　で　も　あった.
Besides being a businessman, he was a musician.

Chūkoku   shĭtá   ué   ni   kané   wo   kuremáshĭta.　　**Besides** advising, he gave
忠告　した　上　に　金　を　呉れました.　　me money.
(*lit.* Advice gave; besides money gave me.)

Eigó   wo   yóku   hanásu   ué   ni   shiná-go   wo   shĭtté   imásŭ.
英語　を　よく　話す　上　に　支那語　を　知っています.
Besides speaking English well, he knows Chinese.

Anáta   no   hoká   ni   wa   koré   wo   shĭtté   imasén.　　No one **besides** you,
あなたの　外　に　は　これ　を　知って　いません.　　knows this.

As a conjunction corresponding in meaning to *moreover*, **besides** may be
translated by *soré ni* それに.

Asokó   e   ikú   ni   wa   ososugimásŭ;   soré ni   watashí   wa   taihén   tsŭkárete
あそこ　へ　行く　に　は　おそすぎます,　それ　に　私　は　大変　つかれて
imásŭ.　　It is too late to go there; **besides**, I am very tired.
います.　　(*osoí* おそい late, *ososugíru* おそすぎる to be too late)

To Have Something Done

The expression *to have something done* is translated by the subordinate of the principal verb, followed by *moraú* 貰う (*lit.* to receive), which, when in the desiderative form, may be followed by *désŭ.* This construction may be said to be a polite form of the causative.

Kinō   konó   hakó   wo   naóshĭte   morattá.　　Yesterday I had this box
きのうこの　箱　を　直して　　貰った.　　mended.
(*lit.* Yesterday, this box having mended, I received.)

Itté   anáta   no   bóshi   wo   kírei   ni   shĭté   moraí   nasái.
行って貴方　の　帽子　をきれいに　して　貰い　なさい.
Go and have your hat cleaned. (*lit.* Go, your hat cleanly having done, receive.)

Hankechĭ ga kitanái kará aratté morai nasái.
ハンケチ が 汚い から 洗って 貰い なさい.
As your handkerchief is dirty, better have it washed.
(*lit.* Handkerchief dirty because, having washed, receive.)

Konó shigotó wo anáta no sokkishá ni shĭté moraitái désŭ.
この 仕事 を 貴方 の 速記者 に して 貰いたい です.
I wish to have this work done by your stenographer.
(*lit.* This work, your stenographer by, having done, wish to receive is.)

Such constructions as "I had this letter delivered at ten o'clock,"
for instance, are generally avoided in Japanese, in favour of a more
simple construction.

Konó tegamí wo jūji ni uketorimáshĭta.   I received this letter at ten
この 手紙 を 十時 に 受取りました.   o'clock.
(*lit.* This letter, ten o'clock at, I received.)

Causative Verbs

Causative verbs are used when one wishes to express one of the
following meanings: *to cause one to do something, to make one do
something, to permit to do* or *to let do,* and *to have done.*

Verbs of Class I form the causative by adding **saseru** させる to
the simple stems, and verbs of Class II, by adding **seru** せる to
the *a*-stems.

See **phonetic rules** on Causative verbs, Page 687.

Saserŭ させる corresponds to the following expressions:

to make (a person) do	to cause (a person) to do
to force (a person) to do	to induce (a person) to do
to let (a person) do	to allow (a person) to do

Class I

mĭru	見る	to see	*mi*	見	*misaséru*	見させる	to cause to see
déru	出る	to go out	*de*	出	*desaséru*	出させる	to cause to go out

Class II

káku	書く	to write	*kaka*	書か	*kakaséru*	書かせる	to cause to write
dásu	出す	to take out	*dasa*	出さ	*dasaséru*	出させる	to cause to take out
mátsu	待つ	to wait	*mata*	待た	*mataséru*	待たせる	to cause to wait
yómu	読む	to read	*yoma*	読ま	*yomaséru*	読ませる	to cause to read
tóru	取る	to take	*tora*	取ら	*toraséru*	取らせる	to cause to take
kaú	買う	to buy	*kawa*	買わ	*kawaserŭ*	買わせる	to cause to buy

Irregular Verbs

surú	する	to do	*saserŭ*	させる	to cause to do
kúru	来る	to come	*kosaséru*	来させる	to cause to come
shinú	死ぬ	to die	*shinaserŭ*	死なせる	to cause to die

Saserú させる *to cause to do* etc., is the causative of **surú** する *to do*, as the first irregular form above shows, and *seru* せる is its abbreviated form, used as a suffix for the formation of the causative of verbs of Class II.

Thus, in analysing the word **misaséru** 見させる *to cause to see*, for instance, we find that it is composed of **mi**=*seeing* and **saseru**=*to cause to do* or *to have done*. **Misaséru** 見させる then, translated literally, corresponds to *seeing to have done* or *to have done seeing*=to cause to see.

In the case of a verb of Class II, **kakaséru** 書かせる *to cause to write* for instance, we find that the verb is composed of **kaka**=*writing* and **seru**=*to cause to do* or *to have done*. **Kakaséru** 書かせる then, translated literally, corresponds to *writing to have done* or *to have done writing*=to cause to write.

Saseru was, most likely, abbreviated to **seru** for the verbs of Class II, for euphonic reason. In fact, were we to use *saseru* also for verbs of Class II, we should have such unharmonious sounds as *kasasaseru* 貸ささせる instead of *kaséru* 貸させる to cause to lend, *dasasaseru* 出ささせる instead of *dasaséru* 出させる to cause to take out or put out, etc.

It may be of interest for the student to know that at the present day there are some Japanese, perhaps not well acquainted with the grammatical rules of their mother tongue, who would say *matasaséru* instead of *mataséru* to cause to wait, *yomasaséru* instead of *yomaséru* to cause to read, etc.

Causative verbs are conjugated like verbs of Class I ending in **eru,** like **tabéru** 食べる to eat.

kakaséru 書かせる to cause to write

Present	*kakasemásŭ*	書かせます	Future	*kakasemashō* 書かせましょう
Past	*kakasemáshĭta* 書かせました		Subord.	*kakásete* 書かせて

Saserú させる to cause to do

Present	*sasemásŭ*	させます	Future	*sasemashō* させましょう
Past	*sasemáshĭta*	させました	Subord.	*sasaté* させて

Examples

*Mēdo ni konó kozútsumi wo **dasásete** kudasái.* **Have** the maid **post**
メードに この 小包 を 出させて 下さい. this parcel.

(*lit.* The maid by, this parcel cause to post please.—*dásu* 出す to post)

*Watashí no kutsú wo anáta no kutsuyá-san **ni naosásete** kudasái.*
私 の 靴 を 貴方 の 靴屋さん に なおさせて 下さい.
Have my shoes **mended** by your shoemaker.

(*lit.* My shoes, your shoemaker by, cause to mend please.)

Anó shōnin wa ítsumo umái kotó bákari itté kyakú ni monó wo
あの 商人 は いつも 旨い 事 ばかり言って 客 に 物 を
kawaserú *no ga jōzu désŭ.* That merchant is very clever at saying things
買わせる の が 上手 です. to **make** his customers **buy** his goods.

(*lit.* That merchant always nice things only saying, to his customers things to cause to buy is clever.)

Anó hǐtó ni konó shorúi wo **kakáseta** *no wa watashí désǔ.*
あの 人 に この 書類 を 書かせた の は 私 です.

It is I who **made** that person **write** this document.
(*lit.* That man by, this document that caused to be written person, I was.—
no wa after **kakáseta** stands for *the person who......*)

Watashí wa ítsumo uchí no kodomotachí **ni** *wa tamé ni náru hon*
私 は いつも うち の 子供達 に は ため に なる 本
bákari **yomasemásǔ.**   I always **let** my children **read** only useful books.
ばかり 読ませます.

(*lit.* I, always, my children by, useful books only let read.—*tamé ni náru* useful)

Konó tegamí wo watashí **ni** **kakásete** *kudasái.*   **Let** me **write** this
この 手紙 を 私 に 書かせて 下さい.   letter.

(*lit.* This letter, me by, cause to write please.=Let me write......)

Konó shigotó wo anáta no tamé ni watashí **ni** *saseté kudasái.*
この 仕事 を あなた の ため に 私 に させて 下さい.
Let me **do** this work for you.

(*lit.* This work, for you, me by, let do please.—*shigotó wo surú* to work;
shigotó wo saserú to cause to do work, to let work)

From some of the above examples it may be seen that the person that
suffers the action indicated by the causative verb takes the particle **ni** に.

Often, when in English one would say that *a person had a work done*, an
active, a passive, or a causative verb may be used. In Japanese only an
active or passive verb is used instead.

Tokugawá sandái shōgun Iémitsu ga Nikkō no Otamayá wo **tatemáshita.**
徳川 三代 将軍 家光 が 日光 の 御霊屋 を 建てました.

Iemitsu, the third Tokugawa shogun, built the Nikko Temple. *or* Iemitsu,
the third Tokugawa shogun, caused the Nikko Temple to be built.
(*lit.* Tokugawa third shogun Iemitsu Nikko Temple built.)

Nikkō no Otamayá wa Tokugawá sandái shōgun Iémitsu ni yotté
日光 の 御霊屋 は 徳川 三代 将軍 家光 によって
tateraremáshǐta.[1] The Nikko Temple was built by Iemitsu, the third Tokugawa
建てられました.   shōgun.

(*lit.* Nikko Temple, Tokugawa third shogun by, was built.)

Ni yotté によって is a literary expression corresponding to **by.**
Note that the passive construction as used in the above and similar cases,
is of the literary style and is generally avoided in ordinary conversation.

Vocabulary

Nouns					
booty	*emonó*	エモノ	cannon	*taihō*	大砲
breath	*kokyū*	呼吸	century	*séiki*	世紀
			civilization	*bumméi*	文明

---
1 *tatéru* to build, *tateraréru* to be built

cock	ondorí	オンドリ		stupendous	subarashíi	スバラシイ
end (the)	owarí	終オリ		Western	Taiséi	泰タイ西セイ
enterprise	kigyō	企キ業ギョウ			**Verbs**	
era	jidái	時ジ代ダイ		to advise	susume·rú	ススメル
Europe	Ōshū	欧オウ州シウ		to announce	tsuge·rú	告ツゲル
fortitude	níntai	忍ニン耐タイ		to blow	narasú	鳴ナラス
great man	ijín	偉イ人ジン		to crow	tokí wo tsŭkúru	
hand-shake	ákŭshu	握アク手シュ				時ヲツクル
hardship	kónnan	困コン難ナン		to endure	hé·ru	経ヘル
statesman	seijiká	政セイ治ジ家カ		to occur	okóru	起オコル
siren	sáiren	サイレン		to shoot	útsu	ウツ
	Adjectives			to strengthen	tsuyomé·ru	強ツョメル
great	idái-na	偉イ大ダイナ		to use	tsŭkaú	使ツカウ
impolite	shitsúrei	失シツ礼レイ			**Adverbs**	
important	jūyō-na	重ジウ要ヨウナ		almost	hotóndo	殆ホトンド

after breakfast *asashokú-go;* a spoonful *sají ni íppai;* living thing *séibutsu;* to live, to exist *ikíru;* to breathe *kokyŭ surú;* to graduate *sotsugyō surú;* to run away, to flee *nigéru;* commerce and industry *shōkōgyō;* to study, to learn *manabú;* modern Japan, the present Empire of Japan *Géndai Nihón;* Osaka Castle *Ōsaka-jō;* fishing village *gyosón; o-jigí wo shi-áu* to bow at each or one another; *teppō* gun

Exercise *Renshū* 練習

1. Ondorí wa ása sánji góro ni tokí wo tsŭkuríhajimerú. Mukashí tokéi ga nákatta tokí ni hĭtó wa ondorí no tokí wo tsŭkúru kotó ni yotté sōchō no jikán wo shittá. **2.** Tōkyō Yokohamá no daijíshin wa sen-kyū-hyakú-ni-jū-san-nen kúgatsu tsuitachí no shōgo sampún máe ni okorimáshĭta. **3.** Watashí wa hotóndo maigetsú Atami e ikimásŭ. **4.** Ishá wa watashí ni mái-ása shokugó ni konó kusurí wo sají ni íppai nómu yō ni susumemáshĭta. **5.** Súbete no séibutsu wa ikíru tamé ni kokyŭ wo séneba-naránu.[1] **6.** Kónnan wo héru góto-ni warewaré no níntai wa tsuyomarimásŭ. **7.** Issén-kyū-hyakú-san-jū-yo-nen máde Tōkyō de wa mái-nichí hirú no jū-ni-ji ni taihō wo útta monó déshĭta. Sen-kyū-hyakú-san-jū-go-nen no hajimé kará sen-kyū-hyaku yonjū ninen máde taihō wo útsu kawarí ni ōkina sáiren wo narashĭté hirú no jikán wo tsugemáshĭta. Génzai de wa rajió de shōgo no jíkoku ga shirasareté imásŭ. **8.** Nihón-jin ga áu to Ōbei-jin no surú ákŭshu no kawarí ni o-jigí wo shi-aimásŭ. **9.** Sen-go-hyakú-yon-jū-nínen ni Porutogarú-jin ga Nihón ni kĭtá máe ni wa Nihón-jin wa teppō wo tsŭkaú kotó wo shirimasén déshĭta. **10.** Itsu Shiná-go wo naraimáshĭta ka.—Jū-nen ízen Shiná e ikú máe ni Nihón de naraimáshĭta. Senséi wa Shiná-jin de Pékin daigakú wo sotsugyō shĭtá katá déshĭta. **11.** Keikán ga tōchaku shĭtá máe ni dorobō wa emonó

---

1 *kokyŭ wo séneba-naránu* must breathe (*séneba-naránu* is the literary form of *shinákereba narimasén*=must—See page 365.)

wo mótte nígete shimaimáshĭta. **12.** Tokugawá jidái ni wa Nihón-jin wa Nihón wo déru kotó wo yurusaremasén[1] déshĭta ga sen-happyakú-rokú-jū-hachí-nen ichí-gatsú ni Tokugawá jidái no owarí ga kitá nochí takŭsán no Nihón-jin ga Méiji Tennō no go-shōrei[2] ni yorí taiséi bumméi no kenkyū oyobí yōshiki[3] shōkōgyō-hō wo manabú tamé ni Ōshū ya Ameriká e yukimáshĭta. Kónnichi Nihón wa sekái no yūsū-na[4] shōkōgyō kokú[5] no hĭtótsu de arimásŭ. **13.** Odá Nobunagá, Toyotomí Hideyoshí, Tokugawá Ieyasú wa yūmei na seijiká de átta bákari de náku,[7] konó sannín wa Nihón no undá móttomo idái-na bushō de arimásŭ. Dái-jū-rokú séiki ni óite[8] hachí-nen-kan ni áitsuide[9] umaretá konó san íjin wa kíndai Nihón no kisó wo tsukútta_no de arimáshĭta. **14.** Hideyoshí no idái-na kigyō no hĭtótsu no uchí no[10] Ōsaka-jō[11] wa soré wo tsŭkúru no ni sū-nen mo kakátta.[12] Konó subarashíi shiró no dekíru máe Ōsaka wa chiisái gyosón de átta ga shiró no dékita nochí wa jūyō-na tokái to nátta. **15.** Hĭtó wo mataséru no wa taihén shitsúrei désŭ.

1. おんどりは朝三時頃に時をつくり初める. 昔時計がなかった時に人はおんどりの時をつくる事によって早朝の時間を知った. **2.** 東京横浜の大地震は千九百廿三年九月朔日の正午三分前に起りました. **3.** 私は殆ど毎月熱海へ行きます. **4.** 医者は私に毎朝食後にこの薬をさじに一杯のむようにすすめました. **5.** すべての生物は生きるために呼吸をせねばならぬ. **6.** 困難をへる毎に我々の忍耐は強まります. **7.** 一千九百卅四年迄東京では毎日昼の十二時に大砲をうったものでした. 千九百卅五年の初めから千九百四十二年まで大砲をうつ代りに大きなサイレンを鳴らして昼の時間を告げました. 現在ではラジオで正午の時刻が知らされています. **8.** 日本人が会うと欧米人のする握手の代りにお辞儀をし合います. **9.** 千五百四十二年にポルトガル人が日本に来た前には日本人は鉄砲を使う事を知りませんでした. **10.** いつ支那語を習いましたか. 一十年以前支那へ行く前に日本で習いました. 先生は支那人で北京大学を卒業した方でした. **11.** 警官が到着した前に泥棒はえものを持って逃げてしまいました. **12.** 徳川時代には日本人は日本を出る事を許されませんでしたが千八百六十八年一月に徳川時代の終りが来たのち沢山の日本人が明治天皇の御奨励により泰西文明の研究及び洋式商工業法を学ぶために欧州やアメリカへ行きました. 今日, 日本は世界の有数な商工業国の一つであります.

---

1 *yurúsu* to permit, *yurusaréru* to be permitted   2 *shōrei* encouragement; *go-shōrei ni yorí* by the encouragement   3 Western methods   4 *yūsū-na* most   5 *shōkōgyō kokú* commercialized and industrialized countries   6 *undá* that ever had, that produced; *umú* to give birth, to bear   7 *bákari de náku* besides   8 *ni óite* in (literary style)   9 *áitsuide* in succession, one after the other; *hachí nen-kan ni áitsuide* within eight years of one another   10 *hĭtótsu no uchí no* one of......   11 *Ōsaka-jō* Osaka castle The building of the great castle of Osaka was among the mightiest of all Hideyoshi's undertakings. It was built in the year 1585.   12 *kakátta* it took; *sū-nen kakátta* it took several years; *mo* is here used for emphasis

13. 織田信長, 豊臣秀吉, 徳川家康は有名な政治家であったばかりで
なくこの三人は日本の生んだ最も偉大な武将であります. 第十六世紀
に於て八年間に相次いで生れたこの三偉人は近代日本の基礎を作った
のでありました. 14. 秀吉の偉大な企業の一つのうちの大阪城はそれ
を造るのに数年もかゝった. このすばらしい城の出来る前大阪は小さ
い漁村であったが城の出来た後は重要な都会となった. 15. 人を待た
せるのは大変失礼です.

1. Cocks begin to crow at about three o'clock in the morning. In ancient
times, when there were no clocks or watches of any kind, people understood
the early morning time by the cock crowing. 2. The great earthquake in
Tokyo and Yokohama occurred on September 1st, 1923, three minutes to noon.
3. I go to Atami almost every month. 4. The doctor has advised me to
drink a spoonful of this medicine every morning after breakfast. 5. Every
living thing must breathe in order to live. 6. Every hardship endured
strengthens our fortitude. 7. Until 1934, they used to shoot a cannon in
Tokyo every day at 12 o'clock noon. From the beginning of 1935, until 1942,
instead of shooting a cannon, they blew a huge siren to announce the noon
hour. The noon hour is now announced by radio. 8. When Japanese meet,
instead of shaking hands as Western people do, they bow at each other.
9. Before the Portuguese came to Japan in the year 1542, the Japanese did
not know the use of fire arms. 10. When did you learn Chinese?—I learned
it here in Japan ten years ago, before I went to China. My teacher was
a Chinese who graduated at the Peking University. 11. Before the police
arrived the thief got away with his booty. 12. During the Tokugawa Era
no Japanese was allowed to leave Japan, but after the Tokugawa Era came
to an end in January 1868, many Japanese, encouraged by the Emperor Meiji,
went to Europe and America to study Western civilization and learn Western
methods of commerce and industry. To-day Japan is one of the most commercialized and industrialized countries in the world. 13. Oda Nobunaga, Toyotomi
Hideyoshi, and Tokugawa Ieyasu, besides being famous statesmen, are the
three greatest generals Japan has ever had. These three great men, who
were born in the XVI century within eight years of one another, laid the
foundation of modern Japan. 14. Among the greatest of Hideyoshi's undertakings was the great Osaka castle, which he caused to be built within a
few years. Before the erection of this stupendous Castle, Osaka wa small
fishing village, but after the Castle was built, the village became a important city. 15. It is very impolite to let people wait for us.

Forty-fourth Lesson　第四十四課

Potential Mood
Can

Can and its equivalent, *to be able to*, are translated by *dekíru* 出来る.

Present

Positive		Negative	
dekimásŭ 出来ます	I can	*dekimasén* 出来ません	I cannot
dekíru 出来る	I am able	*dekínai* 出来ない	I am not able

Past

dekimáshĭta 出来ました	I could	*dekimasén déshĭta* 出来ません でした	I could not
dékita 出来た	I was able	*dekínakatta* 出来なかった	I was not able

Future

dekimashō 出来ましょう		*dekimasén deshō* 出来ませんでしょう	
dekíru deshō 出来るでしょう	I shall be able	*dekimasumái* 出来ますまい	I shall not be able
dekíru darō 出来る だろう		*dekínai darō* 出来ないだろう	
		dekinakarō 出来なかろう	

The verb which in English follows **can** or **to be able to** is used in the simple present, followed by the expression *kotó ga dekíru* 事が出来る. (*lit.* The thing can be done.) *Ga* is used instead of *wo* because the word *kotó* is in the nominative case. See Lesson 50 for another form of the potential mood.

Arúku kotó ga dekimásŭ. 歩く 事 が 出来ます.	I can walk. (*lit.* To walk the thing can be done.)
Arúku kotó ga dekimasén. 歩く 事 が 出来ません.	I cannot walk.
Arúku kotó ga dekimáshĭta. 歩く 事 が 出来ました.	I was able to walk.
Arúku kotó ga dekimasén déshĭta. 歩く 事 が 出来ません でした.	I couldn't walk.
Arúku kotó ga dekimashō. 歩く 事 が 出来ましょう.	I shall be able to walk.
Konó kabán wo hakobú kotó ga dekimásŭ ka. この 鞄 を 運ぶ 事 が 出来ます か.	Can you carry this suit-case?

Soré wa amari omói kará hakobú kotó ga dekimasén.
それ は 余り 重い から 運ぶ 事 が 出来ません.
As it is too heavy I **cannot** carry it.
(*lit.* That, too heavy because, to carry the thing cannot.)

Kinō ténki ga wárukatta nóde Yasukuní Jínja e sampái ni yuku[1] kotó
きのう 天気 が 悪かった ので 靖国 神社 へ 参拝 に 行く 事
ga dekimasén déshita.   As the weather was bad yesterday I **could not go**
が 出来ません でした.   and worship·at the Yasukuni shrine.
(*lit.* Yesterday the weather was-bad because, Yasukuni Shrine to, to worship,
to go the thing could not.)

Tōkyō kará Nikkō máde arúite ikú kotó ga dekíru deshō ka.
東京 から 日光 迄 歩いて 行く 事 が 出来る でしょうか.
Shall we be able to walk from Tokyo to Nikko? (*lit.* From Tokyo, Nikko to,
walking the thing can, will it be?=......will it be possible?)

Iié, dekinai deshō, amarí tōi kará.   No, we shall not be able, as
いゝえ, 出来ない でしょう, 余り 遠い から.   it is too far.

In some cases the verb that in English would follow the auxiliary **can** is
omitted in Japanese. This omission occurs when the meaning of the sentence
is easily understood without the principal verb.

Anáta wa koré ga dekimásŭ ka.   **Can** you do this?
貴方 は これ が 出来ます か.   (*lit.* You this can?)

Iié, dekimasén. いゝえ, 出来ません.   No, I cannot.

Eigó ga dekimásŭ ka. 英語が出来ますか.   **Can** you speak English?

Hái, dekimásŭ. はい, 出来ます.   Yes, I **can**.

Iié, dekimasén. いゝえ, 出来ません.   No, I **cannot**.

Note that when the principal verb is omitted as in the above two questions,
the object is followed by *ga.* However, if the principal verb is not omitted
the object is regularly followed by *wo.*

Anáta wa koré wo surú kotó ga dekimásŭ ka.   **Can** you do this?
貴方 は これ を する 事 が 出来ます か.
(*lit.* You, this to do, the thing can?)

Eigó wo hanásu kotó ga dekimásŭ ka.   **Can** you speak English?
英語 を 話す 事 が 出来ます か.
(*lit.* English to speak, the thing can?)

Konó shigotó wo ashĭtá máde ni surú kotó ga dekimásŭ ka.
この 仕事 を あした 迄 にする 事 が出来ます か.   **Can** you do this
(*lit.* This work to-morrow by, to do the thing can?)   work by to-
or *Konó shigotó ga ashĭtá máde ni dekimásŭ ka.*   morrow?
この 仕事 が あした 迄 に 出来ます か.
(*lit.* This work to-morrow by, can?—*máde ni* by, not later than......)

---

1 *sampái ni yukú* to go and worship at (a shrine), to pay homage to, to **pay**
reverence at (a tomb), to visit the Imperial tomb

May

In Lesson 26 it was stated that the affirmative subordinate, followed by *mo yoroshii* もよろしい or *mo ii* もいゝ, has the concessive meaning of **may**.

Kómban sampó ni dekaketé mo yoroshii désŭ ka.
今晩　散歩　に　出かけて　も　よろしい　です　か.
May I go out for a walk to-night?

Yoroshii (désŭ). よろしい（です）.　　You **may**.

When **may** indicates probability the principal verb is used in the probable future or in the simple present, followed by *ka-mo shiremasén* かも知れません or the less polite *ka-mo shirenái (désŭ)* かも知れない（です）.

The syllable *ka* か of either expression may be said to have the same value as the particle used at the end of an interrogation in place of a question mark, and *mo shiremasén* も知れません or *mo shirenái* も知れない, translated literally, correspond to *whether yes or no (mo* も*) it is not known* (*shiremasén* 知れません or *shirenái* 知れない). Since *ka* か corresponds to a question mark, when using either expression, it should be pronounced with a slight interrogative tone before uttering *mo shiremasén* or *mo shirenái*.

Anáta ga ossháru kotó wa hontō deshō.　　What you say **may** be true.
貴方　がおっしゃる事　は　本当　でしょう.
(*lit.* You say thing true will probably be.)

Anáta ga osshátta kotó wa hontō ka-mo shiremasén.
貴方　がおっしやった事　は　本当　かも　知れません.　　⎫
Kimí ga ittá kotó wa hontō ka-mo shirenái.　　　　　　　⎬ What you said **may** be true.
君　が　云った事　は　本当　か　も　しれない.　　　　　⎭
(*lit.* You said thing, true is?, whether yes or no it is not known.)

Chichí wa ashĭtá Kōbe kará kúru ka-mo shiremasén.
父　は　あした　神戸　から　来る　かも　知れません.
Our father **may** come from Kobe to-morrow. (*lit.* Our father to-morrow Kobe from, comes?, whether yes or no it is not known.)

Kómban tsŭkí ga kása[1] wo kité imásŭ kará myōnichi wa áme ga fúru deshō.
今晩　月　が　暈　を　着ていますから　明日　は　雨　が　降るでしょう.
As the moon has a ring around it to-night, it **may** rain to-morrow.

Tábun sō ittá ka-mo shirenái.　　Perhaps I **may** have said so.
多分　そう云った　かも　知れない.
(*lit.* Perhaps so I-said?, wheather yes or no it is not known.)

The **negative** of **may**, when expressing improbability or doubt, is generally formed by the negative present of the principal verb followed by *deshō* でしょう or *darō* だろう or by *ka-mo shiremasén* かも知れません or *ka-mo shirenái* かも知れない. Any of these expressions may be followed by *to omoimásŭ* と思います if doubtful emphasis is to be expressed.

---

1 *kása* a halo, ring, corona, *kité* sub. of *kirú* to wear, *kása wo kirú* lit. to wear ring＝to have a ring around.

Anó katá wa kónai ka-mo shiremasén (or *kónai deshō,* etc.)
あの 方 は 来ない かも 知れません （来ないでしょう）.
He may not come, (*kónai* 来ない negative of *kúru* 来る to come)

Sonná kotó wa okoránai deshō to omoimásŭ (......*ka-mo shirenái*).
そんな 事 は 起こらないでしょうと 思います （かも 知れない）.
Such a thing may not happen.

(*okoránai* 起こらない neg. of *okóru* 起こる to happen)

A pleonastic expression that is sometimes used with *ka-mo shiremasén*
かも知れません is *kotoni-yorú to* 事によると corresponding to *perhaps,
possibly, may be.*

Kotoni-yorú to ashĭtá o-tazuné surú ka-mo shiremasén. or
事による とあした お訪ね する かも 知れません.

Ashĭtá kotoni-yorú to o-tazuné surú ka-mo shiremasén.
あした 事による と お訪ね する かも 知れません.
I may **possibly** call on you to-morrow. (*o-tazuné surú* to visit)

Kyō watashí no senséi wa kimasén déshĭta, kotoni-yorú to go-byōki
きょう 私 の 先生 は 来ません でした 事による と 御病気
ka-mo shiremasén.   To-day my teacher hasn't come; **maybe** he is ill.
かも 知れません.   (*lit.* maybe ill?, whether yes or no it is not known.)

When **may** indicates purpose, it is generally translated by *tamé
ni* ために.

Watashí wa chíshiki wo masŭ tamé ni benkyō sñmásŭ.
私 は 知識 を 増す ため に 勉強 します.
I study that I **may** increase my knowledge. (*chíshiki* knowledge, *masŭ* to increase)

Hĭtó wa ikíru tamé ni tabemásŭ.   People eat that they **may** live.
人 は 生きる ため に 食べます.

When **may** expresses a wish, it may be translated by *yō-ni* よ
うに, in which case the principal verb will be used in its simple
present form or in the present with the suffix *másŭ* ます.

Kámisama ga anáta wo mamóru (or *mamorimásŭ*) *yō-ni.*
神様 があなた を まもる （まもります） ように.
May God protect you. (*mamóru* to protect)

Anáta ga ítsudemo kōfuku de áru (or *de arimásŭ*) *yō-ni.*
あなた が いつでも 幸福 で ある （であります） ように.
May you be always happy. (*kōfuku* happy)

A more formal version of the first example would be:
Kámisama ga anáta wo o-mamorí kudasaimásŭ yō-ni.
神様 があなた を おまもり 下さいます ように.

and a more emphatic form of the second example is:
Anáta ga ítsudemo kōfuku de arú kotó wo inorimásŭ.
あなた が いつでも 幸福 で ある 事 を 祈ります.
(*lit.* You, always happy to be, the thing I pray.)

Might

When **might**, indicating present or future probability, is used as if suggesting or actually expressing someone's opinion, it may be translated by the simple present of the principal verb followed by *ka-mo shiremasén (shirenái)* かも知れません (知れない) and, if emphasis is to be expressed, *to omoimásŭ* may be added.

Koré wa anáta no ka-mó shirenái (to omoimásŭ). This **might** be
これ は あなたの かも 知れない（と 思います.）   yours.
(In the above example the verb *désŭ* です after *no* の is omitted.)

Káre wa jikí-ni gaikokú e ikú ka-mo shirenái (to omoimásŭ).
彼 は 直きに 外国 へ行く かも 知れない（と 思います.）
I think he **might** go abroad soon.

Kómban anó katá wa kúru ka-mo shirenái to omoimásŭ ka.
今晩 あの 方 は 来る かも 知れない と 思います か.
Do you think he **might come** to-night?

Kúru ka-mo shiremasén. 来るかも知れません. He **might** come.

Sonná baai ni wa jūdai-na kotó ga okóru ka-mo shiremasén.
そんな 場合 に は 重大な 事 が 起こる かも 知れません.
In that case something serious **might** happen. (*wa*=emphatic particle)

Sonná machigaí wa dáre de mo surú ka-mo shiremasén.
そんな 間違い は 誰 で も する かも 知れません.
Such mistake **might** (may) be made by anybody.

Sonó inú wo ijimeté wa ikemasén, kuitsŭkú ka-mo shiremasén kara.
その 犬 をいじめてはいけません, くいつく かも 知れません から.
Don't tease that dog, as he **might** bite you.

When **might** is used with the unexpressed meaning of *I wonder* or without the idea of someone's opinion, then only the probable future of the principal verb is used. If, however, **might** is used in the interrogative, as if asking someone's opinion, the probable future is followed by *to omoimásŭ* と思います.

Sonná baái ni dónna kotó ga okóru deshō ka.
そんな 場合 に どんな 事 が 起こる でしょうか.
What **might happen** in that case? (Here *I wonder* is understood.)

Sonná baai ni wa dónna kotó ga okóru deshō to omoimásŭ ka.
そんな 場合 に は どんな 事 が 起こる でしょうと 思います か.
What might happen in that case? (=What do you think might happen......)

The **negative of might** is generally formed, as in the case of the negative of **may**, by the present of the principal verb followed by any of the expressions *ka-mo shiremasén, ka-mo shirenái, deshō* or *darō*, to which *to omoimásŭ* may be added.

Anó katá wa kónai ka-mo shiremasén to omoimásŭ. He **might**
あの 方 は 来ない かも 知れません と 思います.   **not** come.

Sonná kotó wa okoránai deshō. Such a thing **might not** happen.
そんな 事 は起こらないでしょう.

Must

When **must** indicates obligation or necessity, it may be translated by the simple stem of verbs of Class I and the *a*-stem of verbs of Class II, followed by *nákereba narimasén* なければなりません or *nákereba naránai* なければならない, *nákereba ikemasén* なければいけません or *nákereba ikenái* なければいけない.

Nákereba なければ corresponds to *if it isn't* or *if it doesn't* and each one of the following words correspond to *won't do*. The expressions with *narimasén* なりません and *ikemasén* いけません are more polite than the others with *naránai* ならない and *ikenái* いけない.

For the first persons singular and plural, only *nákereba narimasén* or *nákereba naránai* is used, while both *nákereba narimasén* (*naránai*) and *nákereba ikemasén* (*ikenái*) are used for the second and third persons.

Nákereba ikemasén (*ikenái*) has a stronger idea of obligation than *nákereba narimasén* (*naránai*).

The verb that in English follows **must** will be, in Japanese, in its **simple stem** if it belongs to **Class I**, and in its *a*-stem if it belongs to **Class II**.

Mi-nákereba narimasén.　　I must see.
見なければ　なりません.　　(*mi* 見 is the stem of *míru* 見る to see)

Káre wa tabé-nákereba ikemasén.　He must eat. (*tabé* 食べ stem of
彼　は　食べなければ　いけません.　　*tabéru* 食べる to eat)

Kaká-nákereba narimasén.　　I must write.
書かなければ　なりません.　　(*kaká* 書か stem of *káku* 書く to write)

Káre wa matá-nákereba ikenái.　He must wait. (*matá* 待た stem of
彼　は　待たなければ　いけない.　　*mátsu* 待つ to wait)

Irregular verbs

Shi-nákereba narimasén.　　I must do.
しなければ　なりません.　　(*shi* し stem of *surú* する to do)

Shigotó wo shi-nákereba narimasén.　I must work. (*lit.* Work if I
仕事　を　しなければ　なりません.　　don't, it won't do.)

Ko-nákereba ikemasén.　　He must come.
来なければ　いけません.　　(*ko* 来 stem of *kúru* 来る to come)

In the above examples the hyphen between the principal verb and the expression corresponding to *must*, has been used for the convenience of the student.

Osói kará kaerá-nákereba narimasén.　As it is late we must go home.
遅い　から　帰らなければ　なりません.
　　(*lit.* Late because, return if we don't it won't do.)

Osói kará kaerá-nákereba narimasén.　⎫ As it is late you, he, they,
遅い　から　帰らなければ　なりません.　⎪ must go home.
Osói kará kaerá-nákereba ikemasén.　⎬ (*kaerá* stem of
遅い　から　帰らなければ　いけません.　⎭ *kaeru* to return)

Nihón-go   wo   ryūchō   ni   hanásu   ni   wa[1]   *yóku   benkyō   shi-nákereba*
日本語　を　流ちょう　に　話す　に　は　よく　勉強　しなければ
narimasén.   In order to speak Japanese fluently you **must** study hard.
なりません.   (*lit.* Japanese-language fluently to speak in order to, well study
                        doing if you don't it won't do.)

The negative of **must** is formed by the subordinate of the principal verb,
followed by *wa narimasén* はなりません, *wa naránai* はならない, or
wa ikemasén はいけません, *wa ikenái* はいけない, as already shown in
Lesson 25.

Yobirín wo narasazú ni háitte wa ikemasén. You **mustn't** enter with-
呼鈴　を　鳴らさず　に　入って　は　いけません.   out ringing the bell.
   (*lit.* Bell without-ringing, entering won't do.)

Watashí no taipuraitā wo tsŭkatté wa ikemasén. You **mustn't** use
私　のタイプライターを　使って　は　いけません.   my typewriter.
   (*lit.* My typewriter using won't do.)

Hĭtó ga hanashí wo shĭté irú tokí ni jamá wo shĭté wa narimasén.
人　が　話　を　している　時　に　邪广　を　して　は　なりません.
One **must not** interrupt people when they are speaking.
   (*lit.* People talk doing are when, hindrance doing won't do.)

Must not may also be translated by the negative of the principal
verb, followed by *yō-ni* ように. This form is considered more polite
than the one with *narimasén* or *ikemasén.*

Yō-ni corresponds to *so as to, in order to, so that one may* and other
expressions of similar meaning. See *yō-ni*, Lesson 39, page 304.

Hĭtó ga hanashí wo shĭté irú tokí ni jamá wo shinái yō-ni.
人　が　話　を　している　時　に　邪广　を　しない　ように.
One **must not** interrupt people when they are speaking.
   (*lit.* People talk doing are when, hindrance not to do so as to.)

When speaking to another person, *negaimásŭ* 願います, *I beg of you,*
may follow *yō-ni* when one wishes to be still more polite. This construction
would correspond to *please,* followed by the imperative.

Watashi ga benkyō shĭté irú tokí ni sonná ni otó wo sasenái yō-ni
私　が　勉強　している　時　にそんな　に　音　をさせないように
negaimásŭ.   **Please** do not make such a noise when I am studying.
願います.   (*lit.* I, study doing am when, such noise not to cause to do
                  (*sasenái*) so as to, I beg of you.)

O-wasuré monó (no) nái yō-ni negaimásŭ.   **Please** do not forget
お忘れ　物　(の) ない　ように　願います.   anything.
   (*lit.* Forgotten things there are not in order to, I beg of you.)

When **must** indicates inference, the strongest probability, or almost certainty,
it is translated by *ni chigái ga arimasén* に違いがありません or *ni chigái
ga nái* (*désŭ*) に違いがない (です). Note that *ga* is emphatic and may be
omitted.

_____

1 *Ni wa* after the simple present means *in order to.*

The syllable *ni* に of the two expressions is the abbreviation of *ni tsúite* について (=about, concerning, with reference to); *chigái* 違い means *mistake* and *arimasén* ありません, as well as *nái* ない, stands for *there is not.* Thus, *ni chigái ga arimasén* に違いがありません or *ni chigái nái* に違いない corresponds to *there is no mistake about it.*

Anó katá wa Fújita Hákase ni chigái ga arimasén.
あの 方 は 藤田 博士 に 違い が ありません.

   That man **must be** Doctor Fujita. (*lit.* That man, Doctor Fujita, there is no mistake about it.—*Hákase* academic title)

Koré wa tomodachí no hon ni chigái nái (désŭ).   This **must be** my
これ は 友達 の 本 に 違い ない (です).   friend's book.

   (*lit.* This, my friend's book, there is no mistake about it.)

Kono nyūsu wa hontō de áru ni chigái nái.   This news **must be**
このニュース は 本当 である に 違い ない.   true.

   (*lit.* This news true is, there is no mistake about it.)

Ought

When **ought** is used in the meaning of *to be bound in duty, by moral obligation* or *by ideal necessity*, it may be translated, in increasing degree of emphatic force, by *hazú* 筈, *béki* べき, *béki hazú* べき筈, followed by *désŭ* です or *déshĭta* でした, according to whether one refers to the present or the past.

The verb that in English is used in its infinitive form after **ought**, is used, in Japanese, in its simple present.

Kodomó wa oyá ni shĭtagáu hazú désŭ.   Children **ought to** be obedient
子供 は 親 に 従う 筈 です.   to their parents.

(*shĭtagáu* to obey, to be obedient to...., to yield to persuasion, etc.)

Watashí wa imá-goró asokó e tsúite irú béki hazú désŭ.
私 は 今頃 あそこへ着いている べき 筈 です.

I ought to be there now. (*lit.* I, about now, there having arrived ought to.— *tsúite irú* to have arrived)

Sonó shigotó wa zuttó máe ni shĭté áru béki hazú déshĭta.
その 仕事 は ずっと 前 に してある べき 筈 でした.

   The work **ought to** have been done long ago.—(*shĭté áru*=being done)

The verb *surú* する when followed by *béki* べき may be abbreviated to *su* す.

Watashí wa náni wo subéki (surú béki) désŭ ka.   What **ought I to** do?
私 は 何 を すべき (するべき) です か.

Kimí wa soré wo subéki désŭ.   You **ought to** do it.
君 はそれ を すべき です.

Anáta wa ojisán ni sōdan subéki déshĭta.   You **ought to** have consulted
あなた は伯父さんに 相談 すべき でした.   with your uncle.

The negative form of **ought** is generally translated by *hazú* 筈,
béki べき, *béki hazú* べき筈 followed by *de wa arimasén* で
はありません or *de wa nái* ではない, when referring to the present,
or by *de wa arimasén déshìta* ではありませんでした or *de
wa nákatta* ではなかった when referring to the past.

Káre wa sō iú béki de wa nái.　　He **ought not** to say so.
彼　は　そう云うべき　で　は　ない.

Watashí wa sokó e ikú béki de wa nákatta.　　I **ought not** to have
私　は　そこ　へ　行く　べき　で　は　なかった.　　gone there.

When **ought** is used in the sense of *being proper, just, justifiable,*
reasonable, merited, due, it may be translated by *atarimaé* 当り前,
corresponding in meaning to such mentioned words.

Otōsan ni sōdan surú no ga atarimaé désŭ. (or *hazú désŭ*, etc.)
お父さんに　相談　する　の　が　当り前　です.（筈です）

　　You **ought to** consult your father. (......*ni sōdan surú* to consult)

Sō iú hĭtó ga seikō surú no wa atarimaé désŭ. (or *surú hazú désŭ*, etc.)
そういう人　が　成功　するの　は　当り前　です.　（する　筈　です）

　　Such a man **ought to** succeed. (*seikō surú* to succeed)
　　(*lit.* Such a man success to make is justifiable, merited, due, etc.)

When **ought** suggests *logical consequence hazú* 筈 may be used.

Torí náraba tobú hazú désŭ.　　If it is a bird it **ought to** fly.
鳥　ならば　飛ぶ　筈　です.　　(Bird if is, to fly ought to.)

Ought may be translated also by the progressive form of a verb
followed by *ii* (good).

Ten-in wa imá-goró mō kité ité ii (or *kité irú*) *hazú désŭ.*
店員　は　今頃　もう来て　いていゝ　（来ている）　筈　です.

　　The shopman **ought to** have arrived by now.
　　(*lit.* The shopman, about now, already, being coming ought.—*kité ité* 来て
　いて progressive form of *kité irú* to have come)

Ought may be translated also by the present subjunctive of *surú*
する (*suréba* すれば) followed by *yói* よい (it is good) or *yókatta*
よかった, according to whether one refers to the present or the past.

Soré wa máe ni suréba yói (or *yói désŭ*.)　　That **ought to** be done
それ　は　前　に　すれば　よい　（よい　です）.　　before.

Soré wa máe ni suréba yókatta (or *yói déshita*).　　That **ought to** have
それ　は　前　に　すれば　よかった　（よいでした）.　　been done before.

The negative of the above is formed by the negative of *surú* する (*shinái*
しない or *shinákatta* しなかった) followed by *hō ga yói* 方がよい or *hō
ga yókatta* 方がよかった, according to whether one refers to the present or
the past.

*Soré wa máe ni **shinái hō ga yói** (désŭ).* That **ought not** to be
それ は 前 に しない 方 が よい （です）. done before.

*Soré wa máe ni **shinái hō ga yókatta.*** That **ought not** to have
それ は 前 に しない 方 が よかった. been done before.

Ought and **ought not** may be translated also as **must** and **must not** are translated, that is, with *narimasén* なりません, *naránai* ならない, *ikemasén* いけません, *ikenái* いけない, and their past forms when referring to the past.

*Soré wo súgu ni **shi-nákute wa narimasén.*** It **ought to** be done
それ を すぐ に しなくて は なりません. at once.

(*lit.* That, at once, not being done won't do.)

*Soré wo **yurúshĭte oité wa ikemasén.*** That **ought not** to be allowed.
それ を 許して おいて は いけません.

(*yurúshĭte okú* 許しておく to allow a matter to stand)

*Otōtosan wa sonná kotó wo **itté wa narimasén.***
弟さん は そんな 事 を 云っては なりません.

Your younger brother **ought not** to say such things.

When **ought** suggests probability, besides being translated by *hazú* 筈, *béki* べき, etc., may be translated by the simple present of a verb followed by *to omoimásŭ* と思います, *deshō* でしょう or *deshō to omoimásŭ.* でしょうと思います.

*Anáta no umá wa **kátsu to omoimásŭ** (kátsu deshō, kátsu hazú désŭ,* etc.)
あなたの 馬 は 勝つ と 思います（勝つでしょう, 勝つ 筈 です）

Your horse **ought to win.**

Inside

Inside, when used as an adverb or preposition, is translated by *no náka de* の中で, *no náka e* の中へ, *no náka ni* の中に. See Lesson 17 page 94 for the use of the postpositions *de* で and *ni* に. *No naka e* is used when the expression is followed by a verb indicating motion towards a place.

*Eki no **náka de** mátte imásŭ.* I shall wait for you **inside** the station.
駅 の 中 で 待っています.

*Dáre de mo anó o-terá **no náka** e ikemásŭ.* Anybody may (can) go
誰 で も あの お寺 の 中 へ 行けます. **inside** that temple.

*Anáta no jibikí wa anó hikidashí **no náka** ni háitte[1] imásŭ.*
貴方 の 字引 は あの 引出し の 中 に 入って います.

Your dictionary is **inside** that drawer.

When used as a noun, meaning *the inside, the inner part,* the word **inside** is translated by *uchigawá* 内側 or *náibŭ*[2] 内部.

---

1 *háitte irú* to contain, to be included **2** *náibu* (Lit. style)

*Konó hakó no **uchigawá** wa akái.*
この 箱 の 内側 は 赤い.　　｜ This box is red **inside.**

*Konó hako no **náibu** wa akái.*　　｛ The **inside** of this box is red.
この 箱 の 内部 は 赤い.　　｜

Outside

Outside, used as an adverb or preposition, is translated by *no sóto de* の外で, *no sóto ni* の外に, *no sóto e* の外へ. When used as a noun, meaning *the outside, the external part*, it is translated by *sotogawá* 外側, or by *gáibu* 外部 in literary style.

*Anáta no tomodachí ga yūbin-kyokú **no sóto de** mátte imásŭ.*
貴方 の 友達 が 郵便局 の 外 で 待っています.
Your friend is waiting for you **outside** the post-office.

*Kōshū-dénwa wa éki **no sóto ni** arimásŭ.*   A telephone booth is
公衆 電話 は 駅 の 外 に あります.   **outside** the station.
(*kōshū* public, of or for the public; *kōshū-dénwa* public telephone)

*Kono tatémono wa **sotogawá** ga rénga de **uchigawá** wa ki désŭ.*
この 建物 は 外側 が れんが で 内側 は 木 です.
This building is brick **outside** and wood **inside.**

*Konó tatémono wa **gáibu** ga rénga de **náibu** wa ki désŭ. (Lit.)*
この 建物 は 外部 が れんが で 内部 は 木 です.
This building is brick **outside** and wood **inside.**

Vocabulary

Nouns					
animal	dōbutsu	動物	skilled	jōzu-na	上手ナ
chess	shōgi	将棋	**Verbs**		
comfort	ánraku	安楽	to be late	okure·rú	遅レル
camel	rakudá	ラクダ	to bite	kuitsŭkú	クイツク
draughts	seiyō-go	西洋碁	to borrow	kari·rú	借リル
education	kyōiku	教育	to close	shimé·ru	シメル
food	tabemonó	食物	to express	hyōgen surú	表現スル
meaning	ími	意味	to lose	nakŭsú	失クス
poem	shi	詩	to mend	shūzen surú	修繕スル
purpose	mokutekí	目的	to remember	oboé·ru	覚エル
safe	kínko	金庫	to use	tsŭkaú	使ウ
writer	sakŭshá	作者	**Adverbs**		
Adjectives			clearly	hakkíri-to	ハッキリト
permanent	eizokutekí no	永続的ノ	otherwise	sámonai-to	サモナイト
ignorant	múgaku no	無学ノ	uselessly	mudá-ni	ムダニ

foreign language *gaikokú-go*; most, general, usual, the average *taitéi no*; human being, man, a mortal, a person *ningén*; by to-morrow *ashǐtá máde ni*; to play chess *shōgi wo sásu*; great poet *dái-shijín*; to bear in mind, to be versed in *wakimáeru*; to take off (shoes, socks, clothes) *núgu*; to leave open *akebanashí*; to find, come across *miatarú*; to waste *mudá ni tsükaú*; hardly *métta ni* with negative verb; to be locked with key *kagí ga kakátte irú*; to put on the light *dentō* or *akarí wo tsükéru*; to put off the light *dentō* or *akarí wo kesú*; to light a lamp *akarí wo tsükéru* (*dentō* electric light or lamp, *akarí* any kind of light); to extinguish, put out, to blow out *kesú*; postoffice *yūbin-kyokú*; brick *rénga*; money *kínsen* (Lit.); lasting *nágaku tsuzukú*; to be found *miatarú*

Exercise   *Renshū*   練習

1. Benkyō sézu ni gaikokú-go wo yóku obóeru kotó wa dekínai.   2. Taitéi no dōbutsu wa séigo[1] sū-jitsú[2] de arúku kotó ga dekimásŭ ga ningén wa sū-ka-getsú tatáneba[3] arúku kotó ga dekimasén.   3. Rakudá wa shi-go-nichí no aidá tabemonó to mizú náshi de ikú kotó ga dekimásŭ.   4. Watashí no furúi kutsú wo ashǐtá máde ni shūzen surú kotó ga dekí-nákereba[4] atarashíi no wo issokú[5] kaimásŭ.   5. Shōgi wo sásu kotó ga dekimásŭ ka.—Iié, dekimasén, kéredomo seiyō-go wa dekimásŭ.   6. Itarī no daishijín Dánte wa kyū-sái[6] no tokí súdeni[7] yói shi wo tsükúru kotó ga dekimáshǐta.   7. Hyakú-nen guraí máe máde wa taitéi no hǐtó wa múgaku de yómikaki[8] ga dekimasén déshǐta.   Kónnichi de wa ikubún[9] de mo gakkō kyōiku wo ukénai[10] kodomó wa métta ni imasén.   8. Gaikokú-go wo manabú ómona mokutekí[11] wa sonó kotobá de káitari hanáshǐtari[12] shǐté jibún wo hakkíri to hyōgen surú kotó no[13] dekíru kotó désŭ.   9. Anáta no jibikí wo chottó no aidá[14] haishakú[15] shǐté mo yói désŭ ka.—Hái, anáta no o-sükí-na daké nágaku[16] o-mochí ni nátte[17] mo yoroshíi désŭ.   10. Sámuku narimáshǐta.   Kómban yukí ga fúru ka-mo shiremasén. (Daibú sámuku narimáshǐta.   Kómban átari[18] yukí[19] ka-mo shiremasén.)   11. Isogánai[20] to kishá ni norí-okuréru ka-mo shiremasén yo.   12. Jōzu-na sakŭshá wa kotobá no ími wo yóku wakimáeru[21] oráneba naránu[22].   13. Kínsen de eizokutekí no ánraku wa kaerú[23] ka-mo shirenái ga nágaku tsuzukú kōfuku wa kaenái.   14. Nihón no ié ni agarú[24] máe ni wa kutsú wo nugáneba narimasén.   15. Súgu ni o-dekaké nasái.   Sámonai-to jimúsho ni osokú narimásŭ yo.   16. Ima anáta to go-isshó ni yukú kotó ga dekimasén.   Watashí wa imōto wo gakkō e tsureté yuká-nákereba narimasén

---

1 '*séigo* after birth   **2** *sū-jitsú* a few days   **3** *tátsu* to pass, to elapse, said of time; *tatáneba* contracted form of *tatánakereba* unless (time) elapses; *sū-ka-getsú tatánakereba* unless several months pass   **4** if you cannot make   **5** one pair   **6** *kyū-sái* nine years old   **7** already   **8** *yómikaki* to read and write   **9** *ikubún* some   **10** *ukénai* negative of *ukéru* to receive; *kyōiku wo ukénai kodomó* boy that does not receive education   **11** *ómona* chief, principal, main; *ómona mokutekí* main purpose   **12** *káitari hanáshǐtari shǐté* writing and speaking   **13** *no* is sometimes used to indicate the nomínative instead of *ga* as in this sentence.   **14** *chottó no aidá* for a while   **15** *haishakú surú* is the polite verb for *to borrow* instead of *karirú*   **16** *o-sükí na daké nágaku* as long as you like   **17** *o-mochí ni náru* polite form for *mótsu*, to have   **18** *átari* about   **19** the verb *fúru* has been omitted; *yuki ga fúru* to snow   **20** *isógu* to hurry; *isogánai to* if you do not hurry   **21** *wakimáete* well acquainted   **22** *oráneba naranú* must   **23** *kaerú* can be bought, *kaerú* is the potential form of *kaú*, to buy   **24** *agarú* to enter (a house)

kará.   **17.** Anáta no tegamí wo jū-ji no kishá de dashitái no náraba ni-jī-kán háyaku ni kakasé-nákereba[1] narimasén.   **18.** Háitta áto to wo akebanashí ni shĭté wa ikemasén.   Shimé-nákereba ikemasén ne.   **19.** Watashí no saifú ga dóko ni mo miatarimasén.   Nakushĭtá ni chigái arimasén.   **20.** Mudá ni o-kané wo tsŭkaú béki de wa arimasén.   **21.** Anáta wa mótto yóku shĭtté irú béki hazú désŭ. (shĭtté irú *to know*)   **22.** Kimí wa watashitachí to isshó ni kúru béki hazú désŭ.   **23.** Anáta wa nihóngo wo benkyō subéki hazú désŭ.   **24.** Kimí wa jimúsho e sonná ni osokú kúru hazú de wa nái.   **25.** Anáta wa sō shi-nákereba narimasén.   **26.** Anáta wa sō itté wa ikenái.   **27.** Watashí wa sō surú béki hazú déshĭta.   **28.** Anáta wa sonná kotó guraí shĭtté irú (or shĭtté ité íi) hazú déshĭta.   **29.** Gekijō ni háitte pŭroguramú wo dōzo moratté kité kudasái.   **30.** Dóko de watashí wo mátte imáshĭta ka.—Anó tatémono no sotó de matté imáshĭta.   **31.** Dōzo dentō wo tsŭkéte kudasái. —Dōzo keshĭté kudasái.—O-yasumí nasái.

1. 勉強せずに外国語をよく覚える事はできない. **2.** 大抵の動物は生後数日で歩く事ができますが人間は数ヶ月たたねば歩く事ができません. **3.** ラクダは四五日の間食物と水なしで行く事ができます. **4.** 私の古い靴をあした迄に修繕する事ができなければ新しいのを一足買います. **5.** 将棋を差す事ができますか.—いゝえ，できませんけれども西洋碁はできます. **6.** イタリーの大詩人ダンテは九才の時すでによい詩をつくる事ができました. **7.** 百年ぐらい前までは大抵の人が無学で読み書きができませんでした.今日では幾分でも学校教育を受けない子供はめったにいません. **8.** 外国語を学ぶ主な目的はその言葉で書いたり話したりして自分をはっきりと表現する事のできる事です. **9.** 貴方の字引を一寸の間拝借してもよいですか.—はい，貴方のお好きなだけ長くお持ちになってもよろしいです. **10.** 寒くなりました，今晩雪が降るかも知れません（大分寒くなりました，今晩あたり雪かも知れません）. **11.** 急がないと汽車に乗り遅れるかも知れませんよ. **12.** 上手な作者は言葉の意味をよくわきまえておらねばならぬ. **13.** 金銭で永続的の安楽は買えるかも知れないが長く続く幸福は買えない. **14.** 日本の家に上がる前には靴を脱がねばなりません. **15.** 直ぐにお出かけなさい.さもないと事務所に遅くなりますよ. **16.** 今，貴方と御一緒に行く事ができません，私は妹を学校へ連れて行かなければなりませんから. **17.** 貴方の手紙を十時の汽車で出したいのならば二時間早くに書かせなければなりません. **18.** 入ったあと戸を開け放しにしてはいけません.しめなければいけませんね. **19.** 私の財布がどこにも見当りません失くしたに違いありません. **20.** 無駄にお金を使うべきではありません. **21.** あなたはもっとよく知っているべき筈です. **22.** 君は私達と一緒に来るべき筈です.

---

1 *kakaséru* to cause to write, to have (something) written

23. あなたは日本語を勉強すべき筈です. **24.** 君は事務所へそんなに
おそく来る筈ではない. **25.** あなたはそうしなければなりません.
26. あなたはそう云ってはいけない. **27.** 私はそうするべき筈でした.
28. あなたはそんな事ぐらい知っている（知っていていゝ）筈でした.
29. 劇場に入ってプログラムをどうぞ貰って来て下さい. **30.** どこで
私を待っていましたか.—あの建物の外で待っていました. **31.** どうぞ
電燈をつけて下さい.—どうぞ消して下さい.—お休みなさい.

1. Without studying we cannot learn a foreign language well. **2.** Most
animals can walk a few days after they are born, but man cannot walk until
he is several months old. **3.** Camels can go without food and water for four
or five days. **4.** If you cannot mend my old shoes by to-morrow, I shall buy
a new pair. **5.** Can you play chess?—No, I cannot but I can play draughts.
6. Dante, the greatest of Italian poets, was able to compose good poems when
he was a nine years old boy. **7.** Until about a hundred years ago, most
people were ignorant and could neither read nor write; to-day there is hardly
a boy that has not had some school education. **8.** The main object of the
study of a foreign language is that one may be able to express oneself clearly,
whether in writing or in speaking. **9.** May I borrow your dictionary for a
while?—Yes, you may have it as long as you like. **10.** It is getting cold;
to-night it may snow. **11.** If you do not hurry you may miss the train.
12. The skilled writer must have an intimate acquaintance with the meaning
of words. **13.** With money one may buy permanent comfort, but not lasting
happiness. **14.** Before entering a Japanese house, one must take off one's
shoes. **15.** You must leave at once, otherwise you will arrive late at the office.
16. I cannot go with you now, I must accompany my little sister to school.
17. If you wish your letters to go by the ten o'clock train, you must have
them written two hours earlier. **18.** You mustn't leave the door open after
you enter; you must close it. **19.** I cannot find my purse anywhere; I must
have lost it. **20.** You ought not to spend your money uselessly. **21.** You
ought to know better. **22.** You ought to come with us. **23.** You ought to
study Japanese. **24.** You ought not to come to the office so late. **25.** You
ought to do so. **26.** You ought not to say so. **27.** I ought to have done so.
28. You ought to have known such a thing. **29.** Go inside the theatre and
get a program. **30.** Where were you waiting for me?—I was waiting for
you outside that building. **31.** Put on the (electric) light, please.—Put it off.
—Good night.

Forty-fifth Lesson 第四十五課

Potential Mood (continued)
Could

As the past of *can*, **could** is translated by *dekimáshǐta* 出来ました or *dékita* 出来た, as shown in the previous lesson.

Anó ojōsan wa san-sái no tokí ni oyógu kotó ga dekimáshǐta.
あのお嬢さんは 三才 の 時 に 泳ぐ 事 が 出来ました.
That girl **could** swim when three years old.

Tsǔkárete imáshǐta kará mō soré-íjō arúku kotó ga dekimasén déshǐta.
疲れて いましたからもうそれ以上歩く 事 が 出来ません でした.
I was tired and **could not** walk any longer.
(*lit.* Being tired was because, farther that more, to walk the thing could not.)

When **could** is used in the **conditional present** it may be translated by *kotó ga dekíru deshō* (or *darō*) *ni* 事が出来るでしょう(だろう)に, and the verb preceding *could* in its simple form. This construction is generally used when the sentence is introduced by an *if-clause*.

Yóku benkyō suréba nihón-go wo ni-nen ínai de obóeru kotó ga
よく 勉強 すれば 日本語 を 二 年 以内 で 覚える 事 が
dekíru deshō ni.   If you studied hard you **could learn** the Japanese
出来る でしょうに.   language in two years.
(*lit.* Well study if you did Japanese language two years within to learn could.)

Anó katá wa hóshikattara anó jidōsha wo kaú kotó ga dekíru deshō ni.
あの 方 は欲しかったらあの自動車 を 買う 事 が 出来る でしょうに.
He **could buy** that motocar if he wanted to.

When **could** does not depend on an *if-clause* and is in reference to the present or future, the present or future of *dekíru* 出来る is used.

In referring to the present, **could,** in this case, may be replaced by **can** without alteration of meaning.

Kómban takú e kúru kotó ga dekimásǔ ka.
今晩 宅 へ 来る 事 が 出来ます か.
Could (can) you **come** this evening to my home?

Konó toránku wo hakobú kotó ga dekimásǔ ka.
この トランク を 運ぶ 事 が 出来ます か.
Could (can) you **carry** this trunk?

Amari omói kará dekimasén. I **could** (can) **not** because it is too
あまり 重い から 出来ません.　heavy.

Yamá no chōjō máde kómban tōchaku surú kotó ga dekíru deshō ka.
山 の 頂上 まで 今晩 到着 する 事 が 出来るでしょうか.
Could we reach the top of the mountain by to-night?

Mótto háyaku arúkeba dekíru deshō. We **could** if we walked faster.
もっと 早く 歩けば 出来るでしょう.

The **conditional past perfect** with **could** may be translated by
the simple present followed by *kotó ga dékita deshō ni* 事が出
来たでしょうに or by the gradually less polite forms *kotó ga dékita
de arō ni* 事が出来たであろうに, *kotó ga dékita darō ni* 事が出来た
だろうに.

This construction may be used when the sentence or clause with
could suggests the contrary.

Náze watashí ni sō iimasén déshĭta ka. Watashí wa íkura-ka o-kané
なぜ 私 にそう云いませんでしたか.　私 は 幾らか お金
wo kasú kotó ga dékita deshō ni. Why did you not tell me so? I **could**
を 貸す 事 が 出来た でしょうに.　**have lent** you some money.

Yōfukuya wa watashí no yōfuku wo senshū máde ni shiagéru kotó ga
洋服屋 は 私 の 洋服 を 先週 までに 仕上げる 事 が
dékita deshō ni. My tailor **could have finished** my suit by last week.
出来た でしょうに.　(but he didn't finish it for some reason or other)

Could followed by the perfect tense of the verb **to do** in the passive form,
besides being translated by the same construction described above, may be
translated by the past of *dekíru* 出来る followed by *deshō ni* でしょうに.

Sonó shigotó wa mótto yóku dékita deshō ni (or......*surú kotó ga*
その 仕事 は もっと よく 出来た でしょうに　（する 事 が
dékita deshō ni). That work **could have been done** better.
出来たでしょうに).

However, if the verb **to do** is used in its active voice then *shĭtá deshō
ni* したでしょうに is used instead of *dékita deshō ni* 出来たでしょうに. Also
in this case the construction with *kotó ga* 事が may be used.

Sonó baaí ni dáre de-mo onají yō-ni shĭtá deshō ni (or......*surú*
その 場合 に 誰 でも 同じ ように した でしょうに　（する
kotó ga dékita deshō ni). In that case anybody **could have done** the
事 が 出来たでしょうに).　same. (*Sonó baaí ni* In that case......)

May

May followed by the perfect tense generally indicates probability
and may be translated by the past of the principal verb, followed
by *deshō* でしょう or *darō* だろう, *ka-mo shiremasén* かも知
れません or *ka-mo shirenái* かも知れない.

Konó haná wo dáre ga okuttá deshō ka.
この　花　を　誰　が　送った　でしょうか.
Who **may have sent** these flowers? *or* I wonder who may have......

Tábun anáta no séito ga okuttá ka-mo shiremasén.
たぶん　あなた　の　生徒　が　送った　かも　知れません.
Perhaps one of your pupils **may have sent** them.

Kutsúya wa mō anáta no kutsú wo tsŭkŭtta ka-mo shiremasén.
靴屋　は　もうあなた　の　靴　を　つくった　かも　知れません.
Our shoemaker **may have finished** your shoes already.

When more probability is to be expressed, that is, when **may** is
emphasized, *déshĭta* でした may be added to the expression *ka-mo
shiremasén* (*shirenái*) かも知れません (知れない).

Watashí wa sō ittá ka-mo shiremasén déshĭta.   I **may** have
私　は　そう云ったかも　知れません　でした.   said so.

The **negative** of **may** followed by the perfect tense may be formed
by the negative past of the principal verb, followed, as in the case
of the positive form, by *deshō* (*darō*) でしょう (だろう), or by
ka-mo shiremasén (*shirenái*) かも知れません (知れない).

Anó shōnen wa hontō no kotó wo iwanákatta deshō (or *iwanákatta*
あの　少年　は　本当　の　事　を　云わなかったでしょう (云わなかった
ka-mo shiremasén).   The boy may not have told the truth. (*iwanákatta* 云わ
かも　知れません).   なかった negative of *iŭ* 云う to say, to tell)

Anó katá wa anáta no kangáe wo wakará-nákatta ka-mo shiremasén.
あの　方　はあなた　の　考え　を　わからなかった　かも　知れません.
He may not have understood your idea. (*wakáru* わかる to understand)

*Taifū no tamé ni sonó fúne wa máda shuppán shinákatta ka-mo
台風　の　ために　あの　船　は　まだ　出帆　しなかった　かも
shiremasén.*   On account of the typhoon the ship may not have left yet.
知れません.

Might

When **might**, followed by the perfect tense of a verb indicates
probability or is used with hypothetical meaning, it may be translated
by the past tense of the principal verb followed by *ka-mo shiremasén* (*shirenái*) かも知れません(知れない), to which expressions
déshĭta nóni でしたのに, or either *déshĭta* でした or *nóni* の
に only, may be added if emphasis is to be expressed.

Anáta wa éki e takŭshī de itté itára go-ji no resshá de táteta ka-mo
あなた　は　駅　ヘタクシーで行っていたら五時の　列車　で　立てた　かも
shiremasén déshĭta nóni.   If you had gone to the station by taxi you
知れません　でした　のに.   might have left by the five o'clock train.
(*itté irú* 行っている to have gone, *resshá* 列車 train, *táteta* 立てた past of
tatéru 立てる to be able to leave)

Soré wo máe ni watashí ni hanashimáshĭta náraba náni-ka go-chūkoku
それ を 前 に 私 に 話しました ならば 何か 御忠告
wo shĭté agereretá ka-mo shiremasén déshĭta nóni.
を して 上げられた かも 知れません でした のに.
If you had told me that before I might have given you some advice.

Sonná machigaí wa dáre de mo shĭtá ka-mo shiremasén (*nóni*).
そんな 間違い は 誰 で も した かも 知れません （のに）.
Such mistakes might have been made by anybody.

When someone's opinion is considered, the past of the principal verb may be followed by *deshō to omoimásŭ* でしょうと思います. If, however, nobody's opinion is considered, the past of the principal verb is generally followed only by *deshō* でしょう.

Sonná baaí ni dónna kotó ga okótta deshō ka.   What might have happened
そんな 場合にどんな 事 が起こったでしょうか.   in that case?
(=I wonder what might have happened in that case.)

Sonná baaí ni dónna kotó ga okótta deshō to omoimásŭ ka.
そんな 場合 に どんな 事 が 起こったでしょうと 思います か.
What might have happened in that case? (=What do you think might have happened in that case?)

Dónna kotó ga okótta deshō ka dáre mo wakarimasén.
どんな 事 が 起こったでしょうか 誰 も 分かりません.
Nobody knows what might have happened.

The expression *ka-mo shiremasén* かも知れません after the past tense of the principal verb may be used also when expressing one's own opinion, as in the following example:

Sonná baaí ni jūdai-na kotó ga okótta ka-mo shiremasén.
そんな 場合 に 重大な 事 が 起こった かも 知れません.
In such case something serious might have happened (*So I think* is implied.)

The negative of **might** followed by the perfect tense is, in most cases, obtained by the negative past of the principal verb followed by *ka-mo shiremasén* (*shirenái*) かも知れません（知れない）.

Káre wa sō iwanákatta ka-mo shiremasén.   He might not have
彼 は そう 云わなかった かも 知れません.   said so.

Káre wa sonó ten wo kangáe-nákatta ka-mo shirenái.
彼 は その 点 を 考えなかった かも 知れない.
He might not have thought of that point.

Must

When **must,** followed by the perfect tense of a verb, indicates inference, it may be translated by the past tense of the principal verb followed by *ni chigái arimasén* に違いありません or *ni chigái nái* に違いない.

Koré wa zuttó máe ni okótta ni chigái arimasén.
これ は ずっと 前 に 起こった に 違い ありません.
This **must** have happened a long time ago. (*okóru* 起こる to happen)

Anó katá wa náni-ka utagatté itá ni chigái nái.
あの 方 は 何か うたがっていた に 違い ない.
He **must** have suspected something. (*utagaú* うたがう to suspect)

Anó katá wa kishá ni norí-okúreta ni chigái arimasén.
あの 方 は 汽車 に 乗りおくれた に 違い ありません.
He **must** have missed the train. (*norí-okuréru* のりおくれる to fail to catch, to miss, as a train, a boat)

Watashí no tebúkuro ga miemasén; nakushítá ni chigái arimasén.
私 の 手袋 が 見えません, なくした に 違い ありません.
I cannot find my gloves; I **must** have lost them. (*nakusú* なくす to lose)

Watashí wa máe ni konó michí wo mimasén déshita; saikín dékita ni
私 は 前 にこの 道 を 見ません でした, 最近 できた に
chigái arimasén.   I haven't seen this street before; they **must** have made
違い ありません.   it recently. (*michí* street, *saikín* recently)

The **negative** of **must** followed by the perfect tense of a verb and indicating inference, is obtained by the negative past of the principal verb followed by *ni chigái arimasén* (*nái*) に違いありません (ない).

Anó katá wa anáta ga ittá kotó wo wakará-nákatta ni chigái
あの 方 は あなた が 云った 事 を わからなかった に 違い
arimasén.   He **must** not have understood what you said.
ありません.   (*wakáru* わかる to understand)

Anó katá wa náni-mo utagawá-nákatta ni chigái nái.
あの 方 は 何も うたがわなかった に 違い ない.
He **must** not have suspected anything.

Káre wa éki e máda tsúká-nákatta ni chigái arimasén.
彼 は 駅 へ まだ 着かなかった に 違い ありません.
He **must** not have arrived at the station yet. (*tsukú* 着く to arrive)

Ought

Ought followed by the perfect tense and suggesting duty, moral obligation or desirability, may be translated by the simple present of the principal verb followed by either one of the expressions *hazú* 筈, *béki* べき, *béki hazú* べき筈 and, in decreasing degree of politeness, by *de arimáshita* でありました, *déshita* でした, *de átta* であった.

Anáta wa só iú béki hazú de arimáshita (or *déshita, de átta*).
あなた は そう云うべき 筈 で ありました (でした, であった).
You **ought** to have said so.

Koré wa máe ni sareté irú béki de átta.   This **ought** to have been
これ は 前 に されて いる べき であった.   done before.

   (*sareté irú* されている passive of *surú* する to do)

Sakúban kúrabu e ikú béki hazú déshita.   Last night I **ought** to have
昨晩 クラブへ 行く べき 筈 でした.   gone to the club.

Go-tōchaku wo dempō de watashí ni shiraserú béki hazú déshita.
御到着 を 電報 で 私 に 知らせる べき 筈 でした.
You **ought** to have informed me of your arrival by telegram.

Anó jimúin wo yatóu máe ni anáta wa káre no sainō wo tamésu
あの 事務員 を やとう 前 にあなた は 彼 の 才能 を 試す

béki de átta.   Before employing that clerk you **ought** to have tried his
べき であった.   ability. (*sainō* talent, ability; *tamésu* to try, to test)

Karé wa ishá ni náru béki déshita.   He **ought** to have been
彼 は 医者に なる べき でした.   a doctor.

Anó dáiku ga dónna-ni háyaku shigotó wo shǐtá ka wo anáta wa
あの 大工 が どんなに 早く 仕事 を した か をあなた は

míru béki déshita.   You **ought** to have seen how quickly that carpenter
見る べき でした.   could work!

   (*dónna-ni......ka* corresponds to **how,** and the following *wo* puts the preceding
   clause in the accusative governed by *míru* 見る to see)

The **negative** form of **ought** followed by the perfect tense and
suggesting duty, moral obligation or desirability, is generally obtained
by the simple present of the principal verb followed by *hazú* 筈,
béki べき, *béki hazú* べき筈 and *de wa arimasén déshita* で
はありませんでした or *de wa nákatta* ではなかった.

   Anáta wa sō iú béki házu de wa arimasén déshita (or *de*
   あなた は そう云うべき 筈 で は ありません でした   (で
   wa nákatta).   You **ought** not to have said so.
   は なかった).

   Anó katá wa anó mōshikomi wo sonná ni háyaku shōdaku subéki de
   あの 方 はあの 申込み をそんなに 早く 承諾 すべき で

   wa arimasén déshita (or *de wa nákatta*). He **ought not** to have accepted
   は ありません でした   (で はなかった).   the proposal so quickly.

   (*mōshikomi* proposal; *shōdaku surú* to accept)

   Káre wa jibún no musŭkó wo sonná ni bassú-béki de wa nákatta.
   彼 は 自分 の 息子 をそんなに 罰すべき で は なかった.

   He **ought not** to have punished his son so severely. (*bassúru* 罰する to punish;
   ru before *beki* has been dropped for euphonic reason)

   Koré wa máe ni sarerú béki hazú de wa nákatta.
   これ は 前 に される べき 筈 で は なかった.
   This **ought not** to have been done before. (*sarerú* passive of *surú*)

Then

Then and **and then,** with the meaning of *afterwards,* is translated by *soré kará* (after that). If a verb precedes *soré kará,* it is put in the *subordinate.*

Watashí wa Teikokú Hóteru de chūjiki[1] *wo shĭté* **soré kará** *Ginzá e*
私 は 帝国 ホテル で 中食 を して それ から 銀座 へ
ikimáshĭta. I had my lunch at the Imperial Hotel and **then** went to Ginza.
行きました. (*Ginza* a well-known Tokyo thoroughfare)

When **then** means *at that time,* it is translated by *sonó toki* その時 or *sonó tōji* その当時.

Sonó toki náni wo shĭté irasshaimáshĭta ka. What were you doing **then**?
その 時 何 をしていらっしゃいましたか. (......at that time?)

Benkyō shĭté imáshĭta. 勉強していました. I was studying.

Watashí wa **sonó tōji** *honnó*[2] *kodomó déshĭta.* I was only a boy **then**.
私 は その 当時 ほんの 子供 でした. (......in those days.)

When **then** means *therefore,* its translation is omitted in Japanese, as it may be in English, without much prejudice to the meaning.

Móshi anáta wa sonó jíjitsu wo go-zónji náraba soré wo watashí ni
若し 貴方 は その 事実 を 御存じ ならば それ を 私 に
hanasá-nákereba ikemasén. If you know the facts **then** you must tell me.
話さなければ いけません.
(If you the facts know, them to me if you don't tell it won't do.)

Then is translated by *déwa* when it corresponds to one of the expressions *for this reason, in consequence, as a consequence, so well then, in that case.*

Mō kaerá-nákereba narimasén. Now I must go back.
もう 帰らなければ なりません. (Now, if I don't return won't do.)

Déwa myōnichi matá o-me ni kakarimashō. **Then** I shall see you
では 明日 又 お目 にかかりましょう. again to-morrow.

Déwa getsuyōbi máde sayōnara. **Then,** goodbye until Monday.
では 月曜日 まで さようなら.

Watashí wa késa háyaku kará yasúmazu[3] *ni aruki-tsuzuketé imáshĭta.*
私 は けさ 早く から 休まず に 歩き 続けて いました.
I have been walking since early this morning without any rest.

Déwa o-tsŭkaré ni chigái arimasén. **Then** you must be tired.
では お疲れ に 違い ありません.

Until then or **by that time** is translated by *sonó toki máde (ni)*
その時迄 (に).

---

1 *chūjiki wo surú* to have lunch   **2** *honnó......déshĭta* was only......   **3** *yasúmazu* without resting

Again

Again may be translated by *matá* or *soshǐté matá* そして又 (and again), *fǔtatabí* 再び (a second time), *ni-do to* 二度と (twice), or *mō ichí-do* もう一度 (once more).

Watashí wa késa anáta no ókǔsan ni Teikokú Hóteru no sóba de o-me
私　は　けさ　貴方　の　奥さん　に　帝国　ホテル　の　側　で　お目

ni kakári soshǐté matá gógo shibaí de o-me ni kakarimáshǐta.
に　かかり　そして　又　午後　芝居　で　お目　に　かかりました.

I met your wife in the morning near the Imperial Hotel, then I met her **again** in the afternoon at the theatre.

Mō ichí-do itté kudasái. もう一度言って下さい.　　Please say it **again**.

Watashí wa sokó ni fǔtatabí yukimasumái.
私　は　そこ　に　再び　行きますまい.
　　　　　　　　　　　　　　　　　　　　　　I shall probably not go
Watashí wa ni-do to sokó e yukimasumái.　　there **again**.
私　は　二　度　と　そこ　へ行きますまい.

Sometimes one hears both expressions, *ni-do to fǔtatabí*, used together in the same sentence, especially when emphasis is upon the word *again*.

Idiomatic usage:

as long again	*baí nagái*	倍長い
as many again	*baí ōi*	倍多い
now and again	*tokidoki*	時々
once again	*imá ichí-do*	今一度
once and again	*saisaí*	再々
over again	*kurikaeshí*	繰り返し
over and over again	*kurikaeshí kurikaeshí*	繰り返し繰り返し
time and again	*shíbashiba*	屢々

Káre wa kaifukú shimáshǐta. 彼は回復しました.　He is well **again**.
　(*kaifukú surú* 回復する to recover from sickness)

Watashí wa soré wo mō ichí-do yarinaoshimáshǐta.　I made it all
私　は　それ　を　もう　一度　やりなおしました.　　over **again**.
　(*yarinaósu* やりなおす to make over, to recommence, to do over again, etc.)

Káre wa tabitabí soré wo iimáshǐta.　He mentioned it **again** and
彼　は　度々　それ　を　云いました.　　**again**.

Soré wa aré yóri mō hambún hodó ōkíi désǔ.　It is half as large
それ　は　あれ　より　もう　半分　ほど大きい　です.　　**again** as that.

Towards

Towards is translated by *no hō e* の方へ when it indicates direction, by *mukátté* 向って, *ni ménshǐte* に面して, when it means *facing a place*, and by *ni táishǐte* に対して when used abstractly.

Ni ménshǐte is a literary expression.

*Watashí wa omiyá **no hō** e arúite ikimáshǐta.*   I walked **towards**
私 は お宮 の 方 へ 歩いて 行きました.   the shrine.

*Watashí no bessō wa úmi e **mukatté** imásǔ.*
私 の 別荘 は 海 へ 向って います.   } My villa looks

*Watashí no bessō wa úmi **ni ménshǐte** imásǔ.*   **towards** the sea.
私 の 別荘 は 海 に 面して います.   }

*Rōjin **ni táishǐte** wa shínsetsu de nákereba ikemasén.*
老人 に 対して は 親切 で なければ いけません.

We must be kind to (**towards**) the aged.

    (*lit.* The aged towards, kind if we are not, it won't do.)

Vocabulary

Nouns

ability	sainō	才能		telescope	bōenkyō	望遠鏡 / テレスコープ
air	kūki	空気			**Adjectives**	
alarm	keihō	警報		clever	tákumi-na	巧ミナ
astronomy	temmóngaku	天文学		delighted	ureshǐi	嬉シイ
bell	yobirín	呼鈴		ˡimperfect	fukánzen-na	不完全ナ
beverage	nomímono	飲物			**Verbs**	
defense	béngo	弁護		to accept	shōdaku surú	承諾スル
fireman	shōbōfu	消防夫		to finish	shiagé·ru	仕上ゲル
imprisonment	chōeki	懲役		to get tired	tsǔkaré·ru	疲レル
judge	saibánkan	裁判官		to scratch	hikkáku	ヒッカク
lawyer	bengóshi	弁護士		to remain	taizaí surú	滞在スル
mail	yūbin	郵便		to ring	narasú	ナラス
phenomenom	genshō	現象		to swim	oyógu	泳グ
permission	kyóka	許可		to tease	ijime·rú	虐メル
science	kagakú	科学			**Adverbs**	
sky	kūchū	空中		easily	zōsa náku	造作ナク
sweat	áse	汗		really	jissaí	実際
tent	ténto	テント				

    celestial body *tentái;* streetcar fare *denshachín;* to live, to have life *ikíru;* to pitch *harú;* to pitch a tent *ténto wo harú;* to remain, stop *todomáru;* pitch dark *makkúra;* to lose, to miss one's way *michí ni mayóu;* to condemn *senkokú surú,* letter-box *yūbin-bakó;* postman *yūbin-haitatsú;* to deliver *haitatsú surú;* to work, to function, take effect *kikú;* to burn completely *zenshō surú;* to come running *kákete kúru;* to perspire *áse wo káku;* to become acquainted with *o-chikazukí ni náru;* Art Exhibition *Bíjitsu Tenrankái*

Exercise *Renshū* 練習

1. Hĭtó wa shokúmotsu náshi de san-shi-shū-kan íkite irú kotó ga dekíru ga kūki náshi de wa ni-fun-kan yóri nágaku wa ikirarénai.[1] Kūki wa hĭtó ni shokúmotsu ya nomímono yóri mo mótto hitsuyō désŭ. **2.** Bōenkyō náshi de wa temmóngaku wa fukánzen-na kagakú de átta de arō[2] shi[3] warewaré wa takŭsán no kūchū no genshō wo wakáru kotó ga dekínakatta de arō shi matá tentái no shizénkai[4] mo shirú kotó ga dekínakatta de arō. **3.** Itsu matá o-idé ni naréru[5] deshō ka.—Raishū no doyōbi ni ukagaú kotó ga dekíru deshō. **4.** Dóno kuraí o-kané wo kashĭté kudasáru kotó ga dekíru deshō ka.—Oyosó go-man-yen bakarí kasú kotó ga dekimashō ga getsumatsú máe wa damé désŭ.[6] **5.** Tsŭkaremáshĭta ; kokó ni káette kúru nóni[7] ni-jíkan mo arukimáshĭta.— Náze arúite kimáshĭta ka. Dénsha de kúru kotó ga dékita deshō ni, dekimasén déshĭta ka.—Hái, dénsha de kúru kotó ga dékita no désŭ ga kané wo wasuré denshachín wo haráu kotó ga dekimasén déshĭta kará. **6.** Anó néko wo ijimeté wa ikemasén hikkáku ka-mo shiremasén kará. **7.** Ténto wo hatté ashĭtá no ása máde kokó ni todomátta hō ga yói. Konná makkúra-na ban ni koré íjō arúkeba michí ni mayóu ka-mo shirenái. **8.** Kimí no bengóshi no tákumi-na béngo ga nákattara[8] saibankán wa kimí ni shūshin chōeki[9] wo senkokú shĭtá ka-mo shirenákatta. **9.** Yūbin-bakó ni tegamí ga áru ka míte irasshái. Yūbin-haitatsú ga mō yūbin wo haitatsú shĭte áru ka-mo shiremasén. **10.** Shōbófu wa zōsa náku anó káji wo keshĭtá deshō ni. Dága[10] keihō ga yóku kikanákatta nóde ié ga hotóndo zenshō shĭtá tokí ni shōbófu wa tōchaku shimáshĭta. **11.** Anáta wa kákete kitá ni chigái arimasén kaó ga akákute áse wo káite imásŭ.—Hái, kákete kimáshĭta. Osokú nátta to omoimáshĭta nóde. **12.** Kimí wa dekakerú máe ni shújin no kyóka wo éru béki[11] de átta. **13.** Dáre-ka yobirín wo narashimáshĭta ; o-ishasán ni chigái nái désŭ. **14.** Konó monzén ni chūsha[12] shĭté wa ikemasén. **15.** Watashí ga gekijō wo déta tokí wa jū-ji góro dátta ni chigái arimasén. **16.** Káre wa átari[13] wo míte itá no náraba anó shinkō[14] shĭté kitá resshá no akarí wo míta ni chigái nái. **17.** Kinō anáta ga Uenó Kōen e irasshátta tokí ni Bíjutsu Tenránkai wo gorán ni narimáshĭta ka.—Iié, mimasén déshĭta.—Zéhi gorán nasái ; jissaí hijō ni omoshirói désŭ kará. **18.** Anáta wa anó mōshikomi[15] wo shōdaku subéki hazú déshĭta. **19.** Káre wa ishá ni náru béki hazú déshĭta. **20.** Káre wa hōritsŭka ni náru benkyō wo subéki de wa nákatta. **21.** Dáre démo jibún no kókka no hōritsu wo shĭtté ité soré ni shĭtagaú béki désŭ.

1. 人は食物なしで三四週間生きている事ができるが空気なしでは
二分間より長くは生きられない. 空気は人に食物や飲物よりも，もっ
と必要です． 2. 望遠鏡なしでは天文学は不完全な科学であったであ
ろうし我々は沢山の空中の現象を解る事ができなかったであろうし又

---

1 *ikíru* to live ; *ikiraréru* can live, to be able to live ; see Lesson 52 for this form of the potential **2** *de átta de arō* would be **3** and, besides **4** nature **5** *naréru* to be able to **6** *damé* useless, impossible ; *damé désŭ* cannot **7** *nóni* in order to **8** without **9** *shūshin chōeki* life sentence **10** *dága* however, but **11** *kyóka wo éru* to get permission **12** *chūsha surú* to park **13** *átari* vicinity, surroundings **14** *shinkō surú* to advance, to approach **15** proposal

天体の自然界も知る事ができなかったであろう．　**3.** いつ又お出でに
なれるでしょうか．—来週の土曜日に伺う事ができるでしょう．　**4.** ど
の位お金を貸して下さる事ができるでしょうか．—凡そ五万円ばかり貸
す事ができましょうが月末前はだめです．　**5.** 疲れました，こゝに帰
って来るのに二時間も歩きました．—なぜ歩いて来ましたか，電車で来
る事ができたでしょうに，できませんでしたか．—はい，電車で来る事
ができたのですが金を忘れ電車賃を払う事ができませんでしたから．
6. あの猫を虐めてはいけませんひっかくかも知れませんから．　**7.** テ
ントを張ってあしたの朝までこゝに止まった方がよい，こんなまっくら
な晩にこれ以上歩けば道に迷うかも知れない．　**8.** 君の弁護士の巧
みな弁護がなかったら裁判官は君に終身懲役を宣告したかも知れなか
った．　**9.** 郵便箱に手紙があるか見ていらっしゃい．郵便配達がもう郵
便を配達してあるかも知れません．　**10.** 消防夫は造作なくあの火事を
消したでしょうに，だが警報がよく利かなかったので家が殆ど全焼し
た時に消防夫は到着しました．　**11.** 貴方は駆けて来たに違いありませ
ん顔が赤くて汗をかいています．—はい，駆けて来ました，遅くなった
と思いましたので．　**12.** 君は出かける前に主人の許可をえるべきで
あった．　**13.** 誰か呼鈴をならしました，お医者さんに違いないです．
14. この門前に駐車してはいけません．　**15.** 私が劇場を出た時は十時
頃だったに違いありません．　**16.** 彼はあたりを見ていたのならばあの
進行して来た列車のあかりを見たに違いない．　**17.** きのう，あなたが
上野公園へいらっしゃった時に美術展覧会を御らんになりましたか．
—いゝえ，見ませんでした．—是非御らんなさい，実際，非常に面白いで
すから．　**18.** あなたはあの申込みを承諾すべき筈でした．　**19.** 彼は医
者になるべき筈でした．　**20.** 彼は法律家になる勉強をすべきではなか
った．　**21.** 誰でも自分の国家の法律を知っていてそれに従うべきです．

---

1. Man could live without food for three or four weeks, but without air he
could not live longer than a couple of minutes. Air is more necessary to man
than food and drink. **2.** Without the telescope astronomy would be an imperfect
science; we could not have understood many of the phenomena of the sky
and could not have known the nature of the celestial bodies. **3.** When could
you come to see me again?—I could come next week on Saturday. **4.** How
much money could you lend me?—I could lend you about fifty thousand yen,
but not before the end of the month. **5.** I feel tired; I have walked for
two hours in order to come back here.—Why did you come on foot? You
could have taken the street-car, couldn't you?—Yes, I could have come by
the street-car, but I have forgotten my money and could not pay the fare.
6. Don't tease that cat; he might scratch you. **7.** It is better to pitch our
tent and remain here until to-morrow morning. In such a dark night we
may get lost if we walk longer. **8.** Without the clever defence of your lawyer

the judge might have condemned you to life imprisonment. **9.** See if there are any letters in the letter-box; the postman may have delivered the mail already. **10.** The firemen might have extinguished the fire without difficulty, but as the alarm did not function properly (translate: *yoku* well) they arrived after the house was almost completely burned down. **11.** You must have run; your face is red and perspiring.—Yes, I have run because I thought I was late. **12.** Before going out you ought to have asked your master's permission. **13.** Someone has rung the bell; it must be the doctor. **14.** Cars must not be parked in front of this gate. **15.** When I left the theatre it must have been about ten o'clock. **16.** If he had looked he must have seen the lights of the approaching train. **17.** When you went to Ueno Park yesterday, did you visit the Art Exibition?—No, I didn't.—You ought to have visited it. It is really very interesting. **18.** You ought to have accepted that proposal. **19.** He ought to have been a medical doctor. **20.** He ought not to have studied to become a lawyer. **21.** Every man ought to know and obey the laws of his country.

Forty-sixth Lesson　第四十六課

Potential with There To Be

There can be, an expression that generally indicates a probable condition, may be translated by the present of *irú* いる, *óru* おる, *áru* ある, as the case may be, followed, in a decreasing degree of probability, by *to omoimásŭ* と思います (so I think), *deshō* でしょう (the suffix indicating probable future), *deshō to omoimásŭ* でしょうと思います or by *ka-mo shiremasén* かも知れません (=......? whether yes or no it is not known—See Page 375) followed by *to omoimásŭ* と思います if there is more doubt about the thing spoken of.

irú (óru, áru) to omoimásŭ いる(おる，ある)と思います.	
irú (óru, áru) deshō いる(おる，ある)でしょう.	
irú (óru, áru) deshō to omoimásŭ いる(おる，ある)でしょうと　思います.	there can be
irú (óru, áru) ka-mo shiremasén いる(おる，ある)　かも　知れません.	
irú (óru, áru) ka-mo shiremasén to omoimásŭ いる(おる，ある)　かも　知れません　と　思います.	

The present of *irú, óru, áru* with the suffix *másŭ* ます, used in polite speech, has been omitted in the above and in the following explanations for brevity's sake.

For the same reason also the form in *darō* だろう, instead of *deshō* で
しょう, has been omitted.

Jimúsho ni wa máda jimúin ga **irú** *to omoimásŭ* (or *irú* **deshō,** etc.)
事務所 に は まだ 事務員 が いる と 思います   (いる でしょう).
   There can still **be** some clerks at the office.

In interrogative sentences **there can be** is generally translated by the probable
future:

Konó hakó no náka ni náni ga **áru** **darō.**   What **can there be** in
この 箱 の 中 に 何 が ある だろう.   this box?

There cannot be is generally translated by the negative present of *irú* い
る, *óru* おる, *áru* ある (*imasén* いません, *orimasén* おりません, *arimasén* ありません or the less polite *inái* いない or *nái* ない), when one is
almost sure that the thing spoken of does not exist, followed by *to omoimásŭ*
と思います if more doubt is to be expressed.

Kūki ga nákereba seiméi wa **nái.**   **There cannot be** life without air.
空気 が 無ければ 生命 は ない.
   (*lit.* Air if there is not, life there isn't.)

Konó shigotó ni wa náni mo ríeki ga **arimasén.**
この 仕事 に は 何 も 利益 が ありません.
   There cannot be any profit in this business.

Ima jimúsho ni wa dáre mo **imasén** (*to omoimásŭ*).
今 事務所 に は 誰 も いません (と 思います).
   There cannot be anybody at the office now.

There could be may be translated by *irú* いる, *óru* おる, *áru* ある, followed
by *ka-mo shiremasén* かも知れません, and **there could not be** may be
translated by the negative form of the same verbs followed by *to omoimásŭ*
と思います when the two expressions refer to a probable present or future
condition.

There may be, as well as **there might be,** in the meaning of *perhaps there
is* or *are*, is generally translated like *there can be*, that is, by the present of
irú, óru, áru, followed, in a decreasing order of probability, by *to omoimásŭ*
と思います, *deshō* でしょう, *deshō to omoimásŭ* でしょうと思います or
by *ka-mo shiremasén* かも知れません, followed by *to omoimásŭ* と思い
ます if there is still more doubt about the thing spoken of.

irú (*óru, áru*) *to omoimásŭ* いる(おる, ある)と思います
iru (*óru, áru*) *deshō* いる(おる, ある)でしょう
irú (*óru, áru*) *deshō to omoimásŭ*
いる (おる, ある)でしようと 思います   **there may**
irú (*óru, áru*) *ka-mo shiremasén*   (might)
いる (おる, ある) かも 知れません   **be**
irú (*óru, áru*) *ka-mo shiremasén to omoimásŭ*
いる (おる, ある) かも 知れません と 思います

Kómban árashi ga **áru** *to omoimásŭ* (or *áru deshō,* etc.).
今晩 嵐 が ある と 思います   (あるでしょう).
   There may be a storm to-night.

*Ráigetsu uchí no kínjo ni o-matsurí ga **áru deshō** to omoimásŭ.*
来月　うちの　近所　に　お祭り　が　あるでしょうと　思います.
There may be a festival in our neighbourhood next month.

*Yūbinbako wo míte irasshái. Tegamí ga **áru ka-mo shiremasén.***
郵便箱　を見ていらっしゃい.　手紙　が　ある　かも　知れません.
Go and see the mail box. **There may** (might) **be** some letters.

*Móttomo mazushíi hĭtó no atamá no náka ni démo tensái ga **áru ka-mo***
最も　貧しい　人　の　頭　の　中　にでも　天才　が　ある　かも
shiremasén. **There may be** genius even in the mind of the poorest man.
知れません.　　(*lit.* The most poor man's mind in even, genius there may
be.—*démo* でも even, *tensái* 天才 genius)

The negative form **there may not be,** as well as **there might not be,** are
generally translated by the negative present of *irŭ* いる, *óru* おる, *áru* あ
る, followed, as in the above case of *there may be,* by **to omoimásŭ** と思い
ます, *deshō* でしょう, etc.

<blockquote>

imasén (orimasén, arimasén) **to omoimásŭ**
いません(おりません, ありません)と　思います

imasén (orimasén, arimasén) **deshō**
いません(おりません, ありません)でしょう

imasén (orimasén, arimasén) **deshō to omoimásŭ**　**there may** (might)
いません(おりません, ありません)でしょうと思います　　**not be**

imasén (orimasén, arimasén) **ka-mo shiremasén**
いません(おりません, ありません)かも　知れません
(to omoimásŭ)
(と　思います)

</blockquote>

The less polite forms with *inái* いない, *nái* ない, have been omitted for
brevity's sake.

There may (or **might**) **have been,** in the meaning of *perhaps there was* or
were, is generally translated by the past of *irŭ* いる, *óru* おる, *áru* ある
(*itá* いた, *ótta* おった, *átta* あった) followed, in a decreasing order of
probability, by **to omoimásŭ** と思います, *deshō* でしょう, *deshō to
omoimásŭ* でしょうと思います, or by *ka-mo shiremasén* かも知れません
followed by **to omoimásŭ** と思います if there is still more doubt about the
thing spoken of.

<blockquote>

itá (átta) **to omoimásŭ** いた(あった)と思います

itá (átta) **deshō** いた(あった)でしょう

itá (átta) **deshō to omoimásŭ**　　**there may**
いた(あった)でしょうと　思います　　(**might**)
　　　　　　　　　　　　　　　　　　have been
itá (átta) **ka-mo shiremasén** (*to omoimásŭ*)
いた(あった)かも　知れません　(と　思います)

</blockquote>

Anó yakyū ni dóno kurai hĭtó ga itá to omoimásŭ ka.
あの　野球　に　どの　位　人　が　いたと　思います　か.
How many people do you think there may have been at the baseball game?

Sanzén nin gurai itá deshō to omoimásŭ. **There may** (might)
三千　人　位　いたでしょうと　思います.　　**have been** 3,000 people.

*Sakúban kaminarí ga narimáshĭta kará chikáku-ni árashi ga **átta deshō**.*
昨晩　　雷　　が　なりました　から　　近く　に　　嵐　があったでしょう.
I heard thunders last night. **There may have been** a storm not far from here.
(*lit.* Last-night thunders resounded because, near here storm there was
perhaps.)

When **there might have been** refers to the possibility of existence of the
thing spoken of, even though to all appearances did not exist, then, only
itá (átta) ka-mo shiremasén いた（あった）かも知れません is used.

Sokó ni dáre mo imasén déshĭta ga dáre ka itá ka-mo shiremasén.
そこ　に　誰　も　いませんでした　が　誰　か　いた　かも　　知れません.
There was nobody there, but **there might have been** somebody.

*Sokó ni náni mo arimasén déshĭta ga náni ka **átta ka-mo shiremasén**.*
そこ　に　何　もありませんでした　が　何　かあった　かも　　知れません.
There was nothing there, but **there might have been** something.

The same expression *itá (átta) ka-mo shiremasén* or *shirenái* is used
to translate **there might be** when in reference to the past.

*Sonó tetsúzuki ni náni ka machigái ga **átta ka-mo shirenái** to*
その　　手続　に　何　か　　間違い　が　あった　かも　　知れない　と
watashí wa utagattá.   I suspected **there might be** some error
私　　は　　疑った.   in the proceedings.
(*tetsúzuki* proceedings, *utagattá* past of *utagaú* 疑う to suspect)

There may (might) not have been, in the meaning of *perhaps there was* or
were not, is generally translated by the negative past of *irú* いる, *óru* おる,
áru ある (*inákatta* いなかった, *oránakatta* おらなかった, *nákatta* なかった),
followed, in decreasing order of probability, by *to omoimásŭ* と思います,
deshō でしょう, *deshō to omoimásŭ* でしょうと思います, *ka-mo shiremasén* かも知れません, followed by *to omoimásŭ* と思います if there is
still more doubt about the thing spoken of.

inákatta (oránakatta, nákatta) **to omoimásŭ** いなかった（おらなかった, なかった）と　思います	
inákatta (oránakatta, nákatta) **deshō** いなかった（おらなかった, なかった）でしょう	
inákatta (oránakatta, nákatta) **deshō to omoimásŭ** いなかった（おらなかった, なかった）でしょうと思います	**There may** (might) **not have been**
inákatta (oránakatta, nákatta) **ka-mo shiremasén** いなかった（おらなかった, なかった）かも　知れません (*to omoimásŭ*) （と　　思います）	

*Sonná ni takŭsán hĭtó ga **inákatta to omoimásŭ** (or **inákatta**
そんな　に　沢山　人　が　いなかった　と　思います　（いなかった
deshō, etc.)   **There may** (might) **not have been** so many people.
でしょう）.

*Sonná ni takŭsán monó ga **nákatta ka-mo shiremasén** (or **deshō***
そんな に 沢山 物 が なかった かも 知れません （でしょう

to omoimásŭ, etc.) **There may** (might) **not have been** so
と 思います） many things.

When **there may be** is used with the idea of *probability*, it may be translated also by ***arí úru*** ありうる followed by ***deshō*** でしょう or ***ka-mo shiremasén*** かも知れません. ***Arí úru*** is an expression of the literary style.

*Warewaré ga yokí shinái yō-na tokoró ni tómi ga **arí úru deshō***
我々 が 予期 しないような 所 に 富 が ありうるでしょう

(or *arí úru ka-mo shiremasén*). **There may be** wealth where we
（ありうる かも 知れません）. least expect it.

    (*lit.* We, in do-not-expect-like place, wealth there may be.—*yokí surú* 予期 する to expect, *tómi* 富 wealth)

If more probability is expected, ***ari úbeki*** ありうべき is used instead of *arí úru* ありうる. Both expressions indicate probability, likelihood, possibility.

*Soré wa **arí úru** (arí úbeki) kotó désŭ.*　That may (should) be possible.
それ は あり うる（ありうべき）事 です.　That is almost sure.

The negative form of ***arí úru*** ありうる is ***ari énai*** ありえない and ***ari ubekarazáru*** ありうべからざる is the negative form of *arí úbeki* ありうべき. *Arí ubekarazáru* is an emphatic expression used in literary style.

*Soré wa **arí énai** kotó désŭ.* or *Soré wa **arí ubekarazáru** kotó désŭ.*
それ は ありえない 事 です.　それ は あり うべからざる 事 です.
That is impossible.　That cannot be.

There must be is generally translated as follows:

1. By the present of *irŭ* いる, *óru* おる, *áru* ある, followed by ***ni chigái ga arimasén*** に違いがありません or ***ni chigái nái*** に違いない, when there isn't any doubt about the thing spoken of.

2. By the present of *irŭ* いる, *óru* おる, *áru* ある, followed by ***to omoimásŭ*** と思います, when *there must be* is used in English as equivalent to *I am almost sure that there is.* If the thing spoken of suggests a little less probability than "almost assuredness," the probable future of *irú, óru, áru* may be used.

3. By the negative present subjunctive of *irú* いる, *óru* おる, *áru* ある, followed by ***narimasén*** なりません when the condition spoken of is considered as an obligation.

irŭ (*óru, áru*) ***ni chigái ga arimasén***
いる（おる, ある）に 違い が ありません

irŭ (*óru, áru*) ***to omoimásŭ*** いる（おる, ある）と思います

irŭ (*óru, áru*) ***deshō*** (*to omoimásŭ*)
いる（おる, ある）でしょう（と 思います）

inákereba (*oránakereba, nákereba*) ***narimasén***
いなければ（おらなければ, なければ）なりません

there must be

Anó oká no ué ni hĭtó ga **irŭ ni chigái ga arimasén,** *koyá kará*
あの 丘 の 上 に 人 が いるに 違い が ありません, 小屋 から

déte irú kemurí ga miemásŭ kará.   **There must be** people on that hill, for
出ている 煙 が 見えます から.   I can see smoke coming out of the hut.

(*oká* hill, *koyá* hut, *kemurí* smoke).

Anó heyá ni nezumí ga **irú ni chigái nái** (*désŭ*).
あの 部屋 に ねずみ が いる に 違い ない (です).

There must be a rat in that room.

Sĕndai-yukí no resshá ga mō ichí dái **áru to omoimásŭ.**
仙台行 の 列車 が もう 一 台 あると 思います.

There must be another train for Sendai.

(*lit.* Sendai going train, more one conveyance there is, so I think.)

Mon ni wa ítsumo mómban ga **orá-nákereba narimasén.**
門 に は いつも 門番 が おらなければ なりません.

There must always **be** a watchman at the gate.

(*lit.* At the gate, always, watchman if there is not it won't do.)

Konó tsŭkué no ué ni wa ítsumo pen to ínki ga **oité nákereba**
この 机 の 上 に は いつも ペン とインキが おいて なければ

narimasén.   On this desk **there must** always **be** pen and ink.
なりません.   (*lit.* On this desk, always, pen and ink being put if it isn't won't do.)

There must not be may be translated as follows:

1. By the subordinate of *irŭ* いる, *óru* おる, *áru* ある, followed by *wa ikemasén* はいけません, when the condition or the thing spoken of has the idea of a command, an injunction or a warning.

2. By the negative present or the negative of the probable future of *irú* いる, *óru* おる, *áru* ある, followed by **to omoimásŭ** と思います, when *must not be* expresses an almost sure guess that is the result of a logical conclusion.

3. By the negative of the probable future of *irú* いる, *óru* おる, *áru* ある, if the thing spoken of suggests a little less probability than an almost sure guess.

Watashí no rúsu ni watashí no shosaí ni dáre mo **ité wa ikemasén.**
私 の 留守 に 私 の 書斎 に 誰 も いて は いけません.

There must not be anybody in my study when I am out.

(*watashí no rúsu ni* during my absence, *shosaí* study room)

Sonná ni yóru osokú takŭsán hĭtó ga tōri ni **inái to omoimásŭ**
そんな に 夜 おそく 沢山 人 が 通り にいないと 思います

(or **inái deshō,** etc.)   **There must not be** many people in the street so late
(いないでしょう)   at night.

When **there must not be** implies the idea of *not being put* or *placed*, the subordinate of *okŭ* おく to put (*oité* おいて) is used instead, followed by *wa ikemasén* はいけません.

Anó tēburu no ué ni náni mo **oité wa ikemasén.**
あのテーブルの 上 に 何 も おいては いけません.

There must not be anything on that table. (*lit.* On that table nothing putting, *or* being put, won't do.—Note the double negative)

There must have been is generally translated as follows:

1. By the past of *irú* いる, *óru* おる, *áru* ある followed by *ni chigái ga arimasén* に違いがありません or *ni chigái nái* に違いない, when there isn't any doubt about the thing spoken of.

2. By the past of *irú* いる, *óru* おる, *áru* ある, followed by *to omoimásŭ* と思います when **there must have been** is used in the meaning of *I am almost sure that there was* or *were*.

3. By the past of *irú* いる, *óru* おる, *áru* ある followed by *deshō* でしょう or *darō* だろう if the thing spoken of suggests a little less probability than " almost assuredness," followed by *to omoimásŭ* と思います if the probability is still less.

> *itá* (*átta*) *ni chigái ga arimasén*
> いた(あった)に 違い が ありません
>
> *itá* (*átta*) *to omoimásŭ* いた(あった)と思います
>
> *itá* (*átta*) *deshō* (*to omoimásŭ*)
> いた(あった)でしょう(と思います)

there must have been

Yūbe uchí no kínjo ni káji ga átta ni chigái nái. Watashí wa
ゆうべうち の 近所 に 火事 が あった に 違い ない. 私 は

nedokó ni háitte kará jikí ni kasái-keihō wo kikimáshĭta kará.
寝床 に 入って から ぢき に 火災警報 を 聞きました から.

There must have been a fire in our neighbourhood last night, as I heard the fire alarm soon after I went to bed.

(*lit.* Last night, in our neighbourhood a fire there was, no mistake about it. I to bed entering after, soon fire alarm heard because.)

Kinō o-ténki ga yókatta kará anó keibá ni takŭsán no hĭtó ga itá
きのうお天気 が よかった から あの 競馬 に 沢山 の 人 が いた

to omoimásŭ (or *itá deshō* etc.)
と 思います （いたでしょう）.

As the weather was fine yesterday, **there must have been** many people at the horse races.

There must not have been is generally translated by the negative past of *irú* いる, *óru* おる, *áru* ある followed by *ni chigái ga arimasén* に違いがありません, *to omoimásŭ* と思います, *deshō* でしょう or *deshō to omoimásŭ* でしょうと思います.

> *inákatta* (*oránakatta, nákatta*) *ni chigái ga arimasén* (or *chigái nái*)
> いなかった(おらなかった, なかった)に違い が ありません （違い ない)
>
> *inákatta* (*oránakatta, nákatta*) *to omoimásŭ*
> いなかった(おらなかった, なかった)と 思います
>
> *inákatta* (*oránakatta, nákatta*) *deshō* (*to omoimásŭ*)
> いなかった(おらなかった, なかった)でしょう(と 思います)

Ame ga furimáshĭta kará, anó keibá ni takŭsán hĭtó ga inákatta
雨 が 降りました から, あの 競馬 に 沢山 人 が いなかった

deshō (*to omoimásŭ*). Because of the rain **there must not have been** many
でしょう(と 思います). people at the horse races. (*keibá* horse races)

There ought to be, when implying *duty, moral obligation* or *ideal necessity,* may be translated by *irú* いる, *óru* おる, *áru* ある followed by *hazú* 筈, *béki* べき, *béki hazú* べき筈 and *désŭ* です or *déshĭta* でした according to whether one refers to the present or the past.

Konó kōsaten ni wa kōtsū-shingō ga áru béki-hazú désŭ.
この　交叉点　に　は　交通信号　が　ある　　べき筈　　です.
There ought to be traffic signals at this crossing.

When **there ought to be** implies *probability,* it may be translated by *irú* いる, *óru* おる, *áru* ある followed by *to omoimásŭ* と思います, *deshō* でしょう, *deshō to omoimásŭ* でしょうと思います, besides *hazú* 筈, etc.

Sonó enkái ni wa takŭsán gaikokujín ga irú to omoimásŭ (or *irú*
その　宴会　に　は　沢山　　外国人　が　いると　　思います　　　（いる
hazú désŭ).　**There ought to be** many foreigners at the party.
筈　です).

Ashĭtá no kaigō ni yokyō ga áru deshō to omoimásŭ.
あした　の　会合　に　余興　が　あるでしようと　　思います.
There ought to be some fun at to-morrow's meeting. (*yokyō* fun)

There ought not to be, when implying *duty, moral obligation* or *ideal necessity,* is generally translated by *irú* いる, *óru* おる, *áru* ある followed by *hazú ga nái* 筈がない, *béki-hazú ga nái* べき筈がない or *béki de wa nái* べきではない when referring to the present. When referring to the past *nákatta* なかった is used instead of *nái* ない. In polite speech, *arimasén* ありません, *arimasén déshĭta* ありませんでした are used instead of *nái* ない, *nákatta* なかった.

When the same negative expressions indicate *probability,* the forms with *hazú* 筈, *to omoimásŭ* と思います or *deshō* でしょう may be used, but not the forms with *béki* べき or *béki-hazú* べき筈.

Sonná kanemochí no kuní ni wa bimbōnin ga hĭtóri mo irú hazú ga nái.
そんな　金持　の　国に　は　貧乏人　が　一人　も　いる　筈　が　ない.
In such a wealthy country **there ought not to be** any poor.

Konó áme de anó keibá ni wa takŭsán hĭtó ga inái to omoimásŭ
この　雨　であの　競馬に　は　沢山　　人　がいないと　　思います
(or *irú hazú ga nái*).　On account of the rain **there ought not to be**
（いる　筈　が　ない.）　　many people at the horse races.

So *Sō*

In the following common expressions the English adverb **so** corresponds exactly, in meaning as well as in sound, to the Japanese *sō* そう.

Is it **so**? *Sō désŭ ka.* そうですか.—　　It is so. *Sō désŭ.* そうです.

It isn't **so.** *Sō de wa arimasén.* そうではありません.

(colloq. *Sō jā arimasén.* そうぢゃありません.)

It may be **so**. *Tábun sō désŭ.* たぶんそうです.

Do you think **so**? *Sō omoimásŭ ka.* そう思いますか.

Yes, I think **so**. *Hái, sō omoimásŭ.* はい，そう思います.

No, I do not think **so**. *Iié, sō omoimasén.* いいえ，そう思いません.

It seems **so**. *Sō miemásŭ.* そう見えます. or *Sōrashii désŭ.* そうらしいです.

Did he tell you **so**? *Sō iimáshĭta ka.* そう云いましたか.

Yes, he told me **so**. *Hái, sō iimáshĭta.* はい，そう云いました.

Why **so**? *Náze sō désŭ ka.* なぜそうですか.

How **so**? *Dōshĭte sō désŭ ka.* どうしてそうですか.

If **so**. *Móshi sō náraba.* 若しそうならば.

The expressions **Sō désŭ ka** そうですか given at the beginning of the above list, is very often used by Japanese people, and with some of them as often or more so, as are the expressions *I see, You don't say*, etc., uttered by some English speaking people while listening to somebody's talk.

In the following examples the English **so** is variously translated according to its different equivalents given in parentheses.

(in that manner) **sonó yō-ni** そのように

Sonó yō-ni *furumátte wa ikemasén.* You must not behave **so**.
その ように 振舞って は いけません. (*furumáu* 振舞う to behave)

(thus) **konó yō-ni** このように, **konná fū-ni** こんな風に

Konná fū-ni *nasái.* こんな風になさい. Do it **so**.

(to that extent, in that degree) **soré hodó** それ程, **sonná ni** そんなに

Sonná ni *háyaku hanasánai de kudasái.* Don't speak **so** fast.
そんな に 早く 話さない で 下さい.

Sonná ni そんなに corresponds also to *so much* and *so many* when referring to abstract things. When referring to material things *so much* or *so many* is translated by **sonná ni takŭsán** そんなに沢山, **sonná ni ōzei** そんなに大勢.

To wo shiméru tokí ni **sonná ni** *otó wo tátete wa ikemasén.*
戸 を しめる 時 に そんな に 音 を 立てて は いけません.
You must not make **so much** noise when you close the door.

Watashí wa ízen sonó machí de **sonná ni** *ōzei no hĭtó wo mimasén*
私   は 以前その 町 で そんな に 大勢 の 人 を見ません
déshĭta. I never saw **so many** people in the street before.
でした. (N. B.—*ōzei* used only referring to people.)

Dōzo, **sonná ni takŭsán** *o-satō wo kōhĭ ni irenái de kudasái. i.*
どうぞ, そんな に 沢山 お砂糖 を コーヒーに入れないで 下さい. ‥
Please do not put **so much** sugar into the coffee.

(very, extremely) **hijō ni** 非常に, **taihén** 大変, **jitsŭ ni** 実に, **hontō ni** 本当に

Anáta wa **hijō ni** *shínsetsu désŭ.* You are **so** kind.
あなた は 非常 に 親切 です.

Hontō ni go-shínsetsu-samá. 本当に御親切さま.   It is **so** kind of you.

Soré wo kiité jitsú ni ureshíi désŭ.   I am **so** glad to hear it.
それ を 聞いて 実 にうれしいです.

Atamá ga taihén itái désŭ. 頭が大変痛いです.   My head aches **so.**

O-me ni kakátte taihén ureshíi désŭ.   I am **so** glad to see (meet) you.
お目 にかかって 大変 うれしい です.

   (*o-me ni kakáru* お目にかかる polite for *áu* 会う to meet)

(therefore) **soré-de** それで

Shachō wa rúsu dĕshĭta, soré-de hishó ni aimáshĭta.
社長 は 留守 でした，それで 秘書 に 会いました.
The president was out, **so** I met the secretary.

(consequently) **shĭtagátte** 従って

Sonó shiná wa jōtō, shĭtagátte nedán mo takái désŭ.
その 品 は 上等，従って 値段 も 高い です.
The article is of fine quality, **so** the price is high.

(then, well) **déwa** では

Déwa, kimí wa Yōroppa e ikú no désŭ ne.   **So** you are going to
では，君 はヨーロッパへ行くの です ね.   Europe.

(as......so) **to onají yō-ni** と同じように

Anáta ga watashí ni táishĭte surú to onají yō-ni watashí mo anáta
あなたが 私 に 対して する と 同じ ように 私 も あなた
ni táishĭte shimásŭ.   As you treat me **so** I will treat you.   (*lit.* You, me
に 対して します.   toward, to do the same as, I also you toward do.

Idioms :

You don't say **so!** *Másaka.* まさか.

......and **so** forth.   ......and **so** on.   ......*nádo* 等, (written style) ......*tō* 等

Just **so.** *Mattakú sonó tōri.* 全くその通り.
(in the aforesaid state or condition).

It is better **so.** *Sonó mamá no hō ga íi désŭ.* そのままの方がいいです.

Be **so** kind as to do **so.** *Dōzo, sō shĭté kudasái.* どうぞそうして下さい.

Some

Some is variously translated according to its different acceptations.

(a little. a few) *sŭkóshi* 少し

Sŭkóshi kugí ga hoshíi. 少し釘が欲しい.   I want (wish) **some** nails.

Sŭkóshi kané wo káre ni kashimáshĭta.   I lent him **some** money.
少し 金 を 彼 に 貸しました.

(considerable) *kánari no* (colloq.) かなりの, *sōtō no* (Lit.) 相当の

Koré wo surú ni wa kánari (sōtō) no yūki ga irimásŭ.
これ を する に は かなり (相当) の 勇気 が 要ります.
One needs **some** courage to do this. (*yūki* courage)

(about, more or less) *oyosó* (colloq.) 凡そ, *yáku* (Lit.) 約

Oyosó *yónjikken no murá.*   A village of **some** forty houses.
凡そ　四十軒　の　村.   (*ken* 軒 numerative to count houses)

Oyosó *hyaká satsú no hon.* 凡そ百冊の本.   **Some** 100 books.

Yáku *ni-jū máiru.* 約二十哩.   **Some** 20 miles.

(in some measure, to some extent, partially, partly) *ikubún* 幾分, *ikubunká*
幾分か, *áru téido máde* 或程度まで, *tashō* (Lit.) 多少

Káre no ninkí wa ikubún(ka) óchite kimáshĭta.
彼　の　人気　は　　幾分(か)　落ちて　来ました.

His popularity has declined to **some** extent. (*óchite kúru* 落ちて来る to
decrease, *óchite* 落ちて subord. of *ochíru* 落ちる to fall)

Káre no seikō wa tashō kōun ni yorimásŭ.   **Some** of his success is
彼　の　成功　は　多少　幸運　に　よります.   due to luck.

(*kōun* 幸運 luck, *ni yorú* による to be due to, to be caused by)

Tashō *na-ga-shireté irú hĭtó.*   A man of **some** note.
多少　名が知れて　いる　人.   *na-ga-shirerú* 名が知れる to be famous

shūnyū no ikubún (ka) wo chochikú surú   to save **some** part of
収入　の　幾分　(か)　を　貯蓄　する   one's income

(undetermined) *nan-toká* 何とか

Nan-toká *nogaréru michí wo mitsŭké-nákereba narimasén ne.*
何んとか　のがれる　途　を　見つけなければ　なりません　ね.

We must find **some** way out of it.

(*nogaréru* to escape, *nogaréru michí* a way of escape; *mitsŭkerú* to find)

(some instances, some people) *áru hĭtóbito* 或人々, (according to some) *ni*
yorú to によると

Aru *hĭtóbito wa káre wo kichigái to omótte imásŭ.*
或　人々　は　彼　を　気違い　と　思って　います.

Some people think he is crazy. (*kichigái* crazy)

Hĭtó *ni yorú to* *káre wa kichigái désŭ.*   According to **some** people
人　に　よると　彼　は　気違い　です.   he is crazy.

(a certain unknown) *áru* ある when referring to people, *itsŭka* いつか when
referring to days

Itsŭka *o-tazuné shimásŭ.*   **Some** day I shall visit you.
いつか　お訪ね　します.

Aru *fujín ga sō hanashimáshĭta.*   **Some** lady told me so.
或　婦人　が　そう　話しました.

Something

This word, used as a noun indicating an undetermined thing, may
be translated by *náni-ka* 何か.

Tēburu no ué ni **náni-ka** *arimásŭ.*   There is **something** on the table.
テーブル の 上 に　何か　あります.

Senséi wa **náni-ka** *yónde imásŭ.*   The teacher is reading **something.**
先生 は　何か　読んでいます.

Náni-ka *tabéru monó wo kudasái.*   Give me **something** to eat.
何か　食べる　物　を　下さい.

Soré ni wa **náni-ka** *hen-na tokoró ga arimásŭ.*   There is **something**
それ に は　何か　変な　ところ　があります.   strange about it.

Soré ni wa **náni-ka** *fukákujitsu-na tokoró ga arimásŭ.*
それ に は　何か　不確実な　ところ　が あります.
　　　There is **something** uncertain about it. (*fukákujitsu-na* uncertain)

In some cases, *something* may be translated by **áru-kotó** (*áru* 或
る some, *kotó* 事 an abstract thing).

taisetsú-na **áru-kotó** 大切な或る事 **something** important

When referring to abstract things, **kotó** 事, without the preceding **áru,**
may be used.

Anáta ni hanashitái **kotó** *ga arimásŭ.*   I have **something** to tell you.
あなた に 話したい　事　が あります.
　　　(*lit.* To you I-wish-to-tell thing there is.)

íi **kotó** いい事 **something** good

When referring to material things, instead of *kotó,* **monó** 物 is used.

íi **monó** いい物 **something** good

hoká no **monó** ほかの物 **something** else

In the meaning of *nearly, about,* **something** may be translated by **zattó** ざ
っと in colloquial speech or by **yáku** 約 in literary style.

Káre wa **zattó** *(yáku) hyakú man yen tamemáshĭta.*
彼　は ざっと　(約)　百　万　円　貯めました.
　　　He saved **something** like a million.

In the meaning of *nearly* and *above,* and in more colloquial speech, **something** may be translated by **káre-koré** かれこれ.

Mō **káre-koré** *jū-ji ni chigái nái.*   It must be **something** like
もう　かれこれ　十時 に ちがい ない.   ten o'clock.

Idioms:

Káre wa **tashō** *shijín désŭ.*   He is **something** of a poet.
彼　は　多少　詩人　です.

Káre wa jibún wo **táishĭta** *jímbutsu to omótte imásŭ.*
彼　は　自分 を　大した　人物　と 思って います.
　　　He thinks himself **something.**
　　　(*jímbutsu* a personage, a man of high caliber, *táishĭta* important)

Káre wa burōkā ka **náni-ka** *désŭ.*   He is a broker or **something**
彼　はブローカーか　何か　です.   like.

something like (*ikubún*)......*no yō-na* (幾分)......のような
　　　　　　　　(*tashō*).........*no yō-na* (多少)......のような

Sonó dōbutsu wa (tashō) kumá no yō déshĭta.   That animal was **some-**
その　動物　は　(多少)　熊　のようでした.   **thing like** a bear.

Soré wa (ikubún) sensú no yō-na katachí désŭ.   It is shaped **something**
それ　は　(幾分)　扇子　のような　形　です.   **like** a fan.

something else (=another thing) *hoká no monó* ほかの物

Nái yóri mashí désŭ.   **Something** is better than nothing.
無い　より　増し　です.   (*mashí* something a little better)

Nothing

In Lesson 18 it has been said that **nothing** or **not anything**, used
in the meaning of *naught*, may be translated by *náni mo* 何も
followed by a negative verb, as in the following examples:

Watashí wa náni mo iú kotó ga arimasén.   I have **nothing** to say.
私　は　何　も　云う事　がありません.
(I, nothing to say thing haven't.)

Watashí wa náni-mo tabéru monó ga arimasén.   I have **nothing**
私　は　何も　食べる　物　がありません.   to eat.

Below are given representative sentences showing how to translate
nothing in some of its other acceptations, besides various Japanese
idiomatic equivalents.

(gratis, gratuitously) *táda de* 只で

Koré wo táda de agemashō.   I will give this to you **for nothing.**
これ　を　只　で上げましょう.

Táda de soré wo te ni iremáshĭta.   I got it **for nothing.** (*te ni irerú*
只　でそれ　を　手　に　入れました.   手に入れる to obtain)

(without any reason, for nothing) *riyū náku* 理由なく

riyū náku okóru 理由なくおこる   to get angry **for nothing**

Sonó kodomotachí wa riyū náku kenká shĭtá.   Those children quarreled
その　子供達　は　理由　なく　けんかした.   **for nothing.**

(trifle) *tsumaránai kotó* つまらない事, *nán-de mo* 何んでも with negative
verb

Kárera no kurō wa watashí no ni kuraberéba nan-demó arimasén.
彼等　の　苦労　は　私　の　に　比べれば　何んでも　ありません.
Their trouble is **nothing** to mine.
(*lit.* Their trouble, to mine if compared, nothing is not.)

(of no consequence) *nan-demó* 何んでも with negative verb

Káre ni tótte issén yen wa nan-demó nái.   One thousand yen is
彼　にとって一千　円　は　何んでも　ない.   **nothing** to him.

Idiomatic usage.

Káre ni wa shinshirashíi tokoró ga zen-zen nái.   He has **nothing** of the
彼　に　は　紳士らしい　所　が　全々　ない.   gentleman in him.
(*lit.* In him, gentleman-like trait at all there isn't.)

Mu kará wa náni-monó mo shōjinai.   Mere **nothing** cannot produce
無 から は　　何物　　も 生じない.   anything.

　　(*lit.* Nothing from, *-mu* nothing, nothing is produced. *shōjiru* to produce)

Chíshiki ni kuraberéba kínsen wa monó no kázu de wa nái.
知識 に 比べれば　金銭 は　　物　の　数　で　は　ない.
Money is **nothing** compared to knowledge.

　　(*monó no kázu de wa nái* to count for nothing.—*lit.* To knowledge if com-
　　pared, money, of things number is not.)

*Káre wa tóru ni **taranái monó** désŭ.*   He is a mere **nothing**.
彼　は とる に 足らない　者　です.

　　(*tóru ni* とるに to take, *taranái* 足らない is not worthwhile)

*Anó seijiká wa **munōsha** désŭ.*   That politician is a (mere) **nothing**.
あの 政治家 は　　無能者　です.   (*munōsha* incapable person)

(to come to nothing) *mudá ni owarú* 無駄に終る (*mudá ni* in vain, in
nothing, *owarú* to end)

(idem, in Lit. style) *suihō ni kisú* 水泡に帰す (*suihō* bubbles, *kisú* to come to)

*Sonó keikakú wa **suihō ni kishimáshĭta**.*   The scheme has come to
その　計画　は　水泡 に　　帰しました.   **nothing.**

(to have **nothing** to do with)......*ni sŭkóshi mo kankéi ga nái* ......に
少しも関係がない (*lit.* ......with it even a little relation—connection—there
isn't)

*Soré wa konó jíken ni **sŭkóshi mo** kankéi ga **arimasén.***
それ は この 事件 に　少し　も　関係　が ありません.
That has **nothing** to do with this matter. (*jíken* a matter, an affair)

(to treat lightly, to make **nothing** of) ......*wo nan-tomó omowánai*......
を何んとも思わない

*Káre wa jibún no byōki no kotó wo **nan-tomó omowánai*** (or
彼　は 自分 の 病気 の　事　を　何んとも　　　思わない
omótte imasén).   He makes **nothing** of his sickness.
(思っていません). (*byōki no kotó* sickness thing or matter)

*Watashí wa káre ga iú kotó wo **nan-tomó** omoimasén.*
私　は 彼　が 云う事　を　何んとも 思いません.
I can make **nothing** of what he says.

(to fail to perform or to use) ......*wo shippái surú* ......を失敗する

*Káre wa anó shigotó wo **shippái shimáshĭta**.*   He could make **nothing**
彼　はあの 仕事 を　　失敗　しました.   of the job.

(in no degree, not at all) *sŭkóshi mo*......*náku* 少しも......なく

sŭkóshi mo osoréru kotó náku   **nothing** daunted (*osoréru* to fear)
少し　も おそれる 事　なく

chittó mo kamawánai ちっともかまわない to care **nothing** about
nothing like......

Soré wa kitái shĭtá to wa mattakú chigattá monó ni narimáshĭta.
それ は 期待 した と は　全く　ちがった もの に なりました.
It was **nothing like** what we expected. (*lit.* That, we expected, completely
different thing became. *kitái surú* 期待する to expect)

Koré wa aré ni wa **zuttó otorimásŭ.**   This is **nothing like** as good
これ は あれに は ずっと 劣ります.   as that.

　　(*lit.* This, to that, by far is inferior.—*otóru* 劣る to be inferior)

Koré ijō no **monó wa nái.**   There is **nothing like** this. (*lit.* This,
これ 以上の 　もの 　は 　ない.   more than, a thing there is not.)

nothing but......

Káre wa ikkái no tobakushí **ni suginai.**   He is **nothing but** a gambler.
彼 は 一介の とばく師 に 過ぎない.

　　(*ikkái no* 一介の mere, *ni suginai* に過ぎない to be no more than, to be
　　nothing but)

Konó hyōmen ni wa jūsho **daké káku kotó.**
この 　表面 　には 　住所 　だけ 書く 　事.

Write **nothing but** the address on this side.

　　(*lit.* This side on, address only, to write the thing.—Abbreviated style.)

Konó sekái wo sukuú monó wa heiwá **ígai** *ni wa nái.*
この 　世界 を 　救う 　もの は 　平和 以外 に は 　ない.

Nothing but peace can save the world. (*sukuú* to save, *ígai* except)

Forty-seven Lesson　第四十七課

Subjunctive Mood

There are several forms of subjunctive present in Japanese.
The form most used in ordinary conversation is formed by adding
nára なら or **náraba** ならば to the *simple present* of all verbs,
with or without **móshi** 若し or **moshi mo** 若しも at the beginning
of the *if-clause*, as already shown in Lesson 32. In literary style
náreba なれば instead of *náraba* is used.

See *phonetic rule*, Page 688.

Ima éki e **ikú náraba** *anáta wa kyūkō*[1] *de tatéru*[2] *deshō.*
今 　駅 へ 行く 　ならば 貴方 は 　急行 　で 立てるでしょう.

If you **go** to the station now you may leave by the express train.

Móshi *íchiba*[3] *e* **ikú nára** *yasái wo sŭkóshi katté kité kudasái.*
若し 　市場 　へ 行く 　なら 野菜 を 　少し 買って来て 下さい.

If you **go** to the market please buy some vegetables.

By using the present of the indicative with the suffix **másŭ** and
followed by **nara(ba),** a more polite form of the subjunctive is obtained.

Kyō Gaimushō[4] *e* **irasshaimásŭ náraba** *Gaimudáijin*[5] *ni o-me ni*
きょう 外務省 　へいらっしゃいます ならば 　外務大臣 に お目に
kakaremásŭ.[6]   **If you go** to the Foreign Office to-day you will be able to meet
かゝれます.   the Foreign Minister.

---

1 express train　**2** *tatéru* to be able to leave　**3** market　**4** Foreign Office　**5** Foreign
Minister　**6** *o-me ni kakaréru* お目にかゝれる to be able to meet

Nára was the hypothetical form of the verb *náru* (to be) of the written language, and means *if it be, if it is*. *Nára* is still used without a verb in some expressions as *o-iriyō nára* お入用なら if necessary; *soré nára* それ なら if it be so, if it is so, then; *sayō-nára* 左様なら if it be so = good-bye.

Another form of subjunctive present used in ordinary conversation is formed by adding the suffix *reba* れば to the *simple verbal stem* of verbs of Class I, and *ba* to the *e-stem* of verbs of Class II.

Class I

míru	見る	to see	*mi*	見	*míreba*	見れば	If I see
tabéru	食べる	to eat	*tabe*	食べ	*tabéreba*	食べれば	If I eat

Class II

káku	書く	to write	*kake*	書け	*kákeba*	書けば	If I write
dásu	出す	to put out	*dase*	出せ	*dáseba*	出せば	If I put out
tátsu	立つ	to stand	*tate*	立て	*táteba*	立てば	If I stand
yómu	読む	to read	*yome*	読め	*yómeba*	読めば	If I read
áru	ある	to be	*are*	あれ	*áreba*	あれば	If there be (is)
kaú	買う	to buy	*kae*	買え	*kaéba*	買えば	If I buy

See next lesson for the present subjunctive of *to have, to be*, and *there to be*.

Irregular Verbs

kúru	来る	to come	*kure*	来れ	*kúreba*	来れば	If I come
surú	する	to do	*sure*	すれ	*suréba*	すれば	If I do

Kúru and *surú* are conjugated regularly in this second form of the subjunctive.

See **phonetic rule** on the above form of the subjunctive, page 664.

Examples

*Móshi konó kusurí[1] wo **nómeba** kimochí ga yóku náru deshō.*
若し この 薬 を のめば 気持 が よく なるでしょう.
If you drink this medicine you will feel well.

*Móshi anáta ga Nihón-go wo **hanáseba** Nihón ni súmu kotó ga mótto*
若し 貴方 が 日本語 を 話せば 日本 に 住む 事 がもっと
tanóshiku narimásŭ. **If you speak** Japanese you will have greater joy in
楽しく なります. living in Japan.

*Chottó o-machí nasái; íma kokó ni o-kané wo mótte **iréba**[2] sŭkóshi*
一寸 お待ち なさい, 今 ここ に お金 を 持って いれば 少し
agemashō. Wait a moment; **if I have** money with me I shall give you some.
上げましょう. (Wait a moment; now, here money if I have some I shall give.)

---

1 medicine **2** *iréba* is the subjunctive of *irŭ*

Negative Form

The negative of the two preceding forms of the present of the subjunctive is obtained by adding **masén nára (ba), nái nára (ba),** or **nákereba,** to the simple stem of verbs of Class I. Verbs of Class II have *masén nára (ba)* added to the *i-stem* and *nái nára (ba)* or *nákereba* to the *a-stem.*

Nái nára (ba) or *nákereba* is the negative form of the subjunctive present of *áru (if there be, or is, not),* as shown in the following list.

The termination **ba** may be omitted after **nára.**

Class I

míru 見る	**mi**	見	*mimasén nára (ba)*	見ませんなら(ば)	If I do
to see			*mínai nára (ba)*	見ないなら(ば)	not see
			mí-nákereba	見なけれ(ば)	
tabéru 食べる	**tabe**	食べ	*tabemasén nára (ba)*	食べませんなら(ば)	If I do
to eat			*tabénai nára (ba)*	食べないなら(ば)	not eat
			tabé-nákereba	食べなければ	

Class II

káku 書く	**kaki** 書き	*kakimasén nára (ba)*	書きませんなら(ば)	if I do
to write	**kaka** 書か	*kakánai nára (ba)*	書かないなら(ば)	not write
		kaká-nákereba	書かなければ	
kasú 貸す	**kashi** 貸し	*kashimasén nára (ba)*	貸しませんなら(ば)	if I do
to lend	**kasa** 貸さ	*kasanái nára (ba)*	貸さないなら(ば)	not lend
		kasá-nákereba	貸さなければ	
tátsu 立つ	**tachi** 立ち	*tachimasén nára (ba)*	立ちませんなら(ば)	if I do
to stand	**tata** 立た	*tatánai nàra (ba)*	立たないなら(ば)	not stand
		tatá-nákereba	立たなければ	
yómu 読む	**yomi** 読み	*yomimasén nára (ba)*	読みませんなら(ば)	if I do
to read	**yoma** 読ま	*yománai nára (ba)*	読まないなら(ば)	not read
		yomá-nákereba	読まなければ	
tóru 取る	**tori** 取り	*torimasén nára (ba)*	取りませんなら(ば)	if I do
to take	**tora** 取ら	*toránai nára (ba)*	取らないなら(ば)	not take
		torá-nákereba	取らなければ	

Irregular Verbs

áru ある	**ari** あり	*arimasén nára (ba)*	ありませんなら(ば)	if there
there is		*nái nára (ba)*	無いなら(ば)	is not
		nákereba	無ければ	

kúru 来る	*ki*	来	*kimasén nára (ba)*	来ませんなら（ば）	
to come	*ko*	来	*kónai nára (ba)*	来ないなら（ば）	if I do not come
			ko-nákereba	来なければ	
surú する	*shi*	し	*shimasén nára (ba)*	しませんなら（ば）	
to do			*shinái nára (ba)*	しないなら（ば）	if I do not do
			shi-nákereba	しなければ	

Móshi mo hon wo takúsán **yománai náraba** *monoshiri ni náru kotó*
若し も 本 を 沢山 読まない ならば 物識り に なる 事
ga dekimasén. **If we do not read** many books we cannot become learned.
が 出来ません.

Móshi myō-ása máde ni chichí kará tegamí ga **ko-nákereba** *watashí*
若し 明朝 迄 に 父 から 手紙 が 来なければ 私
wa chichí wo tazúnete mimashō. If I do not receive a letter from my father
は 父 を 訪ねて見ましょう. by to-morrow morning I shall go and visit
him. (*tazunéru* to call-on a person)

When two subjunctive clauses follow each other, the verb of the first one
is used in the subordinate, the verb of the second clause only being put in
the subjunctive mood.

Anáta wa **tsŭkárete ité**[1] *watashitachí to isshó ni* **dekaketáku nái**
貴方 は 疲れて いて 私達 と 一緒 に 出かけたく ない
náraba *uchí ni ité mo yoroshíi désŭ.*
ならば うち にいて も よろしい です.

If you are tired and (if you) do not wish to come out with us, it is all right
to stay at home. (*lit.* You being tired, us together with, wishful-to-go-out if
you are not, at home staying even, allright is.)

Móshi konó pan ga amári **katákute taberarénai náraba** *nokóshŭte*
若し この パン が 余り 堅くて 食べられない ならば 残して
okí nasái. Watashí ga yawarakái no wo mótte kimásŭ.
おきなさい. 私 が 柔かい の を 持って 来ます.

If this bread is too hard and you cannot eat it, just leave it. I will bring you
some soft bread (a softer kind).

A third form of the present subjunctive is formed by adding **to**
と or **to suréba** とすれば to the simple present of all verbs.

míru 見る *míru* **to** 見ると *míru* **to suréba** 見るとすれば if I see
káku 書く *káku* **to** 書くと *káku* **to suréba** 書くとすれば if I write

The negative is formed by adding **nái to** or **nái to suréba** to
the *simple stem* of verbs of Class I, and to the **a-stem** of verbs of
Class II.

míru 見る	*mi*	見	*mínai to*	見ないと	if I do
			mínai to suréba	見ないとすれば	not see
káku 書く	*kaka*	書か	*kakánai to*	書かないと	if I do
			kakánai to suréba	書かないとすれば	not write

---

1 *tsukárete irú* to be tired

Note than when one uses the form with *to* と only, the verb in the clause following the *if-clause* is in the present tense, while when *to suréba* is used the verb in the clause following the *if-clause* is in the future.

If the present tense be used, the sentence indicates greater probability, with almost certainty that the predicted event will happen, while if the future be used, the predicted event is seen to be more uncertain.

*Amé wo amarí takŭsán **tabéru to** ha wo **itamemásŭ.***
飴 を 余り 沢山 食べる と 歯 を 痛めます.
If you eat too much candy you will spoil your teeth.

*Amé wo amarí takŭsán **tabéru to suréba** ha wo **itaméru deshō.***
飴 を 余り 沢山 食べる と すれば 歯 を 痛める でしょう.
If you eat too much candy you will spoil your teeth.

*Kómban konó tegamí wo **kakánai to** ashĭtá wa isogáshikute káku himá*
今晩 この 手紙 を 書かない とあした は 忙がしくて 書く 暇
*ga **arimasén.***   If I don't write this letter to-night I shall have no time to
が ありません.   write it to-morrow because I shall be busy.
   (*lit.* To-night this letter do not write if, to-morrow being busy, to write time there is not.)

*Kómban konó tegamí wo **kakánai to suréba** ashĭtá wa isogáshikute káku*
今晩 この 手紙 を 書かない と すれば あした は 忙がしくて 書く
*himá ga **arimasén deshō.***   (Same translation as in the above example.)
暇 が ありませんでしょう.

A fourth form of the subjunctive present is obtained by the subordinate of the principal verb, followed by *iréba* いれば, *irú to* いると, *irú to suréba,* or *irú to surú nára* (*ba*). The negative form is obtained by adding *inákereba* いなければ, *inái to* いないと, or *irú to shinái nára* (*ba*) to the subordinate. This form of subjunctive with the subordinate is used when the verb placed after *if* indicates a progressive action.

Míru 見る To See

míte iréba	見ていれば	} if I see
míte irú to (suréba)	見ていると(すれば)	if I watch
míte irú to surú nára (ba)	見ているとするなら(ば)	} if I am watching
míte inákereba	見ていなければ	} if I do not see
míte inái to	見ていないと	if I do not watch
míte irú to shinái nára (ba)	見ているとしないなら(ば)	} if I am not watching

Káku 書く To Write

káite iréba	書いていれば	} if I write
káite irú to (suréba)	書いていると(すれば)	if I am writing
káite irú to surú nára (ba)	書いているとするなら(ば)	}
káite inákereba	書いていなければ	} if I do not write
káite inái to	書いていないと	if I am not writing
káite irú to shinái nára (ba)	書いているとしないなら(ば)	}

Anó uekiyá wa watashí ga **mite** **irú** *to yóku hatarakimásŭ ga* **mite**
あの 植木屋 は 私 が 見て いると よく 仂きます が 見て
inái *to súgu namakemásŭ.*   If I am watching that gardener he works well, but
いないと すぐ なまけます.   if I do not watch him he soon becomes idle.

or As long as I keep watching that gardener he works well, but if I do not
keep on watching him he soon becomes idle.

This form of the subjunctive is followed by **surú náraba** when the *if-clause*
is followed by another clause indicating a logical consequence.

Anó otokó ga sonná ni yóku **hataraité** **irú** *to* **surú** **náraba** *byōki*
あの 男 がそんな に よく 仂いて いると する ならば 病気
de wa nái.   If that man is working so hard he must not be sick.
で は ない.

Another form of subjunctive present is obtained by adding **masú-**
reba ますれば to the simple verbal stem of verbs of Class I, and
to the *i*-stem of verbs of Class II. The negative form is obtained
by adding **masén náraba** ませんならば to the verbal stem, as
already shown in this lesson.

This form of the subjunctive is the most polite.

mimasúreba	見ますれば	if I see, if I watch
mimasén náraba	見ませんならば	if I do not see, if I do not watch
kakimasúreba	書きますれば	if I write
kakimasén náraba	書きませんならば	if I do not write

Anáta ga suisenjō[1] wo **kudasaimasúreba** *watashí wa taihén arigátaku[2]*
貴方 がすいせん状を 下さいますれば 私 は 大変 ありがたく
zonjimásŭ.   If you give me a recommendation I shall feel very much obliged
存じます.   to you. (*lit.* You recommendation if you favour me with, I very
         thankful feel.)

Below are given examples of the present subjunctive of verbs of
Class I and Class II in all its various forms.

Class I

Positive		**Míru** 見る	Negative	
if I see, if I watch			if I do not see (*or* watch)	
mimásŭ nára (ba)	見ますなら(ば)		*mimasén nára (ba)*	見ませんなら(ば)
mimasúreba	見ますれば		*mimasén nára (ba)*	見ませんなら(ば)
míru nára (ba)	見るなら(ば)		*mínai nára (ba)*	見ないなら(ば)
míreba	見れば		*mi-nákereba*	見なければ
míru to	見ると		*mínai to*	見ないと
míru to suréba	見るとすれば		*mínai to suréba*	見ないとすれば
míte iréba	見ていれば		*míte inákereba*	見ていなければ
míte irú to	見ていると		*míte inái to*	見ていないと
míte irú to surú nára (ba)	見ていると する なら (ば)		*míte irú to shinái nára (ba)*	見て いると しない なら (ば)

---

1 recommendation **2** *arigatái* to be thankful, grateful, obliged; *arigátaku zonjíru*
polite form for *to be thankful*, etc.

Polite Form

gorán asobaséba	御覧遊ばせば	*gorán asobasá-nákereba*	御覧遊ばさなければ
gorán ni náreba	御覧になれば	*gorán ni naráneba*	御覧にならねば

Class II

Positive   *Káku* 書く   Negative

Positive		Negative	
if I write		if I do not write	
kakimásŭ nára (ba)	書きますなら（ば）	*kakimasén nára (ba)*	書きませんなら（ば）
kakimasúreba	書きますれば	*kakimasén nára (ba)*	書きませんなら（ば）
káku nára (ba)	書くなら（ば）	*kakánai nára (ba)*	書かないなら（ば）
kákeba	書けば	*kaká-nákereba*	書かなければ
káku to	書くと	*kakánai to*	書かないと
káku to suréba	書くとすれば	*kakánai to suréba*	書かないとすれば
káite iréba	書いていれば	*káite inákereba*	書いていなければ
káite irú to	書いていると	*káite inái to*	書いていないと
káite irú to surú nára (ba)		*káite irú to shinái nára (ba)*	
書いていると する なら （ば）		書いていると しない なら （ば）	

Polite Form

o-kakí asobaséba	お書き遊ばせば	*o-kakí asobasá-nákereba*	お書き遊ばさなければ
o-kakí ni náreba	お書きになれば	*o-kakí ni naráneba*	お書きにならねば

Subjunctive Present of True Adjectives

The formation of the subjunctive present of true adjectives is obtained in the following ways:

Positive		Negative	
if it is cold, if I am cold		if it isn't cold, if I am not cold	
samúi nára (ba)	寒いなら（ば）	*sámuku nái nára (ba)*	寒くないなら（ば）
sámukereba	寒ければ	*sámuku nákereba*	寒くなければ
samúi to	寒いと	*sámuku nái to*	寒くないと
samúi to suréba	寒いとすれば	*sámuku nái to suréba*	寒くないとすれば

Polite Form

o-samúi nára (ba)	*o-samukú arimasén nára (ba)*
お寒い なら （ば）	お寒く ありませんなら（ば）

Examples

*Móshi konó hon ga **omoshirói náraba** watashí wa kaimashō.*
若し この 本 が 面白い ならば 私 は買いましょう.
If this book is interesting I will buy it.

*Móshi koré ga **takái to suréba** hoká ni yasúi monó wa arimasén.*
若し これ が 高い と すれば 外 に 安い 物 はありません
If this is dear we haven't anything else cheaper.

Móshi   sonó   íe   ga   yásuku   nái   náraba   kawanái   hō   ga   yói   désŭ.
若し   その   家   が   安く   ない   ならば   買わない   方   が   よい   です.
If that house is not cheap it is better not to buy it.
   (*lit.* If that house cheaply if it is not, not to buy the way good is.)

O-yú   ga   átsuku   nákereba   o-cha   wa   yóku   demasén.
お湯   が   熱く   なければ   お茶   は   よく   出ません.
If the water is not hot you cannot make good tea.
   (If the hot-water is not hot the tea well does not come out.)

N. B.   The subject of an if-clause is followed by *ga*.

In Japanese the subjunctive present is used only when the hypothesis expressed by the *if-clause* may be already existent, or when the hypothesis expressed, although still unrealized, brings, when realized, the certain occurrence of the condition or action expressed by the dependent clause.

For instance, if one says " If I have money I shall lend you some," the condition of having money may already exist, and upon the realization that one has the money the loan will be made.

When one says " If it does not rain soon our crop will be lost," although what is said in the *if-clause* is not based upon a present reality, but on a future probability, one is sure that the prediction expressed in the dependent clause will be realized unless it rains.

In all cases similar to the two above, the *if-clauses* may be translated by the Japanese present of the subjunctive.

On the other hand, if one says " If you meet Mr. Tanaka tell him that I wish to see him," meeting Mr. Tanaka is still in the future and is based on chance, on probability, and one cannot be sure that on meeting Mr. Tanaka the person spoken to will tell him the speaker's desire to see him. In similar cases the Japanese do not use the present subjunctive, but the past subjunctive as given in Lesson 49.

If the student carefully considers the examples given in this lesson and in the following exercise, the use of the present subjunctive will appear clear in its various applications.

Unless, Provided That, Though, Although

There is no corresponding Japanese word to the English **unless**. Its meaning has to be expressed by the negative of the subjunctive of the verb that in English follows the said conjunction.

Anó   hĭtó   ga   Eigó   wo   hanasánai   náraba   watashí   wa   anó   hĭtó   wo
あの   人   が   英語   を   話さない   ならば   私   は   あの   人   を
ryōkai[1]   *surú   kotó   ga   dekimasén.*   **Unless** he speaks English I cannot under-
了解   する   事   が   出来ません.   stand him.

Zen   kókka   ga   tagái   ni   shinrái   shiawánai   náraba   konó   sekái   ni   jizokutekí[2]
全   国家   が   互いに   信頼   しあわない   ならば   この   世界   に   持続的
heiwá[3]   *wa   nái   de   arō.*   **Unless** all nations trust one another there cannot be
平和   は   無い   であろう.   lasting peace in this world.
   (*lit.* All nations, mutually trust if they do not, in this world lasting peace
   there will not be.—*tagái ni* mutually; *shinrái shiáu* to trust one another)

---

1 *ryōkai surú* to understand   **2** lasting   **3** peace

Also **provided** or **provided that** has no corresponding Japanese word. Their meaning is expressed by the positive form of the subjunctive of the verb that in English follows either of the said conjunctions.

*Anáta ga san man yen **dásu náraba** watashí no inú wo urimashō*
貴方 が 三 万 円 出す ならば 私 の 犬を売りましょう.
Provided you give me 30,000 yen I shall sell my dog.

N. B. The subject of a clause introduced by *unless*, *provided* or *provided that* is followed by *ga.*

Although or **though** is translated by the subordinate of the verb or adjective followed by *mo.* See Lessons 26, page 173 and Lesson 27, page 184.

*Anó hĭtó wa **wákakute mo** gakŭshikí ga arimású.*
あの 人 は 若くて も 学識 が あります.
Although he is young he is learned. (*gakŭshikí* learning)

Subjunctive Present of the
Desiderative

The subjunctive present of the desiderative is obtained in the following ways:

Positive	*Míru* 見る	Negative
if I wish to see		if I do not wish to see
mitái nára (ba) 見たいなら(ば)		*mítaku nái nára (ba)* 見たくないなら(ば)
mítakereba 見たければ		*mítaku nákereba* 見たくなければ
mitái to omóeba 見たいと 思えば		*mitái to omowá-nákereba* 見たいと 思わなければ

Polite Form

gorán ni naritái nára(ba) 御覧 になりたい なら(ば)		*gorán ni naritáku nái nára(ba)* 御覧 に なりたくない なら(ば)

Káku 書く

Positive	Negative
if I wish to write	if I do not wish to write
kakitái nára (ba) 書きたいなら(ば)	*kakitáku nái nára(ba)* 書きたくない なら(ば)
kakitákereba 書きたければ	*kakitáku nákereba* 書きたくなければ
kakitái to omóeba 書きたいと 思えば	*kakitái to omowá-nákereba* 書きたいと 思わなければ

Polite Form

o-kakí ni naritái nára(ba) お書きに なりたい なら(ば)	*o-kakí ni naritáku nái nara(ba)* お書きに なりたくない なら(ば)

*Móshi Nihón-go wo yóku **oboetái** **náraba** isshōkemmei[1] ni benkyō*
若し　日本語　を　よく　覚えたい　ならば　一生懸命　に　勉強
shinákereba narimasén.   If you wish to learn Japanese well you must study
しなければ　なりません.   hard. (*obóeru* 覚える to learn)

 *Móshí íma kaimonó ni **dekaketáku** **nái** **náraba** myōnichi de mo*
若し　今　買物　に　出かけたく　ない　ならば　明日　で　も
yoroshíi désŭ.   If you don't wish to go out now for shopping you may go to-
よろしいです.   morrow.

 (*kaimonó ni* for shopping, *dekakerú* でかける to go out)

Enough

 Enough is translated by the word *jūbun* 充分, by the verb *tarirú* 足りる *to be sufficient, to be enough*, or by the expression *mō takŭsán* もう沢山 *already much* (=it is already much, now it is enough).

Jūbun no o-kané wo mótte imásŭ.   I have **enough** money.
充分　の　お金　を　持って　います.

*Zémbu no okyakŭsamá ni isú ga **tarirú** **ka** dō ka shirimasén.*
全部　の　お客様　に　椅子　が　足りる　か　どうか　知りません.
! do **not** know whether there are **enough** chairs for all the guests.
 (*lit.* All the guests for, chairs are sufficient?, how is it I don't know.)

*Móshi kamí ga **tará-nákereba** itté mótto katté irasshái.*
若し　紙　が　足らなければ　行ってもっと買っていらっしゃい.
 If there is not **enough** paper go and buy some more.
  (*lit.* If paper if is not sufficient, go, more buy please.)

*Arigatō, **mō takŭsán** itadakimáshĭta.*   No, thank you, I have **enough.**
ありがとう, もう　沢山　いただきました.　(Thanks, already much received.)

Idiomatic Usage

Sámuku wa arimasén ka.   Are you warm **enough?**
寒く　はありませんか.   (*lit.* Coldly are you not?)

O-réi no mōshi-agé yō mo arimasén.   I can never thank you **enough.**
お礼　の　申上げ　よう　も　ありません.
 (*o-réi* return thanks; *mōshi-agerú* 申上げる to say, to tell; *yō* the way; *lit.*
 Return thanks to say, the way there isn't.)

Dōzo, michí wo oshieté kudasái.   Be kind **enough** to show me the way.
どうぞ, 道　を　教えて　下さい.   (*lit.* Please, the way show me.)

Zŭibun nágaku taizái itashimáshĭta.   We have stayed long **enough.**
ずいぶん　長く　滞在　いたしました.
 (*lit.* Extremely long the sojourn we made.—*taizái itasú* 滞在いたす=*taizái
 surú* 滞在する to sojourn)

Káno-jo wa kánari yóku utaimáshĭta.   She has sung well **enough.**
彼女　は　かなり　よく　歌いました.
 (*lit.* She, considerably well sang.—*utaú* 歌う to sing)

---

1 *isshōkemmei* as hard as one can, with all one's might

Vocabulary

Nouns

birthday	tanjōbi	誕タ生ジョ日ビ
business	jigyō	事ジ業ギョ
crop	toriiré	取トリ入イレ
damage	songái	損ソ害ガイ
depression	{fushín	不フ振シン
	fukéiki	不フ景ケ気キ
ill luck	fúun	不フ運ウン
investment	tōshi	投トウ資シ
invitation	manekí	招マネキ
misery	fukō	不フ幸コウ
need	iriyō	入イリ用ヨウ
offer	mōshiide	申モウシ出イデ
quantity	bunryō	分ブン量リョ
studio	kyōjujo	教キョ授ジュ所ジョ
violinist	{teikinká	提テイ琴キン家カ
	baiorinnísŭto	バイオリンニスト
waiter	kyūji	給キュ仕シ
wealth	tómi	富トミ

Adjectives

helpful	kan-yō-na	肝カン要ヨウナ
influential	yūryoku-na	有ユウ力リクナ

moderate	tékido no	適テ度ドノ
profitable	yūri ni	有ユウ利リニ

Verbs

to accept	azukáru	与アヅカル
to acquire	eraré·ru	得エラレル
to ascribe	séi ni surú	セイニスル
to continue	tsuzukú	続ツク
to fail	shippái surú	失シッ敗パイスル
to follow	shĭtagáu	従シガウ
to gain	mōke·ru	儲モウケル
to hurt	gaisú·ru	害ガイスル
to improve	kōjō surú	向上スル
to invite	manéku	招マク
to recommend	suisén surú	推スイ薦センスル
to repent	kōkai surú	後コウ悔カイスル
to treat	atsŭkaú	扱アツカウ
to throw away	sŭte·rú	捨ステル
to try	kokoromí·ru	試コロミル

Adverbs

never	kesshĭté	決ケッシテ
recently	saikín	最サイ近キン
surely	kittó	キット

miserable, wretched *hisán-na*; condition, situation, circumstance *kyōgū*; unfortunate, unlucky, ill-starred *fúun no*; to make efforts *doryokú surú*; capital, funds *shihón*; to invest (capital) *tōshi surú*; to double, to increase twofold *ni-bái ni surú*; to eat too much *kashokú surú*; winter coat *fuyú no gaitō*; good business *shōbai hanjō*; to be based upon *motozúku*; position, employment *tsŭtomeguchí*; to take a trip round the world *sekái man-yū wo surú*; change, alteration *hénka*; present, of the present time *génkon no*; to succeed in, to be successful *seikō surú*

Exercise *Renshū* 練習

1. Ōku no hĭtóbito wa jibúntachi no hisán-na kyōgū wo fúun no séi ni shimásŭ. Konná hĭtótachi wa sonó fukō no shin no gen-in[1] de áru tokoró no[2] kyōgū wo kōjō surú tamé ni kesshĭté doryokú wo shimasén. Móshi ware-waré ga kōjō[3] wo kokorómínai náraba[4] warewaré no seikatsú ni kan-yō-na

---

1 *shin no gen-in* the only cause   **2** *tokoró no* which   **3** *kōjō* improvement   **4** *koko-romínai náraba* if we do not try; *kokoromíru* to try, to have a try at

hénka wo motarásu[1] kotó ni seikō shịnái de arō. **2.** Wakái[2] uchí ni benkyō shinái náraba toshí wo tótte kará[3] kōkai surú deshō. **3.** Móshi watashí no jigyō ni anáta no shihón wo tōshi nasáru[4] náraba san-yo-nen ínai ni[5] soré wo ni-bái ni shimásŭ ga.—Go-shínsetsu no o-mōshiide[6] wa taihén arigatái désŭ ga génkon no jigyō fushín no tamé mōkeru dókoro[7] ka shihón wo minná ushinawanái to mo[8] kagirimasén to omoimásŭ.—Soré wa anáta no go-zúii[9] désŭ ga móshi anáta ga watashí no chūkoku ni shĭtagawaréru[10] náraba anáta no tōshi wa kittó[11] taihén yūri-ni náru deshō ni. **4.** Móshi konó áme ga mō futsŭká guraí tsuzukú náraba múgi no toriiré ni hijō-na songái wo ukéru deshō. **5.** Súbete no shokúmotsu wa móshi tékido-no bunryō wo tabéru náraba kenkō ni yói ga ikáni[12] kenkō ni yói shokúmotsu de mo kashoku suréba kenkō wo gaishimásŭ. **6.** Koréra no gaikokú zasshí wo sŭtenái de kudásai. Móshi o-iriyō de nákereba[13] watashí ni kudásai. Watashí wa gaikokú zasshí wo yómu no ga sŭkí désŭ.—Yorokónde sashiagemásŭ. **7.** Ashĭtá wa watashí no tanjōbi désŭ kará tomodachí wo shokují ni uchí e manekimásŭ. O-isogáshiku nákereba dōzo okŭsamá to go-isshó ni oidé kudásai.—Go-shínsetsu-na o-manekí ni azukaremasén[14] de zannén désŭ.[15] Názenaraba watashí wa kázoku no monó[16] wo myōasa Karuizawá e tsureté mairá-nákereba narimasén nóde. Kázoku no monó wa natsú-jū Karuizawá de sugósu[17] tsumorí désŭ. **8.** Móshi konó nikú ga amarí katákereba meshiagaranái hō ga yói désŭ. Náni ka hoká no monó[18] wo mótte kúru yō ni kyūji ni iimashō. **9.** Móshi omoté ga sámukereba atarashíi fuyú no gaitō wo kitá[19] hō ga yói deshō. **10.** Móshi o-kané wo mōketai náraba hataraká-nákereba narimasén. Hatarakazú shĭté[20] tómi wa eraremasén. **11.** Anáta no ojōsan ga vaiorín wo o-narái ni naritái náraba Komerī Sénséi no tokoró e o-yarí ni náru[21] no ga yoroshíi deshō. Sénséi wa Itarī kará saikín koráre, yūmei-na teikinká da sō désŭ. Sénséi wa Uenó Kōen no sóba ni kyōjujo wo mótte oraremásŭ. **12.** O-kyakŭsamá wo yóku atsŭkawá-nákereba ni-do to[22] shinamonó wo kái ni kité kuremasén. Shōbai hanjō wa kyakú atsŭkái no yói[23] kotó ni motozukimásŭ. **13.** Kimbén de nái to shippái surú ka-mo shirenái. **14.** Bóku ga kimí wo yobá-nákereba[24] kité wa ikemasén. **15.** Móshi dáre-ka yūryoku-na hĭtó ga anáta wo suisén surú náraba anó tsutomeguchí ga eraréru deshō ni. **16.** Móshi anáta ga hyakumán yen dásu náraba watashí wa anó yō-na[25] ié wo tatéru kotó ga dekimásŭ. **17.** Watashí wa jūbun-na o-kané ga dékita tokí ni sekái man-yū wo shimashō.

---

1 *motarásu* to bring; *motarásu kotó ni* in bringing   **2** *wakái uchí ni* while you are young   **3** *toshí wo tótte kará* when you are old   **4** *tōshi nasáru* polite for *tōshi surú* to invest   **5** *ínai ni* in, within   **6** *go-shínsetsu no o-mōshiide* your kind offer   **7** *mōkeru dókoro ka=mōkeru kawarí ni* instead of gaining   **8** *ushinawanái to mo kagirimasén* might lose   **9** *go-zúii désŭ* do as you wish   **10** *shĭtagawaréru* polite verb for *shitagáu* to follow   **11** *kittó* I assure you   **12** *ikáni* even   **13** *o-iriyō de nákereba* if you don't need   **14** *azukaremasén* cannot accept   **15** *zannén désŭ* I am sorry   **16** *kázoku no monó* the people of my family   **17** *sugósu* to spend, to pass; *natsú-jū sugósu* to spend the summer   **18** *náni ka hoká no monó* something else   **19** *kitá* from *kiru* to wear   **20** *hatarakazú shĭté* without working   **21** *o-yarí ni náru* to send   **22** *ni-do to* again   **23** *kyakú atsŭkái no yói* good service to customers; *atsŭkái* treatment   **24** *yobá-nákereba* unless I call you   **25** *anó yō na* such; *anó yō na ié* such a house

1. 多くの人々は自分達の悲惨な境遇を不運のせいにします. こんな人達はその不幸の真の原因である所の境遇を向上するために決して努力をしません. 若し我々が向上を試みないならば我々の生活に肝要な変化をもたらす事に成功しないであろう.　2. 若いうちに勉強しないならば年を取ってから後悔するでしょう.　3. 若し私の事業に貴方の資本を投資なさるならば三四年以内にそれを二倍にしますが.—御親切の御申し出では大変ありがたいですが現今の事業不振のため, 儲ける所か資本を皆失わないとも限りませんと思います.—それは貴方の御随意ですが若し貴方が私の忠告に従われるならば貴方の投資はきっと大変有利になるでしょうに.　4. 若しこの雨がもう二日位続くならば麦の取入れに非常な損害を受けるでしょう.　5. すべての食物は若し適度の分量を食べるならば健康によいが如何に健康によい食物でも過食すれば健康を害します.　6. これ等の外国雑誌を捨てないで下さい. 若しお入用でなければ私に下さい. 私は外国雑誌を読むのが好きです.—喜んで差上げます.　7. あしたは私の誕生日ですから友達を食事にうちへ招きます. お忙しくなければどうぞ奥様と御一緒にお出で下さい.—御親切なお招きにあづかれませんで残念です. 何故ならば私は家族の者を明朝軽井沢へ連れて参らなければなりませんので. 家族の者は夏中軽井沢で過すつもりです.　8. 若しこの肉が余りかたければ召し上らない方がよいです. 何かほかの物を持って来るように給仕に言いましょう.　9. 若しおもてが寒ければ新らしい冬の外套を着た方がよいでしょう.　10. 若しお金を儲けたいならば働かなければなりません. 働かずして富は得られません.　11. 貴方のお嬢さんがヴァイオリンをお習いになりたいならばコメリー先生の所へおやりになるのが宜しいでしょう. 先生はイタリーから最近来られ, 有名な提琴家だそうです. 先生は上野公園のそばに教授所を持っておられます.　12. お客様をよく扱わなければ二度と品物を買いに来てくれません. 商売繁昌は客扱いのよい事にもとづきます.　13. 勤勉でないと失敗するかも知れない.　14. 僕が君を呼ばなければ来てはいけません.　15. 若し誰か有力な人が貴方を推薦するらばあの勤め口が得られるでしょうに.　16. 若し貴方が百万円だすならば私はあのような家を建てる事ができます.　17. 私は充分なお金ができた時に世界漫遊をしましょう.

1. Many people ascribe their miserable condition to bad luck. These people, however, never make any effort to improve their condition, which is the only cause of their misery. If we do not try we shall never succeed in bringing any helpful change in our lives. 2. If you do not study while you are young you will repent when you are older. 3. If you invest your capital in my business I shall double it in three or four years.—I thank you very much for your kind offer, but on account of the present business depression I am afraid

I might lose all my capital instead of gaining.—Well, you may do as you wish, but I assure you that if you follow my advice your investment will be very profitable. **4.** If this rain continues for another two days the wheat crop will be greatly damaged. **5.** All food is healthful if we eat it in moderate quantity, but even the most healthful food will hurt us if we eat too much of it. **6.** Don't throw away these foreign magazines; if you do not need them give them to me. I like to read foreign magazines.—I will give them to you with pleasure. **7.** To-morrow being my birthday I shall have a few friends at home for a dinner party. If you are not busy, please come with your wife and join us.—I am sorry, I cannot accept your kind invitation because to-morrow morning I have to accompany my family to Karuizawa, where they will spend the summer. **8.** If this meat is too tough don't eat it; I will tell the waiter to bring something else. **9.** If it is cold outside it is better that you wear your new winter coat. **10.** If people wish to earn money they must work. No wealth is acquired without work. **11.** If your daughter wishes to learn to play the violin you may send her to Professor Comelli. He has just come from Italy, and people say he is a celebrated violinist. He has his studio near Ueno Park. **12.** Unless you give good service to your customers they will not come back to buy your goods. Good business is based upon good service. **13.** We shall fail unless we are industrious. **14.** Do not come unless I call you. **15.** You may obtain that position provided some influential person recommends you. **16.** I can build such a house provided you give me 1,000,000 yen. **17.** When I have enough money I shall take a trip around the world.

Forty-eighth Lesson　第四十八課

Subjunctive (continued)

Present and Past

The Japanese form of the subjunctive present as given in the previous lesson is, in most cases, used to translate also the English subjunctive past.

Note that in order to simplify grammatical explanations, the forms of the subjunctive given in the following two pages will be called **subjunctive present**, even though they are used to translate both the English subjunctive present and past.

In the next lesson will be given the conjugation of verbs in the forms which, to simplify gramatical explanations, are classified as **subjunctive past.**

The conjugation of the subjunctive of *to have, to be* and *there to be,* being anomalous, we will give it in all its varied forms.

To Have　*mótsu* 持つ

if I have, if I had	if I have (had) not
mótte orimásŭ nára(ba)	*mótte orimasén nára(ba)*
持っております なら(ば)	持っておりません なら(ば)
mótte imásŭ nára(ba)	*mótte imasén nára(ba)*
持っています なら(ば)	持っていません なら(ば)
mótte irú nára(ba)	*mótte inái nára(ba)*
持っている なら(ば)	持っていない なら(ば)
mótte iréba	*mótte inákereba*
持っていれば	持っていなければ

Polite Form

if you have *or* had, if he has *or* had, etc.	if you have *or* had not, if he has *or* had not, etc.
o-mochí ni narimásŭ nára(ba)	*o-mochí ni narimasén nára(ba)*
お持ち に なります なら(ば)	お持ち に なりません なら(ば)
o-mochí nára(ba)	*o-mochí ni nará-nákereba*
お持ち なら(ば)	お持ち に ならなければ

To Be　*de áru* である

if I am, if I were	if I am (were) not
de arimásŭ nára(ba)	*de arimasén nára(ba)*
であります なら(ば)	でありません なら(ば)
de arimásŭ to suréba	*de arimasén to suréba*
であります と すれば	でありません と すれば
de áru nára(ba)	*de nái nára(ba)*
である なら(ば)	で ない なら(ば)
de áru to suréba	*de nái to suréba*
である と すれば	で ない と すれば

Polite Form

de gozaimásŭ nára(ba)	*de gozaimasén nára(ba)*
で 御座います なら(ば)	で御座いません なら(ば)

There To Be　*ga áru* がある

if there is, if there were	if there is (were) not
ga arimásŭ nára(ba)	*ga arimasén nára(ba)*
が あります なら(ば)	が ありません なら(ば)
ga arimásŭ to suréba	*ga arimasén to suréba*
が あります と すれば	が ありません と すれば
ga áru nára(ba)	*ga nái nára(ba)*
が ある なら(ば)	が ない なら(ば)
ga áreba があれば	*ga nákereba* がなければ
ga áru to suréba	*ga nái to suréba*
が あると すれば	が ない と すれば

Polite Form

ga gozaimásŭ nára(ba)	*ga gozaimasén nára(ba)*
が 御座います なら(ば)	が御座いません なら(ば)

To Work *hatarakú* 仂く

if I work, if I worked	if I do (did) not work
hatarakimásŭ nára(ba)	*hatarakimasén nára(ba)*
仂きます　なら（ば）	仂きません　なら（ば）
hatarakimasúreba	*hatarakimasén nára(ba)*
仂きますれば	仂きません　なら（ば）
hatarakú nára(ba)	*hatarakanái nára(ba)*
仂く　なら（ば）	仂かない　なら（ば）
hatarakéba 仂けば	*hataraká-nákereba* 仂かなければ
hatarakú to 仂くと	*hataraká-nái to* 仂かないと
hatarakú to suréba	*hataraká-nái to suréba*
仂く　と すれば	仂かない　と すれば
hataraité iréba	*hataraité inákereba*
仂いて　いれば	仂いて　いなければ
hataraité irú to	*hataraité inái to*
仂いて　いると	仂いて　いないと
	hataraité inái to surú nára(ba)
hataraité irú to surú nára(ba)	仂いて　いないと する　なら(ば)
仂いて　いると する なら(ば)	*hataraité irú to shinái nára(ba)*
	仂いて　いるとしない なら(ば)

Polite Form

o-hataraki ni náreba	*o-hataraki ni naráneba*
お仂き　に　なれば	お仂き　に　ならねば

Conditional Past

The Japanese *conditional past* is obtained by the future form followed or not by the postposition *ni*.

We remind the student that although this verbal form is classified as *conditional past*, it refers to the present.

To Have *mótsu* 持つ

Positive	Negative
I should (you would, etc.) have	I should (you would, etc.) not have
mochimásŭ deshō (ni)	*mochimasén deshō (ni)*
持ちますでしょう(に)	持ちませんでしょう(に)
mochimashō (ni)	*mochimasén deshō (ni)*
持ちましょう(に)	持ちませんでしょう(に)
mótsu deshō (ni)	*motánai deshō (ni)*
持つ でしょう(に)	持たないでしょう(に)
mótsu darō (ni)	*motánai darō (ni)*
持つ だろう(に)	持たないだろう(に)

I should have, etc.

mótte irú deshō (ni)
持つているでしょう(に)

mótte irú darō (ni)
持つているだろう(に)

I should not have, etc.

mótte inái deshō (ni)
持つていないでしょう(に)

mótte inái darō (ni)
持つていないだろう(に)

Polite Form

o-mochí ni náru déshō (ni)
お持ち に なるでしょう(に)

o-mochí ni narimasén deshō (ni)
お持ち になりませんでしょう(に)

To Be *désŭ* です

Positive	**Negative**
I should (you would, etc.) be	I should not (you would, etc.) be
deshō (ni) でしょう(に)	*nái deshō (ni)* ないでしょう(に)
darō (ni) だろう(に)	*nái darō (ni)* ないだろう(に)

Polite Form

gozaimashō (ni)
御座いましょう(に)

gozaimasén deshō (ni)
御座いませんでしょう(に)

There To Be *ga áru* がある, *ga óru* がおる

there would be

ga áru (irú, óru) deshō (ni)
がある(いる, おる)でしょう(に)

ga áru (irú, óru) darō (ni)
がある(いる, おる)だろう(に)

there would not be

ga nái (inái) deshō (ni)
がない(いない)でしょう(に)

ga nái (inái) darō (ni)
がない(いない)だろう(に)

Polite Form

ga gozaimásŭ deshō (ni)
が御座いますでしょう(に)

ga gozaimasén deshō (ni)
が御座いませんでしょう(に)

To Work *hatarakú* 仂く

I should (you would, etc.) work

hatarakimashō (ni)
仂きましょう (に)

hatarakú deshō (ni)
仂く でしょう(に)

hatarakú darō (ni)
仂く だろう(に)

I should not (you would, etc.) work

hatarakimasén deshō (ni)
仂きません でしょう(に)

hataraká-nái deshō (ni)
仂かない でしょう(に)

hataraká-nái darō (ni)
仂かない だろう(に)

Polite Form

o-hatarakí ni náru deshō (ni)
お仂き に なるでしょう(に)

o-hatarakí ni naránai deshō (ni)
お仂き に ならないでしょう(に)

To Do surú する

I should (you would, etc.) do	I should (you would, etc.) not do
shimashō (*ni*)	*shimasén deshō* (*ni*)
しましょう(に)	しませんでしょう(に)
surú deshō (*ni*)	*shinái deshō* (*ni*)
するでしょう(に)	しないでしょう(に)
surú darō (*ni*)	*shinái darō* (*ni*)
するだろう(に)	しないだろう(に)

Polite Form

nasaimashō (*ni*)	*nasaimasén deshō* (*ni*)
なさいましょう(に)	なさいませんでしょう(に)

Conditional Past of True Adjectives
It Is Cold *Samúi* 寒い

it would be cold I should be cold, etc.	it would not be cold I should not be cold, etc.
samúi deshō (*ni*)	*sámuku-nái deshō* (*ni*)
寒いでしょう(に)	寒くないでしょう(に)
samúi darō (*ni*)	*sámuku-nái darō* (*ni*)
寒いだろう(に)	寒くないだろう(に)

Polite Form

o-samúi deshō (*ni*)	*o-sámuku-nái deshō* (*ni*)
お寒いでしょう(に)	お寒くないでしょう(に)

Examples

Watashí wa takŭsán o-kané wo mótte irú náraba sekái man-yū[1] wo
私 は 沢山 お金 を 持って いる ならば 世界 漫遊 を
surú deshō (ni).   If I had much money I should make a trip around
する でしょう (に).   the world.

Móshi yói tomodachí ga nái to suréba sázo[2] sabishíi deshō (ni).
若し 良い 友達 が ない と すれば さぞ 淋しい でしょう(に).
If we had no good friends we should certainly feel lonesome.

Móshi anó otokó ga báka de nái náraba kimí no iú kotó ga
若し あの 男 が ばか で ない ならば 君 の 言う事 が
wakárn deshō (ni).   If that man were not a fool he would understand
解る でしょう (に).   what you say.

Móshi mótto yói senséi ni tsŭkŭ[3] náraba háyaku Nihón-go wo obóeru
若し もっとよい 先生 に つく ならば 早く 日本語 を 覚える
deshō (ni).   If I had a better teacher I should learn Japanese quickly.
でしょう (に).   (*lit.* If more good teacher under, to study if, quickly Japanese
language should learn.)

---

1 *sekái man-yū* a trip around the world   **2** *sázo* certainly   **3** *senséi ni tsŭkŭ* to
study under a teacher

*Kyō anáta ga Kasumichō no íchiba e **ikéba** nan de mo yásuku*
きょう 貴方 が 霞町 の 市場 へ 行けば 何ん で も 安く
kaerú[1] **deshō.**   If you went to-day to the Kasumichō market you could buy
買える でしょう.   anything cheap.

*Itsumo isshōkemmei **hatarakú náraba** tsúi-ni[2] wa mokŭtekí wo **togéru***
いつも 一生懸命 仂く ならば 遂に は 目的 を 遂げる
deshō.   If we always worked hard we should at last succeed in our purpose.
でしょう.   (*togéru* to realize, to accomplish)

*Anáta ga chūjitsu[3] ni **tsŭtoménai to suréba** anáta no shújin wa*
貴方 が 忠実 に 勤めない と すれば 貴方 の 主人 は
gekkyū[4] *wo **agenái deshō.***   If you didn't (*or* do not) perform your duties
月給 を 上げないでしょう.   faithfully your master wouldn't raise your
                         salary. (*tsŭtoméru* to serve an office)

*Okadá San ga mótto yói enzetsú wo **suréba** kittó tōshi[5] no shichō*[6]
岡田 さん が もっと 良い 演説 を すれば きっと 当市 の 市長
*ni **tōsen**[7] **surú deshō.***   If Mr. Okada delivered better speeches he would
に 当選 する でしょう.   surely be elected mayor of our city.

A verb or adjective in the subjunctive may be followed by *ga, nóni,* or *monó wo.* This occurs when the sentence has an unexpressed adversative or concessive idea, which, were it to be expressed, would introduce a contrary statement, a declaration of doubt concerning the possibility of fulfilling a condition, or an expression of regret.

*Anó hĭtó wa o-saké wo yóseba íi **ga.***   It would be well for that person
あの 人 は お酒 を よせば いゝ が.   (*or* him) to give up drinking.
(That person the wine if he should give up good, but......)

The expression *nóni* or *monó wo* emphasizes the idea of hopelessness as to the unexpressed situation. For this reason it is rarely used with the first person.

*Minná ga ikú no désŭ kará kimí mo ikú hō ga íi **nóni*** (*or monó wo*).
みんな が 行くの ですから 君 も 行く方 がいゝのに   (もの を).
As all are going it would be well if you too could go.
(Supposing that the person spoken to is not able to go on account of conditions that cannot be altered.)

By placing *íi* or *yókatta* after *ga, nóni,* or *monó wo,* such optative English expressions as *if only, would that, I wish that,* are rendered.

*Mō sŭkóshi yásukereba íi **ga*** (*or noni, monó wo*).
もう 少し 安ければ いい が   (のに, もの を).
I wish it were a little cheaper. (......but it isn't, so that I shall not buy it.)

*Ame ga yaméba íi **ga*** (*nóni, monó wo*).   If only it would clear off!
雨 が やめば いゝ が (のに, もの を).
(*lit.* The rain if stopped good, but......—*yamú* やむ to cease, discontinue, etc.)

---

1 *kaerú* to be able to buy **2** *tsúi-ni* at last **3** *chūjitsu ni* faithfully **4** salary
5 *tōshi* our city **6** mayor **7** *tōsen surú* to be elected

Honda Kun wa Ōsaka e tátsu kotó wo bóku ni itté kureréba yókatta
本田　君　は　大阪　へ　立つ　事　を　僕　に言って呉れゝばよかった

nóni.　　　　I wish Mr. Honda had told me that he was going to Osaka.
のに.　　　　(*lit.* Mr. Honda to Osaka to depart, the fact to me saying if he favoured,
was good, but......)

The subjunctive often refers to time and corresponds to *when,
while,* or *as soon as* followed by a verb, especially the subjunctive
formed by the simple present followed by *to.*

Shokují ga súmu to (or *súmeba*) *súgu ni o-dekaké ni narimásŭ ka.*
食事　が　すむ　と　（すめば）直ぐ　に　お出かけ　に　なります　か.
Will you go out as soon as you finish your meal?
(*lit.* The meal when you finish—*or* if you finish—soon going out becomes?)

Sakurá no haná ga sakú to (or *sakéba*) *máinichi nan zen to iú*
桜　の　花　が　咲く　と　（咲けば）毎日　何　千という

hĭtó[1] ga Uenó Kōen e o-hanamí ni ikimásŭ.
人　が　上野　公園　へ　お花見　に行きます.
When the cherry blossoms are in bloom thousands upon thousands of people
go to Ueno Park to view them. (*o-hanamí ni ikú* to go flower-viewing)

The negative present subjunctive followed by *ikenái* いけない,
or *naránai* ならない, may be translated by *must.*

Anáta wa chokín wo shinákereba ikemásén.　　You must save your money.
貴方　は　貯金　を　しなければいけません.
(*lit.* You saving if you do not do, it won't do.)

The present subjunctive preceded by *sáe* さえ means *if only, provided.*

Kimí ga shusseki sáe suréba íi.　　Your attendance only will suffice.
君　が　出席　さえ　すれば　いい.　　(You attendance if only do, good.)

Kimí ga chūi sáe surú náraba konná kotó wa okoránai deshō ni.
君　が　注意さえ　する　ならば　こんな　事　は起こらないでしょうに.
If only you were careful such things would not happen.

In Japanese the subjunctive is often used when there is no hypothetical idea in the corresponding English translation.

Koré wo míreba yasashíi yō désŭ ga tsŭkúru no wa muzukashíi désŭ.
これ　を　見れば　易しいようですが　造る　の　はむづかしい　です.
To look at it it seems easy, but it is really difficult to make it.
(*lit.* This if we look, easy-like is, but to make it difficult is.)

Anáta ga ossháru kotó kará handán suréba hontōrashíi hanashí no yō
あなた　がおつしやる事　から　判断　すれば本当らしい　話　のよう

désŭ　　Judging from what you say, it seems to be a true story.
です.　　　　(*lit.* You to say things from, judgement if we do, true-like story
similar is.—*handán surú* 判断する to judge, *handán* 判断 judgement, conclusion, estimation)

---

1 *nan zen to iú hĭtó* thousands upon of thousands of people

Uketamawáreba[1] *anáta no imōtosan ga go-byōki da sō désŭ ne.*
承れば　　　　貴方　の　妹さん　が　御病気　だそうです　ね.
I hear that your sister has been ill, has she not?
(*lit.* If I hear, your sister is ill, it is said, is it not?)

Tōkyō mo[2] *kawaréba kawattá monó désŭ.*　　How Tokyo has changed!
東京　も　　変れば　　変った　もの　です.
(*lit.* Tokyo, if it changes, it changed.)

Nedán mo[2] *yásukereba shiná mo*[2] *íi désŭ.*　　The price is cheap and
値段　も　　安ければ　　品　も　いいです.　　the quality good.
(*lit.* The price if it is cheap, the goods are good.)

The subjunctive is invariably used in such constructions of the comparative degree as "*the more, the merrier,*" "*the greater, the better,*" etc., as in the following cases:

1. If it is a verb that is in the first clause of the comparison, the verb is used in the subjunctive present immediately followed by its simple present form and the comparative word *hodó* 程, as in the following examples:

Míreba míru hodó sŭkí ni narimásŭ.　　The more I look, the more
見れば　見る　程　好き　に　なります.　　I like it.
(*lit.* If I look, to look more fond I become.—*sŭkí ni náru* to get to like, to become fond of)

Konó e wa yóku míreba míru hodó kírei désŭ.
この　絵　は　よく　見れば　見る　程　きれい　です.
The more carefully one looks at this picture the prettier it is.
(*lit.* This picture well if one looks, to look more pretty is.)

Káre wa móteba mótsu hodó mótto hoshigarimásŭ.
彼　は　持てば　持つ　程　もっと　欲しがります.
The more he has, the more he wants. (*hoshigáru* to desire)
(*lit.* He, if he has, to have more, more he desires—*or* wants.)

Nobáseba nobásu hodó surŭ no ga iyá ni narimásŭ.
延ばせば　延ばす　程　する　の　が　嫌　に　なります.
The longer you put it off, the less inclined will you be to do it.
(*lit.* If you postpone, more to postpone, to do things, you become averse to. *iyá-ni-náru* 嫌になる to get a distaste for, to develop a dislike to, to be disgusted with, etc.)

Benkyō suréba surŭ hodó takŭsán oboemásŭ.　　The more we study,
勉強　すれば　する　程　沢山　覚えます.　　the more we learn.
(*lit.* Study if we do, to do more, much we learn.—*obóeru* 覚える to learn)

2. If instead of a verb it is a true adjective that has to be considered, the adjective is used in the subjunctive present, followed by its original form and *hodó* 程, as shown below:

Háyakereba hayái hodó íi désŭ.　　The sooner, the better.
早ければ　早い　程　いいです.
(*lit.* If it is early, more early good is.)

---

1 *uketamawáru* 承る to hear, to listen to, to be told　**2** *mo* is here used as an emphatic word

Ōkereba *ōi* *hodó* *íi* *désŭ.*   The more, the better.
多ければ 多い　程　いいです.

>   (*lit.* If it is much, plenty more, it is good.—*ōkereba* 多ければ is the subjunc-
>   tive present of *ōku* 多く, which is the adverbial form of *ōi* 多い much,
>   many, plenty of, numerous, etc.)

Monó *ga* *utsŭkŭshikereba* *utsŭkushíi* *hodó* *hĭtó* *wa* *issō* *soré* *wo*
物　が　　美しければ　　　　美しい　　程　人　は一そうそれ を
konomimásŭ.   The nicer a thing is, the more we like it. (*lit.* A thing if beauti-
好みます.   ful, beautiful more, people still more like it.—*issō* 一そう still
                   more, *konómu* 好む to like, to be fond of, etc.)

3. If instead of a true adjective it is a quasi-adjective that has to be considered, the latter is not altered and is not repeated, as shown in the following
example.

Kírei *de* *áreba* *áru* *hodó* *íi* *désŭ.*   The prettier it is, the better.
きれい　で あれば ある　程　いいです.

>   (*lit.* Pretty if it is, to be more good is.—*kírei* きれい is a quasi-adjective.)

Vocabulary

	Nouns			**Adjectives**	
appearance	*mikaké*	見ミ掛カケ	complicated	*komiittá*	込コミ入イツタ
centre	*chūshin*	中チュウ心シン	healthy	*jōbu-ni*	丈ジョウ夫ブニ
convenience	*tsugō*	都ツ合ゴウ	simple	*kantán*	簡カン単タン
correspondent	*tsūshingakari*	通ツウ信シン係ガカリ	strange	*hen-na*	変ヘンナ
cultivation	*kōsaku*	耕コウ作サク	tolerant	*kandái-na*	寛カン大ダイナ
difficulty	*kónnan*	困コン難ナン		**Verbs**	
fertilizer	*hiryō*	肥ヒ料リョウ	to attend	*shussekí surú*	出席スル
gymnastics	*taisō*	体タイ操ソウ	to complain	*kobósu*	コボス
interpreter	*tsūyaku*	通ツウ訳ヤク	to complete	*kanséi surú*	完カン成セイスル
intolerance	*kyōryō*	狭キョウ量リョウ	to decay	*otoróe·ru*	衰オトロエル
land	*jímen*	地ヂ面メン	to employ	*saiyō surú*	採サイ用ヨウスル
mind	*séishin*	精セイ神シン	to revolve	*kaitén surú*	廻カイ転テンスル
question	*shitsumón*	質シツ問モン	to send	*yokósu*	寄ヨ越コス
space	*yóchi*	余ヨ地チ	to use	*shiyō surú*	使シ用ヨウスル
talent	*sainō*	才サイ能ノウ		**Adverbs**	
vocalist	*seigakŭka*	声セイ楽ガク家カ	around	*shūi*	周シュウ囲イ
warning	*keikokú*	警ケイ告コク	really	{*jíjitsu*	事ジ実ジツ
				{*jissai*	実ジツ際サイ

the world, the human society, people *yonónaka*; vocal music *seigakú*; conservatory
of music *ongakú gakkō*; immediate answer *sokutō*; to give an immediate, prompt
answer *sokutō surú*; Spanish language *Supéin-go*; the earth, the globe *chikyū*;
agricultural produce *nōsakubutsu*; to do gymnastics, to do physical exercises *taisō*
wo surú; position, employment *kuchí*; thought, opinion *íken:* to express in words

iiarawásu; to type *taipuraitā de útsu:* to warn *keikokú wo surú;* to neglect *orósoka ni surú;* to hear, to be told *uketamawáru*

Exercise *Renshū* 練習

1. Móshi mo súbete no hĭtó ga mótto kandái de áru náraba konó yonónaka wa mótto kōfuku deshō ni. Ōku no fukō wo tsŭkúru no wa kyōryō to iú monó désŭ. **2.** Móshi jūbun no o-kané ga áru náraba watashí wa musŭmé wo Itarī e ongakú kenkyū kanséi ni yarú[1] deshō. Musŭmé wa seigakú ni sainō ga arimásŭ[2] kará móshi yūmei-na Itarī no ongakú gakkō de manabú náraba rippá-na seigakŭká ni náru deshō. **3.** Mótto o-kanemochí nára anáta wa dō shimásŭ ka.—Hen-na shitsumón désŭ ne. Sokutō wa dekimasén. Watashí wa jíjitsu watashí ga mótto kanemochí nára dō surú darō to kangáeta kotó wa arimasén. Móshi mo watashí ga kanemochí ni náreba sonó tokí ni sonó tómi wo dō surú ka wo kangáeru deshō. **4.** Anó otokó wa ítsumo bimbō da to koboshimásŭ ga móshi anó hĭtó ga hontō-ni bimbō náraba anná ōki-na utsŭkushíi ié ni sumawánai deshō ni. **5.** Móshi kokó no mawarí[3] ni ki ga íkura ka áreba mótto utsŭkúshiku miéru deshō ni. **6.** Móshi anáta ga Nihón-go wo shĭtté irú náraba watashí no jimúsho de tsūshingákari ni saiyō surú deshō ni. **7.** Watashí wa Sŭpéin-go wo wasuré hajimemáshĭta.[4]—Móshi máinichi san-jíppun guraí náni-ka Sŭpéin-go no hon wo o-yomí ni náreba o-wasuré ni naránai deshō. **8.** Taiyō wa taihén ōkikute móshi sonó chūshin ni chikyū ga irareraté mo sonó shūi[5] wo tsŭkí ga kaitén surú daké no[6] hirói yóchi ga arimásŭ. **9.** Móshi zémbu no nōfu ga jímen no kōsaku ni hiryō wo shiyō surú náraba konó kuní no nōsakubutsu wa sonó zen jūmin[7] no tamé ni jūbun de arō. **10.** Anáta ga móshi mái-asa ni-jíppun guraí taisō wo nasáru[8] náraba mótto jōbu-ni náru deshō ni. **11.** Warewaré wa hatarakanái to séishin ga otoroemásŭ. **12.** Ima anáta wa Nihón ni imásŭ nóde Nihón-go wo benkyō surú nóni[9] go-tsugō[10] ga yói deshō. **13.** Kimí wa sū-ka-kokú no kotobá[11] wo shĭtté irú kará dóko-ka ōki-na kaishá no tsūshingákari ka tsūyaku ka no kuchí wo mitsŭkerú nóni wa tsugō ga yói deshō. **14.** Nihón-go ga yóku hanásetara yói no da ga. Watashí wa Nihón-go de jibún no íken wo iiarawásu nóni máda íkuraka kónnan wo kanjimásŭ[12]. **15.** Anó hĭtó ga tegamí wo yokóseba yói ga. **16.** Anáta ga takú no konná-ni chikáku-ni súnde irassháru kotó wo mótto máe ni shĭtté iréba yókatta nóni. **17.** Konó tegamí wo taipuraitā de úttara súgu-ni mótte kité kudasái. **18.** Anáta ga anó hĭtó ni keikokú sáe shĭté kudasáreba yói nóni. **19.** Konó kikái wa mikaké wa kantán désŭ ga jissaí wa komiitté imásŭ[13]. **20.** Kiitá tokoró ni yoréba[14] kimí wa kokó

---

1 *kanséi ni yarú* to send (somebody) to complete (something)   **2** *sainō ga arimásŭ* talented   **3** *kokó no mawarí ni* around here   **4** *wasuré hajiméru* to begin to forget **5** *sonó shūi* around it (around the earth)   **6** *daké no* as far as   **7** *zen jūmin* all the inhabitants   **8** *taisō wo nasáru* polite form of *taisō wo surú* to do gymnastics. **9** *benkyō surú nóni* to study   **10** *go-tsugō ga yói deshō* it would be well for you **11** *sū-ka-kokú no kotobá* several foreign languages; *sū* several, *ka* numerative for country, *kokú* country, *kotobá* language   **12** *kónnan wo kanjirú* to find difficulties **13** *komí-irú* to be complicated   **14** *ni yoréba* according to; *kiitá tokoró ni yoréba* according to what I have heard

sū-ka-getsú jimúsho no shigotó wo orósoka-ni shǐté irú sō désǔ[1] ne. **21.** Uke-tamawáreba[2] anáta wa jikí ni Nihón wo o-tachí ni náru sō désǔ ne. Hontō désǔ ka.—Hái, hontō désǔ. Ráigetsu Ōshū e ikimásǔ. **22.** Konó bashó mo kawaréba kawattá monó désǔ ne. **23.** Konó kotobá wa yóku benkyō suréba surú hodó náo[3] muzukáshiku narimásǔ.

1. 若しもすべての人がもっと寛大であるならばこの世の中はもっと幸福でしょうに．多くの不幸をつくるのは狭量というものです．**2.** 若し充分のお金があるならば私は娘をイタリーへ音楽研究完成にやるでしょう．娘は声楽に才能がありますから若し有名なイタリーの音楽学校で学ぶならば立派な声楽家になるでしょう．**3.** もっとお金持なら貴方はどうしますか．—変な質問ですね，即答はできません．私は事実私がもっと金持ならどうするだろうと考えた事はありません．若しも私が金持になればその時にその富をどうするかを考えるでしょう．**4.** あの男はいつも貧乏だとこぼしますが若しあの人が本当に貧乏ならばあんな大きな美しい家に住まわないでしょうに．**5.** 若しこの廻りに木がいくらかあればもっと美しく見えるでしょうに．**6.** 若し貴方が日本語を知っているならば私の事務所で通信係に採用するでしょうに．**7.** 私はスペイン語を忘れ始めました．—若し毎日卅分位何かスペイン語の本をお読みになればお忘れにならないでしょう．**8.** 太陽は大変大きくて若しその中心に地球が入れられてもその周囲を月が廻転するだけの広い余地があります．**9.** 若し全部の農夫が地面の耕作に肥料を使用するならばこの国の農作物はその全住民のために充分であろう．**10.** 貴方が若し毎朝廿分位体操をなさるならばもっと丈夫になるでしょうに．**11.** 我々は働かないと精神が衰えます．**12.** 今，貴方は日本にいますので日本語を勉強するのに御都合がよいでしょう．**13.** 君は数ヶ国の言葉を知っているからどこか大きな会社の通信係か通訳かの口を見つけるのには都合がよいでしょう．**14.** 日本語がよく話せたらよいのだが，私は日本語で自分の意見を云い表わすのにまだいくらか困難を感じます．**15.** あの人が手紙をよこせばよいが．**16.** 貴方が宅のこんなに近くに住んでいらっしゃる事をもっと前に知っていればよかったのに．**17.** この手紙をタイプライターで打ったらすぐに持って来て下さい．**18.** 貴方があの人に警告さえして下さればよいのに．**19.** この機械は見掛けは簡単ですが実際は込み入っています．**20.** 聞いた所によれば君はこゝ数か月事務所の仕事をおろそかにしているそうですね．**21.** 承れば貴方はぢきに日本をお立ちになるそうですね．本当ですか．—はい，本当です．来月欧州へ行き

---

1 *irú sō desǔ* you have been (according to what I have heard) **2** *uketama-wáreba* I hear that, I am told that **3** *náo* the more

ます. **22.** この場所も変れば変ったものですね. **23.** この言葉はよく
勉強すればする程なおむづかしくなります.

1. If all people were more tolerant this world would be much happier. It
is intolerance that causes much of our unhappiness. **2.** If I had enough
money I should send my daughter to Italy to complete her study of music.
She has a talent for singing and if she were in one of the famous Italian
conservatories of music she would become a good singer. **3.** What would you
do if you were richer?—This is a strange question and I cannot give you
an immediate answer. I really never thought what I would do if I were
richer. If I become rich then I shall think what to do with my wealth.
4. That man always complains that he is poor, but if he really were poor
he would not live in such a large and beautiful house. **5.** If there were some
trees around this place it would look much more attractive. **6.** If you knew
Japanese I should employ you as correspondent in my office. **7.** I am forgetting all the Spanish I knew.—If you read some Spanish books for half an
hour every day you would not forget it. **8.** The sun is so large that if the
earth were placed in its center, there would be ample room for the moon to
revolve round it inside the sun. **9.** If all farmers used fertilizer in the cultiva-
tion of their land the agricultural produce of this country would be sufficient
for all the inhabitants. **10.** If you did some physical exercise for about twenty
minutes every morning you would become healthier. **11.** If we did not work
our mind would fall into decay. **12.** Now that you are in Japan it would
be well for you to study Japanese. **13.** As you know several foreign languages
it would be well for you to find a position as correspondent or interpreter in
some large firm. **14.** I wish I could speak Japanese well. I still find some
difficulty in expressing my thoughts in Japanese. **15.** If he only would write
to me! **16.** I wish I had known before that you were living so near to my
house. **17.** As soon as you have typewritten these letters bring them to me.
18. If only you had warned him! **19.** To look at this machine it seems
simple but it is really complicated. **20.** Judging from what I have heard,
you have been neglecting your office work for several months. **21.** I hear
that you will soon leave Japan; is it true?—Yes, it is true; I shall go to
Europe next month. **22.** How this place has changed! **23.** The more diligently
I study this language the more difficult I find it.

Forty-ninth Lesson 第四十九課

Subjunctive (continued)
Present Perfect and Past Perfect

The present and past perfect of the English subjunctive have a common conjugation in Japanese.

N. B. For the sake of grammatical explanations we shall call this conjugation **subjunctive past,** even though it is used to translate both the *present* and *past perfect* of the English subjunctive mood.

To Have *mótsu* 持つ

Positive	**Negative**
if I have (had) had	if I have (had) not had
......*wo mótte itá nára(ba)*	......*wo mótte inákatta nára(ba)*
......を 持っていた なら（ば）	......を 持っていなかったなら（ば）
......*wo mótte itá to suréba*	......*wo mótte inákatta to suréba*
......を 持っていた と すれば	......を 持っていなかったと すれば
......*ga átta náraba*	......*ga nákatta nára (ba)*
......があった ならば	......がなかった なら（ば）

Polite Form

......*wo o-mochí ni nátte itá nára (ba)*	......*wo o-mochí ni nátte inákatta nára (ba)*
......を お持ちになっていたなら（ば）	......をお持ちになっていなかったなら（ば）
......*wo mótte oráreta[1] nára(ba)*	......*wo mótte orárénakatta nára(ba)*
......を 持っておられた なら（ば）	......を 持っておられなかったなら（ば）

To Be *de áru* である

if I have (had) been	if I have (had) not been
......*de arimáshĭta nára(ba)*	......*de arimasén déshĭta nára(ba)*
......でありました なら（ば）	......でありませんでした なら（ば）
......*de arimáshĭta to suréba*	......*de arimasén déshĭta to suréba*
......でありました と すれば	......でありませんでした と すれば
......*de átta[2] nára(ba)*	......*de nákatta nára(ba)*
......であった なら（ば）	......でなかった なら（ば）
......*de átta to suréba*	......*de nákatta to suréba*
......であったと すれば	......でなかった と すれば
......*dáttara* ......だったら	......*de nákattara* ......でなかったら

---

1 *oráreta* is used instead of *itá* in polite speech—The conjugation with *oráreta* is about as polite as the one with the verb preceded by the honorific **o** **2** *de átta* may be contracted in **dátta**

Polite Form

......*de gozaimáshĭta nára(ba)* 　　　　......*de gozaimasén déshĭta nára(ba)*
......で 御座いました なら（ば）　　　　......で御座いませんでした なら（ば）

There To Be　*ga áru* がある

if there has (had) been　　　　　　if there has (had) not been
......*ga arimáshĭta nára(ba)* 　　　　......*ga arimasén déshĭta nára(ba)*
......が ありました なら（ば）　　　　......がありません でした なら（ば）
......*ga arimáshĭta to suréba* 　　　　......*ga arimasén déshĭta to suréba*
......が ありました と すれば　　　　......がありません でした と すれば
......*ga átta nára(ba)* 　　　　　　......*ga nákatta nára(ba)*
......があったなら（ば）　　　　　　......がなかった なら（ば）
......*ga átta to suréba* 　　　　　　......*ga nákatta to suréba*
......があったと すれば　　　　　　......がなかった と すれば

Polite Form

......*ga gozaimáshĭta nára(ba)* 　　　　......*ga gozaimasén déshĭta nára(ba)*
......が 御座いました なら（ば）　　　　......が御座いませんでした なら（ば）

To Do　*surú* する

if I have (had) done　　　　　　　if I have (had) not done
shimáshĭta nára(ba) 　　　　　　*shimasén déshĭta nára(ba)*
しました なら（ば）　　　　　　しません でした なら（ば）
shimáshĭtara しましたら　　　　　　*shimasén déshĭtara* しませんでしたら
shĭtá nára(ba) したなら(ば)　　　　*shinákatta nára (ba)* しなかったなら(ば)
shĭtára したら　　　　　　　　*shinákattara* しなかったら

Polite Form

nasaimáshĭta nára (ba) 　　　　　*nasaimasén déshĭta nára (ba)*
なさいましたなら（ば）　　　　　なさいませんでした なら（ば）

To work　*hatarakú* 仂く

if I have (had) worked　　　　　　if I have (had) not worked
hatarakimáshĭta nára(ba) 　　　　*hatarakimasén déshĭta nára(ba)*
仂きました　なら(ば)　　　　　仂きません　でした なら(ば)
hataraitá nára(ba) 　　　　　　*hataraká-nákatta nára(ba)*
仂いた　なら(ば)　　　　　　仂かなかった　なら(ば)
hataraité itá nára(ba) 　　　　　*hataraité inákatta nára(ba)*
仂いて いた なら(ば)　　　　　仂いて いなかったなら(ば)
hatarakimáshĭtara 　　　　　　*hatarakimasén déshĭtara*
仂きましたら　　　　　　　　仂きません　でしたら
hataraitára(ba) 　　　　　　　*hataraká-nákattara(ba)*
仂いたら（ば）　　　　　　　仂かなかったら（ば）

Polite Form

o-hataraki ni narimáshĭta nára (ba)　　*o-hataraki ni narimasén déshĭta nára (ba)*
お仂き に なりました なら（ば）　　お仂き に なりませんでした なら（ば）

Subjunctive Perfect of True Adjective

if it has (had) been cold if I have (had) been cold	if it has (had) not been cold if I have (had) not been cold
sámuku arimáshĭtara(ba) 寒く ありましたら（ば）	*sámuku arimasén déshĭtara(ba)* 寒く ありません でしたら（ば）
sámukatta nára(ba) 寒かった なら（ば）	*sámuku nákatta nára(ba)* 寒く なかった なら（ば）
sámukattanara(ba) 寒かったなら（ば）	*sámuku nákattara(ba)* 寒く なかったら（ば）

Polite Form

o-samū gozaimáshĭta nára (ba) お寒う 御座いました なら（ば）	*o-samū gozaimasén déshĭta nára (ba)* お寒う御座いません でした なら（ば）
o-samukattára (ba) お寒かったら（ば）	*o-samukú nákattara (ba)* お寒く なかったら（ば）

Conditional Past Perfect

To Have   *mótsu* 持つ

I should have had	I should not have had
mótte itá deshō (ni) 持っていたでしよう（に）	*mótte inákatta deshō (ni)* 持っていなかったでしよう（に）
mótte itá de arō (ni) 持っていた であろう（に）	*mótte inákatta de arō (ni)* 持っていなかったであろう（に）
mótte itá darō (ni) 持っていただろう（に）	*mótte inákatta darō (ni)* 持っていなかっただろう（に）

Polite Form

o-mochí ni nátte itá deshō (ni) お持ち になっていたでしよう（に）	*o-mochí ni naránakatta deshō (ni)* お持ち に ならなかったでしよう（に）

To Be *de áru* である

I should have been	I should not have been
de átta deshō (ni) であったでしよう（に）	*de nákatta deshō (ni)* で なかったでしよう（に）
de átta darō (ni) であっただろう（に）	*de nákatta darō (ni)* で なかった だろう（に）
de áttarō (ni) であったろう（に）	*de nákattarō (ni)* でなかったろう（に）

Polite Form

de gozaimáshĭta deshō (ni) で 御座いましたでしよう（に）	*de gozaimasén déshĭta deshō (ni)* で 御座いませんでしたでしよう（に）

There To Be *áru* ある

there would have been	there would not have been
átta deshō (ni) あったでしよう(に)	*nákatta deshō (ni)* なかったでしよう(に)
átta de arō (ni) あったであろう(に)	*nákatta de arō (ni)* なかったであろう(に)
átta darō (ni) あっただろう(に)	*nákatta darō (ni)* なかっただろう(に)
áttarō (ni) あったろう(に)	*nákattarō (ni)* なかったろう(に)

Polite Form

gozaimashĭta deshō (ni) 御座いましたでしよう(に)	*gozaimasén déshĭta deshō (ni)* 御座いませんでしたでしよう(に)

To Do *surú* する

I should have done you would have done, etc.	I should not have done you would not have done, etc.
shimáshĭta deshō (ni) しましたでしよう(に)	*shimasén déshĭta deshō (ni)* しません でしたでしよう(に)
shĭtá deshō (ni) したでしよう(に)	*shinákatta deshō (ni)* しなかったでしよう(に)
shĭtá de arō (ni) した であろう(に)	*shinákatta de arō (ni)* しなかった であろう(に)
shĭtá darō (ni) した だろう(に)	*shinákatta darō (ni)* しなかっただろう(に)

Polite Form

nasaimáshĭta deshō (ni) なさいましたでしよう(に)	*nasaimasén déshĭta deshō (ni)* なさいませんでしたでしよう(に)

To Work *hatarakú* 仂く

I should have worked you would have worked, etc.	I should not have worked you would not have worked, etc.
hatarakimáshĭta deshō (ni) 仂きました でしよう(に)	*hatarakimasén déshĭta deshō (ni)* 仂きません でしたでしよう(に)
hatarakimáshĭta darō (ni) 仂きました だろう(に)	*hatarakimasén déshĭta darō (ni)* 仂きません でした だろう(に)
hataraitá deshō (ni) 仂いた でしよう(に)	*hataraká-nákatta deshō (ni)* 仂かなかった でしよう(に)
hataraitá darō (ni) 仂いた だろう(に)	*hataraká-nákatta darō (ni)* 仂かなかった だろう(に)

Polite Form

o-hatarakí ni narimáshĭta deshō (ni) お仂き になりましたでしよう(に)	*o-hatarakí ni narimasén déshĭta deshō (ni)* お仂き になりませんでしたでしよう(に)
o-hatarakí ni nátta deshō (ni) お仂き になったでしよう(に)	*o-hatarakí ni naránakatta deshō (ni)* お仂き に ならなかったでしよう(に)

Conditional Past Perfect of True Adjectives

it would have been cold I should have been cold, etc.	it would not have been cold I should not have been cold, etc.
sámukatta deshō (*ni*) 寒かった でしよう(に)	*sámuku nákatta deshō* (*ni*) 寒く なかったでしよう(に)
sámukatta darō (*ni*) 寒かった だろう(に)	*sámuku nákatta darō* (*ni*) 寒く なかっただろう(に)
sámukattarō (*ni*) 寒かったろう(に)	*sámuku nákattarō* (*ni*) 寒く なかったろう(に)

Polite Form

o-samū gozaimáshĭta deshō (*ni*) お寒う 御座いましたでしよう(に)	*o-samū gozaimasén déshĭta deshō* (*ni*) お寒う 御座いません でしたでしよう(に)
o-samukattá deshō (*ni*) お寒かったでしよう(に)	*o-samukú nákatta deshō* (*ni*) お寒く なかったでしよう(に)

Examples

*Móshi watashí ga mótto o-kané wo **mótte itá náraba** anó yōkandate-*
若し　私　がもっと　お金　を　持って いた　ならば　あの　洋館建
*káoku[1] wo **kattá deshō ni.***   If I had had more money I should have
家屋　を　買った でしよう に.   bought that foreign-style house.

*Móshi watashí ga mō ni-ka-getsú nágaku Parí ni **orimáshĭta náraba***
若し　私　がもう　二ヶ月　長く　巴里に　おりました　ならば
*Kokusaí Bíjitsu Tenrankái wo **mita deshō ni.***
国際　美術　展覧会　を　見た でしよう に.
If I had been in Paris two months longer I should have seen the International Art Exhibition.

*Bóku ga kimí **dátta to shĭtára** sonó jidōsha wo **kawá-nákatta deshō.***
僕　が　君　だったと　したら　その　自動車　を　買わなかったでしよう.
If I had been you I should not have bought that motor-car.

*Anó yakaí[2] ni mótto takŭsán o-kyakŭsamá ga **itá náraba** mótto*
あの 夜会 に もっと 沢山　お客様　が いた ならば もっと
omoshírokatta deshō ni.   If there had been more guests the evening party
面白かった でしよう に.   would have been more interesting.

*Anáta ga Ōsaka ni irasshátta kotó wo **shĭtté orimáshĭta náraba***
貴方　が　大阪　にいらっしやった事　を　知って　おりました　ならば
*o-tegamí wo **dáshĭte itá deshō ni.***
お手紙　を　出して いたでしよう に.
If I had known that you were in Osaka I should have sent a letter to you.

*Móshi anáta ga gakkō de kimbén **dátta náraba** konó mondaí wo*
若し　貴方　が　学校　で　勤勉　だった　ならば　この　問題　を
wakátta deshō ni.   If you had been more diligent at school you would
わかった でしよう に.   have understood this exercise.

---

1 *yōkandate-káoku* foreign-style house   **2** evening party

*Anáta wa wakái tokí ni yóku benkyō **shĭté itá náraba** íma wa*
貴方 は 若い 時 に よく 勉強 して いた ならば 今 は
*yói íchi[1] ga **eráreta deshō ni.***
よい 位置 が 得られた でしよう に.

If you had studied well when you were young you would now have a good
position. (*eráreta* past of *eráreru* passive of *éru* 得る to get, to obtain, to
acquire) (*lit.* You, young when, well study if you had done, now good position would have been acquired.—acquired for you, to your advantage, etc.,
is here understood.)

*O-ténki ga **yókatta náraba** Fújisan no chōjō[2] e tassúru[3] kotó ga*
お天気 が よかった ならば 富士山 の 頂上 へ 達する 事 が
dekimáshĭtarō ni. If the weather had been fine we could have reached
出来ましたろう に. the top of Mount Fuji.

In Japanese the past subjunctive is often used for the present, and
vice versa, and likewise the forms given for the past and the past
perfect of the conditional often do not correspond to the tenses used
in the corresponding English translation.

Were we to explain the use of these tenses in every particular
case, the explanations would rather confuse the mind of the student.
It is only by practice that one can imitate the Japanese in using
them with assurance. Therefore, until that practice is acquired, we
advise the student to use the tenses of the subjunctive and conditional
according to the rules given in these last three lessons, which will
enable him to avoid mistakes.

For the sake of illustration we shall give below some examples in which
the tenses used in the Japanese sentence and in the English translation do
not correspond.

*Móshi Tanaka San ni **átta náraba** yoroshikú[4] itté kudasái.*
若し 田中 さん に 会った ならば よろしく 云って下さい.
If you meet Mr. Tanaka give him my best regards.

*Empitsú ga mótto **hóshĭkattara** sonó hikidashí ni takŭsán háitte imásŭ.*
鉛筆 が もっと 欲しかったら その 引出し に 沢山 入っています.
If you want more pencils there are plenty in that drawer.

*Móshi kyūkō ni **maniawá-nákattara**[5] jidōsha de ikú hō ga yoroshíi deshō.*
若し 急行 に 間に合わなかったら 自動車で行く方がよろしいでしょう.
If you do not catch the express train you had better go by motor-car.

*Kyō móshi áme ga **furá-nákatta náraba** tomodachí ga ái ni kúru*
きょう若し 雨 が 降らなかった ならば 友達 が 会いに 来る
darō ni. If it did not rain our friend would come to see us to-day. (*fúru*
だろう に. 降る to fall, to come down; *áme ga fúru* 雨が降る to rain)

---

1 position, situation **2** top (of a mountain) **3** to reach **4** The word *yoroshikú,*
which means *well,* is the adverbial form of *yoroshíi,* a synonym of *yói* and * íi.*
Yoroshikú is frequently used for sending or giving greetings. *Dōzo, Miwatá San ni
yoroshikú itté kudasái.* Please remember me to Mr. Miwata, *or* Please give my best
regards to Mr. Miwata. The expression *itté kudasái* is often omitted: *Mínasan ni
yoroshikú.* Remember me to everybody. *Yanái San ga yoroshikú to osshaimáshĭta*
Mr. Yanai wished to be remembered to you. **5** *maniáu* 間に合う to be in time for
(a train, etc.)

Should

When **should** has the idea of moral obligation it is translated like *ought,* that is, by adding to the simple present of the verb one of the expressions *béki* べき, *hazú* 筈, or *béki hazú* べき筈, followed by *désŭ* です or *de wa nái* ではない, according to whether the verb is used in the positive or negative form.

De arimásŭ であります and *de wa arimasén* ではありませ ん are used, in polite speech, instead of *désŭ* and *de wa nái.*

> *Watashí wa íma ginkō ni **yukú-béki** (**hazú**) **désŭ** ga jikán ga arimasén.*
> 私　は　今　銀行　に　行くべき　（筈）　です　が　時間がありません.
> I **should** go to the bank, but I have no time.

When **now,** as in the above example, or a word referring to the future, is used in the clause containing *should,* the present of *to be* is placed after *béki,* but if one uses a word indicating a period of time that is still in progress, as *this morning, to-day,* etc., then either the present or the past of *to be* may be used, and if the word indicating time refers to the past, the past tense of *to be* should be used.

> *Watashí wa ashĭtá ginkō ni yukú-**béki** **hazú** **désŭ** ga jikán ga nái*
> 私　は　あした　銀行　に　行くべき　筈　です　が　時間　がない
> *kará yamemashō.* To-morrow I **should** go to the bank, but as I shall not have
> から止めましよう。 time I shall give up going.

> *Watashí wa késa ginkō ni yukú-**béki** **hazú** **déshĭta** (or *désŭ*) ga jikán*
> 私　は　けさ　銀行　に　行くべき　筈　でした　（です）が　時間
> *ga mō nái kará yamemásŭ.* This morning I **should** go to the bank, but as
> が　もうない　から　止めます。 I have no time now I shall give up going.

> *Watashí wa kinō ginkō ni yukú-**béki** **hazú** **déshĭta** ga jikán ga*
> 私　は　きのう　銀行　に　行くべき　筈　でした　が　時間　が
> *arimasén déshĭta kará yamemáshĭta.*
> ありませんでした　から　止めました。
> Yesterday I **should have** gone to the bank, but as I had no time I gave up going.

In place of *béki, hazú,* or *béki hazú* one may use the word *no* の

> *Watashí wa késa ginkō ni yukú **no** déshĭta ga jikán ga arimasén*
> 私　は　けさ　銀行　に　行く　の　でした　が　時間　がありません
> *kará yamemásŭ.* This morning I **should** go to the bank, but as I have no
> から　止めます。 time I give it up.

The expressions *béki, hazú,* or *béki hazú* are also used when *should* is in the negative form.

> *Késa anáta wa háisha ni yukú **no** (or yukú-béki, yukú-béki hazú)*
> けさ　貴方　は　歯医者　に　行く　の　（行くべき，行くべき　筈）
> *de wa **nákatta** (or **nái**) no désŭ ka.* **Should** you **not** go to the dentist
> で　は　なかった　（ない）　の　です　か. this morning?

Kyō gakkō ni **yukú-béki** (or **yukú-béki hazŭ**) *de wa nái no désŭ ka.*
きょう学校 に 行くべき 　（行くべき 　筈） で は ないの です か.
Should you **not go** to school to-day?

Kodomó wa yóru sonná ni osokú **kitakú**[1] **su-béki de wa nái.**
子供 は 夜 そんな に 遅く 帰宅 　すべき で は ない.
Our children **should not come back** home so late at night.

Kimí wa jimúsho e sonná ni osokú **kúru hazú de wa nái.**
君 は 事務所 へそんな に 遅く 来る 筈 で は ない.
You **should not come** to the office so late.

Watashí wa anná zeitakú-na[2] *kimonó wo* **kaú hazú de wa arimasén**
私 はあんな 贅沢 な 着物 を 買う 筈 で は ありません
déshĭta ga amari kírei déshĭta nóde katté shimaimáshĭta.
でした が 余り きれい でした ので 買って しまいました.
I **should not have bought** such an expensive kimono, but it was so pretty that
I bought it at last. (*lit.* I such expensive kimono, to buy should have not,
but too beautiful was because, buying I ended by.)

When *should* in the negative, instead of indicating strong obligation, refers more to convenience, as to something which should not
be done, then besides **béki** one may use the verb in the negative,
followed by **hō ga ii** 方がいゝ (*lit.* the way is good).

Yakú ni tatánu[3] *monó wo* **kaú-béki de wa arimasén.**
役 に 立たぬ 物 を 買うべき で は ありません.
Useless things should not be bought. *or* We **should not buy** useless things.

or *Yakú ni tatánu monó wo* **kawanái hō ga íi.**
役 に 立たぬ 物 を 買わない 方 が いい.
(*lit.* Useless things not to buy the way is good.=We shouldn't buy useless
things.)

Would

When **would** indicates volition, it is translated by the future if in
English it may be replaced by *will* without prejudice to the meaning
of the sentence.

Móshi watashí ga konó jidōsha wo gojū-man yen de teikyō suréba **o-kai**
若し 私 がこの 自動車 を 五十万 円 で 提供 すればお買い
ni náru deshō ka. **Would you buy** this motor-car if I offered to sell it to
に なる でしようか. you for 500,000 yen?—*teikyō surú* 提供する to offer
(*lit.* If I, this motor-car 500,000 yen for, offer if I do, would you buy?)

Kaú deshō. 買うでしよう. Yes, I **would buy** it.

When **would** indicates intention it is translated by **tsumori** つも
り or **ki** 気. **Tsumori** つもり, means *intention*.

---

1 *kitakú surú* to return home   **2** *zeitakú-na* expensive, luxurious, sumptuous, lavish
3 *yakú ni tátsu* to be of use; *yakú* use; *yakú ni* for use; *tatánu* negative of *tátsu*;
yakú ni tatánu useless

Móshi kimí ga hatarakú **tsumorí** (or *ki*) *náraba konó shi de shokugyō*
若し　君　が　仂く　　つもり　　（気）ならば　この　市　で　　転業
wo mitsŭkerú kotó ga dekíru deshō ni.   If you **would** work you could find
を　見つける　事　が　出来るでしよう に.   a position in this city.
       (*lit.* If you, to work intention if had, this city in, a position to find, the thing
       could.)

Móshi Furukawá San ga go-jibún no uchí wo urú **tsumorí** (*ki*) *náraba*
若し　　古川　さんが　御自分　の　家　を　売る　つもり　（気）ならば
takŭsán no hĭtó ga kaitagáru deshō ni.
沢山　の　人　が　買いたがるでしよう に.
       If Mr. Furukawa **would** offer his house for sale, a great many people would
       like to buy it.

When **would** indicates habit it is translated by the expression
kotó mo áru, placed after a verb in the simple present.

Anó otokó wa shōgi wo sáshĭte sū-jikán sugósu ***kotó mo arimásŭ.***
あの　男　は　将棋　を　差して　数時間　すごす　事　も　あります.
       That man **would** spend whole hours playing chess.
       (That man, chess playing, several hours to spend the fact even there is.)

The expression **Would you mind if**......, used to ask a person's
consent for doing something, is generally rendered by the subordinate
of the verb that follows such an expression and ***mo kamaimasén
ka*** placed immediately after.

Tabakó wo ***nónde mo kamaimasén ka.***   Would you mind if I smoke?
タバコ　を　のんで　も　かまいません　か.   Would you mind my smoking?
       (*lit.* Tobacco, smoking even, don't you mind?—*kamáu* かまう to mind, to
       care about, to be concerned about, to give heed to, etc.)

Mádo wo ***aketé mo kamaimasén ka.***   Would you mind if I open
窓　を　開けて　も　かまいません　か.   the window?
       (*lit.* The window, opening even, don't you mind?)

When, however, the action is supposed to be performed by the
person spoken to, a different construction is necessary, as in such
sentences like the following one:

Dōzo, mō ichí-do kurikaeshĭté ***itadakemasén ka.***   Would you mind
どうぞ,　もう　一度　くりかえして　頂けません　か.   repeating it?
       (*lit.* Please, again one time, repeating don't you oblige me?—*kurikaesú* く
       りかえす to repeat, to do—something—over again, etc.)

Vocabulary

	Nouns				
			discovery	*hakkén*	発見
chess	*shōgi*	将棋	drawer	*hikidashí*	引出
crowd	*gunshū*	群集	education	*kyōiku*	教育
criminal	*hánnin*	犯人	environment	*kyōgū*	境遇

exception	*reigái*	例外	peevish	*okorippói*	怒リッポイ
genius	*tensái*	天才	unknown	*míchi*	未知
knowledge	*chíshiki*	知識	**Verbs**		
male servant	*kyūji*	給仕	to acquire	*é·ru*	得ル
measles	*hashĭká*	ハシカ	to encounter	*deaú*	出会ウ
patient	*kanjá*	患者	to follow	*shĭtagáu*	従ウ
predicament	*kukyō*	苦境	to go around	*megurú*	廻ル
savage	*yabanjín*	野蛮人	to hide	{ *himé·ru*	秘メル
top	*chōjō*	頂上		*kakúsu*	隠ス
Adjectives			to judge	*handán surú*	判断スル
imbecile	*teinō-na*	低能ナ	to repeat	*kurikaesú*	クリカエス
instructive	*yūeki-na*	有益ナ	to survive	*seizán surú*	生キ残スル

extensive travels *dái ryokō*; learned person *gakŭshá*; unhappiness, misery *fukō*; general manager *sō-shiháinin*; to lynch *shikéi ni surú*; position, situation, circumstance *tachibá*; to escape, to get away, to get out of, to get rid of *nogaréru*; the best, the highest good *saizén*; to develop *hattatsú surú*; to bring up, to breed, to rear *sodatéru*; to take a rest *yasúmu*; to reach, to arrive *tōchaku surú*; character, disposition *seishitsú*; to predominate *kachí wo séi surú*; to play chess *shōgi wo sásu*

Exercise   *Renshū*   練習

1. Móshi ningén ni ōki-na fúne ga nákatta náraba konó sekái no sū-ka-sho[1] wa máda warewaré ni míchi[2] de átta deshō. Hĭtó wa ōki-na fúne wo tsŭkúru kotó ga dékita tokí ni yattó[3] sekái wo megurú hakkén no dái ryokō wo hajimetá no de arimáshĭta. **2.** Móshi watashí ga chiisái tokí ni koréra no yūeki-na hon ga átta náraba watashí wa íma gakŭshá ni nátte itá deshō ni. Watashí wa chiisái tokí ni chíshiki wo étakatta no déshĭta ga fukō-ni shĭté[4] amarí yūeki-na hon wo mótte imasén déshĭta. **3.** Sakúban kimí wa warewaré to isshó-ni ótta náraba uchí no kaishá no sō-shiháinin ni o-me ni kakátta deshō ni. Sō-shiháinin wa késa Shanhái e o-tachí ni nátte shimaimáshĭta. **4.** Móshi asokó ni jūbun no keikán ga inákatta náraba gunshū wa hánnin wo shikéi ni shóshĭta[5] deshō ni. **5.** Móshi watashí wa anáta no go-chūkoku ni shĭtagátte itá náraba íma konná kurushíi tachibá[6] ni wa naránakatta deshō ni.—Anáta ga shinákatta kotó wo ímasara[7] kangáete mo shĭkatá ga arimasén. Ima wa anáta no kukyō kará nogaréru ni wa náni wo suréba saizén de áru ka wo kangáeru béki désŭ. **6.** Móshi mo ishá ga maniáu jikán[8] ni kónakatta nára anó kanjá wa táshĭka-ni shindá deshō. **7.** Súbete no hĭtó wa taitéi

---

1 *sū-ka-sho* several parts; *sū* several, *ka* numerative, *sho* abbreviation of *bashó* place, part   **2** *míchi de áru* to be unknown, *míchi* unknown, strange   **3** *yattó* only, just   **4** *fukō-ni shĭté* unfortunately   **5** *shikéi ni shósu* used in formal speech instead of *shikéi ni surú* to lynch   **6** *kurushíi* painful; *kurushíi tachibá* a trying position, situation   **7** *Imasara* may be used to translate the expressions *now, no longer,* and *after so long a time,* whenever they refer to something that is or seems too late to do or alter.   **8** *maniáu jikán* in time

onají guraí no chinō wo mótte umareté kimásŭ. Warewaré no chinō wo chigattá téido ni hattatsú[1] saséru no wa kyōiku to kyōgū to de arimásŭ. Móshi warewaré ga yabanjín no náka de sodateráreta[2] náraba warewaré no chinō wa yabanjín no chinō wo ryōga[3] shinái deshō. Móshi reigái ga áru to suréba soré wa tensái to téinō désŭ. **8.** Watashí wa tsŭkaremáshĭta kará yasumimashō. Watashí no neté irú aidá ni móshi dáre-ka kimáshĭta náraba rúsu désŭ to itté kudasái. **9.** Mótto kamí ga o-iriyō náraba kyūji wo o-yobí kudasái. Sō suréba kyūji wa mótto mótte mairimásŭ. **10.** Móshi yukí ga furánakatta náraba watashitachí wa kyō no gógo anó yamá no chōjō ni tōchaku surú kotó ga dékita deshō ni. **11.** Watashí wa kómban tegamí wo káku hazú désŭ ga zutsū ga sŭkóshi shimásŭ kará netái no désŭ. Myōnichi kaki-mashō. **12.** Hikawá Marú wa kinō Yokohamá ni tsŭkú hazú déshĭta ga kōkai-chū[4] tsuyói árashi ni deaimáshĭta tamé ni yūgata máe ni wa nyūkō[5] shinái deshō. **13.** Anáta wa Fukúi San no okŭsán no tokoró e itté wa ikemasén. Anó katá no kodomosán ga hashĭká[6] wo shĭté imásŭ kará móshi anáta ga anó katá no o-takú e ukagaú náraba kansén[7] surú ka-mo shiremasén. **14.** Hĭtó no mikaké de hĭtó wo handán shĭté wa narimasén. Tokí ni yoréba[8] iyá-na kaó de mo shínsetsu-na seishitsú wo hímete óri shínsetsu-sō-na[9] kaó ga taihén okorippói seishitsú wo kakushĭté irú ka-mo shiremasén. **15.** Káita monó wa nan de mo yóku kurikaeshĭté yómu shūkan wo tsŭkurubéki désŭ. **16.** Móshi anáta ga anó katá no tokoró e itté o-mé ni kakáru náraba anó katá wa kittó anáta wo tasŭkéte kudasáru deshō. **17.** Jínrui no rekishí ni óite[10] zen wa yūsei wo shímete irú, jíjitsu,[11] móshi sō de nákatta to suréba bumméi wa seizán shinákatta de arō.

1. 若し人間に大きな船が無かったならばこの世界の数ヶ所はまだ我々に未知であったでしょう．人は大きな船を造る事が出来た時にやっと世界を廻る発見の大旅行をはじめたのでありました．**2.** 若し私が小さい時にこれ等の有益な本があったならば私は今，学者になっていたでしょうに．私は小さい時に知識を得たかったのでしたが不幸にして余り有益な本を持っていませんでした．**3.** 昨晩，君は我々と一緒におったならばうちの会社の総支配人に御目にかゝったでしょうに．総支配人はけさ，上海へお立ちになってしまいました．**4.** 若しあそこに充分の警官がいなかったならば群集は犯人を私刑に処したでしょうに．**5.** 若し私は貴方の御忠告に従っていたならば今こんな苦しい立場にはならなかったでしょうに．—貴方がしなかった事を今更考えても仕方がありません．今は貴方の苦境から逃れるには何をすれば最善であるかを考えるべきです．**6.** 若しも医者が間に合う時間に来

---

1 *téido* degree, extent, measure; *hattatsú saséru* to cause to develop 2 *sodate-raréru* to be brought up 3 *ryōga surú* to surpass; *ryōga shinái deshō* would not be above 4 *kōkai-chū* during her voyage, on her way; *kōkai* voyage, *chū* during 5 *nyūkō surú* to enter a port 6 *hashiká wo surú* to have the measles 7 *kansén surú* to catch (a disease) 8 *tokí ni yoréba* sometimes 9 *shínsetsu-sō-na* kind-looking 10 *ni óite* in (in formal speech) 11 *jíjitsu* indeed

なかったならばあの患者はたしかに死んだでしょう．　**7.** すべての人は大抵同じ位の知能を持って生れて来ます．我々の知能を違った程度に発達させるのは教育と境遇とであります．若し我々が野蛮人の中で育てられたならば我々の知能は野蛮人の知能を凌駕しないでしょう．若し例外があるとすればそれは天才と低能です．　**8.** 私は疲れましたから休みましょう．私の寝ている間に若し誰か来ましたならば留守ですと言って下さい．　**9.** もっと紙がお入用ならば給仕をお呼び下さい．そうすれば給仕はもっと持って参ります．　**10.** 若し雪が降らなかったならば私達はきょうの午後あの山の頂上に到着する事が出来たでしょうに．　**11.** 私は今晩手紙を書く筈ですが頭痛が少ししますから寝たいのです．明日書きましょう．　**12.** 氷川丸はきのう横浜に着く筈でしたが航海中強い嵐に出合いましたために夕方前には入港しないでしょう．**13.** 貴方は福井さんの奥さんの所へ行ってはいけません．あの方の子供さんがはしかをしていますから若し貴方があの方のお宅へ伺うならば感染するかもしれません．　**14.** 人の見掛けで人を判断してはなりません．時によればいやな顔でも親切な性質を秘めており親切そうな顔が大変怒りっぽい性質をかくしているかもしれません．　**15.** 書いた物は何んでもよく繰りかえして読む習慣を作るべきです．　**16.** 若し貴方があの方の所へ行ってお目にかゝるならばあの方はきっと貴方を助けて下さるでしょう．　**17.** 人類の歴史に於いて善は優勢を占めている，事実，若しそうでなかったとすれば文明は生残しなかったであろう．

1. If man had not had large ships several parts of the world would still be unknown to us. It was only when man could build large ships that he began his extensive travels of discovery around the world. **2.** If I had had all these instructive books when I was a boy I should be a learned man now. When I was a boy I liked to acquire knowledge, but unfortunately I had very few instructive books to read. **3.** If you had been with us last night you would have met the general manager of our company. He left this morning for Shanghai. **4.** If there had not been enough policeman the crowd would have lynched the criminal. **5.** If I had followed your advice I should not now be in such a trying position.—It's no use thinking of what you did not do; you should now think of what is best to do to get out of your predicament. **6.** If the doctor had not come in time the patient would certainly have died. **7.** All people are born with more or less the same degree of intelligence. It is education and the environment in which we live that develops our intelligence to different degrees. If we had been brought up among savages our intelligence would not be above that of savages. When there are exceptions we have the genius or the imbecile. **8.** I am tired; I am going to take a rest. If somebody comes while I am sleeping say that I am out. **9.** If you need more paper call the boy and he will bring you more. **10.** If it had not snowed we could reach the top of the mountain this afternoon. **11.** I should write some letters to-night, but as I have a slight headache and wish to go to bed, I shall write them to-morrow. **12.** The Hikawa Maru should have arrived at Yokohama yesterday, but on account of heavy storms which she encountered on her way she will not arrive in port before evening. **13.** You shouldn't go to Mrs. Fukui's. Her children have the measles and you might catch them if you go to her house. **14.** We should not judge people by their appearance. Sometimes a disagreeable face may hide a kind character, while a kind-looking face may conceal the most peevish disposition. **15.** We should make it a practice to read and re-read everything that we write. **16.** If you would go to see him I am sure that he would help you. **17.** In the history of mankind it is the good that predominates; indeed, if it had not been so civilization would not have survived.

Fiftieth Lesson 第五十課

Passive Voice *Judō-tai* 受_{ジュ}動_{ドウ}態_{タイ}

The passive voice is formed by adding **areru** to the simple present of the verbs of Class I after dropping the termination **u,** and to the simple (consonant) stem of verbs of Class II.

Note that the suffix *areru* has the stress on its final *u* (*arerú*) when preceded by a verb whose simple present is stressed on its last syllable, while the stress falls on the *e* of the said suffix (*aréru*) when it is in combination with verbs whose simple present has the stress on its second last syllable, as shown below.

See *phonetic rule*, Page 688.

Class I

míru	見る	*mir*	*miraréru*	見られる	to be seen, watched
tabéru	食べる	*taber*	*taberaréru*	食べられる	to be eaten

Class II

1.	*káku*	書く	*kak*	*kakaréru*	書かれる	to be written
2.	*korosú*	殺す	*koros*	*korosarerú*	殺される	to be killed
3.	*mátsu*	待つ	*mat*	*mataréru*	待たれる	to be waited for
4.	*nusúmu*	盗む	*nusum*	*nusumaréru*	盗まれる	to be robbed
5.	*shikarú*	叱る	*shikar*	*shikararerú*	叱られる	to be scolded
6.	*kiraú*	嫌う	*kiraw*	*kirawarerú*	嫌われる	to be disliked

Verbs of *group 3*, as **mátsu**, drop the final letters **su**, and verbs of *group 6*, as **kiraú**, change the termination **u** into **w**, before adding *areru*.

The termination **areru** is derived from **ar**, the simple stem of **aru** *there is*, and the verb **eru** *to get*, so that **taberaréru** literally means *to get the being eaten* or *to get an eating*, that is, the active for *to get eaten* or *to be eaten*. Thus the Japanese passive verb corresponds to certain idioms used in English, as in the expressions *to get a beating*, *to get a scolding*, instead of *to be beaten*, *to be scolded*.

Passive Conjugation

The conjugation of passive verbs in **areru** is formed according to the rules given for the conjugation of the verbs of Class I.

Indicative

Present

miraremásŭ 見られます	⎱ I am seen	*miraremasén* 見られません	⎱ I am not seen
miraréru 見られる	⎰ I am watched	*mirarénai* 見られない	⎰ I am not watched

Past

miraremáshĭta 見られました	⎫ I was seen	*miraremasén déshĭta* 見られませんでした	⎫ I was not seen
miráreta 見られた	⎬ I have been seen / I had been seen	*miraré-nákatta* 見られなかった	⎬ I have (or had) not been seen

Future

I shall be seen	I shall not be seen
miraremashō 見られましよう	*miraremasén deshō* 見られませんでしよう
miraréru deshō (darō) 見られるでしよう(だろう)	*mirarénai déshō (darō)* 見られないでしよう(だろう)

Subjunctive

Present

if I am (were) seen	if I am (were) not seen
miraremásŭ nára(ba) 見られます なら (ば)	*miraremasén nára(ba)* 見られません なら (ば)
miraréru nára(ba) 見られる なら (ば)	*mirarénai nára(ba)* 見られない なら (ば)
miraráre (ba) 見られれ(ば)	*miraré-nákereba* 見られなけれ(ば)
miraréru to 見られると	*mirarénai to* 見られないと

if I am (were) seen

miraréru to suréba 見られるとすれば

mirárete irú to 見られていると

mirárete irú to suréba
見られている と すれば

mirárete iréba 見られていれば

mirárete irú to surú nára(ba)
見られている と する なら (ば)

if I am (were) not seen

mirarénai to suréba 見られないとすれば

mirárete inái to 見られていないと

mirárete inái to suréba
見られていないと すれば

mirárete inákereba 見られていなければ

mirárete irú to shinái nára(ba)
見られていると しない なら (ば)

Past

if I have (had) been seen

miraremáshĭta nára(ba)
見られました なら (ば)

miraremáshĭtara(ba)
見られましたら (ば)

miráreta nára(ba)
見られた なら (ば)

mirárete itá nára(ba)
見られていた なら (ば)

miráretara(ba)
見られたら (ば)

if I have (had) not been seen

miraremasén déshĭta nára(ba)
見られませんでした なら (ば)

miraremasén déshĭtara(ba)
見られませんでしたら (ば)

miraré-nákatta nára(ba)
見られなかったなら (ば)

mirárete inákatta nára(ba)
見られていなかったなら (ば)

miraré-nákattara(ba)
見られなかったら(ば)

Nihón de wa gaikokú-go no uchí de Eigó ga ichibán ōku hanasaremásŭ.
日本 では 外国語 のうちで 英語が 一番 多く 話されます.
In Japan, among foreign languages, English is spoken most.

Conditional

Past

I should be seen

miraremásŭ deshō (ni)
見られますでしよう(に)

miraréru deshō (ni)
見られるでしよう(に)

mirárete irú deshō (ni)
見られているでしよう(に)

I should not be seen

miraremasén deshō (ni)
見られませんでしよう(に)

mirarénai deshō (ni)
見られないでしよう(に)

mirárete inái deshō (ni)
見られていないでしよう(に)

Past Perfect

I should have been seen

miraremáshĭta deshō (ni)
見られましたでしよう(に)

miráreta deshō (ni)
見られたでしよう(に)

I should not have been seen

miraremasén déshĭta deshō (ni)
見られませんでしたでしよう(に)

miraré-nákatta deshō (ni)
見られなかったでしよう(に)

For brevity, the forms of the conditional with *darō* have been omitted.

The person who receives or suffers the action expressed by the passive verb is regularly used in the nominative and take *ga* or *wa*, as the case may be.

Kodomó ***ga*** *korosaremáshĭta.*   A child has been killed.
子供　が　殺されました.

Watashí ga íma súnde irú ié ***wa*** *jū-nen máe ni tateráreta monó désŭ.*
私　が　今　住んでいる家　は　十年　前　に　建てられた　もの　です.
The house in which I am now living was built ten years ago.
(*lit.* I now-living-am house, ten years before was built, thing is.)

Tsugí no Orimpíkku[1] taikái ***wa*** *sen-kyū-hyaku-rokujū-yo nen ni Tōkyō de*
次　のオリムピック大会　は　千九百六十四　年　に　東京　で
hirakaréru[1] deshō.   The next Olympic Games will probably be held in Tokyo
開かれる　でしよう.　　in 1964.

The person or thing by whom or by which somebody receives or suffers the action indicated by the passive verb, is followed by the particle *ni*, corresponding, in this case, to the English by.

Anó séito wa ***senséi*** *ni homeraréru to yokí[2] shĭté itá nóni káette*
あの　生徒　は　先生　に　ほめられる　と　予期　して　いた　のに　却って
shikararemáshĭta.[3]   That pupil was expecting to be praised by his teacher, but
叱られました.　　was scolded instead.
(*lit.* That pupil, teacher by, to be praised, so anticipation made although,
instead was scolded.—*nóni* although, in spite of the fact that....)

Senjitsú Nakanó kojíin[4] de míta kawaíi kodomó wa áru kanemochí no
先日　中野　孤児院　で　見た　可愛い　子供　は　ある　金持　の
fujín *ni morawaremáshĭta.[5]*   The lovely child we saw the other day at the Na-
婦人　に　貰われました.　　kano orphanage was adopted by some rich lady.
(*lit.* The other day, Nakano orphanage at, saw lovely child, some rich lady
by was adopted.—*moraú* 貰う to get, to receive, to obtain—to adopt a child
kodomó wo moraú 子供を貰う)

Tōkyō Keibá[6] Kúrabu[7] ga kyónen kattá anó yūmei-na umá ga ashĭtá
東京　競馬　クラブ　が　去年　買ったあの　有名　な　馬　が　あした
Mitsui kōshaku[8] *ni sambyakú-man yen de uraréru deshō.*
三井　侯爵　に　三百万　円　で　売られるでしよう.
The famous horse which the Tokyo Horse Race Club bought last year, will
be sold to-morrow to Marquis Mitsui for ¥ 3,000,000.

Instead of *ni* placed after the person or thing from which one receives the passive action, one may sometimes use *kará.*

Watashí wa yókú benkyō shĭtá nóde ***senséi*** ***kará*** *homeraremáshĭta,*
私　は　よく　勉強　した　ので　先生　から　ほめられました,
kéredomo otōto wa namáketa[9] nóde shikararemáshĭta.
けれども　弟　は　なまけた　ので　叱られました.

---

1 *Orimpíkku taikái* Olympic games; *hiráku* to hold, to open **2** *yokí surú* to expect, anticipate **3** *káette* instead, on the contrary; *shikarú* to scold **4** orphanage **5** *moraú* to adopt **6** *keibá* horse-race **7** club **8** marquis **9** *namakéru* to be idle, to be lazy

I was praised by my teacher for having studied well, but my younger brother was scolded for his laziness. (I, well as I studied, by my teacher I was praised, but my younger brother, as he was lazy, was scolded.)

When the passive verb has a complement, this is regularly expressed by the accusative.

*Watashí wa **súri**[1] ni tokéi **wo** suraremáshǐta.*   I have been robbed of my
私 は すり に 時計 を すられました.   watch by a pickpocket.
I have had my watch stolen by a pickpocket.

*Anó hǐtó wa **inú ni** ashí **wo** kamitsǔkaremáshǐta.*[2]   He has had his leg
あの 人 は 犬 に 足 を かみつかれました.   bitten by a dog.
He was bitten in the leg by a dog.

Generally speaking the passive voice is not used so much in Japanese as it is in English, an active construction usually being preferable, especially when the receiver or the sufferer of the action expressed by the passive verb is an inanimate object.

It would be difficult to give definite rules on this subject, as the use of the active or passive construction depends in Japanese, as it does in English, on various circumstances. Sometimes the active construction is better than a passive one, and sometimes not. However, while a passive construction in Japanese may be incorrect, an active construction is always correct. We, therefore, advise the student not to use the passive construction too often, especially when referring to inanimate objects, and to use instead an active construction until he has acquired a sufficient practical knowledge of the language.

Below we will give a few more practical examples showing active sentences changed into passive ones.

A. *Anó dorobō ga nigéru tokí **keikán ga** mimáshǐta nóde súgu **tsǔkamae-***
あの 泥棒 が 逃げる 時 警官 が 見ました ので 直ぐ つかまえ
máshǐta.[3]   While that thief was running away a policeman saw him and soon
ました.   caught him.

P. *Anó dorobō wa nigéru tokí **keikán ni** miráreta nóde súgu tsǔkamae-*
あの 泥棒 は 逃げる 時 警官 に 見られた ので 直ぐ つかまえ
raremáshǐta.   While that thief was running away he was seen by a policeman
られました.   and was soon caught (by him).

A. *Tokugawá-gun wa Ōsaka-jō wo **kakondá**.*[4]   The Tokugawa army besieged
徳川 軍 は 大阪城 を 囲んだ.   the Osaka castle.

P. *Ōsaka-jō wa Tokugawá-gun **ni** **kakomaretá**.*
大阪城 は 徳川 軍 に 囲まれた.
The Osaka castle was besieged by the Tokugawa army.

A. *Shiró wo **torimáshǐta**.*   城を取りました.   They took the castle.

P. *Shiró wa **toraremáshǐta**.*   城は取られました.   The castle was taken.

---

1 pickpocket   **2** *kamitsǔkú* to bite   **3** *tsǔkamaerú* to catch, seize   **4** *kakomú* to surround, to besiege

A. *Anó wakái ki wo uchí no niwá e uekaemáshĭta*[1] *soshĭté furúi hō wo*
あの 若い 木 を うち の 庭 へ 植えかえましたそして 古い 方 を
kirimáshĭta.   We transplanted the young tree in our garden and
伐りました.   cut down the old one.

P. *Anó wakái ki wa uchí no niwá e* **uekaeraremáshĭta** *soshĭté furúi*
あの 若い 木 は うち の 庭 へ 植えかえられました そして 古い
hō wa **kirárete** *shimaimáshĭta.*   The young tree was transplanted in our
方 は 伐られて しまいました.   garden and the old one was cut down.

Anomalous Passive Verbs

koraréru	来られる	to be (*or* have) come	from *kúru*	来る	to come
osowarú	教わる	to be taught	from *oshierú*	教える	to teach
seraréru	せられる	to be done	from *surú*	する	to do
sarerú	される				

It is a peculiarity of the Japanese language that passives can be
formed also from intransitives as in the case of **kúru** 来る *to come.*
Japanese passive-intransitive verbs, however, correspond to English
expressions that have an active meaning.

hĭtó ni koraréru   to get guests, to have a coming
人 に 来られる   (generally said of an unwelcome visit)

áme ni furaréru   to get wet by the rain (to get a falling
雨 に 降られる   from rain, to get rained upon)

hĭtó ni shinarerú   to lose somebody by death
人 に 死なれる   (to get a dying from somebody)

kinén sarerú 記念される   to be remembered, to be commemorated

Ainikú Honda San **ni koráreta** *nóde shokují wo surú kotó ga dekimasén*
あいにく 本多 さん に 来られた ので 食事 を する 事 が出来ません
déshĭta.   I could not take my meal because unfortunately I received a visit
でした.   from Mr. Honda. (*ainikú* unfortunately, *shokují* meal)

Watashitachí wa kinō ensokú ni ittá nóni **áme ni furaremáshĭta.**
私達 は きのう 遠足 に行ったのに 雨 に 降られました.
    Yesterday we went to a picnic but unfortunately we were caught by the rain.
    (*lit.* We yesterday, to a picknick went, but rain unfortunately-fell-on-us.)

Meiji Tennō wa kindaí Nihón wo hajimetá génshu toshĭté zen-nihónjin
明治 天皇 は 近代 日本 を 始めた 元首 として 全日本人
kará eíkyū ni kinén sarerú deshō.
から 永久 に 記念 されるでしょう.

    The Emperor Meiji will forever be remembered by all Japanese as the sovereign
    who inaugurated modern Japan. (*lit.* Meiji Emperor modern Japan that began
    sovereign as, all Japan by forever remembrance will be done.)

---

1 *uekáeru* to transplant

Tennō emperor, *kindaí* modern, *hajimetá* past of *hajimerú* 始める to begin; in this case *hajimetá* modifies the word *sovereign* and corresponds to *who* or *that began*; *génshu* a sovereign; *toshĭté* as, *zen* all, *kará* by, *eikyū ni* forever

Tōshi no shichō wa shōjiki[1] de sonó ué jizenká[2] de arimásŭ kará **minná**
当市 の 市長 は 正直 で その 上 慈善家 でありますから みんな
ni *taihén* **sonkéi[3] sareté imásŭ.**   The mayor of our town is much respected
に 大変 尊敬 されて います.   by everybody for his honesty and
                                                  charitableness.

Anó onná-no-ko no ryōshin ga chūi[4] shĭté itá náraba anó onná-no-ko
あの 女の子 の 両親 が 注意 して いた ならば あの 女の子
wa yūkai[5] **sarenákatta deshō ni.**
は 誘拐 されなかった でしよう に.
That little girl would not have been kidnapped if her parents had watched her.
  (*lit.* That girl's parents, watch if they had done, that girl kidnapping would-
  not-have-been-done, *or* that girl would not have been kidnapped.)

In many cases the English passive verb corresponds to an intransitive verb in Japanese.

sawágu 騒ぐ to be excited   **matomarú** まとまる to be settled
kimarú 決る {to be decided   **bikkúri surú** {to be surprised
                 {to be arranged   びっくり する   {to be frightened

Sonó rōdō sōgi[6] wa shachō no chōtei[7] de **matomarimáshita.[8]**
その 労仂 争議 は 社長 の 調停 で まとまりました.
That labour dispute was settled by the mediation of the director of the company.

Inú ga hóeta[9] nóde dorobō wa **bikkúri[10] shĭté** *nigemáshĭta.*
犬 が 吠えた ので 泥棒 は びっくり して 逃げました.
The burglar was frightened away by the barking of a dog.
  (*lit.* The dog barked because, the thief being frightened, ran away.)

Sonó shirasé wo kiité **bikkúri shimáshĭta.**   I was much surprised to
その 知らせ を 聞いてびっくり しました.   hear that news.
  (*lit.* That news hearing—or upon hearing—I was astonished.)

When *surú*, in compounds, takes the form of *jiru* or *zuru* (Lit.), its passive is *jirareru* じられる or *zerareru* ぜられる.

kinjirú 禁じる	} to prohibit	*kinjirarerú* 禁じられる	} to be prohibited
kinzurú 禁ずる		*kinzerarerú* 禁ぜられる	
fūjiru 封じる	} to seal a letter	*fūjiraréru* 封じられる	} to be sealed
fūzuru 封ずる		*fūzeraréru* 封ぜられる	

---

1 honesty **2** charitableness **3** *sonkéi surú* to respect **4** *chūi surú* to watch
5 *yūkai surú* to kidnap **6** *sōgi* dispute; *rōdō sōgi* labour dispute **7** *shachō* director
of a company, *chōtei* mediation **8** *matoméru* to settle **9** *hoéru* to bark **10** *bikkúri*
surú to be surprised, astonished, amazed, startled, etc.

meijirú 命じる	} to order		*meijirarerú* 命じられる	} to be ordered	
meizurú 命ずる			*meizerarerú* 命ぜられる		
omonjíru 重んじる	} to honour to value		*omonjiraréru* 重んじられる	} to be honoured to be valued	
zonjíru 存じる	to think, know		*zonjiraréru* 存じられる	to be thought, known	

Nihón de wa miseinenshá[1] no kitsuén wa hōritsu de kinjirareté imásŭ.
日本 で は 未成年者 の 喫煙 は 法律 で 禁じられて います.

In Japan people under age are prohibited by law from smoking.
(*lit.* In Japan, under-age-people's smoking, by law is prohibited.)

Nihón de wa ínochi yóri mo méiyo ga omonjiraremásŭ.
日本 で は 命 より も 名誉 が 重じられます.

In Japan one's honour is valued more than one's life.
(*lit.* In Japan, life more than, honour is valued.)

Vocabulary

Nouns

atom	*génshi*	原子	rubber	*gómu*	ゴム
ball	*bōru (tamá)*	ボール(球)	tribe	*shúzoku*	種族
conflagration	*taiká*	大火	triumph	*shōri*	勝利
elephant	*zō*	象	**Adjectives**		
finger	*yubí*	指	principal	*shúgi*	主義
fur	*ke*	毛	pure	*junsuí*	純粋
game	*yūgi*	遊戯	**Verbs**		
graphite	*kokuén*	黒鉛	to compose	*naritatsú*	成立ツ
honey	*hachimitsú*	蜂蜜	to discover	*hakkén surú*	発見スル
indifference	*mutónjaku*	無頓着	to kill	*korosú*	殺コス
iron	*tetsú*	鉄	to practice	*jikkō surú*	実行スル
ivory	*zōge*	象牙	to reduce	*genjí·ru*	減ジル
lead	*namarí*	鉛	to show	*shimesú*	示ス
luster	*kōtaku*	光沢	to sow	*máku*	蒔ク
mahogany	*mahoganī*	マホガニー	to use	*mochii·rú*	用イル
pain	*kutsū*	苦痛	to value	*hyōka surú*	評価スル
permanence	*fuhén*	不変	**Adverbs**		
pleasure	*kairakú*	快楽	completely	*mattakú*	全ク
power	*nōryoku*	能力	principally	*ómo-ni*	主ニ
			universally	*híroku*	広ク

---

1 *miseinén* minority; *miseinenshá* people under age

ancient times *kódai;* permanent *eikyū-fuhén;* to be valued *tōtobaréru;* to value *tōtobu;* South America *Nambéi;* cane sugar *satōkibi-tō;* beet sugar *satōdaikon-tō;* matter, substance *busshitsú;* to sweeten *amamí wo tsŭkéru;* platinum *hakkín, pŭrachiná;* mountains, mountain ranges *sammyakú;* to mine *saikutsú surú;* working implements *shigotó dōgu;* large quantity *tairyō;* cotton cloth *mémpu;* to export *yushutsú surú;* to import *yunyū surú;* manufacturing, working (noun) *kakō;* artistic object *bijitsuhín;* to transplant *ishokú surú;* a great part *daibúbun;* several *sŭkai ni watattá;* severe earthquake shocks *gekishín;* unprecedented *mizōu no*

Exercise   *Renshū* 練習

1. Kódai kará ōgon[1] wa sonó eikyū-fuhén no iró to kōtaku to no tamé ni tōtobárete imásŭ. **2.** Gómu wa Ameriká ga hakkén sarerú zuttó ízen-ni Nambéi no áru Indiyán no shúzoku ni yotté[2] yūgi yō[3] no bōru wo tsŭkúru nóni mochiirareté[4] imáshĭta. Konó riyū[5] de gómu wa *Indiyan gómu* toshĭté[6] shirarerú[7] yō-ni narimáshĭta. **3.** Mahoganī wa móto Jamáika kará kitá monó de arimásŭ. Ima, mahoganī wa súbete no kuní de kágu wo tsŭkúru nóni mochiirareté imásŭ. **4.** Chiizú wa náni kará tsŭkuraremásŭ ka.—Chiizú wa gyūnyū kará tsŭkuraremásŭ. **5.** Mukashí, satōkibi-tō ya satōdaikon-tō ga máda shirareté inákatta jidái ni[8] wa shokúmotsu ni amamí wo tsŭkéru tamé ni hachimitsú ga mochiirareté imáshĭta. **6.** Hakkín (Pŭrachiná) wa ómo-ni Roshiyá to Kariforuniyá no áru sammyakú kará saikutsú[9] saremásŭ. **7.** Tetsú wa ō-mukashí kará shigotó dōgu wo tsŭkúru tamé ni Ōshū ya Ajiyá de mochiirareté imásŭ. **8.** Tairyō no watá ga mái-nen Ameriká kará Nihón e yunyū saremásŭ. Mémpu ga Nihón de tsŭkurárete Shína, Indo, Afŭriká, Ōshū nádo[10] e yushutsú saremásŭ. **9.** Nan-zen[11] to iú zō ga mái-nen sonó zōge no tamé ni korosaremásŭ.[12] Zōge wa ō-mukashi kará kakō sareté[13] bijitsuhín ni sareté imásŭ. **10.** Ameriká de wa komé wa ishokú sarezú ni[14] futsū no hataké ni tsŭkuraremásŭ.[15] Nihón de wa komé wa taitéi makáreta nochí[16] shi-go-shū-kan guraí de ishokú saremásŭ. **11.** Jūrui[17] no kawá wa sonó ke ni yotté hyōka[18] saremásŭ. **12.** Shokúmotsu wo tabéru nóni híroku mochiirareté íru fōku wa Yōroppa de wa honnó[19] ni-hyáku nen guraí máe ni shiyō saré-hajimemáshĭta.[20] Sonó ízen ni Yōroppa no hĭtóbito wa shokúmotsu wo tabéru nóni yubí wo tsŭkatté imáshĭta. **13.** Shína de wa Seirekí ízen issén nen íjō mo máe[21] kará shokují ni[22] háshi ga shiyō saré-hajimemáshĭta. Shína no Chūo (Seirekí-zen 1154–1122) wa shokúmotsu wo tabéru nóni háshi wo saishó-ni[23] mochiitá to omowárete[24] imásŭ. **14.** Busshitsú wa génshi kará

---

1 *ōgon* gold, in literary style   2 *ni yotté* by   3 *yō* use; *yūgi yō no bōru* ball to be used for games=play ball   4 *mochiirarerú* to be used   5 *riyū* reason; *konó riyū de* for this reason   6 *toshité* as   7 *shirarerú* passive of *shirú* to know   8 *shirareté inákatta jidái ni* when......were not yet known   9 *saikutsú sarerú* to be mined, to be obtained by mining   10 *nádo* etcetera.   11 *nan-zen* thousands   12 *korosarerú* passive of *korosú* to kill.   13 *kakō sarerú* to be worked   14 *ishokú sarezú ni* without transplanting   15 *tsŭkurarerú* to be made, here used for *to be cultivated*   16 *makáreta nochí* after the seeds have been sown   17 *jūrui* animals   18 *hyōka sarerú* to be valued   19 *honnó* only   20 *shiyō saré-hajimemáshĭta* began to be used   21 *issén nen íjō mo máe* more than one thousand years before   22 *shokují ni* for eating   23 *saishó-ni* first (adv.)   24 *saishó-ni mochiitá to omowárete imásŭ* is supposed to have first used

naritatté imásŭ. **15.** Móshi donná shúrui[1] no dōgu mo nákatta náraba warewaré no shigotó no nōryoku wa taihén genjirareta[2] deshō. **16.** Monó wo
káku ni tekíshĭta[3] empitsú ga tsŭkuráreta no wa kokuén ga hakkén saretá
nochí no kotó de arimásŭ. Mukashí hĭtóbito wa junsúi no namarí ya gin de
tsŭkútta empitsú wo shiyō shimáshĭta. **17.** Issen-kyū-hyakú-ni-jū-san nen ni
Tōkyō no daibúbun wa mizōu no táika ni yotté mattakú hakái saremáshĭta.[4]
Sonó táika wa sū-kái ni watattá gekishín no nochí súgu ni okorimáshĭta.
18. Sŭtoá-tetsúgaku wa kairakú ya kutsū ni táishĭte[5] mutónjaku wo shimesú
kotó wo shúgi to shĭté jikkō shimásŭ. Sŭtoá-tetsúgaku wa seirekí san-séiki
ízen ni Girishá de Shitoumú no Zenō ni yotté sōshi saremáshĭta[6] ga soré wa
ni-séiki go[7] Rōma de okonawaretá máde wa[8] shōri wo emasén[9] déshĭta.

1. 古代から黄金はその永久不変の色と光沢とのために貴ばれてい
ます.　**2.** ゴムはアメリカが発見されるずっと以前に南米のあるイン
ディヤンの種族によってゆうぎ用のボールを造るのに用いられていま
した.　この理由でゴムはインディヤンゴムとして知られるようになり
ました.　**3.** マホガニーは, 元, ヂャマイカから来たものであります.
今, マホガニーはすべての国で家具を造るのに用いられています.
4. チーズは何から造られますか.—チーズは牛乳から造られます.
5. 昔, 砂糖黍糖や砂糖大根糖がまだ知られていなかった時代には食物
に甘味をつけるために蜂蜜が用いられていました.　**6.** 白金(プラチ
ナ)は主にロシアとカリフォルニヤの或る山脈から採掘されます.
7. 鉄は大昔から仕事道具を造るために欧州やアジヤで用いられてい
ます.　**8.** 大量の綿が毎年アメリカから日本へ輸入されます.　綿布が
日本で造られて支那, 印度, アフリカ, 欧州等へ輸出されます.　**9.** 何
千という象が毎年その象牙のために殺されます.　象牙は大昔から加工
されて美術品にされています.　**10.** アメリカでは米は移植されずに普
通の畑に作られます.　日本では米は大抵播かれた後四五週間ぐらいで
移植されます.　**11.** 獣類の皮はその毛によって評価されます.　**12.** 食
物を食べるのに広く用いられているフォークはヨーロッパではほんの
二百年ぐらい前に使用され始めました.　その以前にヨーロッパの人々
は食物を食べるのに指を使っていました.　**13.** 支那では西暦以前一千
年以上も前から食事に箸が使用され始めました.　支那の紂王(西暦前
1154—1122)は食物を食べるのに箸を最初に用いたと思われています.
14. 物質は原子から成立っています.　**15.** 若しどんな種類の道具も無
かったならば我々の仕事の能力は大変減じられたでしょう.　**16.** 物を
書くに適した鉛筆が造られたのは黒鉛が発見された後の事でありま

1 *donná shúrui* any kind　**2** *genjirarerú* to be reduced　**3** *tekíshĭta* suitable; *teki-súru* to be suitable　**4** *hakái sarerú* to be destroyed　**5** *táishite* to, against　**6** *sōshi sarerú* to be founded　**7** *ni-séiki go* after two centuries　**8** *okonawaretá máde wa* until it was practiced　**9** *éru* to achieve, to obtain

す．昔，人々は純粋の鉛や銀で造った鉛筆を使用しました．　**17.** 一千九百廿三年に東京の大部分は未曽有の大火によって全く破壊されました．その大火は数回にわたった激震ののち直ぐに起りました．　**18.** ストア哲学は快楽や苦痛に対して無頓着を示す事を主義として実行します．ストア哲学は西歴三世紀以前にギリシヤでシトウムのゼノーによって創始されましたがそれは二世紀後ローマで行われた迄は勝利を得ませんでした．

1. Since ancient times gold has been valued on account of its permanent colour and luster.　**2.** Long before America was discovered, rubber was used by certain Indian tribes of South America to make play balls. This is the reason why this product became known as Indian rubber.　**3.** Mahogany originally came from Jamaica. Now mahogany is used in all countries for making furniture.　**4.** What is cheese made from?—Cheese is made from milk.　**5.** Formerly, when cane and beet sugar were not yet known, honey was used for sweetening food.　**6.** Platinum is obtained principally from some mountains in Russia and California.　**7.** Iron has been used in Europe and Asia since very ancient times for making implements.　**8.** Cotton in large quantities is imported into Japan from America every year. Cotton cloth is made in Japan and exported to China, India, Africa, and Europe.　**9.** Thousands of elephants are killed every year for their ivory. Ivory has been worked into artistic objects since very ancient times.　**10.** In America rice is cultivated in ordinary fields without transplanting. In Japan rice is generally transplanted four or five weeks after it has been sown.　**11.** Skins of animals are valued according to their fur.　**12.** Forks, which are universally used in eating food, began to be used in Europe only about two hundred years ago. Before that, people in Europe used their fingers for eating food.　**13.** In China chopsticks began to be used for eating more than one thousand years before Christ. Cheo-tsin, a ruler in China (B. C. 1154-1122), is supposed to have first used chopsticks for eating food.　**14.** Matter is composed of atoms.　**15.** If we had no tools of any kind our power to work would be greatly reduced.　**16.** It was only after graphite was discovered that suitable writing pencils were made. In ancient times people used pencils made of pure lead or silver.　**17.** In 1923 a large part of Tokyo was completely destroyed by an unprecedented conflagration which started immediately after several severe earthquake shocks.　**18.** Stoicism has as a principle or practice the showing of indifference to pleasure or pain. Stoicism was founded in Greece by Zeno of Citum three centuries before Christ, but it did not achieve its triumph until it was practiced in Rome, two centuries later.

Fifty-first Lesson　第五十一課

Potential Mood　*Kanō-hō* 可ヵ能ノ法ホウ

In lessons 44 and 45 it is stated that by the expression *kotó ga dekíru,* placed after the simple present of the verb, the potential form denoting capacity is obtained.

*Anó shōnen wa Shiná-go wo **hanásu** kotó ga **dekimásŭ.***
あの　少年　は　支那語　を　話す　こと　が　出来ます.
That boy can speak Chinese.

*Konná sawagashíi[1] tokoró de wa benkyō wo **surú** kotó ga **dekimasén.***
こんな　騒がしい　ところ　で　は　勉強　を　する　事　が　出来ません.
I cannot study in such a noisy place.

Nouns denoting action, such as *benkyō* in the above example, may be followed immediately by *ga dekíru,* without *wo surú kotó.*

*Konná sawagashíi tokoró de wa **benkyō ga dekimasén.***
こんな　騒がしい　ところ　で　は　勉強　が　出来ません.
(*lit.* In such a noisy place study cannot, *or* can't be done.)

The potential of verbs of Class I, denoting capacity or possibility, may also be expressed by their passive form. (See previous lesson.)

der.aréru　出られる　to be able to go out
miraréru　見られる　to be able to see
taberaréru　食べられる　to be able to eat

*Anó tokoró kará Fújisan ga **miraremásŭ.***
あの　所　から　富士山　が　見られます.

*Anó tokoró kará Fújisan wo **míru** kotó ga dekimásŭ.*
あの　所　から　富士山　を　見る　事　が　出来ます.

} From that place Mt. Fuji can be seen. You (I, we, they *or* one) **can see** Mount Fuji from that place.

*Konó mon kará **deraremasén.***
この　門　から　出られません.

*Konó mon kará **déru** kotó ga dekimasén.*
この　門　から　出る　事　が　出来ません.

} You (I, we, they *or* one) **cannot go out** from this gate.

*Konó kudámono wa máda aói kará **taberaremasén.***
この　果物　は　まだ　青い　から　食べられません.

or *Konó kudámono wa máda aói kará **tabéru** kotó ga dekimasén.*
この　果物　は　まだ　青い　から　食べる　事　が　出来ません.

This fruit is still green, and **cannot be eaten.** (*lit.* This fruit, still green because cannot be eaten. or......to eat the thing cannot.)

---

1 noisy

Árashi no tamé ni kómban dekakeraremasén.

あらし の ため に 今晩 出かけられません.

or *Árashi no tamé ni kómban dekakerú kotó ga dekimasén.*

あらし の ため に 今晩 出かける 事 が 出来ません.

On account of the storm we cannot go out to-night.

(*lit.* Storm on account of to-night we cannot go out.)

The common potential form of verbs of Class II is obtained by adding the termination *eru* to the *simple (consonant) stem*. The termination *eru* means *to obtain, to get*.

All potentials in *eru* are conjugated according to the rules given for the conjugation of verbs of Class I.

To write   *káku* 書く   To be able to write   *kakéru* 書ける

Indicative Present

I can write	I cannot write
kakemásŭ 書けます	*kakemasén* 書けません
kakéru 書ける	*kaké-nái* 書けない

Past

I could (was able to) write	I could not (was not able to) write
kakemáshĭta 書けました	*kakemasén déshĭta* 書けませんでした
káketa 書けた	*kaké-nákatta* 書けなかった

Future

I shall be able to write	I shall not be able to write
kakemashō 書けましょう	*kakemasén deshō* 書けませんでしょう
kakéru deshō 書けるでしょう	*kaké-nái deshō* 書けないでしょう

Probable Past

he probably was able to write	he probably was not able to write
kakemáshĭta deshō	*kakemasén déshĭta deshō*
書けましたでしょう	書けませんでしたでしょう
kakemashĭtarō	*kakemasén deshĭtarō*
書けましたろう	書けませんでしたろう
káketa deshō 書けたでしょう	*kaké-nákatta deshō* 書けなかったでしょう

The forms in *darō* have been omitted for brevity's sake.

Subjunctive Present

if I am (were) able to write	if I am (were) not able to write
kakemásŭ nára(ba)	*kakemasén nára(ba)*
書けます なら (ば)	書けません なら (ば)
kakéreba 書ければ, etc.	*kaké-nákereba* 書けなければ, etc.

Past

if I have (had) been able to write	if I have (had) not been able to write
kakemáshĭta nára(ba)	*kakemasén déshĭta nára(ba)*
書けました なら (ば)	書けません でした なら (ば)
káketa nára(ba), etc.	*kaké-nákatta nára(ba)*, etc.
書けた なら (ば)	書けなかった なら (ば)

Conditional Past

I should be able to write	I should not be able to write
kakemashō (*ni*)	*kakemasén deshō* (*ni*)
書けましょう(に)	書けませんでしょう(に)
kakéru deshō (*ni*)	*kaké-nái deshō* (*ni*)
書けるでしょう(に)	書けないでしょう(に)

Past Perfect

I should have been able to write	I should not have been able to write
kakemáshǐta deshō (*ni*)	*kakemasén déshǐta deshō* (*ni*)
書けましたでしょう(に)	書けません でしたでしょう(に)
kákete itá deshō (*ni*)	*kákete inákatta deshō* (*ni*)
書けていたでしょう(に)	書けていなかったでしょう(に)
káketa deshō (*ni*)	*kaké-nákatta deshō* (*ni*)
書けたでしょう(に)	書けなかったでしょう(に)

The negative form of the potential mood is formed also by the verb *kanéru* かねる, placed after the simple stem of verbs of Class I and the *i*-stem of verbs of Class II. This negative form is generally used in formal spoken or written style. Note that *kanéru* has the negative meaning of *not to be able to*, and is used only as an auxiliary verb after verbal stems.

dekakerú to go out	*dekaké-kanemásŭ*	出かけかねます	I am not able to go out
hanásu to speak	*hanashí-kanemáshǐta*	話しかねました	I was not able to speak

Verbs of Class II

In Their Potential Form

kógu	漕ぐ	to row		*yómu*	読む	to read
kogéru	漕げる	to be able to row		*yoméru*	読める	to be able to read
kasú	貸す	to lend		*yabúru*	破る	to tear
kaserú	貸せる	to be able to lend		*yaburéru*	破れる	to be able to tear
mátsu	待つ	to wait		*kaú*	買う	to buy
matéru	待てる	to be able to wait		*kaerú*	買える	to be able to buy

The subject (in English) of *to be able* or *can*, is in Japanese, when expressed at all, either placed in the *nominative* with *wa,* or, when emphasized, in the *dative* with *ni wa.*

Watashí *wa íma isogashíi kará* **deraremasén.**   As I am busy I am
私　　は　今　忙がしい　から　出られません.   unable to go out.
 (*lit.* I now busy because, to go out is not possible.)

Konó nikú wa amarí katái kará **watashí ni wa taberaremasén.**
この　肉　は　余り　硬い　から　　私　　に　は　　食べられません.
 This meat is too tough; I cannot eat it.
 (*lit.* This meat too tough because,—as for me—it cannot be eaten.)

Anáta wa koré ga **yomemásŭ** *ka.* **Watashí ni wa yomemasén.**
貴方　は　これ　が　読めます　か.　　私　に　は　　読めません.
Can you **read** this?   (As for me) I cannot read it.
    (*lit.* You, this can be read?—As for me—it cannot be read.)

The particle *ni* followed by *wa* in the last two examples may be paraphrased by *As for me, As far as I am concerned*, etc.

The object is in the accusative case with *wo* when it is followed by the simple present of the verb, plus *kotó ga dekíru,* but with *ga* if the verb is in the potential form obtained with the termination *areru* or *eru.*

Watashí wa **kanji**[1] *wo máda* **káku kotó ga dekimasén.**
私　は　漢字　を　まだ　書く　事　が　出来ません.
    (*lit.* I, Chinese characters, yet to write the thing is not possible.)

or *Watashí wa* **kanjí ga máda kakemasén.**   I **cannot** yet write the
   私　は　漢字　が　まだ　書けません.   Chinese characters.
    (*lit.* I, Chinese characters yet are not possible to be written.)

O-kané wo wasuretá nóde sonó e **wo kaú kotó ga dekimasén déshǐta.**
お金　を　忘れた　ので　その絵を　買う　事　が　出来ません　でした.
    (*lit.* The money I forgot because, that picture to buy the thing was not possible.)

or *O-kané wo wasuretá nóde sonó e* **ga kaemasén déshǐta.**
   お金　を　忘れた　ので　その絵　が　買えません　でした,
    As I had forgotten the money I **could not buy** that picture.
    (*lit.* The money I forgot because, that picture could not be bought.)

Among all the verbs of Class I *míru* 見る is the only one that forms its potential irregularly by adding the termination *eru* (*miéru* 見える), instead of *areru.*

Among the verbs of Class II there are the following exceptions:
Surú and **kúru** have no potential in *eru.* The potential of *surú* is formed by the circumlocution with *dekíru: surú kotó ga dekíru* to be able to do.

The potential of **kúru** is formed by adding **areru** to the irregular stem *kor: koraréru* to be able to come.

Kíkú to hear, has two potential forms: **kikoerú** and **kikerú** to be able to hear.

Watashí no heyá no mádo kará Fújisan ga yóku **miemásŭ.**
私　の　部屋の　窓　から　富士山　が　よく　見えます.
From the window of my room I **can** clearly **see** Mount Fuji.
    (*lit.* My room's window from, Mt. Fuji well can be seen.)

Me wo tojíru[2] *to* **miemasén.**   If we close our eyes we **cannot see.**
眼　を　閉ぢると　見えません.   (*lit.* The eyes if we close, it cannot be seen.)

---

1 Chinese character **2** *tojíru* to close

Kómban kumótte[1] *irú kará hoshí ga* **miemasén.**   As to-night is cloudy
今晩 曇って いるから 星 が 見えません.   we **cannot see** the stars.
or As to-night is cloudy the stars are not visible.

Mótto ōkii kóe de itté kudasái; anáta no iú kotó ga **kikoemasén** *kará.*
もっと大きい声 で云って下さい，貴方 の云う事 が 聞こえません から.
I **cannot** hear what you say; speak louder. (With big voice speak please,
your to say things are not heard because. *or* ...... cannot be heard because.)

To be able to see is also translated by *me ga miéru* 眼が見える *the eyes
can see,* and *to be able to hear* is translated by *mimi ga kikoerú* 耳が聞こ
える, *the ear can hear.*

Anó otokó wa tsúmbo[2] *déshĭta ga shújitsu*[3] *wo shĭté kará mimí ga* **kikoemásŭ.**
あの 男 は つんぼ でしたが 手術 をしてから 耳 が 聞こえます.
That man was deaf, but since he had his ears operated on he **can hear.**
(*lit.* That man deaf was, but operation doing after, the ears are able to hear.)

Umi no fukái[4] *tokoró ni wa me ga* **miénai** *sakaná ga takŭsán imásŭ.*
海 の 深い 所 に は 眼 が 見えない 魚 が 沢山 います.
Deep in the sea there are many fishes that **cannot see.**
(*lit.* The sea's deep place in, eyes are not able to see fishes, many there are.)

The idea of not being able to do what one would like to do, or ought to
do, is expressed by the simple present of the principal verb, followed by *ni*
or *nimo* and the potential of the same verb. The simple present of the
verb, plus *nimo,* corresponds to the subordinate of the desiderative followed
by *mo.*

Sekái man-yū[5] *ni dekaketái ga ryohí*[6] *ga arimasén kará* **dekakéru nimo**
世界 漫遊 に出かけたいが 旅費 がありませんから 出かける にも

dekakeraremasén. (or *dekaketákute mo dekakeraremasén.*)
出かけられません.   （出かけたくて も 出かけられません.）
I should like to take a trip around the world, but as I have no money for the
necessary expenses I **am unable to go.** (*lit.* World trip on I wish to go, but
traveling expenses there aren't because, even wishing to go, it is not possible
to go.—*dekakerú* to go out, start off, set off, etc.)

Ikura hóshikute mo kané ga nákereba **kaú ni kawaremasén** (*kaitákute*
いくら 欲しくて も 金 が 無ければ 買う に 買われません（買いたくて

mo kawaremasén).   No matter how much you may desire it, you **cannot buy** it
も 買われません）.   without money. (*kaú* to buy, *kawarerú* to be able to buy)
(*lit.* However much you may wish, money if you have not, wishing to buy
even, cannot be bought, *or* one is not able to buy.)

Possibility is also expressed by the verb followed by the expression *ka-mo
shiremasén* かも知れません, which means *one cannot know whether,* equivalent
to *may be, perhaps.*

---

1 *kumóru* to be cloudy   **2** deaf   **3** *shújitsu wo surú* to perform an operation
4 deep   **5** *sekái* world, *man-yū* trip   **6** travelling expenses

Mótto yói ishá ni kakátte itá náraba anó byōnin wa **tasŭkátta ka-mo**
もっとよい医者 にかかっていたならば あの 病人 は 助かった かも
shiremasén.   If they had had a better doctor the patient **might** perhaps have
知れません.   **been saved.** (*ishá ni kakáru* to consult a doctor)
       (*lit.* More good doctor if they had consulted, that patient might have been
       saved.—*tasŭkáru* 助かる to be saved, to be spared, etc.)

The passive or potential in *areru* is used also as a polite form, indicating
action by the second or third person. When such verbs are used in polite
speech they are considered active verbs.

Ima anó jidōsha ni **noraréru** *o-katá wa miyasamá de arimásŭ.*
今 あの 自動車 に 乗られる お方 は 宮様 で あります.
    The person who is now entering the motor-car is an Imperial prince.
    (*lit.* Now that motor-car on goes person Imperial prince is.)

The potential in *areru* is often used in the written style or in general
statements, whether written or spoken.

So......That

This expression is often translated by the potential, followed by *yō
ni* ように or *hodó* 程 and the adjective.

Háha no aijō[1] wa **hakarénai[2]** *hodó* (or *yō-ni*) *fukái.*
母 の 愛情 は はかれない 程 （ように）深い.
    A mother's love is so deep that one **cannot measure** it.
    (*lit.* Mother's love, not to be able to measure-like, is deep.)

Konó kurumí[3] wa **warenái[4]** *hodó* (or *yō-ni*) *katái.*
この くるみ は 割れない 程 （ように）堅い.
    This walnut is so hard that it **cannot be cracked.**
    (*lit.* This walnut not to be able to crack-like, is hard.)

There are verbs that express the idea of possibility without being used in
the potential form. When such verbs follow the expression **so......that,** they
are used in their ordinary negative conjugation.

Sonó jishín no sangái[5] wa sōzō[6] mo **tsŭkánai[7]** *hodó ōkikatta.*
その 地震 の 惨害 は 想像 も つかない 程 大きかった.
    The devastation caused by the earthquake was so great that one **cannot
imagine** it. (*lit.* That earthquake's devastation, imagination even not to be
able-like, was great.)

If the verb that follows **so......that** is not in the potential mood, the expression is translated in various ways, as shown in the following representative
examples.

Sonó shōsetsu wa minná ga **yomitagáru** *hodó omoshirói désŭ.*
その 小説 は みんな が 読みたがる 程 面白い です.
    That novel is so interesting that everybody likes to read it.
    (*lit.* That novel, everybody wish to read-like, interesting is.)

---

1 love   **2** *hakáru* to measure   **3** walnut   **4** *warú* to crack   **5** devastation   **6** imagination   **7** *sōzō ga tsŭkú* or *dekíru* to be able to imagine; *sōzō ga tsŭkánai* to be unable
to form idea of; *mo* after *sōzō* means even; *ga* after *sōzō* is omitted because *mo* is
used

Fújisan wa dáre démo **homéru hodó** *utsŭkushíi désŭ.*

富士山 は 誰 でも ほめる 程 美しい です.

Mount Fuji is so beautiful that everybody admires it.

(*lit.* Mt. Fuji, everybody to admire-like, beautiful is.)

Amarí o-fŭtorí[1] *ni* **naráreta nóde** *chottó wakarimasén déshĭta.*

あまり お肥り に なられた ので 一寸 わかりません でした.

You have become so fat that I could not recognize you at once.

(*lit.* Too fat you became because, for a moment I didn't understand=didn't recognize you.)

A passive verb preceded by **can** and **could** may be translated by the passive form in *areru,* but an active construction is preferred whenever possible.

Jōzu-na kutsúya wa ichí-nichí ni kutsú wo issokú **tsŭkŭru kotó ga**

上手な 靴屋 は 一日 に 靴 を 一足 造る 事 が

dekimásŭ. or *Jōzu-na kutsúya wa ichí-nichí ni kutsú wo issokú*

出来ます. 上手 な 靴屋 は 一日 に 靴 を 一足

tsŭkuremásŭ. A skilful shoemaker **can make** a pair of shoes in one day.

造れます. A pair of shoes **can be made** in one day by a skilful shoemaker.

Konó hon wa dóko no hon-ya démo **utté imásŭ.** This book is sold at

この 本 は どこ の 本屋 でも 売っています. any bookseller's.

(This book at any bookseller they sell.)

Konó hon wa dóko no hon-ya démo **kaemásŭ.** This book can be bought

この 本 は どこ の 本屋 でも 買えます. at any bookseller's.

Kinō sonó shigotó wo oerú kotó ga **dekínakatta.**

きのうその 仕事 を 終える 事 が 出来なかった.

We (or they) **could not** finish that work yesterday.

(*lit.* Yesterday that work to finish the thing could not.)

Kinō sonó shigotó wa **oerarenákatta.** That work **could not be**

きのうその 仕事 は 終えられなかった. **finished** yesterday.

A passive verb preceded by **may** or **might,** is used in the simple present, followed by *ka-mo shiremasén.*

Tábun anó gaké[3] *kará úmi ga* **miéru ka-mo shiremasén.**

たぶんあの 崖 から 海 が 見える かも 知れません.

Perhaps the sea **may be seen** from that cliff.

The probable future may be used instead of the above construction, if one wishes to express less doubt as to the result.

Konó shinamonó wa kōkoku[4] *wo suréba súgu ni* **urerú deshō.**

この 品物 は 広告 を すれば 直ぐ に 売れるでしょう.

If you advertise these goods they may soon be sold.

Anywhere and Not......Anywhere

Anywhere is translated by *dóko de-mo* 何処でも or *dóko ní-mo* 何処にも, *dóko ni de-mo* 何処にでも (with positive verb), and **not......anywhere** by *dóko de-mo* 何処でも or *dóko ní-mo* 何処にも (with negative verb).

---

1 *futori* 肥り fat **2** *oerú* 終える to finish, *oerarerú* can be finished **3** cliff **4** *kōkoku surú* to advertise

Kikú wa Nihón no **dóko ni de-mo** *arimásŭ.* Chrysanthemums are found
菊 は 日本 の どこ に でも あります.   **anywhere** in Japan.

Kō iú yō na shinamonó wa shínai de[1] wa **dóko ni-mo** *utté inái deshō.*
こういうような 品物 は 市内 で はどこにも売っていないでしょう.
This kind of goods is not sold **anywhere** in this city.

Somewhere

dóko ni ka どこにか or **dóko ka ni** どこかに *áru tokoró ni* 或る所に

Konó kuní no **dóko ka ni** *kínzan[2] ga arimásŭ.*
この 国 の どこ か に 金山 が あります.
Somewhere in this country there are gold mines.

Dóko ni imáshĭta ka.   どこにいましたか.   Where have you been?

Aru tokoró ni *imáshĭta.* 或る所にいました.   I have been **somewhere.**

Everywhere

itarú tokoró ni 到る処に, **dóko de-mo** どこでも, **dóko ni de-mo** どこにでも

Matsú no ki[3] wa Nihón-jŭ[4] **itarú tokoró ni** *(dóko démo, dóko ni démo)*
松 の 木 は 日本中 到る 処 に (どこ でも, どこ に でも)
miraréru deshō.   Pine-trees may be seen **everywhere** in Japan.
見られるでしょう.

Totemó (emphatic word)

The word *totemó* is often used before the negative potential to
emphasize it.

Watashí wa konó tegamí wo **totemó** *hon-yakú* **dekimasén.**
私 は この 手紙 を とても 翻訳 できません.
I cannot possibly translate this letter. (*hon-yakú surú* to translate)

Konó utá wa muzukáshikute **totemó** *utaemasén.*
この 歌 は むづかしくて とても 歌えません.
This song is difficult and I cannot sing it at all.
(This song being difficult at all I cannot sing.)

The word *totemó* is used in a great many cases, without being followed
by the potential.

Totemó tasŭkaránai.   とても助からない.   It is beyond help.

Totemó yarikirénai.   とてもやり切れない.   I couldn't stand it.

Sonná kotó wa **totemó** *dekínai.*   It is quite impossible.
そんな 事 は とても 出来ない.

Totemó nozomí ga nái.   It is beyond hope. *or* There is no
とても 望み が ない.   possible hope in the wide world.

---

1 *shínai de* in the city   **2** gold mine   **3** *mátsu-no-ki* pine-tree   **4** *jŭ* throughout;
Nihón-jŭ throughout Japan

Anó fujín wa **totemó** *shi-jū ni wa miemasén.*
あの 婦人 は とても 四十 に は 見えません.
That lady hardly looks to be forty.

Nihón-go de wa **totemó** *anáta ni kanaimasén.*[1]
日本語 では とても 貴方 に かないません.
I cannot equal you in Japanese.

(*lit.* In Japanese language, by any possibility, for you am not a match.—......
ni kanaimasén to be no match for)

Anó hĭtó wa **totemó** *tasŭkaránu*[2] *to akiramemáshĭta.*[3]
あの 人 は とても 助からぬ と 諦めました.
He gave up all hope of life.

(*lit.* That person, by-any-possibility cannot-be-saved, so he resigned himself)

The word **totemó** is also used to translate the adverbs and adjectives *very, awfully, mighty, unspeakably, stunning, ripping, striking,* and some other words indicating high degree.

Anó onná wa **totemó** *bimbō désŭ.*
あの 女 は とても 貧乏 です.
She is very (awfully) poor.

Konó kusurí wa **totemó** *yóku kikimásŭ.*[4]
この 薬 は とても よく 利きます.
This medicine has a marvellous effect.

Anó rōjin wa **totemó** *kanemochí désŭ.*
あの 老人 は とても 金持 です.
That old man is very rich.

Watashí wa kómban **totemó** *tsŭkaremáshĭta.*
私 は 今晩 とても 疲れました.
I am awfully tired to-night.

Idioms

Shikatá ga arimasén (or *nái*).
仕方 がありません (ない).
It can't be helped.

Sō surú yóri shikatá ga nái.
そう する より 仕方 が ない.
I can't help doing so.

Warawazú ni wa iraremasén.
笑わず に はいられません.
I can't help laughing.

(*lit.* Without laughing I am not able to be.) (*waraú* 笑う to laugh, *warawazú* not to laugh, *irarerú* to be able to be)

Sonó shōtai wo shōchí surú yóri hoká ni shikatá ga arimasén.
その 招待 を 承知 するより 外 に 仕方 がありません.
I can't help accepting the invitation. (*lit.* The invitation to accept than, differently there is no help.—*shōchi surú* to accept)

Anó shōnen wo shikarazú ni wa iraré-nákatta.
あの 少年 を 叱らず に はいられなかった.
I couldn't help scolding that boy.

(*lit.* That boy without scolding I was not able to be.)

Vocabulary

Nouns

armour	*búki*	武器	diver	*sensúifu*	潜水夫
destroyer	*kuchikukán*	駆逐艦	ether	*tenkū*	天空

---

1 *kanáu* to equal, to match **2** *tasŭkáru* to be saved, to be rescued **3** *akiraméru* to give up, to resign oneself to (one's fate) **4** *kikú* to do (a person) good

festival	*sairéi*	祭サイ礼レイ
fishes	*gyórui*	魚ギョ類ルイ
kick	*kerí*	蹴ケリ
lemonade	*remónsui*	レモン水スイ
	remonēdo	レモネード
mile	*máiru*	哩マイル
ostrich	*dachō*	駝ダ鳥チヨウ
owl	*fukurō*	梟フクロウ
permission	*kyóka*	許キョ可カ
speed	*sokuryokú*	速ソク力リョク
steam	*jōki*	蒸ジョウ気キ
tropics	*nettái*	熱ネッ帯タイ
vocabulary	*tangó*	単タン語ゴ
	Adjectives	
annual	*reinén-no*	例レイ年ネンノ
deaf	*mimí ga tōi*	耳ミガ遠トオイ
low-minded	*asamashíi*	浅アサマシイ
marine	*kaiséi*	海カイ棲セイ
special	*tokubetsú*	特トク別ベツ
unspeakable	*góngo dōdan-na*	言語道断ナ
virtuous	*tokutakái*	徳トク高タカイ
visible	*me ni miéru*	眼ニ見エル
	Verbs	
to express	*hyōgen surú* (Lit.)	表ヒョウ現ゲンスル
	arawásu	現アラワス
to increase	*zōdai surú*	増ゾウ大ダイスル
to navigate	*tsūkō surú*	通ツウ航コウスル
to reach	*tassúru*	達タッスル
to recognize	*miwake·rú*	見ミ分ワケル
therefore	*soré-yué*	ソレ故ユエ
through	*tsūjite*	通ツウジテ

to make speed *sokuryokú wo dásu;* the bottom of the water (sea, river, pond, etc.) *suitéi;* agricultural products *nōsakubutsú;* to travel across *ōdan surú;* electric power *dénryoku;* acoustic instrument *den-on-ki;* nevertheless *soré ni mo-kakawarazú;* coral insect *sangochū;* bottom of the sea *kaitéi;* to build up *kizukí agerú; mimí no tōi hĭtó* deaf person; noble *kedakái,* nobly *kedákaku*

Exercise *Renshū* 練習

1. Kotobá wo shiranákute wa kangáe wo hyōgen surú kotó ga dekimasén. Soré-yué, móshi gaikokú-go de jibún no kangáe wo yóku arawashitái náraba tángo wo yóku benkyō shinákereba narimasén. **2.** Watashí wa móshi yūgata kōhī wo nomimásŭ to yábun yóku nemuraremasén. **3.** Kuchikŭkán wa búki wo mótte imasén ga dái sokuryokú wo dásu kotó ga dekimásŭ. **4.** Nihón no kawá wa[1] ōki-na fúne wa tsūkō surú kotó ga dekimasén názenaraba Nihón no kawá wa amarí fukáku arimasén kará. **5.** Táda manabú kotó wo tsūjite nómi[2] hĭtó wa iká-ni shĭté[3] kedákaku tokutákaku ikíru ka[3] wo shirú kotó ga dekimásŭ. **6.** Sensúifu wa ikkái-ni[4] go-rokú-ji-kan suitéi ni[5] irú kotó ga dekimásŭ. **7.** Hiryō no shiyō ni yotté[6] nōsakubutsu wo zōdai surú kotó ga dekimásŭ. **8.** Shokúbutsu wa ningén ya dōbutsu to onáji yō-ni kūki náshi de wa ikiraremasén. **9.** Jidōsha ya hikōki ga hatsuméi sarerú máde hĭtó wa rakudá náshi de sabakú wo koerarenákatta. **10.** Oyosó yon-jū nen máe kishá wa ichí-jikán go-jū máiru yóri mo háyaku hashiremasén déshĭta. Kónnichi wa ichí-jikán ni-hyakú máiru íjō no sokuryokú de hashíru kotó ga dekíru

---

1 Sometimes, as in this case, *wa,* instead of *wo,* indicates the accusative. **2** *tsūjite nómi* only through **3** *iká-ni shĭté......ka* how, *iká-ni shĭté kedákaku ikíru ka* how to live nobly **4** *ikkái-ni* at a time **5** *suitéi ni* under the water **6** *hiryō* fertilizer, *shiyō ni yotté* by the use

resshá ga arimásŭ. **11.** Jōki to dénryoku náshi de jinrúi¹ wa kokó² isséiki-han ni okéru² shúju³ no dái hakkén wo surú⁴ kotó ga dekínakatta. **12.** Tokubetsú no den-on-ki wo shiyō shĭté⁵ mimí no tōi⁶ hĭtóbito wa kikú kotó ga dekimásŭ. **13.** Fukurō wa néko to onáji yō-ni⁷ yóru míru kotó ga dekimásŭ. **14.** Gyórui wa me ni miéru mimí wa arimasén ga soré nímo-kakawarazú kikú kotó ga dekimásŭ. **15.** Ashĭtá Nikkō e itté reinén no sairéi wo mitái no désŭ ga shújin ga o-rúsu de raishū máe ni wa o-kaerí ni narimasén kará watashí wa dekaketé yukú kyóka⁸ ga itadakemasén. **16.** Watashí ga dónna ni yóku hataraité mo⁹ uchí no shiháinin wa kesshĭté manzokú no¹⁰ yō-ni miemasén.¹¹ **17.** Hikarí wa ichí-byō kan ni jū-hachí-man-rokŭ-sen máiru no sokuryokú de tenkū wo hashirimásŭ.¹² Takŭsán no hoshí wa sonó hikarí ga warewaré ni tassúru nóni¹³ sū-sen nen mo kakáru hodó tōi désŭ.—Taiyō no hikarí wa chikyū ni tassúru nóni hachí fun guraí kakarimásŭ. Taiyō wa chikyū kará dóno kuraí tōi désŭ ka. **18.** Dachō no ashí wa hijō ni tsúyoku sonó hĭtó-kerí de¹⁴ hĭtó wo korosú kotó ga dekíru hodó désŭ. **19.** Konó remonēdo wa noménai hodó atsúi désŭ.¹⁵ **20.** Móshi to wo shiménai to inú ga nigemásŭ yo. **21.** Anó máigo¹⁶ no shōnen ga konó hen ni imáshĭta. **22.** Bánana wa nettái no dóko ni de-mo seichō shimásŭ. **23.** Anáta no pin wo hōbō sagashimáshĭta ga mitsŭkerú kotó ga dekimasén. **24.** Anó hĭtó ga Eigó wo hanásu tóki ni watashí wa chottó mo wakarimasén. **25.** Anáta wa sukkári¹⁷ o-kawari ni narimáshĭta watashí wa anáta wo dō shĭté mo miwakeraremasén¹⁸ déshĭta. **26.** Anó otokó wa góngo dōdan-na hodó asamashíi. **27.** Sangochū wa saishō¹⁹ kaiséi dōbutsu désŭ ga shikáshi²⁰ kaitéi kará shimá wo kizukí-agerú kotó ga dekimásŭ.

1. 言葉を知らなくては考えを表現する事ができません．それ故，若し，外国語で自分の考えをよく現わしたいならば単語をよく勉強しなければなりません．**2.** 私はもし夕方コーヒーを飲みますと夜分よくねむられません．**3.** 駆逐艦は武器を持っていませんが大速力を出す事ができます．**4.** 日本の川は大きな船は通航する事ができません．なぜならば日本の川は余り深くありませんから．**5.** 唯学ぶ事を通じてのみ人は如何にして気高く徳高く生きるかを知る事ができます．**6.** 潜水夫は一回に五六時間水底にいる事ができます．**7.** 肥料の使用によって農作物を増大する事ができます．**8.** 植物は人間や動物と同じように空気なしでは生きられない．**9.** 自動車や飛行機が発明されるまで人はらくだなしでさばくを越えられなかった．**10.** 凡そ四十年

---

1 man **2** *kokó* last, *kokó isséiki-han ni okéru* in the last century and a half **3** *shúju* many **4** *dái hakkén* great discovery, *hakkén surú* to discover **5** *shiyō shĭté* with **6** When qualifying a noun the word *mimí ga tōi*, deaf, changes *ga* into *no* **7** *to onáji yō* ni as well as **8** *yukú kyóka* permission to go **9** *dónna ni*+subordinate +*mo* no matter how+verb **10** *manzokú no* satisfied **11** *yō-ni miéru* to seem **12** *hashirú* to travel **13** *tassúru nóni* in order to reach **14** *hitó-kerí de* with a kick **15** *noménai hodó atsúi désŭ* is so hot that I cannot drink it **16** *máigo ni náru* to be missing; *máigo* missing child; *máigo no* missing **17** *sukkári* a great deal **18** *miwakerarenái* not to be able to recognize **19** *saishō* smallest **20** *ga shikáshi* yet

前汽車は一時間五十哩よりも速く走れませんでした. 今日は一時間二百哩以上の速力で走る事ができる列車があります. **11.** 蒸汽と電力なしで人類はこゝ一世紀半に於ける種々の大発見をする事ができなかった. **12.** 特別の伝音器を使用して耳の遠い人々は聞く事ができます. **13.** 梟は猫と同じように夜見る事ができます. **14.** 魚類は眼に見える耳はありませんがそれにも拘わらず聞く事ができます. **15.** あした日光へ行って例年の祭礼を見たいのですが主人がお留守で来週前にはお帰りになりませんから私は出かけて行く許可がいただけません. **16.** 私がどんなによく伹いてもうちの支配人は決して満足のように見えません. **17.** 光は一秒間に十八万六千哩の速力で天空を走ります. 沢山の星はその光が我々に達するのに数千年もかゝる程遠いです. 太陽の光は地球に達するのに八分位かゝります. 太陽は地球からどの位遠いですか. **18.** 駝鳥の足は非常に強くその一蹴りで人を殺す事ができるほどです. **19.** このレモネードは飲めないほど熱いです. **20.** 若し戸をしめないと犬が逃げますよ. **21.** あの迷子の少年がこの辺にいました. **22.** バナゝは熱帯のどこにでも生長します. **23.** 貴方のピンを方々探しましたが見つける事ができません. **24.** あの人が英語を話す時に私は一寸も解りません. **25.** 貴方はすっかりお変りになりました私は貴方をどうしても見分けられませんでした. **26.** あの男は言語道断なほど浅ましい. **27.** 珊瑚虫は最小海棲動物ですが併し海底から島を築き上げる事ができます.

1. We cannot express thoughts without knowing words. Therefore if we wish to express our thoughts well in a foreign language we must study thoroughly the vocabulary. **2.** If I drink coffee in the evening I cannot sleep well at night. **3.** The destroyers have no armour but they can make great speed. **4.** Large vessels cannot navigate the rivers of Japan because they are not deep enough. **5.** Only through learning can a man know how to live nobly and virtuously. **6.** A diver can remain under water for five or six hours at a time. **7.** We can increase agricultural production by the use of fertilizers. **8.** Plants, like men and animals, cannot live without air. **9.** Until motorcars and airplanes were invented men could not cross deserts without camels. **10.** About forty years ago trains could not travel faster than fifty miles an hour. To-day there are trains that can travel at the speed of over two hundred miles an hour. **11.** Without steam and electric power man could not have made many of the great discoveries of the last century and a half. **12.** With special acoustic instruments deaf people can hear. **13.** Owls, as well as cats, can see at night. **14.** Fishes have no visible ears, but they can hear nevertheless. **15.** I should like to go to Nikko to-morrow and see the annual festival, but as my master is away and will not return before next week, I cannot obtain permission to go. **16.** No matter how well I work, my manager never seems to be satisfied. **17.** Light travels through the ether at the speed of 186,000 miles a second. Many stars are so far away that their light takes several thousands of years to reach us.—The light of the sun takes about eight minutes to reach the earth. How far away is the sun from the earth? **18.** The feet of an ostrich are so powerful that with a kick it can kill a man. **19.** This lemonade is so hot that I cannot drink it. **20.** If you do not close the door the dog may run away. **21.** The missing boy was seen somewhere around this place. **22.** Bananas grow anywhere in the tropics. **23.** I have looked for your pin everywhere but I cannot find it. **24.** When that man speaks English I cannot understand him at all. **25.** You have changed a great deal; I couldn't possibly recognize you. **26.** That man is unspeakably low-minded. **27.** Coral insects are some of the smallest marine creatures, yet they can build up islands from the bottom of the sea.

Fifty-second Lesson　第五十二課

Reflexive Pronouns and Reflexive Verbs

Reflexive Pronouns

Hanshá Daiméishi 反射代名詞

The word *self* is usually rendered by *jibún* 自分, from *ji* 自 *self* and *bun* 分 *part*, and by *jishin* 自身, from *shin* 身 *body*. *Jibún,* however, is more colloquial than *jishin,*

Jibún or *jishin* is generally followed by *de* で when this postposition corresponds to **by** as in *by oneself*, etc.

In speaking respectfully to the second person or of the third person the honorific *go* 御 is prefixed.

> *jibún de*　自分で ⎫ (by) myself, yourself, himself, herself
> *jishin de*　自身で ⎭ (by) ourselves, yourselves, themselves

> *Watashí wa soré wo jibún de mótte kimáshǐta.*　I brought it myself.
> 私　は それ を 自分　で 持って　来ました.

> *Jibún de ikí nasái.* 自分で行きなさい.　Go yourself.

> *Anó hǐtó wa jibún de kónakereba ikemasén.*　He must come himself.
> あの　人　は　自分　で　来なければいけません.

When *jishin* is immediately preceded by a personal pronoun it does not take the nominative particle.

> *Watashí jishin de soré wo mótte kimáshǐta.*　I brought it myself.
> 私　　自身　で それ を 持って　来ました

When using *jishin* the personal pronoun may be repeated in emphatic statements, in which case the first personal pronoun takes the nominative particle *wa* or *ga,* according to the rules given for their respective use.

Watashí wa watashí jíshin de soré wo shimáshĭta.   I did it myself.
私　　は　　私　　自身　　で　それ　を　しました.

Note that *jishin de* may be used only when preceded by a noun or pronoun, while *jibún de* may be used without being preceded by any word.

Watashí jíshin de soré wo shimáshĭta.
私　　　自身　　で　それ　を　　しました.   ⎫
Jibún de soré wo shimáshĭta.   ⎬ I did it myself.
自分　で　それ　を　しました.   ⎭

Both *jishin* and *jibún* may be preceded by the honorific *go* when politely speaking to the second or of the third person.

Go-jibún de sore wo nasaimáshĭta.   You did it yourself.
御自分　で　それ　を　なさいました.   (He did it himself.)

To avoid ambiguity when using *jibún* or *jíshin,* it is advisable to have both expressions preceded by the noun or pronoun they are related to.

Watashí wa jibún de soré wo shimáshĭta.   I did it myself.
私　　は　自分　で　それ　を　　しました.
Anáta wa go-jibún de soré wo nasaimáshĭta.   You did it yourself.
貴方　は　　御自分　で　それ　を　なさいました.
Yamadá San wa go-jibún de soré wo nasaimáshĭta.
山田　さん　は　　御自分　で　それ　を　なさいました.
Mr. Yamada did it himself.

By using both *jibún* and *jíshin* we obtain a more emphatic form of the personal pronoun.

Anáta wa jibún jíshin de soré wo shimáshĭta.   You did it yourself.
貴方　は　自分　自身　で　それ　を　しました.

The polite form of the same sentence would be:

Anáta wa go-jibún de soré wo nasaimáshĭta.
貴方　は　　御自分　で　それ　を　なさいました.   ⎫
Anáta wa go-jíshin de soré wo nasaimáshĭta.   ⎬ You did it yourself.
貴方　は　　御自身　で　それ　を　なさいました.   ⎭
Anáta wa go-jibún jíshin de soré wo nasaimáshĭta.
貴方　は　　御自分　自身　で　それ　を　なさいました.

Anó hĭtó wa jibún de (jíshin de) kimáshĭta.
あの　人　は　自分　で　（自身　で）来ました.   ⎫
Anó katá wa go-jibún de (go-jíshin de) irasshaimáshĭta.   ⎬ He came himself.
あの　方　は　御自分　で　（御自身　で)いらっしっいました.   ⎭
Káre wa káre jíshin de kimáshĭta.
彼　は　彼　自身　で　来ました.

Watashitachí   wa   jibuntachí   de   konó   ki   wo   uemáshĭta.
私達　　は　　自分達　　で　この　木　を　植えました.

Watashitachí   wa   jishin   de   konó   ki   wo   uemáshĭta.
私達　　は　　自身　　で　この　木　を　植えました.

Watashitachí   wa   watashitachí   jíshin   de   konó   ki   wo   uemáshĭta.
私達　　は　　私達　　　自身　　で　この　木　を　植えました.

We planted these trees ourselves.

Anáta   wa   jibún   de   (jíshin   de)   ikimáshĭta   ka.
貴方　は　自分　で　（自身　　で）行きました　か.

Anáta   wa   jibún   jishin   de   ikimáshĭta   ka.
貴方　は　自分　自身　で　行きました　か.

Anáta   wa   anáta   jíshin   de   ikimáshĭta   ka.
貴方　は　貴方　　自身　で　行きました　か.

Anáta   wa   go-jibún   de   (go-jíshin   de)   oidé   nasaimáshĭta   ka.
貴方　は　御自分　　で　（御自身　　で)お出でなさいましたか.

Did you go yourself?

The same construction is used when in English the reflexive pronoun is immediately preceded by the personal pronoun.

Watashí   wa   jibún   de   anó   táishō   ni   o-hanashí   shimáshĭta.
私　は　自分　であの　大将　に　お話し　しました.

Watashí   wa   jíshin   de   anó   táishō   ni   o-hanashí   shimáshĭta.
私　は　自身　であの　大将　に　お話し　しました.

Watashí   wa   jibún   jishin   de   anó   táishō   ni   o-hanashí   shimáshĭta.
私　は　自分　自身　であの　大将　に　お話し　しました.

Watashí   wa   watashí   jíshin   de   anó   táishō   ni   o-hanashí   shimáshĭta.
私　は　私　　自身　であの　大将　に　お話し　しました.

I myself spoke to the general.

Anó   hĭtó   wa   jibún   de   watashí   ni   sō   hanashimáshĭta.
あの　人　は　自分　で　私　にそう　話しました.

Anó   katá   wa   go-jíshin   de   watashí   ni   sō   o-hanashí   ni   narimáshĭta.
あの　方　は　御自身　で　私　にそう　お話し　になりました.

He himself told me so.

Jibún or *jíshin* followed by *no* corresponds to the emphatic possessive adjective.

jibún no	自分の	my, your, his, own
jíshin no	自身の	her, our, own
jibún jíshin no	自分自身の	their own

Note that *jishin no* as an emphatic pronoun is sparingly used.

Anó   hĭtó   wa   jibún   no   monó   wo   jibún   de   kowashimáshĭta.
あの　人　は　自分　の　物　を　自分　で　こわしました.

He himself broke his own things.

Anó   hĭtó   wa   jibún   no   ié   wo   tatemáshĭta.　　That man built his
あの　人　は　自分　の　家　を　建てました.　　　own house.

Generally *jibún no* or *jíshin no* are not used as pronouns.

Koré wa dáre no ié désŭ ka.   Whose house is this?
これ は 誰 の 家です か.

Jibún no ié désŭ.   自分の家です.   ⎫
Watashí jíshin no ié désŭ.   私自身の家です.   ⎬ My own house.

Jibún, followed by *wa* or *ga* is, in rare cases, used as a simple personal pronoun.

Ashĭtá jibún wa Ōsaka e ikimásŭ.   To-morrow I shall go to Osaka.
あした 自分 は 大阪 へ行きます.

Koré wa jibún ga warúi no désŭ.   It is my fault. (idiom)
これ は 自分 が 悪い の です.   (*lit.* This, I bad am.)

Reflexive Verbs   *Hanshá Dōshi* 反射動詞

Reflexive verbs in Japanese are formed by using *jibún wo* 自分を, *jíshin wo* 自身を, or *jibún jíshin wo* 自分自身を before a verb.

jibún wo homéru   自分をほめる   ⎫
jíshin wo homéru   自身をほめる   ⎬ to praise oneself
jibún jíshin wo homéru   自分自身をほめる   ⎭

Watashí wa jibún wo homemásŭ.   ⎫
私 は 自分 を ほめます.   ⎪
Watashí wa watashí jíshin wo homemásŭ.   ⎬ I praise myself
私 は 私 自身 を ほめます.   ⎪
Watashí wa jibún jíshin wo homemásŭ.   ⎭
私 は 自分 自身 を ほめます.

Anáta wa (go-) jibún wo homemásŭ.   ⎫
貴方 は (御) 自分 を ほめます.   ⎪
Anáta wa (go-) jíshin wo homemásŭ.   ⎬ you praise yourself
貴方 は (御) 自身 を ほめます.   ⎪
Anáta wa (go-) jibún jíshin wo homemásŭ.   ⎭
貴方 は (御) 自分 自身 を ほめます.

Most of the English reflexive verbs have no corresponding reflexive forms in Japanese. Sometimes they are translated by intransitives, transitives, and sometimes by compounds with *surú*.

kakuréru	隠れる	to hide oneself
unuborerú	うぬぼれる	to flatter oneself
karadá wo araú[1]	体を洗う	to wash oneself
kimonó wo kirú[2]	着物を着る	to dress oneself
kubí wo kukurú[3]	首を括る	to hang oneself
dekishí surú	溺死する	to drown oneself

---

1 *araú* to wash   **2** *kirú* to put on, to don   **3** *kubí* neck, *kukurú* to cord

Watashí wa kimonó wo kimásŭ. 私　は　着物　を　着ます.	I dress myself.
Anáta wa kimonó wo kimásŭ. 貴方　は　着物　を　着ます.	You dress yourself.
Káre wa kimonó wo kimásŭ. 彼　は　着物　を　着ます.	He dresses himself.
Watashidómo wa kimonó wo kimásŭ. 私共　は　着物　を　着ます.	We dress ourselves.
Anátatachi wa kimonó wo kimásŭ. 貴方達　は　着物　を　着ます.	You dress yourselves.
Anó-hĭtótachi wa kimonó wo kimásŭ. あの人達　は　着物　を　着ます.	They dress themselves.

The expression *by oneself* is translated by *hĭtóri de* 一人で.

Anáta no chiisái musŭmesán wa hĭtóri de uchí e kaerimáshĭta.
貴方　の　小さい　娘さん　は　一人　で　家　へ　帰りました.
Your little daughter returned home by herself.

Sometimes *hĭtóri de* is used to translate English reflexive verbs.

hĭtóri de asobú 一人　で　遊ぶ	} to amuse oneself } to play by oneself

Anáta no oí wa niwá de hĭtóri de asondé imásŭ.
貴方　の　甥　は　庭　で　一人　で　遊んで　います.
Your nephew is amusing himself in the garden.

Have To plus the Infinitive

To have, followed by an *infinitive* is translated like *must*, that is, by *nákereba narimasén* なければなりません or *nákereba naránai* なければならない.

Watashí wa kómban máde ni tegamí wo yon-tsŭ kaká-nákereba
私　は　今晩　迄　に　手紙　を　四通　書かなければ
narimasén.   I **have to write** four letters by to-night. (*lit.* I, to-night until,
なりません.   letters four, if I don't write it won't do.)

Watashí wa kinō Yokohamá ni iká-nákereba naránakatta.
私　はきのう　横浜　に　行かなければ　ならなかった.
I **had to go** to Yokohama yesterday.

Anáta wa konó ié ni táishĭte íkura harawá-nákereba naránakatta
貴方　は　この　家　に　対して　幾ら　払わなければ　ならなかった
no désŭ ka.   How much **had you to pay** for this house?
の　ですか.

Watashí wa soré ni táishĭte ¥3,000,000 (sambyakú man yen) harawá-
私　はそれ　に　対して　　三百　万　円　払わ
nákereba naránakatta no déshĭta.   I **had to pay** ¥3,000,000 for it.
なければ　ならなかった　の　でした.

Do Not Have To and Need Not

Both expressions are translated by *hitsuyō wa* (or *ga*) *arimasén* 必要は（が）ありません (there is no need).

Hitsuyō 必要 means *necessity, requirement, indispensability,* etc.

Anáta wa dekaketakú-nái náraba dekakerú hitsuyō wa arimasén.
貴方　は　出かけたくない　ならば　出かける　必要　は　ありません.
You **do not have to** go out if you do not wish to.
(*lit.* You, if don't wish to go out necessity there is not.)

These negative expressions may also be translated by the negative subordinate of the verb, followed by *mo yói* もよい, with or without *désŭ.*

Anáta wa dekaketakú-nái náraba dekaké-nákute mo yói désŭ.
貴方　は　出かけたくない　ならば　出かけなくて　も　よい　です
You **do not have to** go out if you do not wish to.
(*lit.* You, if do not wish to go out, not going out even good is.)

To Be plus the Infinitive

To be followed by an *infinitive* is translated by *hazú désŭ* 筈です when referring to the present, and by *hazú déshĭta* 筈でした, or *hazú ni nátte imáshĭta* 筈になっていました when referring to the past. *Hazú* means *to be expected, to be due, ought to be.*

Watashí wa ashĭtá kōen surú hazú désŭ.　　I am (due) to give
私　は　あした　講演　する　筈　です.　　a lecture to-morrow.
(*lit.* I, to-morrow to give a lecture am due to.—*kōen surú* to give a lecture)

Káre wa kyō kúru hazú désŭ.　　He is expected to-day.
彼　は　きょう　来る　筈　です.　　(*lit.* He to-day to come is expected.)

Sonó kekkón shikí wa myōchō áru hazú désŭ.　The wedding is to take
その　結婚　式　は　明朝　ある　筈　です.　place to-morrow morning.
(*lit.* The wedding ceremony to-morrow morning to be is expected.—*kekkón* wedding, *shikí* ceremony, *myōchō* to-morrow morning)

Watashí wa imagoró asokó ni irú hazú désŭ.　I ought to be there
私　は　今頃　あそこ　に　いる　筈　です.　　by now.
(*lit.* I, about now, there to be to ought to.—*imagoró* about this time, etc.)

Ráigetsu Yōroppa e káeru hazú désŭ.　　I am to return to Europe
来月　ヨーロッパへ　帰る　筈　です.　　next month.

Watashí wa Nihón-go no kéiko wo ukéru hazú ni nátte imáshĭta
私　は　日本語　の　稽古　を　受ける　筈　に　なって　いました
ga jikán ga arimasén déshĭta.　　I had to take a Japanese lesson
が　時間　が　ありませんでした.　　but I had no time.

Vocabulary

Nouns			**Adjectives**		
ability	shúwan	手腕	annoying	urusái	煩サイ
chance	kikái	機会	customary	higoró-no	日頃ノ
consideration	jukkō	熟考	difficult	nan	難
destiny	úmmei	運命		kónnan	困難
discouragement	rakŭtán	落胆	true	shin no	真ノ
failure	shippái	失敗	**Verbs**		
fault	kettén	欠点	to approach		
			to get near	chikazúku	近ヅク
man of ability	shuwanká	手腕家	to catch, seize	tsŭkámu	ツカム
master	áruji	主	to choose	erábu	エラブ
misfortune	sainán	災難	to find	mitsŭke·rú	見付ケル
occupation	shokugyō	転業	**Adverbs**		
responsibility	sekinín	責任	at last	yattó	ヤット
tub	óke	桶	daily	nichijō-no	日常ノ
will	íshi	意志	undoubtedly	kittó	キット

to fall into misfortune *sainán ni ochiirú;* to receive attention, to be cared for *kamátte kurerú;* self-sufficient *dokuritsú-dóppo;* to care, to mind *kamáu;* to take responsibility *sekinín wo oú;* to blame *semé wo oú;* to be disgusted *aisó wo tsŭkasú;* to be discouraged *rakŭtán surú;* to take courage, to be courageous *shikkári surú;* to take care of *sewá wo surú;* to retire from a post, to leave one's employment *shirizóku;* to swim across *oyogikirú;* to try to swim across *oyogikirō to surú;* to drown oneself *dekishí surú;* to file (letters) *tojikomú;* to get rid of *nogaréru;* literary work *sakuhín;* question, problem *mondaí*

Exercise *Renshū* 練習

1. Konó yo-no-naká no ōku no hĭtó wa jibún jíshin no kotó bákari kangae-másŭ. Kō iú hĭtótachi wa shin-no tomó[1] ga arimasén kará sainán ni ochiittá tokí ni dáre mo kamátte[2] kurenái deshō. **2.** Watashí no musŭkó wa máda taihén wakái (chiisái) ga nan démo jibún de shimásŭ. Musŭkó wa kittó dokuritsú-dóppo no otokó ni náru deshō. **3.** Kimí ni okótta kotó ni táishĭte[3] wa dáre mo sekinín wo oú kotó ga dekimasén. Táda[4] kimí jíshin ga jibún no shippái ni táishĭte semé wo oú nómi[4] désŭ. Kimí wa jibún jishin no úmmei no áruji de arimásŭ. **4.** Watashí no itóko wa kanemochi de shuwanká désŭ ga amarí jibún jíshin no kotó bákari wo kangáete irú yō ni miemásŭ. **5.** Sonná ni jibún ni aisó wo tsŭkasú monó de wa arimasén. Ummei[5] no seisúi[5] wa dáre ni démo áru to iú kotó wo anáta wa yóku shĭtté irú hazú désŭ. Rakŭtán shĭté wa ikemasén; shikkári shi nasái. Anáta wa kikái ga chikazúita tokí ni tsŭkámu kotó ga máda dekimásŭ yo. **6.** Uchí no obāsan

---

1 *shin-no tomó* true friend **2** *dáre mo kamátte kurenái deshō* nobody will pay attention **3** *ni táishite* for; *kimí ni okótta kotó ni táishĭte* for what has happened to you **4** *táda, nómi* only, merely, solely **5** *úmmei* destiny, fortune; *seisúi* the ups and downs; *úmmei no seisúi* the ups and downs of fortune

wa jibún no sewá wo yóku shimásŭ. Obāsan wa kyū-jū-go sái désŭ ga máda jōbu de shikkári[1] shĭté imásŭ. **7.** Konó hon wo dō shimashō. Anáta ni agemashō ka.—Go-jibún de soré wo mitsŭketá no désŭ kará anáta ga tótte okí nasái. **8.** Konó o-káshi wa taihén oishíi désŭ. Dóko de o-kái ni narimáshĭta ka.—Kattá no de wa arimasén. Watashí ga jibún de tsŭkurimáshĭta. **9.** Watashí no yūjin wa yóku jukkō no nochí kaishá wo shirizóki jibún no shōbai wo hajimemáshĭta. Kaishá no monó wa dáre démo watashí no yūjin wa shōbai ni taisúru[2] shúwan ga nái to omoimáshĭta ga yūjin wa dái seikō shimáshĭta. **10.** Anó sakŭshá wa tanín no[3] sakuhín no kettén wo mitsŭké jibún no sakuhín bákari wo homemásŭ. **11.** Natsú takŭsán no Nihón-jin wa higoró-no ōkii furó-óke[4] de nichijō no furó ni háiru kawarí-ni chíisa-na tarái no náka de o-yu de karadá wo araimásŭ. Konó natsú no furó wa "gyōzui" to yobareté imásŭ.[5] **12.** Sakújitsu kodomó ga konó kawá wo oyogi-kirō to shimáshĭta ga yóku oyógu kotó ga dekimasén deshĭta nóde dekishí shimáshĭta. **13.** Jínsei[6] ni okéru shokugyō wo eránda áto hĭtó wa tsugí ni soré to onáji guraí no nan-mondaí[7] wo kangaé-nákereba narimasén. Soré wa seikō[8] no hōhō de arimásŭ. **14.** Kómban náni ka nasáru kotó ga arimásŭ ka.—Hái, jimúsho e shigotó ni kaerá-nákereba narimasén.—Móshi go-yō ga nákatta náraba go-isshó ni sampó ni yukaremásŭ nóni.—Dōmo arigatō. Ashĭtá no ban wa himá désŭ. **15.** Bōya, náze naité irú no.—Dátte konó pan ga kirái.—Kirái náraba tabénakute mo íi no désŭ yo. **16.** Ima náni wo itashimashō ka.—Anáta wa sonó tegamí wo tojikomá-nákereba ikemasén.—Sonó áto náni wo itashimashō ka.—Sonó áto wa uchí e káette mo yoroshíi désŭ. **17.** Konó sentakú wo minná shinákereba ikemasén ka.—Minná dekí-nákereba sentakuyá wo yobí nasái. **18.** Yattó anó urusái hĭtó kará nogarereraremáshĭta.[10] **19.** Tsuyói íshi[11] no chikará ga nákereba kitsuén no shūkan wo yamerú no wa kónnan désŭ.

1. この世の中の多くの人は自分自身の事ばかり考えます. こういう人達は真の友がありませんから災難におちいった時に誰もかまってくれないでしょう. **2.** 私の息子はまだ大変若い (小さい) が何んでも自分でします. 息子はきっと独立独歩の男になるでしょう. **3.** 君に起こった事に対しては誰も責任をおう事ができません. 唯君自身が自分の失敗に対して責めを負うのみです. 君は自分自身の運命の主であります. **4.** 私のいとこは金持で手腕家ですが余り自分自身の事ばかりを考えているように見えます. **5.** そんなに自分に愛想をつかすものではありません. 運命の盛衰は誰にでもあるという事を貴方はよく知っている筈です. 落胆してはいけません, しっかりしなさい. 貴方は機会が近づいた時につかむ事がまだできますよ. **6.** うちのおばあさんは自分の世話をよくします. おばあさんは九十五才ですがまだ丈夫

---

1 *shikkári shĭté irú* to be strong 2 *ni taisúru* for 3 *tanín no* other people's 4 *furó-óke* bath tub 5 *yobareté imásŭ* is called 6 *jínsei* life ; *jínsei ni okéru* in life 7 *nan-mondaí* difficult problem 8 *seikō* success ; *seikō no hōhō* the way to succeed 9 slang for *because* 10 *nogarerar éru* to be able to get rid of 11 *íshi no chikará* will power

でしっかりしています. **7.** この本をどうしましょう. 貴方に上げま
しょうか.—御自分でそれを見つけたのですから貴方がとっておきな
さい. **8.** このお菓子は大変おいしいです. どこでお買いになりまし
たか.—買ったのではありません私が自分で造りました. **9.** 私の友人
はよく熟考ののち, 会社を退き自分の商売を始めました. 会社の者は
誰でも私の友人は商売に対する手腕がないと思いましたが友人は大成
功しました. **10.** あの作者は他人の作品の欠点を見つけ自分の作品ば
かりをほめます. **11.** 夏, 沢山の日本人は日頃の大きいふろ桶で日常
のふろに入る代りに小さなたらいの中でお湯で体を洗います. この夏
のふろは "行水" と呼ばれています. **12.** 昨日子供がこの川を泳ぎき
ろうとしましたがよく泳ぐ事ができませんでしたので溺死しました.
13. 人生に於ける転業をえらんだあと, 人は次にそれと同じぐらいの
難問題を考えなければなりません. それは成功の方法であります.
14. 今晩何かなさる事がありますか.—はい, 事務所へ仕事に帰らなけ
ればなりません.—若し御用がなかったならば御一緒に散歩に行かれ
ますのに.—どうもありがとう. あしたの晩は暇です. **15.** 坊や, なぜ
泣いているの.—だってこのパンが嫌い.—嫌いならば食べなくてもい
ゝのですよ. **16.** 今, 何を致しましょうか.—貴方はその手紙をとじ込
まなければいけません.—そのあと何を致しましょうか.—そのあとは
家へ帰ってもよろしいです. **17.** この洗濯をみんなしなければいけま
せんか.—みんな出来なければ洗濯屋を呼びなさい. **18.** やっとあのう
るさい人から逃れられました. **19.** 強い意志の力がなければ喫煙の
習慣をやめるのは困難です.

1. Many people in this world think only of themselves. Such people have
no true friends, and they find themselves alone when they are struck by
misfortune. **2.** My son is still very young, yet he does everything by himself.
He will undoubtedly be a self-sufficient man. **3.** Nobody can be held responsible for what has happened to you. You have only yourself to blame for
your failure. You are the master of your own destiny. **4.** My cousin is rich
and a man of ability but he seems to think too much of himself. **5,** You
should not be so disgusted with yourself. You know very well that the wheel
of Fortune turns around for everybody. Don't be discouraged, but be brave;
you may yet get your chance when it comes near you. **6.** My grandmother
looks after herself very well. She is now ninety-five years old but is still
healthy and strong. **7.** What shall I do with this book? Shall I give it to
you?—You yourself found it, so you should keep it. **8.** This cake is very
delicious; where did you buy it?—I did not buy it; I made it myself.
9. After careful consideration my friend left our company and opened his
own business. Everybody in the company thought that he had no ability
for business, but he has made a big success. **10.** That writer finds fault with
everybody else's work and praises only his own. **11.** In summer, many

Japanese wash themselves with hot water in small tubs, instead of taking their daily hot bath in the customary large tubs. This kind of summer bath is called " gyōzui." **12.** Yesterday a boy tried to swim across this river, but as he could not swim well he drowned himself. **13.** Having chosen an occupation in life, one has next to consider a no less difficult question : the means of obtaing success. **14.** Have you anything to do to-night?—Yes, I have to return to the office to work.—If you had nothing to do we could go out together for a walk.—Thank you just the same. To-morrow night I shall be free. **15.** Why are you crying, my boy.—Because I don't like this bread. —Well, you do not have to eat it if you do not like it. **16.** What am I to do now?—You have to file those letters.—And what am I to do after?—After that you may go home. **17.** Am I supposed to do all this washing?—If you cannot do it all, call a laundry-man. **18.** At last I got rid of that annoying person. **19.** It is difficult to get rid of the habit of smoking unless one has great will power.

Fifty-third Lesson　第五十三課

Reciprocal Pronouns
Sōgo-dái-méishi 相ゾ互ヺ代名詞

Each other and **one another** are rendered by *tagái ni* 互に; besides, the verb *áu* 合う *to agree*, which in this case has the function of an auxiliary, is generally added to the simple stem of verbs of Class I and to the *i*-stem of verbs of Class II. *Au* is regularly conjugated according to the required tenses.

Note that *tagái ni* is an emphatic expression and may be omitted whenever emphasis is not required. The reciprocity of the action is understood by the auxiliary *áu,* placed after the verbal stem.

aisúru 愛する	to love	*tagái ni aishí-áu* 互 に 愛し合う	}to love each other }to love one another
iú 言う	to say	*iú-áu* 言い合う	}to say to each other }to say to one another
nagéru 投げる	to throw	*tagái ni nagé-áu* 互 に 投げ合う	}to throw at each other }to throw at one another
tasŭkéru 助ける	to help	*tagái ni tasŭké-áu* 互 に 助け合う	}to help each other }to help one another
o-sejí wo iú お世辞を言う	to flatter	*tagái ni o-sejí wo iú-áu* 互 にお世辞を言い合う	}to flatter each other }to flatter one another

Anó otokó-no-kodomotachí wa **tagái ni** *ishí wo* **nagé-atté** *imáshĭta.*
あの　男の子供達　は　互　に　石　を　投げ合って　いました.
Those boys were throwing stones at one another (at each other).

Hĭtó **wa** **tagái** **ni** **aishi** **awá-nákereba** *narimasén.*   People must love
人　は　互　に　愛し　合わなければ　なりません.   one another.

O-tagái **ni** *sayōnara* *wo* **ií-aimáshĭta.**   We said good-bye
お互　に　左様なら　を　言い合いました.   to each other.

Konó gakkō de wa séito ga minná **o-tagái** **ni** **tasŭké-aimásŭ.**
この　学校　で　は　生徒　が　みんな　お互　に　助け合います.
In this school all students help one another.

Sonó fŭtarí no musŭmetachí wa ítsumo **tagái** **ni** *o-seji wo ií-aimásŭ.*
その　二人　の　娘達　は　いつも　互　にお世辞　を言い合います.
Those two girls always flatter each other.

Reciprocal pronouns may also be translated by the word **dōshi**
同士, from *dō* 同 *same, together,* and **shi** 士 *fellow.* The particle *de*
generally follows **dōshi.**

Tomodachí **dōshi** *de kenká wo surú no wa yóku nái désŭ.*
友達　同士　でけんか　を　する　の　は　よくない です.
Friends should not quarrel among themselves (with one another).
   (*lit.* Friends, with one another, quarrel to do the thing, good is not.)

Genjí[1] to Héike[1] wa katakí **dōshi** *de átta.*
源氏　と　平家　は　敵　同士　であった.
The Genji and Heike families were enemies. (were enemies of each other)

Indefinite Pronouns
Fŭtéi-dái-méishi 不ブ定テイ代名詞

The words **man, one,** and **people,** when used as indefinite pronouns,
are translated by **hĭtó** 人.

Hĭtó wa jibún no gímu wo shirá-nákereba narimasén.
人　は　自分　の　義務　を　知らなければ　なりません.
One should know one's own duty.

Hĭtó wa shi shĭté[2] mo na wa nokóru.[3]   **Man** dies, but his
人　は　死して　も　名　は　残る.   name remains.

Hĭtó wa fuyúkai-na kotó wo kiraimásŭ.   **People** dislike unpleasant
人　は　不愉快　な　事　を　嫌います.   things.
   One dislikes unpleasant things. (*lit.* Man unpleasant things dislikes.)

We, as an indefinite pronoun may be translated by **warewaré**
我々, as well as by **hĭtó,** as in the above examples. *Warewaré* is
more emphatic than *hĭtó.*

Warewaré (hĭtó) wa mazushíi[4] hĭtóbito wo tasŭké-nákereba narimasén.
我々　（人）　は　貧しい　人々　を　助けなければなりません.
We must help the poor. (*lit.* We, poor people if do not help won't do.)

---

1 *Genjí* and *Héike* are the names of two powerful families of the 12th century,
who bitterly fought against each other for military and political supremacy. **2** *shi*
surú to die (in formal speech or literary style), *shi* death, *shi shĭté mo* even dying
3 *nokóru* to remain, to be left over or behind **4** poor

The world, as well as **people,** may be translated by *sejín* 世人, which is the literal translation of the two indefinite English words.

Sejín wa tsúne ni ijín[1] wo sambí[2] surú.　　**The world** (people) always
世人 は 常 に 偉人 を 讃美 する.　　admire great men.

Also *the world* may be translated by *hìtó.*

The indefinite expressions *they say that......,* and *they tell me that ......,* etc., are translated by *to iú kotó désŭ* という事です (*so to say the thing is*), by *hanashí désŭ* 話です (*the talk is*), or by *sŏ désŭ* そうです (*so it is, so it appears*).

Tokugawá kōshaku wa ráigetsu Fŭransú e irassháru to iú kotó désŭ
　徳川　　公爵　は　来月　フランスへいらっしゃるという　事　です.
(or *irassháru sŏ désŭ.*) They say that Prince Tokugawa will go to France
いらっしゃるそうです.　　next month.

Anáta wa Itarī-go wo hanásu kotó ga dekíru sŏ désŭ ne.
貴方 はイタリー語を 話す 事 が 出来る そう です ね.
They tell me that you can speak Italian.

Sometimes, in familiar speech, the word *ne,* at the end of a sentence, as in the last of the above two examples, gives a vague idea of uncertainty to the thing that has been said or told.

Sŏ désŭ is used also when the above indefinite expressions are used in the past tense. Sometimes, however, *sŏ déshìta,* instead of *sŏ désŭ,* may be used.

Sakúban Nihón-bashí no sóba ni káji ga átte ié ga sū-ken yaketá[3] sŏ désŭ
昨晩　　日本橋　のそば に火事があって家が　数軒　焼けたそうです
(or *sŏ déshìta*).　　They told me that last night a fire burned down several
（さう　でした）.　　houses near Nihon-bashi.

Anáta wa go-kekkón[4] nasátta sŏ désŭ ne (or *sŏ déshìta ne*).
貴方 は　御結婚 なさったそう です ね　（さう でした ね）.
They told me that you have married.

Across

When **across** indicates position without motion, it is translated by *no mukō* の向こう or *no mukō gawá* の向こう側 placed after the noun it modifies.

Yamadá Hákase[5] wa dóko ni súnde imásŭ ka.　　Where does Dr. Yamada
山田 博士 は どこ に住んでいますか.　　live?

Anó katá wa konó michí no mukō (gawá) ni súnde imásŭ.
あの 方 は この 道 の 向こう （側） に住んでいます.
He lives **across** this street.

---

1 great man　**2** *sambí surú* to admire　**3** *yakerú* to burn down　**4** *kekkón surú* to marry, *go-kekkón nasáru* polite form　**5** *Hákase* is used as a title for people who have taken the highest degree conferred by a university or college, as doctor of law, of medicine, etc.

When *across* is used after a verb of motion, it is translated by the verb *yokogíru* 横ぎる (to go across).

Hĭtóri no onná-no-ko ga Sumidagawá wo yokogítte oyogimáshĭta.
一人 の 女の子 が 隅田川 を 横ぎって 泳ぎました.
A girl swam **across** the Sumida river. (*oyógu* to swin)

Jidōsha ga ōi kará michí wo yokogíru no wa kikén[1] désŭ.
自動車 が多いから 道 を 横ぎる の は 危険 です.
As there are many motor-cars, it is dangerous **to go across** the street.

Watashí wa nóhara wo yokogítte chikámichi[2] wo ikimáshĭta.
私 は 野原 を 横ぎって 近道 を 行きました.
I went by a short-cut **across** the field. (*lit.* I, the field crossing, shortcut I went.
—*chikámichi wo ikú* or *surú* to take a short cut)

Sometimes the verb itself embodies the meaning of *across*, in which case it has no corresponding word in the translation.

Sumidagawá ni wa takŭsán no hashí ga kakátte[3] imásŭ.
隅田川 に は 沢山 の 橋 が かかって います.
There are a great many bridges **across** the Sumida river.
(*lit.* On Sumida river many bridges are laid across.)

To come across in the sense of *to meet a person by accident* is translated by *ni deaú* に出会う to happen to meet.

Watashí wa Tōkyō Ekí e ittá tokí ni anáta no móto no Nihón-go no
私 は 東京 駅 へ行った時 に 貴方 の 元 の 日本語 の
senséi ni deaimáshĭta.   When I went to Tokyo station I **came across**
先生 に 出会いました.   your former Japanese teacher.
(*lit.* I, Tokyo station went when, your former Japanese-language teacher met.)

Through

When *through* indicates position without motion it is translated by *kará* から or *no aidá kará* の間から, placed after the noun it modifies.

Anó mátsu no edá no aidá kará íma mángetsu ga miemásŭ.
あの 松 の 枝 の 間 から 今 満月 が 見えます.
We can now see the full moon **through** the branches of the pine-trees.
(*lit.* Those pine-trees' branches through, now full moon is seen.)

Sonó jidōsha jíko[4] ga okótta tokí watashí wa chōdo mádo kará mite
その 自動車 事故 が起こった時 私 は 丁度 窓 から 見て
imáshĭta.   When that motor-car accident happened I was just then looking
いました.   **through** the window. (*lit.* That motor-car accident occurred
when, I, just then, window from looking was.)

When *through* is used instead of *by means of*, *through the efforts of*, and similar expressions, it is translated by *de* で or *ni yotté* によって.

---

1 danger, peril **2** short-cut **3** *kakáru* to be laid across **4** accident

Maedá San no sewá[1] de (or *jínryoku de*) *watashí wa konó tsŭtomeguchí[2]*
前田 さん の 世話 で （尽力 で） 私 は この 勤口
ga arimáshĭta.   I got this position **through** the assistance of Mr. Maeda.
が ありました.   (*lit.* Mr. Maeda's assistance by, I this position had.)

Some Japanese verbs embody the idea of *through*, in which case
this word is not translated.

Anó kodomó wa anáta no ié no mádo e ishí wo nagekomimáshĭta.[3]
あの 子供 は あなた の 家 の 窓 へ 石 を 投げこみました.
That boy threw a stone **through** the window of your house.
(*lit.* That boy, your house window to, stone threw through.)

Sumidagawá wa Tōkyō tónai[4] wo nagárete[5] imásŭ.
隅田川 は 東京 都内 を 流れて います.
The Sumida river flows **through** Tokyo city.
(*lit.* Sumida river, Tokyo city-inside flowing is.)

Through, preceded by a transitive verb, is translated by *tsuranúite*
or *tōshĭte*. *Tsuranúite* is the subordinate of *tsuranúku* 貫く
to go through something, and *tōshĭte* is the subordinate of *tōsu*
通す *to run, pass, etc. (anything) through.*

Anáta wa sonná ni ga[6] wo tōshĭte (tsuranúite) wa ikemasén.
貴方 は そんな に 我 を 通して （貫いて） は いけません.
You mustn't push through your own stubbornness.
(*lit.* You, such stubborness running through won't do.)

When preceded by an intransitive verb, *through* may be translated
by *tsuranúite, tōshĭte,* or by *tōtte* 通って from *tōru* 通る, *to
pass through, to pass by.*

Sumidagawá wa Tōkyō tónai wo tsuranúite (tōshĭte or tōtte)
隅田川 は 東京 都内 を 貫いて （通して 通って）
nagárete imásŭ.   The Sumida river passes **through** the city of Tokyo.
流れて います.   (*lit.* Sumida river, Tokyo city-inside going through flowing is.)

Any of the three expressions *tsuranúite, tōshĭte* and *tōtte* may be
used to translate **through** preceded by an intransitive verb if it
expresses a progressive action, as the flowing of a river, etc. However,
when the action occurs suddenly, then only *tsuranúku* is generally
used, as in the following example:

Dangán ga káre no muné wo tsuranúita.
弾丸 が 彼 の 胸 を 貫いた.
A bullet **went through** his chest. (*dangán* bullet, *muné* chest)

Sometimes a verb followed by *through* is translated into Japanese
by different expressions.

---

1 *sewá* or *jínryoku* assistance   2 *position*   3 *nagekomú* to throw into, through
4 *tónai* inside the city; *to* metropolis; *nái* inside   5 *nagaréru* to flow, to stream
6 *ga* stubbornness

Anó rōfujin wa iró-iró no kurō¹ wo shĭté kimáshĭta.
あの 老婦人 は 色々 の 苦労 を して 来ました.
That old lady has passed **through** many difficulties.
　(*lit.* That old lady various difficulties experienced.)

Sonó akambō wa yodōshi² nakiakashimáshĭta.³　That baby cried all night
その 赤ん坊 は 夜通し 泣きあかしました.　**through.**

Watashí wa yodōshi ókite imáshĭta.　I was awake all night **through.**
私 は 夜通し おきていました.

The Same

The same, when corresponding in meaning to *identical*, is generally translated by **onaji** 同じ in colloquial speech, and, in literary style, by **dōitsu** 同一, sometimes abbreviated into **dō** 同, by **dōji** 同時 and by **dōyō** 同よう.

the same thing	{ **onaji** *monó*	同じ物
	dōitsu *no monó*	同一の物
of the same kind	{ **onaji** *shurúi*	同じ種類
	dō-*shurúi*	同種類
all (quite) the same	*mattakú* **onaji**	全く同じ
just the same	*chōdo* **onaji**	丁度同じ
at the same time	{ **onaji** *tokí ni*	同じ時に
	dōji *ni*	同時に
in the same way	{ **onaji** *hōhō de*	同じ方法で
	dōyō *na hōhō de*	同ような方法で

Anó shōnentachi to shōjotachi wa **onaji** *gakkō e ikimásŭ.*
あの 少年達 と 少女達 は 同じ 学校 へ 行きます.
Those boys and girls go to **the same** school.

Anáta wa watashí to **onaji**-*toshí désŭ.*　You are of **the same** age as
あなた は 私 と 同じ年 です.　myself.

Chichí no kenkō wa máe to **onaji** *désŭ.*　My father's health is just
父 の 健康 は 前 と 同じ です.　**the same** as before.

Watashitachí wa **onaji** *tēburu ni suwarimáshĭta.*　We sat at **the same**
私達 は 同じ テーブル に 坐りました.　table.

Anáta wa jū-nen máe to chōdo **onaji** *désŭ.*　You look just **the same**
あなた は 十年 前 と 丁度 同じ です.　as ten years ago.

In the meaning of *unchanged*, the expression **the same** is generally translated by **kawarimasén** 変りません or **kawaranái** 変らない.

Byōnin wa késa to hotóndo **kawaranái.**　The patient is almost **the**
病人 は けさと 殆ど 変らない.　**same** as this morning.
　(*lit.* The patient, this morning-like, practically is unchanged.)

---

1 *kurō* troubles, hardships, difficulties; *kurō wo shĭté kúru* to experience difficulties
2 *yodōshi* all night long, all night through　3 *nakiakásu* to cry all night through

Káre no watashí ni táisuru táido wa ítsumo **kawaranái.**
彼　の　私　に　対する　態度　は　いつも　変らない.
He has been always **the same** to me. (*táido* attitude, behaviour)
(*lit.* He, to me towards, attitude always does not change.)

Anáta wa jū-nen máe to chittómo **kawarimasén.**
あなた　は　十年　前　とちっとも　変りません.
You look just **the same** as ten years ago.
(*lit.* You ten years ago as, at all haven't changed.)

In the sense of *still, yet,* the expression **the same** may be translated by **yahári** やはり (likewise, as well, etc.)

Káre wa sŭkóshi namakemonó désŭ ga **yahári** *watashí wa káre wo*
彼　は　少し　なまけ者　です　が　やはり　私　は　彼　を
sŭkí désŭ.   He is a little bit lazy, but I like him all **the same.**
好き　です.

Idiomatic usage:

It is the same to me.   *Watashí mo sonó tōri désŭ.*   私もその通りです.
It is the same old trick.   *Yóku áru furúi te désŭ.*   よくある古い手です.
It is all the same to me.   *Watashí wa dóchira de mo kamaimasén.*
                             私　は　どちら　で　も　かまいません.

Such

The usual translation of **such** is **konná** こんな, **anná** あんな and **sonná** そんな.

Konná is used when referring to things near the speaker, **anná** when referring to things far from the speaker and the person spoken to, and **sonná** when referring to things nearer to the person spoken to than to the speaker.

All three expressions are also used when referring to abstract things.

Watashí wa **anná** *rikō-na kodomó wo míta kotó ga arimasén.*
私　は　あんな　利口な　子供　を　見た　事　がありません.
I never saw **such** a clever boy.
(*lit.* I, **such** a clever boy I saw the fact there is not.)

Konná *kiré wo urimásŭ ka.*   Do you sell **such** cloth?
こんな　切れ　を　売ります　か.

Anná *hirói kawá wa oyogí-kiremasén.*[1]   I cannot swim across **such**
あんな　広い　河　は　泳ぎきれません.   a wide river.

Sonná *shigotó wa dekimasén.*   I cannot do **such** work.
そんな　仕事　は　出来ません.

Sonná *bakágeta gíron wo kiitá kotó ga arimasén.*   I never heard **such**
そんな　ばかげた　議論　を　聞いた　事　がありません.   foolish arguments.
(*lit.* Such foolish arguments I heard the fact there is not.—*gíron* discussion, arguments)

---

1 *oyogí-kirú* to swim across; *oyogí kiremasén* cannot be swum across

Such is idiomatically translated in various ways, as shown in the following representative examples.

Sō iŭ hĭtótachi wa kikén désŭ.   **Such** people are dangerous.
そう いう 人達 は 危険 です.   (*sō iŭ* so called=such)

Senséi ya dendōshi no yō-na shokugyō.   **Such** occupations as teacher or
先生 や 伝道師 の ような 転業.   missionary. (*yō-na* like)

Anáta wa watashí wo hijō-ni bikkúri sasemáshĭta.   You gave me **such**
あなた は 私 を 非常に びっくりさせました.   a fright.
    (*bikkúri saserú* びっくりさせる to frighten, *hijō-ni* much, very much)

Tóttemo subarashíi déshĭta.   We had **such** a wonderful time. (*tóttemo*
とっても 素晴しい でした.   very much; *subarashíi* splendid etc.)

Káre wa soré wo shinjíru hodó no báka de wa nái.
彼 はそれ を 信じる 程 の ばか で はない.
He is not **such** a fool as to believe that.
    (*lit.* He, that to believe as, fool is not.—*shinjíru* to believe)

Tsŭkué, tēburu, isú sonó-ta no ruijí kágu.   Desks, tables, chairs and
机, テーブル, 椅子 その他 の 類似 家具.   **such like** furniture.

Watashí wa kinō chōdo koré to onaji no wo kaimáshĭta.
私 はきのう丁度 これ と 同じ の を 買いました.
I bought just **such** another yesterday.

Mā, nan to iŭ kodomó darō!   **Such** a child! *or* What a child!
まあ, 何んという 子供 だろう.   (In rather bad sence.)
    (*lit.* Well, what kind of a boy will he be!?)

Taihén-na usótsŭki.   He is **such** a liar. (*taihén-na* awful, dreadful,
大変 な うそつき.   extraordinary, etc.)

Sŭ-ken no ié ga fukí-tobasáreta hodó no sugói bakuhatsŭ-ryokú déshĭta.
数軒 の 家 が 吹きとばされた 程 の すごい 爆発力 でした.
Such was the force of the explosion that several houses were blown off.
    (*Sŭ* several, *ken* numerative for houses, *fukí-tobásu* 吹きとばす to blow off,
    fukí-tobasaréru 吹きとばされる to be blown off, *bakuhatsú* explosion,
    ryokú force, *sugói* すごい dreadful, terrible, etc.)

such and such...... | *koré-koré no* (colloq.)   これこれの
                          | *shiká-jiká no* (Lit.)   しかじか(の)

such and such persons   *dáre-dáre*   誰々

Sonó kozútsumi no naiyō wa shiká-jiká désŭ.   The contents of this parcel
その 小包 の 内容は しかじか です.   are **such and such.**

Dáre-dáre e shiká-jiká no kingakú no shiharaí......
誰々 へ しかじか の 金額 の 支払
The payment of **such and such** sums to **such and such** persons......

Yonónaka wa konná monó désŭ.   **Such** is life. (*yonónaka* the world, society,
世の中 は こんな もの です.   the public, the times, etc.)

Vocabulary

	Nouns		Alps	*Arupŭsú*	アルプス
ability	*nōryoku*	能力	boatman	*sendō*	船頭

				Adjectives		
brain	*zunō*	頭脳				
canal	*únga*	運河	cultured	*monoshirí*	物識
change (improvement)	*kaizén*	改善	different	*kotonátta*	異ナッタ
			disgusting	*iyána*	嫌ナ
change (modification)	*kairyō*	改良	material	*busshitsú*	物質
			mental	*seishinteki*	精神的
direction	*hōkō*	方向	principal	*jūyō-na*	重要ナ
lakes	*koshō*	湖沼	powerful	*kyōryoku-na*	強力ナ
limitation	*han-i*	範囲		Verbs		
long life	*nagaikí*	長生				
Mars	*Kásei*	火星	to advance	*shímpo surú*	進歩スル
matter	*jíbutsu*	事物	to cut	*kaisetsú surú*	開設スル
mountain	*sangakú*	山岳	to divert	*nagaré wo henkō surú*	
nature	*shizénkai*	自然界			流レヲ変更スル
need	*hitsujuhín*	必需品	to keep	*tamótsu*	保ツ
planet	*yūsei*	遊星	to live	*kurasú*	暮ス
railway	*tetsudō*	鉄道	to try	*yatté mí·ru*	ヤッテ見ル
rivers	*kásen*	河川		Adverbs		
selfishness	*rikóshin*	利己心				
source	*gensén*	源泉	ever	*kátsute*	カツテ
understanding	*chíshiki*	知識	generally	*gáishǐte*	概シテ
vegetable	*shokúbutsu*	植物	likely	*rashíi*	ラシイ
width	*hírosa*	広サ	scarcely	*karōjite*	辛ウジテ
youth	*wákasa*	若サ	sincerely	*seijitsú-ni*	誠実ニ
			suitably	*tekitō-ni*	適当ニ
			the most	*jitsú-ni*	実ニ

hári ni íto wo tōsu   to **run** a thread **through** a needle
針 に 糸 を 通す

paipú ni mizú wo tōsu   to **let** water **run through** a pipe
パイプ に 水 を 通す

hǐtó wo mon wo tōsu   to **let** a person **go through** the gate
人 を 門 を 通す

hǐtó ga mon wo tōru   a person **goes through** the gate
人 が 門 を 通る

   to be able to obtain *éru kotó ga dekíru*; to change for the better, to improve *kaizén surú*; to improve the quality of, to produce a better kind of *kairyō surú*; to tunnel, to make a tunnel *tonnerú wo ugátsu*; to dig, to pierce, to cut through *ugátsu*; to fasten, to connect, to join *tsunagú*; to read well, to read carefully *jukudokú surú*; to write well, to write in good style *fudé ga tátsu*; to quarrel with one another *tagái ni arasói-áu*; to be opened, inaugurated *hirakaréru*; to be run over *hikaréru*; to reveal *akíraka ni náru*; to make good, to achieve *monógoto wo shǐtogéru*; state, condition of things *jōtai*; physical work *kínniku rōdō*; commonplace, commonest *heiheibombón no*; a man of ideas *chibō no jímbutsu*

Exercise *Renshū* 練習

1. Yatté míru máde wa náni ga dekíru ka wakarimasén. **2.** Warewaré wa seikatsú ni hitsuyō-na monó[1] wo éru tamé ni tsuchí ni mattakú tayótte[2] imásŭ. Warewaré ga i-shokú-jū[3] sonó-ta no[4] busshitsú seikatsú hitsujuhín wo éru kotó ga dekíru gensén wa hoká ni arimasén. **3.** Konó sekái wa kátsute chibō no jímbutsu[5] ni yotté osameráreta gótoku[6] kónnichi mo osamerárete imásŭ. **4.** Jinrúi wa konó sekái ni sumitsuité írai,[7] nagái toshitsukí[8] no aidá ni ōku no hénka wo motaráshĭta. Shokubutsurúi ya dōbutsurúi no kairyō, kásen no nagaré no henkō, koshō no haisuí, sangakú ni tonnerú wo ugáchi, matá úmi to úmi wo tsunagú[9] únga no kaisetsú wo shĭté kitá. **5.** Nihyakú nen ámari máe máde ningén no busshitsú no honséi ni kánshite no[10] chíshiki wa Girishájin ya Rōmajin nádo no to hotóndo onají kuraí[11] na monó de átta. **6.** Hĭtó ga móshi seishintekí no shigotó wo sézu kínniku rōdō bákari wo surú náraba sonó hĭtó wa zunō dáke wo tsŭkattá hodó[12] nagaikí wo shinái darō to iwareté imásŭ. **7.** Móshi rekishí to soré kará sekái no kotonátta kuní no hĭtóbito no fūshū wo yóku kenkyū surú náraba hĭtó wa ryokō sézu tómo[13] táshĭka ni monoshirí ni náru deshō. **8.** Hĭtó wa jibún no nōryoku no han-i wo shirubéki[14] désŭ. **9.** Seishintekí ni wákasa wo tamótsu ni wa[15] hĭtó wa chitekí kúnren[16] wo shinákereba narimasén. **10.** Tekitō-ni shokú wo tóru monó[17] wa gáishĭte kenkō ni kuraserú[18] yō désŭ shi jukudokú surú monó wa yóku fudé ga tatsurashíi désŭ. **11.** Rikóshin no nái mokutekí wo mótsu hĭtó wa sekén ga nan to iú tómo[19] seikō shimásŭ. **12.** Tetsudō, sempakú soshĭté hikōki wa sekái no súbete no bubún wo tagái ni chikazukemáshĭta.[20] **13.** Móshi hĭtóbito ga mótto kandái de seijitsú ni tasŭké-áu náraba konó yo wa mótto sumí-yói tokoró[21] to náru deshō ni. **14.** Keitéi shímai[22] ga tagái ni arasói-áu hodó iyá-na kotó wa ta[23] ni arimasén. **15.** Naganén[24] no aidá yūmei-na Shimpurón Sandō wa Arupŭsú wo koerú jūyō-na michí de arimáshĭta ga sen-kyū-hyakú-rokú nen Shimpurón tonnerú ga hirakárete írai konó michí wa amarí tsŭkawaré nakú[25] narimáshĭta. **16.** Sobiēto Rempō (So-ren) wa Ajiyá wo koeté Taiheiyō ni máde nóbite imásŭ. **17.** Anó inú wa michí wo hashĭtté koeté itá tokí ni jidōsha ni hikaremáshĭta. **18.** Anó sendō wa

---

1 *seikatsú ni hitsuyō-na monó* things which we need for our life=on which we live **2** *mattakú* wholly, *tayótte irú* to depend on **3** *i-shokú-jū*=clothing (*i*), food (*shokú*), and shelter (*jū*) **4** *sonó-ta no* others **5** man (*lit.*) **6** *gótoku* as; *osameráreta gótoku* as it has been ruled **7** *sumitsuité írai* originally found **8** *toshitsŭkí* years; *nagái toshitsŭkí no aidá ni* in the course of ages **9** *úmi to úmi wo tsunagú* from sea to sea **10** *busshitsu no honséi* the nature of matter; *ni kanshité no* of **11** *hotóndo onají kuraí* scarcely further **12** *tsŭkattá hodó* as if he used **13** emphatic particle meaning *even* **14** *shirubéki désŭ* should know **15** *tamótsu ni wa* in order to keep **16** *chitekí kúnren* intellectual exercise **17** *tekitō ni shokú wo tóru monó wa* the man who eats well (properly, suitably) **18** *kenkō ni kuraserú yō* is able to live in good health, or well **19** *séken* people, the world; *séken ga nan to iú tómo* whatever the world may say **20** *chikazukéru* to cause to approach; *tagái ni chikazukemáshĭta* has approached each other **21** *mótto sumí yói tokoró* a better place to live in **22** *keitéi shímai* brothers and sisters **23** *ta ni* other, else; *hodó iyána kotó wa ta ni arimasén* there is nothing more disgusting than **24** *naganén* many years; *naganén no aidá* for thousands of years **25** *amarí tsukawaré nái* to be little used

dóko ni súnde imásŭ ka.—Kawá mukō ni súnde imásŭ. **19.** Konó kosúi no hírosa wa dóno kuraí arimásŭ ka. *or* Kosúi no mukō gishí máde[1] dóno kuraí arimásŭ ka.—Mukō (*or* Mukō gishí) máde go-máiru arimásŭ. **20.** Móshi watashitachí ga me de míru bákari de nákŭ[2] kokóro no me wo tōshĭte monó wo míru náraba heiheibombón no monó de mo jitsú-ni subarashíi monó désŭ. **21.** Kyōryoku-na bōenkyō wo tōshĭte Kásei wo chūibukaku kenkyū shĭtá tokí ni Kásei wa chikyū ni yóku nitá shizén kōsei[3] wo mótte irú kotó ga akíraka ni narimáshĭta. **22.** Súbete no yūsei wa onáji hōkō ni unkō shimásŭ.[4] **23.** Yo-ji ni ukagaú kawarí ni go-ji de wa go-tsugō ga waruí desŭ ka—Dō itashimáshĭte. Onají de gozaimásŭ. **24.** Anná kitanarashíi otokó wo kesshĭte míta kotó ga arimasén. **25.** Mokŭtekí wo togéru[5] tamé ni wa zenryō de átte yói kotó wo séneba narimasén.

1. やって見る迄は何が出来るか解りません. **2.** 我々は生活に必要な物を得るために土に全く頼っています. 我々が衣食住其他の物質生活必需品を得る事ができる源泉は外にありません. **3.** この世界はかつて知謀の人物によって治められた如く今日も治められています. **4.** 人類はこの世界に住みついて以来, 長い年月の間に多くの変化をもたらした. 植物類や動物類の改良, 河川の流れの変更, 湖沼の排水, 山岳にトンネルをうがち又海と海をつなぐ運河の開設等をしてきた. **5.** 二百年余り前まで人間の物質の本性(ほんしょう)に関しての知識はギリシヤやローマ人などのと殆んど同じくらいなものであった. **6.** 人が若し, 精神的の仕事をせず筋肉労伤ばかりをするならばその人は頭脳だけを使った程長生きをしないだろうと言われています. **7.** 若し歴史とそれから世界の異った国の人々の風習をよく研究するならば人は旅行せずとも確かに物識りになるでしょう. **8.** 人は自分の能力の範囲を知るべきです. **9.** 精神的に若さを保つには人は智的訓練をしなければなりません. **10.** 適当に食を取る者は概して健康に暮せるようですし熟読する者はよく筆が立つらしいです. **11.** 利己心の無い目的を持つ人は世間が何んと云うとも成功します. **12.** 鉄道, 船舶そして飛行機は世界のすべての部分を互に近づけました. **13.** 若し, 人々がもっと寛大で誠実に助け合うならばこの世はもっと住みよい所となるでしょうに. **14.** 兄弟姉妹が互に争い合うほど嫌な事は他にありません. **15.** 長年の間有名なシンプロン山道はアルプスを越える重要な道でありましたが千九百六年シンプロントンネルが開かれて以来この道はあまり使われなくなりました. **16.** ソヴィエート連邦(ソ連)はアジヤを越えて太平洋に迄のびています. **17.** あの犬は道を走って越えていた時に自動車にひかれました. **18.** あの船頭はどこに住んでいますか.—川向こうに住んでいます. **19.** この湖水の広さはどの位あり

---

1 *mukō gishí máde* to the other side=across 2 *bákari de nákŭ* not only 3 *shizén kōsei* physical constitution 4 *unkō surú* to travel (of heavenly bodies) 5 *mokŭteki wo togéru* to make good; *mokŭtekí* purpose, *togéru* to accomplish

ますか．　湖水の向こう岸までどの位ありますか．—向こう　（向こう岸）
まで五哩あります．　　20.　若し，私達が眼で見るばかりでなく心の眼を
通して物を見るならば平々凡々の物でも実にすばらしいものです．　　21.
強力な望遠鏡を通して火星を注意深く研究した時に火星は地球によく似
た自然構成を持っている事が明らかになりました．　22. すべての遊星
は同じ方向に運行します．　23. 四時に伺う代りに五時では御都合が
悪いですか.—どう致しまして．同じで御座います．　24. あんな汚らし
い男を決して見た事がありません．　25. 目的を遂げるためには善良で
あって善い事をせねばなりません.

1. We do not know what we can do until we try. 2. We are wholly
dependent on the earth for that on which we live (for what we live on).
There is no other source from which we can obtain food, shelter, clothing,
and the other needs of our material life. 3. The world is ruled to-day, as it
ever has been ruled, by men of ideas. 4. In the course of ages man has
done much to change the world he originally found. He has modified vegetable
and animal life, diverted rivers, drained lakes, tunnelled mountains, and cut
canals from sea to sea. 5. Little more than two hundred years ago man had
advanced scarcely further in the understanding of the nature of matter than
had the Greeks and the Romans. 6. It is said that if a man performs only
physical work and does no mental work, he will probably not live so long
as if he used his brain. 7. Without traveling one may be truly cultured if
one studies well the history and the customs of the peoples of the different
countries of the world. 8. A man should understand well the limitations of
his ability. 9. To keep strong in mind a man must have intellectual exercise.
10. We may say that just as the man who eats well is likely to live well,
so the man who reads well is likely to write well. 11. The man with an
unselfish purpose succeeds, whatever the world may say. 12. Railways, ships
and airplanes have brought all parts of the world to within a short distance
from each other. 13. If people were more tolerant and sincerely helped one
another this world would be a much better place to live in. 14. Nothing is
more disgusting than to see brothers and sisters quarreling with one another.
15. For thousands of years the famous Simplon Pass was the principal route
across the Alps, but since 1906, when the Simplon tunnel was opened, the
pass has been very little used. 16. The Union of Soviet Socialist Republics
extends across Asia to the Pacific. 17. That dog was run over by a motor-car
while running across the road. 18. Where does the boatman live?—He lives
across the river. 19. How wide is this lake? *or* How far is it across the
lake?—It is five miles across. 20. The commonest things are the most wonderful, if we look at them not merely through the eyes of our head, but also
through the eyes of our mind. 21. When carefully studied through a powerful
telescope Mars reveals itself as having a physical constitution very like that
of the earth. 22. All planets travel in the same direction. 23. Is it inconvenient for you if I come at five instead of four o'clock?—Not at all; it is
just the same to me. 24. I never saw such a dirty man. 25. Man must be
good and do good in order to make good.

Fifty-fourth Lesson 第五十四課

Infinitives *Futeihō* 不ッ定ティ法ホウ

In Lesson 36, page 273 (which see), it has been stated that, placed after a verb of motion, an infinitive indicating purpose is translated by its corresponding Japanese verbal *stem* followed by *ni*.

*Akabō[1] ga kabán wo **tóri ni** kimáshĭta.*   The porter has come **to get**
赤帽　が　鞄　を　取り　に　来ました.   the trunk.

In the same lesson it has been stated also that, placed after a verb that is not of motion, an infinitive with the implied meaning of purpose is translated by the *simple present* of the corresponding Japanese verb, followed by *tamé ni*.

Manabú tamé ni *gakkō e yukimásŭ.*   We go to school **to learn.**
学ぶ　ため　に　学校　へ　行きます.

Yasúmu tamé ni *kokó ni todomarimashō.*   Let us stop here **to rest.**
休む　ため　に　ここ　にとどまりましょう.

We shall now give in this lesson the rules for the translation of the infinitive when used in other cases.

When an infinitive follows the means, instrument, or agent, and is preceded by such verbs as *to want, to need, to desire, to wish,* **nóni** のに, instead of *ni* に or **tamé ni** ために, may be used.

*Tegamí wo **káku nóni** (tamé ni or ni) kamí ga irimásŭ.*
手紙　を　書く　のに　(ため　に　, に)　紙　が　いります.
We need paper (in order) **to write** a letter.

*Konó tegamí wo **fújiru**[2] **nóni** (tamé ni or ni) fūrō[3] ga hoshii désŭ.*
この　手紙　を　封じる　のに　(ため　に　, に)封ろうが欲しいです.
I wish to have some wax **to seal** this letter.

With other verbs, the expression **nóni** is generally used.

*Konó hakó ni kugí wo **útsu nóni** kanazuchí[4] wo mótte kité kudasái.*
この　箱　に　釘　を　打つ　のに　金鎚　を　持って来て　下さい.
Please, bring me a hammer **to nail** this box.

When an infinitive is used subjectively it is translated by the *simple present*, followed by **kotó wa** 事は or **to iú kotó wa** という事は. The expression **to iú** is used to emphasize the idea expressed by the infinitive.

*Oshierú (**to iú**) kotó wa tōtoi[5] shokugyō[6] de arimásŭ.*
教える　(と　いう)　事　は　尊い　転業　であります.
To teach is a noble profession.

---

1 porter   **2** *fújiru* to seal   **3** wax   **4** *kugí wo útsu* to nail (*kugí* nail, *útsu* to strike;) *kanazuchí* hammer   **5** noble   **6** occupation, profession

Arúku (to iú) kotó wa kenkō[1] ni yói undō désŭ.
歩く（と いう）事 は 健康 によい 運動 です.
To walk is a healthful exercise. (*kenkō ni yói* healthful)

When two or more infinitives are the subject of the same finite verb, the expression *to iú* is generally omitted, because if it were used the sentence would sound too stiff.

Kangáeru kotó to hanásu kotó wa ningén no saidái[2] tokkén[3] de arimásŭ.
考える 事と 話す 事 は 人間 の 最大 特権 であります.
To think and **to speak** are the greatest privileges of man.

Note that when an infinitive is the subject of a verb, the corresponding Japanese expression is followed by *wa* or *ga,* according to the rules already given for the use of these two postpositions.

Ayamachí wo surú[4] kotó wa ningén de ári, *yurúsu[5] kotó wa* kámi
過ち を する 事 は 人間 であり, 許す 事 は 神
de áru. **To err** is human; **to forgive** is divine. (*ayamachí* error, fault)
で ある. (*ningén* a human being, man; a mortal)

Míru kotó ga dekínai no wa hijō ni kanashíi kotó ni chigainái.
見る 事 が 出来ないの は 非常 に 悲しい 事 にちがいない.
It must be very sad **not** to be able **to see.**

Sometimes an infinitive subject may be expressed by *a noun.*

Konó jimúsho de wa kitsuén[6] wa kinjiraretė imásŭ.
この 事務所 で は 喫煙 は 禁じられて います.
In this office it is prohibited **to smoke.** (*kinjirarerú* to be prohibited)

The expression *to iú* is omitted when an infinitive is preceded by *there is,* also when the infinitive is used objectively.

Náni mo surú kotó ga arimasén.   There is nothing **to do.**
何 も する 事 がありません.

Benkyō surú kotó ga sŭkí désŭ.   I like **to study.**
勉強 する 事 が 好き です.

Instead of *kotó* one may use *no,* especially when the infinitive is in the objective case. Note that the expressions *kotó, to iú kotó,* and *no,* placed after the verb, serve to substantivize it.

Anó hĭtó wa okāsan to *sampó surú no ga* sŭkí désŭ.
あの 人 は お母さんと 散歩 する の が 好き です.
He likes **to take walks** with his mother.

Anó kodomó wa asobú no wo sŭkimasén.   That boy does not like
あの 子供 は 遊ぶ の を 好きません.   **to play.**

The postposition *wo* is regularly used after an infinitive in the accusative.

---

1 health **2** *saidái* the greatest **3** privilege **4** *ayamachí wo surú* to err **5** *yurúsu* to forgive **6** *kitsuén* smoking (tobacco)

*Bóku ga sonó kodomotachí to **ikú no wo** chichí wa kinjimáshǐta.*
僕 が その 子供達 と 行く の を 父 は 禁じました.
My father has forbidden me **to go** with those children.

*Anó hǐtó wa watashí ni **hanásu no wo** kiraimásǔ.*   He dislikes **to**
あの 人 は 私 に 話す の を 嫌います.   **speak** to me.

*Yūkan-na[1] héishi wa **shinú kotó wo** osoremasén.[2]*
勇敢 な 兵士 は 死ぬ 事 を 恐れません.
A courageous soldier fears not **to die.**

Kotó or **no,** but not *to iú kotó,* is often used when an infinitive is preceded by the verb *to be,* with an adjective or a participial adjective.

*Anó shōnen wa gakká wo **manabú no** ga taihén osói désǔ.*
あの 少年 は 学課 を 学ぶ の が 大変 遅い です.
That boy **is** very **slow to learn** his lessons.

*Konó usugurái[3] akari de wa **yómu kotó** ga **dekimasén.***
この うす暗い あかり で は 読む 事 が 出来ません.
In this dim light I **am unable to read.**

*Anáta no senséi wo sonná ni háyaku **hōmon[4] surú no** wa yoroshikú*
貴方 の 先生 を そんなに 早く 訪問 する の は よろしく
nái to omoimásǔ.   I think that it **is not proper to visit** your teacher so early.
ない と 思います.   (*lit.* Your teacher so early to visit, proper is not, so I think.)

An infinitive preceded by the verb *to be,* with an adjective, may be translated in the tense proper in English were the infinitive idea expressed by a finite verb. However, the construction with **kotó** may also be used.

*Mō ichí-do **o-me ni kakáreba** (kakáru kotó ga dekíreba) **ureshíi** désǔ.*
もう 一度 お目 に かかれば (かかる 事 が出来れば) 嬉しい です.
I **shall be glad to meet** (if I meet) you again.

The infinitive preceded by **to be** may, in some cases, be translated by what in Japanese corresponds to an English relative construction.

*Yamá no chōjō[5] ni **tōchaku shǐtá no wa** watashí ga **saishó[6]** déshǐta.*
山 の 頂上 に 到着 した の は 私 が 最初 でした.
I **was first to arrive** at the top of the mountain.
(*lit.* At the top of the mountain that arrived, I was the first.)

When immediately preceded by a finite verb, an infinitive may be translated in the tense that would be proper were the infinitive expressed by a finite verb preceded by the conjunction *that.*

*Anó otokó wa anó tegamí wo **káita kotó** wo hitéi[7] shimáshǐta.*
あの 男 は あの 手紙 を 書いた 事 を 否定 しました.
That man denied **to have written** that letter.＝That man denied that he had written that letter.

---

1 *yūkan-na* courageous   **2** *osoréru* to fear   **3** dim   **4** *hōmon surú* to visit   **5** top
6 the first   **7** *hitéi surú* to deny

Káre wa jibún no káoku ni **hōka shĭtá**[1] **kotó** *wo mitomemáshĭta.*[2]

彼 は 自分 の 家屋 に 放火 した 事 を 認めました。

He admitted **to have set fire** to his own house.=He admitted that he had set fire to his own house. (*káoku* literary expression for *house*)

After such verbs as *to acknowledge, to acclaim, to proclaim,* and similar ones, the infinitive *to be,* followed by an object, is omitted in Japanese, as it may be omitted in English.

Wareware wa wareware no shidōsha[3] *to shĭté saijakunenshá*[4] *wo* **shōnin**

我々 は 我々 の 指導者 として 最若年者 を 承認

shimáshĭta.[5]   We acknowledged the youngest man (to be) our leader.

しました.   (*lit.* We, our leader as, youngest man acknowledged.)

Shiháinin wa watashí wo jibún no hishó[6] *ni* **shĭté kuremáshĭta.**

支配人 は 私 を 自分 の 秘書 に して くれました.

My manager has kindly appointed me his private secretary.

Preceded by a finite verb, the infinitive *to be,* followed by an adjective, is translated by **désŭ to** or by the less polite expression **da to.**

Anó otokó wa hijō nĭ shōjiki **désŭ to** *omoimásŭ.*

あの 男 は 非常に 正直 です と 思います.

I believe that man **to be** very honest.

Konó hōchi wa úso **da to** *omoimásŭ.*   I believe this news **to be** untrue.

この 報知 は 嘘 だ と 思います.

Anó otokó wa hijō ni kanemochí **da to** *hĭtóbito wa omótte imásŭ.*

あの 男 は 非常に 金持 だ と 人々 は 思って います.

People think that man **to be** very rich.

Note that **da to** followed by the verb **omóu** may be used in good conversation. Compare this use of **da to** with the use of the shorter past form followed by **tokí ni.** (Lesson 30, page 203)

Instead of *désŭ to* or *da to,* the infinitive **to be** may be translated by **de arú to.**

Anó onná wa kichigái[7] **de áru to** (or *da to, désŭ to*) *hamméi*[8] *shimáshĭta.*

あの 女 は 気違い で あると （だと，ですと） 判明 しました.

That woman proved **to be** insane.

If an infinitive, preceded by a finite verb, may be used in English in the form of direct speech, the direct speech is generally used in the Japanese translation. In this case, the expression corresponding to the infinitive is followed by **to.**

(1) *Nihón-go wo* **naraō to** *késshin*[9] *shimáshĭta.*   I have decided **to learn**

日本語 を 習おう と 決心 しました.   Japanese.

    (*lit.* The Japanese language "I will learn" so I have decided.)

---

1 *hōka surú* to set fire **2** *mitomerú* to admit **3** leader **4** youngest man **5** *shōnin surú* to acknowledge. **6** *hishó* secretary, *hishó ni surú* to appoint as secretary **7** insane **8** *hamméi surú* to prove **9** *késshin surú* to decide

Mótto **benkyō shimásŭ to** *senséi ni yakŭsokú*[1] *shimáshĭta.*

もっと　勉強　します　と　先生　に　約束　しました.

I promised my teacher **to study** more.
   (*lit.* "More I study" so to the teacher I promised.)

Anó hĭtó wa jū-man yen **kashĭté kuré to** *watashí ni tanomimáshĭta.*

あの　人　は　拾万　円　貸して　くれ　と　私　に　頼みました.

That man asked me **to lend** him a hundred thousand yen.
   (That man "¥ 100,000 yen lend me" so to me asked.)

Chichí wa kómban Ōsaka kará **kŭru to** *omoimásŭ.*

父　は　今晩　大阪　から　来る　と　思います.

We expect our father **to arrive** to-night from Osaka.
   (*lit.* "Our father to-night from Osaka comes" so we think.)

Káre wa **kŭru to** *yakŭsokú shimáshĭta.*   He promised **to come.**

彼　は　来る　と　約束　しました.

   (*lit.* He, "I come" so—promise made.)

Káre wa bóku wo **ŭtsu to** *odokashimáshĭta.*   He threatened **to beat** me.

彼　は　僕　を　打つ　と　おどかしました.

   (*lit.* He, me "I beat" so he threatened.)

When the infinitive is translated by the future, instead of using the form with *mashō,* as used in example (**1**), the future form in *yō* or *ō* is generally used.

It has been stated, in Lesson 32, page 229, that this form of future is considered vulgar, but it is used in good conversation when translating an infinitive. Compare this rule with the one given in Lesson 30, page 203, for the use of the short form of the *past* followed by *tokí ni.*

Anó hĭtó wa shōnen wo **sukuō**[2] *to kokoromimáshĭta.*[3]

あの　人　は　少年　を　救おう　と　試みました.

He attempted **to rescue** the boy.
   (*lit.* He "The boy I will rescue" so he attempted.)

Anó hĭtotachí wa sókoku[4] *wo* **sŭteyō to** *késshin shimáshĭta.*

あの　人達　は　祖国　を　捨てようと　決心　しました.

They decided **to abandon** their country.
   (*lit.* They "The country we will abandon" so they decided.)

Watashí no tomodachí wa watashí wo **tasŭkeyō to** *doryokú*[5] *shimáshĭta.*

私　の　友達　は　私　を　助けようと　努力　しました.

My friend endeavoured **to help** me. (*tasŭkéru* 助ける to help)
   (*lit.* My friend, me "I will help" so he endeavoured.)

This construction is used also for the desiderative.

Mōrisu San wa Nihón-go wo **naraō** (or **naraitái**) *to omoimáshĭta.*

モーリスさん　は　日本語　を　習おう　（習いたい）　と　思いました.

Mr. Morris desired to study Japanese. (*naráu* 習う to learn, to study)
   (*lit.* Mr. Morris "Japanese language I will study" so he thought.)

---

1 *yakŭsokú surú* to promise **2** *sukuú* to rescue **3** *kokoromíru* to attempt **4** *sókoku* one's homeland; *sŭterú* 捨てる to abandon **5** *doryokú surú* to endeavour

Shiháinin wa atarashíi sokkishá[1] *wo **yatoō**[2] (**yatoitái**) **to** omótte imásŭ.*
支配人　は　新しい　速記者　を　雇おう（雇いたい）と　思っています.
My manager wishes to engage a new stenographer.
(*lit.* The manager " new stenographer I will engage " so he thinks.)

Instead of **to** after the verb, one may use the expression **yō-ni,** in which case the infinitive is translated by the *simple present.*

*Táishō wa jibún no gúntai ni **shingún surŭ**[3] **yō-ni** (or **shiró to**)*
大将　は　自分　の　軍隊　に　進軍　する　ように　（しろ　と）
meijimáshĭta.[4]　The general commanded his troops **to advance.** (*lit.* The general
命じました.　　to his troops, advance in order to make, ordered.)

*Watashí wa Tanaká San ni uchí ni **ité kudasáru yō-ni** (**kudasái***
私　は　田中　さん　に　うち　に　いて　下さる　ように　（下さい
to) *negaimáshĭta.*　I begged Mr. Tanaka **to remain** at my home.
と）願いました.

*Chichí wa bóku wo daigakú e **iréru yō-ni** (**ireyō to**) késshin shimáshĭta.*
父　は　僕　を　大学　へ　入れるように（入れようと）決心　しました.
My father decided **to send** me to the University.

Bázoku[5] *wa warewaré ni kané wo zémbu **watasŭ**[6] **yō-ni** (**watasé***
馬賊　は　我々　に　金　を　全部　渡す　ように　（渡せ
to) *kyōsei*[7] *shimáshĭta.*　The bandits forced us **to give** them all our money.
と）強制　しました.

An infinitive preceded by the verbs *to prefer, to be better, to be advisable*, and other of similar meaning, may be translated by a finite verb followed by **hō ga ii** 方がいゝ, or **hō ga yói** 方がよい (the way is good).

*Kómban watashí wa uchí ni **irŭ hō ga yói** désŭ.*
今晩　私　はうち　に　いる　方　が　よい　です.
To-night I **prefer to remain** at home.
(*lit.* To-night I at home to remain the way is good.)

Anó hĭtó wo gomakásu[8] *yóri wa jíjitsu*[9] *wo **hanáshĭta hō ga íi** deshō.*
あの　人　を　ごまかす　より　は　事実　を　話した　方がいいでしょう.
It **would be better to tell** him the truth than to deceive him.
(*lit.* That person, to deceive than, the truth told the way good will be.)

When an infinitive in the passive voice has the value of **can,** it is translated by the *potential.*

Watashí ga o-hanashí shĭtá anó e wa Bíjitsu Tenrankái[10] *de **miraremásŭ.***
私　が　お話し　したあの絵　は　美術　展覧会　で　見られます.
The picture I have spoken of **is to be seen** (can be seen) at the Art Exhibition.

An infinitive without **to** placed after verbs of perception, such as *to behold, to feel, to hear, to observe, to perceive, to see, to notice, to watch*, are regularly translated by the *simple present*, followed by

1 stenographer　2 *yatóu* to engage　3 *shingún surú* to advance　4 *meijirú* to command　5 bandit　6 to give　7 *kyōsei surú* to force　8 to deceive　9 truth　10 *Bíjitsu Tenrankái* Art Exhibition

wa, ga, or *wo,* as the case may require. *No* generally precedes the particle indicating the case.

Morí de torí ga naité[1] irú no ga kikoemáshĭta.　**I heard** birds **sing**
森　で　鳥　が　鳴いて　いる　の　が　聞こえました.　　in the woods.

Takŭsán no hĭtó ga anó o-terá e háiru no wo mimáshĭta.
沢山　の　人　が　あの　お寺　へ　入る　の　を　見ました.
We observed many people **enter** the temple.

Ryōshitachi[2] wa shíshi[3] ga sonó aná[4] kará déte kurú no wo
猟師達　は　しし　が　その　穴　から　出て　来る　の　を
mimáshĭta.　The hunters **saw** a lion **come out** of his lair.
見ました.

Inú ga hoéru[5] no wo kikimáshĭta.　**I heard** a dog **bark.**
犬　が　吠える　の　を　聞きました.

Absolute infinitives are translated according to their equivalents.

Hontō no kotó wo iéba (or *iú to) bóku wa kimí no e wo sŭkimasén.*
本当　の　事　を云えば　（云うと）僕　は　君　の絵を好きません.
To tell you the truth (If I am to tell you the truth) I do not like your painting.
(*lit.* True thing if I tell, I your painting don't like.)

See Lesson 22 for the translation of infinitives placed after the adverb *how,* and Lesson 44, page 360 for the infinitives without the particle *to* preceded by *can, may, might, must,* and *ought.*

Vocabulary

Nouns

accused (the)	*hikokú*	被ヒ告コク
body	*shíntai*	身シン体タイ
captain	*táii*	大タイ尉イ
citizen	*shímin*	市シ民ミン
duty	*gímu*	義ギ務ム
exercise	*kúnren*	訓クン練レン
expectation	*mikomí*	見ミ込コミ
fibre	*sen-i*	繊セン維イ
fishing	*gyoryō*	漁ギョ猟リョウ
gendarme	*kémpei*	憲ケン兵ペイ
glow-worm	*hótaru*	螢ホタル
government	*séifu*	政セイ府フ
help	*tetsudái*	手テ伝ツダイ
law	*hōritsu*	法ホウ律リツ
liberty	*jiyū*	自ジ由ユウ

passenger	*senkyakú*	船セン客キャク
passport	*ryokōken*	旅リョ行コウ券ケン
prison	*keimushó*	刑ケイ務ム所ショ
(prison) cell	*dokubō*	独ドク房ボウ
prisoner	*shūjin*	囚シュウ人ジン
resources	*zaigén*	財ザイ源ゲン
route	*kōtsūro*	交コウ通ツウ路ロ
sale	*baikyakú*	売バイ却キャク
ship-canal	*únga*	運ウン河ガ
welfare	*annéi*	安アン寧ネイ

Adjectives

financial	*keizaiteki*	経ケイ済ザイ的テキ
innocent	*múzai*	無ム罪ザイ
intellectual	*chiteki*	知チ的テキ
physical	*taiikú*	体タイ育イク

Verbs

to assist	*joryokú surú*	助力スル

---

1 *nakú* to sing (of bird)　**2** hunters　**3** lion　**4** lair　**5** to bark

to attack	*shūgeki surú*	襲撃スル		to prevent	*bōshi surú*	防ボ止シスル
to attempt	*kuwadate·rú*	企クダテル		to request	*yōkyū surú*	要ヨ求キスル
to carry	*hakobú*	運ハブ		to shorten	*chikamè·ru*	近チカメル
to declare	*senkokú surú*	宣セ告コクスル		to spin	*tsumúgu*	紡グ
to defend	*mamóru*	守マル		to support	*shíji surú*	支シ持ジスル
to enact	*seiteí surú*	制セ定テイスル		**Adverbs**		
to listen to	*ukagaú*	伺ウガウ		eagerly	*nésshin-ni*	熱ネッ心シンニ
to move	*ugóku*	動ウゴク		frantically	*nekkyōteki-ni*	熱狂的ニ
to order	*meiji·rú*	命メイジル		still	*imadá-ni*	未イマダニ
to plough	*tagayásu*	タガヤス		sufficiently	*jūbun-na*	充ジュウ分ブンナ

true liberty *shin no jiyū*; physical exercise *taiikú undō*; to keep, to preserve *tamótsu*; to be together with *taizá surú*; intellectual exercise *chitekí kúnren*; learned people, the wise, thinkers *shikishá*; custom officer *zeikanrí*; to applaud *hákushu wo surú*; to expect, to anticipate *mikomú*; anticipation *mikomí*; to accost *kotobá wo kakèru*; to yield, to discharge, to emanate *hassúru*; North Star *Hokkyóku-séi*; naked eye *nikugán*; foreign countries *shogaikokú*; welfare (well being) of the people, national welfare *mimpukú*

Exercise *Renshū* 練習

1. Ningén ga omóu mamá ni[1] ikíru no wa shin no jiyū de wa arimasén. Hĭtó wa hōritsu ni yotté[2] ikínakereba narimasén. **2.** Hĭtó wa shíntai wo tsúyoku surú tamé ni[3] taiikú undō ga hitsuyō to onájiku[4] séishin wo wákaku tamótsu tamé ni[5] chitekí kúnren wo okonawanéba[6] narimasén. **3.** Nihón de wa gyoryō wa mukashí kará okonawareté itarashíi[7] désŭ. **4.** Hatarakú kotó wa ningén no móttomo taisetsú-na gímu no hĭtótsu de arimásŭ. **5.** Tabéru kotó to nerú kotó wa ikíru tamé ni hitsuyō désŭ. **6.** Watashí wa shikishá to taizá surú tokí jibún de hanásu yóri mo shikishagatá no ossháru kotó wo ukagaú no ga sŭkí désŭ. **7.** Dōzo, Imamurá San e denwá wo kákete myōchō jū-ji ni watashí no jimúsho e o-mié ni náru[8] yō-ni itté kudasái. **8.** Mádo wo aráu yō-ni mēdo ni iimáshĭta ka.—Iié, iú no wo wasuremáshĭta. **9.** Sekái no ōku no tokoró de wa[9] imadá-ni ni[10] wo hakobú tetsudái ya tochí wo tagayásu nóni umá to ushí ni tayótte[11] imásŭ. **10.** Zeikanrí ga funé ni kité zen-senkyakú ni toránku ya kabán wo akerú yō-ni iimáshĭta. **11.** Saibankán wa hikokú wo múzai de áru to senkokú shimáshĭta. **12.** Anáta wa hontō-ni o-uchí wo urú tsumorí désŭ ka.—Sā![12] mótte itái no désŭ ga uranái wáke[13] ni wa ikanái no désŭ, názenaraba watashí wa keizaitekí zaigén wo zémbu nakushĭté shimaimáshĭta kará. **13.** Shūjin wa dokubō no mádo kará nigeyō to kuwadatemáshĭta. **14.** Kōensha ga hanasō to shĭtá tokí ni chōshu

---

1 *omóu mamá ni* as he thinks; *mamá* as **2** *ni yotté* according to **3** *tsúyoku surú tamé ni* to keep strong **4** *hitsuyō to onájiku* just as necessary; *hitsuyō* necessity **5** *wákaku tamótsu tamé ni* (in order) to keep young **6** *okonaú* to do, to act; *okonawanéba narimasén* must have **7** *okonawareté itarashíi désŭ* seems to have been practiced **8** *o-mié ni náru* to come **9** *ōku no tokoró de wa* in most places **10** *ni* or *nimotsu* load **11** *tayóru* to depend upon **12** well (interj.) **13** *uranái wáke ni wa ikanái* (*lit.*) not to sell the reason won't go=I must sell

wa nekkyōteki-ni hakŭshú wo shimáshĭta. **15.** Anáta wa go-jibún no nōjō no baikyakú kará íkura o-uketorí ni náru mikomí désŭ ka.—Sŭkúnaku tómo[1] san-jū-man yen uketorú tsumorí désŭ. **16.** Eki e tsúita tokí ni kémpei ga watashí ni kotobá wo káke watashí no ryokō-ken wo miséru yō-ni yōkyū shimáshĭta. **17.** Nakanó San ni watashí wo go-ji ni Teikokú Hóteru de mátsu yō-ni itté kudasái. **18.** Anáta to go-isshó ni íma dekakeraremásŭ. **19.** Taisén únga wa kōtsūro wo chikaméru tamé ni tsŭkuraremásŭ. **20.** Watá wa súbete no sen-i no náka de íto ni ichibán tsumugí yasúi désŭ. **21.** Anchū ni[2] okareréba hótaru wa hĭtó ga soré ni yotté monó wo yómu kotó ga déki matá tokéi no jíkan wo míru nóni jūbun-na hodó tsuyói[3] hikarí wo hasshimásŭ. **22.** Hokkyóku-séi wa nikugán ni wa kesshĭte ugokánu[4] yō-ni miemásŭ. **23.** Sōchō[5] tekí wo shūgeki surú yō-ni wága táii wa meijimashĭta. **24.** Jū-shichí séiki no hajimé ni Nihón séifu wa Nihón-jin ga shogaikokú e yukú no wo bōshi surú tamé no hōritsu wo seitéi shimashĭta. **25.** Káku[6] kokumín wa nésshin ni rikō subéki yottsú no gímu ga arimásŭ. Soréra wa kókka no hōritsu wo tsŭkúru nóni joryokú surú kotó, kákuji no gyōmu[7] wo mótte kuní wo shíji shi ittán kankyū[8] áreba yóku kuní wo mamóru kotó, hōritsu ni shĭtagáu kotó soshĭté mimpukú no tamé ni hōritsu no shikkō wo tasŭkéru[9] kotó de arimásŭ.

1. 人間が思うまゝに生きるのは真の自由ではありません. 人は法律によって生きなければなりません. **2.** 人は身体を強くするために体育運動が必要と同じく精神を若く保つために知的訓練を行わねばなりません. **3.** 日本では漁猟は昔から行われていたらしいです. **4.** 仂く事は人間の最も大切な義務の一つであります. **5.** 食べる事と寝る事は生きるために必要です. **6.** 私は識者と対座する時自分で話すよりも識者方のおっしゃる事を伺うのが好きです. **7.** どうぞ今村さんへ電話を掛けて明朝十時に私の事務所へ御見えになるように云って下さい. **8.** 窓を洗うようにメードに言いましたか. —いゝえ, 言うのを忘れました. **9.** 世界の多くの所ではいまだに荷を運ぶ手伝いや土地をたがやすのに馬と牛にたよっています. **10.** 税関吏が船に来て全船客にトランクや鞄を開けるように言いました. **11.** 裁判官は被告を無罪であると宣告しました. **12.** 貴方は本当にお家を売るつもりですか. —さあ, 持っていたいのですが売らない訳にはゆかないのです, なぜならば私は経済的財源を全部なくしてしまいましたから. **13.** 囚人は独房の窓から逃げようと企てました. **14.** 講演者が話そうとした時に聴衆は熱狂的に拍手をしました. **15.** 貴方は御自分の農場の売却から幾らお受け取りになる見込みですか. —少なくとも三十万円受け取るつもりです.

---

1 *sŭkúnaku tómo* at least   2 *anchū ni* in the dark; *anchū ni okareréba* if placed in the dark   3 *jūbun-na hodó tsuyói* strong enough   4 *kesshĭte ugokánu* not to move at all   5 *sōchō* early in the morning   6 *káku* every   7 *kákuji no gyōmu wo mótte* with one's work; *kákuji* each, *gyōmu* work   8 *ittán kankyū áreba* in case of emergency; *ittán* once, *kankyū* emergency, *áreba* if there is   9 *shikkō wo tasŭkéru* to help to administer

16. 駅へ着いた時に憲兵が私に言葉をかけ私の旅行券を見せるように要求しました．**17.** 中野さんに私を五時に帝国ホテルで待つように言って下さい．**18.** 貴方と御一緒に今出かけられます．**19.** 大船運河は交通路を近めるために造られます．**20.** 綿はすべての繊維の中で糸に一番紡ぎ易いです．**21.** 暗中におかれゝばほたるは人がそれによって物を読む事が出来又時計の時間を見るのに充分なほど強い光を発します．**22.** 北極星は肉眼には決して動かぬように見えます．**23.** 早朝敵を襲撃するように我が大尉は命じました．**24.** 十七世紀の初めに日本政府は日本人が諸外国へ行くのを防止するための法律を制定しました．**25.** 各国民は熱心に履行すべき四つの義務があります．それ等は国家の法律をつくるのに助力する事，各自の業務を以って国を支持し一旦緩急あればよく国を守る事法律に従う事そして民福のために法律の執行を助ける事であります．

1. To live as a man wishes is not true liberty. Man must live according to law. **2.** Just as to keep strong in body a man needs physical exercise, so to keep young in mind a man must have intellectual exercise. **3.** In Japan fishing seems to have been practiced from earliest times. **4.** To work is one of the most important duties of man. **5.** To eat and sleep is necessary in order to live. **6.** When I am with learned people I prefer to listen to what they say, rather than to speak myself. **7.** Please telephone to Mr. Imamura and tell him to come to my office to-morrow morning at ten o'clock. **8.** Did you tell the maid-servant to wash the windows?—No, I forgot to tell her. **9.** In many parts of the world man still depends entirely upon the horse and the ox to help to carry loads and to plough the land. **10.** A custom officer came on board and asked all passengers to open their trunks and valises. **11.** The judge declared the accused to be innocent. **12.** Do you really intend to sell your house?—Well, I should like to keep it, but I am forced to sell it, because I have exhausted all my financial resources. **13.** A prisoner attempted to escape from the window of his cell. **14.** When the orator began to speak, the audience applauded frantically. **15.** How much do you expect to receive from the sale of your farm?—I expect to receive at least three hundred thousand yen. **16.** When I arrived at the station a gedarme accosted me and requested me to show him my passport. **17.** Tell Mr. Nakano to wait for me at five o'clock at the Imperial Hotel. **18.** I am now ready to go with you. **19.** Ship canals are made to shorten routes. **20.** Cotton is the easiest of all fibers to spin into thread. **21.** Placed in the dark, the glow worm yields a light strong enough to enable us to read print or to tell the time by a watch. **22.** The North Star appears to the naked eye never to move at all. **23.** Our captain ordered us to attack the enemy early in the morning. **24.** Early in the 17th century, the Japanese government enacted laws devised to prevent the Japanese from visiting foreign countries. **25.** Every citizen has four duties which he ought to fulfil eagerly. They are: to assist in making his country's laws; to support his country with his work and defend it when necessary; to obey its laws; to help to administer its laws for the general good of the people.

Fifty-fifth Lesson 第五十五課

Participles *Búnshi* 分ブ詞シ

Some of the previous lessons have shown how to translate participles when used to form the progressive conjugation and the compound tenses of verbs.

When otherwise used, participles are translated into Japanese in various ways, according to their English equivalents.

Cause or Reason

A participle indicating cause or reason is translated into Japanese by the same construction used in translating a verb preceded by *as* or *because*.

*Konó mizunomí[1] wa tetsú de **dékite imásŭ kará** (or **nóde**) kowaremasén.*
この 水呑み は 鉄 で 出来て います から （ので）こわれません.
Being made (Because it is made) of iron this tumbler will not break.

*Ima o-kané ga **arimasén kará** (**nóde**) náni mo kaú kotó ga dekimasén.*
今 お金 が ありません から （ので） 何 も 買う 事 が出来ません.
Not having (As I have not) now money with me I cannot buy anything.

*Anó hĭtó wa anná ni **hashítte imásŭ kará** súgu ni uchí e tsŭkú deshō.*
あの 人 はあんなに 走って います から 直ぐ に 家へ着くでしょう.
Running as he does he will soon reach home.
As he is running so (*fast* understood) he will soon reach home.

Ichí nichí-jū arukidōshi déshĭta kará (nóde) sukkári tsŭkaremáshĭta.
一 日中 歩き通し でした から （ので）すっかり 疲れました.
Having (As I had) walked the whole day I was exhausted.

The suffix *dōshi*, as used in the last example, indicates continuation, progression, and corresponds to the expressions *all through, throughout*. It is placed after the simple stem of verbs of Class I and the *i*-stem of verbs of Class II. Ex: *Arukidōshi* to walk the whole distance; *shaberidōshi* to keep talking; *tabedōshi* to keep on eating. (*arúku* to walk, *shabéru* to talk or gossips, *tabéru* to eat)

Concession or Contrast

The participles *granting* and *admitting*, which, with concessive meaning, are sometimes used at the beginning of a sentence, are translated by a finite verb and one of the expressions *to shĭté-mo* としても, *karí ni......to shĭté-mo* 仮に......としても, or *tatoé...... tówa-ié* たとえ......とは言え, as shown below. Each of the given

---

1 tumbler, drinking vessel (*mizú* water, *nomi* from *nómu* to drink)

expressions corresponds to *although;* the first one is the least emphatic.

Kari ni kimí ga jíko bōei[1] no tamé ni okonattá[2] **to shⁱté-mo** kimí wa
仮 に 君 が 自己 防衛 の ため に 行った と しても 君 は
kimí no mōshitate[3] wo shōmei surú[4] shōnin[5] ga arimasén.
君 の 申立て を 証明 する 証人 がありません.

Granting that you acted in self-defence, you have no witness to testify to your assertion.

Watashí no keikakú[6] ga kanzén[7] de nái **to shⁱté-mo** náo kátsu[8] watashí wa
私 の 計画 が 完全 でないと しても なお 且つ 私 は
soré wo jikkō[9] ni utsusō to[10] omoimás^u.   (*jikkō ni utsúsu* to put into
それ を 実行 に 移そう と 思います.   practice)

Admitting that my plan is not perfect yet, I shall now begin to put it into practice.
     (My plan perfect is not although, yet I it in practice I put so I think.)

Tatoé kimí wa jibún jíshin no doryokú[11] de kanemochí ni nátta **tówa-ié**
たとえ 君 は 自分 自身 の 努力 で 金持 になったとは言え
kimí no yoséi[12] wo itazurá[13] ni sugóshⁱte[14] wa naránai.
君 の 余生 を 徒ら に 過して は ならない.

Granting that you have become rich through your own efforts, you should not spend the rest of your life in idleness.

When a participle is used with a contrasting meaning, it is translated by a finite verb, followed by the expression **tówa-ié** とは言え, which also means *although.*

Kizutsúita[15] **tówa-ié** anó yūkan-na bokusā wa tatakaí tsuzukemáshⁱta.
傷ついた とは言え あの 勇敢 なボクサー は 闘い 続けました.

(Although) **wounded,** that brave boxer continued to fight.

Condition

A participle, used with the implied meaning of a condition, is translated into Japanese by the subjunctive, as may be done in English.

Konó yamá no chōjō e **noboréba** *mizuúmi[16] ga miemás^u.*
この 山 の 頂上 へ 登れば 湖 が 見えます.

Climbing (If you climb) to the top of this mountain you will see a lake.

Háyaku **hashíreba** *anó hⁱtó ni oits^ukimás^u.[17]*
速く 走れば あの 人 に 追いつきます.

Running (If you run) fast you will catch up with him.

Shōjiki ni **okonaéba** *minná kará sonkéi saremás^u.[18]*
正直 に 行えば みんな から 尊敬 されます.

Acting (If you act) honestly you will deserve respect from all.

---

1 *jíko* self, *bōei* defence   **2** *okonaú* to act   **3** assertion   **4** *shōmei surú* to prove
5 witness   **6** plan   **7** perfect   **8** *náo kátsu* yet   **9** practice   **10** *utsúsu* to put   **11** effort
12 *yósei* the rest of one's life   **13** idleness   **14** *sugósu* to spend   **15** *kizutsúita*
wounded, *kizutsúku* to get wounded   **16** lake   **17** *oitsúku* to overtake   **18** *sonkéi
sarerú* to be respected, *sonkéi* respect

Mō sŭkóshi yásuku **teikyō suréba**[1] *konó shiná wa tayásuku urerú deshō ni.*
もう 少し 安く 提供 すれば この 品はたやすく売れるでしように.
Offered (If they were offered) a little cheaper these goods would sell easily.

Time

Participles having the implied meaning of time are translated into Japanese according to the equivalent English expressions.

Hashí wo **watatté itá tokí ni** *watashí wa Nihón-go no senséi ni*
橋 を 渡って いた 時 に 私 は 日本語 の 先生 に
o-mé ni kakarimáshĭta.   **Crossing** (While I was crossing) the bridge I met
お目 に かかりました.   my Japanese teacher.

Kitaku[2] **shĭté kará** *doá no kagí wo nakushĭtá kotó ni ki ga tsŭkimáshĭta.*
帰宅 して から ドアの 鍵 を なくした 事 に 気 が つきました.
Having (After I had) **reached** my house I noticed that I had lost the door
key. (*nakusú* to lose, *ki ga tsŭkú* to notice)

Shigotó wo **oeté kará** *sampó ni dekakemáshĭta.*
仕事 を 終えて から 散歩 に 出かけました.
Having finished (After I had finished) my work I went out for a walk.

The participles which, placed after the nouns they qualify, may be, in English, changed into relative clauses, are translated by what corresponds in Japanese to a relative construction.

Kaisén wo **arawáshĭta e.**   A picture **representing** (that represents)
海戦 を 現わした 絵.   a naval battle. (*arawásu* to represent)

Inaká ni **sŭnde irú monó** *wa tokái ni* **sŭnde irú** *monó yóri mo*
田舎 に 住んで いる 者 は 都会 に 住んで いる 者 より も
mótto kenkó désŭ.   People **living** (who live) in the country are healthier than
もっと 健康 です.   those **living** in a city.

Ima **hanáshĭte irú hĭtó wa** *dái-yūbenka désŭ.*
今 話して いる 人 は 大雄弁家 です.
The man (who is) **speaking** now is a great orator.

Nambéi de **hanasárete irú kotobá** *wa Sŭpéin-go to Porutogarú-go désŭ.*
南米 で 話されて いる 言葉 はスペイン語と ポルトガル語です.
The languages (that are) **spoken** in South America are Spanish and Portuguese.

Kinō **shinsŭi**[3] **shĭta fŭne** *wa Nihón no saidái-kyū shōsen no náka no*
きのう 進水 した 船 は 日本 の 最大級 商船 の 中 の
hĭtótsu désŭ.   The ship (that was) **launched** yesterday is one of the largest of
一つ です.   the Japanese merchant vessels. (*saidái* largest; *kyū* class)

Kyōto-séi no (**Kyōto de dékita**) *shikkí*[4] *wa sekái-jū de yūmei désŭ.*
京都製 の (京都 で 出来た) 漆器 は 世界中 で 有名 です.
The lacquered wares (that are) **made** in Kyoto are famous all over the world.

---

1 *teikyō surú* to offer   **2** *kitakú=ki* from *káeru+takú* home; *kitakú surú* to return home, to come home   **3** *shinsúi surú* to launch   **4** *shikkí* lacquered ware

In the preceding lesson it has been stated that an infinitive without *to*, placed after verbs of perception, such as *to behold, to feel, to hear, to observe, to perceive, to see, to notice, to watch,* are regularly translated by the simple present, followed by *wa, ga,* or *wo,* as the case may require. The same construction is used to translate also the participles placed after the same verbs of perception.

Yamá no kánata ni[1] **súgata wo kesú**[2] *tsŭki wo nagamemáshĭta.*
山 の 彼方 に 姿 を 消す 月 を 眺めました.
We beheld the moon **disappearing** (disappear) beyond the mountains.

Dáre ka sukuí[3] *wo* **motómete irú no** *ga kikoemáshĭta.*
誰 か 救い を 求めて いる の が 聞こえました.
We heard somebody **crying** (cry) for help. (*motoméru* to call for)

Shōnendan ga yaéi[4] *kará* **hikiagéru**[5] **no** *wo mimáshĭta.*
少年団 が 野営 から 引きあげる の を 見ました.
We observed the boy scouts **leaving** (leave) their camp.

Umá ga suishá-goyá[6] *no hō e* **hashítte ikú no** *wo mimáshĭta.*
馬 が 水車小屋 の 方へ 走って 行く の を 見ました.
I saw a horse **running** (run) towards the water-mill.

Tomodachí wa bóku ga tomodachí no ushiró kará **arúite ittá no ni**
友達 は 僕 が 友達 の 後 から 歩いて 行ったのに
ki ga tsŭkimasén[7] *déshĭta.*   My friend did not notice me **walking** (walk)
気 が つきません でした.   after him.

The following are among the English verbs which may be immediately followed by a present participle:

to arrive	*tsukú*	着く	to keep (on)	*tsuzukú*	続く
to cease	*tomarú*	止まる	to lie (down)	*yokotawáru*	横たわる
to come	*kúru*	来る	to meet	*áu*	会う
to continue	*tsuzukú*	続く	to remain	*todomáru*	留まる
to go	*ikú*	行く	to run	*hashíru* (Lit.)	走る
				kakéru (Colloq.)	駈ける
to go on	*tsuzukerú*	続ける	to stand	*tátsu*	立つ

The participles that follow this class of verbs are generally used in the subordinate.

Onná-no-ko ga watashí no hō e **kákete kimáshĭta.** A girl **came running**
女の子 が 私 の 方へ 駈けて 来ました.   towards me.

Tsŭkáreta rōdōshatachi wa jímen no ué ni **yokotawátte néte imáshĭta.**
疲れた 労伤者達 は 地面 の 上 に 横たわって ねて いました.
The tired workmen **lay sleeping** on the ground.

---

1 *kánata ni* beyond   **2** *súgata wo kesú* to disappear   **3** *sukuí* help   **4** *yaéi* camp
5 *hikiagéru* to leave   **6** *suishá-goyá* water-mill   **7** *ki ga tsukú* to notice

A participle preceded by the verb *to continue* and its synonyms *to go on*, *to keep on*, or by *to remain*, is translated by the simple stem of verbs of Class I and the *i*-stem of verbs of Class II, followed by the verb *tsuzukerú to continue.*

iú 言う to say   *iitsuzukéru* 言い続ける to continue saying

tátsu 立つ to stand   *tachitsuzukerú* 立ち続ける to remain standing

Anó hǐtó wa **tachitsuzuketé** *imáshǐta.*   He remained standing.
あの 人 は 立ち続けて いました.

Kyōshi wa seikō wa níntai[1] ni motozúku[2] to iitsuzúkete imáshǐta.
教師 は 成功 は 忍耐 に もとづく と 言い続けて いました.
The teacher **went on saying** that success depends on perseverance.

Anó hǐtó wa watashí wo **mitsuzuketé** *imáshǐta.*   He **kept on looking**
あの 人 は 私 を 見つゞけて いました.   at me.

If the present participle embodies the implied meaning of *while*, the expression *no ni のに* is placed after the verb in the progressive form.

Watashí wa áni ga áni no sensėi to **arúite irú** *no ni aimáshǐta.*
私 は 兄 が 兄 の 先生 と 歩いて いる の に会いました.
I met my brother **walking** with his teacher.

Sometimes, in English, a participle may serve to join an introductory clause to the principal clause of a sentence, thus avoiding the use of the conjunction *and*. The introductory clause thus formed has the emphasis upon the action intended to be emphatic. Ex:

I took some money out of my pocket **and** gave it to the beggar.
Taking some money out of my pocket I gave it to the beggar.

In such a case the participle is translated into Japanese by the subordinate.

Watashí wa pokétto kará íkuraka no kané wo **toridashǐté** *kojikí ni*
私 は ポケットから 幾らか の 金 を 取り出して 乞食 に
yarimáshǐta.   Translation of the preceding two sentences.—(*lit.* I, pocket from,
やりました.   some money taking out, to the beggar gave.)

Ryōshi wa iwá kagé ni **mi wo kakúshǐte**[3] *kumá no chikazúku no wo*
猟師 は 岩 かげ に 身 を かくして 熊 の 近づく の を
machimáshǐta.   The hunter, **hiding himself** behind a rock, waited for the approach
待ちました.   of the bear. *or* The hunter hid himself behind a rock and waited
         for the approach of the bear.

If the participle is in the perfect tense it is translated by the past, followed by *nóde* or *kará.*

---

1 *níntai ni* in perseverance   **2** *motozúku* to depend on   **3** *mi wo kakúsu* to hide oneself

Rōdōshatachi wa shigotó wo **oetá nóde** (**kará**) *uchí e káette ikimáshĭta.*
労佽者達　は　仕事　を　終えた ので（から）　家 へ帰って行きました.
The workmen, **having finished** their work, went home.
The workmen finished their work **and** went home.

Participles sometimes used after the conjunctions *when, while, whether, though,* and *as if* are translated by their equivalent constructions with finite verbs.

Anáta no gakkō no sóba wo **tótta tokí ni** *anáta no senséi ni o-mé*
あなたの　学校　の　側　を　通った　時　にあなたの　先生　に お目
ni kakarimáshĭta. **While passing** by your school I met your teacher.
に かゝりました.　　(*lit.* Your school's vicinity passed when, your teacher met.)

Anó otokó wa takŭsán **dokŭshó surŭ**[1] *ga sŭkóshi kirí oboemasén.*
あの　男　は　沢山　読書　する　が　少し　きり覚えません.
That man, **though reading** much, learns but little.

Tomodachí wa **káeru tsumori no yō-ni** *tachiagarimáshĭta.*
友達　は　帰る　　つもり　の　ように　立ち上がりました.
My friend rose **as if intending** to leave.
(*lit.* My friend, to return of intention-like, rose.)

A participle may sometimes be translated by an idiomatic expression.

Séi-u ni[2] **kakawarazŭ**[3] *watashí wa go-ji ni dekakemásŭ.*
晴雨　に　かかわらず　私　は　五時　に 出かけます.
Whether raining or not I will go out at five o'clock.

Impersonal absolute participles are translated in different ways according to their different meanings. Below are the most common of this class of participles:

concerning	*ni tsúite*	について
considering	⎰*kangáereba*	考えれば
	⎱*......no warí ni*	......の割に
excepting	*......wo nozoité*	......を除いて
generally speaking	*gáishĭte iéba*	概して言えば
strictly speaking	*gemmitsú ni iéba*	厳密に言えば
regarding	*ni tsúite*	について
judging from	*gaikén kará handán shĭté* (or *suréba*)	
appearance	外見　から　判断　して　（すれば）	

Zannén nágara anáta no go-yōkyū[4] *ni* **tsúite** *wa anáta wo go-manzokŭ*[5]
残念　ながら　貴方　の　御要求　に　ついて　は　貴方　を　御満足
saserú kotó ga dekimasén. **Concerning** your request, I am sorry to say that
させる　事　が 出来ません.　I cannot satisfy you.
(*lit.* I am sorry but, concerning your request, you to satisfy, I cannot.—
*Zannén nágara......*I am sorry but......)

---

1 *dokushó surú* to read　**2** *séi* fine weather, *u* rain, *séi u ni* in fine weather or rain
3 *kakawarazú* in spite of　**4** *yōkyū* request　**5** *manzokú saserú* to satisfy

Anó hĭtó no dái zaisán[1] wo **kangáereba** *anó hĭto wa anná sómatsu-na[2]*
あの 人 の 大 財産 を 考えれば あの 人 はあんな 粗末な

ié ni sumubéki de wa arimasén.   **Considering** his great wealth, he should
家 に 住むべき で はありません.   not live in that miserable house.

Gáishĭte iéba *hĭtó wa jibún no katéi wo aishimásŭ.*
概して 言えば 人 は 自分 の 家庭 を 愛します.
Generally speaking people love their homes.

Gaikén kará handán suréba *anó hĭtó wa shōjiki-monó ni miemásŭ.*
外見 から 判断 すれば あの 人 は 正直者 に 見えます.
Judging from appearances, he seems to be an honest man.

Fŭtarí **wo nozoité** *zémbu no séito wa kyōshitsu ni imáshĭta.*
二人 を 除いて 全部 の 生徒 は 教室 に いました.
Excepting two, all the students were in the class room.

Past participles denoting a permanent habit, state or character, may be translated by the same construction used to translate relative clauses. Some of these participles are translated by a noun used as an adjective.

kyōiku no áru shōnen	教育のある少年	an educated boy
yóku narasáreta dōbutsu	よく馴らされた動物	a well-trained animal
taiekí shōkō	退役将校	a retired officer

Adjectives formed from nouns to which the termination **ed** is added are translated by the Japanese word corresponding to the English adjective without the terminal *ed*, followed by the qualified noun. **No** is sometimes used to join the adjectival expression to the qualified noun.

akahigé no otokó	赤ひげの男	a red-bearded man
katamé no onná	片眼の女	a one-eyed woman
ashí no nagái shōnen	足の長い少年	a long-legged boy
ki-gikú	黄菊	a yellow-coloured chrysanthemum
kedakái hĭtó	気高い人	a noble-minded person

Vocabulary

Nouns					
battle	*kássen[3]*	合ッ戦セン	giraffe	*kirín*	麒キ麟リン
bridge	*hashí*	橋シ	house	*káoku*	家カ屋オク
bush	*yabú*	ヤブ	mechanics	*kikáigaku*	機キ械カイ学ガク
			occupation	*tsutoméguchi*	勤ツト口グチ
engine	*hatsudōki*	発ハツ動ドウ機キ	old age	*rōnen*	老ロウ年ネン
	énjin	エンヂン	performance	*ensō*	演エン奏ソウ
hare	*usagí*	兎ウサギ	seat	*zaseki*	座ザ席セキ

1 *zaisán* wealth   **2** *sómatsu-na* miserable   **3** *Kássen* is used when referring to ancient wars, while *sentō* is used when referring to modern battles.

shoulder	*káta*	肩カタ	to insult	*bujokú surú*	侮辱スル
statesman	*iséisha*	為イ政イ者シャ	to lead	*michibíku*	導チミビク
Verbs			to notice	*mikake·rú*	見ミカケル
to carry	*hakobikómu*	運ハコビ込ゴム	to occupy	*fusagarú*	フサガル
	katsúgu	カツグ	to pass by	*tsūka surú*	通ツウ過カスル
to connect	*tsunagú*	ツナグ	to represent	*arawásu*	現アラワス
to explode	*bakuhatsú surú*	爆バク発ッスル	**Adverbs and Prepositions**		
to fear	*osoré·ru*	恐オソレル	along	*ni sōte*	ニ沿ウテ
to fulfil	*hatásu*	果ハタス	easily	*tayásuku*	タヤスク

to do, to fulfil one's duty *gímu wo hatásu*; to return home *kitakú surú*; to miss the mark *uchisokonáu*; to notice, to remark, to become conscious of *ki ga tsúku*; to rise, to get up, to stand up *tachiagarú*; to buy, to obtain, to purchase *motoméru*; to sleep well *jukusúi surú*; good (character) *zenryō-na*; one's superior *meué*

Exercise   *Renshū*   練習

1. Jibún no gímu wo hatáseba nanigotó mo osoréru kotó wa arimasén.
2. O-takú kará tōku ni súnde orimásŭ nóde koré íjō tabí-tabí[1] wa ukagaemasén.[2]
3. Anáta wa kikáigaku wo yóku go-zónji désŭ kará súgu ni yói tsŭtoméguchi ga áru deshō. 4. Sonná ni nágaku Nihón ni o-sumái désŭ kará Nihón-go wo yóku go-zónji no hazú désŭ ne. 5. Mokuzō[3] náraba káoku wa tayásuku yakerú deshō. 6. Tatoé anáta ga yóku benkyō surú to shǐté mo senséi náshi de wa Nihón-go wa yóku oboeraremasén. 7. Yūbe jukusúi shimasén déshǐta nóde kyō watashí wa taihén nemutái désŭ. 8. Bujokú saretá[4] nóde sonó zenryō-na fujín wa hǐtokotó mo iwazú ni heyá wo demáshǐta. 9. Yóku hatarakú náraba anáta wa konó shigotó wo futsŭká-kan de oerú kotó ga dekíru deshō. 10. Ima o-ishá no tokoró e irassháru náraba o-ishá wa uchí ni oraréru deshō. 11. O-takú no sóba wo tōtta tokí ni[5] anáta no níisan ga gaikokú-fujín to hanáshǐte itá no wo mimáshǐta. 12. Hitsuyō-na hon wo motómete kará kitakú shimáshǐta. 13. Watashí wa Bíjitsu Tenrankái de Sekigahará dái-kássen wo arawáshǐta e wo mimáshǐta. 14. Chiisái murá wo tsūka shǐté kará watashitachí no jidōsha no énjin ga bakuhatsú shimáshǐta. 15. Nyūyōku no Hadosón-gawá no ryōgan[6] wo tsunagú hashí wa hijō-ni nagái désŭ. 16. Tonarí no heyá de dáre ka arúite irú no ga kikoemásŭ. Dáre désŭ ka.—Jochū ga heyá wo sōji shǐté irú no désŭ. 17. Yokohamá e ikú tokí ni watashí wa hikōki ga jū-go-dái úmi no hō e tondé ikú no wo mimáshǐta. 18. Kawá ni sōte arúite itá tokí ni usagí ga ni-hikí yabú no hō e hashítte ikú no wo mikakemáshǐta. Watashí wa usagí wo uchimáshǐta ga uchisokonatté shimaimáshǐta. 19. Zasekí ga zémbu fusagatté itá nóde watashitachí wa ensō-chū[7] hajimé kará owarí máde tachidōshi déshǐta. 20. Hǐtó ga watashí no ushiró ni tátte ité watashí no shǐté itá kotó wo míte

---

1 *koré íjō tabí-tabí* oftener   2 *ukagaerú* to be able to call; *ukagaú* to call, to visit   3 *mokuzō* made of wood   4 *bujokú sarerú* to be insulted   5 *tōtta tokí ni* when I passed   6 *ryōgan* both banks, both sides of a river   7 *ensō-chū* during the performance

itá no ni ki ga tsŭkimasén déshĭta. **21.** Kimí no meué ni átta tokí áisatsu wo surú monó désŭ yo. **22.** Anó otokó wa adakámo[1] hanashí wo surú tsumorí no yō-ni[1] tachiagarimáshĭta ga hĭtókoto mo iwazú ni súgu matá koshikake-máshĭta. **23.** Otōto ga tsŭkárete itá yō-ni miemáshĭta kará nerú yō-ni chūkoku shimáshĭta. **24.** Gáishĭte iéba samúi kuní ni súmu hĭtóbito wa atatakái kuní ni súmu hĭtóbito yóri mo mótto tsuyói désŭ. **25.** Rōnen no warí ni[2] chichí wa taihén jōbu désŭ. **26.** Móttomo ashí no nagái dōbutsu wa kirín désŭ. **27.** Watashí ga yondá tokí nagái higé no otokó wa zubón no pokétto kará te wo dashinágara susundé kimáshĭta[3] soshĭté watashí no kabán wo káta ni katsúide nímotsu no heyá ni hakobikomimáshĭta. **28.** Méiji Tennō wa "Tánka" to shĭté shirareté irú Nihón no mijikái shi no go-tannō-na on-katá[5] de araseraremáshĭta.[6] Gyósei[7] no náka no hĭtótsu ni "Yóki[8] wo tóri, áshiki[9] wo sŭteté, totsukuní[10] ni, otoránu[11] kuní to násu[12] yóshi-mo-gána[13]" to o-yomí ni nararemáshĭta.[14]

1. 自分の義務を果たせば何事もおそれる事はありません. **2.** お宅から遠くに住んでおりますのでこれ以上度々は伺えません. **3.** 貴方は機械学をよく御存じですから直ぐによい勤口があるでしょう. **4.** そんなに長く日本にお住まいですから日本語をよく御存じの筈ですね. **5.** 木造ならば家屋はたやすく焼けるでしょう. **6.** たとえ，貴方がよく勉強するとしても先生なしでは日本語はよく覚えられません. **7.** ゆうべ熟睡しませんでしたのできょう私は大変ねむたいです. **8.** 侮辱されたのでその善良な婦人は一言も云わずに部屋を出ました. **9.** よく仂くならば貴方はこの仕事を二日間で終える事が出来るでしょう. **10.** 今，お医者の所へいらっしゃるならばお医者はうちにおられるでしょう. **11.** お宅のそばを通った時に貴方の兄さんが外国婦人と話していたのを見ました. **12.** 必要な本を求めてから帰宅しました. **13.** 私は美術展覧会で関ガ原大合戦を現わした絵を見ました. **14.** 小さい村を通過してから私達の自動車のエンヂンが爆発しました. **15.** 紐育のハドソン河の両岸をつなぐ橋は非常に長いです. **16.** 隣りの部屋で誰か歩いているのが聞こえます. 誰ですか.—女中が部屋を掃除しているのです. **17.** 横浜へ行く時に私は飛行機が十五台海の方へ飛んで行くのを見ました. **18.** 川に沿うて歩いていた時に兎が二匹やぶの方へ走って行くのを見かけました. 私は兎をうちましたがうち

---

1 *adakámo......yō-ni* as if **2** *warí ni* considering; *rōnen no warí ni* considering his old age **3** *susundé kúru* to advance **4** *saidái* biggest; *saidái kyōkoku* most powerful country **5** *shi no go-tannō-na on-katá* an accomplished writer of poems; *go-tannō* accomplished; *on-katá* personage **6** *araseraremáshĭta* from *araseraréru*, respectful form of *de áru* to be **7** *gyósei* an Emperor's poems. **8** *yóki* the good; *yóki wo tóri* taking the good **9** *áshiki* the bad; *áshiki wo sŭteté* throwing away what is bad **10** *totsŭkuní* foreign countries. **11** *otóru* to be inferior; *otoránu* not to be inferior **12** *násu* to make **13** *yóshi-mo-gána* oh, how I wish......! **14** *o-yomí ni náru* to compose (a poem); *nararéru* polite form for *náru*

そこなってしまいました. **19.** 座席が全部ふさがっていたので私達は演奏中はじめから終りまで立ち通しでした. **20.** 人が私の後に立っていて私のしていた事を見ていたのに気がつきませんでした. **21.** 君の目上に会った時挨拶をするものですよ. **22.** あの男はあだかも話しをするつもりのように立ち上がりましたが一言も云わずに直ぐ又腰掛けました. **23.** 弟が疲れていたように見えましたから寝るように忠告しました. **24.** 概して言えば寒い国に住む人々は暖かい国に住む人々よりももっと強いです. **25.** 老年の割に父は大変丈夫です. **26.** 最も足の長い動物は麒麟（きりん）です. **27.** 私が呼んだ時長いひげの男はズボンのポケットから手を出しながら進んで来ました，そして私の鞄を肩にかついで荷物の部屋に運び込みました. **28.** 明治天皇は「短歌」として知られている日本の短かい詩の御堪能な御方であらせられました. 御製の中の一つに「よきを取り悪しきを捨てゝ外つ国に劣らぬ国となすよしもがな」とお詠みになられました.

1. Doing one's duty, one need not fear anything. **2.** Living far from your house, I am unable to visit you oftener. **3.** Knowing mechanics so well you will soon find a good occupation. **4.** Having lived in Japan for so long, you should know the Japanese language well. **5.** Made of wood, houses will easily burn. **6.** Even admitting that you study hard, you cannot learn the Japanese language well without a teacher. **7.** Not having slept well last night, I feel very sleepy to-day. **8.** Insulted, the good lady left the room without saying a word. **9.** Working hard, you could finish this work in two days. **10.** Going to the doctor's now, you will find him at home. **11.** Passing by your house, I saw your brother speaking to a foreign lady. **12.** Having bought the books that I needed, I returned home. **13.** At the Art Exhibition I have seen a picture representing the great battle of Sekigahara. **14.** Having passed through a small village, the engine of our motor-car exploded. **15.** The bridges connecting the two sides of the Hudson River in New York are very long. **16.** I hear somebody walking in the next room. Who is it?—It is our maid-servant cleaning it. **17.** Going to Yokohama, I saw fifteen aeroplanes flying towards the sea. **18.** While walking along the river, I noticed two hares running towards the bush. I shot at them but missed them. **19.** As all seats were occupied, we remained standing during the whole performance. **20.** I had not noticed that a man stood behind me watching what I was doing. **21.** Meeting your superiors, you should salute them. **22.** That man rose as if intending to speak but he soon sat down again without saying a word. **23.** Seeing that my younger brother was tired, I advised him to go to bed. **24.** Generally speaking, people living in cold countries are stronger than those living in warm countries. **25.** Considering his old age, my father is very strong. **26.** The longest-legged animal is the giraffe. **27.** The long-bearded man, taking his hands out of his trousers pockets, advanced on my summon, and throwing my trunk over his shoulders, carried it into the luggage room. **28.** The Emperor Meiji was an accomplished writer of the short Japanese poems which are known as *tanka*. In one of these poems he wrote: "Oh, how I wish to make this country inferior to none, adopting that which is good, and rejecting that which is bad."

Fifty-sixth Lesson 第五十六課

Gerunds *Dōshikei Meishí* 動詞形名詞

As a rule, a gerund used as the subject or the object to a verb is translated by the simple present of the corresponding Japanese verb followed by **kotó** or by the colloquial expression **no.**

> *Arúku kotó (no) wa kenkō ni yói undō désu.*
> 歩く 事 (の) は 健康 に よい 運動 です.
> **Walking** is a healthful exercise.

> *Watashí wa inaká wo arúku no (kotó) ga sŭkí désŭ.*
> 私 は 田舎 を 歩く の (事) が 好き です.
> I enjoy **walking** in the country.

> *Nemurú kotó (no) wa ikíru tamé ni hitsuyō désŭ.* **Sleeping** is
> ねむる 事 (の) は 生きる ため に 必要 です. necessary to life.
> (*lit.* To sleep the thing, to live for necessary is)

> *Watashí wa natsú kógai de nerú no (kotó) ga sŭki désŭ.*
> 私 は 夏 戸外 で ねる の (事) が 好き です.
> In summer I like **sleeping** in the open air.—*kógai* open air

As in English so in Japanese, a gerund may be substituted by a noun:

> *Suimín (=nemurú kotó) wa ikíru tamé ni hitsuyō désŭ.* **Sleep** is
> 睡眠 (ねむる事) は 生きる ため に 必要 です. necessary to life.

When the gerund is complement to a verb, only **kotó** may be used in the Japanese translation.

> *Watashí no sŭkí-na tanoshimí wa arúku kotó désŭ.*
> 私 の 好きな 楽み は 歩く 事 です.
> My favorite recreation is **walking.**

When a gerund is used subjectively the expression **to iú** may precede **kotó,** if emphasis is to be expressed.

> *Arúku to iú kotó wa kenkō ni yói undō désu.*
> 歩く と いう 事 は 健康 に よい 運動 です.

Note that what has been said in Lesson 54, page 480 for the use of **to iú kotó** when translating infinitives, applies also to the translation of gerunds.

Examples

*Shiháinin wa kōjō wo nichiyōbi ni **heisá surú**[1] **kotó** wo teián*[2]
支配人 は 工場 を 日曜日 に 閉鎖 する 事 を 提案
shimáshĭta.　The manager proposed **closing** his factory on Sunday.
しました.

*Anó morí wo **tōru**[3] **no** (**kotó**) wo sakéru*[4] *kotó ga dekimasén déshĭta.*
あの 森 を 通る の (事) を さける 事 が 出来ませんでした.
We could not avoid **passing** through that forest.

*Hondá San wa sonó mondaí ni **tazusawarú**[5] **kotó** (**no**) wo kotowari-*
本田 さん は その 問題 に たづさわる 事 (の) を 断り
máshĭta.　Mr. Honda declined **having** anything **to do** with that matter.
ました.

When a gerund, followed by an object, qualifies a preceding noun, neither *kotó* nor *no* is used, and the order of the words in the Japanese translation is just the opposite of the order required for the English construction.

> *Kínu wo tsŭkúru gíjitsu.* 絹を造る技術.
> Silk　to　make　art. = The art of making silk.

For euphonic reason, the repetition of **kotó** in the same sentence is generally avoided, although it is grammatically correct.

*Anó katá ga **dekakerú no** (**kotó**) wo **tomerú kotó** ga dekimasén*
あの 方 が 出かける の (事) を 止める 事 が 出来ません
déshĭta.　We could not prevent his **going out.**
でした.　(*lit.* That person the going out, to stop the thing could not.)

We remind the student that the potential may be translated only with **kotó,** so that **no** cannot be used after *tomerú* (not to be able to stop) in the above example.

The construction with *kotó* or *no* is used also when translating a gerund in the perfect tense, but in this case the verb is in the past.

*Watashí no bengóshi wa machigái wo **shĭtá kotó** (**no**) wo mitome-*[6]
私 の 弁護士 は 間違い を した 事 (の) を 認め
máshĭta.　My lawyer admitted **having made** a mistake.
ました.　(*lit.* My lawyer, mistake made, the fact admitted.)

*Sō **ittá kotó** (**no**) wo kōkai shimáshĭta.*　I repent **having spoken** in
そう言った 事 (の) を 後悔 しました.　this way.

*Watashí wa máe ni anó fujín ni **o-me** ni **kakátta kotó** wo*
私 は 前 に あの 婦人 に お目 に かかった 事 を
obóete imásŭ.
覚えています.

I remember having met that lady before.—*o-me ni kakáru* to meet
(*lit.* I, before, that lady met, the fact remember.—*obóeru* to remember)

---

1 *heisá surú* to close　**2** *teián surú* to propose　**3** to pass by, along, through
4 to avoid　**5** *tazusawarú* to have something to do with, meddle in, to be a party to
6 *mitomerú* to admit

*Anó daigakú e nyūgakú[1] wo **kobamáreta**[2] kotó (**no**) wo zannén ni*
あの　大学　へ　入学　を　拒まれた　　事　（の）　を　残念　に

omoimásŭ.[3]　　　　I regret **having been refused** admission to that university.
思います.　　　　　　　(*lit*. To that university the admission that-was-refused the fact
　　　　　　　　　　　　　　ragrettably I think.)

When a present gerund is used in English instead of the perfect,
the past tense is required in Japanese.

*Watashí wa shōnen jídai ni konó ié wo **míta** kotó (**no**) wo obóete imásŭ.*
私　は　少年　時代に　この家　を　見た　　事　（の）　を　覚えています.
I remember **seeing** (having seen) this house when I was a boy.

The simple present followed by **kotó** or **no** is also used to translate
a gerund when it is the object of one of the prepositions **at, from,
in, of, to,** which are omitted in the Japanese translation.

*Anó fujín wa Nihón-go wo **oshierú** kotó (**no**) ga jōzu désŭ.*
あの　婦人　は　日本語　を　教える　事　（の）　が　上手　です.
That lady is clever **at teaching** the Japanese language.

*Ani wa bóku ga **gaishutsú surú**[4] kotó (**no**) wo samatagemáshĭta.[5]*
兄　は　僕　が　外出　する　事　（の）　を　妨げました.
My brother prevented me **from going out.**

*Itóko ga anó warúi otokó to isshó ni **dekakerú** kotó (**no**) wo omói*
いとこが　あの　悪い　男　と　一緒　に　出かける　事　（の）　を　思い

todomarasemáshĭta.[6]　　I prevented my cousin **from going** out with that bad man.
止まらせました.　　　　　(*lit*. My cousin, that bad man with, to go out the fact I
　　　　　　　　　　　　　　caused to give up.)

*Watashitachí wa Fújisan e **noború** kotó (**no**) ni seikō shimáshĭta.*
私達　　は　富士山　へ　登る　事　（の）に　成功　しました.
We succeeded **in climbing** Mount Fuji.

*Konó hon wo **yómu** kotó (**no**) wa taihén omoshirói déshĭta.*
この　本　を　読む　事　（の）　は　大変　面白い　でした.
I have found much pleasure **in reading** this book.

*Watashí wa shōsetsu wo **yómu** kotó (**no**) ga sŭki désŭ.*
私　は　小説　を　読む　事　（の）　が　好き　です.
I am fond **of reading** novels.

*Watashidómo wa konó jigyō ni **seikō surú** kotó (**no**) wo kakŭshín[7]*
私共　　は　この　事業　に　成功　する　事　（の）　を　確信

shĭté imásŭ.　　　We are confident **of succeeding** in this enterprise. (*lit*. We, this
して　います.　　　　enterprise in, success make, the fact are convinced of.)

*Kishá ga déru máe ni éki e **tsŭkú** kotó (**no**) wa táshĭka désŭ.*
汽車　が　出る　前　に　駅へ　着く　事　（の）　は　確か　です.
We are certain **of reaching** the station before the train leaves.

---

1 entrance, admission into a school　**2** *kobámu* to refuse, to reject; *kobamaréru*
to be refused　**3** *zannén ni omóu* to regret　**4** *gaishutsú surú* to go out (of doors)
5 *samatagerú* to prevent, to keep somebody from doing something　**6** *omoí-todo-máru* to give up (the idea of), to desist from; *omoi-todomaraséru* to cause to give
up, etc.　**7** *kakushín surú* to be confident of, to be convinced of, to be certain of

*Konó onná-no-ko wa jíbun de kimonó wo **kirú kotó** (**no**) ga máda*
この　女の子　は　自分　で　着物　を　着る　事　（の）が　まだ

dekimasén.　　This girl is still incapable **of dressing herself.**
出来ません.　　(*kimonó wo kirú* to dress oneself)

*Watashí wa anáta no yūjin de **áru kotó** (**no**) wo hokorí[1] to shimásŭ.*
私　は　貴方　の　友人　で　ある　事　（の）を　誇り　と　します.
I am proud **of being** your friend.

*Sonó rōjin wa hĭtóri de **irú kotó** (**no**) ni nárete imásŭ.*
その　老人　は　一人　で　いる　事　（の）に　なれて　います.
That old man is well used **to being** alone. (*naréru* to be used to)

Also when preceded by a preposition, a present gerund, used instead
of the perfect, is translated by the past of the verb, followed by
kotó or ***no***.

*Anáta ga **hazukashimeráreta**[2] **kotó** (**no**) wo zonjimasén déshĭta.*
貴方　が　辱しめられた　事　（の）を　存じません　でした.
I was not aware of your **being** (having been) **wronged.**

*Sonó séito wa senséi no kanjō wo **gáishĭta**[3] **kotó** (**no**) wo kōkai[3]*
その　生徒　は　先生　の　感情　を　害した　事　（の）を　後悔

shimáshĭta.　　The student repented **of offending** (having offended) his teacher.
しました.　　　(*lit.* The student, the teacher's feelings injured, the fact repented.)

The possessive, which in English is sometimes used before a gerund,
is not translated into Japanese.

*O-sakí e **háiru** kotó (no) wo o-yurushí[5] kudasái.*　**Please excuse my entering**
お先　へ　入る　事　（の）を　お許し　下さい.　　before you.

*Anó katá ga kómban **oidé ni náru kotó** (**no**) wa táshĭka de wa arimasén.*
あの　方　が　今晩　お出でに　なる　事　（の）は　確か　ではありません.
His **coming** to-night is not certain. (*oidé ni náru* polite form of *kúru* to come)

*Kimí no nĭisan ga tádachi-ni[6] bóku ni o-kané wo **harátte kurerú kotó***
君　の　兄さんが　直ちに　僕　に　お金　を　払って　くれる　事

wo shuchō[6] shimásŭ.　　I insist on your elder brother's **paying me** immediately.
を　主張　します.　　(*lit.* Your elder brother, immediately, the money paying and give me, I insist.)

*Watashidómo ga Ōshū e **yukú kotó** (**no**) wa íma wa kakujitsú[7] désŭ.*
私共　が　欧洲　へ　行く　事　（の）は　今　は　確実　です.
Our **going** to Europe is now a certainty.

*Máe ni o-tégami wo **sashiagemasén**[8] **déshĭta kotó** (**no**) wo o-yurushí*
前　に　お手紙　を　差上げません　でした　事　（の）を　お許し

kudasái.　　Pardon my **not having written** to you before. (*lit.* Before, letter didn't
下さい.　　let you have, the fact pardon please.—*yurushí* pardon, forgiveness)

---

1 *hokorí to surú* to be proud　**2** *hazukashiméru* to put (a person) to shame, to
humiliate, to abuse, to wrong　**3** *gaisúru* to injure, to hurt, to offend　**4** *kōkai surú*
to repent　**5** *yurushí* permission, *yurúsu* to permit　**6** *tádachi-ni* immediately; *shuchō*
surú to insist　**7** certainty　**8** *sashiagerú* to let a person have, to offer, to give (a
present, etc.)

The following is a more idiomatic translation of the last two examples:

Watashidómo no Ōshū-yukí wa íma kakujitsú désŭ.
私共　の　欧洲行　は　今　確実　です.

Máe ni o-tégami wo sashiagemasén de shitsúrei shimáshĭta.
前　に　お手紙　を　差上げません　で　失礼　しました.

When the possessive is used before a gerund in a clause indicating a logical consequence of what is stated in the preceding clause, the whole sentence is translated by the same construction that should be used if in English an adverb of reason, *as* or *because*, were used.

*Konó ié wa **jōbu désŭ kará** taoréru[1] kikén[2] wa arimasén.*
この　家　は　丈夫　です　から　倒れる　危険　は　ありません.
This house is strong; there is no danger of its falling.
(**As this house is strong,** there is no danger of **its falling.**)

*Konó torí wa yóku **nárete[3] imásŭ kará** nigéru shimpái wa*
この　鳥　は　よく　馴れて　います　から　逃げる　心配　は
arimasén.   This bird is well trained; there is no fear of its flying away.
ありません.   (**As this bird is well trained,** there is no fear of **its flying away.**)

Kará, nóde, or ***kotó ni táishĭte*** may be used to translate a gerund whenever it is in a clause indicating a consequence of the fact expressed in the principal clause. Also in this case the adverb of reason, *because*, is implied.

Note that ***kotó ni táishĭte*** means "*for the thing*" (lit. *to the thing for*).

*Watashí ga anó hĭtó wo **tasŭkéta nóde** (**kará** or **kotó ni táishĭte**)*
私　が　あの　人　を　助けた　ので（から　，事　に　対して）
anó hĭtó wa kanshá shimáshĭta.   That man thanked me **for helping** him.
あの　人　は　感謝　しました.
(*lit.* I, that person helped because, that person thanked.—*tasŭkéru* to help, *kanshá surú* to express one's thanks)

Anó yūkan-na seinén wa kawá de oboré-káketa fŭtarí no kodomó wo
あの　勇敢　な　青年　は　川　で　溺れかけた　二人　の　子供　を
***tasŭkéta kará** (**nóde** or **kotó ni táishĭte**) hōbi wo ataeraremáshĭta.*
助けた　から（ので，　事　に　対して）ほう美を　与えられました.
The brave young man was rewarded **for having saved** two children from drowning in the river. (*lit.* The brave young man, in the river that began to drown two children saved because, reward was given.—*oboré-kakéru* to begin to drown, *hōbi* reward, *ataerarerú* to be given)

The expression ***kotó ni táishĭte*** belongs to the literary style, so that it is avoided in statements of ordinary occurrence, as in the following sentence:

---

1 to fall, to come down, to collapse **2** danger **3** *narásu* to train, to tame; *naréru* to be trained

Miúra San ga taihén yóku **utattá kará** (**nóde**) *watashitachí wa*
三浦　さん　が　大変　よく　歌った　から　（ので）　私達　は

homemáshĭta.　We praised Miss Miura **for singing** so well.
ほめました.　(*utaú* to sing, *homéru* to praise)

The expression **kotó ni táishĭte** means also "*against the thing*" and placed after the simple present of a verb may be used to translate a gerund when the preceding verb has the implied meaning of *against*. In this case the expression *kotó ni táishĭte* may be replaced by **ni tsúite,** which corresponds to the preposition **concerning.**

Anó hĭtó ni o-kané wo **kasú kotó ni táishĭte** (**ni tsúite**) *watashí*
あの　人　に　お金　を　貸す　事　に　対して　（に　ついて）　私

wa izón ga arimasén.　I have no objection **to lending** him money.
は　異存　が　ありません.　(I have no objection **against lending** him money.)

(*lit.* To that man, money to lend the thing against, I objection have not.)

Anáta ga konó hon wo go-shuppán[1] **nasáru ni tsúite** (**kotó ni**
貴方　が　この　本　を　御出版　なさる　に　ついて　（事　に

táishĭte) *watashí wa hantái[2] shimasén.*　I do not object to **your publish-**
対して）　私　は　反対　しません.　**ing** this book.

(*lit.* You, this book to publish against, I opposition do not make.)

In various cases peculiar constructions are used to translate clauses or sentences containing gerunds. Below we shall give the most common of these cases.

Shínjitsu[3] wo **iú ni** *koshĭtá[4] kotó wa arimasén.*　There is nothing like
真実　を　言う　に　こした　事　はありません.　**telling** the truth.

Watashí wa ása háyaku **benkyō surú** *shūkan désŭ.*
私　は　朝　早く　勉強　する　習慣　です.

I am in the habit of **studying** early in the morning.

Háha **ni átta** *yorokobí wa táishĭta[5] monó déshĭta.*　My joy at **seeing** my
母　に会った　喜び　は　大した　もの　でした.　mother was great.

(*lit.* Mother met, joy great thing was.—*ni áu* to meet, to see)

Anáta ni tsúite no yói shirasé[6] wo **kiité** *ureshíi déshĭta.*
貴方　についての　よい　知らせ　を　聞いて　嬉しい　でした.

We were pleased at **hearing** good news about you.

Konó hon wa **yómu** *kachi[7] ga arimásŭ.*　This book is worth **reading.**
この　本　は　読む　価値　が　あります.

Ku-ji no resshá ni maniaimasén déshĭta.　We **failed in catching**
九時　の　列車　に間に合いませんでした.　the nine o'clock train.

(*lit.* Nine o'clock train for, we were not in time.—*ni maniáu* to be in time for)

---

1 *go-shuppán nasáru* polite form of *shuppán surú* to publish　**2** *hantái surú* to oppose, to object to (against)　**3** truth　**4** *kosú* to surpass, to be better than　**5** great　**6** news　**7** *káchi ga áru* to be worth

Nigéru dókoro[1] *ka sonó ryokōsha wa náifu wo te ni shĭté yajū*[2] *no*
逃げる どころ か その 旅行者 は ナイフ を 手 に して 野獣 の
hō e mukatté ikimáshĭta.   Far from **running away,** the traveller went towards
方 へ 向って 行きました.   the wild animal with a knife in his hand.

> (*lit.* To run away far from, the traveler, knife in hand doing, the wild
> animal's direction to, facing went.—*nigéru* to run away)

Resshá ni nori-okuréru[3] *shimpái no tamé*[4] *watashi wa hasshá*[5] *yóri*
列車 に 乗りおくれる   心配 の ため 私 は 発車 より
mo han-jikán máe ni éki e ikimáshĭta.
も 半時間 前 に 駅 へ 行きました.

> For fear **of missing the train** I went to the station half an hour before its
> departure. (*lit.* The train to miss for fear, I, departure than, half hour before
> to the station went.)

Konó otokó-no-katá ni ízen o-me ni kakátta obóe ga arimasén.
この 男の方 に 以前 お目 に かかった 覚え が ありません.

> I do not remember **having met** this man before.

Sonná bakágeta[6] *kotó wo kikú to warawazú*[7] *ni wa iraremasén.*
そんな ばかげた 事 を 聞くと 笑わず に は いられません.

> When I hear such nonsense I cannot help **laughing.**

> (*lit.* Such silly thing hear when, without laughing cannot be.—*iraréru* to
> be able to be)

Kómban ojí wa kisō mo arimasén.   There is no hope of my uncle's
今晩 伯父 は 来そう も ありません.   **coming** to-night.

> (*lit.* To-night my uncle doesn't seem to come.—*kisō* seems to come; *ki*
> stem of *kúru* to come, *sō* suffix meaning "it seems," "it looks as if," etc.)

A gerund preceded by the preposition **by** is translated by the
simple present, followed by *kotó ni yotté.*

Benkyō surú kotó ni yotté manabimásŭ.   **By studying** we learn.
勉強 する 事 に よって 学びます.

Sometimes the verb used in the gerund may be omitted, in which
case only *ni yotté* is used.

Benkyō ni yotté manabimásŭ. 勉強によって学びます.

A gerund preceded by the preposition **for,** with the implied meaning of purpose, is translated by the simple present, followed by
tamé ni or *nóni.*

Perū de wa nímotsu[8] *wo umpán surú*[9] *tamé ni (nóni) ráma wo*
ペルーで は 荷物 を 運搬 する ため に (のに) らま を
tsŭkaimásŭ.   In Peru people use the llama **for carrying** loads.
使います.

---

1 *dókoro ka* far from (*lit.* instead of)   **2** wild animal   **3** *nori-okuréru* to miss (a
train, tram)   **4** *shimpái no tamé* for fear   **5** departure   **6** *bakágeta* silly; *bakágeta
kotó* nonsense   **7** *warawazú ni wa* without laughing, *iraremasén* cannot be   **8** load
9 *umpán surú* to carry

Bijitsu Tenrankái e nyūjō[1] surú nóni (tamé ni) go-jū yen harawá-
美術　展覧会　へ　入場　する　のに　（ため　に）五十　円　払わ

nákereba narimasén déshǐta.　　I had to pay 50 yen **for entering**
なければ　なりません　でした.　　the Art Exhibition.

For is translated by *tamé no monó* when, preceded by *to be,*
it is followed by a gerund that has no object.

Konó mizú wa nómu tamé no monó de wa arimasén.
この　水　は　飲む　ため　の　もの　で　はありません.

This water is not **for drinking.** (*lit.* This water to drink for, thing is not.)

Koré wa nomímizu de wa arimasén. (more idiomatic)
これ　は　飲水　で　はありません.　*nomímizu* drinking water

A gerund preceded by **on** or **upon** is translated by the simple
present, followed by one of the expressions *ya ína ya* や否や, *to
súgu* と直ぐ, *totán ni* とたんに *Totán ni* is more colloquial than
the other two expressions. Any of the three expressions corresponds
to **as soon as, hardly......when, just as,** etc.

Jōsen[2] surú ya ína ya (to súgu) watashí wa kyūyū[3] ni aimáshǐta.
乗船　する　や　否　や（と　直ぐ）　私　は　旧友　に会いました.

On going on board the ship I met my old friend.

(*lit.* Embarcation to do as soon as, I old friend met.)

Resshá kará déru ya ína ya (totán ni) sonó eigá haiyū[4] wa gunshū[5]
列車　から　出る　や　否　や（とたんに）その　映画　俳優　は　群集

ni kangéi[6] saremáshǐta.　　**Upon coming out** of the train the movie star was
に　歓迎　されました.　　welcomed by the crowd.

(*lit.* The train from to come out as soon as, the movie star by the crowd
was welcomed.)

A gerund may sometimes be translated by the subordinate.

Benkyō shǐté manabimásǔ. 勉強して学びます.　　By studying we learn.

Watashí no itóko wa warúi sakaná wo tábete byōki ni narimáshǐta.
私　のいとこ　は　悪い　魚　を　食べて　病気　に　なりました.

My cousin got sick **from eating** bad fish.

(*lit.* My cousin bad fish having eaten, sick became.)

Onoráto San wa Tōkyō de watashí ni átte bikkúri shimáshǐta.
オノラートさん　は　東京　で　私　に会ってびっくり　しました.

Mr. Onorato was surprised **at seeing** me in Tokyo.

(*lit.* Mr. Onorato, in Tokyo, me meeting, was surprised.)

Sometimes a noun is used to translate a gerund.

---

1 *nyūjō surú* to enter (public places)　**2** *jōsen surú* to go on board　**3** *kyūyū* old
friend　**4** *eigá haiyū* movie star　**5** crowd　**6** *kangéi surú* to welcome

jōzu-na **utaikatá**　上手な歌い方　　good singing

Katō San wa shikén no **seikō** *wo akiramemáshĭta.*
加藤 さん は 試験 の 成功 を あきらめました.

Mr. Kato despaired **of succeeding** in his examination.
(*lit*. Mr. Kato, examination's success, despaired of.—*akiraméru* to despair of)

In rare cases the simple stem of verbs of Class I, but more frequently the *i*-stem of verbs of Class II, are used to translate a gerund.

hajimé　初め　beginning (from *hajimerú* to begin)

hanami　花見　flower-viewing (*haná+mi* simple stem of *míru* to see)

torí no **saezurí**　the singing of a bird
鳥 の さえずり　　(*saezúru* to sing, said of birds)

Nōfutachi wa **mugímaki**[1] *wo oemáshĭta.*　The farmers have finished sowing
農夫達 は 麦まき を 終えました.　their wheat. (*máku* to sow)

The expression **yō-ni,** placed after the simple present of a verb, is sometimes used to translate a gerund.

Iwatá San wa o-saké wo **nómu yō-ni** *nátte kará katéi wo kaerimimasén.*[2]
岩多 さん は お酒 を 飲む ようになってから 家庭をかえりみません.

Since he took **to drinking,** Mr. Iwata has been neglecting his family.
(*lit*. Mr. Iwata, wine to drink-like having become because, the family doesn't think of.)

Yánushi wa anáta ga tádachi-ni[3] *yáchin wo* **haráu yō-ni** (or *kotó*
家主 は あなた が 直ちに 家賃 を 払う ように 　（事

wo) *shuchō*[4] *shĭté imásŭ.*　The landlord insists **on** your **paying** the house rent
を） 主張 して います.　immediately.

N. B. For the translation of gerunds preceded by the prepositions *after, before, besides, by, instead of,* and *without,* we refer the student to the index.

Vocabulary

Nouns						
art	*gíjitsu*	技術	gill	*erá*	エラ
bamboo	*také*	竹	monk	*shūdōsō*	修道僧
birth	*kōtan*	降誕	opinion	*íken*	意見
breathing	*kokyū*	呼吸	particular	*shōsai*	詳細
cause	*gen-in*	原因	past	*káko*	過去
confidence	*kakushín*	確信	present	*génzai*	現在
future	*mírai*	未来	process	*hōhō*	方法
			pupil(eye)	*hĭtomí*	瞳

1 *múgi* wheat, *mugímaki* wheat sowing　2 *kaerimíru* to think of　3 *tádachi-ni* immediately　4 *shuchō surú* to insist (on)

secret	*himitsú*	秘ヒ密ミッ		to express	*nobé·ru*	述ノベル
silkworm	*káiko*	蚕カイ		to guard	*kanshí surú*	監カ視シスル
swimmer	*suiéisha*	水スィ泳エィ者シャ		to hurt	*kizutsúké·ru*	キヅツケル
swimming	*suiéi*	水泳		to learn	*obóe·ru*	覚オボエル
typist	*taipísŭto*	タイピスト		to manufacture	*seizō surú*	製セィ造ゾゥスル
Adjectives				to rear	*káu*	飼カウ
disagreeable	*fuyúkai-na*	不愉快ナ		to resign	*jishokú surú*	辞ジ職スル
doubtful	*utagawashíi*	疑ウタガワシイ		to transmit	*tsŭtae·rú*	伝ヅタエル
foreign	*kokúgai-no*	国コク外ガイノ		to trust	*shinjí·ru*	信シンジル
ignorant	*mukyōiku*	無ム教キョ育イク		**Adverbs**		
lowly	*iyashíi*	卑イヤシイ		as a rule	*ippán-ni*	一ィッ般パンニ
Verbs				closely	*genjū-ni*	厳ゲン重ジゥニ
to benefit	*ekí-súru*	益エキスル		secretly	*hisóka-ni*	密ヒソカニ

to introduce *shōkai surú*, to be introduced *shōkai sarerú*; to carry away *hakobidásu*; bamboo tube *také-zutsú*; the interior, the inner part *náibu*; to fit, to suit, to be adapted, fitted *tekisúru*; to present, to offer (to sovereings and princes of the blood) *kenjō surú*; to be ashamed *hajíru*; to get, to obtain, to receive *éru*; right, not mistaken, not wrong *tadashíi*; to refrain from *sashihikaerú*; to remake, to re-do *yarinaósu*; to charge (price) *seikyū surú*; to look back *furikáeru*; to worry *shimpai surú*; power, capacity *nōryoku*

Exercise *Renshū* 練習

1. Kínu wo tsŭkúru gíjitsu wa Shína de wa ō-mukashí kará shirareté imáshĭta. Káiko wo káu hōhō to kínu wo seizō surú hōhō wa Kirisŭtó kōtan go[1] gohyakú-gojū nen Rōma kōtei Jusuchinián no jidái ni fŭtarí no Pérusha[2] no shūdōsō ni yotté Yōroppa e shōkai saremáshĭta. Konó shūdōsō-tachí wa Shína de kínu no seizōhō wo narátta no déshĭta. Shína de káiko-ga[3] no tamágo wo te ni iré[4] soré wo také-zutsú ni kakúshĭte hisóka-ni Konsutanchinōpuru[5] e hakobidáshi Rōma kōtei ni soré wo kenjō shimáshĭta. Shinájin wa kínu no kenkyū[6] no himitsú wo dekíru daké[7] genjū-ni kanshí shi kokúgai no hĭtóbito ga soré wo shirú no wo konomimasén déshĭta. **2.** Fukurō no hĭtomí wa yóru míru no ni tekíshĭte imásŭ. **3.** Gyórui wa me ni miéru[8] mimí ga arimasén ga erá ga arimásŭ; konó erá wa kokyū to soshĭté náibu ni áru mimí e otó wo tsŭtaerú tamé ni tsŭkawareté[9] imásŭ. **4.** Ō-mukashí Yōroppa de wa ippán-ni kanemochí wa taihén mukyōiku de monó wo yómu kotó ga dekimasén déshĭta shi kō iú hĭtótachi wa yómi-kakí[10] wa hijō ni iyashíi shokugyō to omótte imáshĭta. **5.** Kimí wa anná kotó wo shĭtá kotó wo hajimasén ka.—Chittó-mo.[11]

---

1 *go* after; *Kirisŭtó kōtan go* after the birth of Christ **2** Persia **3** *káiko-ga* silkworm moth **4** *te ni irerú* to get (*lit.* to put in the hand) **5** Constantinople **6** *kínu no kenkyū* treatment of silk (treating silk) **7** *dekíru daké* as possible; *dekíru daké genjū ni* as closely as possible **8** *me ni miéru* visible **9** *tsŭkawarerú* to be used **10** *yómi-kakí* reading and writing **11** *chittó mo* not in the least

Soré dókoroka[1] bóku wa ā[2] shǐtá kotó wo tadashíi to omótte imásǔ. **6.** Konó mondaí ni tsúite mótto shōsai wo éru máde watashí wa jibún no íken wo nobéru no wo sashihikaemashō. **7.** Anó otokó wo shínjita no wa watashí ga wárukatta[3] to íma wakarimáshǐta. **8.** Konó hashí no na wo go-zónji désǔ ka. —Iié, watashí wa konó hashí wo ízen míta kotó sáe[4] obóete imasén. Saikín tsǔkuráreta ni chigái nái désǔ ne. **9.** Konó furúi gaitō no yarinaoshí ni kimí no yōfukuya wa íkura seikyū shimáshǐta ka.—Atarashíi no wo tsǔkúru no to hotóndo onají guraí[5] seikyū shimáshǐta. **10.** Suiéijitsu wa móshi mo naraō to surú suiéisha ga kakushín wo móteba háyaku oboeraremásǔ. **11.** Anáta no atarashíi jigyō no seikō wa utagawashíi désǔ. **12.** Konó shorúi wo káita kotó ni táishǐte watashí wa taipísǔto ni ni-sen yen haraimáshǐta. **13.** Anó fujín ga nakushǐtá inú wo watashí ga mitsǔketé agetá nóde[6] watashí ni sen-yen kuremáshǐta. **14.** Watashí ga gakká wo yóku benkyō shǐtá nóde senséi wa homemáshǐta. **15.** Anó fuyúkai-na otokó no tamé ni harakú no wa iyá ni narimáshǐta. Asú[7] wa jishokú shimashō. **16.** Watashí no yūjin no Duránte San wa Nihón-ga[8] wo benkyō surú tsumorí de Nihón e kimáshǐta. **17.** Káko wo furikáettari matá mírai ni tsǔkí-susúndari[9] shǐté shimpaí wo surú no wa ningén no nōryoku désǔ. Móshi ningén ga génzai dáke kirí kangaerarénai náraba ningén wa shimpaí no gen-in[10] ga nái deshō. **18.** Hǐtó wo tomó toshǐté[11] ekí surú chikará no nái ningén démo hǐtó wo tekí toshǐté[12] kizutsǔkéru chikará wo mótte irú ka-mo shiremasén.

1. 絹を造る技術は支那では大昔から知られていました. 蚕を飼う方法と絹を製造する方法はキリスト降誕後五百五十年, ローマ皇帝ジュスチニアンの時代に二人のペルシャの修道僧によってヨーロッパへ紹介されました. この修道僧達は支那で絹の製造法を習ったのでした. 支那で蚕蛾の卵を手に入れそれを竹筒にかくして密かにコンスタンチノーブルへ運び出しローマ皇帝にそれを献上しました. 支那人は絹の研究の秘密を出来るだけ厳重に監視し国外の人々がそれを知るのを好みませんでした. **2.** ふくろうの瞳は夜見るのに適しています. **3.** 魚類は目に見える耳がありませんがえらがありますこのえらは呼吸とそして内部にある耳へ音を伝えるために使われています. **4.** 大昔, ヨーロッパでは一般に金持は大変無教育で物を読む事が出来ませんでしたしこうゆう人達は読み書きは非常にいやしい転業と思っていました. **5.** 君はあんな事をした事を恥ぢませんか.—ちっとも. それどころか僕はあゝした事を正しいと思っています. **6.** この問題についてもっ

---

1 *soré dókoroka* instead of that=on the contrary   2 *ā* such; *ā shǐtá kotó* such a thing   3 *wárukatta* I was wrong, from *warúi* to be wrong   4 *sáe* even; *ízen míta kotó sáe* even to have seen it before   5 *hotóndo onají gurai* almost the same   6 *mitsǔketé agetá nóde* for having found; *agetá* from *agerú*, indicates favour towards a person   7 *asú* to-morrow   8 *Nihón-ga* the Japanese art of painting (lit. Japanese pictures)   9 *mírai ni tsǔkí-susumú* to look forward; *mírai ni* in the future; *tsǔkí* from *tsukú* to push; *susumú* to march   10 *shimpaí no gen-in* cause for worry   11 *hǐtó wo tomó toshité* as a friend   12 *hǐtó wo tekí toshité* as an enemy

と詳細をえるまで私は自分の意見をのべるのをさしひかえましょう. **7.** あの男を信じたのは私が悪かったと今わかりました. **8.** この橋の名を御存じですか.—いゝえ, 私はこの橋を以前見た事さえ覚えていません. 最近造られたにちがいないですね. **9.** この古い外套のやり直しに君の洋服屋は幾ら請求しましたか.—新らしいのをつくるのと殆ど同じぐらい請求しました. **10.** 水泳術は若しも習おうとする水泳者が確信をもてば早く覚えられます. **11.** 貴方の新しい事業の成功は疑わしいです. **12.** この書類を書いた事に対して私はタイピストに弐千円払いました. **13.** あの婦人が失くした犬を私が見つけて上げたので私に千円くれました. **14.** 私が学課をよく勉強したので先生はほめました. **15.** あの不愉快な男のために仂くのはいやになりました. あすは辞払しましよう. **16.** 私の友人のデュランテさんは日本画を勉強するつもりで日本へ来ました. **17.** 過去をふり返ったり又未来に突き進んだりして心配をするのは人間の能力です. 若し, 人間が現在だけきり考えられないならば人間は心配の原因がないでしよう. **18.** 人を友として益する力のない人間でも人を敵としてきづつける力をもっているかもしれません.

1. The art of making silk has been known in China since very ancient times. The process of rearing the silkworms, and the manner of making the silk was introduced into Europe by two Persian monks at the time of the Roman Emperor Justinian, 550 years after the birth of Christ. These two monks had learned how to manufacture silk in China. There they got a supply of eggs of the silk moth, hid them in a hollow bamboo, and then carried them secretly to Constantinople and presented them to the Roman Emperor. The Chinese guarded the secret of treating silk as closely as possible and did not want people of other countries to know it. **2.** The pupil of the owl's eye is adapted for seeing at night. **3.** Fishes have no visible ears, but they have gills which are used both for breathing and for transmitting sounds to their internal ears. **4.** In ancient times in Europe the rich man was, as a rule, very ignorant, and far from being able to read, he considered reading and writing too lowly an occupation for him. **5.** Are you not ashamed of having done such a thing?—Not in the least. I still think I was right in doing it. **6.** I shall refrain from expressing an opinion on this matter until I receive further particulars. **7.** I now realize that I was wrong in trusting that man. **8.** Do you know the name of this bridge?—No, I don't even remember having seen it before. It must have been built recently. **9.** How much did your tailor charge for redoing your old overcoat?—He charged me nearly as much as I should pay for having a new one made. **10.** The art of swimming is acquired quickly if the would-be swimmer has confidence in himself. **11.** Your succeeding in your new undertaking is doubtful. **12.** I paid the typist two thousand yen for writing this document. **13.** That lady gave me 1,000 yen for having found the dog she had lost. **14.** My teacher praised me for having studied my lesson well. **15.** I am tired of working for that disagreeable man. To-morrow I shall resign. **16.** My friend Mr. Durante has come to Japan with a view to studying the Japanese art of painting. **17.** It is man's power of looking back to the past and forward to the future that makes worry possible. If man could think only of the present he would not have any cause for worry **18.** A man who has no power to benefit us as a friend, may have the power of injuring us as an enemy.

Fifty-seventh Lesson 第五十七課

Adverbs *Fukushi* 副詞

In previous lessons the adverbs of time, place, degree, quantity, in their most common uses, and those obtained by modifying the ending of true adjectives, have been illustrated.

In this lesson other English expressions and their corresponding Japanese translation are given, classified under the group of *true adverbs*, while in the following lesson will be given groups of Japanese adverbs classified according to their common characteristics.

True Adverbs

To this group belong words which, whatever their origin may have been, are now used exclusively or mostly as adverbs.

***about:** approximately, nearly *gurai* ぐらい, *oyosó* 凡そ, *káre-koré* かれこれ (*colloq.*); *yáku* 約 (*Lit.*); here and there *achirá-kóchira* あちらこちら; somewhere round, near *sokorá átari ni* そこら当りに.—See also Lesson 24, page 158.

ichí-jikán gurai no uchí ni   一時間ぐらいのうちに   in **about** an hour

oyosó (*yáku*) *ni máiru* or *ni máiru gurai*   **about** two miles
凡そ (約) 二 哩,   二 哩, ぐらい

káre gurai no nenréi   彼ぐらいの年齢   **about** his age

Káre-koré jikán désŭ. かれこれ時間です.   It is **about** time.

Sokorá-átari-ni áru deshō.   You may find it **about**.
そこら当りに   あるでしょう.

About is variously translated when modifying certain verbs, a few of which are given below:

to face about	*tenkái saserú*	転回させる
to get about	*ugóki mawarú*	動きまわる

to loiter about	*burat̆sŭkí arúku*	ぶらつき歩く
to take turns about	*rimbán-ni surú*	輪番にする
to walk about	*arúki-mawarú*	歩きまわる
to wander about	*samayói arúku*	さまよい歩く

Idiomatic usage:

daitái jūbun だいたい充分   just **about** enough

Hihō ga séken ni hiromátte irú.   The sad news is going **about**.
悲報 が 世間 に 広まって いる.

(*hihō* sad news; *séken* the world, the public; *ni* among; *hiromáru* to spread)

about as......*oyosó* (*yáku*) *onají guraí*...... 凡そ（約）同じぐらい

hóbo onají guraí (*Lit.*)   ほぼ同じぐらい

***abundantly** *tak̆ŭsán* (*ni*) colloq. 沢山(に); *dossári* どっさり (*slang*); *hōfu-ni* 豊富に (*Lit.*); *obitad̆áshiku* おびただしく (innumerably—*Lit.*)

***after all,** eventually *ts̆ŭmari* つまり; finally, ultimately *kekkyok̆ŭ* 結局; in the end *shosén* 所詮; at last *tōtō* 到頭 (colloq.), *ts̆úi-ni* 遂に (*Lit.*)

Ts̆úmari, sonó kanjō wo watashí ga haráeba íi no dés̆ŭ.
つまり, その 勘定 を 私 が 払えばいいの です.
After all, I'd better pay the bill.

Kekkyok̆ú, watashí wa asokó e ikanái kotó ni kimemáshĭta.
結局, 私 は あそこへ行かない 事 に 決めました.
I have decided, **after all,** not to go there.—*kotó ni kimerú* to decide

Kekkyok̆ú, kamaimasén deshō. **After all,** what does it matter?
結局, かまいませんでしょう. **After all** it is nothing to worry about.

kamáu かまう to mind, to care about, to trouble oneself about, etc.

Shosén, anó byōnin wa naoránai to kázoku wa akirámete imás̆ŭ.
所詮, あの 病人 は なおらないと 家族 は あきらめています.
The family have given up hope that the patient would recover **after all.**

akiraméru あきらめる to give up (an idea), to be resigned to (a loss, etc.)

Tōtō, nagái áme ga yamimáshĭta.   The long spell of rain has stopped
到頭, 長い 雨 が 止みました.   **after all.**

Ts̆úi ni, kanashíi kekká ga kitá.   **After all,** the sad end came.
遂 に, 悲しい 結果 が 来た.   *kekká* result, consequence, outcome

Tōtō seikō shimáshĭta. とうとう成功しました.   I succeeded **after all.**

***again** *matá* 又 (colloq.); *imá-ichidó* 今一度 (=once more, *Lit.*); *f̆ŭtatabí* 再び (*Lit.*); **again** and **again** *ík̆udo-mo* 幾度も; now and **again** *tokidoki* 時々; once **again** *mō-ichidó* もう一度; over and over **again** *nándomo* 何度も; to be well **again** *kaifuk̆ú surú* 回復する; back **again** (to the original place) *motó no tokoró e* もとの所へ *motó e* もとへ.

***almost** *taigái* 大概 (=very nearly, colloq.); *ōkata* 大方 (=almost nearly, colloq.); *hotóndo* 殆ど (*Lit.*); *sundé-no-kotó de* すんでの事で (*slang*)

Watashí wa sundé-no-kotó de hikí-korosaréru tokoró déshĭta.
私 は すんでの事 で ひき殺される ところ でした.
I was **almost** run over. (*hikí-korósu* ひき殺す to kill by running over)

*Sonó shigotó wa **hotóndo** (taigái, ōkata) dékite imásŭ.*

その　仕事　は　　殆ど　　（大概，　大方）　出来て　います.

The work is **almost** done.

*****along,** in a line with the length of something *sottá* そった, from *soú* そう to be parallel to, alongside with, etc.; some way on *zuttó* ずっと.

*Kosuí ni **sottá** go-rokú ken no ié.*   A few houses **along** by the lake.

湖水　に　そった　　五六　　軒　の　家.

(*kosuí* lake, *ken* numerative for counting houses)

zuttó yūgata ni ずっと夕方に   **along** towards evening

Idiomatic usage.

Káre wa dō shĭté kurashĭté imásŭ ka.   How is he getting **along**?

彼　は　どうして　暮らしています　か.   (*dō shĭté* how?, in what way?)

(*lit.* He, how does he make a living?—*kurasú* 暮らす to subsist, support oneself)

Go-benkyō wa sonó-go ikága désŭ ka.   How are you getting **along** with

御勉強　は　その後　いかが　です　か.   your studies?

(Your study, lately how is?)

Watashí wa tomodachí wo tsureté kimáshĭta.   I have brought my friend

私　は　　友達　　を　　つれて　来ました.   **along.**

(*lit.* I, my friend bringing with, came.—*tsureté kúru* つれて来る to bring with)

Sā, watashí to isshó ni irasshái.   Come **along** with me.

さあ，　私　と　一緒にいらっしゃい.   (Well, with me together, come.)

Sóra, hashítte ikí-nasái.   Now, run **along**.

そら，　走って　行きなさい.   (Now, running go.—*hashíru* 走る to run, to rush)

*****all along** (=all the time) *zuttó* ずっと, (from the beginning) *hajimé kará* 初めから; (continuously) *hiki-tsuzúite* 引きつづいて; (from end to end) *hashí kará hashí máde* 端から端まで

*****already,** beforehand *maé-mótte* 前以って (*colloq.*), *kánete* かねて (*Lit*); even now, by this time *íma-démo* 今でも; in good time, thus early *háyaku-mo* 早くも; a while ago, quite a while ago *tokkú-ni* とっくに (*colloq.*—this expression is a synonym of *mō* もう, and *mō tokkú-ni* may be used for emphasis)—See also Lesson 31, page 218.

Kánete (maé-mótte) go-tsúchi shimáshĭta tōri.   As I have **already**

かねて　（前以って）　御通知　しました　通り.   informed you.

(*tsúchi surú* 通知する to give—a person—notice that, to inform of, etc.)

Súgu irasshái, íma-démo osói désŭ yo.   Go at once; it is **already** late.

すぐいらっしゃい，今でも　おそいです　よ.   (*yo* emphatic expression)

Keikán wa sonó toki háyaku-mo keikái shĭté imáshĭta.

警官　は　その　時　　早くも　　警戒　して　いました.

The policemen had, at that time, **already** taken precautions.

(*keikán* 警官 policeman; *keikái surú* 警戒する to take precautions, to give warning)

Tokkú-ni (Mō) dékite imásŭ.   It is **already** done.

とっくに　（もう）出来て　います.

Mō tokkú-ni ikú toki désŭ.   It is **already** (high) time for you to go.

もう　とっくに　行く　時　です.

already known *kichí no* 既知の (*Lit.*)

an already known fact *kichí no jíjitsu* 既知の事実

***always *ítsu-mo* いつも (*colloq.*); *ítsu-de-mo* いつでも (*colloq.* and emphatic); *shijū* 始終 (=all the time); *tsúne-ni* 常に (*Lit.*); *heizéi* 平生 (usually, *Lit.*)

***anyhow, by any means *dō shĭté mo* どうしても (*colloq.*), *nán-to shĭté mo* 何んとしても (*Lit.*); in any case *dōse* どうせ (*colloq.*), *izuré ni shĭté mo* いづれにしても (*Lit.*); at any rate *to-ni-kakú* とにかく; one way or the other *donó michí* どのみち (*colloq.*), *izuré* いづれ (*Lit.*)

> *Nán-to shĭté mo sonó shinamonó wo kaimásŭ.*   I will buy that thing
> 何んと して も その 品物 を 買います.   **anyhow.**

> *Izuré ni shĭté mo* (or *Dōse*) *watashí wa dekaké-nákereba narimasén.*
> いづれ に して も (どうせ) 私 は 出かけなければなりません.
> I must go out **anyhow.** (*dekakerú* 出かける to go out, to set out, etc.)

> *To-ni-kakú sō itashimashō.*   I will do so **anyhow.**
> とにかく そう致しましょう.

> *Izuré* (*Donó-michí*) *ashĭtá máde ni go-henjí itashimásŭ.*
> いづれ (どのみち) あした 迄 に 御返事 いたします.
> **Anyhow,** I will give you an answer by to-morrow.

***awfully *taihén-(ni)* 大変 (に), *totemó* とても (*colloq.*)

> *Anó inú wa totemó kitanai.*   That dog is **awfully** dirty.
> あの 犬 は とても 汚い.

***case, in any case (=anyhow) *to-mo-kakú* ともかく, *to-ni-kakú* とにかく; *to-mo-kakú mo* ともかくも (emphatic); in case of, in the event of......*no baai ni wa* ......の場合には (*colloq.*), ...*no sái ni wa* ......の際には (*Lit.*)

> *káji no baai* (*sái*) *ni wa*...... 火事の場合 (際) には...... in **case** of fire
> *masaká-no-tokí* (or *baai*) *ni* まさかの時 (場合) に in **case** of need
> *kesshĭté......nái* 決して......ない in no **case,** never

> *jū-chū hákku* 十中八九   in nine **cases** out of ten
> (*chū* among, *hákku*=*hachi*+*ku*; *lit.* in 8 or 9 **cases** out of 10)

> *Sonó keikakú wa jū-chū hákku seikō surú to omoimásŭ.*
> その 計画 は 十中 八九 成功 する と 思います.
> I think the plan will succeed in nine **cases** out of ten.
> (*keikakú* plan, *seikō surú* to succeed)

***certainly (in answering) *Hái, sonó tōri désŭ.* はい, その通りです. (Yes), **certainly.**—*Ii désŭ tómo.* いいですとも; Yes, by all means. No doubt *táshĭka-ni* たしかに; of course *mochíron* 勿論

***course, of course *mochíron* 勿論; *iú-máde-mo nákŭ* 言うまでもなく (=needless to say); *murón* 無論 (*Lit.*—generally used by men)

> *Kaigō ni kimásŭ ka.*—*Mochíron.*   Will you come to the meeting?—
> 会合 に 来ます か.   勿論.   **Of course.**

Of course, moreover, is translated by *tómo* とも, an expression used in translating also the adverb *certainly.* Note that *tómo* is used in familiar speech.

Soré wa daijōbu désŭ ka.—Ē, daijōbu désŭ **tómo.**
それ は 大丈夫 です か. ええ, 大丈夫 です とも.

Is it safe?—**Of course.** Oh, yes, it is safe.

***enough** (See Lesson 47, page 408)

sure enough *an-no-jō* 案のじょう (colloq.) ; *hatáshĭte* 果して (Lit')

An-no-jō (hatáshĭte) sonó kodomó wa sokó ni imáshĭta.
案のじょう（果して）その 子供 は そこ に いました.

Sure enough, there was the child.

strange **enough** *jitsŭ-ni fushigí-na kotó ni* 実に不思議な事に

(*jitsú-ni* truly, *fushigí-na* strange, mysterious, wondrous)

***even** *mo* も, *de mo* でも, *máde mo* 迄も. The three expressions are here given in their increasing degree of emphatic force. However, while *de mo* でも and *máde mo* 迄も may be used with positive as well as negative verbs, *mo* も, in the signification of **even,** is almost always used with negative verbs.

Chotto **mo** *nemurimasén déshĭta.*   I didn't sleep **even** a moment.
一寸 も ねむりません でした.

Anó hĭtó wo ichí-do **mo** *míta kotó ga nái.*   I haven't seen him
あの 人 を 一度 も 見た こと が ない.   **even** once.

Kodomó **de mo** *shĭtté imásŭ.*   **Even** children know it.
子供 で も 知って います.

Watashí no kimonó **máde mo** *nusumaremáshĭta.*   **Even** my clothes
私 の 着物 まで も ぬすまれました.   were stolen.

Káre wa jíjitsu **máde mo** *shinjimasén déshĭta.*   He didn't believe **even**
彼 は 事実 まで も 信じません でした.   the actual fact.

Even is also translated by *sáe* さえ, *de sáe* でさえ, *de sáe mo* でさえも and by *súra* すら, *de súra* ですら, *de súra mo* ですらも. The expressions are given in their increasing emphatic force, and the first three are rather of the better speech, while the other three belong to the literary style.

Káre wa jibún no namaé **sáe** *kakemasén.*   He cannot write **even** his
彼 は 自分 の 名前 さえ 書けません.   own name.

sonó tokí **de sáe** or *sonó tokí* **de mo**   **even** then
その 時 でさえ,   その 時 で も

Kodomó **de sáe mo** *yóku dekimásŭ.*   **Even** a child can do it well.
子供 でさえ も よく 出来ます.

Káre wa shōnin wo tsureté kité **súra mo** *shinji-yō-to shinákatta.*
彼 は 証人 を つれて 来て すら も 信じようと しなかった.
He would not believe it **even** after I brought witnesses.

In slang, **even** may be translated by *dátte* だって.

Toshiyori **dátte** *(de mo, de sáe) anó yamá e ikemásŭ.*
年寄り だって（で も, でさえ）あの 山 へ 行けます.

Even old people can go to that mountain.

***event,** at all events, in some way or other *izuré* いずれ, *to-ni-kakú* とにかく

***finally,** lastly *sáigo-ni* 最後に ; at last (colloq.) *yōyaku* ようやく, *tōtō* と

うとう, *Lit. tsúi-ni* 遂に ; ultimately *kekkyokú* 結局

***firstly,** first of all *mázu* 先づ ; in the first place (emphatic) *mázu dái-ichi ni* 先づ第一に ; at the beginning *saishó-ni* 最初に, (emphatic) *mázu saishó-ni* 先ず最初に

***greatly,** very much *hijō-ni* 非常に, (*Lit.*)*hanahadá* はなはだ, *ōi-ni* 大いに *ōi-ni* (*hanahadá, hijō-ni*) *sonkéi sarerú* (*Lit.*) to be **greatly** respected 大いに (はなはだ, 非常に) 尊敬 される

***generally,** universally, in general *ippán-ni* 一般に ; extensively, everywhere *amanéku* あまねく ; in a general sense *daitái-ni* (*óite*) 大体に (於いて) ; broadly speaking, as a rule (*colloq.*) *futsū* 普通, (*Lit.*) *gáishite* 概して

Nihónjin wa ippán-ni (*daitái, gáishite*) *hayá-oki désŭ.*
日本人 は 一般に (大体, 概して) 早起き です.

The Japanese are **generally** early risers.
(*hayá-oki* from *hayái* early and *okíru* to get up)

Uchí de wa daitái shichí-ji ni yūshoku wo tabemásŭ.
うち で は 大体 七時 に 夕食 を 食べます.

We **generally** dine at seven.
(*yūshoku* dinner, supper, evening meal ; *yūshoku wo tabéru* to dine)

***hardly,** harshly *kibíshiku* きびしく ; unkindly *fushínsetsu-ni* 不親切に ; severely *hídoku* ひどく ; strenuously *honé-ótte* 骨おって ; with difficulty *kurushínde* 苦しんで ; barely (*colloq.*) *yattó* やっと, (*Lit.*) *karōjite* 辛うじて ; almost not, scarcely *hotóndo* ...... 殆ど and negative verb ; seldom *métta-ni* めったに and negative verb

Yattó (*Karōjitte*) *shōri wo éta.*   Victory was **hardly** won.
やっと (辛うじて) 勝利 をえた.   (*shōri* victory, *éru* える to gain, win)

Karōjite shi wo manukaremáshĭta.   He **hardly** escaped death.
辛うじて 死 を まぬかれました.   (*manukarerú* to escape—death, etc.)

Anó hĭtó wo hotóndo obóete imasén.   I **hardly** remember him.
あの 人 を 殆ど 覚えていません.   (*obóeru* 覚える to remember)

Káre wa métta-ni éiga e ikimasén.   He **hardly** ever goes to the cinema.
彼 は めったに 映画へ行きません.

Watashí ga hanásu ka hanasánai uchí ni káre wa itté shimaimáshĭta.
私 が 話す か 話さない うち に 彼 は行ってしまいました.

I had **hardly** spoken to him before he was gone.

Note that the construction of the last example is idiomatic.

***indeed,** in truth (*colloq.*) *makotó-ni* 誠に, (*Lit.*) *jitsú-ni* 実に ; in fact *jissái-*(*ni*) 実際 (に) ; really *mattakú* 全く ; Well, it is true. *Naruhodó.* なるほど.

Káre wa mattakú (*makotó-ni, jitsú-ni, jissái*) *erái hĭtó désŭ.*
彼 は 全く (誠に, 実に, 実際) 偉い 人 です.

He is **indeed** a remarkable man. (*erái* great, celebrated, remarkable, etc.)

Jissái mattakú, mattakú jissái!   **Indeed** and **indeed!**
実際　　全く,　　　全く　　実際.　　　(very emphatic)

Hái, mattakú sō désŭ. or *Jissái sō désŭ tómo.*
はい,　全く　そうです.　　実際 そう です とも.

  Yes, indeed! (Second translation is emphatic)

Mattakú (*Jitsú-ni*) *hidói átsusa désŭ.*   Very hot, **indeed.**
全く　　（実に）　ひどい　暑さ　です.

Hontō-ni arígatō gozaimásŭ.   Thank you very much **indeed.**
本当に ありがとうございます.

Watashí wa hontō-ni (*jissái, mattakú*) *ureshíi désŭ.*   I am very glad
私　は　本当に　（実際,　全く）　うれしい です.   **indeed.**

Naruhodó, ossháru tōri désŭ.   **Indeed,** you are right.
なるほど, おっしゃる通り です. (*lit.* Indeed, you say the same is.)

*****just,** hardly, scarcely *yattó* やっと; entirely *mattakú* 全く; exactly *chōdo*
丁度; only *honnó* ほんの; just a little *honnó sŭkóshi* ほんの少し

Watashí wa yattó sonó resshá ni maniaimáshĭta.   I **just** caught the
私　は　やっと その　列車　に　間に合いました.   train.

(*maniáu* 間に合う to be in time for, *maniawánai* to be too late for)
mattakú onají or *chōdo onají* 全く同じ,　丁度同じ   **just** the same

Kánojo wa honnó sŭkóshi kigén ga wárukatta.   She was **just** a little
彼女　は　ほんの　少し　きげん　が　悪かった.   displeased.

Chōdo níji désŭ. 丁度二時です.   It is **just** two o'clock.

When **just** is used to emphasize, it may be translated by *tōri* 通り.

Hontō ni anáta no ossháru tōri désŭ.   It is **just** as you say.
本当 に あなた のおっしゃる通り です.

Idiomatic usage:

Mā, chottó sōzō shĭté gorán nasái.   **Just** fancy! (*chottó* just a little,
まあ, 一寸そうぞうしてごらんなさい.   *sōzō surú* to imagine, fancy)

Súgu itashimásŭ. すぐいたします.   I will do it **just** now.

*****last,** after all others (*colloq.*) *ichibán owari-ni* 一番終りに, (*Lit.*) *sáigo-ni*
最後に; most lately *saikín* 最近, *sáigo-ni* 最後に

Káre wa ichibán owari-ni (*sáigo-ni*) *kimáshĭta.*   He came **last.**
彼　は　一番　終りに　（最後に）来ました.

Yōroppa e saikín (*sáigo-ni*) *irasshátta no wa ítsu déshĭta ka.*
ヨーロッパへ 最近　（最後に）いらっしゃったのは いつ でした か.

  When did you **last** go to Europe? (*lit.* To Europe lastly, your having gone,
  when was?—*irasshátta no wa* is here used as a noun)

*****little,** a little (See Lesson 10, page 56)

***likewise,** as well *yahári* やはり, (*familiar speech*) *yappári* やっぱり; also *matá* 又; similarly *onájiku* 同じく; equally *dōyō-ni* 同ように

***means,** by all means, surely *kanarazú* 必ず, at any cost *dō-shité mo* どうしても; without fail *zéhi* ぜひ; in any way *nanibún* 何ぶん

by means of......, with the help of...... ......*ni yotté* ......によって

by no means *kesshité*......*de wa nái* 決して......ではない

Káre wa tsŭkiátte kesshité yúkai-na hĭtó de wa nái.
彼 はつき合って 決して ゆかいな 人 で は ない.

He is **by no means** a pleasant man to deal with. (*tsŭkiáu* つき合う to deal with)

***more.**—See Lesson 39, page 299 and Lesson 41, page 328

***moreover,** again *matá* 又; on top of it *sonó ué* その上; (*emphatic*) *sonó ué matá* その上又

***namely** (*colloq.*) *ii-káereba* 云いかえれば, (*Lit.*) *sunáwachi* 即ち

Fŭtarí no chiisái onnanokó, sunáwachi Hanakó to Kikukó.
二人 の 小さい 女の子, 即ち 花子 と 菊子.

Two little girls, **namely,** Hanako and Kikuko.

***naturally,** of course *mochiron* 勿論; needless to say *murón* 無論; as a matter of fact *tōzen,* (*Lit.*) 当然; automatically, spontaneously *shizén-ni* 自然に,; by nature *umaretsŭki* 生れつき; without concealment *ari-no-mamá-ni* ありのままに; without affectation *kidorazú-ni* 気取らずに; with ease *rakú-rakú-to* らくらくと; unaffectedly *shizén-ni* 自然に

Kánojo wa shizén ni utaimásŭ. She sings **naturally.**
彼女 は 自然 に 歌います.

***no** (See **Yes,** Lesson 14 and this lesson, page 527)

***nothing** (always with negative verbs): (*colloq.*) *sŭkóshi-mo* 少しも; (*slang*) *chittó-mo* ちっとも

Soré wa sŭkóshi-mo yakú ni tatánai. That helps **nothing.**
それ は 少しも 役 に 立たない.

(*yakú ni tátsu* 役に立つ to be useful, *yakú ni tatánai* to be useless)

Chittó-mo kamawánai. I (you, we, etc.) care **nothing.**
ちっとも かまわない.

Táishĭta kotó de wa nái. It is **nothing** much.
大した 事 で は ない.

***notwithstanding,** all the same, still *yahári* やはり, (*colloq.*) *yappári* やっぱり; in spite of *ni-mo kakawarazú* にもかかわらず; nevertheless *soré démo* それでも

***off**—See Lesson 60, page 554.

***only**—The following representative examples will show the various ways in which this adverb may be translated. See also Lesson 19, page 110.

Dempō wa kinō útta bákari désŭ.   I sent the telegram **only** yesterday.
電報 は きのう打ったばかり です.

Watashí wa ichí-do daké sonó hĭtó ni aimáshĭta.   **Only** once I met
私 は 一度 だけ その 人 に 会いました.   that person.

Káre kóso sonó chíi ni tekíshĭta jímbutsu désŭ.   He is the **only** man
彼 こそ その 地位 に 適した 人物 です.   for that position.

(*chíi* a position, office, post; *tekisúru* 適する to be fit, to suit, as for service, for a given purpose, etc.; *jímbutsu* a person, a man, a man of worth, etc.)

hĭtótsu kiri	一つきり	**only** one
hĭtóri kiri	一人きり	**only** one person
Míta kiri désŭ.	見たきりです.	I **only** saw him (it).
hĭtoríkko	一人っ子	an **only** child
táda hĭtóri no itóko	ただ一人のいとこ	an **only** cousin

Nihón no kānēshon wa utsŭkushíi ga, táda oshíi kotó ni kaorí ga arimasén.
日本 のカーネーションは美しいが, ただおしい事 に 香りがありません.

Japanese carnations are lovely; **only,** they have no fragrance.
(*oshíi kotó ni* it is a pity, it is regrettable; *kaorí* smell, fragrance)

In more colloquial speech, instead of *táda* one may use *tattá* たった, which expression seems to be more emphatic.

Tattá íma soré wo kikimáshĭta.   **Only** now I heard of it.
たった 今 それ を 聞きました.

To give more emphasis, both *tattá* and *kiri* may be used in the same sentence:

Tattá ichí-do míta kiri désŭ.   I have **only** seen him (it) once.
たった 一度 見た きり です.

bákari de náku......mo ばかりでなく......も	} **not only......but**
daké de náku......mo だけでなく......も	

Soré wo míta bákari de náku, tábe mo shimáshĭta yo.
それ を 見た ばかり で なく, 食べ も しました よ.

    I **not only** saw it **but** ate it. (*yo* colloquial emphatic particle)

Táda Nihón-go wo hanásu bákari de náku káku kotó mo dekimásŭ.
ただ 日本語 を 話す ばかり で なく 書く 事 も 出来ます.

    I **not only** can speak Japanese, **but** I can **also** write it.

Only preceded by the subjunctive may be translated by *sáe* さえ.

Jūbun kané sáe áreba.   **If** I **only** had enough money.
充分 金 さえ あれば.

Soré wo shirí sáe suréba. それを知りさえすれば. **If** I **only** knew it.

Sŭkóshi namakéru kotó sáe nákereba, káre wa íi untenshú désŭ.
少し　なまける　事　さえ　なければ，　彼　は　いい　運転手　です.

He is a good driver, **only** that he is a little lazy.

(*namakéru* to be idle, lazy; *untenshú* driver, motorman)

Wakátte sáe itára. わかってさえいたら. **If** I had **only** known !

O-machí kudasarí sáe suréba, shiháinin wa mairimásŭ.
お待ち　下さり　さえ　すれば，　支配人　は　参ります.

Our manager is coming, **if** you will **only** wait.

Note that the verb before *sáe* is used in its *i*-stem.

Mā̆, kangáete mo gorán nasái. **Only** fancy ! *or* Just fancy !
まあ，　考えて　も　ごらんなさい.

After the figure of a sum of money, **only** is translated by *nári* 也.

Kin go-man yen nári. 金五万円也. Fifty thousand yen **only.**

The word *kin* 金, which means *money*, is generally put before a figure indicating a sum of money, to prevent possible alterations.

*****originally,** formerly *móto* 元; from the first, by origin *hónrai* 本来; at first *saishó wa* 最初は; primarily *gánrai* 元来 (*Lit.*); from the beginning *hajimé kará* 始めから, *móto kará* 元から; creatively *dokusōteki-ni* 独創的に

*****part,** partly *ikubŭn no* いく分の; in part *ichí-bubún* 一部分; to some extent *áru téido* ある程度

Ikubŭn no shínjitsu wo fukúmu uwasá. A rumour that is **part** truth.
いく分　の　真実　を　ふくむ　うわさ.

(*shínjitsu* truth; *fukúmu* to contain, hold, have; *uwasá* rumour)

Soré wa ichí-bubún ki de ichí-bubún wa ishí de dékite imásŭ.
それ　は　一部分　木　で　一部分　は　石　で　出来ています.

It is made **part** of wood and **part** of stone.

*****passably,** tolerably *kánari* かなり; moderately *futsū-ni* 普通に

*****perhaps,** probably *tábun* 多分; possibly *osóraku* おそらく; maybe *hyottó surú-to* ひょっとすると (*colloq.*); might be *kotoni-yorú-to* 事によると (*colloq.*); possibly, probably *arúiwa* あるいは (*Lit.*)

*****plenty,** abundantly *takŭsán* 沢山 (*colloq.*), *hōfu-ni* 豊富に (*Lit.*); fully *jūbunni* 充分に

*****positively,** surely *kanarazú* 必ず; certainly *táshĭka-ni* たしかに; decisively *danzén-to* 断然と; firmly *katakú* かたく

*****presently,** soon, pretty soon *jikí-ni* じきに (*colloq.*), *yagaté* やがて (*Lit.*);

before long *hodónaku* 程なく; at present *génzai* 現在: at the present moment, now *mókka* 目下 (*Lit.*)

***probably, perhaps *tábun* 多分; most likely *taitéi* 大抵; likely *osóraku-wa* おそらくは; maybe *arúiwa* あるいは

***quite, entirely *sukkári* すっかり; completely *mattakú* 全く (*colloq.*), *kanzén-ni* 完全に (*Lit.*); actually *jissái* 実際, practically *jijitsú-jō* 事実上; almost, very nearly *hotóndo* 殆ど; very *taihén* 大変 (*colloq.*), *hijō-ni* 非常に (*Lit.*)

> *Watashí wa taihén génki désŭ.*   I am quite well.
> 私   は   大変 元気 です.

> *totemó takŭsán*   とても沢山   quite a lot
> *Mattakú sō désŭ.*   全くそうです.   Quite so.
> *Yoroshíi désŭ.*   よろしいです.   Quite right (All right.)

***rate, at all events, at any rate *tómokaku* とも角; at least *sŭkúnaku tómo* 少なくとも; in that case, at that rate *sonná wáke náraba* そんなわけならば: in this way, at this rate *konná-fū-ni* こんな風に

***scarcely, with difficulty, hardly *yattó* やっと (*colloq.*), *karójite* 辛うじて (*Lit.*); probably not *osóraku......nái* おそらく......ない; certainly not *hotóndo......nái* 殆ど......ない

> *Byōnin wa yattó (karójite) hanásu kotó ga dekimáshĭta.*
> 病人 は やっと(辛うじて) 話す 事 が 出来ました.
> The patient could scarcely speak.

> *Osóraku káre ga sonná kotó wo ittá hazú ga nái.*
> おそらく 彼 が そんな 事 を 云った 筈 が ない.
> He can scarcely have said such a thing.

> *Watashí wa káre wo hotóndo shiranái.*   I scarcely know him.
> 私   は 彼 を   殆ど   知らない.

***somewhat, in some degree *yáya* やゝ; to some extent *ikubún-ka* 幾分か: a little *sŭkóshi* 少し (*colloq.*), *shōshō* 少々 (*Lit.*); more or less *tashō* 多少

> *Kánojo wa yáya (ikubún-ka, sŭkóshi, shōshō, tashō) tamerátte hanáshĭta.*
> 彼女 は やや (幾分か,   少し,   少々,   多少)ためらって 話した.
> She spoke somewhat hesitantly. (*tameráu* ためらう to hesitate)

***still, yet, at present *máda* まだ; even now *ima (de) mo* 今 (で) も; as previously *jūzen dōri* 従前通り (*Lit.*); more *mótto* もっと (*colloq.*), *sárani* 更に (*Lit.*); nevertheless *soré ni-mo kakawarazú* それにもかかわらず; after that *yahári* やはり; for all that *soré-démo* それでも

> *Konó kikái wa máda tsŭkaemásŭ.*   This machine is still usable.
> この 機械 は まだ 使えます.   (*tsukaerú* to be of service)

> *Anáta wa sèi ga takái ga, o-níisan wa mótto (sára-ni) takái désŭ.*
> 貴方 は 背 が 高い が, お兄さん は もっと   (更に) 高い です.
> You are tall but your elder brother is still taller.

Káre wa kanemochí désŭ ga **soré ni-mo kakawarazú** (*yahári, soré-*
彼　は　金持　です　が　それ　にも　かかわらず　(やはり, それ
démo) *mótto hoshigátte imásŭ.*　He is rich (and) **still** he craves for more.
でも) もっと 欲しがっています.　　(*hoshigáru* to desire strongly, etc.)

***that**, to that extent **sonná-ni** そんなに; so much **soré daké** それだけ

Watashí wa **sonná-ni** *tōku máde wa arukemasén déshĭta.*
私　は　そんなに　遠く　まで　は　歩けません　でした.
I could not walk **that** far. (*arukéru* 歩ける to be able to walk)

Káre wa **soré daké** *kiri shimasén déshĭta.*　He has done only **that**
彼　は　それ　だけ　きりしません　でした.　　　much.

***then**, Well, then......**Sáte** さて; about that time **sonó-kóro** その頃 (*colloq.*),
tōji 当時 (*Lit.*); on the spot **sonó-ba-de** その場で; next **kóndo wa** こん度
は; directly after that **soré kará** それから; moreover, besides **sonó ué** その上;
in that case **soré-déwa** それでは or **déwa** では

Sonó kóro (*tōji*) *wa bukká ga amarí sagátte imasén déshĭta.*
その　頃　(当時)　は　物価　が　あまり下がっていませんでした.
Prices were not so low **then.** (*sagáru* to drop; *bukká* prices of commodities)

Atsúi gyūnyŭ wo íppai nónde, **soré kará** *nemáshĭta.*
熱い　牛乳　を　一杯　飲んで, それ　から　寝ました.
I drank a glass of hot milk and **then** I went to bed.

Sonó ué watashí wa ginkō e ikanákereba narimasén.
その　上　私　は　銀行　へ 行かなければなりません.
Then I have to go to the bank.

Soré-déwa kimí no sŭkí-na yō ni nasái.　Take your own way **then.**
それでは　君　の　好きな　ようになさい.

Déwa yoroshíi désŭ, anáta wa sokó e kyō ikú hitsuyō ga arimasén.
では　よろしい　です, 貴方　は　そこ へきょう行く　必要　がありません.
All right **then,** you need not go there to-day. (*hitsuyō* necessity)

***up**—There is no Japanese word corresponding to this adverbial particle, used to
qualify many verbs. The combination of an English verb and the particle **up** is
generally translated into Japanese by a single word. A few of such combinations
are given below:

Motion upward.

to come up	*agarú*	上がる
to fly up	*tobí-agarú*	飛び上がる
to stand up	*tachí-agarú*	立ち上がる
to throw up	*nagé-agerú*	投げ上げる
high up in the air	*sóra tákaku*	空高く

Kokó e agatté irasshái. ここへ上がっていらっしゃい.　　Come up here.

Indicating or approaching completion, totality, finality, etc:

to bring up (a child)	(*kodomó wo*) *sodatéru*	(子供を) 育てる
to catch up (to overtake)	*oitsúku*	追いつく
to stay up (awake)	*ókite irú*	起きている
to stay up all night	*hĭtobán-jū ókite irú*	一晩中おきている
to get up (from bed)	*okíru*	起きる
to get up (from chair)	*tachí-agarú*	立ち上がる

Késa háyaku okimáshǐta.   I **was up** early this morning.
けさ 早く 起きました.

Taiyō wa mō agatté imásǔ.   The sun **is up** already.
太陽 は もう上がって います.

to bring up	*Toránku wo mótte kité kudasái.*	**Bring up my**
mótte kúru	トランク を 持って 来て 下さい.	**trunk.**
to cut up	*Nikú wo kizamú yō-ni ryōrinin ni itté kudasái.*	Tell the cook to
kizamú	肉 を きざむ ように 料理人 に云って下さい.	cut up the meat.
to give up	*Ojí wa sakunén shōbai wo yamemáshǐta.*	My uncle **gave up** his
yamerú	伯父 は 昨年 商売 を やめました.	business last year.
to put up	*Konó e wo kabé ni kákete kudasái.*	**Put up** this picture on
kakéru	この 絵 を かべ に かけて 下さい.	the wall.
to take up	*Kodomó wo dakiágete kudasái.*	**Take up** the child.
dakiagéru	子供 を 抱き上げて 下さい.	

As synonym of certain English expressions.

(above)	*ni-sen yen íjō* 二千円以上	from 2,000 yen **up**
(dear)	*Sakaná no nedán wa takái désǔ.*	The price of fish is **up.**
	魚 の 値段 は 高い です.	
(from......to)	*Jimúin kará shachō máde.*	**From** a clerk **up** to president.
	事務員 から 社長 まで.	
(increase)	*Saikin bukká ga agarimáshǐta.*	Prices have gone **up** lately.
	最近 物価 が 上がりました.	(*bukká* prices of commodities)
(since)	*kodomó jídai kará* 子供時代から	**from** childhood **up**
up-to-date	(until to-day) *kyō máde* きょう迄	
	(modern) *gendái-fū-no* 現代風の	
	(latest, newest) *saishín no* 最新の	

*****usually,** generally *daitái* 大体; as a rule *taitéi* 大抵; at all times *tsúne-ni* 常に (*Lit.*); always *ítsumo* いつも (*colloq.*), *heizéi* 平生 (*Lit.*); commonly *tsūjō wa* 通常は (*Lit.*), *totemó* とても (*slang*); ordinarily *tsúrei wa* 通例は
*****very,** exceedingly *taihén* 大変 (*colloq.*), *hijō-ni* 非常に (*Lit.*); extremely *kiwámete* 極めて (*Lit.*); awfully *hídoku* ひどく; quite *shigokú* 至極 (*Lit.*) very, very much *dōmo* どうも (*slang*); not very *amari* あまり or *sahodó* さ ほど followed by a negative verb

Koré wa taihén (hijō-ni, kiwámete, totemó, shigokú) bénri désǔ.
これ は 大変 (非常に, 極めて, とても, 至極) 便利 です.
   This is **very** convenient.

Dōmo arigatō. どうもありがとう.   Thank you **very** much.

Dōmo sumimasén.   I am **very** sorry. or Please excuse me.
どうも すみません.

Kyō wa, dōmo atsúi désǔ. きょうはどうも暑いです.   It's **very** hot to-day.

Nihón-go wa dōmo muzukashíi désǔ.   The Japanese language is **very**
日本語 は どうも むずかしい です.   difficult.

Kánojo wa amari yóku utaimasén déshǐta.   She did **not** sing **very**
彼女 は あまり よく 歌いません でした.   well.

*Kyō, káre wa **amari** génki de wa **nái**.* He is **not very** well to-day.
きょう，彼 は あまり 元気 で は ない.

*Sonó kodomó wa **sahodó** byōki de wa **arimasén**.* The child is **not
very** sick.
その 子供 は さほど 病気 で は ありません.

*****way,** in some **way,** in one **way** or another *dō-niká* どうにか; in a **way**＝more
or less, in some measure *chottó* 一寸 (*colloq.*), *ikubún* 幾分 (*Lit.*);

*Anó e wo **chottó** (ikubún) súki désŭ.* I like that picture in a **way.**
あの 絵 を 一寸 （幾分） 好き です.

to have one's own **way** *omói-dōri ni surú* 思い通りにする

Hĭtó wa nan-demó omói-dōri ni surú kotó wa dekínai.
人 は 何んでも 思い通り に する 事 は 出来ない.
One cannot have one's own **way** in everything.

*****well,** generally translated by *yóku*

The adverb *yóku* よく *well*, from *yói* よい *good*, is very often
used in ordinary conversation, and corresponds to rather many
English words, as shown below. The underlying meaning of *yóku*
よく however, corresponds, in most cases, to *well*.

well, nicely, right(ly), truly

Yóku dekimáshĭta. よく出来ました. It is **well** done.

Yóku kákete imásŭ. よく書けています. It is **nicely** written.

thoroughly, fully, quite

Yóku shirabemáshĭta. よく調べました. I examined it **thoroughly.**

*Anáta wa soré wo **yóku** shĭtté imásŭ ne.* You know it quite
貴方 は それ を よく 知って います ね. **well.**

skilfully, carefully

Yóku chūi shĭté kudasái. Please do it **carefully.**
よく 注意 して 下さい. (*chūi surú* to pay attention, etc.)

closely, exactly

*Konó mondaí ni tsúite watashí wa **yóku** shirimasén.*
この 問題 について 私 は よく 知りません.
I do not know **exactly** about this matter.

idiomatic usage

yóku kangáeru	よく考える	to consider **well**
yóku míru	よく見る	to look at a thing **closely**
hĭtó ni yóku surú	人によくする	to be kind (**good**) to a person
hĭtó wo yóku iú	人をよく云う	to speak **well** of a person
yóku hatarakú	よく仂く	to work **faithfully**
yóku nemurú	よくねむる	to sleep **soundly** (well)
yóku áru kotó	よくある事	a common affair
(*kenko ga*) *yóku nái*	（健康が）よくない	to be **unwell** (*kenkō* health)
(*kenkō ga*) *yóku náru*	（健康が）よくなる	to become **better** (in health)

yóku áu   よく合う   to fit **well**

Watashí no atarashíi kutsú wa yóku aimásŭ.   My new shoes fit **well**.
私　の　新しい　靴　は　よく　合います.

Yamadá-kun wa yóku gakkō wo yasumimásŭ.   Mr. Yamada **often** stays
山田君　は　よく　学校　を　休みます.   away from school.

Nísan nichí yasúmeba yóku narimásŭ.   A few days rest will **put** me
二三　日　休めば　よく　なります.   **right**.

Ikkágetsu go-sen yen de yóku kuraserú monó désŭ ne.   (*kuraserú* to be able
一ヵ月　五千　円　で　よく　暮らせる　もの　です　ね.   to live, subsist)
I wonder **how** he can manage to live on 5,000 yen a month.

Watashitachí wa éiga e yóku ikimásŭ.   We **often** go to the cinema.
私達　は　映画へ　よく　行きます.

Sakunén wa taifū ga yóku arimáshĭta.   Last year we had **often** (or
昨年　は　台風　が　よく　ありました.   many) typhoons.

Soré wa káre no yóku tsŭkaú kōjitsu désŭ.   It was his **usual** excuse.
それ　は　彼　の　よく　使う　口実　です.   (*kōjitsu* excuse)

Kodomó wa yóku tabemásŭ. 子供はよく食べます.   Children eat **much**.

Konó amé-furi ni yóku oidé kudasaimáshĭta.
この　雨降り　に　よくお出で下さいました.   (*amé-furi* a rainfall)
It is **very kind of you** to have come in such a rainy day.
    (*oidé kudasáru* to favour the speaker with a visit—polite speech)

Anó jíko de káre wa yóku shinanákatta monó désŭ.
あの事故で彼　は　よく　死ななかった もの　です.
It is a miracle that he was not killed in that accident.
    (*shinanákatta* negative past of *shinú* to die)

Yūbe yóku nemurimasén déshĭta.   I didn't sleep **well** last night.
ゆうべ よく ねむりません でした.   (*nemurú* to sleep)

Sonó mendō-na mondaí ni tsúite yóku kangaemáshĭta.   (*kangáeru* to
そのめんどうな 問題 について よく 考えました   think, consider)
I have considered **well** that troublesome matter.

Hĭtó ni yóku shinái to hĭtó mo yóku shĭté kuré-nái monó désŭ.
人　に　よく　しないと　人　も　よく　してくれない　もの　です.
If you are not kind to people they will not be good to you.

***while,** once in a while *tamá-ni-wa* たまには. See also Lesson 31, page 214
    Tamá-ni-wa, asokó e itté mo watashí wa kamaimasén.
    たまには,　あそこへ行っても　私　は　かまいません.
    Once in a **while** I don't mind to go there.

***why,** (interrogation) *náze* なぜ (*colloq.*), *dōshite* どうして (*slang*); for what
reason *dō-iŭ wáke de* どういう訳で; what for, for what *nán-no-tamé ni* 何
んのために. See also Lesson 17.

***within,** On the inside, internally *uchigawá* 内側, *náibu* 内部. *Uchigawá*
refers to material things, *náibu* to both material and abstract things.—See also Lesson
31, page 214

Sonó hakó no **uchigawá** *wa mekkí shĭté arimásŭ*. That box is gilted
その 箱 の 内側 は めっき して あります. **within.**

(*mekkí surú* めっきする to plate, to gild)

Sonó mádo wa **uchigawá** *kará akimásŭ*. The window opens from
その 窓 は 内側 から 開きます. **within.**

To wa **uchigawá** *kará kagí ga kakátte imásŭ*. The doors are locked
戸 は 内側 から 鍵 がかかっています. **within.**

Reikán wa **náibu** *kara déte kimásŭ*. Inspirations come from **within.**
霊感 は 内部 から 出て 来ます. (*reikán* inspiration)

(indoors) **okúnai-ni** 屋内に, *okúnai-ni háiru* 屋内に入る to go **within**

Okúnai-ni *dáre mo imasén déshĭta*. There was nobody **within.**
屋内に 誰 も いませんでした.

Idiomatic Usage

within hearing *kikoerú tokoró* 聞こえる所
within law *hōritsu no han-inái* 法律の範囲内 (*han-i* 範囲 the limits, bounds, extent,
  etc.; *nái* 内=*inái* within)
to keep within the law *hōritsu kará hazurenái*[1] *yō-ni surú*
            法律 から はづれない ように する
within one's income *jibún no shūnyū no han-inái* 自分の収入の範囲内
within sight of......*miéru tokoró* 見える所
a task well within one's powers *rikiryō*[2] *de jūbun dekíru shigotó*
            力量 で 充分 出来る 仕事

***yes, See Lesson 14, page 74 and Lesson 62, page 599.

In formal and very polite speech, yes is translated by *Sayō de gozaimásŭ*
左様でございます and *Sō de gozaimásŭ* そうでございます is used in less polite
speech.

In still less polite speech *Sayō désŭ* 左様です may be used, while *Sō désŭ* そ
うです is used in ordinary speech.

Note that the single word *Sayō* 左様 for yes may be used by men, but such
usage is considered of a rather old style of speech.

Okakurá San wa anáta no senséi désŭ ka. Is Mr. Okakura your teacher?
岡倉 さん は 貴方 の 先生 ですか。

Sayō de gozaimásŭ. Yes, he is.
左様 で ございます。

Sayō de wa gozaimasén. No, he is not.
左様 で は ございません。

Both *hái* はい and *iié* いゝえ may be used concurrently with the above expre‧
ssions; in this case, however, the expressions acquire emphatic force, as in the
following examples.

Anáta wa Hirotá San de gozaimásŭ ka. Are you Mr. Hirota?
貴方 は 広田 さん で ございますか。

Hái, sayō de gozaimásŭ. Yes, I am.
はい 左様 で ございます。

Iié sayō de wa gozaimasén. No, I am not.
いゝえ左様 で は ございません

***yet, see page 596

---

1 *hazurenái* negative of *hazurerú* はづれる to be contrary to, to deviate from
2 *rikiryō* capacity, ability

Fifty-eighth Lesson 第五十八課

Adverbs (continued) Fukushí 副詞

In this lesson are given Japanese adverbs used in ordinary conversation, divided into groups according to their characteristics.

Adverbs formed by means of the postposition *ni* に.

betsudán-ni 別段に	exceptionally	*jiki-ni* じきに	immediately
betsú-ni 別に	particularly	*jissái-ni* 実際に	actually
búrei-ni 無礼に	impolitely	*jitsú-ni* 実に	really
chokŭsetsú-ni 直接に	directly	*kakubetsú-ni* 格別に	exceptionally
dandán-ni だんだんに	gradually	*kakujitsú-ni* 確実に	certainly
fuchūi-ni 不注意に	carelessly	*kansetsú-ni* 間接に	indirectly
fuséi-ni 不正に	unjustly	*kari-ni* かりに	temporarily
fushigí-ni 不思議に	strangely	*keisotsú-ni* 軽卒に	recklessly
futsū-ni 普通に	commonly	*ketteiteki-ni* 決定的に	definitely
gehin-ni 下品に	vulgarly	*kii-ni* 奇異に	queerly
hen-ni 変に	strangely	*kōfuku-ni* 幸福に	happily
hígoto-ni 日毎に	day by day	*kóto-ni* 殊に	especially
hijō-ni 非常に	unusually	*makotó-ni* 誠に	actually
hi-mashí-ni 日ましに	day by day	*maré-ni* 稀に	rarely
hōgai-ni 法外に	unreasonably	*meikakú-ni* 明確に	distinctly
hontō-ni 本当に	actually	*métta-ni* めったに	seldom
ippán-ni 一般に	generally	*mukōmizu-ni* 向う見ずに	recklessly
ízen-ni 以前に	formerly	*múri-ni* 無理に	forcibly

múyami-ni むやみに	blindly	**shízuka-ni** 静かに	quietly
nóbetsu-ni のべつに	continually	**sōgo-ni** 相互に	mutually
ói-ói-ni おいおいに	gradually	**sonó ué-ni** その上に	besides
o-maké-ni おまけに	into the bargain	**súgu-ni** すぐに	at once
ombín-ni おんびんに	peaceably	**tádachi-ni** 直ちに	immediately
reigai-ni 例外に	exceptionally	**tagai-ni** 互いに	mutually
rinji-ni 臨時に	temporarily	**tamá-ni** たまに	occasionally
saiwai-ni 幸いに	fortunately	**táshĭka-ni** 確かに	certainly
sáki-ni 先に	formerly	**téinei-ni** 丁寧に	politely
shiawasé-ni 幸せに	happily	**tóku-ni** 特に	especially
shidai-ni 次第に	gradually	**tsugí-ni** 次に	next
shikíri-ni しきりに	frequently	**tsúi-ni** 遂に	finally
shitsúrei-ni 失礼に	impolitely	**tsúne-ni** 常に	ordinarily
shizén-ni 自然に	spontaneously	**yōi-ni** 容易に	easily

yatará-ni　やたらに　　recklessly

Adverbs characterized by their ending syllable *ri* り.

Adverbs belonging to this class may be followed by the postposition **to** と, in which case they are emphatic.

*****bikkúri** びっくり; *bikkúri surú* びっくりする to get frightened

　Inú ga hóeta nóde dorobō wa **bikkúri** *shĭté nigemáshĭta.*
　犬 が 吠えた ので 泥棒 は びっくり して 逃げました.
　　The burglar was frightened away by the barking of the dog.
　(*hoéru* to bark, *nigéru* run away)

*****bon-yári** (*to*) ぼんやり (と) dimly, vacantly

　Kasumí no náka ni shimá ga **bon-yári** (*to*) *míeta.* (*kasumí* haze, mist;
　かすみ の 中 に 島 が ぼんやり (と) 見えた. *míeta* was seen)
　　The island was seen **dimly** through the haze.

*****chirári** (*to*) ちらり (と) with one glance, cursorily

　Kinō, anó katá wo **chirári** (*to*) *mimáshĭta.* **I glanced at** him
　きのう, あの 方 を ちらり (と) 見ました. yesterday.

******dosári*** (*to*) どさり（と）with a thud

Káre wa omói fukuró wo yuká ni ***dosári*** (*to*) otóshĭta.
彼　は　重い　袋　を　床　に　どさり（と）おとした.
He dropped the heavy bag on the floor **with a thud.** (*otósu* to drop
fukuró bag; *yuká* floor)

******hakkíri*** (*to*) はっきり（と）clearly, exactly

Káre wa soré wo ***hakkíri*** (*to*) iimáshĭta.　　He said it **clearly.**
彼　は　それ　を　はっきり（と）云いました.

Watashí wa ***hakkíri*** (*to*) wakarimáshĭta.　　I understood **exactly.**
私　は　はっきり（と）わかりました.

******hirári*** (*to*) ひらり（と）with alacrity

Kishú ga umá kará ***hirári*** (*to*) órita.　　(*kishú* jockey)
騎手　が　馬　から　ひらり（と）降りた.
The jockey sprang off his horse. (*órita* past of *oríru* to alight)

******honnóri*** (*to*) ほんのり（と）slightly, faintly

Sóra ga ***honnóri*** (*to*) akarukú nátta.　　The sky became **faintly** light.
空　が　ほんのり（と）あかるくなった.　　(*akarukú náru* to become light)

Kánojo no hō ga ***honnóri*** (*to*) akakú nátta.　　Her cheeks got **slightly**
彼女　のほおが　ほんのり（と）赤く　なった.　　red. (*hō* cheek)

******kitchíri*** (*to*) きっちり（と）to a T, perfectly, tightly

Sonó tebúkuro wa ***kitchíri*** (*to*) átte irú.　　Those gloves fit **to a T.**
その　手袋　は　きっちり（と）合っている.　　(*átte* from *áu* 合う to fit)

Dōzo, sonó hakó ni fŭtá wo ***kitchíri*** (*to*) shĭté kudasái.　Please cover that
どうぞ,その　箱　にふたを　きっちり（と）して　下さい.　　box **tightly.**

******kossóri*** (*to*) こっそり（と）stealthily

Káre wa ***kossóri*** (*to*) heyá kará déte ittá.　　He **sneaked out** of
彼　は　こっそり（と）へや　から　出て行った.　　his room.

******kossóri*** (*to*) *arúku* こっそり（と）歩く to walk **stealthily**

******mekkíri*** (*to*) めっきり（と）noticeably, remarkably

Byōnin wa konogoró ***mekkíri*** (*to*) yowarimáshĭta.　　(*yowáru* よわる
病人　は　この頃　めっきり（と）よわりました.　　to grow weak)
The patient has become **noticeably** weak of late.

Atsusa wa ***mekkíri*** (*to*) tsúyoku nátta.　　The heat has become
暑さ　は　めっきり（と）強く　なった.　　**remarkably** severe.

******nikkóri*** (*to*) にっこりと（said of smile）

nikkóri (*to*) waraú にっこり（と）笑う to break into a smile

******nossóri*** (*to*) のっそり（と）unwieldily, sluggishly

nossóri (*to*) heyá ni háitte kúru のっそり（と）へやに入って来る to hulk
into a room

******patchíri*** (*to*) ぱっちり（と）(said of large, bright eyes)

me wo ***patchíri*** (*to*) *akerú* 目をぱっちりと開ける to open one's eyes **wide**

patchíri (*to*) *shĭtá me* ぱっちり（と）した目 bright, clear eyes

******sappári*** (*to*) さっぱり（と）cleanly, entirely, not the least, at all

O-fúro ni háitte karadá ga **sappári** *shimáshĭta.*　After taking a bath my
お風呂 に 入ってからだ が　さっぱり　しました.　body felt **refreshed.**
(*o-fúro ni háiru* to take a bath—*lit.* to enter a bath)

Watashí wa sonná kotó wo **sappári** *(to) shirimasén.*
私　は そんな 事 を　さっぱり（と）知りません.
I am **entirely** in the dark about such a matter.

Káre wa **sappári** *(to) Nihón-go wo shiranái.*　He has **not the least**
彼　は　さっぱり（と）日本語 を 知らない.　knowledge of Japanese.

sappári *(to) shĭtá fukusō wo shĭté irú* さっぱり（と）した服そうをしている
to be **cleanly** (neatly) dressed (*fukusō* style of dress, attire)

Anó katá wa konó-goró **sappári** *(to) kimasén.*　He has not been coming
あの 方 は この 頃　さっぱり（と）来ません.　here lately **at all.**

***sarári** *(to)* さらり（と）entirely, without regret

tabakó wo **sarári** *(to) yamerú* たばこをさらり（と）やめる to give up
smoking **entirely**

nozomí wo **sarári** *(to) sŭterú* 望みをさらり（と）すてる to give up one's hope
entirely (without regret)

***shikkári** *(to)* しっかり（と）firmly, strongly

shikkári *(to) mótte irú* しっかり（と）持っている to hold **firmly**

shikkári *(to) musubú* しっかり（と）むすぶ to tie **strongly**

***sukkári** *(to)* すっかり（と）entirely, quite, right to the end

Anó musŭmé wa **sukkári** *(to) otoná ni nátta.*　That girl has **quite**
あの　娘　は　すっかり（と）おとな に なった.　grown up.

Watashí wa konó hon wo **sukkári** *(to) yomimáshĭta.*
私　は この 本 を　すっかり（と）読みました.
I have read this book **right to the end.**

sukkári *(to) damé ni náru* すっかり（と）だめになる to get **entirely** rotten

***tappúri** *(to)* たっぷり（と）full, fully, plentifully, abundantly

kyōmi **tappúri** 興味たっぷり to be **full** of interest

tappúri *ichí-nichí* たっぷり一日 a **full** day

Dōzo, gyūnyū wo **tappúri** *(to) kákete kudasái.*　Please put milk
どうぞ, 牛乳 を　たっぷり（と）かけて 下さい.　**abundantly.**

***ukkári** *(to)* うっかり（と）absentmindedly, unconsciously

Kánojo wa sonó himitsú wo **ukkári** *(to) shabétta.*　She told that secret
彼女 は その 祕密 を うっかり（と）しやべった.　**unconsciously.**

ukkári *(to) shĭté irú* うっかり（と）している to be **absentminded**

***yukkúri** *(to)* ゆっくり（と）slowly

yukkúri *(to) arúku* ゆっくり（と）歩く to walk **slowly**

yukkúri *(to) nemurú* ゆっくり（と）ねむる to have a **good** sleep

yukkúri *(to) kangáeru* ゆっくり（と）考える **to take time** to think

The particle **to** と is used at the end of certain short words with which it forms another class of adverbs. In this case the particle **to** と is not omitted and often coalesces with the word to which it is attached.

***chantó** ちゃんと exactly, precisely, properly, just, right

Keisán wa **chantó** *átte imásŭ.*   The accounts tally **exactly.**
計算 は ちゃんと 合っています。

Watashí wa shuppatsú no yōi ga **chantó** *dékite imásŭ.*   (*yōi* 用意
私 は 出発 の用意 が ちゃんと 出来ています。   preparations)
I am **quite** ready for departure. (*shuppatsú* departure)

Sonó kaikéi-gákari wa shiharaí wo **chantó** *shimásŭ.*   (*shiharaí* payment)
その 会計係 は 支払 を ちゃんと します。
The accountant makes the payments **punctually.**

Sonó heyá wa **chantó** *katazúite imásŭ.*   The room is in **perfect** order.
その へや は ちゃんと 片づいて います。   (*katazúku* to be put in order)

***chottó** ちょっと (一寸) briefly, just a moment

Chottó *o-machí kudasái.*   ちょっと(一寸)お待ち下さい。   ⎫ Please wait a
Dōzo, **chottó** *mátte kudasái.* どうぞ，一寸待って下さい。   ⎭ moment.

Konó pen wo **chottó** *taméshĭte-míte kudasái.*   **Just** try on this pen.
この ペン を ちょっと ためして見て 下さい。   (*taméshite míru* to try)

Chottó *míru to, soré wa yosasō désŭ.*   At **first** sight it looks good.
一寸 見る と，それ は よさそうです。

Kánojo wa **chottó** *utá ga jōzu désŭ.*   She is **something** of a singer.
彼女 は ちょっと 歌 が 上手 です。

Káre wa **chottó** *shĭtá zaisán wo tsŭkútta.*   He made a **snug** fortune.
彼 は 一寸 した 財産 を つくった。

chottó shĭtá *kazé*   一寸した風邪   a **slight** cold

chottó shĭtá *yadoyá* 一寸した宿屋 a **decent-looking** inn

***gyottó** ぎよっと, said of a state of consternation

gyottó surú ぎよっとする   to be frightened, to be startled

gyottó shĭté ぎよっとして   frightened, struck with terror

Sonó jíko no arísama wo míte **gyottó** *shimáshĭta.*
その 事故 の ありさま を 見てぎよっと しました。
I was frightened at the sight of that accident.

***hattó** はっと, said of surprise

hattó surú はっとする   to be taken aback

hattó shĭté はっとして   in surprise

***hottó surú** ほっとする to give a sigh of relief

Soré wo kiité **hottó** *shimáshĭta.*   I **felt relieved** upon hearing that.
それ を 聞いてほっと しました。

***hyoí-to** ひよいと accidentally, suddenly

hyoí-to *mi wo kawasú* ひよいと身をかわす   to dodge oneself

*Ii kangáe ga **hyoí-to** atamá ni ukandá.*   A good idea (suddenly) flashed
いい 考え が ひよいと 頭 にうかんだ.   across my mind.

(*ukabú* うかぶ to come across one's mind, to occur to a person, etc.)

*****hyottó** ひょっと by chance, possibly

Hyottó *anó katá ni deaimáshĭta.*   I came across him **by chance.**
ひょっとあの 方 に 出会いました.   (*ni deaú* to happen to meet)
*Senséi wa **hyottó** shĭtára o-dekaké ka-mo shirenái.*
先生 は ひょっと したら お出かけ かも 知れない.
The teacher may **possibly** have gone out.

*****jittó** じっと firmly, steadily, with concentration

jittó *mitsumerú*   じっと見つめる   to gaze at, to look **fixedly** at
jittó *shĭté irú*   じっとしている   to remain motionless, keep still
*Konó kodomó wa kesshĭté **jittó shĭté** imasén.*   This child never keeps
この 子供 は 決してじっと して いません.   **quiet.**

*****kichín-to** きちんと exactly, to a T, good, straight, precisely, neatly

kichín-to *haráu*   きちんと払う   to pay **exactly**
*kutsú ga **kichín-to** áu*   靴がきちんと合う   shoes fit **to a T**
kichín-to *shĭté irú*   きちんとしている   to be in **good** order
kichín-to *suwarú*   きちんと坐る   to sit **straight**
kichín-to *ni-ji ni*   きちんと二時に   **precisely** at two o'clock
*Kánojo wa **kichín-to** shĭtá fukusō wo shĭté irú.*   She is **neatly**
彼女 は きちんと した 服そう を して いる.   dressed.

*****kittó** きっと surely, never fail, certainly

*Káre wa **kittó** shikén ni gōkaku surú deshō.*   He will be **sure** of success
彼 は きっと 試験 に 合格 するでしょう.   in the examinations.
Kittó *anó otokó wa dorobō ni chigáinái.*   **Undoubtedly,** that man is
きっとあの 男 は 泥棒 にちがいない.   a thief.
Kittó *irasshái yo!* きっといらっしゃいよ.   **Never fail** to come.
Kittó *kimásŭ.* きっと来ます.   **Certainly** I will come.

*****mótto** もっと more, some more

Mótto *kudasái.*   もっと下さい.   Give me **some more.**
Mótto *tábete kudasái.*   もっと食べて下さい.   Eat more. or Have **some more.**
Mótto *kaitái désŭ.*   もっと買いたいです.   I want to buy **some more.**
Mótto *arukimashō.*   もっと歩きましょう.   Let's walk **farther.**
Mótto *ii.*   もっといい.   Better.
Mótto *warúi.*   もっと悪い.   Worse.

*****páppa-to** ぱっぱと—**páppa-to** *tabakó wo fukásu* ぱっぱとたばこを吹か
す to puff away at one's pipe

*Kané wo **páppa-to** tsŭkaú* 金をぱっぱと使う   to spend money **wantonly**

*****patán-to** ぱたんと with a snap, with a bang (of a little explosion, etc.)

*To ga **patán-to** shimátta.*   The door **snapped to.**
戸 が ぱたんと しまった.   The door shut **with a bang.**

*****pishári-to** ぴしゃりと with a slam

    pishári-to mádo wo shiméru   to shut a window **with a slam**
    ぴしゃりと 窓 を しめる

    pishári-to útsu ぴしゃりと打つ   to slap

*****pitári-to** ぴたりと happening unexpectedly, tightly

    pitári-to tomarú   ぴたりと止る   to stop **suddenly**
    pitári-to to wo shiméru ぴたりと戸をしめる   to shut the door **tightly**
    pitári-to tsŭkú   ぴたりとつく   to stick **closely**

*****pon-to** ぽんと said of a little explosion, of a little blow

    pon-to káta wo tatáku ぽんと肩をたたく   to tap on the shoulder
    pon-to hizá wo útsu   ぽんとひざを打つ   to smack one's knees
    *inú ni bisŭkétto wo **pon-to** nágete yarú*   to throw a biscuit to a dog
    犬 にビスケットを ぽんと 投げて やる

    (*nagéru* 投げる to throw, hurl, cast; *yarú* to give to an inferior)

*****tóbotobo-to** とぼとぼと totteringly

    *Sonó rōjin wa heyá kará **tóbotobo-to** déte ittá.*
    その 老人 は へや から とぼとぼと 出て行った.
    The old man went out **trudgingly** from the room.

*****ton-to** とんと absolutely, at all, clean

    *Soré wo surú jikán ga **ton-to** arimasén.*   I have **absolutely** no
    それ を する 時間 が とんと ありません.   time to do it.

    *Káre wa watashí wo **ton-to** obóete imasén déshĭta.*
    彼 は 私 を とんと 覚えていません でした.

    He didn't remember me **at all.**

    *Sóre wo **ton-to** wasureté imáshĭta.*   I have **clean** forgotten it.
    それ を とんと 忘れて いました.

    *Iwamotó San wa dóko de umaretá ka **ton-to** shirimasén.*
    岩元 さん は どこ で 生れた か とんと 知りません.
    I haven't the **least** idea where Mr. Iwamoto was born.

*****zuttó** ずっと all the way, all through, very much

    *Watashí wa natsú yasumí-jū **zuttó** Karuizawá ni imáshĭta.*
    私 は 夏 休中 ずっと 軽井沢 に いました.
    I stayed at Karuizawa **all through** the summer vacation.

By reduplicating certain nouns, the stems of adjectives and the present tense of verbs, another class of adverbs is formed. Some of these adverbs are followed by *ni* or *to,* while some others are used without any postposition.

chikái 近い near; *chikajiká ni* 近々に within a few days, after a short time
dan 段 a step; *dandán* (*ni* or *to*) 段々 (に, と) step by step, gradually, by and by

iró 色 colour, sort; **iroiró** 色々 variously, in various ways

kasanéru 重ねる to pile up; **kasanegásane** 重ね重ね repeatedly

kowái 怖い frightful; **kowagowá** 怖々 timidly, with fear

míru 見る to see; **míru-míru** 見る見る while looking at, visibly, in an instant

nakú 泣く to cry; **nakú-nakú** 泣く泣く with tears

ori 折 occasion; **ori-ori** 折々 from time to time

osoréru 恐れる to fear; **osorú-osorú** 恐る恐る timidly, trembling with fear

Watashí wa dandán Nihón-go ga wakátte kimásŭ.
私 は 段々 日本語 が 解って きます.
Gradually I am beginning to understand Japanese.

Fúne wa míru-míru uchí ni shizumimáshĭta.[1]　The boat sank in an
舟 は 見る見る 内 に 沈みました.　instant.

The subordinate, especially in the negative, often corresponds to an adverbial expression. The following subordinates are constantly used as adverbs:

awaté 慌てて in a hurry, in confusion, frightened, from *awaterú* to be flurried, to be in a hurry, to be confused, to be frightened

hajimete 初めて for the first time, at first

hikitsuzúite 引続いて in succession, (*hikitsuzúku* 引続く to continue)

isandé 勇んで boldly, courageously, (from *isamú* 勇む to be emboldened)

káette 却って on the contrary, rather, even

kamáwazu 構わず carelessly (from *kamáu* 構う to care for, to mind)

kasanetté 重ねて again, repeatedly (from *kasanerú* 重ねる to pile up)

kawatté 代って instead (from *kawarú* 代る to change)

kiwámete 極めて positively (from *kiwaméru* 極める to determine)

kokoróete 心得て deliberately, knowingly (from *kokoroéru* 心得る to know)

kokorozúkazu 心付かず without perceiving (from *kokorozúku* 心付く to pay attention to)

mukōmizu ni 向う見ずに rashly, heedlessly (from *mukō wo míru* 向うを見る to see what is before one)

ochitsuité 落着いて with composure, calmly (from *ochitsŭkú* 落着く to be tranquil, quiet)

oshité 押して by force, compulsively (from *osú* 押す to push, to press)

sadámete 定めて surely, no doubt (from *sadaméru* 定める to fix, to settle)

shíite 強いて with violence, urgently (from *shiíru* 強いる to force)

tsutsushinde 謹んで respectfully (from *tsutsushímu* 謹しむ to be cautious, discreet)

Awateté resshá wo nori machigaemáshĭta.[2]　**In my hurry** I took the
慌てて 列車 を 乗り 間違えました.　wrong train.

---

1 *shizumú* to sink　**2** *machigáeru* to mistake, to make a mistake; *nori* from *norŭ* to get on, into (train, motor-car, etc.)

*Kanemochí wa kanarazushimó kōfuku de wa náku **káette** tokí-dokí bimbōnin*
金持　は　必ずしも　　幸福　では　なく　却って　　時々　　貧乏人
no kōfuku wo urayamimásŭ.   The rich are not always happy; **on the contrary**
の　幸福　をうらやみます.   they sometimes envy the happiness of the poor.
(*kanemochí wa* the rich, *kanarazushimó....náku* not always)

Adverbial expressions are frequently formed by combining *náku*
with substantives. Some of these expressions have the particle *mo*
invariably placed before *náku,* some are always without it, while
others may have it only when they are to be made emphatic.

ma-mo-náku 間も無く immediately, from *ma* interval
wáke-mo-náku 訳も無く unreasonably, without any reason, from *wáke*
  reason (*mo* always used)—*wáke-náku* 訳無く (without *mo* も) easily
(*go*) *enryó-náku* (御) 遠慮無く without reserve (*mo* always omitted)
hodó (*mo*) *náku* 程 (も) 無く in no time, from *hodó* quantity
machigái (*mo*) *náku* 間違い (も) 無く ⎫
sō-i (*mo*) *náku*   相違 (も) 無く ⎭without fail, surely
omoigaké (*mo*) *náku* 思いがけ (も) 無く unexpectedly
oshigé-(*mo*) *náku* 惜気(も) 無く ungrudgingly, from *oshíi* grudge and *ke*
  indication, symptom
táema (*mo*) *náku* 絶え間 (も) 無く uninterruptedly, from *taemá* cessation
zōsa (*mo*) *náku* 造作 (も) なく without trouble, easily

Fifty-ninth Lesson   第五十九課

Prepositions *Zenchíshi* 前置詞

In previous lessons it has been shown how to translate English
prepositions in their commonest uses.

In this and next lessons, besides giving examples showing how to
translate the prepositions that have not been illustrated yet, we shall
give examples showing how to translate the prepositions already
illustrated in this book in their new applications.

Note that in various cases a preposition is not translated into
Japanese, especially when placed after a verb, as it may be seen
from some of the following examples.

About

*Konó katákake[1] wo anáta no kubí no **mawarí ni** o-kaké nasái.*
この　肩掛　を　貴方　の　くび　の　まわり　に　お掛けなさい.
  Put this shawl **about** your neck. (*lit.* This shawl, your neck around, put)
*Ōzei no hĭto ga watashí no **mawarí ni** oshiyosemáshĭta.[2]*
大勢の　人　が　私　の　まわり　に　押しよせました.
  Many people crowded **about** me.

———————
1 shawl **2** *oshiyoséru* to press, to crowd

Heyá no achí-kóchi[1] ni hon ga arimáshĭta. There were books all
部屋 の あちこち に 本 が ありました. **about** the room.

Anó fujíntachi wa anáta no kotó wo hanáshĭte imásŭ.
あの 婦人達 は 貴方 の 事 を 話して います.
Those ladies are speaking **about** you.
(*lĭt.* Those ladies, your things are talking.)

Inaká átari wo umá de norí-mawashimashō.[2] Let us take a ride **about**
田舎 あたり を 馬 で 乗りまわしましょう. the country.
(*lĭt.* Country environs, by horse, let's ride about.)

Anáta no kodomosán-gatá wa uchí no niwá no hen de asondé imásŭ.
貴方 の 子供さん方 は うちの 庭 の 辺 で 遊んでいます.
Your children are playing **about** my garden.
(*lĭt.* Your children, my house's garden's vicinity in, playing are.)

Otōto wa kekkón surú tokoró désŭ. or *Otōto wa jikí ni kekkón shimásŭ.*
弟 は 結婚 する 所 です. 弟 は じきに 結婚 します.
My younger brother is **about** to be married.

Anó jíken[3] ni tsúite anáta no go-íken[4] wa dō désŭ ka.
あの 事件 に ついて 貴方 の 御意見 は どう です か.
What is your opinion **about** that matter?
(*lĭt.* That matter regarding, your opinion how is?)

Anó dái-kásai ni tsúite okikí ni narimáshĭta ka.
あの 大 火災 に ついて お聞きに なりました か.
Have you heard **about** the great fire?

Soré ni tsúite nan-ni mo kikimasén déshĭta. I have heard nothing
それ に ついて 何んに も 聞きません でした. **about** it.

Watashí ga ryōkai[5] surú kotó no dekínai nanimonó ka[6] ga anó otokó ni
私 が 了解 する 事 の出来ない 何物 か があの 男 に
arimásŭ. There is something **about** that man that I cannot make out.
あります. (*lĭt.* I, understand thing that cannot, something in that man there is.)

Minná ga homéru sonó e ni wa náni ga áru no désŭ ka.
みんな が ほめる その 絵 に は 何 が ある の です か.
What is there **about** that picture that everybody admires?

Anáta wa náni wo shĭté imásŭ ka. What are you **about?**
貴方 は 何 を して います か. (*lĭt.* What are you doing?)

Watashí wa jibún ga náni wo shĭté itá no ka shirimasén déshĭta.
私 は 自分 が 何 を していたの か 知りません でした.
I did not know what I was **about.**
(*lĭt.* I myself, what doing was?, didn't know.)

Sonó jíken wa kō iú fū ni okorimáshĭta.[7] The matter came **about** in
その 事件 は こういう風 に 起こりました. this way.

Ikuraka mochí-awasé ga arimásŭ ka. Have you any money **about** you?
幾らか 持ち合わせ が あります か.

---

1 *achí-kóchi* here and there **2** *norimawásu* to ride about **3** matter **4** opinion
5 *ryōkai surú* to understand **6** *nanimonó ka* something **7** *okóru* to happen, **to**
come about

(*lit.* Some things on hand have you?—*mochí-awaserú* 持ち合わせる to have with one, to happen to have, *mochí-awasé* things on hand)

Sokó e jū-ji-góro ni tsŭkimásŭ.   I shall arrive there at **about**
そこ へ 十時 頃 に 着きます.   ten o'clock.

Above

Ima wa hyōten[1] íjō jū-go-do désŭ.   It is now fifteen degrees **above**
今 は 氷点 以上 十五度 です.   freezing-point.

    (*lit.* Now, freezing point more than fifteen degrees is.)

Koré wa watashí ga náni yóri mo sŭkí-na monó désŭ.
これ は 私 が 何 より も 好きな 物 です.

    This is what I prefer **above** all.

    (*lit.* This, I, anything more than, being fond of thing is.)

Kimí no okonaí[2] wa hínan no ten[3] ga arimasén.   Your behaviour is
君 の 行い は 非難 の 点 が ありません.   **above** reproach.

Yói hyōban[4] wa tómi[5] íjō désŭ.   A good name is **above** wealth.
よい 評判 は 富 以上 です.   (Good name, wealth more than, is.)

Anáta no gakŭsetsú[6] wo watashí wa ryōkai[7] dekimasén.
貴方 の 学説 を 私 は 了解 できません.

    Your theory is **above** my comprehension.

    (*lit.* Your theory, I comprehension cannot.)

Watashí no yūjin wa sonná hiretsú[8] de wa arimasén.
私 の 友人 は そんな 卑劣 で は ありません.

    My friend is **above** any such meanness.   (My friend so mean is not.)

Sanó San no ókŭsan wa keiyakú[9] íjō ni ichi-man-yen yokéi ni kudasaimáshĭta.
佐野さんの 奥さん は 契約 以上に 一万円 余計 に 下さいました.

    Mrs. Sano gave me 10,000 yen **over and above** what we had agreed upon.

    (*lit.* Mr. Sano's wife, agreement more than, ten thousand yen in excess gave me.)

Náni wa sáte-okí shōjiki de áre.   **Above** all be honest.
何 は さておき 正直 であれ.   (*lit.* Anything setting aside be honest.)

(*sáte-okú* さておく to let alone, to set aside)

Káre wa yon-jissái íjō ni chigái nái.   He must be **above** forty.
彼 は 四十才 以上に 違い ない.   (*sái* numerative for years of age)

    (*lit.* He forty years more than, there is no mistake.)

Kánojo wa míbun fusōō ni kurashĭté imásŭ.   She lives **above** her means.
彼女 は 身分 不相応 に 暮らして います.

    (*lit.* She, social standing, disproportionately living is.)

Kaibatsú ni-sen mētoru.   Two thousand metres **above** sea-level.
海抜 二千 メートル.   (*kaibatsú* above sea-level)

above mentioned *jōki no* 上記の, **above** stated *jōjutsu no* 上述の, as mentioned **above** *jōki no gótoku* 上記の如く

---

1 freezing point   2 behaviour   3 *hínan no ten* point of reproach; *hínan* reproach, *ten* point   4 name   5 wealth   6 theory   7 comprehension   8 *hiretsú* meanness   9 agreement

After

Ishii San ga anáta no ámpi[1] wo tazunemáshĭta.   Mr. Ishii asked me
石井 さん が 貴方 の 安否 を 尋ねました.   **after** your health.
    (*lit.* Mr. Ishii, your health made inquiry for.—*tazunéru* 尋ねる to make
inquiry for)

Raineru San wa saishín[2] ryūkō[3] no yōfuku wo kité imáshĭta.
ライネル さん は 最新 流行 の 洋服 を 着て いました.
Mrs. Reinel was dressed **after** the newest fashion.

Watashí ga kaimonó wo surú aidá ákachan ni ki wo tsŭkéte kudasái.
私 が 買物 を する 間 赤ちゃん に 気 を つけて 下さい.
Look **after** the baby while I am shopping.
    (*lit.* I, shopping make while, to the baby be very attentive.—*ki wo tsŭkéru*
to be very attentive to, to rivet one's attention upon)

Watashí wa anó katá ni tegamí wo **áto-kará-áto-kará** *kakimáshĭta*
私 はあの 方 に 手紙 を 後から後から 書きました
ga henjí wo hĭtótsu mo uketorimasén déshĭta.   I wrote him letter **after** letter,
が 返事 を 一つ も 受取りませんでした.   but received no answer.
    (*lit.* I, to that person, letters one after the other wrote, but answers, one
even did not receive.—*áto-kará-áto-kará* one after the other)

Ōsaka wa Tōkyō ni tsugú dái-tokái désŭ.   Osaka is the largest city
大阪 は 東京 に 次ぐ 大都会 です.   **after** Tokyo.
    (*lit.* Osaka, to Tokyo next, big city is.—*tsugú* 次ぐ to come after=next)

Kánojo wa obasán no na wo tótte Hanakó to nazukeráreta.
彼女 はおばさんの 名 をとって 花子 と 名づけられた.
She was called Hanako **after** her aunt.
    (*lit.* She, aunt's name taking, Hanako, so was named.—*nazukéru* 名づける
to name, christen, *nazukeraréru* to be christen, to be named)

Káre wa watashí ga tsúite kará kimáshĭta.   He arrived **after** me.
彼 は 私 が 着いて から 来ました.
(He, I having arrived after, came.)

Idioms:

After you, please.   *Dōzo, o-sakí e.* どうぞ, お先へ.
day **after** day (*Lit.*) *hibi* 日々; (*colloq.*) *kúru-hi mo kúru-hi mo* 来る日も来る日も
time **after** time (*Lit.*) *íkutabi mo* 幾度も; (*colloq.*) *nan-do mo* 何度も
wave **after** wave *namí matá namí* 波又波
a picture **after** Picasso *Pikáso-ryū no e* ピカソ流の絵
after all (*Lit.*) *kekkyokú* 結局, (*colloq.*) *yahári* やはり, (*slang*) *yappári* やっぱり
After all is said and done. *Tóya-káku itté mo kekkyokú.* とやかく云っても結局.

Against

Anó kabé **ni** *yorikakátte[4] wa ikemasén.*   Don't lean **against** that wall.
あの 壁 によりかかっては いけません.

---

1 health, well-being   **2** latest   **3** fashion   **4** *yorikakáru* to lean against

Fúne wa iwá[1] ni shōtotsu[2] shimáshǐta.   The ship struck **against** a rock.
船 は 岩 に 衝突 しました.

Kandá San wa o-tōsan no íshi[3] ni hánshǐte (somúite) gaikokú e
神田 さん は お父さんの 意志 に 反して （背いて） 外国 へ
ikimáshǐta.   Mr. Kanda went abroad **against** his father's will.
行きました.   (*lit.* Mr. Kanda father's will against abroad went.)

Sumikurá San no jinkakú[4] ni táishǐte wa náni mo mōshiageru[5] kotó
住倉 さんの 人格 に 対して は 何 も 申し上げる 事
ga arimasén.   I have nothing to say **against** Mr. Sumikura's character.
がありません.

Chōshū wa enzetsushá no hatsugén[6] ni táishǐte kōgi shimáshǐta.[7]
聴衆 は 演説者 の 発言 に 対して 抗議 しました.
The audience protested **against** the speaker's utterances.

Sonó kikén[8] ni táishǐte anó hǐtó ni keikokú shimáshǐta.[9]
その 危険 に 対して あの 人 に 警告 しました.
I warned him **against** the danger.

Along

Watashí wa kawá no doté[10] ni sotté arúite imáshǐta.
私 は 川 の 土手 に そって 歩いていました.
I was walking **along** the river bank.

Anó hǐtó wa ítsumo watashí wo damasō[11] to shǐté[12] imáshǐta.
あの 人 は いつも 私 を だまそう と していました.
He was all **along** trying to deceive me.
        (*lit.* That person, always me will deceive, so trying was.)

Amid, Amidst

Watashí wa mukōmizu no[13] otokotachí no náka ni irú kotó wo shǐtté
私 は 向う見ず の 男達 の 中 に いる 事 を 知って
imáshǐta.   I knew I was **amid** unscrupulous men.
いました.

Among, Amongst

Múchi no[14] hǐtóbito no aidá (náka or uchí) de meishín[15] wa ryūkō shimásǔ.[16]
無知 の 人々 の 間 （中, うち） で 迷信 は 流行 します.
Among ignorant people superstition prevails.

Bóku no hon no náka (uchí) ni kudaranái monó wa arimasén.
僕 の 本 の 中 （うち） に 下らない 物 は ありません.
Among my books you will not find any that are frivolous.

Sonó kodomotachí no aidá ni (or Sonó kodomotachí ni) konó o-káshi
その 子供達 の 間 に （その 子供達 に） この お菓子
wo wákete[17] yarí nasái.   Divide this cake **among** those children.
を 分けて やりなさい.

---

1 rock **2** *shōtotsu surú* to strike against **3** will **4** character **5** to say (pol.)
6 utterance **7** *kōgi surú* to protest **8** danger **9** *keikokú surú* to warn **10** bank
(of a river) **11** *damásu* to deceive **12** *to surú* after a verb means *to try to do*
(*something*) **13** *mukōmizu no* unscrupulous **14** *múchi no* ignorant **15** superstition
16 *ryūkō surú* to prevail **17** *wakéru* to divide

Nakamá-dōshi **de** (or *Nakamá no aidá de*) *kenká surú no wa yóku nái.*
仲間同士　で　（仲間　の　間　で）けんか　する　の　は　よくない.
You should not quarrel **among** yourselves. (*lit.* Comrades among, quarrel the
doing, good is not. *nakamá* companion, comrades; *dōshi* fellow)

Yonín kyōdai **no uchí** *de sōryō ga ichibán kashikói désŭ.*
四人　兄弟　の　うち　で　総領　が　一番　かしこい　です.
Among the four brothers the eldest is the cleverest. (*sōryō* the eldest son)
among others *kótoni* 殊に (*colloq.*), *nakanzúku* 就中 (*Lit.*)

Around or Round

Chikyū wa taiyō **no shūi** (or **mawarí**) *wo unkō shimásŭ.*[1]
地球　は　太陽　の　周囲　　　（周り）　を　運行　します.
The earth moves **round** the sun.

Wakái ongakŭká[2] **no mawarí ni** (or **shūi ni**) *sū-nin no fujín ga*
若い　音楽家　の　まわり　に　（周囲　に）　数人　の　婦人　が
tatté imáshĭta.   Several ladies stood **around** the young musician.
立っていました.

Watashí wa go-ji **góro-ni** *kaerimásŭ.*   I'll be back **around** five.
私　は　五時　頃に　帰ります.

Yūbinkyoku wa kádo wo **magattá tokoró ni** *arimásŭ.*
郵便局　は　角　を　曲がった　ところ　に　あります.
The postoffice is **around** the corner. (*lit.* Postoffice, the corner rounded, in
place is.—*magarú* 曲がる to turn, to round)

Watashitachí wa oká kará **átari no** *késhiki wo homemáshĭta.*
私達　は　丘　から　あたり　の　景色　を　ほめました.
From the hill we admired the scenery **around.** (*lit.* We, from the hill, the
surroundings' scenery admired.—*homéru* ほめる to admire, to praise)

Ga ga akarí no **mawarí** *wo tondé irú.*   Moths fly **around** lights.
蛾　が　あかりの　まわり　を　飛んでいる.　　　(*mawarí* the environs)

Mēdo wa uraniwá no **hen ni** *imásŭ.*   The maid is **around** the backyard.
メード　は　裏庭　の　辺　に　います.　　　(*hen ni* in the vicinity)

to sit **around** the stove ⎰ *sŭtōbu wo kakondé suwarú* ストーヴをかこんで坐る
　　　　　　　　　　　　　⎱ *sŭtōbu no mawarí ni suwarú* ストーヴのまわりに坐る

(*kakomú* かこむ to surround, to encircle, *suwarú* 坐る to sit or squat down,
mawarí ni in the neighbourhood, round, around, about)

to travel around the world ⎰ *sekái man-yū wo surú* 世界漫遊をする
　　　　　　　　　　　　　⎱ *sekái-jū wo ryokō surú* 世界中を旅行する

(*man-yū* a tour, a pleasure trip, a travel; *-jū* through, throughout)

---

1 *unkō surú* to move round (of celestial bodies)   **2** musician

At

Anáta no okāsan wa mádo no sóba ni suwatté imáshĭta.
貴方 のお母さんは 窓 の そば に 坐って いました.
Your mother was sitting at the window. (*sóba ni* near)

Takŭsán no hĭtó ga sonó kaigō[1] ni imáshĭta.   Many people were at
沢山 の 人 が その 会合 に いました.   the meeting.

Hanadá San ga irasshátta tokí ni watashí wa shokují wo shĭté imáshĭta.
花田 さん がいらっしゃった時に 私 は 食事 を していました.
When Mr. Hanada came I was at dinner. (*shokují wo surú* to dine)

Anó misé de mugiwará-bōshi wo gohyakú-yen de utté imásŭ.
あの 店 で 麦わら帽子 を 五百円 で 売っています.
In that store they are selling straw hats at 500 yen each.

Konó ié wa sambyakú man yen ni hyōka sareté[2] imásŭ.
この 家 は 三百 万 円 に 評価 されて います.
This house is valued at 3,000,000 yen.

Bóku ga anó rōjin wo warattá nóde anó hĭtó wa bóku ni nigái kaó
僕 があの 老人 を 笑った のであの 人 は 僕 に 苦い 顔
wo shimáshĭta.[3]   The old man frowned at me for laughing at him.
を しました.
(*lit.* I, that old man laughed because, that man at me bitter face made.)

Watashitachí wa kippō[4] ni kyōki shimáshĭta.[5]   We were rejoiced at the
私達 は 吉報 に 狂喜 しました.   good news.

Ikattá[6] torá wo míte watashitachí wa furuemáshĭta.[7]
怒った 虎 を 見て 私達 は ふるえました.
We trembled at the sight of the enraged tiger.

Totsuzén[8] no bakuhatsú ni minná odorokimáshĭta.   Everybody was alarmed at
突然 の 爆発 にみんなおどろきました.   the sudden explosion.
(*odoróku* おどろく to be alarmed, astonished, surprised, impressed, etc.)

Kimí no shitsúrei-na[9] furumái[10] ni odorokimásŭ.   I am astonished at your
君 の 失礼 な 振舞い におどろきます.   disrespectful behaviour.

Sonó inú wa bóku ga yobú to kimáshĭta.   The dog came at my call.
その 犬 は 僕 が 呼ぶ と 来ました.
(*lit.* The dog, I called when, came.)

Watashí wa anáta no otōsan ni ojí no tokoró de o-mé ni kakarimáshĭta.
私 はあなた のお父さんに伯父の ところ で お目 に かかりました.
I met your father at my uncle's. (*ojí no tokoró de* at my uncle's place)

Náni wo míte imásŭ ka. 何を見ていますか.   What are you looking at?

Common verbs followed by *at*

to aim at a target *mató wo neraú* 的をねらう

----

1 meeting **2** *hyōka surú* to value **3** *nigái kaó wo surú* to frown at **4** good
news **5** *kyōki surú* to rejoice at **6** *ikarú* to be, get angry **7** *furuerú* to tremble
8 sudden **9** *shitsúrei-na* disrespectful **10** behaviour

to frown **at** a person   *hǐtó ni máyu wo hisoméru* 人に眉をひそめる

to glance **at** a person   *hǐtó wo chirári-to míru* 人をちらりと見る

to grumble **at** a person   *hǐtó ni guchí wo iú* 人にぐちを云う

to hint **at** a thing   *kotó wo honomekásu* 事をほのめかす

to jeer **at** a person   *hǐtó wo hayashí-taterú* 人をはやし立てる

to jump **at** a proposal   *mōshikomi ni tobitsúku* 申込みにとびつく

to knock **at** the door   *to wo tatáku* 戸をたたく

to laugh **at** a person   *hǐtó wo azawaraú* 人をあざ笑う

to look carefully **at** a person   *hǐtó wo yóku mǐru* 人をよく見る

to stare **at** a person   *hǐtó wo mitsumerú* 人を見つめる

to throw a stone **at** a bird   *torí ni ishí wo nagéru* 鳥に石を投げる

Beneath

Hiyoké no shǐtá de yasumimashō.   Let us rest **beneath** the shade.
日除け の 下 で 休みましょう.

Anáta no okonai wa anáta no igén wo sonjimáshǐta.   Your conduct was **be-**
貴方 の 行い は 貴方 の 威厳 を 損じました.   **neath** your dignity.

(*igén* dignity; *sonjíru* to harm, damage, mar)

Beside

Shiná fujín ga watashí no sóba ni suwatté imáshǐta.
支那 婦人 が 私 の そば に 坐って いました.

A Chinese lady was sitting **beside** me.

Besides (See page 279)

Anó hǐtó wa monó wo nusumáreta[1] bákari de náku ōda saremáshǐta.[2]
あの 人 は 物 を 盗まれた ばかり で 無く 殴打 されました.

Besides being robbed he was beaten.

Chichí wa anáta ni konó tegamí no hoká ni kozútsumi wo watashimasén[3]
父 は 貴方にこの 手紙 の 外 に 小包 を 渡しません

déshǐta ka.   Didn't my father give you a parcel **besides** this letter?
でした か.

Between (See also Lesson 19)

Between is generally translated by *no aidá* の間, but sometimes it is omitted in the translation.

Sonó mondaí wo watashitachí no aidá de kaiketsú shimáshǐta.
その 問題 を 私達 の 間 で 解決 しました.

We settled the matter **between** ourselves. (*kaiketsú surú* to settle)

Sonó mondaí wa chichioyá to musúkó no aidá de kaiketsú saremáshǐta.
その 問題 は 父親 と 息子 の 間 で 解決 されました.

The matter was settled **between** father and son.

---

1 *monó wo nusumaréru* to be robbed of something   **2** *ōda surú* to assail with blows, to beat   **3** *watasú* to hand (over), to deliver, to give

fŭtarí **no aidá wo** *sáku*   to come **between** two persons
二人 の 間 を さく   (*sáku* to split, to sever)

ryōkyokutan **no aidá wo** *tóru*   to take **between** the two extremes
両極端 の 間 を とる   (*ryōkyokutan* both extremes)

Watashidómo no ensokú ni shi-go-jū-nin no hĭtó ga orimáshĭta.
私共 の 遠足 に 四五十人 の 人 が おりました.
There were **between** forty and fifty people at our picnic.

Watashitachí **daké no aidá no hanashí désŭ** *ga Káneda San wa*
私達 だけ の 間 の 話 です が 金田 さん は
watashí ga shĭttá uchí de ichibán no usótsŭki désŭ.
私 が 知った うち で 一番 の うそつき です.
Between ourselves, Mr. Kaneda is the greatest liar I have ever known.
(*lit.* **Between** ourselves only the talk is, but Mr. Kaneda I have-known
among first liar is.)

Beyond or Past

Watashí no uchí wa soréra no oká no **kánata (mukō)** *ni arimásŭ.*
私 の 家 はそれ等 の 丘 の 彼方 （向う） に あります.
My house is **beyond** those hills.

Anáta no okonái wa shōsan[1] **íjō** *désŭ.*   Your deed is **beyond** praise.
貴方 の 行い は 賞讃 以上 です.

But

Hĭtóri wo **nozoité** *zémbu no monó ga watashí no mōshiide*[2] *wo shōchi*[3]
一人 を 除いて 全部 の 者 が 私 の 申出で を 承知
shimáshĭta.   All **but** one accepted my proposal.
しました.   (*nozoité* except, save, but, exclusive of)

Watashí **no hoká** *wa miná ikimáshĭta.*   They are all gone **but** me.
私 の 外 は 皆 行きました.   (*no hoká* except, but)

Anó misé **no hoká** *de wa dóko démo soré wo kaemasén.*
あの 店 の 外 では どこ でも それ を 買えません.
You can't buy it anywhere **but** in that shop. (*dóko démo* anywhere)

Káre wa ayamáru yóri **hoká** *nákatta.*   What could he do **but** apologize.
彼 は あやまる より 外 なかった.   (*ayamáru* to apologize)
(*lit.* He, to apologize than, other thing there was not.)

Soré **daké** *wa iyá désŭ.*   Anything **but** that. (*lit.* That only, distasteful,
それ だけ は いや です.   undesirable, hateful, etc., is.)

Táda ichí-do kirí.   ただ一度きり.   Never **but** once.

Owarí kará ni-bammé. 終りから二番目.   The last **but** one.

By (See passive voice, page 436)

Sonó shōsetsu wa wakái fujín **ni yotté** *kakaremáshĭta.*
その 小説 は 若い 婦人 に よって 書かれました.
That novel was written **by** a young lady.   (*kakaréru* to be written)

Watashĭtachí wa miná hi **no sóba ni** *suwatté imáshĭta.*   We were all sitting
私達 は 皆 火 のそば に 坐って いました.   **by** the fire.

Nihón de satō wa kin **de** *uraremásŭ.*   In Japan sugar is sold **by** the kin.
日本 で 砂糖 は 斤 で 売られます.   (one *kin*=1.32 lbs.)

---

1 praise **2** proposal **3** *shōchi surú* to accept, to consent to, to agree to

Anáta no o-koé de anáta wo súgu ni wakarimáshǐta.   I soon recognized you
貴方 の お声 で 貴方 を 直ぐに わかりました.   **by** your voice.

Anó shōnen wa kimi yóri mo zuttó rikó désǔ.   That boy is cleverer than
あの 少年 は 君 よりも ずっと 利口です.   you **by** a good deal.

Keikán wa sonó dorobō no udé wo tsǔkamaemáshǐta.
警官 は その 泥棒 の うで を つかまえました.
The policeman caught the thief **by** the arm. (*tsǔkamaerú* to catch, seize)

For (See pages 103 and 213)

Sonó rōfujin wa kanashimí no tamé ni kuchí ga kikemasén déshǐta.
その 老婦人 は 悲しみ の ため に 口 が 利けません でした.
The old lady could not speak **for** grief. (*kikerú* to be able to operate)
(*lit.* The old lady, grief on account of, the mouth couldn't operate. *kanashǐmí*
grief)

Satō San no musǔkosán wa toshi no warí ni séi ga takái désǔ.
佐藤 さん の 息子さん は 年 の 割 に 背 が 高い です.
Mr. Satō's son is tall **for** his age. (*no warí ni* in proportion to)

Watashí jíshin no tamé ni wa shimpaí wa arimasén ga anáta no
私 自身 の ため に は 心配 は ありませんが 貴方 の
tamé ni watashí wa yūryo shimásǔ.   As **for** myself I have no anxiety,
ため に 私 は 憂慮 します.   but **for** you I have apprehension.
(*yūryo surú* to have apprehension, to be anxious)

Konó bōshi wo go-hyakú yen de motomemáshǐta.[1]   I bought this hat **for**
この 帽子 を 五百 円 で 求めました.   five hundred yen.

Watashí wa anó nōfu ni anó hǐtó no umá ippikí ni táishǐte jípu
私 はあの 農夫 に あの 人 の 馬 一匹 に 対して ジープ
ichí-dái yarimáshǐta.   I gave that farmer a jeep **for** his horse.
一台 やりました.

Konó búnshō wo ichí-go ichí-go eiyakú shi-nasái.
この 文章 を 一語 一語 英訳 しなさい.
Translate this sentence into English word **for** word.
(*ichí-go ichí-go* word for word; *eiyakú* English translation)

Nimán yen no kogítte.   A cheque **for** 20,000 yen.
弐万 円 の 小切手.   (*kogítte* cheque)

Káre wa sonó kawaisō-na shōjo no yōbō wo azakerimáshǐta.
彼 は その 可愛相な 少女 の 容ぼう を あざけりました.
He derided that poor girl **for** her appearance. (*yōbō* looks, countenance)
(*lit.* He, that poor girl's appearance derided.—*azakerú* to deride)

"*Jínrui ga tsǔkuráreta sōzōdekiúru mokutekí wa nan no tamé de átta*
"人類 が 造られた 想像できうる 目的 は 何ん の ため であった
ka, móshi jínrui ga kōfuku de áru tamé de nái náraba." *to Kārairú*
か, 若し 人類 が 幸福 で ある ため で ないならば "とカーラィル
wa tōta.   "**For** what imaginable purpose was man made if not to be happy?"
は 問うた.   asked Carlyle. (*jínrui* man, human being; *tsǔkuraréru* 造られる
to be made; *sōzōdekiúru* imaginable; *mokutekí* purpose; *kōfuku*
happiness; *tōta* past of *toú* 問う to ask)

---

1 *motoméru* to obtain, to purchase, polite expression for *to buy*

From (See pages 95 and 288)

*Watashí no nakamá[1] wa jibún no mokutekí[2] wo watashí **ni** kakŭshimáshĭta.[3]*
私 の 仲間 は 自分 の 目的 を 私 に かくしました.
My comrade concealed his intention **from** me.

*Anó hĭtó wa ippán no[4] shūkan[5] **kará** hanárete[6] imáshĭta.*
あの 人 は 一般 の 習慣 から はなれて いました.
He departed **from** the general custom.

Ōarashi no tamé ni gakkō e ikaremasén déshĭta. (Great storm on account
大嵐 の ため に 学校 へ行かれませんでした. of to school couldn't go.)
I was kept **from** going to school on account of the great storm.

Keikán wa watashitachí no tsūkō[7] wo tomemáshĭta.   A policeman prevented
警官 は 私達 の 通行 を 止めました.   us **from** passing.

Kinō watashí wa gakkō wo yasumimáshĭta.[8]   Yesterday I was absent
きのう 私 は 学校 を 休みました.   **from** school.

*Warúi kazé **ni** nayánde imásŭ.*   I am suffering **from** a bad cold.
悪い 風邪 に 悩んで います.
  (*kazé* a cold; *nayámu* to suffer from—*lit.* Bad cold **from,** suffering am.)

*Konó oká **kará** shĭtá no umí ga miemásŭ.*   **From** this hill we can see
この 丘 から 下 の 海 が 見えます.   the ocean below.

*Chichí wa jigyō **kará** intái shĭtái no désŭ.*   My father wishes to retire
父 は 事業 から 引退したいの です.   **from** business.

*Go-setsuméi[9] **kará míreba** sonó fujín wa hijō ni kanemochí ni chigái*
御説明 から 見れば その 婦人 は 非常に 金持 に 違い
arimasén ne.   **From** your description that lady must be extraordinarily rich.
ありませんね.

Konó mondaí ni tsúite no watashí no íken wa anáta no to hijō ni chigaimásŭ.
この 問題 についての 私 の意見は 貴方 のと非常に 違います.
My opinion on this subject is very different **from** yours.

Anáta no gímu wa watashí no to zenzén chigaimásŭ.   Your duty is distinct
貴方 の 義務 は 私 のと 全然 違います.   **from** mine.
  (*lit.* Your duty and mine entirely differ.)

*Warewaré wa jínsei[10] ni óite nayamí **kará** kanzén ni nogaréru kotó*
我々 は 人生 に於て 悩み から 完全に 逃れる 事
wa dekinai.   We cannot be completely free **from** trouble in life.
は 出来ない.   (*lit.* We in life from trouble entirely to escape cannot.)

Koréra no shinamonó wa zeikín wo ménjo[11] sareté imásŭ.
これ等 の 品物 は 税金 を 免除 されて います.
These goods are exempted **from** taxation.

---

1 comrade **2** intention **3** *kakúsu* to conceal, to hide **4** *ippán no* general **5** custom
6 *hanaréru* to depart from **7** the passing (of a street) **8** *yasúmu* to be absent,
miss (school) **9** description **10** *jínsei* life; *jinsei ni óite* in life **11** *ménjo surú* to
exempt from; *ménjo sarerú* to be exempted from

This last sentence may be translated as follows:

Konó shinamonó wa menzeihín désŭ.   (*menzeihín* articles exempt from
この　品物　は　免税品　です.　　　taxation)

Vocabulary

Nouns

ability	{ rikiryō	力量^{リキリョウ}
	{ sainō	才能^{サイノウ}
barrier	kyōkai	境界^{キョウカイ}
basis	kisó	基礎^{キソ}
branch	bun-ya	分野^{ブンヤ}
celebration	o-iwái	お祝^{イワ}イ
ceremony	gíshiki	儀式^{ギシキ}
cleanliness	seiketsú	清潔^{セイケツ}
cost	kéihi	経費^{ケイヒ}
currency	tsūka	通貨^{ツウカ}
delight	yorokobí	喜^{ヨロコ}ビ
feather	hané	羽^ネ
greatness	idaisá	偉大^{イダイ}サ
health	kenkō	健康^{ケンコウ}
land	rikú	陸^{リク}
language	géngo	言語^{ゲンゴ}
learning	gakujitsú	学術^{ガクジツ}
name	na	名^ナ
navy	káigun	海軍^{カイグン}
ornament	kyōyō	教養^{キョウヨウ}
phase	hōmen	方面^{ホウメン}
rank	kaikyū	階級^{カイキュウ}
riding	jōyō	乗用^{ジョウヨウ}
sacredness	shinséi	神聖^{シンセイ}
study	bengakú	勉学^{ベンガク}
tail	o	尾^オ
telegraph	denshín	電信^{デンシン}

thought	shisō	思想^{シソウ}
tradition	densetsú	伝説^{デンセツ}
width	habá	幅^{ハバ}
wireless	musén	無線^{ムセン}

Adjectives

artistic	geijitsuteki	芸術的^{ゲイジツテキ}
intellectual	chitekí	知的^{チテキ}
natural	tennén no	天然^{テンネン}ノ
scientific	kagakuteki	科学的^{カガクテキ}
universal	sekaitekí	世界的^{セカイテキ}

Verbs

to achieve	tassú·ru	達^{タッ}スル
to broaden	hiroge·rú	拡^{ヒロ}ゲル
to complete	shunkō surú	竣工スル
to discover	hakkén surú	発見^{ハッケン}スル
to express	arawásu	表^{アラ}ワス
to found	kensetsú surú	建設^{ケンセツ}スル
to get cool	samé·ru	冷^サメル
to get warm	atatamáru	温^{アタタ}マル
to serve	yakú ni tátsu	役^{ヤク}ニ立^タツ
to spoil	sonjí·ru	損^{ソン}ジル
to surpass	ryōga surú	凌駕^{リョウガ}スル
to tell	katarú	語^{カタ}ル

Adverbs

ceaselessly	kandán-náku	間断^{カンダン}ナク
commercially	shōgyōjō (ni)	商業上^{ショウギョウジョウ}(ニ)
in succession	tsuzuité	続^{ツヅ}イテ

to support, to hold *sasaerú*; to observe (a festival) *okonaú*; to be crowded (of people) *nigiwáu*; to revolve one time *isshū surú*; to level *heitán ni surú*; open air *kógai*; wireless telegraphy *musén-dénshin*; great scientist *dái-kagakŭshá*; captain (navy) *kaigán-táisa*; rear-admiral *kaigán-shōshō*; vice-admiral *kaigán-chūjō*; admiral *kaigán-taishō*; admiral of the fleet *génsui*; above the sea *kaibatsú*; basin (of river) *ryūiki*; commerce of the world *sekái shōgyō*; bathing, taking a bath *nyūyoku*: to have a bath *nyūyoku surú*

Exercise   *Renshū* 練習

1. Nihón ni wa " onagadorí " to yobarerú o no jū-ni fíto[1] guraí nagái torí ga imásŭ. Konó torí ga kógai wo arúku tokí ni wa hĭtó ga torí no hané wo sonjínai tamé ni[2] sonó o wo sasaemásŭ. **2.** Musén-dénshin wa Itarī no dái-kagakŭshá Gurierumó Marukoní ni yotté sen happyakú hachí-jū-ku nen ni hakkén saremáshĭta, ga soré wa honnó[3] jū-nen guraí nochí ni wa shōgyōjō ni mochií hajimeraremáshĭta[4]. **3.** Káigun ni óite kaigún-táisa íjō no kaikyū wa kaigún-shōshō, kaigún-chūjō, kaigún-taishō oyobí[5] génsui de arimásŭ. **4.** Fújisan wa kaibatsú ichí-man-ni-sen-sámbyaku-hachi-jū-naná fíto arimásŭ. **5.** Arekisandā Daiō[6] wa jibún no na ni chinánda[7] tokoró no Ejipŭtó no Arekisandoriyá wo kensetsú shimáshĭta. **6.** Nihón de wa ichí-gatsú no tsŭkí wa tsugí kará tsugí e to[8] tsuzuité okonawarerú[9] iró-iró no gíshiki ya o-iwái de nigiwaimásŭ. **7.** Nambéi Taiheiyō kaigán ittái ni watatté[10] Andesú to yobarerú takái sammyakú ga hashítte imásŭ. **8.** Chikyū wa sámbyaku rŏku-jū-go-nichi rokú jíkan de táiyō no mawarí wo isshū shimásŭ. **9.** Tōkyō no íma no Uenó-éki wa issén-kyū-hyakú-san-jū-ni nen sán-gatsú ni kéihi ni-hyakú-shichi-jū-man yen de shunkō shimáshĭta. **10.** Kawá wa kandán náku sonó ryūiki wo hirogé matá heitán ni surú hatarakí wo shĭté imásŭ.[11] **11.** Kásen wa rikú no okuchí to úmi to no aidá no tennén no michí de arimásŭ. **12.** Sangakú wa shíba-shíba ni-ka-kokú[12] no áida ni kyōkai wo tsŭkúru. **13.** Géngo wa kotobá ni yotté shisō wo arawashimásŭ. **14.** Rikú wa úmi yóri mo hirú háyaku atatamári yóru háyaku samemásŭ. **15.** Reonarudó da Vínchi wa sekaitekí no tensái de átta soshĭté chitekí, kagakutekí, geijitsŭtekí katsudōryoku no arayúru hōmen ni[13] óite idái-sa wo kachiéta. Ikánaru[14] gaku-jitsú no bun-ya mo káre ga rikái dekínu monó wa nái yō ni míeta.[15] **16.** Kin to gin wa sekái shōgyōjō ni óite tsūka no kisó to shĭté tsŭkawarerú kotó ni yotté[16] jūdai-na yakuwarí[17] wo enjité[18] imásŭ. **17.** Indo de sáru wa shinseishí sareté imásŭ[19] názenaraba furúi densetsú ga sáru no kamí ga Indo kokumín

---

1 Several words indicating European measures are used in Japan, with some phonetic alteration. The most common of these are : *fíto* 呎 for foot or feet, *yádo* 碼 for yard, *máiru* 哩 for mile; *póndo* 封度 unit of weight; *póndo* 磅 pound, monetary unit; *mētoru* 米 metre; *kiromētoru* 粁 kilometre; *gúramu* 瓦 gram; *kirogúramu* 瓩 kilogram. **2** *sonjí-nái tamé ni* in order not to spoil   **3** only   **4** *mochií hajiméru* to begin to use   **5** *oyobí* and, in formal speech   **6** *Arekisandā Daiō* Alexander the Great; *daiō* great sovereign   **7** *jibún no na ni chinánda* after his own name   **8** *tsugí kará tsugí e to* one after the other   **9** *okonawarerú* to be observed   **10** *ittái ni watatté* along **11** *hatarakí wo shĭté irú* to be at work   **12** *ni-ka kokú* two countries   **13** *arayúru hōmen ni óite* every, in every phase; *arayúru* every, in formal style   **14** *ikánaru* any; with negative verb : not any; *ikánaru gakujitsú no bun-ya* any branch of learning   **15** *káre ga rikái dekínu monó wa nái yō ni míeta* no branch of learning seemed to surpass his ability (*lit.* he understanding that could not thing there is not it seemed.) **16** *tsŭkawarerú kotó ni yotté* for the purpose of being used, to be used   **17** *jūdai-na yakuwarí* important part   **18** *enjíru* to play, to take part   **19** *shinseishí sareté imásŭ* is considered sacred

no tamé ni idainá shigotó wo surú no wo tasŭkéta to katatté imásŭ nóde.
18. Arabiyá de rakudá wa jōyō to nímotsu umpán[1] ni híroku shiyōsareté imásŭ.
19. Afuriká wa kitá kará minamí e go-sen máiru nágasa ga ári nishí kará
higashí e yon-sen máiru habá ga arimásŭ. **20.** Seiketsujō to kenkōjō[2] to
kará míte[2] nyūyoku wa hitsuyō désŭ. **21.** Bengakú wa yorokobí to kyōyō to
sainō to no tamé ni yakú ni tachimásŭ.

1. 日本には「尾長鶏」と呼ばれる尾の十二呎位長い鶏がいます．この
鶏が戸外を歩く時には人が鶏の羽を損じないためにその尾を支えま
す．**2.** 無線電信はイタリーの大科学者グリエルモ・マルコニによって
千八百八十九年に発見されましたがそれはほんの十年位のちには商業
上に用い始められました．**3.** 海軍に於て海軍大佐以上の階級は海軍
少将，海軍中将，海軍大将及び元帥であります．**4.** 富士山は海抜一万
二千三百八十七呎あります．**5.** アレキサンダー大王は自分の名に因
んだところの埃及(ｴｼﾞ)のアレキサンドリヤを建設しました．**6.** 日本
では一月の月は次から次へと続いて行われる色々の儀式やお祝いで賑
わいます．**7.** 南米太平洋海岸一帯にわたってアンデスと呼ばれる高
い山脈が走っています．**8.** 地球は三百六十五日六時間で太陽の周り
を一周します．**9.** 東京の今の上野駅は一千九百卅二年三月に経費弐
百七拾万円で竣工しました．**10.** 川は間断なくその流域を拡げ又平坦
にする伽きをしています．**11.** 河川は陸の奥地と海との間の天然の道
であります．**12.** 山岳はしばしば二ヵ国の間に境界をつくる．**13.** 言
語は言葉によって思想を現わします．**14.** 陸は海よりも昼はやく温
まり夜はやく冷めます．**15.** レオナルド・ダ・ヴィンチは世界的の天
才であったそして知的，科学的，芸術的活動力のあらゆる方面に於て
偉大さをかち得た．如何なる学術の分野も彼が理解出来ぬものはない
ように見えた．**16.** 金と銀は世界商業上に於て通貨の基礎として使わ
れる事によって重大な役割を演じています．**17.** 印度で猿は神聖視さ
れています，なぜならば古い伝説が猿の神が印度国民のために偉大な
仕事をするのを助けたと語っていますので．**18.** アラビアで駱駝は乗
用と荷物運搬に広く使用されています．**19.** アフリカは北から南へ五
千哩長さがあり西から東へ四千哩幅があります．**20.** 清潔上と健康上
とから見て入浴は必要です．**21.** 勉学は喜びと教養と才能とのために
役に立ちます．

---

1 *nímotsu umpán* carrying loads **2** *jō* or *jō kará* affixed to a word means *from
the point of view of*; *mite* seeing; *Seiketsujō to kenkōjō to kará mite* seen from the
point of view of cleanliness and health

1. In Japan there are birds called *onagadori*, whose tails are as much as twelve feet long. When these birds walk about in the open air, train-bearers[1] support their tails, so that the feathers may not be spoiled. **2.** Wireless telegraphy was invented by the great Italian scientist Guglielmo Marconi, in 1889, but it was only about ten years later that it began to be in commercial use. **3.** In the navy, above the captain the ranks are: rear-admiral, vice-admiral, admiral, and admiral of the fleet. **4.** Mount Fuji rises 12,387 feet above the level of the sea. **5.** Alexander the Great founded the city of Alexandria in Egypt, which he called after his own name. **6.** In Japan the month of January is crowded with all sorts of ceremonies and celebrations which are observed one after another in succession. **7.** Along the whole length of the Pacific coast of South America runs a continuous belt of high mountains called the Andes. **8.** The earth revolves round the sun once in 365 days and six hours. **9.** The present Ueno station in Tokyo was completed in March 1932 at a cost of ¥ 2,700,000.[2] **10.** A river is ceaselessly at work broadening and levelling its basin. **11.** Rivers are natural roads between the sea and the interior of a country. **12.** Mountains frequently form a barrier between two countries. **13.** Language is the expressing of thoughts by means of words. **14.** Land heats more rapidly by day and cools more rapidly by night than sea. **15.** Leonardo da Vinci was a universal genius and achieved greatness in every phase of intellectual, scientific, and artistic activity. No branch of learning seemed to be beyond his reach. **16.** Gold and silver play an important part in the commerce of the world by serving as the basis of the currency. **17.** In India the monkey is sacred because an old tradition tells that a monkey god helped to do a great work for the people of the country. **18.** In Arabia camels are widely used both for riding and carrying loads. **19.** Africa is 5,000 miles long from North to South, and 4,000 miles broad from west to east. **20.** From the point of view of cleanliness and health, a bath is a necessity. **21.** Studies serve for delight, for ornament, and for ability.

---

1 translate *hĭtó* (person) **2** In 1932 the Japanese currency was gold standard.

Sixtieth Lesson 第六十課

Prepositions (continued) *Zenchíshi* 前ゼ置ヂ詞シ (続)
In (See also Lesson 11 and 17)

Onoráto San wa watashí no shin no yūjin désŭ.　I found a true friend
オノラートさんは　私　の　真　の　友人　です.　**in** Mr. Onorato.
(*lit.* Mr. Onorato my true friend is.)

Zen sekái no bumméi wa híbi[1] shímpo shíté imásŭ.
全　世界　の　文明　は　日々　進歩　して　います.
The whole world is advancing **in** civilization.
(*lit.* The civilization of the whole world is advancing day by day.)

Anó kuní no jinkō wa genshō shitsútsu[2] arimásŭ.　That country is decreas-
あの　国　の　人口　は　減少　しつつ　あります.　ing **in** population.
(*lit.* The population of that country is decreasing.)

Bóku no gakuyū[3] wa sūgaku[4] ga hiídete[5] imásŭ.　My schoolmate excells
僕　の　学友　は　数学　が　秀でて　います.　**in** mathematics.
(*lit.* My schoolmate mathematics excelling is.)

Koréra no yōfuku wa táda ōkisa ga chigaú daké désŭ.　These suits differ
これ等　の　洋服　は　ただ大きさが　違う　だけ　です.　only **in** size.
(*lit.* These suits only the size is different.)

Watashí wa Nihón-go ga taihén shímpo shimáshĭta.　I have greatly improved
私　は　日本語　が　大変　進歩　しました.　**in** Japanese.
(*lit.* I the Japanese language much have improved.)

Soréra no ni-ken no ié wa katachí ga nité imásŭ.
それ等　の　二軒　の　家　は　形　が　似て　います.
Those two houses resemble each other **in** style.
(*lit.* Those two houses the styles resemble.)

Watashí no itóko wa watashí yóri mo chishiki[6] ga sugúrete[7] imásŭ.
私　のいとこ　は　私　よりも　知識　が　すぐれて　います.
My cousin surpasses me **in** knowledge.
(*lit.* My cousin more than I knowledge surpasses.)

Watashí wa shosai[8] de jibún no hon wo seitón shĭté[9] imáshĭta.
私　は　書斎　で　自分　の　本　を　整頓　して　いました.
I was engaged arranging my books **in** the library.
(*lit.* I, in the library my own books was arranging.)

Mánshū wa kōbutsu[10] no shigén[11] ni tónde imásŭ.[12]
満洲　は　鉱物　の　資源　に　富んで　います.
Manchuria is fertile **in** mineral resources.
(*lit.* Manchuria in mineral resources is fertile.)

---

1 *híbi* day by day　**2** *genshō* decrease; *genshō surú* to decrease, *genshō shitsútsu*
is decreasing　**3** schoolmate　**4** mathematics　**5** *hiíderu* to excel　**6** knowledge
7 *sugúreru* to surpass　**8** private library　**9** *seitón surú* to arrange, to put in good
order　**10** mineral　**11** resources　**12** *tónde irú* to be fertile, rich

Watashí wa séiji[1] ni kyōmi[2] ga arimasén.   I am not interested **in**
私　は　政治　に　興味　がありません.   politics.
    (*lit.* I in politics interest have not.)

Fujíkake San wa shikén ni seikō shimáshĭta.   Mr. Fujikake was success**ful**
藤掛　さん　は　試験　に　成功　しました.   **in** his examination.
   (Mr. Fujikake in examination succeeded.)

Emason San no ókŭsan wa Nihón-go wo hanásu no ga taihén jōzu désŭ.
エマソンさん　の　奥さん　は　日本語　を　話す　の　が　大変　上手　です.
   Mrs. Emmerson is very skilful **in** speaking Japanese.
   (Mr. Emmerson's wife the Japanese language to speak very skilful is.)

Idioms

busō[3] shĭté irú	武装している	to be **in** arms
kikén no náka ni irú	危険の中にいる	to be **in** danger
kenkō[4] de áru	健康である	to be **in** good health
jōkigen[5] de áru	上機嫌である	to be **in** good humour
komátte irú	困っている	to be **in** trouble
kōbutsu ni toboshíi	鉱物に乏しい	to be poor **in** minerals
atamá ga tarinái	頭が足りない	to be poor **in** intellect
sūgaku no atamá ga amari nái		to be poor **in** mathematics
数学　の　頭　が　あまりない		

Hachí ga kodomó no kaó wo sashimáshĭta.   A wasp stung the child **in**
蜂　が　子供　の　顔　を　さしました.   the face. (*sásu* to sting)

tori ga sóra wo tobú 鳥が空を飛ぶ   birds fly **in** the sky

búnsho de	文書で	**in** writing
himitsú ni	秘密に	**in** secret
hisóka ni	密かに	**in** private
naishó de (ni)	内証で（に）	**in** confidence

Into

Mizú wa netsú[6] ni yotté jōki[7] ni kawarimásŭ.[8]   Water is changed **into**
水　は　熱　によって蒸気に　変ります.   steam by heat.
    (*lit.* Water by heat into steam is changed.)

Ikutsu ka no chiisái nagaré[9] ga Sumidá-gawá e nagarekomimásŭ.[10]
幾つ　か　の　小さい　流れ　が　隅田川　へ　流れ込みます.
   Several small streams flow **into** the Sumida river.
    (*lit.* Several small streams into the Sumida river flow.)

yottsú no bubún ni wakéru 四つの部分に分ける   to divide **into** four parts
dōsatsu[11] surú   洞察する   to see **into** a subject

---

1 politics   **2** interest   **3** armament   **4** good health   **5** good humour   **6** heat
7 steam   **8** *kawarú* to be changed   **9** stream   **10** *nagarekomú* to flow (into)
11 insight, penetration

Prepositions (continued) 553

kotobá de arawásu[1] 言葉で表わす to put a thought **into** language

machigái[2] *wo surú* 間違いをする to be led **into** error

Of (See also Possessive Case, Lesson 13)

Konó shínshi wa furúi buké[3] *no de*[4] *désŭ.* This gentleman comes **of** an
この 紳士 は 古い 武家 の 出 です. ancient samurai family.

(*lit.* This gentleman old samurai family's origin is.)

Anó toshitótta[5] *konáya wa haién*[6] *de shinimáshĭta.* The old miller died
あの 年取った 粉屋 は 肺炎 で 死にました. **of** pneumonia.

(*lit.* The old miller of pneumonia died.)

Watanabê San wa tsuyói íshi[7] *no hĭtó désŭ.* Mr. Watanabe is a man
渡辺 さん は 強い 意志 の 人 です. **of** strong will.

(*lit.* Mr. Watanabe strong will man is.)

Watashí wa chokorēto hĭtó-hakó wo tomodachí ni okurimáshĭta.
私 はチョコレート 一箱 を 友達 に 送りました.

I sent my friend a box **of** chocolate.

(*lit.* I chocolate one-box to my friend sent.)

Konó hakó wa tetsú de dékite imásŭ. This box is made **of** iron.
この 箱 は 鉄 で 出来ています. (This box with iron is made.)

Watashí no umá wa ashí ga íppon bíkko[8] *désŭ.* My horse is lame **of**
私 の 馬 は 足 が 一本 びっこ です. one leg.

(My horse one leg lame is.)

Ima watashí wa o-kané ni fusokú[9] *shĭté imásŭ.* I am now short **of**
今 私 は お金 に 不足 して います. money.

(*lit.* Now in money short I am.)

Konó chihō wa shokúbutsu ga háete[10] *imasén.* This region is bare **of**
この 地方 は 植物 が 生えていません. vegetation.

(*lit.* This region vegetation growing is not.)

hĭtó wo wáruku iú 人を悪く云う to speak ill **of** a person

Out of

Sonó ijín wa mazushíi ié no de déshĭta. That great man came **out of**
その 偉人 は 貧しい 家 の 出 でした. a poor family.

(*lit.* That great man poor family's origin was.—*de* origin, birth, stock)

Dánte no sakuhín kará nuitá issetsú. A passage **out of** Dante.
ダンテ の 作品 から 抜いた 一節. (*sakuhín* literary work)

(*nuitá* past of *nukú* 抜く to extract; *issetsú* a literary passage)

Káre wa soré wo karabakó de tsŭkurimáshĭta. He made it **out of**
彼 は それ を 空箱 で つくりました. an empty box.

Sonó gasú tánku no bakuhatsú wa sonó shi no sóto de okorimáshĭta.
その ガスタンクの 爆発 は その 市 の 外 で 起こりました.

The gas tank exploded **out of** the city. (*bakuhatsú surú* to explode)

---

1 to show **2** error **3** *samurai* (warrior) family **4** *de* origin, birth, stock **5** old
6 pneumonia **7** will **8** lame **9** *fusokú surú* to be short of; *fusokú* shortage
10 *haéru* to grow

Tōkyō **kará** *go-máiru gurai déta tokoró* (or *de* で, as the case may be).
東京 から 五哩 ぐらい 出た ところ.
Some five miles **out of** Tokyo. (*déta* from *déru* to go out of)

Sakaná wa mizú náshi de wa ikirarénai.   Fish cannot live **out of** the
魚 は 水 無し で は生きられない.   water.
    (*lit.* Fish without water cannot live.)

Ki wa tochí **kará** *haemásŭ.*   Trees grow **out of** the earth.
木 は 土地 から 生えます.   (Trees from the ground grow.)

Bóku wa kesshōten[1] ni íki wo kitté[2] tōchaku shimáshĭta.
僕 は 決勝点 に 息 を 切って 到着 しました.
I arrived at the finish **out of** breath.
    (*lit.* I at the finish breath panting I arrived.)

Ima takŭsán no hĭtó ga shitsugyō[3] shĭté imásŭ.   Many people are now
今 沢山 の 人 が 失業 して います.   **out of** work.

Konó yōfuku wa ryūkō[4] ókure[5] désŭ.   This dress is **out of** fashion.
この 洋服 は 流行 後れ です.   (This dress fashion is behind.)

Kimi no yashin[6] wa tasserarenái.[7]   Your ambition is **out of** reach.
君 の 野心 は 達せられない.   (Your ambition cannot be reached.)

Jibō-jíki[8] **kará**[9] *anó hĭtó wa suishí[10] shiyō to kuwadatemáshĭta.[11]*
自暴自棄 から あの 人 は 水死 しようと 企てました.
Out of desperation he attempted to drown himself.
    (Desperation out of, he, I will drown myself, so trying attempted.)

kōkishın kará (or *de*)	好奇心から（で）	**out of** curiosity
jidái ókure no	時代おくれの	**out of** date
utagái mo náku	うたがいもなく	**out of** doubt
kikoenái tokoró ni	聞こえない所に	**out of** hearing
hitsuyō kará (*colloq.*)	必要から	**out of** necessity
hitsuyōjō (*Lit.*)	必要上	**out of** necessity
te no todokánai tokoró ni	手のとどかない所に	**out of** reach
hōgai na	法外な	**out of** reason
shinagiré	品切れ	**out of** stock
mondaí-gaí de	問題外で	**out of** the question
shió ga kírete irú	塩が切れている	to be **out of** salt

Sáru monó wa híbi-ni útoshi. (prov.)   **Out of** sight, **out of** mind.
去る 者 は 日々に うとし.   (*híbi* day by day, *sáru* to leave)
    (*lit.* Goes away person, day by day is estranged.)

Off

Watashitachí no fúne wa Yokohamá-kō-gái ni teihakŭ[12] shimáshĭta.
私達 の 船 は 横浜港外 に 碇泊 しました.
Our ship anchored **off** Yokohama harbour.
    (*lit.* Our ship, Yokohama harbour outside at, anchored.)

---

1 the goal, the finish line   **2** *íki wo kíru* to pant, to gasp   **3** *shitsugyō surŭ* to be out of work   **4** fashion   **5** *okurerŭ* to be behind   **6** ambition   **7** *tassúru* to reach **8** desperation   **9** out of   **10** to drown oneself   **11** *kuwadaterŭ* to attempt   **12** *teihakŭ surŭ* to anchor

Bōshi ga fukitobasaremáshĭta.[1] My hat was blown **off** my head.
帽子 が 吹きとばされました.

Kishú[2] *wa umá kará ᴄchimáshĭta.* The jockey fell **off** his horse.
騎手 は 馬 から 落ちました.

Ato tattá isshūkan de fuyú-yasumí. Winter vacation is only a week **off.**
あとたった 一週間 で 冬休み.

 (*lit.* In another week, winter-rest.—*fuyú* winter ; *yasumí* rest)

To no hándoru ga toremáshĭta. The handle of the door came **off.**
戸 の ハンドル が とれました (*toréru* to come off)

Botán ga toremáshĭta. ボタンがとれました. A button has come **off.**

Dóno kuraí hedatátte imásŭ ka. How far **off** is it? (*hedatátte* from
どの 位 へだたっています か. *hedatáru* to be separated from)

Go máiru hedatátte (or *hanárete*) *imásŭ.* It is five mile **off.**
五 哩 へだたって (はなれて) います.

Hijō-ni tōku désŭ. 非常に遠くです. It is a great way **off.**

to be **off** *dekakerú* 出かける

Mō dekakerú jikán désŭ. もう出かける時間です. It is time to be **off.**

to bite **off** *kamikirú* かみきる

to cool **off** *saméru* さめる

to cut **off** *kiritorú* 切りとる

to cut **off** on the telephone *denwá wo kíru* 電話をきる

to cut **off** one's connections *kankéi wo tátsu* 関係をたつ

to fly **off** *tobí-sáru* 飛びさる

to get **off** a car *kurumá kará oríru* 車から降りる

to put **off** *nobásu* のばす

to put **off** one's departure *shuppatsú wo nobásu* 出発をのばす

to put **off** one's hat *bōshi wo tóru* 帽子をとる

to put **off** one's shoes *kutsú wo núgu* 靴をぬぐ

to run **off** *hashirí sarú* 走り去る

to see **off** *miokurú* 見送る

to see a friend **off** on a journey *ryokō ni ikú tomodachí wo miokurú* 旅行に行く
友達を見送る

to wear **off** *surikirerú* すりきれる

ten per cent **off** *ichí waribikí* 一割引

off limits *tachiirí kinshí* 立入禁止

off duty *hibán* 非番

On, Upon

(See Lesson 11, page 63 and Lesson 42, page 338)

Rōma wa Tibā-gawá ni nozondé[3] *imásŭ.* Rome is **on** the Tiber.
ローマ はティーバー河 に のぞんで います.

---

1 *fukitobasarerú* to be blown off ; *fukitobasú* to blow off **2** jockey **3** *ni nozondé*
on ; *nozomú* to border on

Watashí no obāsan wa ítsu-démo onají kotó **ni tsúite**[1] *hanashimásŭ.*
私 のおばあさんは いつでも 同じ 事 に ついて 話します.
My grandmother always speaks **on** the same subject.

Anó fujín wa koyubí[2] **ni** *daiyamóndo no yubiwá wo hameté*[3] *imáshĭta.*
あの 婦人 は 小指 にダイヤモンドの 指輪 を はめて いました.
That lady had a diamond ring **on** her little finger.

Watashí wa taisetsú-na jíken **ni** *tazusawatté*[4] *imásŭ.*   I am engaged **upon** an
私 は 大切 な 事件 に 携わって います.   important affair.

Watashí wa anáta **ni** *tayorimásŭ.*[5]   I shall depend **upon** you.
私 は 貴方 に たよります.

Dáre démo jibún jíshin **ni** *tayorubéki désŭ.*   Every man should depend
誰 でも 自分 自身 に たよる可き です.   **upon** himself.

Anáta wa táshĭka-ni[6] *súgu watashí* **kará** *no táyori*[7] *wo kikú deshō.*
貴方 は 確か に すぐ 私 から の 便り を聞くでしょう.
You may depend **upon** soon hearing from me.
(*lit.* You surely soon from me news will hear.)

Táda konó jōken[8] **de** *nómi*[9] *anáta no o-mōshiide*[10] *wo o-hikiuké*[11] *shimashō.*
ただ この 条件 で のみ 貴方 の お申出で を お引受けしましょう.
Only **upon** this condition shall I accept your offer.
(*lit.* Only this condition upon only your offer I shall accept.)

Watashí wa yasái wo tábete seikatsú[12] *shĭtá monó désŭ.*
私 は 野菜 を 食べて 生活 した もの です.
I used to live **on** vegetables. (I vegetables eating lived the thing is.)

Imōto wa baiorín wo taihén jōzu ni hikimásŭ.[13]   My younger sister plays
妹 はバイオリンを 大変 上手 に 弾きます.   very well **on** the violin.
(My younger sister the violin very well plays.)

Anó oká no **ué ni** *chiisái koyá ga arimásŭ.*   There is a small hut **on**
あの 丘 の 上 に 小さい 小屋 が あります.   that hill.

Konó shigotó wo anáta no **tamé ni** *shimásŭ.*   I will do this work **on**
この 仕事 を 貴方 の ため に します.   your account.
(This work for you I do.)

Káre wa shirói kinují **ni** *Fújisan wo kakimáshĭta.*
彼 は 白い 絹地 に 富士山 を かきました.
He drew Mount Fuji **on** white silk cloth. (*kinují* silk cloth)

Anó hĭtó wa watashí no senaká **wo** *uchimáshĭta.*   He gave me a blow
あの 人 は 私 の 背中 を 打ちました.   **on** the back.
(*lit.* That man my back struck.—*útsu* 打つ to strike, hit, beat)

Sonná genshukú-na[14] *baái*[15] **ni oité**[16] *hĭtóbito wa utattári odottári subéki*
そんな 厳しゅくな 場合 に 於て 人々 は 歌ったり踊ったりすべき
de wa nái.   **On** such solemn occasions people should not sing and dance.
で は ない.

---

1 about   **2** little finger   **3** *hameté irú* to wear   **4** *tazusawarú* to be engaged upon
5 *tayóru* to depend upon   **6** *táshĭka-ni* surely   **7** a letter; news   **8** condition   **9** *táda
......de nómi* only upon (emphatic and formal)   **10** offer   **11** *o-hikiuké surú=hikiukéru*
to accept   **12** *seikatsú surú* to live   **13** *hikú* to play   **14** *genshukú-na* solemn
15 occasion   **16** *ni oité* on

Over (See page 64)

Watashí wa yon-jū-sái íjō désŭ.   I am **over** forty years old.
私 は 四十才 以上 です.

*Watashí wa mıgı no me no **ué ni** chiisái kizú-ató¹ ga arimásŭ.*
私 は 右 の 眼 の 上 に 小さい 傷あと が あります.
I have a small scar **over** my right eye.

*Watashí no ié wa kawá no **mukō ni** arimásŭ.*   My house is **over**
私 の 家 は 川 の 向こう に あります   the river.

*Onají tegamí wo **ni-do** taipuraitā de utáneba² narimasén déshĭta.*
同じ 手紙 を 二度タイプライターで打たねば なりません でした.
I had to type the same letters **over** again.

Bóku wa kakíne³ wo tobí-koemáshĭta.   I jumped **over** the fence.
僕 は 垣根 を 飛び越えました.

Kaigí⁴ wa Inoué Shí⁵ nı yotte shikaisaremáshĭta.⁶
会議 は 井上 氏 によって 司会されました.
The conference was presided **over** by Mr. Inoue.

Asokó no chiisái ié ga miemásŭ ka.   Do you see a small house **over**
あそこ の 小さい 家 が 見えます か.   there?
   (*lit.* That small house do you see?—*Asokó no* that there.)

Nomí-nàgara sonó mondai ni tsúite gíron shimashō.
飲みながら その 問題 について 議論しましょう.
Let us discuss the matter **over** a glass of wine. (*nomí-nágara* while drinking;
   mondaí matter; *gíron* argument, discussion; *gíron surú* to discuss)

Koréra no ringó wa fuyú-jū motanai deshō.   These apples will not keep
これら の りんご は 冬中 もたないでしょう.   **over** the winter.
   (*fuyú* winter, *fuyú-jū* through all winter; *motánai* do not keep)

Isói-de shimbún nı zattó me wo tōshimáshĭta.   I hastily ran **over**
急いで 新聞 に ざっと 目 を 通しました.   the newspaper.
   (*zattó* briefly, roughly; *me wo tōsu* 目を通す to read roughly)

Tōkyō Hóteru ni ippakú shimáshĭta.   I stayed at Tokyo Hotel **over**night.
東京 ホテル に 一泊 しました.   (*ippakú surú* to stay overnight.)

Sonó kodomó wa jidōsha de hikí-korosáreta.   The child was run **over**
その 子供 は 自動車 で ひき殺された   by a motorcar.
   (*hikí-korosaréru* passive of *hikí-korósu* to kill by running over)

Watashí wa úmi wo miwatasú no ga sŭkí désŭ.   (*miwatasú* to look out
私 は 海 を 見渡す の が 好き です.   over, as the sea, etc.)
I never get tired of looking out **over** the sea.

yamá no chōjō ni kúmo ga kakáru   clouds hang **over** the summit of
山 の 頂上 に 雲 が かかる   mountains

karadá-jū 体中   all **over** the body

shindá-ko no toshí wo kazóeru   to cry **over** split milk
死んだ子 の 年 を かぞえる
   (*lit.* dead child's age to count=useless thing to do)

---

1 *kizú-ató* scar **2** *taipuraitā de útsu* to type **3** fence **4** conference **5** *Shi*
used instead of *San* in formal speech **6** *shikaisarerú* to be presided over

Ningén wa bambutsú[1] wo osamemásŭ.   Man rules **over** all other creatures.
人間 は 万物 を 治めます.   (*lit.* Man all creatures rules over.)

Through (See Lesson 53, page 471)

Watashí wa natsú-jū inaká de kurashimáshǐta.
私 は 夏中 田舎 で 暮らしました.
I lived in the country **through** the whole summer.

Anó hǐtó wa zenshōgai[2] wo tsūjíte hijō ni shōjiki-na shōnin déshǐta.
あの 人 は 全生涯 を 通じて 非常 に 正直 な 商人 でした.
He was a very honest merchant **through** life.

Hanamurá San ga shikén ni seikō shinákatta no wa taimán[3] no tamé
花村 さん が 試験 に 成功しなかった の は 怠慢 の ため
déshǐta.   It was **through** negligence that Mr. Hanamura did not succeed in his
でした.   examination.

Watashí wa gaimudáijin ni tsūyaku[4] wo tōshǐte hanashimáshǐta.
私 は 外務大臣 に 通訳 を 通して 話しました.
I spoke to the Foreign Minister **through** an interpreter.

Rikotekí yokubō kará no kaihō ni yótte eraréru tokoró no nyūwa,
利己的 欲望 から の 解放 に よって得られる ところ の 柔和,
ochitsúkǐ, awaremí wa Tōyō no idái-na shūkyō Bukkyō no komponteki
落つき, 憐み は 東洋 の 偉大な 宗教 仏教 の 根本的
oshǐé de áru.   Gentleness, serenity, compassion, **through** liberation from selfish
教 である.   craving—these are the fundamental teachings of the great Oriental religion of Buddhism.
(*lit.* Selfish craving from liberation through to be obtained, **which** gentleness,
serenity, compassion Oriental great religion Buddhism fundamental teachings **are.**—*rikotekí* selfish, *yokubō* craving, *kará no* from, *kaihō* liberation,
ni yotté through, *eraréru* to be obtained, *tokoró no* which, *nyūwa* gentleness, *ochitsúkí* serenity, *awaremí* compassion, *Tōyō* Oriental, *idái-na* great,
shūkyō religion, *Bukkyō* Buddhism, *komponteki* fundamental, *oshǐé* teachings,
de áru are)

Throughout

Mokujōya San wa ichí-nen-jū Kamakurá ni súnde imásŭ.
黙城谷 さん は 一年中 鎌倉 に 住んでいます.
Mr. Mockjoya lives in Kamakura **throughout** the year.

Sonó hōdō[5] wa tádachi ni zénkoku[6] ni hiromarimáshǐta.[7]
その 報道 は 直ち に 全国 に 広まりました.
The news soon spread **throughout** the country.

To (See Lesson 17, page 95)

Issén yen wa fugō[8] ni wa nan-demó arimasén.
一千 円 は 富豪 に は 何んでも ありません.
One thousand yen is nothing **to** a millionaire.

---

1 *bambutsú* all creatures **2** all life **3** negligence **4** interpreter **5** news **6** *zénkoku*
ni throughout the country; *zénkoku* the whole country **7** *hiromáru* to spread
8 millionaire

Sonná hon wa dáre ni mo yūeki[1] de wa arimasén.
そんな 本 は 誰 に も 有益 で はありません.
Such books are not useful to anybody.

Kodomó wa tabitabí ryōshin no chūkoku ni mimí wo kashimasén.[2]
子供 は 度々 両親 の 忠告 に 耳 を 貸しません.
Children are often deaf to their parents' advices.
(*lit.* Children often to parents' advices do not listen.)

Anáta no kotobá wa kyozetsú[3] ni hĭtoshíi[4] désŭ. Your words are equiva-
貴方 の 言葉 は 拒絶 に 等しい です. lent to a refusal.

Go-sen yen no bakkín[5] ni shoseraremáshĭta.[6] We were sentenced to a
五千 円 の 罰金 に 処せられました. fine of 5,000 yen.

San ga ku ni taisúru[7] gótoku[8] san-jū ga kyū-jū ni táishĭte imásŭ.
三 が 九 に 対する 如く 三十 が 九十 に 対して います.
As three is to nine so is thirty to ninety.
(*lit.* Three to nine against as thirty to ninety against is.)

Anó otokó wa anáta no tamé ni bōshi wo tótta[9] to omoimásŭ.
あの 男 は 貴方 の ため に 帽子 を とった と 思います.
I believe that man took off his hat to you.
(*lit.* That man for you hat took off I think.)

Anáta wa anó go-fujín to dónna go-kankéi[10] désŭ ka.
貴方 は あの 御婦人 と どんな 御関係 です か.
What relation are you to that lady?
(*lit.* You and that lady what relations are?)

Watashí wa kánojo no ottó désŭ. I am her husband.
私 は 彼女 の 夫 です.

Koré wa aré to tōtei hikakú[11] ga dekimasén. This can hardly be
これ は あれ と 到底 比較 が 出来ません. compared to that.
(*lit.* This and that hardly comparison can't be made.)

Duranté San wa Itarī Taishikán no ittō shokikán désŭ. (*ittō shokikán* first
デュランテさんはイタリー大使館 の 一等 書記官 です. secretary)
Mr. Durante is first secretary to the Italian Embassy.

Komatsú San wa Ōsaka shichō no hishó[12] désŭ.
小松 さん は 大阪 市長 の 秘書 です.
Mr. Komatsu is private secretary to the mayor of Osaka.
(*lit.* Mr. Komatsu of Osaka mayor the secretary is.)

Anó yō-na hĭtóbito wa kókka[13] no idái-na méiyo[14] désŭ.
あのような 人々 は 国家 の 偉大な 名誉 です.
Such men are a great honour to their country.

Tsuyói íshi wa daijigyō no yōso[15] désŭ. Strong will is essential to
強い 意志 は 大事業 の 要素 です. great achievement.
(*lit.* Strong will an essential of great achievement is.)

---

1 useful **2** *mimí wo kasú* to listen to, *lit.* to lend one's ears **3** refusal **4** equivalent
5 fine **6** *bakkín ni shoseraréru* to be fined **7** against **8** as **9** *tóru* to take off
10 *kankéi* connection **11** comparison **12** private secretary **13** country **14** *méiyo*
honour; *idái-na* great **15** an essential element, an important factor, a requisite

Wága rentái[1] *wa Sapporó yukí wo meizeraremáshĭta.*[2]
わが　連隊　は　札幌　行　を　命ぜられました.
Our regiment has been ordered to Sapporo.
(*lit.* Our regiment Sapporo going was ordered.)

Anáta no yokín gakú[3] *wa yon-jū man yen désŭ.*   Your saving account
貴方　の　預金　額　は　四十　万　円　です.   amounts to 400,000 yen.
(*lit.* Your deposit account is 400,000 yen.)

Konó shokúmotsu wa mazúi désŭ.   This food is disagreeable to the taste.
この　食物　は　まづい　です.   (This food is tasteless.)

Anáta no go-shínsetsu-na go-énjo wo jitsú-ni arigátaku zonjimásŭ.
貴方　の　御親切　な　御援助　を　実に　ありがたく　存じます.
I feel very grateful to you for your kind assistance.
(*lit.* Your kind assistance indeed thankful I feel.)

Towards (See Lesson 45, page 381)

Meué[4] *ni táishĭte wa ingín ni*[5] *furumawáneba*[6] *narimasén.*
目上　に　対して　はいんぎんに　振舞わねば　なりません.
One must behave respectfully towards one's superiors.

Ōta San no ókŭsan wa go-kínjo no mazushíi-hĭtóbito[7] *ni táishĭte*
太田　さん　の　奥さん　は　御近所　の　貧しい人々　に　対して
taihén nasaké-bukái[8] *déshĭta.*   Mrs. Ota was very charitable towards the poor
大変　情深い　でした.   in her neighbourhood.

Shizén-kái[9] *ni okéru*[10] *súbete no monó wa kanséi*[11] *ni mukaú*[12] *keikō*[13]
自然界　に　於ける　すべての　物　は　完成　に　向かう　傾向
ga arimásŭ.   In everything in nature there is a tendency towards perfection.
が　あります.   (*keikō* tendency)

Yūgata góro[14] *hidói árashi ga okorimáshĭta.*   Towards the evening a severe
夕方　頃　ひどい　嵐　が　起こりました.   storm broke out.
(*lit.* About evening severe storm occurred.)

Yūjin ga watashí ni o-kané wo kashĭté kuré to tanónda tokí ni
友人　が　私　に　お金　を　貸して　くれ　と　頼んだ　時　に
warewaré no hanashí wa owarí ni chikazúite[15] *imáshĭta.*
我々　の　話　は　終り　に　近づいて　いました.
It was towards the end of our conversation that my friend asked me for
money. (My friend to me "Please lend me money" so, when he asked our
conversation towards the end getting near was.)

Rāshi San wa mō-gakkō[16] *wo kōen surú*[17] *tamé ni jū-man yen kífu*
ラーシ　さん　は　盲学校　を　後援　する　ため　に　十万　円　寄附
shimáshĭta.[18]   Mr. Larsh contributed 100,000 yen towards the support of the
しました.   school for the blind.

---

1 regiment   **2** *meizúru* to order   **3** *yokín* deposit; *gakú* amount; *yokín gakú* saving
amount   **4** superiors   **5** *ingín ni* respectfully   **6** *furumáu* to behave   **7** *mazushíi-*
hĭtóbito poor people   **8** charitable   **9** *shizén-kái* nature   **10** *ni okéru* in, (literary
speech)   **11** perfection   **12** *ni mukaú* towards, (literary speech)   **13** *keikō* inclination
14 about   **15** *chikazúku* to approach   **16** *mō-gakkō* school for the blind   **17** *kōen*
surú to support   **18** *kífu surú* to contribute

Under (See Lesson 11, page 64)

Nihón de fujín wa nijissái íka[1] de wa ryōshin no shōdaku[2] náshi
日本 で 婦人 は 二十才 以下 で は 両親 の 承諾 なし
de kekkón ga dekimasén.　In Japan women under 20 years of age cannot
で 結婚 が 出来ません.　marry without their parents' consent.

Anó otokó wa giméi no motó ni[3] ni-jū nen ikimáshĭta.
あの 男 は 偽名 の 下 に 二十 年 生きました.
That man lived under a false name for twenty years. (*giméi* false name)

Nihón no gakkō wa zémbu Mombushō[4] no kantokú[5] no motó ni arimásŭ.
日本 の 学校 は 全部 文部省 の 監督 の 下 にあります.
All Japanese schools are under the control of the Department of Education.

Tomodachí to iú kōjitsu[6] no motó ni anó hĭtó wa watashi wo
友達 という 口実 の 下 に あの 人 は 私 を
uragirimáshĭta.[7]　Under the pretext of being my friend, that man betrayed me.
裏切りました.

Koréra no kodomotachí wa watashí no sewá[8] ni nátte[9] imásŭ.
これ等 の 子供達 は 私 の 世話 に なっています.
These children are under my care.

Watashí no mókka no jōtai[10] de wa sonó yakŭsokú wo hatásu[11] kotó
私 の 目下 の 状態 で は その 約束 を 果す 事
ga dekimasén.　Under my present circumstances I am unable to fulfil that
が 出来ません.　promise.

Kutsū[12] arúiwa fukō[13] no tokí ni wa shímbō[14] séneba narimasén.
苦痛 或は 不幸 の 時 に は 辛抱 せねば なりません.
Under pain or misfortune we must have patience.

Uchí wa íma shŭzenchū[15] désŭ.　My house is now under repairs.
家 は 今 修繕中 です.

Konó kaishá wa gaikokú no keiéi[16] désŭ.　This firm is under foreign
この 会社 は 外国 の 経営 です.　administration.

Up (See Lesson 57, page 523)

Motion Upward

yamá ni noború　山に登る　to go up a mountain
nagaré wo kogí-noború[17]　流れを漕ぎ上る　to row up a stream

With (See Lesson 14, page 79)

Anó otokó to[18] wa nan no kankéi[19] mo arimasén.
あの 男 と は 何んの 関係 もありません. } I have no connection
Anó otokó to wa sŭkóshi mo kankéi[19] ga arimasén.　whatever with that
あの 男 と は 少し も 関係 がありません. } man.
(That man and I even a little connection there is not.)

---

1 under　**2** consent　**3** *motó ni* under　**4** Department of Education　**5** control
6 pretext　**7** *uragíru* to betray　**8** care　**9** *sewá ni náru* to be under the care of
someone　**10** *mókka no* present, *jōtai* circumstances　**11** to fulfil　**12** pain　**13** misfortune　**14** *shímbō surú* to be patient　**15** *shūzen* repairs; *chū* affixed to a noun is
used to translate under in the meaning of *undergoing*　**16** administration　**17** *nagaré*
stream; *kogí-noború* to row, to sail up　**18** *watashí* after *to* is here omitted; this
omission occurs sometimes in similar phrases　**19** connection

Watashitachi wa tomodachi no omoshirói hanashí ni támashii wo
私達　は　友達　の　面白い　話　に　魂　を
ubawaremáshĭta.[1]　　We were charmed **with** our friend's interesting story.
うばわれました.　(*lit.* We our friend's interesting story by, our soul was snatched.)

Anáta no go-íken ni wa dōi[2] *dekí-kanemásŭ.*[3]　　I do not agree **with** your
貴方　の　御意見　に　は　同意　出来かねます　　opinion.

Aburá wa mizú ni mazaránai.　　Oil does not mix **with** water.
油　は　水　に　まざらない.　　(*mazáru* to get mixed)

Kawaisō-na kodomotachi wa sámusa ni furueté[4] *imáshĭta.*
かわいそうな　子供達　は　寒さ　にふるえて　いました.
The poor children were shivering **with** cold.

Anáta wa taihén rakú ni[5] *Nihón-go wo manandé irú yō ni miemásŭ.*
貴方　は　大変　楽　に　日本語　を　学んで　いるように　見えます.
You seem to be learning the Japanese language **with** great facility.

Shōjiki ni iéba[6] *watashí wa kimí no chikágoro no*[7] *shigotó-burí*[8] *ga*
正直　に　云えば　私　は　君　の　近頃　の　仕事ぶり　が
ki ni irimasén.[9]　　To be frank **with** you, I do not like the way you have been
気に入りません.　　working lately.

Sonó hihō[10] *de hĭtóbito wa kanashimí*[11] *ni utaremáshĭta.*[12]
その　悲報　で　人々　は　悲しみ　に　打たれました.
At the sad news all people were overcome **with** grief.

Go-irái[13] *ni ōjite*[14] *watakŭshidómo no shinamonó no mihón*[15] *hĭtókumi*[16]
御依頼　に　応じて　私共　の　品物　の　見本　一組
wo go-sōfu mōshiagemáshĭta.[17]　　In compliance **with** your request we have sent
を　御送附　申上げました.　　you a set of samples of our goods.

Anáta no níisan ga tsutsumí[18] *wo wakí no shĭtá*[19] *ni kakaeté*[20] *purattóhōmu*[21]
貴方　の兄さん　が　包み　を　脇　の　下　に　抱えてプラットホーム
ni tátte imáshĭta.　　Your brother was standing on the platform **with** a bundle
に立っていました.　　under his arm.

Kázoku zentái wa kyōki[22] *shimáshĭta.*　　The whole family were mad **with**
家族　全体　は　狂喜　しました.　　joy.

Kojikí wa ryō-te[23] *wo hizá*[24] *no ué ni oité*[25] *bénchi ni koshí wo kákete*[26]
乞食　は　両手　を　膝　の　上　においてベンチに　腰　を　かけて
imáshĭta.　　The beggar was seated on a bench **with** his hands resting on his knees.
いました.　　(The beggar both hands on knees resting, on bench was sitting.)

---

1 *támashii wo ubáu* to charm; *támashii* soul; *ubáu* to snatch　**2** agreement
3 *dekikanerú* to be unable, not to be possible　**4** *furuerú* to shiver　**5** *rakú ni* easily
6 *shōjiki ni iéba* honestly if I say=to be frank with you　**7** *chikágoro no* lately
8 the way of working　**9** *ki ni irú* to like　**10** sad news　**11** grief　**12** *útsu* to strike;
utaréru to be struck　**13** your request　**14** in compliance with　**15** samples　**16** a set
of　**17** *go-sōfu mōshiageru=sōfu surú* to send　**18** *tsutsumí* bundle　**19** *wakí* arm;
wakí no shĭtá ni under the arm　**20** *kakaerú* to carry　**21** platform　**22** *kyōki surú*
to be mad with joy; *kázoku* family; *zentái* all　**23** *ryō-te* both hands　**24** knees
25 *okú* to put, to rest　**26** *koshí wo kakéru* to sit; *bénchi* bench

Wága shōkai wa táezu[1] ōkina chūmon wo ukemásŭ.[2]
わが 商会 は 絶えず 大きな 注文 を 受けます.
Large orders are continually placed **with** our firm.
  (*lit.* Our firm continually large orders receives.)

jidōsha ni gasorín wo irerú   to feed a motocar **with** gasolin
自動車 に ガソリン を 入れる

Seijitsú to chōwa shinái súbete no kōdō wa, fúwa, sonshitsú soshĭté
誠実 と 調和 しない すべて の 行動 は, 不和, 損失 そして
kónran nádo ni itarú.   Every act not in harmony **with** truth leads to discord,
混乱 など に 至る.   loss and confusion.

(*seijitsú* truth, *to* with, *chōwa* harmony, *shinái* does not, *súbete* every, *kōdō* act,
fúwa discord, *sonshitsú* loss, *soshĭté* and, *kónran* confusion, *nádo ni* etcetera, *itarú*
to lead—Note that in the above sentence, the use of *nádo* is pleonastic but may
suggest the idea that there might be some other bad effect.)

Within

(See Adverbs, Lesson 57, page 526)

(not beyond) *han-i nái de*   範囲内で
hōritsu no han-i nái de   法律の範囲内で   **within** the law
shūnyū no han-i nái de   収入の範囲内で   **within** one's income
(in the limits of) *ínai* 以内, followed or not by *ni* に or *de* で as the case
may be

Watashí no uchí wa éki kará ni máiru ínai désŭ.
私 のうち は 駅 から 二 哩 以内 です
My house is **within** two miles of the station.

Ichí-ji-kan ínai de konó shigotó wo oemásŭ.   I'll finish this work **within**
一 時間 以内 でこの 仕事 をおえます.   an hour.

Ichí-ji-kan ínai ni modorimásŭ.[3]   I shall be back **within** an hour.
一時間 以内 に 戻ります.

Referring to abstract things only *ni* に may be used:

Konó shigotó wa kimí no chikará ni oyobimasén.[4]   This work is not **within**
この 仕事 は 君 の 力 に 及びません.   your power.
  (*lit.* This work in your power does not reach.)

within hearing of *kikoerú tokoró de* 聞こえるところで

Without

(See Lesson 25, page 167 and Lesson 39, page 310)

Ōzei no hĭtó ga kyūjō[5] no mon no sóto ni tátte imáshĭta.
大勢 の 人 が 宮城 の 門 の 外 に 立っていました.
Many people stood **without** the gate of the Imperial Palace.

Wága gen[6]-náikaku[7] kakuryōtachi[8] wa reigái nákŭ[9] erái séijika[10] désŭ.
わが 現 内閣 閣僚達 は 例外 なく 偉い 政治家 です
  The ministers of our present government are, **without exception,** clever
  statesmen.

---

1 continually **2** *ukéru* to receive **3** *modóru* to return, to be back **4** *oyobú* to
reach, to attain to, to come to **5** Imperial Palace **6** present **7** government **8** *kakuryō* minister **9** without exception **10** *séijika* statesman; *erái* clever

Uchí no jimúsho no fútari no jimúin ga kyō **yokokú**[1] *náshi ni*
うち の 事務所 の 二人 の 事務員 が きょう 予告 なし に
káiko saremáshǐta.[2] Two employees of our office were dismissed to-day **without**
解雇 されました. **notice.**

Kóndo no getsuyōbi ni **kittó**[3] (or **machigái**[3] **náku**) *mō ichí-do o-tazuné*
今度 の 月曜日 にきっと （間違い なく）もう 一度 お訪ね
shimásǔ. We shall come and visit you again next Monday, **without fail.**
します.

Kimí no áto wo tsǔkéta[4] *hǐtó wa* **táshǐka-ni** *tantéi déshǐta.*
君 の 後 を つけた 人 は 確か に 探偵 でした.
The man who followed you was a detective, **without doubt.**
(*lit.* Your back followed man surely detective was.)

Vocabulary

Nouns			Adjectives		
colonel	*rikugún-táisa*	陸軍大佐	excessive	*kádo no*	過度ノ
depth	*fukása*	深サ	muscular	*kínniku*	筋肉ノ
diver	*sensúifu*	潜水夫	violent	*monosugói*	物凄イ
freshness	*shinsensá*	新鮮サ		*mōretsu-na*	猛烈ナ
gambling	*tobakú*	賭博	wealthy	*monomochí*	物持
heart	*shinzō*	心臓	**Verbs**		
impression	*inshō*	印象	to increase	*kuwawarú*	加ワル
instinct	*honnō*	本能	to leave	*nokósu*	残ス
intercourse	*kōsai*	交際	to look for	*motomé·ru*	求メル
islands	*shotō*	諸島	to lose	*ushinaú*	失ナウ
land	*rikuchí*	陸地	to love	*aisúru*	愛スル
living	*seikatsú*	生活	to spin	*tsumúgu*	紡グ
origin	*kígen*	起源	to spread	*hiromáru*	広マル
pressure	*atsuryokú*	圧力	to stick	*shūchaku surú*	執着スル
puppy	*koinú*	仔犬	**Adverbs**		
ruled (the)	*hitōchisha*	被統治者	easily	*tayásuku*	タヤスク
ruler	*tōchisha*	統治者	especially	*tóku-ni*	特ニ
rumour	*uwasá*	噂	largely	*ōi-ni*	大イニ
spirit	*séishin*	精神	only	*wázuka-ni*	僅カニ
strain	*kinchō*	緊張	really	*itsú-ni*	実ニ
strength	*kiryokú*	気力			

to show. to appear, to come out *arawásu*; to take care of, to look after, to be in
charge of *sewá surú*; to attack, to strike *osoú*; to be helpless, to be at a loss *komáru*;
a little girl *osanái shōjo*; summer *káki* (in literary style)

---

1 *yokokú* notice, previous notice **2** *káiko surú* to dismiss **3** *kittó* surely; *machi-*
gái náku without mistake = without fail **4** *áto wo tsǔkéru* to follow

indepedent country *dokuritsú-kokú*; legend *mukashí-bánashi*; iron chain *tetsú no kusarí*; suspension bridge *tsurí-bashí*; raw cotton *watá*; way, manner, method *hōhō* : entrance (to a place) *nyūjō*; free of charge *muryō*; all property *zenzáisan*; Philippine Islands *Hirippín Guntō*; outlook on life *jinséikan*; diver's dress *sensúifuku*; summer *káki* (Lit.)

Exercise　*Renshū*　練習

1. Ningyō wo aisúru kotó wa[1] jitsú ni boséi no honnō de átte soré wa osanái shōjo no jíbun kará[2] súde-ni arawárete imásŭ. **2.** Inú wo yóku sewá surú monó[3] wa inú wa koinú no jidái ni[4] shínsetsu-ni shĭté yarú[5] to soré ga inú no seishitsú-ni ōki-na hénka[6] wo ataerú[7] to iú kotó wo shĭtté imásŭ. **3.** Hígai wo tomonáu[8] árashi ga tóku-ni káki tabitabí Nihón no minamí kaigán wo osoimásŭ. **4.** Higashí Himarayá no dokuritsú-kokú Būtan ni mukashí-bánashi no náka ni mo sonó kígen ga wakaránai hijō ni furúi tetsú no kusarí no tsurí-bashí ga arimásŭ. **5.** Dénki ga ningén ni shiyō sarerú[9] yō-ni nátta no[10] wa yattó[11] hyakú nen guraí máe désŭ. **6.** Watá wa tayásŭku íto ni tsumugemásŭ. **7.** Sáru wo toraéru nóni[12] iró-iró no hōhō ga arimásŭ. Sáru wa naká-naká no dorobō désŭ kará tabemonó ga toréru tokoró e wa dóko e démo yukimásŭ kara. **8.** Chikyū no hyōmen no wázuka naná-bun no ni[13] ga rikuchí désŭ. **9.** Konó rōjin wa ítsu-démo tabakó no niói ga shimásŭ. **10.** Anó bimbō-na onná wa hĭtorí-musŭkó wo nakushĭtá kanashimí no tamé ni shinimáshĭta. **11.** Nichiyōbi ni wa anó hakubutsukán wa nyūjō muryō désŭ. **12.** Anó otokó wa monomochí no ié[14] ni umaremáshĭta ga tobakú de zenzáisan wo ushinatté shimaimáshĭta. **13.** Taiheiyō de ichibán fukái tokoró wa Nihón no hokú-tō[15] okí[16] to Mariyán Shotō okí to soshĭté Hirippín Guntō no náka no ōkina shimá de áru Mindanaó no higashí de arimásŭ. **14.** Séishin no chikará to shinsensá to wa ōi-ni kákuji no[17] jinseikán ni yorimásŭ.[18] **15.** Séifu no seikō to iú monó wa mattakú sonó tōchisha to hitōchisha no seishitsú to nōryoku ni yorú. **16.** Yamá no ué de hitsují no ban wo surú hitsujikái wa inú náshi de wa komarimásŭ. **17.** Mōretsu-na arúi wa kádo no kinnikú undō wa shinzō no omoí fután désŭ.[19] **18.** Monosugói káji ga Hakodaté wo osottó[20] irú to iú uwasá ga shichū ni[21] hiromarimáshĭta. **19.** Kaigún-táisa wa rikugún-táisa to onají désŭ. **20.** Noruwējin ga motoméru seikatsú wa rikú de nákú[22] úmi de arimásŭ. **21.** Ichíji ni[23] shūchaku shĭté soré wo yóku surú monó wa[24] tabitabí seikō shimásŭ. **22.** Sensúifuku wa ichí-ji ni[25] go-rokú

---

1 *ningyō wo aisúru kotó wa* to love dolls=the love of dolls　**2** *osanái shōjo no jíbun kará* in little girls　**3** *monó* people, persons; *inú wo yóku sewá surú monó wa* people who have much to do with dogs　**4** *jidái ni* at the time; *koinú no jidái ni* in their puppy days　**5** *shínsetsu ni shĭté yarú* (used when speaking to, or of inferiors) =*shínsetsu ni surú* to do a kindness, to treat kindly　**6** *ōki-na hénka* what a difference, a big difference　**7** *ataerú* makes　**8** *hígai wo tomonáu* destructive; *hígai* damage; *tomonáu* to cause　**9** *shiyō sarerú* to be used　**10** *yō ni nátta no wa* that has become　**11** only　**12** *toraéru nóni* in order to catch　**13** *naná-bun no ni* two sevenths　**14** *monomochí no ié* rich family　**15** *hokú-tō* north-east　**16** off　**17** *kákuji no* his; *kákuji* each person, each one, every individual　**18** *ni yorimásŭ* to be conditioned by　**19** *omoí fután* heavy burden=a strain of the heart (lit. heart strain)　**20** *osoú* to rage　**21** *shichū ni* in the city　**22** *rikú de nákú* not to the land　**23** *ichíji ni* to one thing　**24** *soré wo yóku surú monó wa* a man who does it well; *shūchaku surú* to adhere, cling to　**25** *ichí-ji ni* at a time

jikán kaitéi ni irarerú yō ni dékite imásŭ. 23. Mizú no atsuryokú wa mizú no
tukása ni yotté kuwawarimásŭ. 24. Ippán ni, Nihón-jin to no kōsai wa
sonó shakaitekí tokushitsú[1] de gaijín ni taihén yói inshō wo nokósu to iwareté
imásŭ.[2]

1. 人形を愛する事は実に母性の本能であってそれは幼い少女の時
分からすでに現われています. 2. 犬をよく世話する者は犬は仔犬の
時代に親切にしてやるとそれが犬の性質に大きな変化を与えるという
事を知っています. 3. 被害を伴う嵐が特に夏季度々日本の南海岸を
おそいます. 4. 東ヒマラヤの独立国ブータンに昔話の中にもその起
源が判らない非常に古い鉄の鎖の吊橋があります. 5. 電気が人間に
使用されるようになったのはやっと百年ぐらい前です. 6. 綿はたや
すく糸に紡げます. 7. 猿を捕えるのに色々の方法があります. 猿は
なかなかの泥棒で食物が取れる所へはどこへでも行きますから.
8. 地球の表面の僅か七分の二が陸地です. 9. この老人はいつでもた
ばこの臭いがします. 10. あの貧乏な女は一人息子をなくした悲しみ
のために死にました. 11. 日曜日にはあの博物館は入場無料です.
12. あの男は物持の家に生れましたが賭博で全財産を失ってしまいま
した. 13. 太平洋で一番深い所は日本の北東沖とマリヤン諸島沖とそ
してヒリッピン群島の中の大きな島であるミンダナオの東でありま
す. 14. 精神の力と新鮮さとは大いに各自の人生観によります.
15 政府の成功というものは全くその統治者と被統治者の性質と能力
による. 16. 山の上で羊の番をする羊飼いは犬なしでは困ります.
17. 猛烈な或は過度の筋肉運動は心臓の重い負担です. 18. 物すごい
火事が函館をおそっているという噂が市中に広まりました. 19. 海軍
大佐は陸軍大佐と同じです. 20. ノルウェー人が求める生活は陸でな
く海であります. 21. 一事に執着してそれをよくするものは度々成功
します. 22. 潜水服は一時に五六時間海底にいられるようにできてい
ます. 23. 水の圧力は水の深さによって加わります. 24. 一般に日本
人との交際はその社会的特質で外人に大変よい印象を残すと云われて
います.

1. The love of dolls is really the mother-instinct showing itself already in
little girls. 2. Everyone who has much to do with dogs knows what a difference
kindness shown to them in their puppy days makes in their dispositions.
3. Destructive storms frequently visit the southern coast of Japan, especially
in summer. 4. In Bhutan, an independent kingdom in the Eastern Himalayas,
there is a suspension bridge with iron chains of such antiquity that its origin
is lost in legends. 5. The introduction of electricity into the service of man
dates back barely one hundred years. 6. Raw cotton is easily spun into yarn.

1 *shakaitekí tokushitsú* social qualities 2 *iwareté imásŭ* it is stated

7. There are all sorts of ways of catching monkeys, for they are great thieves, and will go wherever food is to be got. **8.** Only two sevenths of the earth's surface consists of land. **9.** This old man always smells of tobacco. **10.** That poor woman died of sorrow for the loss of her only son. **11.** On Sundays you may enter the Museum free of charge. **12.** That man was born of a wealthy family, but he lost all his property in gambling. **13.** In the Pacific the greatest depths are off the north-east of Japan, off the Marianne Islands and east of Mindanao, one of the largest of the Philippine Islands. **14.** The strength and freshness of a man's spirit are largely conditioned by his outlook on life. **15.** The success of any government entirely depends on the character and ability of the rulers and the ruled. **16.** The shepherd who watches his flock upon the mountain would be helpless without his dog. **17.** Violent or excessive muscular exercise is a strain upon the heart. **18.** A rumour has spread through the city that a violent fire is raging in Hakodate. **19.** A captain in the navy is equivalent to a colonel in the army. **20.** It is to the sea and not to the land that the Norwegians look for a living. **21.** Success often comes to a man who sticks to one thing and does it well. **22.** The diver's dress enables a man to keep under water for five or six hours at a time. **23.** The pressure of water increases with the depth. **24.** As a general rule, it may be stated that intercourse with the people of Japan leaves Western people very favorably impressed with the social qualities of the inhabitants of the island empire.

Sixty-first Lesson 第六十一課

Conjunctions *Setsuzokushi* 接ッ続ッ詞シ

The Japanese translation of most of the English conjunctions has been given already in their usual applications. In this lesson, besides presenting them again in new applications, we shall treat those conjunctions still to be illustrated.

N. B. See index for the conjunctions not included in this lesson.

Also (see only)

The most usual translation of **also** is *mo*. (See Lesson 20, page 121)

Anáta no yūjin wa hōbi wo moraŭ[1] deshō soshĭté anáta mo.
貴方 の 友人 は ほおびを 貰う でしょうそして 貴方 も.
Your friend shall be rewarded, and you **also**.

This conjunction is made emphatic by the addition of the word *matá* 亦.

---

1 *hōbi wo moraŭ* to be rewarded, *hōbi* reward, *moraŭ* to receive

Watashí **mo matá** *mótte ımású.*   I **also** have it.
私　　も　　亦　持っています.

In formal speech **also** may be translated by *yahári* やはり.
Yahári, however, is used in ordinary conversation as well, especially
by men, and is altered into *yappári* やっぱり in familiar speech
by both men and women. **Yahári** is generally accompanied by **mo.**

   Yahári *anáta* **mo** *dekimású.* やはり貴方も出来ます.   You **also** can do it.

Also is, moreover, translated by the expressions **démo** でも, **sáe**
さえ, and **dátte** だって, all used in ordinary conversation.

Note that words preceding the expressions corresponding to *also*
reject the case-particle.

   Anáta **démo** *dekimású.*   貴方でも出来ます.   ⎫
   Anáta **sáe** *dekimású.*   貴方さえ出来ます.   ⎬You **also** can do it.
   Anáta **dátte** *dekimású.*   貴方だって出来ます.   ⎭

To render the conjunction **also** more emphatic, **dátte** may be used
concurrently with *yahári.*

   Wareware **dátte** *yahári* sō *désū.*   That is **also** the case with us.
   我々　だって　やはり　そうです.   (*lit.* Even with us also so is.)

As a synonym of *moreover*, **also** may be translated by **sonó ué**
その上 (=on top of that).

   Senséi wa bóku ni konó hon to **sonó ué** *mannenhitsú wo kudasaimáshīta.*
   先生　は　僕　にこの　本　とその　上　万年筆　を　下さいました.
   The teacher gave me this book and **also** a fountain pen.

Although
(See **though,** page 589, also Lesson 26 page 173
and Lesson 47, page 406)

As an adversative conjunction, **although** is translated by *ga* が.

   Yattó[1] tsŭkí wa agarimáshĭta[2] **ga** *hotóndo kúmo[3] ni kakusárete[4] imáshĭta.*
   やっと　月　は　上がりました　が　殆ど　雲　にかくされていました.
   At last the moon arose, **although** it was almost hidden by clouds.

And (See index)

When joining a series of nouns, pronouns, or numerals given as
a complete list, the conjunction **and** is translated by *to* と, repeated
after each word. (See Lessons 1, 3 and 8, page 48) After the last
word *to* may be omitted, but when used, it precedes the case-particle
or preposition.

---

1 at last   **2** *agarú* to rise   **3** cloud   **4** *kakúsu* to hide

Kinō depāto[1] *de kutsú issokú* **to** *bōshi* **to** *shátsu* (**to**) **wo** *kaimáshĭta.*
きのうデパートで　靴　一足　と　帽子　と　シャツ　(と)　を　買いました.
Yesterday, at a department store, I bought a pair of shoes, a hat, **and** some shirts.

Anáta **to** *watashí* (**to**) *wa íi tomodachí désŭ.*　You **and** I are good
貴方　と　私　(と)　は　いい　友達　です.　friends.

To is also used to join substantivized infinitives and gerunds, but not finite verbs, which are joined by the alternative form (Lesson 37, page 280), or by the subordinate (See Lesson 26).

Bansán[2] *no áto de o-kyakŭsamatachí wa* **nóndari odottári** *shi-hajime-*
晩餐　の　後　で　お客様達　は　飲んだり　踊ったり　し始め
máshĭta.　After dinner the guests began to drink **and** dance.
ました.　(*nómu* 飲む to drink, *odorú* 踊る to dance)

When the list of objects is not given as a complete one, *ya* や instead of *to* is used except after the last word. (See Lesson 10, page 58)

Dáno だの, which, as already stated (Lesson 10, page 58), may be used in place of *ya*, corresponds also to the expressions *etcetera, and the like, and so forth, and what not.*

Sokó ni wa bará **dáno** *tsúbaki*[3] **dáno** *yurí*[4] **dáno** *ga kírei ni saité*[5]
そこ　に　は　ばら　だの　椿　だの　百合　だの　がきれいに咲いて
ımáshĭta.　In that place, roses, camelias, lilies **and so forth** were blooming
いました.　beautifully.

Often in ordinary conversation the enumeration is followed up by **nádo** 等, which also means *and so forth*. Both words are used to make a statement more emphatic. In literary style, the Chinese character corresponding to **nádo** is generally pronounced **tō.**

Anó misé de wa hōki[6] *ya* (or **dáno**) *hatakí*[7] *ya* (or **dáno**) *haké*[8]
あの　店　で　はほおき　や　(だの)　はたき　や　(だの)　はけ
nádo *wo utté imásŭ.*　In that shop they sell brooms, dusters, brushes **and**
等　を　売っています.　**so forth.**

In some cases, **to** or **nádo** is used in sentences which, translated into English, have not the idea expressed by *and so forth*, as in the following example:

Aru hĭtóbito wa **seikō, kénryoku,**[9] **tómi,**[10] **gakŭshiki**[11] **tō** (*nádo*)
或　人々　は　成功,　権力,　富,　学識　等　(等)
wo amarí doryokú[12] *sézu ni*[13] *hikiyoséru*[14] *ka no kan ga*[15] *áru ni hikikáete*[16]
を　余り　努力　せず　に　引きよせる　か　の　観　が　あるに引きかえて

---

1 department store; in large cities a department store is generally called *depāto*
2 formal dinner taken in the evening　**3** camelia　**4** lily　**5** *sakú* to bloom　**6** broom
7 duster　**8** brush　**9** power　**10** wealth　**11** attainment　**12** effort　**13** *sézu ni*
without doing　**14** to attract　**15** *kan ga áru* to seem　**16** *ni hikikáete* while

ta no[1] *hĭtóbito ni wa soré wo wága monó ni surú*[2] *tamé ni zetsudái*
他 の 人々 に は それ を わが 物 に する ため に 絶大

na kónnan[3] *ga tomonáu.*   Some men seem to attract success, power, wealth,
な 困難 が 伴う.   attainments with very little effort, while others
conquer them with great difficulty.

(*lit.* Some people success, power, wealth, attainments and so forth, too much
efforts without doing attract, the fact seems, while to other people, those
things to make their own great difficulties go with.—*ka* か after *hikiyoséru*
corresponds to a question mark, and *no* の stands for *the fact*)

And may be translated by *shi* し, placed after adjectives or the
present, past and future of verbs. *Shi,* which is often in combination with *mo*......*mo*......, marks the translation from one to another
of two coordinated clauses.

Kyōto ni **mo** *ikimáshĭta* **shi** *Nára ni* **mo** *ikimáshĭta.*
京都 に も 行きました し 奈良 に も 行きました.
I went to Kyōto **and** Nara, too.

Sonó kimonó wa iró **mo** *yói* **shi** *gará* **mo** *yói désŭ.*
その 着物 は 色 も よい し 柄 も よい です.
The colour **and** design of that kimono are nice.

(*yói shi,* or *íi shi* may be contracted into *yóshi.*)

And is further translated by the expressions printed in heavy type
in the following representative examples:

Ato de íppai nomaséru[4] **kará** *yóku hatarakí nasái.*
あと で 一杯 飲ませる から よく 倔き なさい.
Work hard **and** I shall treat you to a drink afterwards.

Anná ni kanemochí de áru **nímo kakawarazú** *kojikí no yō-na*
あんな に 金持 で ある にも かかわらず 乞食 のような
seikatsú wo shĭté imásŭ.   So rich, **and** lives like a beggar.
生活 を して います. (*lit.* So rich is notwithstanding, poor like life does.)

Go-ryōshin **narabí** *ni minasama ni dōzo yoroshikú.*
御両親 並び に 皆様 にどうぞよろしく.
Please give my best regards to your parents **and** all.

Nihón san-kéi[5] *wa Matsushimá, Miyajimá* **oyobí**[6] *Ama-no-hashidaté de*
日本 三景 は 松島, 宮島 及び 天の橋立 で
arimásŭ.   The three famous beauty spots in Japan are Matsushima, Miyajima
あります.   **and** Ama-no-hashidate.

Soré wa Eigó de káite áru **shikámo** *hetá-na Eigó de.*[7]
それ は 英語 で書いてある 而も 下手な 英語 で.
It is written in English, **and** poor English at that.

---

1 *ta no* other (adj.) **2** *wága monó ni surú* to make something one's own, to
conquer **3** *zetsudái-na* great, *kónnan* difficulty **4** to offer a drink **5** *kéi* scenery,
scene **6** *oyobí* lit. expression **7** *Káite áru* after *de* is here omitted for not repeating
the same verb. In similar sentences omissions of this kind are grammatically correct.

Anó hǐtó wa anó tokí sō omói **shikáshǐte**[1] *íma mo sō omótte imásǔ.*

あの　人　は あの　時　そう思い　　而して　　今　も そう思っています.

He thought so then, **and** thinks so now.

Iku máiru **mo** *íku máiru* **mo** *sabakú wo arukimáshǐta.*

幾　　哩　も　幾　　哩　も　沙漠　を　歩きました.

We walked miles **and** miles through the desert.

Hiratá Shi wa shibáraku[2] *no aidá sōridaijin*[3] **ken** *gaimudaijín*[4] *déshǐta.*

平田　氏　は　暫く　の　間　総理大臣　兼　外務大臣　でした.

For sometime Mr. Hirata was the Premier **and** Minister of Foreign Affairs.

Sonó hon wa omoshíroku **kátsu** *kyōkunteki*[5] *de arimásǔ.*

その　本　は　面白く　且つ　教訓的　で あります.

That book is interesting **and** instructive. (*lit.* That book interestingly, besides, instructive is.—*kátsu* is an expression of the literary style corresponding to besides, moreover, furthermore, etc.)

Two or more adjectives qualifying a noun may be used in their original form or may be used in the subordinate except the last one that remains unaltered.

ōkii tsuyói inú　　大きい強い犬
ōkikute tsuyói inú　大きくて強い犬 } a large **and** strong dog

Samǔi kurái ban déshǐta.　　寒い暗い晩でした. } It was a cold **and**
Sámukute kurái ban déshǐta. 寒くて暗い晩でした. } dark night.

When a noun is qualified by both true adjectives and quasi-adjectives, the subordinate is not used.

kírei-na chiisái inú　きれいな小さい犬　　a pretty **and** small dog

As

See Lesson 39, page 301 for the use of **as** in its comparative applications.

When this conjunction indicates the way or manner, it may be translated by the word **tōri** 通り instead of the expression **yō-ni** ように.

Náze watashí ga ittá **tōri** *ni* (or **yō-ni**) *shimasén ka.*

なぜ　私　が 云った通り に　　（ように）しません か.

Why don't you do **as** I told you?

Note that the particle *ni* may follow **tōri,** as in the above example, or be omitted; however, when *désǔ* or *déshǐta* follows **tōri** the particle *ni* is invariably omitted.

Máe ni mōshǐta **tōri** *désǔ.*　　　　　It is just **as** I said before.

前　に　申した　通り です.

Ossháru **tōri** *désǔ.* おっしゃる通りです.　It is **as** you say.

Tōri is also used to translate the expression **according to.**

---

1 *shikáshǐte* may be replaced by *soshǐté* (See *soshǐte* Lesson 3, page 31 and **Lesson 8,** page 48)　**2** for sometime　**3** Premier　**4** Foreign minister　**5** instructive

chŭmon[1] *no* **tōri** or *chŭmon-dōri*   according to order
注文　　の　　通り,　　　注文通り

yakŭsokú no **tōri** or *yakŭsokú-dōri*   according to promise
約束　　の　通り,　　　　約束通り

Go-chūmon no **tōri** *shinamonó wo o-okurí shimáshĭta.*
御注文　　の　　通り　　品物　　を　お送り　しました.
We sent the goods to you **according to** your order.

In commercial letter-style the above sentence should be written:

Go-chūmon **ni** *ōji shinamonó wo o-okurí mōshimáshĭta.*
御注文　　に　応じ　品物　　を　お送り　申しました.

Tōri is used in various common expressions, a few of which are the following:

ítsumo no **tōri**	いつもの通り	the same **as** usual (**as** always)
mígi[2] *no* **tōri**	右の通り	**as** stated above (**as** on the right)
sa[2] *no* **tōri**	左の通り	**as** stated below (**as** on the left)

As is translated by **gótoku** 如く in formal style.

heizéi[3] *no* **gótoku**	平生の如く	**as** usual
jōki[4] *no* **gótoku**	上記の如く	**as** stated above
ōse[5] *no* **gótoku**	仰せの如く	**as** you say

As is further translated by the expression in heavy type in the following typical examples:

Anáta no go-seikō wa issō[6] *go-rippá-na*[7] *monó désŭ* **názenaraba** *séken*
貴方　の　御成功　は　一層　御立派な　もの　です　なぜならば　世間
de wa anáta ga **shippaí** *nasáru*[8] *to omótte imáshĭta* **kará.**
で　は　貴方　が　失敗　なさる　と　思って　いました　から.
Your success is the more creditable **as** people thought you would fail.
(your success the more fine thing is because people you fail so they thought.)

Mújaki[9] **sō** *ni míete mo anó onná wo shínjite*[10] *wa ikemasén.*
無邪気　そうに　見えて　も　あの　女　を　信じて　は　いけません.
Don't trust that woman, innocent **as** she looks.

Tokéi ga **chōdo** *jū-ji wo útta*[11] **toki ni** *resshá wa tōchaku shimáshĭta.*
時計　が　丁度　十時　を　打った　時　に　列車　は　到着　しました.
The train arrived **as** the clock struck ten.

As if

The expression **as if** is translated by **yō-ni** ように when placed before a verb, by **yō-na** ような when before a noun, and by **yō** before *désŭ* or *déshĭta.*

---

1 order (of goods)   **2** When referring to letters, what is *above* for us, is *on the right* for Japanese, and what is *below* is *on the left; migi* right, *sa* left. **3** usually, always **4** above stated **5** command, order, what one says **6** the more **7** *rippá-na* fine, creditable **8** *séken* people, the world: *shippái nasáru=shippái surú* to fail **9** innocent **10** *shinjíru* to trust **11** *útsu* to strike

When emphasis is to be expressed, the expression *chōdo* 丁度 or *marú-de* まるで may be correlated with *yō-ni, yō-na,* or *yō.*

Konó mozō-shinjú[1] no kubikazarí[2] wa hommonó[3] no yō-ni miemásŭ.
この　模造真珠　の　くび飾　は　本物　の　ように見えます.
This imitation pearl necklace looks **as if** it were genuine.

Anó hĭtó wa nan de mo shĭtté irú yō-na kotó wo iimásŭ.
あの　人　は　何んで　も　知っているような　事　を云います.
He speaks **as if** he knew everything.

Nambú San wa o-rúsu no yō désŭ.　　It looks **as if** Miss Nambu were
南部　さん　は　お留守　の　よう　です.　　not at home.

Anó hĭtó wa marú-de jibún de míte kitá yō-na kotó wo iimásŭ.
あの　人　は　まるで　自分　で　見て　来た　ような　事　を云います.
He talks **as if** he had been there and had seen it himself.
(That person really himself having seen came like the things says.)

Anáta no go-shújin wa marú-de (chōdo) kyōjin[4] no yō déshĭta.
貴方　の　御主人　は　まるで　（丁度）　狂人　のようでした.

Anáta no go-shújin wa kyōjin no yō déshĭta.
貴方　の　御主人　は　狂人　のよう　でした.
Your master looked **as if** he were mad.

As long as or So long as *aidá wa*

Isshó ni irú aidá wa kówaku[5] arimasén.　　We have nothing to fear, **so**
一緒　に　いる　間　は　怖く　ありません.　　**long as** we stay together.
(Together we are as long as fear there is not.)

Watashí no íkite irú aidá wa anáta no tomodachí désŭ.
私　の生きている　間　は　貴方　の　友達　です.
You shall have a friend in me **as long as** I live.

As soon as

As soon as is translated by *shídai* 次第, *ya-ínaya* や否や, *to súgu-ni* とすぐに (page 587), and by the subjunctive (page 418). *Ya-ínaya* indicates almost simultaneous actions, while when using *shídai* or the subjunctive, a short delay may intervene between the two occurrences.

Hayashí San ga kitára súgu ni dekakemashō.　　We shall leave **as soon**
林　さんが　来たら　すぐ　に出かけましょう.　　**as** Mr. Hayashi comes.

Takú ga kaerí shídai o-ukagaí shimásŭ.　　I shall visit you **as soon as**
宅　が　帰り　次第　お伺い　します.　　my husband comes back.

Dempō wo uketorú ya-ínaya éki e ikimáshĭta.
電報　を　受取る　や否や　駅　へ行きました.
I went to the station as soon as I received your telegram.

---

1 *mozō* imitation, *shinjú* pearl **2** *kubikazarí* necklace **3** genuine article **4** mad person **5** *kowái* fearful

Note that *shídai* is placed after the simple stem of verbs of Class I and the *i*-stem of verbs of Class II.

Because

Besides being translated by *kará, nóde,* or *názenaraba* (See Lesson 17, page 97), *because of* or *on account of* is translated by *no tamé ni* のために in ordinary speech, and by *yué wo mótte* 故を以って in formal speech.

Ōyama   kyōju   wa   rōnen[1]   no   yué   wo   mótte   taishokú[2]   shimáshĭta.
大山　　教授　は　老年　の　故　を　以って　　退転　　しました.
Professor Ōyama retired because of his old age.

Kinō   áme   no   tamé   ni   ensokú   ni   ikaremasén   déshĭta.
きのう　雨　の　ため　に　　遠足　に行かれませんでした.
Yesterday I could not go out on the picnic **because** of the rain.
(*ensokú ni ikú* to go out on a picnic, *ikarerú* to be able to go)

In familiar speech, **because of,** *owing to* etc., may be translated by *séi* せい, as in the following examples:

Warúi   ténki   no   séi   de   káre   no   ryōmachi   ga   okorimáshĭta.
悪い　　天気　の　せいで　　彼　　のリョウマチが　おこりました.
Because of the bad weather he had an attack of rheumatism.
(*ryōmachi* rheumatism, *ryōmachi ga okóru* to have an attack of rheumatism)

Anó   katá   ga   ibyō   de   kurushímu   no   wa   amarí   tabéru   séi   désŭ.
あの　方　が　胃病　で　　苦しむ　　の　は　あまり　食べる せい です.
He suffers from stomach trouble **because** he eats too much.
(*ibyō* stomach trouble, *kurushímu* to suffer from)

Before

Before is translated by *máe, máe ni, ízen ni* and *nái uchí ni.* See pages 95 and 349.

Hi ga dénai uchí ni shuppatsú[3] shimáshĭta.   We left **before** the sun
日　が 出ない うち に　　出発　　しました.   rose.

Takŭsán arukánai uchí ni tsŭkaremáshĭta.[4]   I had not walked far **before**
沢山　 歩かない うち に　 疲れました.   I began to feel tired.
(Much before I didn't walk I got tired.)

In some cases *before* is not translated.

Súgu ni machigái wo mitsŭkemáshĭta.   It was not long **before** I found
すぐ に　間違い　を　見つけました.   my mistake.
(Soon the mistake I found.)

---

1 old age **2** *taishokú surú* to retire from public service **3** *shuppatsú surú* to leave
4 *tsukaréru* to get tired

Besides

Besides being translated by *hoká ni,* as shown on page 352, this conjunction may be translated by *soré-ni,* and *o-maké ni.*

Senshū éiga e ikimasén déshĭta názenaraba senshū no pŭroguramú wo
先週　映画　へ行きませんでした　なぜならば　先週　の　プログラム　を

sŭkimasén déshĭta, soré-ni himá mo arimasén déshĭta kará.
好きません でした，それに　暇　もありません でした から.

Last week I did not go to the cinema because I did not like the program; **besides** I had no time to go.

Anó hĭtó wa udé¹ mo áru shi o-maké ni kané mo arimásŭ.
あの　人　は　腕　も　あるし　おまけ　に　金　も　あります.

He has good abilities, and plenty of money **besides.**

(That person ability also has, besides money also has.)

Both......and

These correlative conjunctions are translated by *mo......mo,* by *shi,* which is generally accompanied by *mo,* and by *kátsu.*

Mohidīn San wa binwanká² de kátsu seiryokŭká³ désŭ.
モヒディーンさんは　敏腕家　で　且つ　精力家　です.

Miss Mohideen is **both** capable **and** energetic.

Horií San wa doitsú-go mo eigó mo wakarimásŭ.
堀井 さん は ドイツ語 も 英語 も 解ります.

Mr. Horii knows **both** German **and** English.

Watashí no uchí ni wa néko mo irú shi inú mo imásŭ.
私　のうちには　猫　もいるし犬　も　います.

In my house I have **both** cat **and** dog.

When **both** is synonymous of *both the two,* it may be translated, in colloquial speech, by *fŭtarí tomó* 二人とも when referring to people and by *fŭtatsú tomó* 二つとも when referring to things. In literary style, *nágara* ながら is used instead of *tomó.*

Sonó fujintachí wa fŭtarí tomó (nágara) akaí bōshi wo kabútte imáshĭta.
その　婦人達　は　二人　とも（ながら）赤い　帽子 をかぶっていました.

Both ladies wore red hats. (*kabúru* かぶる to wear, to put on)

Mádo wa fŭtatsú tomó (nágara) shimátte imásŭ.　　**Both** windows are
窓　は　二つ　とも（ながら）しまって います.　　closed.

When **both** is used only for emphasis, it may be omitted in the translation, as in the following examples:

Konó kirejí wa yókute yasúi désŭ.　　This cloth is (**both**) good **and** cheap.
この 切れ地 は よくて 安い です.　　(*lit.* This cloth good cheap is.)

---

1 *udé* arm; *udé ga áru* to have ability　**2** a capable person, a go-getter　**3** *séiryoku* energy; *seiryokŭká* energetic person

Ani to imōto wa (*fŭtarí tomó*) *Nambéi ni imásŭ.*

兄 と 妹 は （二人 とも） 南米 に います.

(**Both**) my elder brother **and** my younger sister are in South America.

But

It has already been stated that as an adversative conjunction, **but** is translated by *ga, kéredomo, shikáshi,* or *shikáshi nágara.* See Lesson 14, page 77. This conjunction is also translated in other ways, as shown in the following examples:

Hĭtótsu kirí (or *shĭká*) *mótte imasén.*   I have **but** one.

一つ きり （しか） 持っていません.   (One except I have not.)

Anó hĭtó wa máda hon-no kodomó désŭ.   He is nothing **but** a child.

あの 人 は まだ ほんの 子供 です. (That person still mere child is.)

Konó kodomó wa naité bákari imásŭ.   This child does nothing **but** cry.

この 子供 は 泣いて ばかり います.   (This child crying only is.)

Anáta no hoká ni tayóru[1] hĭtó ga arimasén.   I have no one **but** you

貴方 の 外 に 頼る 人 がありません.   to turn to for help.

     (*lit.* You except to rely upon person I have not.)

Hoká no kotó náraba tónikaku[2] koré dáke wa iyá désŭ.

外 の 事 ならば とにかく これ だけ は いや です.

I will do anything **but** this.

     (Another thing if it is, at all events this only I don't like.)

Sō surú hoká ni shikatá[3] ga arimasén déshĭta.   There was nothing for

そうする 外 に 仕方 がありませんでした.   it **but** to do so.

     (*lit.* So to do that except, way there was not.)

Taichō no meiréi[4] ni shitagáwazu[5] ni wa iraremasén déshĭta.

隊長 の 命令 に 従わず に はいられません でした.

We couldn't **but** obey our captain's orders. (To our captain's orders without obeying we could not.—*irarerú* potential form of *irú*, to be able to.)

Anó hĭtó wa namáke sáe[6] shinákereba íi hĭtó désŭ.

あの 人 は なまけ さえ しなければ いい 人 です.

But for his idleness he would be a good man.

     (*lit.* That person idle provided he were not, good person is.)

Wágako[7] ni hĭtó-me[8] ái sáe suréba watashí wa anshín[9] shimásŭ.

わが子 に 一目 会いさえ すれば 私 は 安心 します.

If I could **but** see my child my mind would be at ease.

     [(To) my child once provided I meet my mind feels at ease.]

Anó hĭtó ga watashí no iú kotó wo kiité sáe kurerú náraba

あの 人 が 私 の 云う 事 を 聞いてさえ くれる ならば

---

1 *tayóru* to rely upon; *tayóru hĭtó* a person to rely upon   **2** at all events   **3** way **4** order   **5** *shitagáu* to obey   **6** *sáe* followed by the subjunctive means *provided, if only, if......but*   **7** my child   **8** *hĭtó-me* one glance＝once   **9** *anshín surú* to be at ease

watashí no keppakú[1] *wo wakátte kurerú deshō.*
私 の 潔白 を 解って くれるでしょう.

If he would **but** listen to me he would be convinced of my innocence.

    (*lit.* That person my said thing if he listens, my innocence would understand.)

But is translated by ***nágara*** in the following idiomatic expressions:

Go-kurō nágara......   I am sorry to trouble you, **but**...... (*lit.* Your trouble,
御苦労 ながら......   **but**=I know it is troublesome for you, **but**......)

Go-mendō nágara......   御面倒ながら......

    (*lit.* Your nuisance, annoyance, **but**=I know it is annoying for you, **but**......)

O-ki-no-dokú nágara......   I am very sorry for you, **but**......
御気の毒 ながら......

    (*ki* mind, *dokú* poison; *ki+no+dokú=ki-no-dokú,*=poison for your mind;
    *o-ki-no-dokú nágara......*I know it is like poison for your mind, but......)

Shitsúrei nágara......   Pardon me, **but**......

    (Impolite, **but**=I know it is impolite, **but**......)

Zannén nágara......   残念ながら......   I regret **but**......)

Zannén nágara *kómban ukagaú*[2] *kotó ga dekimasén.*
残念 ながら 今晩 伺う 事 が 出来ません.
I am sorry, **but** I cannot come to-night.

Go-mendō *nágara konó hagakí*[3] *wo dáshĭte*[4] *kudasái.*
御面どう ながら この はがき を 出して 下さい.
I am sorry to trouble you, **but** will you please mail this post-card?

O-ki-no-dokú-samá nágara *go-irái*[5] *ni wa ōji-kanemásŭ.*[6]
御気の毒さま ながら 御依頼 に は 応じかねます.
I am sorry, **but** I cannot oblige you.

    (*lit.* I am very sorry for you, **but** to your request I cannot accept.)

In epistolary style, whether for private or commercial correspondence, the idea expressed in the last example was generally written as follows:

*Zannén nágara go-irái ni wa ōji-kane*sōro.* 残念ながら御依頼には応じかね候.

Note that ***sōro,*** as used in the last example, instead of the suffix ***másŭ,*** was common in epistolary style until the end of World War II, especially in official or commercial correspondence, but its usage is now considered obsolete.

Having now made the above remark on epistolary style, it will not be out of place to give here the almost general form of the introduction, beginning of the body, and salutation of Japanese letters.

Haikéi, kiká masú-masú go-han-éi no dan gáshi-tatematsurimásŭ.
拝啓, 貴下 益々 御繁栄 の 段 賀し奉ります.

    Dear Sir, I respectfully offer you my congratulation on your being in great prosperity. (*lit.* Dear Sir, you very much in prosperity I congratulate you.)

---

1 innocence   **2** to visit   **3** post-card   **4** *dásu* to mail, to post   **5** *irái* request
6 *ōji-kanéru* not to be able to accept

haikéi Dear Sir, [My] Dear Mr.......Dear Madam, Gentleman; *kiká* you; *masú-masú* more and more; *go-han-éi* prosperity; *dan* in; *han-éi no dan* in prosperity; *gasúru* to congratulate; *tatematsúru* to present, to offer; *gáshi-tatematsúru* to offer congratulation

It is understood that the idea of prosperity is expressed in the above introduction only for formality's sake.

The Complimentary Close

Sō-Sō tónshu   匆々頓首   Yours truly
   (*sō-sō* in haste; *tónshu* I bow to you)

Sō-Sō kéigu   匆々敬具   Yours respectfully
   (*kéigu* I respectfully finished)

Keihakú   敬白   Yours respectfully, Yours sincerely
   (*keihakú* I have said respectfully)

Tónshu saí-haí   頓首再拝   I am, Sir, your obedient servant
   (*tónshu* to bow, *saí* twice, *haí* to bow) *or* Yours very respectfully

Note that all the words in the above four expressions of salutation are used only in the epistolary language.

Either (See also Lesson 38, page 291)

Used before a noun, **either** may be translated by *dóchira no* ど ちらの in positive sentences and by *dóchira-ka no* どちらかの in interrogative sentences.

Anáta wa **dóchira no** *hakó wo tótte mo yoroshíi désŭ.* You may take
あなた は　どちら　の　箱　をとっても よろしい です. **either** box.

Dóchira no *hon mo sŭkimasén.* I don't like **either** book.
どちら　の　本　も　好きません.

Dóchira-ka no *e wo kudasaimásŭ ka.* Will you give me **either**
どちらか　の　絵を　下さいます　か.   picture?

Káre wa **dóchira no** *tō e mo tōhyō wo hikaemáshĭta.*
彼　は　どちら　の　党へ　も　投票　を ひかえました.
  He abstained from voting for **either** party. (*tōhyō* vote, *hikaéru* hold back)

dóchira no *baaí ni mo* どちらの場合にも in **either** case

Dóchira *de mo yoroshíi désŭ.* どちらでもよろしいです. **Either** will do.

As a synonym of *each of two*, **either** may be translated by *ryōhō no* 両方の.

Mon no **ryōhō no** *kawá ni tátte irú ishidōró.*
門　の　両方　の　側　に立っている石どうろう. (*mon* gate, *ishidōró*
  The stone lanterns standing on **either** side of the gate. stone lantern)

The expression **not either** may be translated by *mo* も followed by a negative verb.

Káre ga ikanái nará watashí **mo** *ikimasén.* If he does not go, I shall
彼　が行かないなら　私　も　行きません. not go **either**.

Either......or

These correlative conjunction are translated by *ka......ka* か......か, *ka arúiwa......ka* か或は......か, as already shown in Lesson 38, page 292, or by *mo......mo.*

Dóchira no bōshi ga watashí ni niáu to omoimásŭ ka.
どちら の 帽子 が 私 に 似合うと 思います か.
Which hat do you think will suit me?

Kurói no mo nezumí-iró no mo anáta ni yóku niaimásŭ.
黒い の も 鼠色 の も 貴方 に よく似合います.
I think that **either** the black one **or** the grey one will suit you well.

Else

In ordinary conversation, **else** or **or else** is translated by *de nákereba* でなければ or *sámo-nákereba* さもなければ, and by *sámo-nákuba* さもなくば in formal speech.

Anó katá wa shin no kanashimí[1] wo mótte irú ni chigái arimasén
あの 方 は 真 の 悲しみ を 持って いる にちがいありません
sámo-nákereba anná ni wa nakanái deshō. (*nakú* to weep)
さもなければ あんなに は 泣かないでしょう.
She must have some real sorrow; **else** she would not weep as she does.

Káre wa fuzákete[2] irú ni chigainái de nákereba kichigái[3] désŭ.
彼 は ふざけて いる に 違いない で なければ 気違い です.
He must be joking, or **else** he is mad.

Even

In Lesson 26, page 173, it has been stated that **even if** may be translated by the subordinate followed by *mo.* In ordinary conversation, this conjunctional expression is furthermore translated by *tatoé* たとえ, *démo* でも, or *tómo* とも. *Tatoé* is generally used concurrently with *démo* or *tómo*; *démo* may be used after nouns or true adjectives, while *tómo* is used after the simple present of verbs or the adverbial form of true adjectives.

Tatoé anáta ga sŭkánai démo shikatá ga arimasén. (*sŭkánai* not
たとえ 貴方 が 好かない でも 仕方 がありません. to like)

Tatoé anáta ga sŭkánaku tómo shikatá ga arimasén.
たとえ 貴方 が 好かなく とも 仕方 がありません.
I can't help it **even** if you do not like it.

Tákaku tómo kaimásŭ. **Even** dear I will buy it.
高く とも 買います. (*takái* dear)

Ame démo ikimásŭ. 雨でも行きます. } I will go **even** if it
Ame ga fúru tómo ikimásŭ. 雨が降るとも行きます. } rains.

1 *shin no* real; *kanashimí* sorrow **2** *fuzákéru* to joke, *fuzákete irú* to be joking **3** mad, crazy

In formal speech **even if** may be translated by **yóshi** よし, **yoshiyá** よしや, or **yoshímba** よしんば. Men, however, may use these words in ordinary conversation as well.

Note that these three expressions are generally used concurrently with **tómo,** while **démo** is preferably used with **tatoé.**

Yoshiyá *zen-káiin*[1] *ga sorowánaku*[2] **tómo** *shō*[3] *kúji ni kaikái*[4] *shimásŭ.*
よしや　全会員　が　そろわなく　とも　正　九時　に　開会　します.
The meeting will start at 9 o'clock sharp, **even if** all the members are not here.

Idiomatic and emphatic :

even then	*sonó toki de sáe* (or **démo**)	その時でさえ（でも）
even now	*íma de sáe* (or **démo**)	今でさえ（でも）
even so	*sō to shĭté* **mo**	そうとしても
even to the end	*owarí máde* **mo**	終りまでも

Káre wa jíjitsu **sáe** *mo hitéi shĭtá.*   He denied **even** the facts.
彼　は　事実　さえ　も　否定　した.   (*hitéi surú* to deny)

Sō to shĭté **mo** *anó hĭtó wo shinjimasén.*   **Even** so I don't trust him.
そうと　して　も　あの　人　を　信じません.

For (See pages 103 and 213)

As a conjunction, **for** is translated by **kará** から, the same as *because.*

Seiukéi[5] *ga sagátte*[6] *imásŭ* **kará** *áme deshō.*   It will rain, **for** the baro-
晴雨計　が　下がっています　から　雨　でしょう.   meter is falling.

Anó hĭtó wa kowagátte[7] *imásŭ* **kará** *bōken*[8] *wa shinái deshō.*
あの　人　は　こわがって　います　から　冒険　は　しないでしょう.
He will not venture, **for** he is afraid.

Just as

Just as is translated by **totán (ni)** とたん（に）, **chŏdo......no toki** 丁度......の時, or by **tokoró e** ところへ. When referring to a past event, the verb preceding *totán ni* or *tokoró* may be used either in the simple present or in the past. In ordinary conversation, the short form of the past is used with any of the three expressions, while the past with the suffix *máshĭta* is generally used in formal speech.

Watashí ga háiru (or *háitta*) **totán** *ni anó hĭtó wa déte ikimáshĭta.*
私　が　入る　（入った）とたん　に　あの　人　は　出て行きました.
He went out **just as** I entered.

---

1 *zen* all, whole ; *kaíin* members   **2** *soróu* to complete, *sorowánaku* without being complete   **3** sharp   **4** *kaikái surú* to open a meeting   **5** barometer   **6** *sagáru* to fall, go down   **7** *kowagáru* to be afraid   **8** *bōken* venture ; *bōken wo surú* to venture ; *wa* may be used instead of *wo* in emphatic statements

Dekakeyō to surú (or *shǐtá*) ***tokoró*** *e dempō ga kimáshǐta.*
出かけようと する （した） ところ へ 電報 が 来ました.
Just as I was going out a telegram came.

*Resshá ga **chōdo** ugokí-kaketá[1] **toki** ni éki e tōchaku shimáshǐta.*
列車 が 丁度 動きかけた 時 に 駅 へ 到着 しました.
We arrived at the station **just as** the train began to move.

Neither......nor, Neither

The alternative conjunctions **neither......nor** are translated by ***mo***
......***mo*** も......も, placed after the words indicating the things taken
into consideration, followed by a negative verb.

*Watashí wa kánojo no na **mo** toshí **mo** shirimasén.* (*na* name, *toshí*
私 は 彼女 の 名 も 年 も 知りません. age)
I know **neither** her name **nor** her age.

*Káre wa kané **mo** nákereba atamá **mo** nái.* He has no money
彼 は 金 も なければ 頭 も ない. **nor** brain **neither.**

*Anáta **mo** watashí **mo** sonó hǐtó ni átta kotó ga nái.*
貴方 も 私 も その 人 に会った 事 が ない.
Neither you **nor** I have met that man.

When **neither** is used without the correlative *nor*, and with the
understood meaning of *neither the one nor the other*, it is generally
translated by ***dóchira no*** どちらの.

***Dóchira no** hanashí mo hontō de wa arimasén.* **Neither** story is true.
どちら の 話 も 本当 で はありません.

***Dóchira no** baai démo watashí wa sanséi shimasén.* In **neither** case
どちら の 場合 でも 私 は 賛成 しません. can I agree.

The expression **neither of them** is translated by ***dóchira mo*** どちらも.

*Kárera no **dóchira mo** watashí wo mi-oboeté imasén déshǐta.*
彼等 の どちら も 私 を 見覚えていません でした.
Neither of them recognized me. (*mi-oboerú* to call to mind, etc.)

When **neither** is followed by an auxiliary that takes the place of a verb
used in a preceding clause, it is translated by ***mo***.

*Anáta no otōsan ga irassharánai náraba watashi **mo** mairımasen.*
貴方 のお父さんがいらっしゃらないならば 私 も まいりません.
If your father does not go, **neither** shall I.

Nevertheless

This conjunction may be translated by ***nímo kakawarazú*** にも
かかわらず, ***ga*** が, ***shikáshi*** 併し, or ***shikáshi nágara*** 併しな
がら. ***Ga*** and ***nímo kakawarazú*** are the most colloquial of
the four expressions.

---

1 *ugokí-kakerú* to begin to move

Anó e ni wa íkuraka kettén[1] *ga arimásŭ* **shikáshi nágara** (or
あの 絵 に は 幾らか 欠点 が あります 併し ながら (
shikáshi, ga) *aré wa konó tenrankái ni shuppín*[2] *saretá uchí de ichibán*
併し, が）あれ は この 展覧会 に 出品 された うち で 一番
íi désŭ.   That painting has some imperfections; **nevertheless** it is the best ever
いいです.   shown in this exhibition.

Tabakó wa kenkō ni gái ga áru to iú kotó wo dáre de mo shĭtté
たばこ は 健康 に 害 が あるという事 を だれ で も 知って
irú **nímo kakawarazŭ́** *námbyaku-man to iú hĭtó ga tabakó wo sutté*
いる にも かかわらず 何百万 という人 が たばこ をすって
imásŭ.   Everybody knows that tobacco is harmful to health, **nevertheless** millions
います.   of people smoke it. (*kenkō ni* to health, *gái* injury, harm, *to iú kotó*
            wo the fact, *dáre de mo* everybody, *shĭtté irú* know, *námbyaku-man*
            millions, *námbyaku* hundreds, *man* ten thousand, *to iú* emphatic expres-
            sion, *hĭtó* people, *suú* to breathe in, to inhale, *tabakó wo suú* to smoke)

In colloquial speech, **nevertheless** is generally translated by *démo*
でも.

Anó shigotó wo kirái **démo** (*nímo kakawarazú*) *shinákereba naránai no désŭ.*
あの 仕事 をきらい でも （にも かかわらず）しなければならないのです.
I dislike that work, **nevertheless** I have to do it.

Notwithstanding

As a conjunction, **notwithstanding** is translated by *nímo kakawarazú* にもかかわらず.

Anná ni kanemochí **nímo kakawarazú** *anó hĭtó wa kōfuku de wa*
あんなに 金持 にも かかわらず あの 人 は 幸福 で は
arimasén.   He is not happy, **notwithstanding** that he is so rich.
ありません.

As an adverb, used as a synonym of *nevertheless*, **notwithstanding** is omitted
in the Japanese translation, as in the following example:

Nan to osshátte mo watashí wa soré wo shimásŭ.
何ん とおっしゃっても 私 は それ を します.
Whatever you may say I will do it, **notwithstanding.**
(*nan to osshátte mo* whatever you may say)

Often

In the sense of *frequently*, this expression is generally translated
by *tabítabi* 度々 or *shibashiba* 屢々 as said in Lesson 15.
However, when emphasis is to be expressed, that is, when **often** is
used in the sense of *very frequently*, it may be translated by *nan-
do démo* 何度でも or *íku-do démo* 幾度でも. The same translations correspond also to **as often as**; however, when the same expression is used in the sense of *every time*, it is generally translated
by *tabí ni* 度に, pronounced *tambí ni* たんびに in emphatic colloquial speech.

---

1 imperfection   **2** *shuppín surú* to show at an exhibition, to exhibit

*Anó jimúsho e ikú **tabí ni** ítsumo anó rōjin wo mimásŭ.*
あの 事務所 へ行く 度 に いつも あの 老人 を 見ます.
I invariably see that old man **as often as** (*or* every time) I go to that office.

*Anáta no o-sŭkí na daké **tabítabi** (**íku-do démo**) uchí e irassái.*
貴方 の お好き な だけ 度々 (幾度 でも)うちへいらっしゃい.
You may come to my house **as often as** you wish.

Only (See Adverbs, Lesson 57, page 519)

The expression *not only......but also* is generally translated by *......**bákari de náku......mo** ばかりでなく......も. **Matá** また* may follow *mo* も when emphasis is to be expressed.

*Taiyō wa warewaré ni hikarí **bákari de náku** netsú **mo** ataemásŭ.*
太陽 は 我々 に 光り ばかり で なく 熱 も 与えます.
Not only does the sun give us light, **but** it gives us also heat.
(*taiyō* the sun; *hikarí* light; *netsú* heat; *ataerú* to give)

*Anó kanemochí no rōjin wa kojíin e kané **bákari de náku** káre no*
あの 金持 の 老人 は 孤児院へ 金 ばかり で なく 彼 の
*bessō **mo matá** ataemáshĭta.*   That rich old man **not only** gave his money
別荘 も また 与えました.   to the orphanage **but** gave **also** his villa.

*Soré ni tsúite kiitá **bákari de náku** watashí **mo** mimáshĭta.*
それ に ついて聞いた ばかり で なく 私 も 見ました.
I **not only** heard about it, **but** I **also** saw it. (*kiitá* past of *kikú* to hear)

In some cases *matá* may follow immediately *bákari de náku*, as in the following example:

*Anó kōen[1] wa kyōmi[2] ga nái **bákari de náku matá** nagá-sugimáshĭta.[3]*
あの 講演 は 興味 がない ばかり で なく また 長すぎました.
The lecture was **not only** devoid of interest, **but also** too long.

Or

Besides being translated by *to* and *soretómo* (See Lesson 18, page 102), this conjunction is translated by *ka* か, *arúiwa* 或は, and *matá-wa* 又は.

*Konó heyá wa hachí-jō **ka** jū-jō désŭ.*   This room has eight **or** ten
この 部屋 は 八畳 か 十畳 です.   mats.[4]

*Fŭtatsú **arúiwa** mittsú de jūbun désŭ.*   Two **or** three will be enough.
二つ 或は 三つ で 充分 です.

*Ushí **arúiwa** umá nádo ga nákatta to shĭta náraba, nōsaku[5] ni taihén*
牛 或は 馬 等 がなかった と した ならば, 農作 に 大変
fúben déshĭta deshō.   If there had not been horses **or** oxen, farming would
不便 でしたでしよう.   have been greatly handicapped.

*Kyō no gógo **matá-wa** myōnichi no gozén ni ikimásŭ.*
きょうの 午後 又は 明日 の 午前 に 行きます.
I shall go there this afternoon **or** to-morrow morning.

---

1 lecture 2 *kyōmi ga áru* interesting, to be interesting; *kyōmi ga nái* uninteresting, without interest 3 *nagá-sugirú* to be too long 4 The size of a Japanese room is calculated by the number of standard sized mats (each about 3 by 6 feet) its floor is composed of. 5 farming (subst.)

Matá-wa is used also like the English **or,** at the beginning of a sentence that ends in a question or in an expression of doubt.

Otogí-bánashı wo shimashō ka. Matá-wa watashí no Afŭriká ryokōdan[1]
おとぎ話　をしましょうか。　又は　　私　のアフリカ　旅行談
wo shimashō ka.　　　Shall I tell you a fairy tale? **Or** shall I tell you of my
をしましょうか.　　　　travels in Africa?

In formal speech, **or** is translated by *móshikuwa* 若しくは.

Fŭtatsú móshikuwa mittsú de jūbun désŭ.　Two **or** three will be
二つ　　若しくは　　三つ　で　充分　です.　　enough.

When **or** is used with the meaning of *otherwise*, it is translated by *sámo-nái-to* さもないと.

Yóku benkyō shi-nasái, sámo-nái-to rakudái shimásŭ yo.
よく　勉強　しなさい，　さもないと　落第　します　よ.
Study hard, **or** you will fail in the examination.

Otherwise

When corresponding in meaning to *under other conditions* or *in different circumstance*, **otherwise** may be translated by *de nái to* でないと, *de nákereba* でなければ, or by *sámo-nái-to* さもないと.

Ki wo tsŭké nasái, de nái to (de nákereba or sámo-nái-to)
気　を　つけなさい，で　ない　と　（で　なければ，　　さもない　と）
méiwaku ga kakarimásŭ yo.　Be careful, **otherwise** you will get into trouble.
迷惑　が　かかります　よ.　　（*ki wo tsŭkéru* to be careful）
　　（*méiwaku ga kakáru* to get into trouble）

Below, in parentheses, the other corresponding English meanings of **otherwise** and their Japanese translation, are given with examples:

(in another manner or way) *sonó hoká no hōhō de* その外の方法で

Anó senséi wa séito ni han wo shimesú yóri hoká no hōhō de wa
あの　先生　は　生徒に　範　を　しめす　より　外　の　方法　で　は
oshienái.　That teacher teaches his students any **otherwise** than by example.
教えない.

(differently) *betsú no yō-ni* 別のように, *betsú no hōhō de* 別の方法で

Watashí wa betsú no yō-ni kangaemásŭ.　I think **otherwise.**
私　は　別　の　ように　考えます.

Koré wa zenzén betsú no hōhō de shinákereba naránai.
これ　は　全々　別　の　方法　で　しなければ　ならない.
This must be done quite **otherwise.**

(contrarily) *dóchira-ka to-iéba* どちらかと云えば

Watashí wa dóchira-ka to-iéba íma dekakerú hō ga íi désŭ.
私　は　どちらか　といえば　今　出かける　方　がいいです.
I would rather go out than **otherwise.**

---

1 *ryokō* travel, *dan* story; *Afŭriká ryokōdan* a story about travelling in Africa (if not) *móshi sō shinákattara*   若しそうしなかったら

Watashí wa súgu ikimáshĭta, *móshi sō shinákattara* resshá ni
私　は　すぐ　行きました，　若し　そう　しなかったら　列車　に
ma-ni-awánakatta no déshĭta.　I went at once, **otherwise** I should have missed
間に合わなかった　の　でした.　　　the train.

(in other respects) *hoká no ten de* 外の点で

Sonó *hoká no ten de* wa kōfuku-na seikatsú.　An **otherwise** happy
その　外　の　点　で　は　幸福な　　生活.　　life.

(and otherwise) *sonó ta iró-iró* その他色々

Káre wa jogén ya *sonó ta iró-iró* no kotó de watashí wo énjo
彼　は　助言　や　その　他　色々　の　事　で　私　　を　援助
shĭté kuremáshĭta.　He helped me with advice and **otherwise**.
して　くれました.　　(*énjo surú* to help, assist; *jogén* advice)

(or otherwise) *matá wa sonó hantái* またはその反対

Soré ga hitsuyō de áru ka *matá wa sonó hantái* de áru ka wa
それ　が　必要　である　か　また　は　その　反対　である　か　は
watashí no kan shĭtá kotó de wa arimasén.　I am not concerned with its
私　の　関　した　事　で　はありません.　necessity or **otherwise.**

(*hitsuyō* necessity; *kan shĭtá* from *kan súru* to concern)

Idiomatic usage:

Watashí wa warawazáru wo énakatta.　I could do no **otherwise** than
私　は　笑わざる　をえなかった.　　laugh.

(*warawazáru* literary form of *warawazú* without laughing)

Hoká ni betsudán o-isogashikú nákereba......　If you are not **otherwise**
外　に　別段　お忙しく　なければ......　engaged......

Kashikói hĭtó mo áru ga sō de nái hĭtó mo áru.　Some are wise, some
かしこい　人　も　あるがそうでない　人　も　ある.　are **otherwise.**

(*lit.* Wise people also there are, people that are not so, also there are.)

The meaning of this last example is also expressed by the following proverb:

Mekurá sen-nin, meakí sen-nin. めくら千人，めあき千人.

(*mekurá* blind people, *sen-nin* a thousand, *meakí* people that can see)

Provided

This conjunction is translated by the subjunctive (See Lesson 47,
page 406), or by *sáe* followed by the subjunctive. (Lesson 48, page 418)

Móshi rinjí[1] *tetsudái*[2] *ga áru náraba* watashí wa anó shigotó wo
若し　臨時　手伝い　が　ある　ならば　私　は　あの　仕事　を
raishū máde ni oerú deshō.　I shall finish that work by next week, **provided**
来週　まで　に終えるでしょう.　I get extra help.

A verb preceding *sáe* is used in its simple stem if it belongs to
Class I, and in the *i*-stem if it belongs to Class II.

---

1 extra   **2** help

Anáta no musŭkosán ga bóki[1] wo shĭtté i-sáe suréba watashí no
貴方　の　息子さん　が　簿記　を　知って　いさえ　すれば　私　の
jimúsho de yatoimashō.[2]   I shall employ your son in my office **provided** he
事務所　で雇いましょう.   knows bookkeeping. (The *i* before *sáe* is the
   simple stem of *irú*.)

Since

As a synonym of *because*, **since** may be translated by *kará* から,
nóde ので or *názenaraba* なぜならば.

Hitsuyō ga nái to omoimáshĭta kará (or *nóde*) *asokó e ikimasén déshĭta.*
必要　がないと　思いました　から　（ので)あそこへ行きませんでした.
I did not go there **since** I didn't think it necessary.
    (*lit.* Necessity there isn't, so I thought because, there didn't go.)

Kará or *nóde* may be used concurrently with *názenaraba*, in
which case the sentence becomes emphatic:

Asokó e ikimasén déshĭta, názenaraba hitsuyō ga nái to omoimáshĭta kará.
あそこへ行きませんでした,なぜならば　必要　がないと　思いました　から.

Note that *kará* and *nóde* are placed at the end of the clause dependent
on *because*, while *názenaraba* is placed at its beginning, as shown in the
two above examples.

In long sentences the use of *názenaraba* would render their construction too heavy and too stiff from a Japanese point of view, in which
case the construction with *kará* or *nóde* is preferred, as in the
following example:

Anó yamá wa chōbō ga hírokatta kará (or *nóde*) *wareware no kansatsú*
あの　山　は　眺望　が　広かった　から　　（ので)　我々　の　観察
ni wa hijō ni tekíshĭte imáshĭta.   (*chōbō* view, *hirói* wide, *kansatsú* observa-
には　非常に　適して　いました.   tion; *tekísu* to be suitable)
   That mountain, **since** it commands a wide view, was very suitable for our
   observation.

As an equivalent of *inasmuch as* or *seeing that*, **since** is translated
by *ijō* 以上:

Watashitachí ga soré wo shĭtté irú ijō, káre ni soré ni tsúite hana-
私達　　が　それ　を　知っている以上,　彼　にそれ　について　話
sáneba narimasén.   **Since** we know it, we must tell him about it.
さねば　なりません.   (*lit.* We, that we know since, to him that about must tell.)
Anáta ga kattá ijō, harawá-nákereba ikemasén.   **Since** you bought it, you
あなた　が　買った以上,　払わなければ　いけません.   must pay.

Used instead of *ago* or *before*, **since** is translated by *máe ni* 前に:

San nen máe ni káre no otōsan wa nakunarimáshĭta.
三　年　前　に　彼　のお父さんは　亡くなりました.
   It is three years **since** his father died.

---

1 bookkeeping   **2** *yatóu* to employ

Soré wa zuttó máe ni okorimáshĭta. It happened long since.
それ は ずっと 前 に 起こりました.

The expression *not long since* may be translated by *saikín* 最近 (=recently):

Soré wa saikín okorimáshĭta. That happened **not long since.**
それ は 最近 起こりました

So

(See Lesson 39, pp 302–304 on Comparison, and Lesson 46, page 392)

When used with the meaning of *therefore*, this conjunction is translated by *kará* から.

Mō osói désŭ kará netá hō ga íi désŭ. It is now late, **so** it is better
もう遅い です から 寝た 方 がいいです. to go to bed.

No sooner, Sooner

No sooner is translated by *to súgu* と直ぐ, or *ya ína-ya* や否や.

Nedokó ni háiru to súgu sū-hatsú no jūsei[1] wo kikimáshĭta.
寝床 に 入る と すぐ 数発 の 銃声 を 聞きました.
No sooner had I gone to bed **than** I heard several reports of gun.

Anó hĭtó wa watashí wo míru ya ína-ya nigedashimáshĭta.[2]
あの 人 は 私 を 見る や 否や 逃げ出しました.
No sooner did he see me **than** he ran away.

Káre wa kūkō ni tsŭkú ya-ína-ya byóki ni nátta. (*kūkō* airport, *tsŭkú*
彼 は 空港 に 着く や否や 病気 になった. to arrive)
He had **no sooner** arrived at the airport **than** he fell sick.

Iú to súgu shĭté shimaimáshĭta. **No sooner** said **than** I have done it.
云うと すぐ して しまいました.

No sooner is also translated by *totán ni* とたんに, which expression gives, more than the other two, the idea that on the very moment one thing ends another begins, as in the following example:

Umarerú totán-ni warewaré wa nakihajiméru. **No sooner** are we born
生れる とたんに 我々 は 泣きはじめる. **than** we begin to weep.
(*umarerú* to be born, *nakihajiméru* to begin to weep, *nakú* to weep, cry)

The expression **would sooner......than** may be translated by *kurai náraba* 位ならば, corresponding to *rather, sooner than.*

Soré wo surú kurai náraba jishokú surú hō ga mashí désŭ.
それ を する 位 ならば 辞職 する 方 が まし です.
I **would sooner** resign **than** do it.
(*jishokú* resignation, *mashí-na* better, preferable)

Idioms

Sooner or later. *Osokaré háyakare.* おそかれ早かれ.
The **sooner** the better. *Hayái hodó íi désŭ.* 早い程いいです.

---

1 *jūsei* report of a gun; *hatsú* numerative for counting gunshots **2** *nigedasú* to run away

Still

When this word joins its original meaning of continuance to that of opposition it is translated by *nóni* のに. In this case, *nóni* corresponds to *in spite of the fact that....*

Anó hĭtó wa warúi kotó wo shimashĭta **nóni** *jibún wa tadashíi to*
あの 人 は 悪い 事 を しました のに 自分 は 正しい と
omótte imásŭ.   He did wrong, still he thinks he is right. (*lit.* That man bad
思って います.   thing did, still himself is right so thinking is.)

In the meaning of *even more* or *yet*, **still** is generally translated by *mótto* もっと in colloquial speech and *issō* 一層 in literary style.

Kimí wa séi ga takái ga, o-níisan wa **mótto** *takái.*
君 は 背 が 高い が, お兄さん は もっと 高い.
    You are tall, but your elder brother is **still** taller.

As a synonym of *nevertheless*, **still** is translated by *ni mo kaka-warazú* にもかかわらず.

Anó rōjin wa kanemochí de áru **ni mo kakawarazú** *mótto hoshigátte*
あの 老人 は 金持 である にも かかわらず もっと 欲しがって
imásŭ.   That old man is rich, (and) **still** he craves for more.
います.

In the meaning of *as used to be*, **still** may be translated by *yappári* やっぱり in colloquial speech and by *yahári* やはり in more formal speech.

Anáta wa **yahári** *Nihón-go wo benkyō shĭté imásŭ ka.*
あなた は やはり 日本語 を 勉強 して いますか.
    Are you **still** studying Japanese?

still more (much more) *máda mótto* まだもっと

Soré wa **máda mótto** *arimásŭ.*   There are **still more.**
それ は まだ もっと あります.

still less *máshĭte* まして+negative verb

Anáta ga dekínai náraba **máshĭte** *watashí ni wa dekimasén.*
あなた が 出来ない ならば まして 私 には 出来ません.
    If you cannot do it, **still** less ought I.

Suppose

Suppose or **supposing** is translated by the subjunctive, preceded or not by *tatóe-ba* たとえば.

Tatóe-ba watashí ga hiyō[1] wo **móteba** *anáta wa sonó shigotó wo*
たとえば 私 が 費用 を 持てば 貴方 は その 仕事 を
hikiukemásŭ[2] ka.   **Suppose** I were to bear the expense, would you undertake
引受けます か.   the work?—

---

1 *hiyō* expense; *hiyō wo mótsu* to bear the expense   **2** *hikiukéru* to undertake, to accept

or *Watashí ga hiyō wo **móteba** anáta wa sonó shigotó wo hikiukemásŭ ka.*
私　が　費用　を　持てば　貴方　は　その　仕事　を　引受けます　か.

or *Watashí ga hiyō wo **mótsu to surébα** anáta wa sonó shigotó wo*
私　が　費用　を　持つ　と　すれば　貴方　は　その　仕事　を

hikiukemásŭ ka.　　Suppose I were to bear the expense, would you undertake
引受けます　か.　　the work?

That

When used as a conjunction of quotation before any verb meaning *to say*, or *to think*, **that** is translated by *to* と, which, however, cannot be omitted like its English equivalent.

*Ikeda San wa kómban kúrabu e korarénai **to** iimáshĭta.*
池田　さん　は　今晩　クラブ　へ　来られない　と　云いました.
Mr. Ikeda told me **that** he cannot come to the club to-night.

*Uchí no o-tonarí wa súgu ni Tōkyō wo tátsu **to** omoimásŭ.*
うち　の　お隣り　は　直ぐ　に　東京　を　立つ　と　思います.
I think **that** our neighbour will soon leave Tokyo.

When **that** is preceded by a present participle of quotation, which, in its turn, is preceded by an introductory clause, *to* is followed by *iú* いう or *no* の.

*Anáta no otōsan ga Chichibú Marú de tsŭkú **to iú** shirasé no dempō*
貴方　のお父さんが　秩父　丸　で　着く　という知らせ　の　電報
ga chōdo íma kimáshĭta.　　I just received a telegram announcing **that** your
が　丁度　今　来ました.　　father will arrive by the Chichibu Maru.

*Hatakeyamá San ga getsumatsú ni go-jōkyō[1] nasáru **to iú** (or **to no**)*
畠山　さん　が　月末　に　御上京　なさる　という　（と　の）
tegamí ga kimáshĭta.　　I received a letter from Miss Hatakeyama stating **that**
手紙　が　来ました.　　she would arrive in Tokyo at the end of the month.

Saitō kyōju[2] wa gaikokujín ni Tōkyō Gaikokugó-gakkō de Nihón-go wo
斎藤　教授　は　外国人　に　東京　外国語学校　で　日本語　を
*oshierú **to no** kotó désŭ.*　　They say **that** Professor Saito is going to teach
教える　と　の　事　です.　　Japanese to foreigners at the Tōkyō School of
　　Foreign Languages.

When the reported speech is expressed with some doubt, the conjunction **that** may be translated by *to ka* とか.

*Kúru **to ka** iimáshĭta.*　　He said, I think, **that** he would come.
来る　と　か　云いました.

If it is a statement that is expressed with doubt, **that** is translated by *ka to* かと, *ka* corresponding to a question mark (?), and *to* to *so*.

---

1 *jōkyō surú* to come up to the capital; *jō* come up, *kyō* capital; the word **Tōkyō** is composed of **tō** east, and **kyō** capital=*the eastern capital*. In 1868, the Emperor Meiji left his ancestral residence in Kyōto, the former capital of Japan, to be reenthroned and reside in the then city of **Yedo,** which, being east of the old capital, was renamed **Tōkyō,** or the "Eastern capital." **2** professor

    Kaō ka to omoimásŭ.   I think **that** I shall probably buy it.
    買おうか と 思います.   (*lit.* I shall buy?, so I think)

The expression **so that** or **in such manner that** may be translated
by *yō-ni* ように.

    Káre wa mitsŭkaranái[1] *yō-ni hisónde*[1] *imáshĭta.*   He lay low so **that** he
    彼 は 見つからない ようにひそんでいました.   would not be discovered.

Yō-ni may be used to avoid two imperatives.

    Jochū ni súgu káeru **yō-ni** *itté kudasái.*   Tell the maid-servant to come
    女中 に すぐ 帰る ように云って下さい.   back soon.
        (*lit.* To the servant soon to return-like, tell please.)

When **so that** indicates result or degree, it is translated by *hodó*
(ni) 程 (に).

    Konó umá wa tátte irú kotó ga dekínai **hodó** *bíkko*[2] *désŭ.*
    この 馬 は 立っている 事 が 出来ない 程 びっこ です.
    This horse is so lame **that** he can hardly stand.
        (*tátte irú kotó ga dekínai* cannot stand)

    Yūbe shibaí ni wa zasekí[3] *ga hĭtótsu mo nái* **hodó** *ōzei hĭtó ga*
    ゆうべ 芝居 に は 座席 が 一つ も ない 程 大勢 人 が
    imáshĭta.
    いました.

or *Yūbe shibaí ni amarí takŭsán hĭtó ga imáshĭta nóde zasekí wo tóru*
    ゆうべ 芝居 に 余り 沢山 人 が いましたので 座席 を とる
    kotó ga dekimasén déshĭta.   There were so many people at the theatre last
    事 が 出来ません でした.   night **that** we could not get any seats.

That or **in order that** placed before *may* or *might*, followed by
another verb, is translated by *tamé (ni)* ため (に).

    Hĭtó wa seikatsú wo tatéru[4] *tamé ni hatarakimásŭ.*
    人 は 生活 を 立てる ため に 働きます.
    People work **that** they **may** earn a living.

Then

This conjunction is translated by *sorenára (ba)* それなら (ば),
which, in familiar speech, is altered into *sonnára* そんなら, and
by *sō iú wáke nára (ba)* そういう訳なら (ば).

    Watashí wa soré wo shĭtté imásŭ.—Sorenára (ba) anáta wa watashidómo
    私 はそれ を 知っています.—それなら (ば) 貴方 は 私共
  ni hanasá-nákereba narimasén.   I know it.—**Then** you must tell us.
  に 話さ なければ なりません.

Though

It has been already stated that the subordinate of verbs and

----

1 *mitsŭkerú* to discover, to find out; *hisómu* to lurk **2** lame **3** seat **4** *seikatsú*
wo tatéru to earn a living

adjectives followed by *mo,* gives the concessive idea conveyed by *though* or *although,* followed by a verb. See Lesson 26, page 173 and Lesson 27, page 184.

1. *Ojíisan wa taihén toshí wo tótte ité mo háyaku okimásŭ.*
おぢいさんは　大変　年　を取っていて　も　早く　起きます.
 Though my grandfather is very old, he gets up early.
 (*toshí wo tóru* to become old, *toshí wo tótte irú* to be old.)

When *though* and *although* may be replaced by the adversative **however,** without altering the meaning of the sentence, they are translated by *tówa-ié* とは云え, while when they may be replaced by the participles *admitting* or *granting,* or by the expression *notwithstanding the fact that,* they may be translated by *tówa-ié* とは云え, *karí ni* かりに (or *tatoé* たとえ)......*tówa-ié* とは云え, *tóshǐte-mo* としても, or *karí ni......tóshǐte-mo* かりに......としても.

2. *Matsuí San wa daigakú wo sotsugyō shǐtá[1] tówa-ié chūgakŭsei[2] yóri*
松井　さん　は　大学　を　卒業　した　とは云え　中学生　より
mo gakŭshikí[3] ga áru to wa miemasén.
も　学識　が　あると　は　見えません.
 Though Mr. Matsui was graduated at the university, he does not seem to have more knowledge than a middle school boy. (Mr. Matsui graduated at the university, however he does not......)
  (lit. Mr. Matsui university graduated **though,** middle school student more than, knowledge has, so is not seen.)

3. *Jōdan[4] tóshǐte-mo* (or *tówa-ié*) *sonná kotó wo iú béki de wa nái.*
冗談　としても　　　（とは云え）そんな　事　を云うべき　で　はない.
Karí ni jōdan tówa-ié (or *tóshǐte-mo*) *sonná kotó wo iú béki de wa nái.*
かり　に　冗談　とは云え　　　（としても）そんな　事　を云うべきではない.
Tatoé jōdan tówa-ié sonná kotó wo iú béki de wa nái.
たとえ　冗談　とは云えそんな　事　を云うべきで　は　ない.
 Though it is a joke you should not say such a thing.
  (Granting, or admitting that it is a joke, you should not say such things.)

4. *Karí ni watashí ga Komurá San ni anó katá no jímen[5] ni táishǐte*
かり　に　私　が　小村　さんにあの　方　の　地面　に　対して
tadái no kingakú[6] wo dásu tóshǐte-mo (or *dasō to itté mo*) *anó hǐtó*
多大　の　金額　を　出す　としても　　　（出そうと云っても）あの　人
wa uranái deshō. **Though** I offered Mr. Komura a large sum of money for
は　売らないでしょう. his plot of land he would not sell it. (Notwithstanding the fact that I offered, etc.)

Instead of *tóshǐte-mo,* one may use **démo** or **nímo** in ordinary speech, and **nímo-séyo** にもせよ, in formal speech.

 Karí ni jōdan démo (*nímo* or *nímo-séyo*) *sonná kotó wo iú béki*
かり　に　冗談　でも　（にも,　　　にもせよ）そんな　事　を云うべき

---

1 *sotsugyō surú* to be graduated **2** middle school student **3** knowledge **4** joke
5 plot of land **6** *tadái no kingakú* a large sum of money; *tadái* large, *kingakú* sum of money

de wa nái.   **Though** it is a joke you should not say such a thing.
で は ない.   (See example 3.)

When **though** has the meaning of the adversative *but* or *however*, it is translated by *ga* が, *shikáshi* 併し, or *tówa-ié* とは云え.

Watashí no kodomó wa máda osanái[1] *ga* (*shikáshi* or *tówa-ié*) *gakkō*
私　の　子供　は　まだ　幼い　が　（併し，　　とは云え）学校
e yarimashō.[2]　**Though** my child is still young, I shall send him to school.
へやりましょう.　(*lit.* My boy still young but to school I will send.)

When **though** may be replaced by one of the expression *in spite of* and *in spite of the fact that,* it is translated by *nímo kakawarazú* にもかかわらず.

Kikén[3] *wo keikokú saretá* **nímo kakawarazú** *watashitachí wa kakō*[4]
危険　を　警告　された　にも　　かかわらず　　私達　　は　火口
no fuchí[5] *e yukimáshĭta.*　We went to the edge of the crater, **though** we had
の　縁　へ行きました.　　been warned of the danger. (We went to the edge
of the crater, in spite of the fact that we had been warned against the danger.)

Yoshidá San wa watashí ga anó hĭtó ni aitakunái no (or *kotó*) *wo*
吉田　さんは　私　があの　人　に会いたくないの　　（事）　を
shĭtté irú **nímo kakawarazú** *watashí no jimúsho e ni-do mo kimáshĭta.*
知っている　にも　　かかわらず　　私　　の事務所へ二度　も　来ました.
Mr. Yoshida came to my office twice, **though** he knew I did not want to meet
him. (Mr. Yoshida came to my office twice, in spite of the fact that......)

Nímo kakawarazú or *tówa-ié* may be used, in concessive clauses, instead of the subordinate followed by *mo*.

Ojíisan wa taihén toshí wo tótte ité mo háyaku okimásŭ.
おじいさんは　大変　年　を取っていて　も　早く　起きます.
Ojíisan wa taihén toshí wo tótte irú tówa-ié háyaku okimásŭ.
おじいさんは　大変　年　を取っている とは云え　早く　起きます.
Ojíisan wa taihén toshí wo tótte irú nímo kakawarazú háyaku okimásŭ.
おじいさんは大変　年　を取っているにも　　かかわらず　早く　起きます.
Though my grandfather is very old, he gets up early. (See example 1)

Instead of using the subordinate, one may use the stem of the verb, followed by *tsutsu* つつ. The suffix *tsutsu* is used after the simple stem of verbs of Class I and the *i*-stem of verbs of Class II.

Osói to shĭtté ité mo dekakemáshĭta.
遅い と 知っていて も 出かけました.
Osói to shirítsutsu dekakemáshĭta.
遅い と 知りつつ 出かけました.
⎱ I went out **though** I knew
⎰ it was too late.

Byōnin[6] *wa jibún no byōjō*[7] *wa zetsubō*[8] *to wa shirítsutsu* (*mo*) (or
病人　は　自分　の　病状　は　絶望　と　は　知りつつ　（も）

---

1 young　**2** *gakkō e yarú* to send to school　**3** *kikén* danger; *kikén wo keikokú surú* to warn of a danger　**4** *kakō* crater　**5** *fuchí* edge　**6** patient　**7** condition of a disease　**8** hopeless

shĭtté ité mo) *náo ta no ishá ni shinsatsú shĭté*[1] *moraitái to nozomimáshĭta.*[2]
(知っていても)なお他の医者に　診察　して　貰いたい　と　望みました.

The patient wished to be examined by another doctor, though he knew his
case was hopeless.

Though may be translated also by *nágara,* placed after nouns,
or, like the suffix *tsutsu,* after the simple stem of verbs of Class I
and the *i*-stem of verbs of Class II.

*Byōnin wa jibún no byōjō wa zetsubō to wa shir*ı *nágara náo ta no*
病人　は　自分　の　病状　は　絶望　と　は　知り　　ながら　なお他の
ishá ni shinsatsú shĭté moraitái to nozomimáshĭta.　　　(See previous
医者に　診察　して　貰いたい　と　望みました.　　　　　　example.)

Bímbō nágara manzokú shĭté imásŭ.　　**Though** I am poor, I am satisfied.
貧乏　ながら　満足　して　います.

Till, Until (See Lesson 17, page 95)

Till or **until** is translated by *máde* when referring to time or
place, and by *hodó* ほど when referring to an event that is the
final result of a progressive action.

Akarukú náru máde me ga sámete[3] *ımáshĭta.*　　I was awake **till** it was
明るく　なる　迄　目　が　覚めて　いました.　　light

Koyá no yáne[4] *zentái ga tondá*[5] *hodó kazé ga tsúyoku fukimáshĭta.*[6]
小屋　の　屋根　全体　が　飛んだ　ほど　風　が　強く　吹きました.

The wind beat violently against the hut **till** the whole roof was blown off.

Sometimes, in the same sentence, the conjunction *till* or *until* may
refer both to time and to the final result of an action, in which
case both *máde* and *hodó* may be used.

Tsŭkárekitta hodó (or *máde*) *arukimáshĭta.*　　I walked **until** I was
疲れ切った　ほど　　　（迄）　歩きました.　　exhausted.

　　　(*tsŭkárekitta* past of *tsŭkaré-kirú* to be tired out, to be exhausted)

In this case, if we use *hodó,* we immediately think of the exhausted
condition of the speaker, without giving much thought to the time
when he became exhausted, while if we use *máde* we immediately
think of the time that it took the speaker to get exhausted.

Unless (See Lesson 47, page 406)

In the meaning of *if not* or *supposing that not,* **unless** is, in most
cases, rendered in Japanese by the subjunctive of the verb dependent
on the said conjunction:

---

1 *shinsatsú surú* to examine a patient; *shinsatsú shĭté moraú* to be examined by
a doctor　**2** *nozomú* to wish　**3** *me ga saméru* to be awake　**4** roof　**5** *tobú* to fly
to be blown off　**6** *fukú* to blow

Tádachin₁ kyūjo[1] *ga* **kónai₁ náraba** (or **to**) *wareware wa gáshi surú*[2]
直ちに　救助　が　来ない　ならば　　（と）　　我々　は　餓死　する
deshō.　　We shall starve to death **unless** relief is soon brought to us.
でしょう.　　(At once relief if it does not come we shall starve to death.)

Mótto **hatarakanái to** (or **náraba**) *anáta wa táshĭka-ni shippái shimásŭ.*
もっと　働かない　　と　　（ならば）　貴方　は　確かに　　失敗　します.
Unless you work harder, you will certainly fail.

In the meaning of *except that*, **unless** may be translated by ......**no hoká wa** ......の外は.

Yamú-wo-énai tokí **no hoká wa** *watashí wa káigai e ikimasén.*
やむをえない　時　の　　外　は　　私　は　海外　へ行きません.
Unless absolutely compelled, 1 will not go abroad. (*yamú-wo-énai* やむをえない necessary, unavoidable; *tokí* moment, occasion etc.; *káigai* abroad)

When (See Lesson 22, page 145)

This conjunction is translated by *tokí ni* 時に, when it refers to time, by *nóni* のに, when it has the meaning of *while, whereas,* or *although,* and by *kará* から, when it means *after.*

Hara San no kotó wo chōdo hanáshĭte itá **tokí ni** *anó katá wa*
原　さんの　事　を　丁度　話して　いた　時　に　あの　方　は
yobirín wo oshimáshĭta.[3]　　We were just speaking of Mr. Hara, **when** he rang
呼鈴　を　押しました.　　the bell.

O-kané ga nái **nóni** *dō-shĭté anó ié wo kaú kotó ga dekimashō.*
お金　が　無い　のに　どうしてあの　家　を　買う　事　が出来ましょう.
How can 1 buy that house **when** I have no money.

Shikén no júmbi[4] *wo shinákereba naránai* **nóni** *anó hĭtó wa asondé*
試験　の　準備　を　しなければ　ならない　のに　あの　人　は　遊んで
bákarí imásŭ.　　He keeps playing **when** he should prepare for the examinations.
ばかり　います.

Ebisawá San wa gakkō wo déte **kará** *Mitsúi Ginkō e tsŭtomemáshĭta.*
海老沢　さん　は　学校　を　出て　から　三井　銀行　へ　勤めました.
When Mr. Ebisawa left school, he was engaged at the Mitsui Bank.
(*tsutoméru* 勤める to be in the service of, to take service under, etc.)

Rōma ni **irú tokí** *wa Rōmajin no yō-ni shinásái.*
ローマ　に　いる　時　は　ローマ人　のようにしなさい.
When in Rome do as the Romans do.

The above sentence is the literal translation of the original proverb, well known among foreigners. However, it has its Japanese counterpart in the following sentence:

---

1 *kyūjo* relief　**2** *gáshi surú* to starve to death　**3** *yobirín wo osú* to push, to ring the bell; *yobirín* bell, *osú* to push　**4** *júmbi* (*wo*) *surú* to prepare; *shikén no júmbi wo surú* to prepare for examinations

Gō[1] ni itté wa gō ni shītagae.[2]   If you go to the country do as country
郷 に入っては 郷 に 従え.   people do.

(*lit.* To the country having gone, to the country conform.)

Whenever

This conjunction is translated by *toki itsu-démo* 時いつでも.

Anáta ga dekaketái **toki** *itsu-démo go-isshó ni ikaremásŭ.*
貴方 が出かけたい 時 いつでも 御一緒 に 行かれます.
I am ready to accompany you, whenever you wish to go.

Kyōto e ikú **toki** *itsu-démo áni no ié ni tomarimásŭ.*
京都 へ行く 時 いつでも 兄 の 家 に 泊ります.
Whenever I go to Kyoto I stay at my elder brother's.

Where

As a conjunction **where** is translated by *sokó ni* そこに or *tokoró* 所.

Ugóite[3] wa ikemasén; **sokó ni** *irasshái.*   Don't move; stay **where**
動いて は いけません,そこ にいらっしゃい.   you are.

(*lit.* Moving won't do; there stay.)

Kokó ga bōto wo karirú[4] kotó no dekíru **tokoró** *désŭ ka.*
ここ が ボートを 借りる 事 の できる 所 ですか.
Is this the place **where** we can hire a boat?

(*lit.* Here boat to hire the thing we can, place is?)

Séishin[5] ittō nanigotó-ka narazarán.[6]   } **Where** there is a will
精神 一到 何事 か 成らざらん.   } there is a way.

(*lit.* The mind once decided, nothing cannot be done.) } (The first sentence is
                                                   } the idiomatic translation
Ishi ga áru **tokoró** *ni wa michí ga arimásŭ.* } of the saying; the second
意志 が ある 所 に は 道 が あります.   } is the literal translation
                                                   } of the English original.)
(*lit.* Will **where** there is road there is.)   }

Wherever

This conjunction may be translated by *itsu-démo* いつでも or
dóko e......mo どこへ......も.

Watashí wa **itsu-démo** *konó kyōfu[7] ni osowaremásŭ.[8]* } These fears
私 は いつでも この 恐怖 に おそわれます   } pursue me
(*lit.* I, always, by these fears I am stricken.)   } **wherever** I
                                                             } go.
Watashí wa **dóko e itté mo** *konó kyōfu ni osowaremásŭ.* }
私 は どこ へ行っても この 恐怖 に おそわれます. }
(*lit.* I, **wherever** going by these fears I am stricken.) }

---

1 country **2** *shitagáu* to conform to, to comply with **3** *ugóku* to move **4** to
hire, to borrow **5** mind, spirit, soul **6** *narazarán=naránaku wa nái=naránai
kotó wa nái* not to become thing there is not; *narazarán* is a double negative with
emphasized positive meaning, in rare cases used in literary style **7** fear **8** *osoú*
to attack

Whether (See Lesson 32, page 233)

This conjunction may be translated by subordinates standing in pairs, and by *ka* か, *ka dō ka* かどうか, or *ka dō désŭ ka* かどうですか, placed after a finite verb.

Yásukutte mo yásuku-nákutte mo watashí wa soré wo kaimasén.
安くって も 安くなくって も 私 は それ を買いません。
Whether it is cheap or not I will not buy it.

Nikú ga nietá[1] ka (or *ka dō ka, ka dō désŭ ka*) *míte kudasái.*
肉 が 煮えた か (か どうか, か どう です か) 見て 下さい。
See **whether** the meat is cooked.

Watashí no e wo anáta wa sŭkí désŭ ka (ka dō ka, ka dō désŭ
私 の絵を 貴方 は 好きです か (か どうか, か どう です
ka) soshŭté tenrankái ni soré wa shuppín surú káchi ga áru[2] ka (ka
か) そして 展覧会 に それ は 出品 する 価値 が ある か (か
dō ka, ka dō désŭ ka) hakkíri itté kudasái.
どうか, か どう です か) はっきり云って下さい。

Tell me frankly **whether** you like my painting, and **whether** it is worth showing it at the Exhibition. (*tenrankái* exhibition, *shuppín surú* to exhibit)

While (See Lesson 31, page 214)

While is translated by *uchí wa* うちは or *aidá wa* 間は, when it has the meaning of *as long as*.

Seiméi ga áru aidá (uchí) wa kibō[3] ga arimásŭ.   **While** there is life
生命 が ある 間 (うち) は 希望 が あります。   there is hope.

When **while** has the meaning of *during the time that*, it is translated by *aidá (ni)* 間 (に) or *toki (ni)* 時 (に).

Anó senséi ni tsúite benkyō shŭté ıtá aidá (toki) ni watashí wa
あの 先生 に ついて 勉強 して いた 間 (時) に 私 は
takŭsán oboemáshŭta.[4]   I learned much **while** I was studying with that teacher.
沢山 覚えました。

(*lit.* That teacher with, study was doing while, I much learned.)

Also when it denotes the simultaneousness of two events, it is translated by *tokí (ni)* 時 (に) or *aidá (ni)* 間 (に).

Chikyū no hambún ga hirú no tokí (aidá) ni ta no[5] hambún wa
地球 の 半分 が 昼 の 時 (間) に 他 の 半分 は
yóru désŭ.   **While** one half of the earth has day, the other half has night.
夜 です。   (*lit.* The earths' half, day while, other half night.)

When *while* denotes an action that occurs, or may occur while another action takes place, *uchí ni* うちに is used.

---

1 *nirú* to boil, to cook **2** *káchi ga áru* worth, to be worth **3** hope **4** *obóeru* to remember, to learn **5** *ta no* other

*Kurumá   ga   tomaranái   **uchí   ni**   tobiórite*[1]   *wa   ıkemasén.*
車　が　止まらない　うち　に　飛び降りて　は　いけません.
Don't jump off the car **while** it is in motion.
   (*lit.* The car does not stop while to jump off won't do.)

When **while** means *on the contrary*, this conjunction is translated
by *nóni hikikáete* のに引換えて.

*Anó   hĭtó   ga   anná   ni   kimbenká-na   **nóni   hikikáete**   anó   hĭtó   no*
あの　人　が　あんなに　勤勉家な　のに　引換えて　あの　人　の
otōto   wa   ítsumo   namákete   imásŭ.   His younger brother is always idle, **while**
弟　は　いつも　なまけて　います.   he is such an industrious man.
   (*anná-ni* such, *kimbenká-na* industrious, *namakéru* to be idle, lazy)

When indicating *space of time*, **while** may be translated by *shibáraku* しばらく.

shibáraku   áto   de   after a **while**
しばらく　あと　で

Shibáraku   mátte   kudasái.   Wait a **while.**
しばらく　待って　下さい.

Shibáraku   anó   katá   ni   aimasén.   I haven't seen him for a **while.**
しばらく　あの　方　に会いません.

   Ma-mo-nakú 間もなく   In a little **while.**
   Tokí-dokí 時々   Once in a **while.**
   nagái aidá 長い間   a long **while**

As a synonym of *whereas*, **while** may be translated by *nóni* のに.

*Aru   hĭtóbito   wa   kanemochí   de   áru   **nóni**   áru   hĭtóbito   wa   bímbō   de   áru.*
或　人々　は　金持　である　のに　或　人々　は　貧乏　である.
Some men are rich **while** others are poor. (*kanemochí* rich, *bímbō* poor)

*Káre   wa   tsŭkaú   kané   ga   nái   **nóni**   kánojo   wa   kaú   monó   ga   nái.*
彼　は　使う　金　が　ない　のに　彼女　は　買う　もの　が　ない.
While he has no money to spend, she has nothing to spend money on.
   (*tsŭkaú* to spend, to use; *kaú* to buy; *kaú monó* things to buy)

Yet

When **yet** is used as a synonym of *however* or *but* connecting
opposed facts, ideas, etc., it may be translated by *ga* が, *shikáshi*
しかし, *kéredomo* けれども, *nóni* のに, *démo* でも or *tówa-ié*
とは云え.

Shínjitsu[2] *wo   hanashimáshĭta   ga (nóni)   anó   hĭtó   wa   shinjimasén*[3] *déshĭta.*
真実　を　話しました　が　(のに)あの　人　は　信じません　でした.
I told him the truth, **yet** he would not believe me.

---

1 *tobıoríru* to jump off   **2** truth   **3** *shinjíru* to believe

Shikō[1] *wa miemasén* **shikáshi** (*ga, tówa-ié*) *jínsei ni óite náni ka*
思考　は　見えません　併し　（が，とは云え）人生　に　於て　何　か

yūeki-na[2] *kotó wo nashitogerú*[3] *no wa táda shikō ni yoru*[4] *bákari désŭ.*
有益な　　事　を　成し遂げる　の　は　ただ　思考　に　よる　ばかり　です.

Thoughts are invisible, and **yet,** it is only by thought that we succeed in
doing anything useful in life. (*lit.* Thoughts are not seen, however, in man's
life something useful things to succeed in only by thought is.—*jínsei* human
life, existence, etc.)

Oji wa toshiyorí **démo** *génki désŭ.*　　My uncle is old, **yet** active.
伯父　は　年寄り　でも　元気　です.

Below, in parentheses, are given other meanings in which **yet**
may be used and their corresponding Japanese translations:

(already) *mō* もう

　Mō ikú jikán désŭ ka. もう行く時間ですか.　　Is it time to go **yet**?

　Mō gakkō wa hajimarimáshĭta ka.　　Has the school begun **yet**?
　もう　学校　は　始まりました　か.

(still more) *mótto* もっと

　Kinō wa samúi déshĭta ga kyō wa **mótto** *samúi désŭ.*
　きのう　は　寒い　でした　がきよう　は　もっと　寒い　です.
　It was cold yesterday but to-day it is colder **yet.**

(even) *sáe mo* さえも

　Káre wa anáta ga ittá kotó wo shinjínai bákari de náku shōko **sáe**
　彼　は　貴方　が　云った　事　を　信じない　ばかり　で　なく　証拠　さえ

mo *shinjimasén déshĭta.*　　He did not believe what you said, nor **yet** the
も　信じません　でした.　　　　evidence.

　Káre wa joryokú dókoroka kané **sáe mo** *ukénai deshō.*
　彼　は　助力　どころか　金　さえ　も　受けないでしょう.

He will not accept help nor **yet** money.　(*lit.* He help in no wise, money
even will not accept.—*joryokú* help, assistance; *dókoroka* in no wise, far
from, not at all)

(notwithstanding) *ni-mo kakawarazú* にもかかわらず

　Soré wa hijō-ni hen **ni-mo kakawarazú** *hontō désŭ.*
　それ　は　非常に　変　にも　　かかわらず　本当　です.
　It is very strange, **yet** it is true.

　Káre wa watashí ni áu yakŭsokú wo shĭtá **ni-mo kakawarazú** *kité*
　彼　は　私　に会う　約束　を　した　にも　　かかわらず　来て

imasén.　　He is not here, **yet** he promised to meet me. (*yakŭsokú* promise)
いません.

Idiomatic usage:

　　　yet more *máda-máda* まだまだ

　　　yet again *mō ichí-do* もう一度

　Máda-máda surú kotó ga takŭsán arimásŭ.　　**Yet more** remains to
　まだまだ　　する　事　が　沢山　あります.　　　　be done.

_____

1 thought　**2** *yūeki-na* useful　**3** to succeed　**4** *ni yorú* by

Sixty-second Lesson　第六十二課

Interjections　*Kantōshi*　間ヵン投トゥ詞シ

The Japanese interjections may be divided into two groups: **1**) words reproducing mere sounds expressive of emotions; **2**) expressions consisting of words borrowed from other parts of speech.

Group 1

A あっ Expressing sudden perception, surprise, pain.

A o-kané wo wasuretá. あっ お金 を 忘れた.	Oh! I have forgotten my money.
A itái. あっ痛い.	Ouch! It hurts!
A saifú ga nakunattá. あっ 財布 が 失くなった.	My God! The purse is gone!
A káji da. あっ火事だ.	Oh look! There is a fire.

Ā あー Expressing disappointment, sorrow, admiration, alarm, delight.

Ā ureshíi.	あー嬉しい.	How glad I am!
Ā soré wa sŭtekí.	あーそれはすてき.	Oh! That's grand!
Ā naruhodó.	あー成程.	Oh, I see!
Ā sō désŭ ka.	あーそうですか.	Oh, indeed!
Ā taihén.	あー大変.	Heaven and earth!
Ā kawái sō ni.	あーかわいそうに.	Ah, poor fellow!
Ā atsúi.	あー暑い.	How hot!
Ā anó hĭto wa mō imasén. あーあの 人 は もういません.		Alas! He is no more.
Ā ryōshin ga íkite itá náraba. あー 両親 が 生きていた ならば.		Would that I had my parents living!

Ō おゝ O! Oh! How! Ouch!

Ō samúi.	おゝ寒い.	How cold!
Ō itái.	おゝ痛い.	Ouch! It hurts!
Ō iyá da bakabakashíi. おゝいや だ 馬鹿々々しい.		Ugh! How foolish it is!
Ō sō désŭ ka.	おゝそうですか.	Well, is that so?

Ē えゝ Well......? What......?

Ē nan désŭ ka.	えゝ何んですか.	Well, what is it?
Ē nan to iimáshĭta ka.	えゝ何んと云いましたか.	What did you say?

Ē anó hǔtó wa shinimáshǐtatte.[1]　　Did you say he died?!
えゝあの 人 は 死にましたって.

Ē えゝ O yes! Yes! Well! Let me see. Er—Hum! What!

Ē machigaináku ikimásǔ.　　　O yes, I will be there without fail.
えゝ 間違いなく 行きます.

Ē íi désǔ tómo. えゝいゝですとも.　Yes, with pleasure. Certainly.

Ē sō désǔ ka. えゝそうですか.　Is it?—Is that so?

Ē Expressing surprise, anger, hate, despite. Pshaw! Yah! Hang it! O.

Ē dō-démo katté ni shinasái. O well, I don't care; do as you please.
えゝ どうでも 勝手 に しなさい.　(Well, whatever way as you wish do.)

Mā まあ corresponds to *just, come,* or the emphatic *do.*

Mā íppai o-nomí nasái. まあ一杯お飲みなさい.　Come, have a drink.

Mā íppai yaritamáe.　Come, have a drink. (used among men only)
まあ 一杯 やり給え.

Mā o-machí kudasái.　まあお待ち下さい.　Just wait, please.

Mā yatté gorán nasái. まあやって御らんなさい.　Just try it.

Mā o-shizuká ni.　まあお静かに.　Do be quiet!

Mā o-kaké kudasái.　まあおかけ下さい.　Do sit down.

Mā まあ well, I think, I should say, it would seem, say.

Mā ikazuní okimashō.　　Well, I would rather not go.
まあ 行かずにおきましょう.

Mā yóku irasshaimáshǐta.　　Well, well, I am glad you have
まあ よくいらっしゃいました.　come.

Mā sonná ími deshō.　　Well, it means something like
まあ そんな 意味でしょう.　that.

Teradá San wa mā gakǔshá no hō deshō.　Mr. Terada is a scholar,
寺田 さん は まあ 学者 の 方でしょう.　it seems.

Mā arúite ikú kotó ni shimashō.　I think I had better go on foot.
まあ 歩いて 行く 事 にしましょう.

Dóko ka kaigán e.— Mā Kamakurá e démo yukimashō ka.
どこ か 海岸 へ.—まあ 鎌倉 へ でも 行きましょうか.
　Let's go to the sea side; say Kamakura.

Mā Oh! O dear! O dear me! O my! Good gracious! Indeed! my word!

Mā odoróita. まあ驚いた.　　O what a surprise!

---

1 The termination *tte* after a verb indicates surprise. *Hébi wo tabemáshǐta.* 蛇を
食べました. I ate a snake.—*Ē hébi wo tabemáshitatte.* ええ蛇を食べましたって. What
did you say? You ate a snake?!

Mā dō shĭtá no désŭ ka.   Good Lord, what is it?
まあ どうした の です か.

Mā nan no otó deshō.   Oh dear, what can that noise be?
まあ 何ん の 音 でしょう.

Naruhodó 成程 I see, quite true, indeed (used by men only).

Naruhodó sō iú wáke désŭ ka.   I see, that's the reason.
成程 そういう 訳 です か.

Naruhodó koré wa tsumaránai hon désŭ.   This book is really very dull
成程 これ は つまらない 本 です.   to read.

Naruhodó, yói hōhō désŭ ga jikkō wa kónnan désŭ.
成程, よい 方法 です が 実行 は 困難 です.
A good plan to be sure, but it is hard to practice.

Naruhodó, kimí no iú kotó wa móttomo désŭ.   Indeed, you are right.
成程, 君 の 云う 事 は 尤も です.

Ne ね In familiar use, *ne* characterizes the speech of women and children.

Placed at the end of a sentence, *ne* has generally an interrogative force, and corresponds to the English *is it? isn't it? isn't that so? doesn't it*, etc.

Omoshirói désŭ ne. 面白いですね.   It is interesting, isn't it?

Kírei désŭ ne. きれいですね.   It's pretty, isn't it?

Koré wa kimí no désŭ ne.   This is yours, I suppose.
これ は 君 の です ね.

Kyō wa ku-gatsú-tsuitachí désŭ ne.   To-day is the first of September,
きょう は 九月朔日 です ね.   isn't it?

Anáta wa sázo tsŭkáreta deshō ne.   You must be very tired, I dare
貴方 は さぞ 疲れた でしょうね.   say.

Ne may follow any word in a sentence to maintain the attention of the person spoken to, to what one is saying, but some people use it very often, without necessity, and just for habit. In this case it corresponds to the pleonastic use of the English *you see*, or *you know*.

In familiar speech, *anó-ne* あのね, or simply *ne,* like the English *I say*, attracts attention to what is to be said.

Ne anáta ね貴方 corresponds to *dear*, or *my dear* said by a wife to her husband.

Sŏ désŭ ne そうですね is sometimes used when politely agreeing with what somebody says, or when one is perplexed or considering what answer one had better give. In the latter case, *ne* corresponds to *Let me see*.

Anáta wa dótchi wo o-kaí ni narimásŭ ka.   Which do you want
貴方 は どっち を お買い に なります か.   to buy?

Sō désŭ ne. Ōkii no wo kaimashō. Let me see. I'll buy
そう です ね. 大きいの を買いましょう. the big one.

Óya おや Oh! Oh dear! Dear me! O my! Good heavens! Mercy
on me! By Jove! Lord!

Óya, mā.   おやまあ.   Dear me! O my!
Óya, denwá désŭ. おや電話です. Goodness! There's the phone!
Óya, óya, nan désŭ ka. おやおや何んですか. O my, how is that?
Óya, jū-ichí-ji désŭ. おや十一時です. Why! It is eleven.
Óya, óya, sonó ié no banchí wo wasuremáshĭta. By Jove, I forgot the
おや, おや, その 家 の 番地 を 忘れました. number of the house.

Sā さあ Come; now; well; here; there; ah!

Sā kói. さあこい.   Come on! (challenge)
Sā minná de yarimashō. Come, let us all do it.
さあ みんな でやりましょう.
Sā dōzo o-hairí kudasái. O do come in.
さあ どうぞ お入り 下さい.
Sā surú ka shinái ka henjí wo shi nasái. Come, now! Say whether
さあ する か しない か 返事 を しなさい. you will do it or not.
Sā Yokohamá e kimáshĭta. Well, here we are in Yokohama.
さあ 横浜 へ 来ました.
Sā kimi no o-kané désŭ. Here is your money.
さあ 君 の お金 です.
Sā okí nasái. さあ起きなさい. Wake up there.
Sā sokó désŭ mondai wa. There, that's the point.
さあ そこ です 問題 は.
Inoué San wa nan sái guraí deshō.—Sā wakarimasén ne.
井上 さん は 何 才ぐらいでしょう.—さあ 分りません ね.
 How old do you think Mr. Inoue is?—Well, I can't tell.

In rather vulgar speech, this interjection is used by men, when speaking
among themselves, in the meaning of *Indeed!, I say!, You know!, I assure
you.*, etc.

Dái sŭkí désŭ sā! 大好きですさあ. **Indeed** (Sure) I do like it.
Murón sā!   無論さあ.   **Certaily** (Of course) it is!
Káre wa kúru to sā. 彼は来るとさあ. He says he would come.

Group 2

Yo よ This interjection is often used in familiar speech as in the
following examples.

Kón-ya kittó ki-nasái yo! Be sure to come to-night.
こんや きっと来なさい よ. (*kón-ya* to-night, *kittó* surely)

Wasurenái de asokó e ikí-nasái **yo!**   Don't forget to go there.
忘れない　であそこへ行きなさいよ

Namákete irú to rakudái surú **yo!**   If you are idle, you will fail
なまけて いると 落第 する よ.　　(in the examination).

　(*namakéru* to be idle, lazy, *rakudái surú* to fail in an examination)

Táshĭka ni sonná kotó wa áru hazú ga nái **yo!**   It can't be true,
たしか にそんな 事 は ある 筈 が ない よ.　 I am sure.

　(*lit.* Surely, such a thing ought not to be.—*táshĭka ni* surely)

Yō よう In familiar speech, this interjection may be used in the meaning of **Bravo!**, or **Well done!**

Yō, *Fujiwará!* よう, 藤原.　　Bravo Fujiwara!

Yō, *umái zo!*　　Well done, boys!
よう, うまいぞ.

In good speech, **yō** is used in the following expression:

Yō *kóso.* ようこそ.　　You are welcome!

By itself, **yō** is used in vulgar speech as a hailing expression, and corresponds to **Say! Hullo!**

Ze! ぜ **Zo!** ぞ—Both interjections have emphatic force and they are used in vulgar, but friendly, speech, by men and boys when speaking among themselves. In meaning they correspond to *I assure you, I warn you,* etc.

Kazé wo hikú **ze** (or **zo**).　　You will catch a cold, **I warn you.**
かぜ を 引くぜ （ぞ）.

Abunái **ze** (or **zo**). 危ないぜ （ぞ）.　　**Mind you,** it is dangerous.

Kimí wa uchí e káetta hō ga íi **ze** (or **zo**).　　**I advise you** to go
君 は うち へ 帰った 方 がいいぜ　　（ぞ）.　　home.

Ára あら is generally used by women.

Ára nan deshō, jishín deshō ka.　　There! What's that! An earth-
あら 何んでしょう, 地震 でしょうか.　　quake?

Ára ára asokó wo gorán nasái.　　Look, look over there.
あら あらあそこ を 御らん なさい.

Ára nan no otó deshō.　　Hark! What's the sound?
あら 何んの 音でしょう.

Áre あれ There! Look! Listen! Hark.

Áre, asokó e Nodá San ga ikimásŭ.　　Look, there goes Mrs. Noda!
あれ, あそこ へ 野田 さん が 行きます.

Dōmo どうも This word is used to emphasize.

Dōmo *arigatō.* どうもありがとう.　　I thank you very much.

Dōmo *wakarimasén.*　　I am sure I don't understand.
どうも 分りません.

Dōmo *komarimáshĭta.*　　I am in a fix.
どうも 困りました.

Dōmo   *o-sewá-samá*   *déshĭta.*   I am very much obliged to you.
どうも　　お世話様　　でした.

Dōmo   *shikatá*   *ga*   *arimasén.*   There is no help for it.
どうも　仕方　が ありません.

Dōmo   *anó*   *otokó*   *ga*   *ayashíi désŭ.*   That man is really suspicious.
どうも あの 男 が 怪しい です.

Dōmo   *Nihón-go*   *wa*   *muzukashíi désŭ.*   The Japanese language is really
どうも　日本語　は むづかしい です.   difficult.

Háte (na) はて (な) This interjection is used generally by men,
and indicates perplexity.

Háte   *dō*   *shĭtá*   *monó*   *deshō*   *ka.*   Well, what am I to do now?
はて どうした もの でしょうか.

Háte   *na*   *saifú*   *wo*   *dóko*   *e*   *oitá*   *káshira.*   Let me see; where did I leave
はて な 財布 を どこへおいたかしら.   my purse.

Móshi-móshi もしもし This word is used to draw attention.

Móshi-móshi,   *anáta*   *wa*   *náni*   *ka*   *o-otoshí*   *ni*   *narimáshĭta.*
もしもし,　　貴方　は　何　か　お落し　に　なりました.
Say, you have dropped something.

Móshi-móshi   *kokó*   *wa*   *nan*   *to*   *iú*   *machí*   *désŭ*   *ka.*
もしもし　こゝ は 何んと 云う 町 です か.
Excuse me, but what's the name of this street?

Móshi-móshi is used also when speaking to someone over the
telephone, as in the following example:

The caller: *Móshi-móshi,*   *Aóyama,*   *fŭtá-sen-go-hyakú-hachí-jū-go-ban*   *désŭ*   *ka.*
もしもし,　　青山,　　　　二千五百八十五番　　　　です か.

or *Móshi-móshi,*   *Aóyama*   *ni-go-hachí-go*   *désŭ*   *ka.*   Is that *Aoyama*
もしもし,　　青山　2-5-8-5　です か.　　2585?

(Tokyo telephone system is divided into 92 districts, one of which is called
Aoyama.)

The called party; *Hái, sō désŭ.* はい, そうです.   Yes, (it is).

The caller: *Móshi-móshi,*   *dónata*   *désŭ*   *ka.*   Who is speaking?
もしもし,　　どなた です か.

The called party: *Móshi-moshí,*   *kochirá*   *wa*   *Nákasu*   *désŭ.*   Miss Nakasu
もしもし,　　こちら は 中須 です.   speaking.

Sóra そら There; Here! Now! Come!

Sóra denwá désŭ. そら電話です.   Here goes the telephone.

Sóra káji da. そら火事だ.   Hark! A fire!

Sóra kói. そら来い.   Come on!

Sóra gorán nasái. そら御覧なさい.   I told you!

A few more interjections are used by some Japanese, however,
being these considered vulgar, they have been omitted in this lesson.

READING EXERCISES

Yomikatá Renshū
読方　　練習

In the following 22 pages the Reading Pieces are given in roman letters with explanatory notes, while their transliteration with Japanese symbolic characters is given from page 630 to 646.

See additional Reading Exercises Page 651–670 and 759–761.

Japanese Imperial decrees, like the following rescript, were, until the end of the Pacific War in 1945, written in elevated literary style, and contained a great many words which were not used in conversation.

To-day, however, Japanese Imperial decrees are issued in a language very much near to good spoken speech.

Below, the Imperial Rescript on Education, given out by the Emperor Meiji in the year 1890, is reproduced because it is a good example of Japanese highly worded old literature and also because it has been of historical importance for the Japanese nation.

① KYŌIKU CHOKUGÓ[1]

Chin[2] omō[3] ni[3] wága kōso kōsō[4] kuní wo hajimurú kotó kōen ni[5] tokú wo tatsúru kotó shinkō nári.[6] Wága shimmín yóku chū ni yóku kō ni[7] okuchō kokóro wo ítsu ni shǐté[8] yóyo sonó bi wo naséru wa[9] koré wága kokutái no séika ni shǐté[10] kyōiku no engén matá jitsú ni kokó ni sónsu.[11] Nanjí shimmín fúbo ni kō ni keitéi ni yū ni[12] fūfu ái-wáshi hōyū ái-shínji[13] kyōken onoré wo jíshi[14] hakuái shū ni oyoboshí[15] gakú wo osáme gyō wo narái[16] mótte chinō wo keihatsú shi tókki wo jōju

---

[1] *kyōiku* education, *chokugó* Imperial message, Imperial rescript; *Kyōiku Chokugó* Imperial Rescript on Education   [2] *Chin* this was how the Emperor referred to Himself. *Chin* used to be the *We* of Western sovereigns.   [3] *omō ni=omóu ni* We think, We consider; *Chin omō ni* We consider that=**Know ye, Our subjects :**   [4] *wága* our, *kōso kōsō* Imperial Ancestors   [5] *kuní* Our Empire, *hajimurú kotó* have founded, *kōen* vast and far reaching, *kōen ni* on a basis broad and everlasting; *Wága kōso kōsō kuní wo hajimurú kotó kōen ni* **Our Imperial ancestors have founded our Empire on a basis broad and everlasting**   [6] *tokú* virtue, *tatsúru* to implant, *shinkō* deeply and firmly; *tokú wo tatsúru kotó shinkō nári* **and have deeply and firmly implanted virtue**   [7] *wága shimmín* Our subjects, *yóku* well, *chū ni* in loyalty, *kō ni* in filial piety   [8] *okuchō* the whole nation, *kokóro* mind, *ítsu ni surú* to unite; *okuchō kokóro wo ítsu ni shǐté* the whole nation being united in one mind; *Wága shimmín yóku chū ni yóku kō ni okuchō kokóro wo ítsu ni shǐté* **Our subjects ever united in loyalty and filial piety**   [9] *yóyo* from generation to generation, *sonó bi* its beauty, *naséru* to illustrate; *yóyo sonó bi wo naséru wa* **have from generation to generation illustrated the beauty thereof.**   [10] *wága* our, *kokutái* the character of the Empire, *séika* glory, *séika ni shǐté* in glory; *koré wága kokutái no séika ni shǐté* **This is the glory of the fundamental character of our Empire;**   [11] *engén* source, *matá* also, *jitsú ni* surely, *kokó ni sónsu* herein lies; *kyōiku no engén matá jitsú ni kokó ni sónsu* **and herein also lies the source of our education**   [12] *nanjí shimmín* Ye, our subjects, *fúbo* parents, *kō ni* to be filial, *keitéi* brothers, *yū* friends; *nanjí shimmín fúbo ni kō ni keitéi ni yū ni* **Ye, our subjects, be filial to your parents, affectionate to your brothers and sisters ;**   [13] *fūfu* husband and wife, *ái-wasurú* to be harmonious, *hōyū* friend, *ái-shinjíru* to be true to one another; *fūfu ái-wáshi hōyū ái-shínji* **as husbands and wives be harmonious, as friends true ;**   [14] *kyōken* modesty, *onoré* I, *onoré wo jíshu* to keep oneself; *kyōken onoré wo jíshi* **bear yourself in modestly and moderation ;**   [15] *hakuái* benevolence, *shū ni* to all, *oyobosú* to extend; *hakuái shū ni oyoboshí* **extend your benevolence to all ;**   [16] *gakú* learning, *osaméru* to pursue, *gyō* arts, occupation, *gyō wo naráu* to cultivate arts, to learn one's occupation; *gakú wo osáme gyō wo narái* **pursue learning and cultivate arts**

shi¹ susundé kōeki wo hiróme séimu wo hiráki² tsúne ni kokkén wo omónji kokuhō ni shǐtagái³ ittán, kankyū áreba⁴ giyū kō ni hōji⁵ mótte tenjō mukyū no kōun wo fúyoku subéshi.⁶ Kakú no gótoki wa hǐtóri Chin ga chūryō no shimmín tarú nóminarazu matá mótte⁷ nanjí sósen no ifū wo kenshō surú ni tarán.⁸

Konó michí wa jitsú ni⁹ wága kōso kōsō no íkun ni shǐté¹⁰ shíson shimmín no tomó ni júnshu subéki tokoró¹¹ koré wo kókon ni tsūjite ayamárazu koré wo chūgai ni hodokoshité motórazu.¹² Chin nanjí shimmín to tomó ni¹³ kenkén fukuyō shǐté miná sonó tokú wo ítsu ni sen kotó wo koinegáu.¹⁴

Méiji ni-jū-san-nen jū-gatsú san-jū-nichí¹⁵

GYÓMEI GYÓJI¹⁶

---

¹ *mótte* and, *chinō* knowledge, *keihatsú surú* to develop, *tókki* moral power, *jōju surú* to perfect ; *mótte chinō wo keihatsú shi tókki wo jōju shi* **and thereby develop intellectual faculties and perfect moral power ;** ² *susundé* furthermore, *kōeki* public good, *hiroméru* to spread, to advance, *séimu* common interest, *hiráku* to promote ; *susundé kōeki wo hiróme séimu wo hiráki* **furthermore advance public good and promote common interest ;** ³ *tsúne ni* always, *kokkén* Constitution, *omonjíru* to respect, *kokuhō* laws, *shǐtagáu* to observe ; *tsúne ni kokkén wo omónji kokuhō ni shǐtagái* **always respect the Constitution and observe the laws ;** ⁴ *ittán* once, *kankyū* emergency, *ittán kankyū áreba* **should emergency arise,** ⁵ *giyū* courage, *kō* public good=State, *hōjiru* to sacrifice oneself ; *giyū kō ni hōji* **offer yourself courageously to the State ;** ⁶ *mótte* and thus, *tenjō* heaven and earth, *mukyū no* eternal, *kōun* the prosperity of the Imperial Throne, *fuyokú surú* to guard and maintain ; *mótte tenjō mukyū no kōun wo fuyokú subéshi* **and thus guard and maintain the prosperity of our Imperial Throne coeval with heaven and earth,** ⁷ *Kakú no gótoki wa* so, *hǐtóri* only, *chūryō* good and faithful, *táru=de áru* to be, ...*nóminarazu matá mótte* not only....but ; *Kakú no gótoki wa hǐtóri Chin ga chūryō no shimmín tarú nóminarazu matá mótte* **So that ye not only be Our good faithful subjects, but....** ⁸ *sósen* ancestors, *ifū* traditions, *kenshō surú* to render illustrious, *tarán=tarú* to be worth ; *nanjí sósen no ifū wo kenshō surú ni tarán.* **but render illustrious the best traditions of your forefathers.** ⁹ *Konó michí wa jitsú ni* This way indeed=**The Way here set forth is indeed** ¹⁰ *wága kōso kōsō no* by Our Imperial Ancestors, *íkun* the teaching of the departed, *ni shǐté=de arimásŭ ; wága kōso kōsō no íkun ni shǐté* **the teaching bequeathed by Our Imperial Ancestors** ¹¹ *shisón* descendants, *tomó ni* together with, *júnshu subéki tokoró* to be observed ; *shisón shimmín no tomó ni júnshu subéki tokoró* **to be observed alike by Their Descendents and the subjects** ¹² *kókon* all ages, *ni tsūjite* through, *ayamárazu* infallible, *chūgai* home and abroad, *hodokosú* to give, *motóru* to conflict with ; *koré wo kókon ni tsūjite ayamárazu koré wo chūgai ni hodokoshité motórazu* **infallible for all ages and true in all places** ¹³ *Chin nanjí shimmín to tomó ni* **In common with you, Our subjects** ¹⁴ *kenkén fukuyō surú* to keep something carefully in one's mind, *tokú* virtue, *ítsu ni sen kotó wo* together, *koinegáu* wish ; *kenkén fukuyō shǐté miná sonó tokú wo ítsu ni sen kotó wo koinegáu* **It is Our wish to lay it to heart in all reverence in common with you, Our subjects, that we may all thus attain to the same virtue.** ¹⁵ *Méiji ni-jū-san-nen jū-gatsú san-jū-nichí* **The 30th day of the 10th month of the 23rd year of Meiji.** ¹⁶ *Gyómei* The Emperor's name, *Gyóji* Imperial Seal

② Momotarō no Hanashí[1]

Mukashí mukashí ojíisan to obāsan[2] ga arimáshĭta. Ojíisan wa máinichí yamá e shibakarí[3] ni ikimáshĭta, obāsan wa kawá e sentakú[4] ni ikimáshĭta.

Aru hi[5] obāsan ga kawá de sentakú wo shĭté irú to[6] kawakamí[7] kará ōkina momó ga dómburiko dómburiko to nagárete[8] kimáshĭta. Obāsan wa sonó momó wo hirotté[9] uchí e mótte kaerimáshĭta. Ojíisan ga yamá kará káetta tokí sonó momó wo misemáshĭta.[10] Ojíisan wa " Koré wa koré wa mezurashíi[11] ōki-na momó da ne " to itté yorokobimáshĭta.[12] Obāsan ga momó wo kirō to surú to[13] momó ga fŭtatsú ni wareté[14] náka kará otokonokó ga umaremáshĭta.[15] Momó kará umaremáshĭta kará[16] Momotarō to na wo tsŭkemáshĭta.[17] Momotarō wa ōkiku nátte taisō tsúyoku narimáshĭta.[18]

Aru hi Momotarō wa ojíisan to obāsan ni " Watashí wa Oní-ga-Shimá[19] e oní wo séibatsu[20] ni ikitái désŭ. Dōzo kibidángo[21] wo koshiraeté kudasái" to iimáshĭta. Obāsan wa kibidángo wo koshiraeté yarimáshĭta.[22] Momotarō wa sonó kibidángo wo koshi ni tsŭkéte[23] isamáshiku[24] dekakemáshĭta. Sŭkóshi ikú to[25] mukō kará[26] inú ga kimáshĭta. " Momotarō San, dóko e irrasshaimásŭ ka." " Oní-ga-Shimá e oní wo séibatsu ni ikimásŭ." " O-koshí ni tsŭkéta monó wa nan désŭ ka." " Nippónichí no[27] kibidángo désŭ." " Hĭtótsu kudasái. O-tómo shimashō."[28] Momotarō wa inú ni kibidángo wo hĭtótsu yarimáshĭta. Inú wa yorokónde kérai ni narimáshĭta.[29] Sorekará Momotarō to inú ga sŭkóshi ikú to

---

[1] *momó* peach, *Tarō* a common Japanese name given to persons of masculine sex, *Momotarō* Peach-boy, *hanashí* story ; *Momotarō no hanashí* The story of Momotarō [2] *Mukashí mukashí* Once upon a time, *ojíisan* an old man, *obāsan* an old woman [3] *shibakarí* gathering firewood, *shibakarí ni* in order to gather firewood [4] *sentakú* washing; *sentakú ni* for washing [5] *áru hi* one day [6] *sentakú wo shĭté irú to* while she was washing [7] upper reaches of a river, upstream, *kawakamí kará* from upstream [8] *dómburiko dómburiko* up and down, when moved by water ; *nagáreru* to float; *dómburiko dómburiko to nagárete kimáshĭta* came floating up and down the water [9] *hiroú* to pick up [10] showed(him) [11] extraordinary, unusual [12] *yorokóbu* to be glad [13] *kirō to surú to* as she was going to cut [14] *fŭtatsú ni warerú* to split in two (intransitive) [15] *umarerú* to be born [16] *momó kará* from a peach, *umaremáshĭta kará* as he was born [17] *na wo tsŭkéru* to name ; *Momotarō to na wo tsŭkemáshĭta* named him Momotarō [18] *taisō tsúyoku narimáshĭta* became very strong [19] Devil's Island [20] *oní* devil, *séibatsu ni* to conquer [21] *kíbi* millet *dángo* dumplings [22] *koshiraeté yarú* to make and give [23] *koshí* waist, *koshí ni tsŭkéte* hanging it to his waist [24] gallantly [25] *sŭkóshi ikú to* after walking for a while [26] *mukō kará* from the opposite side [27] *Nippón ichí no* the best in Japan [28] *o-tómo surú* to accompany [29] *kérai* follower; *kérai ni narimáshĭta* became his follower

Momotarō wa oni no taishō to tatakaimashita. (Page 609)

....momo ga futatsu ni warete naka kara otokonoko ga umare-
mashita.   (Page 608)

Momotarō wa sono takaramono wo kuruma ni tsumimashita.
(Page 609)

sáru[1] ni aimáshĭta. Sáru wa inú to onáji kotó wo Momotarō ni kikimáshĭta.[2] Momotarō wa sáru ni mo kibidángo wo hĭtótsu yarimáshĭta.
Sáru wa yorokónde Momotarō no kérai ni narimáshĭta. Momotarō to
inú to sarú to ga mō sŭkóshi ittá tokí ni kijí[3] ni aimáshĭta. Konó kijí
mo máe no inú ya sarú to onáji kotó wo iimáshĭta nóde[4] Momotarō wa
kibidángo wo hĭtótsu yarimáshĭta. Kijí wa yorokónde Momotarō no
kérai ni narimáshĭta. Momotarō wa, inú, sáru, kijí wo tsureté Oní-ga-
Shimá e tsŭkimáshĭta.[5]

Oní wa tetsú no mon wo shikkári shímete imáshĭta kará[6] Momotarō
wa háiru[7] kotó ga dekimasén déshĭta. Sokodé kijí wa tónde itté[8] ué
kará tekí no yōsu wo shirabemáshĭta.[9] Sáru wa mon wo nobotté[10] náka
e háiri,[11] mon no kagí wo hazushĭté[12] mon wo akemáshĭta. Momotarō
to inú wa isshó ni semeirimáshĭta.[13] Kijí wa tobimawátte[14] oní no me wo
tsuttsukimáshĭta.[15] Sáru wa oní wo hikkakimáshĭta.[16] Inú wa oní e kui-
tsŭkimáshĭta.[17] Momotarō wa oní no táishō to tatakaimáshĭta.[18] Momotarō ga taihén tsuyói nóde[19] oní no táishō wa tōtō kōsan shimáshĭta.[20]
"Mō kesshĭté warúi kotó wo shimasén kará[21] dōzo ínochi wo tasŭkéte
kudasái" to negaimáshĭta.[22]

Momotarō wa oní no táishō wo yurúshite yarimáshĭta.[23] Oní no
táishō wa o-réi ni iró-iró no takaramonó wo sashidashimáshĭta.[24]
Momotarō wa sonó takaramonó wo kurumá ni tsumimáshĭta.[25] Inú
ga sonó kurumá wo hikimáshĭta,[26] Sáru ga áto wo oshimáshĭta.[27] Kijí
ga tsuná wo hikimáshĭta.[28]- Soshĭté isamáshiku uchí e kaerimáshĭta.
Ojíisan to obāsan wa taihén yorokobimáshĭta. Sorekará minná kōfuku
ni kurashimáshĭta.[29]

---

[1] *sáru* monkey [2] *Sáru wa inú*…. The monkey asked the same thing that the dog
had asked [3] pheasant [4] *onaji kotó wo iimáshĭta nóde* having said the same thing
[5] *tsureté* taking with, *tsŭkú* to arrive [6] *tetsú no mon* iron gate, *shikkári shiméru* to
close firmly, *shímete imáshĭta kará* as they had closed firmly [7] to enter [8] *sokodé* then,
tónde itté having flown [9] *ué kará* from above, *tekí* enemy, *yōsu* condition, *shirabéru*
to examine, to observe [10] *noború* to climb [11] *náka e háiri* entered inside and
[12] *kagí wo hazusú* to unlock [13] *isshó ni* together; *semeirú* to break into, to raid
[14] *tobimawáru* to fly about [15] *me* eye, *tsuttsúku* to peck [16] *hikkáku* to scratch
[17] *kuitsŭkú* to bite [18] *táishō* chief, leader; *tatakaú* to fight [19] *tsuyói nóde* being
strong [20] *tōtō* at last, *kōsan surú* to surrender [21] *mō* again, *kesshĭté* never, *warúi
kotó wo shimasén kará* as I shall not do anything bad [22] *ínochi* life, *tasŭkéru* to
spare, *negáu* to beseech [23] *yurúshĭte yarú* to pardon, to grant a request [24] *o-réi*
return present, *iró-iró* various, *takaramonó* treasures, *sashidasú* to offer [25] *kurumá*
cart, *tsumú* to load [26] *hikú* to pull [27] *áto wo* from behind, *osú* to push [28] *tsuná*
rope, *hikú* to tug, to pull [29] *kōfuku ni* happily, *kurasú* to live

③ Hanasaká-Jijíi¹ no Hanashí

Mukashí áru tokoró ni² yói ojíisan ga arimáshĭta. Ojíisan wa inú wo ippikí kátte imáshĭta.³ Inú no namaé wa "Póchi" to iimáshĭta.⁴ Ojíisan wa Póchi wo taihén kawaigátte imáshĭta.⁵ Póchi mo ojíisan wo sŭkí déshĭta.

Aru hi Póchi ga hataké no súmi de "Ojíisan, kokó wo horí nasái, wan-wan" to hoemáshĭta.⁶ Ojíisan ga sokó wo hóru to tsuchí no náka kará⁷ takaramonó ga takŭsán demáshĭta. Tonarí no yokú-no-fukái⁸ ojíisan ga soré wo míte "Dōzo watashí ni Póchi wo kashĭté kudasái" to iimáshĭta. Sokodé konó yokú-no-fukái ojíisan wa Póchi wo múri ni hoesasemáshĭta.⁹ Soshĭté sokó wo horimáshĭta¹⁰ ga tsuchí no náka kará kitanái monó¹¹ ga demáshĭta. Yokú-no-fukái ojíisan wa okótte¹² Póchi wo koroshimáshĭta.¹³ Yói ojíisan wa soré wo hijō ni kanashimimáshĭta.¹⁴ Soshĭté Póchi no o-haká wo táte, sonó ué ni ki wo íppon uemáshĭta.¹⁵ Konó ki wa zun-zun ōkiku narimáshĭta.¹⁶ Yói ojíisan wa konó ki wo kítte soré de úsu wo tsŭkurimáshĭta.¹⁷ Sonó úsu no náka de o-komé wo tsŭkú to o-komé ga minná kin ni narimáshĭta.¹⁸ Yokú-no-fukái ojíisan wa soré wo míte sonó úsu wo karí ni kimáshĭta.¹⁹ Soshĭté sonó úsu de o-komé wo tsúita tokí ni o-komé wa kitanái monó

---

¹ *hanasaká=haná wo sakaserú* to cause flowers to bloom; *Hanasaká-Jijíi* The old man that caused flowers to bloom ² *áru tokoró ni* in a certain place ³ *inú wo káu* to keep a dog; *Ojíisan....imáshĭta* The old man was keeping a dog ⁴ *Inú....iimáshĭta* The dog was called Pochi. ⁵ *kawaigáru* to love ⁶ *hataké* field, *súmi* corner, *wan-wan* bow-wow, *hoéru* to bark, *hóru* to dig; *Aru hi....wan-wan* One day, at the corner of a field, the dog said (bowwowed): Master, dig here. Note that in Japanese an old man may properly be adressed as "*Ojíisan*"=old man.⁷ *tsuchí* soil, earth; *tsuchí no náka kará* from the earth ⁸ *tonarí* neighbour, *yokú-no-fukái* avaricious, *kasú* to lend ⁹ *múri ni* forcibly, *hoesaséru* to cause to bark ¹⁰ *Soshĭté....*Then he dug there. ¹¹ *kitanái monó* dirty things ¹² *okóru* to get angry ¹³ killed ¹⁴ *kanashímu* to be grieved; *Yói....kanashimimáshĭta* The good old man was much grieved on account of that. ¹⁵ *haká* grave, *haká wo tatéru* to construct a tomb, *uerú* to plant; *Soshĭté....uemáshĭta.* Then he planted a tree on Pochi's grave. ¹⁶ *zun-zun* quickly; *Konó....*This tree soon became big. ¹⁷ *úsu* mortar; *Yói....*The good old man made a mortar out of that tree. ¹⁸ *o-komé wo tsŭkú* to beat, to pound rice dough—In Japan rice dough used to be pounded in a mortar to make it firmer. With rice dough various kinds of cake are made. *Sonó úsu....narimáshĭta.* When he pounded the rice dough that was in the mortar, it became all gold. ¹⁹ *karí ni kimáshĭta* came to borrow

....o-kome wa kitanai mono ni narimashita.
(Page 610)

....o-kome ga minna kin ni narimashita.
(Page 610)

.....soko wo horimashita ga tsuchi no naka
kara kitanai mono ga demashita.

(Page 610)

Ojiisan ga soko wo horu to tsuchi no naka kara
takara mono ga takusan demashita.

(Page 610)

Suruto kareki no eda ni hana ga kirei ni sakimashita. (Page 611)

Urashima Tarō wa hijō ni yorokonde kame no senaka ni norimashita.
(Page 612)

....Urashima wa totsuzen shiraga no ojiisan ni natte shimaimashita.
(Page 613)

ni narimáshĭta kará[1] yokú-no-fukái ojíisan wa taisō okótte úsu wo moshĭté shimaimáshĭta.[2] Yói ojíisan wa sonó haí wo moratté soré wo makimáshĭta.[3] Surutó karekí-no-edá ni haná ga kírei ni sakimáshĭta.[4] Sonó tokí chōdo tonosamá ga sokó wo o-tōri ni nátte sonó haná wo taihén homemáshĭta soshĭté yói ojíisan ni takŭsán hōbi wo ataemáshĭta.[5] Soré wo míta yokú-no-fukái ojíisan wa[6] súgu ni mané wo shĭté haí wo makimáshĭta ga haí wa tonosamá no me no náka e hairimáshĭta.[7] Tonosamá wa taihén okótte konó yokú-no-fukái ojíisan wo rō ni ireté shimaimáshĭta.[8]

A Children's Song

This is the beginning of a song telling the story of Hanasaká-Jijíi.

Urá no hataké de Póchi ga nakú[9]
うら の 畑 で ポチ が なく
Shōjiki jíisan hóttareba[10]
正直 じいさんほったれば
Ōban kóban ga záku-záku záku-záku.[11]
大判 小判 が ざく ざく ざく ざく。
Ijíwaru jíisan Póchi karité[12]
いじ悪 じいさん ポチ 借りて
Soré de hataké wo hóttarebá[13]
それ で 畑 を ほったれば
Kawará ya setokaké gára-gára gára-gára.[14]
瓦 や せとかけ がら がら がら がら。

---

[1] Soshĭté....kará Then, as the rice became a dirty thing after beating it....[2] mosú to burn; yokú....shimaimáshĭta The avaricious man became angry and burnt the mortar. [3] hai ashes, máku to scatter; Yói....The good old man, having received the ashes, scattered them around. [4] surutó thereupon, karekí dead tree, edá branch of a tree, sakú to bloom; Thereupon, flowers bloomed beautifully on the branches of the dead trees. [5] tonosamá a lord, o-tōri ni nátte while passing, homéru to admire, hōbi reward, ataerú to give; Sonó tokí....ataemáshĭta. Just at that moment a lord passed by and much admired those flowers, and he gave a reward to the good old man. [6] Soré wo....The avaricious man, who saw that.... [7] mané wo surú to imitate; súgu....he immediately scattered ashes, but they entered the lord's eyes. [8] rō prison, ireté shimaú to end by putting into; Tonosamá....The lord became angry and put the avaricious old man into prison. [9] In the backfield Pochi is barking; urá back, hataké field, nakú to bark [10] The honest old man when he digs (there); jíisan short for ojíisan old man, hóru to dig, hóttareba when he digs [11] large gold coins (and) small gold coins (come out) jingling (and) jingling; ōban large gold coin, kóban small gold coin, záku-záku jingling (onomatopoetic expression) [12] The wicked old man Pochi having borrowed; ijíwaru wicked, karirú to borrow [13] and then in the field when he digs; soré de and then [14] pieces of tiles and broken pieces of china (come out) rattling (and) rattling; kawará tiles, setokaké broken pieces of china, gára-gára rattling (onomatopoetic expression)

④ Urashimá Tarō no Hanashí

NOTE. Urashima Taro is considered the Rip Van Winckle of Japan, and is supposed to have lived at the Sea-God's Palace three hundred years, which long period of time Urashima thought had not been longer than a few days.

Mukashí, Urashimá Tarō to iú ryōshi ga arimáshǐta.[1] Aru hi hamabé wo tōtte irú to[2] kodomotachí ga ōzei atsumátte sawáide imáshǐta.[3] Míru to kodomotachí wa ippikí no ōkina káme wo tsŭkamaeté ijimeté imá-shǐta[4]. Urashimá Tarō wa soré wo taihén kawaisō ni omótte kodomo-tachí ni "Sonná ni káme wo ijimeté wa ikenái" to iimáshǐta[5] ga kodomotachí wa kikimasén[6] déshǐta. Soshǐté masú-masú káme wo ijime-máshǐta kará[7] Urashimá Tarō wa "Sorenára watashí ga sonó káme wo kaō" to itté káme wo kaitorimáshǐta.[8] Soshǐté sonó káme wo úmi e hanáshǐte yarimáshǐta.[9]

Soré kará ni-san-nichí nochí Urashimá Tarō ga fúne ni nótte tsurí wo shǐté irú to[10] "Urashimá San, Urashimá San" to yóbu kóe ga shi-máshǐta.[11] Dáre ka to omótte furikáette míru to soré wa ōki-na káme déshǐta.[12] Sonó káme wa fúne no sóba e oyóide kimáshǐta.[13] Soshǐté ureshisō ni o-jigí wo shimáshǐta.[14] "Konó aidá wa arigatō gozaimáshǐta.[15] Watashí wa anáta ga tasŭkéta káme désŭ.[16] Dōzo watashí no senaká ni o-nori kudasái.[17] Watashí wa anáta wo Ryūgū e o-tsuré shimásŭ" to iimáshǐta.[18] Urashimá Tarō wa hijō ni yorokónde káme no senaká ni norimáshǐta. Soré kará káme wa úmi no sokó e[19] oyóide ikimáshǐta. Kaitéi wa jitsú ni kírei déshǐta.[20] Mamónaku Urashimá Tarō to káme

---

[1] *ryōshi* fisherman ; *Mukashí*....Once upon a time there was a fisherman called Urashima Tarō. [2] *hamabé* seaside, beach; *tōtte irú to* while he was passing=while he was walking along [3] *atsumátte* gathering, *atsumáru* to gather (v. i.), *sawágu* to make noise [4] *tsŭkamaerú* to hold, *ijimerú* to tease ; *Míru to*....When he looked, the children were holding and teasing a large turtle. [5] *kawaisō ni omóu* to pity ; *Urashimá....to iimáshǐta.* Urashimá Taro, pitying it, said to the children : You shouldn't tease it in such a way. [6] *kikú* to listen to [7] *Soshǐté....kará* As they teased the turtle more and more [8] *kaú* and *kaitóru* to buy ; *Urashimá....kaitori-máshǐta.* "Then I shall buy the turtle," said Urashimá Taro, and bought it. [9] *úmi* sea, *hanáshǐte yarú* to let free [10] *fúne ni norú* to be in a boat, *tsurí wo surú* to fish ; *Soré....irú to* Then two or three days later, while Urashima was fishing in a boat.... [11] "*Urashimá San*....a voice called "Urashimá San, Urashimá San." [12] *furikáeru* to turn one's head ; *Dáre....déshǐta.* Wondering who it was, and upon turning his head (he saw that) it was the large turtle. [13] *oyógu* to swim ; *Sonó*....The turtle swam to the boat. [14] *ureshisō ni* delightfully, *o-jigí wo surú* to bow [15] *konó aidá* the other day ; "*Konó*....*gozaimáshǐta.* I thank you for what you did the other day. [16] *tasŭkéru* to save ; *Watashí....désŭ.* I am the turtle you helped. [17] *senaká* back, *norú* to ride ; *Dōzo....kudasái.* Please ride on my back. [18] *Ryūgū* the Sea-God's Palace ; *Watashí....iimáshǐta.* He said : I shall take you to the Sea-God's Palace. [19] *úmi no sokó e* to the bottom of the sea [20] *kaitéi* the bottom of the sea, *jitsú ni* really ; *Kaitéi....déshǐta.* The bottom of the sea was really beautiful.

wa rippá-na Ryūgū e tsŭkimáshĭta.[1] Ryūgū ni wa utsŭkushíi Otóhime-Samá[2] ga orimáshĭta. Otóhime-Samá wa Urashimá Tarō ni takŭsán no go-chisō wo shimáshĭta.[3] Urashimá wa uchí e káeru no wo wasureté mái-nichí tanóshiku kurashimáshĭta.[4] Sonó uchí ni Urashimá wa ryō-shin no kotó wo kangáe uchí e kaerítaku narimáshĭta.[5] Aru hi Otó-hime-Samá ni " Dōmo nágaku oséwa ni narimáshĭta. Iró-iró arigatō gozaimáshĭta. Watakŭshí wa kyō uchí e kaerimásŭ " to iimáshĭta.[6] Surutó Otóhime-Samá wa kírei-na hakó wo o-miyagé ni Urashimá ni kuremáshĭta.[7] Soshĭté " Konó hakó wa kesshĭté aketé wa ikemasén " to iimáshĭta.[8]

Urashimá wa sonó hakó wo kakaeté káme no senaká ni notté káette ikimáshĭta.[9] Urashimá ga móto no hamabé ni tsúita tokí sokó no yōsu wa zémbu kawatté imáshĭta.[10] Jibún no ié mo ryōshin mo tomo-dachí mo miatarimasén déshĭta.[11] Urashimá Tarō wo obóete irú hĭto wa hĭtóri mo imasén déshĭta.[12] Urashimá wa yumé no yō ni omoimá-shĭta.[13] Soshité achirá-kochirá wo arukimáshĭta.[14] Dan-dan kanashikú narimáshĭta nóde Otóhime-Samá kará morattá hakó wo aketé mimá-shĭta.[15] Surutó náka kará shirói kemurí ga tachinoborimáshĭta.[16] Sonó kemurí ga Urashimá no kaó ni kakátta[17] tokí ni Urashimá wa totsuzén shiragá no ojíisan ni nátte shimaimáshĭta.

---

[1] *mamónaku* soon, *rippá-na* magnificent, *tsŭkú* to arrive   [2] *Otóhime-Samá* the princess of Sea-God's Palace   [3] *takŭsán no go-chisō wo surú* to give a big feast   [4] *Urashimá....kurashimáshĭta.* Urashima, forgetting to go back home, was living happily every day.   [5] *Sonó uchí ni* By and by, *ryōshin* parents, *uchí e kaeritáku narimáshĭta*, began to wish to go home   [6] *Iró-iró....iimáshĭta.* and he said: I thank you very much for everything. To-day I shall go back home.   [7] *Surutó* Thereupon, *hakó* box, *o-miyagé ni* as a present, *kuremáshĭta* gave   [8] *Soshĭté....iimáshĭta.* Then she said: You must never open this box.   [9] *kakaerú* to carry; *Urashimá....iki-máshĭta.* Urashima, riding on the turtle's back, went back with the box.   [10] *motó no hamabé* the same beach, *yōsu* condition, *zémbu kawatté imáshĭta* had entirely changed; *Urashimá....imáshĭta.* When Urashima returned to the same beach, con-ditions there had entirely changed.   [11] *miatarú* to be found; *Jibún....déshĭta.* His home, parents, and friends could not be found.   [12] *Urashimá....déshĭta.* There wasn't even one person who remembered Urashima.   [13] Urashima thought it was all a dream.   [14] *achirá-kochirá* here and there, *arúku* to walk   [15] *Dan-dan* Little by little, *kanashikú náru* to become sad; *Dan-dan....mimáshĭta.* As he was becoming sad, he opened and looked in the box that he received from the princess.   [16] *shirói kemurí* white smoke, *tachinoború* to rise up   [17] *kaó* face, *kakáru* to envelop, *totsuzén* suddenly, *shiragá no ojíisan* a white-haired old man, *ni nátte shimaimáshĭta* becoming ended = became at last

⑤ Níntoku Tennō[1] no O-hanashí

Níntoku Tennō wa Nihón no dái jū-rokú dái no Tennō Héika[2] de tai-hén nasaké-bukái on-katá de irasshaimáshĭta.[3]

Aru ása Tennō wa góten no takái tokoró e o-agarí ni nátte[4] shihō wo gorán ni narimáshĭta.[5] Sonó tokí chōdo jimmín wa ása no góhan wo takú jikán déshĭta ga dóko no ié kará mo kemurí ga agarimasén dé-shĭta.[6] Tennō wa soré wo fushigí ni o-omoí ni nátte kínji no monó ni o-tazuné ni narimáshĭta.[7] Kínji no monó wa "Konogoró wa o-komé ga taihén fusakú de jimmín wa taisō mazushíi kurashí wo shĭté imásŭ" to mōshiagemáshĭta tokoró[8] Tennō wa "Soré wa kawaisō désŭ. Soré de wa koré kará san-nen no aidá sozéi wo osamenákute mo yoroshíi" to ōse ni narimáshĭta.[9] Jimmín wa námida wo nagáshĭte yorokobimá-shĭta.[10]

San-nen no nochí Tennō ga góten no takái tokoró e o-agarí ni nari-máshĭta tokí[11] dóko no ié kará mo kemurí ga tachí-nobotté imáshĭta.[12] Sonó tokí Tennō wa o-sobá no Kōgō ni "Ā, Chin wa tomimáshĭta" to ōse ni narimáshĭta.

---

[1] The Emperor Nintoku ruled over Japan at the beginning of the 4th century A. D. [2] *dái-jū-rokú-dái no Tennō Héika* the sixteenth Emperor [3] *nasaké-bukái on-katá* kind hearted person, merciful person, *de irasshaimáshĭta* equivalent to *déshĭta* [4] *áru ása* one morning, *góten* palace, *takái tokoró e* to a high place, *o-agarí ni náru* polite form for *agarú* to go up [5] *shihō* four directions, *gorán ni narimáshĭta* he looked (polite); *shihō....he* looked around in all directions [6] *góhan wo takú* to boil rice; *jíkan* time, *kemurí* smoke, *agarú* to rise; *Sonó....agarimasén déshĭta.* It was then just the time when people boil their morning rice (the rice for breakfast), but no smoke was rising from any house. [7] *fushigí ni omóu* to wonder, *kínji no monó* attendants, *o-tazuné ni náru* polite for *tazunéru* to ask; *Tennō....narimáshĭta.* The Emperor, wondering what was the reason of that, inquired of his attendants about it. [8] *konogoró* recently, *fusakú* bad crop, *taisō* very, *mazushíi* poor, *kurashí* living, *mōshiageru* to say; *Kínji....tokoró* When his attendants said to him; On account of the recent bad crop the people have been living in very poor condition.... [9] *sozéi* taxes, *osaméru* to pay, *ōse ni náru* formal for *iú* to say; *Tennō....narimáshĭta.* the Emperor said: It is a pity; for three years they need not pay taxes. [10] *námida* tears, *nagásu* to run down; *námida wo nagáshĭte* with tears; *Jimmín....* The people wept for joy. [11] *San-nen....tokí* Three years later, when the Emperor went to the upper part (lit. high place) of his palace [12] *tachí-noború* to rise up; *dóko....imáshita.* smoke was rising up from every house. [13] *o-sobá* near, *tómu* to be wealthy, to be rich; *Sonó....narimáshĭta.* Then the Emperor said to the Empress, who was near him: Oh, I have become rich!

....doko no ie kara mo kemuri ga tachi-nobotte imashita.

(Page 614)

(His Majesty the Emperor, holding the umbrella, saluting the cheering crowd.)

Kōgō ga sonó o-kotobá no ími wo o-ukagái mōshiagemáshĭta tokí[1] Tennō wa "Jimmín ga tómu no wa Chin ga tómu no to onají désŭ. Jimmín wa kuní no motó désŭ" to ōse ni narimáshĭta.[2] Soshĭté áto san-nen-kan jimmín kará sozéi wo o-torí ni narimasén de[3] hitásura jimmín no kōfuku wo o-kangaé asobasaremáshĭta.[4] Rokú-nen no nochí jimmín wa susundé sozéi wo o-torí kudasáru yō-ni o-negái mōshiage-máshĭta.[5] Soshĭté jimmín wa yorokónde rippá-na góten wo Tennō no tamé ni tsŭkúri ítsŭ-máde-mo Tennō no go-jintokú (go-nintokú) wo kanshá shimáshĭta.[6]

KIMI-GA-YO

(The Japanese National Anthem)

Kimí ga yo wa[7]

Chiyó ni yáchiyo ni[8]

Sazaré-ishí no iwaó to nárite[9]

Koké no músu máde.[10]

君<ruby>き<rt></rt></ruby>が代<ruby>よ<rt></rt></ruby>

君<ruby>き<rt></rt></ruby>が代<ruby>よ<rt></rt></ruby>は千代<ruby>ち<rt></rt></ruby>に
八千代<ruby>ちよ<rt></rt></ruby>にさゞれ石<ruby>いし<rt></rt></ruby>の
巌<ruby>いわお<rt></rt></ruby>となりて
苔<ruby>こけ<rt></rt></ruby>のむすまで

---

[1] *ími* meaning, *o-ukagái mōshiageru* very polite for *ukagaú* to ask; *Kōgō....tokí* When the Empress asked the meaning of those words [2] *tómu* to become rich, *kuní no motó* the foundation of the country; *Tennō....narimáshĭta.* the Emperor said: When the people are rich, we also are rich (lit. The people to be rich we to be rich is the same). The people are the foundation of the country. [3] *Soshĭté....de* Then for another three years he did not take any taxes from his people, [4] *hitásura* earnestly, *kōfuku* welfare, *o-kangaé asobasaremáshĭta; hitásura....*and earnestly thought of their (lit. the people's) welfare [5] *susúnde* voluntarily, *o-torí kudasáru yō ni* to accept; *Rokú-nen....mōshiagemáshĭta.* After six years the people voluntarily begged to accept the taxes [6] *jintokú (nintokú)* benevolence, *kanshá surú* to thank; *Soshĭté....shimáshĭta.* Then the people felt happy and forever thanked the benevolence of their Emperor by building for him a splendid palace. [7] *kimí* sovereign, *ga* is here used to indicate the genitive case, and corresponds to *no, yo* era or rule; *Kimí ga yo wa* **May the dynasty endure** [8] *chiyó* one thousand years, *ni* yea, *yáchiyo* eight thousands years, *ni* for; *Chiyó ni yáchiyo ni* **a thousand, yea, eight thousand years** [9] *sazaré-ishí* pebble, *no* is here used instead of *ga*; *iwaó* rock, *nárite=nátte* subordinate of *náru* to become; *sazaré-ishí no iwaó to nárite* **until the time when the grains of sand** [10] *koké* moss, *koké no músu máde* mossy, covered with moss, *máde* until; *koké no músu máde.* **changed to rocks, are clothed with moss.**

⑥　　" Banzái " no Kígen[1]

Méiji-Taitéi wa iró-iró no go-rippá-na kotó wo Nihón no tamé ni asobasaremáshĭta.[2] Sonó náka no hĭtótsu wa kempō wo hajímete o-tsŭkurí ni nátta kotó désŭ.[3]

Nihón kempō wa Méiji ni-jū-ni-nen ni-gatsú jū-ichí nichí (Kigénsetsu) ni happú seraremáshĭta.[4] Sonó yokujitsú Méiji Tennō, Kōgō ryō héika wa Tōkyō shímin no o-negái wo o-yurushí ni nátte Uenó Kōen no shukugá-shikí ni o-nozomí ni narimáshĭta.[5]

Konó tokí ōzei no jimmín wa omówazu " Banzái " to sakénde o-mukaé mōshiagemáshĭta.[6] Koré ga " Banzái " wo sakébu yō-ni nátta hajimé de arimásŭ.[7]

---

[1] The word *banzái*, which, as the English *hurrah!* or *long live....!*, is used as a shout of joy and salutation, is composed of *ban* (ten thousand) and *sái* (year). *Banzái no kígen* The origin of " banzai." [2] *Taitéi* the Great Emperor, *iró-iró* various, *go-rippá-na* splendid, *kotó* things, *Nihón* Japan, *tamé ni* for, *asobasarerú* to deign to do; *Méiji....asobasaremáshĭta.* The Great Emperor Meiji did various splendid things for Japan. [3] *kempō* constitution, *o-tsŭkurí ni nátta* polite form for *tsŭkurimáshĭta*=did; *Sonó....désŭ.* One of them is the promulgation of the Constitution. [4] *happú surú* to promulgate, *happú seraremáshĭta* polite form for *happú surú* to promulgate; *Kigénsetsu* Empire Day; *Nihón....seraremáshĭta.* The Constitution of Japan was promulgated on the 11th of February of the 22nd year of Meiji (1889). [5] *yokujitsú* the following day, *Kōgō* the Empress, *ryō héika* both Majesties, *Tōkyō shímin no o-negái* the request of the Tōkyō citizens, *o-yurushí ni náru* polite form for *yurúsu* to grant, *Uenó Kōen* one of the largest parks in Tōkyō, *shukugá-shiki* celebration, *o-nozomí ni náru* polite form for *nozomú* to attend; *Sonó....narimáshĭta.* The following day, Their Majesties the Emperor and the Empress granted the request of the Tōkyō citizens by attending a celebration that was held at Ueno Park. [6] *omówazu* spontaneously, *sakénde* with a shout, *o-mukaé mōshiageru* very polite for *mukaerú* to welcome; *Konó....mōshiagemashĭta.* On this occasion many people spontaneously shouted " Banzai," [7] *sakébu* to shout; *Koré....arimásŭ.* This was how the shout of joy " Banzai " originated.

Onná no ushiró-súgata wo miokutté itá o-Shaká-Samá no me ni námida ga yadóte imáshita. (Buddha, with tears in his eyes, gazed after the woman until she was out of sight.) Page. 619.

The colossal bronze image of Buddha, cast in 1252 A.D.—Height 43 feet, circumference 97 feet, length of face 7.7 feet, of eye 3.3 feet, of ear 6.6 feet, of nose 2.8 feet. Weight 210,000 pounds.—

⑦   O-Shaká-Samá to Karashí no Tsúbu[1]

Mukashí O-Shaká-Samá no tokoró e hǐtóri no onná ga jibún no shindá akambō wo daité kimáshǐta.[2] Soshǐté, konó onná wa O-Shaká-Samá ni "Dōzo, watashí no akambō wo ikí-kaerásete kudasái" to nakí-nagará negaimáshǐta.[3]

Sonó tokí, O-Shaká-Samá wa shízuka-ni unazúite "Déwa, hǐtó-tsumamí no karashí no tsúbu wo hǐtó kará moratté,[4] shindá akambō no kaó ni kaké-nasái. Sō suréba akambō wa ikí-kaerú.[5] Tádashi, sonó karashí no tsúbu wa, kesshǐté dáre-mo shindá kotó no nái uchí no hǐtó kará morawá-nákereba naránai" to osshaimáshǐta.[6]

Koré wo kiité, onná wa taihén yorokóbi,[7] akambō no shigái wo kakaeté, ōisogi de, machí e ikimáshǐta.[8] Soshǐté sassokú, áru íe e itté,[9] "Sumimasén ga, karashí no tsúbu wo hǐtó-tsumamí itadakitái désǔ" to tano-

---

[1] *Sháka* is the Japanese name for Buddha, *O* and *Samá* are used as honorifics. The Indian name for Buddha is *Sakyamuni*. ... *karashí* mustard, *tsúbu* grain; *O-Shaká Samá to Karashí no Tsúbu* Buddha and the Mustard Grain   [2] *Mukashí*, Once upon a time, *hǐtóri no onná* a woman, *jibún no* her own, *shindá* past of *shinú* to die, *akambō* baby, *daité* sub. of *dakú* to carry in one's arms; *Mukashí, O-Shaká-Samá no tokoró e hǐtóri no onná ga jibún no shindá akambō wo daité kimáshǐta.* Once upon a time, a woman, carrying her dead baby, went to Buddha's place.   [3] *soshǐté* and, then, *ikí-kaerásete* sub. of *ikí-kaeraserú* causative of *ikí-kaerú* to revive, *nakú* to cry, weep, *nakí-nagará* while weeping, *negaimáshǐta* past of *negáu* to beg, to beseech; *Soshǐté, konó onná wa O-Shaká-Samá ni "Dōzo, watashí no akambō wo ikí-kaerásete kudasái" to nakí-nagará negaimáshǐta.* And in tears, she beseeched Buddha (with these words): "I pray, restore my child to life."   [4] *Sonó tokí* Then, *shízuka-ni* calmly, *unazúite* sub. of *unazúku* to nod, bow one's head in assent, *Déwa* Well, well then, *hǐtó-tsumamí* a pinch of, *moratté* sub. of *moraú* to get, to receive, obtain; *Sonó tokí, O-Shaká-Samá wa shízuka-ni unazúite "Déwa, hǐtó-tsumamí no karashí no tsúbu wo hǐtó kará moratté,* Then, Buddha calmly nodding (said): "Well, get from someone a pinch of mustard grains (and)....   [5] *kaó* face, *kakéru* to sprinkle, *Sō suréba* If you do so; *shindá akambō no kaó ni kaké-nasái. Sō suréba, akambō wa ikikaerú.* sprinkle them over the face of the dead child. In this way your child will return to life.   [6] *tádashi* provided that, on condition that, *kesshǐté* never, on no account, by no means, *dáre mo shindá kotó no nái uchí* a house where nobody died, *morawá-nákereba naránai* must be obtained, given, *ossháru* to say; *Tádashi, sonó karashí no tsúbu wa, kesshǐté dáre-mo shindá kotó no nái uchí no hǐtó kará morawá-nákereba naránai to osshaimáshǐta.* However, the mustard grains must be had, by all means, only from a person in whose family no death occurred."   [7] *kiité* having heard, sub. of *kikú* to hear, *yorokóbi*, short for *yorokobimáshǐta* was glad; *Koré wo kiité, onná wa taihén yorokóbi,* Upon hearing this, the woman was very glad (and)....   [8] *kakaeté* sub. of *kakaerú* to hold, carry in one's arms, *ō-ísogi de* in a great hurry, *machí* town; *akambō no shigái wo kakaeté, ō-ísogi de, machí e ikimáshǐta.* .....carrying the body of her dead baby in her arms, rushed to the town.   [9] *sassokú* at once, *áru* a certain, *íe* house, *itté* sub. of *ikú* to go; *Soshǐté, sassokú, áru íe e itté* Then she went to a certain house....

mimáshĭta.[1] Sonó ié no hĭtó ga, "Sā, sā, dōzo, go-enryonáku o-mochí nasái" to ittá tokí ni,[2] onná wa tamerái-nágara, "Chottó, ukagaimásŭ ga, o-takú de wa imá-máde ni, dónata-ka nakunarimáshĭta ka" to tazunemáshĭta.[3]

Konó ié no hĭtó wa, "Mochíron, uchí no toshiyorí ya shínrui no monó ga shinimáshĭta yo" to kotaemáshĭta.[4]

Surutó onná wa tanónda karashí no tsúbu wo morawazú-ni, déte-itté shimaimáshĭta.[5] Onná wa, isóide tsugí no ié e itté, máe to onají kotó wo kikimáshĭta[6] ga, yappári, sokó no uchí de mo, iró-iró no hĭtó ga shindé imáshĭta nóde, karashí no tsúbu wo moraemasén déshĭta.[7]

---

[1] *sumimasén ga,* Excuse me, *itadakitái* I wish to have, wish to be given, *tanomimáshĭta* past of *tanómu* to beg, entreat, beseech ; "*Sumimasén ga, karashí no tsúbu wo hĭtó-tsumamí itadakitái dĕsŭ" to tanomimáshĭta.* (and) entreatingly said : "Pardon me, but I should like to have a pinch of mustard grains." [2] *Sā, sā* certainly, *go-enryonáku* at your convenience, as you wish, unreservedly, *o-mochí nasái* take (them), *to ittá tokí ni* when he said ; *Sonó ié no hĭtó ga, "Sā, sā, dōzo, go-enryonáku o-mochí nasái" to ittá tokí ni,* When the man of that house had said : "Certainly, please, take (as many) as you like," [3] *tamerái-nágara* hesitatingly, *tameráu* to hesitate, *chottó* a moment, just a minute, *ukagaú* to inquire, *Chottó, ukagaimásŭ ga* Excuse me but,....*o-takú* your home, your family, *imá-máde ni* up to now, *nakunarú* to die, *tazunéru* to ask, to inquire ; *onná wa tamerái-nágara, "Chottó, ukagaimásŭ ga, o-takú de wa imá-máde ni, dónata-ka nakunarimáshĭta ka" to tazunemáshĭta.* Excuse me, but did anyone of your family die before now?" [4] *mochíron* Of course, *uchí no toshiyorí* the old folks of our family, *shínrui* relatives, *monó* persons, *shinú* to die, *kotaéru* to answer, *yo* emphatic particle ; *Konó ié no hĭtó wa' "Mochíron, uchí no toshiyorí ya shínrui no monó ga shinimáshĭta yo" to kotaemáshĭta.* The man of the house replied : "Of course, our old folks and relatives have passed away." [5] *Surutó* thereupon, *tanónda* past of *tanómu* to ask for, *morawazú-ni* without taking, *moraú* to get, receive, accept, take, *déte-ikú* to leave, go away, *shimaimáshĭta* past of *shimaú* to end by, *déte-itté shimaimáshĭta* left, went away ; *Surutó, onná wa tanónda karashí no tsúbu wo morawazú-ni, déte-itté shimaimáshĭta.* Thereupon, the woman went away without taking any grains. [6] *isóide* in a hurry, *tsugí no* next, *máe to* as before, *onají kotó* the same thing, *kikú* to ask, inquire ; *Onná wa, isóide tsugí no ié e itté, máe to onají kotó wo kikimáshĭta....*In a hurry she went to the next house and asked the same thing as before [7] *ga* but, however, *yappári* also, likewise, as well, *iró-iró* several, *shindé imáshĭta* died, *nóde* as, because, *moraerú* to be able to obtain ; *ga, yappári, sokó no uchí de mo, iró-iró no hĭtó ga shindé imáshĭta nóde, karashí no tsúbu wo moraemasén déshĭta.* however, as in that house also, like in the first one, several people had died, she could not get any grains.

Shikáshi, onná wa, shimbō-zúyoku, machí-jū no ié wo nokórazu tazú-nete mimáshĭta[1] ga, hĭtó ga kesshĭté shinanákatta to iú ié wa íkken mo arimasén déshĭta.[2]

Yūgata, onná wa, tsŭkáre-kitté, o-Shaká-Samá no tokoró e káette ikimáshĭta.[3] Sonó tokí, o-Shaká-Samá wa, yasashikú, "Omaé to onají kanashimí wo hoká no hĭtó mo mótte irú no désŭ" to osshaimáshĭta.[4]

Onná wa damátte, jibún no akambō no shigái wo daité, bóchi no hō e shió-shió-to tachí-satté ikimáshĭta.[5] Onná no ushiró-súgata wo mi-okutté itá o-Shaká-Samá no me ni námida ga yadótte imáshĭta.[6]

---

[1] *shimbō-zúyoku* patiently, *machí-jū* the whole town, *-jū* throughout, all over, etc., *nokórazu* all through, without exception, etc., *tazunéru* to make inquiry for, to be in search for, *tazúnete-míru* to try to ask; *Shikáshi, onná wa, shimbō-zúyoku, machí-jū no ié wo nokórazu tazúnete mimáshĭta....* Still, patiently did she try to inquire at every house in the whole town.... [2] *shinanákatta* negative past of *shinú* to die, *íkken mo* even one house; *ga, hĭtó ga kesshĭté shinanákatta to iú ié wa ikkén mo arimasén déshĭta.* however, houses in which no person had died there were none. [3] *yūgata* evening, in the evening, *tsŭkáre-kitté* sub. of *tsŭkáre-kirú* to be dead tired, to be exhausted, *káette* sub. of *káeru* to return, *káette-ikú* to go back; *Yūgata, onná wa, tsŭkáre-kitté, o-Shaká-Samá no tokoró e káette ikimáshĭta.* In the evening, in exhausted condition, she went again to Buddha. [4] *yasashikú* kindly, *omaé* you, expression used when speaking to an inferior, *kanashimí* sorrow, grief, mourning, *hoká no* other, *mótte irú* have; *Sonó tokí, o-Shaká-Samá wa, yasashikú, "Omaé to onají kanashimí wo hoká no hĭtó mo mótte irú no désŭ" to osshaimáshĭta.* Then Buddha kindly said: Also other people have the same grief that you have. [5] *damátte* in silence, without uttering a word, *daité* sub. of *dakú* to hold, carry in one's arms, *bóchi* burial ground, cemetery, *shió-shió-to* sorrowfully, *tachí-satté* sub. of *tachí-sarú* to depart from, to take one's leave; *Onná wa damátte, jibún no akambō no shigái wo daité, bóchi no hō e shió-shió-to tachí-satté ikimáshĭta.* Without saying a word, (and) with the dead baby in her arms, she sadly went towards the burial ground. [6] *ushiró-súgata* one's retreating figure, *ushiró* the back, *mi-okutté* sub. of *mi-okurú* to gaze after a person until he is out of sight, to follow a person with one's eyes; *itá* that was, past of *irú* to be, *námida* tears, *yadóru* to lodge, to dwell; *Onná no ushiró-súgata wo mi-okutté itá o-Shaká-Samá no me ni námida ga yadótte imáshĭta.* Buddha, with tears in his eyes, gazed after the woman until she was out of sight.

NOTE. The following historical narration tells of the vengeance taken by 47 loyal retainers, at the beginning of the 18th century, upon a high official of the Japanese feudal government for having insulted their master and caused his untimely death by harakiri.

For over one long year, these men pretended to have lost interest in their master's unjust death, but though scattered here and there in the country so as not to arise suspicion, they maintained constant contact among themselves, secretly plotting and scheming their revenge. At last, one snowy night of the month of December 1703, everything being ready to the minutest details, they attacked the mansion of the high official, captured and beheaded him.

Their master having been avenged, the 47 masterless samurai surrendered themselves to the Government authorities, who ordered them to commit harakiri.

They were then, and are still, buried in the same cemetery where their master's ashes were interred.

To fully understand the significance of this story, it must be borne in mind that at that time, harakiri or self disemboweling, was considered, when ordered by some authority, as an "honorable punishment," or the mildest punishment that could be given to an offender, and not as a punishment administered to a criminal, who, was then beheaded. And when harakiri was performed upon oneself by one's own will for some reason or other, it was considered as the "noblest of all noble deaths."

This historical event has impressed the mind of the Japanese so much, and the admiration for the loyalty of the 47 warriors has been so great, that since it occurred their tombs have been daily visited by many people from all parts of the country, who, devoutedly adorn them with incense sticks and flowers.

In the grounds of the cementry there is a building where the armour and weapons used by the 47 warriors on the fatal night are kept and exhibited to the public.

Every country has had heroes whose deeds are told in books, and a few of them are, besides, still remembered one day each year with official ceremonies, but it is only in Japan that a deed involving the voluntary sacrifice of 47 men secretly bound with one another for over one year with the sole purpose of avenging their wronged master, has struck the imagination and the feelings of the people so much as to make their burial place an object of daily pilgrimage for over two centuries and a half.

In this constant pilgrimage one may see the popular reproof of wrong doing and praise for those who try to right it.

This story should be then considered from its moral rather than its romantic side.

⑧   Shi-jū-shichí Shi no Hanashí[1]

Génroku[2] jū-yo nen (A. D. 1702) sángatsu[3], Kyōto kará chokushí ga Edo-jō e kúru kotó ni narimáshĭta.[4] Tokugawá go-dái shōgun wa chokushí wo mukaerú tamé ni[5] settaiyakú wo Asanó to iú wakái daimyō ni meijimáshĭta.[6]

Sonó tōji,[7] shōgun-ke no gitenchō de átta Kíra to iú rōjin wa[8] hijō-ni yokú ga fukáku,[9] shokkén wo riyō shĭté,[10] hĭtóbito kará wáiro wo takŭsán tótte orimáshĭta.[11] Chokushí-séttai to iú taiyakú wo hajímete meijiraretá Asanó wa[12] iró-iró muzukashíi gíshiki ni tsúite gitenchō Kíra ni shidō wo tanomimáshĭta,[13] ga Kíra wa kesshĭté Asanó ni gíshiki ni tsúite oshiemasén déshĭta.[14] Soré wa Asanó ga tadashíi hĭtó deshĭta

---

[1] *shi-jū-shichí* 47, *shi* samurai or warrior, *hanashí* a story; *Shi-jū-shichí shi no hanashĭ* The story of the forty-seven samurai   [2] *Génroku* name of a Japanese era (1688~1703)   [3] *jū-yo nen* 14th year, *sángatsu* March; *Génroku jū-yo nen sángatsu* The third month of the fourteenth year of Genroku era   [4] *Kyōto kará* from Kyoto, *chokushí* imperial envoy, *Edó* old name of Tokyo until 1868, *jō* castle, *Edo-jō* the castle where the military rulers of Japan were established, *kúru kotó ni narimáshĭta.* was decided to send. *Kyōto kará chokushí ga Edó-jō e kúru kotó ni narimáshĭta.* was decided to send from Kyoto, an imperial envoy to Edo castle   [5] *Shōgun* is the designation of the military rulers who in fact superseded the authority of the emperors from 1605 to 1868. go-dái the fifth, *mukaerú tamé ni* for receiving; *Tokugawá go-dái shōgun wa chokushí wo mukaerú tamé ni* Tokugawa shogun the fifth, in order to receive the envoy....   [6] *settaiyakú* reception committee, *daimyō* feudal lord, *ni meijirú* to appoint; *settaiyakú wo Asanó to iú wakái daimyō ni meijimáshĭta.....* appointed the young lord Asano a reception committee.   [7] *sonó tōji* in those days   [8] *-ke* house, family, *gitenchō* master of ceremony, *de átta* that was, *to iú* by the name of, *rōjin* old man: *shōgun-ke no gitenchō de átta Kíra to iú rōjin wa* an old man by the name of Kira, who was master of ceremony of the Shogun's household   [9] *yokú ga fukáku* avaricious; *hijō-ni yokú ga fukáku* (and) was very avaricious   [10] *shokkén* authority, *riyō surú* to take advantage; *shokkén wo riyō shĭté* taking advantage of his authority   [11] *wáiro* bribe, *wáiro wo tóru* to receive bribe; *hĭtóbito kará wáiro wo takŭsán tótte orimáshĭta.* used to receive from people much bribe.   [12] *settái* reception, *taiyakú* important duty, *hajímete* for the first time, *meijiraretá* who was appointed; *Chokushí-settái to iú taiyakú wo hajímete meijiraretá Asanó wa....* Asano, who for the first time was appointed to the important duty of reception committee   [13] *iró-iró* various, *muzukashíi* difficult, *gíshiki* ceremony, formalities, *ni tsúite* about, *shidō* guidance, direction, coaching, *tanómu* to ask; *iró-iró muzukashíi gíshiki ni tsúite gitenchō Kíra ni shidō wo tanomimáshĭta* asked master of ceremonies Kira about the various difficult formalities (that had to be complied with)   [14] *kesshĭté* by no means, not in the least, *oshierú* to teach, instruct; *ga Kíra wa kesshĭté Asanó ni gíshiki ni tsúite oshiemasén déshĭta.* however, Kira would by no means instruct Asano about the (prescribed) ceremonial.

kará Kíra ni wáiro wo tsŭkaimasén déshĭta nóde.¹

Aru hi, denchū de, Kíra ga Asanó wo hijō-ni bujokú shimáshĭta kará,²
Asanó wa kátto nári, dénchū ni mo kakawarazú, Kíra ni kirí-tsŭkemá-
shĭta.³ Shikáshi, ta no daimyō ni tomerareté Kíra wo korosú kotó ga
dekimasén déshĭta.⁴ Tōji, Edo-jō-chū de wa kataná wo nukú kotó wa
genkín sareté óri,⁵ móshi, sonó hō wo okáseba⁶ gembatsú ni shoseraréru no déshĭta kará⁷ Asanó wa sonó hi no yóru ni seppukú wo
saseraremáshĭta.⁸ Sonó ué, Asanó-ke wa danzetsú, káre no shiró wa
torí-ageraré, kéraitachi wa zémbu rōnin ni narimáshĭta.⁹

---

¹*Soré wa....déshĭta nóde* That fact occurred because...., *tadashíi* honest, upright,
wáiro wo tsŭkaú to use, offer bribe; *Soré wa Asanó ga tadashíi hĭtó déshĭta kará
Kíra ni wáiro wo tsŭkaimasén déshĭta.* That was in consequence of the fact that
Asano, being an upright man, would not give any bribe. ²*Aru hi* One day, *dénchū de*
in the (Shogun's) palace, *bujokú surú* to insult; *Aru hi, dénchū de, Kíra ga Asanó
wo hijō-ni bujokú shimáshĭta kará....*One day, in the (Shogun's) palace, having Kira
greatly insulted Asano.... ³*kátto* all of a sudden, *kátto náru* to burst into a passion,
ni mo kakawarazú in spite of the fact that he was, *kirí-tsŭkerú* to slash at (a person);
Asanó wa kátto nári, dénchū ni mo kakawarazú, Kíra ni kirí-tsŭkemáshĭta. Asano,
bursting into a passion (and) in spite of the fact that he was in the (Shogun's) palace,
slashed at Kira (with his sword). ⁴*ta no* another, *tomerarerú* to be stopped, held,
ni tomerareté being held by, *korosú* to kill; *Shikáshi, ta no daimyō ni tomerareté
Kíra wo korosú kotó ga dekimasén déshĭta.* However, having been held by another
daimyo he could not kill Kira. ⁵*tōji* in those days, *chū* inside of, *Edo-jō-chū* in Edo
palace, *kataná* sword, *nukú* to unsheath, *genkín sarerú* to be strictly prohibited; *Tōji,
Edo-jō-chū de wa kataná wo nukú kotó wa genkín sareté óri,....* (As) in those days
unsheathing one's sword inside the Yedo palace was strictly prohibited.... ⁶*móshi*
if, *hō* law, *okásu* to break, to violate; *móshi sonó hō wo okáseba* (and) if (someone)
broke that law.... ⁷*gembatsú* severe punishment, *ni shoseraréru* passive of *ni shosúru*
to condemn to, *déshĭta kará* because, as;....*gembatsú ni shoseraréru no déshĭta kará
....*one would be condemned to severe punishment.... ⁸*sonó hi* that day, *yóru ni*
at night, *seppukú* harakiri, *saserarerú* passive of *saserú* to cause or make a person
do;....*Asanó wa sonó hi no yóru ni seppukú wo saseraremáshĭta.....*on the night
of that (very) day Asano was obliged to commit harakiri. (See note.) ⁹*Sonó ué*
moreover, *danzetsú* extinction short for *danzetsú shimáshĭta* past of *danzetsú surú*
to become extinct, *shiró* castle, *torí-agerarerú* passive of *torí-agerú* to take away
from, dispossess, expropriate, *kérai* retainer, vassal, *zémbu* all, *rōnin* masterless samurai,
ni narimáshĭta became; *Sonó ué, Asanó-ke wa danzetsú, káre no shiró wa torí-
ageraré, kéraitachi wa zémbu rōnin ni narimáshĭta.* Moreover, the Asano family
became extinct, his castle was confiscated and all his retainers became masterless.

The high official Kira captured by the avenging retainers. Page 623.—This picture is a photolithographic reproduction, in reduced size, of a woodblock print by a famous Japanese artist of the beginning of last century. The original is now at the Tsubouchi Memorial Theatre Museum at the Waseda University, Tokyo.

The fortyseven loyal warriors on their way to their former master's tomb to announce their accomplished vengeance. Page 623.—This picture is a photolithographic reproduction, in reduced size, of a woodblock print by a famous Japanese artist of the beginning of last century. The original is now at the Tsubouchi Memorial Museum at the Waseda University, Tokyo.

Sonogó, Asanó no móto karō Ōishi to sonó chōnan¹ oyobí chūgi-na
kérai awásete shi-jū-shichí méi wa² hijō-na kurō wo shǐté tsúi-ni³ Asanó
seppukú-go ichí-nen shichí-ka-getsú-me no áru ō-yukí no yonaká ni,⁴
Kíra no yashikí ni uchí-itté,⁵ Kíra no samuraitachí to tatakaí, tōtō, Kíra
no kubí wo uchí-torimáshǐta.⁶

Sonó yoaké ni, Ōishi wo sentō ni ikkō wa,⁷ Asanó no haká no áru
Sengakují e yukí,⁸ Kíra no kubí wo shújin no bozén ni suemáshǐtá.⁹
Kōshǐte, kárera wa chikará wo awásete shújin no adá wo rippá-ni
uchimáshǐta.¹⁰

Shibáraku nochí ni, shi-jū-shichí shi wa shízuka-ni seppukú shimáshǐta

---

¹ *sonogó* after sometime, *móto* former, *karō* chief retainer, minister of a daimyo,
chōnan eldest son; *Sonogó, Asanó no móto karō Ōishi to sonó chōnan* . . . . After
sometime, Asano's former chief retainer Oishi, his eldest son. . . . ² *oyobí* and, as well
as, *chūgi-na* loyal, *kérai* retainer, *awáseru* to join together, *méi* numerative for persons,
used in literary style; *oyobí chūgi-na kérai awásete yon-jū-shichí méi wa* . . . . as well
as (some) loyal retainers, joining together, (formed a combination of) forty-seven
persons. . . . ³ *hijō-na* great, *kurō* hardships, *kurō wo surú* to undergo, suffer hardships,
tsúi-ni at last; *hijō-na kurō wo shǐté, tsúi-ni* . . . . (who, after) undergoing great hardships
. . . . ⁴ *seppukú* harakiri, disembowelment, -*go* after, *ichí nen* one year, *shichí-ka-getsú-me*
the seventh month, -*me* postposition used to render a number ordinal, *áru* a certain,
ō-yukí heavy snow, *yonaká* night; *Asanó seppukú-go ichí nen shichí-ka-getsú-me no
áru ōyuki no yonaká ni* . . . . on a snowy night, one year and seven months after Asano's
harakiri. . . . ⁵ *yashikí* mansion, *uchí-irú* to attack, break into, raid into; *Kíra no
yashikí ni uchí-itté,* . . . . broke into Kira's mansion. . . . ⁶ *to tatakaú* to fight with, *tōtō*
at last, finally, *kubí* head, *uchí-torú* to kill, *kubí wo uchí-torú* to cut off someone's
head; *Kíra no samuraitachí to tatakaí, tōtō, Kíra no kubí wo uchí-torimáshǐta.*
fought against his (Kira's) retainers (and) at last (they caught) Kira and cut off his
head. ⁷ *Sonó yoaké* That daybreak *sentō ni* in the lead, *ikkō* the party; *Sonó yoaké
ni, Ōishi wo sentō ni ikkō wa,* . . . . At daybreak, with Oishi in the lead, the party (of
the 47 retainers). . . . ⁸ *haká* grave, *no áru* where there is *Sengakují* Sengakuji temple,
yuki went (and). . . . *Asanó no haká no áru Sengakují e yukí* . . . . went to Sengakuji
temple where there is Asano's grave. . . . ⁹ *bozén* in front of a tomb, *suerú* to place;
Kíra no kubí wo shújin no bozén ni suemáshǐta. (and) placed Kira's head in front
of their (former) master's tomb. ¹⁰ *Kōshǐte* Thus, *chikará* efforts, *adá* revenge,
vengeance, retaliation, *adá wo útsu* to take revenge on an enemy, *hǐtó no adá wo
útsu* to avenge a person's murder (*lit.* to strike, hit, beat a person's enemy), *rippá-ni*
brilliantly, magnificently, grandly, etc,; *Kōshǐte, kárera wa chikará wo awásete shújin
no ada wo rippá-ni uchimáshǐta.* Thus, they, combining their efforts, took a brilliant
revenge upon their master's enemy.

nóde, shújin no haká no áru Sengakují ni hōmuraremáshǐta.[1]

Sonó tokí kará, kónnichi máde, máinichi tasū no hǐtóbito ga kárera no haká ni máiri,[2] bozén no sénkō no kemurí ga táeta hi ga arimasén.[3]

---

[1] *Shibáraku nochí ni* Sometime after, *shízuka-ni* calmly, *seppukú surú* to perform harakiri, to disembowel oneself ; *hōmuru* to bury, *hōmuraréru* to be buried; *Shibáraku nochí ni, shi-jū-shichí shi wa shízuka-ni seppukú shimáshǐta nóde, shújin no haká no áru Sengakují ni hōmuraremáshǐta.* Sometime later, the forty-seven samurai, having calmly performed harakiri, were laid to rest at Sengakuji temple, in which there is the grave where their master is buried. [2] *Sonó tokí kará* Since then, *kónnichi máde* until to-day, *tasū no* many, a large number, a multitude, *máiru* to visit, worship at (a temple, a grave, etc.) ; *Sonó tokí kará kónnichi máde, máinichi tasū no hǐtóbito ga kárera no haká ni máiri,* Since then, every day, a large number of people have been visiting their graves [3] *bozén* before a grave, *sénkō* incense, *kemurí* smoke, *táeta* past of *taéru* to go out, to pass by, *hi* day ; *bozén no sénkō no kemurí ga táeta hi ga arimasén.* and no day passes by without (seeing) the smoke of insence (burning) before them.

The great vendetta described above took place on December 15th, 1703, and it was on February 4th 1704 that the 47 loyal retainers were ordered to end their life by harakiri, on the ground that they had violated the laws of the land, which prohibited vendetta.

In the evening of that fatal fourth day of February the bodies of the 47 brave men were taken to Sengakuji temple for burial, and according to their will, they were laid to rest near the tomb of their master.

The sympathy of the people at large and all high government officials was for the 47 masterless samurai, because the way they worked out their course with sincerity of purpose in defiance of all hardships and difficulties, was regarded as a typical example of fidelity to one's lord and master. Even Shogun Tsunayoshí, the actual ruler of Japan at that time, was anxious to save them from death but in vain. However sympathetic he may have been, he couldn't set the precedent of disregarding the laws already established by his own government.

The anniversary of the death of the 47 faithful warriors is observed at Sengakuji temple every year on February 4th, with impressive ceremonies devotionally witnessed by people of all walks of life, who on that occasion gather at the temple grounds in larger crowds than on usual days, attracted there by an impulse that urges them to pay homage to the spirit of the brave men who more than two centuries and a half ago sacrificed their life to avenge their unjustly wronged master.

The deeds of the fortyseven faithful samurai have been immortalized by the most famous Japanese dramatists of the XVIII century in a great many literary works that have been popular to this day among Japanese of all classess and which are often played on the stage and shown on the screen of crowded theatres and cinemas every year all·over the country, especially in December, the annual return of the month of the historical event.

JAPANESE NEWSPAPER STYLE

The current style of written language as used in Japanese newspapers is, generally speaking, different from the spoken language as well as from the literary style. In most cases, news are printed in abbreviated form, comparable to the abbreviated style of headlines of items in newspapers of Western countries.

To the beginner, the abbreviated form will seem rather difficult to master, however, as with everything else, by practice one may overcome the difficulty.

Just to give the student an idea of such a style, we reproduce, here below, a few pieces of news taken from one of the leading Tokyo daily newspapers.

⑨ ## NAGÁSAKI-SHI GASÚ-TÁNKU BAKUHATSÚ[1]
Jūshōsha go-jū-méi íjō[2]

Kyō, gógo ichí-ji Nagásaki-shi de gasú tánku ga bakuhatsú shi,[3] jū-shōsha go-jū-méi íjō wo dáshǐta.[4] Kásei wa shōbō no funtō de ni-ji-han góro ni chin-atsú seráreta ga,[5] bakuhatsú gen-in wa mókka torishirabé-chū.[6]

---

[1] *Nagásaki* name of a port city, *-shi* city, *gásu* gas, *tánku* tank, *bakuhatsú* explosion [2] *jūshōsha* severely wounded person, *go-jū* fifty, *méi* literary numerative for counting persons, *íjō* more than, over [3] *kyō gógo* afternoon, p. m., *ichí-ji* one o'clock; *shi* after *bakuhatsú* stem of *shimáshǐta* past of *surú* [4] *dásu* to turn out, to produce, to cause [5] *kásei* fire, blaze, *shōbō* firemen, *funtō* hard struggle, strenuous efforts, *ni-ji-hán* half past two, *góro* about, *chin-atsú* subjugation, suppression, *chin-atsú surú* to suppress, subdue, etc., *seráreta* past of *seráreru* passive of *surú*, *ga* but [6] *gen-in* the cause, origin, *mókka* at the present moment, now (Lit.), *tori-shirabé* investigation, inquiry, *-chū* in the course of, under, in process, etc.

GAS TANK EXPLOSION IN NAGASAKI
Over 50 persons severely wounded

To-day, at one p. m. in Nagasaki city, a gas tank exploded causing severe wounds to more than fifty persons.

Thanks to (*lit.* By) the firemen's strenuous efforts the consequent blaze was extinguished at about 2.30.

The cause of the explosion is now under investigation.

⑩ **AKITÁ-KEN NOSHIRÓ-SHI DE TAIKÁ¹**
Sen-sámbyaku-ko yakí enshō
Gózen yo-ji génzai³
Hankágai wo shōdo ni⁴

(Noshiró) Hatsŭká gógo jū-ichí-ji go-fun, Akitá-ken Noshiró-shi Hataké-machí no Tanaká Tétsu San (32) katá fukín kará shukká,⁵ ni-jū mētoru no tōfū ni aoráre, hi-no-te wa⁶ shínai zúi-ichí no hankágai Hataké-machí wo yakí-tsŭkúshi, Sakaé-machí, Tomí-machí ni moé-utsútte,⁷ sára-ni Yanagí-machí no Suzukí byōin, Mainichí Shimbún-sha Noshiró shíbu nádo wo hĭtó-namé ni shi,⁸ sára-ni Shin-Yanagí-machí ni moé-utsútta ga, shōka yōsui ga kírete⁹ shizén shōka wo mátsu bákari,¹⁰ ni-jū-ichí nichí gózen yo-ji génzai, sen sámbyaku-ko wo zenshō shĭté náo enshō-chū de áru.¹¹

---

¹*Akita* name of a Japanese prefecture, *ken* prefecture, *taiká* conflagration, disastrous fire ²*sen-sámbyaku* one thousand three hundred, *ko* literary numerative for counting houses instead of the colloquial *ken; yakí=yakimáshĭta* past of *yakú* to burn, *enshō* a spreading fire ³*gózen* A. M., forenoon, *yo-ji* four o'clock, *génzai* at present, the present time, up to now ⁴*hankágai=hanká-na* bustling, busy, *gái* street, district, town; *shōdo* burnt ground, scorched earth; *shōdo ni* turned into a wilderness of cinders and ashes, gutted ⁵*gógo* afternoon, *fun* minute, *Hataké* proper name (of a street) *machí* street, *Tanaká Tétsu* person's name, 32 *san-jū-ni* thirty-two years old, *katá* house, home, *fukín* neighbourhood, vicinity, *kará* from, *shukká* outbreak of fire, *shukká surú* a fire breaks out ⁶*ni-jū mētoru* twenty meters, *tōfū* east wind (*tō* east, *fū* wind) *ni* by, *aoráre* stem of *aoraréru* to be fanned, *hí-no-te* flames ⁷*shínai* in the city, (*shi* city, *nái* inside), *zúi-ichí* in literary speech this expression means "the best," "the most," No. 1, etc., *yakí-tsŭkúshi* stem of *yakí-tsŭkúsu* to burn up, to raze to the ground, etc., *Sakaé* and *Tomí* names of streets, *moé-utsútte* sub. of *moé-utsúru* to catch fire, to spread to ⁸*sára-ni* moreover, *Yanagí-machi* Yanagi Street (*machi* street), *byōin* hospital, *Mainichí* title of one of the leading Japanese newspapers, *shimbún-sha* newspaper office, *shíbu* branch, *nádo* etc., *hĭtó-namé ni shi* licked up, wiped out, burnt up (*hĭtó* one, *namé* a lick, *ni* by, with, *shi* stem of *surú*) ⁹*Shin-Yanagí* name of another street, *moé-utsútta* past of *moé-utsúru* to catch fire, *shōka* fire extinguishing, *yōsui* service or city water, *shōka yōsui* water available for extinguishing a fire, *kírete* sub. of *kiréru* to run out, to be exhausted ¹⁰*shizén* spontaneous, *mátsu* to wait, *bákari* only ¹¹*ni-jū-ichí-nichí* the 21st, *gózen* A. M., in the morning, *yo-ji* four o'clock, *zenshō* total destruction by fire, *zenshō shité* sub. of *zenshō surú* to be entirely destroyed by fire, *náo* still, *enshō* the spread of a fire, *-chū* in process of, in the course of, in progress, etc., *de áru* is

⑩ CONFLAGRATION IN NOSHIRO CITY, AKITA PREFECTURE

1,300 houses burnt by spreading fire up to 4 a. m.

Busy streets turned into cinders and ashes

(Noshiro) On the evening of the 20th, at five minutes past eleven, a fire broke out in a place near the house of (a certain) Mr. Tetsu Tanaka, 32 years old, (situated at) Hatake Street in Noshiro city, Akita prefecture.

Fanned by a 20-meter a second east wind, the fire razed the busiest street (of the city, called) Hatake and spread to Sakae and Tomi streets; moreover, the flames consumed (*lit.* licked up) Suzuki Hospital, the Noshiro branch of the Mainichi newspaper office (situated) in Yanagi Street (and) spread to Shin-Yanagi Street. (Unfortunately) the supply of the city water having been exhausted (there is nothing to do) but wait (that the fire will) spontaneously burn itself out. At four o'clock in the morning of the 21st the fire has already completely destroyed 1,300 houses, and is still spreading.

⑪ SÓREN, JINKŌ-EISÉI NI SEIKŌ
Soviet Union,   artificial satellite   succeeds

Kokú-kokú, chijō e tsuyói démpa—(Jūgatsu itsŭká-zuké, Asahí Shimbún)
every minute   earth to, powerful electric waves—(October   5th   dated,   Asahi   newspaper)

(Róndon, yokká hátsu. A. P.) Mosukō Hōsō wa yokká yo no eigó hōsō de, Tásu.
(London,   4th   despatch, A. P.)   Moscow Radio   4th evening English broadcast in, Tass

tsūshin   no happyō to-shīté, Sóren ga dōjitsu,   sekái de saishó no jinkō-eiséi
correspondence announcement   as,   Soviet Union same day, the world in   first   artificial satellite

no uchiagé ni seikō shītá to hōjita.
launching in success made so reported.

The Soviet Union succeeds (in launching) **an artificial satellite.**

Every minute powerful electric waves (are transmitted) **to the earth.**

October 5th (1957), Asahi newspaper.—London, 4th, A. P.—Radio Moskow has, on the evening of the 4th, broadcast, in English language, that according to an announcement by the official Tass, the Soviet Union has succeeded, on the same day, in launching the first artificial satellite.

⑪ SÓREN NO JINKŌ-EISÉI DÁI-NI-GŌ
Soviet Union's   artificial satellite   second

Go-hyakú-hachí kiroguramú, inú nosé—Isshū-go mo inú wa kenzai—
508   kilos,   dog aboard—One whirl-after   dog   alive and well—

Hyakú-ni fun de isshū,   kōdo wa sén-go-hyakú kiró.
102   minutes in one revolution, altitude   1,500   kilos.

(Jū-ichí-gatsú yokká-zuké, Asahí Shimbún)—Sobiéto nyūsu, Tōkyō—Mikká gózen
November   4th dated, Asahi   newspaper—Soviet   news,   Tokyo—3rd   a. m.

hachí-ji yon-jū-go fun (Nihón jikṅn mikká gógo ni-ji yon-jū-go fun) no Mosukō
8 o'clock   45   minutes (Japan-time   3rd   p. m. 2 o'clock   45   minutes   Moscow

hōsō   ni-yoréba, dōjitsu,   Sóren ga   jinkō-eiséi dái-ni-gō no uchiagé ni seikō
broadcast according to same day, Soviet Union artificial satellite 2nd   launching in success

shītá to happyō shitá.
made so announcement made.

⑪ THE SOVIET UNION'S SECOND ARTIFICIAL SATELLITE

(Weighing) **508 kilos, with dog aboard.—After the first whirl around the world the dog was still alive and well.—In 102 minutes** (the satellite) **makes one revolution at the altitude of 1,500 kilometres.**

November 4th (1957), Asahi Shimbun.—Soviet News, Tokyo.—According to Radio Moscow's broadcast, on the 3rd (of November 1957) at 8.45 a. m. (Japanese time 2.45 p. m.) the Soviet Union has succeeded, on the same day, in launching the second artificial satellite.

See the news of the cosmic flight and landing of the two Soviet astronauts Valery Bykovsky and Valentina Tereshkova as it was announced by the Japanese newspaper " Mainichi Shimbun," Page 759-761.

⑫ TÉNKI YOHŌ[1]

Hónjitsu, kitá nóchi minamí no kazé,[2] haré tokidokí kumorí,[3] nitchū atsúi,[4] myōnichi nan-tō no kazé, háretari kumóttari.[5]

---

[1] *ténki* weather, *yohō* forecast [2] *hónjitsu* to-day, *kitá* north, *nochí* later, after, *minamí* south, *kazé* wind, [3]*haré* stem of *haréru* to clear up and short for *haremásǔ, tokidokí* occasionally, *kumorí* stem of *kumóru* to be or become cloudy and short for *kumorimásǔ* [4] *nitchū* daytime, *atsúi* very warm [5] *myōnichi* to-morrow, *nan-tō* south-east, *háretari* at times clear, *kumóttari* at times cloudy (*haré* stem of *haréru* to clear up, *kumorí* stem of *kumóru* to become cloudy, followed by the suffix *tari* for alternative construction)

WEATHER FORECAST

To-day: North wind, later South wind, clear sky, occasionally cloudy, very warm in the daytime. To-morrow SE wind, sometimes clear, sometimes cloudy.

⑬ BURAJIRÚ TÁISHI SHINNINJŌ[1]

Konó-hodó chakunín shǐtá chū-Nichí Burajirú Kokú no Roberutó Gonzaresú Táishi wa,[2] futsǔká gógo san-ji Kōkyo wo otozúre Tennō Héika ni shinninjō wo teishutsú shǐtá.[3]

---

[1] *Burajirú* Brazil, *táishi* ambassador, *shinninjō* credentials [2] *konó-hodó* recently, *chakunín shǐtá* past of *chakunín surú* to arrive at one's post, *chū-Nichí* staying in Japan (*chū* in, staying in, *Nichí* Japan)—*chū* prefixed to *Nichí*, corresponds to the preposition *to* in such expressions as "ambassador *to* England" etc., *Kokú* country, state [3]*futsǔká* the second of the month, *gógo* afternoon, p. m., *san-ji* three o'clock, *Kōkyo* the Imperial Palace, *otozúre=otozuremáshǐta* past of *otozuréru* to visit, *Tennō* the Emperor, *Héika* His or Her Majesty, *Tennō Héika* His Majesty the Emperor, *teishutsú* presentation, *teishutsú surú* to present, submit

BRAZILIAN AMBASSADOR PRESENTS CREDENTIALS

(His Excellency) Roberto Gonzales, Brazilian Ambassador to Japan, who recently arrived (in Tokyo) to take up his post, visited, on the 2nd inst. at 3 p. m., the Imperial Palace and presented his credentials to His Majesty the Emperor.

READING EXERCISES

IN JAPANESE CHARACTERS

The reading pieces in the following seventeen pages (630–646) given in Japanese characters with and without *furigana*, have their corresponding transliteration with roman letters and English translation from page 606 to page 628. For ready reference, corresponding numbers have been given to the reading pieces in Japanese characters and in their transliteration.

See Addenda.. **Page 649**

⑫　天気予報

本日、北のち南の風、晴、時

時曇、日中暑い。

明日、南東の風、晴れたり

曇ったり。

⑬　ブラジル大使信任状

このほど着任した駐日ブラジル国のロ

ベルト・ゴンザレス大使は二日午後三時

皇居を訪れ、天皇陛下に信任状を呈出し

た。

⑫　天気予報

本日、北のち南の風、晴、時

時曇、日中暑い。

明日、南東の風、晴れたり

曇ったり。

⑬　ブラジル大使信任状

このほど着任した駐日ブラジル国のロ

ベルト・ゴンザレス大使は二日午後三時

皇居を訪れ、天皇陛下に信任状を呈出し

た。

⑪

ソ連、人工衛星に成功

刻々、地上へ強い電波

（十月五日附、朝日新聞）

【ロンドン、四日発、A・P】モスクワ放送は四日夜の英語放送で、タス通信の発表として、ソ連が同日、世界で最初の人工衛星の打上げに成功したと報じた。

ソ連の人工衛星第二号

五〇八キログラム、犬乗せ、
一周後も犬は健在、
百二分で一周、高度は千五百キロ

（十一月四日附、朝日新聞）

【ソビエト・ニュース＝東京】三日午前八時四十五分（日本時間三日午後二時四十五分）のモスクワ放送によれば、同日、ソ連が人工衛星第二号の打上げに成功したと発表した。

⑩

秋田県能代市で大火

千三百戸焼き延焼

午前四時現在＝繁華街を焦土に

【能代】二十日午後十一時五分、秋田県能代市畠町の田中鉄さん（三二）方付近から出火、二十メートルの東風にあおられ、火の手は市内随一の繁華街畠町を焼き尽し、栄町、富町に燃え移って、さらに柳町の鈴木病院、毎日新聞社能代支部などをひとなめにし、さらに新柳町に燃え移ったが、消火用水が切れて自然消火をまつばかり、二十一日午前四時現在千三百戸を全焼してなお延焼中である。

⑨

長崎市ガスタンク爆発

重傷者五十名以上

今日午後一時長崎市でガスタンクが爆発し重傷者五十名以上を出した。

火勢は消防の奮闘で二時半頃に鎮圧せられたが爆発原因は目下取調べ中。

⑨

長崎市ガスタンク爆発

重傷者五十名以上

今日午後一時長崎市でガスタンクが爆発し重傷者五十名以上を出した。

火勢は消防の奮闘で二時半頃に鎮圧せられたが爆発原因は目下取調べ中。

夜に切腹をさせられました。その上浅野家は断絶、彼の城は取り上げられ、家来達は全部浪人になりました。その後、浅野の元家老大石とその長男及び忠義な家来合せて四十七名は非常な苦労をして、遂に浅野切腹後一年七か月目の或る大雪の夜中に、吉良の屋敷に討ち入って吉良の侍達と戦い、とうとう吉良の首を打ち取りました。その夜明けに大石を先頭に一行は浅野の墓のある泉岳寺へ行き、吉良の首を主人の墓前にそえました。

こうして彼等は力を合せて主人の仇を立派にうちました。しばらく後に四十七士は静かに切腹しましたので、主人の墓のある泉岳寺にほうむられました。その時から今日まで毎日多数の人々が彼等の墓にまいり、墓前のせんこうの煙がたえた日がありません。

⑧ 四十七士の話

元禄十四年（Ａ・Ｄ・一七〇二）三月、京都から勅使が江戸城へ来る事になりました。徳川五代将軍は勅使をむかえるために接待役を浅野と云う若い大名に命じました。その当時将軍家の儀典長であった吉良と云う老人は非常に慾が深く転権を利用して人々からわいろを沢山とっておりました。勅使接待という大役をはじめて命じられた浅野は色色むずかしい儀式について儀典長吉良に指導をたのみましたが、吉良は決して浅野に儀式について教えませんでした。それは浅野が正しい人でしたから吉良にわいろをつかいませんでしたので。或る日、殿中で吉良が浅野を非常に侮辱しましたから吉良に、浅野はかっとなり、殿中にもかかわらず、吉良に切りつけました。しかし、他の大名にとめられて、吉良を殺す事ができませんでした。当時、江戸城中では刀を抜く事は厳禁されており、もしその法をおかせば厳罰に処せられるのでしたから。浅野はその日の

ちろん、うちの年寄やしんるいの者が死にましたよ」とこたえました。

すると女はたのんだからしつぶをもらわずに、出て行ってしまいました、女は急いで次の家へ行って、まえと同じことをききましたが、やっぱり、そこの家でも、いろいろの人が死んでいましたので、からしのつぶをもらえませんでした。

しかし、女は、しんぼうづよく、町中の家をのこらずたずねて見ました、が、人が決して死ななかったという家は一軒もありませんでした。

夕方、女はつかれきって、おしゃかさまのところへ帰って行きました。

その時、おしゃかさまは、やさしく「お前と同じかなしみをほかの人も持っているのです。」とおっしゃいました。

女はだまって、自分のあかんぼうのしがいをだいて、ぼちの方へしおしおと立ち去って行きました。女のうしろすがたを見おくっていたおしゃかさまの目に涙がやどっていました。

⑦ おしゃかさまとからしのつぶ

昔、おしゃかさまのところへ一人の女がじぶんの死んだあかんぼうを死んだあかんぼうをだいて来まし
た。そして、この女はおしゃかさまに「どうぞ私のあかんぼうを生きかえらせて下さ
い」と泣きながらねがいました。

その時、おしゃかさまはしずかにうなずいて「では、一つまみのからしのつぶを人
からもらって、死んだあかんぼうのかおにかけなさい。そうすればあかんぼうは生き
かえる。但し、そのからしのつぶは、決してだれも死んだことのない家の人からもら
わなければならない」とおっしゃいました。

これをきいて、女は大変よろこび、あかんぼうのしがいをかかえて、大急ぎで、町
へ行きました。そして、さっそく、ある家へ行って、「すみませんがからしのつぶを一
つまみいただきたいです」とたのみました。その家の人が「さあ、さあ、どうぞごえ
んりょなくお持ちなさい。」と云った時に、女はためらいながら、「一寸うかがいますが、
お宅では今までに、どなたか亡くなりましたか」とたずねました。この家の人は「も

むのと同じです。人民は国の本です」と仰せになりました。そしてあと三年間人民か

ら租税をお取りになりませんでひたすら人民の幸福をお考え遊ばされました。六年の

後人民は進んで租税をおとり下さるようにお願い申し上げました。そして人民はよろ

こんで立派な御殿を天皇のためにつくりいつまでも天皇の御仁徳を感謝しました。

⑥ 「万歳」の起源

明治大帝は、色々の御立派な事を日本のために遊ばされました。その中の一つは、憲

法を初めておつくりになった事です。日本憲法は明治二十二年二月十一日（紀元節）に

発布せられました。その翌日明治天皇皇后両陛下は、東京市民のお願いをお許しにな

って上野公園の祝賀式におのぞみになりました。この時大勢の人民は、思わず、「万歳」

と叫んでお迎え申し上げました。これが「万歳」を叫ぶようになった初めであります。

⑤ 仁徳天皇のお話

仁徳天皇は日本の第十六代の天皇陛下で大変なさけぶかい御方でいらっしゃいました。或る朝、天皇は御殿の高い処へお上りになって四方をごらんになりました。その時丁度人民は朝の御飯をたく時間でしたがどこの家からも煙が上りませんでした。天皇はそれをふしぎにお思いになって近侍の者にお尋ねになりました。近侍の者は「この頃はお米が大変不作で人民は大層貧しい暮しをしております」と申し上げましたところ天皇は「それはかわいそうですそれではこれから三年の間、租税をおさめなくてもよろしい」と仰せになりました。人民は涙を流してよろこびました。

三年の後天皇が御殿の高い処へお上りになりました時どこの家からも煙が立ちのぼっていました。その時天皇はお側の皇后に「あゝ朕は富みました」と仰せになりました。皇后がその御言葉の意味を御伺い申し上げました時、天皇は、「人民が富むのは朕が富

間もなく浦島太郎と亀は立派な龍宮へ着きました。

乙姫様は浦島太郎に沢山の御馳走をしました。浦島は家へ帰るのを忘れて、毎日楽しく暮らしました。その内に浦島は両親の事を考え家へ帰りたくなりました。ある日、乙姫様に「どうも長くお世話になりました。色々ありがとうございました。私はきょううちへ帰ります」と言いました。すると乙姫様はきれいな箱をお土産に浦島にくれました。そして「この箱は決して開けてはいけません」と言いました。浦島はその箱をかゝえて、亀の背中に乗って帰って行きました。

時そこの様子は全部かわっていました。自分の家も両親も友達も見当りませんでした。浦島がもとの浜辺に着いた時この様子は全部かわっていました。自分の家も両親も友達も見当りませんでした。浦島がもとの浜辺に着いた浦島太郎を覚えている人は一人もいませんでした。浦島は夢のように思いました。そして あちらこちらを歩きました。だんゝ悲しくなりましたので乙姫様からもらった箱を開けて見ましたすると中から白い煙が立ちのぼりました。その煙が浦島の顔にかゝった時に浦島はとつぜんしらがのおじいさんになってしまいました。

④ 浦島太郎の話

昔、浦島太郎という漁師がありました。或日浜辺を通っていると、子供達が大勢集っててさわいでいました。見ると子供達は、一匹の大きな亀をつかまえていじめていました。浦島太郎はそれを大変かわいそうに思って子供達に「そんなに亀をいじめてはいけない」と言いましたが、子供達は聞きませんでした。そしてますます亀をいじめましたから浦島太郎は「それなら、私がその亀を買おう」と言って亀を買取りました。

そしてその亀を海へ放してやりました。

それから二三日後、浦島太郎が舟に乗って釣りをしていると『浦島さん〳〵』と呼ぶ声がしました。誰かと思って振り返って見るとそれは大きな亀でした。その亀は舟のそばへ泳いできました。そしてうれしそうにおじぎをしました。「この間はありがとうございました。私はあなたが助けた亀です。何卒私の背中にお乗り下さい。私はあなたを龍宮へお連れします」と言いました。浦島太郎は非常によろこんで亀の背中に乗りました。それから亀は海の底へ泳いで行きました。海底はじつにきれいでした。

ガ、ソレヲ見テ、「ドウゾ私ニポチヲ貸シテ下サイ」ト云イマシタ。ソコデコノ慾ノ深

イオジイサンハポチヲムリニ吠エサセマシタ。ソシテソコヲ掘リマシタガ土ノ中カラ

汚イ物ガ出マシタ。慾ノ深イオジイサンハ、怒ッテポチヲ、殺シマシタ。ヨイオジイ

サンハソレヲ非常ニ悲シミマシタ。ソシテ、ポチノオ墓ヲ立テソノ上ニ木ヲ一本植エ

マシタ。コノ木ハズンズン大キクナリマシタ。ヨイオジイサンハコノ木ヲ切ッテソレ

デ臼ヲツクリマシタ。ソノ臼ノ中デオ米ヲツクト、オ米ガミンナ金ニナリマシタ。慾

ノ深イオジイサンハ、ソレヲ見テ、ソノ臼ヲ借リニ来マシタ。ソシテソノ臼デオ米ヲ

ツイタ時ニオ米ハ汚イモノニナリマシタダカラ慾ノ深イオジイサンハ大層怒ッテ臼ヲモ

シテシマイマシタ。ヨイオジイサンハソノ灰ヲモラッテ、ソレヲマキマシタ。スルト

枯木ノ枝ニ花ガキレイニ咲キマシタ。ソノ時、丁度殿様ガソコヲオ通リニナッテソノ

花ヲ大ヘンホメマシタソシテヨイオジイサンニ沢山ホウビヲアタエマシタ。ソレヲ見

タ慾ノ深イオジイサンハ直グニマネヲシテ灰ヲマキマシタガ灰ハ殿様ノ眼ノ中ヘ入リ

マシタ。殿様ハ大変怒ッテコノ慾ノ深イオジイサンヲ牢ニ入レテシマイマシタ。

タ。桃太郎ハ鬼ノ大将ト戦イマシタ。桃太郎ガ大変ツヨイノデ鬼ノ大将ハトウ〳〵降

参シマシタ。「モウ決ッシテ悪イ事ヲシマセンカラドウゾ命ヲタスケテ下サイ」トネガ

イマシタ。桃太郎ハ鬼ノ大将ヲ許シテヤリマシタ。鬼ノ大将ハオ礼ニ色々ノ宝物ヲサ

シダシマシタ。桃太郎ハソノ宝物ヲ車ニツミマシタ。犬ガソノ車ヲヒキマシタ。猿ガ

後ヲ押シマシタ。雉子ガ綱ヲヒキマシタ。ソシテ勇マシク家ヘ帰リマシタ。オジイサ

ントオバアサンハタイヘンヨロコビマシタ。ソレカラ皆幸福ニ暮ラシマシタ。

③ 花咲カジジイノ話

昔、或ル所ニ、ヨイオジイサンガアリマシタ。オジイサンハ、犬ヲ一匹飼ッテイマシ

タ。犬ノ名前ハ「ポチ」ト云イマシタ。オジイサンハ ポチヲ大変カワイガッテイマ

シタ。ポチモオジイサンヲ好キデシタ。

或ル日、ポチガ畑ノスミデ「オジイサン、コヽヲ、掘リナサイワン〳〵」ト吠エマシタ。

オジイサンガソコヲ掘ルト土ノ中カラ宝物ガ沢山出マシタ。隣ノ慾ノ深イオジイサン

「鬼ガ島ヘ鬼ヲ征伐ニ行キマス」

「オ腰ニツケタモノハ何デスカ」

「日本一ノキビダンゴデス」

「一ッ下サイオトモシマショウ」

桃太郎ハ犬ニキビダンゴヲ一ッヤリマシタ。犬ハヨロコンデ家来ニナリマシタ。ソレカラ桃太郎ト犬ガ少シ行クト猿ニ会イマシタ。猿ハ犬ト同ジ事ヲ桃太郎ニキ、マシタ。桃太郎ハ猿ニモキビダンゴヲ一ッヤリマシタ。猿ハヨロコンデ桃太郎ノ家来ニナリマシタ。

桃太郎ト犬ト猿トガモウ少シ行ッタ時ニ雉子ニ会イマシタ。コノ雉子モ前ノ犬ヤ猿ト同ジ事ヲ云イマシタノデ桃太郎ハキビダンゴヲ一ッヤリマシタ。雉子ハヨロコンデ桃太郎ノ家来ニナリマシタ。

桃太郎ハ犬、猿、雉子ヲツレテ鬼ガ島ヘ着キマシタ。鬼ハ鉄ノ門ヲシッカリシメテイマシタカラ桃太郎ハ入ル事ガ出来マセンデシタ。

ソコデ雉子ハ飛ンデ行ッテ上カラ敵ノ様子ヲシラベマシタ。猿ハ門ヲ登ッテ中ヘ入リ門ノ鍵ヲハズシテ門ヲ開ケマシタ。桃太郎ト犬ハ一緒ニ攻メ入リマシタ。雉子ハ飛ビマワッテ鬼ノ目ヲツツキマシタ。猿ハ鬼ヲヒッカキマシタ。犬ハ鬼ヘクイツキマシ

② 桃太郎ノ話

昔々、オジイサントオバアサンガアリマシタ。オジイサンハ毎日山ヘシバカリニ行キマシタ。オバアサンハ川ヘ洗濯ニ行キマシタ。或ル日、オバアサンガ川デ洗濯ヲシテイルト川上カラ大キナ桃ガドンブリコ〳〵ト流レテ来マシタ。オバアサンハソノ桃ヲ拾ッテウチヘモッテ帰リマシタ。オジイサンガ山カラ帰ッタ時ソノ桃ヲ見セマシタ。

オジイサンハ「コレハ〳〵メズラシイ大キナ桃ダネ」トイッテヨロコビマシタ。オバアサンガ桃ヲ切ロウトスルト桃ガ二ツニワレテ中カラ男ノ子ガ生レマシタ。桃カラ生レマシタカラ桃太郎ト名ヲツケマシタ。桃太郎ハ大キクナッテ大層ツョクナリマシタ。

或日、桃太郎ハオジイサントオバアサンニ「私ハ鬼ガ島ヘ鬼ヲ征伐ニ行キタイデス。ドウゾキビダンゴヲコシラエテ下サイ」ト云イマシタ。オバアサンハキビダンゴヲコシラエテヤリマシタ。桃太郎ハソノキビダンゴヲ腰ニツケテ勇マシク出カケマシタ。

少シ行クト向コウカラ犬ガキマシタ。

「桃太郎サン、ドコヘイラッシャイマスカ」

① 勅語

朕惟フニ我ガ皇祖皇宗國ヲ肇ムルコト宏遠ニ德ヲ樹ツルコト深厚ナリ我ガ臣民克ク忠ニ克ク孝ニ億兆心ヲ一ニシテ世々厥ノ美ヲ濟セルハ此レ我ガ國體ノ精華ニシテ教育ノ淵源亦實ニ此ニ存ス爾臣民父母ニ孝ニ兄弟ニ友ニ夫婦相和シ朋友相信シ恭儉己レヲ持シ博愛衆ニ及ボシ學ヲ修メ業ヲ習ヒ以テ智能ヲ啓發シ德器ヲ成就シ進デ公益ヲ廣メ世務ヲ開キ常ニ國憲ヲ重シ國法ニ遵ヒ一旦緩急アレバ義勇公ニ奉ジ以テ天壤無窮ノ皇運ヲ扶翼スベシ是ノ如キハ獨リ朕ガ忠良ノ臣民タルノミナラズ又以テ爾祖先ノ遺風ヲ顯彰スルニ足ラン斯ノ道ハ實ニ我ガ皇祖皇宗ノ遺訓ニシテ子孫臣民ノ俱ニ遵守スベキ所之ヲ古今ニ通ジテ謬ラズ之ヲ中外ニ施シテ悖ラズ朕爾臣民ト俱ニ拳々服膺シテ咸其德ヲ一ニセンコトヲ庶幾ウ

明治二十三年十月三十日

御名御璽

読方練習

ヨミ カタ レン シュウ

In the Preceding seventeen pages (630–646) are given reading pieces in Japanese characters with and the without *furigana*. Their transliteration in roman letters and corresponding English translation are given from page 606 to page 628.

READING EXERCISES

(Addenda)

THE NEW CONSTITUTION OF JAPAN

THE NEW CONSTITUTION OF JAPAN

On November 3rd 1946, the New Constitution of Japan was promulgated, and on May 3rd 1947 it was formally enforced.

This event, of historical and international importance, symbolizes the final acceptance by Japan of a fundamental character which conclusively establishes the bases of a completely democratic and peaceful government and society, such as Japan has never before been able successfully to attain.

The constitution under which Japan was governed before, was promulgated by the Emperor Meiji in 1888 ; however, although it first set the nation along the path of enlightened progress, it was unfortunately thwarted from fruition until the end of the Pacific War in 1945, owing to its weakness which lent itself readily to being abused and subverted by misguided leaders of the country.

The New Constitution is a revolutionary improvement on the old one, as it gives the Japanese people the highest powers of the Government, and by it, Japan enters a new era in her history.

With the new Constitution finally gone into effect, the first and fundamental phase of Japan's reformation has at last been completed, and the nation has begun its progress on a new road of development. Indeed, the great event marks a revolutionary turning point in the whole cause of the nation's century-long history, and for the first time the fundamental law has inequivocably ensured the sovereignty of the people's will, has ensured respect for the inalianable and natural rights of human beings, has provided for a political system consciously designed to give effect to the people's sovereign will and to safeguard their natural rights, and has moreover committed the nation to international peace.

Realizing the importance of this historical event, which is destined to bring a great change in the social life of the Japanese people and to have international repercussions, the authors of this book have thought of supplementing this new edition with the following pages on the New Constitution, in order that the foreign student of things Japanese may be acquainted with it while studying the language.

Tranliteration in *romaji* of the preamble to the chapters of the new Constitution of Japan enforced on the 3rd of May 1947.

See Japanese text in kanji, page 665 and the official English translation, page 653.

NIPPON KOKU KEMPŌ[1]

Nippon kokumin[2] wa, seitō ni senkyo sareta kokkai ni okeru[3] daihyō-sha wo tsūjite kōdō shi,[4] warera to warera no shison no tame ni,[5] sho-kokumin to no[6] kyōwa ni yoru seika to,[7] waga kuni zendo ni watatte[8] jiyū no motarasu keitaku wo kakuho shi,[9] seifu no kōi ni yotte[10] futa-tabi sensō no sanka ga okoru koto no nai yō ni[11] suru koto wo ketsui shi,[12] koko ni shuken ga kokumin ni sonsuru koto wo sengen shi,[13] kono kempō wo kakutei suru.[14]

Somo-somo kokusei wa,[15] kokumin no genshuku na shintaku ni yoru mono de atte,[16] sono ken-i wa kokumin ni yurai shi,[17] sono kenryoku wa kokumin no daihyō-sha ga kore wo kōshi shi,[18] sono fukuri wa koku-min ga kore wo kyōju suru.[19] Kore wa jinrui-fuhen no genri de ari,[20] kono kempō wa, kakaru genri ni motozuku mono de aru.[21] Warera wa kore ni hansuru issai no kempō, hōrei oyobi shōchoku wo haijo suru.[22]

Nippon kokumin wa, kōkyū no heiwa wo nengan shi,[23] ningen sōgo

---

[1] *koku* country, nation ; *kempō* constitution [2] *kokumin* people [3] *seitō ni* duly ; *senkyo suru* to elect ; *senkyo sareru* to be elected ; *kokkai* the Diet ; *ni okeru* (lit. style) in [4] *daihyōsha* representative ; *tsūjite* through ; *kōdō suru* to act ; *kōdō shi* acting [5] *shison* posterity ; *no tame ni* for [6] *sho-kokumin* all peoples, all nations ; *to no* with [7] *kyō* cooperation ; *wa* peace ; *kyōwa* peaceful cooperation ; *ni yoru* by, through ; *seika* the fruits ; *to* and [8] *zendo* land, country ; *ni watatte* throughout [9] *jiyū* liberty, freedom ; *motarasu* to bring, carry, bear ; *keitaku* blessing ; *kakuho suru* to secure [10] *seifu* government ; *kōi* action ; *ni yotte* through [11] *futatabi* again ; *sanka* horrors : *okoru* to occur ; *koto no nai yō ni* lit. transl.: the fact there-is-not-like ; *futatabi sensō no sanka ga okoru koto no nai yō ni* that never again the horrors of war occur [12] *ketsui suru* to resolve [13] *koko ni* herewith ; *shuken* sovereignty ; *sonsuru* there to be ; *sengen suru* to ordain [14] *kakutei suru* to establish

[15] *somo-somo* emphatic expression ; *kokusei* government [16] *genshuku na* sacred ; *shintaku* trust ; *ni yoru mono de aru* to be founded upon [17] *ken-i* authority ; *ni yurai suru* to derive from [18] *sono* of which ; *kenryoku* power ; *kōshi suru* to exercise [19] *fukuri* benefit ; *kyōju suru* to enjoy [20] *jinrui* human being ; *fuhen* everlasting ; *jinrui-fuhen no* universal ; *genri* principle [21] *kakaru* such ; *motozuku* to base upon ; *motozuku mono de aru* to be based, founded upon [22] *hansuru* to be against ; *issai no* all ; *hōrei* laws ; *oyobi* (lit. style) and ; *shōchoku* rescript ; *haijo suru* to reject [23] *kōkyū no* eternal ; *heiwa* peace ; *nengan suru* to desire

no kankei wo shihai suru[1] sūkō na risō wo fukaku jikaku suru no de atte,[2] heiwa wo aisuru sho-kokumin[3] no kōsei to shingi ni shinrai shite,[4] warera no anzen to seizon wo hoji shiyō to ketsui shita.[5]

Warera wa, heiwa wo iji-shi,[6] sensei to reijū, appaku to henkyō wo chijō kara[7] eien ni jokyo shiyō to tsutomete iru[8] kokusai shakai ni oite,[9] meiyo aru chii wo shimetai to omou.[10] Warera wa, zen-sekai no kokumin ga, hitoshiku kyōfu to ketsubō kara manukare,[11] heiwa no uchi ni seizon suru[12] kenri wo yūsuru koto wo kakunin suru.[13]

Warera wa, izure no[14] kokka mo, jikoku no koto nomi ni sennen shite[15] takoku wo mushi shite wa naranai no de atte,[16] seiji dōtoku no hōsoku wa,[17] fuhenteki na mono de ari,[18] kono hōsoku ni shitagau koto wa,[19] jikoku no shuken wo iji shi,[20] takoku to taitō kankei ni tatō to suru[21] kakkoku no sekimu de aru to shinzuru.[22]

Nippon kokumin wa, kokka no meiyo ni kake,[23] zenryoku wo agete[24] kono sūkō na risō to mokuteki wo tassei suru koto wo chikau.[25]

---

[1] *ningen* human ; *sōgo no* mutual ; *kankei* relations ; *shihai suru* to control   [2] *sūkō na* lofty, high ; *risō* ideal ; *jikaku suru* conscious ; *de atte* being   [3] *aisuru* to love; *heiwa wo aisuru sho-kokumin* all peace-loving peoples   [4] *kōsei* justice ; *shingi* good faith ; *shinrai suru* to rely upon   [5] *anzen* |security ; *seizon* survival ; *hoji suru* to keep, hold ; *ketsui suru* to determine   [6] *iji suru* to preserve ; *iji-shi* preserving   [7] *sensei* tyranny ; *reijū* slavery ; *appaku* oppression ; *henkyō* intolerance ; *chijō* the earth   [8] *eien ni* for ever, for all time ; *jokyo suru* to banish : *tsutomeru* to make efforts ; *tsutomete iru* have been making efforts   [9] *kokusai* international ; *shakai* society ; *ni oite* (lit. style) in   [10] *meiyo aru* honoured ; *chii* place ; *shimeru* to occupy ; *shimetai to omou* to desire to occupy   [11] *zen-sekai* the whole world ; *hitoshiku* all ; *kyōfu* fear ; *ketsubō* want ; *manukareru* to free from   [12] *heiwa no uchi ni* in peace ; *seizon suru* to live   [13] *kenri* the right ; *yūsuru* to have ; *kakunin suru* to confirm (=to recognize and acknowledge)   [14] *izure no* all   [15] *jikoku* one's own country : *koto* affairs ; *nomi ni* only ; *sennen suru* to concentrate : *sennen shite* with devotion   [16] *takoku* other countries ; *mushi suru* to ignore, to disregard ; *shite wa naranai* must not   [17] *seiji* political : *dōtoku* morality ; *hōsoku* laws   [18] *fuhenteki na* univesral ; *mono de ari* it is   [19] *shitagau* to obey ; *kono hōsoku ni shitagau koto wa* obedience to such laws   [20] *shuken* sovereignty ; *iji suru* to sustain   [21] *taitō* equal ; *kankei* relationship ; *tatō to suru* trying to (*tatō* from *tatsu* to ﹛stand ﹜up)   [22] *kakkoku* all nations ; *sekimu* responsibility ; *shinzuru* to believe (=to hold) ; *to* so   [23] *meiyo* honour ; *kokka no meiyo* national honour ; *ni kake* upon   [24] *zenryoku* full strength ; *agete* with ; *zenryoku wo agete* determined will and full resources   [25] *risō* a principle ; *mokuteki* purpose ; *tassei suru* to attain ; *chikau* to pledge

Official translation of the preamble to the chapters of the new Constitution of Japan.
See its original text, page 665, and its transliteration in *romaji*, page 651.

We, the Japanese people, acting through our duly elected representatives in the National Diet, determined that we shall secure for ourselves and our posterity the fruits of peaceful cooperation with all nations and the blessings of liberty throughout this land, and resolved that never again shall we be visited with the horrors of war through the action of goverment, do proclaim the sovereignty of the people's will and do ordain and establish this Constitution, founded upon the universal principle that goverment is a sacred trust, the authority for which is derived from the people, the powers of which are exercised by the representatives of the people, and the benefits of which are enjoyed by the people ; and we reject and revoke all constitutions, laws, ordinances, and rescripts in conflict herewith.

Desiring peace for all time and fully conscious of the high ideals controlling human relashionship now stirring mankind, we have determined to rely for our security and survival upon the justice and good faith of the peace-loving peoples of the world. We desire to occupy an honoured place in an international society designed and dedicated to the preservation of peace, and the banishment of tyranny and slavery, oppression and intolerance for all time from the earth. We recognize and acknowledge that all peoples have the right to live in peace, free from fear and want.

We hold that no people is responsible to itself alone, but that laws of political morality are universal, and that obedience to such laws is incumbent upon all peoples who would sustain their own sovereignty and justify their sovereign relationship with other peoples.

To these high principles and purposes we, the Japanese people, pledge our national honor, determined will and full resources.

Below is the transliteration in *romaji* of the Imperial rescript read by the Emperor of Japan at the historic first session of the National Diet under the new Constitution enforced on May 3rd 1947.

See the original text, page 511, and its English translation, page 499.

CHOKUGO[1]

Honjitsu,[2] Dai-ikkai kokkai[3] no kaikai-shiki[4] ni nozomi,[5] zen kokumin wo daihyō suru[6] shokun to[7] ichidō ni kaisuru[8] koto wa, watakushi[9] no fukaku yorokobi to suru tokoro de aru.[10]

Nippon koku kempō ni akiraka de aru yō ni,[11] Kokkai wa kokken no saikō-kikan[12] de ari, kuni no yui-itsu no rippō-kikan[13] de aru. Shitagatte,[14] waga kuni kongo no hatten no kiso[15] wa, itsu ni Kokkai no tadashii un-ei ni son suru.[16]

Ima-ya,[17] waga kuni wa, katsute-nai shinkoku na keizai-kiki ni chokumen shite iru.[18] Kono toki ni atari,[19] wareware Nippon kokumin ga shin ni ittai to natte,[20] kono kiki wo koppuku shi,[21] minshu-shugi ni motozuku[22] heiwa-kokka no kensetsu ni seikō suru[23] koto wo, setsu ni nozomu mono de aru.[24]

---

[1] *Chokugo* Imperial Rescript   [2] *honjitsu* (formal speech) to-day   [3] *dai-ikkai* the first session ; *kokkai* national assembly, the Diet   [4] *kaikai* opening ; *shiki* ceremony ; *kaikai-shiki* opening ceremony   [5] *ni nozomi* (lit. style) at   [6] *zen* entire, all ; *kokumin* nation, the people of the country ; *daihyō suru* to represent ; *zen-kokumin wo daihyō suru* to represent the entire nation   [7] *shokun to* (lit. style) with you   [8] *ichidō* a room, a hall ; *ni* in ; *kaisuru* to meet, to join ; *ichidō ni kaisuru* to meet in one (the same) room   [9] *watakushi* (ordinary speech) I—Note that this is the first time that the Emperor of Japan refers to himself by this personal pronoun in an Imperial rescript. Compare with *Chin*, We, in the Rescript on Education by the Emperor Meiji (See p. 470), by which word the emperors of Japan used to refer to themselves until the new Constitution was proclaimed in 1947.   [10] *fukaku* deeply (very) ; *yorokobi* pleased ; *to suru tokoro de aru* (lit. style) I am   [11] *Nippon-koku* the Japanese country ; *kempō* constitution ; *akiraka de aru* clear, distinct, plain ; *de aru* it is ; *yō ni* as ; *Nippon-koku kempō ni akiraka de aru yō ni* As it is clearly set forth in the Japanese Constitution   [12] *kokken* state power ; *saikō* highest, supreme ; *kikan* organ, means, medium ; *kokken no saikō-kikan* the supreme organ of state power   [13] *yui-itsu* the only, the sole ; *rippō* law ; *de aru* is ; *kuni no yui-itsu no rippō-kikan de aru* is the sole law-making authority (organ) of the country   [14] *shitagatte* therefore   [15] *waga* (lit. stile) our ; *kongo* no (l.s.) future ; *hatten* development ; *kiso* the foundation, the base, basis ; *waga kuni kongo no hatten no kiso wa* the basis of the future development of our country   [16] *itsu ni* entirely ; *tadashii* right, righteous, just ; *un-ei* operation   [17] *ima-ya* (lit. & formal) Now   [18] *katsute-nai* not once, at no time=unprecedented in history ; *shinkoku na* serious, grave, severe ; *keizai* economy ; *kiki* crisis ; *keizai kiki* economic crisis ; *chokumen shite iru* faced with ; *chokumen suru* to face, to be confronted by   [19] *kono toki ni atari* at this juncture   [20] *shin ni* really ; *ittai to natte* uniti·g as one man   [21] *koppuku suru* to surmount ; *kono kiki wo koppuku shi* surmounting this crisis   [22] *minshu-shugi* democracy ; *motozuku* to be based on, to be founded on   [23] *heiwa kokka* a nation of peace ; *bunka kokka* a nation of culture ; *kensetsu* construction, establishment ; *seikō suru* to succeed in, to win success, to accomplish (one's purpose)   [24] *setsu ni* earnestly ; *nozomu* to hope

Below is the translation of the Imperial rescript read by the Emperor of Japan at the historic first session of the National Diet under the new Constituation enforced on May 3rd, 1947.

See the original text, page 667, and its transliteration in *romaji*, page 654.

IMPERIAL RESCRIPT

I am very pleased to attend to-day the opening ceremony of the First Session of the Diet and to meet in one room with you who represent the entire nation.

As set forth plainly in the Constitution of Japan, the Diet is the highest organ of state power and the sole law-making authority of the State. The future development of our nation depends, therefore, entirely upon the right operation of the Diet.

Japan is now faced with an economic crisis unparalleled in history. It is my earnest hope that at this juncture we, the Japanese people, shall surmount this crisis by uniting really as one man and succeed in constructing a nation of peace, a nation of culture, founded upon democracy.

On the 3rd of May 1947, the new Constitution of Japan was enforced, and on that great event an impressive ceremony was held in Tokyo.

Below is, in romaji, the description of the celebration given by the Yomiuri, one of the leading newspapers in Japan.

See the full English translation, page 658. and the Japanese text in kanji, page 669

SHINSEI NIPPON NO REKISHI HIRAKU[1]

SHIN KEMPŌ NI CHIKAU CHŪSEI[2]

Fū-u wo tsuki Kyūjō mae hiroba no seiten.[3]

Ei-en naru jiyū to heiwa ni shōchō sareru[4] kaguwashiki bunka kokka kensetsu e[5] no tainin wo otta shijō kūzen no shukuten[6] "Shin Kempō shikō kinen shiki" wa[7] mikka asa jū-ji han kara Kyūjō mae hiroba de okonawareta.[8]

Kono hi Tōkyō wa fūsoku jū mētoru wo koeru hageshii fū-u de atta.[9] Sono yokonaguri no rei-u wo tsuite[10] ku-ji chikaku kara kasa no retsu ga[11] shikijō e en-en to tsuzuku.[12]

Teikoku mae sankaisha wa sono sū sudeni ichi man.[13] Takamatsu-no-miya, Kaya-no-miya-Kunihisa-ō ryō denka,[14] Kempō fukyū-kai yaku-in, kakuryō, kaku-tō daihyō-ra no kaobure ga sorou to[15] jū-ji han,

---

[1] *shinsei* a new life, a new birth; *rekishi* history; *hiraku* (v.i.) to open   [2] *kempō* constitution; *chikau* to pledge; *chūsei* fidelity, allegiance; *chikau chūsei* oath of allegiance   [3] *fū-u* wind and rain; *tsuki* amidst; *Kyūjō* the Imperial Palace; *hiroba* plaza, public square; *seiten* grand celebration   [4] *ei-en naru* perpetual; *jiyū* freedom; *heiwa* peace; *ni* in; *shōchō suru* to symbolize   [5] *kaguwashiki* brilliant; *bunka* culture; *kokka* nation; *kensetsu* construction; *e* for, towards   [6] *tainin* great task, important mission; *tainin wo ou* to be charged with; *shijō* in history; *kūzen no* unprecedented; *shukuten* commemoration, ceremony   [7] *shikō* enforcement; *kinen shiki* commemorative ceremony   [8] *mikka* the third of the month; *okonawareru* to be held   [9] *fūsoku* the velocity of the wind; *koeru* to be over (more); *hageshii* violent, strong   [10] *yokonaguri no* driving, strong; *rei-u* chilly rain; *tsuite* through, amidst   [11] *chikaku kara* about; *kasa* umbrella; *retsu* a row, a line, queue   [12] *shikijō* the place where a ceremony is held; *e* in; *en-en to* windingly; *tsuzuku* to go on, to continue   [13] *teikoku* the appointed time; *sankaisha* attendance; *sono sū* its number; *sudeni* already   [14] *Takamatsu-no-miya* Prince Takamatsu; *Kaya-no-miya-Kunihisa-ō* Prince Kaya Kunihisa-ō; *ryō* both; *denka* Imperial Highness   [15] *fukyū* popularization; *kai* society; *yakuin* member; *kakuryō* Cabinet minister; *kaku-tō* each political party (*kaku* each, all; *tō* political party); *daihyō* representative, delegate; *ra* suffix indicating plural number; *kaobure* personnel; *sorou* to show oneself up, to appear *to* when

Kempōfukyū-kai kaichō Ashida Hitoshi-shi no aisatsu de[1] kaikai ga ogosoka ni senserareta.[2] Ozaki Yukio-shi, Yoshida shusō, Yasui To-chiji no kangeki ni[3] furueru shukuji ga tsuzuku.[4]

Bankan wo ichi-go chi-go ni komete[5] ima-zo go-jū-hachi nen no Teikoku Kempō kara eibetsu shite[6] shuken wo kokumin ni torimodosu rekishi-teki shunkan de aru.[7]

Kinen kokuminka "Warera no Nippon" no gasshō ga nagare[8] Kempō Daijin no Kanamori Kokumusō no heishiki no aisatsu ga owaran to suru toki,[9] totsuzen Kimigayo ga sōsare,[10] ame de go-rinseki wo o-toriyame to natte ita[11] Tennō Heika ga niwaka ni go-shusseki ni narareta.[12] O-hitori de kasa wo sasareta mama[13] dan-jō ni tatareru to banzai, banzai no koe ga kisezushite waki okotte[14] Yoshida shusō no banzai shōwa wa aratamete yari-naosareru[15] nekkyō buri no uchi ni Heika ni wa jū-ichi-ji kikkari o-kaeri ni natta.[16]

Wazuka[17] san-jippun, shikamo fū-u no naka no shikiten de atta ga[18] kaishū ichi-dō shimijimi to akaruku atatakai mono ga mune ippai in natta.[19] Atarashii rekishi no asa no seiten de atta.[20]

---

[1] *kaichō* president; *shi* (suffix) Mister; *aisatsu* address; *de* with [2] *kaikai* opening of a ceremony; *ogosoka ni* solemnly; *sensuru* to announce [3] *shusō* the Premier; *To-chiji* the Governor of the Metropolis (*To* metropolis); *kangeki* deep emotion; *ni* with [4] *furueru* to tremble; *shukuji* congratulary speech; *tsuzuku* to proceed, to continue [5] *bankan* a flood of emotion; *ichi-go ichi-go* each word; *ni* in; *komete* putting, from *komeru* to put into [6] *ima-zo* this very moment (*zo* emphatic particle); *Teikoku Kempō* Imperial Constitution; *eibetsu suru* to bid farewell [7] *shuken* sovereignty; *torimodosu* to restore; *rekishi-teki* historical; *shunkan* moment [8] *kinen* commemorative; *kokuminka* folk song (*kokumin* people, *ka* song); *gasshō* choir, chorus; *nagare* flowing, from *nagareru* to flow [9] *daijin* minister; *kokumusō* minister of State (Note that *Kanamori*, a minister of State, was nicknamed "Minister of the Constitution" as he was at the head of the body that formulated the new constitutional laws of Japan.); *heishiki* closing ceremony; *owaran to suru toki* when it was towards the end (*owaran* from *owaru* to end) [10] *totsuzen* suddenly; *Kimigayo* name of the Japanese national anthem; *sōsareru* to be played [11] *ame de* on account of the rain; *rinseki* presence; *go-rinseki* the august presence (of the Emperor); *toriyameru* to cancel, to omit; *o-toriyame to natte ita* it was cancelled [12] *niwaka ni* all at once; *shusseki narareru* respectful form of *shusseki suru* to attend [13] *o-hitori de* by himself; *kasa* umbrella; *mama* while [14] *dan-jō* a stand, platform; *ni tatareru* to stand on; *to* when; *koe* voice, shout; *kisezushite* spontaneously; *waki okoru* to gush out [15] *shōwa* formal cheers; *aratameru* to renew; *yarinaosu* to try again, to repeat [16] *nekkyō* enthusiasm, excitement; *nekkyō buri no uchi ni* in great excitement; *kikkari* sharp; *o-kaeri ni natta* left, from *kaeru* to leave, to return [17] *wazuka* only [18] *shikamo* moreover; *shikiten* ceremony; *atta ga* it was but [19] *kaishū* the attendance; *ichi-dō* the whole; *kaishū ichi-dō* everyone present; *shimijimi to* impressively; *akaruku* bright: *mono* feelings; *mune* the bosom, the chest; *mune ippai ni natta* the bosom (the heart) became full (of bright and warm feelings) [20] *atarashii* new: *rekishi* history; *asa* morning (dawn)

658

NOTE. The words in parenthesis given in the following translation have no corresponding expressions in the Japanese text, but have been added in order to make the meaning of the sentences clear to the student.

The style used in Japanese newspapers is, rather often, not so clear to Occidental people, whose languages are always expressed according to set rules and in a way that their expressions leave no doubt as to the meaning they are supposed to convey. The Japanese newspaper style does not follow the grammatical rules of the spoken language, but seems to leave something to the imagination and intuition of the reader, and to have missing links between the clauses of compound sentences.

It is said that this style has been adopted in order to give the news in brief form, but it certainly is a great obstacle to render the Japanese language uniform in its diction and grammar.

A NEW LIFE FOR JAPAN HAS STARTED

OATH OF ALLEGIANCE TO THE NEW CONSTITUTION GREAT CELEBRATION HELD AT IMPERIAL PALACE PLAZA IN WIND AND RAIN.

The ceremony of the enforcement of the New Constitution, unprecedented in the history (of our country), and involving the great task of building a brilliant cultural nation symbolical of perpetual freedom and peace, was held at about half past ten in the Imperial Palace Plaza.

This day Tokyo had a violent wind (blowing) at the velocity of more than ten metres (a minute, accompanied by) driving rain. In the chilly rain, rows (and rows) of winding umbrellas were (seen) heading towards the place where the ceremony was to be held.

Before the appointed time, the number of the people (assembled there) was already about ten thousand.

The opening ceremony was solemnly announced at half past ten, at the appearance of Their Highnesses Prince Takamatsu, Prince Kaya Kunihisa, members of the Society for the Popularization of the Constitution, Cabinet ministers and representatives of all political parties, with an address (delivered) by the President of the Society for the Popularization of the Constitution, Mr. Hitoshi Ashida.

With deep emotion, Mr. Yukio Ozaki, Premier Yoshida and the Tokyo Governor Yasui followed (one after the other) with congratulatory speeches.

It was (indeed) an epoch-making moment (when the speakers), putting great emotion in each word (they uttered, told the people) to bid farewell to their fifty-eight years old Imperial Constitution and have the sovereignty (of the country) restored (in their hands).

(While the strains of) the folk song "Our Japan" (composed to commemorate the occasion) sung by a chorus were flowing (to the ears of all present), and when the state minister Kanamori, (nicknamed) the Minister of the Constitution, was at the end of his address (delivered) at the close of the ceremony, the Kimigayo (the Japanese national anthem) was played and His Majesty the Emperor, whose august presence had been cancelled on [account of the rain, suddenly appeared. (While) holding himself an umbrella, and when he stood on the stand (specially prepared for the occasion), shouts of "Banzai, banzai!" spontaneously gushed out of the crowd, and so excited they were that Premier Yoshida had to give the start for new formal cheers, and (while these were being shouted) His Majesty, sharp at eleven o'clock, left.

It was only a thirty minutes' ceremony in wind and rain, but everyone present had his heart impressively filled with bright and warm feelings. It was (indeed) a very significant ceremony of the dawn of the new history (of Japan).

NOTE. In order that the student may have a clear view of the construction of the sentences in Japanese newspapers, the above reading piece is again given, in the next page, is romaji with the English translation under each word.

SHINSEI NIPPON NO REKISHI HIRAKU
New life   Japan   of   history   opens

SHIN KEMPŌ NI CHIKAU CHŪSEI
New   Constitution   to   pledge   fidelity

Fū-u   wo tsuki   Kyūjo   mae   hiroba   no   seiten.
Wind and rain   amidst   Imperial Palace   before   plaza   of grand celebration.

Ei-en naru jiyū   to   heiwa   ni   shōchō   sareru   kaguwashiki
Perpetual   freedom   and   peace   in   symbol   to be made   brilliant

bunka   kokka   kensetsu   e   no   tainin wo   otta
culture   nation   construction   for   of   the great task   charged with

shijō   kūzen no   shukuten   Shin   Kempō   shikō
in history   unprecedented   ceremony   New   Constitution   enforcement

kinen-shiki wa   mikka   asa   jū-ji   han   kara
the commemoration   the third day   morning   ten o'clock   half   from

Kyūjō   mae   hiroba   de   okonawareta.
Imperial Palace   front of   plaza   in   was held.

Kono hi   Tōkyō wa   fūsoku   jū   mētoru wo   koeru
This day   Tokyo   the velocity of the wind   ten   metres   to be over

hageshii   fū-u   de atta.   Sono   yokonaguri no   rei-u wo
violent   wind and rain   was.   That   driving   chilly rain

tsuite   ku-ji   chikaku   kara   kasa no   retsu ga
through   nine o'clock   nearly   from   umbrellas-of   rows

shikijō   e   en-en to   tsuzuku.
the place of the ceremony   in   windingly   continue.

Teikoku   mae   sankaisha wa   sono   sū   sudeni
The appointed time   before   the attendance   its   number   already

ichi-man.   Takamatsu-no-miya,   Kaya-no-miya-Kunihisa-ō   ryō
ten thousand.   Takamatsu Prince,   Kaya Prince Kunihisa   both

denka   Kempō   fukyū-kai   yakuin   kakuryō,
highnesses.   Constitution   popularization society   members,   Cabinet ministers,

kaku-tō   daihyō-ra   no kaobure ga   sorou   to
each political party   representatives   of personnel   appear   when

jū-ji   han,   Kempō   fukyū-kai   kaichō   Ashida
ten o'clock   half,   Constitution   popularization society   president   Ashida

Hitoshi-shi   no   aisatsu   de   kaikai ga   ogosoka ni
Hitoshi Mister   of   address   with   opening of the ceremony   solemnly

senserareta.   Ozaki   Yukio-shi,   Yoshida   shusō,   Yasui
was announced.   Ozaki   Yukio-Mr.   Yoshida   Premier,   Yasui

To-chiji   no   kangeki ni   furueru   shukuji ga
Governor of the metropolis   of   deep emotion   to tremble   congratulatory speech

tsuzuku.
proceeds.

Bankan wo   ichi-go   ichi-go   ni   komete   ima-zo
A flood of emotion   one word   one word   in   putting   this very moment

go-jū-hachi   nen   no   Teikoku   Kempō   kara   eibetsu   shite
fifty-eight   years   of   Imperial   Constitution   from   farewell   doing

shuken wo   kokumin   ni   torimodosu   rekishi-teki   shunkan
the sovereignty   people   to   to restore   historical   moment

de aru.
is.

Kinen   kokuminka   "Warera no   Nippon"   no   gasshō ga
Commemorative   folk song   "Our   Japan"   of   the chorus

nagare   Kempō   Daijin   no   Kanamori   Kokumusō   no
flowing   Constitution   Minister   of   Kanamori   Minister of State   of

heishiki   no   aisatsu ga   owaran to   suru   toki,   totsuzen
closing ceremony   of   the address   at the end   to be   when,   suddedly

Kimigayo ga   sōsare,   ame   de   go-rinseki wo   o-toriyame
National Anthem   being played,   rain   by   the August presence   cancelled

to natte ita	Tennō	Heika ga	niwaka ni	go-shusseki
that had been	the Emperor	His Majesty	all at once	his presence

ni narareta.	O-hitori de	kasa wo	sasareta	mama	dan-jō
made.	By himself	the umbrella	held	while	platform

ni	tatareru	to	banzai,	banzai	no	koe ga	kisezushite
on	to stand	when	hurrah,	hurrah	of	the voice	spontaneously

waki okotte	Yoshida	Shusō	no	banzai	shōwa wa	aratamete
gushing forth	Yoshida	Premier	of	cheers	the formality	renewing

yari-naosareru	nekkyō	buri no uchi ni	Heika ni wa[1]
to be tried again	enthusiasm	while it was continuing.	His Majesty

jū-ichi ji	kikkari	o-kaeri	ni natta.
eleven o'clock	sharp	his return	made.

Wazuka	san-jippun,	shikamo	fū-u	no	naka no
Only	thirty minutes,	moreover	wind and rain	of	in the midst

shikiten	de atta	ga	kaishū	ichi-dō	shimijimi to	akaruku
ceremony	was	but	attendance	the whole	impressively	bright

atatakai	mono ga	mune	ippai ni	natta.	Atarashii	rekishi
warm	the feeling	bosom	full	became.	New	history

no	asa	no	seiten	de atta.
of	morning (dawn)	of	grand celebration	it was.

---

1 *ni wa* emphatic sign of the nominative

READING EXERCISES

IN JAPANESE CHARACTERS

See Additional Reading Pieces Page 759—761

Below is the official text of the preamble to the chapters of the new Constitution of Japan, enforced on the 3rd of May 1947.
See the same text with *furigana*, page 666,

日本國憲法

日本國民は、正當に選擧された國會における代表者を通じて行動し、われらとわれらの子孫のために、諸國民との協和による成果と、わが國全土にわたつて自由のもたらす惠澤を確保し、政府の行爲によつて再び戰爭の慘禍が起ることのないようにすることを決意し、ここに主權が國民に存することを宣言し、この憲法を確定する。そもそも國政は、國民の嚴肅な信託によるものであつて、その權威は國民に由來し、その權力は國民の代表者がこれを行使し、その福利は國民がこれを享受する。これは人類普遍の原理であり、この憲法は、かかる原理に基くものである。われらは、これに反する一切の憲法、法令及び詔勅を排除する。

日本國民は、恒久の平和を念願し、人間相互の關係を支配する崇高な理想を深く自覺するのであつて、平和を愛する諸國民の公正と信義に信賴して、われらの安全と生存を保持しようと決意した。われらは、平和を維持し、專政と隷從、壓迫と偏狹を地上から永遠に除去しようと努めてゐる國際社會において、名譽ある地位を占めたいと思う。われらは、全世界の國民が、ひとしく恐怖と缺乏から免かれ、平和のうちに生存する權利を有することを確認する。

われらは、いづれの國家も、自國のことのみに專念して他國を無視してはならないのであつて、政治道德の法則は、普遍的なものであり、この法則に從うことは、自國の主權を維持し、他國と對等關係に立とうとする各國の責務であると信ずる。

日本國民は、國家の名譽にかけ、全力をあげてこの崇高な理想と目的を達成することを誓う。

For the convenience of the student, the official Japanese text of the preamble to the chapters of the new Constitution of Japan, given on page 665, is here reprinted with *furigana*.

日本國憲法

日本國民は、正當に選擧された國會における代表者を通じて行動し、われらとわれらの子孫のために、諸國民との協和による成果と、わが國全土にわたつて自由のもたらす惠澤を確保し、政府の行爲によつて再び戰爭の慘禍が起ることのないやうにすることを決意し、ここに主權が國民に存することを宣言し、この憲法を確定する。そもそも國政は、國民の嚴肅な信託によるものであつて、その權威は國民に由來し、その權力は國民の代表者がこれを行使し、その福利は國民がこれを享受する。これは人類普遍の原理であり、この憲法は、かかる原理に基くものである。われらは、これに反する一切の憲法、法令及び詔勅を排除する。

日本國民は、恒久の平和を念願し人間相互の關係を支配する崇高な理想を深く自覺するのであつて、平和を愛する諸國民の公正と信義に信頼して、われらの安全と生存を保持しようと決意した。われらは、平和を維持し、專制と隷從、壓迫と偏狹を地上から永遠に除去しようと努めてゐる國際社會において、名譽ある地位を占めたいと思ふ。われらは、全世界の國民が、ひとしく恐怖と缺乏から免かれ、平和のうちに生存する權利を有することを確認する。

われらは、いづれの國家も、自國のことのみに專念して他國を無視してはならないのであつて、政治道德の法則は普遍的なものであり、この法則に從ふことは、自國の主權を維持し、他國と對等關係に立たうとする各國の責務であると信ずる。

日本國民は、國家の名譽にかけ、全力をあげてこの崇高な理想と目的を達成することを誓ふ。

Below is the Imperial rescript read by the Emperor of Japan at the historic first session of the National Diet under the new Constitution enforced on May 3rd, 1947.

See the same text with *furigana*, page 668, its transliteration in *romaji*, page 654 and its official English translation, page 655.

勅　語

本日、第一回國會の開會式に臨み、全國民を代表する諸君と一堂に會することは、わたくしの深く喜びとするところである。

日本國憲法に明らかであるように、國會は、國權の最高機關であり、國の唯一の立法機關である。したがって、わが國今後の發展の基礎は、一に國會の正しい運營に存する。

今や、わが國は、かつてない深刻な經濟危機に直面してゐる。この時に當り、われわれ日本國民が眞に一體となつて、この危機を克服し、民主主義に基く平和國家・文化國家の建設に成功することを、切に望むものである。

For the convenience of the student, the text of the Imperial rescript given on page 511, is reprinted below with *furigana*.

See transliteration in *romaji*, page 654, and English translation, page 655.

勅語

本日第一回國會の開會式に臨み、全國民を代表する諸君と一堂に會することは、わたくしの深く喜びとするところである。

日本國憲法に明らかであるように、國會は、國權の最高機關であり、國の唯一の立法機關である。したがって、わが國今後の發展の基礎は、一に國會の正しい運營に存する。

今や、わが國は、かつてない深刻な經濟危機に直面してゐる。この時に當り、われわれ日本國民が眞に一體となつて、この危機を克服し、民主主義に基く平和國家・文化國家の建設に成功することを切に望むものである。

Description of the celebration held in Tokyo on May 3rd, 1947, on the occasion of the enforcement of the New Constitution, as it appeared in the *Yomiuri*, one of the leading newspapers in Japan.

See the same piece of news with *furigana*, page 670, its transliteration in *romaji*, page 656, and its English translation, page 658,

新 生 日 本 の 歴 史 ひ ら く

新憲法に誓う忠誠

風雨を衝き宮城前廣場の盛典

永遠なる自由と平和に象徴される香わしき文化國家建設への大任を負つた史上空前の祝典 〝新憲法施行記念式〟 は三日朝十時半から宮城前廣場で行われた

この日東京は風速十メートルをこえるはげしい風雨であつた、その横なぐりの冷雨をついて九時ちかくからカサの列が式場へえんえんとつづく、定刻前参会者はその数すでに一万、高松宮、賀陽宮邦壽王両殿下、憲法普及会役員、閣僚、各党代表らの顔ぶれがそろうと十時半、憲法普及会々長芦田均氏のあいさつで開会がおごそかに宣せられた、尾崎行雄氏、吉田首相、安井都知事の感激にふるえる祝辞がつづく、万感を一語一語にこめていまぞ五十八年の〝帝國憲法〟から永別して主権を國民にとりもどす歴史的瞬間である、記念國民歌「われらの日本」の合唱が流れ〝憲法大臣〟の金森國務相の閉式のあいさつが終らんとするとき、とつぜん「君が代」が奏され、雨で御臨席をお取止めとなつていた天皇陛下がにわかに御出席になられた、お一人で傘をさされたまゝ壇上に立たれると万歳、万歳の声が期せずして湧き起つて吉田首相の万歳唱和は改めてやり直される熱狂ぶりのうちに陛下には十一時きつかりお帰りになつた、わずか卅分、しかも風雨の中の式典であつたが会衆一同しみじみと明るく温いものが胸いつぱいになつた新しい歴史の朝の盛典であつた。

NOTE. For the convenience of the student, the reading piece given on page 669. is here repeated with *furigana*.

新生日本の歴史ひらく

新憲法に誓う忠誠

風雨を衝き宮城前廣場の盛典

永遠なる自由と平和に象徴される香わしき文化國家建設への大任を負った史上空前の祝典〝新憲法施行記念式〟は三日朝十時半から宮城前廣場で行われた

この日東京は風速十メートルをこえるはげしい風雨であつた。その横なぐりの冷雨をついて九時ちかくからカサの列が式場へえん〳〵とつゞく、定刻前参会者はその数すでに一万、高松宮、賀陽宮邦壽王両殿下、憲法普及会役員、閣僚、各党代表らの顔ぶれがそろうと十時半、憲法普及会々長芦田均氏のあいさつで開会がおごそかに宣せられた。尾崎行雄氏、吉田首相、安井都知事の感激にふるえる祝辞がつゞく、万感を一語一語にこめていまぞ五十八年の〝帝國憲法〟から永別して主權を國民にとりもどす歴史的瞬間である。記念國民歌「われらの日本」の合唱が流れ〝憲法大臣〟の金森國務相の閉式のあいさつが終らんとするとき、とつぜん「君が代」が奏され、雨で御臨席をお取止めとなつていた天皇陛下がにわかに御出席になられた。お一人で仐をさされたま〻壇上に立たれると万歳、万歳の声が期せずして湧き起つて吉田首相の万歳唱和は改めてやり直される熱狂ぶりのうちに陛下には十一時きっかりお帰りになつた。わずか卅分、しかも風雨の中の式典であつたが会衆一同しみじみと明るく温いものが胸いつぱいになつた新しい歴史の朝の盛典であつた。

読方練習
ヨミカタレンシュウ

日本国憲法
NIPPON KOKU KEMPŌ
The Constitution of Japan.

In the preceding twentyone pages (649–670) is given the original texts in kanji, their transliteration with roman characters and full English translation, of the Preamble to the New Constitution of Japan, the Imperial Rescript read by the Emperor at the historic first session of the National Diet under the New Constitution and the press comment on the memorable event appeared in one of the leading Japanese newspapers.

ACCENTUATION

ACCENTUATION

ACCENTUATION

In considering and studying the rules on accentuation illustrated
in this chapter, the student should refer, for better understanding,
to the indicated lessons and pages.

Lesson 15, page 84

The stress on the *a* of *másŭ* and on the *e* of *masén* is regularly maintained
on the same vowels when used as verbal suffixes.

míru 見る	to see	*mimásŭ* 見ます	I see	*mimasén* 見ません	I do not see
tabéru 食べる	to eat	*tabemásŭ* 食べます	I eat	*tabemasén* 食べません	I do not eat
hanásu 話す	to speak	*hanashimásŭ* 話します	I speak	*hanashimasén* 話しません	I do not speak

Note that for brevity's sake the English translation of the inflected expressions will be given only in the first person singular.

Lesson 16, page 88

The stress on the first *a* of *máshĭta* is regularly maintained on the same
vowel when used as a suffix to form the past tense of verbs.

míru	見る	to see	*mimáshĭta*	見ました	I saw
tabéru	食べる	to eat	*tabemáshĭta*	食べました	I ate
hakobú	運ぶ	to carry	*hakobimáshĭta*	運びました	I carried
hanásu	話す	to speak	*hanashimáshĭta*	話しました	I spoke

Lesson 20, page 119

The stress laid on the *u* of the suffixes *yasúi* 易い and *nikúi* 難い and
on the second last *i* of the suffix *rashíi* らしい is maintained on the same
vowels when combined with the words they modify,

míru 見る	to see	*miyasúi* 見易い	easy to see
		minikúi 見難い	difficult to see
wakáru 解る	to understand	*wakariyasúi* 解り易い	easy to understand
		wakarinikúi 解り難い	difficult to understand
		wakarurashíi 解るらしい	it seems it can be understood
otokó	男 man	*otokorashíi*	男らしい manly
kodomó	子供 child	*kodomorashíi*	子供らしい childish

Lesson 21, page 128

Adjectives of quality and their Adverbial form

1. True adjectives accentuated on their terminal *i* are stressed on the terminal *u* of their adverbial form.

akaruí	明るい	bright		*akarukú*	明るく	brightly
kuraí	暗い	dim		*kurakú*	暗く	dimly
kanashií	悲しい	sad		*kanashikú*	悲しく	sadly
omoí	重い	heavy		*omokú*	重く	heavily
karuí	軽い	light (not heavy)		*karukú*	軽く	lightly

2. Most true adjectives accentuated on the syllable next to their terminal *i* have, when in adverbial form, the stress transposed on the second last syllable of their stem.

Stem

atsúi	暑い	hot	*atsu*	暑	*átsuku*	暑く	hotly
hirói	広い	wide	*hiro*	広	*híroku*	広く	widely
isogashíi	忙しい	busy	*isogashi*	忙し	*isogáshiku*	忙しく	busily
kitanái	汚い	dirty	*kitana*	汚	*kitánaku*	汚く	dirtily

The relatively few true adjectives belonging to this second group which do not follow the stated rule, do not change the position of their stress when in their adverbial form.

hikúi	低い	humble, low		*hikúku*	低く	humbly
shimeppói	湿っぽい	damp		*shimeppóku*	湿っぽく	damply
kashikói	賢い	wise		*kashikóku*	賢く	wisely
yasuppói	安っぽい	cheap		*yasuppóku*	安っぽく	cheaply

Also true adjectives formed by only one stressed syllable immediately followed by *i,* as *yói* for instance, do not change the position of their stress when in adverbial form.

kói	濃い	thick (liquid, colours)		*kóku*	濃く	thickly
tōi	遠い	far (adj.)		*tōku*	遠く	far (adv.)
yói	良い	good		*yóku*	良く	well

Lesson 21, page 130

Accentuation of Past Form of True Adjectives

1. The past form of true adjectives accentuated on their terminal *i,* as *amai, osoi,* is stressed on the vowel at the end of their stem.

		Stem		Past Form	
amai 甘い	sweet	*ama* 甘		*amákatta* 甘かった	it was sweet
abunai 危ない	dangerous	*abuna* 危な		*abunákatta* 危なかった	it was dangerous

akarui 明るい	bright	*akaru* 明る	*akarúkatta* 明るかった	it was bright
katai 固い	hard	*kata* 固	*katákatta* 固かった	it was hard
kurai 暗い	dark	*kura* 暗	*kurákatta* 暗かった	it was dark
tsumetai 冷たい	cool	*tsumeta* 冷た	*tsumetákatta* 冷たかった	it was cool
osoi 遅い	late	*oso* 遅	*osókatta* 遅かった	it was late

2. True adjectives accentuated on the syllable next to their terminal *i*, have, when in adverbial form, the stress laid on the second last syllable of their stem.

		Stem	Past Form	
atsúi 暑い	hot	*atsu* 暑	*átsukatta* 暑かった	it was hot
erái 偉い	famous	*era* 偉	*érakatta* 偉かった	it was famous
hosói 細い	thin	*hoso* 細	*hósokatta* 細かった	it was thin
isogashíi 忙しい	busy	*isogashi* 忙し	*isogáshikatta* 忙しかった	it was busy
umái 旨い	tasty	*uma* 旨	*úmakatta* 旨かった	it was tasty
samúi 寒い	cold	*samu* 寒	*sámukatta* 寒かった	it was cold

The few true adjectives belonging to this second group which do not follow the stated rule, maintain the stress on the last vowel of their stem when in past form.

			Stem		Past Form		
chikái	近い	near	*chika*	近	*chikákatta*	近かった	it was near
fukái	深い	deep	*fuka*	深	*fukákatta*	深かった	it was deep
fŭtói	太い	thick	*futo*	太	*fŭtókatta*	太かった	it was thick

Also true adjectives formed by only one accented syllable immediately followed by *i*, do not alter the position of their stress when in their past form.

kói	濃い	dense	*kókatta*	濃かった	it was dense
tōi	遠い	far	*tōkatta*	遠かった	it was far
yói	良い	good	*yókatta*	良かった	it was good

Lesson 21, page 133

Negative conjugation with *Nai* and *Nakatta*

Verbs that in their simple present form are stressed on the second last syllable, as *míru*, *kógu* for instance, are stressed on the terminal vowel of their simple stem if they belong to Class I and of their *a*-stem if they belong to Class II, when combined with *nai* ない or *nakatta* なかった.

		Stem				
míru 見る	to see	*mi* 見	*mínai* 見ない	I do not see	*minakatta* 見なかった	I did not see
kógu 漕ぐ	to row	*koga* 漕が	*kogánai* 漕がない	I do not row	*kogánakatta* 漕がなかった	I did not row
hanásu 話す	to speak	*hanasu* 話さ	*hanasánai* 話さない	I do not speak	*hanasánakatta* 話さなかった	I did not speak

However, the negative form of verbs whose simple present has the stress on their final *u*, as *irú*, *kasú* for instance, have the stress on the first syllable of either suffix.

		Stem				
irú いる	to be	*i* い	*inái* いない	I am not	*inákatta* いなかった	I was not
kaú 買う	to buy	*kawa* 買わ	*kawanái* 買わない	I do not buy	*kawanákatta* 買わなかった	I did not buy
kasú 貸す	to rent	*kasa* 貸さ	*kasanái* 貸さない	I do not rent	*kasanákatta* 貸さなかった	I did not rent

Lesson 21, page 135

Nagative of verbs formed with the suffix *nu*.

Verbs whose simple present is accentuated on their final *u*, have their negative form in *nu* accentuated on the *u* of the said suffix. Verbs whose simple present is accentuated on its second last syllable, have their negative form in *nu* accentuated on the final vowel of their stem, as shown in the following examples. For comparison, the negative form in *nai* is also given.

		Stem		Negative Form	
tobú 飛ぶ	to fly	*toba* 飛ば	*tobanái*	飛ばない	not to fly,
			tobanú	飛ばぬ	do not fly, does not fly, etc.
hatarakú 仂く	to work	*hataraka* 仂か	*hatarakanái*	仂かない	not to work,
			hatarakanú	仂かぬ	do not work, does not work, etc.
káku 書く	to write	*kaka* 書か	*kakánai*	書かない	not to write,
			kakánu	書かぬ	do not write, does not write, etc.
tabéru 食べる	to eat	*tabe* 食べ	*tabénai*	食べない	not to eat,
			tabénu	食べぬ	do not eat, does not eat, etc.

Lesson 22, page 138

Desiderative Conjugation

The suffix *tái* たい always maintains the stress on the *a* when it is combined with the simple stem of verbs of Class I and the *i*-stem of verbs of Class II to form the affirmative present of the desiderative conjugation.

		Stem		
míru 見る	to see	*mi* 見	*mitái* 見たい	I wish to see
yómu 読む	to read	*yomi* 読み	*yomitái* 読みたい	I wish to read
hanásu 話す	to speak	*hanashi* 話し	*hanashitái* 話したい	I wish to speak
kaú 買う	to buy	*kai* 買い	*kaitái* 買いたい	I wish to buy
tobú 飛ぶ	to fly	*tobi* 飛び	*tobitái* 飛びたい	I wish to fly

The suffix *tákatta* たかった is always stressed on its first *a* when it is combined with the simple stem of verbs of Class I and the *i*-stem of verbs of Class II to form the affirmative past of the desiderative conjugation.

		Stem	**Past Form**	
míru 見る	to see	*mi* 見	*mitákatta* 見たかった	wished to see
tabéru 食べる	to eat	*tabe* 食べ	*tabetákatta* 食べたかった	wished to eat
kaú 買う	to buy	*kai* 買い	*kaitákatta* 買いたかった	wished to buy
yómu 読む	to read	*yomi* 読み	*yomitákatta* 読みたかった	wished to read
hanásu 話す	to speak	*hanashi* 話し	*hanashitákatta* 話したかった	wished to speak

The suffix *taku* たく is always stressed on its *a* when it is combined with the simple stem of verbs of Class I and the *i*-stem of verbs of Class II to form their adverbial form.

				Adverbial Form	
míru	見る	to see		*mitáku*	見たく
tabéru	食べる	to eat		*tabetáku*	食べたく
yómu	読む	to read		*yomitáku*	読みたく
hanásu	話す	to speak		*hanashĭtáku*	話したく

mitáku-nái	見たくない	I, you, etc., do not wish to see
mitáku-nákatta	見たくなかった	I, you, etc., did not wish to see
hanashĭtáku-nái	話したくない	I, you, etc., do not wish to speak
hanashĭtáku-nákatta	話したくなかった	I, you, etc., did not wish to speak

Lesson 23, page 150

Subordinate

1. The subordinate of verbs that are accentuated on the last syllable of their simple present, as *agarú* 上がる *to go up*, for instance, is always stressed on its terminal *e agatté* 上がって *going up*.

araú	洗う	to wash	*aratté*	洗って	washing
asobú	遊ぶ	to play	*asondé*	遊んで	playing
dekakerú	出掛ける	to go out	*dekaketé*	出掛けて	going out
hajimerú	始める	to begin	*hajimeté*	始めて	beginning
kaú	買う	to buy	*katté*	買って	buying

2. Verbs accentuated on the second last syllable of their simple present, as *arúku to walk*, for instance, do not change the position of the stress in their subordinate form.

arúku	歩く	to walk	*arúite*	歩いて	walking
chikazúku	近づく	to approach	*chikazúite*	近づいて	approaching
erábu	選ぶ	to choose	*eránde*	選んで	choosing
hanásu	話す	to speak	*hanáshite*	話して	speaking

3. Most verbs whose simple present ends in *éru*, as *atsuméru* 集める *to gather*, for instance, have, in their subordinate form, the stress on the syllable that precedes the one of which the accentuated *e* of the termination *éru* is a part.

atsuméru	集める	to gather	*atsúmete*	集めて	gathering
homéru	ほめる	to praise	*hómete*	ほめて	praising
miséru	見せる	to show	*mísete*	見せて	showing

Note that causative verbs formed with *saseru* させる and *seru* せる (See page 354) as well as passive verbs formed with the suffix *areru* (See page 436), follow the rule of this third group in the formation of their subordinate as given above.

4. There are several verbs ending in *eru* like those of group 3 above, and in *iru* preceded by a stressed *a*, as *kangáeru* 考える *to think*, *háiru to enter*, etc., which maintain the stress on the same letter *a* in their subordinate form.

háiru	入る	to enter	*háitte*	入って	entering
kangáeru	考える	to think	*kangáete*	考えて	thinking
kotáeru	答える	to answer	*kotáete*	答えて	answering
machigáeru	間違える	to mistake	*machigáete*	間違えて	mistaking

Lesson 25, page 167

Negative Subordinate

Verbs whose simple present is accentuated on their terminal *u,* as *asobú* 遊ぶ *to play, dekakerú* 出掛ける *to go out*, for instance, have their negative subordinate forms stressed on the syllable *na* of the suffix *nákute* なくて, on the *a* of the suffix *nái* ない and on the suffix *zu* ず.

asobú 遊ぶ	to play	*asobanákute* *asobanái de* *asobazú ni*	遊ばなくて 遊ばないで 遊ばずに	}not playing not having played without playing
dekakerú 出掛ける	to go out	*dekakenákute* *dekakenái de* *dekakezú ni*	出掛けなくて 出掛けないで 出掛けずに	}not going out not having gone out without going out
hatarakú 仂く	to work	*hatarakanákute* *hatarakanái de* *hatarakazú ni*	仂かなくて 仂かないで 仂かずに	}not working not having worked without working

Verbs whose simple present is accentuated on their second last syllable have their negative subordinate form stressed on the terminal vowel of their simple stem if they belong to Class I, as *tabéru,* and on the terminal vowel of the *a*-stem if they belong to Class II, as *hanásu,* followed by *nai de* ないで or *nakute* なくて.

Stem

tabéru 食べる	to eat	*tabe* 食べ	*tabénakute* *tabénai de*	食べなくて 食べないで	}not eating not having eaten wihtout eating
hanásu 話す	to speak	*hanasa* 話さ	*hanasánakute* *hanasánai de*	話さなくて 話さないで	}not speaking not having spoken without speaking

However, when followed by *zu ni,* the stress is laid on the second last syllable of their stem in case of verbs of Class I, as *tabéru* for instance, but in case of verbs of Class II, as *hanásu,* the position of the stress is not altered.

Stem

tabéru 食べる	to eat	*tabe* 食べ	*tábezu ni*	食べずに	}not eating not having eaten without eating
hanásu 話す	to speak	*hanasa* 話さ	*hanásazu ni*	話さずに	}not speaking not having spoken without speaking

If the stem of a verb is of only one syllable, the stress is maintained on it in all three forms of the negative subordinate, as in:

Stem

míru 見る	to see	*mi* 見	*mínakute* *mínai de* *mízu ni*	見なくて 見ないで 見ずに	}not seeing not having seen without seeing

Also verbs accentuated on the third last syllable of their simple present, as *háiru* for instance, have their negative subordinate form stressed on the terminal vowel of their stem, when followed by the suffix *nakute* or *nai de*

	Stem		
háiru to enter 入る	*haira* 入ら	*hairánakute* 入らなくて	not entering
		hairánai de 入らないで	not having entered without entering

The stress, however, remains unaltered when the stem is followed by the suffix *zu ni.*

háirazu ni 入らずに not entering etc.

Lesson 27, page 181

Subordinate of True Adjectives

True adjectives accentuated on their terminal *i* have their subordinate stressed on the second last vowel of their original form.

akaruí 明るい bright	*akarúkute* 明るくて being bright
kuraí 暗い dark	*kurákute* 暗くて being dark
omoí 重い heavy	*omókute* 重くて being heavy

True adjectives accentuated on the syllable next to their terminal *i* have their subordinate form accentuated on the preceding syllable, as in the following example:

atsúi 暑い hot	*átsukute* 暑くて being hot
samúi 寒い cold	*sámukute* 寒くて being cold

Lesson 29 page 185

Subordinate of Verbs in Desiderative Form

Verbs of Class I are stressed on the terminal vowel of their simple stem when followed by the suffix *takute* たくて, while verbs of Class II, in their *i*-stem form, are combined with the same suffix *takute* with the stress on the *a.*

	Stem			
míru 見る	to see	*mi* 見	*mítakute*	見たくて wishing to see
tabéru 食べる	to eat	*tabe* 食べ	*tabétakute*	食べたくて wishing to eat
tobú 飛ぶ	to fly	*tobi* 飛び	*tobitákute*	飛びたくて wishing to fly
hanásu 話す	to speak	*hanashi* 話し	*hanashitákute*	話したくて wishing to speak
agarú 上がる	to go up	*agari* 上がり	*agaritákute* 上がりたくて	wishing to go up
hashíru 走る	to run	*hashiri* 走り	*hashiritákute* 走りたくて	wishing to run

Lesson 30, page 202
Short Form of Past Tense of Verbs

The stress on this past form of verbs is laid on the same syllable that is stressed in their subordinate form.

		Subordinate		Past	
míru 見る	to see	*míte* 見て	seeing	*míta* 見た	saw
tabéru 食べる	to eat	*tábete* 食べて	eating	*tábeta* 食べた	ate
dekakerú 出掛ける	to go out	*dekaketé* 出掛けて	going out	*dekaketá* 出掛けた	went out
tobú 飛ぶ	to fly	*tondé* 飛んで	flying	*tondá* 飛んだ	flew
káku 書く	to write	*káite* 書いて	writing	*káita* 書いた	wrote
hatarakú 仂く	to work	*hataraité* 仂いて	working	*hataraitá* 仂いた	worked
háiru 入る	to enter	*háitte* 入って	entering	*háitta* 入った	entered

Lesson 30, page 202
Negative form of verbs with the suffix *nakatta*.

The negative suffix *nakatta* has the stress on the *a* of its first syllable when added to the stem of verbs of both Class I and II accentuated on their terminal *u*. For comparison also the short form of the positive past is given below:

		Positive Past		Nagative Past	
irú (there) いる	to be	*itá* いた	(there)was	*inákatta* いなかった	there was not
dekakerú 出かける	to go out	*dekaketá* 出かけた	when out	*dekakenákatta* 出かけなかった	didn't go out
kasú 貸す	to lend	*kashitá* 貸した	lent	*kasanákatta* 貸さなかった	didn't lend
tobú 飛ぶ	to fly	*tondá* 飛んだ	flew	*tobanákatta* 飛ばなかった	didn't fly

With verbs of Class I and II whose simple present is stressed on the second or third last syllable, the stress is maintained on the terminal vowel of their stem as shown below:

		Stem	Positive Past		Negative Past	
míru 見る	to see	*mi* 見	*míta* 見た	saw	*minákatta* 見なかった	didn't see
tabéru 食べる	to eat	*tabe* 食べ	*tábeta* 食べた	ate	*tabénakatta* 食べなかった	didn't eat
káku 書く	to write	*kaka* 書か	*káita* 書いた	wrote	*kakánakatta* 書かなかった	didn't write

mátsu 待つ	to wait	*mata* 待た	*mátta* 待った	waited	*matánakatta* 待たなかった	didn't wait
yómu 読む	to read	*yoma* 読ま	*yónda* 読んだ	read	*yománakatta* 読まなかった	didn't read
káeru 帰る	to return	*kaera* 帰ら	*káetta* 帰った	returned	*kaeránakatta* 帰らなかった	didn't return

Lesson 32, page 223

The future form obtained with the suffix *mashō*, the shorter forms obtained with the suffix *yō* and by changing the terminal *u* of the simple present of verbs of Class II, as well as the expressions *deshō* and *darō*, are always accentuated on their final vowel *ō*.

míru	見る	to see	*mimashō* *míru deshō* *míru darō* *miyō*	見ましょう 見るでしょう 見るだろう 見よう	} I shall see, you will see, etc.
káku	書く	to write	*kakimashō* *káku deshō* *káku darō* *kakō*	書きましょう 書くでしょう 書くだろう 書こう	} I shall write, You will write, etc.

Lesson 32, page 226

The future forms obtained with the negative suffixes *masumái* ますまい or *nái* まい, are stressed on the *a* next to the terminal *i* of either suffix.

káku	書く	to write	*kakimasumái* *kakumái*	書きますまい 書くまい	} I shall (probably) not write, etc.
míru	見る	to see	*mimasumái* *mimái*	見ますまい 見まい	} I shall (probably) not see, etc.

Lesson 37, page 280

Alternative

Verbs of both Class I and Class II whose simple present is accentuated on their terminal *u*, and which, according to given rules, have their subordinate accentuated on the terminal *e*, have their **affirmative alternative form** stressed on the *a* of either suffix *tari* and *ari*.

		Subordinate		Alternative	
dekakerú 出掛ける	to go out	*dekaketé* 出掛けて	going out	*dekaketári* 出掛けたり	sometimes going out, sometimes …………
kaú 買う	to buy	*katté* 買って	buying	*kattári* 買ったり	sometimes buying, sometimes …………
tomarú 止まる	to stop (intr.)	*tomatté* 止まって	stopping	*tomattári* 止まったり	sometimes stopping, sometimes …………
hakobú 運ぶ	to carry	*hakondé* 運んで	carrying	*hakondári* 運んだり	sometimes carrying, sometimes …………

Verbs of both Class I and Class II whose simple present is accentuated on the second or third last syllable, have their **affirmative alternative form** stressed on the same vowel that is accentuated in their subordinate form.

		Subordinate		Alternative	
míru 見る	to see, look	*míte* 見て	seeing	*mítari* 見たり	sometimes looking, sometimes............
homéru ほめる	to praise	*hómete* ほめて	praising	*hómetari* ほめたり	sometimes praising, sometimes..............
háiru 入る	to enter	*háitte* 入って	entering	*háittari* 入ったり	sometimes entering, sometimes..............
yómu 読む	to read	*yónde* 読んで	reading	*yóndari* 読んだり	sometimes reading, sometimes..............
hanásu 話す	to speak	*hanáshĭte* 話して	speaking	*hanáshĭtari* 話したり	sometimes speaking, sometimes.............

As to the **negative alternative form** of verbs of Class I, whose simple present is accentuated on the second last syllable, the stress is laid on the last letter of their simple stem, while the negative alternative form of verbs of Class II, similarly accentuated on their second last syllable, is stressed on the final *a* of their *a*-stem, stems which are combined with the suffix *nakattari*

		Stem	Positive and Negative Alternative	
míru 見る	to see, look		*mítari* 見たり	sometimes looking.
		mi 見	*mínakattari* 見なかったり	sometimes not looking
homéru ほめる	to praise		*hómetari* ほめたり	sometimes praising.
		home ほめ	*homénakattari* ほめなかったり	sometimes not praising
káku 書く	to write		*káitari* 書いたり	sometimes writing,
		kaka 書か	*kakánakattari* 書かなかったり	sometimes not writing
hanásu 話す	to speak		*hanáshĭtari* 話したり	sometimes speaking,
		hanasa 話さ	*hanasánakattari* 話さなかったり	sometimes not speaking
gomakásu ごまかす	to cheat		*gomakáshitari* ごまかしたり	sometimes cheating
		gomakasa ごまかさ	*gomakasánakattari* ごまかさなかったり	sometimes not cheating

With verbs of both Class I and II whose simple present is accentuated on the *u* of their last syllable, the stress is laid on the *a* of the first syllable of the negative alternative suffix *nakattari,* as in the following examples:

		Stem	Positive and Negative Alternative	
asobú 遊ぶ	to play		*asondári* 遊んだり	sometimes playing
		asoba 遊ば	*asobanákattari* 遊ばなかったり	sometimes not playing
kimerú 決める	to decide		*kimetári* 決めたり	sometimes deciding
		kime 決め	*kimenákattari* 決めなかったり	sometimes not deciding
tomarú 止まる	to stop		*tomattári* 止まったり	sometimes stopping
		tomara 止まら	*tomaranákattari* 止まらなかったり	sometimes not stopping

Lesson 40, page 319

Imperative Forms

Verbs of Class I accentuated on the terminal *u* of their simple present, have their imperative form ending in *ro* and *yo* stressed on the *o* of either suffix.

agerú 上げる	to raise	*Ageró.* 上げろ.	*Ageyó.* 上げよ.	Raise!
dekakerú 出掛ける	to go out	*Dekakeró.* 出掛けろ.	*Dekakeyó.* 出掛けよ.	Go out!
katamerú 固める	to harden	*Katameró.* 固めろ.	*Katameyó.* 固めよ.	Harden!

However, verbs of the same Class I accentuated on their second last syllable have the imperative form in *ro* stressed on the terminal syllable of their simple stem, while the form in *yo* is stressed on the second last syllable of the simple stem.

		Stem	Imperative		
atsuméru 集める	to gather	*atsume* 集め	*Atsuméro.* 集めろ.	*Atsúmeyo.* 集めよ.	Gather!
hiroméru 広める	to widen	*hirome* 広め	*Hiroméro.* 広めろ.	*Hirómeyo.* 広めよ.	Widen!
miséru 見せる	to show	*mise* 見せ	*Miséro.* 見せろ.	*Míseyo.* 見せよ.	Show!
todokéru 届ける	to deliver	*todoke* 届け	*Todokéro.* 届けろ.	*Todókeyo.* 届けよ.	Deliver!

Verbs of Class II accentuated on the last syllable of their simple present have the imperative form ending in *yo* stressed on the terminal *e* of their *e*-stem, while verbs accentuated on the second last syllable do not change the position of the stress when used in their imperative form with *yo.*

As it has been stated in Lesson 40, page 319, the *e*-stem of verbs of Class II by itself. without any suffix, may be used as a form of imperative.

		Stem	**Imperative**	
asobu	to play	*Asobé*	*Asobéyo*	Play !
遊ぶ		遊べ	遊べよ	
hataraku	to work	*Hataraké*	*Hatarakéyo*	Work !
仂く		仂け	仂けよ	
hanásu	to speak	*Hanáse*	*Hanáseyo*	Speak !
話す		話せ	話せよ	
erábu	to choose	*Erábe*	*Erábeyo*	Choose !
選ぶ		選べ	選べよ	
isógu	to hurry	*Isóge*	*Isógeyo*	Hurry !
急ぐ		急げ	急げよ	
shitagáu	to obey	*Shitagáe*	*Shitagáeyo*	Obey !
従う		従え	従えよ	

The imperative form of verbs of Class I, obtained by combining their simple stem with the suffix *na,* and the imperative form of verbs of Class II obtained by combining their *i*-stem with the same suffix, have the stress on the terminal *a* of the combined expressions.

		Stem		
miru	to look	*mi*	*Miná.*	Look !
見る		見	見な.	
tabéru	to eat	*tabe*	*Tabená.*	Eat !
食べる		食べ	食べな.	
asobú	to play	*asobi*	*Asobiná.*	Play !
遊ぶ		遊び	遊びな.	
hataraku	to work	*hataraki*	*Hatarakiná.*	Work !
仂く		仂き	仂きな.	
hanásu	to speak	*hanashi*	*Hanashiná.*	Speak !
話す		話し	話しな.	
isógu	to hurry	*isogi*	*Isoginá.*	Hurry !
急ぐ		急ぎ	急ぎな.	
shitagáu	to obey	*shitagai*	*Shitagainá.*	Obey !
従う		従い	従いな.	

Lesson 43, page 354

Causative Verbs

Verbs of both Class I and II whose simple present is stressed. on the last syllable. have their causative form stressed on the terminal *u* of the suffixes *saserú* させる and *serú* せる.

ageru	上げる	to raise	*agesaserú*	上げさせる	to cause to raise
yameru	止める	to give up	*yamesaserú*	止めさせる	to cause to give up
tobú	飛ぶ	to fly	*tobaserú*	飛ばせる	to cause to fly
hataraku	仂く	to work	*hatarakaserú*	仂かせる	to cause to work

Verbs of both Class I and II whose simple present is stressed on the second last syllable, have their causative form stressed on the *e* of the suffix *saséru* させる or *séru* せる.

miru	見る	to look	*misaséru*	見させる	to cause to look
tabéru	食べる	to eat	*tabesaséru*	食べさせる	to cause to eat
káku	書く	to write	*kakaséru*	書かせる	to cause to write
hanásu	話す	to speak	*hanasaséru*	話させる	to cause to speak

Causative verbs formed with the suffix *saseru* or *seru* follow, in their inflectional changes, the same rules of accentuation as applied to verbs of Class I.

Lesson 47, page 399
Subjunctive

Verbs of both Class I and II do not alter the position of their stress as laid on their simple present form when inflected with the suffix *reba* or *ba*.

míru	見る	to look, see	*míreba*	見れば	if I see
tabéru	食べる	to eat	*tabéreba*	食べれば	if I eat
yobú	呼ぶ	to call	*yobéba*	呼べば	if I call
hatarakú	仂く	to work	*hatarakéba*	仂けば	if I work
káku	書く	to write	*kákeba*	書けば	if I write
hanásu	話す	to speak	*hanáseba*	話せば	if I speak

Lesson 50, page 436
Passive Voice

The suffix *areru,* used to form the passive voice, is stressed on its final *u* (*arerú*) when used to modify a verb whose simple present is stressed on its last syllable, but it is stressed on *e* of its second last syllable when it modifies a verb whose simple present is also stressed on its second last syllable.

korosú	殺す	to kill	*korosarerú*	殺される	to be killed
shikarú	叱る	to scold	*shikararerú*	叱られる	to be scolded
míru	見る	to see	*miraréru*	見られる	to be seen
tabéru	食べる	to eat	*taberaréru*	食べられる	to be eaten
káku	書く	to write	*kakaréru*	書かれる	to be written
nusúmu	盗む	to steal	*nusumaréru*	盗まれる	to be stolen

ACCENTUATION
ON
VERBAL FORMS

NOTE. In the following 67 pages are given the salient features of the accentuation on verbal forms. For the other important characteristics of the accentuation on verbal forms, as well as the accentuation on words of the other parts of speech, see pp. 675–688.

ACCENTUATION ON VERBAL FORMS

Japanese verbs, considered from the changes in accentuation that they undergo in their various conjugational forms, may be divided into four groups:

GROUP ONE.—Verbs belonging to this group are characterized by their simple present stressed on the last syllable and by their subordinate stressed on its terminal *e,* as in *akerú* 開ける to open—*aketé* 開けて opening, *araú* 洗う to wash—*aratté* 洗って washing, etc.

GROUP TWO.—Verbs belonging to this group are characterized by their simple present stressed on the second last syllable, which is also the affected syllable of their subordinate form, as in *abúru* 焙る to roast—*abútte* 焙って roasting, *chigíru* ちぎる to tear off—*chigítte* ちぎって tearing off, etc.

GROUP THREE.—Verbs belonging to this group are characterized by their ending in the syllable *ru* preceded by a stressed *e* or *i,* as in *arataméru* 改める to reform, *dekíru* 出来る to be able, etc. The subordinate of such verbs is stressed on the syllable that precedes the one stressed in the simple present form, as in *aratámete* 改めて reforming, *dékite* 出来て being able to do, etc.

GROUP FOUR.—To this group belong a small number of verbs characterized by their simple present ending in *ru* or *su* preceded by two vowels, as in *káeru* 帰る to go back. *káesu* 返す to give back, *otoróeru* 衰える to become weak, etc.

The stress on the simple present of verbs of this group falls on the first of the two vowels, which is also the one stressed in their subordinate form, as in *káette* 帰って going back, *káeshite* 返して giving back, *otoróete* 衰えて becoming weak. etc.

GROUP ONE
Main Characteristics

Simple Present: Stressed on the last syllable.

Subordinate
}Positive: Stressed on its terminal letter *e.*
}Negative: Stressed on the *a* of the suffix *nákute* なくて.

Negative
with *nai* and
nakatta
}Present: Stressed on the *a* of the suffix *nái* ない.
}Past: Stressed on the *a* of the first syllable of the suffix *nákatta* なかった.

GROUP ONE	SUBORDINATE Positive	Negative	NEGATIVE Present	Past
abarerú 暴れる behave violently	abareté 暴れて	abarenákute 暴れなくて	abarenái 暴れない	abarenákatta 暴れなかった
abirú 浴びる pour (water) on oneself	abité 浴びて	abinákute 浴びなくて	abinái 浴びない	abinákatta 浴びなかった
abiserú 浴びせる pour (water) upon	abiseté 浴びせて	abisenákute 浴びせなくて	abisenái 浴びせない	abisenákatta 浴びせなかった
agarú 上る go, come up	agatté 上って	agaranákute 上らなくて	agaranái 上らない	agaranákatta 上らなかった
agerú 上げる give, offer	ageté 上げて	agenákute 上げなくて	agenái 上げない	agenákatta 上げなかった
akerú 開ける open	aketé 開けて	akenákute 開けなくて	akenái 開けない	akenákatta 開けなかった
akirerú 呆れる be amazed	akireté 呆れて	akirenákute 呆れなくて	akirenái 呆れない	akirenákatta 呆れなかった
akogarerú 憧れる yearn after	akogareté 憧れて	akogarenákute 憧れなくて	akogarenái 憧れない	akogarenákatta 憧れなかった
amaerú 甘える be coquettish	amaeté 甘えて	amaenákute 甘えなくて	amaenái 甘えない	amaenákatta 甘えなかった
amayakasú 甘やかす fondle	amayakashité 甘やかして	amayakasanákute 甘やかさなくて	amayakasanái 甘やかさない	amayakasanákatta 甘やかさなかった
aomukú 仰むく look upward	aomuité 仰むいて	aomukanákute 仰むかなくて	aomukanái 仰むかない	aomukanákatta 仰むかなかった
aradaterú 荒立てる aggravate	aradateté 荒立てて	aradatenákute 荒立てなくて	aradatenái 荒立てない	aradatenákatta 荒立てなかった
arasú 荒す devastate	arashité 荒して	arasanákute 荒さなくて	arasanái 荒さない	arasanákatta 荒さなかった
araú 洗う wash; cleanse	aratté 洗って	arawanákute 洗わなくて	arawanái 洗わない	arawanákatta 洗わなかった
arerú 荒れる become rough	areté 荒れて	arenákute 荒れなくて	arenái 荒れない	arenákatta 荒れなかった

692

GROUP ONE	SUBORDINATE		NEGATIVE	
	Positive	Negative	Present	Past
asobaserú 遊ばせる let (a boy) play	asobaseté 遊ばせて	asobasenákute 遊ばせなくて	asobasenái 遊ばせない	asobasenákatta 遊ばせなかった
asobú 遊ぶ amuse oneself	asonde 遊んで	asobanákute 遊ばなくて	asobanái 遊ばない	asobanákatta 遊ばなかった
ataerú 与える give	ataeté 与えて	ataenákute 与えなくて	ataenái 与えない	ataenákatta 与えなかった
atarú 当る strike (against)	atatté 当って	ataranákute 当らなくて	ataranái 当らない	ataranákatta 当らなかった
ategaú あてがう apply (a thing to)	ategatté あてがって	ategawanákute あてがわなくて	ategawanái あてがわない	ategawanákatta あてがわなかった
aterarerú 当てられる be affected by	aterareté 当てられて	aterarenákute 当てられなくて	aterarenái 当てられない	aterarenákatta 当てられなかった
aterú 宛てる address	ateté 宛てて	atenákute 宛てなくて	atenái 宛てない	atenákatta 宛てなかった
atsukaú 扱う treat, handle	atsukatté 扱って	atsukawanákute 扱わなくて	atsukawanái 扱わない	atsukawanákatta 扱わなかった
awaterú 慌てる be confused	awateté 慌てて	awatenákute 慌てなくて	awatenái 慌てない	awatenákatta 慌てなかった
burasagarú ぶら下がる hang down	burasagatté ぶら下がって	burasagaranákute ぶら下がらなくて	burasagaranái ぶら下がらない	burasagaranákatta ぶらさがらなかった
burasagerú ぶら下げる hang, suspend v. tr.	burasageté ぶら下げて	burasagenákute ぶら下げなくて	burasagenái ぶら下げない	burasagenákatta ぶら下げなかった
buratsukú ぶらつく loiter	buratsuité ぶらついて	buratsukanákute ぶらつかなくて	buratsukanái ぶらつかない	buratsukanákatta ぶらつかなかった
butsukarú ぶつかる strike, hit	butsukatté ぶつかって	butsukaranákute ぶつからなくて	butsukaranái ぶつからない	butsukaranákatta ぶつからなかった
butsukerú ぶつける throw, fling at	butsuketé ぶつけて	butsukenákute ぶつけなくて	butsukenái ぶつけない	butsukenákatta ぶつけなかった
chijimarú 縮まる be shortened	chijimatté 縮まって	chijimaranákute 縮まらなくて	chijimaranái 縮まらない	chijimaranákatta 縮まらなかった
chijimerú 縮める shrink v. tr.	chijimeté 縮めて	chijimenákute 縮めなくて	chijimenái 縮めない	chijimenákatta 縮めなかった
chijimú 縮む shrink v. i.	chijindé 縮んで	chijimanákute 縮まなくて	chijimanái 縮まない	chijimanákatta 縮まなかった
chijirasú 縮らす crinkle	chijiraseté 縮らせて	chijirasanákute 縮らさなくて	chijirasanái 縮らさない	chijirasanákatta 縮らさなかった
chijirerú 縮れる be frizzled	chijireté 縮れて	chijirenákute 縮れなくて	chijirenái 縮れない	chijirenákatta 縮れなかった

| GROUP ONE | SUBORDINATE | | NEGATIVE | |
	Positive	Negative	Present	Past
chirabarú 散らば る disperse	chirabatté 散らばって	chirabaranákute 散らばらなくて	chirabaranái 散らばらない	chirabaranákatta 散らばらなかった
chirakasú 散らか す scatter v. t.	chirakashité 散らかして	chirakasanákute 散らかさなくて	chirakasanái 散らかさない	chirakasanákatta 散らかさなかった
chirasú 散らす strew v. tr.	chirashité 散らして	chirasanákute 散らさなくて	chirasanái 散らさない	chirasanákatta 散らさなかった
chirú 散る fall, disperse	chitté 散って	chiranákute 散らなくて	chiranái 散らない	chiranákatta 散らなかった
dakú 抱く hold in arms	daité 抱いて	dakanákute 抱かなくて	dakanái 抱かない	dakanákatta 抱かなかった
darakerú だらけ る feel languid	daraketé だらけて	darakenákute だらけなくて	darakenái だらけない	darakenákatta だらけなかった
deaú 出会う happen to meet	deatté 出会って	deawanákute 出会わなくて	deawanái 出会わない	deawanákatta 出会わなかった
dekakerú 出掛ける take an outing	dekaketé 出掛けて	dekakenákute 出掛けなくて	dekakenái 出掛けない	dekakenákatta 出掛けなかった
dekiagarú 出来上る be completed	dekiagatté 出来上って	dekiagaranákute 出来上らなくて	dekiagaranái 出来上らない	dekiagaranákatta 出来上らなかった
dokerú どける remove	doketé どけて	dokenákute どけなくて	dokenái どけない	dokenákatta どけなかった
dokú どく move aside	doité どいて	dokanákute どかなくて	dokanái どかない	dokanákatta どかなかった
fukú 拭く wipe, mop	fuité 拭いて	fukanákute 拭かなくて	fukanái 拭かない	fukanákatta 拭かなかった
fukuramasú 脹らます swell (v. tr.)	fukuramashité 脹らまして	fukuramasanákute 脹らまさなくて	fukuramasanái 脹らまさない	fukuramasanákatta 脹らまさなかった
fukuramú 脹らむ swell (v. i.)	fukurandé 脹らんで	fukuramanákute 脹らまなくて	fukuramanái 脹らまない	fukuramanákatta 脹らまなかった
fukurerú 脹れる swell (v. i.)	fukureté 脹れて	fukurenákute 脹れなくて	fukurenái 脹れない	fukurenákatta 脹れなかった
furerú 触れる touch, feel	fureté 触れて	furenákute 触れなくて	furenái 触れない	furenákatta 触れなかった
furú 振る wave (a flag)	futté 振って	furanákute 振らなくて	furanái 振らない	furanákatta 振らなかった
furuerú 震える tremble, quiver	furueté 震えて	furuenakuté 震えなくて	furuenái 震えない	furuenákatta 震えなかった
fusagarú 塞がる fill, close	fusagatté 塞がって	fusagaranákute 塞がらなくて	fusagaranái 塞がらない	fusagaranákatta 塞がらなかった

GROUP ONE	SUBORDINATE Positive	Negative	NEGATIVE Present	Past
fusagú 塞ぐ close, shut	fusaidé 塞いで	fusaganákute 塞がなくて	fusaganái 塞がない	tusaganákatta 塞がなかった
genjirú 減じる substract	genjité 減じて	genjinákute 減じなくて	genjinái 減じない	genjınákatta 減じなかった
gūsurú 遇する treat	gūshité 遇して	gūshinákute 遇しなくて	gūshinái 遇しない	gūshinákatta 遇しなかった
habakarú 憚る be afraid	habakatté 憚って	habakaranákute 憚らなくて	habakaranái 憚らない	habakaranákatta 憚らなかった
hajimarú 始まる begin (v. i.)	hajimatté 始って	hajimaranákute 始まらなくて	hajimaranái 始まらない	hajimaranákatta 始まらなかった
hajimerú 始める begin (v. tr.)	hajimeté 始めて	hajimenákute 始めなくて	hajimenái 始めない	hajimenákatta 始めなかった
hakobú 運ぶ carry	hakondé 運んで	hakobanákute 運ばなくて	hakobanái 運ばない	hakobanákatta 運ばなかった
hakú 穿く put on (shoes)	haité 穿いて	hakanákute 穿かなくて	hakanái 穿かない	hakanákatta 穿かなかった
hamerú 嵌める put on (ring)	hameté 嵌めて	hamenákute 嵌めなくて	hamenái 嵌めない	hamenákatta 嵌めなかった
harú 貼る stick, plaster	hatté 貼って	haranákute 貼らなくて	haranái 貼らない	haranákatta 貼らなかった
hashagú はしゃ ぐ frolic	hashaidé はしゃいで	hashaganákute はしゃがなくて	hashaganái はしゃがない	hashaganákatta はしゃがなかった
hashorú 端折る tuck up (skirt)	hashotté 端折って	hashoranákute 端折らなくて	hashoranái 端折らない	hashoranákatta 端折らなかった
hatarakú 働く work, toil	hataraité 働いて	hatarakanákute 働かなくて	hatarakanái 働かない	hatarakanákatta 働かなかった
hazurerú 外れる be off, miss	hazureté 外れて	hazurenákute 外れなくて	hazurenái 外れない	hazurenákatta 外れなかった
hazusú 外す unfasten, undo	hazushite 外して	hazusanákute 外さなくて	hazusanái 外さない	hazusanákatta 外さなかった
hekomú 凹む sink, collapse	hekondé 凹んで	hekomanákute 凹まなくて	hekomanái 凹まない	hekomanákatta 凹まなかった
herasú 減らす decrease v. tr.	herashité 減らして	herasanákute 減らさなくて	herasanái 減らさない	herasanákatta 減らさなかった
hikú 引く draw, pull	hiité 引いて	hikanákute 引かなくて	hikanái 引かない	hikanákatta 引かなかった
hirogerú 拡げる extend, expand v. tr.	hirogeté 拡げて	hirogenákute 拡げなくて	hirogenái 拡げない	hirogenákatta 拡げなかった
hiroú 拾う pick up	hirotté 拾って	hirowanákute 拾わなくて	hirowanái 拾わない	hirowanákatta 拾わなかった
hodokosú 施す give in charity	hodokoshité 施して	hodokosanákute 施さなくて	hodokosanái 施さない	hodokosanákatta 施さなかった

GROUP ONE	SUBORDINATE Positive	Negative	NEGATIVE Present	Past
hōjirú 報じる return, requite	hōjité 報じて	hōjinákute 報じなくて	hōjinái 報じない	hōjinákatta 報じなかった
horobirú 滅びる go to ruin	horobité 滅びて	horobinákute 滅びなくて	horobinái 滅びない	horobinákatta 滅びなかった
horobosú 滅ぼす destroy	horoboshité 滅ぼして	horobosanákute 滅ぼさなくて	horobosanái 滅ぼさない	horobosanákatta 滅ぼさなかった
hōrú 放る throw, hurl	hōtté 放って	hōranákute 放らなくて	hōranái 放らない	hōranákatta 放らなかった
ijimerú 虐める tease, torment	ijimeté 虐めて	ijimenákute 虐めなくて	ijimenái 虐めない	ijimenákatta 虐めなかった
ikimú いきむ strain (oneself)	ikindé いきんで	ikimanákute いきまなくて	ikimanái いきまない	ikimanákatta いきまなかった
ikú 行く go, proceed	itté 行って	ikanákute 行かなくて	ikanái 行かない	ikanákatta 行かなかった
imashimerú 戒める admonish	imashimeté 戒めて	imashimenákute 戒めなくて	imashimenái 戒めない	imashimenákatta 戒めなかった
irerú 入れる put in, bring in	ireté 入れて	irenákute 入れなくて	irenái 入れない	irenákatta 入れなかった
irú 居る be; exist	ité 居て	inákute 居なくて	inái 居ない	inákatta 居なかった
isamerú 諫める remonstrate	isameté 諫めて	isamenákute 諫めなくて	isamenái 諫めない	isamenákatta 諫めなかった
isamú 勇む be in high spirits	isandé 勇んで	isamanákute 勇まなくて	isamanái 勇まない	isamanákatta 勇まなかった
itadakú 載く be given	itadaité 載いて	itadakanákute 載かなくて	itadakanái 載かない	itadakanákatta 載かなかった
itarú 至る go, proceed	itatté 至って	itaranákute 至らなくて	itaranái 至らない	itaranákatta 至らなかった
itasú 致す do	itashité 致して	itasanákute 致さなくて	itasanái 致さない	itasanákatta 致さなかった
iú 言う say, tell	itté 言って	iwanákute 言わなくて	iwanái 言わない	iwanákatta 言わなかった
junjirú 準じる be proportionate to	junjité 準じて	junjinákute 準じなくて	junjinái 準じない	junjinákatta 準じなかった
kabirú 黴る get musty	kabité 黴て	kabinákute 黴なくて	kabinái 黴ない	kabinákatta 黴なかった
kaburerú かぶれる have a rash	kabureté かぶれて	kaburenákute かぶれなくて	kaburenái かぶれない	kaburenákatta かぶれなかった
kaerú 代える exchange, barter	kaeté 代えて	kaenákute 代えなくて	kaenái 代えない	kaenákatta 代えなかった

| GROUP ONE | SUBORDINATE | | NEGATIVE | |
	Positive	Negative	Present	Past
kagú 嗅ぐ smell, scent v. tr.	kaide 嗅いで	kaganákute 嗅がなくて	kaganái 嗅がない	kaganákatta 嗅がなかった
kakaerú 抱える embrace	kakaete 抱えて	kakaenákute 抱えなくて	kakaenái 抱えない	kakaenákatta 抱えなかった
kakagerú 掲げる put up, hoist	kakagete 掲げて	kakagenákute 掲げなくて	kakagenái 掲げない	kakagenákatta 掲げなかった
kakerú 欠ける break v. i.	kakete 欠けて	kakenákute 欠けなくて	kakenái 欠けない	kakenákatta 欠けなかった
kakomú 囲む enclose, hem in	kakonde 囲んで	kakomanákute 囲まなくて	kakomanái 囲まない	kakomanákatta 囲まなかった
kakú 欠く lack, want v. i.	kaite 欠いて	kakanákute 欠かなくて	kakanái 欠かない	kakanákatta 欠かなかった
karasú 枯らす let dry	karashite 枯らして	karasanákute 枯らさなくて	karasanái 枯らさない	karasanákatta 枯らさなかった
karerú 枯れる wither	karete 枯れて	karenákute 枯れなくて	karenái 枯れない	karenákatta 枯れなかった
kanjirú 感じる feel, be conscious of	kanjite 感じて	kanjinákute 感じなくて	kanjinái 感じない	kanjinákatta 感じなかった
karú 刈る cut, clip, crop	katte 刈って	karanákute 刈らなくて	karanái 刈らない	karanákatta 刈らなかった
karirú 借りる borrow	karite 借りて	karinákute 借りなくて	karinái 借りない	karinákatta 借りなかった
kasanarú 重なる be piled up	kasanatte 重なって	kasanaranákute 重ならなくて	kasanaranái 重ならない	kasanaranákatta 重ならなかった
kasanerú 重ねる pile up v. tr.	kasanete 重ねて	kasanenákute 重ねなくて	kasanenái 重ねない	kasanenákatta 重ねなかった
kasú 貸す lend, loan	kashite 貸して	kasanákute 貸さなくて	kasanái 貸さない	kasanákatta 貸さなかった
kasumerú 掠める rob, plunder	kasumete 掠めて	kasumenákute 掠めなくて	kasumenái 掠めない	kasumenákatta 掠めなかった
kasumú 霞む be hazy	kasunde 霞んで	kasumanákute 霞まなくて	kasumanái 霞まない	kasumanákatta 霞まなかった
katamarú 固まる become hard	katamatte 固まって	katamaranákute 固まらなくて	katamaranái 固まらない	katamaranákatta 固まらなかった
katamerú 固める harden v. tr.	katamete 固めて	katamenákute 固めなくて	katamenái 固めない	katamenákatta 固めなかった
katarú 語る talk, narrate	katatte 語って	kataranákute 語らなくて	kataranái 語らない	kataranákatta 語らなかった
kaú 買う buy, purchase	katte 買って	kawanákute 買わなくて	kawanái 買わない	kawanákatta 買わなかった
kawarú 代る replace	kawatte 代って	kawaranákute 代らなくて	kawaranái 代らない	kawaranákatta 代らなかった

GROUP ONE	SUBORDINATE Positive	Negative	NEGATIVE Present	Past
kawaru 変る change v. i., be altered	kawatté 変って	kawaranákute 変らなくて	kawaranái 変らない	kawaranákatta 変らなかった
kayoú 通う go to and back	kayotte 通って	kayowanákute 通わなくて	kayowanái 通わない	kayowanákatta 通わなかった
kazarú 飾る ornament, adorn	kazatté 飾って	kazaranákute 飾らなくて	kazaranái 飾らない	kazaranákatta 飾らなかった
kemurú 煙る smoke v. i., be smoky	kemutté 煙って	kemuranákute 煙らなくて	kemuranái 煙らない	kemuranákatta 煙らなかった
kenasú 貶す speak ill of	kenashité 貶して	kenasanákute 貶さなくて	kenasanái 貶さない	kenasanákatta 貶さなかった
keshikakerú 嗾け る instigate	keshikaketé 嗾けて	keshikakenákute 嗾けなくて	keshikakenái 嗾けない	keshikakenákatta 嗾けなかった
kesú 消す put out, extinguish	keshité 消して	kesanákute 消さなくて	kesanái 消さない	kesanákatta 消さなかった
kezurú 削る shave (wood), whittle	kezutté 削って	kezuranákute 削らなくて	kezuranái 削らない	kezuranákatta 削らなかった
kikú 聞く hear, listen to	kiité 聞いて	kikanákute 聞かなくて	kikanái 聞かない	kikanákatta 聞かなかった
kikú 利く take effect, act on	kiité 利いて	kikanákute 利かなくて	kikanái 利かない	kikanákatta 利かなかった
kimarú 定まる be decided	kimatté 定まって	kimaranákute 定まらなくて	kimaranái 定まらない	kimaranákatta 定まらなかった
kimerú 決める decide v. tr.	kimeté 決めて	kimenákute 決めなくて	kimenái 決めない	kimenákatta 決めなかった
kinjirú 禁じる forbid, ban	kinjité 禁じて	kinjinákute 禁じなくて	kinjinái 禁じない	kinjinákatta 禁じなかった
kiraú 嫌う dislike, detest	kiratté 嫌って	kirawanákute 嫌わなくて	kirawanái 嫌わない	kirawanákatta 嫌わなかった
kirú 着る put on, have on (dress)	kité 着て	kinákute 着なくて	kinái 着ない	kinákatta 着なかった
kiserú 着せる dress, clothe	kiseté 着せて	kisenákute 着せなくて	kisenái 着せない	kisenákatta 着せなかった
kitaerú 鍛える forge, temper	kitaeté 鍛えて	kitaenákute 鍛えなくて	kitaenái 鍛えない	kitaenákatta 鍛えなかった
kizamú 刻む cut, mince, hash	kizandé 刻んで	kizamanákute 刻まなくて	kizamanái 刻まない	kizamanákatta 刻まなかった

| GROUP ONE | SUBORDINATE | | NEGATIVE | |
	Positive	Negative	Present	Past
kizasú 兆す show signs of	kizashité 兆して	kizasanákute 兆さなくて	kizasanáι 兆さない	kizasanákatta 兆さなかった
koerú 越える go over, go across	koeté 越えて	koenákute 越えなくて	koenái 越えない	koenákatta 越えなかった
kogomú 踞む lean (over)	kogondé 踞んで	kogomanákute 踞まなくて	kogomanái 踞まない	kogomanákatta 踞まなかった
kojitsukerú こじつける strain (the interpretation)	kojitsuketé こじつけて	kojitsukenákute こじつけなくて	kojitsukenáι こじつけない	kojitsukenákatta こじつけなかった
kongarakarú こんがらかる get entangled	kongarakatté こんがらかって	kongarakaranákute こんがらからなくて	kongarakaranái こんがらからな い	kongarakaranákatta こんがらからなかっ た
kōrasú 凍らす freeze, refrigerate	kōrashité 凍らして	kōrasanákute 凍らさなくて	kōrasanái 凍らさない	kōrasanákatta 凍らさなかった
korobasú 転ばす roll (over)	korobashité 転ばして	korobasanákute 転ばさなくて	korobasanái 転ばさない	korobasanákatta 転ばさなかった
korobú 転ぶ tumble (down)	korondé 転んで	korobanákute 転ばなくて	korobanái 転ばない	korobanákatta 転ばなかった
korosú 殺す kill, slay	koroshité 殺して	korosanákute 殺さなくて	korosanái 殺さない	korosanákatta 殺さなかった
kōrú 凍る freeze v. i., be frozen	kōtté 凍って	kōranákute 凍らなくて	kōranái 凍らない	kōranákatta 凍らなかった
koshiraerú 拵える make, manufacture	koshiraeté 拵えて	koshiraenákute 拵えなくて	koshiraenái 拵えない	koshiraenákatta 拵えなかった
kosú 越す cross, go across	koshité 越して	kosanákute 越さなくて	kosanái 越さない	kosanákatta 越さなかった
kubomú 窪む become hollow	kubondé 窪んで	kubomanákute 窪まなくて	kubomanái 窪まない	kubomanákatta 窪まなかった
kuchirú 朽ちる rot, decay	kuchité 朽ちて	kuchinákute 朽ちなくて	kuchinái 朽ちない	kuchinákatta 朽ちなかった
kudarú 下る come (or go) down	kudatté 下って	kudaranákute 下らなくて	kudaranái 下らない	kudaranákatta 下らなかった
kudasú 下す let down, lower	kudashite 下して	kudasanákute 下さなくて	kudasanái 下さない	kudasanákatta 下さなかった
kugirú 区切る punctuate	kugitté 区切って	kugiranákute 区切らなくて	kugiranái 区切らない	kugiranákatta 区切らなかった
kukerú 絎ける blind-stitch	kuketé 絎けて	kukenákute 絎けなくて	kukenái 絎けない	kukenákatta 絎けなかった

| GROUP ONE | SUBORDINATE | | NEGATIVE | |
	Positive	Negative	Present	Past
kukurú 括る bind, tie up	kukutté 括って	kukuranákute 括らなくて	kukuranái 括らない	kukuranákatta 括らなかった
kumú 汲む draw, ladle	kundé 汲んで	kumanákute 汲まなくて	kumanái 汲まない	kumanákatta 汲まなかった
kuraberú 較べる compare, contrast	kurabeté 較べて	kurabenákute 較べなくて	kurabenái 較べない	kurabenákatta 較べなかった
kuramú 眩む get giddy	kurandé 眩んで	kuramanákute 眩まなくて	kuramanái 眩まない	kuramanákatta 眩まなかった
kurasú 暮らす live, make a living	kurashité 暮らして	kurasanákute 暮らさなくて	kurasanái 暮らさない	kurasanákatta 暮らさなかった
kurerú 暮れる grow dark	kureté 暮れて	kurenákute 暮れなくて	kurenái 暮れない	kurenákatta 暮れなかった
kurerú 呉れる give, let have	kureté 呉れて	kurenákute 呉れなくて	kurenái 呉れない	kurenákatta 呉れなかった
kusunerú くすねる pilfer, purloin	kusuneté くすねて	kusunenákute くすねなくて	kusunenái くすねない	kusunenákatta くすねなかった
kutsurogú 寛ぐ be at ease	kutsuroidé 寛いで	kutsuroganákute 寛がなくて	kutsuroganái 寛がない	kutsuroganákatta 寛がなかった
kuwadaterú 企てる plan, scheme, plot	kuwadateté 企てて	kuwadatenákute 企てなくて	kuwadatenái 企てない	kuwadatenákatta 企てなかった
kuwaerú 加える add up, sum up	kuwaeté 加えて	kuwaenákute 加えなくて	kuwaenái 加えない	kuwaenákatta 加えなかった
kuwaerú 啣える take in one's mouth	kuwaeté 啣えて	kuwaenákute 啣えなくて	kuwaenái 啣えない	kuwaenákatta 啣えなかった
kuwawarú 加わる join (in), take part in	kuwawatté 加わって	kuwawaranákute 加わらなくて	kuwawaranái 加わらない	kuwawaranákatta 加わらなかった
magarú 曲る bend, curve v.i.	magatté 曲って	magaranákute 曲らなくて	magaranái 曲らない	magaranákatta 曲らなかった
magerú 曲げる bend, curve v. tr.	mageté 曲げて	magenákute 曲げなくて	magenái 曲げない	magenákatta 曲げなかった
magotsukú まごつく be flurried, confused	magotsuité まごついて	magotsukanákute まごつかなくて	magotsukanái まごつかない	magotsukanákatta まごつかなかった
makerú 負ける be defeated, beaten	maketé 負けて	makenákute 負けなくて	makenái 負けない	makenákatta 負けなかった

GROUP ONE	SUBORDINATE Positive	Negative	NEGATIVE Present	Past
makú 巻く wind, twine v. tr.	maité 巻いて	makanákute 巻かなくて	makanái 巻かない	makanákatta 巻かなかった
makurú 捲くる roll up v. tr.	makutté 捲くって	makuranákute 捲くらなくて	makuranái 捲くらない	makuranákatta 捲くらなかった
manabú 学ぶ learn, be taught	manandé 学んで	manabanákute 学ばなくて	manabanái 学ばない	manabanákatta 学ばなかった
manerú 真似る imitate, copy	maneté 真似て	manenákute 真似なくて	manenái 真似ない	manenákatta 真似なかった
manukarerú 免かれる escape (death), be saved from	manukarete 免かれて	manukarenákute 免かれなくて	manukarenái 免かれない	manukarenákatta 免かれなかった
marumerú 丸める make round, curl	marumeté 丸めて	marumenákute 丸めなくて	marumenái 丸めない	marumenákatta 丸めなかった
masú 増す increase, swell v. i.	mashité 増して	masanákute 増さなくて	masanái 増さない	masanákatta 増さなかった
matomarú 纒まる be settled, be completed	matomatté 纒まって	matomaranákute 纒まらなくて	matomaranái 纒まらない	matomaranákatta 纒まらなかった
matomerú 纒める to bring (a matter) to conclusion	matometé 纒めて	matomenákute 纒めなくて	matomenái 纒めない	matomenákatta 纒めなかった
matsurú 祭る deify, enshrine	matsutté 祭って	matsuranákute 祭らなくて	matsuranái 祭らない	matsuranákatta 祭らなかった
maú 舞う dance, flutter about	matté 舞って	mawanákute 舞わなくて	mawanái 舞わない	mawanákatta 舞わなかった
mawarú 回る go round, revolve v. i.	mawatté 回って	mawaranákute 回らなくて	mawaranái 回らない	mawaranákatta 回らなかった
mawasú 回す turn, revolve v. tr.	mawashité 回して	mawasanákute 回さなくて	mawasanái 回さない	mawasanákatta 回さなかった
meawaserú 娶せる marry, give in marriage to	meawaseté 娶せて	meawasenákute 娶せなくて	meawasenái 娶せない	meawasenákatta 娶せなかった
megumú 恵む bestow a favor on	megundé 恵んで	megumanákute 恵まなくて	megumanái 恵まない	megumanákatta 恵まなかった
meijirú 命じる command, order	meijité 命じて	meijinákute 命じなくて	meijinái 命じない	meijinakatta 命じなかった

| GROUP ONE | SUBORDINATE | | NEGATIVE | |
	Positive	Negative	Present	Past
migakú 磨く polish, brighten	migaité 磨いて	migakanákute 磨かなくて	migakanái 磨かない	migakanákattə 磨かなかった
mikomú 見込む expect, anticipate	mikondé 見込んで	mikomanákute 見込まなくて	mikomanái 見込まない	mikomanákattə 見込まなかった
mikosú 見越す forecast, foresee	mikoshité 見越して	mikosanákute 見越さなくて	mikosanái 見越さない	mikosanákatta 見越さなかった
mikubirú 見くびる disparage, think meanly of	mikubitté 見くびって	mikubiranákute 見くびらなくて	mikubiranái 見くびらない	mikubiranákattə 見くびらなかった
mimaú 見舞う ask after (a person's health)	mimatté 見舞って	mimawanákute 見舞わなくて	mimawanái 見舞わない	mimawanákatta 見舞わなかった
minasú 見做す regard, (as), consider	minashité 見做して	minasanákute 見做さなくて	minasanáɪ 見做さない	minasanákatta 見做さなかった
minorú 実る bear fruit, fructify	minotté 実って	minoranákute 実らなくて	minoranái 実らない	minoranákattə 実らなかった
mitaterú 見立てる diagnose, select	mitatete 見立てて	mitatenákute 見立てなくて	mitatenai 見立てない	mitatenákatta 見立てなかった
mitomerú 認める see, witness, notice	mitometé 認めて	mitomenákute 認めなくて	mitomenái 認めない	mitomenákattə 認めなかった
mitorerú 見惚れる gaze upon in rapture	mitorete 見惚れて	mitorenákute 見惚れなくて	mitorenái 見惚れない	mitorenákatta 見惚れなかった
mitsugú 貢ぐ give financial aid	mitsuidé 貢いで	mitsuganákute 貢がなくて	mitsuganái 貢がない	mitsuganákattə 貢がなかった
mitsukarú 見付かる be found out, be detected	mitsukatté 見付かって	mitsukaranákute 見付からなくて	mitsukaranái 見付からない	mitsukaranákatta 見付からなかった
mitsukerú 見付ける find (out), discover	mitsuketé 見付けて	mitsukenákute 見付けなくて	mitsukenáɪ 見付けない	mitsukenákatta 見付けなかった
mitsumerú 見詰める gaze, stare at	mitsumete 見詰めて	mitsumenákute 見詰めなくて	mitsumenái 見詰めない	mitsumenákatta 見詰めなかった
mitsumorú 見積もる estimate (at), value (at)	mitsumotte 見積もって	mitsumoranákute 見積もらなくて	mitsumoranái 見積もらない	mitsumoranákattə 見積もらなかった

GROUP ONE	SUBORDINATE		NEGATIVE	
	Positive	Negative	Present	Past
miwakerú 見分ける distinguish (from)	miwaketé 見分けて	miwakenákute 見分けなくて	miwakenái 見分けない	miwakenákatta 見分けなかった
mochiirú 用いる use, make use of	mochiité 用いて	mochiinákute 用いなくて	mochiinái 用いない	mochiinákatta 用いなかった
moerú 燃える burn, blaze	moeté 燃えて	moenákute 燃えなくて	moenái 燃えない	moenákatta 燃えなかった
momarerú 揉まれる to be jostled	momareté 揉まれて	momarenákute 揉まれなくて	momarenái 揉まれない	momarenákatta 揉まれなかった
momú 揉む rub, massage	monde 揉んで	momanákute 揉まなくて	momanái 揉まない	momanákatta 揉まなかった
moraú 貰う be given, receive	moratté 貰って	morawanákute 貰わなくて	morawanái 貰わない	morawanákatta 貰わなかった
motenasú もてなす treat, fete (a person)	motenashite もてなして	motenasanákute もてなさなくて	motenasanái もてなさない	motenasanákatta もてなさなかった
moyasú 燃やす burn, commit to flames	moyashité 燃やして	moyasanákute 燃やさなくて	moyasanái 燃やさない	moyasanákatta 燃やさなかった
mukaerú 迎える meet, invite	mukaeté 迎えて	mukaenákute 迎えなくて	mukaenái 迎えない	mukaenákatta 迎えなかった
mukaú 向かう face, front, be opposite	mukatte 向かって	mukawanákute 向かわなくて	mukawanái 向かわない	mukawanákatta 向かわなかった
mukerú 向ける turn, point at	muketé 向けて	mukenákute 向けなくて	mukenái 向けない	mukenákatta 向けなかった
mukú 剥く peel (an orange), hull (rice)	muité 剥いて	mukanákute 剥かなくて	mukanái 剥かない	mukanákatta 剥かなかった
mukurerú むくれる get angry, be sour	mukureté むくれて	mukurenákute むくれなくて	mukurenái むくれない	mukurenákatta むくれなかった
musaború 貪る covet, crave	musabotte 貪って	musaboranákute 貪らなくて	musaboranái 貪らない	musaboranákatta 貪らなかった
musebú 咽ぶ be choked with	musende 咽んで	musebanákute 咽ばなくて	musebanái 咽ばない	musebanákatta 咽ばなかった
muserú 咽せる be choked (with)	museté 咽せて	musenákute 咽せなくて	musenái 咽せない	musenákatta 咽せなかった
mushirú 毟る pluck, pick, pull	mushitté 毟って	mushiranákute 毟らなくて	mushiranái 毟らない	mushiranákatta 毟らなかった

GROUP ONE	SUBORDINATE Positive	Negative	NEGATIVE Present	Past
musubú 結ぶ tie, join	musundé 結んで	musubanákute 結ばなくて	musubanái 結ばない	musubanákatta 結ばなかった
nagusamerú 慰める comfort, console	nagusameté 慰めて	nagusamenákute 慰めなくて	nagusamenái 慰めない	nagusamenákatta 慰めなかった
nakaserú 泣かせる let cry, move to tears	nakasete 泣かせて	nakasenákute 泣かせなくて	nakasenái 泣かせない	nakasenákatta 泣かせなかった
nakerú 泣ける be moved to tears	naketé 泣けて	nakenákute 泣けなくて	nakenái 泣けない	nakenákatta 泣けなかった
nakú 泣く weep, cry, sob 泣いて	naite	nakanákute 泣かなくて	nakanái 泣かない	nakanákatta 泣かなかった
nakusú 失くす lose, be deprived of	nakushité 失くして	nakusanákute 失くさなくて	nakusanái 失くさない	nakusanákatta 失くさなかった
naraberú 並べる arrange, place in order	narabeté 並べて	narabenákute 並べなくて	narabenái 並べない	narabenákatta 並べなかった
narabú 並ぶ be in a row	narandé 並んで	narabanákute 並ばなくて	narabanái 並ばない	narabanákatta 並ばなかった
narasú 鳴らす ring, sound (a bell, horn) v. tr.	narashité 鳴らして	narasanákute 鳴らさなくて	narasanái 鳴らさない	narasanákatta 鳴らさなかった
narú 鳴る sound, ring, peal v. i.	natté 鳴って	naranákute 鳴らなくて	naranái 鳴らない	naranákatta 鳴らなかった
nedarú ねだる tease, importune	nedatté ねだって	nedaranákute ねだらなくて	nedaranái ねだらない	nedaranákatta ねだらなかった
negirú 値切る beat down the price	negitté 値切って	negiranákute 値切らなくて	negiranái 値切らない	negiranákatta 値切らなかった
nekaserú 寝かせる send (a person) to sleep	nekaseté 寝かせて	nekasenákute 寝かせなくて	nekasenái 寝かせない	nekasenákatta 寝かせなかった
nemurú 眠る sleep, fall asleep	nemutté 眠って	nemuranákute 眠らなくて	nemuranái 眠らない	nemuranákatta 眠らなかった
neraú 狙う take aim, take good aim	neratté 狙って	nerawanákute 狙わなくて	nerawanái 狙わない	nerawanákatta 狙わなかった
nerú 寝る sleep, fall asleep	neté 寝て	nenákute 寝なくて	nenái 寝ない	nenákatta 寝なかった

GROUP ONE	SUBORDINATE		NEGATIVE	
	Positive	Negative	Present	Past
nigirú 握る clasp, clench	nigitté 握って	nigiranákute 握らなくて	nigiranái 握らない	nigiranákatta 握らなかった
nirú 煮る boil, cook	nité 煮て	ninákute 煮なくて	ninái 煮ない	ninákatta 煮なかった
niserú 似せる imitate, copy	niseté 似せて	nisenákute 似せなくて	nisenái 似せない	nisenákatta 似せなかった
noború 昇る rise, ascend	nobotté 昇って	noboranákute 昇らなくて	noboranái 昇らない	noboranákatta 昇らなかった
noborerú 逆上せる be dizzy, feverish	noboseté 逆上せて	nobosenákute 逆上せなくて	nobosenái 逆上せない	nobosenákatta 逆上せなかった
norú 乗る ride (horse, bicycle)	notté 乗って	noranákute 乗らなくて	noranái 乗らない	noranákatta 乗らなかった
noserú 乗せる put, lay (a thing) on	noseté 乗せて	nosenákute 乗せなくて	nosenái 乗せない	nosenákatta 乗せなかった
nozokú 覗く look, get a peep	nozoité 覗いて	nozokanákute 覗かなくて	nozokanái 覗かない	nozokanákatta 覗かなかった
nozomú 臨む look out upon	nozonde 臨んで	nozomanákute 臨まなくて	nozomanái 臨まない	nozomanákatta 臨まなかった
nozomú 望む desire, hope	nozonde 望んで	nozomanákute 望まなくて	nozomanái 望まない	nozomanákatta 望まなかった
nukarú ぬかる be muddy, be slushy	nukatté ぬかって	nukaranákute ぬからなくて	nukaranái ぬからない	nukaranákatta ぬからなかった
nukasú 抜かす omit, leave out	nukashité 抜かして	nukasanákute 抜かさなくて	nukasanái 抜かさない	nukasanákatta 抜かさなかった
nukerú 抜ける come out, slip out	nuketé 抜けて	nukenákute 抜けなくて	nukenái 抜けない	nukenákatta 抜けなかった
nukú 抜く draw out	nuité 抜いて	nukanákute 抜かなくて	nukanái 抜かない	nukanákatta 抜かなかった
nurasú 濡らす wet, moisten	nurashité 濡らして	nurasanákute 濡らさなくて	nurasanái 濡らさない	nurasanákatta 濡らさなかった
nurerú 濡れる get wet, be damp	nureté 濡れて	nurenákute 濡れなくて	nurenái 濡れない	nurenákatta 濡れなかって
nurú 塗る paint, plaster	nutté 塗って	nuranákute 塗らなくて	nuranái 塗らない	nuranákatta 塗らなかった
oborerú 溺れる drown, be drowned	oboreté 溺れて	oborenákute 溺れなくて	oborenái 溺れない	oborenákatta 溺れなかった

GROUP ONE	SUBORDINATE Positive	Negative	NEGATIVE Present	Past
ochiburerú 落ちぶれる be ruined, fall low	ochibureté 落ちぶれて	ochiburenákute 落ちぶれなくて	ochiburenái 落ちぶれない	ochiburenákatta 落ちぶれなかった
ochiirú 陥る fall into, run into	ochiitte 陥って	ochiiranákute 陥らなくて	ochiiranái 陥らない	ochiiranákatta 陥らなかった
odokasú 脅かす threaten, intimidate	odokashité 脅かして	odokasanákute 脅かさなくて	odokasanái 脅かさない	odokasanákatta 脅かさなかった
odokerú おどける jest, crack a joke	odoketé おどけて	odokenákute おどけなくて	odokenái おどけない	odokenákatta おどけなかった
odomú 澱む precipitate, settle v. i.	odonde 澱んで	odomanákute 澱まなくて	odomanái 澱まない	odomanákatta 澱まなかった
odorú 踊る dance, jump, leap	odotté 踊って	odoranákute 踊らなくて	odoranái 踊らない	odoranákatta 踊らなかった
odosú 威す threaten, menace	odoshite 威して	odosanákute 威さなくて	odosanái 威さない	odosanákatta 威さなかった
oerú 終える finish, complete	oete 終えて	oenákute 終えなくて	oenái 終えない	oenákatta 終えなかった
oginaú 補う supply, make up for	oginatté 補って	oginawanákute 補わなくて	oginawanái 補わない	oginawanákatta 補わなかった
ogorú 奢る be extravagant	ogotte 奢って	ogoranákute 奢らなくて	ogoranái 奢らない	ogoranákatta 奢らなかった
ojikerú 怖ける fear, be afraid of	ojiketé 怖けて	ojikenákute 怖けなくて	ojikenái 怖けない	ojikenákatta 怖けなかった
okonaú 行う do, act	okonatté 行なって	okonawanákute 行わなくて	okonawanái 行わない	okonawanákatta 行わなかった
okonawarerú 行われる be put into practice	okonawarete 行われて	okonawarenákute 行われなくて	okonawarenái 行われない	okonawarenákatta 行われなかった
okotarú 怠る neglect (one's duties)	okotatté 怠って	okotaranákute 怠らなくて	okotaranái 怠らない	okotaranákatta 怠らなかった
okú 置く put, place	oité 置いて	okanákute 置かなくて	okanái 置かない	okanákatta 置かなかった
okurerú 後れる be late, be delayed	okureté 後れて	okurenákute 後れなくて	okurenái 後れない	okurenákatta 後れなかった

GROUP ONE	SUBORDINATE		NEGATIVE	
	Positive	Negative	Present	Past
okurú 送る send, forward	okutté 送って	okuranákute 送らなくて	okuranái 送らない	okuranákatta 送らなかった
oshierú 教える teach, instruct	oshieté 教えて	oshienákute 教えなくて	oshienái 教えない	oshienákatta 教えなかった
osoú 襲う attack, assail	osotté 襲って	osowanákute 襲わなくて	osowanái 襲わない	osowanákatta 襲わなかった
osowarerú 襲われる be attacked	osowareté 襲われて	osowarenákute 襲われなくて	osowarenái 襲われない	osowarenákatta 襲われなかった
osowarú 教わる be taught, learn	osowatté 教わって	osowaranákute 教わらなくて	osowaranái 教わらない	osowaranákatta 教わらなかった
osú 押す push, thrust	oshité 押して	osanákute 押さなくて	osanái 押さない	osanákatta 押さなかった
otoshiirerú 陥れる entrap, ensnare	otoshiireté 陥れて	otoshiirenákute 陥れなくて	otoshiirenái 陥れない	otoshiirenákatta 陥れなかった
oú 追う drive away	otté 追って	owanákute 追わなくて	owanái 追わない	owanákatta 追わなかった
owarú 終る end, come to an end	owatté 終って	owaranákute 終らなくて	owaranái 終らない	owaranákatta 終らなかった
oyobosú 及ぼす exert, cause (harm)	oyoboshité 及ぼして	oyobosanákute 及ぼさなくて	oyobosanái 及ぼさない	oyobosanákatta 及ぼさなかった
oyobú 及ぶ reach, attain to	oyondé 及んで	oyobanákute 及ばなくて	oyobanái 及ばない	oyobanákatta 及ばなかった
sagasú 探す search, look for	sagashite 探して	sagasanákute 探さなくて	sagasanái 探さない	sagasanákatta 探さなかった
sagurú 探る search, look for	sagutté 探って	saguranákute 探らなくて	saguranái 探らない	saguranakatta 探らなかった
sakú 咲く bloom, blossom	saité 咲いて	sakanákute 咲かなくて	sakanái 咲かない	sakanákatta 咲かなかった
samatagerú 妨げる disturb, hinder	samatageté 妨げて	samatagenákute 妨げなくて	samatagenái 妨げない	samatagenákatta 妨げなかった
sarasú 晒す bleach, refine	sarashite 晒して	sarasanákute 晒さなくて	sarasanái 晒さない	sarasanákatta 晒さなかった
saraú さらう carry off, snatch, away	saratté さらって	sarawanákute さらわなくて	sarawanái さらわない	sarawanákatta さらわなかった

GROUP ONE	SUBORDINATE Positive	Negative	NEGATIVE Present	Past
sasaerú 支える support, prop	sasaeté 支えて	sasaenákute 支えなくて	sasaenái 支えない	sasaenákatta 支えなかった
sasagerú 捧げる lift up, hold up	sasageté 捧げて	sasagenákute 捧げなくて	sasagenái 捧げない	sasagenákatta 捧げなかった
saserú させる make (a person do)	saseté させて	sasenákute させなくて	sasenái させない	sasenákatta させなかった
sasoú 誘う invite, ask	sasotté 誘って	sasowanákute 誘わなくて	sasowanái 誘わない	sasowanákatta 誘わなかった
sassurú 察する guess, presume	sasshité 察して	sasshinákute 察しなくて	sasshinái 察しない	sasshinákatta 察しなかった
sasurú さする pat, stroke	sasutté さすって	sasuranákute さすらなくて	sasuranái さすらない	sasuranákatta さすらなかった
satorú 悟る see, perceive	satotté 悟って	satoranákute 悟らなくて	satoranái 悟らない	satoranákatta 悟らなかった
satosú 諭す adomonish, remonstrate	satoshité 諭して	satosanákute 諭さなくて	satosanái 諭さない	satosanákatta 諭さなかった
sawarú 触る touch, feel	sawatte 触って	sawaranákute 触らなくて	sawaranái 触らない	sawaranákatta 触らなかった
sawarú 障る hinder, interfere with	sawatté 障って	sawaranákute 障らなくて	sawaranái 障らない	sawaranákatta 障らなかった
shagamú 蹲む squat down, crouch	shagandé 蹲んで	shagamanákute 蹲まなくて	shagamanái 蹲まない	shagamanákatta 蹲まなかった
sharerú 洒落る to dress oneself up	shareté 洒落て	sharenákute 洒落なくて	sharenái 洒落ない	sharenákatta 洒落なかった
shikarú 叱る scold, chide	shikatté 叱って	shikaranákute 叱らなくて	shikaranái 叱らない	shikaranákatta 叱らなかった
shikú 敷く spread (mats, sheets, etc.)	shiité 敷いて	shikanákute 敷かなくて	shikanái 敷かない	shikanákatta 敷かなかった
shimaú 仕舞う finish, conclude	shimatté 仕舞って	shimawanákute 仕舞わなくて	shimawanái 仕舞わない	shimawanákatta 仕舞わなかった
shimesú 示す show, indicate	shimeshité 示して	shimesanákute 示さなくて	shimesanái 示さない	shimesanákatta 示さなかった
shimesú 湿す wet, moisten	shimeshité 湿して	shimesanákute 湿さなくて	shimesanái 湿さない	shimesanákatta 湿さなかった
shinabirú 萎びる wither, shrivel	shinabité 萎びて	shinabinákute 萎びなくて	shinabinái 萎びない	shinabinákatta 萎びなかった
shinaserú 死なせる cause to die	shinaseté 死なせて	shinasenákute 死なせなくて	shinasenái 死なせない	shinasenákatta 死なせなかった

GROUP ONE	SUBORDINATE Positive	Negative	NEGATIVE Present	Past
shinobú 忍ぶ bear, stand (pain)	shinondé 忍んで	shinobanákute 忍ばなくて	shinobanái 忍ばない	shinobanákatta 忍ばなかった
shinú 死ぬ die, pass away	shindé 死んで	shinanákute 死ななくて	shinanái 死なない	shinanákatta 死ななかった
shirarerú 知られる become known	shirareté 知られて	shirarenákute 知られなくて	shirarenái 知られない	shirarenákatta 知られなかった
shiraserú 知らせる let (a person) know	shiraseté 知らせて	shirasenákute 知らせなくて	shirasenái 知らせない	shirasenákatta 知らせなかった
shirerú 知れる become known	shireté 知れて	shirenákute 知れなくて	shirenái 知れない	shirenákatta 知れなかった
shirú 知る know, be aware of	shitté 知って	shiranákute 知らなくて	shiranái 知らない	shiranákatta 知らなかった
shirusú 記す write down, inscribe	shirushité 記して	shirusanákute 記さなくて	shirusanái 記さない	shirusanákatta 記さなかった
shitaú 慕う yearn for, long for	shitatté 慕って	shitawanákute 慕わなくて	shitawanái 慕わない	shitawanákatta 慕わなかった
shizumerú 沈める sink, submerge v. tr.	shizumeté 沈めて	shizumenákute 沈めなくて	shizumenái 沈めない	shizumenákatta 沈めなかった
shizumú 沈む sink, be submerged v. i.	shizundé 沈んで	shizumanákute 沈まなくて	shizumanái 沈まない	shizumanákatta 沈まなかった
soerú 添える add to, attach to	soeté 添えて	soenákute 添えなくて	soenái 添えない	soenákatta 添えなかった
somarú 染まる dye, take color v. i.	somatté 染まって	somaranákute 染まらなくて	somaranái 染まらない	somaranákatta 染まらなかった
somerú 染める dye, colour (pictures) v. tr.	someté 染めて	somenákute 染めなくて	somenái 染めない	somenákatta 染めなかった
soshirú そしる slander, vilify	soshitté そしって	soshiranákute そしらなくて	soshiranái そしらない	soshiranákatta そしらなかった
sosogú 注ぐ pour into, sprinkle	sosoidé 注いで	sosoganákute 注がなくて	sosoganái 注がない	sosoganákatta 注がなかった
soú 添う accompany	sotté 添って	sowanákute 添わなくて	sowanái 添わない	sowanákatta 添わなかった

GROUP ONE	**SUBORDINATE** Positive	Negative	**NEGATIVE** Present	Past
sugarú 縋る cling to, hang on	sugatté 縋って	sugaranákute 縋らなくて	sugaranái 縋らない	sugaranákatta 縋らなかった
sukuú 掬う scoop, dip, ladle	sukutté 掬って	sukuwanákute 掬わなくて	sukuwanái 掬わない	sukuwanákatta 掬わなかった
sukuú 救う rescue from (danger)	sukutté 救って	sukuwanákute 救わなくて	sukuwanái 救わない	sukuwanákatta 救わなかった
surú する do, make	shité して	shinákute しなくて	shinái しない	shinákatta しなかった
susugú 濯ぐ wash, rinse	susuidé 濯いで	susuganákute 濯がなくて	susuganái 濯がない	susuganákatta 濯がなかった
susumerú 進める advance, put forward	susumeté 進めて	susumenákute 進めなくて	susumenái 進めない	susumenákatta 進めなかった
susumerú 勧める recommend, advise	susumeté 勧めて	susumenákute 勧めなくて	susumenái 勧めない	susumenákatta 勧めなかった
susumú 進む advance, go forward	susundé 進んで	susumanákute 進まなくて	susumanái 進まない	susumanákatta 進まなかった
sutarerú 廃れる go out of use	sutareté 廃れて	sutarenákute 廃れなくて	sutarenái 廃れない	sutarenákatta 廃れなかった
suterú 捨てる throw away, abandon	suteté 捨てて	sutenákute 捨てなくて	sutenái 捨てない	sutenákatta 捨てなかった
suú 吸う inhale, imbibe	sutté 吸って	suwanákute 吸わなくて	suwanái 吸わない	suwanákatta 吸わなかった
suwarú 座る sit down, squat down	suwatté 座って	suwaranákute 座らなくて	suwaranái 座らない	suwaranákatta 座らなかった
tadarerú 爛れる be sore, break out in sores	tadareté 爛れて	tadarenákute 爛れなくて	tadarenái 爛れない	tadarenákatta 爛れなかった
tairagerú 平らげる subdue, subjugate	tairageté 平らげて	tairagenákute 平らげなくて	tairagenái 平らげない	tairagenákatta 平らげなかった
takarú たかる swarm, gather v. i.	takatté たかって	takaranákute たからなくて	takaranái たからない	takaranákatta たからなかった
takú 焚く burn, kindle	taité 焚いて	takanákute 焚かなくて	takanái 焚かない	takanákatta 焚かなかった

GROUP ONE	SUBORDINATE		NEGATIVE	
	Positive	Negative	Present	Past
tamarú 溜る collect, gather v. i.	tamatté 溜って	tamaranákute 溜らなくて	tamaranái 溜らない	tamaranákatta 溜らなかった
tamerú 溜める accumulate, amass v. tr.	tameté 溜めて	tamenákute 溜めなくて	tamenái 溜めない	tamenákatta 溜めなかった
tanjirú 嘆じる lament, bewail, regret	tanjité 嘆じて	tanjinákute 嘆じなくて	tanjinái 嘆じない	tanjinákatta 嘆じなかった
tarirú 足りる be enough, suffice	tarité 足りて	tarinákute 足りなくて	tarinái 足りない	tarinákatta 足りなかった
tarú 足る be enough, suffice	tatté 足って	taranákute 足らなくて	taranái 足らない	taranákatta 足らなかった
tarumú 弛む slacken, be loosened	tarundé 弛んで	tarumanákute 弛まなくて	tarumanái 弛まない	tarumanákatta 弛まなかった
tasú 足す add, made up (for)	tashité 足して	tasanákute 足さなくて	tasanái 足さない	tasanákatta 足さなかった
tatakaú 戦う fight, make war	tatakatté 戦って	tatakawanákute 戦わなくて	tatakawanái 戦わない	tatakawanákatta 戦わなかった
tatamú 畳む fold (clothes)	tatandé 畳んで	tatamanákute 畳まなくて	tatamanái 畳まない	tatamanákatta 畳まなかった
tazusawarú 携わる participate in	tazusawatté 携わって	tazusawaranákute 携わらなくて	tazusawaranái 携わらない	tazusawaranákatta 携わらなかった
tenjirú 転じる turn round, revolve v. tr.	tenjité 転じて	tenjinákute 転じなくて	tenjinái 転じない	tenjinákatta 転じなかった
tobasú 飛ばす let fly, make fly	tobashité 飛ばして	tobasanákute 飛ばさなくて	tobasanái 飛ばさない	tobasanákatta 飛ばさなかった
tobú 飛ぶ fly, take to the wing	tondé 飛んで	tobanákute 飛ばなくて	tobanái 飛ばない	tobanákatta 飛ばなかった
todokórú 滞る stagnate, be stagnant	todokótté 滞って	todokóranákute 滞らなくて	todokóranái 滞らない	todokoranákatta 滞らなかった
tōjirú 投じる throw, cast away	tōjité 投じて	tōjinákute 投じなくて	tōjinái 投じない	tojinákatta 投じなかった
ₒomarú 泊る stop (at, in), lodge (in)	tomatté 泊って	tomaranákute 泊らなくて	tomaranái 泊らない	tomaranákatta 泊らなかった

| GROUP ONE | SUBORDINATE | | NEGATIVE | |
	Positive	Negative	Present	Past
tomarú 止まる stop, come to a stop	tomatte 止まって	tomaranákute 止まらなくて	tomaranái 止まらない	tomaranákatta 止まらなかった
tomerú 止める stop, put a stop to v. tr.	tometé 止めて	tomenákute 止めなくて	tomenái 止めない	tomenákatta 止めなかった
torawarerú 捕われる be caught, be arrested	torawareté 捕われて	torawarenákute 捕われなくて	torawarenái 捕われない	torawarenákatta 捕われなかった
tōzakerú 遠ざける keep away from	tōzaketé 遠ざけて	tozakenákute 遠ざけなくて	tōzakenái 遠ざけない	tōzakenákatta 遠ざけなかった
tsuburerú 潰れる be crushed, collapse	tsubureté 潰れて	tsuburenákute 潰れなくて	tsuburenái 潰れない	tsuburenákatta 潰れなかった
tsubusú 潰す crush, smash	tsubushité 潰して	tsubusanákute 潰さなくて	tsubusanái 潰さない	tsubusanákatta 潰さなかった
tsugerú 告げる tell, let (a person) know	tsugeté 告げて	tsugenákute 告げなくて	tsugenái 告げない	tsugenákatta 告げなかった
tsugú 次ぐ rank next to	tsuidé 次いで	tsuganákute 次がなくて	tsuganái 次がない	tsuganákatta 次がなかった
tsūjirú 通じる pass, put through	tsūjité 通じて	tsūjinákute 通じなくて	tsūjinái 通じない	tsujinákatta 通じなかった
tsukamarú 捕まる be caught, be arrested	tsukamatté 捕まって	tsukamaranákute 捕まらなくて	tsukamaranái 捕まらない	tsukamaranákatta 捕まらなかった
tsukaú 使う use, make use of	tsukatté 使って	tsukawanákute 使わなくて	tsukawanái 使わない	tsukawanákatta 使わなかった
tsukawasú 遣わす send, dispatch	tsukawashité 遣わして	tsukawasanákute 遣わさなくて	tsukawasanái 遣わさない	tsukawasanákatta 遣わさなかった
tsukerú 漬ける soak (in), steep (in)	tsuketé 漬けて	tsukenákute 漬けなくて	tsukenái 漬けない	tsukenákatta 漬けなかった
tsukirú 尽きる become exhausted	tsukité 尽きて	tsukinákute 尽きなくて	tsukinái 尽きない	tsukinákatta 尽きなかった
tsumamú 抓む pick, take a pinch of	tsumandé 抓んで	tsumamanákute 抓まなくて	tsumamaná 抓まない	tsumamanákatta 抓まなかった
tsumazukú 躓く take a false step	tsumazuité 躓いて	tsumazukanákute 躓かなくて	tsumazukanái 躓かない	tsumazukanákatta 躓かなかった

GROUP ONE	SUBORDINATE		NEGATIVE	
	Positive	Negative	Present	Past
tsumorú 積もる accumulate, be piled up	tsumotté 積もって	tsumoranákute 積もらなくて	tsumoranái 積もらない	tsumoranákatta 積もらなかった
tsumú 積む pile up, stack v. i.	tsundé 積んで	tsumanákute 積まなくて	tsumanái 積まない	tsumanákatta 積まなかった
tsumú 摘む pick, pluck, pull out v. tr.	tsundé 摘んで	tsumanákute 摘まなくて	tsumanái 摘まない	tsumanákatta 摘まなかった
tsunagarú 繋がる be connected, hicht (in, to)	tsunagatté 繋がって	tsunagaranákute 繋がらなくて	tsunagaranái 繋がらない	tsunagaranákatta 繋がらなかった
tsunagú 繋ぐ tie, connect, tether	tsunaidé 繋いで	tsunaganákute 繋がなくて	tsunaganái 繋がない	tsunaganákatta 繋がなかった
tsuranarú 連なる range, lie in a row	tsuranatté 連なって	tsuranaranákute 連ならなくて	tsuranaranái 連ならない	tsuranaranákatta 連ならなかった
tsuranerú 連ねる link, join, put in a row	tsuraneté 連ねて	tsuranenákute 連ねなくて	tsuranenái 連ねない	tsuranenákatta 連ねなかった
tsurerú 連れる take (with), bring (with)	tsureté 連れて	tsurenákute 連れなくて	tsurenái 連れない	tsurenákatta 連れなかった
tsurú 釣る angle (for fish)	tsutté 釣って	tsuranákute 釣らなくて	tsuranái 釣らない	tsuranákatta 釣らなかった
tsutaerú 伝える convey, report, transmit	tsutaeté 伝えて	tsutaenákute 伝えなくて	tsutaenái 伝えない	tsutaenákatta 伝えなかった
tsutawarú 伝わる be handed down	tsutawatté 伝わって	tsutawaranákute 伝わらなくて	tsutawaranái 伝わらない	tsutawaranákatta 伝わらなかった
tsuzukú 続く continue, keep on	tsuzuité 続いて	tsuzukanákute 続かなくて	tsuzukanái 続かない	tsuzukanákatta 続かなかった
uerú 植える plant (a tree)	ueté 植えて	uenákute 植えなくて	uenái 植えない	uenákatta 植えなかった
ukaberú 浮べる float, set (a ship) afloat	ukabeté 浮べて	ukabenákute 浮べなくて	ukabenái 浮べない	ukabenákatta 浮べなかった
ukabú 浮ぶ float (on water, in air)	ukandé 浮んで	ukabanákute 浮ばなくて	ukabanái 浮ばない	ukabanákatta 浮ばなかった

| GROUP ONE | **SUBORDINATE** | | **NEGATIVE** | |
	Positive	Negative	Present	Past
ukagaú 伺う call on (a person)	ukagatté 伺って	ukagawanákute 伺わなくて	ukagawanái 伺わない	ukagawanákatta 伺わなかった
ukagaú 窺う watch for (a chance)	ukagatté 窺って	ukagawanákute 窺わなくて	ukagawanái 窺わない	ukagawanákatta 窺わなかった
ukarerú 浮かれる make merry, be gay	ukareté 浮かれて	ukarenákute 浮かれなくて	ukarenái 浮かれない	ukarenákatta 浮かれなかった
uketorú 受取る receive, accept 受取って	uketotté	uketoranákute 受取らなくて	uketoranái 受取らない	uketoranákatta 受取らなかった
ukú 浮く float, become buoyant	uité 浮いて	ukanákute 浮かなくて	ukanái 浮かない	ukanákatta 浮かなかった
umarerú 生れる be born, see the light	umareté 生れて	umarenákute 生れなくて	umarenái 生れない	umarenákatta 生れなかった
umarú 埋まる be filled up 埋まって	umatté	umaranákute 埋まらなくて	umaranái 埋まらない	umaranákatta 埋まらなかった
umú 産む bear, give birth to	undé 産んで	umanákute 産まなくて	umanái 産まない	umanákatta 産まなかった
unasarerú うなされる have a nightmare	unasareté うなされて	unasarenákute うなされなくて	unasarenái うなされない	unasarenákatta うなされなかった
unuborerú 自惚れる be vain, be conceited	unuboreté 自惚れて	unuborenákute 自惚れなくて	unuborenái 自惚れない	unuborenákatta 自惚れなかった
urerú 売れる sell, be in demand	ureté 売れて	urenákute 売れなくて	urenái 売れない	urenákatta 売れなかった
urotsukú うろつく loiter, wander (about)	urotsuité うろついて	urotsukanákute うろつかなくて	urotsukanái うろつかない	urotsukanákatta うろつかなかった
urú 売る sell, deal in (goods)	utté 売って	uranákute 売らなくて	uranái 売らない	uranákatta 売らなかった
ushinaú 失う lose, miss (a chance)	ushinatté 失って	ushinawanákute 失わなくて	ushinawanái 失わない	ushinawanákatta 失わなかった
usuragú 薄らぐ thin, grow pale v. i.	usuraidé 薄らいで	usuraganákute 薄らがなくて	usuraganái 薄らがない	usuraganákatta 薄らがなかった
utagaú 疑う doubt, be doubtful of	utagatté 疑って	utagawanákute 疑わなくて	utagawanái 疑わない	utagawanákatta 疑わなかった

GROUP ONE	SUBORDINATE Positive	Negative	NEGATIVE Present	Past
utaú 歌う sing, chant	utatté 歌って	utawanákute 歌わなくて	utawanái 歌わない	utawanákatta 歌わなかった
utsumukú 俯向く look downward	utsumuité 俯向いて	utsumukanákute 俯向かなくて	utsumukanái 俯向かない	utsumukanákatta 俯向かなかった
uttaerú 訴える go to law (with a person)	uttaeté 訴えて	uttaenákute 訴えなくて	uttaenái 訴えない	uttaenákatta 訴えなかった
uzukumarú 蹲る crouch, squat down	uzukumatté 蹲って	uzukumaranákute 蹲らなくて	uzukumaranái 蹲らない	uzukumaranákatta 蹲らなかった
uzumorerú 埋もれる be buried, be covered with	uzumoreté 埋もれて	uzumorenákute 埋もれなくて	uzumorenái 埋もれない	uzumorenákatta 埋もれなかった
wabirú 詫びる apologize for (a fault)	wabité 詫びて	wabinákute 詫びなくて	wabinái 詫びない	wabinákatta 詫びなかった
wakú 沸く boil, grow hot	waité 沸いて	wakanákute 沸かなくて	wakanái 沸かない	wakanákatta 沸かなかった
waraú 笑う laugh, smile	waratté 笑って	warawanákute 笑わなくて	warawanái 笑わない	warawanákatta 笑わなかった
warawasú 笑わす move to laughter	warawashité 笑わして	warawasanákute 笑わさなくて	warawasanái 笑わさない	warawasanákatta 笑わさなかった
warerú 割れる split, cleave v. i.	wareté 割れて	warenákute 割れなくて	warenái 割れない	warenákatta 割れなかった
warú 割る divide, cut, halve v. tr.	watté 割って	waranákute 割らなくて	waranái 割らない	waranákatta 割らなかった
wasurerú 忘れる forget, be forgetful of	wasureté 忘れて	wasurenákute 忘れなくて	wasurenái 忘れない	wasurenákatta 忘れなかった
watarú 渡る go over, go across	watatté 渡って	wataranákute 渡らなくて	wataranái 渡らない	wataranákatta 渡らなかった
watarú 亙る range (from A to B, etc.) v. i.	watatté 亙って	wataranákute 亙らなくて	wataranái 亙らない	wataranákatta 亙らなかった
watasú 渡す hand over (to), deliver	watashité 渡して	watasanákute 渡さなくて	watasanái 渡さない	watasanákatta 渡さなかった
wazurawasú 煩わす trouble, keep (a person) busy	wazurawashité 煩わして	wazurawasanákute 煩わさなくて	wazurawasanái 煩わさない	wazurawasanákatta 煩わさなかった

GROUP ONE	SUBORDINATE		NEGATIVE	
	Positive	Negative	Present	Past
yakerú	yaketé	yakenákute	yakenái	yakenákatta
焼ける	焼けて	焼けなくて	焼けない	焼けなかった
burn, be burned v. i.				
yakú	yaité	yakanákute	yakanái	yakanákatta
焼く	焼いて	焼かなくて	焼かない	焼かなかった
burn, roast v. tr.				
yamerú 止める	yameté	yamenákute	yamenái	yamenákatta
give up, stop 止めて		止めなくて	止めない	止めなかった
yamú	yandé	yamanákute	yamanái	yamanákatta
止む	止んで	止まなくて	止まない	止まなかった
stop, subside v. i.				
yararerú	yararreté	yararenákute	yararenái	yararenákatta
やられる	やられて	やられなくて	やられない	やられなかった
be done, have (anything done)				
yarú 遣る	yatté	yaranákute	yaranái	yaranákatta
give, let have 遣って		遣らなくて	遣らない	遣らなかった
yaserú	yaseté	yasenákute	yasenái	yasenákatta
痩せる	痩せて	痩せなくて	痩せない	痩せなかった
get lean, lose weight				
yawageru	yawarageté	yawaragenákute	yawaragenái	yawaragenákatta
和らげる	和らげて	和らげなくて	和らげない	和らげなかった
soften (one's voice)				
yawaragú	yawaraidé	yawaraganákute	yawaraganái	yawaraganákatta
和らぐ	和らいで	和らがなくて	和らがない	和らがなかった
soften, become mild				
yobú 呼ぶ	yondé	yobanákute	yobanái	yobanákatta
call, call out to 呼んで		呼ばなくて	呼ばない	呼ばなかった
yogorerú 汚れる	yogoreté	yogorenákute	yogorenái	yogorenákatta
become dirty 汚れて		汚れなくて	汚れない	汚れなかった
yogosú 汚す	yogoshité	yogosanákute	yogosanái	yogosanákatta
stain, blemish 汚して		汚さなくて	汚さない	汚さなかった
yorú 寄る	yotté	yoranákute	yoranái	yoranákatta
approach 寄って		寄らなくて	寄らない	寄らなかった
yusuburú	yusubutté	yusuburanákute	yusuburanái	yusuburanákatta
揺すぶる	揺すぶって	揺すぶらなくて	揺すぶらない	揺すぶらなかった
shake, swing v. tr.				
yusugú 濯ぐ	usuidé	yusuganákute	yusuganái	yusuganákatta
wash out, rinse 濯いで		濯がなくて	濯がない	濯がなかった
yusurú 強請る	yusutté	yusuranákute	yusuranái	yusuranákatta
extort (money) 強請って		強請らなくて	強請らない	強請らなかった
yuú 結う	yutté	yuwanákute	yuwanái	yuwanákatta
dress (hair) 結って		結わなくて	結わない	結わなかった
yuzurú 譲る	yuzutté	yuzuranákute	yuzuranái	yuzuranákatta
hand over 譲って		譲らなくて	譲らない	譲らなかった

GROUP TWO

Main Characteristics

Simple Present : Stressed on the second last syllable.

Subordinate
{ **Positive :** Stressed on the same syllable as the one accentuated in its simple present form.
Negative : Stressed on the terminal *a* of the verbal *a*-stem.

Negative Form
{ with *nai* ない : Stressed on the terminal *a* of the verbal *a*-stem.
with *nakatta* なかった : Stressed on the terminal *a* of the verbal *a*-stem.

GROUP TWO	SUBORDINATE		NEGATIVE	
	Positive	Negative	Present	Past
abáku 発く disclose, divulge	abáite 発いて	abakánakute 発かなくて	abakánai 発かない	abakánakatta 発かなかった
abúru 焙る roast, broil, grill, toast	abútte 焙って	aburánakute 焙らなくて	aburánai 焙らない	aburánakatta 焙らなかった
aégu 喘ぐ pant., gasp (for breath)	aéide 喘いで	aegánakute 喘がなくて	aegánai 喘がない	aegánakatta 喘がなかった
ajiwáu 味わう taste, appreciate	ajiwátte 味わって	ajiwawánakute 味わわなくて	ajiwawánai 味わわない	ajiwawánakatta 味わわなかった
akináu 商う sell, deal in, trade in	akinátte 商って	akinawánakute 商わなくて	akinawánai 商わない	akinawánakatta 商わなかった
amásu 余す leave (over), spare	amáshite 余して	amasánakute 余さなくて	amasánai 余さない	amasánakatta 余さなかった
ámu 編む knit, crochet	ánde 編んで	amánakute 編まなくて	amánai 編まない	amánakatta 編まなかった
anadóru 侮る despise, scorn	anadótte 侮って	anadoránakute 侮らなくて	anadoránai 侮らない	anadoránakatta 侮らなかった
aógu 扇ぐ fan (a fire, a person)	aóide 扇いで	aogánakute 扇がなくて	aogánai 扇がない	aogánakatta 扇がなかった
arasóu 争う dispute, argue	arasótte 争って	arasowánakute 争わなくて	arasowánai 争わない	arasowánakatta 争わなかった
arawásu 現わす show (anger, etc)	arawáshite 現わして	arawasánakute 現わさなくて	arawasánai 現わさない	arawasánakatta 現わさなかった
arúku 歩く walk, go on foot	arúite 歩いて	arukánakute 歩かなくて	arukánai 歩かない	arukánakatta 歩かなかった

GROUP TWO	SUBORDINATE Positive	Negative	NEGATIVE Present	Past
asebámu 汗ばむ be slightly sweaty	asebúnde 汗ばんで	asebamánakute 汗ばまなくて	asebamánai 汗ばまない	asebamánakatta 汗ばまなかった
aséru 焦る be in a hurry	asétte 焦って	aseránakute 焦らなくて	aseránai 焦らない	aseránakatta 焦らなかった
ashiráu あしらう treat, handle	ashirátte あしらって	ashirawánakute あしらわなくて	ashirawánai あしらわない	ashirawánakatta あしらわなかった
atsumáru 集まる gather, collect	atsumátte 集まって	atsumaránakute 集まらなくて	atsumaránai 集まらない	atsumaránakatta 集まらなかった
áu 会う meet, interview	átte 会って	awánakute 会わなくて	awánai 会わない	awánakatta 会わなかった
awarému 憐れむ pity, have mercy	awarénde 憐れんで	awaremánakute 憐れまなくて	awaremánai 憐れまない	awaremánakatta 憐れまなかった
ayabúmu 危ぶむ fear, doubt	ayabúnde 危ぶんで	ayabumánakute 危ぶまなくて	ayabumánai 危ぶまない	ayabumánakatta 危ぶまなかった
ayakáru あやかる resemble, to take after	ayakátte あやかって	ayakaránakute あやからなくて	ayakaránai あやからない	ayakaránakatta あやからなかった
ayamáru 謝る apologize	ayamátte 謝って	ayamaránakute 謝らなくて	ayamaránai 謝らない	ayamaránakatta 謝らなかった
ayamáru 誤る mistake, err	ayamátte 誤って	ayamaránakute 誤らなくて	ayamaránai 誤らない	ayamaránakatta 誤らなかった
ayashímu 怪しむ doubt, question	ayashínde 怪しんで	ayashimánakute 怪しまなくて	ayashimánai 怪しまない	ayashimánakatta 怪しまなかった
ayásu あやす nurse, humour (a baby)	ayáshite あやして	ayasánakute あやさなくて	ayasánai あやさない	ayasánakatta あやさなかった
ayatsúru 操る handle, manage	ayatsútte 操って	ayatsuránakute 操らなくて	ayatsuránai 操らない	ayatsuránakatta 操らなかった
azamúku 欺く deceive, cheat	azamúite 欺いて	azamukánakute 欺かなくて	azamukánai 欺かない	azamukánakatta 欺かなかった
azukáru 預かる take charge of	azukátte 預かって	azukaránakute 預からなくて	azukaránai 預からない	azukaránakatta 預からなかった
bakásu 化かす bewitch, enchant	bakáshite 化かして	bakasánakute 化かさなくて	bakasánai 化かさない	bakasánakatta 化かさなかった
barásu ばらす pull down (a house), disjoint	baráshite ばらして	barasánakute ばらさなくて	barasánai ばらさない	barasánakatta ばらさなかった
bundóru 分捕る capture, seize	bundótte 分捕って	bundoránakute 分捕らなくて	bundoránai 分捕らない	bundoránakatta 分捕らなかった

GROUP TWO	SUBORDINATE		NEGATIVE	
	Positive	Negative	Present	Past
bútsu 打つ beat, strike	bútte 打って	butánakute 打たなくて	butánai 打たない	butánakatta 打たなかった
chakásu 茶化す make fun of, laugh away	chakáshite 茶化して	chakasánakute 茶化さなくて	chakasánai 茶化さない	chakasánakatta 茶化さなかった
chibashíru 血走る become bloodshot	chibashítte 血走って	chibashiránakute 血走らなくて	chibashiránai 血走らない	chibashiránakatta 血走らなかった
chigíru ちぎる tear off, tear (to pieces)	chigítte ちぎって	chigiránakute ちぎらなくて	chigiránai ちぎらない	chigiránakatta ちぎらなかった
chigíru 契る pledge, vow, swear	chigítte 契って	chigiránakute 契らなくて	chigiránai 契らない	chigiránakatta 契らなかった
chikáu 誓う swear, pledge	chikátte 誓って	chikawánakute 誓わなくて	chikawánai 誓わない	chikawánakatta 誓わなかった
chikayóru 近寄る go (come) near	chikayótte 近寄って	chikayoránakute 近寄らなくて	chikayoránai 近寄らない	chikayoránakatta 近寄らなかった
chikazúku 近づく approach, get near	chikazúite 近づいて	chikazukánakute 近づかなくて	chikazukánai 近づかない	chikazukánakatta 近づかなかった
chimayóu 血迷う be beside oneself	chimayótte 血迷って	chimayowánakute 血迷わなくて	chimayowánai 血迷わない	chimayowánakatta 血迷わなかった
chinámu 因む be connected with	chinánde 因んで	chinamánakute 因まなくて	chinamánai 因まない	chinamánakatta 因まなかった
dakitsúku 抱き付く cling to, embrace	dakitsúite 抱き付いて	dakitsukánakute 抱き付かなくて	dakitsukánai 抱き付かない	dakitsukánakatta 抱き付かなかった
damáru 黙る become silent	damátte 黙って	damaránakute 黙らなくて	damaránai 黙らない	damaránakatta 黙らなかった
damásu 騙す deceive, cheat	damáshite 騙して	damasánakute 騙さなくて	damasánai 騙さない	damasánakatta 騙さなかった
dásu 出す take out, put out	dáshite 出して	dasánakute 出さなくて	dasánai 出さない	dasánakatta 出さなかった
déru 出る come (go) out	déte 出て	dénakute 出なくて	dénai 出ない	dénakatta 出なかった
donáru 奴鳴る cry, shout, roar	donátte 奴鳴って	donaránakute 奴鳴らなくて	donaránai 奴鳴らない	donaránakatta 奴鳴らなかった
doyásu どやす drub, beat	doyáshite どやして	doyasánakute どやさなくて	doyasánai どやさない	doyasánakatta どやさなかった

GROUP TWO	SUBORDINATE Positive	Negative	NEGATIVE Present	Past
egáku 描く	egáite 描いて	egakánakute 描かなくて	egakánai 描かない	egakánakatta 描かなかった
draw, picture, paint				
egúru 抉る	egútte 抉って	eguránakute 抉らなくて	eguránai 抉らない	eguránakatta 抉らなかった
scoop out, gouge				
erábu 選ぶ	eránde 選んで	erabánakute 選ばなくて	erabánai 選ばない	erabánakatta 選ばなかった
choose, prefer				
eragáru 偉がる	eragátte 偉がって	eragaránakute 偉がらなくて	eragaránai 偉がらない	eragaránakatta 偉がらなかった
be self important				
éru 得る	éte 得て	énakute 得なくて	énai 得ない	énakatta 得なかった
obtain, acquire				
fukásu 蒸かす	fukáshite 蒸かして	fukasánakute 蒸かさなくて	fukasánai 蒸かさない	fukasánakatta 蒸かさなかった
steam v. tr.				
fúku 吹く	fúite 吹いて	fukánakute 吹かなくて	fukánai 吹かない	fukánakatta 吹かなかった
blow, breathe out				
fukúmu 含む	fukúnde 含んで	fukumánakute 含まなくて	fukumánai 含まない	fukumánakatta 含まなかった
keep in one's mouth				
funsúru 扮する	fúnshite 扮して	funshínakute 扮しなくて	funshínai 扮しない	funshínakatta 扮しなかった
dress (up), garb oneself (in)				
fúru 降る	fútte 降って	furánakute 降らなくて	furánai 降らない	furánakatta 降らなかった
fall (rain), descend				
fuségu 防ぐ	fuséide 防いで	fusegánakute 防がなくて	fusegánai 防がない	fusegánakatta 防がなかった
defend (oneself)				
futóru 肥る	futótte 肥って	futoránakute 肥らなくて	futoránai 肥らない	futoránakatta 肥らなかった
fatten, grow stout				
fuyásu 殖やす	fuyáshite 殖やして	fuyasánakute 殖やさなくて	fuyasánai 殖やさない	fuyasánakatta 殖やさなかった
increase, multiply				
gambáru 頑張る	gambátte 頑張って	gambaránakute 頑張らなくて	gambaránai 頑張らない	gambaránakatta 頑張らなかった
persist in, insist on				
gomakásu 誤魔化す	gomakáshite 誤魔化して	gomakasánakute 誤魔化さなくて	gomakasánai 誤魔化さない	gomakasánakatta 誤魔化さなかった
cheat, deceive				
gyosúru 御する	gyóshite 御して	gyoshínakute 御しなくて	gyoshínai 御しない	gyoshínakatta 御しなかった
manage, handle				

720

	SUBORDINATE		NEGATIVE	
	Positive	Negative	Present	Past
habúku 省く exclude, eliminate	habúite 省いて	habukánakute 省かなくて	habukánai 省かない	habukánakatta 省かなかった
hagemásu 励ます encourage, spur (on)	hagemáshite 励まして	hagemasánakute 励まさなくて	hagemasánai 励まさない	hagemasánakatta 励まさなかった
hagému 励む strive (labour) for	hagénde 励んで	hagemánakute 励まなくて	hagemánai 励まない	hagemánakatta 励まなかった
hágu 剥ぐ tear off, strip off	háide 剥ぐ	hagánakute 剥がなくて	hagánai 剥がない	hagánakatta 剥がなかった
hajíku 弾く fillip, flip, snap	hajíite 弾いて	hajikánakute 弾かなくて	hajikánai 弾かない	hajikánakatta 弾かなかった
hakadóru 捗取る advance, progress	hakadótte 捗取って	hakadoránakute 捗取らなくて	hakadoránai 捗取らない	hakadoránakatta 捗取らなかった
hakáru 計る measure, gauge	hakátte 計って	hakaránakute 計らなくて	hakaránai 計らない	hakaránakatta 計らなかった
háku 掃く sweep, brush	háite 掃いて	hakánakute 掃かなくて	hakánai 掃かない	hakánakatta 掃かなかった
háku 吐く vomit, spew	háite 吐いて	hakánakute 吐かなくて	hakánai 吐かない	hakánakatta 吐かなかった
hanásu 話す speak, talk	hanáshite 話して	hanasánakute 話さなくて	hanasánai 話さない	hanasánakatta 話さなかった
hanikámu はにかむ be shy, look abashed	hanikánde はにかんで	hanikamánakute はにかまなくて	hanikamánai はにかまない	hanikamánakatta はにかまなかった
haóru 羽織る put on, fling over	haótte 羽織って	haoránakute 羽織らなくて	haoránai 羽織らない	haoránakatta 羽織らなかった
harásu 晴らす dispel (doubts)	haráshite 晴らして	harasánakute 晴らさなくて	harasánai 晴らさない	harasánakatta 晴らさなかった
haráu 払う pay, settle (account)	harátte 払って	harawánakute 払わなくて	harawánai 払わない	harawánakatta 払わなかった
hasámu 挟む put between, hold between	hasánde 挟んで	hasamánakute 挟まなくて	hasamánai 挟まない	hasamánakatta 挟まなかった
hashíru 走る run, rush, dart	hashítte 走って	hashiránakute 走らなくて	hashiránai 走らない	hashiránakatta 走らなかった
hatáku はたく dust, beat, strike	hatáite はたいて	hatakánakute はたかなくて	hatakánai はたかない	hatakánakatta はたかなかった

GROUP TWO	SUBORDINATE Positive	Negative	NEGATIVE Present	Past
hatásu 果す carry out, accomplish	hatáshite 果して	hatasánakute 果さなくて	hatasánai 果さない	hatasánakatta 果さなかった
háu 這う crawl, grovel	hátte 這って	hawánakute 這わなくて	hawánai 這わない	hawánakatta 這わなかった
hayamáru 早まる be hasty, be rash	hayamátte 早まって	hayamaránakute 早まらなくて	hayamaránai 早まらない	hayamaránakatta 早まらなかった
hayáru 流行る be in fashion	hayátte 流行って	hayaránakute 流行らなくて	hayaránai 流行らない	hayaránakatta 流行らなかった
hedatáru 距たる be distant (from)	hedatátte 距たって	hedataránakute 距たらなくて	hedataránai 距たらない	hedataránakatta 距たらなかった
hetsuráu へつらう flatter, adulate	hetsurátte へつらって	hetsurawánakute へつらわなくて	hetsurawánai へつらわない	hetsurawánakatta へつらわなかった
hibíku 響く sound, resound	hibíite 響いて	hibikánakute 響かなくて	hibikánai 響かない	hibikánakatta 響かなかった
higámu 僻む become jaundiced	higánde 僻んで	higamánakute 僻まなくて	higamánai 僻まない	higamánakatta 僻まなかった
hikáru 光る shine, glitter	hikátte 光って	hikaránakute 光らなくて	hikaránai 光らない	hikaránakatta 光らなかった
hikkáku 引っ搔く scratch, claw	hikkáite 引っ搔いて	hikkakánakute 引っ搔かなくて	hikkakánai 引っ搔かない	hikkakánakatta 引っ搔かなかった
hikkomásu 引っ込ます draw in, withdraw	hikkomáshite 引っ込まして	hikkomasánakute 引っ込まさなくて	hikkomasánai 引っ込まさない	hikkomasánakatta 引っ込まさなかった
hinéru 捻る twirl, twist	hinétte 捻って	hineránakute 捻らなくて	hineránai 捻らない	hineránakatta 捻らなかった
hippáru 引っ張る pull, draw, drag	hippátte 引っ張って	hipparánakute 引っ張らなくて	hipparánai 引っ張らない	hipparánakatta 引っ張らなかった
hiráku 開く open, uncover	hiráite 開いて	hirakánakute 開かなくて	hirakánai 開かない	hirakánakatta 開かなかった
hiraméku 閃く flash, flicker v.i.	hiraméite 閃いて	hiramekánakute 閃めかなくて	hiramekánai 閃めかない	hiramekánakatta 閃めかなかった
hishígu 拉ぐ crush, smash	hishíide 拉いで	hishigánakute 拉がなくて	hishigánai 拉がない	hishigánakatta 拉がなかった
hisómu 潜む lurk, lie concealed	hisónde 潜んで	hisománakute 潜まなくて	hisománai 潜まない	hisománakatta 潜まなかった
hitáru 浸る soak v.i., to be soaked	hitátte 浸って	hitaránakute 浸らなくて	hitaránai 浸らない	hitaránakatta 浸らなかった

GROUP TWO	SUBORDINATE Positive	Negative	NEGATIVE Present	Past
hitásu 浸す soak, moisten v. tr.	hitáshite 浸して	hitasánakute 浸さなくて	hitasánai 浸さない	hitasánakatta 浸さなかった
hiyakásu 冷やかす banter, jeer at	hiyakáshite 冷やかして	hiyakasánakute 冷やかさなくて	hiyakasánai 冷やかさない	hiyakasánakatta 冷やかさなかった
hizamazúku 跪く kneel (down)	hizamazúite 跪いて	hizamazukánakute 跪かなくて	hizamazukánai 跪かない	hizamazukánakatta 跪かなかった
hodóku 解く undo, untie	hodóite 解いて	hodokánakute 解かなくて	hodokánai 解かない	hodokánakatta 解かなかった
hokóru 誇る boast of, brag of	hokótte 誇って	hokoránakute 誇らなくて	hokoránai 誇らない	hokoránakatta 誇らなかった
hohoému ほほ笑む smile, begin to bloom	hohoénde ほほ笑んで	hohoemánakute ほほ笑まなくて	hohoemánai ほほ笑まない	hohoemánakatta ほほ笑まなかった
hōmúru 葬る bury, inter	hōmútte 葬って	hōmuránakute 葬らなくて	hōmuránai 葬らない	hōmuránakatta 葬らなかった
honomekásu 仄めかす show faintly	honomekáshite 仄めかして	honomekasánakute 仄めかさなくて	honomekasánai 仄めかさない	honomekasánakatta 仄めかさなかった
hóru 彫る carve, tattoo	hótte 彫って	horánakute 彫らなくて	horánai 彫らない	horánakatta 彫らなかった
hóru 掘る dig, delve	hótte 掘って	horánakute 掘らなくて	horánai 掘らない	horánakatta 掘らなかった
hoshigáru 欲しがる desire, want	hoshigátte 欲しがって	hoshigaránakute 欲しがらなくて	hoshigaránai 欲しがらない	hoshigaránakatta 欲しがらなかった
hósu 干す dry, desiccate	hóshite 干して	hosánakute 干さなくて	hosánai 干さない	hosánakatta 干さなかった
ibáru 威張る be proud, to be haughty	ibátte 威張って	ibaránakute 威張らなくて	ibaránai 威張らない	ibaránakatta 威張らなかった
ibúsu 燻す smoke, fumigate	ibúshite 燻して	ibusánakute 燻さなくて	ibusánai 燻さない	ibusánakatta 燻さなかった
idómu 挑む challenge (to fight)	idónde 挑んで	idománakute 挑まなくて	idománai 挑まない	idománakatta 挑まなかった
ikásu 生かす revive, keep alive	ikáshite 生かして	ikasánakute 生かさなくて	ikasánai 生かさない	ikasánakatta 生かさなかった
inanáku 嘶く neigh, whinny	inanáite 嘶いて	inanakánakute 嘶かなくて	inanakánai 嘶かない	inanakánakatta 嘶かなかった

GROUP TWO	SUBORDINATE Positive	Negative	NEGATIVE Present	Past
inóru 祈る pray (to), say a prayer	inótte 祈って	inoránakute 祈らなくて	inoránai 祈らない	inoránakatta 祈らなかった
irodóru 彩る color, paint	irodótte 彩って	irodoránakute 彩らなくて	irodoránai 彩らない	irodoránakatta 彩らなかった
iroméku 色めく color, be tinged	iroméite 色めいて	iromekánakute 色めかなくて	iromekánai 色めかない	iromekánakatta 色めかなかった
irozúku 色付く color, become colored	irozúite 色付いて	irozukánakute 色付かなくて	irozukánai 色付かない	irozukánakatta 色付かなかった
íru 煎る parch (beans), fire (tea)	ítte 煎って	iránakute 煎らなくて	iránai 煎らない	iránakatta 煎らなかった
isógu 急ぐ make haste, hasten	isóide 急いで	isogánakute 急がなくて	isogánai 急がない	isogánakatta 急がなかった
itagáru 痛がる complain of pain	itagátte 痛がって	itagaránakute 痛がらなくて	itagaránai 痛がらない	itagaránakatta 痛がらなかった
itámu 痛む feel a pain	itánde 痛んで	itamánakute 痛まなくて	itamánai 痛まない	itamánakatta 痛まなかった
itawáru 労わる pity, care for	itawátte 労わって	itawaránakute 労わらなくて	itawaránai 労わらない	itawaránakatta 労わらなかった
itonámu 営む perform, hold (a ceremony)	itonánde 営んで	itonamánakute 営まなくて	itonamánai 営まない	itonamánakatta 営まなかった
itsuwáru 偽る tell a lie, feign	itsuwátte 偽って	itsuwaránakute 偽らなくて	itsuwaránai 偽らない	itsuwaránakatta 偽らなかった
iwáu 祝う congratulate (a person on)	iwátte 祝って	iwawánakute 祝わなくて	iwawánai 祝わない	iwawánakatta 祝わなかった
iyagáru 嫌がる dislike, hate, grudge	iyagátte 嫌がって	iyagaránakute 嫌がらなくて	iyagaránai 嫌がらない	iyagaránakatta 嫌がらなかった
iyashímu 卑しむ despise, disdain	iyashínde 卑しんで	iyashimánakute 卑しまなくて	iyashimánai 卑しまない	iyashimánakatta 卑しまなかった
iyásu 癒す heal (a person of a wound)	iyáshite 癒して	iyasánakute 癒さなくて	iyasánai 癒さない	iyasánakatta 癒さなかった
izanáu 誘う invite, entice	izanátte 誘って	iazanawánakute 誘わなくて	izanawánai 誘わない	izanawánakatta 誘わなかった

724

| | SUBORDINATE | | NEGATIVE | |
GROUP TWO	Positive	Negative	Present	Past
jirásu	jiráshite	jirasánakute	jirasánai	jirasánakatta
焦らす	焦らして	焦らさなくて	焦らさない	焦らさなかった
irritate, provoke				
kabáu	kabátte	kabawánakute	kabawánai	kabawánakatta
庇う	庇って	庇わなくて	庇わない	庇わなかった
protect (the weak)				
kabúru	kabútte	kaburánakute	kaburánai	kaburánakatta
被る	被って	被らなくて	被らない	被らなかった
put on, wear (on the head)				
kagayáku	kagayáite	kagayakánakute	kagayakánai	kagayakánakatta
輝く	輝いて	輝かなくて	輝かない	輝かなかった
shine, sparkle, gleam				
kagíru 限る	kagítte	kagiránakute	kagiránai	kagiránakatta
limit, restrict 限って		限らなくて	限らない	限らなかった
kajíru	kajítte	kajiránakute	kajiránai	kajiránakatta
齧る	齧って	齧らなくて	齧らない	齧らなかった
gnaw, nibble (at)				
kakáru	kakátte	kakaránakute	kakaránai	kakaránakatta
掛かる	掛かって	掛からなくて	掛からない	掛からなかった
hang (on, from), be suspended				
káku	káite	kakánakute	kakánai	kakánakatta
掻く	掻いて	掻かなくて	掻かない	掻かなかった
scratch (one's head)				
káku	káite	kakánakute	kakánai	kakánakatta
書く	書いて	書かなくて	書かない	書かなかった
write, compose, (a poem)				
kakúsu 隠す	kakúshite	kakusánakute	kakusánai	kakusánakatta
hide, conceal 隠して		隠さなくて	隠さない	隠さなかった
kamáu	kamátte	kamawánakute	kamawánai	kamawánakatta
構う	構って	構わなくて	構わない	構わなかった
mind, care about				
kanashímu	kanashínde	kanashimánakute	kanashimánai	kanashimánakatta
悲しむ	悲しんで	悲しまなくて	悲しまない	悲しまなかった
grieve, be sad				
kanáu	kanátte	kanawánakute	kanawánai	kanawánakatta
適う	適って	適わなくて	適わない	適わなかった
suit (one's fancy)				
karakáu	karakátte	karakawánakute	karakawánai	karakawánakatta
からかう	からかって	からかわなくて	からかわない	からかわなかった
banter, tease, make fun of				
karamáru	karamátte	karamaránakute	karamaránai	karamaránakatta
絡まる	絡まって	絡まらなくて	絡まらない	絡まらなかった
twine round, twist about v. i.				

GROUP TWO	SUBORDINATE Positive	Negative	NEGATIVE Present	Past
karámu 絡む coil around, get twisted	karánde 絡んで	karamánakute 絡まなくて	karamánai 絡まない	karamánakatta 絡まなかった
kasámu 嵩む grow bulky, swell	kasánde 嵩んで	kasamánakute 嵩まなくて	kasamánai 嵩まない	kasamánakatta 嵩まなかった
kaségu 稼ぐ earn	kaséide 稼いで	kasegánakute 稼がなくて	kasegánai 稼がない	kasegánakatta 稼がなかった
kashikomáru 畏まる obey (with respect)	kashikomátte 畏まって	kashikomaránakute 畏まらなくて	kashikomaránai 畏まらない	kashikomaránakatta 畏まらなかった
kashizúku 侍く wait upon, attend on	kashizúite 侍いて	kashizukánakute 侍かなくて	kashizukánai 侍かない	kashizukánakatta 侍かなかった
katamúku 傾く incline (to), tilt	katamúite 傾いて	katamukánakute 傾かなくて	katamukánai 傾かない	katamukánakatta 傾かなかった
kátsu 勝つ win, vanquish	kátte 勝って	katánakute 勝たなくて	katánai 勝たない	katánakatta 勝たなかった
katsúgu 担ぐ carry on the shoulder	katsúide 担いで	katsugánakute 担がなくて	katsugánai 担がない	katsugánakatta 担がなかった
káu 飼う keep (an animal)	kátte 飼って	kawánakute 飼わなくて	kawánai 飼わない	kawánakatta 飼わなかった
kawaigáru 可愛がる love, pet, be attached (to)	kawaigátte 可愛がって	kawaigaránakute 可愛がらなくて	kawaigaránai 可愛がらない	kawaigaránakatta 可愛がらなかった
kawakásu 乾かす dry, desiccate	kawakáshite 乾かして	kawakasánakute 乾かさなくて	kawakasánai 乾かさない	kawakasánakatta 乾かさなかった
kawáku 乾く dry, be dry, dry up v. i.	kawáite 乾いて	kawakánakute 乾かなくて	kawakánai 乾かない	kawakánakatta 乾かなかった
kayugáru 痒がる complain of itching	kayugátte 痒がって	kayugaránakute 痒がらなくて	kayugaránai 痒がらない	kayugaránakatta 痒がらなかった
kegásu 汚す make unclean, soil	kegáshite 汚して	kegasánakute 汚さなくて	kegasánai 汚さない	kegasánakatta 汚さなかった
kéru 蹴る kick (at), hack	kétte 蹴って	keránakute 蹴らなくて	keránai 蹴らない	keránakatta 蹴らなかった
kiraméku 輝く glitter, sparkle	kiraméite 輝いて	kiramekánakute 輝かなくて	kiramekánai 輝かない	kiramekánakatta 輝かなかった
kirásu 切らす run out of, be short of	kiráshite 切らして	kirasánakute 切らさなくて	kirasánai 切らさない	kirasánakatta 切らさなかった

GROUP TWO	SUBORDINATE		NEGATIVE	
	Positive	Negative	Present	Past
kíru 切る cut, chop, hash	kítte 切って	kiránakute 切らなくて	kiránai 切らない	kiránakatta 切らなかった
kitásu 来たす cause, bring about	kitáshite 来たして	kitasánakute 来たさなくて	kitasánai 来たさない	kitasánakatta 来たさなかった
kiwamáru 極まる end, reach the extreme	kiwamátte 極まって	kiwamaránakute 極まらなくて	kiwamaráni 極まらない	kiwamaránakatta 極まらなかった
kizukáu 気遣う be anxious (about, for)	kizukátte 気遣って	kizukawánakute 気遣わなくて	kizukawána 気遣わない	kizukawánakatta 気遣わなかった
kizúku 築く build, construct	kizúite 築いて	kizukánakute 築かなくて	kizukánai 築かない	kizukánakatta 築かなかった
kobósu 零す spill, drop, spill (milk)	kobóshite 零して	kobosánakute 零さなくて	kobosánai 零さない	kobosánakatta 零さなかった
kogásu 焦がす burn, scorch, singe	kogáshite 焦がして	kogasánakute 焦がさなくて	kogasánai 焦がさない	kogasánakatta 焦がさなかった
kógu 漕ぐ row (boat), paddle	kóide 漕いで	kogánakute 漕がなくて	kogánai 漕がない	kogánakatta 漕がなかった
koinegáu 希う beg, request, entreat	koinegátte 希って	koinegawánakute 希わなくて	koinegawánai 希わない	koinegawánakatta 希わなかった
kokorozásu 志す plan, intend (to go abroad)	kokorozáshite 志して	kokorozasánakute 志さなくて	kokorozasánai 志さない	kokorozasánakatta 志さなかった
komáru 困る be distressed, be troubled	komátte 困って	komaránakute 困らなくて	komaránai 困らない	komaránakatta 困らなかった
kómu 込む be crowded, be packed	kónde 込んで	kománakute 込まなくて	kománai 込まない	kománakatta 込まなかった
kōmúru 蒙る get, receive (a favour)	kōmútte 蒙って	kōmuránakute 蒙らなくて	kōmuránai 蒙らない	kōmuránakatta 蒙らなかった
konómu 好む like, fancy, be fond of	konónde 好んで	konománakute 好まなくて	konománai 好まない	konománakatta 好まなかった
korásu 懲らす chastise, discipline	koráshite 懲らして	korasánakute 懲らさなくて	korasánai 懲らさない	korasánakatta 懲らさなかった

GROUP TWO	SUBORDINATE		NEGATIVE	
	Positive	Negative	Present	Past
kóru 凝る grow stiff, have stiff shoulder	kótte 凝って	koránakute 凝らなくて	koránai 凝らない	koránakatta 凝らなかった
kosúru 擦る rub, scour, scrub	kosútte 擦って	kosuránakute 擦らなくて	kosuránai 擦らない	kosuránakatta 擦らなかった
kotonáru 異なる differ (from), vary	kotonátte 異なって	kotonaránakute 異ならなくて	kotonaránai 異ならない	kotonaránakatta 異ならなかった
kotowáru 断る decline, beg off	kotowátte 断って	kotowaránakute 断らなくて	kotowáraı 断らない	kotowaránakatta 断らなかった
kowagáru 怖がる fear, dread, be scared	kowagátte 怖がって	kowagaránakute 怖がらなくて	kowagáraı 怖がらない	kowagaránakatta 怖がらなかった
kowásu 毀す break, demolish	kowáshite 毀して	kowasánakute 毀さなくて	kowasánai 毀さない	kowasánakatta 毀さなかった
koyásu 肥す manure, fertilize	koyáshite 肥して	koyasánakute 肥さなくて	koyasánai 肥さない	koyasánakatta 肥さなかった
kozúku 小突く poke, thrust, push	kozúite 小突いて	kozukánakute 小突かなくて	kozukánai 小突かない	kozukánakatta 小突かなかった
kubáru 配る distribute, allot	kubátte 配って	kubaránakute 配らなくて	kubaránai 配らない	kubaránakatta 配らなかった
kuchizusámu 口吟む hum (a tune)	kuchizusánde 口吟んで	kuchizusamánakute 口吟まなくて	kuchizusamánai 口吟まない	kuchizusamánakatta 口吟まなかった
kudáku 砕く break (into pieces)	kudáite 砕いて	kudakánakute 砕かなくて	kudakánai 砕かない	kudakánakatta 砕かなかった
kudasáru 下さる give, bestow (on)	kudasátte 下さって	kudasaránakute 下さらなくて	kudasaránai 下さらない	kudasaránakatta 下さらなかった
kugúru 潜る pass through, dive	kugútte 潜って	kuguránakute 潜らなくて	kuguránai 潜らない	kuguránakatta 潜らなかった
kujíku 挫く crush, sprain, wrench	kujíite 挫いて	kujikánakute 挫かなくて	kujikánai 挫かない	kujikánakatta 挫かなかった
kumóru 曇る become cloudy	kumótte 曇って	kumoránakute 曇らなくて	kumoránai 曇らない	kumoránakatta 曇らなかった
kúmu 組む braid, construct	kúnde 組んで	kumánakute 組まなくて	kumánai 組まない	kumánakatta 組まなかった

GROUP TWO	SUBORDINATE		NEGATIVE	
	Positive	Negative	Present	Past
kurumáru くるまる be wrapped up, in	kurumátte くるまって	kurumaránakute くるまらなくて	kurumaránai くるまらない	kurumaránakatta くるまらなかった
kurúmu くるむ wrap (in), tuch up (in)	kurúnde くるんで	kurumánakute くるまなくて	kurumánai くるまない	kurumánakatta くるまなかった
kurushímu 苦しむ suffer (from), feel pain	kurushínde 苦しんで	kurushimánakute 苦しまなくて	kurushimánai 苦しまない	kurushimánakatta 苦しまなかった
kurúu 狂う go mad, lose one's head	kurútte 狂って	kuruwánakute 狂わなくて	kuruwánai 狂わない	kuruwánakatta 狂わなかった
kusáru 腐る rot, decompose, decay	kusátte 腐って	kusaránakute 腐らなくて	kusaránai 腐らない	kusaránakatta 腐らなかった
kusásu くさす speak ill of, decry	kusáshite くさして	kusasánakute くささなくて	kusasánai くささない	kusasánakatta くささなかった
kusubúru 熏ぶる smoke, smolder	kusubútte 熏ぶって	kusuburánakute 熏ぶらなくて	kusuburánai 熏ぶらない	kusuburánakatta 熏ぶらなかった
kuttsúku くつ付く stick to, adher to	kuttsúite くつ付いて	kuttsukánakute くつ付かなくて	kuttsukánai くつ付かない	kuttukánakatta くつ付かなかった
kuwásu 食わす feed, suppart	kuwáshite 食わして	kuwasánakute 食わさなくて	kuwasánai 食わさない	kuwasánakatta 食わさなかった
kuyámu 悔む repent (of), regret	kuyánde 悔んで	kuyamánakute 悔まなくて	kuyamánai 悔まない	kuyamánakatta 悔まなかった
kuyashigáru 口惜しがる be mortified	kuyashigátte 口惜しがって	kuyashigaránakute 口惜しがらなくて	kuyashigaránai 口惜しがらない	kuyashigaránakatta 口惜しがらなかった
kuzúsu 崩す destroy, demolish	kuzúshite 崩して	kuzusánakute 崩さなくて	kuzusánai 崩さない	kuzusánakatta 崩さなかった
mabúsu 塗す cover (something with)	mabúshite 塗して	mabusánakute 塗さなくて	mabusánai 塗さない	mabusánakatta 塗さなかった
machigáu 間違う be mistaken, wrong, incorrect	machigátte 間違って	machigawánakute 間違わなくて	machigawánai 間違わない	machigawánakatta 間違わなかった
madowásu 惑わす puzzle, perplex, mislead	madowáshite 惑わして	madowasánakute 惑わさなくて	madowasánai 惑わさない	madowasánakatta 惑わさなかった
majiwáru 交わる associated with, keep company with	majiwátte 交わって	majiwaránakute 交わらなくて	majiwaránai 交わらない	majiwaránakatta 交わらなかった

GROUP TWO	SUBORDINATE Positive	Negative	NEGATIVE Present	Past
makanáu 賄う board, supply with food	makanátte 賄って	makanawánakute 賄わなくて	makanawánai 賄わない	makanawánakatta 賄わなかった
máku 撒く scatter, sprinkle	máite 撒いて	makánakute 撒かなくて	makánai 撒かない	makánakatta 撒かなかった
máku 蒔く sow (seeds)	máite 蒔いて	makánakute 蒔かなくて	makánai 蒔かない	makánakatta 蒔かなかった
mamóru 守る protect, defend, watch (over)	mamótte 守って	mamoránakute 守らなくて	mamoránai 守らない	mamoránakatta 守らなかった
manéku 招く invite, beckon (to)	manéite 招いて	manekánakute 招かなくて	manekánai 招かない	manekánakatta 招かなかった
masáru 勝る surpass, excel, be better than	masátte 勝って	masaránakute 勝らなくて	masaránai 勝らない	masaránakatta 勝らなかった
matagáru 跨る get astride (of a horse)	matagátte 跨って	matagaránakute 跨らなくて	matagaránai 跨らない	matagaránakatta 跨らなかった
matágu 跨ぐ bestride, straddle	matáide 跨いで	matagánakute 跨がなくて	matagánai 跨がない	matagánakatta 跨がなかった
mátsu 待つ wait, watch for	mátte 待って	matánakute 待たなくて	matánai 待たない	matánakatta 待たなかった
mayóu 迷う be puzzled, be at a loss	mayótte 迷って	mayowánakute 迷わなくて	mayowánai 迷わない	mayowánakatta 迷わなかった
mayowásu 迷わす puzzle, bewilder	mayowáshite 迷わして	mayowasánakute 迷わさなくて	mayowasánai 迷わさない	mayowasánakatta 迷わさなかった
medátsu 目立つ be conspicuous, be attractive	medátte 目立って	medatánakute 目立たなくて	medatánai 目立たない	medatánakute 目立たなかった
megúmu 芽ぐむ bud, sprout, put forth shoots	megúnde 芽ぐんで	megumánakute 芽ぐまなくて	megumánai 芽ぐまない	megumánakatta 芽ぐまなかった
megurásu 回らす enclose (with, in)	meguráshite 回らして	megurasánakute 回らさなくて	megurasánai 回らさない	megurasánakatta 回らさなかった
mekásu めかす primp, deck up	mekáshite めかして	mekasánakute めかさなくて	mekasánai めかさない	mekasánakatta めかさなかった
metóru 娶る marry (a woman)	metótte 娶って	metoránakute 娶らなくて	metoránai 娶らない	metoránakatta 娶らなかった

GROUP TWO	SUBORDINATE		NEGATIVE	
	Positive	Negative	Present	Past
mezásu	mezáshite	mezasánakute	mezasánai	mezasánakatta
目指す	目指して	目指さなくて	目指さない	目指さなかった
aim at, have an eye to				
michibíku 導く	michibíite	michibikánakute	michibikánai	michibikánakatta
guide, lead	導いて	導かなくて	導かない	導かなかった
midásu	midáshite	midasánakute	midasánai	midasánakatta
乱す	乱して	乱さなくて	乱さない	乱さなかった
put out of order				
míru 見る	míte	mínakute	mínai	mínakatta
see, look at	見て	見なくて	見ない	見なかった
mitásu 満たす	mitáshite	mitasánakute	mitasánai	mitasánakatta
fill (up), supply	満たして	満たさなくて	満たさない	満たさなかった
modóru	modótte	modoránakute	modoránai	modoránakatta
戻る	戻って	戻らなくて	戻らない	戻らなかった
go (come) back, turn back				
modósu 戻す	modóshite	modosánakute	modosánai	modosánakatta
return, put back 戻して	戻さなくて	戻さない	戻さなかった
mogáku	mogáite	mogakánakute	mogakánai	mogakánakatta
踠く	踠いて	踠かなくて	踠かない	踠かなかった
struggle, wriggle				
mógu	móide	mogánakute	mogánai	mogánakatta
捥ぐ	捥いで	捥がなくて	捥がない	捥がなかった
wrest from, break off				
mogúru 潜る	mogútte	moguránakute	moguránai	moguránakatta
dive into water 潜って	潜らなくて	潜らない	潜らなかった
morásu	moráshite	morasánakute	morasánai	morasánakatta
洩らす	洩らして	洩らさなくて	洩らさない	洩らさなかった
let leak, give exit to (steam)				
móru 洩る	mótte	moránakute	moránai	moránakatta
leak, be leaky 洩って	洩らなくて	洩らない	洩らなかった
motarásu	motaráshite	motarasánakute	motarasánai	motarasánakatta
齎す	齎して	齎さなくて	齎さない	齎さなかった
bring, bring about (on)				
motozúku	motozúite	motozukánakute	motozukánai	motozukánakatta
基く	基いて	基かなくて	基かない	基かなかった
be based on, be founded on				
mótsu 持つ	mótte	motánakute	motánai	motánakatta
have, hold, take 持って	持たなくて	持たない	持たなかった
mukúmu	mukúnde	mukumánakute	mukumánai	mukumánakatta
むくむ	むくんで	むくまなくて	むくまない	むくまなかった
swell, become swollen				
músu	múshite	musánakute	musánai	musánakatta
蒸す	蒸して	蒸さなくて	蒸さない	蒸さなかった
steam, heat with steam				

| GROUP TWO | SUBORDINATE | | NEGATIVE | |
	Positive	Negative	Present	Past
nabíku	nabíite	nabikánakute	nabikánai	nabikánakatta
靡く	靡いて	靡かなくて	靡かない	靡かなかった
flutter, wave, stream				
nabúru	nabútte	naburánakute	naburánai	naburánakatta
なぶる	なぶって	なぶらなくて	なぶらない	なぶらなかった
play with, ridicule				
nagabíku	nagabíite	nagabikánakute	nagabikánai	nagabikánakatta
長引く	長引いて	長引かなくて	長引かない	長引かなかった
be prolonged, drag on				
nagásu	nagáshite	nagasánakute	nagasánai	nagasánakatta
流す	流して	流さなくて	流さない	流さなかった
dash, pour, let flow				
nagéku	nagéite	nagekánakute	nagekánai	nagekánakatta
嘆く	嘆いて	嘆かなくて	嘆かない	嘆かなかった
sigh, be grieved				
nágu	náide	nagánakute	nagánai	nagánakatta
凪ぐ	凪いで	凪がなくて	凪がない	凪がなかった
become calm (of wind)				
nagúru	nagútte	naguránakute	naguránai	naguránakatta
殴る	殴って	殴らなくて	殴らない	殴らなかった
beat, strike, knock				
najímu	najínde	najimánakute	najimánai	najimánakatta
馴染む	馴染んで	馴染まなくて	馴染まない	馴染まなかった
become familiar				
namáru	namátte	namaránakute	namaránai	namaránakatta
訛る	訛って	訛らなくて	訛らない	訛らなかった
speak with an accent				
naóru	naótte	naoránakute	naoránai	naoránakatta
直る	直って	直らなくて	直らない	直らなかった
recover (from illness)				
naósu	naóshite	naosánakute	naosánai	naosánakatta
直す	直して	直さなくて	直さない	直さなかった
repair, mend, put in order				
narásu	naráshite	narasánakute	narasánai	narasánakatta
馴らす	馴らして	馴らさなくて	馴らさない	馴らさなかった
tame, domesticate				
narásu 均す	naráshite	narasánakute	narasánai	narasánakatta
level (off, over)	均して	均さなくて	均さない	均さなかった
naráu	narátte	narawánakute	narawánai	narawánakatta
習う	習って	習わなくて	習わない	習わなかった
learn, study, be taught				
naráu	narátte	narawánakute	narawánai	narawánakatta
倣う	倣って	倣わなくて	倣わない	倣わなかった
imitate, emulate (a person)				

GROUP TWO	SUBORDINATE		NEGATIVE	
	Positive	Negative	Present	Past
náru なる become, be	nátte なって	naránakute ならなくて	naránai ならない	naránakatta ならなかった
náru なる bear (fruit,) grow (on a tree)	nátte なって	naránakute ならなくて	naránai ならない	naránakatta ならなかった
násu 為す do, practice	náshite 為して	nasánakute 為さなくて	nasánai 為さない	nasánakatta 為さなかった
nasúru 擦る rub on, spread over	nasútte 擦って	nasuránakute 擦らなくて	nasuránai 擦らない	nasuránakatta 擦らなかった
nayamásu 悩ます afflict, torment	nayamáshite 悩まして	nayamasánakute 悩まさなくて	nayamasánai 悩まさない	nayamasánakatta 悩まさなかった
nayámu 悩む be troubled with	nayánde 悩んで	nayamánakute 悩まなくて	nayamánai 悩まない	nayamánakatta 悩まなかった
nebáru 粘る be sticky, be adhesive	nebátte 粘って	nebaránakute 粘らなくて	nebaránai 粘らない	nebaránakatta 粘らなかった
negáu 願う request, beg	negátte 願って	negawánakute 願わなくて	negawánai 願わない	negawánakatta 願わなかった
nekómu 寝込む fall (fast) asleep	nekónde 寝込んで	nekománakute 寝込まなくて	nekománai 寝込まない	nekománakatta 寝込まなかった
néru 練る knead (dough)	nétte 練って	neránakute 練らなくて	neránai 練らない	neránakatta 練らなかった
netámu 妬む be jealous of	netánde 妬んで	netamánakute 妬まなくて	netamánai 妬まない	netamánakatta 妬まなかった
nibúru 鈍る become dull, blunt	nibútte 鈍って	niburánakute 鈍らなくて	niburánai 鈍らない	niburánakatta 鈍らなかった
nigásu 逃がす let go, let escape	nigáshite 逃がして	nigasánakute 逃がさなくて	nigasánai 逃がさない	nigasánakatta 逃がさなかった
nigiwáu 賑わう be prosperous, thrive	nigiwátte 賑わって	nigiwawánakute 賑わわなくて	nigiwawánai 賑わわない	nigiwawánakatta 賑わわなかった
nigóru 濁る become muddy (turbid)	nigótte 濁って	nigoránakute 濁らなくて	nigoránai 濁らない	nigoránakatta 濁らなかった
nigósu 濁す make (water) muddy	nigóshite 濁して	nigosánakute 濁さなくて	nigosánai 濁さない	nigosánakatta 濁さなかった
nijímu 滲む blot, spread, smudge	nijínde 滲んで	nijimánakute 滲まなくて	nijimánai 滲まない	nijimánakatta 滲まなかった

GROUP TWO	SUBORDINATE		NEGATIVE	
	Positive	Negative	Present	Past
nikúmu 憎む hate, detest, abominate	nikúnde 憎んで	nikumánakute 憎まなくて	nikumánai 憎まない	nikumánakatta 憎まなかった
nináu 担う carry on one's shoulder	ninátte 担って	ninawánakute 担わなくて	ninawánai 担わない	ninawánakatta 担わなかった
nióu 匂う smell, scent, be fragrant	niótte 匂って	niowánakute 匂わなくて	niowánai 匂わない	niowánakatta 匂わなかった
nirámu 睨む glare at, scowl at	niránde 睨んで	niramánakute 睨まなくて	niramánai 睨まない	niramánakatta 睨まなかった
nobásu 延ばす lengthen, postpone	nobáshite 延ばして	nobasánakute 延ばさなくて	nobasánai 延ばさない	nobasánakatta 延ばさなかった
nokóru 残る be left over, remain	nokótte 残って	nokoránakute 残らなくて	nokoránai 残らない	nokoránakatta 残らなかった
nokósu 残す leave, keep back	nokóshite 残して	nokosánakute 残さなくて	nokosánai 残さない	nokosánakatta 残さなかった
noméru のめる fall (tumble) foward	nométte のめって	nomeránakute のめらなくて	nomeránai のめらない	nomeránakatta のめらなかった
nómu 飲む drink, swallow, gulp down	nónde 飲んで	nománakute 飲まなくて	nománai 飲まない	nománakatta 飲まなかった
nonoshíru 罵る speak ill of, use abusive language	nonoshítte 罵って	nonoshiránakute 罵らなくて	nonoshiránai 罵らない	nonoshiránakatta 罵らなかった
noróu 呪う curse, utter curses against	norótte 呪って	norowánakute 呪わなくて	norowánai 呪わない	norowánakatta 呪わなかった
nosabáru のさばる have things one's own way	nosabátte のさばって	nosabaránakute のさばらなくて	nosabaránai のさばらない	nosabaránakatta のさばらなかった
núgu 脱ぐ take off (shoes)	núide 脱いで	nugánakute 脱がなくて	nugánai 脱がない	nugánakatta 脱がなかった
nugúu 拭う wipe, mop	nugútte 拭って	nuguwánakute 拭わなくて	nuguwánai 拭わない	nuguwánakatta 拭わなかった
nukazúku 額づく bow, kotow	nukazúite 額づいて	nukazukánakute 額づかなくて	nukazukánai 額づかない	nukazukánakatta 額づかなかった
nurúmu ぬるむ become tepid	nurúnde ぬるんで	nurumánakute ぬるまなくて	nurumánai ぬるまない	nurumánakatta ぬるまなかった

GROUP TWO	SUBORDINATE		NEGATIVE	
	Positive	Negative	Present	Past
nusúmu 盗む steal, rob, purloin	nusúnde 盗んで	nusumánakute 盗まなくて	nusumánai 盗まない	nusumánakatta 盗まなかった
núu 縫う sew, stitch	nútte 縫って	nuwánakute 縫わなくて	nuwánai 縫わない	nuwánakatta 縫わなかった
obusáru 負ぶさる ride on one's back	obusátte 負ぶさって	obusaránakute 負ぶさらなくて	obusaránai 負ぶさらない	obusaránakatta 負ぶさらなかった
obúu 負ぶう take (something) on one's back	obútte 負ぶって	obuwánakute 負ぶわなくて	obuwánai 負ぶわない	obuwánakatta 負ぶわなかった
odorokásu 驚かす surprise, astonish	odorokáshite 驚かして	odorokasánakute 驚かさなくて	odorokasánai 驚かさない	odorokasánakatta 驚かさなかった
odoróku 驚く be surprised, astonished	odoróite 驚いて	odorokánakute 驚かなくて	odorokánai 驚かない	odorokánakatta 驚かなかった
ogámu 拝む worship, do reverence to	ogánde 拝んで	ogamánakute 拝まなくて	ogamánai 拝まない	ogamánakatta 拝まなかった
okásu 犯す commit, perpetrate	okáshite 犯して	okasánakute 犯さなくて	okasánai 犯さない	okasánakatta 犯さなかった
okóru 怒る be offended, get angry	okótte 怒って	okoránakute 怒らなくて	okoránai 怒らない	okoránakatta 怒らなかった
okóru 起る happen, come to pass	okótte 起って	okoránakute 起らなくて	okoránai 起らない	okoránakatta 起らなかった
okósu 興す revive, resuscitate	okóshite 興して	okosánakute 興さなくて	okosánai 興さない	okosánakatta 興さなかった
okósu 起す wake up, awaken	okóshite 起して	okosánakute 起さなくて	okosánai 起さない	okosánakatta 起さなかった
omóu 思う think, believe	omótte 思って	omowánakute 思わなくて	omowánai 思わない	omowánakatta 思わなかった
orósu 下ろす take down, lower	oróshite 下ろして	orosánakute 下ろさなくて	orosánai 下ろさない	orosánakatta 下ろさなかった
óru 織る weave	ótte 織って	oránakute 織らなくて	oránai 織らない	oránakatta 織らなかった
osamáru 納まる be paid, be restored	osamátte 納まって	osamaránakute 納まらなくて	osamaránai 納まらない	osamaránakatta 納まらなかった

GROUP TWO	SUBORDINATE		NEGATIVE	
	Positive	Negative	Present	Past
ossháru 仰しゃる say, tell, talk	osshátte 仰しゃって	ossharánakute 仰しゃらなくて	ossharánai 仰しゃらない	ossharánakatta 仰しゃらなかった
otóru 劣る be inferior to, be worse than	otótte 劣って	otoránakute 劣らなくて	otoránai 劣らない	otoránakatta 劣らなかった
otósu 落す drop, let fall	otóshite 落して	otosánakute 落さなくて	otosánai 落さない	otosánakatta 落さなかった
oyógu 泳ぐ swim, sail	oyóide 泳いで	oyogánakute 泳がなくて	oyogánai 泳がない	oyogánakatta 泳がなかった
rikímu 力む strain oneself	rikínde 力んで	rikimánakute 力まなくて	rikimánai 力まない	rikimánakatta 力まなかった
sabáku 裁く judge, decide (on a case)	sabáite 裁いて	sabakánakute 裁かなくて	sabakánai 裁かない	sabakánakatta 裁かなかった
sabishigáru 寂し がる feel lonely	sabishigátte 寂しがって	sabishigaránakute 寂しがらなくて	sabishigaránai 寂しがらない	sabishigaránakatta 寂しがらなかった
sadamáru 定まる be decided, be determined	sadamátte 定まって	sadamaránakute 定まらなくて	sadamaránai 定まらない	sadamaránakatta 定まらなかった
saegíru 遮る interrupt (a person)	saegítte 遮って	saegiránakute 遮らなくて	saegiránai 遮らない	saegiránakatta 遮らなかった
saezúru 囀る sing, chirp	saezútte 囀って	saezuránakute 囀らなくて	saezuránai 囀らない	saezuránakatta 囀らなかった
sagáru 下がる hang down, pend, dangle	sagátte 下がって	sagaránakute 下がらなくて	sagaránai 下がらない	sagaránakatta 下がらなかった
sakanobóru 溯る go upstream, ascend (a river)	sakanobótte 溯って	sakanoboránakute 溯らなくて	sakanoboránai 溯らない	sakanoboránakatta 溯らなかった
sakaráu 逆らう oppose, go against (the will of)	sakarátte 逆らって	sakarawánakute 逆らわなくて	sakarawánai 逆らわない	sakarawánakatta 逆らわなかった
sakébu 叫ぶ shout, cry, exclaim	sakénde 叫んで	sakebánakute 叫ばなくて	sakebánai 叫ばない	sakebánakatta 叫ばなかった
sáku 裂く tear, rend, split	sáite 裂いて	sakánakute 裂かなくて	sakáai 裂かない	sakánakatta 裂かなかった
samásu 覚ます awake, undeceive	samáshite 覚まして	samasánakute 覚まさなくて	samasánai 覚まさない	samasánakatta 覚まさなかった
samayóu 彷徨う wander about	samayótte 彷徨って	samayowánakute 彷徨わなくて	samayowánai 彷徨わない	samayowánakatta 彷徨わなかった

GROUP TWO	SUBORDINATE		NEGATIVE	
	Positive	Negative	Present	Past
samugáru 寒がる complain of the cold	samugátte 寒がって	samugaránakute 寒がらなくて	samugaránai 寒がらない	samugaránakatta 寒がらなかった
sáru 去る leave, go away	sátte 去って	saránakute 去らなくて	saránai 去らない	saránakatta 去らなかった
sasayáku 囁く whisper, murmur	sasayáite 囁いて	sasayakánakute 囁かなくて	sasayakánai 囁かない	sasayakánakatta 囁かなかった
sásu 刺す pierce, thrust	sáshite 刺して	sasánakute 刺さなくて	sasánai 刺さない	sasánakatta 刺さなかった
sasuráu さすらう wander, roam	sasurátte さすらって	sasurawánakute さすらわなくて	sasurawánai さすらわない	sasurawánakatta さすらわなかった
sawagásu 騒がす disturb, perturb	sawagáshite 騒がして	sawagasánakute 騒がさなくて	sawagasánai 騒がさない	sawagasánakatta 騒がさなかった
sawágu 騒ぐ make a noise	sawáide 騒いで	sawagánakute 騒がなくて	sawagánai 騒がない	sawagánakatta 騒がなかった
sekásu 急かす hurry, rush v. tr.	sekáshite 急かして	sekasánakute 急かさなくて	sekasánai 急かさない	sekasánakatta 急かさなかった
séku 急く hurry, hasten	séite 急いて	sekánakute 急かなくて	sekánai 急かない	sekánakatta 急かなかった
semáru 迫る press, urge (a person to do)	semátte 迫って	semaránakute 迫らなくて	semaránai 迫らない	semaránakatta 迫らなかった
séru 競る compete, make a bid	sétte 競って	seránakute 競らなくて	seránai 競らない	seránakatta 競らなかった
shabéru 喋る chat, talk, gabble	shabétte 喋って	shaberánakute 喋らなくて	shaberánai 喋らない	shaberánakatta 喋らなかった
shakúru しゃくる scoop, dip, ladle	shakútte しゃくって	shakuránakute しゃくらなくて	shakuránai しゃくらない	shakuránakatta しゃくらなかった
shibáru 縛る bind, tie, fasten	shibátte 縛って	shibaránakute 縛らなくて	shibaránai 縛らない	shibaránakatta 縛らなかった
shibóru 絞る wring, squeeze	shibótte 絞って	shiboránakute 絞らなくて	shiboránai 絞らない	shiboránakatta 絞らなかった
shibúru 渋る hang back	shibútte 渋って	shiburánakute 渋らなくて	shiburánai 渋らない	shiburánakatta 渋らなかった
shigéru 繁る grow thick, be luxuriant	shigétte 繁って	shigeránakute 繁らなくて	shigeránai 繁らない	shigeránakatta 繁らなかった

GROUP TWO	SUBORDINATE		NEGATIVE	
	Positive	Negative	Present	Past
shikómu 仕込む train, bring up, breed	shikónde 仕込んで	shikománakute 仕込まなくて	shikománai 仕込まない	shikománakatta 仕込まなかった
shikujíru しくじ る fail, blunder	shikujítte しくじって	shikujiránakute しくじらなくて	shikujiránai しくじらない	shikujiránakatta しくじらなかった
shikúmu 仕組む contrive, scheme	shikúnde 仕組んで	shikumánakute 仕組まなくて	shikumánai 仕組まない	shikumánakatta 仕組まなかった
shimáru 締まる be shut, tighten	shimátte 締まって	shimaránakute 締まらなくて	shimaránai 締まらない	shimaránakatta 締まらなかった
shinógu 凌ぐ endure, bear	shinóide 凌いで	shinogánakute 凌がなくて	shinogánai 凌がない	shinogánakatta 凌がなかった
shirámu 白む grow light, turn gray	shiránde 白んで	shiramánakute 白まなくて	shiramánai 白まない	shiramánakatta 白まなかった
shirizóku 退く retreat, recede	shirizóite 退いて	shirizokánakute 退かなくて	shirizokánai 退かない	shirizokánakatta 退かなかった
shitagáu 従う obey (an order, a person)	shitagátte 従って	shitagawánakute 従わなくて	shitagawánai 従わない	shitagawánakatta 従わなかった
shitashímu 親しむ grow intimate with	shitashínde 親しんで	shitashimánakute 親しまなくて	shitashimánai 親しまない	shitashimánakatta 親しまなかった
shizumáru 静まる become quiet, calm down	shizumátte 静まって	shizumaránakute 静まらなくて	shizumaránai 静まらない	shizumaránakatta 静まらなかった
sógu 殺ぐ chip, slice off	sóide 殺いで	sogánakute 殺がなくて	sogánai 殺がない	sogánakatta 殺がなかった
somúku 背く go against (one's principles)	somúite 背いて	somukánakute 背かなくて	somukánai 背かない	somukánakatta 背かなかった
sorásu 逸らす turn (one's eyes)	soráshite 逸らして	sorasánakute 逸らさなくて	sorasánai 逸らさない	sorasánakatta 逸らさなかった
soróu 揃ふ become complete	sorótte 揃って	sorowánakute 揃わなくて	sorowánai 揃わない	sorowánakatta 揃わなかった
soyógu そよぐ rustle, sway, swing	soyóide そよいで	soyogánakute そよがなくて	soyogánai そよがない	soyogánakatta そよがなかった
suberásu 滑らす let slip	suberáshite 滑らして	suberasánakute 滑らさなくて	suberasánai 滑らさない	suberasánakatta 滑らさなかった
subéru 滑る slide, glide	subétte 滑って	suberánakute 滑らなくて	suberánai 滑らない	suberánakatta 滑らなかった

GROUP TWO	SUBORDINATE Positive	SUBORDINATE Negative	NEGATIVE Present	NEGATIVE Past
sugómu 凄む scare with violence	sugónde 凄んで	sugománakute 凄まなくて	sugomána 凄まない	sugománakatta 凄まなかった
sugósu 過ごす pass, spend	sugóshite 過ごして	sugosánakute 過ごさなくて	sugosánai 過ごさない	sugosánakatta 過ごさなかった
sumásu 済ます finish, conclude	sumáshite 済まして	sumasánakute 済まさなくて	sumasánai 済まさない	sumasánakatta 済まさなかった
súmu 済む end, terminate, be concluded	súnde 済んで	sumánakute 済まなくて	sumánai 済まない	sumánakatta 済まなかった
súmu 住む live, dwell, reside	súnde 住んで	sumánakute 住まなくて	sumánai 住まない	sumánakatta 住まなかった
súru 刷る print, put in print	sútte 刷って	suránakute 刷らなくて	suránai 刷らない	suránakatta 刷らなかった
tadásu 正す correct, rectify (an error)	tadáshite 正して	tadasánakute 正さなくて	tadasánai 正さない	tadasánakatta 正さなかった
tadóru 辿る follow (a road), trace (a path)	tadótte 辿って	tadoránakute 辿らなくて	tadoránai 辿らない	tadoránakatta 辿らなかった
tagáu 違う differ (from), vary	tagátte 違って	tagawánakute 違わなくて	tagawánai 違わない	tagawánakatta 違わなかった
tagayásu 耕す till, plow, cultivate	tagayáshite 耕して	tagayasánakute 耕さなくて	tagayasánai 耕さない	tagayasánakatta 耕さなかった
tagúru 手繰る draw in, reel in	tagútte 手繰って	taguránakute 手繰らなくて	taguránai 手繰らない	taguránakatta 手繰らなかった
takabúru 高ぶる be proud, be haughty	takabútte 高ぶって	takaburánakute 高ぶらなくて	takaburánai 高ぶらない	takaburánakatta 高ぶらなかった
takamáru 高まる rise, be raised, swell	takamátte 高まって	takamaránakute 高まらなくて	takamaránai 高まらない	takamaránakatta 高まらなかった
takurámu 企らむ scheme, plan, contrive	takuránde 企らんで	takuramánakute 企らまなくて	takuramánai 企らまない	takuramánakatta 企らまなかった

| GROUP TWO | SUBORDINATE | | NEGATIVE | |
	Positive	Negative	Present	Past
tameráu ためらう hesitate, waver	tamerátte ためらって	tamerawánakute ためらわなくて	tamerawánai ためらわない	tamerawánakatta ためらわなかった
tamesu 試す try, attempt, test	taméshite 試して	tamesánakute 試さなくて	tamesánai 試さない	tamesánakatta 試さなかった
tanómu 頼む beg, ask, request	tanónde 頼んで	tanománakute 頼まなくて	tanománai 頼まない	tanománakatta 頼まなかった
tanoshímu 楽しむ take pleasure in	tanoshínde 楽しんで	tanoshimánakute 楽しまなくて	tanoshimánai 楽しまない	tanoshimánakatta 楽しまなかった
taósu 倒す bring down, level	taóshite 倒して	taosánakute 倒さなくて	taosánai 倒さない	taosánakatta 倒さなかった
tarasu 滴らす drop, let drop 滴らして	taráshite	tarasánakute 滴らさなくて	tarasánai 滴らさない	tarasánakatta 滴らさなかった
tashinámu 嗜む have a taste for, like	tashinánde 嗜んで	tashinamánakute 嗜まなくて	tashinamánai 嗜まない	tashinamánakatta 嗜まなかった
tasukáru 助かる be saved, survive (disaster)	tasukátte 助かって	tasukaránakute 助からなくて	tasukaránai 助からない	tasukaránakatta 助からなかった
tatáku 叩く strike, beat, knock	tatáite 叩いて	tatakánakute 叩かなくて	tatakánai 叩かない	tatakánakatta 叩かなかった
tatáru 祟る bring evil upon	tatátte 祟って	tataránakute 祟らなくて	tataránai 祟らない	tataránakatta 祟らなかった
tatazúmu 佇む stand for a while, linger	tatazúnde 佇んで	tatazumánakute 佇まなくて	tatazumánai 佇まない	tatazumánakatta 佇まなかった
tatematsúru 奉る offer, present	tatematsútte 奉って	tatematsuránakute 奉らなくて	tatematsuránai 奉らない	tatematsuránakatta 奉らなかった
tátsu 立つ stand up, rise	tátte 立って	tatánakute 立たなくて	tatánai 立たない	tatánakatta 立たなかった
tattóbu 貴ぶ value, set a value on	tattónde 貴んで	tattobánakute 貴ばなくて	tattóbanai 貴ばない	tattobánakatta 貴ばなかった
tayásu 絶やす exterminate, extirpate	tayáshite 絶やして	tayasánakute 絶やさなくて	tayasánai 絶やさない	tayasánakatta 絶やさなかった
tayóru 頼る rely on, place confidence on	tayótte 頼って	tayoránakute 頼らなくて	tayoránai 頼らない	tayoránakatta 頼らなかった

GROUP TWO	SUBORDINATE Positive	Negative	NEGATIVE Present	Past
tebanásu 手放す let go one's hold	tebanáshite 手放して	tebanasánakute 手放さなくて	tebanasánai 手放さない	tebanasánakatta 手放さなかった
tekozúru 手古ずる not to know what to do with	tekozútte 手古ずって	tekozuránakute 手古ずらなくて	tekozuránai 手古ずらない	tekozuránakatta 手古ずらなかった
temadóru 手間取る take time, be delayed	temadótte 手間取って	temadoránakute 手間取らなくて	temadoránai 手間取らない	temadoránakatta 手間取らなかった
terásu 照らす shine on, light on	teráshite 照らして	terasánakute 照らさなくて	terasánai 照らさない	terasánakatta 照らさなかった
téru 照る shine, blaze away	tétte 照って	teránakute 照らなくて	teránai 照らない	teránakatta 照らなかった
tetsudáu 手伝う assist, help	tetsudátte 手伝って	tetsudawánakute 手伝わなくて	tetsudawánai 手伝わない	tetsudawánakatta 手伝わなかった
todóku 届く reach, attain to	todóite 届いて	todokánakute 届かなくて	todokánai 届かない	todokánakatta 届かなかった
todorokásu 轟かす let resound all over	todorokáshite 轟かして	todorokasánakute 轟かさなくて	todorokasánai 轟かさない	todorokasánakatta 轟かさなかった
todoróku 轟く roar, peal	todoróite 轟いて	todorokánakute 轟かなくて	todorokánai 轟かない	todorokánakatta 轟かなかった
togarásu 尖らす sharpen, point	togaráshite 尖らして	togarasánakute 尖らさなくて	togarasánai 尖らさない	togarasánakatta 尖らさなかった
togáru 尖る be pointed, sharp	togátte 尖って	togaránakute 尖らなくて	togaránai 尖らない	togaránakatta 尖らなかった
tokásu 溶かす melt, dissolve	tokáshite 溶かして	tokasánakute 溶かさなくて	tokasánai 溶かさない	tokasánakatta 溶かさなかった
tóku 解く untie, unsew	tóite 解いて	tokánakute 解かなくて	tokánai 解かない	tokánakatta 解かなかった
tomonáu 伴なう accompany, go with	tomonátte 伴なって	tomonawánakute 伴なわなくて	tomonawánai 伴なわない	tomonawánakatta 伴なわなかった
tómu 富む be rich, abound in	tónde 富んで	tománakute 富まなくて	tománai 富まない	tománakatta 富まなかった
tomuráu 弔う mourn (for the dead)	tomurátte 弔って	tomurawánakute 弔わなくて	tomurawánai 弔わない	tomurawánakatta 弔わなかった
tóru 取る take, seize	tótte 取って	toránakute 取らなくて	toránai 取らない	toránakatta 取らなかった

GROUP TWO	SUBORDINATE		NEGATIVE	
	Positive	Negative	Present	Past
totonóu 整う be prepared, be ready	totonótte 整って	totonowánakute 整わなくて	totonowánai 整わない	totonowánakatta 整わなかった
tsudóu 集う gather, collect	tsudótte 集って	tsudowánakute 集わなくて	tsudowánai 集わない	tsudowánakatta 集わなかった
tsubomáru 窄ま る shut, close	tsubomátte 窄まって	tsubomaránakute 窄まらなくて	tsubomaránai 窄まらない	tsubomaránakatta 窄まらなかった
tsubuyáku 呟く mutter (to oneself)	tsubuyáite 呟いて	tsubuyakánakute 呟かなくて	tsubuyakánai 呟かない	tsubuyakánakatta 呟かなかった
tsukámu 掴む seize, catch	tsukánde 掴んで	tsukamánakute 掴まなくて	tsukamánai 掴まない	tsukamánakatta 掴まなかった
tsukasadóru 司る rule, govern	tsukasadótte 司って	tsukasadoránakute 司らなくて	tsukasadoránai 司らない	tsukasadoránakatta 司らなかった
tsukuróu 繕う repair, mend, patch up	tsukurótte 繕って	tsukurowánakute 繕わなくて	tsukurowánai 繕わない	tsukurowánakatta 繕わなかった
tsukúru 作る make, create	tsukútte 作って	tsukuránakute 作らなくて	tsukuránai 作らない	tsukuránakatta 作らなかった
tsukúsu 尽す exhaust, render	tsukúshite 尽して	tsukusánakute 尽さなくて	tsukusánai 尽さない	tsukusánakatta 尽さなかった
tsumáru 詰まる be stopped up, be full	tsumátte 詰まって	tsumaránakute 詰まらなくて	tsumaránai 詰まらない	tsumaránakatta 詰まらなかった
tsumúgu 紡ぐ spin, make yarn	tsumúide 紡いで	tsumugánakute 紡がなくて	tsumugánai 紡がない	tsumugánakatta 紡がなかった
tsunóru 募る raise (subscription)	tsunótte 募って	tsunoránakute 募らなくて	tsunoránai 募らない	tsunoránakatta 募らなかった
tsuranúku 貫く pierce, penetrate	tsuranúite 貫いて	tsuranukánakute 貫かなくて	tsuranukánai 貫かない	tsuranukánakatta 貫かなかった
tsutomáru 勤ま る be fit for	tsutomátte 勤まって	tsutomaránakute 勤まらなくて	tsutomaránai 勤まらない	tsutomaránakatta 勤まらなかった
tsutsúku つつく pick (at), poke (at)	tsutsúite つついて	tsutsukánakute つつかなくて	tsutsukánai つつかない	tsutsukánakatta つつかなかった
tsutsúmu 包む wrap, cover	tsutsúnde 包んで	tsutsumánakute 包まなくて	tsutsumánai 包まない	tsutsumánakatta 包まなかった
tsutsushímu 慎む be discreet, be cautious	tsutsushínde 慎んで	tsutsushimánakute 慎まなくて	tsutsushimánai 慎まない	tsutsushimánakatta 慎まなかった

GROUP TWO	SUBORDINATE		NEGATIVE	
	Positive	Negative	Present	Past
ubáu 奪う take (by force)	ubátte 奪って	ubawánakute 奪わなくて	ubawánai 奪わない	ubawánakatta 奪わなかった
udáru 茹だる be boiled	udátte 茹だって	udaránakute 茹だらなくて	udaránai 茹だらない	udaránakatta 茹だらなかった
ugátsu 穿つ dig, cut through, pierce	ugátte 穿って	ugatánakute 穿たなくて	ugatánai 穿たない	ugatánakatta 穿たなかった
ugokásu 動かす move, remove	ugokáshite 動かして	ugokasánakute 動かさなくて	ugokasánai 動かさない	ugokasánakatta 動かさなかった
uketamawáru 承る hear, listen to	uketamawátte 承って	uketamawaránaku- te 承らなくて	uketamawará- nai 承らない	uketamawaránakat- ta 承らなかった
uméku 呻く groan, moan	uméite 呻いて	umekánakute 呻かなくて	umekánai 呻かない	umekánakatta 呻かなかった
úmu 膿む form pus, suppurate	únde 膿んで	umánakute 膿まなくて	umánai 膿まない	umánakatta 膿まなかった
unagásu 促す urge, press, demand	unagáshite 促して	unagasánakute 促さなくて	unagasánai 促さない	unagasánakatta 促さなかった
unáru 唸る groan, moan	unátte 唸って	unaránakute 唸らなくて	unaránai 唸らない	unaránakatta 唸らなかった
unazúku うなずく nod, bow in assent	unazúite うなずいて	unazukánakute うなずかなくて	unazukánai うなずかない	unazukánakatta うなずかなかった
unéru うねる undulate, meander	unétte うねって	uneránakute うねらなくて	uneránai うねらない	uneránakatta うねらなかった
uragíru 裏切る betray, turn traitor	uragítte 裏切って	uragiránakute 裏切らなくて	uragiránai 裏切らない	uragiranakatta 裏切らなかった
urámu 怨む feel resentment at (something)	uránde 怨んで	uramánakute 怨まなくて	uramánai 怨まない	uramánakatta 怨まなかった
urayámu 羨む envy, be jealous of	urayánde 羨んで	urayamánakute 羨まなくて	urayamánai 羨まない	urayamanakatta 羨まなかった
urúmu 潤む be wet, be dimmed	urúnde 潤んで	urumánakute 潤まなくて	urumánai 潤まない	urumánakatta 潤まなかった
uruóu 潤う be moistened	uruótte 潤って	uruowánakute 潤わなくて	uruowánai 潤わない	uruowánakatta 潤わなかった
usobúku 嘯く roar, howl	usobúite 嘯いて	usobukánakute 嘯かなくて	usobukánai 嘯かない	usobukánakatta 嘯かなかった

| GROUP TWO | SUBORDINATE | | NEGATIVE | |
	Positive	Negative	Present	Past
utómu 疎む neglect, treat coldly	utónde 疎んで	utománakute 疎まなくて	utománai 疎まない	utománakatta 疎まなかった
útsu 打つ strike, hit	útte 打って	utánakute 打たなくて	utánai 打たない	utánakatta 打たなかった
utsúru 移る remove (to a place)	utsútte 移って	utsuránakute 移らなくて	utsuránai 移らない	utsuránakatta 移らなかった
utsúsu 移す remove (to, into), transfer	utsúshite 移す	utsusánakute 移さなくて	utsusánai 移さない	utsusánakatta 移さなかった
wakáru 解る understand, make out	wakátte 解って	wakaránakute 解らなくて	wakaránai 解らない	wakaránakatta 解らなかった
waméku 喚く cry, scream	waméite 喚いて	wamekánakute 喚かなくて	wamekánai 喚かない	wamekánakatta 喚かなかった
yabúru 破る tear, rend, rip	yabútte 破って	yaburánakute 破らなくて	yaburánai 破らない	yaburánakatta 破らなかった
yadóru 宿る take shelter	yadótte 宿って	yadoránakute 宿らなくて	yadoránai 宿らない	yadoránakatta 宿らなかった
yadósu 宿す give shelter	yadóshite 宿して	yadosánakute 宿さなくて	yadosánai 宿さない	yadosánakatta 宿さなかった
yakúsu 訳す translate	yakúshite 訳して	yakusánakute 訳さなくて	yakusánai 訳さない	yakusánakatta 訳さなかった
yámu 病む fall ill, be laid up	yánde 病んで	yamánakute 病まなくて	yamánai 病まない	yamánakatta 病まなかった
yasúmu 休む take a rest	yasúnde 休んで	yasumánakute 休まなくて	yasumánai 休まない	yasumánakatta 休まなかった
yatóu 雇う employ, engage	yatótte 雇って	yatowánakute 雇わなくて	yatowánai 雇わない	yatowánakatta 雇わなかった
yodómu 淀む stagnate, settle	yodónde 淀んで	yodománakute 淀まなくて	yodománai 淀まない	yodománakatta 淀まなかった
yokósu 寄越す send, forward	yokóshite 寄越して	yokosánakute 寄越さなくて	yokosánai 寄越さない	yokosánakatta 寄越さなかった
yokotawáru 横たわる lie (down), couch	yokotawátte 横たわって	yokotawaránakute 横たわらなくて	yokotawaránai 横たわらない	yokotawaránakatta 横たわらなかった
yokubáru 欲張る be avaricious	yokubátte 欲張って	yokubaránakute 欲張らなくて	yokubaránai 欲張らない	yokubaranakatta 欲張らなかった
yómu 読む read, peruse	yónde 読んで	yománakute 読まなくて	yománai 読まない	yománakatta 読まなかった

GROUP TWO	SUBORDINATE		NEGATIVE	
	Positive	Negative	Present	Past
yorokóbu	yorokónde	yorokobánakute	yorokobánai	yorokobánakatta
喜ぶ	喜んで	喜ばなくて	喜ばない	喜ばなかった
be glad (of), rejoice				
yoroméku	yoroméite	yoromekánakute	yoromekánai	yoromekánakatta
よろめく	よろめいて	よろめかなくて	よろめかない	よろめかなかった
stagger, totter				
yósu	yóshite	yosánakute	yosánai	yosánakatta
止す	止して	止さなくて	止さない	止さなかった
stop, leave off				
yóu	yótte	yowánakute	yowánai	yowánakatta
酔う	酔って	酔わなくて	酔わない	酔わなかった
get drunk, intoxicated				
yowáru	yowátte	yowaránakute	yowaránai	yowaránakatta
弱る	弱って	弱らなくて	弱らない	弱らなかった
weaken, grow weak				
yowásu	yowáshite	yowasánakute	yowasánai	yowasánakatta
酔わす	酔わして	酔わさなくて	酔わさない	酔わさなかった
make drunk				
yuraméku	yuraméite	yuramekánakute	yuramekánai	yuramekánakatta
揺らめく	揺らめいて	揺らめかなくて	揺らめかない	揺らめかなかった
flicker, quiver				
yurúgu	yurúide	yurugánakute	yurugánai	yurugánakatta
揺ぐ	揺いで	揺がなくて	揺がない	揺がなかった
shake, waver				
yurúmu	yurúnde	yurumánakute	yurumánai	yurumánakatta
緩む	緩んで	緩まなくて	緩まない	緩まなかった
loosen, get loose				
yurúsu	yurúshite	yurusánakute	yurusánai	yurusánakatta
許す	許して	許さなくて	許さない	許さなかった
permit, pardon, approve				
zawaméku	zawaméite	zawamekánakute	zawamekánai	zawamekánakatta
ざわめく	ざわめいて	ざわめかなくて	ざわめかない	ざわめかなかった
be noisy, rustle				
zokusúru	zokúshite	zokusánakute	zokusánai	zokusánakatta
属する	属して	属さなくて	属さない	属さなかった
belong to, be one of				
zurásu	zuráshite	zurasánakute	zurasánai	zurasánakatta
ずらす	ずらして	ずらさなくて	ずらさない	ずらさなかった
work down (the trousers)				

GROUP THREE
Main Characteristic

Simple Present : Ending in *ru* preceded by a stressed *e* or *i*.

Subordinate
- **Positive :** Stressed on the syllable preceding the one accentuated in the simple present.
- **Negative :** Stressed on the same syllable as the one accentuated in the simple present.

Negative form
- with *nai* ない
- with *nakatta* なかった

Stressed on the last syllable of the simple stem preceding either suffix.

GROUP THREE	SUBORDINATE Positive	Negative	NEGATIVE Present	Past
akiraméru 諦らめる resign oneself to	akirámete 諦らめて	akiraménakute 諦らめなくて	akiraménai 諦らめない	akiraménakatta 諦らめなかった
akíru 飽きる grow tired	ákite 飽きて	akínakute 飽きなくて	akínai 飽きない	akínakatta 飽きなかった
anjíru 案じる be anxious	ánjite 案じて	anjínakute 案じなくて	anjínai 案じない	anjínakatta 案じなかった
aozaméru 青ざめる turn pale	aozámete 青ざめて	aozaménakute 青ざめなくて	aozaménai 青ざめない	aozaménakatta 青ざめなかった
arataméru 改める reform, alter	aratámete 改めて	arataménakute 改めなくて	arataménai 改めない	arataménakatta 改めなかった
aséru 褪せる fade, discolor	ásete 褪せて	asénaknte 褪せなくて	asénai 褪せない	asénakatta 褪せなかった
atataméru 温める warm, heat	atatámete 温めて	atataménakute 温めなくて	atataménai 温めない	atataménakatta 温めなかった
atsuméru 集める collect, gather	atsúmete 集めて	atsuménakute 集めなくて	atsuménai 集めない	atsuménakatta 集めなかった
awaséru 合わせる put together	awásete 合わせて	awasénakute 合わせなくて	awasénai 合わせない	awasénakatta 合わせなかった
azukéru 預ける give into keeping	azúkete 預けて	azukénakute 預けなくて	azukénai 預けない	azukénakatta 預けなかった
bakéru 化ける appear in disguise	bákete 化けて	bakénakute 化けなくて	bakénai 化けない	bakénakatta 化けなかった
bokéru 耄ける grow senile	bókete 耄けて	bokénakute 耄けなくて	bokénai 耄けない	bokénakatta 耄けなかった
chigiréru ちぎれる be torn to piece	chigírete ちぎれて	chigirénakute ちぎれなくて	chigirénai ちぎれない	chigirénakatta ちぎれなかった
chikazukéru 近づける allow to come near	chikazúkete 近づけて	chikazukénakute 近づけなくて	chikazukénai 近づけない	chikazukénakatta 近づけなかった

GROUP THREE	SUBORDINATE Positive	Negative	NEGATIVE Present	Past
daréru だれる grow listless	dárete だれて	darénakute だれなくて	darenai だれない	darenakatta だれなかった
dekíru 出来る be done, can	dékite 出来て	dekínakute 出来なくて	dekínai 出来ない	dekínakatta 出来なかった
enjíru 演じる perform, play	enjite 演じて	enjínakute 演じなくて	enjínai 演じない	enjínakatta 演じなかった
fuéru 殖える increase	fúete 殖えて	fuénakute 殖えなくて	fuénai 殖えない	fuénakatta 殖えなかった
fūjíru 封じる seal (a letter)	fūjite 封じて	fujínakute 封じなくて	fūjínai 封じない	fūjínakatta 封じなかった
fukaméru 深める deepen, heighten	fukámete 深めて	fukaménakute 深めなくて	fukaménai 深めない	fukaménakatta 深めなかった
fukumaséru 含ませる soak (a thing with water)	fukumásete 含ませて	fukumasénakute 含ませなくて	fukumasénai 含ませない	fukumasenakatta 含ませなかった
fukumeru 含める include	fukúmete 含めて	fukuménakute 含めなくて	fukuménai 含めない	fukumenakatta 含めなかった
fumaéru 踏まえる step on	fumáete 踏まえて	fumaénakute 踏まえなくて	fumaénai 踏まえない	fumaénakatta 踏まえなかった
fuzakéru ふざける joke, jest	fuzákete ふざけて	fuzakénakute ふざけなくて	fuzakénai ふざけない	fuzakénakatta ふざけなかった
hagéru 禿げる grow bald	hágete 禿げて	hagénakute 禿げなくて	hagénai 禿げない	hagénakatta 禿げなった
haguréru 逸れる lose sight of (one's companion)	hagúrete 逸れて	hagurénakute 逸れなくて	hagurénai 逸れない	hagurénakatta 逸れなかった
hajíru 恥じる feel shame at	hájite 恥じて	hajínakute 恥じなくて	hajínai 恥じない	hajínakatta 恥じなかった
hanaréru 離れる separate, part from	hanárete 離れて	hanarénakute 離れなくて	hanarénai 離れない	hanarénakatta 離れなかった
hanéru 跳ねる leap, spring	hánete 跳ねて	hanénakute 跳ねなくて	hanénai 跳ねない	hanénakatta 跳ねなかった
hayaméru 早める hasten, put up speed	hayámete 早めて	hayaménakute 早めなくて	hayaménai 早めない	hayaménakatta 早めなかった
hazukashiméru 辱める put to shame	hazukashímete 辱めて	hazukashiménakute 辱めなくて	hazukashiménai 辱めない	hazukashiménakatta 辱めなかった
hedatéru 距てる part, set apart	hedátete 距てて	hedaténakute 距てなくて	hedaténai 距てない	hedaténakatta 距てなかった
héru 経る pass	héte 経て	hénakute 経なくて	hénai 経ない	hénakatta 経なかった

GROUP THREE	SUBORDINATE		NEGATIVE	
	Positive	Negative	Present	Past
hiidéru 秀でる surpass	hiídete 秀でて	hiidénakute 秀でなくて	hiidénai 秀でない	hiidénakatta 秀でなかった
hikaéru 控える draw in, refrain	hikáete 控えて	hikaénakute 控えなくて	hikaénai 控えない	hikaénakatta 控えなかった
hinekuréru ひねくれる become crooked	hinekúrete ひねくれて	hinekurénakute ひねくれなくて	hinekurénai ひねくれない	hinekurénakatta ひねくれなかった
hirakéru 開ける become civilized	hirákete 開けて	hirakénakute 開けなくて	hirakénaɪ 開けない	hirakénakatta 開けなかった
hiroméru 広める extend, widen	hirómete 広めて	hiromenakute 広めなくて	hiroménaɪ 広めない	hiroménakatta 広めなかった
hisoméru 潜める conceal, hide	hisómete 潜めて	hisoménakute 潜めなくて	hisoménai 潜めない	hisomenakatta 潜めなかった
hodokéru 解ける come loose	hodókete 解けて	hodokénakute 解けなくて	hodokénai 解けない	hodokénakatta 解けなかった
hoéru 吠える bark	hóete 吠えて	hoénakute 吠えなくて	hoénai 吠えない	hoénakatta 吠えなかった
hokorobíru 綻びる be unsewn, bigin to open	hokoróbite 綻びて	hokorobínakute 綻びなくて	hokorobínai 綻びない	hokorobínakatta 綻びなかった
homéru 褒める praise, extol	hómete 褒めて	homénakute 褒めなくて	homénai 褒めない	homénakatta 褒めなかった
ikéru 埋ける bury (a thing in the ground)	íkete 埋けて	ikénakute 埋けなくて	ikénai 埋けない	ikénakatta 埋けなかった
ikíru 生きる live, exist	íkite 生きて	ɪkínakute 生きなくて	ikínai 生きない	ikinakatta 生きなかった
íru 射る shoot (on arrow)	íte 射て	ínakute 射なくて	ínai 射ない	ínakatta 射なかった
jiréru 焦れる fret	jírete 焦れて	jirénakute 焦れなくて	jirénai 焦れない	jirénakatta 焦れなかった
kabuséru 被せる cover	kabúsete 被せて	kabusénakute 被せなくて	kabusénai 被せない	kabusénakatta 被せなかった
kaerimíru 顧みる look back	kaerímite 顧みて	kaeriminakute 顧みなくて	kaerimínai 顧みない	kaeriminakatta 顧みなかった
kakéru 駆ける run	kákete 駆けて	kakénakute 駆けなくて	kakénai 駆けない	kakénakatta 駆けなかった
kakuréru 隠れる hide oneself	kakúrete 隠れて	kakurénakute 隠れなくて	kakurénai 隠れない	kakurénakatta 隠れなかった
kamaéru 構える build, construct	kamáete 構えて	kamaénakute 構えなくて	kamaénai 構えない	kamaénakatta 構えなかった

GROUP THREE	SUBORDINATE		NEGATIVE	
	Positive	Negative	Present	Past
kanaéru 叶える grand, answer	kanáete 叶えて	kanaénakute 叶えなくて	kanaénai 叶えない	kanaenakatta 叶えなかった
kanéru 兼ねる combine (one thing with another)	kánete 兼ねて	kanénakute 兼ねなくて	kanénai 兼ねない	kanenakatta 兼ねなかった
karaméru 搦める bind	karámete 搦めて	karaménakute 搦めなくて	karaménai 搦めない	karamenakatta 搦めなかった
kasuréru 掠れる be grazed	kasúrete 掠れて	kasurénakute 掠れなくて	kasurénai 掠れない	kasurénakatta 掠れなかった
katamukéru 傾け る incline	katamúkete 傾けて	katamukénakute 傾けなくて	katamukénai 傾けない	katamukénakatta 傾けなかった
katazukéru 片附ける put in order	katazúkete 片附けて	katazukénakute 片附けなくて	katazukénai 片附けない	katazukénakatta 片附けなかった
kazoéru 数える count, reckon	kazóete 数えて	kazoénakute 数えなくて	kazoénai 数えない	kazoenakatta 数えなかった
kegaréru 汚れる get dirty	kegárete 汚れて	kegarénakute 汚れなくて	kegarénai 汚れない	kegarénakatta 汚れなかった
kiwaméru 極める go to the end	kiwámete 極めて	kiwaménakute 極めなくて	kiwaménai 極めない	kiwaménakatta 極めなかった
kiyoméru 清める purify	kiyómete 清めて	kiyoménakute 清めなくて	kiyoménai 清めない	kiyoménakatta 清めなかった
kobíru とびる flatter	kóbite とびて	kobínakute とびなくて	kobínai とびない	kobínakatta とびなかった
koboréru こぼれる fall, drop	kobórete こぼれて	koborénakute こぼれなくて	koborénai こぼれない	koborénakatta こぼれなかった
koéru 肥える grow fat	kóete 肥えて	koénakute 肥えなくて	koénai 肥えない	kaénakatta 肥えなかった
kogaréru 焦がれ る pine for	kogárete 焦がれて	kogarénakute 焦がれなくて	kogarénai 焦がれない	kogarénakatta 焦がれなかった
kojiréru 拗れる be twisted	kojírete 拗れて	kojirénakute 拗れなくて	kojirénai 拗れない	kojirénakatta 拗れなかった
kōjiru 嵩じる grow worse	kōjite 嵩じて	kōjínakute 嵩じなくて	kōjínai 嵩じない	kōjínakatta 嵩じなかった
kokoroéru 心得る know, understand	kokoróete 心得て	kokoroénakute 心得なくて	kokoroénai 心得ない	kokoroénakatta 心得なかった
kokoromíru 試みる try, make a trial	kokorómite 試みて	kokoromínakute 試みなくて	kokoromínai 試みない	kokoromínakatta 試みなかった
komaséru 困ら せる embarrass	komarásete 困らせて	komarasénakute 困らせなくて	komarasénai 困らせない	komarasénakatta 困らせなかった
konéru 捏ねる knead, mix up	kónete 捏ねて	konénakute 捏ねなくて	konénai 捏ねない	konénakatta 捏ねなかった

GROUP THREE	SUBORDINATE		NEGATIVE	
---	Positive	Negative	Present	Past
konjíru 混じる mix, blend	kónjite 混じて	konjínakute 混じなくて	konjínai 混じない	konjínakatta 混じなかった
koraéru 堪らえる bear, endure	koráete 堪らえて	koraénakute 堪らえなくて	koraénai 堪らえない	koraénakatta 堪らえなかった
kosuréru 擦れる be rubbed	kosúrete 擦れて	kosurénakute 擦れなくて	kosurénai 擦れない	kosurénakatta 擦れなかった
kowaréru 毀れる break, fall through	kowárete 毀れて	kowarénakute 毀れなくて	kowarénai 毀れない	kowarénakatta 毀れなかった
kubéru 焼べる burn	kúbete 焼べて	kubénakute 焼べなくて	kubénai 焼べない	kubénakatta 焼べなかった
kudakéru 砕ける break	kudákete 砕けて	kudakénakute 砕けなくて	kudakénai 砕けない	kudakénakatta 砕けなかった
kurushiméru 苦しめる torment	kurushímete 苦しめて	kurushiménakute 苦しめなくて	kurushiménai 苦しめない	kurushiménakatta 苦しめなかった
kutabiréru くたびれる get tired	kutabírete くたびれて	kutabirénakute くたびれなくて	kutabirénai くたびれない	kutabirénakatta くたびれなかった
kuzuréru 崩れる crumble	kuzúrete 崩れて	kuzurénakute 崩れなくて	kuzurénai 崩れない	kuzurénakatta 崩れなかった
makaséru 任せる entrust to	makásete 任せて	makasénakute 任せなくて	makasénai 任せない	makasénakatta 任せなかった
mataséru 待たせる keep waiting	matásete 待たせて	matasénakute 待たせなくて	matasénai 待たせない	matasénakatta 待たせなかった
mazéru 混ぜる mix, mingle	mázete 混ぜて	mazénakute 混ぜなくて	mazénai 混ぜない	mazénakatta 混ぜなかった
mezaméru 目覚める wake up	mezámete 目覚めて	mezaménakute 目覚めなくて	mezaménai 目覚めない	mezaménakatta 目覚めなかった
michíru 満ちる fill	míchite 満ちて	michínakute 満ちなくて	michínai 満ちない	michínakatta 満ちなかった
midaréru 乱れる go out of order	midárete 乱れて	midarénakute 乱れなくて	midarénai 乱れない	midarénakatta 乱れなかった
miséru 見せる show, let see	mísete 見せて	misénakute 見せなくて	misénai 見せない	misénakatta 見せなかった
mōkéru 設ける prepare, establish	mōkete 設けて	mōkénakute 設けなくて	mōkénai 設けない	mōkénakatta 設けなかった
mōkéru 儲ける make, get (a profit), make a good bargain	mōkete 儲けて	mōkénakute 儲けなくて	mōkénai 儲けない	mōkénakatta 儲けなかった
moréru 漏れる leak, get vent	mórete 漏れて	morénakute 漏れなくて	morénai 漏れない	morénakatta 漏れなかった
motaréru 凭れる lean on	motárete 凭れて	motarénakute 凭れなくて	motarénai 凭れない	motarénakatta 凭れなかった

GROUP THREE	SUBORDINATE		NEGATIVE	
	Positive	Negative	Present	Past
motoméru 求める want	motómete 求めて	motoménakute 求めなくて	motoménai 求めない	motoménakatta 求めなかった
motsuréru 縺れる be entangled	motsúrete 縺れて	motsurénakute 縺れなくて	motsurénai 縺れない	motsurénakatta 縺れなかった
mukuíru 報いる reward, recompence	mukúite 報いて	mukuínakute 報いなくて	mukuínai 報いない	mukuínakatta 報いなかった
muréru 蒸れる be steamed	múrete 蒸れて	murénakute 蒸れなくて	murénai 蒸れない	murénakatta 蒸れなかった
nadaméru 宥める soothe	nadámete 宥めて	nadaménakute 宥めなくて	nadaménai 宥めない	nadaménakatta 宥めなかった
nadéru 撫でる stroke, pat	nádete 撫でて	nadénakute 撫でなくて	nadénai 撫でない	nadénakatta 撫でなかった
nagaméru 眺める look at	nagámete 眺めて	nagaménakute 眺めなくて	nagaménai 眺めない	nagaménakatta 眺めなかった
nagaréru 流れる stream	nagárete 流れて	nagarénakute 流れなくて	nagarénai 流れない	nagarénakatta 流れなかった
nagéru 投げる throw	nágete 投げて	nagénakute 投げなくて	nagénai 投げない	nagénakatta 投げなかった
namakéru 懶ける be idle	namákete 懶けて	namakénakute 懶けなくて	namakénai 懶けない	namakénakatta 懶けなかった
naméru なめる lick	námete なめて	naménakute なめなくて	naménai なめない	naménakatta なめなかった
naréru 慣れる be used to	nárete 慣れて	narénakute 慣れなくて	narénai 慣れない	narenakatta 慣れなかった
nazukéru 名付ける name	nazúkete 名付けて	nazukénakute 名付けなくて	nazukénai 名付けない	nazukénakatta 名付けなかった
nenjíru 念じる pray	nénjite 念じて	nenjínakute 念じなくて	nenjínai 念じない	nenjínakatta 念じなかった
nigéru 逃げる run away	nígete 逃げて	nigénakute 逃げなくて	nigénai 逃げない	nigénakatta 逃げなかった
nikumaréru 憎まれる be hated	nikumárete 憎まれて	nikumárenakute 憎まれなくて	nikumaréna 憎まれない	nikumárenakatta 憎まれなかった
ninjíru 任じる appoint (a person mayor)	nínjite 任じて	ninjinakute 任じなくて	ninjinai 任じない	ninjinakatta 任じなかった
nobéru 述べる state, speak	nóbete 述べて	nobénakute 述べなくて	nobenai 述べない	nobenakatta 述べなかった
nobíru 伸びる extend, grow	nóbite 伸びて	nobínakute 伸びなくて	nobínai 伸びない	nobínakatta 伸びなかった
nogaréru 逃れる escape, avoid	nogárete 逃れて	nogarenakute 逃がれなくて	nogarénai 逃がれない	nogarénakatta 逃がれなかった

GROUP THREE	SUBORDINATE Positive	Negative	NEGATIVE Present	Past
nomaréru 飲まれる be swallowed	nomárete 飲まれて	nomarénakute 飲まれなくて	nomarénai 飲まれない	nomarénakatta 飲まれなかった
nugéru 脱げる come off	núgete 脱げて	nugénakute 脱げなくて	nugénai 脱げない	nugénakatta 脱げなかった
ochíru 落ちる fall, drop	óchite 落ちて	ochínakute 落ちなくて	ochínai 落ちない	ochínakatta 落ちなかった
oíru 老いる grow old, age	óite 老いて	oínakute 老いなくて	oínai 老いない	oínakatta 老いなかった
okíru 起きる get up	ókite 起きて	okínakute 起きなくて	okínai 起きない	okínakatta 起きなかった
okoraseru 怒らせる offend	okorásete 怒らせて	okorasénakute 怒らせなくて	okorasénai 怒らせない	okorasénakatta 怒らせなかった
oreru 折れる break, be folded	órete 折れて	orénakute 折れなくて	orénai 折れない	orénakatta 折れなかった
oríru 下りる come down	órite 下りて	orínakute 下りなくて	orínai 下りない	orínakatta 下りなかった
osaméru 治める rule over	osámete 治めて	osaménakute 治めなくて	osaménai 治めない	osaménakatta 治めなかった
osoréru 恐れる fear, dread	osórete 恐れて	osorénakute 恐れなくて	osorénai 恐れない	osorénakatta 恐れなかった
sabíru 錆びる rust	sábite 錆びて	sabínakute 錆びなくて	sabínai 錆びない	sabínakatta 錆びなかった
sadaméru 定める decide	sadámete 定めて	sadaménakute 定めなくて	sadaménai 定めない	sadaménakatta 定めなかった
sagéru 下げる hang	ságete 下げて	sagénakute 下げなくて	sagénai 下げない	sagénakatta 下げなかった
sakéru 避ける avoid	sákete 避けて	sakénakute 避けなくて	sakénai 避けない	sakénakatta 避けなかった
sakinjíru 先んじる go ahead	sakínjite 先んじて	sakinjínakute 先んじなくて	sakinjínai 先んじない	sakinjínakatta 先んじなかった
saméru 冷める cool, abate	sámete 冷めて	saménakute 冷めなくて	saménai 冷めない	saménakatta 冷めなかった
sazukéru 授ける grant, teach	sazúkete 授けて	sazukénakute 授けなくて	sazukénai 授けない	sazukénakatta 授けなかった
seméru 攻める attack	sémete 攻めて	seménakute 攻めなくて	seménai 攻めない	seménakatta 攻めなかった
shibiréru 痺れる become numb	shibírete 痺れて	shibirénakute 痺れなくて	shibirénai 痺れない	shibirénakatta 痺れなかった
shigureru 時雨れる shower	shigúrete 時雨れて	shigurénakute 時雨れなくて	shigurénai 時雨れない	shigurénakatta 時雨れなかった

GROUP THREE	SUBORDINATE Positive	Negative	NEGATIVE Present	Past
shiíru 強いる compel, force	shíite 強いて	shiínakute 強いなくて	shiínai 強いない	shiínakatta 強いなかった
shiitagéru 虐げる oppress	shiitágete 虐げて	shiitagénakute 虐げなくて	shiitagénai 虐げない	shiitagénakatta 虐げなかった
shikéru しける be damp	shíkete しけて	shikénakute しけなくて	shikénai しけない	shikénakatta しけなかった
shiméru 占める occupy	shímete 占めて	shiménakute 占めなくて	shiménai 占めない	shiménakatta 占めなかった
shiméru 締める tie up	shímete 締めて	shiménakute 締めなくて	shiménai 締めない	shiménakatta 締めなかった
shinjíru 信じる believe, trust	shínjite 信じて	shinjínakute 信じなくて	shinjínai 信じない	shinjínakatta 信じなかった
shirabéru 調べる investigate	shirábete 調べて	shirabénakute 調べなくて	shirabénai 調べない	shirabénakatta 調べなかった
shirizokéru 退け る drive back	shirizókete 退けて	shirizokénakute 退けなくて	shirizokénai 退けない	shirizokénakatta 退けなかった
shitagáeru 従える be attended	shitagáete 従えて	shitagaénakute 従えなくて	shitagaénai 従えない	shitagaénakatta 従えなかった
shitsukéru 躾け る breed	shitsúkete 躾けて	shitsukénakute 躾けなくて	shitsukénai 躾けない	shitsukénakatta 躾けなかった
shizuméru 静め る calm, quiet	shizúmete 静めて	shizuménakute 静めなくて	shizuménai 静めない	shizuménakatta 静めなかった
shōjíru 生じる produce	shōjite 生じて	shōjínakute 生じなくて	shōjínai 生じない	shōjínakatta 生じなかった
sobadatéru そば だてる prick up	sobadátete そばだてて	sobadaténakute そばだてなくて	sobadaténai そばだてない	sobadaténakatta そばだてなかった
sodatéru 育てる bring up	sodátete 育てて	sodaténakute 育てなくて	sodaténai 育てない	sodaténakatta 育てなかった
soréru 逸れる miss the mark	sórete 逸れて	sorénakute 逸れなくて	sorénai 逸れない	sorénakatta 逸れなかった
suboméru 窄める make narrower	subómete 窄めて	suboménakute 窄めなくて	suboménai 窄めない	suboménakatta 窄めなかった
sugíru 過ぎる pass, go past	súgite 過ぎて	sugínakute 過ぎなくて	sugínai 過ぎない	sugínakatta 過ぎなかった
sunéru 拗ねる pout, sulk	súnete 拗ねて	sunénakute 拗ねなくて	sunénai 拗ねない	sunénakatta 拗ねなかった
suréru 擦れる rub, chafe	súrete 擦れて	surénakute 擦れなくて	surénai 擦れない	surénakatta 擦れなかった
susukéru 煤ける become sooty	susúkete 煤けて	susukénakute 煤けなくて	susukénai 煤けない	susukénakatta 煤けなかった
tabanéru 束ねる bundle	tabánete 束ねて	tabanénakute 束ねなくて	tabanénai 束ねない	tabanénakatta 束ねなかった

GROUP THREE	SUBORDINATE Positive	Negative	NEGATIVE Present	Past
tabéru 食べる eat, take (food)	tábete 食べて	tabénakute 食べなくて	tabénai 食べない	tabénakatta 食べなかった
taéru 堪える endure, bear	táete 堪えて	taénakute 堪えなくて	taénai 堪えない	taénakatta 堪えなかった
takaméru 高める raise, lift	takámete 高めて	takaménakute 高めなくて	takaménai 高めない	takaménakatta 高めなかった
takéru 長ける excel in	tákete 長けて	takénakute 長けなくて	takénai 長けない	takénakatta 長けなかった
tamagéru 魂消る become astonished	tamágete 魂消て	tamagénakute 魂消なくて	tamagénai 魂消ない	tamagénakatta 魂消なかった
tamukéru 手向け る offer	tamúkete 手向けて	tamukénakute 手向けなくて	tamukénai 手向けない	tamukénakatta 手向けなかった
taoréru 倒れる fall, come down	taórete 倒れて	taorénakute 倒れなくて	taorénai 倒れない	taorénakatta 倒れなかった
taréru 垂れる hang	tárete 垂れて	tarénakute 垂れなくて	tarénai 垂れない	tarénakatta 垂れなかった
tashikaméru 確かめる ascertain, make sure	tashikámete 確かめて	tashikaménakute 確かめなくて	tashikaménai 確かめない	tashikaménakatta 確かめなかった
tashinaméru 窘め る reprove	tashinámete 窘めて	tashinaménakute 窘めなくて	tashinaménai 窘めない	tashinaménakatta 窘めなかった
tasukéru 助ける help, aid	tasúkete 助けて	tasukénakute 助けなくて	tasukénai 助けない	tasukénakatta 助けなかった
tataséru 立たせる make (a person stand)	tatásete 立たせて	tatasénakute 立たせなくて	tatasénai 立たせない	tatasénakatta 立たせなかった
tatéru 立てる stand, build	tátete 立てて	taténakute 立てなくて	taténai 立てない	taténakatta 立てなかった
tatoéru 例える compare	tatóete 例えて	tatoénakute 例えなくて	tatoénai 例えない	tatoénakatta 例えなかった
tawamuréru 戯れ る play	tawamúrete 戯れて	tawamurénakute 戯れなくて	tawamurénai 戯れない	tawamurénakatta 戯れなかった
tazunéru 訪ねる call (a person)	tazúnete 訪ねて	tazunénakute 訪ねなくて	tazunénai 訪ねない	tazunénakatta 訪ねなかった
tazunéru 尋ねる look for, ask	tazúnete 尋ねて	tazunénakute 尋ねなくて	tazunénai 尋ねない	tazunénakatta 尋ねなかった
teréru てれる be shy	térete てれて	terénakute てれなくて	terénai てれない	terénakatta てれなかった
tobokéru とぼける pretend not to know	tobókete とぼけて	tobokénakute とぼけなくて	tobokénai とぼけない	tobokénakatta とぼけなかった

GROUP THREE	SUBORDINATE		NEGATIVE	
	Positive	Negative	Present	Past
togaméru 咎める find fauld with	togámete 咎めて	togaménakute 咎めなくて	togamenai 咎めない	togaménakatta 咎めなかった
togéru 遂げる accomplish	tógete 遂げて	togénakute 遂げなくて	togénai 遂げない	togénakatta 遂げなかった
tojíru 閉じる shut, close	tójite 閉じて	tojínakute 閉じなくて	tojínai 閉じない	tojínakatta 閉じなかった
tojíru 綴じる bind (a book)	tójite 綴じて	tojínakute 綴じなくて	tojínai 綴じない	tojínakatta 綴じなかった
tokéru 溶ける melt	tókete 溶けて	tokénakute 溶けなくて	tokénai 溶けない	tokénakatta 溶けなかった
tonaéru 唱える recite, advocate	tonáete 唱えて	tonaénakute 唱えなくて	tonaénai 唱えない	tonaénakatta 唱えなかった
toraéru 捕える catch	toráete 捕えて	toraénakute 捕えなくて	toraénai 捕えない	toraénakatta 捕えなかった
toréru 取れる come off, come apart	tórete 取れて	torénakute 取れなくて	torénai 取れない	torénakatta 取れなかった
tsukaéru 仕える serve	tsukáete 仕えて	tsukaénakute 仕えなくて	tsukaénai 仕えない	tsukaénakatta 仕えなかった
tsukaréru 疲れる get tired	tsukárete 疲れて	tsukarénakute 疲れなくて	tsukarénai 疲れない	tsukarénakatta 疲れなかった
tsuméru 詰める cram	tsúmete 詰めて	tsuménakute 詰めなくて	tsuménai 詰めない	tsuménakatta 詰めなかった
tsutoméru 努める make an effort	tsutómete 努めて	tsutoménakute 努めなくて	tsutoménai 努めない	tsutoménakatta 努めなかった
tsuyoméru 強める strengthen	tsuyómete 強めて	tsuyoménakute 強めなくて	tsuyoménai 強めない	tsuyoménakatta 強めなかった
ukéru 受ける receive	úkete 受けて	ukénakute 受けなくて	ukénai 受けない	ukénakatta 受けなかった
urotaéru うろたえる be confused	urotáete うろたえて	urotaénakute うろたえなくて	urotaénai うろたえない	urotaénakatta うろたえなかった
uséru 失せる disappear	úsete 失せて	usénakute 失せなくて	usénai 失せない	usénakatta 失せなかった
utaréru 打たれる be struck	utárete 打たれて	utarénakute 打たれなくて	utarénai 打たれない	utarénakatta 打たれなかった
wakaréru 別れる separate (from)	wakárete 別れて	wakarénakute 別れなくて	wakarénai 別れない	wakarénakatta 別れなかった

| GROUP THREE | SUBORDINATE | | NEGATIVE | |
	Positive	Negative	Present	Past
wakéru 分ける divide, part	wákete 分けて	wakénakute 分けなくて	wakénai 分けない	wakénakatta 分けなかった
warubiréru 悪びれる be timid	warubírete 悪びれて	warubirénakute 悪びれなくて	warubirénai 悪びれない	warubirénakatta 悪びれなかった
yaburéru 破れる be torn	yabúrete 破れて	yaburénakute 破れなくて	yaburénai 破れない	yaburénakatta 破れなかった
yasumáseru 休ませる repose	yasumásete 休ませて	yasumasénakute 休ませなくて	yasumasénai 休ませない	yasumasénakatta 休ませなかった
yasuméru 休める repose	yasúmete 休めて	yasuménakute 休めなくて	yasuménai 休めない	yasuménakatta 休めなかった
yatowaréru 雇われる be engaged	yatowárete 雇われて	yatowarénakute 雇われなくて	yatowarénai 雇われない	yatowarénakatta 雇われなかった
yatsuréru 寠れる be worn out	yatsúrete 寠れて	yatsurénakute 寠れなくて	yatsurénai 寠れない	yatsurénakatta 寠れなかった
yokéru 避ける avoid	yókete 避けて	yokénakute 避けなくて	yokénai 避けない	yokénakatta 避けなかった
yoméru 読める be able to read	yómete 読めて	yoménakute 読めなくて	yoménai 読めない	yoménakatta 読めなかった
yowaméru 弱める weaken	yowámete 弱めて	yowaménakute 弱めなくて	yowaménai 弱めない	yowaménakatta 弱めなかった
yudanéru 委ねる entrust with	yudánete 委ねて	yudanénakute 委ねなくて	yudanénai 委ねない	yudanénakatta 委ねなかった
yugaméru 歪める distort	yugámete 歪めて	yugaménakute 歪めなくて	yugaménai 歪めない	yugaménakatta 歪めなかった
yuruméru 緩める loosen	yurúmete 緩めて	yuruménakute 緩めなくて	yuruménai 緩めない	yuruménakatta 緩めなかった
zokusúru 属する belong to	zokúshite 属して	zokushínakute 属しなくて	zokushínai 属しない	zokushínakatta 属しなかった
zonjíru 存じる know	zónjite 存じて	zonjínakute 存じなくて	zonjínai 存じない	zonjínakatta 存じなかった
zurukéru ずるける shirk one's duty	zurúkete ずるけて	zurukénakute ずるけなくて	zurukénai ずるけない	zurukénakatta ずるけなかった

GROUP FOUR

Main Characteristics

Simple Present: Ending in *ru* or *su* preceded by two vowels, the first one of which being accentuated.

Subordinate
Positive: Stressed on the same syllable as the one accentuated in the simple present.
Negative: Stressed on the terminal **e** of the simple stem of verbs of Class I and on the terminal **a** of the **a**-stem of verbs of Class II.

Negative form
with nai　ない
with nakatta なかった
Stressed on the terminal **e** of the simple stem of verbs of Class I and on the terminal **a** of the **a**-stem of verbs of Class II.

| GROUP FOUR | SUBORDINATE | | NEGATIVE | |
	Positive	Negative	Present	Past
áeru 和える	áete 和えて	aénakute 和えなくて	aénai 和えない	aénakatta 和えなかった
dress something with (cooking)				
atsuráeru 誂える order	atsuráete 誂えて	atsuraénakute 誂えなくて	atsuraénai 誂えない	atsuraénakatta 誂えなかった
gottagáesu ごった返す be confused	gottagáeshite ごった返して	gottagaesánakute ごった返さなくて	gottagaesánai ごった返さない	gottagaesánakatta ごった返さなかった
káeru 帰る	káette 帰って	kaeránakute 帰らなくて	kaeránai 帰らない	kaeránakatta 帰らなかった
come or go back (home)				
káesu 返す	káeshite 返して	kaesánakute 返さなくて	kaesánai 返さない	kaesánakatta 返さなかった
give back, return				
káesu 孵す	káeshite 孵して	kaesánakute 孵さなくて	kaesánai 孵さない	kaesánakatta 孵さなかった
hatch, incubate				
kangáeru 考える think, consider	kangáete 考えて	kangaénakute 考えなくて	kangaénai 考えない	kangaénakatta 考えなかった
kotáeru 答える	kotáete 答えて	kotaénakute 答えなくて	kotaénai 答えない	kotaénakatta 答えなかった
answer, give a reply				
kutsugáesu 覆えす upset	kutsugáeshite 覆えして	kutsugaesánakute 覆えさなくて	kutsugaesánai 覆えさない	kutsugaesánakatta 覆えさなかった
machigáeru 間違える	machigáete 間違えて	machigaénakute 間違えなくて	machigaénai 間違えない	machigaénakatta 間違えなかった
make a mistake, err				
máiru 参る go, come, call	máitte 参って	mairánakute 参らなくて	mairánai 参らない	mairánakatta 参らなかった
otoróeru 衰える become weak	otoróete 衰えて	otoroénakute 衰えなくて	otoroénai 衰えない	otoroénakatta 衰えなかった

| GROUP FOUR | SUBORDINATE | | NEGATIVE | |
	Positive	Negative	Present	Past
sonáeru 備える furnish, provide	sonáete 備えて	sonaénakute 備えなくて	sonaénai 備えない	sonaénakatta 備えなかった
totonóeru 整える prepare, put in order	totonóete 整えて	totonoénakute 整えなくて	totonoénai 整えない	totonoénakatta 整えなかった
wakimáeru 弁え る discern	wakimáete 弁えて	wakimaénakute 弁えなくて	wakimaénai 弁えない	wakimaénakatta 弁えなかった

759

Transliteration in roman characters and English translation of the news announcing the joint flight of two Soviet cosmonauts as it appeared in the Japanese daily newspaper "Mainichi Shimbun" on June 17th 1963. See original Japanese text Page 761.

HATSÚ NO JOSÉI UCHŪ-HIKŌSHI TOBÚ[1]
Sóren, Uosutōku Rokú-gō Uchí-agé
Níjūroku-sái no Tereshikowá-jō.[2]

Sénkyūhyaku-rokujūsan nen rokugatsú jūshichi nichí, Mainichí Shimbún.[3] Sobietó Nyūsu—Jūroku nichí,[4] Tōkyō—Jūroku nichí gógo ní-ji hachí-fun Nihón jikán gógo hachí-ji hachí-fun[5] no Mosukō hōsō wa rinjí hōsō de[6] shijō hatsú no joséi uchū-hikōshi dái-ichigō Warenchiná Tereshikowá-jō[7] wo nosetá Uosutōku Rokú-gō ga uchí-ageraretá to happyō shitá.[8]

1 *hatsú no* the first; *joséi* woman; *uchū* universe, the cosmos, *hikōshi* aviator, aviatrix, *uchū-hikōshi* cosmonaut, cosmonette; *tobú* to fly—*Hatsú no joséi uchū-hikōshi tobú.* The first woman cosmonaut flies. 2 *Sóren* abbreviation of *Sobietó Rempō* Soviet Union, *So=Sobietó* Soviet, *Ren=rempō* union; *Uosutōku* Vostok, *Rokú-gō* No. 6, *Uosutōku Rokú-gō* Vostok VI; *uchí-agé* being launched, subordinate of *uchí-agerú* to shoot up, to send up=to launch; *níjūroku* 26, *sái no* years old, *níjūroku-sái no* 26 year-old; *Tereshikowá* name of the aviatrix, *jō* miss, *Tereshikowá-jō* Miss Tereshkova—*Sóren, Uosutōku Rokú-gō Uchí-agé níjūroku-sái no Tereshikowá-jō.* The Soviet Union has launched (spaceship) Vostok VI (carrying inside) twentysix-year old Miss Tereshkova. 3 *sénkyūhyaku-rokujū san* 1963; *nen* year; *rokugatsú*; *Mainichí* name of one of the two leading Japanese newspapers; *shimbún* newspaper— *Sénkyūhyaku-rokujūsan nen rokugatsú jūshichi nichí, Mainichi Shimbun.* The Mainichi newspaper, June 17th 1963 4 *nyūsu* news; *Sobietó Nyūsu* Soviet News; *jūroku* 16, *jūroku nichí* the 16th 5 *gógo* afternoon; *ni-ji* two o'clock; *hachí* eight; *fun* minute; *jikán* time, *Nihón jikán* Japan's time; *hachí-ji* eight o'clock (Japan's time is six hours ahead of Moscow time)—*Jūroku nichí gógo ní-ji hachí fun......* On the afternoon of the 16th (of June), at 8 minutes past 2 (Japan's time 8 minutes past 8 p. m.) 6 *Mósukō* Moscow; *hōsō* broadcast; *rinjí* special; *rinjí hōsō de* by special broadcast—*Mósukō hōsō wa rinjí hōsō de* Moscow broadcasting (station) by special broadcast 7 *shijō* in history; *hatsú no* first; *dái-ichi-gō* No. 1; *Warenchiná* Valentina—*shijō hatsú no joséi uchū-hikōshi dái-ichígō Warenchiná Tereshikowá-jō wo......* the first woman cosmonaut in history Miss Valentina Tereshkova...... 8 *nosetá* that carried, that took on board, past form of *noserú* to carry, to take on board; *uchí-ageraretá* was launched, past of *uchí-agererú* to be launched; *to* so; *happyō shitá* announced, past of *happyō surú* to announce—......*nosetá Uosutōkú Rokú-go ga uchí-ageraretá to happyō shitá.* ......announced (that spaceship) Vostok VI carrying (her) was launched.

English Version; THE FIRST WOMAN COSMONAUT FLIES

The Soviet Union has launched spaceship Vostok VI carrying (inside) twentysix-year old Miss Tereshkova.

The Mainichi Newspaper, June 17th, 1963—Soviet News, Tokyo 16th— On the afternoon of the 16th (of June) at 8 minutes past 2 (Japan's time 8 minutes past 8) Moscow broadcasting station announced that spaceship Vostok VI was launched (into the cosmos) carrying in it twentysix-year old Valentina Tereshkova, the first woman cosmonaut recorded in history.

Transliteration in roman characters and English translation of the news announcing the completion of the joint flight of two Soviet cosmonauts as it appeared in the Japanese daily newspaper "Mainichi Shimbun" on January 17th 1963. See original Japanese text Page 761.

RYŌ EISÉI-SEN BUJÍ CHIJŌ NI KÁERU[1]
Rokú-gō yonjūkyū shū, nanájū jikán gojíppun,[2]
gó-gō hachí-jūni shū, hyakú-jūkyū jikán róppun,[3]
Tereshikowá-jō Bu-chūsa yóri sanjikán sakí.[4]

Sobietó Nyūsu, jū-ku nichí Tōkyō.[5]—Tereshikowá-jō sōjū no[6] Uosutōku Rokú-gō, Bukafusukī chūsa sōjū no Uosutōku gó-gō[7] no kyōdō hikō wa shubí-yóku kanséi saretá.[8]

1*ryō* both; *eiséisen* spaceship, *eiséi* satellite, *sen* ship; *bují* safely; *chijō* ground, earth, *chijō ni* on the ground, on the earth; *káeru* to return—*Ryō eiséi-sen bují chijō ni káeru*. Both spaceships return safely to earth. 2*rokú* VI, *gō* number, *Rokú-gō* short for *Uosutoku Rokú-gō*=Vostok VI; *yonjūkyū* 49; *shū* round, orbit; *nanajū* seventy; *jikán* hour; *gojíppun* fifty minutes—*Rokú-gō yonjūkyū shū, nanájū jikán gojíppun*. Vostok VI (completes) 49 orbits in seventy hours and fifty minutes. 3*gó-gō* short for *Uosutokú gó-gō* Vostok V; *hachijūni* 82; *shū* orbit; *hyakujūkyū* 119; *jikán* hour; *róppun* six minutes—*gó-gō hachijūni shū, hyakú-jūkyū jikán róppun* Vostok V (completes) 82 orbits in 119 hours and six minutes. 4*Tereshikowá-jō* Miss Tereshkowa; *Bu* abbreviation of *Bukofusukī* Bykovsky; *chūsa* lieutenant colonel; *yóri* than; *sanjikán* three hours; *sakí* ahead of—*Tereshikowá-jō Bu-chūsa yóri sanjikán sakí*. Tereshkova (lands) three hours before Lt. Col. Bykovsky. 5*Sobietó Nyūsu* Soviet News; *jūku* 19, *jūku nichí* the 19th (of June) 6*sōjū* handling, control, manipulation, *sōjū no* in control of 7*Bukofusukī Chūsa sōjū no Uosutōku gó-gō*...... and Bykovsky in control of Vostok V...... 8*kyōdō* joint; *hikō* flight; *shubiyóku* successfully; *kanséi* completion, *kanséi surú* to complete, to finish, *kanséi sarerú* to be completed, *kanséi saretá* was completed—*kyōdō hikō wa shubiyóku kanséi saretá*......the joint flight was completed successfully.

English Version
BOTH SPACESHIPS RETURN SAFELY TO EARTH

Vostok VI completes 49 orbits in seventy hours and fifty minutes (while) Vostok V completes 82 orbits in 119 hours and six minutes. Miss Tereshkova (lands) three hours ahead of Lt. Col. Bykovsky.

Soviet News, June 19th (1963)—Miss Tereshkova in control of Vostok VI and Lt. Col. Bykovsky in control of Vostok V have successfully completed their joint flight.

See Pages 759 and 760 for transliteration in roman characters and English translation of the following Japanese text appeared in the "Mainichi Shimbun" of Tokyo on June 17th 1963 on the occasion of the joint flight of the Soviet cosmonaut Bykovsky and cosmonette Tereshkova.

初の女性宇宙飛行士飛ぶ

ソ連、ウォストーク6号打上げ
26才のテレシコワ嬢（一九六三年六月十七日毎日新聞）

〔ソビエト・ニュース＝十六日東京〕十六日午後二時八分（日本時間午後八時八分）のモスクワ放送は臨時放送で史上初の女性宇宙飛行士第一号ワレンチナ・テレシコワ嬢を乗せたウォストーク6号が打上げられたと発表した。

両衛星船無事地上に帰る

6号49周、七〇時間五十分
5号82周、一一九時間六分
テレシコワ嬢ブ中佐より三時間先

〔ソビエト・ニュース＝十九日東京〕テレシコワ嬢操縦のウォストーク6号ブコフスキー中佐操縦のウォストーク5号の共同飛行は首尾よく完成された。

INDEXES

INDEX

of

English Grammatical Subjects and Related Words.

(See Page 781 for **Index of Japanese Words**)

INDEX

of

Japanese Grammatical Words and Phrases

(See Page 736 for Index of English Grammatical Subjects and Related Words)

WORKS ON JAPANESE

BY

MR. AND MRS. ORESTE VACCARI

The authors' motto:

TO DO BETTER WHAT OTHERS DO WELL

STUDYING JAPANESE
WITH VACCARI'S BOOKS
BECOMES A REAL PLEASURE

REMARK

Vaccari's works on Japanese have been recognized by prominent scholars as the best and most thorough for the study of the language, and are being used as text-books in various schools in Japan and universities abroad.

Vaccari's works have the great merit, over any similar works published by other authors, of being the most modern and teaching the Japanese language as it is spoken to-day.

In the last 50 years or so, the Japanese language has undergone profound changes, so that books published a few decades ago by the most prominent orientalists have, to a certain extent, become obsolete.

The Japanese language, unlike the most important European languages which, one might say, were standardized some hundred years ago by great literary geniuses such as Dante, Shakespeare, Cervantes, Goethe, Shiller, and those of the XVI and XVII centuries in France, is still undergoing slight changes in its syntactical, if not grammatical, construction, and many words and expressions considered correct until a few years ago, are, to-day, considered out of date or incorrect.

Therefore, those wishing to learn Japanese as it is spoken to-day, may have their wish satisfied by studying the works illustrated in the following pages.

A feature of all Vaccari's works is that every word and sentence given in the Japanese ideographic script are accompanied by their transliteration with roman letters and English translation, so that they may be used by students wishing to learn the language as it is written by Japanese people as well as by those who wish to learn the language only as it is written with the roman alphabet.

日本語読本

JAPANESE READERS

ENTIRELY RESET—GREATLY ENLARGED EDITION

These Readers will provide the student with the most comprehensive, methodic and thorough book produced until the present day for learning Japanese and for improving and practicing the knowledge of the language that he may have acquired by his previous study.

These Readers are indispensable to the beginner as well as to the advanced student.

These Readers have been compiled in such a manner that they may be used by students wishing to study Japanese as it is written by Japanese people with their ideographic script, as well as by those who wish to learn only the spoken language written with roman letters.

CONTENTS

PART I

How to write *Kana*, How to write *Kanji*, Orthography and Pronunciation of Hepburn and Nippon-siki Spellings, Preliminary Readings, Reading and Conversation in *Kana*, Reading with *Kanji*, Transliteration with Romaji and Full English Translation of all the Reading Exercises.

PART II

Advanced Reading with *Kanji*, Notes illustrating doubtful and difficult passages. Transliteration with Romaji and full English Translation of all Reading Exercises.

Among the **New Features** of the Reset Edition of this book, are the following: The Japanese text of the reading pieces given in symbolic characters throughout the book, has been printed with the 1,850 **kanji** as used at the present time by Japanese newspapers and magazines, following a law approved by the Diet in 1947, which was enacted in order to simplify the Japanese written language.

A graphic accent has been placed on the stressed syllable of words of two or more syllables throughout the book, which will enable the student to acquire a correct pronunciation from the very beginning of his study.

New interesting stories on Things Japanese have been included in the book.

Seventeen colored pictures, some of them reproductions of famous Japanese woodcuts and of some Indian paintings by a noted artist, illustrate passages of some of the reading pieces.

9×6 inches, 650 pages

Price: In Japan ¥1,800, Post. ¥200—Abroad $9.00, Post. $1.00

See next page for the distinctive features of this work, illustrated by **Horace L. Griggs**, a member of the Association of Correctors of the Press (**London**), and the London Society of Compositors.

ASSOCIATION OF
CORRECTORS OF THE PRESS
LONDON

The versatile pens of these indefatigable co-authors, Mr. and Mrs. Vaccari have again been busily employed. This time it is a series of Readers, tentitled "Japanese Readers"

In the early stages of this work the student is introduced to simple, one-character words, given in the *katakana* script, together with its *hiragana* counterpart, romanized transliteration, and English translation.

These syllabics, in Exercise No. 1, are reproduced in an exceptionally large type—a particularly pleasing innovation—as by this means their formation is immediately focused upon the mind, so that, when the student encounters these same characters (but of much smaller dimentions) later on, both in this work and also in other Japanese literature, he will readily identify them.

Following in appropriate sequence are further exercises, treating of words of two, three, four and more characters.

Worthy of special mention are the pages devoted to the *nigori* and *maru*; the former consisting of two dashes and the latter a small circle—the object being, when used in juxtaposition to certain characters, to euphonize words and phrases.

Diphthongs, long vowels, double consonants, and other orthographical peculiarities are also dealt with in rotation, accompanied in every instance by a variety of examples illustrating their usage.

A careful perusal of these diacritical signs and combinations will amply repay the student, for, should he fail to appreciate their correct application, proficiency at least, so far as colloquial Japanese is concerned, will be rendered impossible.

Later, simple *kanji* (Chinese characters) are introduced, gradually increasing—as the exercises progress—in frequency, variety, and intricacy of design.

Whilst on this particular subject, the section entitled, "How to Write Kanji," deserves more than passing reference, Chinese characters are given both in the printed and written forms, followed in many instances by reproduction of the latter, depicting, stroke by stroke, the principle of their construction. It is a remarkable fact that such an essential feature is usually entirely ignored in the average text-book and primer on the Japanese language.

A carefully selected list of the most common kanji, together with their pronunciation and translation, further enriches this most comprehensive work.

These four volumes indeed constitute a veritable vade-mecum for the student of Japanese, and, it matters not what branch of this complex language he may wish to pursue, Mr. and Mrs. Vaccari, with characteristic thoroughness and foresight, appear to have anticipated his requirements.

Colloquial, literary, epistolary, classical, poetical, and newspaper styles—each a separate study in itself—are incorporated in this monumental production, and embrace conversational, topical, commercial, religious, military, historical, allegorical, proverbial and many other subjects and terms and phraseology, indispensable to all whose ambition it is to achieve something really worth while in their efforts to master the intricacies of the Japanese language.

There is no doubt, whatever, that these Japanese Readers cover the same field as would require in the ordinary way at least a dozen different books, so varied are the contents, and, what is more, though replete with examples illustrative thereof, monotonous redundancy has been studiously avoided; and instruction, imparted by the most interesting methods, has remained the paramount factor throughout the entire publication.

HORACE L. GRIGGS
Member of the Association of Correctors
of the Press (London), and the London
Society of Compositors,

PICTORIAL
CHINESE-JAPANESE CHARACTERS

A NEW AND MOST FASCINATING METHOD
TO LEARN IDEOGRAPHS
9×6 inches, 300 pages

Price: In Japan ¥2,000, Post. ¥200—Abroad $10.00, Post. $1.00

The Chinese script, which began to be adopted by the Japanese at the close of the sixth century A. D., was pictorial in origin.

The first made characters were rough outlines of material objects they were intended to represent. By combining two or more of these symbols other characters were made suggesting abstract ideas.

From the time of their creation several thousands of years ago until the second century A. D. when they were finally standardized as they appear in modern times, they underwent gradual changes of form and lost their primitive pictorial appearance.

As they are written at present, the symbolic characters, excepting the simplest ones, appear to be, especially to those who begin their study, but a jumble of lifeless and meaningless strokes put together without connection with the words they are intended to represent.

Viewed in this light, they fail to give lasting impressions upon one's mind. Their study becomes thus a heavy labour and in most cases it is given up as hopeless. It is for this reason that only very few succeed in obtaining a working knowledge of even the small proportion of the characters that are required for practical purposes.

Yet, were one to see the original form of the characters and know the idea that suggested their formation, they would be easily memorized and their acquisition would become a real pleasure.

It is the aim of the authors of this new work to represent the fundamental characters on which the Chinese-Japanese written language is based, in their original form, their gradual alterations and lastly as they are written at present. Moreover, each character will be illustrated with notes and interesting information that will give life to them and render their shape and meaning an unforgettable picture.

A few examples given at the end of this announcement will give an idea of this new work, which will make the study of the symbolic characters accessible to anyone who wishes to learn them.

By this new method the student will not only learn the ideographs in less time than by any other method followed heretofore, but will also learn their ancient form, which, strange as it may sound, will facilitate memorizing the way they are written in modern times instead of becoming an extra study.

It is no exaggeration to add that studying characters by this new method will be as pleasant as reading an interesting novel.

友 yū, *tomo* friend, companion—Originally represented by two hands as of a person extending them to welcome a *friend*, a *companion.* This way of welcoming a dear friend is common also among people of Western countries.

妻 sai, *tsuma* wife—Originally, the idea of a wife was represented by the sketch of a woman with a broom held by a hand, as shown in the first picture. Such a picture was evidently suggested by the universal idea that it is the lot of a *wife* to look after home work, here symbolized by the broom.

夫 fū, *otto* husband—As the first picture clearly shows, the idea of a *husband* was represented by a man with hat on (indicating that he is outside his home) and with arms and legs in motion as if going to do some work or actually doing it.

心　shin, *kokoro* heart—Originally, the **heart** was represented by the rough sketch of its actual shape.

巣　sō, *su* nest—Represented by three birds in a nest on a tree. The modern character still retains much of its original form.

見　ken, *miru* to see—The idea of *seeing* is here well indicated by the sketch of an **eye** on a pair of legs.

馬　ba, *uma* horse—This character was originally represented by the outline of the animal it indicates.

REVISED AND ENLARGED EDITION

当 用 漢 字 集

STANDARD KANJI

AN EASY METHOD TO LEARN
THE 1850 CHINESE-JAPANESE CHARACTERS PRESCRIBED
BY THE MINISTRY OF EDUCATION OF JAPAN
FOR USE IN NEWSPAPERS AND MAGAZINES
with
SEVEN THOUSAND COMPOUND CHARACTER-WORDS
USED IN EVERYDAY LITERATURE
and
AN ADDITIONAL LIST OF 92 CHARACTERS
USED IN WRITING PERSONAL NAMES

9 × 6 inches—500 pages

Price : in Japan ￥ 1,500, Post. ￥ 200—Abroad $ 8.00, Post. $ 1.00

It is a recognized fact that the greatest handicap a student is confronted with when trying to master Japanese language, is the study of *kanji*. Few in fact are those who succeed in learning them well and in sufficient number to overcome the difficulty of reading and understanding Japanese books and newspapers, and until one is in a position to read these one cannot hope to know well the language of the people of Japan.

The difficulty in learning *kanji*, however, will be greatly lessened if they are studied with method.

Although the uninitiated into the study of Japanese do not see any relation between the apparent undecipherable characters, yet there is fundamental relation between them, and this relation is distinctly perceived as soon as the student has learned a few hundred simple characters, these being the components of most of the more complex ones. When this relation has become apparent to the eye, not only will the difficulty of memorizing them be greatly reduced, but studying them will become a pleasant task.

This relation between the *kanji* will be easily detected by the student if he learns them in the order of the number of their strokes, which is the way they have been arranged in this book.

Moreover, each particular symbol, given in brush style and originally written by an expert writer, has been repeated, in printed style, in some of its most common compound character-words, thereby illustrating very clearly the distinction between the printed and manuscript forms, which represents a most important essential to the student.

The symbolic characters are given on the left side of each page, while on the right side is given, in roman letters, their corresponding Japanese transliteration (KUN),[1] its Chinese pronunciation (ON)[1] and the English translation of both single *kanji* and compound character-words.

The 1850 characters contained in this book are the ones prescribed by the Ministry of Education of Japan in November 1947 for use in newspapers and magazines, a measure that was taken in order to simplify the Japanese written language.

Previous to this legislative act, not less that 4000 characters were used for newspapers and magazines, a number that was rather difficult to know well even for many Japanese.

However, now that the number of *kanji* required to read daily newspapers has been reduced to less than half, it will be much easier for the foreign student to attain that degree of knowledge that will give him the capacity and satisfaction of being able to read Japanese daily literature.

At the end of the illustration of the 1850 *kanji*, an index has been added with the characters in the order of the number of their strokes and reference page in order to facilitate their search.

The index of the 1850 characters is given, in brush writing, in kaisho or standard style, in gyōsho or semi-cursive style and in sōsho or cursive style. The student will thus be able to learn the three styles of writing Chinese-Japanese characters if he wishes to do so.

An exclusive and useful feature of this book is the accent placed on the stressed syllable of each transliterated word, which ensures speedy and precise familiarity with the correct Japanese pronunciation.

This book is a valuable contribution towards a better knowledge of the Japanese language among the growing number of foreign students of Japanese.

---

[1] The pronunciation of Chinese-Japanese characters is not invariably the same. Some of them may be read even in seven different ways, and their pronunciation may be of Chinese or Japanese derivation. The sound of kanji of Chinese derivation is called ON, and that of Japanese derivation is called *KUN*.

又

1 又々   2 又頼み
3 又は

matá again, another
yū

1 *matámata* again and again
2 *matadanomí* indirect request
3 *matá wa* or, in other words

八

1 八時   2 八分目
3 八方美人 4 八月
5 八卦   6 八日

yatsú or *yattsú*, *ya*, *yō* eight
hachí eight

1 *hachíji* eight o'clock 2 *hachibum-mé* moderate in quantity 3 *happō-bijin* everybody's friend 4 *hachigatsú* August 5 *hakké* divination 6 *yōka* 8th (of month)

十

1 十時   2 十字軍
3 十字架 4 十月
5 十分   6 十誡

tō, *jū* ten

1 *jūji* ten o'clock   2 *jūjigun* a crusade 3 *jūjika* a cross, the Holy Rood 4 *jūgatsu* October 5 *jíppun* ten minutes 6 *jikkái* the ten commandments

---

七

1 七日   2 七月
3 七五三 4 七輪
5 七福神

nanátsu, *nána*, *shichí* 7, seven

1 *nanoká* or *nanuká* the 7th of the month, seven days 2 *shichí-gatsú* July 3 *shichigosán* the lucky numbers (7, 5, 3) 4 *shichírin* a small portable stove 5 *shichifukujín* the seven gods of Fortune

(SPECIMEN PAGE)

没 (没)

1 没収   2 没我

shizumú to sink (v. i.)
bossúru to set, sink (of the sun)
botsu

1 *bosshū* confiscation, seizure 2 *bótsuga* self-effacement, disinterestedness

---

沈

1 沈没   2 沈黙   3 沈澱
4 沈着   5 沈勇   6 沈痛

shizumú to sink
chin

1 *chimbotsú* sinking
2 *chimmokú* silence
3 *chindén* precipitation, sedimentation
4 *chinchakú* calm (attitude)
5 *chin-yū* cool courage
6 *chintsū* pathetic, grave

汽

1 汽船   2 汽車
3 汽笛   4 汽罐

yúge steam
ki steam

1 *kisén* steamship
2 *kishá* railway train (steam train)
3 *kitekí* steam whistle
4 *kikán* an engine

沖

1 沖天   2 横浜沖
3 沖合   4 沖渡し

okí open sea, offing
chū

1 *chūten no* rising (shooting up) to heaven
2 *Yokohamá-okí* off Yokohama
3 *okiaí* off (shore, etc.)
4 *okiwatashí* free overside

沢 (澤)

1 沢山   2 沢庵
3 光沢   4 潤沢

sawá marsh, swamp
taku

1 *takúsán* much, many
2 *takúan* pickled radish
3 *kōtaku* luster, gloss
4 *juntakú* abundance, luster

決

kessúru to decide, vote on
kesshité never
ketsu

1 決定　2 決心　3 決死

1 *kettéi* decision, settlement
2 *késshin* determination
3 *kesshí* desperate, determined

走

hashíru to run, to flee
sō

1 走程　2 競走　3 逃走

1 *sōtei* course, run, drive 2 *kyōsō* race, run 3 *tōsō* flight, escape

足

ashí foot, limb, step, pace
tarú (lit.), *tarirú* to be sufficient
soku pair (of footgear)
soku

1 足踏　2 足並　3 足跡

1 *ashibumi* step, stepping 2 *ashinamí* pace 3 *ashiáto, sokúseki* (lit.) foot-print

近 (近)

chikái near, close, nearby
kin

1 近眼　2 近所　3 近海
4 近代　5 近刊　6 近頃

1 *kingán* short-sightedness 2 *kínjo* neighbourhood 3 *kinkái* neighbouring sea 4 *kíndai* modern times, modern 5 *kinkán* recent publication 6 *chiká-goro* recently, lately

返 (返)

káesu to return, give back
hen

1 返事　2 返礼　3 返済

1 *henjí* answer 2 *hénrei* return present 3 *hensái* repayment

(SPECIMEN PAGE)

| 誌 | *shirusú* to write down
shi |
| 1 雑誌　　2 日誌 | 1 *zasshí* magazine 2 *nisshí* diary |

| 誠 | *makotó* truth, sincerity
sei |
| 1 誠意　　2 誠実 | 1 *séii* sincerity, faith 2 *seijitsú* sincerity |

| 読(讀) | *yómu* to read, to recite
toku, doku, tō |
| 1 読書　 2 読本　 3 句読 | 1 *dokushó* reading
2 *tokuhón* reader, reading book
3 *kutō* punctuation |

| 誤 | *ayamarí* mistake, error
go |
| 1 誤報　 2 誤字　 3 誤解 | 1 *gohō* misinformation 2 *gojí* a wrong
word (character), misprint 3 *gokái* mis-
understanding |

| 説 | *tóku* to explain, to preach
setsu opinion, theory |
| 1 説教　 2 説明　 3 説諭 | 1 *sekkyō* sermon   2 *setsuméi* explana-
tion 3 *setsúyu* admonition, reproof |

(SPECIMEN PAGE)

英和会話小辞典

The New Up-to-date
ENGLISH-JAPANESE
CONVERSATION-DICTIONARY

(Reset and greatly enlarged Edition)
BY MR. AND MRS. ORESTE VACCARI

This new work is different from ordinary dictionaries in that most of the English words listed in it not only have their Japanese translation with roman letters, but also the Japanese translation of sentences and phrases that one may need in daily conversation.

This Conversation-Dictionary may thus be used even by those who have no knowledge of Japanese.

A feature of this dictionary is that an accent has been put on each word to indicate the stressed syllable, so that it will be easy to know how to pronounce Japanese words correctly.

Many are the Japanese words which, although spelled with the same letters, have different meanings according to the syllable on which the stress is laid. For example: The word íppai with the stress on the first i means *one cup*, while if the stress is laid on the a (ippái) it means *full*. The great importance of the correct stress is thus evident. Long and silent vowels also have been indicated by proper marks.

Another feature is that most verbs listed in this dictionary are given not only in their form corresponding to the English infinitive, but also in their present form of the indicative, so that one may use them even without knowing the rules of the conjugation of Japanese verbs.

These lexicographic innovations, as shown in the following specimen pages, will render this work the most valuable book for foreign tourists in Japan and for all those who wish to learn practical Japanese conversation.

The present reset and enlarged edition of this dictionary contains about one third more words and practical phrases than any of the previous thirteen editions published up to 1957.

POCKET SIZE—Pages 530
Price: In Japan ¥ 540, Post. ¥ 100—Abroad $3.00, Post. $0.75

glass (*material*) garasú; (*for drinking from*) koppú—*Please give me a g. of wine.* Dōzo, budōshu wo íppai kudasái.—*looking g.* kagamí—*eye-glasses* mégane—*window g.* madó-garasú—*g. works* (*factory*) garasú kōjō; (*glassware*) garasú-seihín

glide *v.t.* (*plane down*) kassō surú

glider (*Aviation*) guraidā

globe (*round object*) tamá; (*the earth*) chikyū

globe-fish fúgu

globe-trotter sekái-man-yūsha

gloom (*darkness*) kuragarí; (*sullenness*) inkí; (*melancholy*) yūutsu

gloomy (*dark*) kuraí; (*somber, dusky*) usuguraí; (*depressed*) inkí-na, yūutsu-na; (*of the weather*) uttō-shíi—*Why are you so g. to-day?* Dōshĭte kyō anáta wa sonná 'ni inkí désŭ ka.—*The weather is g. to-day.* Kyŏ wa o-ténki ga uttōshíi désŭ.—*a g. room* usuguraí heyá

glorious (*illustrious, triumphant*) kōei áru; (*majestic*) sōgon-na; (*delightful*) subarashíi

glory (*honor*) kōei; (*splendor*) sōkan; (*brilliant sight*) bikán

glove tebúkuro—*leather gloves* kawá no tebúkuro—*a pair of gloves* tebúkuro hĭtó-kumí

glow (*incandescence*) hakunetsú; (*luminosity*) hakunetsukō

glue *n.* nikawá, norí

to glue *v.t.* norí de tsŭkéru [tsŭkemásŭ]

glutton taishokŭká

glycerine risurín

gnat búyo

gnaw *v.t.* kajíru [kajirimásŭ]

go *v.i.* yukú [yukimásŭ], ikú [ikimásŭ] *Coll.;* máiru [mairimásŭ] (*humble speech*); irassháru (*polite speech*)—*Where are you going?* Dóko e irasshaimásŭ ka.—*I am going to the office.* Jimúsho e ikimásŭ.—*When will you g. to the postoffice?* Itsu yūbinkyoku e ikimásŭ ka.—*I shall g. now.* Ima ikimásŭ.—*G. this way.* Kochirá e irasshái.—*When will you g. to Osaka?* Itsu Ōsaka e irasshaimásŭ ka. —*I shall g. there next week.* Raishū mairimásŭ.—*I wish to g. to Nikko.* Nikkō e ikitái désŭ.—*G. and buy some envelopes.* Fūtō wo katté kité kudasái.—*Let us g. and take a walk.* Sampó ni ikimashō.—*Let us g. up that hill.* Anó oká e noborimashō.—*When did Mr. Imai g. out?* Itsu Imái San wa dekakemáshĭta ka.—*He went out at about ten o'clock.* Jū-ji goró o-dekaké ni narimáshĭta.—*May we g. inside?* Háitte mo yoroshíi désŭ ka.

to go away itté shimáu [shimaimásŭ]; (*return back*) káette shimáu—*to g. back* káeru [kaerimásŭ]—*to g. down* (*from stairs, car, etc.*) oríru [orimásŭ]; (*of trains*) kudarú [kudarimásŭ]—*to g. into* háiru [hairimásŭ]—*to g. out* déru [demásŭ]—*to g. up* noború [noborimásŭ] goal (aim, object of effort) mokŭ-teki; (conclusion) shūkyoku ; (sports) gōru, kesshōten

goat yági—g. milk yági no chi-chí

God (deity) kámi ; (idol) gūzō ; (Christian) Sōzō no kámi—Thank God! Arigatái.—For God's sake. Goshō désŭ kará. (lit. Happiness in the next world.—Buddhist expression)—Do you believe in G.? Anáta wa kámi wo shinjimásŭ ka.—Yes, I believe in G. Hái, (kámi wo) shinjimásŭ.—O God! Kámisama!

goddess me-gamí

godfather nazuké-oyá ; daifú

godmother nazuké-oyá ; daibó

godown kurá

godparents nazuké-oyá

gold kin—Are there any g. mines in Japan? Nippón ni kínzan ga arimásŭ ka.—g. coin kínka—g. foil kimpakú—g. fish kíngyo—g. mine kínzan—g. ring kin yubiwá

golf górufu—to play g. górufu wo surú—Do you play g.? Anáta wa górufu wo nasaimásŭ ka.—Yes, I play it often. Hái, tabí-tabí shi-másŭ—g. club gorufú kúrabu.—g. links gorufujō

good íi, yói—You are a very g. guide. Anáta wa taihén íi gáido or annáinin désŭ—She is g. looking. Anó katá wa kiryō ga íi désŭ.—Is that fruit g.? Sonó kudámono wa íi désŭ ka.—No it is not g. Iié, yóku arimasén.—This medicine will do you g. Konó kúsuri wa yóku

kikú desho.—This food is very g. Konó tabemonó wa taihén kékkō désŭ.--This pen is not g. ; bring me another. Konó pen wa damé désŭ. Hoká no wo mótte kité kudasái.—a g. deal of money takŭsán no okané—a g. many people ōzei no hĭtó

Salutations—G. morning ohayō, ohayō gozaimásŭ.—G. day Kónnichi wa.—G. afternoon. Kónnichi wa.—G. evening Kómban wa.—G. night. (on meeting) Kómban wa.; (on leaving or just before going to bed) O-yasumí nasái.—G. bye Sayónara.

goods shinamonó—fancy g. ko-mámono—foreign g. gaikokú-hin—imported g. yunyūhin—Send these g to my home. Konó shinamonó wo uchí e todókete kudasái.

goose gachō

Gospel—the G. Fukuín—to preach the G. Fukuín wo tóku

gossip n. goshíppu; (idle talk) mudá-bánashi

to gossip v.i. mudá-bánashi wo surú, shabéru [shaberimásŭ]

gout tsŭfū

govern v.t. (to rule) osaméru ; (to control) kánri surú

government (politics) seijí ; (form of polity) seitaí ; (management) kánri ; (governing body) tōchikikan ; (ministry) séifu—the Japanese g. Nippón séifu—g. official kōmuin Lit., o-yakŭnín Coll.

governor (of a province, etc.) chíji ; (of bank) sōsai

仏和会話小辞典

DICTIONNAIRE PRATIQUE
FRANCO-JAPONAIS
POUR LA CONVERSATION

(entièrement mis à jour)

NOUVELLE EDITION
Revisée—Augmentée

Cet ouvrage diffère des dictionnaires ordinaires par le fait que la plupart des mots qui y sont donnés sont accompagnés non seulement de leur équivalent japonais en caractères latins, mais aussi de phrases usuelles qui peuvent être employées facilement dans la conversation de tous les jours.

Ce dictionnaire peut ainsi être utilisé même par ceux qui n'ont aucune connaissance du japonais.

Afin de rendre ce dictionnaire plus pratique encore et plus utile, le signe (') a été employé pour indiquer en chaque mot la syllabe accentuée, de telle sorte que le lecteur peut se rendre compte immédiatement de la prononciation correcte des mots japonais cités.

Il y a beaucoup de mots japonais qui seraient parfaitement homonymes s'ils ne prenaient une signification différente selon la syllabe sur laquelle porte l'accent tonique. Par exemple: le mot **ip'pai** avec l'accent tonique sur le premier **i**, signifie *une tasse*, tandis qu'avec l'accent tonique sur **a** le même mot signifie *plein*. Cet exemple (et l'on pourrait en donner beaucoup d'autres) montre bien l'importance pratique de l'accent tonique en japonais.

Des signes spéciaux ont été employés également pour distinguer les voyelles longues et les voyelles muettes.

A l'aide de ces signes phonétiques, ceux qui se serviront de ce dictionnaire pourront facilement apprendre à prononcer correctement les mots japonais, même s'ils ne se donnent pas la peine d'étudier les règles nombreuses et souvent incertaines de prononciation auxquelles, à defaut de ce dictionnaire, il leur faudrait avoir recours pour parler la langue japonaise de manière à être bien compris des japonais eux-mêmes.

Un autre avantage qui caractérise ce dictionnaire, c'est que tous les verbes sont donnés non seulement avec la forme japonaise correspondant à notre infinitif, mais aussi avec la forme du présent de l'indicatif, de telle sorte que l'on peut employer ces formes directement même si l'on ne connait pas les règles de la conjugaison des verbes.

Toutes ces innovations lexicographiques, telles qu'elles apparaissent dans la page specimen qui suit, feront de cet ouvrage le livre indispensable pour tous les étrangers qui sont dans la necessité de bein parler japonais, et pour ceux-là aussi qui désirent simplement être en mesure de tenir une petite conversation en japonais.

550 pages, 15×11 centimètres—Prix ￥1,000 au Japon
Frais d'envoi ￥ 100—à l'étrager $ 5.00, Frais d'envoi $ 0.75

zuiín—*a. de légation* kōshi-zuiín—
a. de l'air kūgunbukán—*a. commercial* shomúkan—*a. militaire*
rikúgun-bukán—*a. naval* kaigún-
bukán

attachement nésshin, aichakú
attacher (*joindre*) tsükéru
[tsükemásü], musubí-tsükéru — *a.
une chose avec de la colle* náni ka
wo norizuké ni surú

attaque kōgeki—*une* **a.** *de nuit*
yashū—*une* **a.** *générale* sōkōgeki—
une **a.** *aérienne* kūshū—*J'ai eu une*
a. *de rhumatisme.* Ryōmachi ni
kakarimáshïta.

attaquer (*en cachette*) osoú
[osoimásü]; (*assaillir*) kōgeki surú
—*J'ai été* **attaqué** *par un voleur.*
Dorobō ni osowaremáshïta.

attarder temadoraséru [tema-
dorasemásü]
s'attarder temadóru [temadori-
másü]—*s'a. en route* tochū de temadóru

atteindre (*à une hauteur*) todóku
[todokimásü]; (*quelqu'un en mar-
chant*) oitsükú [oitsúkimásü]; (*ar
river à*) ni tassúru [tasshimásü]—
C'est trop haut, je ne puis pas y **atteindre.** Amarí takái désü kará
todokimasén.—*Votre lettre m'a* **at-
teint** *hier.* Sakújitsu o-tegamí wo
itadakimáshïta.—*Il est trop loin,
nous ne pouvons pas l'a.* Anó katá

wa amarí tōku e irasshaimáshïta
kará oitsúku kotó ga dekimasén.—
J'espère pouvoir bientôt **a.** *mon but.*
Mokutekí wo háyakᵉ tasshitái
désü.

attendre mátsu [machimásü]—
Attendez un moment. Chottó
mátte kudasái.—*Attendez-moi s'il
vous plaît.* Shibáraku mátte kudasái.—*Je regrette de vous avoir fait*
a. Dōmo o-machidōsama.—*Atten-
dons un peu plus longtemps.* Mō-
sükóshi machimashō.—*Je ne puis
pas* **a.** *plus longtemps.* Mō mátsu
kotó ga dekimasén.—*J'ai* **attendu**
assez longtemps. Mō jūbun machi-
máshïta. — *Dites-lui s'il vous plaît
d'a.* Anó katá ni mátte kudasáru
yō ni hanáshïte kudasái.—*Combien
de temps avez-vous* **attendu?** Dóno
kurái o-machí ni narimáshïta ka.—
J'ai **attendu** *pendant une demi-
heure.* Sánjippun guraí machimá-
shïta. — *Attendez jusqu'à mon
retour.* Watashí ga káeru máde
mátte kudasái.—*Qu'est-ce que vous*
attendez? Náni wo mátte irasshai-
másü ka.— *Je suis fatigué d'a.*
Machí-kutabiremáshïta. — *Combien
de temps avons-nous à* **a.?** Dóno
kurái matánakereba narimasén ka.
s'attendre machiawaserú [machi-
awasemásü]—*Je ne m'attendais
pas à cela.* Soré wa omói mo yora-

sōsaku, (*de monuments*) kembutsú—
faire une v. hōmon surú, o-tazuné
surú—*Je désire faire une* v. *à* M.
Arita. Arita San wo o-tazuné shitái
désŭ.

UNE VISITE

*Est-ce bien la demeure de M. Mo-
tonari Miwata?* Kochirá wa Miwatá
Motónari San no o-takú désŭ ka.—
M. Miwata demeure-t-il ici? Miwatá
San wa kokó ni súnde irasshaimásŭ
ka.—*Est-ce que M. Miwata est chez lui?*
Miwatá San wa go-zaitakú désŭ ka.
Je désirerais voir M. Miwata. Miwatá San ni o-me ni kakaritái désŭ.—
Voici ma carte. Koré wa watakŭshí
no meishí désŭ.—*Je m'appelle
Brinon.* Watashí no namaé wa
Burinón désŭ.—*Veuillez m'annoncer
à M. Miwata.* Miwatá San ni o-tori-
tsugí negaimásŭ.—*Bonjour M. Miwata.* Kónnichi wa.—*Comment allez-
vous?* Ikága de gozaimásŭ ka.—
Veuillez-vous asseoir (*sur une chaise*).
Dōzo, o-kaké kudasái. (*Si c'est sur
un coussin, dans les maisons japo-
naises*) Dōzo, o-shikí kudasái.—*Je
suis très heureux que vous soyez venu
me voir.* Yóku o-idé kudasai-mashi-
tá.—*Comment va la famille?* Go-
kázoku wa ikága désŭ ka.—*Très
bien, merci.* Arigatō gozaimásŭ. Taihén jōbu désŭ.—*Et comment va
Madame Miwata?* Okŭsama wa

ikága désŭ ka.—*Elle se porte bien.
Elle est allée à Nikko hier.* Tasshá
désŭ. Kanái wa sakújitsu Nikkō e
yukimashíta. — *Vous prendrez bien
une tasse de thé.* Dōzo, o-cha wo meshi-
agatté kudasái.—*Ne vous gênez pas.*
Dōzo, go-enryó náku.—*Mettez-vous
à votre aise, je vous prie.* Dōzo, o-
rakú ni.—*Je vais prendre congé.* O-
itomá itashimásŭ.—*Je reviendrai.*
Matá ukagaimásŭ.—*Vous êtes bien
pressée.* O-isogí ni naránai de kudasái.—*Restez encore un peu, s'il vous
plaît.* Dōzo, mō sŭkóshi irassháite
kudasái.—*J'espère vous revoir bientôt.*
Chikái uchí ni matá o-me ni kakaritái désŭ.—*Faites-moi le plaisir de
revenir.* Matá irasshái. *Mes respects
à Madame.* Okŭsama ni yoroshikú.
Après vous. Dōzo, o-sakí e.—*Soignez
bien votre santé.* Dōzo, o-dáiji ni.—
Au revoir. Sayonará.

visiter (*une personne*) hōmon
surú, tazunéru [tazunemásŭ]; (*des
monuments, etc.*) kembutsú surú

visiteur hōmonsha, raihōsha, o-
kyakusamá

visser nejíru [nejirimásŭ]

vitamine bitámin

vite *adj.* hayái; *adv.* háyaku.—
Ne parlez pas si v. Dōzo, sonná ni
háyaku hanasánai de kudasái.—*Je
ne puis pas travailler plus* v. Koré
yóri háyaku hatarakemasén. —

PAGE SPECIMEN

英和・和英辞典

VACCARI'S CONCISE
ENGLISH-JAPANESE—JAPANESE-ENGLISH
DICTIONARY
(in roman and Japanese symbolic characters)
500 pages—$3^1/_2 \times 2$ inches
Price: in Japan Yen 450, Post. ￥100—Abroad $ 2.50, Post. $ 0.75

This little volume is the first and only English-Japanese and Japanese-English Dictionary that gives the transliteration of Japanese words in roman characters as well as their corresponding Japanese symbolic script, and although small, it contains all the words used in our ordinary daily conversation.

It is, moreover, the only English-Japanese and Japanese-English Dictionary that shows, by a graphic accent, the stressed syllable of the Japanese words formed by two or more syllables, which enables its user to pronounce them correctly.

This Dictionary may thus be used to advantage by those who have no knowledge of Japanese or know too little of it to make themselves understood by Japanese people who can only speak their own native language. It will therefore be useful to tourists visiting Japan during their short stay in the country and to those foreigners who, staying in Japan for a longer period of time do not contemplate starting the methodical study of Japanese.

It may be added however, that, since this little book is the only English-Japanese Japanese-English Dictionary that gives the transliteration in roman characters of the Japanese words as well as their corresponding symbolic script, this new and modest work may be welcomed also by those advanced foreign students of Japanese who haven't reached yet that degree of knowledge that is necessary to acquire in order to be able to use a bilingual dictionary intended for Japanese people in which Japanese words are given only in symbolic characters.

**See next page for specimen of
English-Japanese and Japanese-English parts**

Specimen Pages

daibó 代母 godmother
daibúbun 大部分 the greater part of
daibutsú 大仏 colossal statue of Buddha
daidokoró 台所 kitchen
daigakú 大学 university
daigíshi 代議士 member of the House of Representatives
daihyō 代表 representation
daihyōsha 代表者 representative man
dái-ichí 第一 the first, No. 1
daijí 大事 great thing, serious matter
dáijin 大臣 minister of state
daijōbu 大丈夫 all right. sure. O.K.
daikín 代金 price, cost
daikín-hikikaé 代金引換 C.O.D.
dái-kiraí 大嫌い abhorrence
daikón 大根 garden radish
dáiku 大工 carpenter
daiméishi 代名詞 pronoun
daimyō 大名 feudal lord
dainán 大難 great calamity
dairí 代理 agency, proxy
dairínin 代理人 deputy, agent
dairíseki 大理石 marble
dairí táishi 代理大使 chargé d' affaires
dairitén 代理店 agency
dái-rokkán 第六感 the sixth sense
dái-san 第三 the 3rd, No. 8
dái-senkyóku 大選挙区 the major constituency
daishó 代書 scribe
daishō 代将 brigadier-general
daisū 代数 algebra
dáisuki 大好き to be crazy about
daitaí 大体 generally

Specimen page
of the JAPANESE-ENGLISH part

a—no definite article in Japanese—*a house* uchí—*a horse* umá
abbot (*Buddhist*) sōjō 僧正, (*Christian*) sōinchō 僧院長
abbreviate—(*shorten*) shōryaku surú 省略する
abdomen onaka おなか
abduct (*kidnap*) yūkai surú 誘拐する
ability (*capacity*) shúwan 手腕; (*skill*) giryō 技量
able—*to* ... dekiru 出来る *See* **can**
abnormal (*unusual*) ijō-na 異常な; (*unnatural*) fushizen no 不自然の
abolish haishi surú 廃止する
abound takŭsán áru 沢山ある
about (*referring to time*) góro 頃—*a two o'clock* ni-ji góro (*referring to quantity*) kuraí, guraí 位,—*a. one hundred* hyakú guraí—*a. three days* mikká guraí
above (*higher than, over*) ué ni 上に
abroad (*foreign country*) gaikokú 外国; (*overseas*) káigai 海外—*to go a.* gaikokú e iku.
absence (*being away*) rúsu 留守—*during one's a.* rusuchū 留守中
absent (*away*) rúsu désu 留守です
absentminded (*vacant*) bon-yári ぼんやり
absolutely mattaku desu 全くです
abstain (*from*) yamerú やめる
absurd kōtōmukei-na 荒唐無稽な
abundant takŭsán no 沢山の
accent ákusento アクセント
accident (*incident*) jiken 事件; (*mishap*) jiko 事故

Specimen page
of the ENGLISH-JAPANESE part

JAPANESE IN A HURRY

(Revised and Enlarged)

A QUICK APPROACH TO
JAPANESE LANGUAGE

Containing 100 Short Lessons
on Subjects of Daily Conversation and
1000 Basic Japanese Words

This book is a revision of the 100 lessons which appeared in the *Pacific Stars & Stripes*, among whose readers it soon gained great popularity, an eloquent proof of the effectiveness of its method. Now issued in book form in response to popular demand.

The present edition of **Japanese in a Hurry** contains forty more pages than the previous six editions published in the short period of three years. The additional pages give a most interesting description of the characteristic **Annual Events in Japan.** Eight pictures illustrate some of the described events.

The additional pages alone are worth the price of the book.

POCKET SIZE—210 Pages
Price: In Japan ¥ 450, Post. ¥ 100
Abroad $ 2.50, Post. $ 0.75

LESSON 12

YOU AND I. (ANATA TO WATASHI)

You and I are good friends. **Anáta to watashí-wa íi tomodachí désǔ.**

Are you a Chinese? **Anáta-wa Shiná-jin désǔ ka.**

No, I am a Japanese **Iié, watashí-wa Nihón-jin désǔ.**

How old are you? **Anáta-wa íkutsu désǔ ka.** (You, how many are?)

I am 20 years old. **Watashí-wa ní-jissai désǔ.** (jíssai = jū + sai*)

   In Japanese, the personal pronoun is generally omitted whenever the reference is clear, as in the following examples:

Have you a pencil? **Empḷtsú-wo mótte imásǔ ka.**

   Yes, I have. **Hái, mótte-imásǔ.**

   No, I have not. **Iié, mótte-imasén.**

Did you go to the theatre? **Shibaí e ikimáshïta ka.**

   Yes, I did. **Hái, ikimáshïta.** (Yes, I went.)

   No, I didn't. **Iie, ikimasén déshïta.** (No, I did not go.)

   In answering a question, the principal verb is used in Japanese even when in English it is given by the simple auxiliary **do** or **did**, as in the previous examples.

HE AND SHE

He and she may be translated by **anó ḳatá** (in less polite speech: **ano hïtó**).

Both **anó katá** and **anó hïtó** correspond, translated literally, to "that person."

He (that person) is a trader. **Anó katá-wa bōekishō désǔ.**

She is a teacher. **Anó katá-wa senséi désǔ.**

---

   * In telling somebody's age, the word **sái** (age) is used after the stated number of years.

CORSO COMPLETO

GRAMMATICA

DELLA

LINGUA GIAPPONESE

di ORESTE ed ELISA ENKO VACCARI

"UN MANUALE PIACEVOLE
PER UNA LINGUA DIFFICILE"

(Da un commento sulla prima edizione in inglese della Grammatica
Giapponese di Oreste ed Enko Elisa Vaccari, apparso ne "LA TRIBUNA"
di Roma.

"Questa Grammatica è senza dubbio il miglior manuale per chi
voglia apprendere il giapponese parlato. Ed è anche un eccellente
avviamento per imparare a scriverlo. Famigliarizza lo studioso
anche con i segni cinesi, i quali formano la sostanza lessicale di un
testo nipponico."

"Ogni esercizio è trascritto in caratteri latini, accompagnati dal
testo in scrittura giapponese e dalla traduzione: fornisce cioè tutto
il materiale che può servire ad un autodidatta."

"Numerosissime note lo consigliano su usi, costumi, allusioni
letterarie. Non manca qualche notissima fiaba, come quella di
Momotaro, popolare laggiú quanto Cappuccetto Rosso da noi."

In 8°, di pag. XLV–570, con otto illustrazioni a colori,
una grande carta geografica del Giappone e una pianta
dettagliata della città di Tokio.

Prezzo: (nel Giappone) ¥2,000, Affr. ¥200—Estero $10.00, Affr. $1.00

GIAPPONESE IN FRETTA E FURIA

MANUALETTO DI CONVERSAZIONE
ITALO-GIAPPONESE

200 pagine—15 × 11 centimetri
Prezzo: (nel Giappone) ¥1,000, Affr. ¥100—Estero $5.00, Affr. $0.75

Questo libro, come il suo titolo ben suggerisce, non è stato preparato per uno studio metodico della lingua giapponese. Il suo scopo è più modesto: di dare cioè delle frasi semplici su soggetti di conversazione usuale in modo che la persona che lo usa, sia che essa abbia poca o nessuna conoscenza di giapponese, possa esprimere i suoi pensieri in semplice forma quando desidera parlare con persone del paese del Sol Levante.

Si può aggiungere che questo modesto libro può essere utile anche a chi si trova già avanzato nello studio di giapponese, dato che le frasi che esso contiene sono del discorso di ogni giorno, molte delle quali sono generalmente trascurate ed omesse nei libri per uno studio metodico.

Questo libro è diviso in novanta brevi lezioni, ognuna delle quali tratta un soggetto diverso della vita giornaliera. Nelle ultime dieci lezioni sono dati alcuni dei racconti più popolari nel Giappone in modo che chi usa questo libro può avere un piccolo saggio del folclore giapponese.

Oltre alle novanta lezioni, questo libro contiene "Mille Parole" delle più usuali della lingua giapponese, date tanto in caratteri simbolici che in caratteri latini e con la loro traduzione in italiano, ed una trentina di pagine con la descrizione degli eventi annuali di maggior importanza celebrati nel Giappone. Dieci illustrazioni a colori mostrano scene di alcuni di tali eventi.

Questo volumetto contiene così abbastanza materiale per risolvere le difficoltà linguistiche che si possono presentare a chi, non essendo a conoscenza della lingua giapponese, è nella necessità di doversi esprimere in essa. Ed è anche un buon avviamento per chi desidera iniziare uno studio metodico dell'idioma parlato nel Giappone.

4ª LEZIONE

Piace e Non piace

Mi piace. Sŭkí désŭ. Non mi piace. Sŭkimasén o Kirái désŭ.

Vi piace? Sŭkí désŭ ka. Non vi piace? Sŭkimasén ka o Kirái désŭ ka.

Quale? Dóchira.

L'espressione dóchira si usa quando la cosa alla quale si riferisce non è menzionata.

Quale vi piace? Dóchira-ga sŭki désŭ ka.

Mi piace questo. (Mi piacciono questi.) Koré-ga sŭkí désŭ.

Mi piace quello. (Mi piacciono quelli.) Aré-ga sŭkí désŭ.

Non vi piace questo? (Non vi piacciono questi?) Koré-wo sŭkimasén ka. o Koré-wo kirái désŭ ka.

Vi piace questo quadro? Konó e-wo sŭkí désŭ ka.

Vi piace la cucina italiana? Itari-ryōri-wo sŭkí désŭ ka.

Vi piace la cucina giapponese? Nihón-shokú-wo sŭkí désŭ ka.

Vi piace la cucina straniera? Yōshoku-wo sŭkí désŭ ka?

Si, mi piace. Hái, sŭkí désŭ.

No, nom mi piace. Sŭkimasén.

Quale volete comperare? Dóchira-wo kaimásŭ ka. (Quale comprate?)

Quale è migliore? Dóchira-ga mótto íi désŭ ka. (Quale è piú buono?)

Quando quale è immediatamente seguito dalla parola indicante la cosa di cui si parla, essa viene tradotta da dóno.

Quale libro vi piace? Dóno hon-ga sŭkí désŭ ka.

Quale cappello volete comperare? Dóno bōshi-wo kaimásŭ ka.

Comprerò il cappello nero. Kurói bōshi-wo kaimásŭ.

Il cappello nero è grazioso. Kurói bōshi-wa kírei désŭ.

Quale libro desiderate, questo o quello?

Dóno hon-ga hoshíi désŭ ka, koré désŭ ka, aré désŭ ka.

(SPECIMEN PAGE)

Numero sbagliato. **Bangō ga machigátte imásŭ.**
telefonare **denwá-wo kakéru**
Io telefono, voi telefonate, ecc. **Denwá-wo kakemásŭ.**
Telefonate per favore. **Denwá-wo kákete kudasái.**

59ª LEZIONE

UFFICIO POSTALE—YŪBIN-KYOKÚ

Dove è la Posta Centrale?
Chūō Yūbin-kyokú wa dóko désŭ ka.
Dove si trova l'ufficio postale più vicino?
Ichibán chikái yūbin-kyokú-wa dóko désŭ ka.
(Il primo vicino ufficio postale dove è?)
Desidero inviare questa lettera per espresso.
Konó tegamí-wo sokutatsú de dashitái désŭ.
(Questa lettera, per espresso, desidero inviare.)
Voglio inviare questa lettera per via aerea.
Koré-wo kōkūbin de dashitái désŭ.
(Questa lettera per via aerea desidero inviare.)
Quando verrà consegnata? **Ítsu todóku deshō ka.**
Voglio raccomandare questa lettera.
Konó tegamí-wa kakitomé ni shĭtái désŭ.
(Questa per raccomandata desidero fare.)
Datemi la ricevuta. **Uketorí-wo kudasái.**
Questa lettera via ordinaria.
Konó tegamí-wa futsŭ yūbin désŭ.
Quanto è l'affrancatura di questa lettera?
Konó tegamí no sōryō-wa íkura désŭ ka.
Quanto è il porto per inviare una lettera in Europa via aerea?
Yōroppa e no kōkūbin sōryō-wa íkura désŭ ka.
(In Europa via aerea affrancatura quanto è?)

(SPECIMEN PAGE)

漢字カード

IN PLASTIC AGE
PLASTIC
KANJI CARDS

TO MASTER JAPANESE SYMBOLIC CHARACTERS

Size of the Cards 2×2½ inches
Size of Plastic Filing Cabinet 9×5½×6½ inches—Weight 9 lbs.
Price of the set: in Japan Yen 7,000, Post. ¥ 200—Abroad $ 35.00, Post. $ 200

This new publication brings the study of **Kanji** abreast with the present scientific age. In fact, for the first time, **plastic** has been used to produce the 1850 characters prescribed a few years ago by the Japanese Ministry of Education for use in newspapers and magazines, a measure adopted to simplify the Japanese written language.

In this new, original and pioneering publication, every one of the 1850 characters is given on one side of a **plastic card**, in brush style originally written by an expert calligrapher, while on the reverse side its pronunciation in roman letters and corresponding English meaning are given. Moreover, each character in brush style is repeated below in printed style in its most common compound character-words, whose transliteration in roman letters and English meaning are also given on the reverse side of the cards.

As these compounds words (over 7,000) form a careful selection of the ones used in modern times in books, newspapers and magazines, these **kanji cards** will prove of great advantage to the student who intends learning the Japanese written language.

The **1850 plastic cards** contained in an attractive and specially designed **Plastic Filing Cabinet**, have been divided in two sliding receptacles and in groups according to the number of their strokes. Each division is separated from the next one by partitions indicating the respective number of strokes of the characters.

Before this original publication given in plastic material came out, its authors had published a set of cards printed on paper and contained in a cardboard box. Unfortunately, after being used for sometime, the cards, although printed on resistant paper, became somewhat soiled and worn-out. Moreover, while the former set was restricted to only 1250 characters, which were considered as the most common and essential ones before the measures to simplify the Japanese written language were adopted, the new plastic set contains all the 1850 characters used at the present time for any kind of printed matter. Therefore, these **Plastic Kanji Cards** now published constitute a complete work that will enable the student to learn all that is necessary to read Japanese newspapers, magazines and books.

The double advantage of the new Plastic Cards is that, as one master some characters, they can be placed at the end of their special sections, and just the particular ideographs with which one wishes to deal may be taken out and thoroughly concentrated upon ; moreover the cards will remain always bright and clean, no matter how many times they are used for their study, since they can be wiped whenever they get soiled.

Indeed it may well be said that this really practical "**Plastic Character-card Filing Cabinet**" will prove of great assistance to the student of the Japanese written language, when one considers the distinctive advantages it offers.

A UNIQUE, PIONEERING PUBLICATION

BRUSH UP YOUR JAPANESE

ぶらし あっぷ ゆあー じゃぱにーず

THE BOOK THAT GIVES THE FINISHING TOUCHES
TO ONE'S KNOWLEDGE OF JAPANESE

This original, unique publication will be most welcome to all students of the Japanese language who intend to learn it thoroughly to its minutest particulars, in order to give the finishing touch to their already acquired knowledge.

In fact, this new work constitutes a detailed and most careful analysis of the composition of phrases, sentences and idioms that may appear of difficult understanding and interpretation.

The detailed explanations given in this book of every difficulty that the Japanese language may present to the foreign student, will render its study most pleasant and entertaining, and its knowledge an acquisition possessing critical awareness.

The aim of this new work is different from that of the "Japanese Conversation Grammar" by the same authors, but it may well be considered a most valuable Supplement to it, in that while the said Grammar gives a solid ground and the necessary rules to build up and use intelligibly the Japanese speech, the present book constitutes a critical examination and close scrutiny not only of every one of the gramatical parts of the Japanese language but also an analysis of the many idioms and unusual phrases which, not following grammatical rules are difficult to understand unless explained in detail.

It may here be added that although this new work is intended principally for rather advanced students, yet it may be used to very great advantage even by those who have only elementary knowledge of the language because under each Japanese word of every example given in the book, its English translation has been printed, which renders the construction and the meaning of the sentences clear to anyone, no matter how little or how much one may have studied.

Moreover, in a great number of cases the meaning of each component of compound character-words has been given so that the significance of the symbolic expressions will appear to the student's mind as in colorful pictures, which will be of great assistance in memorizing them besides giving etymological knowledge.

This book is a greatly improved and much enlarged edition of the first fiftytwo lessons that appeared weekly in the daily "Asahi Evening News" of Tokyo, from September the 20th 1958 to September 19th 1959, that is, during one full year, under the title Brush Up Your Japanese. And it was because of the desire expressed by many of the readers of the said newspaper to have the lessons in book form that this work has now been published.

Among the improvements over the lessons appeared in the mentioned newspaper that have been introduced in this book, is the translation of every English example not only in the Japanese trans-literation with roman characters but also in the symbolic script, which could not be done in a newspaper because of the limited space allowed for any periodical feature.

At the end of the fiftytwo lessons contained in this book, a symbolic character has been given, as it appeared in the above mentioned newspaper, in the representation of its original form, in its alterations of forms it underwent through the centuries and as it is represented in modern times.

To make this book more attractive and more useful to those who will use it, besides enlarging it with **additional representative examples,** the following new features have been included:

1. An alphabetic list of the onomatopoetic expressions used by the Japanese at the present time in their daily conversation, with suitable and practical examples showing how to use them.

2. A list of Japanese family and given names with the English corresponding meaning of each of their components, which will greatly facilitate memorizing them.

Anyone using this book will agree that it is really a unique, pioneering publications.

9×6 Inches—350 Pages
Price: in Japan Yen 1,500, Post. Yen 200
Abroad $ 8.00, Post. $ 1.00

LESSON 1—Dái Ikka 第一課

A

★ From A to Z.　　　　　Hajimé　kará　owarí　máde.
　　　　　　　　　　　初め　　から　終り　まで
From beginning to end. Beginning from end till.

　(owarí from owarú 終る to come to an end, a close *or* termination; to be over, to finish, to conclude, etc.)

★ I understood from A. to Z.　Sukkári wakarimásh̆ita.
I perfectly understood.　　　すっかり 分かりました
　　　　　　　　　　　　　　Entirely understood.

　(sukkári すっかり entirely, completely, wholly, thoroughly, totally, etc.; wakarimásh̆ita *past of* wakáru 分かる to understand, grasp, make out, make sense, etc.)

★ In a word, I don't approve of your plan.
Tsúmari (*or* Hĭtó-kuchí ni iéba) go-keikakú ni　sanséi　surú　kotó ga
つまり（　一　口　に言えば）御 計画　に　賛成　する　事　が
In short (One mouth in if said) your-plan to, approval to make, the fact
dekimasén.
出来ません
cannot. [*lit.* If expressed in a few words, to your plan approval cannot. kotó ga substantivizes the verb sanséi surú to approve, give one's approval (to a plan), agree (to a person's opinion, with a person), etc.; kotó ga dekimasén the thing or the doing cannot=it can't be done]

★ At the party I was introduced to a Mr. Inoue.
Anó enkái de Inoué-san tó-ka iú katá ni　shōkai　saremásh̆ita.
あの 宴会 で 井上さん とかいう 方 に　紹介　されました
That party at, Inoue-Mr. so-called person to, introduction I was made.

　(tó-ka iú formed by to *so*, ka interrogative particle and iú *to call*; shōkai surú 紹介する to introduce, present, usher, etc.; shōkai sarerú 紹介され る to be introduced, etc.)

★ You have become quite a stranger　Sukkári o-mikagirí désŭ　　ne.
　　to me.　　　　　　　　　　　すっかり お見限り　です　　ね
　　　　　　　　　　　　　　Entirely deserter you are, I must say.

(SPECIMEN PAGE)

日本語学習レコード

VACCARI'S

JAPANESE ON RECORD

A SET OF THREE RECORDS
THAT BRINGS AN EXPERT JAPANESE TEACHER RIGHT
IN YOUR STUDY TO GIVE YOU PRACTICAL SPOKEN
KNOWLEDGE OF THE LANGUAGE YOU INTEND
TO MASTER

With diligent application and depending on books only, a student may learn perfectly well how to understand the Japanese language in its written form and may even become so proficient in his knowledge as to be able to interpret correctly its most difficult literary passages. However, his knowledge thus acquired would be limited to its theoretical field, and were he to hear spoken words of the written language that he may know to perfection, he wouldn't understand them. In fact, the sound of the spoken words would strike his ears as altogether unfamiliar and they would fail to make any connection with his knowledge accumulated in his brain during his years of study. The same may be said of the study of any other foreign language.

The reason of such a disappointing situation is lack of hearing practice of the spoken language that one knows only theoretically.

The ideal way to remedy such a regrettable situation is to get in contact with persons speaking the language one studies or already knows, and converse with them whenever possible. Unfortunately few are those who find themselves in such a favorable situation.

Most students of a foreign language study it with books and only on rare occasions they have the opportunity of hearing its living sounds.

Fortunately modern science has succeeded in capturing and reproducing human voice mechanically in records, thus enabling the student to hear the recorded voice of an expert teacher at any time of the day whenever he is willing to be taught how to understand the spoken words of the language he is studying.

The set of Vaccari's records will give you such an advantage to complete your study of the Japanese language.

The set of VACCARI'S JAPANESE ON RECORD includes a 110-page book containing the text of the spoken words and sentences reproduced in the three records. The whole set is packed and well protected in a solid cardboard box.

The Japanese words printed in the textbook were spoken by Mr. Hiroshi Tamaoki, a young Japanese well known as a radio and television announcer and commentator. The few English words announcing the titles of the subjects given in the Japanese textbook were spoken by the author.

This is another addition to the long series of books for the study of the Japanese language by Mr. and Mrs. Oreste Vaccari.

Price of the set of the three 10-inch records (33 rpm.)
and the 110-page text-book

(in Japan) ¥ 3,600, Postage ¥ 200, Abroad $17.00, Post. $1.00

エービーシー式漢和英大辭典

A.B.C. JAPANESE-ENGLISH DICTIONARY

REVISED AND ENLARGED

This dictionary is based on the alphabetic system, and not upon the old scheme of the radicals and the number of the remaining strokes of *kanji*, which system has been used, up to now, for the compilation of dictionaries of Chinese-Japanese characters.

Single strokes, characteristic stroke-combinations and basic *kanji* are here classified and arranged in logic progression, in 26 groups, corresponding to the number of the letters of the English alphabet.

After having memorized what might be called the **kanji-alphabet,** every Chinese-Japanese character and every compound kanji-word, can be found, in the dictionary, as easily and with the same mathematical precision as one finds words in dictionaries of the European languages, since each element of every *kanji* has its proper determined place under the letter in which it has been classified.

As practical illustrations of the new system, let us consider the following characters:

印 **in** a seal (for making impressions).

According to the kanji-alphabet the character 印 is formed by the element Ｅ, classified under letter **E,** and by 卩 classified under letter **P.** The character 印 then, corresponds to the hypothetical word **EP** and will, therefore, be found in its fixed place in letter **E** of this dictionary, according to the instructions given in detail at the beginning of the book.

張 **haru** to stretch—The element 弓 is classified under letter **S,** 匡 under **E** and the lower element 𠆢 also under **E.** The character 張 then, corresponds to the hypothetical word **SEE,** and will be found in its fixed place in letter **S.**

The two characters given above have been purposely selected for introduction to the new system, because of the coincidental resemblance of the elements composing them to the shape of the corresponding letters **E, P** and **S** of the English alphabet, which coincidence should make the reader of this outline grasp immediately the idea of the new system for the classification of Sino-

Japanese ideographs.

Once the student has memorized the kanji-alphabet, he will be free from the troublesome, and at times long and uncertain system of the radicals and the counting of the remaining strokes of the *kanji* under consideration, which, if he were to use an ordinary *kanji* dictionary, he would be forced to follow whenever he wished to identify any Chinese-Japanese character or compound kanji-word.

This dictionary contains 12,000 *kanji* with their respective compound words (totalling about 80,000). It is compiled in such a way that it may be used, not only according to the new kanji-alphabet system but also according to the old system of the radicals. Those already familiar with the latter system will thus be enabled to use the book immediately even before having mastered the new one.

Other **main features** of this dictionary are:

1. A history of the Chinese ideographs.

2. The origin of the two Japanese syllabic scripts, *Katakana* and *Hiragana*.

3. Method of writing Japanese syllables and Chinese characters.

4. A list of the 1850 *kanji* approved by the Education Ministry in 1947 as the only official ones to be used by all newspapers, magazines and government documents, in an attempt to symplify the Japanese written language.

5. One Thousand **BASIC KANJI** in the *Kaisho* (modern), *Sosho* (cursive) and *Tensho* (ancient) styles of writing.

As most of them, besides being used as independent characters, are used as components of more complex ones, their study and knowledge will prove of great assistance in mastering the Chinese written symbols.

6. The SENJIMON or Thousand Character Classic (in brush style), with explanatory notes and full English translation.

7. Subject distribution of 60 common symbols.

8. How to "spell" Chinese-Japanese characters.

9. The Emperors of Japan and the Japanese Eras.

10. Besides the inclusion of additional kanji-words, the second edition of this dictionary contains, as a new feature, a list of over two thousand words of foreign origin introduced into the Japanese language, invariably written in katakana characters.

This dictionary may indeed be considered an Encyclopedia of the Japanese language.

In Two Volumes

Strongly bound in half leather and cloth.—**THUMB-INDEXED**

10½×8 inches, 1,900 pages—Net Weight 9½ lbs.

Price: in Japan ¥ 8,000, Post. ¥ 200—Abroad $ 38.00, Post. $ 2.00

Extracts from Press Comments on the
A. B. C. JAPANESE-ENGLISH DICTIONARY

THE LONDON TIMES (LITERARY SUPPLEMENT)

It was because of his own troubles in finding his way through dictionaries of the Japanese language printed in characters that Mr. Vaccari sought for some new method of classifying these. He got what he wanted, and his great dictionary, in the compilation of which "Mrs. Vaccari's deep knowledge of her Japanese mother tongue" has been one of his main resources, is arranged accordingly.

By this new arrangement the fundamental characteristics of all Chinese-Japanese characters have been classified into 26 groups, corresponding to the number of the letters of the English alphabet.

Such is the simple special feature of the work, which contains 12,000 kanji and their 80,000 compound words; but to point this out is not enough to suggest the rich, comprehensive and living effect of the two quarto volumes.

PACIFIC STARS AND STRIPES

The Far East U. S. Army Daily Newspaper:

Oreste and Enko Elisa Vaccari, world-famed linguists and lexicographers, have compiled a Japanese-English Dictionary which employs an ABC system whereby Japanese symbolic characters and words may be found even by a person unfamiliar with the language.

The new work, which provides a faster method of finding words even for Japanese speaking people, is believed to be the largest edition pubished in Japan since the beginning of the Pacific War.

BCON

The Far East Daily of the British Occupation Forces in Japan:

Vaccari has surmounted the difficulty of finding symbolic characters in Japanese dictionaries by a basically new method and using entirely different principles in the classification of ideographs.

Extracts from Press Comments on the
A. B. C. JAPANESE-ENGLISH DICTIONARY

THE NIPPON TIMES
English Daily Newspaper issued in Tokyo.

When the Manchu Emperor Kang Hsi (1662—1723) sanctioned the publication of a dictionary of Chinese characters based on 214 radicals (basic units) and a system of strokes, he laid down a tradition that was to dominate the mind of Chinese, Japanese, Koreans and all people that use Chinese ideographs, for some 350 years.

This practice may be superseded by the monumental work of Mr. and Mrs. Oreste Vaccari. Their "ABC Japanese-English Dictionary" in two quarto volumes may well revolutionize kanji (Chinese-characters) lexicography.

Mr. Vaccari's book will be found amazingly convenient not only by foreign students of kanji but by Japanese as well.

CONTEMPORARY JAPAN
Review of Far East Asiatic Affairs.

A novel system is introduced by Mr. Vaccari in his new Japanese-English dictionary. His system has greatly simplified the troublesome task of looking up Japanese characters in dictionaries.

Mr. Vaccari, author of notable books on Japanese language, has conceived a new system of classifying Japanese characters by their general appearance and outstanding parts, and grouping them into twenty-six divisions, corresponding to the letters of the English alphabet. In each division words are arranged in the order of their complication, or from the simplest to the most complicated.

Alphabetic symbols that stand for the 26 divisions, the author calls "Kanji Alphabet." The list of the Kanji Alphabet will tell any one at a glance in what division the symbol in question is listed. Then it is possible to find any complicated word, without counting its number of strokes.

His system will cut down the time required for looking up words in dictionaries to less than one tenth of what people now spend in using old fashioned dictionaries.

昭和十二年一月十日　初版印刷
昭和十二年一月十五日　発　行

版　所
権　有

◆日本語会話文典◆

昭和三十九年四月十日十九版（改訂新版）発行

著　作　兼 発　行　者	オレステ・ヴァカリ エンコ・エリザ・ヴアカリ

東京都渋谷区原宿二丁目一七〇番地 21 号

印　刷　者	高　橋　武　夫

東京都新宿区市ケ谷加賀町一丁目十二番地

印　刷　所	大日本印刷株式会社

東京都新宿区市ケ谷加賀町一丁目十二番地

発　行　所	ヴァカリ語学研究所

東京都渋谷区原宿二丁目一七〇番地 21 号
電話青山 (401) 2585 番

改訂新版

PRICE (in Japan) Yen 2,000, Post. ¥ 200
Abroad $ 10.00, Post. $ 1.00